SPSS® Reference Guide

SPSS Inc.

SPSS Inc.
444 N. Michigan Avenue
Chicago, Illinois 60611
Tel: (312) 329-2400
Fax: (312) 329-3668

For more information about SPSS® software products, please write or call

Marketing Department
SPSS Inc.
444 North Michigan Avenue
Chicago, IL 60611
Tel: (312) 329-2400
Fax: (312) 329-3668

SPSS® Reference Guide
Copyright © 1990 by SPSS Inc.
All rights reserved.
Printed in the United States of America.

67890   98 97 96 95 94

ISBN 0-13-177858-7

Library of Congress Catalog Card Number: 89-043279

Preface

SPSS® is a comprehensive, integrated system for statistical data analysis. It is available on a wide variety of computers and operating systems, including IBM® PC, PS/2®, and compatible computers running OS/2™; Apple Macintosh® computers; workstations, minicomputers, and larger systems under UNIX® and VAX/VMS™; and many other mainframes. All of these versions contain an SPSS Processor that reads and carries out commands in the well-known SPSS language. No matter which version you use, you can issue the same commands and expect the same results.

This manual is a complete reference to the SPSS command language. It opens with "Universals," which describes the rules of the language and documents those components of the language that appear in many commands, such as the arithmetic, string, date, and other functions available in many data transformation commands. Following "Universals" SPSS commands are presented in alphabetical order. The syntax is illustrated with many examples; and commands that carry out analyses and produce reports are also illustrated with extended, annotated examples.

This manual does **not** provide an overview of SPSS, teach you how to create jobs and interpret output, or show you how to run SPSS on your computer and operating system. See "Manuals for the Base System," below, for information about the manuals that perform those functions.

New Features in This Release. As of Release 4 (the successor to SPSS-X™ Release 3), most versions of the software now also contain an SPSS Manager that helps you build commands and review output. The Manager includes a menu-based command generator, context-sensitive help, an online glossary, extensive editing capabilities, and other features designed to help you work efficiently with SPSS.

In addition to the new SPSS Manager interface available on many systems, Release 4 contains a new procedure for exploring data (EXAMINE), a facility to transpose data files (FLIP), a logistic regression procedure, and a comprehensive matrix manipulation language. (LOGISTIC REGRESSION and MATRIX are part of the Advanced Statistics option on some systems.) For systems where SPSS Graphics is installed, SPSS contains the new GRAPH command that allows you to define a chart and invoke the graphics software from within the SPSS system. In addition, a new option, SPSS Categories™, is available to perform conjoint and correspondence analysis. Finally, the documentation has been fully revised to provide more help for new users and more compact and complete reference material for experienced users.

Manuals for the Base System. Documentation for SPSS Release 4 consists of:

- *SPSS Base System User's Guide* shows how to use SPSS commands to manage and analyze data. It explains many of the statistical concepts involved and includes brief operational instructions for each command.
- *SPSS Reference Guide* documents and gives examples of all of the commands, subcommands, and keywords in the base system and Advanced Statistics option.
- An operations guide tells how to run SPSS on one of the operating systems for which the software is available, and explains any differences between that version of SPSS and the system as documented in the user and reference guides. The following

operations guides are scheduled for availability in 1989 or early 1990: SPSS for OS/2, SPSS for the Macintosh, SPSS for UNIX, SPSS for IBM/CMS™, and SPSS for VAX/VMS.

SPSS Options. The following manuals discuss options available for most versions of SPSS. Advanced Statistics is included with the base system in most versions for larger systems but is a separate option in most personal computer versions of the software.

- *SPSS Advanced Statistics User's Guide* contains discussions of advanced statistical analyses, such as discriminant analysis, nonlinear and logistic regression analysis, and multivariate analysis of variance. In addition to the statistical discussions there is a brief discussion of how to run each command.
- *SPSS Trends* documents SPSS's complete time series analysis and forecasting tool. The Trends option includes curve fitting, smoothing, special regression, seasonal adjustment, and Box-Jenkins/ARIMA modeling procedures. The manual contains sample applications and a complete reference to the commands in the Trends option.
- *SPSS Tables* documents the SPSS TABLES procedure, which presents data in presentation quality tables. TABLES can tabulate multiple variables at once and provides great flexibility for displaying totals, percentages, and other statistics. The *SPSS Tables* manual includes a user's guide and a complete reference to TABLES subcommands.
- *SPSS Categories* documents the three conjoint and four correspondence analysis procedures in this new option. The manual includes illustrative applications and a complete reference to the commands.

The SPSS system is constantly undergoing enhancements. For additional information about your system, including any updates since the printing of the most current version of the manual, use the INFO command documented in this guide. If you would like to be on our mailing list and you did not buy your system directly from us, write to us at the address below. We will send you a copy of our newsletter and let you know about SPSS Inc. activities in your area.

SPSS Inc.
444 North Michigan Ave.
Chicago, IL 60611
Tel: (312) 329-2400
Fax: (312) 329-3668

SPSS Federal Systems
12030 Sunrise Valley Dr.
Suite 300
Reston, VA 22091
Tel: (703) 391-6020
Fax: (703) 391-6002

SPSS Latin America
444 North Michigan Ave.
Chicago, IL 60611
Tel: (312) 329-3556
Fax: (312) 329-3668

SPSS Benelux BV
P.O. Box 115
4200 AC Gorinchem
The Netherlands
Tel: +31.1830.36711
Fax: +31.1830.35839

SPSS UK Ltd.
SPSS House
5 London Street
Chertsey
Surrey KT16 8AP
United Kingdom
Tel: +44.932.566262
Fax: +44.932.567020

SPSS UK Ltd., New Delhi
c/o Ashok Business Centre
Ashok Hotel
50B Chanakyapuri
New Delhi 110 021
India
Tel: +91.11.600121 x1029
Fax: +91.11.6873216

SPSS GmbH Software
Steinsdorfstrasse 19
D-80538 Munich
Germany
Tel: +49.89.211050
Fax: +49.89.2285413

SPSS Scandinavia AB
Gamla Brogatan 36-38
4th Floor
111 20 Stockholm
Sweden
Tel: +46.8.102610
Fax: +46.8.102550

SPSS Asia Pacific Pte. Ltd.
10 Anson Road, #34-07
International Plaza
Singapore 0207
Singapore
Tel: +65.221.2577
Fax: +65.221.9920

SPSS Japan Inc.
AY Bldg.
3-2-2 Kitaaoyama
Minato-ku
Tokyo 107
Japan
Tel: +81.3.5474.0341
Fax: +81.3.5474.2678

SPSS Australasia Pty. Ltd.
121 Walker Street
North Sydney, NSW 2060
Australia
Tel: +61.2.954.5660
Fax: +61.2.954.5616

Contents

Universals
Syntax   1
Files   6
Variables   12
Transformation Expressions   17

Commands
ADD FILES   33
ADD VALUE
LABELS   39
AGGREGATE   41
ALSCAL   48
ANOVA   62
AUTORECODE   69
BEGIN DATA—
END DATA   72
BREAK   74
CLEAR
TRANSFORMATIONS   75
CLUSTER   76
COMMENT   84
COMPUTE   85
CORRELATIONS   92
COUNT   97
CROSSTABS   98
DATA LIST   109
DESCRIPTIVES   122
DISCRIMINANT   127
DISPLAY   141
DOCUMENT   143
DO IF   145
DO REPEAT—
END REPEAT   153
DROP
DOCUMENTS   157
EDIT   158
END CASE   160
END FILE   167
EXAMINE   170
EXECUTE   177
EXPORT   178
FACTOR   182
FILE HANDLE   197
FILE LABEL   198
FILE TYPE—
END FILE TYPE   199
FINISH   212
FLIP   213
FORMATS   216
FREQUENCIES   219
GET   225
GET BMDP   228
GET OSIRIS   232
GET SAS   236
GET SCSS   240

GET TRANSLATE   242
GRAPH   246
HELP   275
HILOGLINEAR   277
HOST   284
IF   285
IMPORT   289
INCLUDE   292
INFO   294
INPUT PROGRAM—END
INPUT PROGRAM   296
KEYED DATA LIST   301
LEAVE   306
LIST   309
LOGISTIC
REGRESSION   312
LOGLINEAR   323
LOOP—END
LOOP   333
Macro Facility   344
MANOVA:
Overview   358
MANOVA:
Univariate   362
MANOVA:
Multivariate   383
MANOVA: Repeated
Measures   392
MATCH FILES   399
MATRIX—
END MATRIX   406
MATRIX DATA   439
MCONVERT   454
MEANS   457
MISSING VALUES   463
MULT RESPONSE   465
N OF CASES   473
NLR   475
NONPAR CORR   489
NPAR TESTS   494
NUMBERED,
UNNUMBERED   506
NUMERIC   507
ONEWAY   509
PARTIAL CORR   517
PLOT   523
POINT   529
PRESERVE   532
PRINT   533

PRINT EJECT   537
PRINT FORMATS   539
PRINT SPACE   541
PROBIT   543
PROCEDURE
OUTPUT   549
PROXIMITIES   550
QUICK CLUSTER   563
RANK   568
RECODE   573
RECORD TYPE   577
REFORMAT   584
REGRESSION   585
REGRESSION:
Residuals   598
RELIABILITY   605
RENAME
VARIABLES   612
REPEATING DATA   613
REPORT   624
REREAD   645
RESTORE   649
SAMPLE   650
SAVE   652
SAVE SCSS   656
SAVE TRANSLATE   658
SELECT IF   661
SET   664
SHOW   676
SORT CASES   680
SPLIT FILE   682
STRING   684
SUBTITLE   686
SURVIVAL   687
TEMPORARY   698
TITLE   700
T-TEST   701
UPDATE   704
VALUE LABELS   710
VARIABLE
LABELS   712
VECTOR   713
WEIGHT   720
WRITE   722
WRITE FORMATS   726
XSAVE   728

Contents

Examples

ALSCAL 735
ANOVA 743
AUTORECODE 744
CLUSTER 747
CORRELATIONS 751
CROSSTABS 753
DESCRIPTIVES 754
DISCRIMINANT 756
EXAMINE 757
FACTOR 761
FREQUENCIES 765
HILOGLINEAR 767

LOGISTIC
REGRESSION 770
LOGLINEAR 774
MANOVA 796
MATRIX 826
MEANS 827
MULT RESPONSE 828
NLR/CNLR 830
NONPAR CORR 843
NPAR TESTS 844
ONEWAY 845
PARTIAL CORR 849

PLOT 851
PROBIT 853
PROXIMITIES 860
QUICK CLUSTER 861
REGRESSION 864
RELIABILITY 867
REPORT 869
SURVIVAL 873
T-TEST 875
References 877

Appendixes

Appendix A   Command Order 881
Appendix B   IMPORT/EXPORT Character Sets 887
Appendix C   Obsolete Specifications 891
Appendix D   Computer Cards 903
Appendix E   906

Index 927

Command Reference

Universals

The first part of the *SPSS Reference Guide* discusses syntax: the rules that apply to SPSS commands. It also explores general topics, such as the types of files used by SPSS, variable-naming conventions, and transformation expressions in SPSS. Following these discussions is an alphabetic reference to SPSS commands.

Syntax

Syntax Diagrams

Each SPSS command described includes a syntax diagram that shows all the subcommands, keywords, and specifications allowed for that command. By remembering the following rules, you can use the syntax diagram as a quick reference for each command.

- Elements shown in capital letters are keywords.
- Elements in lower case describe specifications you supply.
- Elements in boldface type are defaults. Some defaults are indicated with **.
- Special delimiters, such as parentheses, apostrophes, or quotation marks, are required where indicated.
- Elements enclosed in square brackets ([ ]) are optional. When brackets would confuse the format, they are omitted. The command description explains which specifications are required or optional.
- Braces ({ }) indicate a choice between elements.
- The word "varlist" stands for a list of variable names.
- The command terminator is not shown in the syntax diagram.

Command Order

The following rules apply to command order in SPSS:

- Commands that define variables for a session (DATA LIST, GET, MATRIX DATA, etc.) must precede commands that assign labels or missing values to those variables; they must also precede transformation and procedure commands that use those variables.
- Transformation commands (IF, COUNT, COMPUTE, etc.) that are used to define variables must precede commands that assign labels or missing values to those variables, and they must also precede the procedures that use those variables.
- Generally, the logical outcome of command processing determines command order. For example, a procedure that creates new variables on the active system file must precede a procedure that uses those new variables. Although most data transformations do not take effect until the data are read (exceptions are noted below), the result is usually as though the commands took effect when encountered. Thus, the logical outcome of command processing usually determines the order in which transformations are used.
- Some commands can appear only in an *input program* where the cases are being created, other commands can appear only in the *transformation program* after the cases have been created, and still other commands can appear in either program. For example, REREAD and END CASE can be used only to read data records and create cases; SELECT IF can be used only after the cases are created; COMPUTE can be used both to create and to transform cases and can appear in either program. For a discussion of these *program states* and command order, see Appendix A.

In addition to observing the rules above, it is important to distinguish between commands that cause the data to be read and those that do not. Table 1 shows the commands that cause the data to be read.

Table 1 Commands that cause the data to be read*

AGGREGATE	MANOVA
ALSCAL	MATRIX
ANOVA	MCONVERT
AUTORECODE	MEANS
BEGIN DATA	MULTIPLE RESPONSE
CLUSTER	nonlinear regression (CNLR and NLR)
CORRELATIONS	NONPAR CORR
CROSSTABS	NPAR TESTS
DESCRIPTIVES	ONEWAY
DISCRIMINANT	PARTIAL CORR
EXAMINE	PLOT
EXECUTE	PROBIT
EXPORT	PROXIMITIES
FACTOR	QUICK CLUSTER
FLIP	RANK
FREQUENCIES	REGRESSION
GRAPH	RELIABILITY
HILOGLINEAR	REPORT
IMPORT	SAVE, SAVE SCSS, SAVE TRANSLATE
LIST	SORT
LOGISTIC REGRESSION	SURVIVAL
LOGLINEAR	T-TEST

*This table shows the procedures in the SPSS Base and Advanced Statistics options; it does not show commands in other SPSS software options, such as SPSS Tables or SPSS Trends.

Most of the remaining commands (those that do not cause the data to be read) do not take effect immediately; they are processed when encountered in the command sequence and take effect when data are read.

Table 2 Commands that take effect immediately

ADD VALUE LABELS	SPLIT FILE
FORMATS	STRING
LEAVE	VALUE LABELS
MISSING VALUES	VARIABLE LABELS
N OF CASES	VECTOR
NUMERIC	WEIGHT
PRINT FORMATS	WRITE FORMATS

However, transformation commands that alter the active system file dictionary take effect as soon as they are encountered in the command sequence, regardless of conditional statements that precede them. Because these transformations (identified in Table 2) take effect immediately, their order in the command sequence can be misleading. Consider the following:

```
COMPUTE PROFIT=INCOME-EXPENSES.
MISSING VALUES INCOME EXPENSES (0).
LIST.
```

- COMPUTE precedes MISSING VALUES and is processed first; however, SPSS delays its execution until the data have been read.

- MISSING VALUES takes effect as soon as it is encountered.

- LIST causes the data to be read; thus, SPSS executes both COMPUTE and LIST during the same data pass. Because MISSING VALUES is already in effect by this time, all cases with the value 0 for either INCOME or EXPENSES return a missing value for PROFIT.

Even though the MISSING VALUES command follows COMPUTE in the command sequence, it is in effect before COMPUTE is executed. In this example, to prevent the MISSING VALUES command from taking effect before COMPUTE is executed, MISSING VALUES must be positioned after the LIST command. Alternatively, place an EXECUTE command between COMPUTE and MISSING VALUES.

As mentioned above, transformations that alter the dictionary take effect immediately, regardless of the conditional statements that precede them. In the sequence

```
DO IF AGE=99.
MISSING VALUES INCOME EXPENSES (0).
ELSE.
COMPUTE PROFIT=INCOME-EXPENSES.
END IF.
LIST.
```

the MISSING VALUES command is in effect when COMPUTE is executed, even if the condition defined on DO IF is false for all cases.

Commands

Commands are the instructions that you give SPSS to initiate an action. The following rules apply to all SPSS commands:

- Commands begin with a keyword that is the name of the command and often have additional specifications, such as subcommands and user specifications. Refer to the discussion of each command to see which subcommands and additional specifications are required.

- Commands and any command specifications can be entered in upper and lower case. Commands, subcommands, keywords, and variable names are translated to upper case before processing. All user specifications, including labels and data values, preserve upper and lower case.

- Spaces can be added between specifications at any point where a single blank is allowed. In addition, lines can be broken at any point where a single blank is allowed. The exceptions are 1) the END DATA command, which can have only one space between words, and 2) strings specified on commands such as TITLE, SUBTITLE, VARIABLE LABELS, VALUE LABELS, etc., which can be broken across two lines only by specifying a + between string segments (see Strings, below).

- Most two- or three-word commands, such as SORT CASES, VALUE LABELS, or ADD VALUE LABELS, can be abbreviated to a minimum of three letters per word, provided each word of the command is used (SOR CAS, VAL LAB, and ADD VAL LAB are valid abbreviations for SORT CASES, VALUE LABELS, and ADD VALUE LABELS, respectively). END DATA is an exception: you must spell both command keywords in full; END DAT is not a valid abbreviation for END DATA.

- Three-character truncation does not apply to INFO command specifications. Spell out all keywords in full. For procedure names, spell out the first word in full and subsequent words through at least the first three characters.

Commands Run Within SPSS

When you begin an SPSS session and enter and run commands during the session, you are running commands within SPSS. The following rules apply to commands run within SPSS:

- Each command ends with a command terminator. The default command terminator is a period (.). It is best to omit the terminator on BEGIN DATA, however, so that SPSS will treat inline data as one continuous specification.
- The command terminator must be the last non-blank character in a line.
- Commands can begin in any column of a command line and continue for as many lines as needed. The exception is the END DATA command, which must begin in the first column of the first line after the end of data.
- The maximum length of any line in a command is 80 characters, including the prompt and the command terminator.

However, commands in a command file that you specify on the INCLUDE command do not follow the above rules. Commands in that file must follow the same rules as those in a command file processed through your operating system.

Processing Command Files Through Your Operating System

When you create and save an SPSS command file and then submit that file to a batch queue or execute it from your operating system's command prompt, you are running commands through your operating system. (See your SPSS *Operations Guide* for instructions.) The following rules apply when commands are run through your operating system:

- All commands in the SPSS command file must begin in column 1. If multiple lines are used to complete a command statement, column 1 of each continuation line must be blank.
- Command terminators are optional.

Subcommands

Many commands include additional specifications called subcommands for locating data, handling data, and formatting the output display.

- Subcommands begin with a keyword that is the name of the subcommand. Some subcommands include additional specifications.
- A subcommand keyword is separated from its specifications, if any, by an equals sign. The equals sign is usually optional but is required where ambiguity is possible in the specification. To avoid ambiguity, it is best to use the equals signs (and also slashes) as shown in the syntax diagrams in this manual.
- Most subcommands can be named in any order. However, some commands require a specific subcommand order.
- Subcommands are separated from each other by a slash.

Keywords

Keywords are words specially defined by SPSS to identify commands, subcommands, functions, operators, and other specifications.

- Keywords, including commands and subcommands, can often be truncated to the first three characters of each word. An exception is the keyword WITH, which must be spelled in full.
- Some keywords are reserved and cannot be used as variable names. Logical operators (AND, OR, and NOT), relational operators (EQ, GE, GT, LE, LT, and NE), and ALL, BY, TO, and WITH are the reserved keywords.
- Keyword ALL refers to all user-defined variables in the active system file.
- Keyword THRU between two values specifies a range. The range includes the specified values.
- Keyword TO between two variable names specifies an inclusive list of variables.

Values

Values refer to specifications in commands or the data points processed by SPSS.

- A number specified as an argument to a subcommand can be entered with or without leading zeros.

- Data values of numeric variables can be specified as integers or real numbers, with or without leading zeros.
- Whenever values of string (alphanumeric) variables are used in commands, they must be specified within apostrophes or quotation marks, including all blanks.
- String values in data files or entered between BEGIN DATA and END DATA commands do not need to be enclosed in special delimiters (for exceptions, see FREE and LIST format on DATA LIST).
- Blanks within apostrophes or quotation marks are significant.

- Values in the data can include descriptive characters ($, %, etc.), provided data are in fixed format and the correct input format is defined for the associated variable name (see Variable Formats, below).

Delimiters

Delimiters are used to separate data values, keywords, arguments, and specifications.

- A blank is usually used to separate one specification from another, except when another delimiter serves the same purpose or when a comma is required.
- Commas are required to separate arguments to functions. Otherwise, commas are generally valid substitutes for blanks, and vice versa.
- Arithmetic operators ($+$, $-$, $*$, and $/$) serve as delimiters in expressions. Blanks before and after arithmetic operators are optional.
- Special delimiters include parentheses, apostrophes, quotation marks, the slash, and the equals sign. Blanks before and after special delimiters are optional.
- The slash is used primarily to separate subcommands and lists of variables. Although slashes are sometimes optional, it is a good practice to enter them as shown in the syntax diagrams.
- The equals sign is used between a subcommand and its specifications, as in STATISTICS=MEAN, and to show equivalence, as in *old variable list=new variable list*. Equals signs following subcommands are frequently optional, but it is best to enter them.

Strings

The term "string" is used to refer to alphanumeric data or specifications such as titles and labels.

- The values of string variables can contain numbers, letters, and special characters and can be up to 255 characters long. SPSS further differentiates between long strings and short strings. Long strings can be displayed by some procedures and by the PRINT command, and they can be used as "break" variables to define subgroups in REPORT. They cannot, however, be tabulated as long strings in procedures such as CROSSTABS, and they cannot have values declared as missing. Short strings, on the other hand, can be tabulated and can have missing values. The maximum length of a short string depends on the computer and operating system used to run SPSS; it is typically 8 characters.
- Each string specified in a command should be enclosed in a set of either apostrophes or quotation marks.
- String specifications can be broken across command lines only by specifying each string segment within apostrophes or quotes and using a + sign to splice segments. For example, 'one,two' can be specified as 'one,' + 'two'. The + can be specified on either the first or the second line of the broken string.
- System-missing values cannot be generated for string variables read from a raw data file, since any character is a legal string value.
- When a transformation command on a string variable yields a missing or undefined result, a blank value is assigned.
- Blank is therefore defined as the user-missing value for string variables created by transformation commands. If you compute one string variable equal to another, user-missing values will be converted to blanks (but will remain user-missing).

Files

SPSS uses a number of files in its operation. This section provides an overview to the types of files you can use, as well as a discussion of the active system file.

Types of Files

The files that you can use in SPSS are

- *Command file:* Contains the SPSS commands. Command files can be created by a text editor or the *SPSS Manager* (for SPSS versions that use it to enter and run commands). During an SPSS prompted session, you can use the INCLUDE command to process the commands in a command file as an alternative to entering the commands individually.

- *Journal file:* Contains a log of commands entered during an SPSS session, along with any error or warning messages generated by the commands. The journal file can be used as a command file in subsequent sessions.

- *Input data file:* Contains only raw data. Data files can be arranged in almost any format. This file can be imbedded within the SPSS command file, or it can be a separate file on tape or disk.

- *Display file:* Contains the tabular output from SPSS procedures, diagnostic information about the session, and output from any PRINT or WRITE commands that did not send output to a separate output file. This file is formatted for listing at a terminal or on a line printer.

- *Active system file:* Serves as the main input to transformations and procedures. It is created by DATA LIST, GET, IMPORT, MATRIX DATA, or an input program and is modified by transformations and some procedures. It exists only for the duration of the SPSS session but can be saved as a system file or exported as a portable file.

- *Output file:* Contains data formatted for reading by a computer. Some procedures create output files containing matrix or other materials, and the WRITE command produces a data file to your specifications.

- *System file:* A file specifically formatted for use by SPSS, containing both data and the *dictionary* that defines the data to the system. System files speed processing and are required as input for combining files.

- *Portable file:* A system file created by the EXPORT command and formatted for portability to computers other than the one on which it was created.

- *Foreign files:* Files created by other software that can be used by SPSS on some operating systems. Foreign files include dBASE, Lotus, and Multiplan files. See your SPSS *Operations Guide* for the types of foreign files (if any) that SPSS can read and write on your system.

Conventions for naming, printing, deleting, or permanently saving files, and for submitting command files for processing, differ from one computer and operating system to another. See your SPSS *Operations Guide*, or consult the documentation for handling files that was delivered with your system.

SPSS Active System File

Data to be used in SPSS must be defined—that is, it must have names for the variables, formats for reading and displaying values, and (optionally) some labels and missing-value specifications. The essential information can be provided on a DATA LIST command or on one of the other commands that define more complex files. A system file or portable file already contains the necessary definitions, as do most foreign files. Once this information is available, SPSS can build an *active system file,* which is then modified by transformation commands and analyzed by procedure commands.

The active system file is not actually created until SPSS encounters a command (usually a procedure) that causes it to read the data (see Command Order, above). This allows the data to be read and transformed and the first procedure processed with only one pass through the original file. It also ensures that SPSS will not use computer resources to read data and perform transformations before it has received syntactically correct instructions to produce some kind of output.

When SPSS does encounter a procedure command, it executes all of the preceding data definition and transformation commands and performs whatever action the procedure calls for. The active system file is then available for further transformations and procedures, and it remains available until the end of the session or until it is specifically replaced. In addition, some procedures are able to add variables to the active system file, or, in the case of AGGREGATE or procedures that can write out matrix materials, to replace the active system file altogether.

Matrix System Files

Many procedures in SPSS can read raw data and write a representative matrix of the data values to a *matrix system file,* which, like any system file, uses a dictionary to record descriptive information about the matrix data. Matrix system files can be used as input for subsequent analysis.

Table 3 shows the types of matrix materials written by SPSS procedures. The ROWTYPE_ values (discussed below) of each matrix are also included so you see which procedure matrices are readable by other procedures. If a procedure produces more than one type of matrix, the subcommand required or comments on that matrix are included in the table.

Table 3 Types of matrices and their contents

Command	Subcommands/Notes	ROWTYPE_ values*
ALSCAL		PROX
CLUSTER		PROX
CORRELATIONS		MEAN
		STDDEV
		N
		CORR
DISCRIMINANT	/CLASSIFY=POOLED	N (1 per cell)
		COUNT (1 per cell)
		MEAN (1 per cell)
		STDDEV (pooled)
		CORR (pooled)
	/CLASSIFY=SEPARATE, /STATISTICS=BOXM, or /STATISTICS=GCOV	N (1 per cell)
		COUNT (1 per cell)
		MEAN (1 per cell)
		STDDEV (1 per cell)
		CORR (1 per cell)
FACTOR	/MATRIX=OUT(CORR=file) /MATRIX=IN(CORR=file)	CORR
	/MATRIX=OUT(FAC=file) /MATRIX=IN(FAC=file)	FACTOR
MANOVA		N (cell and pooled)
		MEAN (1 per cell)
		STDDEV (pooled)
		CORR (pooled)
NONPAR CORR	/PRINT=SPEARMAN	N
		RHO
	/PRINT=KENDALL	N
		TAUB
ONEWAY	separate variance — can be input and output	MEAN (1 per cell)
		STDDEV (1 per cell)
		N (1 per cell)
	pooled variance — can be input only	MEAN (1 per cell)
		N (1 per cell)
		MSE (pooled)
		DFE (pooled)
PARTIAL CORR		N
		CORR

Continued

Command	Subcommands/Notes	ROWTYPE_ values*
PROXIMITIES		PROX
REGRESSION		MEAN
		STDDEV
		N
		CORR
RELIABILITY		N
		MEAN
		STDDEV
		CORR

*For any command, if /MISSING=PAIRWISE, all N values of ROWTYPE_ will be a matrix of N's. Otherwise, a single vector of N's is used.

- All SPSS procedures that handle matrix materials use the MATRIX subcommand. The MATRIX subcommand specifies the file from which the input matrix is read and/or the file to which the output matrix is written. The MATRIX subcommand standardizes the method each procedure uses to read and write matrices. Though procedures vary in the types of matrix materials they handle, the MATRIX subcommand always uses at least one of two keywords, IN and OUT, to specify the matrix system files.

- MATRIX=IN cannot be used in place of GET or DATA LIST to begin a new SPSS command file. MATRIX is a subcommand on procedures that handle matrix materials, and procedures cannot run before an active system file is defined.

- When MATRIX=IN is used, the active system file does not need to contain the matrix materials. For example, you can perform a series of analyses on one file and then read matrix materials from another file. MATRIX=IN can be used in that context because there is a defined active system file at the time that the procedure specifying the MATRIX subcommand is used.

- The procedures that read matrix materials can read them only if the matrix file is an appropriate matrix system file. For example, NONPAR CORR writes matrix system files, but REGRESSION cannot read them because REGRESSION reads and writes matrices with Pearson's correlation coefficient and NONPAR CORR writes with either Spearman's or Kendall's coefficient.

Format of the Matrix System File

The matrix system file shown in Figure 1 was produced by procedure CORRELATIONS by the commands

```
GET FILE  UNION/KEEP FOOD RENT PUBTRANS TEACHER COOK ENGINEER
SEX.
SORT CASES BY SEX.
SPLIT FILE BY SEX.
CORRELATIONS  FOOD TO ENGINEER /MATRIX OUT(CORRMTX).
```

Figure 2 shows the file's dictionary. Because split-file processing is in effect, separate matrix materials are generated for each split-file variable. The split-file variable is the first variable in the file.

- The matrix system file has two special variables created by SPSS: ROWTYPE_ and VARNAME_. Variable ROWTYPE_ is a string variable with A8 format; in Figure 1, ROWTYPE_ has values MEAN, STDDEV, N, and CORR (for Pearson correlation coefficient). Variable VARNAME_ is a string variable with A8 format whose values are the names of the variables used to form the correlation matrix. In Figure 1, when ROWTYPE_ is CORR, VARNAME_ gives the variable associated with that row of the correlation matrix. The remaining variables in the file are the variables used to form the correlation matrix. Each has an F10.7 format.

- All the procedures that write matrices in SPSS use a format similar to that shown in Figure 1, and all generate the special matrix variables ROWTYPE_ and VARNAME_. Procedures like FACTOR or DISCRIMINANT that can use factor or grouping variables in their analyses include values for those variables with the matrix materials. In addition, procedure FACTOR creates matrix variables named ROWTYPE_ and FACTOR_ for FACTOR-format files. See Table 3 for the types and contents of the matrices that each procedure handles.

Figure 1 A matrix system file (LIST output)

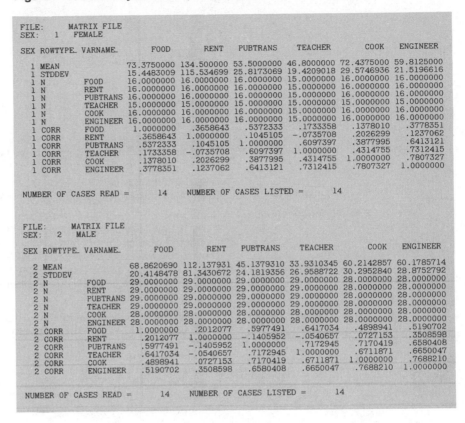

```
FILE:      MATRIX FILE
SEX:   1   FEMALE

SEX ROWTYPE_ VARNAME_        FOOD       RENT     PUBTRANS    TEACHER      COOK     ENGINEER

  1 MEAN                 73.3750000 134.500000 53.5000000 46.8000000 72.4375000 59.8125000
  1 STDDEV               15.4483009 115.534699 25.8173069 19.4209018 29.5746936 21.5196616
  1 N        FOOD        16.0000000 16.0000000 16.0000000 15.0000000 16.0000000 16.0000000
  1 N        RENT        16.0000000 16.0000000 16.0000000 15.0000000 16.0000000 16.0000000
  1 N        PUBTRANS    16.0000000 16.0000000 16.0000000 15.0000000 16.0000000 16.0000000
  1 N        TEACHER     15.0000000 15.0000000 15.0000000 15.0000000 15.0000000 15.0000000
  1 N        COOK        16.0000000 16.0000000 16.0000000 15.0000000 16.0000000 16.0000000
  1 N        ENGINEER    16.0000000 16.0000000 16.0000000 15.0000000 16.0000000 16.0000000
  1 CORR     FOOD         1.0000000   .3658643   .5372333   .1733358   .1378010   .3778351
  1 CORR     RENT         .3658643  1.0000000   .1045105  -.0735708   .2026299   .1237062
  1 CORR     PUBTRANS     .5372333   .1045105  1.0000000   .6097397   .3877995   .6413121
  1 CORR     TEACHER      .1733358  -.0735708   .6097397  1.0000000   .4314755   .7312415
  1 CORR     COOK         .1378010   .2026299   .3877995   .4314755  1.0000000   .7807327
  1 CORR     ENGINEER     .3778351   .1237062   .6413121   .7312415   .7807327  1.0000000


NUMBER OF CASES READ =      14     NUMBER OF CASES LISTED =        14



FILE:      MATRIX FILE
SEX:   2   MALE

SEX ROWTYPE_ VARNAME_        FOOD       RENT     PUBTRANS    TEACHER      COOK     ENGINEER

  2 MEAN                 68.8620690 112.137931 45.1379310 33.9310345 60.2142857 60.1785714
  2 STDDEV               20.4148478 81.3430672 24.1819356 26.9588722 30.2952840 28.8752792
  2 N        FOOD        29.0000000 29.0000000 29.0000000 29.0000000 28.0000000 28.0000000
  2 N        RENT        29.0000000 29.0000000 29.0000000 29.0000000 28.0000000 28.0000000
  2 N        PUBTRANS    29.0000000 29.0000000 29.0000000 29.0000000 28.0000000 28.0000000
  2 N        TEACHER     29.0000000 29.0000000 29.0000000 29.0000000 28.0000000 28.0000000
  2 N        COOK        28.0000000 28.0000000 28.0000000 28.0000000 28.0000000 28.0000000
  2 N        ENGINEER    28.0000000 28.0000000 28.0000000 28.0000000 28.0000000 28.0000000
  2 CORR     FOOD         1.0000000   .2012077   .5977491   .6417034   .4898941   .5190702
  2 CORR     RENT         .2012077  1.0000000  -.1405952  -.0540657   .0727153   .3508598
  2 CORR     PUBTRANS     .5977491  -.1405952  1.0000000   .7172945   .7170419   .6580408
  2 CORR     TEACHER      .6417034  -.0540657   .7172945  1.0000000   .6711871   .6650047
  2 CORR     COOK         .4898941   .0727153   .7170419   .6711871  1.0000000   .7688210
  2 CORR     ENGINEER     .5190702   .3508598   .6580408   .6650047   .7688210  1.0000000


NUMBER OF CASES READ =      14     NUMBER OF CASES LISTED =        14
```

Figure 2 Dictionary of a matrix system file (DISPLAY output)

```
FILE:      MATRIX FILE

           LIST OF VARIABLES ON THE ACTIVE FILE

NAME                                                                      POSITION

SEX                                                                           1
                    PRINT FORMAT: F2
                    WRITE FORMAT: F2

           VALUE    LABEL

             1      FEMALE
             2      MALE

ROWTYPE_                                                                      2
                    PRINT FORMAT: A8
                    WRITE FORMAT: A8

VARNAME_                                                                      3
                    PRINT FORMAT: A8
                    WRITE FORMAT: A8

FOOD     AVG FOOD PRICES                                                      4
                    PRINT FORMAT: F10.7
                    WRITE FORMAT: F10.7

RENT     NORMAL RENT                                                          5
                    PRINT FORMAT: F10.7
                    WRITE FORMAT: F10.7

PUBTRANS  PRICE FOR PUBLIC TRANSPORT                                          6
                    PRINT FORMAT: F10.7
                    WRITE FORMAT: F10.7

TEACHER  NET TEACHER'S SALARY                                                 7
                    PRINT FORMAT: F10.7
                    WRITE FORMAT: F10.7

COOK     NET COOK'S SALARY                                                    8
                    PRINT FORMAT: F10.7
                    WRITE FORMAT: F10.7

ENGINEER  NET ENGINEER'S SALARY                                              9
                    PRINT FORMAT: F10.7
                    WRITE FORMAT: F10.7
```

Variable Order   The following variable order is standard for all matrix system files:

1   Split variables, if any.

2   ROWTYPE_ variable.

3   Factor or grouping variables, if any.

4   VARNAME_ variable (or FACTOR_ variable for FACTOR-format files).

5   Continuous variables used to form the matrix.

Split Files   • When split-file processing is in effect, a full set of matrix materials is written for each split-file group defined by the split variable(s). A split variable cannot have the same variable name as any other variable written to the matrix system file. Not all procedures allow split variables with their matrices.

• If split-file processing is in effect when a matrix is written, the same split file must be in effect when that matrix is read by any procedure.

Additional Statistics   • Some procedures include statistics with their matrix materials. For example, CORRELATION matrices always include the mean, standard deviation, and number of cases used to compute each coefficient, as shown in Figure 1. Other procedures, for example PROXIMITIES and FACTOR, include no statistics with their matrices. See Table 3 for a list of the statistics written by each procedure. Refer to the individual procedure chapter to see what each expects to read from a matrix input file.

Missing Values   • Treatment of missing values in a procedure affects the matrix materials written to the system file. With pairwise treatment of missing values, the procedure includes with the materials a matrix of N's used to compute each coefficient. With any other missing-value treatment, the procedure includes the single N used to calculate all coefficients in the matrix. Figure 1 shows the matrix of N's written by CORRELATIONS when missing values are excluded pairwise from the analysis. Figure 3 shows the single N written by CORRELATIONS when missing values are excluded listwise.

Figure 3 Single N in the matrix system file

```
FILE:      MATRIX FILE
SEX:   1   FEMALE

SEX ROWTYPE_ VARNAME_       FOOD       RENT    PUBTRANS    TEACHER       COOK    ENGINEER

  1 MEAN                73.4666667 136.800000  54.0000000  46.8000000  73.8666667  60.0000000
  1 STDDEV              15.9860058 119.210019  26.6431444  19.4209018  30.0353760  22.2614337
  1 N                   15.0000000  15.0000000  15.0000000  15.0000000  15.0000000  15.0000000
  1 CORR     FOOD        1.0000000    .3652366    .5371597    .1733358    .1358120    .3773434
  1 CORR     RENT         .3652366   1.0000000    .0989524   -.0735708    .1914448    .1213899
  1 CORR     PUBTRANS     .5371597    .0989524   1.0000000    .6097397    .3811372    .6409265
  1 CORR     TEACHER      .1733358   -.0735708    .6097397   1.0000000    .4314755    .7312415
  1 CORR     COOK         .1358120    .1914448    .3811372    .4314755   1.0000000    .7893533
  1 CORR     ENGINEER     .3773434    .1213899    .6409265    .7312415    .7893533   1.0000000


NUMBER OF CASES READ =       9    NUMBER OF CASES LISTED =       9

                                                                           2

FILE:      MATRIX FILE
SEX:   2   MALE

SEX ROWTYPE_ VARNAME_       FOOD       RENT    PUBTRANS    TEACHER       COOK    ENGINEER

  2 MEAN                69.6428571 114.464286  46.1428571  33.7500000  60.2142857  60.1785714
  2 STDDEV              20.3437392  81.8474109  24.0011023  27.4356149  30.2952840  28.8752792
  2 N                   28.0000000  28.0000000  28.0000000  28.0000000  28.0000000  28.0000000
  2 CORR     FOOD        1.0000000    .1752920    .5784136    .6638084    .4898941    .5190702
  2 CORR     RENT         .1752920   1.0000000   -.1817862   -.0491139    .0727153    .3508598
  2 CORR     PUBTRANS     .5784136   -.1817862   1.0000000    .7447511    .7170419    .6580408
  2 CORR     TEACHER      .6638084   -.0491139    .7447511   1.0000000    .6711871    .6650047
  2 CORR     COOK         .4898941    .0727153    .7170419    .6711871   1.0000000    .7688210
  2 CORR     ENGINEER     .5190702    .3508598    .6580408    .6650047    .7688210   1.0000000


NUMBER OF CASES READ =       9    NUMBER OF CASES LISTED =       9
```

In addition to compatible coefficients, the missing-value treatment in the procedure that writes a matrix must be analogous to the treatment used by the procedure that reads the matrix. For example, REGRESSION can read a matrix written by CORRELATIONS but only if the missing-value treatment of both procedures is consistent: either both must reference a matrix of N's, or both must reference a single N. For all procedures, pairwise treatment of missing values generates a matrix of N's; any other treatment of missing values generates a single vector of N's.

Matrix File Dictionaries

As shown in Figure 2, print and write formats of A8 are assigned to the variables that the procedure creates (for example, ROWTYPE_, VARNAME_, and FACTOR_). No labels are assigned to these matrix variables. Print and write formats of F10.7 are assigned to all the continuous variables in the matrix analysis; the names and variable labels defined for these variables in the original data file are retained, but their original values and value labels are dropped because they do not apply to the matrix system file. When split-file processing is in effect, the variable names, variable and value labels, and print and write formats of the split-file variable(s) are read from the dictionary of the original data file.

Procedures read and write square matrices, where each row corresponds to a single case in the matrix system file. For example, the matrix shown in Figure 3 has nine cases. The first three cases, MEAN, STDDEV, and N, have no values for VARNAME_ but do have values for all the variables from FOOD to ENGINEER. The fourth case, CORR, in the matrix generated for split-file 1 (FEMALE) has a value of FOOD for VARNAME_, a value of .3652366 when correlated with variable RENT, a value of .5371597 when correlated with variable PUBTRANS, and so forth.

A matrix system file, therefore, is similar to any SPSS system file. It is a self-documented file containing data and descriptive information. The descriptive information, stored in the file dictionary, includes variable names, variable print and write formats, and optional variable and value labels. You can assign or change the names, labels, and formats of the variables in a matrix system file, just as you can in any system file.

Variables

This section describes rules for defining variables in SPSS.

Variable-Naming Conventions

Variable-naming conventions are the rules used to establish variable names in the active system file dictionary and to refer to variables in commands.

- Variable names are used on SPSS commands to refer to the data values. Variable names can contain up to eight characters, the first of which must be an alphabetic letter or the characters @, #, or $. An underscore can be used within the variable name, as long as the underscore is not the first character.

- A # character in the first position of a variable name defines a scratch variable. (See Scratch Variables, below.)

- A $ in the first position indicates that the variable is a system variable. (See System Variables, below.)

- The period, underscore, and the characters $, #, and @ can be used within variable names. For example, A._$@#1 is a valid variable name.

- Variable names ending with a period should be avoided, since the period will be interpreted as a command terminator when the variable name comes at the end of a command line.

- Variable names can be established on the DATA LIST, KEYED DATA LIST, MATRIX DATA, COMPUTE, RECODE, COUNT, and IF commands. They can be changed with the RENAME VARIABLES command.

- On data definition commands, such as DATA LIST, you can establish names for a set of variables with keyword TO. Specify a character prefix with a numeric suffix before and after keyword TO. The prefix can be any valid name and the number suffixes can be any integers, so long as the first number is smaller than the second. Each variable name, including the number, must not exceed eight characters. For example, ITEM1 TO ITEM5 establishes five variables named ITEM1, ITEM2, ITEM3, ITEM4, and ITEM5.

- With the TO convention, leading zeros used in suffixes are included in the variable name. For example, V001 TO V100 establishes 100 variables, V001, V002, V003, ..., V100. V1 TO V100 establishes 100 variables, V1, V2, V3, ..., V100.

- Keyword TO can also be used on procedures and other commands to refer to a set of consecutive variables on the active system file. AVAR TO VARB refers to the variables AVAR and all other variables up to and including VARB on the active system file. Use the DISPLAY command to see the order of variables on the active system file.

- Reserved keywords that cannot be used as variable names are

ALL AND BY   EQ GE GT   LE
LT   NE   NOT OR TO WITH

System Variables

Special *system variables*, such as the number of cases read by the system, the system-missing value, and the current date, can be used in data transformations.

- The names of system variables begin with a dollar sign ($).

- You cannot modify a system variable or alter its print or write format. Except for these restrictions, you can use system variables anywhere a normal variable is used in the transformation language.

- System variables are not available for procedures.

$CASENUM *Permanent case sequence number.* For each case, $CASENUM is the number of permanent cases read up to and including that case. The format is F8.0.

$SYSMIS *System-missing value.* The format is F1.0 so that it will always display as a period (.).

$JDATE	*Current date in YRMODA format.* The format is F6.0. See YRMODA Function, below.
$DATE	*Current date.* The format is A9 in the form *dd-mmm-yy*.
$TIME	*Current date and time.* $TIME represents the number of seconds from midnight, October 14, 1582 (day 1 of the Gregorian calendar) to the date and time when the data set is read. The format is F20.
$LENGTH	*The current page length.* The format is F11.0. For more information, see SET.
$WIDTH	*The current page width.* The format is F3.0. For more information, see SET.

Scratch Variables

A *scratch variable* can be created by using the # character as the first character of the numeric or string variable name.

- Scratch variables are unavailable for procedures and cannot be saved in a system file.
- Scratch variables cannot be assigned missing values, variable labels, or value labels.
- Scratch variables are initialized to 0 for numeric variables or blank for string variables for the first case and are left across cases with the LEAVE command.
- Scratch variables can be created between procedures but are always discarded as the next procedure begins.
- Once a TEMPORARY command is specified, the scratch variables are discarded.
- Keyword TO cannot be used to refer to scratch variables and permanent variables at the same time.
- Scratch variables cannot be named on a WEIGHT command.

Variable Formats

Values are stored internally in double precision. Values are read according to their *Input* format, which is defined on the DATA LIST or KEYED DATA LIST command.

Values are displayed or printed according to their output format, which is generated automatically, based upon the input format defined on DATA LIST or KEYED DATA LIST. SPSS also generates output formats for numeric variables created on the IF, COUNT, or COMPUTE command. Output formats are used to display values in procedures and to write data to other files.

The input and output formats do not affect the precision of data values stored in memory.

- To see the current format of variables on the active system file, use the DISPLAY command.
- Input formats cannot be changed (though different input formats can be defined for the same data on a subsequent DATA LIST or KEYED DATA LIST command).
- Output formats of numeric variables can be changed with the FORMATS, PRINT FORMATS, or WRITE FORMATS commands. The new formats are in effect only for the current session. To save the new formats, use the SAVE or XSAVE commands.
- Output formats of string variables cannot be changed, though STRING can be used to declare new variables with the desired formats, and COMPUTE can then be used to copy values from existing strings into the new strings. (The STRING command has no default format; a valid string format must be defined for each variable declared on STRING.)

See DATA LIST for information on specifying input data formats. See FORMATS, PRINT FORMATS, and WRITE FORMATS for information on specifying output data formats. See STRING for declaring new string variables.

Format Types

The most commonly used format types are defined below. For complete information on the printable and nonprintable numeric formats, string formats, date and time formats, column binary formats, and unaligned positive integer formats available on your system, see your SPSS *Operations Guide*.

- By default, the DATA LIST and KEYED DATA LIST commands assume that variables are numeric with an F format type. The default width depends on whether data are defined as fixed or freefield (see Variable Widths, below).
- Numeric variables created by COMPUTE, IF, or RECODE commands are assigned a format type F8.2 (or the default format defined on SET FORMAT.)
- Existing string variables transformed with the SPSS transformation language retain their original dictionary formats. String variables declared on STRING and transformed with the SPSS transformation language retain the formats assigned to them on STRING.

The formats below can be specified as input formats or output formats. The formats are shown in FORTRAN-like syntax, where *w* represents the variable width, and *d* represents the number of decimal places. To use these formats with column-style specifications on DATA LIST or KEYED DATA LIST, omit the width specification (because the column locations determine the variable width) and use a comma to separate the format type from the decimal specification. For example, the following format specifications are equivalent

```
DATA LIST / V1 1-6(PCT,2)
            V2 (PCT6.2).
```

DATA LIST defines both variables V1 and V2 in PCT format. Each variable has a total of six columns, two of which are decimal positions. The format of V1 is defined using column-style format specifications; the format of V2 is defined using FORTRAN-like format specifications.

- The variable type cannot be changed from string to numeric, or vice versa.
- The FORMATS, PRINT FORMATS, and WRITE FORMATS commands change only the print and write formats; they do not change the internal representation of a variable.

Implied Decimal Positions

Decimal positions can be *implied* when they are not coded in the data. This can be done only for fixed format data. Decimal places cannot be implied for freefield data.

- By default, SPSS assumes that the data are whole numbers or that decimal points have been recorded in the data file.
- *For fixed data:* If a value has no coded decimal point but the input format specifies decimal positions, the rightmost positions are interpreted as implied decimal digits. For example, if the input format specifies two decimal digits, the value 1234 is interpreted as 12.34; however, the value 123.4 is still interpreted as 123.4.
- *For freefield data:* If a value has no coded decimal point but the input format specifies decimal positions, SPSS reads numbers as whole numbers. Decimal points must be coded in the value if decimal positions are to be read. For example, if the input format specifies two decimal digits, the value 1234 is interpreted as 1234.00; the value 123.4 is interpreted as 123.40.

Common Formats

Aw (Standard Characters). The A format is used to read standard characters. Characters can include any number, letter, or character, including special characters and imbedded blanks. This format defines a variable as a string variable; numbers entered as values for string variables cannot be used in calculations.

Fw.d (Standard Numeric). Each input value can include a maximum of one decimal point. Dollar signs, commas, and percent signs cannot be coded in the data.

F format accepts numbers in scientific notation, provided the data values include E (or D), the sign, and the power of 10. For example, the data value, 543E+3, can be read under an F6 format. If a value is coded in scientific notation, an implied decimal specification is ignored.

The default output formats are type F. Thus, assuming there are no implied decimal positions in the input format, the value 1234 is displayed in output as 1234.

COMMAw.d (Commas in Numbers). As an input format with fixed data, COMMA is identical to F format, except that it can read numeric values with or without imbedded commas. For example, assuming keyword FIXED on DATA LIST, the values 1,234 and 12,34 and 123,4 are all interpreted as 1234; in other words, the commas in the input values are ignored.

As an input format with freefield data, COMMA is identical to F format; thus, commas cannot be coded in the data (a comma in freefield data is interpreted as a delimiter).

The default output formats are COMMA, whether or not the input values have imbedded commas, and whether data are fixed or freefield. Thus, assuming there are no implied decimal positions in the input format, the input value 1234 is displayed in output as 1,234.

DOTw.d (Dots in Numbers). Similar to COMMA format, except the roles of the comma and the dot (period) are reversed. This is useful for reading and displaying numbers according to European conventions.

For input, DOT should be used only with fixed format data.

The default output formats are DOT. Thus, assuming there are no implied decimal positions in the input format, the input value 1234 is displayed as 1.234.

DOLLARw.d (Dollar Sign and Commas in Numbers). As an input format with fixed data, DOLLAR is identical to F format, except that it can read numeric values with or without dollar signs and commas. For example, assuming keyword FIXED on DATA LIST, the values $1,234 and 12,34 and 123,4 are all interpreted as 1234; in other words, dollar signs and commas in the input values are ignored. Only one leading dollar sign with no imbedded blanks can be coded into each value.

As an input format with freefield data, DOLLAR is identical to F format; thus, dollar signs and commas cannot be coded in the data (commas in freefield data are interpreted as delimiters).

The default output formats are DOLLAR, whether or not the input values have imbedded dollar signs and commas, and whether data are fixed or freefield. Thus, assuming there are no implied decimal positions in the input format, the input value 1234 is displayed in output as $1,234. (For information on customizing currency formats for output, see SET.)

PCTw.d (Percent Sign after Numbers). As an input format with fixed data, PCT is identical to F format, except that it can read numeric fields with or without a trailing percent sign. For example, assuming keyword FIXED on DATA LIST, the values 12 and 12% are both interpreted as 12; in other words, percent signs in the input values are ignored. Only one trailing percent sign with no imbedded blanks can be coded into each value.

As an input format with freefield data, PCT is identical to F format; thus, percent signs cannot be coded in the data.

The default output formats are PCT, whether or not the input values have imbedded percent signs, and whether data are fixed or freefield. Thus, assuming there are no implied decimal positions in the input format, the input value 12 is displayed in output as 12%.

PCTw.d format does not compute percentages, it just adds the percent sign to the value. The result of 1 divided by 2, for example, is displayed as 0.5% if PCTw.d format is specified.

Variable Widths

- For input formats with fixed data, the default width depends on whether column-style or FORTRAN-like formats are specified. With column-style specifications, there is no default width; the column locations determine the format width. With FORTRAN-like specifications, the default width is one column. If the actual width is greater than one column, you must specify a maximum width.

- For input formats with freefield data, variables are assumed to be type F numeric values that are eight columns wide, including one decimal point and two decimal digits (format F8.2). If a format type is specified, the default width depends on the format type. For example, the default width for F, A, COMMA, and DOT formats is one column; the default width for PCT and DOLLAR formats is two columns. If the actual width is greater than the default width, you must specify the maximum width.

- By default, numeric variables created with COMPUTE, IF, or RECODE, are assigned an output width of eight characters, including a decimal point and two decimal digits (format F8.2). To change the default format, use SET FORMATS.

- The default width of variables declared on the STRING command depends on the specified format type. For example, the default width for format type A is one column. If the actual width is greater than the default width, you must specify the maximum width after the format specification, as in NAME (A20).

- The width specification for FORTRAN-like formats indicates the total number of columns in the data used to code the variable. For example, F3.2 means a value of three columns, including the decimal digits. It does not mean three whole number digits plus two decimal digits.

- If a format width is specified that does not allow enough room to display the values of a variable, SPSS displays the value without decimal values, commas, dollar signs, or percent signs. When the value cannot be reasonably represented in the width provided, SPSS rounds it, uses scientific notation, or displays asterisks (**) in the available space.

Transformation Expressions

Transformation expressions are used in commands like COMPUTE, IF, DO IF, LOOP IF, SELECT IF, etc. The following sections describe the available operators and the three types of functional expressions: numeric expressions, string expressions, and logical expressions.

Numeric Expressions

Numeric expressions can be used with the COMPUTE command and as part of a logical expression for commands such as IF, DO IF, LOOP IF, SELECT IF, and so forth. Arithmetic expressions can also appear in the index portion of a LOOP command, on the REPEATING DATA command, and on the PRINT SPACES command.

Arithmetic Operations

Arithmetic operators and their meanings are

+   *Addition.* (See also the SUM function, described in Statistical Functions, below.)

−   *Subtraction.*

*   *Multiplication.*

/   *Division.*

**   *Exponentiation.* (See also the SQRT function for taking the square root, described in Arithmetic Functions, below.)

- No two operators can appear consecutively.
- Arithmetic operators cannot be implied. For example, (VAR1)(VAR2) cannot be specified in place of VAR1*VAR2.
- The arithmetic operators and the parentheses serve as delimiters. To improve readability, blanks (not commas) can be inserted before and after an operator
- To form complex expressions, use variables, constants, and functions with the arithmetic operators.
- The order in which SPSS executes operations is: functions, then exponentiation, then multiplication, division, and unary −, then addition and subtraction.
- Operators at the same level are executed from left to right.
- To override the order of operation, use parentheses. Execution begins with the innermost set of parentheses and progresses out.

Numeric Constants

- Constants used in numeric expressions or as arguments to functions can be integer or noninteger, depending on the application or the function.
- You can specify as many digits in a constant as needed, as long as you understand the precision restrictions of your computer.
- Numeric constants can be signed (+ or −) but cannot contain any other special characters such as the comma or dollar sign.
- Numeric constants can be expressed with scientific notation. The exponent for a constant in scientific notation is limited to two digits. The range of values allowed for exponents in scientific notation is from −99 to +99.

Complex Numeric Arguments

- Except where explicitly restricted, complex expressions can be formed by nesting functions and arithmetic operators as arguments to functions.
- The order in which SPSS executes complex numeric arguments is the same as for operations: functions, then exponentiation, then multiplication, division, and unary −, and then addition and subtraction.
- To control the order of execution in complex numeric arguments, use parentheses.

Numeric Functions

Numeric functions can be used in any numeric expression on IF, SELECT IF, DO IF, ELSE IF, LOOP IF, END LOOP IF, and COMPUTE. Numeric functions always return numbers (or the system-missing value whenever the result is indeterminate). The expression to be transformed by a function is called the *argument*. Most functions have a variable name or a list of variable names as arguments.

- In numeric functions with two or more arguments, each argument must be separated by a comma.
- Blanks alone cannot be used to separate each variable name, expression, or constant. For example, to generate the square root of variable X, specify variable X as the argument to the SQRT function, as in SQRT(X).
- Enclose arguments in parentheses, as in TRUNC(INCOME), where the TRUNC function returns the integer portion of variable INCOME.
- Separate multiple arguments with commas, as in MEAN(Q1,Q2,Q3), where the MEAN function returns the mean of variables Q1, Q2, and Q3.

Arithmetic Functions

ABS(arg)	*Absolute value.* ABS(SCALE) is 4.7 when SCALE equals 4.7 or −4.7.
RND(arg)	*Round the absolute value to an integer and reaffix the sign.* RND(SCALE) is −5 when SCALE equals −4.7.
TRUNC(arg)	*Truncate to an integer.* TRUNC(SCALE) is −4 when SCALE equals −4.7.
MOD(arg,arg)	*Remainder (modulo) of the first argument divided by the second.* MOD(YEAR,100) is 83 when YEAR equals 1983.
SQRT(arg)	*Square root.* SQRT(SIBS) is 1.41 when SIBS equals 2.
EXP(arg)	*Exponential.* e *is raised to the power of the argument.* EXP(VARA) is 7.39 when VARA equals 2.
LG10(arg)	*Base 10 logarithm.* LG10(VARB) is .48 when VARB equals 3.
LN(arg)	*Natural or Naperian logarithm (base* e). LN(VARC) is 2.30 when VARC equals 10.
ARSIN(arg)	*Arcsine. The result is given in radians (alias ASIN).* ARSIN(ANG) is 1.57 when ANG equals 1.
ARTAN(arg)	*Arctangent. The result is given in radians (alias ATAN).* ARTAN(ANG2) is .79 when ANG2 equals 1.
SIN(arg)	*Sine. The argument must be specified in radians.* SINE(VARC) is .84 when VARC equals 1.
COS(arg)	*Cosine. The argument must be specified in radians.* COS(VARD) is .54 when VARD equals 1.

All arithmetic functions except MOD have single arguments; MOD has two. The arguments to MOD must be separated by a comma. Arguments can be numeric expressions, as in RND(A**2/B).

Statistical Functions

Each argument to a statistical function (expression, variable name, or constant) must be separated by a comma.

SUM(arg list)	*Sum of the values across the argument list.*
MEAN(arg list)	*Mean of the values across the argument list.*
SD(arg list)	*Standard deviation of the values across the argument list.*
VARIANCE(arg list)	*Variance of the values across the argument list.*
CFVAR(arg list)	*Coefficient of variation of the values across the argument list.* The coefficient of variation is the standard deviation divided by the mean.
MIN(arg list)	*Minimum value across the argument list.*
MAX(arg list)	*Maximum value across the argument list.*

- The *.n* suffix can be used with all statistical functions to specify the number of valid arguments. For example,

MEAN.2(A,B,C,D).

returns the mean of the valid values for variables A, B, C, and D only if at least two of the variables have valid values.
- Keyword TO can be used to reference a set of variables in the argument list.

Missing-Value Functions

Each argument to a missing-value function (expression, variable name, or constant) must be separated by a comma.

VALUE(arg)   *Ignore user-defined missing values.* The argument must be a variable name.

MISSING(arg)   *True or 1 if the value is user-missing or system-missing, false or 0 otherwise.*

SYSMIS(arg)   *True or 1 if the value is system-missing and false or 0 otherwise.*

NMISS(arg list)   *Count of the number of system-missing values in the argument list.*

NVALID(arg list)   *Count of the number of valid values in the argument list.*

- Keyword TO can be used to reference a set of variables in the argument list for functions NMISS and NVALID.
- Functions MISSING and SYSMIS are logical functions, which can be useful short cuts to more complicated specifications on the IF, DO IF, and other conditional commands.

Logical Functions

Each argument to a logical function (expression, variable name, or constant) must be separated by a comma.

RANGE(arg,arg list)   *Return 1 or true if the value of the first argument is in the inclusive range(s). Otherwise, return 0 or false.* The first argument is usually a variable, and the list usually contains pairs of values. NONWORK=RANGE (AGE,1,17,62,99) returns 1 for ages 1 through 17 and 62 through 99 inclusive. The value of NONWORK is 0 for any other values of AGE.

ANY(arg,arg list)   *Return 1 or true if the value of the first argument matches one of the arguments in the list. Otherwise, return 0 or false.* The first argument is usually a variable. PARTIC = ANY(PROJECT,3,4,7,9) returns 1 if the value for variable PROJECT is 3, 4, 7, or 9. PARTIC is 0 for other values of PROJECT.

- Functions RANGE and ANY are logical functions, which can be useful short cuts to more complicated specifications on the IF, DO IF, and other conditional commands.
- Logical functions can be used in COMPUTE applications to create logical variables, which have values 0, 1, or missing.
- Logical functions cannot be used as a number or compared to a number within an expression.

Across-Case LAG Function

LAG(arg,n)   *The value of the variable* n *cases before.* The argument must be a numeric variable; the second argument, if specified, must be a positive integer constant. PREV4=LAG(GNP,4) returns the value of GNP for the fourth case before the current one. The first *n* cases have system-missing values for the lagged variable.

Other Functions

UNIFORM(arg)   *A uniform pseudo random number.* The random number is uniformly distributed with values varying between 0 and the value of the argument. SAMP1 = UNIFORM(150) assigns a value to SAMP1 for each case on the file.

NORMAL(arg)   *A normal pseudo random number.* The random number is randomly distributed with a mean of 0 and a standard deviation equal to the argument. SAMP2 = NORMAL(2.5) assigns a value to each case for the variable SAMP2.

CDFNORM(arg)   *Standard normal cumulative distribution.* This function returns the probability that a random variable with the standard normal distribution (mean of 0 and standard deviation equal to 1) falls below the value of the argument. PROBVAL = CDFNORM(VARA) produces the probability values for PROBVAL based on the values of VARA.

PROBIT(arg)   *Inverse of the standard normal cumulative distribution.* The value of the argument must be a probability greater than 0 and less than 1. The function returns the standard normal value having a cumulative probability equal to the argument. IPROBVAL = PROBIT(VARA/100) computes probit values in the variable IPROBVAL based on the values of VARA divided by 100.

Date and Time Functions

Date and time functions provide aggregation, conversion, and extraction routines for representing dates and time intervals. Each function transforms an expression consisting of one or more arguments. Arguments can be complex expressions, variable names, or constants. Most of the dates and time intervals are internally stored and expressed as the number of seconds either from a particular date or in a time interval.

- In SPSS, a *date* is a floating point number representing the number of seconds (or days for YRMODA) from midnight, October 14, 1582 to a later point in time. Thus, dates represent a particular point in time, stored as the number of seconds to that date. A date includes the time of day, which is the time interval past midnight. When time of day is not given, it is taken as 00:00 and the date is an even multiple of 86,400 (the number of seconds in a day).

- A *time interval* is a floating point number representing the number of seconds in a time period, e.g. an hour, minute, or day. For example, the value representing 5.5 days is 475,200; the value representing the time interval 14:08:17 is 50,897.

- Each date and time function stores the number of seconds or days on the active system file. To display these values as dates or time intervals, use the formats for dates and times described in your SPSS *Operations Guide.*

Both dates and time intervals can be used in arithmetic expressions and produce the following results:

- Date plus or minus date yields a time interval.

- Date plus or minus time interval yields a date.

- Time interval plus or minus time interval yields a time interval.

Both dates and times are represented internally as seconds. In the case of dates, the numbers are very large, and arithmetic overflows may result. For instance, dates in the 20th century are on the order of 10 to the 10th power (11 digits). For that reason, a few precautions are in order:

- Some machine environments cannot accommodate the computation of higher powers of date and time variables. For example, computations higher than the sixth power may cause overflows on IBM machines.

- The magnitude of the values may cause inaccuracies in some statistical procedures. It is advisable to subtract a fixed date if you want to keep seconds as the unit, or to convert days using the XDATE.TDAYS function. REGRESSION, CORRELATIONS, ANOVA, and ONEWAY procedures use an adaptive centering method, so their accuracy will not be affected.

- LIST, REPORT and TABLES are the only procedures that display values in date and time formats. The PRINT and WRITE transformation commands can also display and write date and time formats. However, summary variables in REPORT and calculated variables in TABLES display in F format, regardless of the print formats of variables used as arguments.

• All other procedures use the F format in all cases. The default width and number of decimal places is taken from the print format, but the format type is ignored. For example,

```
COMPUTE DATEVAR=DATE.DMY(01,09,57).
PRINT FORMATS DATEVVAR (DATE9).
FREQUENCIES VARIABLES=DATEVAR.
```

returns the value 11830147200, not 01-SEP-57.

• Changing the print format in no way alters the values that are stored in SPSS. For example, if you assign a print format of DATE9 for a variable read with DATETIME format, the time of day will not display but continues to be part of the value. This means that seemingly identical values can be displayed as separate entries within SPSS procedures.

Aggregation Functions Aggregation functions generate dates and time intervals from values that are not read by SPSS date and time input formats.

• Both DATE and TIME include subfunctions that correspond to the type of values found in the data. The subfunctions are separated from each function by a period and are followed by a left parenthesis, the argument list, and then a right parenthesis.

• The arguments to the DATE and TIME functions must be separated by commas and must contain integer values.

DATE.DMY(d,m,y) *Day, month, year.* Combines a day, month, and year. The value of the argument for day must be expressed as an integer between 1 and 31. The value of the argument for month must be expressed as an integer between 1 and 13 (13 returns January of the following year). Years are expressed in two or four digits. A two-digit specification implies a prefix of 19. For example,

```
COMPUTE BIRTHDAY=DATE.DMY(DAY,MONTH,YEAR).
```

stores the value 1.2E+10 when DAY is 8, MONTH is 11, and YEAR is 57. Procedure LIST displays this value. When followed by a PRINT FORMAT of DATE9, as in

```
PRINT FORMAT BIRTHDAY(DATE9).
```

BIRTHDAY is listed as 08-NOV-57.

DATE.MDY(m,d,y) *Month, day, year.* Combines a month, a day, and a year. This function follows the same rules as DATE.DMY, except for the order of the arguments. For example,

```
COMPUTE BIRTHD=DATE.MDY(MONTH,DAY,YEAR).
```

stores the same value, 1.2E+10. When supplied with an ADATE print format

```
PRINT FORMAT BIRTHD(DATE9).
```

displays 11/08/57.

DATE.YRDAY(y,d) *Combines year and day of the year.* The DATE.YRDAY function combines a day of the year and a year. The argument for year can be expressed as either two or four digits. Two-digit years are assumed to have a prefix of 19. The argument for days can be expressed as any number between and including 1 and 366. For example,

```
COMPUTE WHEN=DATE.YRDAY(1688,301).
```

when combined with a DATE print format produces the date 27-OCT-1688.

DATE.QYR(q,y) *Quarter and year.* Combines a quarter and a year. The argument for quarter must contain digits between and including 1 and 4. The argument for year can contain two or four digits, with two-digit values assumed to have a prefix of 19. For example,

```
COMPUTE QUART=DATE.QYR(QTR,YEAR).
```

using a QDATE print format displays lists 4 Q 57 for a value of 4 for QTR and 57 for YEAR.

　　　Each quarter is assumed to begin on the first day of the first month of the quarter, i.e., the first of January, the first of April, etc. If you provide a DATE print format for the same values, QUART is displayed as 01-OCT-57.

DATE.MOYR(m,y)　　*Month and year.* Combines a month and a year. The value of the argument for month must be expressed as an integer between and including 1 and 12. The argument for year can be expressed as two or four digits. For example,

```
COMPUTE START=DATE.MOYR(MONTH,YEAR).
```

with the MOYR print format lists NOV 57 for value 11 for MONTH and 57 for YEAR.

DATE.WKYR(w,y)　　*Week and year.* Combines a week and a year. The argument for week must contain integer values between and including 1 and 53. The argument for years can be represented by two or four digits. For example,

```
COMPUTE WEEK=DATE.WKYR(WK,YEAR).
```

computes variable WEEK, which with a value of 48 for WK, value 57 for YEAR, and a print format of DATE displays 26-NOV-57.

　　　The DATE.WKYR function computes the date starting the week number for a given year. The first week of each year begins on January 1. By calculating $7*(WEEK value-1)+1$ the function produces the date of the start of the week.

TIME.HMS(h,m,s)　　*Hour, minute, and second.* Combines an hour, minute, and second into a time interval. You can supply from one to three arguments. Trailing arguments can be omitted and default to 0. For example, you can supply arguments for hours and minutes and omit seconds, as in

```
COMPUTE PERIOD1=TIME.HMS(NUMHRS,NUMMIN).
```

The value of the first nonzero argument can spill over into the next higher argument. For example, you could have values of 0 for HRS and 90 for MIN in the following:

```
COMPUTE PERIOD2=TIME.HMS(HRS,MIN).
```

With a TIME print format, the value would be displayed as 01:30.

　　　The last argument can contain a noninteger value, as in

```
COMPUTE PERIOD3=TIME.HMS(HRS).
```

where the value of HRS is 1.5 (trailing arguments of MINUTES and SECONDS are assumed to be 0).

　　　Whenever you supply a nonzero argument to a function, each of the lower-level units must be within the range of -60 to $+60$.

TIME.DAYS(d)　　*Days.* Aggregates days into a time interval. The argument can be expressed as any numeric value. For example,

```
COMPUTE NDAYS=TIME.DAYS(SPELL).
```

with a value of 2.5 for SPELL and a DTIME print format lists the value 2 12:00.

Conversion Functions   The conversion functions convert time intervals from one unit of time to another. Time intervals are stored as the number of seconds in the interval; the conversion functions provide a means for calculating more appropriate units, e.g., converting seconds to days.

Each conversion function consists of the CTIME function followed by a period, the target time unit, and an argument. The argument can be made up of expressions, variable names, or constants. The argument must already be a time interval (see Aggregation Functions, above). Time conversions produce non-integer results, with a default format of F8.2.

CTIME.DAYS(arg)   *Days.* Converts a time interval to the number of days. For example, the aggregation function TIME.HMS (HR,MIN,SEC) produces the interval of 45,030 seconds, when HR equals 12, MIN equals 30, and SEC equals 30. Using the following conversion function

```
COMPUTE
    NDAYS=CTIME.DAYS(TIME.HMS(HR,MIN,SEC)).
```

you obtain a value of .52 for NDAYS for the same values of HR, MIN, and, SEC.

CTIME.HOURS(arg)   *Hours.* Converts a time interval to the number of hours. For example, using the same values as above, you could convert the interval to hours by specifying

```
COMPUTE NHOURS=
    CTIME.HOURS(TIME.HMS(HR,MIN,SEC)).
```

This produces a value of 12.51 for NHOURS.

CTIME.MINUTES(arg)   *Minutes.* Converts a time interval to the number of minutes. Again, given the three variables, HR, MIN, and, SEC, you can convert the interval from seconds to minutes by specifying

```
COMPUTE NMINS=
    CTIME.MINUTES(TIME.HMS(HR,MIN,SEC)).
```

For the values above, this produces a value of 750.50 for NMINS.

Since time and dates are stored internally as seconds, a function that converts to seconds is not necessary.

YRMODA Function   **YRMODA(arg list)**   *Convert year, month, and day to a day number.* The number returned is the number of days since October 14, 1582 (day 1 of the Gregorian calendar).

- Arguments for YRMODA can be variables, constants, or any other type of numeric expression but must yield integers.
- Year, month, and day must be specified in that order.
- The first argument can be any year between 0 and 99, or between 1582 to 47516.
- If the first argument yields a number between 00 and 99, 1900 through 1999 is assumed.
- The month can range from 1 through 13. Month 13 yields the last day of the year—as in YRMODA(YEAR,13,0)— or the first month of the coming year—as in YRMODA(YEAR,13,DAY).
- The day can range from 0 through 31. Day 0 is the last day of the previous month regardless of whether it is 28, 29, 30, or 31. For example, YRMODA(YEAR,MONTH + 1,0) is the last day of variable MONTH.
- Returns a missing value if any of the three arguments is missing.
- Returns a missing value if the arguments do not form a valid date after October 14, 1582.

Extraction Functions

The extraction functions extract subfields from date or time interval values, targeting the day or a time from a date value. This permits you to classify events by day of the week, season, shift, etc.

Each extraction function consists of the function name followed by a period, the subfunction name (what you want to extract), and an argument. The argument can be an expression, variable name, or constant, provided the argument is already in date form.

XDATE.MDAY(arg)

Returns day number in a month. Returns the day number of the date, expressed as an integer between 1 and 31. The date must have occurred after October 14, 1582.

For example, assume that you have a variable called BIRTHDAY read with a DATE20 format, and the value 05-DEC-1954 5:30:15. You can use the XDATE.MDAY function to extract the day number, as in:

```
COMPUTE DAYNUM=XDATE.MDAY(BIRTHDAY).
```

This yields the value 5 for DAYNUM.

XDATE.MONTH(arg)

Returns month number. Returns the month number from a date, expressed as an integer between 1 and 12. The date must have occurred after October 14, 1582. The command

```
COMPUTE MONTHNUM=XDATE.MONTH(BIRTHDAY).
```

extracts the month number 12 from BIRTHDAY, when BIRTHDAY is read in as DATE20 and contains the value 05-DEC-1954 5:30:15.

In addition you could provide a print format of MONTH12, as in

```
PRINT FORMAT MONTHNUM(MONTH12).
```

to spell out the month of DECEMBER.

XDATE.YEAR(arg)

Returns year. Returns a four-digit year from a date. The date must have occurred after October 14, 1582. The command

```
COMPUTE YEAR=XDATE.YEAR(BIRTHDAY).
```

returns the year 1954 when BIRTHDAY has the same values above.

XDATE.HOUR(arg)

Returns hour of the day. Returns the hour from a date (or time of day), expressed as an integer between 0 and 23. For example,

```
COMPUTE HOUR=XDATE.HOUR(BIRTHDAY).
```

returns 5 for the value of BIRTHDAY described above.

XDATE.MINUTE(arg)

Returns minute of the hour. Returns the minute of the hour from a date (or time of day), expressed as an integer from 0 through 59. For example,

```
COMPUTE MIN=XDATE.MINUTE(BIRTHDAY).
```

returns 30 for the value of BIRTHDAY described above.

XDATE.SECOND(arg)

Returns second of a minute. Returns the second of minute from a date or time of day. Expressed as an integer or, if there are fractional seconds, with decimals.

```
COMPUTE SEC=XDATE.SECOND(BIRTHDAY).
```

extracts seconds from the value of BIRTHDAY, resulting in a value of 15.00 for the date above.

XDATE.WKDAY(arg)

Returns day number within a week. Returns the integer number of the day within a week from a date. The date must have occurred after October 14, 1582. The day numbers are from 1 to 7, with Sunday being 1 and Saturday being 7. For example,

```
COMPUTE DAYNAME=XDATE.WKDAY(BIRTHDAY).
```

returns the value 1 for the value of BIRTHDAY of 05-DEC-1954 05:30:15. If you provide a format of WKDAY, as in

```
PRINT FORMAT DAYNAME (WKDAY9).
```

you obtain the value SUNDAY for DAYNAME.

XDATE.JDAY(arg) *Returns day number within a year.* Returns the day of the year, expressed as an integer between 1 and 366. The date must have occurred after October 14, 1582. The command

```
COMPUTE DAYNUM=XDATE.JDAY(BIRTHDAY).
```

returns the value 339 for BIRTHDAY for the date described above.

XDATE.QUARTER(arg) *Returns quarter number within a year.* This function returns the quarter number a date falls in, expressed as 1, 2, 3, or 4. The date must have occurred after October 14, 1582. To find out the quarter in which BIRTHDAY occurred, use

```
COMPUTE Q=XDATE.QUARTER(BIRTHDAY).
```

When BIRTHDAY equals 5-DEC-1954 05:30:15, the value of Q equals 4.

XDATE.WEEK(arg) *Returns week number within a year.* Returns the week number of a date, expressed as an integer between 1 and 53. The date must have occurred after October 14, 1582. The command

```
COMPUTE WEEKNUM=XDATE.WEEK(BIRTHDAY).
```

returns the value 49 for the value of BIRTHDAY described above.

XDATE.TDAY(arg) *Returns number of days in a time interval.* The XDATE.TDAY extraction function returns the number of days in a time period or in the interval from October 14, 1582 to a given date. The value returned is an integer (the fractional portion of a day is ignored). For example,

```
COMPUTE NDAYS=XDATE.TDAY(BIRTHDAY).
```

returns the value 135922, indicating the number of days between October 14, 1582 and December 5, 1954 (the value of BIRTHDAY described above).

XDATE.TIME(arg) *Returns time of day.* This function extracts the time of day from a date, expressed as the number of elapsed seconds since midnight of that date. For example,

```
COMPUTE ELSEC=XDATE.TIME(BIRTHDAY).
```

extracts the value 19815 for the value of BIRTHDAY described above. In addition, you can provide a TIME print format, as in

```
PRINT FORMAT ELSEC(TIME8).
```

to obtain the value 5:30:15 from procedure LIST.

XDATE.DATE(arg) *Returns the date portion of a date.* The XDATE.DATE extraction function returns the integral date portion of a date or the number of elapsed seconds between midnight October 14, 1582 and midnight of the date in question. The date must have occurred after October 14, 1582. To extract the date from variable BIRTHDAY, use

```
COMPUTE BRTHDATE=XDATE.DATE(BIRTHDAY).
PRINT FORMAT BRTHDATE(ADATE8).
```

These two commands produce the value 12/05/54 for the value of BIRTHDAY described above.

Missing Values

- Missing values arise in numeric expressions for reasons other than when SPSS encounters missing values in variables. Certain arithmetic operations, such as division by zero, produce the system-missing value. SPSS also returns a system-missing value for operations that involve functions with arguments that cannot be evaluated.

- Some arithmetic operations involving 0 produce the same results regardless of what values are used. In these cases, SPSS evaluates the operation even when the variables have missing values. These operations are presented in Table 4.

Table 4 Missing-value exceptions in numeric expressions

Expression	Result
0 * missing	= 0
0 / missing	= 0
missing ** 0	= 1
0 ** missing	= 0
MOD(0,missing)	= 0

Missing Values in Arguments

- SPSS tries to evaluate a function using all the information it has and returns the system-missing value only when it doesn't have enough information. Table 5 shows when each function returns a system-missing value.

- Arithmetic functions that take only one argument cannot be evaluated if that argument is missing. The date and time functions cannot be missing on any argument. Otherwise, the result is system-missing. However, statistical functions are evaluated if a sufficient number of arguments are valid.

- The .n suffix can be used with the statistical functions SUM, MEAN, MIN, MAX, SD, VARIANCE, and CFVAR to specify the number of valid arguments you consider acceptable. For example, to compute FACTOR only if a case has valid information for at least two scores, use the .n suffix with the SUM function, as in:

```
COMPUTE FACTOR = SUM.2(SCORE1 TO SCORE3).
```

This command instructs SPSS to sum any two or more valid scores and to return a missing value otherwise.

Domain Errors

Domain errors occur when numeric expressions are mathematically undefined or are numerically unrepresentable on the computer for reasons other than missing data. Two common examples are division by zero and the square root of a negative number. When SPSS detects a domain error in an expression, it issues a warning message and returns the system-missing value for that expression. For example, the command

```
COMPUTE TESTVAR = TRUNC(SQRT(X/Y) * .5).
```

returns system-missing if X or Y is negative or if Y is 0.

The following are domain errors in numeric expressions:

**	*A negative number to a noninteger power.*
/	*A divisor of 0.*
MOD	*A divisor of 0.*
SQRT	*A negative argument.*
EXP	*An argument that produces a result too large to be represented on the computer.*
LG10	*A negative or 0 argument.*
LN	*A negative or 0 argument.*
ARSIN	*An argument whose absolute value exceeds 1.*
NORMAL	*A negative or 0 argument.*
YRMODA	*Arguments that do not form a valid date.*
PROBIT	*A negative argument, zero, or an argument 1 or greater.*

Table 5 Missing values in arguments to functions

Function	Returns system-missing if
ABS (x)	x is missing
ARSIN (x)	
ARTAN (x)	
CDFNORM (x)	
COS (x)	
EXP (x)	
LG10 (x)	
LN (x)	
NORMAL (x)	
PROBIT (x)	
RND (x)	
SIN (x)	
SQRT (x)	
TRUNC (x)	
UNIFORM (x)	
VALUE (x)	x is system-missing
YRMODA (x1,x2,x3)	any x is missing
MOD (x1,x2)	x1 is missing, or x2 is missing and x1 is not 0
MAX.n (x1,x2,...xk)	fewer than n arguments are valid
MEAN.n (x1,x2,...xk)	(NVALID (x1,x2,...xk) < n)
MIN.n (x1,x2,...x1)	default n is 1
SUM.n (x1,x2,...xk)	
CFVAR.n (x1,x2,...xk)	fewer than n arguments are valid
SD.n (x1,x2,...xk)	(NVALID (x1,x2,...xk) < n)
VARIANCE.n (x1,x2,...xk)	default n is 2
LAG (x,n)	x is missing n cases previously (and always for the first n cases)
ANY (x,x1,x2,...xk)	x or all of x1,x2,...xk are missing
RANGE (x,x1,x2,...xk)	x or all of pairs x1,x2, etc. are missing
MISSING (x)	never
NMISS (x1,x2,...xk)	
NVALID (x1,x2,...xk)	
SYSMIS (x)	

String Expressions

Expressions involving string variables can be used in COMPUTE commands and in logical expressions on commands such as IF, DO IF, LOOP IF, SELECT IF, etc.

• A string expression can be a constant enclosed in apostrophes (for example, 'IL'), a string function (see String Functions), or another string variable.

• An expression must return a string if the target variable is string.

• The string returned by a string expression does not have to be the same length as the target variable, but no warning messages are issued if the lengths are not the same. If the target variable in a COMPUTE command is shorter, the result is right-trimmed. If the target variable is longer, the result is right-padded.

String variables, like numeric variables, can be tested in logical expressions.

• String variables must be declared before they can be used in a string expression.

- String variables cannot be compared to numeric variables.
- If strings of different lengths are compared, the shorter string is right-padded with blanks to equal the length of the longer.
- The magnitude of strings can be compared using LT, GT, and so forth, but the success or failure of the comparison depends on the sorting sequence of the particular computer. Use with caution.
- The functions ANY and RANGE can be used instead of more complicated specifications on the IF, DO IF, and other conditional commands. For example, the command

```
SELECT IF (REGION EQ 'NW' OR REGION EQ 'NE' OR REGION EQ 'SE').
```

is equivalent to the command

```
SELECT IF ANY(REGION,'NW','NE','SE').
```

- With functions LPAD, RPAD, LTRIM, and RTRIM, if the length argument (which can be an expression) is illegal or missing, the result is a null string. If the pad or trim is the only operation, the string is then padded to its entire length with blanks. If the operation is nested, the null string is passed to the next nested level.
- The INDEX, RINDEX, and SUBSTR functions can be used to pull out substrings of varying position and length.
- If the result of the SUBSTR function is shorter than LAST, the string is left-justified and padded with blanks.
- If a numeric argument to SUBSTR is illegal or missing, the result is a null string. If SUBSTR is the only operation, the string is then padded to its entire length with blanks. If the operation is nested, the null string is passed to the next nested level.
- If a numeric argument to INDEX or RINDEX is illegal or missing, the result is system-missing.
- When two strings are compared, the case in which they are entered is honored. The LOWER and UPCASE functions are useful for making comparisons of strings regardless of case.
- For certain functions (for example, MIN, MAX, ANY, and RANGE), the outcome will be affected by case, whether the string includes numbers or special characters, and the character set used at your installation. For example, with EBCDIC character sets, lower case precedes upper case in the sort order. Therefore, if NAME1 is in lower case and NAME2 is in upper case, MIN(NAME1,NAME2) will invariably return NAME1 as the minimum. The reverse is true with the ASCII character set, which sorts upper before lower case.
- With LAG, undefined lags for string variables are set to blanks. Thus, if LAG(LNAME,2) is specified, blanks will be returned for the first two cases in the file.
- The second argument of a LAG function must be a positive integer constant.
- When LAG is used with commands that select cases (for example, SELECT IF and SAMPLE), LAG counts cases *after* case selection, even if SELECT IF follows LAG. Therefore, to achieve the desired result, a procedure or EXECUTE may have to be placed between LAG and the commands that select cases.

String Functions

Except where otherwise noted, the target variable for each of the string functions must be a string and must have already been declared. Multiple arguments in a list must be separated by commas.

ANY(arg,arg list)   *Return 1 if the value of the first argument matches one of the arguments in the list. Otherwise, return 0.* For example, ANY(LNAME,'MARTIN','JONES','EVANS') returns 1 for people whose last names are MARTIN, JONES, or EVANS. The target variable must be numeric. ANY is also available as a numeric function.

CONCAT(arg list)

Concatenate the arguments into a string. String variables and strings can be intermixed as arguments. CONCAT(A,'**') creates the string ABCD** for a case with value ABCD for string variable A.

INDEX (a_1,a_2,a_3)

Return a number that indicates the position of the first occurrence of a_2 in a_1. a_1 is the string which will be searched. a_2 is the string variable or string which will be used in the search. If a_3 is not specified, all of a_2 will be used. INDEX(ALPHA6,'**') returns 2 for a case with value X***** for variable ALPHA6. The optional a_3 is the number of characters used to divide a_2 into separate strings to be used for searching. a_3 must be a positive integer and must divide evenly into the length of a_2. The target variable must be numeric. If a_2 is not found within a_1, the value 0 is returned.

LAG(arg,n)

Return the value of the variable n *cases before.* LAG(LNAME,2) returns the value of LNAME for the case that is two cases before the current one. *n* must be a positive integer constant. LAG as a numeric function is also available.

LENGTH(arg)

Return the length of the specified string. The argument can be a string variable or value. LENGTH(LNAME) returns 6 if LNAME has an A6 format. The target variable must be numeric.

LOWER(arg)

Convert upper case to lower case. All other characters remain unchanged. The argument can be a string variable or value. LOWER(NAME1) returns charles if the value of NAME1 is CHARLES.

LPAD (a_1,a_2,a_3)

Pad left. Pad the beginning of a_1 up to the length specified by a_2 using the optional single-character a_3 as the pad character. a_2 must be a positive integer from 1 to 255. The default pad character is a blank. LPAD(ALPHA1,10) adds four leading blanks to the target variable if ALPHA1 has an A6 format. a_3 can be any character enclosed in apostrophes or any expression that yields a single character.

LTRIM (a_1,a_2)

Trim left. Trim the character a_2 from the beginning of a_1. LTRIM(ALPHA3,'0') trims leading zeros from variable ALPHA3. a_2 can be any character enclosed in apostrophes or any expression that yields a single character. The default a_2 is a blank.

MAX(arg list)

Return the maximum value across the argument list. MAX(LNAME,FNAME) selects the name that comes last in the sort order, the first or the last name. MAX is also available as a numeric function.

MIN(arg list)

Return the minimum value across the argument list. MIN(LNAME,FNAME) selects the name that comes first in the sort order, the first or the last name. MIN is also available as a numeric function.

NUMBER(arg,format)

Convert the argument into a number using the format. The argument is string and the format is a numeric format, but the result is numeric. The string is essentially reread using the format and returned as a number. NUMBER (XALPHA,F3.1) converts the string XALPHA to a number using the F3.1 format. Returns the system-missing value if the conversion is invalid.

RANGE(arg,arg list)

Return 1 if the first argument is in any of the inclusive range(s). Otherwise, return 0. The first argument is usually a variable, and the list normally includes pairs of values. RANGE(LNAME,'A','MZZZZZZ') returns 1 for last names which begin with a letter between "A" and "M." The target variable must be numeric. RANGE is also available as a numeric function.

RINDEX (a₁,a₂,a₃) — *Return a number indicating the position of the last occurrence of a_2 in a_1.* a_1 is the string which will be searched. a_2 is the string variable or string which will be used in the search. If a_3 is not specified, all of a_2 will be used. RINDEX(NAME,'N') returns 14 for a case with value STEVEN RACHMAN for variable NAME. The optional a_3 is the number of characters used to divide a_2 into separate strings to be used for searching. a_3 must be a positive integer and must divide evenly into the length of a_2. The target variable must be numeric. If a_2 is not found within a_1, the value 0 is returned.

RPAD (a₁,a₂,a₃) — *Pad right.* Pad the end of a_1 up to the length of a_2 using the optional single-character a_3 as the pad character. a_2 must be a positive integer from 1 to 255. The default pad character is a blank. RPAD(ALPHA2,8,'*') adds two trailing asterisks to the target variable if ALPHA2 has an A6 format. a_3 can be any character enclosed in apostrophes.

RTRIM (a₁,a₂) — *Trim right.* Trim the character a_2 from the end of a_1. RTRIM(ALPHA4,'*') trims trailing asterisks from variable ALPHA4. a_2 can be any character enclosed in apostrophes or any expression that yields a single character. The default a_2 is a blank.

STRING(arg,format) — *Convert the argument into a string using the format.* The argument is numeric and the format is a numeric format, but the result is a string. The number is converted from internal representation according to the format and then stored as a string. STRING (INCOME,DOLLAR8) converts the numeric variable INCOME to the dollar format and returns it as a string value. If the result is shorter than the string variable, it is right-justified. If the result is longer than the string variable, it is right-trimmed.

SUBSTR (a₁,a₂,a₃) — *Substring.* Return the substring of a_1 beginning with the position in a_2 and optionally for a length of a_3. a_2 can be a positive integer from 1 to the length of a_1. a_3, when added to a_2, should not exceed the length of a_1. If a_3 is not specified, the substring is returned up to the end of a_1. SUBSTR(ALPHA6,3) returns the last four characters of ALPHA6 if ALPHA6 has an A6 format. SUBSTR (ALPHA6,3,1) returns the third character of ALPHA6. You can also use the SUBSTR function on the left side of the equals sign to replace a substring in a_1 with a string to the right of the equals sign. a_2 is a positive number that specifies the position of the first character to be replaced and a_3 indicates the length of the replacement string. If you omit a_3 and the string on the right side of the equals sign is shorter than the length of the substring, the result will be right-padded with blanks to the length of the substring. If you omit a_3, and the string on the right side of the equals sign is longer than the length of the substring, the result will be truncated to the length of the substring.

UPCASE(arg) — *Convert lower case to upper case.* The argument can be a string variable or a string. UPCASE(NAME1) returns CHARLES if the value of NAME1 is Charles.

Logical Expressions

Logical expressions can appear on the IF, SELECT IF, DO IF, ELSE IF, LOOP, END LOOP, and COMPUTE commands. SPSS evaluates a logical expression as true or false, or as missing, if it is indeterminate. A logical expression returns 1 if the expression is true, 0 if it is false, or system-missing if it is missing. Thus, logical expressions can be any expressions that yield this three-valued logic.

- The simplest logical expression is a logical variable. A logical variable is any variable that takes on values 1, 0, or system-missing. Logical variables cannot be strings.
- Logical expressions can be simple logical variables or relations, or they can be complex logical tests involving variables, constants, functions, relational operators, logical operators, and nested parentheses to control the order of evaluation.
- A logical expression on an IF command that is true causes the assignment expression to be executed. A logical expression that returns missing has the same effect as one that is false: the value of the target variable is not altered.
- If a logical expression on a DO IF command is true, SPSS executes the commands immediately following the DO IF up to the next ELSE IF, ELSE, or END IF. A false logical expression on a DO IF command causes SPSS to look for the next ELSE IF or ELSE command. A logical expression on a DO IF command that returns missing causes the entire structure to be skipped.
- If the logical expression on a SELECT IF command is true, the case is selected. A logical expression that returns missing has the same effect as one that is false: the case is not selected.
- If an IF logical expression on a LOOP command is true, looping begins (or continues). An IF logical expression on a LOOP command that returns missing has the same effect as one that is false: the structure is skipped. On the END LOOP command, if an IF logical expression is false, control returns to the LOOP command for that structure and looping continues. If it is true, looping stops and the structure is terminated. An IF command that returns a missing value has the same effect as one that is true: the structure is terminated.

Relational Operators

A relation is a logical expression that compares two values using a *relational operator*. In the command

```
IF (X EQ 0) Y=1.
```

variable X and 0 are expressions that yield the values to be compared by the EQ relational operator. Relational operators are

EQ   *Equal to.* Returns true if the expression on the left is exactly equal to the expression on the right.

NE   *Not equal to.* Returns true if the expression on the left does not equal the expression on the right.

LT   *Less than.* Returns true if the expression on the left is less than the expression on the right.

LE   *Less than or equal to.* Returns true if the expression on the left is less than or equal to the expression on the right.

GT   *Greater than.* Returns true if the expression on the left is greater than the expression on the right.

GE   *Greater than or equal to.* Returns true if the expression on the left is greater than or equal to the expression on the right.

- Relational operators can be expressed as symbols or two-letter keywords: = (EQ), ¬= or <> (NE), < (LT), > (GT), <= (LE), and >= (GE).
- The expressions in a relation can be variables, constants, or more complicated arithmetic expressions.
- Blanks (not commas) must be used to separate the relational operator from the expressions. To make the command more readable, use extra blanks or parentheses.
- The result of the logical functions SYSMIS, MISSING, ANY, or RANGE cannot be compared to a number within an expression.

AND and OR Logical Operators

Two or more relations can be logically joined using the *logical operators* AND and OR. Logical operators combine relations according to the following rules:

AND   *Both relations must be true.*

OR   *Either relation can be true.*

- The ampersand (&) symbol is a valid substitute for the logical operator AND. The | (vertical bar) or ¦ (broken vertical bar) symbols are valid substitutes for the logical operator OR.
- Only one logical operator can be used to combine two relations; AND/OR is invalid. However, multiple relations can be combined into a complex logical expression.
- Regardless of the number of relations and logical operators used to build a logical expression, the result is either true, false, or indeterminate because of missing values.
- Operators or expressions cannot be implied. For example, X EQ 1 OR 2 cannot be used in place of X EQ 1 OR X EQ 2.
- The ANY and RANGE functions can be used to simplify complex expressions.

NOT Logical Operator

The NOT logical operator reverses the true/false outcome of the expression that immediately follows.

- The NOT operator affects only the expression that immediately follows, unless more than one expression is enclosed in parentheses.
- The ¬ symbol is a valid substitute for the NOT keyword.

Order of Evaluation

When arithmetic operators and functions are used in a logical expression, the order of operations is exactly the same as for the COMPUTE command: functions and arithmetic operations are evaluated first, then relational operators, then NOT, then AND, and then OR.

- When more than one logical operator is used, AND is evaluated before OR.
- To change the order of evaluation, use parentheses.

Missing Values

If the logic of an expression is indeterminate because of missing values, the expression returns a missing value, and the command is not executed. In a simple relation, the logic is indeterminate if the expression on either side of the relational operator is missing.

Missing Values and Logical Operators

When two or more relations are joined by logical operators AND and OR, SPSS always returns a missing value if all of the relations in the expression are missing. However, if any one of the relations can be determined, SPSS tries to return true or false according to the logical outcomes shown in Table 6. The asterisk flags expressions where SPSS can evaluate the outcome with incomplete information.

Table 6 Logical outcome

Expression	Outcome	Expression	Outcome
true AND true	= true	true OR true	= true
true AND false	= false	true OR false	= true
false AND false	= false	false OR false	= false
true AND missing	= missing	true OR missing	= true*
missing AND missing	= missing	missing OR missing	= missing
false AND missing	= false*	false OR missing	= missing

- When two relations are joined with the AND operator, the logical expression can never be true if one of the relations is indeterminate. The expression can, however, be false.
- If one of the relations is false and the other is missing, the logical expression is evaluated as false and only the DO IF command is skipped.
- When two relations are joined with the OR operator, the logical expression can never be false if one relation returns missing.

Commands

ADD FILES

```
ADD FILES FILE={file}
              {*   }

[/RENAME=(old varlist=new varlist)...]

[/IN=varname]

[/FILE=...]

[/BY varlist]

[/MAP]

[/KEEP={ALL**   }] [/DROP=varlist]
        {varlist}

[/FIRST=varname]  [/LAST=varname]
```
**Default if the subcommand is omitted.

Example:

```
ADD FILES FILE=SCHOOL1 /FILE=SCHOOL2.
```

Overview

ADD FILES combines cases from two to fifty SPSS system files by *concatenating* or *interleaving* cases. When cases are concatenated, all cases from one file are added to the end of all cases from another file. When cases are interleaved, cases in the resulting file are ordered according to the values of one or more key variables.

ADD FILES works with the active system file and with SPSS system files created by the SAVE or XSAVE commands. ADD FILES combines files to produce a new active file. Statistical procedures following ADD FILES use this combined file unless you replace it by building another active file. You must use the SAVE or XSAVE commands if you want to save the file to disk as a system file.

In general, ADD FILES combines files containing the same variables but different cases. See MATCH FILES for combining files containing the same cases but different variables. Also, see UPDATE for updating existing system files. ADD FILES cannot be used to concatenate raw data files. To concatenate raw data files, use DATA LIST within an INPUT PROGRAM structure (see DATA LIST or INPUT PROGRAM for an example). Alternatively, convert the raw data files to system files with the SAVE or XSAVE commands, and then use ADD FILES to combine the system files. On some systems, such as OS/2, the files added can be either SPSS or SPSS/PC+ system files. For more information, see the SPSS *Operations Guide* for your system.

Options

Variable Selection. You can choose which variables from each input file are retained in the new active file.

Variable Names. You can rename variables on each input file before combining the files. This permits you to combine variables that are the same but whose names differ on different input files or to distinguish different variables whose names are the same on different input files.

Variable Flag. You can create a variable that indicates whether a case came from the input file named on the preceding FILE subcommand. When interleaving cases, you can also create a variable that flags the first or last case of a group of cases with the same value on the BY variable.

Variable Map. You can request a map showing all the variables in the new active file, their order, and the input file(s) from which they came.

Basic Specification

- The basic specification is two or more FILE subcommands, each of which specifies a file to be combined into a new active file. If cases are to be interleaved, BY is also required. BY specifies the key variable(s).
- All variables from all input files are included in the new active file unless DROP or KEEP is specified.

Subcommand Order

- RENAME and IN must immediately follow the FILE subcommand to which they apply.
- BY, FIRST, and LAST must be used after all FILE subcommands and their associated RENAME and IN subcommands.
- MAP, DROP, and KEEP must be placed after all FILE and RENAME subcommands.

Syntax Rules

- RENAME can be repeated after each FILE subcommand. RENAME applies only to variables in the file named on the immediately preceding FILE subcommand.
- BY can only be specified once. However, multiple variables can be specified on BY. When BY is used, all files must be sorted in ascending order by the key variable(s) on BY (see SORT).
- FIRST and LAST cannot be used when files are concatenated. They are available only for interleaving cases. (Thus, FIRST and LAST can only be used when BY is used.)
- MAP can be repeated as often as desired.

Operations

- ADD FILES causes all input files named on FILE to be read and builds a new active system file that replaces any active file created earlier in the session. The resulting file is built when the data are read by one of the procedure commands or the EXECUTE, SAVE, or SORT CASES commands.
- The resulting file contains complete dictionary information copied from the input files, including variable names, labels, print and write formats, and missing-value indicators. The resulting file also contains the documents from each of the input files, unless the DROP DOCUMENTS command is used to drop the document text from the resulting file.
- ADD FILES copies all variables in order from the first input file, then all variables in order from the second input file, and so on. Variables that are not common among all files receive the system-missing value for cases that do not contain those variables.
- BY specifies that cases should be interleaved according to a value common to one or more key variables present in all input files. All input files must be sorted in ascending order of the key variables. If BY is not used, SPSS concatenates files.
- If the active file is named as an input file, any N and SAMPLE commands that have been specified are applied to the active file before files are combined.

Limitations

- Maximum 50 files can be combined on one ADD FILES command.
- Maximum 1 BY subcommand. However, BY can specify multiple variables.

- The TEMPORARY command cannot be in effect for any active file that is used as an input file.
- MAP cannot be used for a map of more than 12 files.

Example   `ADD FILES FILE=SCHOOL1 /FILE=SCHOOL2.`

- ADD FILES combines two SPSS system files by concatenating cases. All cases from SCHOOL1 precede all cases from SCHOOL2 in the resulting file.

- If one file has variables that are not included in the other file, those variables receive the system-missing value for all cases that do not have values for the variables that are not in both files.

Example
```
SORT CASES BY LOCATN DEPT.
ADD FILES  FILE=SOURCE /FILE=* /BY LOCATN DEPT
   /KEEP AVGHOUR AVGRAISE LOCATN DEPT SEX HOURLY RAISE /MAP.
SAVE OUTFILE=PRSNNL.
```

- SORT CASES sorts the active file in ascending order by the variables to be named as key variables on ADD FILES.

- ADD FILES specifies two files to be combined: the SOURCE system file and the sorted active file. File SOURCE must also be sorted by LOCATN and DEPT.

- BY indicates that the keys for interleaving cases are the same variables used on SORT CASES: LOCATN and DEPT.

- KEEP specifies the subset and order of variables to be retained on the resulting file.

- MAP provides a listing of the variables in the resulting file and the two input files.

- SAVE saves the resulting file as a new SPSS system file.

FILE Subcommand

FILE identifies each input file to be combined. A separate FILE subcommand must be used to specify each input file.

- An asterisk may be specified on FILE to indicate the current active file.

- The order in which files are named on successive FILE subcommands determines the order of cases on the new active file.

Raw Data Files

To add cases from a raw data file, you must first define the raw data file as the active file by using the DATA LIST command. ADD FILES can then combine the active system file with an SPSS system file.

Example
```
DATA LIST FILE=GASDATA/1 OZONE 10-12 CO 20-22 SULFUR 30-32.
ADD FILES  FILE=PARTICLE /FILE=*.
SAVE  OUTFILE=POLLUTE.
```

- The GASDATA file is a raw data file and is defined on the DATA LIST command.

- The PARTICLE file is a previously saved system file.

- FILE=* on ADD FILES specifies the active file, which is now the gas data. FILE=PARTICLE specifies the PARTICLE system file.

- SAVE saves the resulting active file as a system file with the file name POLLUTE. In file POLLUTE, cases that came from the active file follow all cases that came from file PARTICLE.

RENAME Subcommand

RENAME renames variables on the input files *before* they are processed by ADD FILES. RENAME must follow the FILE subcommand that contains the variables that will be renamed.

- RENAME applies only to the immediately preceding FILE subcommand. To rename variables from more than one input file, enter a RENAME subcommand after each FILE subcommand that has variables to rename.

- Specifications for RENAME consist of a left parenthesis, a list of old variable names, an equals sign, a list of new variable names, and a right parenthesis. The two variable lists must have the same number of variables. If only one variable is renamed, the parentheses are optional.

- More than one such specification can be entered on a single RENAME subcommand, each enclosed in parentheses.

- The TO keyword can be used both to refer to consecutive variables to be renamed (on the left side of the equals sign) and to generate new names (on the right side of the equals sign).

- RENAME takes effect immediately. Any KEEP and DROP subcommands entered prior to a RENAME must use the old names, while KEEP and DROP subcommands entered after a RENAME must use the new names.

- All specifications within a single set of parentheses take effect simultaneously: the specification RENAME (A,B = B,A) is legal and swaps the names of the two variables.

- You can use RENAME to correct a situation where a key variable has different names on different input files. Since BY must be entered last, it always uses the new name of a key variable.

- Variables cannot be renamed to scratch variables.

- Input system files are not changed on disk; only the copy of the file being combined is affected.

Example
```
ADD FILES FILE=CLIENTS /RENAME=(TEL_NO, ID_NO = PHONE, ID)
/FILE=MASTER /BY ID.
```

- ADD FILES adds new client cases from file CLIENTS to existing client cases in file MASTER.

- Two variables on CLIENTS are renamed prior to the match. TEL_NO is renamed PHONE to match the name used for phone numbers on the master file. ID_NO is renamed ID so that it will have the same name as the identification variable in the master file and can be used on the BY subcommand.

- The BY subcommand ensures that cases are ordered according to client ID numbers.

BY Subcommand

BY specifies one or more identification or key variables that determine the order in which cases are added to the resulting file. When BY is specified, cases from one file are matched with cases from other files having the same values for the key variables.

- BY must follow the FILE subcommands and any associated RENAME and IN subcommands.

- BY must specify the names of one or more key variables. The key variables must be present in all input files and have the same names in all input files. The key variables may be string variables (long strings are allowed).

- All input files must be sorted by the key variable(s), in ascending order. If necessary, use SORT CASES before ADD FILES.

- Cases in the resulting file are ordered by the values of the key variable(s). All cases from the first file with a value for the key variable are included in the resulting file followed by all cases from the second file with the same value followed by all cases from the third file with the same value, and so forth. Then all cases from the first file with the next value from the key variable display, and cases from the input files continue to be interleaved according to the value of the key variable(s).

- Missing values on key variables are handled like any other values.

DROP and KEEP Subcommands

DROP and KEEP are used to include only a subset of variables on the new active file. DROP specifies a set of variables to exclude, and KEEP specifies a set of variables to retain. These subcommands apply only to the resulting file and must follow all FILE and RENAME subcommands.

- DROP and KEEP must specify one or more variables. Keyword TO can be used to refer to consecutive variables. If RENAME is used to rename variables, specify the new names on DROP and KEEP.
- Keyword ALL can be specified on KEEP. ALL must be the last specification on KEEP, and it refers to all variables not previously named on KEEP.
- DROP cannot be used with variables created by the IN, FIRST, or LAST subcommand.
- KEEP can be used to change the order of variables in the resulting file. With KEEP, variables are kept in the order they are listed on the subcommand. If a variable is named more than once on KEEP, only the first mention of the variable is in effect; all subsequent references to that variable name are ignored.

Example

```
ADD FILES FILE=PARTICLE /RENAME=(PARTIC=POLLUTE1)
   /FILE=GAS /RENAME=(OZONE TO SULFUR=POLLUTE2 TO POLLUTE4)
   /DROP=POLLUTE4.
```

- The renamed variable POLLUTE4 is dropped from the resulting file. DROP is specified after all the FILE and RENAME subcommands, and it refers to the dropped variable by its new name.

IN Subcommand

IN creates a flag variable in the resulting file that indicates whether a case came from the input file named on the preceding FILE subcommand. IN applies only to the file specified on the immediately preceding FILE subcommand.

- IN has only one specification, the name of the flag variable.
- The variable created by IN has the value 1 for every case that came from the associated input file, or the value 0 if the case came from a different input file.
- Variables created by IN are automatically attached to end of the resulting file and cannot be dropped. If FIRST or LAST are used, the variable created by IN precedes the variable(s) created by FIRST or LAST.

Example

```
ADD FILES  FILE=WEEK10 /FILE=WEEK11 /IN=INWEEK11 /BY=EMPID.
```

- IN creates the variable INWEEK11, which has the value 1 for all cases in the resulting file that came from the input file WEEK11 and the value 0 for those cases that were not in file WEEK11.

Example

```
ADD FILES  FILE=WEEK10 /FILE=WEEK11 /IN=INWEEK11 /BY=EMPID.
SELECT IF  (NOT INWEEK11).
```

- The variable created by IN is used to screen partially missing cases for subsequent analyses.
- SELECT IF selects only the cases in the resulting file for which there are no matching cases in file WEEK11.
- Since IN variables have either the value 1 or 0, they can be used as logical expressions when 1=true and 0=false.

FIRST and LAST Subcommands

FIRST and LAST create logical variables that flag the first or last case of a group of cases with the same value on the BY variables. FIRST and LAST must be placed after all FILE subcommands and their associated RENAME and IN subcommands.

- FIRST and LAST have only one specification, the name of the flag variable.

- FIRST creates a variable with the value 1 for the first case of each group and the value 0 for all other cases.
- LAST creates a variable with the value 1 for the last case of each group and the value 0 for all other cases.
- Variables created by FIRST and LAST are automatically attached to the end of the resulting file and cannot be dropped.

Example

```
ADD FILES  FILE=SCHOOL1 /FILE=SCHOOL2
/BY=GRADE /FIRST=HISCORE.
```

- The variable HISCORE contains the value 1 for the first case in each grade in the resulting file and the value 0 for all other cases.

MAP Subcommand

MAP produces a map showing which variables are in the new active file and from what file or files they may be taken. Variables are listed in the order they exist in the resulting file. MAP has no specifications and must be placed after all FILE and RENAME subcommands.

- Multiple MAP subcommands can be used. Each MAP shows the current status of the active file and reflects only the subcommands that precede the MAP subcommand.
- To obtain a map of the new active file in its final state, specify MAP last.
- If a variable is renamed, its original name is shown in the source file and its new name appears in the resulting file. Variables created by IN, FIRST, and LAST are not included in the map since they are automatically attached to the end of the file and cannot be dropped.
- MAP can be used with the EDIT command to obtain a listing of the variables in the resulting file without actually reading the data and combining the files.
- MAP cannot be used for more than 12 files; the display page is not wide enough.

ADD VALUE LABELS

```
ADD VALUE LABELS varlist value 'label' value 'label'... [/varlist...]
```

Example:
```
ADD VALUE LABELS JOBGRADE 'P' 'Parttime Employee'
                          'C' 'Customer Support'.
```

Overview

ADD VALUE LABELS adds or alters value labels without affecting the value labels that have already been defined for that variable. In contrast, VALUE LABELS adds or alters value labels but deletes all existing value labels for that variable when it does so.

Basic Specification

• The basic specification is a variable name and individual values with associated labels.

Syntax Rules

• Labels can be assigned to values of any previously defined variable. It is not necessary to enter value labels for all of a variable's values.

• Each value label must be enclosed in apostrophes or quotation marks.

• When an apostrophe occurs as part of a label, enclose the label in quotation marks. (You may enclose the label in apostrophes if the internal apostrophe is entered twice with no intervening space.)

• Value labels cannot exceed 60 characters.

• Value labels can contain any characters, including blanks.

• The same labels can be assigned to the same values of different variables by specifying a list of variable names. For string variables, the variables must be of equal length.

• Multiple sets of variable names and value labels can be specified on one ADD VALUE LABELS command as long as each set is separated by slashes.

• To continue a label from one command line to the next, precede the continuation of the label with a plus (+) sign. Each string segment of the label must be enclosed in apostrophes or quotes. To insert a blank between the strings, the blank must be included in the label specification.

• To maintain compatibility with earlier releases of SPSS, the value can be enclosed in parentheses, in which case the label does not need to be enclosed in apostrophes. If you use this syntax, the slash separating the sets of value labels is required, and the label may not contain internal slashes or parentheses.

Operations

• ADD VALUE LABELS takes effect as soon as it is encountered in the command sequence, unlike most transformations, which do not take effect until the data are read. Thus, special attention should be paid to its position among commands. See Universals: Command Order for more information.

• The added value labels are automatically displayed on the output from many procedures and are stored in the active system file dictionary.

• ADD VALUE LABELS can be used for variables that have no previously assigned value labels.

• Labels added to values do not affect those labels previously assigned to other values.

• In the specification, if a value is specified that is longer than the format of the associated variable, SPSS will be unable to read the full value and may not be able to associate the value labels correctly. This occurs even though the values named on ADD VALUE LABELS and the actual values agree.

• If the value specifications for string variables are shorter than the variable being labeled, the value specifications are right-padded without warning.

Limitations
- Each value label can be up to 60 characters long, although most procedures display only 20 characters.
- Some procedures display fewer than 20 characters in labels.
- The TABLES procedure (available in SPSS Tables) will display all 60 characters of a label.

Example
```
ADD VALUE LABELS V1 TO V3 1 'Officials & Managers'
                          6 'Service Workers'
              /V4 'N' 'New Employee'.
```
- Labels are assigned to the values 1 and 6 of the variables between and including V1 and V3 on the active system file.
- Following the required slash, a label for value N of V4 is specified. N is a string value and must be enclosed in apostrophes or quotation marks.
- If labels exist for values 1 and 6 on V1 TO V3 and value N on V4, they are changed in the dictionary. If labels do not exist for these values, new labels are added to the dictionary.
- Existing labels for values other than 1 and 6 on V1 TO V3 and value N on V4 are unaffected.

Example
```
ADD VALUE LABELS  OFFICE88 1 "EMPLOYEE'S OFFICE ASSIGNMENT PRIOR"
 + " TO 1988".
```
- The label for OFFICE88 is the result of concatenating two strings with the plus sign. The blank between PRIOR and TO must be included in the first or second string to be included in the label.

String Value Labels
- Both the values and the labels for short string variables must be enclosed in apostrophes or quotation marks. Labels cannot be added to the values of long string variables.
- The values of a short string variable cannot be longer than the format of the associated variable.
- If labels are to be assigned to a set of string variables, the variables must be of equal length.

Example
```
GET FILE=CITY.
ADD VALUE LABELS  STATE 'TEX' "TEXAS" 'TEN' "TENNESSEE"
                        'MIN' "MINNESOTA".
```
- The GET command gets the system file CITY.
- The ADD VALUE LABELS command assigns labels to three values of variable STATE. Each value and each label is specified in either apostrophes or quotation marks.
- The format for variable STATE must be at least three characters wide, because values TEX, TEN, and MIN are three characters. If the actual format for STATE is fewer than three characters, SPSS issues a warning stating that a value named on ADD VALUE LABELS has more characters than the string variable it labels. Note that this occurs even though the values named on ADD VALUE LABELS and the actual values agree.

Example
```
ADD VALUE LABELS=STATE REGION 'U' "UNKNOWN".
```
- Label UNKNOWN is assigned to value U for both STATE and REGION.
- STATE and REGION must be string variables of *equal* length. If STATE and REGION have *unequal* lengths, a separate specification must be made for each, as in
```
ADD VALUE LABELS STATE 'U' "UNKNOWN" / REGION 'U' "UNKNOWN".
```

AGGREGATE

```
AGGREGATE OUTFILE={file} [/MISSING=COLUMNWISE] [/DOCUMENT]
                {*   }

[/PRESORTED] /BREAK=varlist[({A})][varlist...]
                           {D}

/aggvar['label']aggvar['label']...=function(arguments)[/aggvar...]
```

The following functions are available:

SUM	Sum	MEAN	Mean
SD	Standard deviation	MAX	Maximum
MIN	Minimum	PGT	% of cases gt value
PLT	% of cases lt value	PIN	% of cases between values
POUT	% of cases not in range	FGT	Fraction gt value
FLT	Fraction lt value	FIN	Fraction between values
FOUT	Fraction not in range	N	Weighted n
NU	Unweighted n	NMISS	Weighted n of missing
NUMISS	Unweighted n of missing	FIRST	First nonmissing
LAST	Last nonmissing		

Example:

```
AGGREGATE OUTFILE=AGGEMP /BREAK=LOCATN DEPT /COUNT=N
   /AVGSAL AVGRAISE = MEAN(SALARY RAISE)
   /SUMSAL SUMRAISE = SUM(SALARY RAISE)
   /BLACKPCT 'Percentage Black' = PIN(RACE,1,1)
   /WHITEPCT 'Percentage White' = PIN(RACE,5,5).
```

Overview

AGGREGATE creates a system file from the active system file by aggregating groups of cases into single cases. The values of one or more variables in the active file define the case groups. A series of aggregate functions creates new variables that have one value for each case group. Each function operates on a *source variable* in the active file to create an *aggregated variable* for the system file.

AGGREGATE is often used with the MATCH FILES command to add variables with summary measures (sum, mean, etc.) to a file. Transformations performed on the combined file can store composite summary measures in new variables on the active file. With the REPORT procedure, the composite variables can be used to write reports with nested composite information.

Options

Output File. You can produce either a disk file or a new active file with AGGREGATE.

Case Grouping. You can group cases according to the values of any one or more of the variables in the active file. Variables used to group cases are called *break variables*. A set of cases in the file with identical values for each break variable is called a *break group*. AGGREGATE calculates a single value for each new variable for each break group.

Documentary Text. You can copy documentary text from the original file onto the aggregate file. By default, documentary text is dropped.

Sorting. You can sort the aggregated cases in the output file into either ascending or descending order of the values of each break variable. (AGGREGATE *does not* sort cases in the active file.) If the active file is already sorted by the break variables, you can instruct AGGREGATE to skip this final pass through the file.

Aggregated Variables. You can create aggregated variables using any of 19 aggregate functions. Functions SUM, MEAN, and SD can take only numeric variables as arguments, but all other aggregate functions will accept both numeric and string variables.

Labels and Formats. You can specify variable labels for the aggregated variables. Variables created with functions MAX, MIN, FIRST, and LAST assume the formats and value labels of their respective source variables. All other variables assume the default print formats described under Aggregate Functions, below.

Basic Specification

- The basic specification is OUTFILE, BREAK, and at least one aggregate function. OUTFILE specifies the aggregate file. BREAK names the case grouping variable(s). The aggregate function(s) create the new aggregated variable(s). AGGREGATE creates a new file by aggregating cases according to the variables specified on BREAK. The aggregate file contains the break variables plus the variable(s) created by the aggregate function(s).

Subcommand Order

- OUTFILE must be specified first.
- The aggregate functions must be specified last.
- If specified, DOCUMENT and PRESORTED must precede BREAK.

Operations

- When AGGREGATE produces a system file, the active file remains unchanged and is still available for analysis. When AGGREGATE creates a new active file, it replaces the old active file. Only the new active file is available for analysis.
- AGGREGATE includes the break variables in the file it creates.
- AGGREGATE excludes missing values from all aggregate variable calculations except those involving functions N, NU, NMISS, and NUMISS.
- Unless otherwise specified, AGGREGATE sorts the aggregated cases in the output file in ascending order of the values of the grouping variables. If the active file is already sorted in the order you want your aggregated file, use the PRESORTED subcommand. If PRESORTED is specified, a new aggregate case is created each time a different value or combination of values is encountered on variables named on the BREAK subcommand.
- AGGREGATE ignores split-file processing. To achieve the same effect, name the variable or variables used to split the file as break variables before any other break variables. AGGREGATE produces one file, but the aggregated cases are in the same order as the split files.

Example

```
AGGREGATE OUTFILE=AGGEMP /BREAK=LOCATN DEPT
  /COUNT=N
  /AVGSAL AVGRAISE = MEAN(SALARY RAISE)
  /SUMSAL SUMRAISE = SUM(SALARY RAISE)
  /BLACKPCT 'Percentage Black' = PIN(RACE,1,1)
  /WHITEPCT 'Percentage White' = PIN(RACE,5,5).
```

- AGGREGATE creates the new system file AGGEMP. AGGEMP contains values for the two break variables (LOCATN and DEPT) and all the new aggregate variables (COUNT, AVGSAL, AVGRAISE, SUMSAL, SUMRAISE, BLACKPCT, and WHITEPCT).
- BREAK specifies LOCATN and DEPT as the grouping variables. In the new system file AGGEMP, cases are thus sorted by LOCATN and then are sorted within each value of LOCATN by the values of DEPT. The active system file remains unsorted.
- Variable COUNT is created as the weighted number of cases in each break group. AVGSAL is the mean of SALARY and AVGRAISE is the mean of RAISE. SUMSAL is the sum of SALARY and SUMRAISE is the sum of RAISE. BLACKPCT is the percentage of cases on RACE with the value 1. WHITEPCT is the percentage of cases on RACE with the value 5. (All functions are defined in Aggregate Functions, below.)

Example

```
GET FILE=HUBEMPL /KEEP=LOCATN DEPT HOURLY RAISE SEX.

AGGREGATE OUTFILE=AGGFILE /BREAK=LOCATN DEPT
  /AVGHOUR AVGRAISE=MEAN(HOURLY RAISE).

SORT CASES BY LOCATN DEPT.
MATCH FILES  TABLE=AGGFILE /FILE=* /BY LOCATN DEPT
  /KEEP AVGHOUR AVGRAISE LOCATN DEPT SEX HOURLY RAISE /MAP.

COMPUTE HOURDIF=HOURLY/AVGHOUR.
COMPUTE RAISEDIF=RAISE/AVGRAISE.
LIST.
```

- GET reads the HUBEMPL system file and keeps a subset of variables.
- AGGREGATE creates a file aggregated by LOCATN and DEPT with the two new variables AVGHOUR and AVGRAISE, indicating the means by location and department for HOURLY and RAISE. The aggregated file is saved as the system file AGGFILE. Note that only the aggregated system file AGGFILE is sorted by LOCATN and DEPT; the active system file remains unchanged.
- SORT CASES sorts the active system file in ascending order by the same variables used as AGGREGATE break variables: LOCATN and DEPT.
- MATCH FILES specifies a table lookup match with the AGGFILE system file as the table file and the sorted active system file as the case file.
- BY indicates that the keys for the match are the same variables used on SORT CASES: LOCATN and DEPT.
- KEEP specifies the subset and order of variables to be retained on the resulting file.
- MAP provides a listing of the variables in the resulting file and the two input files.
- The COMPUTE commands calculate the ratios of each employee's hourly wage and raise to the department averages for wage and raise. The results are stored in variables HOURDIF and RAISEDIF.
- LIST displays the resulting file.

OUTFILE Subcommand

OUTFILE specifies whether AGGREGATE should create a new system file or replace the active system file. An asterisk following the equals sign tells AGGREGATE to replace the active system file. OUTFILE must be the first subcommand used on AGGREGATE.

Example
```
AGGREGATE OUTFILE=AGGEMP
  /BREAK=LOCATN
  /AVGSAL = MEAN(SALARY).
```

- OUTFILE creates system file AGGEMP. The active system file remains unchanged and is available for further analysis.
- File AGGEMP contains variables LOCATN and AVGSAL.

BREAK Subcommand

BREAK lists the grouping variables, also called the *break variables*. Each unique combination of values of the break variables defines one break group. A *break group* consists of cases with identical values for each break variable.

- The variables named on BREAK can be any combination of variables from the active system file.
- Unless PRESORTED (see below) is specified, AGGREGATE sorts cases after aggregating. By default, cases are sorted in ascending order of the values of the break variables.
- Sort order can be controlled by specifying an A (for ascending) or D (for descending) in parentheses after any break variables.
- The designations (A) and (D) apply to all preceding undesignated variables.
- AGGREGATE sorts first on the first-named variable, then on the second-named variable within the groups created by the first, and so on.
- Subcommand PRESORTED overrides all sorting specifications.

Example
```
/BREAK=LOCATN DEPT (A) TENURE (D)
```

- BREAK names variables LOCATN, DEPT and TENURE as the break variables.
- Cases in the output file are sorted in ascending order of LOCATN, in ascending order of DEPT within LOCATN, and in descending order of TENURE within LOCATN and DEPT.

DOCUMENT Subcommand

DOCUMENT copies documentation from the original file onto the newly created aggregate file. By default, documents are dropped from the aggregated file, whether the OUTFILE is the active system file or a disk file. DOCUMENT must appear after OUTFILE but before BREAK.

PRESORTED Subcommand

PRESORTED indicates that cases in the active system file are sorted according to the values of the break variables. This prevents AGGREGATE from sorting cases that have already been sorted. PRESORTED can save a considerable amount of processing time by preventing an unnecessary data pass.

- If specified, PRESORTED must precede BREAK. The only specification is keyword PRESORTED. PRESORTED has no additional specifications.
- When PRESORTED is specified, SPSS forms an aggregate case out of each group of *adjacent* cases with the same values for the break variable(s).
- If the active system file is not sorted by the break variables in ascending order and PRESORTED is specified, a warning message is generated but the procedure is executed. Each group of adjacent cases with the same values for break variables form a case in the output file, which may produce multiple cases with the same values for the break variables. In this case, the output file will not be sorted by the break variables.

Example

```
/PRESORTED
/BREAK=LOCATN DEPT
```

- PRESORTED indicates that cases are already sorted by variables LOCATN and DEPT.
- AGGREGATE does not make an extra data pass to sort the cases.

Aggregate Functions

An aggregated variable is created by applying an aggregate function to a variable in the active system file. The variable in the active system file is the *source* variable, and the new aggregated variable is called the *target* variable.

- The aggregate function(s) must be specified last on AGGREGATE.
- The simplest specification is a target variable list, followed by an equals sign, the function keyword, and a list of source variables.
- The number of target variables named must match the number of source variables.
- When several aggregate variables are defined at once, the first-named target variable is a function of the first-named source variable, the second-named target is a function of the second-named source, and so on.
- With the exception of functions MAX, MIN, FIRST, and LAST, which copy complete dictionary information from the source variable, new variables are created with no labels and with default dictionary print and write formats. To label a new variable, place the label in apostrophes immediately following its name. Value labels cannot be assigned on AGGREGATE.
- Print formats are automatically assigned to a target variable according to the function it is based on (see list of functions below). To change print formats or add value labels to an active system file created by AGGREGATE, use the PRINT FORMATS, WRITE FORMATS, FORMATS, or VALUE LABELS commands. If the aggregate file is written to disk, GET the system file, specify the new labels and formats, and resave the file.

The following functions are available:

SUM(varlist)	*Sum across cases.* Dictionary formats are F8.2.
MEAN(varlist)	*Mean across cases.* Dictionary formats are F8.2.
SD(varlist)	*Standard deviation across cases.* Dictionary formats are F8.2.

MAX(varlist)	*Maximum value across cases.* Complete dictionary information is copied from the source variables to the target variables.
MIN(varlist)	*Minimum value across cases.* Complete dictionary information is copied from the source variables to the target variables.
PGT(varlist,value)	*Percentage of cases greater than value.* Dictionary formats are F5.1.
PLT(varlist,value)	*Percentage of cases less than value.* Dictionary formats are F5.1.
PIN(varlist,value1,value2)	*Percentage of cases between value1 and value2 inclusive.* Dictionary formats are F5.1.
POUT(varlist,value1,value2)	*Percentage of cases not between value1 and value2.* Cases where the source variable equals value1 or value2 are not counted. Dictionary formats are F5.1.
FGT(varlist,value)	*Fraction of cases greater than value.* Dictionary formats are F5.3.
FLT(varlist,value)	*Fraction of cases less than value.* Dictionary formats are F5.3.
FIN(varlist,value1,value2)	*Fraction of cases between value1 and value2 inclusive.* Dictionary formats are F5.3.
FOUT(varlist,value1,value2)	*Fraction of cases not between value1 and value2.* Cases where the source variable equals value1 or value2 are not counted. Dictionary formats are F5.3.
N(varlist)	*Weighted number of cases in break group.* Dictionary formats are F7.0 for unweighted files and F8.2 for weighted files.
NU(varlist)	*Unweighted number of cases in break group.* Dictionary formats are F7.0.
NMISS(varlist)	*Weighted number of missing cases.* Dictionary formats are F7.0 for unweighted files and F8.2 for weighted files.
NUMISS(varlist)	*Unweighted number of missing cases.* Dictionary formats are F7.0.
FIRST(varlist)	*First nonmissing observed value in break group.* Complete dictionary information is copied from the source variables to the target variables.
LAST(varlist)	*Last nonmissing observed value in break group.* Complete dictionary information is copied from the source variables to the target variables.

• Functions SUM, MEAN, and SD operate only on numeric source variables. All other functions accept short and long string variables as well as numeric ones.

• The N and NU functions do not require arguments. Without arguments, they return the number of weighted and unweighted cases in a break group. If you supply a variable list, they return the weighted and unweighted number of valid cases for the variables specified.

• For several functions, the argument includes values as well as a source variable designation. PGT, PLT, FGT, and FLT take one value; PIN, POUT, FIN, and FOUT take two values.

• For PIN, POUT, FIN, and FOUT, the first value should be less than or equal to the second. If the first is higher, AGGREGATE automatically reverses them and prints a warning message.

- If the two values are equal, PIN and FIN calculate the percentages and fractions, respectively, of values equal to the argument. POUT and FOUT calculate the percentages and fractions, respectively, of values not equal to the argument.
- Either blanks or commas can be used to separate the components of an argument list. String values specified in an argument should be enclosed in apostrophes. The order used in aggregation functions with string values is alphabetical.

Example
```
AGGREGATE OUTFILE=AGGEMP /BREAK=LOCATN
    /AVGSAL 'Average Salary' AVGRAISE = MEAN(SALARY RAISE).
```

- AGGREGATE defines two aggregate variables, AVGSAL and AVGRAISE.
- AVGSAL is the mean of SALARY for each break group, and AVGRAISE is the mean of RAISE.
- The label Average Salary is assigned to AVGRAISE.

Example
```
AGGREGATE OUTFILE=* /BREAK=DEPT
    /LOWVAC,LOWSICK = PLT (VACDAY SICKDAY,10).
```

- AGGREGATE assigns the percentage of cases with values less than 10 for VACDAY to LOWVAC and for SICKDAY to LOWSICK.

Example
```
AGGREGATE OUTFILE=GROUPS /BREAK=OCCGROUP
    /COLLEGE = FIN(EDUC,13,16).
```

- AGGREGATE assigns the fraction of cases having 13 to 16 years of education to COLLEGE.

Example
```
AGGREGATE OUTFILE=* /BREAK=CLASS
    /LOCAL = PIN(STATE,"IL","IO").
```

- AGGREGATE creates variable LOCAL, which is the percentage of cases in each break group whose two-letter state code represents Illinois, Indiana, or Iowa. (The abbreviation for Indiana, IN, is between IL and IO in an alphabetical sort sequence.)

MISSING Subcommand

By default, AGGREGATE uses all nonmissing values of the source variable to calculate aggregated variables. An aggregated variable will have a missing value only if the source variable is missing for every case in the break group. You can alter the default missing-value treatment by using the MISSING subcommand or by specifying the inclusion of missing values on any function.

- MISSING must precede BREAK. Keyword COLUMNWISE is the only specification available.
- MISSING=COLUMNWISE declares the value of an aggregated variable as missing if the source variable is missing for any case in the break group.
- MISSING does not affect the calculation of the N, NU, NMISS, or NUMISS functions.
- Considerations for missing values do not apply to break variables. Even if a break variable has a system-missing value, cases in that group are processed and the break variable is saved on the file with the system-missing value. Use SELECT IF if you want to eliminate cases with missing values on the break variables.

Including Missing Values

You can force a function to include user-missing values in its calculations by specifying a period after the function name.

- AGGREGATE ignores periods used with functions N, NU, NMISS, and NUMISS if these functions have no argument.
- User-missing values are treated as valid when these four functions are followed by a period and have a variable as an argument. NMISS.(AGE) gives the number of cases for which AGE has the system-missing value only.

The effect of specifying a period with N, NU, NMISS, and NUMISS is illustrated by the following:

N = N. = N(AGE) + NMISS(AGE) = N.(AGE) + NMISS.(AGE)

NU = NU. = NU(AGE)+ NUMISS(AGE) = NU.(AGE) + NUMISS.(AGE)

- The function N (the same as N. with no argument) yields a value for each break group that equals the number of cases with valid values plus the number of cases with user- or system-missing values.
- This in turn equals the number of cases with either valid or user-missing values plus the number with system-missing values.
- The same identities hold for the NU, NMISS, and NUMISS functions.

Example
```
AGGREGATE OUTFILE=AGGEMP /MISSING=COLUMNWISE /BREAK=LOCATN
    /AVGSAL = MEAN(SALARY).
```

- AGGREGATE requests AVGSAL be declared missing for an aggregate case if SALARY is missing for any case in the break group.

Example
```
AGGREGATE OUTFILE=* /BREAK=DEPT
    /LOVAC = PLT.(VACDAY,10).
```

- AGGREGATE sets variable LOVAC to the percentage of cases within each break group with values less than 10 for VACDAY, even if some of those values are defined as user-missing.

Example
```
AGGREGATE OUTFILE=CLASS /BREAK=GRADE
    /FIRSTAGE = FIRST.(AGE).
```

- AGGREGATE assigns the first value of AGE in each break group to variable FIRSTAGE.
- If the first value of AGE in a break group is user-missing, that value will be assigned to FIRSTAGE. However, the value will retain its missing-value status since variables created with FIRST take their dictionary information from their source variables.
- Function LAST with a period operates in parallel fashion.

Comparing Missing Value Treatments

Table 1 demonstrates the effects of the MISSING subcommand and of the period missing-value convention. Each entry in the table is the number of cases used to compute the specified function for variable EDUC, which has 10 nonmissing cases, 5 user-missing cases, and 2 system-missing cases for the group. Note that columnwise treatment produces the same results as the default for every function except the MEAN function.

Table 1   Alternative missing-value treatments

Function	Default	Columnwise
N	17	17
N.	17	17
N(EDUC)	10	10
N.(EDUC)	15	15
MEAN(EDUC)	10	0
MEAN.(EDUC)	15	0
NMISS(EDUC)	7	7
NMISS.(EDUC)	2	2

ALSCAL

```
ALSCAL  VARIABLES=varlist

[/FILE=file]  [CONFIG  [({INITIAL})]]
                        {FIXED  }

              [ROWCONF [({INITIAL})]]
                        {FIXED  }

              [COLCONF [({INITIAL})]]
                        {FIXED  }

              [SUBJWGHT[({INITIAL})]]
                        {FIXED  }

              [STIMWGHT[({INITIAL})]]
                        {FIXED  }

[/INPUT=ROWS ({ALL})]
              { n }

[/SHAPE={SYMMETRIC**}]
        {ASYMMETRIC }
        {RECTANGULAR}

[/LEVEL={ORDINAL**[(([UNTIE] [SIMILAR])]}]
        {INTERVAL[({1})]                   }
        {         {d}                      }
        {RATIO[({1})]                      }
        {        {d}                       }
        {NOMINAL                           }

[/CONDITION={MATRIX       }]
            {ROW          }
            {UNCONDITIONAL}

[/MODEL  ={EUCLID**}]
   or     {INDSCAL }
 METHOD   {ASCAL   }
          {AINDS   }
          {GEMSCAL }

[/CRITERIA=[NEGATIVE] [CUTOFF({0**})] [CONVERGE({.001})]
                              {c  }             {c   }

             [ITER({30})] [STRESSMIN({.005})] [NOULB]
                   {ni}              { s  }

             [DIMENS({2**    })] [DIRECTIONS(r)]
                     {min[,max]}

             [CONSTRAIN]           [TIESTORE(n)]]

[/PRINT=[DATA] [HEADER] [INTERMED]]

[/PLOT=[DEFAULT] [ALL]]

[/OUTFILE=file]

[/MATRIX=IN({file})]
            {*   }
```

**Default if the subcommand is omitted.

Example:

```
ALSCAL VARIABLES=ATLANTA TO TAMPA.
```

ALSCAL was originally designed and programmed by Forrest W. Young, Yoshio Takane, and Rostyslaw J. Lewyckyj, of the Psychometric Laboratory, University of North Carolina.

Overview   ALSCAL uses an alternating least-squares algorithm to perform multidimensional scaling (MDS) and multidimensional unfolding (MDU). You can select 1 of 5 models to obtain stimulus coordinates and/or weights in multidimensional space.

Options   **Data Input.** You can read in-line data matrices, including all types of two- or three-way data, such as a single matrix or a matrix for each of several subjects (see the INPUT subcommand). You can read square (symmetrical or asymmetrical) or rectangular matrices of proximities (see the SHAPE subcommand) and also proximity matrices created by the PROXIMITIES and CLUSTER procedures (see the MATRIX subcommand). Finally, you can read a file of coordinates and/or weights to provide initial or fixed values for the scaling process.

Methodological Assumptions. You can specify data as matrix-conditional, row-conditional, or unconditional (see the CONDITION subcommand). You can treat data as nonmetric (nominal or ordinal) or as metric (interval or ratio). In addition, you can identify ordinal level proximity data as measures of SIMILARITY or DISSIMILARITY and can leave tied observations as tied (discrete) or specify them as untied (continuous).

Model Selection. You can specify most commonly used multidimensional scaling models by selecting the correct combination of ALSCAL subcommands, keywords, and criteria. In addition to the default Euclidean distance model, ALSCAL offers the individual differences (weighted) Euclidean distance model (INDSCAL), the asymmetric Euclidean distance model (ASCAL), the asymmetric individual differences Euclidean distance model (AINDS), and the generalized Euclidean metric individual differences model (GEMSCAL).

Output. You can produce output that includes the raw and scaled input data, intermediate results at each step of the scaling process, missing value patterns, normalized data with means, the squared data with additive constants, each subject's scalar product and individual weight space, plots of linear or nonlinear fit, and plots of the data transformations.

Basic Specification   The basic specification is VARIABLES followed by a variable list. By default, ALSCAL produces a two-dimensional nonmetric Euclidean multidimensional scaling solution. Input is assumed to be one or more square symmetric matrices with data elements that are dissimilarities at the ordinal level of measurement. Ties are not untied, and conditionality is by subject. Values less than 0 are treated as missing. The default output includes the improvement in Young's S-STRESS for successive iterations, two measures of fit for each input matrix (Kruskal's STRESS and the squared correlation, RSQ), and the derived configurations for each of the dimensions.

Subcommand Order   • Subcommands can be named in any order.

Operations   • ALSCAL calculates the number of input matrices by dividing the total number of observations in the data set by the number of observations in each matrix. All matrices must contain the same number of observations. This number depends on the settings on SHAPE and INPUT (if used). For example, if SHAPE= SYMMETRIC or SHAPE=ASYMMETRIC, ALSCAL expects square matrix data, and it sets the number of observations in each matrix equal to the number of variables (stimuli being analyzed). If SHAPE=RECTANGULAR, ALSCAL sets the number of column stimuli equal to the number of variables in the analysis. The number of row stimuli is set equal to the number of rows specified on INPUT. If no INPUT subcommand is specified, ALSCAL uses the number of cases in the input file or, with split files, the number of cases in the first split-file group. (All groups must contain the same number of cases.)

• ALSCAL ignores user-missing values in all variables in the configuration/ weights file (see FILE Subcommand). The system-missing value is an error in the TYPE_ variable and is converted to 0 in the other variables.

• In the case of split files, ALSCAL reads initial or fixed configurations from the configuration/weights file (see the FILE subcommand) for each split-file group. If there is only one initial configuration in the file, ALSCAL rereads these initial or fixed values for successive split-file groups.

Limitations
- Maximum 100 variables on VARIABLES subcommand.
- Maximum six dimensions can be scaled.
- ALSCAL does not recognize data weights created by the WEIGHT command.
- ALSCAL analyses can include no more than 32,767 values in each of the input matrices. Large problems may add significantly to computing time.

Example

```
TITLE AIR DISTANCES AMONG U.S. CITIES.
COMMENT DATA ARE FROM JOHNSON AND WICHERN (1982), PAGE 563.
DATA LIST FREE
  /ATLANTA BOSTON CINCNATI COLUMBUS DALLAS INDNPLIS
    LITTROCK LOSANGEL MEMPHIS STLOUIS SPOKANE TAMPA 1-60.
BEGIN DATA.
   0
1068    0
 461  867    0
 549  769  107    0
 805 1819  943 1050    0
 508  941  108  172  882    0
 505 1494  618  725  325  562    0
2197 3052 2186 2245 1403 2080 1701    0
 366 1355  502  586  464  436  137 1831    0
 558 1178  338  409  645  234  353 1848  294    0
2467 2747 2067 2131 1891 1959 1988 1227 2042 1820    0
 467 1379  928  985 1077  975  912 2480  779 1016 2821    0
END DATA.

ALSCAL VARIABLES=ATLANTA TO TAMPA.
```

- By default, ALSCAL assumes a symmetric matrix of dissimilarities for ordinal level variables. Only values below the diagonal are used. The upper triangle can be left blank. The 12 cities form the rows and columns of the matrix.
- The result is a classical MDS analysis that reproduces a map of the United States (when the output is rotated to the conventional north-south and east-west dimensions).

Missing Values

By default, ALSCAL estimates upper and lower bounds on missing values in order to compute the initial configuration. To prevent this, specify CRITERIA= NOULB. Missing values are always ignored during the iterative process.

VARIABLES Subcommand

VARIABLES identifies the columns in the proximity matrix or matrices that ALSCAL reads.

- VARIABLES is required and can name only numeric variables.
- Each matrix must have at least four rows and four columns.

INPUT Subcommand

ALSCAL reads data row by row, with each case in the active system file representing a single row in the data matrix (VARIABLES specifies the columns). Use INPUT when reading in-line data to specify how many rows are in each matrix.

- The only specification is ROWS(n), where n is the number of rows in each matrix. n must be at least 4.
- If INPUT is omitted, ALSCAL assumes that each case in the active system file represents one row of a single input matrix.
- The number of rows per matrix must divide evenly into the total number of rows in the data.
- With split-file data, the number of rows in the input matrix is the number of cases in each split-file group. All split-file groups must have the same number of rows.

Example

```
ALSCAL VARIABLES=V1 to V7 /INPUT=ROWS(8).
```

- INPUT indicates there are eight rows per matrix, with each case in the active system file representing one row.
- The total number of cases must be divisible by 8.

SHAPE Subcommand

Use SHAPE to specify the structure of the input data matrix or matrices.

• Specify one of the keywords below. SYMMETRIC is the default.

SYMMETRIC   *Symmetric data matrix or matrices.* This is the default. For a symmetric matrix, ALSCAL looks only at the values below the diagonal, so values on and above the diagonal can be left missing.

ASYMMETRIC   *Asymmetric data matrix or matrices.* The corresponding values in the upper and lower triangles are not all equal. The diagonal is ignored.

RECTANGULAR   *Rectangular data matrix or matrices.* The rows and columns represent different sets of items.

Example   `ALSCAL VAR=V1 TO V8 /SHAPE=RECTANGLE.`

• ALSCAL performs a classical MDU analysis, treating the rows and columns as separate sets of items.

LEVEL Subcommand

LEVEL identifies the level of measurement for the values in the data matrix or matrices.

• Specify only one of the keywords defined below. ORDINAL is the default.

• With keyword INTERVAL or RATIO, the degree of a polynomial transformation to be fit to the data can be specified. The degree can be any integer value from 1 to 4, and it must be specified in parentheses after INTERVAL or RATIO. The default value is 1.

ORDINAL[([UNTIE] [SIMILAR])]   *Ordinal level data.* This is the default. It treats the data as ordinal, using Kruskal's (1964) least-squares monotonic transformation. The analysis is nonmetric. By default, the ordinal data is treated as discrete. Ties in the data remain tied throughout the analysis. If you want to regard ordinal data as continuous, specify the UNTIE option, which resolves ties in an optimal fashion. By default ALSCAL treats the data as dissimilarities. Ordinal data can be treated as similarities if the SIMILAR option is specified. UNTIE and SIMILAR cannot be used with the other levels of measurement.

INTERVAL[(d)]   *Interval level data.* This specification produces a metric analysis of the data using classical regression techniques.

RATIO[(d)]   *Ratio level data.* Like INTERVAL, this specification produces a metric analysis.

NOMINAL   *Nominal level data.* ALSCAL treats the data as nominal by using a least»squares categorical transformation (Takane et al, 1977). This option produces a nonmetric analysis of nominal data. It is useful when there are few observed categories, when there are many observations in each category, and when the order of the categories is not known.

Example   `ALSCAL VAR=ATLANTA TO TAMPA /LEVEL=INTERVAL(2).`

• This example identifies the distances between U.S. cities as interval level data. The 2 in parentheses indicates a polynomial transformation with linear and quadratic terms.

CONDITION Subcommand

CONDITION defines which numbers in a data set are comparable. MATRIX is the default.

MATRIX	*Only numbers within each matrix are comparable.* If each matrix represents a different subject, this makes comparisons conditional by subject. This is the default.
ROW	*Only numbers within the same row are comparable.* This specification is appropriate only for asymmetric or rectangular data and cannot be used when MODEL=ASCAL or MODEL=AINDS.
UNCONDITIONAL	*All numbers are comparable.* Comparisons can be made among any values in the input matrix or matrices.

Example

ALSCAL VAR=V1 TO V8 /SHAPE=RECTANGULAR /CONDITION=ROW.

• ALSCAL performs a Euclidean MDU analysis conditional on comparisons within rows.

FILE Subcommand

The proximity data can be read from the active system file or, with the MATRIX subcommand, from a system file created by PROXIMITIES or CLUSTER. FILE causes ALSCAL to read a file containing additional data: an initial or fixed configuration for the coordinates of the stimuli and/or weights for the matrices being scaled. This file can be created with the OUTFILE subcommand or with an SPSS input program.

• The minimum specification is the file that contains the configurations and/or weights.

• FILE can also include a set of optional specifications that define the structure of the configuration/weights file.

• The variables in the configuration/weights file that correspond to successive ALSCAL dimensions must have the names DIM1, DIM2 . . . DIM*r*, where *r* is the maximum number of ALSCAL dimensions. The file must also contain the short string variable TYPE_ to identify the types of values in all the rows.

• Appropriate values for the variable TYPE_, and the order in which they must appear, are CONFIG, ROWCONF, COLCONF, SUBJWGHT, and STIMWGHT. Each value can be truncated to the first three letters. ALSCAL accepts CONFIG and ROWCONF interchangeably.

• Stimulus coordinate values are specified as CONFIG; row stimulus coordinates as ROWCONF; column stimulus coordinates as COLCONF; and subject and stimulus weights, respectively, as SUBJWGHT and STIMWGHT.

• ALSCAL skips unneeded types as long as they appear in the file in their proper order. Generalized weights (GEM) and flattened subject weights (FLA) cannot be initialized or fixed and will always be skipped (these are weights that can be generated by ALSCAL but never entered as input).

The following list summarizes the optional specifications on the FILE subcommand that can be used to define the structure of the configuration/weights file. Each specification can be further identified with option INITIAL or FIXED in parentheses. INITIAL is the default. The FIXED option defines an external or hypothesized structure for stimulus coordinates, subject weights, and/or stimulus weights as in an external unfolding model. This option forces ALSCAL to use the defined structure without modification to calculate the best values for all unfixed portions of the structure.

CONFIG[(option)]	*Read stimulus configuration.* The configuration/weights file contains initial stimulus coordinates. Input of this sort is appropriate when SHAPE=SYMMETRIC or SHAPE= ASYMMETRIC or when the number of variables in a matrix equals the number of variables in the ALSCAL command. The value of the TYPE_ variable must be either CONFIG or ROWCONF for all the stimulus coordinates of the configuration.

ROWCONF[(option)] *Read row stimulus configuration.* The configuration/ weights file contains initial row stimulus coordinates. This specification is necessary if SHAPE=RECTANGULAR. The number of observations equals the number of rows you specify on the INPUT subcommand or, if you do not include INPUT, the number of cases in the proximity file. The value of TYPE_ must be either ROW or CON for the set of coordinates for each row.

COLCONF[(option)] *Read column stimulus configuration.* The configuration/ weights file contains initial column stimulus coordinates. This kind of file can be entered as input only if SHAPE= RECTANGULAR and if the number of observations in the matrix equals the number of variables in the ALSCAL command. The value of TYPE_ must be COL for the set of coordinates for each column.

SUBJWGHT[(option)] *Read subject (matrix) weights.* The configuration/weights file contains subject weights. The number of observations in a subject-weights matrix must equal the number of matrices in the proximity file. Subject weights can be entered as input only if MODEL=INDSCAL, MODEL= AINDS, or MODEL=GEMSCAL. The value of TYPE_ for each set of weights must be SUB.

STIMWGHT[(option)] *Read stimulus weights.* The configuration/weights file contains stimulus weights. This option can be used only if the number of observations in the configuration/weights file equals the number of matrices in the proximity file. Matrix input of this kind is permissible only if MODEL=AINDS or MODEL=ASCAL. The value of TYPE_ for each set of weights must be STI.

If the optional specifications for the configuration/weights file are not included on FILE, ALSCAL sequentially reads the TYPE_ values appropriate to the model and shape according to the defaults in Table 1.

Table 1 Default input values for the FILE subcommand

Shape	Model	Default
SYMMETRIC	EUCLID	CONFIG (or ROWCONF)
	INDSCAL	CONFIG (or ROWCONF) SUBJWGHT
	GEMSCAL	CONFIG (or ROWCONF) SUBJWGHT
ASYMMETRIC	EUCLID	CONFIG (or ROWCONF)
	INDSCAL	CONFIG (or ROWCONF)
	GEMSCAL	CONFIG (or ROWCONF) SUBJWGHT
	ASCAL	CONFIG (or ROWCONF) STIMWGHT
	AINDS	CONFIG (or ROWCONF) SUBJWGHT STIMWGHT
RECTANGULAR	EUCLID	ROWCONF (or CONFIG) COLCONF
	INDSCAL	ROWCONF (or CONFIG) COLCONF SUBJWGHT
	GEMSCAL	ROWCONF (or CONFIG) COLCONF SUBJWGHT

Example	`ALSCAL VAR=V1 TO V8 /FILE=ONE CON(FIXED) STI(INITIAL).`

• ALSCAL reads the configuration/weights file ONE.

• The stimulus coordinates are read as fixed values, and the stimulus weights are read as initial values.

MODEL Subcommand

MODEL (alias METHOD) defines the scaling model for the analysis. The only specification is MODEL (or METHOD) and any one of five scaling and unfolding model types. EUCLID is the default.

EUCLID *Euclidean distance model.* This model is the default. It can be used with any type of proximity matrix.

INDSCAL *Individual differences (weighted) Euclidean distance model.* ALSCAL will scale the data using the weighted individual differences Euclidean distance model, as proposed by Carroll and Chang (1970). This type of analysis can be specified only if the analysis involves more than one data matrix and if more than one dimension is specified on CRITERIA.

ASCAL *Asymmetric Euclidean distance model.* This model (Young, 1975b) can be used only if SHAPE=ASYMMETRIC and if the number of dimensions requested on CRITERIA is greater than one.

AINDS *Asymmetric individual differences Euclidean distance model.* This option combines Young's (1975a) asymmetric Euclidean model with the individual differences model as proposed by Carroll and Chang (1970). This model can only be used when SHAPE=ASYMMETRIC, the analysis involves more than one data matrix, and the number of dimensions on CRITERIA is greater than one.

GEMSCAL *Generalized Euclidean metric individual differences model.* The number of directions for this model is set with the DIRECTIONS option on CRITERIA. The number of directions specified can be equal to but not exceed the group space dimensionality. By default, the number of directions is set equal to the number of dimensions in the solution.

Example	`ALSCAL VARIABLES = V1 TO V6`
	`  /SHAPE = ASYMMETRIC`
	`  /CONDITION = ROW`
	`  /MODEL = GEMSCAL`
	`  /CRITERIA = DIM(4) DIRECTIONS(4).`

• In this example, the number of directions in the GEMSCAL model is set to 4.

CRITERIA Subcommand

Use CRITERIA to control features of the scaling model and to set convergence criteria for the solution. You can specify one or more of the following:

CONVERGE(c) *Stop iterations if the change in S-Stress is less than c.* S-Stress is a goodness-of-fit index. By default, CONVERGE=.001. To increase the precision of a solution, replace c with a smaller number, for example 0.0001. To obtain a less precise solution (perhaps to reduce computing time), specify a larger value, for instance 0.05. Negative values of CONVERGE are not allowed. If CONVERGE=0, the algorithm will iterate 30 times unless a value is specified with the ITER option.

ITER(ni) *Set the maximum number of iterations to ni.* The default value is 30. A higher value will give a more precise solution, but will take longer to compute.

STRESSMIN(s) *Set the minimum stress value to s.* By default, ALSCAL stops iterating when the value of S-STRESS is 0.005 or less. STRESSMIN can be assigned any value from 0 to 1.

NEGATIVE   *Allow negative weights in individual differences models.* By default, ALSCAL does not permit the weights to be negative. To allow negative weights, specify CRITERIA= NEGATIVE. Weighted models include INDSCAL, ASCAL, and AINDS, but not GEMSCAL. The NEGATIVE option will be ignored if MODEL=EUCLID.

CUTOFF(c)   *Set the cutoff value for treating distances as missing to c.* By default, ALSCAL treats all negative similarities (or dissimilarities) as missing and 0 and positive similarities as nonmissing (CUTOFF=0). Changing the CUTOFF value causes ALSCAL to treat similarities greater than or equal to that value as nonmissing. User- and system-missing values are considered missing regardless of the CUTOFF specification.

NOULB   *Do not estimate upper and lower bounds on missing values.* By default, ALSCAL estimates the upper and lower bounds on missing values in order to compute the initial configuration. If CRITERIA=NOULB upper and lower bounds will not be estimated. This specification has no effect during the iterative process, when missing values are ignored.

DIMENS(min[,max])   *Set the minimum and maximum numbers of dimensions in the scaling solution.* By default, ALSCAL calculates a solution with two dimensions. To obtain solutions for other than two dimensions, specify the minimum number and the maximum number of dimensions in parentheses after DIMENS. The minimum and maximum numbers can be integers between 2 and 6. A single value inside the parentheses represents both the minimum and the maximum number of dimensions. Thus, DIMENS(3) is equivalent to DIMENS(3,3). The minimum number of dimensions can be set to 1 only if MODEL=EUCLID.

DIRECTIONS(r)   *Set the number of principal directions in the generalized Euclidean model to r.* This option has no effect for models other than MODEL=GEMSCAL. The number of principal directions can be any positive integer between 1 and the number of dimensions specified on the DIMENS option. By default, ALSCAL will set the number of directions equal to the number of dimensions.

TIESTORE(n)   *Set the amount of storage needed for ties to n.* This option estimates the amount of storage needed to deal with ties in ordinal data. By default, the amount of storage is set to 1000 or the number of cells in a matrix, whichever is smaller. Should this be insufficient, ALSCAL terminates with a message that more space is needed.

CONSTRAIN   *Constrain multidimensional unfolding solution.* The CONSTRAIN option can be used to keep the initial constraints throughout the analysis.

PRINT Subcommand

PRINT specifies output not available by default. You can request any combination of the following:

DATA   *Display input data.* The display includes both the raw data and the scaled data for each subject according to the structure specified on SHAPE.

INTERMED   *Display intermediate steps in the scaling process.* Intermediate steps leading up to the final scaling solution are displayed. Some of the items the INTERMED option displays are the raw data, the missing-value pattern, the data with missing-value estimates, the normalized data and means, the squared data with additive constant estimated, and the scalar product for each subject. This option can produce a great deal of output.

HEADER   *Display a header page.* The header includes the model, output, algorithmic, and data options in effect for the analysis.

- Data options listed by PRINT HEADER include the number of rows and columns, the number of matrices, the measurement level, the shape of the data matrix, the type of data (similarity or dissimilarity), whether ties are left tied or were untied, the conditionality, and the data cutoff value.

- Model options listed by PRINT HEADER are the type of model specified (EUCLID, INDSCAL, ASCAL, AINDS, or GEMSCAL), the minimum and maximum dimensionality, and whether or not negative weights are permitted.

- Output options section specifies whether the output included the session option header and data matrices, whether ALSCAL plotted configurations and transformations, whether it created an output data set, and whether it computed initial stimulus coordinates, initial column stimulus coordinates, initial subject weights, and initial stimulus weights.

- Algorithmic options listed by PRINT HEADER include the maximum number of iterations permitted, the convergence criterion, the maximum S-STRESS value, whether or not missing data are estimated by upper and lower bounds, and the amount of storage allotted for ties in ordinal data.

Example   `ALSCAL VAR=ATLANTA TO TAMPA /PRINT=INTERMED.`

- In addition to the raw data, ALSCAL will display intermediate transformations of the data.

PLOT Subcommand

PLOT plots the multidimensional scaling results. The minimum specification is simply PLOT to produce the defaults.

DEFAULT   *Produce default plots.* These are plots of the stimulus coordinates, the matrix weights (if MODEL=INDSCAL, MODEL=AINDS, or MODEL=GEMSCAL), and the stimulus weights (if MODEL= AINDS or MODEL=ASCAL). The default also includes a scatterplot of the linear fit between the data and the model and, for certain types of data, scatterplots of the nonlinear fit and the data transformation. ALSCAL produces $d*(d-1)/2$ pages of plots for the stimulus space and, when appropriate, for each of the weight spaces, when d is the number of dimensions in the solution.

ALL   *Plot the stimulus space for each matrix.* PLOT=ALL produces a separate plot of each subject's data transformation (if CONDITION= MATRIX or the data are nominal or ordinal) or a plot for each row (if CONDITION=ROW), and, for weighted models, a separate plot of each subject's weight space. This option can produce voluminous output, especially if CONDITION=ROW.

Example   `ALSCAL VAR=V1 TO V8 /INPUT=ROWS(8) /PLOT=ALL.`

- This command produces all the default output. It also produces a separate plot for each subject's data transformation and a plot of V1 through V8 in a two-dimensional space for each subject.

OUTFILE Subcommand

OUTFILE saves coordinate and weight matrices to an SPSS system file. The only specification is the output file.

- The file produced has a format that the FILE subcommand can use to read initial values.

- The output system file has an alphanumeric (short string) variable named TYPE_ that identifies the kind of values in each row, a numeric variable DIMENS that specifies the number of dimensions, a numeric variable MATNUM that indicates the subject (matrix) to which each set of coordinates corresponds, and variables DIM1, DIM2...DIM*r* that correspond to the <r> ALSCAL dimensions in the model.

- The values of any split-file variables are also included in the output file.

The following list indicates the seven different kinds of ALSCAL file output. Only the first three characters of each identifier are written to variable TYPE_ on the SPSS system file. For example, CONFIG becomes CON.

• CONFIG: Stimulus configuration coordinates for SHAPE=SYMMETRIC or SHAPE=ASYMMETRIC.
• ROWCONF: Row stimulus configuration coordinates for SHAPE= RECTANGULAR.
• COLCONF: Column stimulus configuration coordinates for SHAPE= RECTANGULAR.
• SUBJWGHT: Subject (matrix) weights for MODEL=INDSCAL, MODEL= AINDS, or MODEL=GEMSCAL.
• FLATWGHT: Flattened subject (matrix) weights for MODEL=INDSCAL, MODEL=AINDS, or MODEL=GEMSCAL.
• GEMWGHT: Generalized weights for MODEL=GEMSCAL.
• STIMWGHT: Stimulus weights for MODEL=ASCAL or MODEL=AINDS.

The structure of the configuration/weights file produced by OUTFILE is determined by the SHAPE and MODEL subcommands as shown in Table 2.

Table 2 Types of configurations and/or weights in output files

Shape	Model	TYPE_
SYMMETRIC	EUCLID	CON
	INDSCAL	CON
		SUB
		FLA
	GEMSCAL	CON
		SUB
		FLA
		GEM
ASYMMETRIC	EUCLID	CON
	INDSCAL	CON
		SUB
		FLA
	GEMSCAL	CON
		SUB
		FLA
		GEM
	ASCAL	CON
		STI
	AINDS	CON
		SUB
		FLA
		STI
RECTANGULAR	EUCLID	ROW
		COL
	INDSCAL	ROW
		COL
		SUB
		FLA
	GEMSCAL	ROW
		COL
		SUB
		FLA
		GEM

Example   `ALSCAL VAR=ATLANTA TO TAMPA /OUTFILE=ONE.`

• OUTFILE creates the default SPSS configuration/weights file ONE from the previous example of air distances between cities.

MATRIX Subcommand   MATRIX reads SPSS matrix system files. It can read a matrix written by either PROXIMITIES or CLUSTER. MATRIX has one keyword, IN, which must be used to specify the matrix file in parentheses.

- Generally, data read by ALSCAL are already in matrix form. Thus, if the matrix materials are in the active system file, you do not need to use MATRIX to read them. Rather, you can simply use the VARIABLES subcommand to indicate the variables (or columns) to be used. However, if the matrix materials are not in the active system file, MATRIX must be used to specify the matrix system file that contains the matrix.

- MATRIX=IN cannot be used in place of GET or DATA LIST to begin an SPSS session. MATRIX is a subcommand on ALSCAL, and ALSCAL cannot run before an active system file is defined.

- To read a matrix, first GET the matrix file, then specify IN(*) on MATRIX.

- Since ALSCAL does not support case labeling, it ignores values for the ID variable (if present) in a CLUSTER or PROXIMITIES matrix.

- The proximity matrices ALSCAL reads all have ROWTYPE_ values of PROX. No additional statistics are included with these matrix materials.

- ALSCAL ignores unrecognized ROWTYPE_ values in the matrix file. In addition, it ignores variables present in the matrix file that are not specified on the VARIABLES subcommand in ALSCAL. The order of rows and columns in the matrix is unimportant.

- If split-file processing was in effect when the matrix was written, the same split file must be in effect when ALSCAL reads that matrix.

IN   *Read a matrix system file.* If the matrix system file is *not* the current active system file, specify the active system file in parentheses. If the matrix system file *is* the current active system file, enter an asterisk in parentheses (*) to so indicate.

Example   ```
PROXIMITIES V1 TO V8 /ID=NAMEVAR /MATRIX=OUT(*).
ALSCAL VAR=CASE1 TO CASE10 /MATRIX=IN(*).
```

- PROXIMITIES uses V1 through V8 of the active system file to generate a matrix file of Euclidean distances between each pair of cases in the active system file based on the eight variables. The number of rows and columns in the resulting matrix are equal to the number of cases. MATRIX=OUT then replaces the active system file with this new matrix system file.

- MATRIX=IN on ALSCAL reads the matrix system file, which is the new active system file. In this instance, MATRIX is optional because the matrix materials are in the active system file.

- If there were ten cases in the original active system file, ALSCAL performs a multidimensional scaling analysis in two dimensions on CASE1 through CASE10.

**Example**    ```
GET FILE PROXMTX.
ALSCAL VAR=CASE1 TO CASE10 /MATRIX=IN(*).
```

- This example assumes you want to read an existing matrix system file. GET retrieves the matrix system file PROXMTX.

- MATRIX=IN specifies an asterisk because the current active system file is the matrix. MATRIX is optional, however, since the matrix materials are in the active system file.

Example   ```
GET FILE PRSNNL.
FREQUENCIES VARIABLE=AGE.
ALSCAL VAR=CASE1 TO CASE10 /MATRIX=IN(PROXMTX).
```
```

- This example assumes you want to perform a frequencies analysis on file PRSNNL, then use ALSCAL to read a different file. The file you want to read is an existing matrix system file.
- MATRIX=IN specifies a file because the current active system file is PRSNNL. MATRIX=IN must therefore specify the file from which the matrix materials will be read. In this instance, the matrix materials are *not* in the active system file, and MATRIX is therefore required.
- PROXMTX *does not* replace PRSNNL as the active system file.

Specification of Analyses

Table 3 summarizes the types of analyses that can be performed for the major forms of proximity matrices you can use with ALSCAL. Tables 4 and 5 list the specifications necessary to produce these analyses using ALSCAL, depending on whether you want a nonmetric or metric type of analysis. You can, of course, include additional specifications to control the precision of your analysis with CRITERIA.

Table 3 Models for types of matrix input

Matrix mode	Matrix form	Model class	Single matrix	Replications of single matrix	Two or more individual matrices
Object by object	Symmetric	Multi-dimensional scaling	CMDS Classical multidimensional scaling	RMDS Replicated multidimensional scaling	WMDS(INDSCAL) Weighted multidimensional scaling
	Asymmetric single process	Multi-dimensional scaling	CMDS(row conditional) Classical row conditional multidimensional scaling	RMDS(row conditional) Replicated row conditional multidimensional scaling	WMDS(row conditional) Weighted row conditional multidimensional scaling
	Asymmetric multiple process	Internal asymmetric multi-dimensional scaling	CAMDS Classical asymmetric multidimensional scaling	RAMDS Replicated asymmetric multidimensional scaling	WAMDS Weighted asymmetric multidimensional scaling
		External asymmetric multi-dimensional scaling	CAMDS(external) Classical external asymmetric multidimensional scaling	RAMDS(external) Replicated external asymmetric multidimensional scaling	WAMDS(external) Weighted external asymmetric multidimensional scaling
Object by attribute	Rectangular	Internal unfolding	CMDU Classical internal multidimensional unfolding	RMDU Replicated internal multidimensional unfolding	WMDU Weighted internal multidimensional unfolding
		External unfolding	CMDU(external) Classical external multidimensional unfolding	RMDU(external) Replicated external multidimensional unfolding	WMDU(external) Weighted external multidimensional unfolding

Table 4 ALSCAL specifications for nonmetric models

Matrix mode	Matrix form	Model class	Single matrix	Replications of single matrix	Two or more individual matrices
Object by object	Symmetric	Multidimensional scaling	`ALSCAL VAR= varlist.`	`ALSCAL VAR= varlist.`	`ALSCAL VAR= varlist` `/MODEL=INDSCAL.`

	Asymmetric single process	Multidimensional scaling	`ALSCAL VAR= varlist`
			`/SHAPE=ASYMMETRIC`
			`/CONDITION=ROW.`
				`ALSCAL VAR= varlist`
				`/SHAPE=ASYMMETRIC`
				`/CONDITION=ROW.`
					`ALSCAL VAR= varlist`
					`/SHAPE=ASYMMETRIC`
					`/CONDITION=ROW`
					`/MODEL=INDSCAL.`

	Asymmetric multiple process	Internal asymmetric multidimensional scaling	`ALSCAL VAR= varlist`
			`/SHAPE=ASYMMETRIC`
			`/MODEL=ASCAL.`
				`ALSCAL VAR= varlist`
				`/SHAPE=ASYMMETRIC`
				`/MODEL=ASCAL.`
					`ALSCAL VAR= varlist`
					`/SHAPE=ASYMMETRIC`
					`/MODEL=AINDS.`

		External asymmetric multidimensional scaling	`ALSCAL VAR= varlist`
			`/SHAPE=ASYMMETRIC`
			`/MODEL=ASCAL`
			`/FILE=file COLCONF(FIX).`
				`ALSCAL VAR= varlist`
				`/SHAPE=ASYMMETRIC`
				`/MODEL=ASCAL`
				`/FILE=file COLCONF(FIX).`
					`ALSCAL VAR= varlist`
					`/SHAPE=ASYMMETRIC`
					`/MODEL=AINDS`
					`/FILE=file COLCONF(FIX).`

Object by attribute	Rectangular	Internal unfolding	`ALSCAL VAR= varlist`
			`/SHAPE=REC`
			`/INP=ROWS`
			`/CONDITION=ROW.`
				`ALSCAL VAR= varlist`
				`/SHAPE=REC`
				`/INP=ROWS`
				`/CONDITION(ROW).`
					`ALSCAL VAR= varlist`
					`/SHAPE=REC`
					`/INP=ROWS`
					`/CONDITION=ROW`
					`/MODEL=INDSCAL.`

		External unfolding	`ALSCAL VAR= varlist`
			`/SHAPE=REC`
			`/INP=ROWS`
			`/CONDITION=ROW`
			`/FILE=file ROWCONF(FIX).`
				`ALSCAL VAR= varlist`
				`/SHAPE=REC`
				`/INP=ROWS`
				`/CONDITION=ROW`
				`/FILE=file ROWCONF(FIX).`
					`ALSCAL VAR= varlist`
					`/SHAPE=REC`
					`/INP=ROWS`
					`/CONDITION=ROW`
					`/FILE=file ROWCONF(FIX)`
					`/MODEL=INDSCAL.`

Table 5 ALSCAL specifications for metric models

Matrix mode	Matrix form	Model class	Single matrix	Replications of single matrix	Two or more individual matrices

Object by object	Symmetric	Multidimensional scaling	`ALSCAL VAR= varlist`
			`/LEVEL=INT.`
				`ALSCAL VAR= varlist`
				`/LEVEL=INT.`
					`ALSCAL VAR= varlist`
					`/LEVEL=INT`
					`/MODEL=INDSCAL.`

	Asymmetric single process	Multidimensional scaling	`ALSCAL VAR= varlist`
			`/SHAPE=ASYMMETRIC`
			`/CONDITION=ROW`
			`/LEVEL=INT.`
				`ALSCAL VAR= varlist`
				`/SHAPE=ASYMMETRIC`
				`/CONDITION=ROW`
				`/LEVEL=INT.`
					`ALSCAL VAR= varlist`
					`/SHAPE=ASYMMETRIC`
					`/CONDITION=ROW`
					`/LEVEL=INT`
					`/MODEL=INDSCAL.`

	Asymmetric multiple process	Internal asymmetric multidimensional scaling	`ALSCAL VAR= varlist`
			`/SHAPE=ASYMMETRIC`
			`/LEVEL=INT`
			`/MODEL=ASCAL.`
				`ALSCAL VAR= varlist`
				`/SHAPE=ASYMMETRIC`
				`/LEVEL=INT`
				`/MODEL=ASCAL.`
					`ALSCAL VAR= varlist`
					`/SHAPE=ASYMMETRIC`
					`/LEVEL=INT`
					`/MODEL=AINDS.`

		External asymmetric multidimensional scaling	`ALSCAL VAR= varlist`
			`/SHAPE=ASYMMETRIC`
			`/LEVEL=INT`
			`/MODEL=ASCAL`
			`/FILE=file COLCONF(FIX).`
				`ALSCAL VAR= varlist`
				`/SHAPE=ASYMMETRIC`
				`/LEVEL=INT`
				`/MODEL=ASCAL`
				`/FILE=file COLCONF(FIX).`
					`ALSCAL VAR= varlist`
					`/SHAPE=ASYMMETRIC`
					`/LEVEL=INT`
					`/MODEL=AINDS`
					`/FILE=file COLCONF(FIX).`

Object by attribute	Rectangular	Internal unfolding	`ALSCAL VAR= varlist`
			`/SHAPE=REC`
			`/INP=ROWS`
			`/CONDITION=ROW`
			`/LEVEL=INT.`
				`ALSCAL VAR= varlist`
				`/SHAPE=REC`
				`/INP=ROWS`
				`/CONDITION=ROW`
				`/LEVEL=INT.`
					`ALSCAL VAR= varlist`
					`/SHAPE=REC`
					`/INP=ROWS`
					`/CONDITION=ROW`
					`/LEVEL=INT`
					`/MODEL=INDSCAL.`

		External unfolding	`ALSCAL VAR= varlist`
			`/SHAPE=REC`
			`/INP=ROWS`
			`/CONDITION=ROW`
			`/LEVEL=INT`
			`/FILE=file ROWCONF(FIX).`
				`ALSCAL VAR= varlist`
				`/SHAPE=REC`
				`/INP=ROWS`
				`/CONDITION=ROW`
				`/LEVEL=INT`
				`/FILE=file ROWCONF(FIX).`
					`ALSCAL VAR= varlist`
					`/SHAPE=REC`
					`/INP=ROWS`
					`/CONDITION=ROW`
					`/LEVEL=INT`
					`/FILE=file ROWCONF(FIX)`
					`/MODEL=INDSCAL.`

Annotated Example   For a complete example with output, see Examples following the Command Reference.

References
Carroll, J. D. and J. J. Chang. 1970. Analysis of individual differences in multidimensional scaling via an *n*-way generalization of "Eckart-Young" decomposition. *Psychometrika* 35:238-319.

Johnson, R. and D. W. Wichern. 1982. *Applied Multivariate Statistical Analysis.* Englewood Cliffs, N.J.: Prentice-Hall.

Takane, Y., F. W. Young, and J. de Leeuw. 1977. Nonmetric individual differences multidimensional scaling: An alternating least squares method with optimal scaling features. *Psychometrika* 42:7-67.

Young, F. W. 1975. Methods for describing ordinal data with ordinal models. *Journal of Mathematical Psychology* 12:416-436.

Young, F. W. 1987. *Multidimensional Scaling: History, Theory, and Applications.* Edited by R. M. Hamer. Hillside, N.J.: Lawrence Erlbaum Associates.

ANOVA

```
ANOVA [VARIABLES=] varlist BY varlist(min,max)...varlist(min,max)
  [WITH varlist]

  [/COVARIATES={FIRST**}]
               {WITH  }
               {AFTER }

  [/MAXORDERS={ALL** }]
             {n     }
             {NONE  }

  [/METHOD={EXPERIMENTAL**}]
           {UNIQUE       }
           {HIERARCHICAL }

  [/STATISTICS=[MCA] [REG†] [MEAN] [ALL] [NONE]]

  [/MISSING={EXCLUDE**}]
            {INCLUDE  }

  [/FORMAT={LABELS**}]
           {NOLABELS}
```

**Default if the subcommand is omitted.
†REG (table of regression coefficients) is displayed only if the design is relevant.

Example:

```
ANOVA VARIABLES=PRESTIGE BY REGION(1,9) SEX,RACE(1,2)
  /MAXORDERS=2
  /STATISTICS=MEAN.
```

Overview

ANOVA performs analysis of variance for factorial designs. The default is the full factorial model if there are five or fewer factors. Analysis of variance tests the hypothesis that the group means of the dependent variable are equal. The dependent variable is interval level, and one or more categorical variables define the groups. These categorical variables are termed *factors*. ANOVA also allows you to include continuous explanatory variables, termed *covariates*. Other SPSS procedures that perform analysis of variance are ONEWAY, MEANS, and MANOVA. See T-TEST for performing a comparison of two means.

Options

Specifying Covariates. You can introduce covariates into the model by means of the WITH keyword. See VARIABLES Subcommand.

Order of Entry of Covariates. By default, covariates are processed before main effects for factors. You can process covariates with or after main effects for factors. See COVARIATES Subcommand.

Suppressing Interaction Effects. You can suppress the effects of various orders of interaction. See MAXORDERS Subcommand.

Methods for Decomposing Sums of Squares. By default, the classic experimental approach is used. You can request the regression approach or the hierarchical approach. See METHOD Subcommand.

Statistical Display. You can request means and counts for each dependent variable for groups defined by each factor and each combination of factors up to the fifth level. You can request unstandardized regression coefficients for covariates. The coefficients are computed at the point where the covariates are entered into the equation. Thus, their values depend on the type of design you have specified. You can request multiple classification analysis (MCA) results. In the MCA table, effects are expressed as deviations from the grand mean. The table includes a listing of unadjusted category effects for each factor, category effects adjusted for other factors, category effects adjusted for all factors and covariates, and eta and beta values. See STATISTICS Subcommand.

Formatting Options. You can suppress both variable and value labels in the displayed results. See FORMAT Subcommand.

Basic Specification
- The basic specification is a single VARIABLES subcommand with an analysis list. The minimum analysis list specifies a list of dependent variables, the keyword BY, a list of factor variables, and the minimum and maximum integer values of the factors in parentheses.
- By default, the model includes all interaction terms up to five-way interactions. The sums of squares are decomposed using the classical experimental approach, in which covariates, main effects, and ascending orders of interaction are assessed separately in that order. A case that has a missing value for any variable in an analysis list is omitted from the analysis.

Subcommand Order
- The variable list must be first if keyword VARIABLES is omitted from the specification. If keyword VARIABLES= is used, the variable specification does not have to be first.
- Remaining subcommands can be named in any order.

Operations
- A separate analysis of variance is performed for each dependent variable in an analysis list, using the same factors and covariates.
- All ANOVA output, except that produced by STATISTICS=MEANS, fits in 80 columns. If you want to limit the width of the means and counts table, use the SET WIDTH command.

Limitations
- Maximum 5 ANOVA analysis lists.
- Maximum 5 dependent variables per analysis list.
- Maximum 10 independent variables per analysis list.
- Maximum 10 covariates per analysis list.
- Maximum 5 interaction levels.
- Maximum 25 value labels per variable displayed in the MCA table.
- The combined number of categories for all factors in an analysis list plus the number of covariates must be less than the sample size.

Example
```
ANOVA VARIABLES=PRESTIGE BY REGION(1,9) SEX,RACE(1,2)
  /MAXORDERS=2
  /STATISTICS=MEAN.
```
- VARIABLES specifies a three-way analysis of variance: PRESTIGE by RE-GION, SEX, and RACE.
- Variables SEX and RACE both have the values 1 and 2 included in the analysis.
- MAXORDERS pools all three-way interaction terms into the error sum of squares.
- STATISTICS requests the display of a table of cell means of PRESTIGE within the combined categories of REGION, SEX, and RACE.

Example
```
ANOVA VARIABLES=PRESTIGE BY REGION(1,9) SEX,RACE(1,2)
  /RINCOME BY SEX,RACE(1,2).
```
- ANOVA specifies a three-way analysis of variance of PRESTIGE by REGION, SEX, and RACE, and a two-way analysis of variance of RINCOME by SEX and RACE.

VARIABLES Subcommand

VARIABLES specifies the analysis list. The actual keyword VARIABLES may be omitted.

- More than one design can be specified on the same ANOVA command by separating the analysis lists with a slash.
- Variables named before the BY keyword are dependent variables. Value ranges are not specified for dependent variables.

- Variables named after the BY in the analysis list are factor (independent) variables.
- Every factor variable must have a value range indicating its minimum and maximum values. The values must be separated by a space or comma and enclosed in parentheses.
- Variables named after the keyword WITH are covariates.
- Each analysis list can include only one BY and one WITH keyword.
- Factor variables must have integer values. Noninteger values for factors are truncated.
- Cases with values outside the range specified for a factor are excluded from the analysis.
- If two or more factors have the same value range, you can specify the value range once following the last factor to which it applies.

- You can specify a single minimum and maximum value range that encompasses the ranges of all factors in the list. However, this may reduce performance and cause memory problems if the specified range is larger than the actual range.

COVARIATES Subcommand

COVARIATES specifies the order for assessing blocks of covariates and factor main effects.

- By default, ANOVA assesses the covariates before it assesses the factor main effects.
- The order of entry is irrelevant when METHOD=UNIQUE.

FIRST *Process covariates before main effects for factors.* This is the default.

WITH *Process covariates concurrently with main effects for factors.*

AFTER *Process covariates after main effects for factors.*

MAXORDERS Subcommand

MAXORDERS suppresses the effects of various orders of interaction.

- By default, ANOVA examines all the interaction effects up to and including the fifth order.
- The keyword NONE suppresses all interaction terms so only main effects and covariate effects appear in the ANOVA table, with interaction sums of squares pooled into the error (residual) sum of squares.

ALL *Examine all the interaction effects up to and including the fifth order.* This is the default.

n *Examine all the interaction effects up to and including the n-order effect.* For example, if MAXORDERS=3 is specified, ANOVA examines all the interaction effects up to and including the third order. All higher order interaction sums of squares are pooled into the error term.

NONE *Delete all interaction terms from the model.* All interaction sums of squares are pooled into the error sum of squares.

METHOD Subcommand

METHOD controls the method for decomposing sums of squares.

- By default, ANOVA uses the *classic experimental approach* for decomposing sums of squares.
- Optionally, the *regression approach* or the *hierarchical approach* can be used.

EXPERIMENTAL *Classic experimental approach.* This is the default.

UNIQUE *Regression approach.* UNIQUE overrides any keywords on the COVARIATES subcommand. All effects are assessed for their partial contribution, so order is irrelevant. The MCA and MEAN specifications on the STATISTICS subcommand are not available with the regression approach.

HIERARCHICAL *Hierarchical approach.*

Classic Experimental Approach This is the default if the METHOD subcommand is omitted. Each type of effect is assessed separately in the following order (unless WITH or AFTER is specified on the COVARIATES subcommand):

- Effects of covariates.
- Main effects of factors.
- Two-way interaction effects.
- Three-way interaction effects.
- Four-way interaction effects.
- Five-way interaction effects.

The effects within each type are adjusted for all other effects in that type and also for the effects of all prior types (see Table 1).

Regression Approach All effects are assessed simultaneously, with each effect adjusted for all other effects in the model. Some restrictions apply to the use of the regression approach:

- The lowest specified categories of all the independent variables must have a marginal frequency of at least one, since the lowest specified category is used as the reference category. If this rule is not followed, no ANOVA table is produced, and a message is displayed identifying the first offending variable.

- Given an *n*-way crosstabulation of the independent variables, there must be no empty cells defined by the lowest specified category of any of the independent variables. If this restriction is violated, one or more levels of interaction effects are suppressed, and a warning message is issued. However, this constraint does not apply to categories defined for an independent variable but not occurring in the data. For example, given two independent variables, each with categories of 1, 2, and 4, the (1,1), (1,2), (1,4), (2,1), and (4,1) cells must not be empty. The (1,3), (2,3), (3,3), (4,3), (3,1), (3,2), and (3,4) cells are empty by definition, and the (2,2), (2,4), (4,2), and (4,4) cells may be empty, although the degrees of freedom will be reduced accordingly.

To comply with these restrictions, specify precisely the lowest nonempty category of each independent variable. Specifying a value range of (0,9) for a variable that actually has values of 1 through 9 results in an error, and no ANOVA table is produced.

Hierarchical Approach The hierarchical approach differs from the classic experimental approach only in the way it handles covariate and factor main effects. In the hierarchical approach, the factor main effects and the covariate effects are assessed hierarchically; the factor main effects are adjusted only for the factor main effects already assessed, and the covariate effects are adjusted only for the covariates already assessed. The order in which the factors are listed on the ANOVA command determines the order in which they are assessed.

Example `ANOVA VARIABLES=Y BY A,B,C(0,3).`

- ANOVA specifies three factor variables: A, B, and C. Table 1 summarizes the three approaches with respect to this example.
- With the *default classic experimental* approach, each main effect is assessed with the two other main effects held constant, and two-way interactions are assessed with all main effects and other two-way interactions held constant. The three-way interaction is assessed with all main effects and two-way interactions held constant.
- With the *regression approach,* each factor or interaction is assessed with all other factors and interactions held constant.
- With the *hierarchical approach,* the order in which the factors and covariates are listed on the ANOVA command determines the order in which they are assessed in the hierarchical analysis.

Table 1 Terms adjusted for under each option

Effect	Experimental	Unique (Regression)	Hierarchical
A	B,C	ALL OTHERS	NONE
B	A,C	ALL OTHERS	A
C	A,B	ALL OTHERS	A,B
AB	A,B,C,AC,BC	ALL OTHERS	A,B,C,AC,BC
AC	A,B,C,AB,BC	ALL OTHERS	A,B,C,AB,BC
BC	A,B,C,AB,AC	ALL OTHERS	A,B,C,AB,AC
ABC	A,B,C,AB,AC,BC	ALL OTHERS	A,B,C,AB,AC,BC

Summary of Analysis Methods

Table 2 describes the results obtained with various combinations of methods for controlling entry of covariates and decomposing the sums of squares.

Table 2 Combinations of COVARIATES and METHOD subcommands

	Assessments between types of effects	Assessments within the same type of effect
Default	*Covariates* THEN *Factors* THEN *Interactions*	*Covariates:* adjust for all other covariates *Factors:* adjust for covariates and all other factors *Interactions:* adjust for covariates, factors, and all other interactions of the same and lower orders
COVARIATES=WITH	*Factors* and *Covariates* concurrently THEN *Interactions*	*Covariates:* adjust for factors and all other covariates *Factors:* adjust for covariates and all other factors *Interactions:* adjust for covariates, factors, and all other interactions of the same and lower orders
COVARIATES=AFTER	*Factors* THEN *Covariates* THEN *Interactions*	*Factors:* adjust for all other factors *Covariates:* adjust for factors and all other covariates *Interactions:* adjust for covariates, factors, and all other interactions of the same and lower orders
METHOD=UNIQUE	*Covariates, Factors,* and *Interactions* simultaneously	*Covariates:* adjust for factors, interactions, and all other covariates *Factors:* adjust for covariates, interactions, and all other factors *Interactions:* adjust for covariates, factors, and all other interactions
METHOD=HIERARCHICAL	*Covariates* THEN *Factors* THEN *Interactions*	*Covariates:* adjust for covariates that are preceding in the list *Factors:* adjust for covariates and factors preceding in the list *Interactions:* adjust for covariates, factors, and all other interactions of the same and lower orders
COVARIATES=WITH and METHOD=HIERARCHICAL	*Factors* and *Covariates* concurrently THEN *Interactions*	*Factors:* adjust only for preceding factors *Covariates:* adjust for factors and preceding covariates *Interactions:* adjust for covariates, factors, and all other interactions of the same and lower orders
COVARIATES=AFTER and METHOD=HIERARCHICAL	*Factors* THEN *Covariates* THEN *Interactions*	*Factors:* adjust only for preceding factors *Covariates:* adjust for factors and preceding covariates *Interactions:* adjust for covariates, factors, and all other interactions of the same and lower orders

STATISTICS Subcommand

STATISTICS requests additional statistics for ANOVA. STATISTICS can be specified by itself or with one or more keywords.

- By default, ANOVA calculates only the statistics needed for analysis of variance. Optionally, you can request a means and counts table, unstandardized regression coefficients, and multiple classification analysis.

- If STATISTICS is specified without keywords, ANOVA calculates MEAN and REG (each defined below).

- If you specify a keyword or keywords on the STATISTICS subcommand, ANOVA calculates only the additional statistics you request.

MEAN *Means and counts table.* This statistic is not available with METHOD= UNIQUE. See Cell Means, below.

REG *Unstandardized regression coefficients.* Displays unstandardized regression coefficients for the covariates. See Regression Coefficients for the Covariates, below.

MCA *Multiple classification analysis.* The MCA table is not produced when METHOD=UNIQUE. See Multiple Classification Analysis, below.

ALL *Means and counts table, unstandardized regression coefficients, and multiple classification analysis.*

NONE *No additional statistics.* This is the default if the STATISTICS subcommand is omitted.

Cell Means

STATISTICS=MEAN displays the means and counts table. The means and counts of each dependent variable are displayed for each cell as defined by the factors and combinations of factors.

- This statistic is not available with METHOD=UNIQUE.

- For each dependent variable, a separate table is displayed for each effect, showing the means and cell counts for each combination of values of the factors that define the effect, ignoring all other factors.

- If MAXORDERS is used to suppress higher order interactions, cell means corresponding to suppressed interaction terms are not displayed. The means displayed are the observed means in each cell, and they are produced only for dependent variables, not for covariates.

Regression Coefficients for the Covariates

STATISTICS=REG requests the unstandardized regression coefficients for the covariates.

- The regression coefficients are computed at the point where the covariates are entered into the equation. Thus, their values depend on the type of design specified or used as a default by the COVARIATES or METHOD subcommands.

- The coefficients are displayed immediately below the ANOVA summary table in the output.

Multiple Classification Analysis

STATISTICS=MCA produces MCA output, which consists of the grand mean of the dependent variable and a table of category means for each factor expressed as deviations from the grand mean. The latter are sometimes termed *treatment effects.*

- For each category of each factor the MCA table presents the unadjusted mean of the dependent variable expressed as a deviation from the grand mean, the deviation from the grand mean of the category mean adjusted for other factors, and the deviation from the grand mean of the category mean adjusted for both factors and covariates.

- For each factor the complete MCA output displays the correlation ratio (eta) with the unadjusted deviations (the square of eta indicates the proportion of variance explained by all categories of the factor), a partial beta equivalent to the standardized partial regression coefficient that would be obtained by assigning the unadjusted deviations to each factor category and regressing the dependent variable on the resulting variables, the parallel partial betas from a regression that includes covariates in addition to the factors, and the multiple R and R^2 from this regression.

• The results of the MCA table are affected by the form specified for the analysis (or allowed to run by default). For example, if the COVARIATES subcommand is omitted, ANOVA runs the default order for entering covariates, which is COVARIATES=FIRST, and values adjusted for independents don't display. With covariates present in the analysis, COVARIATES=AFTER, or COVARIATES=AFTER and METHOD=HIERARCHICAL, or COVARIATES=WITH and METHOD=HIERARCHICAL must be specified to obtain an MCA table. With a model in which factors are not processed first, effects adjusted only for factors do not appear. The MCA table cannot be produced when METHOD=UNIQUE is in effect.

MISSING Subcommand

Use MISSING to ignore missing-data indicators and to include all cases in the computations.

• By default, a case that is missing for any variable named in the analysis list is deleted for all analyses specified by that list.

EXCLUDE *Exclude missing data.* This is the default.

INCLUDE *Include user-defined missing data.*

FORMAT Subcommand

Use the FORMAT subcommand to suppress variable and value labels. By default, ANOVA displays variable or value labels if they have been defined.

LABELS *Display variable and value labels.* This is the default.

NOLABELS *Suppress variable and value labels.*

Annotated Example

For a complete example with output, see Examples following the Command Reference.

References

Andrews, F., J. Morgan, J. Sonquist, and L. Klein. *Multiple classification analysis.* 2nd ed. 1973. Ann Arbor: Univ. of Michigan.

AUTORECODE

```
AUTORECODE VARIABLES=varlist

/INTO new varlist

[/DESCENDING]

[/PRINT]
```

Example:
```
AUTORECODE VARIABLES=COMPANY /INTO RCOMPANY.
```

Overview

AUTORECODE recodes the values of both string and numeric variables to consecutive integers and puts the new values into a different variable called a *target variable.* AUTORECODE can recode long string variables into numeric variables, using the original string value as a label for the new numeric value. This is especially useful when using long string variables in the TABLES procedure. (See the SPSS TABLES manual for more information.) It is also useful for creating numeric independent (group) variables from string variables for procedures like ONEWAY, ANOVA, MANOVA, and DISCRIMINANT. AUTORECODE can also recode the values of factor variables to consecutive integers, which is the form required by MANOVA, and which reduces the amount of workspace needed by other statistical procedures like ANOVA.

AUTORECODE is similar to the RECODE command because it recodes the values of variables. However, unlike RECODE, AUTORECODE automatically assigns new target values into which the given values are recoded. In RECODE, you must specify the target values.

Options

Displaying Recoded Variables. You can display the values of the original and recoded variables. (See PRINT Subcommand, below.)

Ordering of Values. By default, values are recoded in ascending order (lowest to highest). You can recode values in descending order (highest to lowest). (See DESCENDING Subcommand, below.)

Basic Specification

• The basic specification is two subcommands: VARIABLES and INTO. VARIABLES specifies the variables to be recoded. INTO names the target variables that store the new values. VARIABLES and INTO must name or imply the same number of variables.

Subcommand Order

• VARIABLES must be specified first.
• INTO must immediately follow VARIABLES.
• The order of PRINT and DESCENDING is unimportant, provided each follows INTO.

Syntax Rules

• A variable cannot be recoded into itself. More generally, target variable names must not duplicate any variable names already in the file.

Operations

• The values of each variable to be recoded are sorted and then assigned numeric values. By default, the values are assigned in ascending order: the value 1 is assigned to the lowest nonmissing value of the original variable, the value 2 to the second-lowest nonmissing value, and so on for each value of the original variable.
• Missing values are recoded into missing values higher than any nonmissing values, with their order preserved. For example, if the original variable has 10 nonmissing values, the value of the first missing value is recoded as 11. The value 11 is then a missing value on the new variable.
• Because the values of a variable to be recoded are sorted before they are assigned new values, AUTORECODE does *not* necessarily preserve the order of values as they were entered in the command file.

- Target variables are assigned the same variable labels as the original source variables. To change the variable labels, use the VARIABLE LABELS command after AUTORECODE.

- Value labels are automatically generated for each value of the target variables. If the original value had a label, that label is used for the corresponding new value. If the original value did not have a label, the old value itself is used as the value label for the new value. The old value is formatted according to its defined print format to create the new value label.

- SPLIT FILES specifications in effect before the AUTORECODE command are ignored. However, SELECT IF specifications can precede AUTORECODE.

Example

```
DATA LIST / COMPANY 1-21 (A) SALES 24-28.
BEGIN DATA.
CATFOOD JOY              10000
OLD FASHIONED CATFOOD   11200
  . . .
PRIME CATFOOD            10900
CHOICE CATFOOD          14600
END DATA.

AUTORECODE VARIABLES=COMPANY /INTO=RCOMPANY /PRINT.

TABLES TABLE = SALES BY RCOMPANY
  /TTITLE='CATFOOD SALES BY COMPANY'.
```

- Because TABLES truncates string variables to eight characters, AUTORECODE is used to recode the string variable COMPANY, which contains the names of various hypothetical cat food companies.

- AUTORECODE recodes COMPANY into a numeric variable RCOMPANY. Values of RCOMPANY are consecutive integers beginning with 1 and ending with the number of different values entered for COMPANY. The values of COMPANY are used as descriptive value labels for RCOMPANY's numeric values. The PRINT subcommand displays a table to confirm the recodes.

- Variable RCOMPANY is used as the banner variable in the TABLES procedure to produce a table of sales figures for each cat food company. RCOMPANY's value labels display as column headings in the table and are not truncated, because TABLES does not truncate value labels that are longer than 8 characters.

Example

```
AUTORECODE VARIABLES=REGION /INTO=RREGION /PRINT.
ANOVA Y BY RREGION (1,5).
```

- In statistical procedures, empty cells can reduce performance and increase memory requirements. In this example, assume factor REGION has only five nonempty categories, represented by the numeric codes 1, 4, 6, 14 and 20. AUTORECODE recodes those values into 1, 2, 3, 4, 5 for target variable RREGION. The RECODE command can also be used to do this, but you would have to specify all five recodes. AUTORECODE automatically recodes the original values into consecutive integer values.

- Variable RREGION is used in ANOVA. If the original variable REGION were used, the amount of memory required by ANOVA would be 4429 bytes (because of all the empty cells in REGION). Using variable RREGION, ANOVA only requires 449 bytes of memory (because RREGION has no empty cells).

Example

```
DATA LIST / RELIGION 1-8 (A) Y 10-13.
MISSING VALUES RELIGION (' ').
BEGIN DATA.
CATHOLIC 2013
PROTEST  3234
JEWISH   5169
NONE      714
OTHER    2321
  . . .
END DATA.

AUTORECODE VARIABLES=RELIGION /INTO=NRELIG /PRINT /DESCENDING.
MANOVA Y BY NRELIG(1,5).
```

- Because MANOVA requires consecutive integer values for factor levels, string variable RELIGION is recoded into a numeric variable. Values for RELIGION are first sorted in descending order (Z to A), then assigned values 1, 2, 3, 4, 5, and 6 in target variable NRELIG. Value 6 is assigned to the ' ', specified as a missing value for RELIGION. In the PRINT table, value 6 is displayed as 6M for variable NRELIG to flag it as a user-missing value.

- Values of RELIGION are assigned as value labels to the corresponding new values in NRELIG.

- Target variable NRELIG is then used as a factor variable in MANOVA.

VARIABLES Subcommand

VARIABLES names the variables to be recoded. VARIABLES is required and must be the first subcommand used. The actual keyword VARIABLES is optional.

- Keyword TO can be used to refer to consecutive variables in the active system file.

- The number of variables named or implied on VARIABLES must equal the number of target variables listed on INTO.

- Values from specified variables are recoded and stored in the target variables listed on INTO. Values of the original variables are unchanged.

INTO Subcommand

INTO names the target variables that store the new values. INTO is required and must immediately follow VARIABLES.

- Keyword TO can be used to generate names for target variables.

- The number of target variables named or implied on INTO must equal the number of source variables listed on VARIABLES.

Example

```
AUTORECODE VARIABLES=V1 TO V3 /INTO=NEW_V1 TO NEW_V3 /PRINT.
```

- AUTORECODE sequentially assigns the names implied by the inclusive list on INTO to the variables referenced on VARIABLES.

- INTO immediately follows VARIABLES, which must be the first subcommand specified on AUTORECODE.

PRINT Subcommand

PRINT displays a correspondence table of values for the original values of the source variable(s) and the new values of the target variable(s). The new value labels are also displayed.

- The only specification is keyword PRINT. PRINT has no additional specifications.

- By default, or if the width is set to less than 132, the table is formatted to display in 80 columns. If the width has been previously set to 132 (by the SET WIDTH command), the output is formatted to display in 132 columns.

- Only the first 18 characters of the values for the original variable and the first 48 characters of the value labels for the new variable are displayed.

DESCENDING Subcommand

DESCENDING assigns the values to new variables in descending order (from highest to lowest). The largest value is assigned 1, the second-largest, 2, and so on. The default assigns the variables in ascending order.

- The only specification is keyword DESCENDING. DESCENDING has no additional specifications.

BEGIN DATA— END DATA

```
BEGIN DATA
data records
END DATA
```

Example:

```
BEGIN DATA.
1  3424  274 ABU DHABI 2
2 39932   86 AMSTERDAM 4
3  8889  232 ATHENS
4  3424  294 BOGOTA    3
END DATA.
```

Overview

BEGIN DATA signals the beginning of data lines in a command file, and END DATA signals the end of data lines. Both BEGIN DATA and END DATA must be used when data are entered within the sequence of commands (inline data). BEGIN DATA and END DATA are also used for inline matrix data or matrix materials.

Basic Specification

- The basic specification is BEGIN DATA, the data lines, and END DATA. BEGIN DATA must be by itself on the line that immediately precedes the first data line. END DATA must be by itself on the line that immediately follows the last data line.

Syntax Rules

- BEGIN DATA, the data, and END DATA must precede the first SPSS procedure.
- END DATA must always begin in column 1, be spelled out in full, and have only one space between the words END and DATA. Procedures and additional transformations can follow the END DATA command.
- Data lines must *not* have a command terminator.

Operations

- When SPSS encounters BEGIN DATA, it begins to read and process data on the next input line. All preceding transformation commands are processed as a file is built for use in SPSS procedures.
- Inline data between BEGIN DATA and END DATA must be limited to a maximum of 80 columns. (For the affected IBM implementations, UNNUMBERED must be in effect to read 80 columns. On some systems, the maximum can be fewer than 80 columns.) To read records in excess of 80 columns, data must be stored in an external file that is specified on the FILE subcommand of DATA LIST (or a similar command).
- SPSS continues to evaluate input lines as data until it encounters END DATA, at which point it begins evaluating input lines as SPSS commands.
- No other SPSS commands are recognized between BEGIN DATA and END DATA.
- The INCLUDE command can specify a file that contains BEGIN DATA, data lines, and END DATA, provided the FILE specification is omitted on DATA LIST (or similar command). Data are still considered inline and should be limited to 80 columns.
- When running SPSS from prompts, the prompt DATA> appears immediately after BEGIN DATA is specified. After END DATA is specified, the prompt SPSS> returns.

Example

```
DATA LIST /XVAR 1 YVAR ZVAR 3-12 CVAR 14-22(A) JVAR 24.
BEGIN DATA.
1   3424   274 ABU DHABI 2
2 39932    86 AMSTERDAM 4
3  8889   232 ATHENS
4  3424   294 BOGOTA     3
5 11323   332 HONG KONG 3
6   323   232 MANILA     1
7  3234   899 CHICAGO    4
8 78998  2344 VIENNA     3
9  8870   983 ZURICH     5
END DATA.
MEANS XVAR BY JVAR.
```

• DATA LIST defines the names and column locations of the variables. The FILE subcommand is omitted because the data are inline.

• There are nine cases in the inline data. Each line of data completes a case.

• END DATA begins in column 1, has only a single space between END and DATA, and signals the end of lines of data.

BREAK

```
BREAK
```

Example:

```
VECTOR          #X(10).
LOOP            #I = 1 TO #NREC.
+  DATA LIST       NOTABLE/ #X1 TO #X10 1-20.
+  LOOP            #J = 1 TO 10.
+    DO IF            SYSMIS(#X(#J)).
+       BREAK.
+    END IF.
+    COMPUTE          X = #X(#J).
+    END CASE.
+  END LOOP.
END LOOP.
```

Overview

BREAK controls looping that cannot be fully controlled with the IF clauses on the LOOP and END LOOP commands. Generally, BREAK is used within a DO IF—END IF structure. The expression on the DO IF command specifies the condition in which BREAK is executed.

Basic Specification

• The only specification is the keyword. BREAK has no additional specifications. BREAK must be enclosed within a LOOP structure. Otherwise, an error results.

Operations

• A BREAK command inside a LOOP structure but not inside a DO IF structure terminates the first iteration of the loop for all cases, since no conditions for BREAK are specified.

• A BREAK command within an inner loop terminates only iterations in that structure, not in any outer loop structures.

Example

```
VECTOR          #X(10).
LOOP            #I = 1 TO #NREC.
+  DATA LIST       NOTABLE/ #X1 TO #X10 1-20.
+  LOOP            #J = 1 TO 10.
+    DO IF            SYSMIS(#X(#J)).
+       BREAK.
+    END IF.
+    COMPUTE          X = #X(#J).
+    END CASE.
+  END LOOP.
END LOOP.
```

• Because BREAK is within a DO IF structure, the loop terminates only when there is a system-missing value for any of the variables #X1 to #X10.

CLEAR TRANSFORMATIONS

`CLEAR TRANSFORMATIONS`

Overview

CLEAR TRANSFORMATIONS discards previous transformations in the active file.

Basic Specification

The only specification is the command keyword. CLEAR TRANSFORMATIONS has no additional specifications.

Operations

- CLEAR TRANSFORMATIONS discards all transformation commands that have accumulated since the last procedure.
- CLEAR TRANSFORMATIONS has no effect if a command file is executed through your operating system and generates a warning if present in the file. If journaling is on during an SPSS session and you use CLEAR TRANSFORMATIONS, be sure to delete CLEAR TRANSFORMATIONS and the unwanted transformation commands from the session's journal file if you plan to execute that file through the operating system. Otherwise, the unwanted transformations will cause problems.

Example

```
GET FILE=QUERY.
FREQUENCIES=ITEM1 ITEM2 ITEM3.
RECODE ITEM1, ITEM2, ITEM3 (0=1) (1=0) (2=-1).
COMPUTE INDEXQ=(ITEM1 + ITEM2 + ITEM3)/3.
VARIABLE LABELS INDEXQ 'SUMMARY INDEX OF QUESTIONS'.
CLEAR TRANSFORMATIONS.
DISPLAY DICTIONARY.
```

- The GET and FREQUENCIES commands are executed.
- The RECODE, COMPUTE, and VARIABLE LABELS commands are transformations; their specifications, therefore, do not affect the data until the next procedure is executed.
- The CLEAR TRANSFORMATIONS command discards the specifications made on the RECODE, COMPUTE and VARIABLE LABELS commands.
- The DISPLAY command displays the active file dictionary. Data values and labels are exactly as they were when the FREQUENCIES command was executed. Variable INDEXQ does not exist because the CLEAR TRANSFORMATIONS command discarded the COMPUTE command.

CLUSTER

```
CLUSTER varlist [/MISSING=LISTWISE**] [INCLUDE]

[/MEASURE={SEUCLID** }] [/METHOD={BAVERAGE**}[(rootname)][,...]]
          {EUCLID   }            {WAVERAGE }
          {COSINE   }            {SINGLE   }
          {POWER(p,r)}           {COMPLETE }
          {BLOCK    }            {CENTROID }
          {CHEBYCHEV}            {MEDIAN   }
          {DEFAULT  }            {WARD     }

[/SAVE=CLUSTER({level  })]  [/ID=varname]
              {min,max}

[/PRINT=[CLUSTER({level  })] [DISTANCE] [SCHEDULE**] [NONE]]
                {min,max}

[/PLOT=[VICICLE**[(min[,max[,inc]])])]] [DENDROGRAM] [NONE]]
       [HICICLE[(min[,max[,inc]])])]]

[/MATRIX=[IN({file})] [OUT({file})]]
            {*   }        {*   }
```

** Default if the subcommand is omitted.

Example:

```
CLUSTER V1 TO V4
 /PLOT=DENDROGRAM
 /PRINT=CLUSTER (2 4).
```

Overview

CLUSTER produces hierarchical clusters of items based on their dissimilarity or similarity on one or more variables. Cluster analysis is discussed in Anderberg (1973).

Options

Cluster Measures and Methods. You can use one of six similarity or distance measures and can cluster items using any one of seven methods: single linkage, complete linkage, between- and within-groups average linkage, and median, centroid, and Ward's methods. You can request more than one clustering method on a single CLUSTER command. Some clustering methods are restricted to particular distance metrics. See MEASURE and METHOD subcommands.

Adding Variables to the Active System File. You can save cluster membership for specified solutions as new variables in the active system file. See SAVE Subcommand.

Display and Plots. You can display cluster membership, the distance or similarity matrix used to cluster variables or cases, and the agglomeration schedule for the cluster solution. You can request either a horizontal or vertical icicle plot or a dendrogram of the cluster solution, and you can control the cluster levels displayed on the icicle plot. You can also specify a variable to be used as a case identifier in the display. See PRINT, PLOT, and ID subcommands.

Missing Values. You can include cases with user-missing values for the clustering variables in the analysis. See MISSING Subcommand.

Writing and Reading Matrices. You can write out the distance matrix and use it in subsequent CLUSTER, PROXIMITIES, or ALSCAL analyses. You can also read in matrices produced by other CLUSTER or PROXIMITIES procedures. See MATRIX Subcommand.

Basic Specification

• The basic specification is a variable list. CLUSTER assumes the items being clustered are cases and uses the squared Euclidean distances between cases on the variables in the analysis as the measure of distance.

Subcommand Order

• The variables list must come first.
• Remaining subcommands can be used in any order.

Syntax Rules	• The variables list and subcommands can each be specified once.
	• More than one clustering method can be used on a matrix.

Operations	The CLUSTER procedure involves four steps:

• First, CLUSTER obtains distance measures of similarities between or distances separating initial clusters (individual cases or variables being clustered).

• Second, it combines the two nearest clusters to form a new cluster.

• Third, it recomputes similarities or distances of existing clusters to the new cluster.

• Finally, it returns to the second step until all items are combined in one cluster.

This process yields a hierarchy of cluster solutions, ranging from one overall cluster to as many clusters as there are cases. Clusters at a higher level can contain several lower-level clusters, but within each level, the clusters are disjoint (each item belongs to only one cluster).

• Clustering requires that valid values be present for most items.

• CLUSTER identifies clusters in solutions by sequential integers (1, 2, 3, and so on).

• When a narrow width is defined on the SET command, plots exceeding the defined width are broken into two sections and are displayed one after the other.

• The BOX specification on the SET command controls the character used in the dendrogram.

Limitations	• CLUSTER stores cases and a lower-triangular matrix of proximities in memory. Storage requirements increase rapidly with the number of cases. You should be able to cluster 150 cases using a small number of variables in an 80K workspace.

| **Example** | ```
CLUSTER V1 TO V4
  /PLOT=DENDROGRAM
  /PRINT=CLUSTER (2 4).
``` |

• This example clusters cases based on their values for all variables between and including V1 and V4 on the SPSS active system file.

• The analysis uses the default measure of distance (squared Euclidean) and the default clustering method (average linkage between groups).

• PLOT requests a dendrogram.

• PRINT requests a table that gives the cluster membership of each case for the two-, three-, and four-cluster solutions.

Variable List	When cases are read, the variables list identifies the variables used to compute similarities or distances between cases. When a distance or similarity matrix is read, the variables list uses the names for the items in the matrix.

• The variables list is required when data enterd as input are rare cases and must be specified before the optional subcommands.

• If the data entered as input are matrix materials, the variable list should be omitted. This is true only for matrix input.

MEASURE Subcommand	MEASURE specifies the distance or similarity measure to be used in clustering cases.

• If the MEASURE subcommand is omitted or included with no specifications, squared Euclidean distances are used.

• Only one measure can be specified.

The following measures are available:
```

SEUCLID   *Squared Euclidean distances.* The distance between two cases is the sum of the squared differences in values on each variable. Use SEUCLID with centroid, median, and Ward's methods of clustering. SEUCLID is the default and can also be requested with the keyword DEFAULT.

EUCLID   *Euclidean distances.* The distance between two cases is the square root of the sum of the squared differences in values on each variable.

COSINE   *Cosine of vectors of variables.* This is a pattern similarity measure.

BLOCK   *City-block or Manhattan distances.* The distance between two cases is the sum of the absolute differences in values on each variable.

CHEBYCHEV   *Chebychev distance metric.* The distance between two cases is the maximum absolute difference in values for any variable.

POWER(p,r)   *Distances in an absolute power metric.* The distance between two cases is the *r*th root of the sum of the absolute differences to the *p*th power of values on each variable. Appropriate selection of integer parameters *p* and *r* yields Euclidean, squared Euclidean, Minkowski, city-block, and many other distance metrics.

METHOD Subcommand

The METHOD subcommand specifies one or more clustering methods.

- If the METHOD subcommand is omitted or included with no specifications, the method of average linkage between groups is used.
- Only one METHOD subcommand can be used, but more than one method can be specified on it.
- When you have a large number of items (cases), CENTROID and MEDIAN require significantly more CPU time than other methods.

The following methods can be specified:

BAVERAGE   *Average linkage between groups (UPGMA).* BAVERAGE is the default and can also be requested with the keyword DEFAULT.

WAVERAGE   *Average linkage within groups.*

SINGLE   *Single linkage or nearest neighbor.*

COMPLETE   *Complete linkage or furthest neighbor.*

CENTROID   *Centroid clustering (UPGMC).* Squared Euclidean distances should be used with this method.

MEDIAN   *Median clustering (WPGMC).* Squared Euclidean distances should be used with this method.

WARD   *Ward's method.* Squared Euclidean distances should be used with this method.

Example

```
CLUSTER V1 V2 V3
   /METHOD=SINGLE COMPLETE WARDS.
```

- This example clusters cases based on their values for variables V1, V2, and V3, and uses three clustering methods: single linkage, complete linkage, and Ward's method.

SAVE Subcommand

SAVE allows you to save cluster membership at specified solution levels as new variables on the SPSS active system file.

- The only specification on SAVE is the CLUSTER keyword, followed by an equals sign and either the number of a single cluster solution or a range of solutions separated by a comma or blank. The solution number or range must be enclosed in parentheses.
- Both the CLUSTER keyword and a solution number or range are required. There are no default specifications.

- For each method for which you want to save cluster membership you must specify a rootname on the METHOD subcommand. The METHOD subcommand is therefore required when you use the SAVE subcommand. The rootname is specified in parentheses after the method keyword.
- The solution number or range applies to all methods for which you supply a rootname on METHOD.
- The new variables derive their names from the rootname and the number of the cluster solution.

Example
```
CLUSTER A B C
  /METHOD=BAVERAGE (CLUSMEM)
  /SAVE=CLUSTERS(3,5).
```

- This command creates three new variables, CLUSMEM5, CLUSMEM4, and CLUSMEM3, containing the cluster membership for each case at the five-, four-, and three-cluster solutions.
- The order of the new variables on the active system file will be CLUSMEM5, CLUSMEM4, and CLUSMEM3, since this is the order in which the solutions are obtained.

ID Subcommand

ID names a string variable to be used as the case identifier in cluster membership tables, icicle plots, and dendrograms. If the ID subcommand is omitted, cases are identified by case number.

PRINT Subcommand

PRINT controls the display of cluster output (except plots, which are controlled by the PLOT subcommand).

- If the PRINT subcommand is omitted or included with no specifications, an agglomeration schedule is displayed. If other keywords are specified on PRINT, the agglomeration schedule is displayed only if explicitly requested.
- CLUSTER automatically displays summary information (the clustering method and measure used, the number of cases) for each method named on the METHOD subcommand. This summary is displayed regardless of specifications on PRINT.

You can specify any or all of the following on the PRINT subcommand:

SCHEDULE
Agglomeration schedule. Displays the order in which and distances at which items and clusters combine to form new clusters. It also shows the last cluster level at which an item joined the cluster. SCHEDULE is the default and can also be requested with keyword DEFAULT.

CLUSTER(min,max)
Cluster membership. For each item, the display includes the value of the case identifier (or the variable name if matrix input is used), the case sequence number, and a value (1, 2, 3, etc.) identifying the cluster to which that case belongs in a given cluster solution. Specify either a single integer value in parentheses indicating the number of cluster solutions or a minimum and maximum value in parentheses indicating a range of solutions for which display is desired. If the number of clusters specified exceeds the number produced, the largest number of clusters is used (number of items minus 1). If CLUSTER is specified more than once, the last specification is taken.

DISTANCE
Matrix of distances or similarities between items. DISTANCE displays the matrix read or computed. The type of matrix produced (similarities or dissimilarities) depends upon the measure selected. DISTANCE produces a large volume of output and uses significant CPU time when the number of cases to cluster is large.

NONE
None of the above. NONE overrides any other keywords specified on PRINT.

Example   CLUSTER V1 V2 V3 /PRINT=CLUSTER(3,5).

* This example requests the display of cluster membership for each case for the three-, four-, and five-cluster solutions.

PLOT Subcommand

PLOT controls the plots produced for each method specified on the METHOD subcommand. For icicle plots, PLOT allows you to control the cluster solution at which the plot begins and ends and the increment for displaying intermediate cluster solutions.

* If the PLOT subcommand is omitted or included with no specifications, a vertical icicle plot is produced.
* If keywords are specified on the PLOT subcommand, only those plots requested are produced.
* If there is not enough memory for a dendrogram or an icicle plot, the plot is skipped and a warning is issued.
* A large plot can be avoided by specifying range values or an increment for VICICLE or HICICLE. Smaller plots require significantly less workspace and time.

VICICLE(min,max,inc)   *Vertical icicle plot.* This is the default. The range specifications are optional. If used, they must be integer and must be enclosed in parentheses. *min* is the cluster solution at which to start the display (the default is 1), and *max* is the cluster solution at which to end the display (the default is the number of cases minus 1). If max is greater than the number of cases minus 1, the default is used. *inc* is the increment to use between cluster solutions (the default is 1). If max is specified, min must be specified, and if inc is specified, both min and max must be specified. If VICICLE is specified more than once, the last specification is used.

HICICLE(min,max,inc)   *Horizontal icicle plot.* All specifications for VICICLE apply to HICICLE. If both VICICLE and HICICLE are specified, the range specifications for both are taken from the last one specified. If no range specifications are given for the last instance of VICICLE or HICICLE, defaults are used even if a range is specified for an earlier instance.

DENDROGRAM   *Tree diagram.* The dendrogram is scaled by the joining distances of the clusters.

NONE   *No plots.*

Example   CLUSTER V1 V2 V3 /PLOT=VICICLE(1,20).

* This example produces a vertical icicle plot for the one-cluster through the twenty-cluster solution.

Example   CLUSTER V1 V2 V3 /PLOT=VICICLE(1,151,5).

* This example produces a vertical icicle plot for every fifth cluster solution starting with 1 and ending with 151 (1 cluster, 6 clusters, 11 clusters, and so on).
* In this example, the vertical dimension of the icicle plot fits on a single printed page.

MISSING Subcommand

MISSING controls the treatment of cases with missing values. By default, a case that has a missing value for any variable in the variable list is omitted from the analysis.

LISTWISE   *Delete cases with missing values listwise.* Only cases with nonmissing values on all variables in the variables list are used. LISTWISE is the default and can also be requested with keyword DEFAULT.

INCLUDE   *Include cases with user-missing values.* Only cases with system-missing values are excluded.

MATRIX Subcommand

MATRIX reads and writes SPSS matrix system files. It writes proximity-type matrices that can be used by subsequent CLUSTER procedures or by procedures PROXIMITIES and ALSCAL (see the table of matrix types in Universals: Defining Matrices). It can read a matrix written by a previous CLUSTER or PROXIMITIES procedure.

- Either IN or OUT is required to specify the matrix file in parentheses. When both IN and OUT are used on the same CLUSTER procedure, they can be specified on separate MATRIX subcommands or both on the same subcommand.
- When reading matrix input, you should omit the variable list from the CLUSTER command.
- SPSS reads variable names, variable and value labels, and print and write formats from the dictionary of the matrix system file. By default, all cases in the matrix system file are used in the analysis.
- The order among rows and cases in the input matrix file is unimportant as long as values for split-file variables precede values for ROWTYPE_. CLUSTER ignores unrecognized ROWTYPE_ values.
- MATRIX=IN cannot be used in place of GET or DATA LIST to create an active system file since MATRIX is a subcommand on CLUSTER, and CLUSTER cannot run before an active system file is defined.
- To begin a new session and immediately read a matrix, first GET the matrix file, then specify IN(*) on MATRIX.
- CLUSTER can read a matrix written to the active system file by a previous CLUSTER or PROXIMITIES procedure.
- Documents from the original file will not be included in the matrix file and will not be present if the matrix file becomes the active system file.
- With a large number of cases, the display file wraps and the matrix format is less readable. Nonetheless, the matrix values can still be used as matrix input values.

OUT *Write a matrix system file.* Specify either a file or an asterisk, and enclose the specification in parentheses. If you specify a file, the file is stored on disk and can be retrieved at any time. If you specify an asterisk (*), the matrix system file replaces the active system file but is not stored on disk unless you use SAVE or XSAVE.

IN *Read a matrix system file.* If the matrix system file is *not* the current active system file, specify a file in parentheses. If the matrix system file *is* the current active system file, specify an asterisk in parentheses (*).

Format of the Matrix System File

- The matrix system file includes two special variables created by SPSS: ROWTYPE_ and VARNAME_. Variable ROWTYPE_ is a string variable with value PROX, for proximity measure.
- PROX is assigned value labels containing the distance measure used to create the matrix. It is also assigned a similarity/dissimilarity keyword.
- If reading in a matrix created with MATRIX DATA, you should supply a value label for PROX of either SIMILARITY or DISSIMILARITY so the matrix is correctly identified. If you do not supply a label, CLUSTER assumes DISSIMILARITY.
- The matrix system file includes the case-identifying variable named on the ID subcommand. Up to 20 characters can be displayed for the identifying variable; ID variables longer than 20 characters are truncated. The identifying variable is present only when the ID subcommand is used.
- Variable VARNAME_ follows the case-identifying variable. VARNAME_ is a string variable whose values are the case numbers of the ID variable.
- The remaining variables in the matrix file are the distance variables used to form the matrix.

Split Files and Variable Order

- When split-file processing is in effect, the first variables in the matrix system file will be the split variables, followed by ROWTYPE_, the case-identifier variable (if the ID subcommand is used), VARNAME_, and the distance variable(s).
- A full set of matrix materials is written for each split-file group defined by the split variable(s).

- A split variable cannot have the same name as any other variable written to the matrix system file.
- If split-file processing is in effect when a matrix is written, the same split file must be in effect when that matrix is read by any procedure.

Additional Statistics
- CLUSTER writes a variety of proximity-type matrices. Each has ROWTYPE_ values of PROX. CLUSTER neither reads nor writes additional statistics with its matrix materials.

Missing Values
- Missing-value treatment affects the values written to a matrix system file. When reading a matrix system file, be sure to specify a missing-value treatment on CLUSTER that is compatible with the treatment used to generate the matrix materials.

Example
```
DATA LIST FILE=ALMANAC1 RECORDS=3
    /1 CITY 6-18(A) POP80 53-60
    /2 CHURCHES 10-13 PARKS 14-17 PHONES 18-25 TVS 26-32
       RADIOST 33-35 TVST 36-38 TAXRATE 52-57(2).
N OF CASES 8.

CLUSTER CHURCHES TO TAXRATE
    /ID=CITY
    /MEASURE=EUCLID
    /MATRIX=OUT(CLUSMTX).
```

- CLUSTER reads raw data from file ALMANAC1 and writes one set of matrix materials to file CLUSMTX.
- The active system file is still the file ALMANAC1 defined on DATA LIST. Subsequent commands are executed on ALMANAC1.

Example
```
DATA LIST FILE=ALMANAC1 RECORDS=3
    /1 CITY 6-18(A) POP80 53-60
    /2 CHURCHES 10-13 PARKS 14-17 PHONES 18-25 TVS 26-32
       RADIOST 33-35 TVST 36-38 TAXRATE 52-57(2).
N OF CASES 8.

CLUSTER CHURCHES TO TAXRATE
    /ID=CITY
    /MEASURE=EUCLID
    /MATRIX=OUT(*).
LIST.
DISPLAY DICTIONARY.
```

- CLUSTER writes the same matrix as in the example above. However, the matrix system file replaces the active system file. The LIST and DISPLAY commands are executed on the matrix file, not on the file ALMANAC1.

Example
```
GET FILE=CLUSMTX.
CLUSTER
    /ID=CITY
    /MATRIX=IN(*).
```

- This example assumes you are starting a new session and want to read an existing matrix system file. GET retrieves the matrix system file CLUSMTX.
- MATRIX=IN specifies an asterisk because the current active system file is the matrix system file CLUSMTX. MATRIX=IN must therefore specify the active system file as the file from which the matrix materials will be read.
- If the GET command is omitted, SPSS issues an error message.
- If MATRIX=IN(CLUSMTX) is specified, SPSS issues an error message.

Example
```
GET FILE=PRSNNL.
FREQUENCIES VARIABLE=AGE.

CLUSTER
    /ID=CITY
    /MATRIX=IN(CLUSMTX).
```

- This example assumes you want to perform a frequencies analysis on file PRSNNL and then use CLUSTER to read a different file. The file you want to read is an existing matrix system file.

- The variable list is omitted on the CLUSTER command. By default, all cases are used in the analysis.
- MATRIX=IN specifies a file because the current active system file is PRSNNL. MATRIX=IN must therefore specify the file from which the matrix materials will be read.
- CLUSMTX *does not* replace PRSNNL as the active system file.

Example
```
GET FILE=CRIME.
PROXIMITIES MURDER TO MOTOR
  /ID=CITY
  /MEASURE=PH2
  /MATRIX=OUT(*).
CLUSTER
  /MATRIX=IN(*).
```

- GET defines the data to SPSS.
- PROXIMITIES specifies variables for the analysis and reads the raw data from file CRIME. The ID subcommand specifies CITY as the case-identifying variable. The MATRIX subcommand indicates that the resulting matrix is written to the active system file.
- MATRIX=IN(*) indicates that the active system file contains the matrix. The variable list is omitted on the CLUSTER command. This is recommended because the variables from the PROXIMITIES procedure are now represented by cases in the matrix system file. By default, all cases are used in the analysis. The slash preceding the MATRIX subcommand is required because there is an implied variable list. Without the slash, CLUSTER would attempt to interpret MATRIX as a variable name rather than a subcommand name.

Annotated Example   For a complete example with output, see Examples following the Command Reference.

References   Anderberg, M. J. 1973. *Cluster analysis for applications.* New York: Academic Press.

COMMENT

```
COMMENT text
```

Example:

```
* CREATE A NEW VARIABLE AS A COMBINATION OF TWO OLD VARIABLES.

COMPUTE XYVAR=0.
IF (XVAR EQ 1 AND YVAR EQ 1)XYVAR=1.
```

Overview

COMMENT inserts explanatory text within the command sequence. Comments are included in the command printback on the display file; they do not become part of the information saved on an SPSS system file. To include commentary in the dictionary of a system file, use the DOCUMENT command.

Syntax Rules

- The first line of a comment can begin with the keyword COMMENT or with an asterisk (*).
- Comment text can extend for multiple lines and can contain any characters.
- Comments cannot be imbedded within data lines.
- As an alternative to keyword COMMENT or the asterisk, /* and */ can be used wherever a blank is valid (except within strings) to set off comments within a command (leaving the blank in place before the comment). A comment demarcated by /* and */ cannot be continued on the next line. The most reasonable place for the comment is at the end of the line, in which case the closing */ is optional.

Operations

- Comments are included in the command printback on the display file. They are not saved as part of an SPSS system file.

Example

```
* CREATE A NEW VARIABLE AS A COMBINATION OF TWO OLD VARIABLES;
  THE NEW VARIABLE IS A SCRATCH VARIABLE USED LATER IN THE
SESSION;
  IT WILL NOT BE SAVED WITH THIS FILE.

COMPUTE #XYVAR=0.
IF (XVAR EQ 1 AND YVAR EQ 1) #XYVAR=1.
```

- The three-line comment will be included in the display file but will not be part of the system file dictionary if the active system file is saved.

Example

```
IF (RACE EQ 1 AND SEX EQ 1) SEXRACE = 1  /*WHITE MALES.
```

- The /* and */ method is used for entering a comment. The closing */ is not used because it is optional when the comment is the last specification on the line.

COMPUTE

COMPUTE target variable=expression

Arithmetic Operators:
+   Addition   −   Subtraction
*   Multiplication   /   Division
** Exponentiation

Arithmetic Functions:
ABS(arg)	Absolute value
RND(arg)	Round
TRUNC(arg)	Truncate
MOD(arg)	Modulus
SQRT(arg)	Square root
EXP(arg)	Exponential
LG10(arg)	Base 10 logarithm
LN(arg)	Natural logarithm
ARSIN(arg)	Arcsine
ARTAN(arg)	Arctangent
SIN(arg)	Sine
COS(arg)	Cosine

Statistical Functions:
SUM[.n](arg list)	Sum of values across argument list
MEAN[.n](arg list)	Mean value across argument list
SD[.n](arg list)	Standard deviation of values across list
VAR[.n](arg list)	Variance of values across list
CFVAR[.n](arg list)	Coefficient of variation of values across list
MIN[.n](arg list)	Minimum value across list
MAX[.n](arg list)	Maximum value across list

Missing Value Functions:
VALUE(varname)	Ignore user-missing
MISSING(varname)	True if missing
SYSMIS(varname)	True if system-missing
NMISS(arg list)	Count number missing values across list
NVALID(arg list)	Number of valid values across list

Cross-case Function:

LAG(varname,n)   Return value of variable n cases before

Logical Functions:
RANGE(varname,range)	True if value of variable is in range
ANY(arg,arg list)	True if value of first arg matches arg list

Other Functions:
UNIFORM(arg)	Uniform pseudo random no. between 0 and n
NORMAL(arg)	Normal pseudo random no. with mean of 0 and std dev of n
CDFNORM(arg)	Return probability random variable falls below n
PROBIT(arg)	Inverse of CDFNORM

The values of "arg" can be numeric values, variables, or expressions.

Date and time aggregation functions:
DATE.DMY(d,m,y)	Read day, month, year and return date
DATE.MDY(m,d,y)	Read month, day, year and return date
DATE.YRDAY(y,d)	Read year, day, number and return date
DATE.QYR(q,y)	Read quarter, year and return quarter start date
DATE.MOYR(m,y)	Read month, year and return month start date
DATE.WKYR(w,y)	Read week, year and return week start date
TIME.HMS(h,m,s)	Read hour, minutes, seconds and return time interval
TIME.DAYS(d)	Read days and return time interval

Date and time conversion functions:

YRMODA(yr,mo,da)	Convert year, month, day to day number
CTIME.DAYS(arg)	Convert time interval to days
CTIME.HOURS(arg)	Convert time interval to hours
CTIME.MINUTES(arg)	Convert time interval to minutes

Date and time extraction functions:

XDATE.MDAY(arg)	Return the day of the month
XDATE.MONTH(arg)	Return the month of the year
XDATE.YEAR(arg)	Return the four-digit year
XDATE.HOUR(arg)	Return the hour of a day
XDATE.MINUTE(arg)	Return the minute of an hour
XDATE.SECOND(arg)	Return the second of a minute
XDATE.WKDAY(arg)	Return the weekday number
XDATE.JDAY(arg)	Return the day number of a day in a given year
XDATE.QUARTER(arg)	Return the quarter of a date in a given year
XDATE.WEEK(arg)	Return the week number of a date in a given year
XDATE.TDAY(arg)	Return the number of days in a time interval
XDATE.TIME(arg)	Return the time portion of a given date and time
XDATE.DATE(arg)	Return integral portion of date

String Functions:

ANY(arg,arg list)	Return 1 if value of arg matches value in arg list
CONCAT(arg list)	Join the arguments into a string
INDEX(a1,a2,a3)	Return number indicating position of first occurence of a2 in a1
LAG(arg,n)	Return value of arg n cases before
LENGTH(arg)	Return length of arg
LOWER(arg list)	Convert uppercase letters to lowercase
LPAD(a1,a2,a3)	Left pad beginning of a1 to length a2 with character a3
LTRIM(a1,a2)	Trim character a2 from beginning of a1
MAX(arg list)	Return maximum value of arg list
MIN(arg list)	Return minimum value of arg list
NUMBER(arg,format)	Convert argument into number using format
RANGE(arg,arg list)	Return 1 if value of arg is in inclusive range of arg list
RINDEX(a1,a2,a3)	Return number indicating rightmost occurence of a2 in a1
RPAD(a1,a2,a3)	Right pad end of a1 to length a2 with character a3
RTRIM(a1,a2)	Trim character a2 from end of a1
STRING(arg,format)	Convert argument into string using format
SUBSTR(a1,a2,a3)	Return substring of a1 beginning with position a2 for length a3
UPCASE(arg list)	Convert lowercase letters to uppercase

Example:

```
COMPUTE NEWVAR=RND((V1/V2)*100).
STRING DEPT(A20).
COMPUTE DEPT='PERSONNEL DEPARTMENT'.
```

Overview

COMPUTE creates a new numeric variable or modifies the values of an existing numeric or string variable for each case in the active system file. The variable name on the left of the equals sign is the *target variable.* The variables, values, and specifications on the right side of the equals sign form an *assignment expression.* The assignment expression can specify a constant, or it can specify one or more functions. For a complete discussion of the functions, see Universals: Functions.

Numeric Transformations

Both arithmetic operations and functions can be used in the transformation of numeric variables. The assignment expression can include combinations of arithmetic operations, constants, and functions. Parentheses are used to indicate the order of operations and to enclose the argument for a function.

String Transformations   String variables can be modified but cannot be created. However, a new string variable can first be declared and assigned a width with the STRING command and then assigned values by COMPUTE. A target variable can be set equal to a string constant or to an existing string variable. The functions at the end of the COMPUTE syntax chart labelled "String Functions" are available for string transformations. All other functions are available for numeric transformations only.

Basic Specification   • The basic specification is the target variable, a required equals sign, and the assignment expression. Values of the target variable are calculated according to the specification on the assignment expression.

Syntax Rules   • The target variable must be named first, and the equals sign is required. Only one target variable is allowed per COMPUTE command.

• Numeric and string variables cannot be mixed in an expression. In addition, if the target variable is numeric, the expression must be numeric; if the target variable is a string, the expression must be a string expression.

• Each function must specify at least one argument enclosed in parentheses. If an expression has two or more arguments, each argument must be separated by a comma. Blanks alone *cannot* be used to separate each variable name, expression, or constant. For a complete discussion of the functions and their arguments, see Universals: Functions.

• You can use the TO keyword to reference a set of variables in an argument list with statistical and missing-value functions.

Numeric Variables   • Parentheses are used to indicate the order of transformations and to set off the arguments for a function.

• Numeric functions can take on expressions, enclosed in parentheses, as arguments. Complex expressions can be formed by nesting functions and arithmetic operators as arguments to functions.

String Variables   • String variables can be modified but cannot be created. However, a new string variable can first be declared and assigned a width with the STRING command, then assigned values by COMPUTE.

• String values and constants must be enclosed in apostrophes or quotation marks.

• String variables, like numeric variables, can be tested in logical expressions. However, string variables cannot be compared with numeric variables. Strings of different lengths can be compared using EQ and NE; the shorter string is right-padded with blanks to equal the length of the longer. The magnitude of strings can be compared using LT, GT, and so forth. The success or failure of the comparison depends on the sorting sequence of the particular computer; use with caution.

Operations   • If the target variable already exists, its values are replaced. If the target variable does not already exist, it is created as a new variable. New variables are initialized to the system-missing value for each case unless the LEAVE command is used.

• Invalid syntax stops all processing of COMPUTE. New variables are not created and existing target variables remain unchanged.

Numeric Variables   • New numeric variables created with COMPUTE are assigned a dictionary format of F8.2. Existing numeric variables transformed with COMPUTE retain their original dictionary formats. The format of a numeric variable can be changed with the FORMAT command.

- SPSS returns the system-missing value when it doesn't have enough information to properly evaluate a function. Arithmetic functions that take only one argument cannot be evaluated if that argument is missing. The date and time functions cannot be evaluated if any argument is missing. Statistical functions, however, are evaluated if a sufficient number of arguments are valid. For example, with the command

```
COMPUTE FACTOR = SCORE1 + SCORE2 + SCORE3.
```

variable FACTOR is assigned the system-missing value for any case with a missing value on any one or more score variables. In contrast, with the command

```
COMPUTE FACTOR = SUM(SCORE1 TO SCORE3).
```

a valid value is assigned to FACTOR if at least one of the score values is valid. It is assigned system-missing only when all the score variables are missing.

- All expressions are evaluated in the following order: first, functions, then exponentiation, and then arithmetic operations. The order of operations can be changed by using parentheses.

String Variables

- Existing string variables transformed with COMPUTE retain their original dictionary formats. String variables declared on STRING and transformed with COMPUTE retain the formats assigned to them on STRING.

- The format of string variables cannot be changed. To change the format, declare a new variable of the desired length on the STRING command.

- The string returned by a string expression does not have to be the same length as the target variable, but no warning messages are issued if the lengths are not the same. If the target variable is shorter, the result is right-trimmed. If the target variable is longer, the result is right-padded. String functions are available for padding (LPAD, RPAD), trimming (LTRIM, RTRIM), and selecting a portion of strings (SUBSTR); in this way the lengths can be controlled.

Numeric Examples

The following examples illustrate the use of COMPUTE with numeric variables. For a complete discussion of each function, see Universals: Numeric Functions.

Arithmetic Operations

```
COMPUTE V1=25-V2.
COMPUTE V3=(V2/V4)*100.

DO IF TENURE GT 5.
COMPUTE RAISE=SALARY*.12.
ELSE IF TENURE GT 1.
COMPUTE RAISE=SALARY*.1.
ELSE.
COMPUTE RAISE=0.
END IF.
```

- V1 is computed as 25 minus V2 for all cases. V3 is computed as the percentage V2 is of V4.

- RAISE is computed as 12 percent of SALARY if TENURE is greater than 5. For remaining cases, RAISE is computed as 10 percent of SALARY if TENURE is greater than 1. For remaining cases, RAISE is computed as 0.

Arithmetic Functions

```
COMPUTE WTCHANGE=ABS(WEIGHT1-WEIGHT2).
COMPUTE NEWVAR=RND((V1/V2)*100).
COMPUTE INCOME=TRUNC(INCOME).
COMPUTE MINSQRT=SQRT(MIN(V1,V2,V3,V4)).

COMPUTE TEST = TRUNC(SQRT(X/Y)) * .5.
COMPUTE PARENS = TRUNC(SQRT(X/Y) * .5).
```

- WTCHANGE is computed as the absolute value of WEIGHT1 minus WEIGHT2.

- NEWVAR is computed as a percentage of V2 and is rounded to an integer using the RND function.

- INCOME is truncated to the integer portion of variable INCOME.

- MINSQRT is computed by a complex expression. SQRT computes the square root of V1, the square root of V2, the square root of V3, and the square root of V4. MIN determines the minimum value of the four square roots, and MINSQRT is set equal to that minimum value.

- TEST equals 0.5 for a case with value 2 for X and Y since 2 divided by 2 (X/Y) is 1, the square root of 1 is 1, truncating 1 returns 1, and 1 times 0.5 is 0.5. However, PARENS is equal to 0 for the same case, since SQRT(X/Y) is 1, 1 times 0.5 is 0.5, and truncating 0.5 returns 0.

Statistical Functions
```
COMPUTE NEWSAL = SUM(SALARY,RAISE).
COMPUTE MINVAL = MIN(V1,V2,V3,V4).
COMPUTE MEANVAL = MEAN(V1,V2,V3,V4).
COMPUTE NEWMEAN = MEAN.3(V1,V2,V3,V4).
```

- NEWSAL is computed as the sum of SALARY plus RAISE.

- MINVAL is set equal to the minimum of the values of V1 to V4.

- MEANVAL is computed as the mean of the values of V1 to V4. As long as a case has a valid value on any of the variables V1 to V4, MEANVAL is assigned a valid value. The mean might be computed on one, two, three, or four values.

- By using the *.n* suffix with a statistical function, you can specify the number of valid arguments you consider acceptable. NEWMEAN is computed as the mean of variables V1 to V4 *only* if at least 3 of these variables have valid values. Otherwise, NEWMEAN is assigned system-missing for that case.

Missing Value Functions
```
MISSING VALUE V1 V2 V3 (0).
COMPUTE ALLVALID=V1 + V2 + V3.
COMPUTE UM=VALUE(V1) + VALUE(V2) + VALUE(V3).
COMPUTE SM=SYSMIS(V1) + SYSMIS(V2) + SYSMIS(V3).
COMPUTE M=MISSING(V1) + MISSING(V2) + MISSING(V3).
```

- The MISSING VALUE command declares the value 0 as missing for V1, V2, and V3.

- ALLVALID is computed as the sum of three variables only for cases with valid values for all three variables. ALLVALID is assigned the system-missing value for a case if any variable in the assignment expression has a system-missing or user-missing value.

- The VALUE function overrides user-missing value declarations. Thus, UM is the sum of V1, V2, and V3 for each case, including cases with value 0 (the user-missing value) for any of the three variables. Cases with system-missing values are not included.

- The SYSMIS function on the third COMPUTE returns value 1 if the variable is system-missing. Thus, SM ranges from 0 to 3 for each case, depending on whether the variables V1, V2, and V3 are system-missing for the case.

- The MISSING function on the fourth COMPUTE returns the value 1 if the variable named is system-missing or user-missing. Thus, M ranges from 0 to 3 for each case, depending on whether variables V1, V2, and V3 are user- or system-missing for that case.

- Alternatively, you could use the COUNT command to create variables SM and M.

Example
```
TITLE  'TEST FOR LISTWISE DELETION OF MISSING VALUES'.

DATA LIST /V1 TO V6 1-6.
BEGIN DATA
213 56
123457
123457
9234 6
END DATA.
MISSING VALUES V1 TO V6(6,9).

COMPUTE NOTVALID=NMISS(V1 TO V6).
FREQUENCIES VAR=NOTVALID.
```

- COMPUTE determines the number of missing values in each case. For each case without missing values, the value of NOTVALID is 0. For each case with one missing value, the value of NOTVALID is 1, and so forth. Both system and user-missing values are counted.

• FREQUENCIES generates a frequency table for NOTVALID. The table gives a count of how many cases have all valid values, how many cases have one missing value, how many cases have two missing values, and so forth. Commands in this example can be used to determine whether cases may have been dropped from an analysis that uses listwise deletion of missing values. See VECTOR or LOOP for an example that tells you whether cases have all valid values or at least one missing value but does not count the number of missing values per case.

Across-Case Operations

```
COMPUTE LV1=LAG(V1).
COMPUTE LV2=LAG(V2,3).
```

• LV1 is set equal to the value of V1 for the previous case.

• LV2 is set equal to the value of V2 for three cases previous. The first 3 cases of LV2 receive the system-missing value.

Logical Functions

```
COMPUTE WORKERS=RANGE(AGE,18,65).
COMPUTE QSAME=ANY(Q1,Q2).
```

• WORKERS is 1 for cases with AGE from 18 to 65, 0 for all other valid values, and system-missing for cases with a missing value for AGE.

• QSAME is a dichotomous (two-valued) variable that records 1 for individuals who gave the same response to two agree-disagree questions (assuming the same coding scheme). QSAME is 1 whenever Q1 equals Q2.

Other Functions

```
COMPUTE V1=UNIFORM(10).
COMPUTE V2=NORMAL(1.5).
```

• V1 is set equal to a pseudo-random number from a distribution with values ranging between 0 and the specified value of 10.

• V2 is set equal to a pseudo-random number from a distribution with a mean of 0 and a standard deviation of the specified value of 1.5.

• You can change the seed value of the pseudo-random-number generator with the SEED specification on SET.

Date and Time Aggregation Functions

```
COMPUTE OCTDAY=DATE.YRDAY(1688,301).
COMPUTE QUART=DATE.QYR(QTR,YEAR).
COMPUTE WEEK=DATE.WKYR(WK,YEAR).
```

• OCTDAY is computed as the 301st day of year 1688. With a DATE format, OCTDAY displays as 27-OCT-1688.

• QUART is computed as a given quarter in a given year. The values for quarter are read from variable QTR, and the values for year from variable YEAR. If QTR is 3 and YEAR is 88, QUART with a QDATE format displays as 3 Q 88.

• WEEK takes the value for the week from variable WK, and the value for the year from variable YEAR. If WK is 48 and YEAR is 57, WEEK with a DATE format displays as 26-NOV-57.

Date and Time Conversion Functions

```
COMPUTE NMINS=CTIME.MINUTES(TIME.HMS(HR,MIN,SEC)).
COMPUTE AGER=(YRMODA(1980,08,23)-
YRMODA(YRBIRTH,MOBIRTH,DABIRTH))/365.25.
```

• The CTIME.MINUTES function converts a time interval to the number of minutes. If HR equals 12, MIN equals 30, and SEC equals 30, the TIME.HMS function produces the interval of 45,030, which CTIME.MINUTES converts to an interval measure in minutes. NMINS equals 750.50.

• The YRMODA function converts the current date (in this example, August 23, 1980) and birthdate to a number of days. Birthdate is subtracted from current date and the remainder is divided by the number of days in a year to yield age in years.

Date and Time Extraction Functions

```
COMPUTE MONTHNUM=XDATE.MONTH(BIRTHDAY).
COMPUTE DAYNUM=XDATE.JDAY(BIRTHDAY).
```

• The XDATE.MONTH function reads a date and returns the month number expressed as an integer from 1 to 12. Assuming BIRTHDAY is formatted as DATE20 and contains the value 05-DEC-1954 5:30:15, MONTHNUM equals 12.

• The XDATE.JDAY function returns the day of the year, expressed as an integer between 1 and 366. For the value BIRTHDAY used by the first COMPUTE, DAYNUM equals 339.

String Examples

The examples below illustrate the use of the COMPUTE command with string variables. For a complete discussion of each function, see Universals: String Functions.

Equivalence

```
STRING DEPT(A20).
COMPUTE DEPT='PERSONNEL DEPARTMENT'.
COMPUTE OLDVAR=NEWVAL.
```

- DEPT is a new string variable and can only be specified on COMPUTE after it has been declared on STRING. STRING assigns DEPT a width of 20 characters, and COMPUTE assigns the new variable DEPT the value "PERSONNEL DEPARTMENT" for each case.

- OLDVAR must already exist; otherwise it would have to be declared on STRING. The values of OLDVAR are modified so they equal the values of NEWVAL. NEWVAL must be an existing string variable. If the dictionary width of NEWVAL is longer than the dictionary width of OLDVAR, the modified values of OLDVAR are truncated.

String Functions

```
STRING NEWSTR(A7) / DATE(A8) / #MO #DA #YR (A2).
COMPUTE NEWSTR=LAG(OLDSTR,2).

COMPUTE #MO=STRING(MONTH,F2.0).
COMPUTE #DA=STRING(DAY,F2.0).
COMPUTE #YR=STRING(YEAR,F2.0).
COMPUTE DATE=CONCAT(#MO,'/',#DA,'/',#YR).

COMPUTE LNAME=UPCASE(LNAME).
```

- STRING declares NEWSTR as a new string variable with a width of 7 characters, DATE as a new string variable with a width of 8 characters, and scratch variables #MO, #DA, #YR with a width of 2 characters each.

- The first COMPUTE sets NEWSTR equal to the value of OLDSTR for two cases previous. The first two cases of NEWSTR receive the system-missing value.

- The next set of COMPUTES uses scratch variables #MO, #DA, #YR to convert existing numeric variables MONTH, DAY, and YEAR to temporary string variables so they can be used in the CONCAT function, which concatenates string variables. The fourth COMPUTE in the set calculates the new string variable DATE as the concatenated value of #MO, #DA, and #YR separated by slashes. If #MO is 10, #DA is 16, and #YR is 49, DATE is equal to 10/16/49.

- The final COMPUTE converts lowercase letters for the existing string variable LNAME to uppercase letters.

CORRELATIONS

```
CORRELATIONS [VARIABLES=] varlist [WITH varlist] [/varlist...]

[/MISSING={PAIRWISE**}  [INCLUDE]]
              {LISTWISE  }

[/PRINT={TWOTAIL**}  {NOSIG**}]
         {ONETAIL  }  {SIG    }

[/FORMAT={MATRIX**}]
          {SERIAL  }

[/MATRIX=OUT({*    })]
              {file}

[/STATISTICS=[DESCRIPTIVES]  [XPROD]  [ALL]]
```

**Default if the subcommand is omitted.

Example:

```
CORRELATIONS VARIABLES=FOOD RENT PUBTRANS TEACHER COOK ENGINEER
    /MISSING=INCLUDE.
```

Overview

CORRELATIONS (alias PEARSON CORR) produces Pearson product-moment correlations with significance levels and, optionally, univariate statistics, covariances and cross-product deviations. Other procedures that also produce correlation matrices are PARTIAL CORR, REGRESSION, DISCRIMINANT, and FACTOR.

Options

Types of Matrices. You can specify one or more correlation matrices with one CORRELATIONS command. A simple variable list produces a square matrix. You can also request a rectangular matrix of correlations between specific pairs of variables or between variable lists. See VARIABLES Subcommand.

Significance Levels. By default, CORRELATIONS displays Pearson correlation coefficients based on a one-tailed test. You can request that the significance level be calculated using a two-tailed test. You can also suppress the number of cases and significance level that display for each coefficient. See PRINT Subcommand.

Additional Statistics. In addition to the correlation coefficient, number of cases, and significance level, you can obtain the mean, standard deviation, and number of nonmissing cases for each variable, and the cross-product deviations and covariance for each pair of variables. See STATISTICS Subcommand.

Formatting Options. By default, CORRELATIONS includes redundant coefficients in the correlation and displays in matrix format. You can include only the nonredundant coefficients and display in serial string format. See FORMAT Subcommand.

Matrix Output. CORRELATIONS allows you to write matrix materials to a system file. The matrix materials include the mean, standard deviation, number of cases used to compute each coefficient, and Pearson correlation coefficient for each variable. The matrix system file can be read by several other SPSS procedures. See MATRIX Subcommand.

Basic Specification

• The basic specification is the VARIABLES subcommand, which specifies the variable list to be analyzed. The actual keyword VARIABLES can be omitted. CORRELATION displays a rectangular matrix of correlation coefficients for the analysis list.

Subcommand Order
- VARIABLES must be first.
- Remaining subcommands can be specified in any order.

Operations
- A correlation of a variable with itself is displayed as 1.0000.
- A correlation that cannot be computed is displayed as a period (.).
- Long or short string variables on an analysis list prevent execution of CORRE-LATION.
- The display uses the width set on the SET command.

Limitations
- A maximum of 40 variable lists.
- A maximum of 500 variables total per CORRELATIONS command.
- A maximum of 250 individual elements. Each unique occurrence of a variable name, keyword, or special delimiter counts as 1 toward this total. Variables implied by the TO convention do not count toward this total.

Example

```
CORRELATIONS VARIABLES=FOOD RENT PUBTRANS TEACHER COOK ENGINEER
  /VARIABLES=FOOD RENT WITH COOK TEACHER MANAGER ENGINEER
  /MISSING=INCLUDE.
```

- The first VARIABLES subcommand requests a square matrix of correlation coefficients among variables FOOD, RENT, PUBTRANS, TEACHER, COOK, and ENGINEER.
- The second VARIABLES subcommand requests a rectangular correlation matrix in which variables FOOD and RENT are the rows and COOK, TEACHER, MANAGER, and ENGINEER are the columns.
- MISSING requests that user-missing values be included in the computation of each coefficient.

VARIABLES Subcommand

VARIABLES names the variable list. The actual keyword VARIABLES is optional. If you explicitly specify keyword VARIABLES, an equals sign must precede the variable list.

- A simple variable list produces a square matrix of correlations of each variable with every other variable.
- A list of variables and keyword WITH produces a rectangular correlation matrix. Variables listed before WITH define the rows of the matrix and those listed after WITH define the columns.
- Keyword ALL can be used in an analysis list to refer to all user-defined variables.
- You can specify multiple VARIABLES subcommands on a single CORRELA-TION command. The slash between the subcommands is required; the keyword VARIABLES is not.

PRINT Subcommand

PRINT switches to a two-tailed test and/or suppresses the display of the number of cases and the significance level.

- By default, CORRELATIONS displays Pearson correlation coefficients, single asterisks (*) to denote coefficients significant at a 0.05 level or less, and double asterisks (**) to denote coefficients significant at a 0.01 level or less. Default significances are for two-tailed tests.
- If you specify both FORMAT=SERIAL and PRINT=NOSIG, only FORMAT =SERIAL will be in effect.

The following keywords can be specified:

TWOTAIL *Two-tailed test of significance.* This test is appropriate when the direction of the relationship cannot be determined in advance, as is often the case in exploratory data analysis. This is the default.

ONETAIL   *One-tailed test of significance.* This test is appropriate when the direction of the relationship between a pair of variables can be specified in advance of the analysis.

NOSIG   *Suppress the displaying of the number of cases and significance level.* A single asterisk (*) following a coefficient indicates significance at the 0.05 level or less. Two asterisks (**) following a coefficient indicate significance at the 0.01 level or less. This is the default (unless FORMAT=SERIAL).

SIG   *Display the number of cases and significance level.*

STATISTICS Subcommand

The correlation coefficient, number of cases, and significance level are automatically displayed for every combination of variable pairs in the variable list. STATISTICS obtains additional statistics.

• The statistics for each variable list on the command precede their corresponding correlation matrices.

DESCRIPTIVES   *Mean, standard deviation, and number of nonmissing cases for each variable.* Missing values are handled on a variable-by-variable basis regardless of the missing-value option in effect for the correlations.

XPROD   *Cross-product deviations and covariance for each pair of variables.*

ALL   *All additional statistics available in CORRELATIONS.* Includes the mean, standard deviation, and number of nonmissing cases for each variable. Also includes the cross-product deviations and covariance for each pair of variables.

MISSING Subcommand

MISSING controls missing values.

• By default, CORRELATIONS deletes cases with missing values on a pair-by-pair basis. A case missing for one or both of the pair of variables for a specific correlation coefficient is not used for that coefficient. Since each coefficient is based on all cases that have valid codes on that particular pair of variables, the maximum information available is used in every calculation. This can also result in a set of coefficients based on a varying number of cases.

• The PAIRWISE and LISTWISE keywords are mutually exclusive; however, each can be specified with INCLUDE.

PAIRWISE   *Exclude missing values pairwise.* Cases missing for one or both of a pair of variables for a specific correlation coefficient are excluded from the analysis. This is the default.

LISTWISE   *Exclude missing values listwise.* Each variable listed on a command is evaluated separately. Cases missing on any variable named in a list are excluded from all analyses.

INCLUDE   *Include user-missing values.* User-missing values are included in the analysis.

FORMAT Subcommand

By default, CORRELATIONS includes redundant coefficients in the correlation and displays in matrix format. FORMAT controls matrix format.

MATRIX   *Display in matrix format with redundant coefficients.* This is the default.

SERIAL   *Display in serial string format with nonredundant coefficients.* Nonredundant coefficients are displayed in serial string format with the coefficients from the first row of the matrix displayed first, followed by all the unique (in other words, those not already displayed) coefficients from the second row and so on for all of the rows in the matrix. Each coefficient is identified with the name of the variable for which it was calculated. The number of cases and significance level are displayed below the correlation, just as they are in the matrix form of the output. PRINT=NOSIG cannot be used with SERIAL format and is ignored if it is specified.

MATRIX Subcommand

MATRIX writes matrix materials to a system file. The matrix materials include the mean, standard deviation, number of cases used to compute each coefficient, and Pearson correlation coefficient for each variable. Several other SPSS procedures can read matrix materials produced by CORRELATIONS, including PARTIAL CORR, REGRESSION, FACTOR, and CLUSTER (see the table of matrix types in Universals: Defining Matrices).

- CORRELATIONS can write a correlation matrix for a simple variable list but not for variable lists containing the keyword WITH.

- If you specify more than one matrix on the CORRELATIONS command, only the last variable list that does not use the keyword WITH is written to the matrix system file.

- Keyword OUT specifies the file to which the matrix is written. Specify the matrix file in parentheses.

- Documents from the original file will not be included in the matrix file and will not be present if the matrix file becomes the active system file.

OUT *Write a matrix system file.* Specify either a file or an asterisk, and enclose the specification in parentheses. If you specify a file, the file is stored on disk and can be retrieved at any time. If you specify an asterisk (*), the matrix system file replaces the active system file but is not stored on disk unless you use SAVE or XSAVE.

Format of the Matrix System File

- The matrix system file has two special variables created by SPSS: ROWTYPE_ and VARNAME_. Variable ROWTYPE_ is a short string variable having values MEAN, STDDEV, N, and CORR (for Pearson correlation coefficient). The next variable, VARNAME_, is a short string variable whose values are the names of the variables used to form the correlation matrix. When ROWTYPE_ is CORR, VARNAME_ gives the variable associated with that row of the correlation matrix.

- The remaining variables in the file are the variables used to form the correlation matrix.

Split Files and Variable Order

- When split-file processing is in effect, the first variables in the matrix system file will be split variables, followed by ROWTYPE_, VARNAME_, and the variables used to form the correlation matrix.

- A full set of matrix materials is written for each split-file group defined by the split variable(s).

- A split variable cannot have the same variable name as any other variable written to the matrix system file.

- If a split file is in effect when a matrix is written, the same split file must be in effect when that matrix is read by any procedure.

Additional Statistics

- CORRELATIONS always writes the mean, standard deviation and the number of cases used to compute each coefficient. This information immediately precedes the correlation matrix in the output file.

Missing Values

- With PAIRWISE treatment of missing values (the default), the matrix of N's used to compute each coefficient is included with the matrix materials.

- With LISTWISE treatment, a single N used to calculate all coefficients is included with the matrix materials.

Example

```
GET FILE=CITY /KEEP FOOD RENT PUBTRANS TEACHER COOK ENGINEER.
CORRELATIONS VARIABLES=FOOD TO ENGINEER
    /MATRIX OUT(CORRMAT).
```

- CORRELATIONS reads raw data from the file CITY and writes one set of matrix materials to the file CORRMAT.
- The active system file is still the file CITY. Subsequent commands are executed on the file CITY.

Example

```
GET FILE=CITY /KEEP FOOD RENT PUBTRANS TEACHER COOK ENGINEER.
CORRELATIONS VARIABLES=FOOD TO ENGINEER
    /MATRIX OUT(*).
LIST.
DISPLAY DICTIONARY.
```

- CORRELATIONS writes the same matrix as in the example above. However, the matrix system file replaces the current active system file. The LIST and DISPLAY commands are executed on the matrix file, not on the file CITY.

Example

```
CORRELATIONS VARIABLES=FOOD RENT COOK TEACHER MANAGER ENGINEER
    /FOOD TO TEACHER /PUBTRANS WITH MECHANIC
    /MATRIX OUT(*).
```

- Only the matrix for FOOD TO TEACHER is written to the matrix system file because it is the last variable list that does not use keyword WITH.

Annotated Example

For a complete example with output, see Examples following the Command Reference.

COUNT

```
COUNT varname=varlist(value list) [/varname=...]
```

Numeric Value List Keywords:

LOWEST, LO, HIGHEST, HI, THRU, MISSING, SYSMIS

Example:
```
COUNT TARGET=V1 V2 V3 (2).
```

Overview
COUNT creates a numeric variable that, for each case, counts the occurrences of the same value (or list of values) across a list of variables. The new variable is called the target variable. The variables and values that are counted are the criterion variables and values. Criterion variables can be either numeric or string variables.

Basic Specification
- The basic specification is the target variable, an equals sign, the criterion variable(s), and the criterion value(s) enclosed in parentheses.

Syntax Rules
- Multiple target variables can be created on the same command by using a slash to separate each set of specifications.
- A single target variable must be composed entirely of numeric variables, or entirely of string variables.
- A variable can be specified more than once in the criterion variable list.
- To name consecutive criterion variables that have the same criterion value or values, use keyword TO.
- To count different values for different variables, use multiple variable lists.
- To specify multiple criterion values within a single set of parentheses, separate each value by a comma or space. String values must be enclosed in apostrophes.
- Keywords THRU, LOWEST (LO), HIGHEST (HI), SYSMIS and MISSING can only be used with numeric criterion variables. None of the keywords can be used with string variables.
- SYSMIS counts system-missing values for numeric variables.
- MISSING counts both user- and system-missing values for numeric variables.

Operations
- The target variable is numeric and is initialized to 0 for each case. If the target variable already exists, its previous values are replaced.
- Target variables created with COUNT are assigned a dictionary format of F8.2.
- COUNT ignores the missing-value status of user-missing values. Thus, COUNT counts a value even if that value has been previously declared as missing.
- COUNT does not propagate missing values automatically. The target variable will never be system-missing. To declare missing-value flags, use the RECODE or MISSING VALUE command.

Example
```
COUNT TARGET=V1 V2 V3 (2).
```
- The value of TARGET for each case will be either 0, 1, 2, or 3, depending on the number of times the value 2 occurs across the three variables.
- TARGET is a numeric variable with F8.2 format.

Example
```
COUNT QLOW=Q1 TO Q10 (LO THRU 0)
   /QSYSMIS=Q1 TO Q10 (SYSMIS).
```
- Assuming there are 10 variables between and including Q1 and Q10 on the active system file, QLOW ranges from 0 to 10, depending on the number of times a case has a negative or 0 value across variables Q1 to Q10.

- QSYSMIS ranges from 0 to 10, depending on how many system-missing values are encountered for Q1 to Q10 for each case. User-missing values are not counted.
- Both QLOW and QSYSMIS are numeric variables and have F8.2 formats.

Example

```
COUNT SVAR=V1 V2 ('male  ') V3 V4 V5 ('female').
```

- SVAR ranges from 0 to 5, depending on the number of times a case has a value of male for V1 and V2 and value of female for V3, V4 and V5.
- SVAR is a numeric variable with F8.2 format.

CROSSTABS

General mode:

```
CROSSTABS [TABLES=]varlist BY varlist [BY...] [/varlist...]

[/MISSING={TABLE** }]
         {INCLUDE}

[/FORMAT={LABELS** }   {AVALUE**}   {NOINDEX**}   {TABLES**}   {BOX**}]
         {NOLABELS }   {DVALUE  }   {INDEX    }   {NOTABLES}   {NOBOX}
         {NOVALLABS}

[/CELLS={COUNT**}  [ROW    ]  [EXPECTED]  [SRESID ]]
        {NONE   }  [COLUMN]   [RESID   ]  [ASRESID]
                   [TOTAL ]               [ALL    ]

[/WRITE[={NONE** }]]
        {CELLS  }

[/STATISTICS=[CHISQ]  [LAMBDA]  [BTAU]  [GAMMA]  [ETA ]]
             [PHI  ]  [UC    ]  [CTAU]  [D    ]  [CORR]
             [CC   ]  [NONE  ]  [RISK]  [KAPPA]  [ALL ]
```

Integer mode:

```
CROSSTABS VARIABLES=varlist(min,max) [varlist...]

/TABLES=varlist BY varlist [BY...] [/varlist...]

[/MISSING={TABLE**}]
         {INCLUDE}
         {REPORT }

[/FORMAT={LABELS** }   {AVALUE**}   {NOINDEX**}   {TABLES**}   {BOX**}]
         {NOLABELS }   {DVALUE  }   {INDEX    }   {NOTABLES}   {NOBOX}
         {NOVALLABS}

[/CELLS={COUNT**}  [ROW    ]  [EXPECTED]  [SRESID ]]
        {NONE   }  [COLUMN]   [RESID   ]  [ASRESID]
                   [TOTAL ]               [ALL    ]

[/WRITE[={NONE** }]]
        {CELLS  }
        {ALL    }

[/STATISTICS=[CHISQ]  [LAMBDA]  [BTAU]  [GAMMA]  [ETA ]]
             [PHI  ]  [UC    ]  [CTAU]  [D    ]  [CORR]
             [CC   ]  [NONE  ]  [RISK]  [KAPPA]  [ALL ]
```

**Default if the subcommand is omitted.

Example:

```
CROSSTABS TABLES=FEAR BY SEX
  /CELLS=ROW COLUMN EXPECTED RESIDUALS
  /STATISTICS=CHISQ.
```

Overview   CROSSTABS produces tables showing the joint distribution of two or more variables that have a limited number of distinct values. The frequency distribution of one variable is subdivided according to the values of one or more variables. The unique combination of values for two or more variables defines a cell, the basic element of all tables. To analyze contingency tables using hierarchical log-linear models, use HILOGLINEAR; to analyze contingency tables using a general linear model approach, use LOGLINEAR (both in *SPSS Advanced Statistics User's Guide*).

Options   **Methods for Building Tables.** CROSSTABS operates in two different modes: *general* and *integer*. *General mode* operates via the TABLES subcommand and requires fewer specifications. *Integer mode* operates via the TABLES and VARIABLES subcommands and requires minimum and maximum values for the variables. This mode builds tables more efficiently.

Cell Contents. By default, CROSSTABS displays only the number of cases in each cell. You can request row, column, and total percentages, and also expected values and residuals. See CELLS Subcommand.

Statistics. In addition to the tables, you can obtain measures of association and tests of hypotheses for each subtable. See STATISTICS Subcommand.

Formatting Options. You can control the order in which rows are displayed, and suppress the display of variable labels, value labels, and the table itself. In addition, you can display a list of the tables produced by CROSSTABS with the page number where each table begins. See FORMAT Subcommand.

Writing and Reproducing Tables. You can write cell frequencies to a file and reproduce the original tables. See WRITE Subcommand.

Basic Specification   The basic specification is TABLES with a tables list. The actual keyword TABLES can be omitted in general mode.

- The minimum tables list specifies a list of row variables, the keyword BY, and a list of column variables.
- The default table shows cell counts.

Subcommand Order   • If keyword TABLES is omitted, the table list must be first.
- If keyword TABLES is explicitly used, subcommands can be specified in any order. The exception is in integer mode, where VARIABLES must precede TABLES.

Operations   • If a long string variable is used, only the short-string portion is tabulated.
- Statistics are calculated separately for each two-way table or two-way subtable. Missing values are reported for the table as a whole.
- If only percentages and/or cell counts are requested, the percentages are displayed without a percent sign and blanks are displayed instead of zero values for counts and percents.
- If percentages and any of the expected values or residuals are requested, the percent sign appears next to the percentage and zero values are displayed as zeros.
- Scientific notation is used for cell counts when necessary.
- The display uses the width defined on the SET command.
- The BOX subcommand on SET controls the characters used in the table display.

Specifications for CROSSTABS subcommands depend on whether *general mode* or *integer mode* is used to build tables. Each method has advantages and disadvantages in computational efficiency, available statistics, and additional options.

- General mode permits string or noninteger variables. Ranges do not have to be specified for variables, which makes general mode more convenient. Any defined SPSS variable can be referenced. The order of the variables in the active system file determines the positional order of variables in the tables list.

• Integer mode builds tables more quickly. However, it requires more space if the table has many empty cells. By specifying the appropriate ranges, you can select a subset of values for processing. You can include missing values in tables while excluding them from the calculation of statistics and percentages. Partial and zero-order gammas are available only in integer mode. The order of the variables on VARIABLES determines the positional order of the variables on TABLES.

Limitations

The following limitations apply to CROSSTABS in *general mode*:

• Maximum 200 variables named or implied with the TABLES subcommand.
• Maximum 1000 nonempty rows or columns for each table.
• Maximum 20 tables lists per CROSSTABS command.
• Maximum 10 dimensions per table.
• Maximum 400 value labels displayed on any single table.

The following limitations apply to CROSSTABS in *integer mode*:

• Maximum 100 variables named or implied with the VARIABLES subcommand.
• Maximum 100 variables named or implied with the TABLES subcommand.
• Maximum 1000 nonempty rows or columns for each table.
• Maximum 20 tables lists per CROSSTABS command.
• Maximum 8 dimensions per table.
• No more than 20 rows or columns of missing values can be displayed with MISSING=REPORT.
• Minimum value which can be specified is −99,999.
• Maximum value which can be specified is 999,999.

Example

```
CROSSTABS TABLES=FEAR BY SEX
   /CELLS=ROW COLUMN EXPECTED RESIDUALS
   /STATISTICS=CHISQ.
```

• CROSSTABS generates a bivariate table. Variable FEAR defines the rows of the table and variable SEX defines the columns.
• CELLS requests row and column percentages, expected cell frequencies, and residuals.
• STATISTICS requests the chi-square statistic.

Example

```
CROSSTABS TABLES=JOBCAT BY EDCAT BY SEX BY INCOME3.
```

• This table list produces a subtable of JOBCAT by EDCAT for each combination of values of SEX and INCOME3.

TABLES Subcommand

General Mode

Use TABLES with CROSSTABS in both general and integer mode.

TABLES specifies the table lists. The actual keyword TABLES can be omitted.

• In general mode, both numeric and string variables can be specified. Long strings are truncated to short strings for defining categories.
• Variables named before the first BY in a table list are row variables, and variables named after the first BY in a table list are column variables.
• Variables named after the second (or subsequent) BY are control variables.
• Each subsequent use of the keyword BY in a table list adds a new dimension to the tables requested and introduces a new order of control among the independent variables.
• You can name more than one variable in each dimension.
• You can use keyword ALL to include all user-defined variables in a dimension.

- When the table list specifies two dimensions, tables are produced that crosstabulate the first variable before BY with each variable after BY, then the second variable before BY with each variable after BY, and so forth.
- When the table list specifies more than two dimensions, a two-way subtable is produced for each combination of values of control variables.
- When the table list specifies more than three dimensions, the value of the last variable mentioned changes the most slowly in determining the order in which the tables are displayed.
- You can specify multiple TABLES subcommands on a single CROSSTABS command. The slash between the subcommands is required; the keyword TABLES is not.

Example   CROSSTABS TABLES=FEAR BY SEX BY RACE.

- This example crosstabulates FEAR by SEX, controlling for RACE. In each subtable, FEAR is the row variable and SEX is the column variable.
- A subtable is produced for each value of the control variable RACE.

Example   CROSSTABS TABLES=FEAR BY SEX BY RACE BY DEGREE.

- Assuming variables RACE and DEGREE have two values each, this command produces four subtables.
- The first subtable crosstabulates FEAR by SEX, controlling for the first value of RACE and the first value of DEGREE; the second subtable controls for the second value of RACE and the first value of DEGREE; the third subtable controls for the first value of RACE and the second value of DEGREE; and the fourth subtable controls for the second value of RACE and the second value of DEGREE.

Example   CROSSTABS TABLES=CONFINAN TO CONARMY BY SEX TO REGION.

- This command produces CROSSTABS tables for all the variables between and including CONFINAN and CONARMY by all the variables between and including SEX and REGION.

Integer Mode   To run CROSSTABS in integer mode, the values of all the variables must be integers. Two subcommands are required. VARIABLES specifies all the variables to be used in the CROSSTABS procedure and the minimum and maximum values for building tables. TABLES specifies the table lists. Variables referenced on TABLES must be named on VARIABLES.

- TABLES has the same syntax in integer mode as it has in general mode; however, there is one important difference. In integer mode, the order of the variables implied on TABLES is established by the order of the variables named or implied on VARIABLES. In general mode, the order of variables implied on the table lists is established by their order in the active system file.
- Multiple TABLES subcommands can be used.
- Integer mode can produce more tables in a given amount of core storage space than general mode, and the processing is faster. The values supplied as variable ranges do not have to include all values of the variables; thus, you have control from within CROSSTABS over the tabulated ranges of the variables. Some subcommand and keyword specifications are available only in integer mode.

Example   CROSSTABS VARIABLES=FEAR (1,2) MOBILE16 (1,3)
    /TABLES=FEAR BY MOBILE16.

- VARIABLES names two variables, FEAR and MOBILE16. Values 1 and 2 for FEAR are used in the tables, and values 1, 2, and 3 are used for variable MOBILE16.
- TABLES specifies a bivariate table with two rows (values 1 and 2 for FEAR) and three columns (values 1, 2, and 3 for MOBILE16). FEAR and MOBILE16 can be named on TABLES because they were named on the previous VARIABLES.

VARIABLES **Subcommand**	VARIABLES specifies a list of variables to be used in the crosstabulations. Specify the lowest and highest values in parentheses after each variable. These values must be integers. Noninteger values are truncated.

- Variables can appear in any order. However, the order in which they are named on VARIABLES affects their implied order on TABLES.
- A range must be specified for each variable. Several variables can have the same range.
- CROSSTABS uses the specified ranges to allocate tables. One cell is allocated for each possible combination of values of the row and column variables for a requested table before the data are read. Therefore, if you specify more generous ranges than the variables actually have, you are wasting space. If the table is sparse because the variables do not have values falling throughout the range specified, consider using the general mode or recoding the variables. If the values of the variables fall outside the specified range, cases with these values are considered missing and are not used in the computation of the table.

Example

```
CROSSTABS  VARIABLES=FEAR SEX RACE (1,2)  MOBILE16 (1,3)
   /TABLES=FEAR BY SEX MOBILE16 BY RACE.
```

- VARIABLES defines 1 as the lowest value and 2 as the highest value for FEAR, SEX, and RACE.

CELLS Subcommand

By default, CROSSTABS displays only the number of cases in each cell. Use CELLS to display row, column, or total percentages, and expected values and residuals. These are calculated separately for each bivariate table or subtable.

- CELLS specified without keywords displays cell counts plus ROW, COLUMN, and TOTAL percentages for each cell.
- If CELLS is specified with keywords, CROSSTABS displays only the requested cell information.
- The key located at the top left corner of each table describes the information contained in each cell.
- Scientific notation is used for cell contents when necessary.

COUNT	*Display cell counts.* This is the default if CELLS is omitted.
ROW	*Display row percentages.* Display the number of cases in each cell in a row expressed as a percentage of all cases in that row.
COLUMN	*Display column percentages.* Display the number of cases in each cell in a column expressed as a percentage of all cases in that column.
TOTAL	*Display two-way table total percentages.* Display the number of cases in each cell of a subtable expressed as a percentage of all cases in that subtable.
EXPECTED	*Display expected frequencies.* Display the number of cases expected in each cell if the two variables in the subtable are statistically independent.
RESID	*Display residuals.* Display the difference between the observed cell counts and the expected cell counts.
SRESID	*Display standardized residuals.* (Haberman, 1978).
ASRESID	*Display adjusted standardized residuals.* (Haberman, 1978).
ALL	*Display all cell information.* Display cell count; row, column, and total percentages; expected values; residuals; standardized residuals; and adjusted standardized residuals.
NONE	*Display no cell information.* Use NONE to write the tables to a procedure file without displayed tables. This has the same effect as specifying FORMAT=NOTABLES.

STATISTICS Subcommand

STATISTICS requests measures of association and related statistics. There are no default statistics.

- STATISTICS without keywords displays the chi-square test.
- If STATISTICS is specified with keywords, CROSSTABS calculates only the requested statistics.
- If a range that excludes cases is specified for a variable in integer mode, the excluded cases are *not* used in the calculation of the statistics.
- If user-missing values are included with MISSING, cases with user-missing values are included in the tables as well as in the calculation of statistics.

CHISQ	*Chi-square.* Pearson chi-square, likelihood-ratio chi-square, and Mantel-Haenszel chi-square. Also, for 2 × 2 tables, Fisher's exact test is computed when a table that does not result from missing rows or columns in a larger table has a cell with an expected frequency less than 5; Yates' corrected chi-square is computed for all other 2 × 2 tables. This is the default if STATISTICS is specified with no keywords.
PHI	*Phi and Cramer's V.*
CC	*Contingency coefficient.*
LAMBDA	*Lambda, symmetric and asymmetric, and also Goodman and Kruskal's tau.*
UC	*Uncertainty coefficient, symmetric and asymmetric.*
BTAU	*Kendall's tau-b.*
CTAU	*Kendall's tau-c.*
GAMMA	*Gamma.* Partial and zero-order gammas for 3-way to 8-way tables are available in integer mode only. Zero-order gammas are displayed for 2-way tables and conditional gammas are displayed for 3-way to 10-way tables in general mode.
D	*Somers' d, symmetric and asymmetric.*
ETA	*Eta.* Available for numeric data only.
CORR	*Pearson's r, and Spearman's correlation coefficient.* Available for numeric data only.
KAPPA	*Kappa coefficient* (Kraemer, 1982). Kappa can only be computed for square tables in which the row and column values are identical. If there is a missing row or column, use integer mode to specify the square table since a missing column or row in general mode would keep the table from being square.
RISK	*Relative risk* (Bishop et al., 1975). Relative risk can only be calculated for 2 × 2 tables.
ALL	*All the statistics available for CROSSTABS.*
NONE	*No summary statistics.* This is the default if STATISTICS is omitted.

MISSING Subcommand

By default, CROSSTABS deletes cases with missing values on a table-by-table basis. A case missing on any of the variables specified for a table is not used either in the displayed table or in the calculation of the statistics. Use MISSING to control missing values.

- The only specification is a single keyword. TABLE is the default.
- When multiple table lists are specified, missing values are handled separately for each list.
- The number of missing cases is always displayed at the end of the table, following the last subtable, and after any requested statistics.
- If the missing values are not included in the range specifications on VARIABLES, they are excluded from the table regardless of the keyword you specify on MISSING.

TABLE *Delete cases with missing values on a table-by-table basis.* This is the default.

INCLUDE *Include user-missing values.*

REPORT *Report missing values in the tables.* This option includes missing values in tables but not in the calculation of percentages or statistics. The letter M is used to indicate that cases within a cell are missing. REPORT is available only in integer mode.

FORMAT Subcommand

By default, CROSSTABS displays tables and subtables with variable labels and value labels when they are available. The values for the row variables display in order from lowest to highest and only the first 16 characters of a value label are displayed.

Use FORMAT to modify the default table display.

LABELS *Display both variable and value labels for each table.* This is the default.

NOLABELS *Suppress variable and value labels.*

NOVALLABS *Suppress value labels, display variable labels.*

AVALUE *Display row variables ordered from lowest to highest value.* This is the default.

DVALUE *Display row variables ordered from highest to lowest.*

NOINDEX *Suppress a table index.* This is the default.

INDEX *Display an index of tables.* The index lists all tables produced and the page number where each table begins. The index follows the last page of tables produced by the table list.

TABLES *Display the crosstabs tables.* This is the default.

NOTABLES *Suppress displayed tables.* If STATISTICS is used with FORMAT= NOTABLES, only the statistics are displayed. If STATISTICS is omitted and FORMAT=NOTABLES, CROSSTABS produces no output. Use NOTABLES to write the tables to a procedure file without displayed tables. This has the same effect as specifying CELLS=NONE.

BOX *Use box drawing characters around every cell.* This is the default.

NOBOX *Suppress the box-drawing characters around each cell.* The banner and stub are still separated from the table by box-drawing characters.

WRITE Subcommand

CROSSTABS can write cell frequencies to a file for subsequent use by either SPSS or some other program. It can also use cell frequencies as input to reproduce tables and compute statistics. Use WRITE to write cell frequencies to a procedure output file.

- The only specification is a single keyword. Keyword ALL is available only in integer mode.

- When WRITE is used, the PROCEDURE OUTPUT command is required to specify the procedure output file. PROCEDURE OUTPUT must precede CROSSTABS.

- WRITE has two options for producing an output file of cell frequencies. You can write all the cells of the table, or only the nonempty cells. The file contains one record for each cell; each record contains a split-file group number and a table number, which identify the table, and the cell frequency and values, which identify the cell.

- If both CELLS and ALL are specified, CELLS is in effect and only the contents of the nonempty cells are written to the file.

- Use CELLS to write only nonempty cells. Combinations of values that include a missing value are not written to the output file. If you include missing values in the tables with keyword INCLUDE on MISSING, no values are considered missing and all nonempty cells will be written.

• Keyword ALL writes all defined cells and is available only with integer mode. A record for each combination of values defined by TABLES is written to the output file. If you include missing values in the tables with either keyword INCLUDE or keyword REPORT on MISSING, all defined cells are written whether or not a missing value is involved. If you exclude missing values on a table-by-table basis (the default), no records are written for combinations of values that include a missing value.

• If multiple tables are specified, the tables are written in the same order as they are displayed. The variable in the row variable list changes more slowly and the variable in the last control variable list changes more quickly.

The output record from each cell contains the following information:

Columns	Contents
1–4	Split-file group number, numbered consecutively from 1. Note that this is not the value of the variable or variables used to define the splits.
5–8	Table number. A table is defined by taking one variable from each of the variable lists separated by the keyword BY.
9–16	Cell frequency. The number of times this combination of variable values occurred in the data, or, if case weights are used, the sum of case weights for cases having this combination of values.
17–24	The value of the row variable (the one named before the first BY).
25–32	The value of the column variable (the one named after the first BY).
33–40	The value of the first control variable (the one named after the second BY).
41–48	The value of the second control variable (the one named after the third BY).
49–56	The value of the third control variable (the one named after the fourth BY).
57–64	The value of the fourth control variable (the one named after the fifth BY).
65–72	The value of the fifth control variable (the one named after the sixth BY).
73–80	The value of the sixth control variable (the one named after the seventh BY).

• The split-file group number, table number, and frequency are written as integers.

• If the integer mode of CROSSTABS is used, the values of variables are also written as integers. If the general mode is used, the values are written in accordance with the PRINT FORMAT specified for each variable. Alphanumeric values are written at the left end of any field in which they occur.

Within each table, the records are written in the following order:

the value of the row variable, within
the value of the column variable, within
the value of the first control variable, within

.
.

the value of the fifth control variable

This order implies that the records are written from one column of the table at a time, and the value of the last control variable changes most slowly.

NONE   *Do not write the cell counts to the file.* This is the default.

CELLS   *Write the cell count for nonempty cells to a file.*

ALL   *Write the cell count for all cells to a file.* Available only in integer mode.

Example

```
GET FILE  GSS80.
PROCEDURE OUTPUT  OUTFILE=CELLDATA.
CROSSTABS VARIABLES=FEAR SEX (1,2)
  /TABLES=FEAR BY SEX
  /WRITE=ALL.
```

• CROSSTABS writes a record for each cell in the table FEAR by SEX to the file CELLDATA. Figure 1 shows the contents of the CELLDATA file.

Figure 1 Cell output records

```
1  1      55      1        1
1  1     172      2        1
1  1     180      1        2
1  1      89      2        2
```

Example

```
PROCEDURE OUTPUT  OUTFILE=XTABDATA.
CROSSTABS  TABLES=V1 TO V3 BY V4 BY V10 TO V15
  /WRITE=CELLS.
```

• CROSSTABS writes a set of records for each table to the XTABDATA output file.

• All of the records for the table V1 BY V4 BY V10 are written first, the records for V1 BY V4 BY V11 second, and the records for V3 BY V4 BY V15 last.

WEIGHT Command

You can use the file created by the WRITE subcommand in a subsequent SPSS session to reproduce a table and compute statistics for it. Each record in the file contains all the information used to build the original table.

Example

The following CROSSTABS command reads the CELLDATA file created by the commands in the previous section (see WRITE Subcommand). It reads the cell frequency as a weighting factor (WGHT), the value of the row variable (FEAR), and the value of the column variable (SEX):

```
DATA LIST FILE=CELLDATA
   /WGHT 9-16 FEAR 17-24 SEX 25-32.
VARIABLE LABELS  FEAR 'AFRAID TO WALK AT NIGHT IN NEIGHBOR-
HOODS'.
VALUE LABELS  FEAR 1 'YES' 2 'NO'/ SEX 1 'MALE' 2 'FEMALE'.
WEIGHT  BY WGHT.
CROSSTABS  TABLES=FEAR BY SEX
  /STATISTICS=ALL.
```

• The WEIGHT command recreates the sample size by weighting each of the four cases (cells) by the cell frequency.

Example

This example assumes you do not have the original data used to write the cell frequencies to file CELLDATA. The WEIGHT command is used to reproduce tables and compute statistics for the published tables.

```
DATA LIST  /FEAR 1 SEX 3 WGHT 5-7.
VARIABLE LABELS  FEAR 'AFRAID TO WALK AT NIGHT IN NEIGHBORHOOD'.
VALUE LABELS  FEAR 1 'YES' 2 'NO'/ SEX 1 'MALE' 2 'FEMALE'.

WEIGHT  BY WGHT.
BEGIN DATA
1 1   55
2 1  172
1 2  180
2 2   89
END DATA.

CROSSTABS  TABLES=FEAR BY SEX
  /STATISTICS=ALL.
```

- The values from the table are used as inline data between BEGIN DATA and END DATA.
- Each cell in the table becomes a case, and each record includes the row and column variables, and the cell frequency for weighting.
- You can define the variables for the cell frequency, row value, and column value in any order.

Annotated Example

For a complete example with output, see Examples following the Command Reference.

References

Bishop, Y. M. M., S. E. Feinberg, and P. W. Holland. 1975. *Discrete multivariate analysis: Theory and practice.* Cambridge: MIT Press.

Haberman, S. J. 1978. *Analysis of qualitative data.* Vol. 1. London: Academic Press.

Kraemer, H. C. 1982. Kappa coefficient In *Encyclopedia of statistical sciences.* ed. S. Kotz and N.L. Johnson. New York: John Wiley & Sons.

DATA LIST

```
DATA LIST [FILE=file] [{FIXED}] [RECORDS={1}] [{TABLE  }]
                       {FREE }             {n}   {NOTABLE}
                       {LIST }


          [END=varname]

/{1    } varlist {col location [(format)]    } [varlist ..]
 {rec #}         {(FORTRAN-like format list)}

[/{2    } ...] [/ ...]
  {rec #}
```

Numeric and string formats:

Format	FORTRAN-like format	Data type
(d)	Fw.d	Numeric (default)
(N)	Nw	Restricted numeric
(E,d)	Ew.d	Scientific notation
(COMMA,d)	COMMAw.d	Numeric with commas
(DOT,d)	DOTw.d	Numeric with dots
(DOLLAR,d)	DOLLARw.d	Numeric with commas and dollar sign
(PCT,d)	PCTw.d	Numeric with percent sign
(Z,d)	Zw.d	Zoned decimal
(A)	Aw	String
(AHEX)	AHEXw	Hexadecimal character
(IB,d)	IBw.d	Integer binary
(P,d)	Pw.d	Packed decimal
(PIB,d)	PIBw.d	Unsigned integer binary
(PIBHEX)	PIBHEXw	Hexadecimal unsigned integer binary
(PK,d)	PKw.d	Unsigned packed decimal
(RB)	RBw	Floating point binary
(RBHEX)	RBHEXw	Hexadecimal floating point binary
	Tn	Tabs to column n
	nX	Skips n columns

Some formats may not be available on all implementations of SPSS.

Date and time input formats:

Format	FORTRAN-like format	Data input	Type
(DATE)	DATEw	dd/mmm/yyyy	International date
(ADATE)	ADATEw	mmm/dd/yyyy	American date
(JDATE)	JDATEw	yyddd	Julian date
(QYR)	QYRw	qQyyyy	Quarter and year
(MOYR)	MOYRw	mm/yyyy	Month and year
(WKYR)	WKYRw	wkWKyyyy	Week and year
(DATETIME)	DATETIMEw	dd-mmm-yyyy hh:mm:ss.ss	Date and time
(TIME)	TIMEw	hh:mm:ss.ss	Time
(DTIME)	DTIMEw	ddd hh:mm:ss.ss	Days and time
(WKDAY)	WKDAYw	string	Day of the week
(MONTH)	MONTHw	string	Month

Column binary* and unaligned positive integer binary specifications:
startcolumn:startrow [-endrow]
startcolumn:startrow-endcolumn:endrow
startbyte:startbit [-endbit]
startbyte:startbit-endbyte:endbit

*Column binary files can be read only if MODE=MULTIPUNCH is specified on the FILE HANDLE command.

Example:

```
DATA LIST /ID 1-3 SEX 5 (A) AGE 7-8 OPINION1 TO OPINION5 10-14.
```

Overview
DATA LIST defines a data file containing raw data (numbers and other alphanumeric characters) by assigning names to variables and providing information about column location and format. Data can be inline (entered within the command sequence between the BEGIN DATA and END DATA commands) or stored in an external file.

For information on defining raw matrix materials, see MATRIX DATA. For defining complex data files that cannot be defined with DATA LIST, see FILE TYPE and REPEATING DATA. For information on reading SPSS system files and SPSS portable files, see GET and IMPORT.

SPSS can also read data files created by other software applications. Commands that read these files include GET SCSS, GET SAS, GET BMDP, GET OSIRIS, and GET TRANSLATE. For information on the types of files your system can read, see Appendix E.

Options
Data Source. You can use inline data or data from an external file.

Data Formats. You can define both numeric and string variables, specify decimal places for numeric variables, and specify an array of formats (percent, dollar, date and time, etc.). For a definition of formats A, F, COMMA, DOT, DOLLAR, and PCT, see Universals: Variable Formats. For a definition of all the available formats, see Appendix E. You can also specify column binary and unaligned positive integer binary formats (available only if used with the MODE= MULTIPUNCH setting on the FILE HANDLE command).

Data Organization. You can specify that data be entered in fixed format with values in the same location on the same record for each case, in freefield format with multiple cases per record, or in freefield format with one case on each record. See FIXED, FREE, and LIST keywords.

Multiple Records. For fixed-format data, you can indicate the number of records per case and optionally read only the records you want to analyze. See RECORDS Subcommand.

Summary Table. For fixed format data, you can display a table that summarizes the variable definitions. See TABLE Subcommand.

End-of-File Processing. You can control end-of-file processing by specifying a logical variable that can be used to invoke special processing after all the cases from the input file have been read. See END Subcommand.

Basic Specification
The basic specification is one of the three keywords FIXED (the default), LIST, or FREE followed by a slash and a variable list.

- Format types can be specified in parentheses after each variable name. If a format type is not specified for a variable, the variable receives the default numeric format.
- If data are in an external data file, the FILE subcommand must be used.
- If data are inline, the BEGIN DATA and END DATA commands must be used.

Subcommand Order
- Subcommands can be named in any order. However, all subcommands must precede the first slash, which signals the beginning of data definition.

Syntax Rules
- Two types of format specifications are available: column style format specifications and FORTRAN-like format specifications. The following is an overview of each type. For more information, see Variable Formats, below.
- Column style formats are available only with FIXED format data.
- With FIXED format, column style and FORTRAN-like formats can be mixed on the same DATA LIST.

Column Style Formats
- Data must be in FIXED format. Column locations must be specified after each variable, and the width of a variable is determined by the number of specified columns. Following the column locations, specify the format type in parentheses. If no format type is specified, numeric (F) format is used.

- An abbreviated format can be used for specifying column locations if several variables are recorded in adjacent columns on the same record and have the same width and format type. First list all variable names, then the beginning column location of the first variable in the list, a dash, and the ending column location of the last variable in the list. SPSS equally divides among the variables the total number of columns specified. If the number of columns does not divide equally, an error message is issued.

- Each format type must be specified after the column locations of the variable to which it applies. If the abbreviated form of specifying column locations for adjacent variables is used, the format type applies to all the variables within the specified columns.

- Since variables are located by column positions, the variables can be named in any order on DATA LIST.

FORTRAN-like formats
- Column locations cannot be specified. The width of a variable is determined by the width portion ("w" on the syntax chart) of the format specification.

- A format specification can apply only to one variable.

- The format can be specified in parentheses after the variable to which it applies. Alternatively, a variable list can be followed by a set of format specifications contained in parentheses. There must be one format specification for each variable in the variable list. Format specifications must be separated by at least one space or comma. If no format is specified for a variable, the default F8.2 format is used.

- Variables are located according to the sequence in which they are named on DATA LIST. The order of variables on DATA LIST must therefore correspond to the order of the variables in the data.

Operations
- DATA LIST clears the current active system file to define a new one.

- Variable names are stored in the active file dictionary.

- Formats are stored in the active file dictionary and are used to display and write the values. Use the FORMATS command to change formats of numeric variables defined on DATA LIST.

- By default, variables are assumed to be numeric. Alphabetical and special characters, except the decimal point and leading plus and minus signs, are not valid numeric values and are set to system-missing if encountered in the data.

Fixed-Format Data
- The order of the variables in the active file dictionary is the order in which they are defined in DATA LIST, not their sequence in the input data file. This order is important if you later use the TO convention.

- Blanks to the left or right of a number in the default format are ignored; imbedded blanks are invalid.

- The system-missing value is assigned to a completely blank field for numeric variables. The value assigned to blanks can be changed using the BLANKS specification on the SET command.

- SPSS ignores the data in columns and on records that are not specified on DATA LIST.

Freefield Data
- FREE can read freefield-format data with multiple cases recorded on one record or with one case recorded on more than one record. LIST can read freefield-format data with one case on each record.

FORTRAN-like Formats
- Whereas FORTRAN interprets blanks as zeros, SPSS does not. In SPSS, leading and trailing blanks are ignored.

- SPSS cannot interpret numeric values that contain imbedded blanks. When SPSS encounters a field that contains one or more blanks interspersed among the numbers, it issues a warning message and assigns the system-missing value to that case.

- SPSS is less tolerant than FORTRAN in accepting data values. For example, standard FORTRAN accepts the value 1-1 as $1.0E-1$. However, SPSS accepts this value only if the input format type is for scientific notation. Under standard numeric format (such as F3), SPSS issues an error message indicating an imbedded sign and assigns the system-missing value to that case.

Example

```
TITLE 'COLUMN STYLE FORMAT SPECIFICATIONS'.

DATA LIST /ID 1-3 SEX 5 (A) AGE 7-8 OPINION1 TO OPINION5 10-14.
BEGIN DATA
001 m 28 12212
002 f 29 21212
003 f 45 32145
...
128 m 17 11194
END DATA.
```

- The data are inline between the BEGIN DATA and END DATA commands. Data are in fixed format. Keyword FIXED is not specified because it is the default. Column locations are specified for each variable.
- Variable definition begins after the slash. Variable ID is in columns 1 through 3. Because no format is specified, numeric format is assumed. Variable ID is therefore a numeric variable that is three characters wide.
- Variable SEX is a short string variable in column 5. Variable SEX is one character wide.
- AGE is a two-column numeric variable in columns 7 and 8.
- Variables OPINION1, OPINION2, OPINION3, OPINION4, and OPINION5 are named using the TO convention (see Universals: Variable-Naming Conventions). Each is a one-column numeric variable, with OPINION1 located in column 10 and OPINION5 located in column 14.
- The BEGIN DATA and END DATA commands enclose the inline data. Note that the values of SEX are in lowercase characters and must be specified as such on subsequent commands.

Example

```
TITLE 'MIXING COLUMN STYLE AND FORTRAN-LIKE FORMAT SPECIFICATIONS'.

DATA LIST FILE=PRSNL / LNAME M_INIT STREET (A20,A1,1X,A10)
                       AGE 35-36.
```

- Data are read from file PRSNL.
- FORTRAN-like format specifications are made with FIXED format data. LNAME, M_INIT, and STREET are all string variables. LNAME is twenty characters wide, M_INIT is one character wide, and STREET is ten characters wide. LNAME, M_INIT, and STREET must be adjacent in the data file. The 1X format element defines a blank column between M_INIT and STREET.
- Column style format is used for variable AGE. AGE begins in column 35, ends in column 36, and by default has numeric format.

FILE Subcommand

FILE specifies the data file. FILE is required when data are stored in an external data file. FILE must not be used when the data are stored in a file that is included with an INCLUDE command or when the data are inline (see INCLUDE and BEGIN DATA).

- FILE must be separated from other DATA LIST subcommands by at least one blank or comma.
- FILE must precede the first slash, which signals the beginning of data definition.

FIXED, FREE, and LIST Keywords

FIXED, FREE, or LIST indicates the format of the data. Only one of the three keywords can be used on each DATA LIST. FIXED is the default.

- FIXED, FREE, or LIST must be separated from other DATA LIST subcommands by at least one blank or comma.

- FIXED, FREE, or LIST must precede the first slash, which signals the beginning of data definition.
- With FIXED data, either column style formats, FORTRAN-like formats, or both can be used. With FREE or LIST data, only FORTRAN-like formats can be used.
- With FIXED data, SPSS reads values according to the column locations specified or implied by the format. Values in the data do *not* have to be in the same order as the variables named on DATA LIST and do *not* have to be separated by a space or column.
- With FREE and LIST data, SPSS reads values sequentially in the order in which the variables are named on DATA LIST. Values in the data *must* be in the order in which the variables are named on DATA LIST and *must* be separated by at least one blank or comma.
- With FREE or LIST data, a blank value cannot be used to indicate missing information. A value must be assigned to the missing information with the MISSING VALUES command.
- In FREE format, the end of a data record is the same as a blank or comma. That is, a value cannot be split across records. However, multiple blank columns at the end of a record are interpreted as one delimiter between values.

FIXED   *Fixed-format data.* Each variable is recorded in the same location on the same record for each case in the data. FIXED is the default.

FREE   *Freefield-format data.* The variables are recorded in the same order for each case, but not necessarily in the same locations. More than one case can be entered on the same record. Values are separated by blanks or commas.

LIST   *Freefield data with one case on each record.* The variables are recorded in freefield format as described for keyword FREE except that the variables for each case must be recorded on one record.

Example   TITLE   'DATA IN FIXED FORMAT'.

DATA LIST FILE=HUBDATA FIXED RECORDS=3
  /1 YRHIRED 14-15 DEPT 19 SEX 20.

- FIXED indicates explicitly that the HUBDATA file is in fixed format. Because FIXED is the default, keyword FIXED could have been omitted.
- FIXED is separated from the other subcommands by at least one space. All subcommands precede the first slash.
- Data definition begins after the slash. Because column style formats are used, column locations are required after each variable. Format types are not specified; all the variables are therefore numeric. Variable widths are determined by the column specifications: YRHIRED is two characters wide, DEPT and SEX are each one character wide.

Example   TITLE   'DATA IN FREE FORMAT'.

DATA LIST FREE / POSTPOS NWINS.
BEGIN DATA
2 19 7 5 10 25 5 17 8 11 3 18 6 8 1 29
END DATA.

- Data are inline, so FILE is omitted. Keyword FREE is used because data are in freefield format with multiple cases on a single record. Keyword LIST *cannot* be used to define the data as it is entered. The next example shows the same data recorded in LIST format.
- All of the data are recorded on one record. The first two values build the first case in the active system file. The value 2 is assigned to variable POSTPOS, and the value 19 to NWINS. The second case is built from the next two values in the data, and so forth. Eight cases are built in the active system file.
- Formats are not specified for the variables. Both POSTPOS and NWINS therefore receive the default F8.2 formats.

Example
```
TITLE  'DATA IN LIST FORMAT'.

DATA LIST LIST / POSTPOS NWINS.
BEGIN DATA
2 19
7 5
10 25
5 17
8 11
3 18
6 8
1 29
END DATA.
```

- LIST is used because each case is recorded on a separate record. However, keyword FREE could also be used. The previous example shows the same data defined in FREE format and entered in a form that *cannot* be defined with keyword LIST.

- LIST format requires more records in the data file than FREE. However, it is less prone to errors in data entry. Since FREE format reads the data as one long series of numbers, if you leave out a value in the data, the values after the missing value are assigned to the incorrect variable for all remaining cases. Since LIST format reads a case from each record, the missing value will affect only the one case.

TABLE and NOTABLE Subcommands

TABLE displays a table summarizing the variable definitions supplied on DATA LIST. NOTABLE suppresses the table. TABLE is the default for FIXED format data.

- TABLE and NOTABLE can only be used with FIXED format data.

- TABLE and NOTABLE must be separated from other DATA LIST subcommands by at least one blank or comma.

- TABLE and NOTABLE must precede the first slash, which signals the beginning of data definition.

RECORDS Subcommand

RECORDS indicates the number of records per case for fixed-format data. In the data definition portion of DATA LIST, each record must be preceded by a slash. By default, DATA LIST reads one record per case.

- The only specification is a single integer, which indicates the number of records. The integer must indicate the *total* number of records for each case, even if the data definition portion of DATA LIST does not define all the records.

- RECORDS can be used only with FIXED format data and must be separated from other DATA LIST subcommands by at least one blank or comma.

- RECORDS must precede the first slash, which signals the beginning of data definition. The number of slashes in the data definition cannot exceed the value of the integer specified on RECORDS.

- Optionally, a slash can be followed by the sequence number of the record being defined. DATA LIST reads the sequence number to determine the record number. Thus, if the sequence number is used, you *do not* have to use a slash for any skipped records.

- The sequence number can be omitted in data definition and a slash, alone, used to skip to the next record. The first slash indicates the first (or only) record. The second and any subsequent slashes tell SPSS to skip to a new record. If you skip a record and define the next record, you *must* specify a slash (unless sequence numbers are used) for the skipped record, even if no variables from that record are defined. The slashes can be specified within the variable list or, alternatively, a variable list can be followed by a complete format list that specifies the slashes for the second and subsequent records (see the example below).

- All variables to be read from one record must be defined before proceeding to the next record. Because RECORD can only be used with FIXED data and column locations are therefore provided for each variable, it is not necessary to define all the variables on a given record.

- Variables from each record can be named in any order, regardless of their sequence in the data file.

Example
```
DATA LIST FILE=HUBDATA RECORDS=3
  /2 YRHIRED 14-15 DEPT 19 SEX 20.
```

- DATA LIST defines fixed format data. RECORDS can only be used for fixed-format data.
- RECORDS indicates there are three records per case in the data. Only one record per case is defined in the data definition.
- The sequence number (2) in the data definition indicates that only the second record is being defined. Because the sequence number is provided, a slash is not required for the first record, which is skipped.
- Variables YRHIRED, DEPT, and SEX do not have to be the only variables present on the second record. However, they are the only variables defined by DATA LIST and therefore the only variables read by SPSS.

Example
```
DATA LIST FILE=HUBDATA RECORDS=3
  / /YRHIRED 14-15 DEPT 19 SEX 20.
```

- Data definition is identical to the data definition in the previous example. Because the record sequence number is omitted after the second slash, a slash is required to represent the skipped first record, even though no variables are defined for that record.

Example
```
DATA LIST FILE=HUBDATA RECORDS=3
  /YRHIRED (T14,F2.0) /  /NAME (T25,A24).
```

- RECORDS indicates there are three records for each case in the data.
- YRHIRED is the only variable defined for the first record. YRHIRED begins in column 14 and has format F2.0.
- The second record is skipped. Because the optional record sequence numbers are not specified, a slash must be used to skip the second record.
- NAME is the only variable defined for the third record. NAME begins in column 25 and is a string variable with a width of 24 characters.
- The slashes that indicate the second and third record numbers are specified within the variable list. See the next example, which uses the slashes within the format specifications.

Example
```
DATA LIST FILE=HUBDATA RECORDS=3
  /YRHIRED NAME (T14,F2.0 /  / T25,A24).
```

- Data definition is identical to data definition in the previous example. YRHIRED is located on the first record, and NAME is located on the third record.
- The slashes that indicate the second and third records are specified within the format specifications. The format specifications follow the complete variable list.

END Subcommand

END provides control of end-of-file processing by specifying a variable that is set to a value of 0 until the end of the data file is encountered, at which time this variable is set to 1. The values of all variables named on DATA LIST are left unchanged. The logical variable created with END can then be used on DO IF and LOOP to invoke special processing after all the cases from a particular input file have been built.

- DATA LIST and the entire set of commands used to define the cases must be enclosed within an INPUT PROGRAM—END INPUT PROGRAM structure. The END FILE command must also be used to signal the end of case generation.
- END can only be used with FIXED data. An error is generated if either FREE or LIST is used on a DATA LIST that includes an END subcommand.

Example
```
TITLE  'DEMONSTRATE THE USE OF THE END SUBCOMMAND'.

INPUT PROGRAM.
NUMERIC         TINCOME (DOLLAR8.0).              /* TOTAL
INCOME
LEAVE           TINCOME.
DO IF           $CASENUM EQ 1.
+   PRINT       EJECT.
+   PRINT       / 'NAME         INCOME'/.
END IF
DATA LIST       FILE=INCOME END=#EOF NOTABLE/ NAME 1-10(A) INCOME
16-20(F).
DO IF           #EOF.
+   PRINT       // 'TOTAL       ', TINCOME.
+   END FILE.
ELSE.
+   PRINT       / NAME, INCOME (A10,COMMA8).
+   COMPUTE     TINCOME = TINCOME+INCOME.  /* ACCUMULATE TOTAL INCOME
END IF.
END INPUT PROGRAM.

EXECUTE.
```

- The data definition commands are enclosed within an INPUT PROGRAM—END INPUT PROGRAM structure.
- NUMERIC declares a new numeric value to be created, TINCOME.
- LEAVE tells SPSS to leave variable TINCOME at its value for the previous case as each new case is read, thus accumulating totals across cases.
- The first DO IF structure, enclosing the PRINT EJECT and PRINT commands, tells SPSS to display the headers NAME and INCOME at the top of the display (when $CASENUM equals 1).
- DATA LIST defines variables NAME and INCOME, and it specifies the scratch variable #EOF as the END variable.
- The second DO IF accumulates the variable INCOME into TINCOME by passing control to ELSE as long as #EOF is not equal to 1. At the end of the file, EOF equals 1, and the expression on the DO IF is true. The label TOTAL and the value for TINCOME are displayed, and control is passed to END FILE.

Example
```
TITLE  'CONCATENATE THREE RAW DATA FILES'.

INPUT PROGRAM.
NUMERIC #EOF1 TO #EOF3.  /*THESE WILL BE USED AS THE END= VARIABLES.


DO IF   #EOF1 NE 1.
+    DATA LIST  FILE=ONE END=#EOF1 NOTABLE /1 NAME 1-20(A)
              AGE 21-22 SEX 24(A).
ELSE IF  #EOF2 NE 1.
+    DATA LIST  FILE=TWO  END=#EOF2 NOTABLE / NAME 1-20(A)
              AGE 21-22 SEX 24(A).
ELSE IF  #EOF3 NE 1.
+    DATA LIST  FILE=THREE END=#EOF3 NOTABLE / NAME 1-20(A)
                 AGE 25-26 SEX 29(A).
ELSE.
+    END FILE.
END IF.
END INPUT PROGRAM.

REPORT FORMAT AUTOMATIC LIST /VARS=NAME AGE SEX.
```

- The INPUT PROGRAM contains a DO IF—ELSE IF—END IF structure.
- Scratch variables are used on each END subcommand so the value will not be reinitialized to the system-missing value after each case is built.
- Three files are read, two of which contain data in the same format. The third requires a slightly different format for the data items. All three DATA LIST commands are placed within a LOOP structure that is terminated only when all of the records from the three files have been exhausted.
- END FILE is placed after the ELSE command to trigger end-of-file processing once all data records have been read.

• This application can also be handled by creating three separate system files and using ADD FILES to put them together. The advantage of using the END subcommand on DATA LIST is that additional files are not required to store the separate system files prior to performing the ADD FILES. In addition, the files remain raw data files: they are not converted to system files.

Variable Definition

The variable definition portion of DATA LIST assigns names and formats to the variables in the data. Depending on the format of the file and the variables you want to analyze, additional information may be required.

Variable Names

• Variable names can contain up to eight characters. All variable names must begin with a letter or the @ or # character. A # symbol as the first character of the variable name defines the variable as a scratch variable. System variables (beginning with a $) cannot be defined on DATA LIST. An underscore can be used within a variable name, provided the underscore is not the first character.

• Keyword TO can be used to name consecutive variables in the data. Leading zeros in the number are preserved in the name. X1 TO X100 and X001 TO X100 both generate 100 variable names, but the first 99 names are not the same in the two lists. X01 TO X9 is not a valid specification. For more information on the TO convention and other variable-naming rules, see Universals: Variable-Naming Conventions.

• The order in which variables are named on DATA LIST determines their order in the active file. If the active file is saved as a system file, the variables are saved in this order unless they are explicitly reordered on the SAVE or XSAVE command that saves them.

Example   `DATA LIST FREE / ID SALARY #V1 TO #V4.`

• DATA LIST indicates the data are in freefield format. Six variables are defined: ID, SALARY, #V1, #V2, #V3, and #V4. #V1 to #V4 are scratch variables that are not stored in the active system file. Their values, however, can be used in transformations. Their values cannot be used in procedure commands.

Variable Locations: FIXED Format

• If column style format specifications are used, each variable name must be followed by its column location. If the variable is one column wide, specify the number of the column. If the variable is two or more columns wide, specify the number of the first column followed by a dash (–) and the number of the last column. If FORTRAN-like format specifications are used, column locations are not specified; however the format must correctly locate each variable to be read (see Variable Formats, below).

• An abbreviated format can be used for specifying column locations if several variables are recorded in adjacent columns on the same record and have the same width and format type. First list all variable names, then the beginning column location of the first variable in the list, a dash, and the ending column location of the last variable in the list. SPSS divides the total number of columns specified equally among the variables. If the number of columns does not divide equally, an error message is issued.

• SPSS ignores the data in columns and on records that are not specified on DATA LIST.

• Column style format specifications and FORTRAN-like column specifications can be mixed on the same DATA LIST command.

• In the data, values do not have to be separated by a space or comma. The same column locations can be used to define different variables.

Example
```
DATA LIST  FILE=HUBDATA RECORDS=3
  /1 YRHIRED 14-15 DEPT 19 SEX 20
  /2 SALARY 21-25.
```

• Three variables, YRHIRED, DEPT, and SEX, are defined on the first record of the data file. One variable, SALARY, will be read from columns 21 through 25 on the second record. The total number of records per case is specified as three, even though no variables are defined on the third record. The third record is simply skipped in data definition.

Example   DATA LIST FILE=HUBDATA RECORDS=3
               /1 DEPT 19 SEX 20 YRHIRED 14-15 MOHIRED 12-13 HIRED 12-15
               /2 SALARY 21-25.

- The first two defined variables are DEPT and SEX, located in columns 19 and 20 on record 1. The next three variables, YRHIRED, MOHIRED, and HIRED, are also located on the first record.

- YRHIRED will be read from columns 14 and 15, MOHIRED from columns 12 and 13, and HIRED from columns 12 through 15. The HIRED variable is a four-column variable with the first two columns representing the month when an employee was hired (the same as the MOHIRED variable) and the last two columns representing the year of employment (the same as YRHIRED).

- The order of the variables in the dictionary is the order in which they are defined on DATA LIST, not their sequence on the input data file.

Example   DATA LIST FILE=HUBDATA RECORDS=3
               /1 DEPT 19 SEX 20 MOHIRED YRHIRED 12-15
               /2 SALARY 21-25.

- MOHIRED and YRHIRED are followed by column locations that apply to them both. DATA LIST divides the total number of columns specified equally between the two variables. Thus, each variable has a width of two columns.

- Because no format types are specified, all variables are numeric.

Variable Locations: FREE or LIST Format

- Column locations *cannot* be specified on the data definition portion of DATA LIST. Only FORTRAN-like formats can be specified for the variables (see Variable Formats below). Values are read sequentially in the order variables are named on the variable list.

- In the data, one value is separated from another by blanks or by commas. Any number of consecutive blanks or commas (except blanks or commas specified within a string value) are interpreted as one delimiter. A value cannot be split across records.

- A blank field for a variable causes values from that point on to be assigned to the wrong variable. With LIST format, only one case is affected. With FREE format, all remaining cases are affected.

- String values which contain imbedded blanks or commas must be delimited by apostrophes or quotation marks. The delimiters are not read as part of the string value (see Universals: Strings). An apostrophe can be included in string values by delimiting the value with quotation marks. Quotation marks can be included by delimiting the value with apostrophes.

- Neither commas nor blanks can be used within numeric values.

- If there are not enough values to complete the last case, a warning is issued and the incomplete case is dropped.

Example   DATA LIST LIST / ID (F3.0) NAME (A8).
               BEGIN DATA
               122   SMITH
               234,,,"O'BRIAN"
               354,,,'VAN DYKE'
               END DATA.

- Data are in LIST format, so no column specifications are made. Formats are specified for the variables because the default format F8.2 is inappropriate to the data. There are two defined variables, ID and NAME. ID is a numeric variable three characters wide; NAME is a string variable eight characters wide.

- For the first case in the data, spaces are used as a delimiter between values. For the second and third cases, commas are used as delimiters between values. Multiple commas or spaces that are used as delimiters are interpreted as a single delimiter.

- For the second case, the quotation marks enclosing the string value make it possible to include an apostrophe in the name. Apostrophes enclosing the string value in the third case make it possible to include a space in the name. The space is interpreted as part of the string value, not as a delimiter.

Variable Formats

The following sections discuss the ways to assign input formats on DATA LIST; they do not discuss the format types available in SPSS. See the SPSS *Operations Guide* for complete information on the formats available on your operating system. See FORMATS, PRINT FORMATS, and WRITE FORMATS for information on specifying output data formats.

- **For column-style specifications:** After each variable name, specify the column location(s) and, in parentheses, the format type. To include decimal positions in the format, specify the format type followed by a comma and the number of decimal positions. For example, (DOLLAR) specifies only whole dollar amounts; (DOLLAR,2) specifies DOLLAR format with two decimal positions. The maximum width of the value is determined by the column locations.

- **For FORTRAN-like specifications:** After each variable name, specify the format type and width. To include decimal positions in the format, specify the width followed by a decimal point and the number of decimal positions. For example, (DOLLAR5) specifies a five-column DOLLAR format without decimal positions; (DOLLAR5.2) specifies a five-column DOLLAR format, two columns of which are decimal positions.

- If no format type is specified, variables are assumed to be numeric F format: either signed or unsigned integers or real numbers.

- If a value is encountered which cannot be read according to the format type specified, it is assigned the system-missing value and a warning message is issued.

- Formats for fixed data can be specified with column-style specifications, FORTRAN-like specifications, or a combination of both. Formats for freefield data can only be specified with FORTRAN-like specifications.

- Column binary and unaligned positive integer binary specifications are available. These specifications can only be used if the FILE HANDLE command is used with the MODE=MULTIPUNCH specification.

Numeric Formats

- Format specifications on DATA LIST are input formats. For FORTRAN-like format specifications, the *w* after the format type is the width of the widest value in the data. Based on the width specification and format type, SPSS generates print and write formats (output formats) for each variable. SPSS automatically expands the output format to accommodate punctuation characters such as decimal points, commas, dollar signs, or date and time delimiters. (This is not true when you assign output formats on commands such as FORMATS, PRINT FORMATS, and WRITE FORMATS. SPSS does not automatically expand output formats you assign.)

Implied Decimal Positions

- **For fixed data:** Decimal positions can mean the actual or the implied number of decimal positions. Thus, if decimal positions are specified in the format but are not entered with a value in the data, SPSS automatically interprets the rightmost digits in that value as the decimal digits. A coded decimal point in a data value overrides the number of implied decimal places for that value. For example, (DOLLAR,2) specifies two decimal positions. The value 123 is interpreted as 1.23; however, the value 12.3 is interpreted as 12.3 because the coded decimal position overrides the number of implied decimal positions.

- **For freefield data:** Decimal positions cannot be implied; thus, decimal points must be coded in the data for the digits to be read as decimal digits. If decimal positions are specified in the format, SPSS zero-fills decimal positions for values that do not include a coded decimal point. If a value in the data has more decimal digits than are specified for *d* in the format, the additional decimals are truncated in displayed output (they are not truncated in calculations). For example, F3.1 defines a three-column variable with one decimal place. The value 22 is displayed as 22.0. The value 2.22 is displayed as 2.2 because the second decimal position is truncated in output.

- It is useful to specify the number of decimal digits for two reasons: to indicate where the implied decimal point is placed in fixed data when decimal points are not coded, and to provide the desired printing format even when explicit decimal points are present in data values.

- The table below compares how values are interpreted for fixed and freefield format. Values in the table are for a four-column numeric variable when no decimal places are defined on DATA LIST, and when two decimal places are defined on DATA LIST.

	FIXED		FREEFIELD	
Values in the data file	Default	Two defined decimal places	Default	Two defined decimal places
2001	2001	20.01	2001.00	2001.00
201	201	2.01	201.00	201.00
−201	−201	−2.01	−201.00	−201.00
2	2	.02	2.00	2.00
20	20	.20	20.00	20.00
2.2	2.2	2.2	2.20	2.20
.201	.201	.201	.201	.201
2 01	Undefined	Undefined	Two values	Two values

String Formats

- String (alphanumeric) variables are indicated with an A in parentheses following the column specification. If data are in hexadecimal form, use AHEX format.

- The values of string variables can contain any number, letter, or character, including special characters and imbedded blanks. For further discussion of string variables, see Universals: Strings.

FIXED Data

- For numeric values, blanks to the left and right of a number are ignored; imbedded blanks are errors. By default, SPSS assigns the system-missing value to a completely blank field. The value assigned to blank fields can be changed with the BLANK subcommand on the SET command.

Example

```
DATA LIST
    /MODEL 1 RATE 2-6(PCT,2) COST 7-11(DOLLAR) READY 12-21(ADATE).
BEGIN DATA
1935   7878811-07-1988
2 16754654606-08-1989
3 17684783612-09-1989
END DATA.
```

- Data are inline and in FIXED format (the default). FIXED format can use column-style format specifications, FORTRAN-like format specifications, or both.

- Column-style format specifications are used. Each variable is followed by its column location. After the column location, a format type is specified in parentheses.

- MODEL begins in column 1, is one column wide, and receives the default numeric format F.

- RATE begins in column 2 and ends in column 6. The PCT format is specified, with two decimal places. Note that a comma is used in the format specification to separate the format type from the number of decimal places. Note also in the data that it does not matter where numbers are entered within the column width. Decimal points are not coded in the data for any case; thus, SPSS reads the rightmost digits of the value on each case as decimal digits. The RATE value 935 on the first case in the data is interpreted as 9.35.

- COST begins in column 7 and ends in column 11. The DOLLAR format is specified.

- READY begins in column 12 and ends in column 21. The ADATE (American Date) format is specified.

Example
```
DATA LIST FILE=RAWDATA
     /MODEL (F1) RATE (PCT5.2) COST (DOLLAR5) READY (ADATE10).
```

- FILE indicates that data are in file RAWDATA.

- The data definition is the same as in the preceding example. FORTRAN-like format specifications are used rather than column style. Column locations are not used, but the format specifications must include a width for each format type.

- The width ("w") portion of each format must specify the total number of characters in the widest value. DOLLAR5 format for COST accepts the five-digit value 10000, which displays as $10,000. The specified input format DOLLAR5 generates an output format DOLLAR7. SPSS automatically expands the width of the output format to accommodate the dollar sign and comma in displayed output.

FREE and LIST Data

- Any of the FORTRAN-like format specifications that are available on your implementation of SPSS can be used. Exceptions are the T and X format elements, and the date and time formats.

- A format specification applies only to the immediately preceding variable. However, with keywords FREE and LIST, if you specify a format type for any variable, you must specify an asterisk for all variables preceding it in the list that you want read with the default format type. The asterisk applies to all variables preceding it. Variables at the end of a list that are not given a format are assigned the default format.

- If a string in the data is longer than its specified length, the string is truncated and a warning message is displayed. If the string in the data is shorter, it is right-padded with blanks, and no warning message is displayed.

- String values in the data must be enclosed in apostrophes or quotation marks if the string contains a blank or a comma. Otherwise, the blank or comma is treated as a delimiter between values. Apostrophes can be included in a string by enclosing the string in quotation marks. Quotation marks can be included in a string by enclosing the string in apostrophes.

Example
```
DATA LIST FILE=WINS FREE /POSTPOS NWINS * POSNAME (A24).
```

- The variable POSNAME is specified as a 24-character string. The asterisk preceding POSNAME is required to specify that variables POSTPOS and NWINS are to be read with the default format type. Only one asterisk is required; it applies to all the variables preceding it (unlike other FORTRAN-like format specifications, which apply only to the preceding variable).

Example
```
DATA LIST FILE=WINS FREE /POSTPOS * NWINS (A5) POSNAME (A24).
```

- Both NWINS and POSNAME are alphanumeric. Each requires its own format specification.

- POSTPOS receives the default numeric format F8.2.

DESCRIPTIVES

```
DESCRIPTIVES [VARIABLES=] varname[(zname)] [varname...]

[/MISSING={VARIABLE**}  [INCLUDE]]
             {LISTWISE }

[/SAVE]

[/FORMAT={LABELS**  }  {NOINDEX**}  {LINE**}]
          {NOLABELS }  {INDEX    }  {SERIAL}

[/STATISTICS=[DEFAULT**]  [MEAN**]  [MIN**]   [SKEWNESS]]
              [STDDEV**  ]  [SEMEAN]  [MAX**]   [KURTOSIS]
              [VARIANCE ]  [SUM   ]  [RANGE]  [ALL]

[/SORT=[{MEAN    }]  [{(A)}]]
         {SMEAN   }    {(D)}
         {STDDEV  }
         {VARIANCE}
         {KURTOSIS}
         {SKEWNESS}
         {RANGE   }
         {MIN     }
         {MAX     }
         {SUM     }
         {NAME    }
```

**Default if the subcommand is omitted.

Example:

```
DESCRIPTIVES VARIABLES=FOOD RENT, APPL TO COOK, TELLER, TEACHER
  /STATISTICS=VARIANCE DEFAULT
  /MISSING=LISTWISE.
```

Overview

DESCRIPTIVES computes univariate statistics, including the mean, standard deviation, minimum, and maximum, for numeric variables. Because it does not sort values into a frequency table, DESCRIPTIVES is an efficient means of computing descriptive statistics for continuous variables. Other procedures that display descriptive statistics include FREQUENCIES, MEANS and EXAMINE.

Options

Z Scores. You can compute Z scores (standardized deviation scores from the mean) and add these to the active system file as new variables.

Display Format. You can display statistics in serial format and restrict the width to narrow format regardless of the width defined on SET. DESCRIPTIVES also offers control over the display of variable labels and variable names.

Statistical Display. Optional statistics include the standard error of the mean, variance, kurtosis, skewness, range, and sum. DESCRIPTIVES does not compute the median or mode (see FREQUENCIES or EXAMINE).

Listing Order. You can list variables in ascending or descending alphabetic order or by the numerical value of any of the available statistics. See SORT Subcommand.

Basic Specification

• The basic specification is the VARIABLES subcommand with a list of variables. The actual keyword VARIABLES may be omitted. All cases with valid values for a variable are included in the calculation of statistics for that variable. Statistics include the mean, standard deviation, minimum, maximum, and number of cases with valid values.

Subcommand Order

• Subcommands can be used in any order.

Operations

• If the STATISTICS subcommand is used, only those statistics explicitly requested are displayed.

• If a string variable is specified on the variable list, no statistics are displayed for that variable.

- The available width and the statistics and formats requested determine whether the statistics are displayed in tabular or serial form.
- If there is insufficient width to display the statistics requested, DESCRIPTIVES first truncates the variable label and then adopts serial format.

Limitations

- If there is insufficient memory available to calculate statistics for all variables requested, DESCRIPTIVES truncates the variable list.

Example

```
DESCRIPTIVES VARIABLES=FOOD RENT, APPL TO COOK, TELLER, TEACHER
  /STATISTICS=VARIANCE DEFAULT
  /MISSING=LISTWISE.
```

- DESCRIPTIVES requests statistics for variables FOOD, RENT, all the variables between and including APPL and COOK, and variables TELLER and TEACHER.
- STATISTICS requests the variance and the defaults: mean, standard deviation, minimum, and maximum.
- MISSING specifies that cases with missing values for any variable on the variable list will be omitted from the calculation of statistics for all variables.

Example

```
DESCRIPTIVES VARS=ALL.
```

- DESCRIPTIVES requests statistics for all variables on the active system file.
- Because no STATISTICS subcommand is included, only the mean, standard deviation, minimum, and maximum are displayed.

VARIABLES Subcommand

VARIABLES names the variables to be included in the table. The actual keyword VARIABLES may be omitted. If you explicitly specify keyword VARIABLES, an equals sign must precede the variable list.

- Keyword ALL refers to all user-defined variables on the active system file.
- Variables named more than once appear in the display more than once.
- Only one variable list can be specified.

Z Scores

The Z-score transformation standardizes variables to the same scale, producing new variables with a mean of 0 and a standard deviation of 1. These variables are added to the active system file.

- To obtain Z scores for all specified variables, use the SAVE subcommand.
- To obtain Z scores for a subset of variables, name the new variable in parentheses following the source variable on the VARIABLES subcommand, and do not use the SAVE subcommand. Specify new names individually; a list in parentheses is not recognized.
- When specifying the name of the new variable, you can use any acceptable eight-character variable name, including any of the default variable names, that is not already part of the active file.

Example

```
DESCRIPTIVES VARIABLES=NTCSAL NTCPUR (PURCHZ) NTCPRI (PRICEZ).
```

- DESCRIPTIVES creates Z-score variables for NTCPUR and NTCPRI. No Z-score variable is created for NTCSAL.

SAVE Subcommand

SAVE obtains one Z-score variable for each variable specified on the DESCRIPTIVES variable list. SAVE calculates standardized variables and stores them on the active system file.

- DESCRIPTIVES automatically supplies variable names and labels for the new variables. The new variable name is created by prefixing the letter Z to a maximum of seven characters of the variable name. For example, ZNTCPRI is the Z-score variable for NTCPRI.

- When DESCRIPTIVES creates new Z-score variables, it displays a table containing the source variable name, new variable name, its label, and the number of cases for which it is computed.
- If you specify new names on the VARIABLES subcommand *and* use the SAVE subcommand, DESCRIPTIVES creates one new variable for each variable on the VARIABLES subcommand, using the default names for variables not explicitly assigned names.
- If DESCRIPTIVES cannot use the default naming convention because it would produce duplicate names, it uses an alternative naming convention: first ZSC001 through ZSC099, then STDZ01 through STDZ09, then ZZZZ01 through ZZZZ09, then ZQZQ01 through ZQZQ09.
- When using the SAVE subcommand, you can name the same variable up to nine times in a variable list. If at any time you want to change any of the variable names, whether those DESCRIPTIVES created or those you previously assigned, you can do so with the RENAME VARIABLES command.
- DESCRIPTIVES automatically supplies variable labels for the new variables by prefixing *ZSCORE:* to the first 31 characters of the source variable's label. If it uses a name like ZSC001, it prefixes *ZSCORE(varname)* to the first 31 characters of the source variable's label. If the source variable has no label, it uses *ZSCORE(varname)* for the label.

SAVE   *Add Z scores to the active file for all variables on the DESCRIPTIVES command.* SPSS forms variable names for the new variables, using wherever possible the letter *Z* and the first seven characters of the old variable name.

Example
```
DESCRIPTIVES VARIABLES=ALL
  /SAVE.
```

- SAVE obtains a Z-score variable for all variables in the active file. All Z-score variables receive the default name.

Example
```
DESCRIPTIVES VARIABLES=NTCSAL NTCPUR (PURCHZ) NTCPRI (PRICEZ)
  /SAVE.
```

- DESCRIPTIVES creates Z-score variables PURCHZ and PRICEZ and assigns a default name to the Z-score variable for NTCSAL.

Example
```
DESCRIPTIVES VARIABLES=SALARY86 SALARY87 SALARY88
  /SAVE.
```

- DESCRIPTIVES cannot use the default naming convention because it would produce duplicate names. Thus, it uses the alternative names ZSALARY8, ZSC001, and ZSC002.

FORMAT Subcommand

FORMAT controls the available formatting options.

- By default, DESCRIPTIVES displays the statistics and a 40-character variable label for each variable on one line. If requested statistics do not fit in the available width, DESCRIPTIVES first truncates variable labels to 21 characters and then, if necessary, uses serial format.
- To restrict DESCRIPTIVES output to 80 columns, use the SET WIDTH command. The 80-column format is useful if you are examining displays on short-carriage terminals. However, the number of columns for statistics is severely restricted. If you use the NOLABELS keyword to suppress variable labels, more space is available for statistics. Also, specifying a listwise deletion of missing values on the MISSING subcommand suppresses the column for valid number of cases, providing additional space for statistics.

LABELS   *Display variable labels.* This is the default.

NOLABELS   *Suppress variable labels.*

INDEX   *Display reference indexes.* INDEX displays a positional and an alphabetic reference index following the statistical display. The index shows the page location in the output of the statistics for each variable. The variables are listed by their position in the active system file and alphabetically.

NOINDEX	*Suppress reference indexes.* This is the default.
LINE	*Display statistics in line format.* LINE displays statistics on the same line as the variable name. This is the default.
SERIAL	*Display statistics in serial format.* SERIAL displays statistics below the variable name, permitting larger field widths and more decimal digits for very large or very small numbers. DESCRIPTIVES automatically forces this format if the number of statistics requested does not fit in the column format.

Example

```
SET WIDTH=80.
DESCRIPTIVES VARIABLES=TEACHER FTEX FSALES SECRET
  /STATISTICS=ALL
  /FORMAT=INDEX SERIAL.
```

• SET WIDTH limits output to an 80-column width.

• FORMAT requests reference indexes and displays the statistics in serial-style format.

STATISTICS Subcommand

By default, DESCRIPTIVES displays the mean, standard deviation, minimum, and maximum. Use the STATISTICS subcommand to specify alternative statistics.

• When you use STATISTICS, DESCRIPTIVES displays *only* those statistics you request.

• Keyword ALL obtains all statistics.

• When requesting the default statistics plus additional statistics, you can specify DEFAULT to obtain the default statistics without having to name MEAN, STDDEV, MIN and MAX.

• The median and mode, which are available in FREQUENCIES and EXAMINE, are not available in DESCRIPTIVES. These statistics require that values be sorted, and DESCRIPTIVES does not sort values (the SORT subcommand does not sort values, it simply lists variables in the order you request).

• If you request a statistic that is not available, DESCRIPTIVES issues an error message, and the command is not executed.

• The number of columns needed to display the statistics controls the manner in which they are displayed. The maximum column width for skewness, kurtosis, and their standard error is 10; the maximum width for mean, standard error of the mean, minimum, maximum, and range is 11; the maximum width for standard deviation is 12; the maximum width for variance is 13; the maximum width for sum is 14. These widths include a blank between statistics.

• Except for the minimum and maximum values, DESCRIPTIVES displays all statistics with three positions to the right of the decimal point if it can fit them into the space allocated within the maximum width. Large numbers are rounded to fit the column width. If the integer portion still exceeds the column width, DESCRIPTIVES uses scientific notation. Extremely small numbers are also displayed with scientific notation.

MEAN	*Mean.*
SEMEAN	*Standard error of the mean.*
STDDEV	*Standard deviation.*
VARIANCE	*Variance.*
KURTOSIS	*Kurtosis.* Also displays standard error of kurtosis.
SKEWNESS	*Skewness.* Also displays standard error of skewness.
RANGE	*Range.*
MIN	*Minimum.*
MAX	*Maximum.*
SUM	*Sum.*
DEFAULT	*Mean, standard deviation, minimum, and maximum.* These are the default statistics.
ALL	*All the statistics available to DESCRIPTIVES.*

SORT Subcommand

By default, DESCRIPTIVES lists variables in the order in which they appear on VARIABLES. Use SORT to list variables in ascending or descending alphabetic order or by numeric value of any of the statistics available with DESCRIPTIVES.

- If you specify SORT without any of the optional keywords, variables are sorted by mean in ascending order.
- SORT sorts variables by the value of any of the statistics available with DESCRIPTIVES, but only those statistics specified on STATISTICS are displayed. If you specify SORT without STATISTICS, the default statistics are displayed.

Only one of the following keywords can be specified on SORT:

MEAN	*Sort by mean.* This is the default when SORT is specified without keywords.
SEMEAN	*Sort by standard error of the mean.*
STDDEV	*Sort by standard deviation.*
VARIANCE	*Sort by variance.*
KURTOSIS	*Sort by kurtosis.*
SKEWNESS	*Sort by skewness.*
RANGE	*Sort by range.*
MIN	*Sort by minimum observed value.*
MAX	*Sort by maximum observed value.*
SUM	*Sort by sum.*
NAME	*Sort by variable name.*

Either of the following can be specified with one of the above keywords to determine sort order:

- **(A)** *Sort in ascending order.* This is the default when SORT is specified without keywords.
- **(D)** *Sort in descending order.*

Example
```
DESCRIPTIVES VARIABLES=A B C
 /STATISTICS=DEFAULT RANGE
 /SORT=RANGE (D).
```

- DESCRIPTIVES sorts variables A, B, and C by range in descending order and displays the mean, standard deviation, minimum and maximum values, number of cases, value labels, and the range.

MISSING Subcommand

MISSING controls missing values.

- By default, DESCRIPTIVES deletes cases with missing values on a variable-by-variable basis. A case missing on a variable will not be included in the summary statistics for that variable, but the case *will* be included for variables where it is not missing.
- The VARIABLE and LISTWISE keywords are mutually exclusive; however, each can be specified with INCLUDE.
- When either the keyword VARIABLE or the default missing-value treatment is used, DESCRIPTIVES reports the number of valid cases for each variable. It always displays the number of cases that would be available if listwise deletion of missing values had been selected.

VARIABLE	*Exclude missing values on a variable-by-variable basis.* This is the default.
LISTWISE	*Exclude missing values listwise.* Cases missing on any variable named are excluded from the computation of summary statistics for all variables.
INCLUDE	*Include user-missing values.*

Annotated Example

For a complete example with output, see Examples following the Command Reference.

DISCRIMINANT

This command is included in the SPSS Advanced Statistics option.

```
DISCRIMINANT GROUPS=varname(min,max) /VARIABLES=varlist

[/SELECT=varname(value)]

[/ANALYSIS=varlist(level) [varlist...]]

[/METHOD={DIRECT**}] [/TOLERANCE={0.001}]
         {WILKS   }                {t    }
         {MAHAL   }
         {MAXMINF }
         {MINRESID}
         {RAO     }

[/MAXSTEPS={2v}]
          {m }

[/FIN={1.0}] [/FOUT={1.0}] [/PIN={pi}]
      {fi }        {fo }

[/POUT={po}] [/VIN={0**}]
                   {vi }

[/FUNCTIONS={g-1,100.0,1.0**}] [/PRIORS={EQUAL**    }]
            {nf , cp ,sig }            {SIZE       }
                                       {value list}

[/SAVE=[CLASS=varname] [PROBS=rootname]

       [SCORES=rootname]]

[/ANALYSIS=...]

[/MISSING={EXCLUDE**}]
          {INCLUDE  }

[/MATRIX=[OUT({*   })] [IN({*   })]]
             {file}      {file}

[/HISTORY={STEP**}  {END**  }]
          {NOSTEP}  {NOEND  }

[/ROTATE={NONE**   }]
         {COEFF    }
         {STRUCTURE}

[/CLASSIFY={NONMISSING  }  {POOLED  }  [MEANSUB]]
           {UNSELECTED  }  {SEPARATE}
           {UNCLASSIFIED}

[/STATISTICS=[MEAN  ]  [COV ]  [FPAIR]  [RAW  ]  [ALL]]
             [STDDEV]  [GCOV]  [UNIVF]  [COEFF]
             [CORR  ]  [TCOV]  [BOXM ]  [TABLE]

[/PLOT=[MAP]  [SEPARATE]  [COMBINED]  [CASES]  [ALL]]
```

**Default if the subcommand is omitted.

Example:

```
DISCRIMINANT GROUPS=OUTCOME (1,4)
  /VARIABLES=V1 TO V7
  /SAVE CLASS=PREDOUT.
```

Overview

DISCRIMINANT performs linear discriminant analysis for two or more groups. The goal of discriminant analysis is to classify cases into one of several mutually exclusive groups, based on their values for a set of predictor variables. The classification rule is developed on cases for which group membership is known. The rule can then be used to classify cases for which group membership is not known. The grouping variable must be categorical, and the independent (predictor) variables must be interval or dichotomous, since they will be used in a regression-type equation.

Options   **Variable Selection Method.** In addition to the direct entry method, you can specify any of several stepwise methods for entering variables into the discriminant analysis, based on different statistical criteria.

Case Selection. You can select a subset of cases for analysis within the DISCRIMINANT command.

Prior Probabilities. You can specify prior probabilities for membership in the different groups. These are used in classifying cases.

Saving Variables. You can add new variables to the active system file containing the predicted group membership, the probability of membership in each of the groups, and the scores on the discriminant functions.

Classification Options. You can request that DISCRIMINANT classify only those cases that were not selected for inclusion in the discriminant analysis, or only those cases whose code on the grouping variable fell outside the range analyzed. In addition, you can classify cases on the basis of the separate-group covariance matrices of the functions rather than the pooled within-groups covariance matrix.

Statistical Display. You can request any of a variety of statistics. You can rotate the pattern or structure matrices. You can compare actual with predicted group membership using a classification results table or any of several types of plots or histograms. In addition, you can display the discriminant scores and the actual and predicted group membership for each case.

Basic Specification   The basic specification requires two subcommands:

• GROUPS specifies the variable used to group cases.
• VARIABLES specifies the predictor variables.

DISCRIMINANT enters all variables simultaneously into the discriminant equation (the DIRECT method) provided that they are not so highly correlated that multi-collinearity problems arise. Default output consists of counts of cases in the groups, the method used and associated criteria, and a summary of results including eigenvalues, standardized discriminant function coefficients, and within-groups correlations between the discriminant functions and the predictor variables.

Subcommand Order   • The GROUPS, VARIABLES, and SELECT subcommands must precede any other subcommands and may be entered in any order.

• ANALYSIS must follow. ANALYSIS specifies the predictor variables to be used in a single analysis. The variables must first have been named on the VARIABLES subcommand.

• Remaining subcommands may be used in any order and apply only to the preceding ANALYSIS subcommand. If any of these subcommands are entered before the first ANALYSIS subcommand or if there is no ANALYSIS subcommand, the entire set of variables named on VARIABLES is analyzed.

Operations   • The procedure first estimates one or more discriminant functions that best distinguish among the groups.

• Using these functions, the procedure then classifies cases into groups (if classification output is requested).

• If more than one ANALYSIS command is supplied, these steps are repeated for each requested group of variables.

Limitations   • Only one GROUPS, one SELECT, and one VARIABLES subcommand may be used per DISCRIMINANT command.

• Pairwise deletion of missing data is not available.

Example
```
DISCRIMINANT GROUPS=OUTCOME (1,4)
   /VARIABLES=V1 TO V7
   /STATISTICS=COV GCOV TCOV
   /SAVE CLASS=PREDOUT.
```

- Only cases for which the grouping variable GROUPS has values 1, 2, 3, or 4 will be used in computing the discriminant functions.
- The variables on the active system file between and including V1 and V7 will be used to compute the discriminant functions and to classify cases.
- In addition to the default output, the STATISTICS subcommand requests the display of the pooled within-groups covariance matrix and the group and total covariance matrices.
- Predicted group membership will be saved in the variable PREDOUT, which will be added to the active system file if it does not already exist.

GROUPS Subcommand

GROUPS specifies the name of the grouping variable, which defines the categories or groups to be distinguished. Along with the variable name, you must specify a range of categories.

- GROUPS is required and may be used only once.
- The specification consists of a variable name followed by a range of values in parentheses.
- Only one grouping variable may be specified; its values must be integers. To use a string variable as the grouping variable, first use AUTORECODE to convert the string values to integers, then specify the recoded variable as the grouping variable.
- Empty groups are ignored and do not affect calculations. For example, if there are no cases in Group 2, the value range (1,5) will define only four groups.
- Cases with values outside the value range or with missing values are ignored during the analysis phase but may be classified during the classification phase (if requested).

VARIABLES Subcommand

VARIABLES identifies the predictor variables, which are used to classify cases into the groups defined on the GROUPS subcommand. The list of variables follows the usual SPSS conventions for variable lists.

- VARIABLES is required and may be used only once. Use the ANALYSIS subcommand to obtain multiple analyses.
- Only numeric variables may be used.
- Variables should be suitable for use in a regression-type equation, either measured at the interval level or dichotomous.

SELECT Subcommand

Use SELECT to limit the discriminant analysis to cases with a specified value on any one variable.

- Only one SELECT subcommand is allowed. It may follow the GROUPS and VARIABLES subcommands but must precede any other subcommands.
- The specification is a variable name and a single integer value in parentheses. Multiple variables or values are not permitted.
- The selection variable need not have been named on the GROUPS (or VARIABLES) subcommand.
- Only cases with the specified value on the selection variable are used in the analysis phase.
- By default all cases, whether selected or not, will be classified. Use CLASSIFY= UNSELECTED to classify only the unselected cases.
- When SELECT is used, classification statistics are reported separately for selected and unselected cases, unless CLASSIFY=UNSELECTED is used to restrict classification.

Example

```
DISCRIMINANT GROUPS=APPROVAL(1,5)
  /VARS=Q1 TO Q10
  /SELECT=COMPLETE(1)
  /CLASSIFY=UNSELECTED.
```

- Using only the cases where variable COMPLETE = 1, DISCRIMINANT estimates a function of Q1 TO Q10 that discriminates between the categories 1 to 5 of the grouping variable APPROVAL.
- Because CLASSIFY=UNSELECTED is requested, the discriminant function will be used to classify only the unselected cases, namely the cases for which COMPLETE does not equal 1.

ANALYSIS Subcommand

Use ANALYSIS to request several different discriminant analyses using the same grouping variable, or to control the order in which variables are entered into a stepwise analysis.

- ANALYSIS is optional. By default all variables on the VARIABLES subcommand are included in the analysis.
- The variables named on ANALYSIS must first be specified on the VARIABLES subcommand.
- Keyword ALL includes all variables on the VARIABLES subcommand.
- If keyword TO is used to specify a list of variables on an ANALYSIS subcommand, it refers to the order of variables on the VARIABLES subcommand, which is not necessarily the order of variables in the active system file.

Example
```
DISCRIMINANT GROUPS=SUCCESS(0,1)
  /VARIABLES=V10 TO V15, AGE, V5
  /ANALYSIS=V15 TO V5
  /ANALYSIS=ALL.
```

- The first ANALYSIS will use variables V15, AGE, and V5 to discriminate between cases where SUCCESS=0 and the cases where SUCCESS=1.
- The second ANALYSIS will use all variables on the VARIABLES subcommand.

METHOD Subcommand

Use METHOD to select any of six methods for entering variables into the analysis phase.

- A variable will never be entered into the analysis if it does not pass the tolerance criterion specified on the TOLERANCE subcommand (or the default).
- A METHOD subcommand applies to the *preceding* ANALYSIS subcommand or to an analysis using all predictor variables if no ANALYSIS subcommand has been specified.
- Only one METHOD subcommand can be entered per ANALYSIS.

Any one of the following methods can be entered on the METHOD subcommand:

DIRECT   *At each step, all variables passing the tolerance criteria are entered simultaneously.* This is the default method.

WILKS   *At each step, the variable that minimizes the overall Wilks' lambda is entered.*

MAHAL   *At each step, the variable that maximizes the Mahalanobis' distance between the two closest groups is entered.*

MAXMINF   *At each step, the variable that maximizes the smallest F ratio between pairs of groups is entered.*

MINRESID   *At each step, the variable that minimizes the sum of the unexplained variation for all pairs of groups is entered.*

RAO   *At each step, the variable that produces the largest increase in Rao's V is entered.*

Statistical Criteria for Entry or Removal

In addition to naming a method for variable selection on the METHOD subcommand, you can specify a number of optional subcommands to set other parameters controlling the selection algorithm.

- These subcommands must follow the METHOD subcommand to which they apply and can be entered in any order.

• All of these subcommands except TOLERANCE apply only to the stepwise methods. Therefore, the METHOD subcommand is not required when you specify TOLERANCE.

TOLERANCE Subcommand

The tolerance of a variable that is a candidate for inclusion in the analysis is the proportion of its within-group variance that is not accounted for by other variables currently in the analysis. A variable with very low tolerance is nearly a linear function of the other variables; its inclusion in the analysis would make the calculations unstable. The TOLERANCE subcommand specifies the minimum tolerance a variable can have and still be entered into the analysis.

• The default tolerance is 0.001.

• You can specify any decimal value between 0 and 1 as the minimum tolerance.

FIN Subcommand

FIN specifies the minimum partial F value a variable must have to enter the analysis.

• The default is FIN=1.

• You can set FIN to any nonnegative number.

• PIN overrides FIN if both are specified.

• FIN is ignored if the METHOD subcommand is omitted or if METHOD specifies DIRECT.

PIN Subcommand

PIN specifies the minimum probability of F a variable must have to enter the analysis.

• If the PIN subcommand is omitted, the value of FIN is used.

• You can set PIN to any decimal value between 0 and 1.

• If PIN is specified, FIN is ignored.

• PIN is ignored if the METHOD subcommand is omitted or if METHOD specifies DIRECT.

FOUT Subcommand

As additional variables are entered into the analysis, the partial F for variables already in the equation changes. FOUT is the smallest partial F a variable can have and not be removed from the model.

• The default is FOUT=1.0.

• You can set FOUT to any nonnegative number. However, FOUT should be less than FIN if FIN is also specified.

• POUT overrides FOUT if both are specified.

• FOUT is ignored if the METHOD subcommand is omitted or if METHOD specifies DIRECT.

POUT Subcommand

POUT is the maximum probability of F a variable can have and not be removed from the model.

• By default, a variable is removed if its partial F falls below the FOUT specification.

• You can set POUT to any decimal value between 0 and 1. However, POUT should be greater than PIN if PIN is also specified.

• POUT overrides FOUT if both are specified.

• POUT is ignored if the METHOD subcommand is omitted or if METHOD specifies DIRECT.

VIN Subcommand

The VIN subcommand specifies the minimum Rao's V a variable must have to enter the analysis. When you use METHOD=RAO, variables satisfying one of the other criteria for entering the equation may actually cause a decrease in Rao's V for the equation. The default VIN prevents this but does not prevent the addition of variables which provide no additional separation between groups.

• The default is VIN=0.

• You can specify any value for VIN.

• VIN should be used only when you have specified METHOD=RAO. Otherwise, it is ignored.

MAXSTEPS Subcommand

By default, the maximum number of steps allowed in a stepwise analysis is the number of variables with inclusion levels greater than 1 plus twice the number of variables with inclusion levels equal to 1. This is the maximum number of steps possible without a loop in which a variable is repeatedly cycled in and out. Use MAXSTEPS to decrease the maximum number of steps allowed.

- MAXSTEPS applies only to the stepwise methods.
- MAXSTEPS should be specified after the METHOD subcommand to which it applies.
- The format is MAX=n, where n is the maximum number of steps desired.

FUNCTIONS Subcommand

By default, DISCRIMINANT computes all possible functions. This is either the number of groups minus 1 or the number of predictor variables, whichever is less. Use FUNCTIONS to set more restrictive criteria for the extraction of functions. The FUNCTIONS subcommand has three parameters:

nf *Maximum number of functions.* The default is the number of groups minus 1 or the number of predictor variables, whichever is less.

cp *Cumulative percentage of the sum of the eigenvalues.* The default is 100%.

sig *Significance level of function.* The default is 1.0.

- The parameters must always be specified in the following order: *nf*, *cp*, *sig*. To specify *cp*, you must explicitly specify the default for *nf*. To specify *sig*, you must specify defaults for *nf* and *cp*. Since *nf* is first, it can be specified without *cp* and *sig*.
- If more than one nondefault restriction is specified on the FUNCTIONS subcommand, SPSS uses the first one encountered.

Example

```
DISCRIMINANT  GROUPS=CLASS(1,5)
   /VARIABLES = SCORE1 TO SCORE20
   /FUNCTIONS=4,100,.80.
```

- The first two specifications on the FUNCTIONS subcommand are defaults: the default for *nf* is 4 (5, the number of groups, minus 1), and the default for *cp* is always 100.
- The third specification tells DISCRIMINANT to use fewer than four discriminant functions if the significance level of a function is greater than 0.80.

STATISTICS Subcommand

By default, the following statistics are produced during the analysis phase:

- *Summary table.* A table showing the action taken at every step (for stepwise methods only).
- *Summary statistics.* Eigenvalues, percent of variance, cumulative percent of variance, canonical correlations, Wilks' lambda, chi-square, degrees of freedom, and significance of chi-square are reported for the functions. (Can be suppressed with HISTORY=NOEND.)
- *Step statistics.* Wilks' lambda, equivalent *F*, degrees of freedom, and significance of *F* are reported for each step. Tolerance, *F*-to-remove, and the value of the statistic used for variable selection are reported for each variable in the equation. Tolerance, minimum tolerance, *F*-to-enter, and the value of the statistic used for variable selection are reported for each variable not in the equation. (Can be suppressed with HISTORY=NOSTEP.)
- *Final statistics.* Standardized canonical discriminant function coefficients, the structure matrix of discriminant functions and all variables named in the analysis (whether they were entered into the equation or not), and functions evaluated at group means, are reported following the last step. (These statistics cannot be suppressed.)

In addition, you can request optional statistics on the STATISTICS subcommand. STATISTICS may be specified by itself or with one or more keywords.

- If STATISTICS is specified with no keywords, DISCRIMINANT displays MEAN, STDDEV, and UNIVF (each defined below). If you include a keyword or keywords on STATISTICS, DISCRIMINANT displays only the statistics you request.

MEAN	*Means.* Displays total and group means for all variables named on the ANALYSIS subcommand. This (along with STDDEV and UNIVF) is the default if you specify STATISTICS by itself, with no keywords.
STDDEV	*Standard deviations.* Displays total and group standard deviations for all variables named on the ANALYSIS subcommand. This (along with MEAN and UNIVF) is the default if you specify STATISTICS by itself, with no keywords.
UNIVF	*Univariate* F *ratios.* Displays the analysis of variance *F* statistic for equality of group means for each predictor variable. This is a one-way analysis of variance test for equality of group means on a single discriminating variable. This (along with MEAN and STDDEV) is the default if you specify STATISTICS by itself, with no keywords.
COV	*Pooled within-groups covariance matrix.*
CORR	*Pooled within-groups correlation matrix.*
FPAIR	*Matrix of pairwise F ratios.* Displays the *F* ratio for each pair of groups. This *F* is the significance test for the Mahalanobis' distance between groups. This statistic is available only with the stepwise methods.
BOXM	*Box's M test.* This is a test for equality of group covariance matrices.
GCOV	*Group covariance matrices.*
TCOV	*Total covariance matrix.*
RAW	*Unstandardized canonical discriminant functions.*
COEFF	*Classification function coefficients.* Although DISCRIMINANT does not directly use these coefficients to classify cases, you can use them to classify other samples (see CLASSIFY Subcommand).
TABLE	*Classification results table.* If you include a SELECT subcommand in your specifications, two tables are produced, one for selected cases and one for unselected cases.
ALL	*All optional statistics available for DISCRIMINANT.*

ROTATION Subcommand

The coefficient and correlation matrices may be rotated to facilitate interpretation of results. To obtain a VARIMAX rotation, use the ROTATION subcommand.

COEFF	*Rotate pattern matrix.*
STRUCTURE	*Rotate structure matrix.*

Neither COEFF nor STRUCTURE affects the classification of cases.

HISTORY Subcommand

HISTORY controls output display.

- By default, HISTORY displays both the step-by-step output and the summary table. Its default keywords are STEP and END.
- Keywords NOSTEP and NOEND enable you to reduce the amount of output produced during stepwise analysis.

STEP	*Display step-by-step output.* This (along with END) is the default.
NOSTEP	*Suppress display of step-by-step output.*
END	*Display the summary table.* This (along with STEP) is the default.
NOEND	*Suppress display of the summary table.*

Classification Phase

Once DISCRIMINANT has completed the analysis phase, the results can be used to classify cases.

- Use the PRIORS subcommand to control prior probabilities for classification.
- Use the PLOT subcommand to obtain various statistics and plots for the classification phase.
- Use the CLASSIFY subcommand to control the way cases are handled during the classification phase.

PRIORS Subcommand

By default, DISCRIMINANT assumes equal prior probabilities for groups when classifying cases. You can provide different prior probabilities with the PRIORS subcommand.

- Prior probabilities are used only during classification.
- If you provide unequal prior probabilities, DISCRIMINANT adjusts the classification coefficients to reflect this.
- If adjacent groups have the same prior probability, you can use the notation $n*c$ in the value list to indicate that n adjacent groups have the same prior probability c.
- The value list must name or imply as many prior probabilities as groups.
- You can specify a prior probability of 0. No cases are classified into such a group.
- If the sum of the prior probabilities is not 1, SPSS rescales the probabilities to sum to 1 and issues a warning.

EQUAL   *Equal prior probabilities.* This is the default.

SIZE   *Proportion of the cases analyzed that fall into each group.* If 50% of the cases included in the analysis fall into the first group, 25% in the second, and 25% in the third, the prior probabilities are 0.5, 0.25, and 0.25, respectively. Group size is determined after cases with missing values for the predictor variables are deleted.

Value list   *User-specified prior probabilities.* A list of probabilities summing to 1.0 is specified.

Example
```
DISCRIMINANT  GROUPS=TYPE(1,5)
  /VARIABLES=A TO H
  /PRIORS = 4*.15,.4.
```

- The PRIORS subcommand establishes prior probabilities of 0.15 for the first four groups and 0.4 for the fifth group.

CLASSIFY Subcommand

CLASSIFY determines how cases are handled during the classification phase of DISCRIMINANT.

- By default, all non-missing cases are classified, and the pooled within-groups covariance matrix is used to classify cases.
- The default keywords for CLASSIFY are NONMISSING and POOLED.

NONMISSING   *Classify all cases that do not have any missing values.* Two sets of classification results are produced, one for the selected cases (those specified on the SELECT subcommand) and one for the nonselected cases. This is the default.

UNSELECTED   *Classify only unselected cases.* The classification phase is suppressed for cases selected via the SELECT subcommand.

UNCLASSIFIED   *Classify only unclassified cases.* Cases whose values on the grouping variable fall outside the range specified on the GROUPS subcommand classified as a separate entry in the classification results table. UNCLASSIFIED suppresses classification of cases that fall into the range specified on the GROUPS subcommand and classifies only cases falling outside the range.

POOLED	*Use the pooled within-groups covariance matrix to classify cases.* This is the default.
SEPARATE	*Use separate-group covariance matrices of the discriminant functions for classification.* The separate-group covariance matrices are used for classification. However, since classification is based on the discriminant functions and not the original variables, this option is not equivalent to quadratic discrimination.
MEANSUBSTITUTION	*Substitute means for missing values during classification.* Cases with missing values are not used during analysis. During classification, means are substituted for missing values, and cases containing missing values are classified.

PLOT Subcommand

PLOT enables you to request a listing of classification results for each case and three types of plots to help you examine the effectiveness of the discriminant analysis. See the Annotated Example for examples of this output.

COMBINED	*All-groups plot.* For each case, the first two function values are plotted. A histogram is displayed if only one function is used.
CASES	*For each case, discriminant scores and classification information is displayed.*
MAP	*Territorial map.* A plot of the group centroids and the boundaries used for classification of the groups. Not displayed for a single function.
SEPARATE	*Separate-groups plots.* These are the same types of plots produced by keyword COMBINED. However, separate plots are produced for each group.
ALL	*All plots available for DISCRIMINANT.*

MISSING Subcommand

MISSING controls missing values.

- By default, cases missing on any of the variables named on the VARIABLES subcommand and cases out of range or missing on the GROUPS subcommand are not used during the analysis phase.
- Cases missing or out of range on the GROUPS variable are used during the classification phase.
- Keyword INCLUDE on the MISSING subcommand enables you to include user-missing values in the analysis.

EXCLUDE	*Exclude all missing values.* Both user-missing and system-missing values are excluded from the analysis. This is the default.
INCLUDE	*Include user-missing values.* User-missing values are treated as valid values. Only the system-missing value is treated as missing.

SAVE Subcommand

SAVE allows you to add much of the casewise information produced by PLOT=CASES to the active system file and to specify new variable names for this information.

- Request only the keywords for the results you want saved.
- SAVE applies to the previous ANALYSIS subcommand (or to an analysis of all variables if no ANALYSIS subcommand precedes SAVE).
- To save casewise results from more than one analysis, enter a SAVE command after each, using different rootnames.
- Keywords CLASS, SCORES, and PROBS can be used in any order, but the new variables are always added to the end of the active file in the following order: first the predicted group, then the discriminant scores, then probabilities of group membership.

- Appropriate variable labels are generated automatically for the new variables.
- The CLASS variable will use the value labels (if any) from the GROUP variable specified for the analysis.

CLASS *Save a variable containing the predicted group membership.* Specify a name for this variable after the keyword CLASS.

SCORES *Save the discriminant scores.* One score is saved for each discriminant function derived. Specify a *rootname* up to seven characters long after the SCORES keyword. DISCRIMINANT will use the rootname to form new variable names for the discriminant scores.

PROBS *For each case, save the probabilities of membership in each group.* As many variables are added to each case as there are groups. Specify a *rootname* up to seven characters long after the PROBS keyword. DISCRIMINANT will use the rootname to generate variable names for the new variables.

Example
```
DISCRIMINANT GROUPS=WORLD(1,3)
  /VARIABLES=FOOD TO FSALES
  /SAVE CLASS=PRDCLASS SCORES=SCORE PROBS=PRB.
```

- With three groups, the following variables are added to each case:

Name	Description
PRDCLASS	Predicted group
SCORE1	Discriminant score for Function 1
SCORE2	Discriminant score for Function 2
PRB1	Probability of being in Group 1
PRB2	Probability of being in Group 2
PRB3	Probability of being in Group 3

MATRIX Subcommand

MATRIX reads and writes SPSS matrix system files. The matrix materials can be used in subsequent DISCRIMINANT procedures.

- Either IN or OUT is required to specify the matrix file in parentheses. When both IN and OUT are used on the same DISCRIMINANT procedure, they can be specified on separate MATRIX subcommands or both on the same subcommand.

- In addition to the Pearson correlation coefficients, the matrix materials include weighted and unweighted numbers of cases, means, and standard deviations.

- Documents from the original file will not be included in the matrix file and will not be present if the matrix file becomes the active system file.

- DISCRIMINANT can read correlation matrices written by a previous DISCRIMINANT command or by other procedures. DISCRIMINANT reads only correlation type matrices. If you want to use a covariance type matrix for input in DISCRIMINANT, you must first use the MCONVERT command to change the covariance matrix to a correlation matrix.

- If variable names are the same, DISCRIMINANT can read a matrix from a previous data set to classify data in a new data set.

Matrix Input
- Matrix materials read by DISCRIMINANT must contain records with ROWTYPE_ values MEAN, N or COUNT (or both), STDDEV, and CORR.

- If records with ROWTYPE_ value COUNT (unweighted number of cases) are not in the data, DISCRIMINANT uses information from records with ROWTYPE_ value N (weighted number of cases). Conversely, if the data do not have N values, DISCRIMINANT uses the COUNT values. These records can appear in any order in the matrix input file, with the following exceptions: the order of split file groups cannot be violated, and all CORR vectors must appear consecutively within each split file group.

- If any of the STATISTICS=BOXM, STATISTICS=GCOV, or CLASSIFY= SEPARATE specifications is in effect when DISCRIMINANT writes a matrix system file, then STDDEV and CORR records in the matrix materials are represented within cell data, and separate covariance matrices are written to the file. This means that when the matrix file is used as input for a subsequent

DISCRIMINANT procedure, at least one of the same three specifications must be used on the DISCRIMINANT command that reads the matrix. It doesn't matter which of the three are specified on the DISCRIMINANT command that reads the matrix, and the specification doesn't have to be one that was used on the DISCRIMINANT command that wrote the matrix.

- BOXM and GCOV on the STATISTICS subcommand and SEPARATE on the CLASSIFY subcommand signal DISCRIMINANT that the matrix materials contain separate covariance matrices.

- MATRIX=IN cannot be used in place of GET or DATA LIST to begin a new SPSS command file. MATRIX is a subcommand on DISCRIMINANT, and DISCRIMINANT cannot run before an active system file is defined. To begin a new command file and immediately read a matrix, first GET the matrix file, then specify IN(*) on MATRIX.

OUT   *Write a matrix system file.* Specify either a file or an asterisk, and enclose the specification in parentheses. If you specify a file, the file is stored on disk and can be retrieved at any time. If you specify an asterisk (*), the matrix system file replaces the active system file but is not stored on disk unless you use SAVE or XSAVE.

IN   *Read a matrix system file.* If the matrix system file *is not* the current active file, specify a file in parentheses. If the matrix system file *is* the current active system file, specify an asterisk (*) in parentheses.

Format of the Matrix System File

- The matrix system file has two special variables created by SPSS: ROWTYPE_ and VARNAME_. Variable ROWTYPE_ is a short string variable having values N, COUNT, MEAN, STDDEV, and CORR (for Pearson correlation coefficient). Variable VARNAME_ is a short string variable whose values are the names of the variables used to form the correlation matrix.

- When ROWTYPE_ is CORR, VARNAME_ gives the variable associated with that row of the correlation matrix.

- Between ROWTYPE_ and VARNAME_ is the group variable, which is specified on the GROUPS subcommand of DISCRIMINANT.

- The remaining variables are the variables used to form the correlation matrix.

Split Files and Variable Order

- When split-file processing is in effect, the first variables in the matrix system file will be the split variables, followed by ROWTYPE_, the group variable, VARNAME_, then the variables used to form the correlation matrix.

- A full set of matrix materials is written for each subgroup defined by the split variable(s).

- A split variable cannot have the same variable name as any other variable written to the matrix system file.

- If a split file is in effect when a matrix is written, the same split file must be in effect when that matrix is read into another procedure.

Additional Statistics

DISCRIMINANT always writes the following matrix materials:

- A vector of N's (weighted number of cases) for each cell in the data.

- A vector of counts (unweighted number of cases) for each cell in the data.

- A vector of means for each cell in the data.

- STDDEV (standard deviation) records and CORR (Pearson correlation coefficient) records.

STDDEV and CORR Records

- Records written to the matrix file with ROWTYPE_ values STDDEV and CORR are influenced by the specifications made on the STATISTICS and CLASSIFY subcommands.

- If any of the STATISTICS=BOXM, STATISTICS=GCOV, or CLASSIFY= SEPARATE specifications is in effect, then STDDEV and CORR records represent within-cell data and receive values for the group variable.

- If none of the above specifications is in effect, STDDEV and CORR records represent pooled values.

- When STDDEV and CORR represent pooled values, the STDDEV vector contains the square root of the mean square error for each variable, and STDDEV and CORR records receive the system missing value for the group variable.

Missing Values
- Missing-value treatment affects the values written to a matrix system file. When reading a matrix system file, be sure to specify a missing-value treatment on DISCRIMINANT that is compatible with the treatment used to generate the matrix materials.

Example
```
GET FILE=UNIONBK /KEEP WORLD FOOD SERVICE BUS MECHANIC CONSTRUC
                     COOK MANAGER FSALES APPL RENT.
DISCRIMINANT  GROUPS=WORLD(1,3)
 /VARIABLES=FOOD SERVICE BUS  MECHANIC CONSTRUC COOK
             MANAGER FSALES
 /METHOD=WILKS
 /PRIORS=SIZE
 /MATRIX=OUT(DISCMTX).
```

- DISCRIMINANT reads raw data from file UNIONBK and writes one set of matrix materials to the file DISCMTX.
- The active system file is still the file UNIONBK. Subsequent commands are executed on file UNIONBK.

Example
```
TITLE 'USE MATRIX OUTPUT TO CLASSIFY DATA IN A DIFFERENT FILE'.

GET FILE=UB2 /KEEP WORLD FOOD SERVICE BUS MECHANIC CONSTRUC COOK
  MANAGER FSALES APPL RENT.
DISCRIMINANT  GROUPS=WORLD(1,3)
 /VARIABLES=FOOD SERVICE BUS  MECHANIC CONSTRUC COOK MANAGER
FSALES
 /METHOD=WILKS
 /PRIORS=SIZE
 /MATRIX=IN(DISCMTX).
```

- The new matrix system file created in the previous example is used to classify data from file UB2 by scores derived from file UNIONBK.

Example
```
GET FILE=UNIONBK /KEEP WORLD FOOD SERVICE BUS MECHANIC CONSTRUC
COOK MANAGER FSALES APPL RENT.
DISCRIMINANT  GROUPS=WORLD(1,3)
 /VARIABLES=FOOD SERVICE BUS  MECHANIC CONSTRUC COOK MANAGER FSALES
 /METHOD=WILKS
 /PRIORS=SIZE
 /MATRIX=OUT(*).
LIST.
```

- DISCRIMINANT writes the same matrix as in the example above. However, the matrix system file replaces the active system file.
- The LIST command is executed on the matrix file, not on the file UNIONBK.

Example
```
GET FILE=DISCMTX.
DISCRIMINANT  GROUPS=WORLD(1,3)
 /VARIABLES=FOOD SERVICE BUS  MECHANIC CONSTRUC COOK
MANAGER FSALES
 /METHOD=RAO
 /MATRIX=IN(*).
```

- This example assumes you are starting a new session and want to read an existing matrix system file. GET retrieves the matrix system file DISCMTX.
- MATRIX=IN specifies an asterisk because the current active system file is the matrix system file DISCMTX. MATRIX=IN must therefore specify the active system file as the file from which the matrix materials will be read.
- If the GET command is omitted, SPSS issues an error message.
- If MATRIX=IN(DISCMTX) is specified, SPSS issues an error message.

Example
```
GET FILE=RAWDATA.
DISCRIMINANT GROUPS=variable(min,max) /VAR=varlist
  /CLASSIFY=SEPARATE
  /MATRIX=OUT(*).
DISCRIMINANT GROUPS=variable(min,max) /VAR=varlist
  /STATISTICS=BOXM
  /MATRIX=IN(*).
```

- Because STATISTICS=BOXM is specified on the DISCRIMINANT command that writes the matrix, at least one of the specifications below *must* be specified on the DISCRIMINANT that reads the matrix:

  STATISTICS=BOXM
  STATISTICS=GCOV
  CLASSIFY=SEPARATE

Inclusion Levels

When you specify a stepwise method (any method other than the default METHOD=DIRECT), you can control the order in which variables are considered for entry or removal by specifying *inclusion levels* on the ANALYSIS subcommand. By default, all variables in the analysis are entered according to the criterion requested on the METHOD subcommand.

- An inclusion level is an integer between 0 and 99, specified in parentheses after a variable or list of variables on an ANALYSIS subcommand.
- The default inclusion level is 1.
- Variables with higher inclusion levels are considered for entry before variables with lower inclusion levels.
- Variables with even inclusion levels are entered as a group.
- Variables with odd inclusion levels are entered individually, according to the stepwise method specified on the METHOD subcommand.
- Only variables with an inclusion level of 1 are considered for removal. To make a variable with a higher inclusion level eligible for removal, name it twice on the ANALYSIS subcommand, first specifying the desired inclusion level and then an inclusion level of 1.
- Variables with an inclusion level of 0 are never entered. However, the statistical criterion for entry is computed and displayed.
- Variables which fail the TOLERANCE criterion are not entered regardless of their inclusion level.

The following are some common methods of entering variables along with the ANALYSIS subcommand and inclusion levels that could be used to achieve them. These examples assume that one of the stepwise methods is specified on the METHOD subcommand (otherwise inclusion levels have no effect).

- *Direct.* ANALYSIS=ALL(2) forces all variables into the equation. (This is the default and can be requested with METHOD=DIRECT or simply by omitting the METHOD and ANALYSIS subcommands.)
- *Stepwise.* ANALYSIS=ALL(1) yields a stepwise solution in which variables are entered and removed in stepwise fashion. (This is the default when anything other than DIRECT is specified on the METHOD subcommand.)
- *Forward.* ANALYSIS=ALL(3) enters variables into the equation stepwise, but does not ever remove variables.
- *Backward.* ANALYSIS=ALL(2) ALL(1) forces all variables into the equation and then allows them to be removed stepwise if they satisfy the criterion for removal.

Example
```
DISCRIMINANT GROUPS=SUCCESS(0,1)
  /VARIABLES=A, B, C, D, E
  /ANALYSIS=A TO C (2) D, E (1)
  /METHOD=WILKS.
```

- A, B, and C are entered into the analysis first, assuming that they pass the tolerance criterion. Since their inclusion level is even, they are entered together.

- D and E are then entered stepwise. Whichever of the two minimizes the overall value of Wilks' lambda is entered first.

- After entering D and E, SPSS checks whether the partial F for either one justifies removal from the equation (see the discussion under FOUT and POUT).

Example
```
DISCRIMINANT GROUPS=SUCCESS(0,1)
    /VARIABLES=A, B, C, D, E
    /ANALYSIS=A TO C (2) D, E (1).
```

- Since no stepwise method is specified, inclusion levels have no effect and all variables are entered into the model at once.

Annotated Example   For a complete example with output, see Examples following the Command Reference.

References   Tatsuoka, M.M. 1971. *Multivariate Analysis.* New York: John Wiley & Sons.

DISPLAY

```
DISPLAY [SORTED] [{NAMES**  }] [/VARIABLES=varlist]
                 {INDEX     }
                 {VARIABLES }
                 {LABELS    }
                 {DICTIONARY}
                 {SCRATCH   }
                 {VECTOR    }

                 [MACROS]
                 [DOCUMENTS]
```
**Default if subcommand is omitted.

Example:
```
DISPLAY SORTED DICTIONARY /VARIABLES=DEPT SALARY SEX TO JOBCAT.
```

Overview   DISPLAY exhibits information from the dictionary of the active system file. The information can be sorted, and it can be limited to selected variables.

Basic Specification   • The basic specification is simply the command keyword, which displays an unsorted list of the variables in the active system file.

Syntax Rules   • DISPLAY can be specified by itself or with any of the keywords defined below. If a keyword is specified, DISPLAY exhibits only the requested information.
    • Only one keyword can be specified per DISPLAY command. NAMES is the default. To specify two or more keywords, use multiple DISPLAY commands.

NAMES   *Display variable names.* A list of the variables in the active system file is displayed. The names are not sorted and display in a compressed format, about eight names across the page. This is the default.

DOCUMENTS   *Display the text provided by the DOCUMENT command.* No error message is issued if there is no documentary information in the SPSS system file.

DICTIONARY   *Display complete dictionary information for variables.* Information includes the variable names, labels, sequential position of each variable in the file, print and write formats, missing values, and value labels. Up to 60 characters can be displayed for variable and value labels.

INDEX   *Display the variable names and positions.*

VARIABLES   *Display the variable names, positions, print and write formats, and missing values.*

LABELS   *Display the variable names, positions, and variable labels.*

SCRATCH   *Display scratch variable names.*

VECTOR   *Display vector names.*

MACROS   *Display a list of the currently defined macros.* The variable list is always sorted.

Operations   • DISPLAY directs information to the results file.
    • If SORTED is not specified, information is displayed according to the order of variables in the active system file.

Example
```
GET FILE=HUB.
DISPLAY DOCUMENTS.
DISPLAY DICTIONARY.
```

- DISPLAY exhibits information from the DOCUMENT command and information supplied on the DATA LIST, VARIABLE LABELS, VALUE LABELS, and MISSING VALUES commands of file HUB.

- Each DISPLAY command specifies only one keyword.

- No procedure is needed to execute DISPLAY since DISPLAY gets its information from the dictionary alone.

SORTED Keyword

SORTED alphabetizes the display by variable name. SORTED can precede keywords NAMES, DICTIONARY, INDEX, VARIABLES, LABELS, SCRATCH, or VECTOR.

Example

```
GET FILE=HUB.
DISPLAY DOCUMENTS.
DISPLAY SORTED DICTIONARY.
```

- The first DISPLAY command exhibits the document information, and the second, the complete dictionary information for variables sorted alphabetically by variable name.

VARIABLES Subcommand

VARIABLES (alias NAMES) limits DISPLAY information to a set of specified variables. VARIABLES must be the last specification on DISPLAY and can follow any specification other than DOCUMENTS.

- The only specification is a slash followed by a list of variables. The slash is optional.

- If keyword SORTED is not specified, information is displayed in the order variables are stored in the active system file, regardless of the order the variables are named on VARIABLES.

Example

```
GET FILE=HUB.
DISPLAY SORTED DICTIONARY
   /VARIABLES=DEPT, SALARY, SEX TO JOBCAT.
```

- DISPLAY exhibits dictionary information for only the variables mentioned (or implied by keyword TO) in the variable list and sorts them alphabetically by variable name.

DOCUMENT

```
DOCUMENT text
```

Example:

```
DOCUMENT    THIS FILE CONTAINS A SUBSET OF VARIABLES FROM THE
            GENERAL SOCIAL SURVEY DATA.  FOR EACH CASE IT
            RECORDS ONLY THE AGE, SEX, EDUCATION LEVEL,
            MARITAL STATUS, NUMBER OF CHILDREN,
            AND TYPE OF MEDICAL INSURANCE COVERAGE.
```

Overview

DOCUMENT saves a block of text of any length in an SPSS system file. The text documents information about the system file. The documentation can later be exhibited with the DISPLAY command.

When GET retrieves a system file, or when ADD FILES, MATCH FILES, or UPDATE are used to combine system files, all documents from each specified file are copied into the active system file. DROP DOCUMENTS can be used to drop those documents from the active file. Whether or not DROP DOCUMENTS is used, new documents can be added to the active file with the DOCUMENT command.

Basic Specification

- The basic specification is DOCUMENT followed by a any length of text. The text is stored in the file dictionary when the data are saved in a system file.

Syntax Rules

- The text can be entered on as many lines as needed.
- Blank lines can be used as paragraph separators within the text.
- Multiple DOCUMENT commands can be used within the command sequence. However, the DISPLAY command cannot be used to exhibit the text from a particular DOCUMENT command. DISPLAY shows all existing documentation.

Operations

- The documentation and the date it was entered are saved in the new system file's dictionary. The new documentation is saved along with any documentation already in the active system file.
- If a DROP DOCUMENTS command *follows* a DOCUMENT command anywhere in the command sequence, the documentation specified on the DOCUMENT command is dropped from the active file along with all other documentation.

Example

```
GET FILE=GENSOC /KEEP=AGE SEX EDUC MARITAL CHILDRN MED_INS.
FILE LABEL  GENERAL SOCIAL SURVEY SUBSET.

DOCUMENT    THIS FILE CONTAINS A SUBSET OF VARIABLES FROM THE
            GENERAL SOCIAL SURVEY DATA.  FOR EACH CASE IT
            RECORDS ONLY THE AGE, SEX, EDUCATION LEVEL,
            MARITAL STATUS, NUMBER OF CHILDREN,
            AND TYPE OF MEDICAL INSURANCE COVERAGE.

SAVE OUTFILE=SUBSOC.
```

- GET keeps only a subset of variables from file GENSOC. All documentation from file GENSOC is copied into the active system file.
- FILE LABEL creates a label for the new system file.
- DOCUMENT specifies the new document text. Both existing documents from file GENSOC and the new document text are saved in file SUBSOC.

Example

```
GET FILE=GENSOC /KEEP=AGE SEX EDUC MARITAL CHILDRN MED_INS.

DROP DOCUMENTS.

FILE LABEL  GENERAL SOCIAL SURVEY SUBSET.

DOCUMENT    THIS FILE CONTAINS A SUBSET OF VARIABLES FROM THE
            GENERAL SOCIAL SURVEY DATA.   FOR EACH CASE IT
            RECORDS ONLY THE AGE, SEX, EDUCATION LEVEL,
            MARITAL STATUS, NUMBER OF CHILDREN,
            AND TYPE OF MEDICAL INSURANCE COVERAGE.

SAVE OUTFILE=SUBSOC.
```

- DROP DOCUMENTS drops the documentation from file GENSOC as data are copied into the active file. Only the new documentation is saved on file SUBSOC.

DO IF

```
DO IF [(]logical expression[)]

  transformations

[ELSE IF [(]logical expression[)]]

  transformations

[ELSE IF [(]logical expression[)]]
                   .
                   .
                   .
[ELSE]

  transformations

END IF
```

The following relational operators can be used in logical expressions:

Symbol	Definition	Symbol	Definition
EQ or =	Equal to	NE or a= or <>	Not equal to
LT or <	Less than	LE or <=	Less than or equal to
GT or >	Greater than	GE or >=	Greater than or equal to

The following logical operators can be used in logical expressions:

Symbol	Definition
AND or &	Both relations must be true
OR or | or ¦	Either relation can be true
NOT or ¬ or ~	Reverses the outcome of an expression

Example:

```
DO IF (YRHIRED LT 87).
RECODE RACE(1=5)(2=4)(4=2)(5=1).
END IF.
```

Example:

```
DO IF (YRHIRED GT 87).
COMPUTE            BONUS = 0.
ELSE IF (DEPT87 EQ 3).
COMPUTE            BONUS = .1*SALARY87.
ELSE IF (DEPT87 EQ 1).
COMPUTE            BONUS = .12*SALARY87.
ELSE IF (DEPT87 EQ 4).
COMPUTE            BONUS = .08*SALARY87.
ELSE IF (DEPT87 EQ 2).
COMPUTE            BONUS = .14*SALARY87.
END IF.
```

Overview
The DO IF—END IF structure conditionally executes one or more transformations on the same subset of cases based on one or more logical expressions defined within the structure. The ELSE command can be used within the structure to execute one or more transformations when the logical expression on the DO IF command is not true. The ELSE IF command within the structure provides further control of execution.

The DO IF—END IF structure is best used for executing multiple transformations. Compare with IF, which is most efficient when used to express a single, conditional, COMPUTE-like transformation. Also, compare this structure with the LOOP—END LOOP structure: DO IF—END IF transforms data on *subsets* of cases defined by the logical expressions on the DO IF and ELSE IF commands; LOOP—END LOOP performs repeated transformations on the *same* case.

Options
> **End-of-file Processing.** See END FILE (elsewhere in this manual) for information on use of the DO IF—END IF structure to instruct SPSS to stop reading data before it encounters the end of the file or to signal the end of the file when creating data. See Concatenating Data Files (below) for using the DO IF—END IF structure to gain further control of end-of-file processing.
>
> **Defining Complex File Structures.** A DO IF—END IF structure within an input program can be used to define complex files that cannot be handled by standard file definition facilities. See Complex File Structures, below.

Basic Specification
> • The basic specification is DO IF followed by a logical expression and at least one transformation command. The structure must end with the END IF command, which has no specifications. The DO IF and END IF commands by themselves (without ELSE IF or ELSE) are most frequently used to execute RECODE, COUNT, and multiple COMPUTE transformations conditionally.

Syntax Rules
> • The ELSE IF command is optional and can be repeated as many times as desired within the structure.
>
> • The ELSE command is optional. It can be used only once and must follow any ELSE IF commands.
>
> • The END IF command must follow any ELSE IF or ELSE commands.
>
> • Logical expressions are mandatory on the DO IF and ELSE IF commands. Do not use logical expressions on the ELSE and END IF commands.
>
> • String values used in expressions must be specified in quotes and must include any leading or trailing blanks. Lowercase letters are considered distinct from uppercase letters.
>
> • String variables specified within the structure must already exist. To declare a new string variable, first create the variable with the STRING command, and then specify the new variable within the DO IF—END IF structure.
>
> • DO IF—END IF control structures can be nested to any level permitted by available memory. Also, DO IF—END IF control structures can be nested within LOOP—END LOOP control structures or LOOP structures within DO IF structures.

Flow of Control
> • Missing values returned by the logical expression on the DO IF command or on any ELSE IF commands cause control to pass to the END IF command at that point.
>
> • If the logical expression on the DO IF command is true, the commands immediately following the DO IF are executed up to the next ELSE IF or ELSE in the structure. Control then passes to the first statement following the END IF for that structure.
>
> • If the expression on the DO IF command is false, control passes to the first ELSE IF where the logical expression is evaluated. If this expression is true, commands following the ELSE IF are executed up to the next ELSE IF or ELSE command, and control passes to the first statement following the END IF for that structure.
>
> • If the expressions on the DO IF and the first ELSE IF commands are both false, control passes to the next ELSE IF, where that logical expression is evaluated. If none of the expressions are true on any of the ELSE IF commands, commands following the ELSE command are executed and control falls out of the structure.
>
> • If none of the expressions on the DO IF command or the ELSE IF commands are true and there is no ELSE command, then a case falls through the entire structure with no change.

Logical Expressions
> • Logical expressions can be simple logical variables or relations, or they can be complex logical tests involving variables, constants, functions, relational operators, and logical operators. The logical expressions use any of the numeric or

string functions allowed in COMPUTE transformations (see COMPUTE, and Universals: Functions).

• Parentheses can be used to enclose the logical expression; they can also be used within the logical expression to specify the order of operations. Extra blanks or parentheses can be used to make the expression easier to read.

• Blanks (not commas) must separate relational operators from expressions.

• A relation can include variables, constants, or more complicated arithmetic expressions. Relations cannot be abbreviated: (A EQ 2 OR A EQ 5) is valid, (A EQ 2 OR 5) is invalid.

• A relation cannot compare a string variable to a numeric value or variable, or vice versa. A relation cannot compare the result of the logical functions SYSMIS, MISSING, ANY, or RANGE to a number.

Operations

• DO IF marks the beginning of the control structure and END IF marks the end. Control for a case is passed out of the structure as soon as a logical condition is met on the DO IF, ELSE IF, or ELSE command within the structure. This structure is more efficient than using multiple IF commands, where each IF statement is evaluated by every case in the data.

• A logical expression is evaluated as true, false, or missing. A transformation specified for that logical expression is executed only if the expression is true.

• If SPSS encounters a case with a missing value for the logical expression on the DO IF command, control passes to the first command after END IF. If a case has a missing value for the conditional expression on any subsequent ELSE IF command, control also passes to the first command after END IF.

• If WEIGHT is specified within a DO IF structure, it takes effect unconditionally.

• Commands like SET, DISPLAY, SHOW, and so forth specified within a DO IF structure are invoked once when they are encountered in the command file.

• The DO IF—END IF structure (like LOOP—END LOOP) can encompass transformations such as the DATA LIST, END CASE, END FILE, and REREAD commands, which define complex file structures.

Numeric Variables

• Numeric variables created within a DO IF structure are initially set to the system-missing value. By default, they are assigned an F8.2 format.

• Logical expressions are evaluated in the following order: first numeric functions, then exponentiation, then arithmetic operations, then relations, and finally logical operators. When more than one logical operator is used, NOT is evaluated, then AND, and then OR. You can change the order of operations using parentheses.

String Variables

• New string variables created within a DO IF structure are initially set to a blank value and are assigned the format specified on the STRING command that creates them.

• Logical expressions are evaluated in the following order: first string functions, then relations, then logical operators. When more than one logical operator is used, NOT is evaluated, then AND, and then OR. You can change the order of operations using parentheses.

• If the transformed value of a string variable exceeds the variable's defined format, the transformed value is truncated. If the transformed value is shorter than the format width defined for that variable, the string is right-padded with blanks to the length of the defined format.

Missing Values and Logical Operators

When two or more relations are joined by logical operators AND and OR, SPSS always returns missing if all of the relations in the expression are missing. However, if any one of the relations can be determined, SPSS tries to return true or false according to the logical outcomes shown in Table 1. The asterisk flags expressions where SPSS can evaluate the outcome with incomplete information.

Table 1 Logical outcome

Expression	Outcome	Expression	Outcome
true AND true	= true	true OR true	= true
true AND false	= false	true OR false	= true
false AND false	= false	false OR false	= false
true AND missing	= missing	true OR missing	= true*
missing AND missing	= missing	missing OR missing	'= missing
false AND missing	= false*	false OR missing	= missing

Example

```
DO IF (YRHIRED LT 87).
RECODE RACE(1=5)(2=4)(4=2)(5=1).
END IF.
```

• The logical expression on DO IF specifies individuals hired before 1987. The coding order is reversed for variable RACE for those individuals hired before 1987. The RACE variable for individuals hired in 1987 or later is not recoded.

• The RECODE command is skipped for any case with a missing value for YRHIRED.

Example

```
TITLE 'ILLUSTRATE A ONE-TIME ONLY TRANSFORMATION'.

DATA LIST       FREE / X(F1).
NUMERIC         #QINIT.
DO IF           NOT #QINIT.
+  PRINT EJECT.
+  COMPUTE      #QINIT = 1.
END IF.
PRINT           / X.

BEGIN DATA
1 2 3 4 5
END DATA.
EXECUTE.
```

• This example shows the best mechanism to use for executing a command only once. In this instance, PRINT EJECT is executed only when the value for scratch variable #QINIT is initialized.

ELSE Command

ELSE executes one or more transformations when the logical expression on the DO IF command is not true.

• Only one ELSE command is allowed within the DO IF—END IF structure. If the ELSE IF command is used, ELSE must follow all ELSE IF commands in the structure.

• If the logical expression on the DO IF command is true, SPSS executes the transformation command or commands immediately following the DO IF up to the first ELSE (or ELSE IF). Then control passes to the command following the END IF command.

• If the result of the logical expression is false, then control passes to ELSE (or ELSE IF).

Example

```
DO IF (X EQ 0).
COMPUTE Y=1.
ELSE.
COMPUTE Y=2.
END IF.
```

• Y is set to 1 for all cases with value 0 for X, and Y is set to 2 for cases with any other valid value for X.

• The value of Y is not set to anything by this structure if X is missing.

Example
```
DO IF (YRHIRED GT 87).
COMPUTE              BONUS = 0.
ELSE.
IF (DEPT87 EQ 1) BONUS = .12*SALARY87.
IF (DEPT87 EQ 2) BONUS = .14*SALARY87.
IF (DEPT87 EQ 3) BONUS = .1*SALARY87.
IF (DEPT87 EQ 4) BONUS = .08*SALARY87.
END IF.
```

- If an individual was hired since 1987, the bonus is set to 0 and control passes out of the structure. Otherwise, control passes to the series of IF commands following ELSE.

- For each IF command, SPSS executes each transformation for each case regardless of what has been executed before and what remains to be executed. Compare this structure with ELSE IF in the following section.

Example
```
TITLE  'TEST FOR LISTWISE DELETION OF MISSING VALUES'.

DATA LIST / V1 TO V6 1-6.
BEGIN DATA
123456
     56
1 3456
123456
123456
END DATA.

DO IF NMISS(V1 TO V6)=0.
+  COMPUTE SELECT='V'.
ELSE
+  COMPUTE SELECT='M'.
END IF.

FREQUENCIES VAR=SELECT.
```

- If there are no missing values for any of the variables V1 to V6, COMPUTE sets the value of SELECT equal to V (for valid). Otherwise, COMPUTE sets the value of SELECT equal to M (for missing).

- FREQUENCIES generates a frequency table for SELECT. The table gives a count of how many cases have missing values for at least one variable, and how many cases have valid values for all variables. Commands in this example can be used to determine whether cases may have been dropped from an analysis that uses listwise deletion of missing values. See COMPUTE for an example that counts the number of missing values per case.

ELSE IF Command

ELSE IF controls the flow of execution within the DO IF—END IF structure.

- Multiple ELSE IF commands are allowed within the DO IF—END IF structure.

- If the logical expression on the DO IF command is true, SPSS executes the transformation command or commands immediately following the DO IF up to the next ELSE IF. Then control passes to the command following the END IF command.

- If the result of the logical expression is false, then control passes to ELSE IF.

Example
```
STRING STOCK(A9).
DO IF (ITEM EQ 0).
COMPUTE STOCK='NEW'.
ELSE IF (ITEM LE 9).
COMPUTE STOCK='OLD'.
ELSE.
COMPUTE STOCK='CANCELLED'.
END IF.
```

- STRING declares string variable STOCK and assigns it a width of 9 characters.

- The DO IF—END IF structure sets STOCK equal to NEW when ITEM equals 0; STOCK equal to OLD when ITEM is less than 9 but not equal to 0; and

STOCK to CANCELLED for all valid values of ITEM greater than 9. The value of STOCK is not set at all by this structure if ITEM is missing.

- For cases with value 0 for ITEM, STOCK is set to NEW and control passes out of the structure. Such cases are not reevaluated by the ELSE IF command, even though 0 is less than 9.

- When the logical expression on DO IF is false, control passes to the ELSE IF command, where the second COMPUTE is executed only for cases with ITEM less than or equal to 9. Then control passes out of the structure.

- If the logical expressions on both the DO IF and ELSE IF commands are false, control passes to ELSE, where the third COMPUTE is executed.

Example
```
DO IF (YRHIRED GT 87).
COMPUTE              BONUS = 0.
ELSE IF (DEPT87 EQ 3).
COMPUTE              BONUS = .1*SALARY87.
ELSE IF (DEPT87 EQ 1).
COMPUTE              BONUS = .12*SALARY87.
ELSE IF (DEPT87 EQ 4).
COMPUTE              BONUS = .08*SALARY87.
ELSE IF (DEPT87 EQ 2).
COMPUTE              BONUS = .14*SALARY87.
END IF.
```

- As soon as SPSS processes a case with value 3 for DEPT87 (and hired before 1987), control passes out of the structure. The other three ELSE IF commands are not evaluated for that case. Compare this example with the example shown for the ELSE command in the section above.

- Note the order of departments. If Department 3 were the largest, Department 1 the next largest, and so forth, control will pass out of the structure more quickly for many cases. For a large number of cases or an SPSS command file that will be executed frequently, these efficiency considerations can be important.

Concatenating Data Files

A DO IF—END IF structure with the ELSE IF and ELSE commands can be used within an INPUT PROGRAM. The following example specifies multiple DATA LIST commands for concatenating raw data files. Each DATA LIST command must use an END subcommand. See DATA LIST for more information on the END subcommand.

Example
```
TITLE  'CONCATENATE THREE RAW DATA FILES'.

INPUT PROGRAM.
NUMERIC  #EOF1 TO #EOF3.  /*THESE WILL BE USED AS THE END= VARIABLES.


DO IF   #EOF1 NE 1.
+    DATA LIST  FILE=ONE END=#EOF1 NOTABLE /1 NAME 1-20(A)
             AGE 21-22 SEX 24(A)
ELSE IF   #EOF2 NE 1.
+    DATA LIST  FILE=TWO  END=#EOF2 NOTABLE / NAME 1-20(A)
             AGE 21-22 SEX 24(A).
ELSE IF  #EOF3 NE 1.
+     DATA LIST  FILE=THREE END=#EOF3 NOTABLE / NAME 1-20(A)
                AGE 25-26 SEX 29(A).
ELSE.
+     END FILE.
END IF.
END INPUT PROGRAM.

REPORT FORMAT AUTOMATIC LIST /VARS=NAME AGE SEX.
```

- The DO IF—ELSE IF—ELSE—END IF structure is specified within an INPUT PROGRAM.

- Scratch variables are used on each END subcommand so the value will not be reinitialized to the system-missing value after each case is built.

- Three data files are read, two of which contain data in the same format. The third requires a slightly different format for the data items. All three DATA LIST commands are placed within the DO IF structure.

• END FILE is placed after the ELSE command to trigger end-of-file processing once all data records have been read.

• This application can also be handled by creating three separate system files and using ADD FILES to put them together. The advantage of using the END subcommand on DATA LIST is that additional files are not required to store the separate system files prior to performing the ADD FILES. In addition, the files remain raw data files: they are not converted to system files.

Nested DO IF Structures

To perform transformations involving logical tests on two variables, you can use nested DO IF—END IF structures.

• There must be an END IF command for every DO IF command in the structure.

Example

```
DO IF (RACE EQ 5).                  /*DO WHITES
+  DO IF (SEX EQ 2).                   /*WHITE FEMALE
+  COMPUTE SEXRACE=3.                  /*WHITE FEMALE
+  ELSE.                               /*WHITE MALE
+  COMPUTE SEXRACE=1.                  /*WHITE MALE
+  END IF.                             /*WHITES DONE
ELSE IF (SEX EQ 2).                 /*NONWHITE FEMALE
COMPUTE SEXRACE=4.                  /*NONWHITE FEMALE
ELSE.                               /*NONWHITE MALE
COMPUTE SEXRACE=2.                  /*NONWHITE MALE
END IF.                             /*NONWHITES DONE
```

• This structure creates variable SEXRACE, which indicates both the sex and minority status of an individual.

• An optional plus sign, minus sign, or period in column one allows you to indent commands to emphasize the nested nature of the structures.

Complex File Structures

Some complex file structures may require you to imbed more than one DATA LIST command inside a DO IF structure. For example, consider a data file that has been collected from various sources. The information from each source is basically the same, but it is in different places on the records:

```
111295100FORD        CHAPMAN AUTO SALES
121199005VW       MIDWEST VOLKSWAGEN SALES
11 395025FORD        BETTER USED CARS
11       CHEVY 195005        HUFFMAN SALES & SERVICE
11       VW    595020        MIDWEST VOLKSWAGEN SALES
11       CHEVY 295015        SAM'S AUTO REPAIR
12       CHEVY 210 20        LONGFELLOW CHEVROLET
 9555032 VW                  HYDE PARK IMPORTS
```

In the above file, an automobile part number always appears in columns 1 and 2, and the automobile manufacturer always appears in columns 10 through 14. Otherwise, the location of other information such as the price and quantity depends on both the part number and the type of automobile. The DO IF structure in the following example reads records for part type 11.

Example

```
TITLE  'READING DATA FOR PART TYPE 11'.

INPUT PROGRAM.
DATA LIST FILE=CARPARTS/PARTNO 1-2 KIND 10-14 (A).

DO IF (PARTNO EQ 11 AND KIND EQ 'FORD').
+ REREAD.
+ DATA LIST /PRICE 3-6 (2) QUANTITY 7-9 BUYER 20-43 (A).
+ END CASE.
ELSE IF (PARTNO EQ 11 AND (KIND EQ 'CHEVY' OR KIND EQ 'VW')).
+ REREAD.
+ DATA LIST /PRICE 15-18 (2) QUANTITY 19-21 BUYER 30-53 (A).
+ END CASE.
END IF.
END INPUT PROGRAM.

PRINT FORMATS PRICE (DOLLAR6.2).
PRINT /PARTNO TO BUYER.
WEIGHT BY QUANTITY.
DESCRIPTIVES PRICE.
```

- The first DATA LIST extracts the part number and the type of automobile.
- Depending on the information from the first DATA LIST, the records are reread using one or another format, pulling the price, quantity, and buyer from different places.
- The two END CASE commands limit the active file to only those cases with Part 11 and automobile type Ford, Chevrolet, or Volkswagen. With no END CASE commands, cases would be created in the active file for other part numbers and automobile types with missing values for price, quantity, and buyer.
- The results of the PRINT command are shown in Figure 1.

Figure 1 Printed information for part 11

```
11 FORD   $12.95 100 CHAPMAN AUTO SALES
11 FORD    $3.95  25 BETTER USED CARS
11 CHEVY   $1.95   5 HUFFMAN SALES & SERVICE
11 VW      $5.95  20 MIDWEST VOLKSWAGEN SALES
11 CHEVY   $2.95  15 SAM'S AUTO REPAIR
```

DO REPEAT— END REPEAT

```
DO REPEAT stand-in var={token     } [/stand-in var=...]
                       {value list}

transformation commands

END REPEAT [PRINT]
```

Example:

```
DO REPEAT R=REGION1 TO REGION5.
COMPUTE R=0.
END REPEAT.
```

Overview

The DO REPEAT—END REPEAT structure replicates the same transformation(s) on a specified set of variables, reducing the number of commands you must enter to accomplish the task. This utility does not reduce the number of commands SPSS executes, just the number of commands you enter.

DO REPEAT works by using a *stand-in variable* to represent a *replacement list* of numeric variables, string variables, numeric constants, or strings. The stand-in variable is specified as a place holder on one or more transformation commands within the structure. When the transformation command(s) are replicated, the stand-in variable is replaced, in turn, by each variable or value specified on the replacement list.

If DO REPEAT is used to create new variables, the order in which they are created depends on how the command is specified. Thus, variables created by specifying the TO convention (for example, V1 TO V5) are not necessarily consecutive on the active system file (see PRINT Subcommand, below).

The following commands can be used within the DO REPEAT—END REPEAT structure:

- The DATA LIST command.
- Data transformations COMPUTE, RECODE, IF, COUNT, and SELECT IF.
- Data declarations VECTOR, STRING, NUMERIC, and LEAVE.
- Data definition MISSING VALUES (but not VARIABLE LABELS or VALUE LABELS).
- LOOP structure commands LOOP, END LOOP, and BREAK.
- DO IF structure commands DO IF, ELSE IF, ELSE, and END IF.
- Print and write commands PRINT, PRINT EJECT, PRINT SPACE, and WRITE.
- Format commands PRINT FORMATS, WRITE FORMATS, and FORMATS.

Basic Specification

- The basic specification is DO REPEAT, a stand-in variable followed by a required equals sign and a variable or value list (the replacement list), and at least one transformation command. The structure must end with the END REPEAT command. On the transformation command(s), a single stand-in variable represents every variable or value specified in its replacement list. SPSS replicates the commands between DO REPEAT and END REPEAT once for each variable or value in the replacement list. To display the expanded set of commands SPSS generates from those specified in the structure, specify PRINT on END REPEAT.

Syntax Rules

- Multiple stand-in variables can be specified on the DO REPEAT command. Each stand-in variable must be separated by a slash and must have its own equals sign and associated variable or value list. All the lists must generate the same number of tokens.
- Stand-in variables can be assigned any valid variable names: permanent, temporary, scratch, system, and so forth. A stand-in variable does not exist outside the DO REPEAT—END REPEAT structure and has no effect on variables with the same name that exist outside the structure. However, two stand-in variables cannot have the same name within the same DO REPEAT structure.

- A replacement *variable* list can be a list of new or existing variable names and can be string or numeric. Keyword TO can be used to name consecutive existing variables and to create a set of new variables. If the new variables are string, they must be declared on a STRING command that either precedes DO REPEAT or is included with the commands within the DO REPEAT structure. All replacement variable and value lists must have the same number of items.

- A replacement *value* list can be a list of strings or numeric values, or it can be of the form n_1 TO n_2, where n_1 is less than n_2 and both are integers. (Note that the keyword is TO, not THRU.)

Operations

- DO REPEAT marks the beginning of the control structure and END REPEAT marks the end. Once control passes out of the structure, all stand-in variables defined within the structure cease to exist.

- Numeric variables created within the structure are initially set to the system-missing value. By default, they are assigned an F8.2 format.

- New string variables declared within the structure are initially set to a blank value and are assigned the format specified on the STRING command that creates them.

- The order in which commands are generated is influenced by the manner in which replacement lists are defined. (See the examples shown for the PRINT subcommand below.)

Example

```
DO REPEAT R=REGION1 TO REGION5.
COMPUTE R=0.
END REPEAT.
```

- DO REPEAT defines the stand-in variable R, which represents the variable list REGION1 to REGION5.

- Five variables are initialized to 0 by a single COMPUTE specification that is repeated for each variable in the replacement list. Thus, SPSS generates five COMPUTE commands from the one specified (see the examples shown for the PRINT subcommand, below).

- Stand-in variable R ceases to exist once control passes out of the DO REPEAT structure.

Example

```
COMMENT This example shows a typical application of
        INPUT PROGRAM, LOOP, and DO REPEAT for generating data.
        The data here are random numbers.


TITLE      'CREATE DATA WITHOUT ANY DATA INPUT'.
SUBTITLE   'RANDOM NUMBERS'.

INPUT PROGRAM.
+   LOOP #I = 1 TO 1000.
+      DO REPEAT RESPONSE = R1 TO R400.
+         COMPUTE RESPONSE = UNIFORM(1) > 0.5.
+      END REPEAT.
+      COMPUTE AVG = MEAN(R1 TO R400).
+      END CASE.
+   END LOOP.
+   END FILE.
END INPUT PROGRAM.

FREQUENCIES VARIABLE=AVG
  /FORMAT=CONDENSE
  /HISTOGRAM
  /STATISTICS=MEAN MEDIAN MODE STDDEV MIN MAX.
```

- The INPUT PROGRAM—END INPUT PROGRAM structure defines the bounds of an input program that builds cases from transformation commands.

- The LOOP—END LOOP structure specifies that the commands within the loop be executed 1000 times.
- The DO REPEAT—END REPEAT structure generates 400 variables, each with a 50 percent chance of being 0, and a 50 percent chance of being 1. This is accomplished by specifying a logical expression on COMPUTE that compares the values returned by UNIFORM to the value 0.5. Logical expressions are evaluated as false (0), true (1), or missing. Thus, each random number returned by UNIFORM that is 0.5 or less is evaluated as false and assigned the value 0, and each random number returned by UNIFORM that is greater than 0.5 is evaluated as true and assigned the value 1.
- END CASE builds a case with the variables created within each loop. Thus, the loop structure creates 1000 cases, each with 400 variables.
- The second COMPUTE creates variable AVG which, for each case, is the mean of V1 TO V400.
- END FILE signals the end of the data file generated by the input program.
- FREQUENCIES produces a condensed frequency table, histogram, and statistics for AVG. The histogram for AVG shows a normal distribution.

PRINT Subcommand

PRINT causes SPSS to display the commands it generates from the DO REPEAT—END REPEAT structure. PRINT can be used to verify the order in which commands are executed.

Example

```
DO REPEAT Q=Q1 TO Q5/ R=R1 TO R5.
COMPUTE Q=0.
COMPUTE R=1.
END REPEAT PRINT.
```

- The DO REPEAT—END REPEAT structure initializes one set of variables to 0 and another set to 1.
- Output from the PRINT subcommand is shown in Figure 1. Notice that the COMPUTE commands are generated in such a way that variables are created in alternating order: Q1, R1, Q2, R2, and so forth. If you plan to use the TO convention to refer to Q1 TO Q5 later, you should use two separate DO REPEAT utilities; otherwise, Q1 TO Q5 will include four of the five R variables. Alternatively, use the NUMERIC command to predetermine the order in which variables are added to the active file, or specify the replacement lists as they are shown in the next example.

Figure 1 Display from the PRINT subcommand

```
  2  0          DO REPEAT Q=Q1 TO Q5/ R=R1 TO R5
  3  0          COMPUTE Q=0
  4  0          COMPUTE R=1
  5  0          END REPEAT PRINT

  6  0          +COMPUTE Q1=0
  7  0          +COMPUTE R1=1
  8  0          +COMPUTE Q2=0
  9  0          +COMPUTE R2=1
 10  0          +COMPUTE Q3=0
 11  0          +COMPUTE R3=1
 12  0          +COMPUTE Q4=0
 13  0          +COMPUTE R4=1
 14  0          +COMPUTE Q5=0
 15  0          +COMPUTE R5=1
```

Example

```
DO REPEAT Q=Q1 TO Q5,R1 TO R5/ N=0,0,0,0,0,1,1,1,1,1.
COMPUTE Q=N.
END REPEAT PRINT.
```

- A series of constants are specified as a stand-in value list for N. All the Q variables are initialized first, then all the R variables, as shown in Figure 2. Compare this example to the example above.

Figure 2 Display from the PRINT subcommand

```
  2   0              DO REPEAT Q=Q1 TO Q5,R1 TO R5/ N=0,0,0,0,0,1,1,1,1,1
  3   0              COMPUTE Q=N
  4   0              END REPEAT PRINT

  5   0              +COMPUTE Q1=0
  6   0              +COMPUTE Q2=0
  7   0              +COMPUTE Q3=0
  8   0              +COMPUTE Q4=0
  9   0              +COMPUTE Q5=0
 10   0              +COMPUTE R1=1
 11   0              +COMPUTE R2=1
 12   0              +COMPUTE R3=1
 13   0              +COMPUTE R4=1
 14   0              +COMPUTE R5=1
```

Example
```
DO REPEAT R=REGION1 TO REGION5/ X=1 TO 5.
COMPUTE R=REGION EQ X.
END REPEAT PRINT.
```

• Stand-in variable R represents the variable list REGION1 to REGION5. Stand-in variable X represents the value list 1 to 5.

• The DO REPEAT—END REPEAT structure creates dummy variables REGION1 to REGION5 that measure 1 or 0 for each of 5 regions.

• PRINT on END REPEAT causes SPSS to display the commands generated by the structure, as shown in Figure 3. The plus signs mark the generated commands.

Figure 3 Commands generated by DO REPEAT

```
  2   0   DO REPEAT R=REGION1 TO REGION5/ X=1 TO 5
  3   0   COMPUTE R=REGION EQ X
  4   0   END REPEAT PRINT

  5   0   +COMPUTE REGION1=REGION EQ 1
  6   0   +COMPUTE REGION2=REGION EQ 2
  7   0   +COMPUTE REGION3=REGION EQ 3
  8   0   +COMPUTE REGION4=REGION EQ 4
  9   0   +COMPUTE REGION5=REGION EQ 5
```

DROP DOCUMENTS DROP DOCUMENTS

Overview
DROP DOCUMENTS drops all documentation from the active system file. New documents can be added to the active file with the DOCUMENT command.

When GET retrieves an SPSS system file, or when ADD FILES, MATCH FILES, or UPDATE are used to combine system files, all documents from each specified file are copied into the active file. DROP DOCUMENTS may be used to drop those documents from the active file. Whether or not DROP DOCUMENTS is used, new documents can be added to the active file with the DOCUMENT command.

Basic Specification
• The only specification is the command keywords. DROP DOCUMENTS has no additional specifications.

Operations
• Documention is dropped only from the active file only. The original system file is unchanged.

• If a DROP DOCUMENTS command *follows* a DOCUMENT command anywhere in the command sequence, the documentation specified on the DOCUMENT command is dropped from the active file along with all other documentation.

Example
```
GET FILE=GENSOC /KEEP=AGE SEX EDUC MARITAL CHILDRN MED_INS.

DROP DOCUMENTS.

FILE LABEL   GENERAL SOCIAL SURVEY SUBSET.
DOCUMENT     THIS FILE CONTAINS A SUBSET OF VARIABLES FROM THE
 GENERAL SOCIAL SURVEY DATA.  FOR EACH CASE IT RECORDS ONLY THE
 AGE, SEX. EDUCATION LEVEL, MARITAL STATUS, NUMBER OF CHILDREN,
 AND TYPE OF MEDICAL INSURANCE COVERAGE.
SAVE OUTFILE=SUBSOC.
```

• DROP DOCUMENTS drops the documentation text from file GENSOC. Only the new documentation text is saved on file SUBSOC.

• The original system file GENSOC is unchanged.

EDIT

```
EDIT
```

Example:

```
EDIT.
GET FILE=QUERY.
RECODE ITEM1, ITEM2, ITEM3 (0=1) (1=0) (2=-1).
COMPUTE INDEXQ=(ITEM1 + ITEM2 + ITEM3)/3.
VARIABLE LABELS INDEXQ 'Summary Index of Questions'.
FREQUENCIES=ITEM1 ITEM2 ITEM3.
```

Overview

EDIT causes SPSS to evaluate a sequence of commands without reading the data file. EDIT is available only for executing command files through your operating system. EDIT is not available for commands run during an SPSS session.

Syntax Rules

The minimum specification is simply the command keyword. EDIT has no additional specifications.

Operations

- EDIT checks for syntax errors, and it checks variable names against the DATA LIST and other commands that create variables to ensure that the variables have been defined.

- EDIT will not know whether a DATA LIST command correctly defines the data; EDIT can only determine whether the syntax is correct.

- If data are inline, the BEGIN DATA and END DATA commands must be in their appropriate positions within the sequence of commands.

- EDIT does not check data records.

- EDIT can be positioned anywhere within the sequence of commands and checks all the commands that follow it.

- Some SPSS procedures create variables such as standard scores and residuals and add them to the active system file. The EDIT facility cannot know about these variables and issues error messages when it encounters them in subsequent commands.

- Since EDIT checks variable names, a system file must be available so SPSS can read the dictionary. Alternatively, the data definitions may be replicated for the EDIT session by DATA LIST, NUMERIC, or STRING commands within INPUT PROGRAM and END INPUT PROGRAM. The DATA LIST need not correspond exactly with the data, but it must name all the variables to be used in the remainder of the session in the same order and with the same format as the variables in the system file.

- EDIT *does not* detect every possible error. For example, it will not recognize that a computation is impossible.

- EDIT *does* report on a string variable used where a numeric variable is required and vice versa.

Example

```
EDIT.
DATA LIST   FILE=HUBDATA RECORDS=3
    /1 EMPLOYID 1-5 MOHIRED YRHIRED 12-15 DEPT79 TO DEPT82 SEX 16-20
    /2 SALARY79 TO SALARY82 6-25 HOURLY81 HOURLY82 40-53(2)
       PROMO81 72 AGE 54-55 RAISE82 66-70
    /3 JOBCAT 6 NAME 25-48 (A).
LIST VARIABLES=MOHIRED YRHIRED DEPT82
    SALARY79 TO SALARY82 NAME /FORMAT=NUMBERED.
```

- EDIT ensures that syntax on DATA LIST and LIST is correct, and that all variables specified on LIST have been defined.

- The DATA LIST and LIST commands are not executed, and the data are not read.

Example

```
EDIT.
GET FILE=HUBDATA.
COMPUTE  CASESEQ2=CASESEQ+1.
LEAVE CASESEQ2.
PRINT FORMATS CASESEQ2 (F3).

SELECT IF DEPT82 EQ 4.
LIST VARIABLES=CASESEQ2 MOHIRED YRHIRED DEPT82
     SALARY79 TO SALARY82 NAME /FORMAT=NUMBERED.
```

• All commands following EDIT are checked for syntax errors and for the proper use of existing variables.

• SPSS reads the dictionary of the system file HUBDATA, specified on the FILE subcommand of GET, to check variables used throughout the session.

• Because the COMPUTE command does not execute, CASESEQ2 is not created. However, EDIT is able to recognize CASESEQ2 when it is specified on the LIST command because CASESEQ2 is defined on the COMPUTE command.

• The commands in the session are not executed, and the data are not read.

END CASE

Example:

```
END CASE

TITLE     'RESTRUCTURING A DATA FILE'.
SUBTITLE  'MAKE EACH DATA ITEM INTO A SINGLE CASE'.

INPUT PROGRAM.
DATA LIST /#X1 TO #X3 (3(F1,1X)).

VECTOR V=#X1 TO #X3.

LOOP #I=1 TO 3.
- COMPUTE X=V(#I).
- END CASE.
END LOOP.
END INPUT PROGRAM.

BEGIN DATA
2 1 1
3 5 1
END DATA.
FORMAT X(F1.0).
PRINT / X.
EXECUTE.
```

Overview

END CASE, available only within an INPUT PROGRAM structure, builds cases from the commands that precede it in the program. When it receives control for a case, END CASE signals that the case is complete and immediately passes control for the case out of the input program.

END CASE is especially useful for restructuring files. For example, END CASE can be used with the VECTOR command to build a single case from several records or, conversely, to build several cases from a single record. END CASE can be used with DO REPEAT and END FILE to create data without any data input.

Basic Specification

• The basic specification is simply the command keywords. END CASE has no additional specifications. SPSS abandons default end-of-case processing and defines the end of a case according to the conditions specified for END CASE in the INPUT PROGRAM structure.

Syntax Rules

• END CASE is only available within an INPUT PROGRAM structure and is generally specified within a LOOP structure.

• Multiple END CASE commands may be used within the input program. Each applies only to the transformation or data definition commands executed since the last END CASE command.

Operations

• When END CASE is specified within an INPUT PROGRAM structure, the INPUT PROGRAM acts like an infinite loop; control passes to the commands after END INPUT PROGRAM each time END CASE is executed, and initialization occurs before resumption of the INPUT PROGRAM. If END CASE is not specified within an INPUT PROGRAM structure, an implicit END CASE is assumed, immediately preceding END INPUT PROGRAM; in this instance, the INPUT PROGRAM is still an infinite loop, though that fact is not so obvious as when END CASE is explicitly specified.

• When END CASE builds a case, it immediately passes that case out of the input program. Transformation commands that *follow* END CASE within the input program are therefore executed when a case is being initialized, not when it is complete. This has serious implications for commands that act upon the data, such as COMPUTE. For more information, see END CASE and Other Commands, below.

• Whenever END CASE is used, consider whether the LEAVE command is required. In some instances, scratch variables can be used as an alternative to using LEAVE.

Example

```
TITLE      'RESTRUCTURING A DATA FILE'.
SUBTITLE   'MAKE EACH DATA ITEM INTO A SINGLE CASE'.

INPUT PROGRAM.
DATA LIST /#X1 TO #X3 (3(F1,1X)).

VECTOR V=#X1 TO #X3.

LOOP #I=1 TO 3.
- COMPUTE X=V(#I).
- END CASE.
END LOOP.
END INPUT PROGRAM.

BEGIN DATA
2 1 1
3 5 1
END DATA.
FORMAT X(F1.0).
PRINT / X.
EXECUTE.
```

• INPUT PROGRAM and END INPUT PROGRAM begin and end the block of commands that build cases from the input file. They are required because the END CASE command is used to create multiple cases from single input records.

• DATA LIST defines three variables for the data. In the format specification, the first 3 is a repetition factor that repeats the format that follows it in parentheses 3 times: once for each variable. The specified format is F1, and the element 1X skips 1 column.

• VECTOR creates vector V with the original scratch variables as its three elements. The indexing expression on the LOOP command increments variable #I three times to control the number of iterations per input case and to provide the index for vector V.

• COMPUTE sets X equal to each of the scratch variables. END CASE tells SPSS to build a case. Thus, the first loop for the first case sets X equal to the first element of vector V. Since V(1) references #X1, and #X1 is 2, the value of X is 2. END CASE then builds the case. The END LOOP returns control to the LOOP command since the indexing is not complete. SPSS then sets X to #X2, which is 1, and builds the second case. The third iteration sets X equal to #X3, which is also 1, builds the third case, and terminates the loop. At this point, control is returned to the DATA LIST for the next input case. The six new cases are therefore

```
2
1
1
3
5
1
```

Example
```
TITLE     'RESTRUCTURING A DATA FILE'.
SUBTITLE  'CREATE A SEPARATE CASE FOR EACH BOOK ORDER'.

INPUT PROGRAM.
DATA LIST   /ORDER 1-4 #X1 TO #X22 (1X,11(F3.0,F2.0,1X)).

LEAVE ORDER.
VECTOR BOOKS=#X1 TO #X22.

LOOP #I=1 TO 21 BY 2  IF NOT SYSMIS(BOOKS(#I)).
- COMPUTE ISBN=BOOKS(#I).
- COMPUTE QUANTITY=BOOKS(#I+1).
- END CASE.
END LOOP.
END INPUT PROGRAM.
BEGIN DATA
1045 182 2 155 1 134 1 153 5
1046 155 3 153 5 163 1
1047 161 5 182 2 163 4 186 6
1048 186 2
1049 155 2 163 2 153 2 074 1 161 1
END DATA.

SORT CASES ISBN.
DO IF $CASENUM EQ 1.
- PRINT EJECT /'Order ISBN Quantity'.
- PRINT SPACE.
END IF.

FORMATS ISBN (F3)/ QUANTITY (F2).
PRINT /' ' ORDER ' ' ISBN '  ' QUANTITY.

EXECUTE.
```

- Data are extracted from a file whose records store values for an invoice number, a series of book codes, and quantities of books ordered. Invoice 1045 is for nine books of four different titles: two copies of book 182, one copy each of 155 and 134, and five copies of book 153. The task is to break each individual book order into a record, preserving the order number on each new case.

- INPUT PROGRAM and END INPUT PROGRAM begin and end the block of commands that build cases from the input file. They are required because the END CASE command is used to create multiple cases from single input records.

- DATA LIST specifies ORDER as a permanent variable and defines 22 scratch variables to hold as many alternating book numbers and quantities as will fit within 72 columns. In the format specification, the first element skips 1 space after the value for variable ORDER. The 11 is a repetition factor that repeats the parenthesized format that follows it 11 times: once for each book number and quantity pair. The specified format is F3.0 for book numbers, F2.0 for the quantities, and the element 1X skips 1 column after each quantity value.

- LEAVE preserves the value of variable ORDER across the new cases to be generated.

- VECTOR sets up vector BOOKS with the original scratch variables as its elements. The first element is #X1, the second is #X2, and so forth.

- If the element for vector BOOKS is not system-missing, LOOP initiates the LOOP structure that moves through vector BOOKS picking off the book numbers and quantities. The indexing clause initiates the indexing variable #I at 1, to be increased by 2 to a maximum of 22.

- The first COMPUTE command sets variable ISBN equal to the element in vector BOOKS indexed by #I, which is the current book number. The second COMPUTE sets variable QUANTITY equal to the next element in vector BOOKS, which is the quantity associated with the book number now stored in variable ISBN.

- END CASE tells SPSS to write out a case with the current values of the three variables: ORDER, ISBN, and QUANTITY.

- END LOOP terminates the loop structure and control is returned to the LOOP command, where #I is increased by 2 and looping continues (until #I exceeds 21).

- SORT CASES sorts the new cases by book number in preparation for displaying.
- The DO IF structure encloses a PRINT EJECT command and a PRINT SPACE command to set up titles for the displayed output.
- PRINT FORMATS establishes dictionary print formats for new variables ISBN and QUANTITY. See the output from the PRINT command.
- EXECUTE is shown here as the procedure that processes the cases for displaying; any procedure will do.

Figure 1 PRINT output showing new cases

```
Order ISBN Quantity

1049   74    1
1045  134    1
1045  153    5
1046  153    5
1049  153    2
1045  155    1
1046  155    3
1049  155    2
1047  161    5
1049  161    1
1046  163    1
1047  163    4
1049  163    2
1045  182    2
1047  182    2
1047  186    6
1048  186    2
```

Example

```
TITLE      'CREATE DATA WITHOUT ANY DATA INPUT'.
SUBTITLE   'RANDOM NUMBERS'.

INPUT PROGRAM.
+  LOOP #I = 1 TO 1000.
+     DO REPEAT RESPONSE = R1 TO R400.
+        COMPUTE RESPONSE = UNIFORM(1) > 0.5.
+     END REPEAT.
+     COMPUTE AVG = MEAN(R1 TO R400).
+     END CASE.
+  END LOOP.
+  END FILE.
END INPUT PROGRAM.

FREQUENCIES VARIABLE=AVG
  /FORMAT=CONDENSE
  /HISTOGRAM
  /STATISTICS=MEAN MEDIAN MODE STDDEV MIN MAX.
```

- The INPUT PROGRAM—END INPUT PROGRAM structure defines the bounds of an input program that builds cases from transformation commands.

- The LOOP—END LOOP structure specifies that the commands within the loop be executed 1000 times.

- The DO REPEAT—END REPEAT structure generates 400 variables, each with a 50% chance of being 0, and a 50% chance of being 1. This is accomplished by specifying a logical expression on COMPUTE that compares the values returned by UNIFORM to the value 0.5. Logical expressions are evaluated as false (0), true (1), or missing. Thus, each random number returned by UNIFORM that is 0.5 or less is evaluated as false and assigned the value 0, and each random number returned by UNIFORM that is greater than 0.5 is evaluated as true and assigned the value 1.

- The second COMPUTE creates variable AVG which, for each case, is the mean of V1 TO V400.

- END CASE builds a case with the variables created within each loop and immediately passes the case out of the input program. Thus, END CASE builds 1000 cases, each with 400 variables.

- END FILE signals the end of the data file generated by the input program.

- FREQUENCIES produces a condensed frequency table, histogram, and statistics for AVG. The histogram for AVG shows a normal distribution.

Example
```
TITLE  'CREATE VAR WHICH APPROXIMATES A LOG-NORMAL DISTRIBUTION'.

SET FORMAT=F8.0.

INPUT PROGRAM.
LOOP I=1 TO 1000.
+ COMPUTE SCORE=EXP(NORMAL(1)).
+ END CASE.
END LOOP.
END FILE.
END INPUT PROGRAM.

FREQUENCIES VARIABLES=SCORE /FORMAT=NOTABLE /HISTOGRAM
   /PERCENTILES=1 10 20 30 40 50 60 70 80 90 99
   /STATISTICS=ALL.
```

- The input program creates 1000 cases with a single variable SCORE. Values for SCORE approximate a log-normal distribution.

Example
```
TITLE  'READ A COMPLEX FILE STRUCTURE'.

INPUT PROGRAM.
DATA LIST  /#RECS 1 HEAD1 HEAD2 3-4(A).   /*READ HEADER INFO
LEAVE  HEAD1 HEAD2.

LOOP  #I=1 TO #RECS.
DATA LIST  /INDIV 1-2(1).                  /*READ INDIVIDUAL INFO
PRINT  /#RECS HEAD1 HEAD2 INDIV.
END CASE.                                  /*CREATE COMBINED CASE
END LOOP.
END INPUT PROGRAM.
BEGIN DATA
1 AC
91
2 CC
35
43
0 XX
1 BA
34
3 BB
42
96
37
END DATA.
EXECUTE.
```

- DATA are from a file with header records that indicate how many individual records follow. The 1 in the first column of the first header record (AC), says that only one individual record (91) follows. The 2 in the first column of the second header record (CC) says that two individual records (35 and 43) follow. The next header record has no individual records, indicated by the 0 in column 1, and so on.

- The first DATA LIST reads the expected number of individual records for each header record into temporary variable #RECS. #RECS is then used as the terminal value in the LOOP command to read the correct number of individual records using the second DATA LIST.

- Variables HEAD1 and HEAD2 are the information in columns 3 and 4, respectively, in the header records. The LEAVE command retains HEAD1 and HEAD2 so that this information can be spread to the individual records.

- Variable INDIV is the information from the individual record. INDIV is then combined with #RECS, HEAD1, and HEAD2 to create the new case. Notice in the output from the PRINT command in Figure 2, below, that no case is created for the header record with 0 as #RECS.

- END CASE passes each case out of the input program to the LIST command. Without END CASE, the PRINT command would still display cases as shown in Figure 2 because it is inside the loop. However, only one case per header record would pass out of the input program.

Figure 2 Displayed information for individual records

```
1 A C 9.1
2 C C 3.5
2 C C 4.3
1 B A 3.4
3 B B 4.2
3 B B 9.6
3 B B 3.7
```

END CASE and Other Commands

The END CASE command tells SPSS that it has built a case and to pass it immediately to the procedure. When you use END CASE in an input program, SPSS abandons its default end-of-case processing and gives you total control. In the absence of instructions to the contrary, transformations such as COMPUTE, definitions such as VARIABLE LABELS, and utilities such as PRINT that follow an END CASE inside an input program are executed while a case is being initialized, not when it is complete. For definition commands like VARIABLE LABELS, MISSING VALUES, and PRINT FORMATS, this has no effect since these are merely written into the dictionary. However, for commands that act on the data itself, such as COMPUTE and PRINT, it makes a big difference.

A PRINT command that follows an END CASE command and precedes the END INPUT PROGRAM command displays the cases at initialization using system-missing values for permanent numeric variables, and blanks for permanent string variables. Since the displayed information does not act on the data, it does not affect the outcome of the variable once the data are read. However, a COMPUTE that is executed at initialization does affect the outcome.

Example

```
*   THE COMPUTE AND PRINT COMMANDS THAT FOLLOW END CASE
    IN THIS EXAMPLE ARE MISPLACED.  THEY SHOULD BE SPECIFIED
    AFTER THE END INPUT PROGRAM COMMAND.

INPUT PROGRAM.
DATA LIST  FILE=TESTDATA /#X1 TO #X3 (3(F1,1X)).

VECTOR V=#X1 TO #X3.

LOOP #I=1 TO 3.
COMPUTE X=V(#I).
END CASE.
END LOOP.

COMPUTE Y=X**2.   /* SHOULD COME AFTER INPUT PROGRAM
VARIABLE LABELS X 'TEST VARIABLE' Y 'SQUARE OF X'.
PRINT FORMATS X Y (F2).
PRINT /X Y.       /* SHOULD COME AFTER INPUT PROGRAM
END INPUT PROGRAM.

FREQUENCIES VARIABLES=X Y.
```

- No error or warning is issued in this session, but SPSS displays only two lines with two periods each. These periods are the initialized system-missing values of X and Y for the two original cases.

- After the data are read and the six cases are created, the VARIABLE LABELS and PRINT FORMATS commands have their desired effects, as shown in the FREQUENCIES table in Figure 3. However, because Y is computed from the initialized value of X, it is always system-missing.

- One solution is to specify PRINT and COMPUTE before the END CASE command. The preferred solution is to specify these commands in the transformation program after the END INPUT PROGRAM command, since they operate on the cases created by the input program.

Figure 3 FREQUENCIES output

```
X         TEST VARIABLE

                                                    VALID     CUM
    VALUE LABEL              VALUE  FREQUENCY  PERCENT  PERCENT   PERCENT
                               1        3       50.0     50.0      50.0
                               2        1       16.7     16.7      66.7
                               3        1       16.7     16.7      83.3
                               5        1       16.7     16.7     100.0
                                     _____   _____   _____
                             TOTAL      6      100.0    100.0

VALID CASES     6    MISSING CASES    0
- - - - - - - - - - - - - - - - - - - - - - - - - - - - - - - - - - - - -

Y         SQUARE OF X

                                                    VALID     CUM
    VALUE LABEL              VALUE  FREQUENCY  PERCENT  PERCENT   PERCENT
                               .        6      100.0    MISSING
                                     _____   _____   _____
                             TOTAL      6      100.0    100.0
```

END FILE

END FILE

Example:

```
INPUT PROGRAM.
DATA LIST FILE=PRICES /YEAR 1-4 QUARTER 6 PRICE 8-12(2).
DO IF (YEAR GE 1881). /*STOP READING BEFORE 1881
END FILE.
END IF.
END INPUT PROGRAM.
```

Overview

END FILE, available only within an INPUT PROGRAM structure, tells SPSS to stop reading data before it actually encounters the end of the file. END FILE can also be used with END CASE to concatenate raw data files by causing SPSS to delay end-of-file processing until it has read multiple data files. And END FILE can be used with LOOP and END CASE to generate data without any data input.

Basic Specification

• The basic specification is simply the command keywords. END FILE has no additional specifications. The end of file is defined according to the conditions specified for END FILE in the INPUT PROGRAM structure.

Syntax Rules

• END FILE is only available within an INPUT PROGRAM structure.

• Only one END FILE command can be executed per input program. However, multiple END FILE commands can appear if they are placed within a conditional structure that calls for an end of file whenever any one of a number of possible conditions is met.

Operations

• END FILE excludes the case that causes the end of the file. To include this case, use the END CASE command (see the first two examples below).

Example

```
TITLE  'SELECT CASES'.

INPUT PROGRAM.
DATA LIST FILE=PRICES /YEAR 1-4 QUARTER 6 PRICE 8-12(2).

DO IF (YEAR GE 1881). /*STOP READING BEFORE 1881

END FILE.
END IF.
END INPUT PROGRAM.

LIST.
```

• The input program is defined between the INPUT PROGRAM and END INPUT PROGRAM commands.

• This example assumes that data records are entered chronologically by year. The DO IF—END IF structure specifies an end of file when the first record with a YEAR of 1881 or later is reached.

• LIST executes the input program and lists cases from the active system file. The case for 1881 that caused the end of the file is not included in the active file generated by the input program. To include this case, see the next example.

• As an alternative to an INPUT PROGRAM with END FILE, if you know the exact number of cases you want SPSS to create, you can use N OF CASES to select them. Another alternative is to use SELECT IF to select cases before 1881, but then SPSS would unnecessarily read the rest of the file.

Example
```
TITLE     'SELECT CASES'.
SUBTITLE 'RETAIN THE CASE THAT CAUSES END-OF-FILE'.

INPUT PROGRAM.
DATA LIST FILE=PRICES /YEAR 1-4 QUARTER 6 PRICE 8-12(2).

DO IF (YEAR GE 1881). /*STOP READING BEFORE 1881 (OR AT END OF FILE)
END CASE.             /*CREATE CASE 1881
END FILE.

ELSE.
END CASE.             /*CREATE ALL OTHER CASES
END IF.
END INPUT PROGRAM.

LIST.
```

- The first END CASE forces SPSS to retain the case END FILE uses to determine end-of-file processing. Normally END FILE excludes this case (see the example above).

- The second END CASE command is required because SPSS abandons default end-of-case processing whenever it encounters the END CASE command. The first END CASE specifies only that the final case be passed out of the input program. The second END CASE specifies that all other cases be passed out of the input program as well.

Example
```
TITLE     'CREATE DATA WITHOUT ANY DATA INPUT'.
SUBTITLE  'RANDOM NUMBERS'.

INPUT PROGRAM.
+  LOOP #I = 1 TO 1000.
+      DO REPEAT RESPONSE = R1 TO R400.
+          COMPUTE RESPONSE = UNIFORM(1) > 0.5.
+      END REPEAT.
+      COMPUTE AVG = MEAN(R1 TO R400).
+      END CASE.
+  END LOOP.
+  END FILE.
END INPUT PROGRAM.

FREQUENCIES VARIABLE=AVG
  /FORMAT=CONDENSE
  /HISTOGRAM
  /STATISTICS=MEAN MEDIAN MODE STDDEV MIN MAX.
```

- The INPUT PROGRAM—END INPUT PROGRAM structure defines the bounds of an input program that builds cases from transformation commands.

- The LOOP—END LOOP structure specifies that the commands within the loop be executed 1000 times.

- The DO REPEAT—END REPEAT structure generates 400 variables, each with a 50% chance of being 0, and a 50% chance of being 1. This is accomplished by specifying a logical expression on COMPUTE that compares the values returned by UNIFORM to the value 0.5. Logical expressions are evaluated as false (0), true (1), or missing. Thus, each random number returned by UNIFORM that is 0.5 or less is evaluated as false and assigned the value 0, and each random number returned by UNIFORM that is greater than 0.5 is evaluated as true and assigned the value 1.

- The second COMPUTE creates variable AVG which, for each case, is the mean of R1 TO R400.

- END CASE builds a case with the variables created within each loop and immediately passes the case out of the input program. Thus, END CASE builds 1000 cases, each with 400 variables.

- END FILE defines the created cases as a data file. Without END FILE, SPSS would create cases but not define them as a data file; the FREQUENCIES procedure would therefore generate an error. A procedure cannot run before a file is defined.

- FREQUENCIES produces a condensed frequency table, histogram, and statistics for AVG. The histogram for AVG shows a normal distribution.

Example
```
TITLE   'CONCATENATE THREE RAW DATA FILES'.

INPUT PROGRAM.
NUMERIC  #EOF1 TO #EOF3.   /*THESE WILL BE USED AS THE END= VARIA-
BLES.

DO IF    #EOF1 NE 1.
+    DATA LIST  FILE=ONE END=#EOF1 NOTABLE /1 NAME 1-20(A)
              AGE 21-22 SEX 24(A).
ELSE IF  #EOF2 NE 1.
+    DATA LIST  FILE=TWO  END=#EOF2 NOTABLE / NAME 1-20(A)
              AGE 21-22 SEX 24(A).
ELSE IF  #EOF3 NE 1.
+      DATA LIST  FILE=THREE END=#EOF3 NOTABLE / NAME 1-20(A)
                 AGE 25-26 SEX 29(A).
ELSE.
+      END FILE.
END IF.
END INPUT PROGRAM.

REPORT FORMAT AUTOMATIC LIST /VARS=NAME AGE SEX.
```

- The INPUT PROGRAM contains a DO IF—ELSE IF—END IF structure.

- Scratch variables are used on each END subcommand so the value will not be reinitialized to the system-missing value after each case is built.

- Three data files are read, two of which contain data in the same format. The third requires a slightly different format for the data items. All three DATA LIST commands are placed within the DO IF structure.

- END FILE is placed after the ELSE command to trigger end-of-file processing once all data records have been read.

- This application can also be handled by creating three separate SPSS system files and using ADD FILES to put them together. The advantage of using the END subcommand on DATA LIST is that additional files are not required to store the separate system files prior to performing the ADD FILES. In addition, the files remain raw data files: they are not converted to system files.

EXAMINE

```
EXAMINE VARIABLES=varlist [[BY varlist] [varname BY varname]]

    [/COMPARE={GROUP**  }]
             {VARIABLE}

    [/SCALE={PLOTWISE**}]
            {UNIFORM  }

    [/ID={$CASENUM**}]
         {varname   }

    [/FREQUENCIES [FROM(initialvalue)] [BY(increment)]]

    [/PERCENTILES[(({5,10,25,50,75,90,95})=[{HAVERAGE }] [NONE]]
                    {value list          }   {WAVERAGE }
                                             {ROUND    }
                                             {AEMPIRICAL}
                                             {EMPIRICAL }

    [/PLOT=[STEMLEAF**] [BOXPLOT**] [NPPLOT]]
           [SPREADLEVEL(value)] [HISTOGRAM]
           [{ALL }]
            {NONE}

    [/STATISTICS=[DESCRIPTIVES**] [EXTREME({5})]]
                                          {n}
                [{ALL }]
                 {NONE}

    [/MESTIMATOR=[{NONE**}]]
                  {ALL   }

                [HUBER({1.339})] [ANDREW({1.34 Pi}]
                       {c    }            {c       }

                [HAMPEL({1.7,3.4,8.5})]
                        {a  ,b  ,c   }

                [TUKEY({4.685})]
                       {c    }

    [/MISSING={LISTWISE**} [INCLUDE]]
             {REPORT   }
             {PAIRWISE }
```

**Default if the subcommand is omitted.

Example:

EXAMINE VARIABLES=MIPERGAL BY MODEL,MODEL BY CYLINDERS.

Overview   EXAMINE provides stem-and-leaf plots, boxplots, robust estimates of location, tests of normality and other descriptive statistics and plots. Separate analyses can be obtained for subgroups of cases.

Options   **Cells.** You can subdivide cases into cells based on their values for grouping (factor) variables. See VARIABLES Subcommand.

Output. You can control the display of output (see COMPARE Subcommand) and the scale of plots (see SCALE Subcommand). You can produce frequency tables and control their output format (see FREQUENCY Subcommand). You can specify the computational method and breaking points for percentiles (see PERCENTILES Subcommand) and assign a variable to be used for labeling outliers (see ID Subcommand).

Plots. You can request plots. Available are stem-and-leaf plots, histograms, vertical boxplots, spread-versus-level plots with the Levene test for homogeneity of variance, and normal and detrended probability plots with accompanying tests for normality. See PLOT Subcommand.

Statistics. You can request univariate statistical output (see STATISTICS Subcommand) and maximum-likelihood estimators (see MESTIMATORS Subcommand).

Basic Specification
- The basic specification is VARIABLES and at least one dependent variable.
- For each dependent variable named on VARIABLES, the default output includes univariate statistics (mean, median, standard deviation, standard error, variance, kurtosis, kurtosis standard error, skewness, skewness standard error, sum, interquartile range (IQR), range, minimum, maximum, and 5% trimmed mean), a vertical boxplot, and a stem-and-leaf plot.
- Outliers are labeled on the boxplot with the system variable $CASENUM.

Subcommand Order
- Subcommands can be named in any order.

Limitations
- String variables can be used as factors, but only the first eight characters are used to form cells. String variables are not allowed as dependent variables.

Caution
- Large amounts of output can be produced if many cells are specified. Many factors or factors with many values will result in a large number of separate analyses.

Example

`EXAMINE VARIABLES=ENGSIZE,COST.`

- ENGSIZE and COST are the dependent variables.
- EXAMINE produces univariate statistics, a vertical boxplot, and a stem-and-leaf plot for each dependent variable.

Example

`EXAMINE VARIABLES=MIPERGAL BY MODEL,MODEL BY CYLINDERS.`

- MIPERGAL is the dependent variable. The cell specification follows the first BY keyword. Cases will first be subdivided based on values of MODEL and then subdivided based on the combination of values for MODEL and CYLINDERS. The keyword BY between factors indicates that all possible combinations are to be considered.
- EXAMINE produces univariate statistics, a vertical boxplot, and a stem-and-leaf plot for MIPERGAL for each cell defined by MODEL.
- EXAMINE generates univariate statistics, a vertical boxplot, and a stem-and-leaf plot for MIPERGAL for each combination of values for MODEL and CYLINDERS.
- Assuming there are three values for MODEL and two values for CYLINDERS, this example produces separate output for all cases considered together, for the three cells defined by MODEL and the six cells defined by MODEL and CYLINDERS together.

VARIABLES Subcommand

VARIABLES specifies the dependent variables and the cells. A list of the dependent variables follows VARIABLES. The list of cells follows the first keyword BY.

- Cells formed by the combination of values of several factors are indicated with the keyword BY separating the factor names.
- Each value of a factor produces at least one separate page of output. If factors are combined with the keyword BY, each combination of values will also produce at least one page of output.

Example

`EXAMINE VARIABLES=SALARY,YRSEDUC BY RACE,SEX,DEPT,RACE BY SEX.`

- SALARY and YRSEDUC are dependent variables.
- The cells are formed first for the values of RACE, SEX, and DEPT individually and then by the combination of values for RACE and SEX.
- Univariate statistics, a boxplot, and a stem-and-leaf plot are generated for the sample as a whole and for each cell specified. That is, default output is produced for each separate value of RACE, SEX, and DEPT. In addition, default output is produced for each combination of values for RACE and SEX. If RACE and SEX each have two possible values and DEPT has three possible values, at least 20 pages of output (10 for SALARY and 10 for YRSEDUC) will be produced:

Variable	Pages
RACE	2
SEX	2
DEPT	3
RACE BY SEX	2
OVERALL	1
total	10

COMPARE Subcommand

COMPARE controls how boxplots are displayed. The default is GROUPS.

- COMPARE=VARIABLES and COMPARE=GROUPS are most useful if there is more than one dependent variable and if there is at least one factor in the design.

GROUPS *Boxplots for all cells in same display.* For each dependent variable, boxplots for all groups are displayed together. Comparisons across cells for a single dependent variable are easily made. This is the default.

VARIABLES *Boxplots for all dependent variables in same display.* For each cell, boxplots for all dependent variables are displayed together. Comparisons of distributions of several dependent variables are easily made. This is useful in situations where the dependent variables are repeated measures of the same variable (see the following example), or when the dependent variable has very different values for different cells, and plotting all cells on the same scale would cause information to be lost.

Example
```
EXAMINE VARIABLES=GPA1 GPA2 GPA3 GPA4 BY MAJOR
   /COMPARE=VARIABLE.
```

- The four GPA variables are summarized for each value of MAJOR.

- COMPARE=VARIABLES specifies that output for the four GPA variables be grouped together for each value of MAJOR. Thus, separate plots containing four GPA values are obtained for each of the majors.

Example
```
EXAMINE VARIABLES=GPA1 GPA2 GPA3 GPA4 BY MAJOR /COMPARE=GROUPS.
```

- COMPARE=GROUPS specifies that the boxplots for GPA1 be shown for all majors in the same display, then the values of GPA2 for all majors, and so on.

SCALE Subcommand

SCALE controls whether boxplots, stem-and-leaf plots, and histograms are constructed on the same scale for each cell in the analysis.

PLOTWISE *Construct scales according to the values in each plot.* Boxplots for each cell are constructed on the basis of the values of the dependent variable for cases in that plot only. This is the default.

UNIFORM *Display plots in a common scale.* Scales for boxplots and histograms are the same for each cell in the model. The common scale is constructed on the basis of dependent variable values of all cases.

- EXAMINE does not produce boxplots in a uniform scale for separate dependent variables unless they are plotted in the same plot using COMPARE= VARIABLE.

Example
```
EXAMINE VARIABLES=SALARY BY SEX
   /SCALE=UNIFORM.
```

- The stem-and-leaf plots for SALARY are plotted on the same scale for both values of SEX.

Example
```
EXAMINE VARIABLES=SALARY BONUS BY SEX
   /COMPARE=VARIABLES
   /SCALE=UNIFORM.
```

- SALARY and BONUS are plotted on the same boxplot for each value of SEX. The scale is the same for each boxplot.

ID Subcommand   ID assigns a variable from the active system file to identify the cases in the analysis. By default the system variable $CASENUM is used for labeling boxplots and extreme-case listings.

- The ID variable can be either string or numeric. If it is numeric, value labels are used to label cases. If no value labels exist, the values are used.
- Up to 25 characters of the identifier are displayed adjacent to outliers or in a note in boxplots and for extreme cases if STATISTICS=EXTREME is requested.
- Only one label variable can be specified.

Example   `EXAMINE VARIABLES=SALARY BY RACE BY SEX /ID=LASTNAME.`

- ID displays up to 25 characters of the value of LASTNAME for outliers in the boxplots.

**FREQUENCIES
Subcommand**   The FREQUENCIES subcommand generates frequency tables.

- Frequency tables for values between the FROM cutoff value and the maximum value for the dependent variable are generated. By default, the FROM cutoff value is the minimum.
- If no BY value is specified for the size of increments, EXAMINE selects an increment size.
- Each bin is identified by its center.

FROM(value)   *The lowest value for the frequency table.* The default is the minimum. All cases with values smaller than the FROM cutoff value are included in a separate bin.

BY (increment)   *Specifies the increment for frequency display.* The default increment is the same as that used for the stems in the stem-and-leaf plot. If the increment is 0, a frequency table for each distinct value is produced.

Example   `EXAMINE VARIABLE=DEGREES`
`        /FREQUENCIES FROM (90) BY (10).`

- FREQUENCIES produces a frequency table for the dependent variable DEGREES.
- The FROM cutoff value for the frequency table is 90.
- Since BY specifies increments of 10, the first frequency bin contains all cases with values of 90 or greater, and less than 100. The midpoint of the bin is 95. The next frequency increment contains all cases having a temperature of 100 or more, but less than 110.
- Frequencies continue in increments of 10 until the maximum value for DEGREES is included in a bin.

**PERCENTILES
Subcommand**   PERCENTILES controls method and breaking points for percentile computations. If PERCENTILES is omitted, no percentiles are produced. If PERCENTILES appears without a keyword, the default method is HAVERAGE and the default breaking points are 5, 10, 25, 50, 75, 90, and 95.

- Values for breaking points are specified in parentheses following the subcommand.
- Keywords for computational method or suppressing PERCENTILE output follow the specifications for breaking point values.

In the following formulas, cases are assumed to be ranked in ascending order. W is the sum of the weights for all non-missing cases, p is the specified percentile divided by 100, i is the rank of each case, and X_i is the value of the ith case.

HAVERAGE   *Weighted average at $X_{(W+1)p}$.* The percentile value is the weighted average of X_i and X_{i+1} using the formula $(1-f)X_i + fX_{i+1}$ where

(W+1)p is decomposed into an integer part i and fractional part f. This is the default if PERCENTILES is specified without a keyword.

WAVERAGE	*Weighted average at X_{W_p}.* The percentile value is the weighted average of X_i and X_{i+1} using the formula $(1-f)X_i + fX_{i+1}$ where i is the integer part of Wp, and f is the fractional part of Wp.
ROUND	*Observation closest to Wp.* The percentile value is X_i where i is integer part of (Wp + .5).
EMPIRICAL	*Empirical distribution function.* The percentile value is X_i when the fractional part of Wp is equal to 0. The percentile value is X_{i+1} when the fractional part of Wp is greater than 0.
AEMPIRICAL	*Empirical distribution with averaging.* The percentile value is $(X_i + X_{i+1})/2$ when the fractional part of Wp equals 0. The percentile value is X_{i+1} when the fractional part of Wp is greater than 0.
NONE	*Suppresses the output of percentiles.* This is the default if PERCENTILES is omitted.

Example   EXAMINE VARIABLE=SALARY /PERCENTILES(10,50,90)=EMPIRICAL.

• PERCENTILES produces percentiles using the EMPIRICAL distribution for tenth, fiftieth, and ninetieth percentiles of the distribution of the dependent variable SALARY.

PLOT Subcommand

PLOT controls the output of plots. The default is a vertical boxplot and a stem-and-leaf plot for each dependent variable for each cell in the model. Spread-versus-level plots can be produced only if there is at least one grouping variable present.

BOXPLOT	*Vertical boxplot.* The boundaries of the box are Tukey's hinges. The median is identified by an asterisk. The length of the box is the interquartile range (IQR) computed from Tukey's hinges. Values more than three IQRs from the end of a box are labeled as extreme (E). Values more than 1.5 IQRs but less than 3 IQRs from the end of the box are labeled as outliers (O).
STEMLEAF	*Stem-and-leaf plot.* In a stem-and-leaf plot, each observed value is divided into two components—leading digits (stem) and trailing digits (leaf).
HISTOGRAM	*Histogram.*
SPREADLEVEL(p)	*Spread-versus-level plot.* If the keyword appears alone, a plot is produced of the natural logs of the interquartile ranges against the natural logs of the medians for all cells. If the power for transforming the data(p) is given, the IQR and median of the transformed data are plotted. If p=0 is specified, a natural log transformation of the data is done. The slope of the regression line and Levene's test for homogeneity of variance are also displayed. Levene's test is based on the original data if no transformation is specified and on the transformed data if a transformation is requested.
NPPLOT	*Normal probability and detrended probability plots.* NPPLOT calculates the Shapiro-Wilks statistic and a Kolmogorov-Smirnov statistic with a Lilliefors significance level for testing normality. The Shapiro-Wilks statistic is not calculated when the sample size exceeds 50.
ALL	*All available plots.*
NONE	*Display no plots.*

Example   EXAMINE VARIABLES=CYCLE BY TREATMNT /PLOT=NPPLOT.

• PLOT produces normal probability plots and detrended probability plots for each value of TREATMNT.

Example   `EXAMINE VARIABLES=CYCLE BY TREATMNT /PLOT=SPREADLEVEL(.5).`

- PLOT produces a spead-versus-level plot for medians and interquartile ranges of the square root of CYCLE. Each point on the plot represents one of the TREATMNT groups.

Example   `EXAMINE VARIABLES=CYCLE BY TREATMNT /PLOT=SPREADLEVEL(0).`

- PLOT generates a spread-versus-level plot for the medians and interquartile ranges of the natural log transformed values of CYCLE.

Example   `EXAMINE VARIABLES=CYCLE BY TREATMNT /PLOT=SPREADLEVEL.`

- PLOT generates a spread-versus-level plot for the logs of medians and the logs of the interquartile ranges of CYCLE for each TREATMNT group.

STATISTICS Subcommand

STATISTICS requests univariate statistics and determines how many extreme values are displayed. DESCRIPTIVES is the default. If you request statistics, only the requested statistics are displayed.

DESCRIPTIVE   *Univariate statistics only.* This includes the mean, median, 5% trimmed mean, standard error, variance, standard deviation, minimum, maximum, range, interquartile range, skewness, skewness standard error, kurtosis, and kurtosis standard error. This is the default.

EXTREME(n)   *The n largest and n smallest values.* If *n* is omitted, the five largest and five smallest values are displayed. Extreme values are labeled with their values on the ID variable if the ID subcommand is used or with their values on the system variable $CASENUM if it is not.

ALL   *Univariate statistics and top five and bottom five extreme values.*

NONE   *Display neither univariate statistics nor extreme values.*

Example   `EXAMINE VARIABLE=FAILTIME /ID=BRAND`
              `/STATISTICS=EXTREME(10) /PLOT=NONE.`

- STATISTICS identifies the 10 cases with lowest values on FAILTIME and the 10 cases with highest values on FAILTIME. The output includes 20 cases labeled by the first 15 characters of their values for the variable BRAND.

MESTIMATORS Subcommand

The M-estimators are robust maximum-likelihood estimators of location. Four M-estimators are available. They differ in the weights they apply to the cases. MESTIMATORS with no keywords produces Huber's M-estimator with c= 1.339; Andrew's wave with c=1.34π; Hampel's M-estimator with a=1.7, b=3.4, c=8.5; and Tukey's biweight with c=4.685.

HUBER(c)   *Huber's M-estimator.* This is the default when c=1.339. The value of the weighting constant c can be set by placing the desired value in parentheses following the keyword.

ANDREW(c)   *Andrew's wave estimator.* The default is 1.34π. The value of the weighting constant c can be set by placing the desired value in parentheses following the keyword. Constants are multiplied by Π.

HAMPEL(a,b,c)   *Hampel's M-estimator.* This is the default when a=1.7, b=3.4, and c=8.5. The values of the weighting constants a, b, and c can be set by placing the desired values in the appropriate order in parentheses following the keyword.

TUKEY(c)   *Tukey's biweight estimator.* This is the default when c=4.685. The value of the weighting constant c can be set by placing the desired value in parentheses following the keyword.

ALL   *Output all four above M-estimators.* This is the default when MESTIMATORS is specified with no keyword.

NONE   *Suppress output of M-estimators.* This is the default if MESTIMATORS is omitted.

Example   EXAMINE VARIABLE=CASTTEST /MESTIMATORS.

- MESTIMATORS generates all four M-estimators computed with the default constants.

Example   EXAMINE VARIABLE=CASTTEST /MESTIMATORS=HAMPELS(2,4,8).

- MESTIMATOR produces Hampel's M-estimator. It is computed with the specified weighting constants a=2, b=4, and c=8.

MISSING Subcommand

MISSING controls the processing of missing values in the analysis. The default is LISTWISE. The keywords LISTWISE, PAIRWISE, and REPORT are mutually exclusive; each can be used with INCLUDE.

LISTWISE *Listwise deletion of missing cases.* A case with user-missing or system-missing values on any dependent variable or any factor in the model specification is excluded from the computation of statistics or displaying of plots. This is the default.

REPORT *Report missing values.* User-missing values and system-missing values for dependent variables are reported in frequency output and excluded from statistical computations and graphs. For factor variables, user-missing values and system-missing values are treated as valid factor categories labeled as missing.

PAIRWISE *Pairwise deletion of missing cases.* A case is deleted from the analysis only if it has a user-missing or system-missing value for the dependent variable or factor being analyzed.

INCLUDE *Include user-missing values.* Only system-missing values are excluded from the analysis.

Example   EXAMINE VARIABLES=RAINFALL MEANTEMP BY REGION.

- The absence of the MISSING subcommand produces the default listwise deletion of user-missing and system-missing values. Any case with a user-missing or system-missing value on RAINFALL, MEANTEMP, *or* REGION is excluded from the analysis.

Example   EXAMINE VARIABLES=RAINFALL MEANTEMP BY REGION
                   /MISSING=PAIRWISE.

- MISSING=PAIRWISE requests that only cases with missing values for RAINFALL or REGION be excluded from the analysis of RAINFALL, and only cases with missing values for MEANTEMP or REGION be excluded from the analysis of REGION.

Annotated Example

For a complete example with output, see Examples following the Command Reference.

References

Frigge, M., D. C. Hoaglin, and B. Iglewicz. 1987. Some implementations of the boxplot. In Heiberger, R. M., and M. Martin, ed., *Computer science and statistics proceedings of the 19th symposium on the interface.* Alexandria, Virginia: American Statistical Association.

Hoaglin, D. C., F. Mosteller, J. W. Tukey. 1985. *Exploring data tables, trends, and shapes.* New York: John Wiley & Sons.

Hoaglin, D. C., F. Mosteller, J. W. Tukey. 1983. *Understanding robust and exploratory data analysis.* New York: John Wiley & Sons.

Tukey, John W. 1977. *Exploratory data analysis.* Reading, Mass.: Addison-Wesley.

Velleman, P. F., and D.C. Hoaglin. 1981. *Applications, basics, and computing of exploratory data analysis.* Boston: Duxbury Press.

EXECUTE

EXECUTE

Overview

EXECUTE forces the data to be read and executes the transformations that precede it in the command sequence.

Syntax Rules

- The minimum specification is simply the command keyword. EXECUTE has no additional specifications.

Operations

- EXECUTE causes the data to be read but has no other influence on the session.
- EXECUTE is designed for use with transformation commands and facilities such as ADD FILES, MATCH FILES, UPDATE, PRINT, and WRITE, which do not read the data and are not executed unless followed by a data-reading procedure.

Example

```
DATA LIST  FILE=RAWDATA / 1 LNAME 1-13 (A) FNAME 15-24 (A)
   MMAIDENL 40-55.
VAR LABELS  MMAIDENL 'MOTHER''S MAIDEN NAME'.
DO IF (MMAIDENL EQ 'Smith').
WRITE OUTFILE=SMITHS/LNAME FNAME.
END IF.
EXECUTE.
FINISH.
```

- This example writes to the system file SMITHS the last and first names of all people whose mother's maiden name was Smith.
- DO IF — END IF and WRITE do not read data and are only executed when data are read for the next procedure.
- Because no procedure is desired in this session, EXECUTE is used to read the data and execute all of the preceding transformation commands. Otherwise, the commands would not execute.

EXPORT

```
EXPORT OUTFILE=file

[/TYPE={COMM**}]
       {TAPE  }

[/KEEP={ALL** }]] [/DROP=varlist]
       {varlist}

[/RENAME=(old varlist=new varlist)...]

[/MAP]

[/DIGITS=number]
```

**Default if the subcommand is omitted.

Example:

```
EXPORT OUTFILE=NEWDATA /RENAME=(V1 TO V3=ID, SEX, AGE) /MAP.
```

Overview

EXPORT produces a portable data file. A portable file contains all of the data and dictionary information stored in the SPSS system file from which it was created. Portable files are used for transporting files between installations having different conversions of SPSS (such as for the PRIME, VAX, or HONEYWELL GCOS computers) or for transporting files between SPSS, SPSS/PC+, or other software using the same portable file format. To send data to an installation having the same machine as your own, send an SPSS system file. A system file is cheaper to process than a portable file.

EXPORT is similar to the SAVE command. It can occur in the same position in the command sequence as the SAVE command and saves the current active system file. This includes the results of all permanent transformations and any temporary transformations made just prior to the EXPORT command. The active system file is unchanged after the EXPORT command.

Options

Format. You can control the format of the portable file. See TYPE Subcommand.

Variables. You can save a subset of variables from the active file and rename the variables. You can also produce a record of all variables and their names on the exported file. See the DROP, KEEP, RENAME, and MAP subcommands.

Precision. You can specify the number of decimal digits of precision for the values of all numeric variables. See DIGITS Subcommand.

Basic Specification

• The basic specification is the OUTFILE subcommand with a file specification. All variables from the active file are written to the portable file with their original names, variable and value labels, missing-value flags, and print and write formats.

Subcommand Order

• Subcommands can be named in any order.

Operations

• Portable files are written with 80-character record lengths.
• Portable files may contain some unprintable characters.
• The active system file is still available for SPSS transformations and procedures after the portable file is created.
• The system variables $CASENUM and $DATE are assigned when the file is read by IMPORT. If the WEIGHT command is used, EXPORT specifies the weighting variable in the portable file.

Methods of Transporting Portable Files

Portable files can be transported either on magnetic tape or by a communications program. Each method involves special considerations, discussed below.

Magnetic Tape. Before transporting files on magnetic tape, make sure the receiving installation can read the tape being sent. The following tape specifications for the installation must be known before writing the tape:

- Number of tracks—either 7 or 9.
- Tape density—200, 556, 800, 1600, or 6250 bits per inch (BPI).
- Parity—even or odd. This must be known only when writing a 7-track tape.
- Tape labeling—labeled or unlabeled. Check whether the site can use tape labels. Also make sure that the site has the ability to read multivolume tape files if the file being written uses more than one tape.
- Blocksize—the maximum blocksize the receiving installation can accept.

A tape written with the following characteristics can be read at most installations: 9-track, 1600 BPI, unlabeled, and a blocksize of 3200 characters. However, there is no guarantee that a tape written with these characteristics will be read successfully at a particular receiving installation. The best policy is to know the acceptable characteristics for tapes that a specific receiving installation can read.

Communications Programs. Transmission of a portable file by a communications program may not be possible if the program misinterprets any characters in the file as control characters (for example, as a line feed, carriage return, or end of transmission). This problem can be prevented by specifying TYPE=COMM on EXPORT. This specification replaces each control character with the character 0. The affected control characters are in positions 0–60 of the IMPORT/EXPORT character set (Appendix B).

The line length that the communications program uses must be set to 80 to match the 80-character record length of portable files. A transmitted file must be inspected with an editor for blank lines or special characters inserted by the communications program. These must be edited out prior to reading the file with the IMPORT command.

Character Translation

Portable files are character files, not binary files, and they have 80-character records so they can be transmitted over data links. A receiving installation may not use the same character set as the installation where a portable file was written. If possible, SPSS translates characters in the portable file to the character set of the receiving installation. Depending on the character set in use, some characters in labels and in string data may be lost in the translation. For example, if a file is transported from an installation using a seven-bit ASCII character set to an installation using a six-bit ASCII character set, some characters in the file may have no matching characters in six-bit ASCII. For a character that has no match, SPSS generates an appropriate nonprintable character (the null character in most character sets). For a complete display of the character-set translations available with the IMPORT and EXPORT commands, refer to Appendix B. A blank in a column of the appendix means that there is no matching character for that character set, and an appropriate nonprintable character will be generated by SPSS when you import a file.

File Transfer

The following advice may help ensure successful file transfers by magnetic tape:

- Unless it is certain the receiving computer can read labels written by the originating computer, prepare an unlabeled tape.
- Make sure the record length of 80 is not changed.
- Do not use a separate character translation program. (In particular, do not attempt ASCII/EBCDIC translations; EXPORT/IMPORT takes care of that for you.)
- Make sure the same blocking factor is used when writing and reading a tape. A blocksize of 3200 is frequently a good choice.
- If possible, write the portable file directly to tape. This avoids possible interference from some copy programs. Read the file directly from the tape for the same reason.
- Use the INFO LOCAL command to find out about using SPSS on your particular computer and operating system. INFO LOCAL generally includes additional information about reading and writing portable files.

If you are communicating a portable file via telephone modem, consider using an error-checking communications system such as Kermit.

Example

```
EXPORT OUTFILE=NEWDATA /RENAME=(V1 TO V3=ID,SEX,AGE) /MAP.
```

- The portable file is written to NEWDATA.
- Variables V1, V2, and V3 are renamed ID, SEX, and AGE for the portable file. Their names remain V1, V2, and V3 in the active SPSS file. None of the other variables written to the portable file is renamed.
- MAP requests a display of the variables in the portable file.

OUTFILE Subcommand

OUTFILE specifies the portable file. OUTFILE is the only required subcommand on EXPORT.

TYPE Subcommand

TYPE creates either a communications- or tape-formatted portable file. TYPE can specify one of two keywords, COMM or TAPE. COMM is the default. (See Methods of Transporting Portable Files, above, for more information on magnetic tapes and communications programs.)

- TYPE=COMM removes all control characters and replaces them with the character 0. TYPE=COMM is used to transport portable files by a communications program. This is the default.
- TYPE=TAPE is used to transport portable files on magnetic tape.
- All portable files from releases earlier than SPSS-X 2.1 are in tape format and may not be suitable for transmission by communications programs.

Example

```
EXPORT TYPE=TAPE /OUTFILE=HUBOUT.
```

- File HUBOUT is saved as a tape-formatted portable file.

DROP and KEEP Subcommands

DROP and KEEP save a subset of variables in the portable file.

- DROP excludes a variable or list of variables from the portable file. All variables not named are included in the portable file.
- KEEP includes a variable or list of variables in the portable file. All variables not named are excluded.
- Variables can be specified on DROP and KEEP in any order.
- With the DROP subcommand, the order of variables in the portable file is the same as their order in the active system file.
- With the KEEP subcommand, the order of variables in the portable file is the order they are named on KEEP. Thus, KEEP can be used to reorder variables in the portable file.
- Both DROP and KEEP can be used on the same EXPORT command, provided they do not name any of the same variables.
- To specify a group of consecutive variables in the active system file, use keyword TO.
- The active file is not affected by DROP or KEEP.

Example

```
EXPORT OUTFILE=NEWSUM /DROP=DEPT TO DIVISION.
```

- The portable file is written to file NEWSUM. Variables between and including DEPT and DIVISION in the active file are excluded from the portable file.
- All other variables are saved in the portable file.

RENAME Subcommand

RENAME renames variables being written to the portable file. The renamed variables retain their variable and value labels, missing-value flags, and print formats assigned in the SPSS session.

- To rename a variable, specify the name of the variable in the active system file, a required equals sign, and the new name.

- A variable list can be specified on both sides of the equals sign. The number of variables on both sides must be the same, and the entire specification must be enclosed in parentheses.
- Keyword TO can be used for both variable lists (see Universals: Variable-Naming Conventions).
- If a renamed variable is specified on a subsequent DROP or KEEP subcommand, the new variable name must be used on DROP or KEEP.

Example
```
EXPORT OUTFILE=NEWSUM /DROP=DEPT TO DIVISION
    /RENAME=(NAME,WAGE=LNAME,SALARY).
```

- RENAME renames NAME and WAGE to LNAME and SALARY.
- LNAME and SALARY retain the variable and value labels, missing-value flags, and print formats assigned to NAME and WAGE.

MAP Subcommand

MAP displays any changes that have been specified by the RENAME, DROP, or KEEP subcommands. MAP displays only the changes specified on the subcommands that precede the MAP request.

- MAP can be specified as often as desired.
- When MAP is specified last, it produces a listing of the contents of the portable file.

Example
```
EXPORT OUTFILE=NEWSUM /DROP=DEPT TO DIVISION /MAP
    /RENAME NAME=LNAME WAGE=SALARY /MAP.
```

- The first MAP subcommand produces a listing of the variables in the file after DROP has dropped the specified variables.
- RENAME renames NAME and WAGE.
- The second MAP subcommand shows the variables in the file after renaming. Since this is the last subcommand, the listing will show the variables as they are written in the portable file.

DIGITS Subcommand

DIGITS specifies the degree of precision for all values of noninteger numeric variables written to the portable file.

- DIGITS has the general form DIGITS=n, in which n is the number of digits of precision.
- DIGITS applies to all numbers for which rounding is required.
- Different degrees of precision *cannot* be specified for different variables. Thus, DIGITS should be set according to the requirements of the variable that needs the most precision.
- Default precision methods used by EXPORT work perfectly for integers that are not too large and for fractions whose denominators are products of 2, 3, and 5 (meaning all decimals, quarters, eighths, sixteenths, thirds, thirtieths, sixtieths, and so forth.) For other fractions and for integers too large to be represented exactly in the active system file (usually more than 9 digits, often 15 or more), the representation used in the active file contains some error already, so no exact way of sending these numbers is possible. SPSS sends enough digits to get very close. The number of digits sent in these cases depends on the originating program: on the IBM versions of SPSS, it is the equivalent of 15 decimal digits (in integer and fractional parts combined). If many numbers on a file require this treatment, the file can grow quite large. These numbers take a great deal of space. If you do not need the full precision normally used, you can save some space in the portable file by using the DIGITS subcommand.

Example
```
EXPORT OUTFILE=NEWSUM /DROP=DEPT TO DIVISION /MAP /DIGITS=4.
```

- DIGITS guarantees the accuracy of values to four significant digits.
- For example, 12.34567890876 will be rounded to 12.35.

FACTOR

```
FACTOR VARIABLES=varlist† [/MISSING=[{LISTWISE**}] [INCLUDE]]
                                       {PAIRWISE }
                                       {MEANSUB  }
                                       {DEFAULT  }


        [/WIDTH={132     }]
                {n       }
                {DEFAULT**}

        [/MATRIX=[IN({COR=file})]  [OUT({COR=file})]]
                     {COR=*   }         {COR=*   }
                     {FAC=file}         {FAC=file}
                     {FAC=*   }         {FAC=*   }


        [/ANALYSIS=varlist...]

        [/PRINT=[DEFAULT**] [INITIAL**] [EXTRACTION**] [ROTATION**]

                [UNIVARIATE] [CORRELATION] [DET] [INV]

                [REPR] [AIC] [KMO]

                [FSCORE] [SIG] [ALL]]

        [/PLOT=[EIGEN] [ROTATION (nl,n2)]]

        [/DIAGONAL={value list}]
                   {DEFAULT** }

        [/FORMAT=[SORT] [BLANK(n)] [DEFAULT**]]

        [/CRITERIA=[FACTORS(n)] [MINEIGEN({1.0**})] [ITERATE({25**})]
                                          {eig  }            {ni  }


                [RCONVERGE({0.0001**})] [DELTA({0**})] [{KAISER** }]
                           {rl      }          {d  }    {NOKAISER}

                [ECONVERGE({0.001**})]] [DEFAULT**]
                           {el     }

        [/EXTRACTION={PC**   }] [/ROTATION={VARIMAX**}]
                     {PAF    }             {EQUAMAX  }
                     {ALPHA  }             {QUARTIMAX}
                     {IMAGE  }             {OBLIMIN  }
                     {ULS    }             {NOROTATE }
                     {GLS    }             {DEFAULT  }
                     {ML     }
                     {DEFAULT}

        [/SAVE=[{REG    } ({ALL} rootname)]]
                {BART   }  {n  }
                {AR     }
                {DEFAULT}

        [/ANALYSIS...]

        [/CRITERIA...]     [/EXTRACTION...]

        [/ROTATION...]     [/SAVE...]
```

**Default if the subcommand is omitted.
†Omit VARIABLES with matrix input.

Example:

```
FACTOR VARIABLES=V1 TO V12.
```

Overview   FACTOR performs factor analysis using one of seven extraction methods. FACTOR accepts matrix input in the form of correlation matrices or factor loading matrices and also writes these materials to a system file.

Options   **Analysis Block Display.** You can tailor the statistical display for an analysis block to include correlation matrices, reproduced correlation matrices, and other statistics. You can sort the output in the factor pattern and structure matrices. You can also request scree plots and plots of the variables in factor space for all analyses within an analysis block.

Extraction Phase Options. You can choose among six extraction methods in addition to the default principal components extraction: principal axis factoring, alpha factoring, image factoring, unweighted least squares, generalized least squares, and maximum likelihood. You can supply initial diagonal values for principal axis factoring. You can also select the statistical criteria used in the extraction.

Rotation Phase Options. You can control the criteria for factor rotation. You can also choose among three rotation methods (equamax, quartimax, and oblimin) in addition to the default varimax rotation, or specify no rotation.

Factor Scores. You can save factor scores as new variables in the active system file, using any of three methods.

Display Format. You can control the width of the display within FACTOR.

Writing and Reading Matrices. You can write a correlation matrix or a factor loading matrix. You can read matrix materials written either by a previous FACTOR procedure, or by a procedure that writes matrices with Pearson correlation coefficients.

Basic Specification   • The basic specification is the VARIABLES subcommand with a variable list. FACTOR performs principal components analysis with a varimax rotation on all variables in the analysis using default criteria.

Subcommand Order   • The standard subcommand order is illustrated in Figure 1.

Figure 1 Subcommand order

```
FACTOR VARIABLES=...
       / MISSING=...
       / WIDTH=...
       / MATRIX=...
```

Analysis Block(s)

```
/ ANALYSIS=...
/ PRINT=...
/ PLOT=...
/ DIAGONAL=...
/ FORMAT=...
```

Extraction Block(s)

```
/ CRITERIA=(extraction criteria)
/ EXTRACTION=...
```

Rotation Block(s)

```
/ CRITERIA=(rotation criteria)
/ ROTATION=...
/ SAVE=...
```

- Subcommands listed in the ANALYSIS block apply to all EXTRACTION and ROTATION blocks within that ANALYSIS block. Subcommands listed in the EXTRACTION block apply to all ROTATION blocks within that EXTRACTION block.
- Each ANALYSIS block can contain multiple EXTRACTION blocks, and each EXTRACTION block can contain multiple ROTATION blocks.
- The CRITERIA and FORMAT subcommands remain in effect until explicitly overridden. Other subcommands affect only the block in which they are contained.
- The order of subcommands can be different from the order shown in Figure 1. However, any analysis that can be performed with procedure FACTOR can be performed using this order, repeating ANALYSIS, ROTATION, and EXTRACTION blocks as needed. (If MATRIX=IN is specified, VARIABLES should be omitted.)

Because of this structured syntax, which allows rotation blocks nested within extraction blocks nested within analysis blocks, you can get unexpected results if you specify commands out of order.

- If you enter any subcommand other than the global subcommands (VARIABLES, MISSING, WIDTH, MATRIX) before the first ANALYSIS subcommand, an implicit analysis block including all variables on the VARIABLES subcommand is activated. Factors are extracted and rotated for this implicit block before any explicitly requested analysis block is activated.
- If you enter a SAVE or ROTATION subcommand before the first EXTRACTION in any analysis block, an implicit extraction block using the default method (PC) is activated. Factors are extracted and rotated for this implicit block before any explicitly requested extraction block is activated.
- If you enter CRITERIA *after* an EXTRACTION or ROTATION subcommand, the criteria do not affect that extraction or rotation.

Example
```
FACTOR VAR=V1 TO V12
  /ANALYSIS=V1 TO V8
  /CRITERIA=FACTORS(3)
  /EXTRACTION=PAF
  /ROTATION=QUARTIMAX.
```

- FACTOR extracts three factors using the principal axis method and quartimax rotation.

Example
```
* UNEXPECTED RESULTS IN FACTOR.

FACTOR VAR=V1 TO V12
  /CRITERIA=FACTORS(3)
  /ANALYSIS=V1 TO V8
  /EXTRACTION=PAF
  /ROTATION=QUARTIMAX.
```

- The CRITERIA subcommand activates an analysis block of all twelve variables. FACTOR extracts three factors using the default extraction method (principal components) and rotation (varimax) before entering the analysis block with V1 to V8, where different extraction and rotation methods are requested.

Example
```
* UNEXPECTED RESULTS IN FACTOR.

FACTOR VARIABLES=V1 TO V12
  /SAVE DEFAULT (ALL,FAC)
  /EXTRACTION=PAF
  /ROTATION=OBLIMIN.
```

- The SAVE subcommand activates an extraction block using the default extraction method (principal components) and rotation (varimax). These factors are saved in the active system file as FAC1, FAC2, and so on.
- The next extraction block uses principal axis factoring and oblimin rotation but does not contain a SAVE subcommand, so no factor scores are saved in the active file.

Example   `* UNEXPECTED RESULTS IN FACTOR.`

```
FACTOR V1 TO V12
  /EXTRACTION PAF
  /CRITERIA FACTORS(5).
```

- Since no CRITERIA subcommand precedes EXTRACTION, default criteria are used, and the CRITERIA subcommand is ignored.

Syntax Rules

- The global subcommands VARIABLES, MISSING, and WIDTH can be specified only once and are in effect for the entire FACTOR procedure. WIDTH can be specified anywhere, while VARIABLES and MISSING must precede any of the other subcommands.
- The subcommands ANALYSIS, PRINT, PLOT, DIAGONAL, and FORMAT are *analysis block* subcommands. ANALYSIS specifies a subset of variables; the other subcommands apply to all analyses performed on those variables until another ANALYSIS subcommand is entered.
- You can request more than one analysis block within a FACTOR procedure.
- The subcommands CRITERIA and EXTRACTION are *extraction block* subcommands. EXTRACTION triggers the extraction of factors according to a specified method. CRITERIA can be used one or more times in an extraction block to set parameters governing any subsequent EXTRACTION and ROTATION subcommands.
- You can request more than one extraction block within an analysis block.
- The subcommands SAVE and ROTATION are *rotation block* subcommands. ROTATION triggers a rotation of the factors in the current extraction block, and SAVE adds factor scores for the following rotation to the active system file.
- You can request more than one rotation block within an extraction block.
- You can save factor scores more than once within a rotation block.

Some subcommands (VARIABLES, ANALYSIS, EXTRACTION, SAVE, ROTATION) perform or initiate an action. For any specific analysis, you should enter these subcommands, or as many of them as you need, in the following order:

- VARIABLES causes the calculation of a correlation matrix, which is the basis for all further analysis. If LISTWISE deletion is performed, it is done on all variables in the variable list.
- ANALYSIS initiates an analysis block, in which specifications for the analysis of a subset of variables are collected.
- EXTRACTION triggers the actual extraction of factors.
- SAVE defines new variables containing factor scores and adds them to the active file.
- ROTATION rotates the most recently extracted factors.

Other subcommands set specifications which remain in effect thereafter:

- The FORMAT and CRITERIA subcommands remain in effect until you explicitly change them.
- The PRINT, PLOT, and DIAGONAL subcommands remain in effect for the current analysis block. However, defaults are restored when an ANALYSIS subcommand is subsequently specified.

Operations

- FACTOR builds a correlation matrix of variables named on the VARIABLES subcommand before it produces any factor results.
- The width specified on the WIDTH subcommand, if any, overrides the width defined on SET.

Limitations
- The only required subcommand is VARIABLES (except for matrix input, which does not require the VARIABLES subcommand).
- Only one MISSING and WIDTH subcommand can be in effect for the FACTOR procedure. If either of these is specified more than once, the last specified is in effect for the entire procedure.
- The MATRIX subcommand must precede the ANALYSIS block. Only one IN and one OUT keyword can be in effect for the MATRIX subcommand. If either IN or OUT is specified more than once, FACTOR does not execute. VARIABLES is not required for MATRIX=IN and cannot be specified before MATRIX=IN.
- The CRITERIA subcommand must precede the EXTRACTION subcommand, or it is ignored.
- If the EXTRACTION subcommand is omitted, ROTATION defaults to VARIMAX; otherwise, it defaults to NOROTATE.
- Only one PRINT, PLOT, and DIAGONAL subcommand can be in effect for each ANALYSIS subcommand. If any of these is specified more than once in a given extraction block, the last one specified for that extraction block is in effect.
- Specifications on the CRITERIA subcommand carry over from analysis to analysis until explicitly overridden with a subsequent CRITERIA subcommand.

Example

```
FACTOR VARIABLES=V1 TO V12.
```

- This example produces the default principal components analysis of twelve variables. Those with eigenvalues greater than 1 (the default criterion for extraction) are rotated using varimax (the default rotation method).

VARIABLES Subcommand

VARIABLES names all the variables to be used in the FACTOR procedure. FACTOR computes a correlation matrix that includes all the variables named. This matrix is used by all analysis blocks that follow.

- VARIABLES is required except with matrix input. When FACTOR reads a matrix system file, the VARIABLES subcommand should not be used.
- The specification on VARIABLES is a list of numeric variables.
- Keyword ALL on VARIABLES refers to all variables in the active system file.
- All variables named on subsequent subcommands must first be named on the VARIABLES subcommand.
- There can be only one VARIABLES subcommand, and only the MISSING and WIDTH subcommands can precede it.

MISSING Subcommand

MISSING controls the treatment of cases with missing values.

- MISSING can be specified only once.
- If MISSING is omitted or included without specifications, listwise deletion is in effect.
- MISSING must precede any analysis block subcommands.
- The MISSING specification controls all analyses requested on the FACTOR command.
- The LISTWISE, PAIRWISE, and MEANSUB keywords on MISSING are alternatives describing how missing data should be treated in computing the correlation matrix. Any of these may be requested in combination with INCLUDE, which specifies whether user-missing data should be treated as missing or valid.

The following keywords can be specified on MISSING:

LISTWISE   *Delete cases with missing values listwise.* Only cases with nonmissing values for all variables named on the VARIABLES subcommand are used. Listwise deletion may also be requested with keyword DE-FAULT.

PAIRWISE   *Delete cases with missing values pairwise.* All cases with nonmissing values for each pair of variables correlated are used to compute that correlation, regardless of whether the cases have missing values on any other variable.

MEANSUB   *Replace missing values with the variable mean.* All cases are used after the substitution is made. If INCLUDE is also specified, user-missing values are included in the computation of the means, and means are substituted only for the system-missing value.

INCLUDE   *Include user-missing values.* Cases with user-missing values are treated as valid, regardless of whether LISTWISE, PAIRWISE, or MEANSUB is in effect.

WIDTH Subcommand

WIDTH controls the width of the display.

- WIDTH can be specified anywhere and affects all FACTOR displays. If more than one width is specified, the last is in effect.
- The only specification on WIDTH is an integer ranging from 72 to 132.
- If WIDTH is omitted, the width specified on the SET command is used.
- If WIDTH is entered without specifications, a width of 132 is used.

ANALYSIS Subcommand

The optional ANALYSIS subcommand specifies a subset of the variables named on VARIABLES for use in subsequent analyses. It can also be used to perform different analyses on the same set of variables.

- The specification for ANALYSIS is a list of variables, all of which must have been named on the VARIABLES subcommand.
- Each use of ANALYSIS explicitly initiates an analysis block. The analysis block ends when another ANALYSIS subcommand or the end of the FACTOR procedure is reached.
- Within an analysis block, only those variables named on the ANALYSIS subcommand are available.
- If ANALYSIS is omitted, all variables named on the VARIABLES subcommand are used in all extractions.
- Keyword TO in a variable list on ANALYSIS refers to the order in which variables are named on the VARIABLES subcommand, not to their order in the active system file.
- Keyword ALL refers to all variables named on the VARIABLES subcommand.
- For correlation matrix input, ANALYSIS can specify a subset of the variables in the matrix.
- For either correlation or factor matrix input, the ANALYSIS subcommand defaults to the entire set of variables and may be omitted.

Example
```
FACTOR VARIABLES=V1 V2 V3 V4 V5 V6
     /ANALYSIS=V1 TO V4
     /ANALYSIS=V4 TO V6.
```

- This example specifies two analysis blocks. Variables V1, V2, V3, and V4 are included in the first analysis block. Variables V4, V5, and V6 are in the second analysis block.
- Keyword TO on ANALYSIS refers to the order of variables on the variable list, not the order in the active system file.
- A default principal components analysis with a varimax rotation will be performed for each analysis block.

FORMAT Subcommand

Use FORMAT to reformat the display of factor pattern and structure matrices to increase interpretability.

- FORMAT can be specified once in each analysis block. If more than one FORMAT is encountered in an analysis block, the last is in effect.
- If FORMAT is omitted or included without specifications, variables appear in the order in which they are named and all matrix entries are displayed.
- Once specified, FORMAT stays in effect until it is overridden.

The following keywords may be specified on FORMAT:

SORT   *Order the factor loadings in descending order by the magnitude of the first factor.*

BLANK(n) *Suppress coefficients lower in absolute value than threshold* n.

DEFAULT   *Turn off keywords SORT and BLANK.*

Example

```
FACTOR VARIABLES=V1 TO V12
   /MISSING=MEANSUB
   /FORMAT=SORT BLANK(.3)
   /EXTRACTION=ULS
   /ROTATION=NOROTATE.
```

- This example specifies a single analysis block. All variables between and including V1 and V12 in the active system file are included.
- The MISSING subcommand requests that variable means be substituted for missing values.
- The FORMAT subcommand requests that variables be ordered in factor pattern matrices by descending value of loadings. Factor loadings with an absolute value less than 0.3 will be omitted.
- Factors are extracted using unweighted least squares.
- The factors are not rotated.

PRINT Subcommand

PRINT controls the statistical display for an analysis block, and all extraction and rotation blocks within it.

- If PRINT is omitted or included without keywords, the displays indicated by the keywords INITIAL, EXTRACTION, and ROTATION are produced for the current analysis block.
- If any keywords are specified, only those displays specifically requested are produced for the current analysis block.
- The defaults are reinstated when an ANALYSIS subcommand is encountered.
- The statistics requested include only the variables in the analysis block.
- PRINT can be placed anywhere within the analysis block. If more than one PRINT subcommand is specified, the last encountered is in effect.

The following keywords can be specified on PRINT:

UNIVARIATE   *Valid n's, means, and standard deviations.* (Not available with matrix input.)

INITIAL   *Initial communalities for each variable, eigenvalues of the unreduced correlation matrix for each factor, and percentage of variance for each.*

CORRELATION *Correlation matrix.*

SIG   *Matrix of significance levels of correlations.*

DET   *The determinant of the correlation matrix.*

INV   *The inverse of the correlation matrix.*

AIC   *The anti-image covariance and correlation matrices* (Kaiser, 1970). The measure of sampling adequacy for the individual variable is displayed on the diagonal of the anti-image correlation matrix.

KMO	*The Kaiser-Meyer-Olkin measure of sampling adequacy and Bartlett's test of sphericity.* Tests of significance are not computed with matrix input if an N command is not used.
EXTRACTION	*Factor pattern matrix, revised communalities, the eigenvalue of each factor retained, and the percentage of variance each eigenvalue represents.*
REPR	*Reproduced correlations and residual correlations.*
ROTATION	*Rotated factor pattern and factor transformation matrix, and the factor correlation matrix.*
FSCORE	*The factor score coefficient matrix.* Factor score coefficients are calculated using the method requested on the SAVE subcommand. The default is the regression method.
ALL	*All available statistics.*
DEFAULT	*INITIAL, EXTRACTION, and ROTATION.*

Example
```
FACTOR VARS=V1 TO V12
  /MISS=MEANS
  /PRINT=DEF AIC KMO REPR
  /EXTRACT=ULS
  /ROTATE=VARIMAX.
```

• This example specifies a single analysis block that includes all variables between and including V1 and V12 in the active system file.

• Variable means are substituted for missing values.

• In addition to the default display, the display includes the anti-image correlation and covariance matrices, the Kaiser-Meyer-Olkin measure of sampling adequacy, and the reproduced residual and correlation matrix.

• Factors are extracted using unweighted least squares.

• The factor pattern matrix is rotated using the varimax rotation.

PLOT Subcommand

Use PLOT to request scree plots or plots of variables in rotated factor space.

• If PLOT is omitted, no plots are produced.

• If PLOT is used without specifications, it is ignored.

• PLOT is in effect only for analyses in the analysis block where it is specified. The default (no plots) is reinstated when the next ANALYSIS subcommand is encountered.

• PLOT can be placed anywhere within an analysis block. If more than one PLOT subcommand is specified, the last one encountered is in effect.

The following keywords may be specified on PLOT:

| **EIGEN** | *Display the scree plot* (Cattell, 1966). The eigenvalues from each extraction are plotted in descending order. |
| **ROTATION(n1 n2) (n3 n4)...** | *Plot the variables in factor space for each rotation.* Specify a pair of factor numbers in parentheses for each plot desired. Always enter the ROTATION subcommand explicitly when you enter this keyword on the PLOT subcommand. |

DIAGONAL Subcommand

DIAGONAL specifies values for the diagonal in conjunction with principal axis factoring.

• Only one DIAGONAL subcommand can be specified in each analysis block.

• DIAGONAL is in effect for all PAF extractions within the analysis block.

• DIAGONAL is ignored with extraction methods other than PAF.

• If DIAGONAL is omitted or included without specifications, FACTOR uses the default method for specifying the diagonal.

• Default communality estimates for PAF (and for other methods, except principal components) are squared multiple correlations. If these cannot be computed, the maximum absolute correlation between the variable and any other variable in the analysis is used.

The following may be specified on DIAGONAL:

valuelist *Diagonal values.* The number of values supplied must equal the number of variables in the analysis block. Use the notation n* before a value to indicate the value is repeated *n* times.

DEFAULT *Initial communality estimates.*

Example
```
FACTOR VARIABLES=V1 TO V12
  /DIAGONAL=.56 .55 .74 2*.56 .70 3*.65 .76 .64 .63
  /EXTRACTION=PAF
  /ROTATION=VARIMAX.
```

• A single analysis block includes all variables between and including V1 and V12 in the active system file.
• DIAGONAL specifies 12 values to use as initial estimates of communalities in principal axis factoring.
• The factor pattern matrix is rotated using varimax rotation.

CRITERIA Subcommand

Use CRITERIA to control extraction and rotation criteria.

• CRITERIA can be specified before any implicit or explicit request for an extraction or rotation.
• Only defaults specifically altered are changed.
• Any criterion that is altered remains in effect for *all* subsequent analysis blocks until it is explicitly overridden. CRITERIA subcommands thus have cumulative effects.

The keywords listed below may be specified on CRITERIA.

• The FACTORS, MINEIGEN, and ECONVERGE keywords apply to extractions.
• The RCONVERGE, KAISER, NOKAISER, and DELTA keywords apply to rotations.
• ITERATE applies to both extrations and rotations.

FACTORS(nf) *Number of factors extracted.* The default is the number of eigenvalues greater than MINEIGEN.

MINEIGEN(eg) *Minimum eigenvalue used to control the number of factors extracted.* The default is 1.

ECONVERGE(e1) *Convergence criterion for extraction.* The default is 0.001.

ITERATE(ni) *Number of iterations for the solutions in the extraction or rotation phases.* The default is 25.

RCONVERGE(e2) *Convergence criterion for rotation.* The default is 0.0001.

KAISER *Kaiser normalization in the rotation phase.* This is the default. The alternative is NOKAISER.

NOKAISER *No Kaiser normalization.*

DELTA(d) *Delta for direct oblimin rotation.* DELTA affects the ROTATION subcommand only when OBLIMIN rotation is requested. The default is 0.

DEFAULT *Reestablish default values for all criteria.*

Example
```
FACTOR VARIABLES=V1 TO V12
  /CRITERIA=FACTORS(6)
  /EXTRACTION=PC
  /ROTATION=NOROTATE
  /CRITERIA=DEFAULT
  /EXTRACTION=ML
  /ROTATION=VARIMAX
  /PLOT=ROTATION(1 2) (1 3).
```

- This example initiates a single analysis block that analyzes all variables between and including V1 and V12 in the active system file.
- Six factors are extracted in the first extraction. The extraction uses the default principal components method, and the factor pattern matrix is not rotated.
- The default criteria are reinstated for the second extraction, which uses the maximum likelihood method. The second factor pattern matrix is rotated using the varimax rotation.
- The PLOT subcommand requests plots of the variables in the factor space defined by the first and second factors and of variables in the factor space defined by the first and third factors. The PLOT subcommand applies to both extractions, since there is only a single ANALYSIS block.

EXTRACTION Subcommand

Use EXTRACTION to specify the factor extraction technique to be used.

- Multiple EXTRACTION subcommands can be specified within an analysis block.
- If EXTRACTION is not specified or is included without specifications, the default principal components extraction is used.
- If you specify criteria for EXTRACTION, the CRITERIA subcommand must precede the EXTRACTION subcommand.
- When you specify EXTRACTION, you should always explicitly specify a rotation method (or ROTATION=NOROTATE).

The following extraction techniques may be specified on EXTRACTION:

PC   *Principal components analysis* (Harman, 1967). This is the default. PC can also be requested with keyword PA1 or DEFAULT.

PAF   *Principal axis factoring.* PAF can also be requested with keyword PA2.

ALPHA   *Alpha factoring* (Kaiser, 1963).

IMAGE   *Image factoring* (Kaiser & Caffry, 1965).

ULS   *Unweighted least squares* (Harman & Jones, 1966).

GLS   *Generalized least squares.*

ML   *Maximum likelihood* (Jöreskog & Lawley, 1968).

Example
```
FACTOR VARIABLES=V1 TO V12
  /EXTRACTION=ULS
  /ROTATE=NOROTATE
  /ANALYSIS=V1 TO V6
  /EXTRACTION=ULS
  /ROTATE=NOROTATE
  /EXTRACTION=ML
  /ROTATE=NOROTATE.
```

- This example specifies two analysis blocks.
- In the first analysis block, variables V1 through V12 are analyzed using unweighted least-squares extraction. The factor pattern matrix is not rotated.
- In the second analysis block, variables V1 through V6 are analyzed first with an unweighted least-squares extraction and then with a maximum likelihood extraction. No rotation is performed for either extraction.

ROTATION Subcommand

ROTATION specifies the factor rotation method. It can also be used to suppress the rotation phase entirely.

- You can specify multiple ROTATION subcommands after each extraction.
- Rotations are performed on the matrix resulting from the previous extraction.
- If you omit both the EXTRACTION and ROTATION subcommands, you implicitly initiate a rotation phase with a varimax rotation.
- If you include the ROTATION subcommand without specifications, the default VARIMAX rotation is used.

• If you include an EXTRACTION subcommand but omit the ROTATION subcommand, the rotation phase may be suppressed.

• Keyword NOROTATE on the ROTATION subcommand produces a plot of variables in unrotated factor space if the PLOT subcommand is also included in the analysis block.

The following can be specified on ROTATION:

VARIMAX   *Varimax rotation.* This is the default if EXTRACTION and ROTATION are both omitted or if EXTRACTION is omitted and ROTATION is entered without specifications. Varimax can also be specified with keyword DEFAULT.

EQUAMAX   *Equamax rotation.*

QUARTIMAX   *Quartimax rotation.*

OBLIMIN   *Direct oblimin rotation.* This is a non-orthogonal rotation; thus, a factor correlation matrix will also be displayed. For this method, specify DELTA on the CRITERIA subcommand.

NOROTATE   *No rotation.*

Example

```
FACTOR VARIABLES=V1 TO V12
  /EXTRACTION=ULS
  /ROTATION
  /ROTATION=OBLIMIN.
```

• The first ROTATION subcommand specifies the default varimax rotation.

• The second ROTATION subcommand specifies an oblimin rotation based on the same extraction of factors.

SAVE Subcommand

SAVE allows you to save factor scores from any rotated or unrotated extraction as new variables on the active system file. You can use any of three methods for computing the factor scores.

• SAVE must follow the ROTATE subcommand specifying the rotation for which factor scores are to be saved. If no ROTATE subcommand precedes SAVE, a VARIMAX rotation is used and factor scores are saved for varimax rotated factors.

• If you are replacing the active system file with matrix materials, you cannot use the SAVE subcommand.

• Specifications for SAVE consist of a keyword specifying a method for computing the scores and, in parentheses, the number of scores to save and a rootname with which to form variable names.

• You can specify SAVE more than once in a rotation block. Thus, you can calculate factor scores using different methods for a single rotation.

• Each specification applies to the previous rotation.

• The new variables are added to the end of the active system file.

Keywords to specify the method of computing factor scores are:

REG   *The regression method.*

BART   *The Bartlett method.*

AR   *The Anderson-Rubin method.*

DEFAULT   *The default is the regression method.*

After one of the above keywords, specify in parentheses the number of scores to save and a rootname to use in naming the variables.

• You can specify either an integer or the keyword ALL.

• The maximum number of scores you can specify is the number of factors retained in the solution.

• SPSS forms variable names by appending sequential numbers to the rootname you specify.

- The rootname must begin with a letter and otherwise conform to the rules for SPSS variable names.
- The rootname must be no longer than seven characters. If ten or more scores are being saved, the rootname must be short enough that the variable names formed will not exceed eight characters.
- The new names formed must be unique within the active file.
- FACTOR automatically generates variable labels for the new variables.

Example
```
FACTOR VARIABLES=V1 TO V12
  /CRITERIA FACTORS(4)
  /ROTATION
  /SAVE REG (4,PCOMP)
  /CRITERIA DEFAULT
  /EXTRACTION PAF
  /ROTATION
  /SAVE DEF (ALL,FACT).
```

- Since there is no EXTRACTION subcommand before the first ROTATION, the first extraction will be the default principal components.
- The first CRITERIA subcommand specifies that four principal components should be extracted.
- The first ROTATION subcommand requests the default varimax rotation for the principal components.
- The first SAVE subcommand requests that scores be calculated by the regression method. Four scores will be added to the file: PCOMP1, PCOMP2, PCOMP3, and PCOMP4.
- The next CRITERIA subcommand restores default criteria. Here it implies that subsequent extractions should extract all factors with eigenvalues greater than 1.
- The second EXTRACTION subcommand specifies principal axis factoring.
- The second ROTATION subcommand requests varimax rotation for PAF factors, so the varimax-rotated factor scores are saved. If this subcommand had been omitted, the rotation phase would have been skipped, and scores for unrotated factors would then be added to the file.
- The second SAVE subcommand requests that scores be calculated by the default method (which is the regression method, as before). The number of scores added to the file is the number extracted, and their names are FACT1, FACT2, and so on.

MATRIX Subcommand

MATRIX reads and writes SPSS matrix system files. It writes matrix materials in either the form of a correlation matrix or a factor loading matrix, whichever you specify. It reads matrix materials written either by a previous FACTOR procedure, or by a procedure that writes matrices with Pearson correlation coefficients (see the table of matrix types in Universals: Defining Matrices).

- MATRIX must always appear before the analysis block. If you use both MATRIX keywords (IN and OUT), you can specify them in either order.
- As part of the specification on both IN and OUT, you must indicate the matrix type. The types are COR for correlation matrix, and FAC for factor loading matrix. Indicate the matrix type within parentheses immediately before you identify the matrix file.
- FACTOR generates the matrix from the first analysis block and writes one matrix per split file. You cannot write a matrix from subsequent analysis blocks on the same FACTOR subcommand.
- Documents from the original file will not be included in the matrix file and will not be present if the matrix file becomes the active file.
- FACTOR cannot read split file matrices. In addition, only one MATRIX IN is allowed per FACTOR command. When FACTOR reads matrix materials, it skips vectors that represent mean, standard deviation, and N values.
- MATRIX=IN cannot be used in place of GET or DATA LIST to begin a new SPSS command file. MATRIX is a subcommand on FACTOR and FACTOR

cannot run before an active file is defined. To begin a new command file and immediately read a matrix, first GET the matrix file, then specify IN(COR=*) or IN(FAC=*) on MATRIX.

- The VARIABLES subcommand should not be used with matrix input. If it is used, it must come after the MATRIX subcommand, and it is ignored.

- For correlation matrix input, the ANALYSIS subcommand may specify a subset of the variables in the matrix. For factor matrix input, MATRIX IN reads all the variables in the matrix; it cannot read a subset. For either type of matrix input, the ANALYSIS subcommand defaults to the entire set of variables and may be omitted.

OUT *Write a matrix system file.* Specify the matrix type and the matrix file; enclose the specification in parentheses. For the matrix type, specify COR for a correlation matrix, or FAC for a factor loading matrix. For the matrix system file, specify a file if you want to retain the current active file but store the matrix materials on disk; the matrix system file can be retrieved at any time. Specify an asterisk if you want the matrix materials to replace the active file; the matrix system file is available for analysis but is not stored on disk unless you use SAVE or XSAVE.

IN *Read a matrix system file.* Specify the matrix type and the matrix file; enclose the specification in parentheses. For the matrix type, specify COR for a correlation matrix, or FAC for a factor loading matrix. For the matrix system file, specify a file if the matrix materials *are not* on the current active file. Specify an asterisk if the matrix materials *are* on the current active file.

Format of the Matrix System File

- For correlation matrices, the matrix system file has two special variables created by SPSS: ROWTYPE_ and VARNAME_. Variable ROWTYPE_ is a short string variable with the value CORR (for Pearson correlation coefficient) for each matrix row. The next variable, VARNAME_, is a short string variable whose values are the names of the variables used to form the correlation matrix.

- For factor loading matrices, SPSS generates two special matrix variables named ROWTYPE_ and FACTOR_. The value for ROWTYPE_ is always FACTOR. The values for FACTOR_ are the ordinal numbers of the factors.

- Following the special variables created by SPSS are the variables used to form the matrix.

Split Files and Variable Order

- FACTOR can read and write split-file matrices.

- When split-file processing is in effect, the first variables in the matrix system file will be the split variables, followed by ROWTYPE_, VARNAME_ (or FACTOR_), then the variables used to form the matrix.

- A full set of matrix materials is written for each split-file group defined by the split variable(s).

- A split variable cannot have the same variable name as any other variable written to the matrix system file.

- If a split file is in effect when a matrix is written, the same split file must be in effect when that matrix is read by any other procedure. (As mentioned above, FACTOR cannot read split-file matrices.)

Additional Statistics

- FACTOR writes only CORR values for correlation matrix materials, and FACTOR values for factor loading matrix materials. It neither reads nor writes additional statistics with its matrix materials. (When FACTOR reads matrix materials, it skips vectors that represent mean, standard deviation, and N values.)

Example

```
GET FILE=GSS80 /KEEP ABDEFECT TO ABSINGLE.
FACTOR VARIABLES=ABDEFECT TO ABSINGLE
    /MATRIX OUT(COR=CORMTX).
```

- FACTOR reads raw data from the file GSS80 and writes a factor correlation matrix to file CORMTX.
- The active system file is still file GSS80. Subsequent commands are executed on file GSS80.

Example
```
GET FILE=GSS80 /KEEP ABDEFECT TO ABSINGLE.
FACTOR VARIABLES=ABDEFECT TO ABSINGLE
  /MATRIX OUT(COR=*).
LIST
```

- FACTOR writes the same matrix as in the example above.
- The active system file is replaced with the correlation matrix. The LIST command is executed on the matrix file, not on file GSS80.

Example
```
GET FILE=GSS80 /KEEP ABDEFECT TO ABSINGLE.
FACTOR VARIABLES=ABDEFECT TO ABSINGLE
  /MATRIX OUT(FAC=*).
```

- FACTOR generates a factor-loading matrix, which replaces the active system file.

Example
```
GET FILE=COUNTRY /KEEP SAVINGS POP15 POP75 INCOME GROWTH.
REGRESSION MATRIX OUT(*)
  /VARS=SAVINGS TO GROWTH
  /MISS=PAIRWISE
  /DEP=SAVINGS /ENTER.
FACTOR MATRIX IN(COR=*) /MISSING=PAIRWISE.
```

- The GET command defines the data to SPSS and selects the variables needed for the analysis.
- The REGRESSION command computes correlations among five variables with pairwise deletion. The MATRIX=OUT specification writes a matrix system file and replaces the active system file with the matrix system file.
- The MATRIX IN(COR=*) specification on FACTOR reads the matrix materials REGRESSION has written to the active file. An asterisk is specified because the matrix materials are on the active file. Notice that FACTOR is using pairwise deletion, since that is how the matrix it read was built.
- When FACTOR reads REGRESSION's matrix materials, it ignores the records containing the means, standard deviations, and N's.

Example
```
GET FILE=COUNTRY /KEEP SAVINGS POP15 POP75 INCOME GROWTH.
REGRESSION
  /VARS=SAVINGS TO GROWTH
  /MISS=PAIRWISE
  /DEP=SAVINGS /ENTER.
FACTOR MATRIX IN(COR=CORMTX).
```

- This example assumes you want to perform a regression analysis on file COUNTRY and then use FACTOR to read a different file. The file you want to read is an existing matrix system file.
- MATRIX=IN specifies a file because the current active file is COUNTRY. MATRIX=IN must therefore specify the file from which the matrix materials will be read.
- CORMTX does not replace COUNTRY as the active system file.

Example
```
GET FILE=CORMTX.
FACTOR MATRIX IN(COR=*).
```

- This example assumes you are starting a new session and want to read an existing matrix system file. GET retrieves the matrix system file CORMTX.
- MATRIX=IN specifies an asterisk because the current active system file is the matrix system file CORMTX. MATRIX=IN must therefore specify the active file as the file from which the matrix materials will be read.
- If the GET command is omitted, SPSS issues an error message.
- If MATRIX=IN(CORMTX) is specified, SPSS issues an error message.

Annotated Example For a complete example with output, see Examples following the Command Reference.

References Cattell, R. B. 1966. The meaning and strategic use of factor analysis. In *Handbook of multivariate experimental psychology,* ed. R. B. Cattell. Chicago: Rand McNally.

Harman, H. H. 1967. *Modern factor analysis.* Chicago: University of Chicago Press.

Harman, H. H., and W. H. Jones. 1966. Factor analysis by minimizing residuals (Minres). *Psychometrika* 31: 351-368.

Jöreskog, K. G., and D. N. Lawley. 1968. New methods in maximum likelihood factor analysis. *British Journal of Mathematical and Statistical Psychology* 21: 85-96.

Kaiser, H. F. 1970. A second-generation Little Jiffy. *Psychometrika* 35: 401-415.

Kaiser, H. F. 1963. Image analysis. In *Problems in measuring change,* ed. C. W. Harris. Madison: University of Wisconsin Press.

Kaiser, H. F., and J. Caffry. 1965. Alpha factor analysis. *Psychometrika* 30: 1-14.

FILE HANDLE

```
FILE HANDLE handle / file specifications
```

Specifications differ by implementation of SPSS.

Overview

FILE HANDLE assigns a unique *file handle* to a file, and supplies operating system specifications for the file.

Syntax Rules

- The first specification is an arbitrary file handle. A file handle cannot exceed eight characters and must begin with an alphabetic character (A–Z) or a $, #, or @. It can also contain numeric digits (0–9). It cannot contain imbedded blanks.
- The remaining specifications depend on the type of computer and operating system on which SPSS is run.
- For data files that contain multipunch (column binary) data, the MODE= MULTIPUNCH subcommand is required.
- FILE HANDLE is required for reading IBM VSAM data sets and multipunch data.
- A defined file handle can be specified on the FILE, OUTFILE, MATRIX, or WRITE subcommands of various procedures.

File Specifications

Details on writing the file specifications for your operating system are documented in the SPSS *Operations Guide* delivered with your system. To see those instructions online, run the INFO command with keyword LOCAL.

Operations

- A file handle is used only during an SPSS session. The handle is never saved as part of an SPSS system file.

Example

```
FILE HANDLE ELE48 / MODE=MULTIPUNCH file specifications.
GET FILE=ELE48.
```

- FILE HANDLE defines ELE48 as the handle for the file.
- The MODE subcommand indicates that the file contains multipunch data.
- The file specifications vary according to the operating system on which SPSS is run. For details, see your SPSS *Operations Guide* or the online documentation accessed with keyword LOCAL on the INFO command.
- The FILE subcommand on GET refers to the handle defined on the FILE HANDLE command.

FILE LABEL

```
FILE LABEL label
```

Overview   FILE LABEL provides a descriptive label for a data file.

Syntax Rules   • The only specification is a label up to 60 characters long.

Operations   • The file label is printed on the first line of each page of output displayed by SPSS.
• If the specified label is longer than 60 characters, SPSS truncates the label to 60 characters without warning.
• If the file is saved, the label is included in the dictionary of the system file.

Example
```
FILE LABEL  HUBBARD INDUSTRIAL CONSULTANTS INC. EMPLOYEE DATA.
SAVE OUTFILE=HUBEMPL
   /RENAME=(AGE JOBCAT=AGE80 JOBCAT82) /MAP.
```
• FILE LABEL assigns a file label to the Hubbard Consultants Inc. employee data.
• The SAVE command saves the file as a system file, renaming two variables and mapping the results to assure that the file HUBEMPL has the desired variable names.

FILE TYPE—END FILE TYPE

For FILE TYPE MIXED

```
FILE TYPE MIXED [FILE=file] RECORD=[varname] col loc
[WILD={NOWARN}]
      {WARN  }
```

For FILE TYPE GROUPED

```
FILE TYPE GROUPED [FILE=file] RECORD=[varname] col loc

 CASE=[varname] col loc [WILD={WARN  }] [DUPLICATE= {WARN  }]
                              {NOWARN}               {NOWARN}


 [MISSING={WARN  }] [ORDERED={YES}]
          {NOWARN}            {NO }
```

For FILE TYPE NESTED

```
FILE TYPE NESTED [FILE=file] RECORD=[varname] col loc

 [CASE=[varname] col loc ] [WILD={NOWARN}] [DUPLICATE={NOWARN}]
                                 {WARN  }             {WARN  }
                                                      {CASE  }


 [MISSING={NOWARN}]
          {WARN  }

 END FILE TYPE
```

Example:

```
FILE TYPE  MIXED RECORD=RECID 1-2.
RECORD TYPE 23.
DATA LIST    /SEX 5 AGE 6-7 DOSAGE 8-10 RESULT 12.
END FILE TYPE.

BEGIN DATA
21   145010 1
22   257200 2
25   235  250   2
35   167             300      3
24   125150 1
23   272075 1
21   149050 2
25   134  035   3
30   138             300      3
32   229             500      3
END DATA.
```

Overview

The FILE TYPE—END FILE TYPE structure defines data for any one of three types of complex files: *mixed files*, which contain several types of records that define different types of cases; hierarchical or *nested files*, which contain several types of records with a defined relationship among the record types; or *grouped files*, which contain several records for each case with some records missing or duplicated. A fourth type of complex file, files with *repeating groups* of information, can be read with the REPEATING DATA command.

FILE TYPE must be followed by at least one RECORD TYPE and one DATA LIST command. One set of RECORD TYPE and DATA LIST commands is used to define each type of record in the data.

END FILE TYPE signals the end of file definition.

Input Programs

SPSS builds the active system file dictionary as it encounters commands that create and define variables. At the same time, SPSS builds an *input program* that will construct the cases and an optional *transformation program* that will modify the cases prior to analysis or display. By the time SPSS encounters a procedure command that tells it to read the data, the active file dictionary is ready, and the programs that construct and modify the cases in the active file are built.

The internal input program is usually built from either a single DATA LIST command or from any of the commands that read or combine SPSS system files (for example GET, ADD FILES, MATCH FILES, UPDATE, etc.). The input program can also be built from the FILE TYPE—END FILE TYPE structure used to define nested, mixed, or grouped files. The third type of input program is specified with the INPUT PROGRAM—END INPUT PROGRAM commands.

Within the FILE TYPE structure, the lowest level record in a NESTED file can be read with a REPEATING DATA command rather than a DATA LIST command. Also, any record in a MIXED file can be read with REPEATING DATA.

Input State

There are four program states in SPSS: the *initial state,* in which there is no active file dictionary; the *input state,* in which cases are created from the input file; the *transformation state,* in which cases are transformed; and the *procedure state,* in which procedures are executed. While these states are generally of no real importance to you, when specifying either FILE TYPE—END FILE TYPE or INPUT PROGRAM—END INPUT PROGRAM you must pay attention to which commands are allowed within the input state, which commands can appear only within the input state, and which are not allowed within the input state. See Appendix A for a discussion of the four program states, command precedence, and a table that describes what happens to each command when it is encountered in each of the four states.

Basic Specification

The basic specification is one of the three file type keywords (MIXED, GROUPED, or NESTED, depending on the structure of the data) and the RECORD subcommand. RECORD names the record identification variable and specifies its column location. FILE TYPE GROUPED also requires the CASE subcommand. CASE names the case identification variable and specifies its column location.

FILE TYPE must be followed by at least one RECORD TYPE and one DATA LIST command. END FILE TYPE is required to signal the end of file definition.

- FILE TYPE specifies the type of file, the location of a record type identifier, and optional information on the handling of duplicate, missing, or invalid record types.
- RECORD TYPE specifies the value(s) of the record type identifier (see RECORD TYPE).
- DATA LIST defines variables for the record type specified on the preceding RECORD TYPE command (see DATA LIST).
- Separate associated RECORD TYPE and DATA LIST commands must be used for each defined record type.

The resulting file, the active system file, is always a rectangular file, regardless of the structure of the original data file.

Specification Order

- FILE TYPE must be the first specification. FILE TYPE subcommands can be named in any order.
- Each RECORD TYPE command must precede its corresponding DATA LIST command.
- END FILE TYPE must be the last specification for file definition.

Syntax Rules

- For MIXED files, each DATA LIST can name variables with the same variable name, since each file type defines a separate case.
- For GROUPED and NESTED files, the variable names on each DATA LIST must be unique since a case is built by combining all record types together onto a single record.
- For MIXED files, if the record types have different variables or if they have the same variables recorded in different locations, separate RECORD TYPE and DATA LIST commands are required for each record type.

- For MIXED files, if the same variable is defined for more than one record type, the format type and length of the variable should be defined the same on all DATA LIST commands. SPSS refers to the *first* DATA LIST command that defines a variable for the print and write formats to be included in the dictionary of the active system file.
- For NESTED files, the order of the RECORD TYPE commands defines the hierarchical structure of the file. The first RECORD TYPE defines the highest level record type, the next RECORD TYPE defines the next highest level record, and so forth. The last RECORD TYPE command defines a case in the active system file.
- For NESTED files, the SPREAD subcommand on RECORD TYPE can be used to spread the values in a record type only to the *first* case built from the set of records related to that record type. All other cases built from the same record are assigned the system-missing value for the variables defined on the record type. See RECORD TYPE for more information.
- String values specified on the RECORD TYPE command must be enclosed in apostrophes or quotation marks.

Operations
- By default for MIXED file types, SPSS skips all records that are not specified on one of the RECORD TYPE commands.
- For MIXED files, if different variables are defined for different record types, the variables are assigned the system-missing value for those record types on which the variable is not defined.
- For NESTED files, the first record in the file should be the type specified on the first RECORD TYPE command—the highest level record of the hierarchy. If the first record in the file is not the highest level type, SPSS skips all records until it encounters a record of the highest level type. If MISSING or DUPLICATE have been specified, these records may produce warning messages but will not be used to build a case on the active system file.

Example
```
TITLE       'A MIXED FILE'.
SUBTITLE    'READING ONLY ONE RECORD TYPE'.

FILE TYPE   MIXED RECORD=RECID 1-2.
RECORD TYPE 23.
DATA LIST    /SEX 5 AGE 6-7 DOSAGE 8-10 RESULT 12.
END FILE TYPE.

BEGIN DATA
21   145010 1
22   257200 2
25   235   250   2
35   167           300     3
24   125150 1
23   272075 1
21   149050 2
25   134   035   3
30   138           300     3
32   229           500     3
END DATA.
```

- FILE TYPE begins the file definition for this mixed file and END FILE TYPE indicates the end of the definitions. FILE TYPE specifies a MIXED file type. Data are specified within the command sequence. The record identification variable RECID is located in columns 1 and 2.
- RECORD TYPE determines that only records with value 23 for variable RECID are copied into the active system file. All other records are skipped. SPSS does not issue a warning when it skips records in mixed files.
- DATA LIST defines variables on only those records with the value 23 for variable RECID.

Example

```
TITLE       'A MIXED FILE'.
SUBTITLE    'READING MULTIPLE RECORD TYPES'.

FILE TYPE   MIXED FILE=TREATMNT RECORD=RECID 1-2.
+ RECORD TYPE 21,22,23,24.
+ DATA LIST    /SEX 5 AGE 6-7 DOSAGE 8-10 RESULT 12.
+ RECORD TYPE 25.
+ DATA LIST    /SEX 5 AGE 6-7 DOSAGE 10-12 RESULT 15.
END FILE TYPE.
```

- The variable DOSAGE is read from columns 8–10 on record types 21, 22, 23, and 24 and from columns 10–12 on record type 25. RESULT is read from column 12 on type 21, 22, 23, and 24 records and from column 15 on type 25 records.

- The active system file contains the values for all variables defined on the DATA LIST commands for record types 21 through 25. All other record types are skipped.

Example

```
TITLE       'A GROUPED FILE'.
SUBTITLE    'STUDENT TEST SCORES'.

FILE TYPE GROUPED RECORD=#TEST 6 CASE=STUDENT 1-4.
RECORD TYPE 1.
DATA LIST   /ENGLISH 8-9 (A).
RECORD TYPE 2.
DATA LIST /READING 8-10.
RECORD TYPE 3.
DATA LIST /MATH 8-10.
END FILE TYPE.

BEGIN DATA
0001 1 B+
0001 2  74
0001 3  83
0002 1 A
0002 2 100
0002 3  71
0003 1 B-
0003 2  88
0003 3  81
0004 1 C
0004 2  94
0004 3  91
END DATA.
```

- FILE TYPE identifies the file as a grouped file. As required for grouped files, all records for a single case are together in the data. The record identification variable #TEST is located in column 6. A scratch variable is specified so it won't be saved in the active system file. The case identification variable STUDENT is located in columns 1–4.

- Because there are three record types, there are three RECORD TYPE commands. For each RECORD TYPE there is a DATA LIST to define variables for records with the corresponding record type.

- END FILE TYPE signals the end of file definition.

- SPSS builds four cases — one for each student. Each case receives a value for each defined record type (the test scores). The values for #TEST are not saved in the active system file. Thus, each case in the active file has four variables: STUDENT, ENGLISH, READING, and MATH.

Example

```
TITLE       'A NESTED FILE'.
SUBTITLE    'ACCIDENT RECORDS'.

FILE TYPE NESTED RECORD=6 CASE=ACCID 1-4.
RECORD TYPE 1.
DATA LIST   /ACC_ID 9-11 WEATHER 12-13 STATE 15-16 (A) DATE 18-24(A).
RECORD TYPE 2.
DATA LIST /STYLE 11 MAKE 13 OLD 14 LICENSE 15-16 (A) INSURNCE 18-21(A).
RECORD TYPE 3.
DATA LIST /PSNGR_NO 11 AGE 13-14 SEX 16 (A) INJURY 18
            SEAT 20-21 (A)  COST 23-24.
END FILE TYPE.

BEGIN DATA
0001 1   322 1 IL 3/13/88   /* Type 1:  accident record
0001 2     1 44MI 134M       /* Type 2:    vehicle record
0001 3     1 34 M 1 FR   3   /* Type 3:        person record
0001 2     2 16IL 322F       /*                vehicle record
0001 3     1 22 F 1 FR 11    /*                    person record
0001 3     2 35 M 1 FR  5    /*                    person record
0001 3     3 59 M 1 BK  7    /*                    person record
0001 2     3 21IN 146M       /*                vehicle record
0001 3     1 46 M 0 FR  0    /*                    person record
END DATA.
```

- FILE TYPE identifies the file as a nested file type. The record identifier, located in column 6, is not assigned a variable name. The default scratch variable name ####RECD is therefore used. The case identification variable ACCID is located in columns 1–4.

- Because there are three record types, there are three RECORD TYPE commands. For each RECORD TYPE there is a DATA LIST to define variables for records with the corresponding record type. The order of the RECORD TYPE commands defines the hierarchical structure of the file.

- END FILE TYPE signals the end of file definition.

- SPSS builds a case for each type 3 record (each "person" in the file). There can only be one type 1 and one type 2 record for each type 3 record: each person can be in only one vehicle, and each vehicle can be in only one accident.

Types of Files

The first specification on FILE TYPE is a file type keyword, which defines the structure of the data file. There are three file type keywords: MIXED, GROUPED, and NESTED. Only one of the three types can be specified on FILE TYPE.

MIXED *Data are in a mixed file.* MIXED defines a file in which each record type defines a case. Some information may be the same for all record types but is recorded in different locations. Other information may be recorded only for specific record types. For example, a data file maintained by a hospital may contain a record for each treatment administered to cancer patients, with different data recorded for each type of treatment. FILE TYPE MIXED builds a file in which each of the record types named on a RECORD TYPE command defines a case. You do not need to define all types of records in the file. In fact, FILE TYPE MIXED is very useful for reading only one type of record because SPSS can decide whether to execute the DATA LIST for a record by simply reading the variable that identifies the record type.

GROUPED   *Data are in a grouped file.* GROUPED defines a file in which cases are defined by grouping together record types with the same identification number. Each case usually has one record of each type. FILE TYPE GROUPED builds a file in which all record types are grouped together for each case identification number. All records for a single case must be together in the file. By default, SPSS assumes that the records are in the same sequence within each case.

NESTED   *Data are in a nested file.* NESTED defines a file in which the record types are related to each other hierarchically. Usually, the last record type defined—the lowest level of the hierarchy—defines a case. For example, in a file containing household records and records for each person living in the household, each person record defines a case. However, information from previous record types may be *spread* to each case. For example, a variable from the household record, such as location (CITY), can be included on the person record. The value for CITY for a particular household can be spread to the records for each person in the household. FILE TYPE NESTED defines a file in which the record types are related to each other hierarchically. The record types are grouped together by a case identification number that identifies the highest level—the first record type—of the hierarchy. The last record type described defines a case in the active system file.

Defaults for each File Type   The specifications on the FILE TYPE and RECORD TYPE commands differ for each file type. Table 1 shows the default values for each FILE TYPE keyword for the three types of files. The notation "Not App." indicates that the subcommand is not applicable to that type of file, hence is unavailable.

• RECORD is always required.

• FILE is required unless data are inline (included within the command sequence).

• CASE is required for GROUPED files.

• For GROUPED files, CASE, DUPLICATE, and MISSING can be specified on any of the associated RECORD TYPE commands. However, DUPLICATE= CASE is invalid.

• For NESTED files, CASE and MISSING can be specified on any of the associated RECORD TYPE commands.

• If any of the subcommands CASE, DUPLICATE, or MISSING are specified on a RECORD TYPE command, the default or specification on the FILE TYPE command is overridden only for the record types listed on that RECORD TYPE command. The default or FILE TYPE specification applies to all other record types.

Table 1 Summary of defaults for FILE TYPE subcommands

Subcommand	MIXED	GROUPED	NESTED
FILE	Conditional	Conditional	Conditional
RECORD	Required	Required	Required
CASE	Not App.	Required	Optional
WILD	NOWARN	WARN	NOWARN
DUPLICATE	Not App.	WARN	NOWARN
MISSING	Not App.	WARN	NOWARN
ORDERED	Not App.	YES	Not App.

FILE Subcommand   FILE specifies the data file whenever the data are not inline (included within the command sequence).

Example   `FILE TYPE  MIXED FILE=TREATMNT RECORD=RECID 1-2.`

• Data are in file TREATMNT. File TREATMNT is a mixed file. The record identification variable RECID is located in columns 1 and 2 of each record.

RECORD Subcommand   RECORD defines the record-identification variable and its column location(s) in the data.

• Specifications for the column location(s) of the record identifier are required. The variable name of the identifier is optional.

• If you do not want to save the record type variable, you can assign a scratch variable name by using the # character as the first character of the variable name. If a variable name is not specified on RECORD, the record identifier is defined as the scratch variable ####RECD.

• The value of the identifier for each record type must be unique and must be in the same location on all records. However, records do not have to be sorted according to type.

• A format can be specified for the record identifier, but the format must include column locations. For example, RECORD=V1 1-2(N) is valid, as is RECORD =V1 1-2(F,1), where (F,1) means F format with 1 decimal digit. However, RECORD=V1 (F2.0) is invalid because (F2.0) is a FORTRAN-like format that cannot be used with column locations.

• The letter (A) in parentheses after the column location identifies the record-type variable as a string variable.

Example   `FILE TYPE  MIXED FILE=TREATMNT RECORD=RECID 1-2.`

• The record identifier is variable RECID, located in columns 1 and 2 of the hospital treatment data file.

CASE Subcommand   CASE defines the case-identification variable and its column location(s) in the data. CASE is required for FILE TYPE GROUPED and optional for FILE TYPE NESTED. CASE cannot be used with FILE TYPE MIXED.

• For GROUPED files, CASE is required. Each different value on the case identification variable defines a case in the active system file.

• For NESTED files, CASE is optional and identifies the highest level record of the hierarchy. SPSS issues a warning message for each record with a case identification number not equal to the case identification number on the last highest-level record. However, the record with the invalid case number is used in building the case.

• Specifications for the column location(s) of the case identifier are required. The variable name of the identifier is optional.

• If you do not want to save the case identification variable, you can assign a scratch variable name by using the # character as the first character of the variable name. If a variable name is not specified on CASE, the case identifier is defined as the scratch variable ####CASE.

• A format can be specified for the case identifier, but the format must include column locations. For example, CASE=V1 1-2(N) is valid, as is CASE=V1 1-2(F,1), where (F,1) means F format with 1 decimal digit. However, CASE=V1 (F2.0) is invalid.

• The letter (A) in parentheses after the column location identifies the case-identification variable as a string variable.

• If the case identification number is not in the same columns on all record types, use the CASE subcommand on the RECORD TYPE commands, as well as on the FILE TYPE command (see RECORD TYPE).

Example
```
TITLE      'A GROUPED FILE'.
SUBTITLE   'STUDENT TEST SCORES'.

FILE TYPE GROUPED RECORD=#TEST 6 CASE=STUDENT 1-4.
RECORD TYPE 1.
DATA LIST   /ENGLISH 8-9 (A).
RECORD TYPE 2.
DATA LIST /READING 8-10.
RECORD TYPE 3.
DATA LIST /MATH 8-10.
END FILE TYPE.

BEGIN DATA
0001 1 B+
0001 2  74
0001 3  83
0002 1 A
0002 2 100
0002 3  71
0003 1 B-
0003 2  88
0003 3  81
0004 1 C
0004 2  94
0004 3  91
END DATA.
```

- CASE is required for GROUPED files. CASE specifies variable STUDENT, located in columns 1–4, as the case identification variable.

- The data contain four different values for STUDENT. The resulting file therefore has four cases: one for each value of STUDENT. In a GROUPED file, each different value on the case identification variable defines a case in the active system file.

Example
```
TITLE      'A NESTED FILE'.
SUBTITLE   'ACCIDENT RECORDS'.

FILE TYPE NESTED RECORD=6 CASE=ACCID 1-4.
RECORD TYPE 1.
DATA LIST   /ACC_ID 9-11 WEATHER 12-13 STATE 15-16 (A) DATE 18-24(A).
RECORD TYPE 2.
DATA LIST /STYLE 11 MAKE 13 OLD 14 LICENSE 15-16 (A) INSURNCE 18-21(A).
RECORD TYPE 3.
DATA LIST /PSNGR_NO 11 AGE 13-14 SEX 16 (A) INJURY 18
              SEAT 20-21 (A) COST 23-24.
END FILE TYPE.

BEGIN DATA
0001 1   322 1 IL 3/13/88   /* Type 1:  accident record
0001 2     1 44MI 134M      /* Type 2:  vehicle record
0001 3     1 34 M 1 FR   3  /* Type 3:     person record
0001 2     2 16IL 322F      /*            vehicle record
0001 3     1 22 F 1 FR 11   /*               person record
0001 3     2 35 M 1 FR   5  /*               person record
0001 3     3 59 M 1 BK   7  /*               person record
0001 2     3 21IN 146M      /*            vehicle record
0001 3     1 46 M 0 FR   0  /*               person record
END DATA.
```

- CASE specifies variable ACCID, located in columns 1–4, as the case identification variable. ACCID identifies the highest level of the hierarchy: the level for the accident records.

- As each case is built, the value of the variable ACCID is checked against the value of ACCID on the last highest level record (record type 1). If the values do not match, a warning message is issued. However, the record is used in building the case.

- The data in the example contain only one value for ACCID, which is spread across all cases. In a NESTED file, the lowest level record type determines the number of cases in the active system file. In this example, the active file has five cases because there are five "person" records.

Example

```
TITLE     'A GROUPED FILE'.
SUBTITLE  'SPECIFYING CASE ON THE RECORD TYPE COMMAND'.

FILE TYPE GROUPED FILE=HUBDATA RECORD=#RECID 80 CASE=ID 1-5.
RECORD TYPE 1.
DATA LIST    /MOHIRED YRHIRED 12-15 DEPT79 TO DEPT82 SEX 16-20.
RECORD TYPE 2.
DATA LIST    /SALARY79 TO SALARY82 6-25
              HOURLY81 HOURLY82 40-53(2) PROMO81 72
              AGE 54-55 RAISE82 66-70.
RECORD TYPE 3  CASE=75-79.
DATA LIST    /JOBCAT 6 NAME 25-48 (A).
END FILE TYPE.
```

- CASE on FILE TYPE indicates the case identification number is located in columns 1–5. Columns 1–5 apply only to record types 1 and 2 because the CASE subcommand on the third RECORD TYPE command overrides the case setting for type 3 records. For type 3 records the case identification number is located in columns 75–79.

- The format type of the case identification variable must be the same on all records. Thus, if the case identification variable is defined as a string on the FILE TYPE command, it cannot be defined as a numeric variable on the RECORD TYPE command, and vice versa.

WILD Subcommand

WILD determines whether SPSS issues a warning when it encounters undefined record types in the data file. Regardless of whether SPSS issues the warning, undefined records are not included in the active system file.

- The only specification is a single keyword. NOWARN is the default for MIXED and NESTED files. WARN is the default for GROUPED files.

- WARN cannot be specified if keyword OTHER is specified on the last RECORD TYPE command to indicate all other record types (see RECORD TYPE). SKIP may be used on the RECORD TYPE command to skip specific record types.

NOWARN *Do not issue a warning message.* SPSS simply skips all record types not mentioned on the RECORD TYPE commands and does not display warning messages. This is the default for MIXED and NESTED file types.

WARN *Issue a warning message.* SPSS displays a warning message and the first 80 characters of the record for each record type that is not mentioned on a RECORD TYPE command. This is the default for GROUPED file types.

Example

```
FILE TYPE  MIXED FILE=TREATMNT RECORD=RECID 1-2 WILD=WARN.
```

- WARN is specified on the WILD subcommand. SPSS displays a warning message and the first 80 characters of the record for each record type that is not mentioned on a RECORD TYPE command.

DUPLICATE Subcommand

DUPLICATE determines how SPSS responds when it encounters more than one record of each type for a single case. DUPLICATE is optional for GROUPED and NESTED files. DUPLICATE cannot be used with MIXED files.

- The only specification is a single keyword. NOWARN is the default for NESTED files. WARN is the default for GROUPED files.

- Keyword CASE is available only for NESTED files.

NOWARN *Do not issue a warning message.* SPSS simply skips all duplicate record types when building each case and does not display warning messages. Only the *last* record from a set of duplicates is included in the active system file. This is the default for NESTED files.

WARN *Issue a warning message.* SPSS displays a warning message and the first 80 characters of the last record of the duplicate set of record types. The duplicate record(s) are skipped, and only the *last* record from a set of duplicates is included in the active system file. This is the default for GROUPED files.

CASE   *Build a case in the active system file for the duplicate record(s).* SPSS builds *one* case in the active file for each duplicate record, spreading information from any higher-level records and assigning system-missing values to the variables defined on the lower-level records. This option is available only for NESTED files.

Example

```
TITLE      'A NESTED FILE OF ACCIDENT RECORDS'.
SUBTITLE   'ISSUE A WARNING FOR DUPLICATE RECORD TYPES'.

FILE TYPE NESTED RECORD=6 CASE=ACCID 1-4 DUPLICATE=WARN'.
RECORD TYPE 1.
DATA LIST   /ACC_ID 9-11 WEATHER 12-13 STATE 15-16 (A)
              DATE 18-24 (A).
RECORD TYPE 2.
DATA LIST /STYLE 11 MAKE 13 OLD 14 LICENSE 15-16 (A)
              INSURNCE 18-21 (A).
RECORD TYPE 3.
DATA LIST /PSNGR_NO 11 AGE 13-14 SEX 16 (A) INJURY 18
              SEAT 20-21 (A)  COST 23-24.
END FILE TYPE.

BEGIN DATA
0001 1  322 1 IL 3/13/88   /*              accident record
0001 2      1 44MI 134M     /*              vehicle record
0001 3      1 34 M 1 FR  3  /*               person record
0001 2      1 31IL 134M     /* duplicate vehicle record
0001 2      2 16IL 322F     /*              vehicle record
0001 3      1 22 F 1 FR 11  /*               person record
0001 3      2 35 M 1 FR  5  /*               person record
0001 3      3 59 M 1 BK  7  /*               person record
0001 2      3 21IN 146M     /*              vehicle record
0001 3      1 46 M 0 FR  0  /*               person record
END DATA.
```

• Data show two vehicle records (type 2) above three person records (type 3) in the hierarchy of record types. This implies that an empty (for example, parked) vehicle was involved, or that each of the three persons was in two vehicles, which is impossible.

• Assume no empty vehicles were involved in this accident. That means only one type 2 record is possible for the type 3 records.

• DUPLICATE specifies keyword WARN. SPSS displays a warning message and the first 80 characters of the second of the duplicate set of type 2 records. The duplicate record is skipped, and only the second of the type 2 records from the duplicate set is included in the active system file.

Example

```
TITLE      'A NESTED FILE OF ACCIDENT RECORDS'.
SUBTITLE   'CREATE A CASE FOR EACH DUPLICATE RECORD'.

FILE TYPE NESTED RECORD=6 CASE=ACCID 1-4 DUPLICATE=CASE.
RECORD TYPE 1.
DATA LIST   /ACC_ID 9-11 WEATHER 12-13 STATE 15-16 (A)
              DATE 18-24 (A).
RECORD TYPE 2.
DATA LIST /STYLE 11 MAKE 13 OLD 14 LICENSE 15-16 (A)
              INSURNCE 18-21 (A).
RECORD TYPE 3.
DATA LIST /PSNGR_NO 11 AGE 13-14 SEX 16 (A) INJURY 18
              SEAT 20-21 (A) COST 23-24.

END FILE TYPE.

BEGIN DATA
0001 1  322 1 IL 3/13/88   /*              accident record
0001 2      1 44MI 134M     /*              vehicle record
0001 3      1 34 M 1 FR  3  /*               person record
0001 2      1 31IL 134M     /* duplicate vehicle record
0001 2      2 16IL 322F     /*              vehicle record
0001 3      1 22 F 1 FR 11  /*               person record
0001 3      2 35 M 1 FR  5  /*               person record
0001 3      3 59 M 1 BK  7  /*               person record
0001 2      3 21IN 146M     /*              vehicle record
0001 3      1 46 M 0 FR  0  /*               person record
END DATA.
```

- As in the example above, data show two vehicle records (type 2) above three person records (type 3) in the hierarchy of record types. This implies that an empty (for example, parked) vehicle was involved, or that each of the three persons was in two vehicles, which is impossible.
- Assume a parked vehicle was involved in this accident.
- DUPLICATE specifies keyword CASE. SPSS builds one case in the active system file for the duplicate type 2 record, spreading information to that case from the type 1 record and assigning system-missing values to the variables defined for type 3 records. The second of the type 2 records from the duplicate set is used to build the three cases for the associated type 3 records.

MISSING Subcommand

MISSING determines whether SPSS issues a warning when it encounters a missing record type for a case. Regardless of whether SPSS issues the warning, it builds the case in the active file with system-missing values for the variables defined on the missing record. MISSING is optional for GROUPED and NESTED files. MISSING cannot be used with MIXED files.

- The only specification is a single keyword. NOWARN is the default for NESTED files. WARN is the default for GROUPED files.
- For GROUPED files, SPSS checks whether there is a record for each case identification number. For NESTED files, SPSS verifies that each defined case includes one record of each type.

NOWARN *Do not issue a warning message when a missing record type is encountered for a case.* This is the default for NESTED files.

WARN *Issue a warning message when a missing record type is encountered for a case.* This is the default for GROUPED files.

Example
```
TITLE   'A GROUPED FILE WITH MISSING RECORDS'.

FILE TYPE GROUPED RECORD=#TEST 6 CASE=STUDENT 1-4
                  MISSING=NOWARN.
RECORD TYPE 1.
DATA LIST  /ENGLISH 8-9 (A).
RECORD TYPE 2.
DATA LIST /READING 8-10.
RECORD TYPE 3.
DATA LIST /MATH 8-10.
END FILE TYPE.

BEGIN DATA
0001 1 B+
0001 2  74
0002 1 A
0002 2 100
0002 3  71
0003 3  81
0004 1 C
0004 2  94
0004 3  91
END DATA.
```

- The data contain records for three tests administered to four students. However, not all students took all tests. The first student took only the English and Reading tests. The third student took only the Math test.
- One case in the active system file is built for each of the four students. If a student did not take a test, the system-missing value is assigned in the active file to the variable for the missing test. Thus, the first student has missing values for the Math test, and the third student has missing values for the English and Reading tests.
- Keyword NOWARN is specified on MISSING. Therefore, no warning messages are issued for the missing records.

Example

```
TITLE     'A NESTED FILE WITH MISSING RECORDS'.

FILE TYPE NESTED RECORD=6 CASE=ACCID 1-4 MISSING=WARN.
RECORD TYPE 1.
DATA LIST    /ACC_ID 9-11 WEATHER 12-13 STATE 15-16 (A)
              DATE 18-24 (A).
RECORD TYPE 2.
DATA LIST /STYLE 11 MAKE 13 OLD 14 LICENSE 15-16 (A)
           INSURNCE 18-21(A).
RECORD TYPE 3.
DATA LIST /PSNGR_NO 11 AGE 13-14 SEX 16 (A) INJURY 18
           SEAT 20-21 (A) COST 23-24.
END FILE TYPE.

BEGIN DATA
0001 1  322 1 IL 3/13/88    /*        accident record
0001 3    1 34 M 1 FR  3     /*          person record
0001 2    2 16IL 322F        /*        vehicle record
0001 3    1 22 F 1 FR 11     /*          person record
0001 3    2 35 M 1 FR  5     /*          person record
0001 3    3 59 M 1 BK  7     /*          person record
0001 2    3 21IN 146M        /*        vehicle record
0001 3    1 46 M 0 FR  0     /*          person record
END DATA.
```

- The data contain records for one accident. The first record is a type 1 record, the second record is a type 3 record. However, there is no type 2 record, and therefore no vehicle associated with the first person. The person may have been a pedestrian, but it's also possible that the vehicle record is missing.

- One case in the active system file is built for each type 3 (person) record. The first case has missing values for the type 2 (vehicle) record.

- Keyword WARN is specified on MISSING. Therefore, a warning message is issued for the missing record.

ORDERED Subcommand

ORDERED indicates whether the records are in the same order as they are defined on the RECORD TYPE commands. Regardless of the order of the records in the data file, and regardless of the specification on ORDERED, SPSS builds cases in the active system file with the records in the same order as defined on the RECORD TYPE commands.

- ORDERED can only be used for GROUPED files.

- The only specification is a single keyword. The default is YES.

- If YES is in effect but the records are not in the same order as defined on the RECORD TYPE commands, SPSS issues a warning for each record that is out of order. SPSS still builds cases in the active system file with the records in the same order as defined on the RECORD TYPE commands.

YES *Records for each case are in the same order as they are defined on the RECORD TYPE commands.* This is the default.

NO *Records are not in the same order within each case.*

Example
```
TITLE  'A GROUPED FILE'.

FILE TYPE GROUPED RECORD=#TEST 6 CASE=STUDENT 1-4
  MISSING=NOWARN
  ORDERED=NO.
RECORD TYPE 1.
DATA LIST   /ENGLISH 8-9 (A).
RECORD TYPE 2.
DATA LIST /READING 8-10.
RECORD TYPE 3.
DATA LIST /MATH 8-10.
END FILE TYPE.

BEGIN DATA
0001 2  74
0001 1 B+
0002 3  71
0002 2 100
0002 1 A
0003 2  81
0004 2  94
0004 1 C
0004 3  91
END DATA.
```

- The first RECORD TYPE command specifies record type 1, the second RECORD TYPE command specifies record type 2, and the third RECORD TYPE command specifies record type 3. However, records for each case are not always ordered type 1, type 2, and type 3.

- ORDERED=NO is specified so SPSS builds cases without issuing a warning that they are out of order in the data.

- Regardless of whether YES or NO is in effect for ORDERED, SPSS builds the active system file with cases in the same order in which they are specified on the RECORD TYPE commands.

FINISH

```
FINISH
```

Overview	FINISH causes SPSS to stop reading commands.
Basic Specification	• The only specification is the command keyword. FINISH takes no additional specifications.
Command Files	• FINISH is optional in a command file. Its primary use is to mark the end of a session.
	• FINISH causes SPSS to stop reading commands. Anything following FINISH in the command file is ignored. Any commands following FINISH in an IN-CLUDE file are ignored.
	• Placing FINISH within a DO IF structure to end a session conditionally doesn't work: FINISH is not subject to DO IF and will end the session unconditionally.
Prompted Sessions	• FINISH is required in a prompted session to terminate the session.
	• Because FINISH is an SPSS command, it can be used only after the SPSS> prompt, which expects a procedure name. FINISH cannot be used to end a prompted session from a DATA>, CONTINUE>, HELP>, or DEFINE> prompt.
Operations	• FINISH immediately causes SPSS to stop reading commands.
	• The appearance of FINISH on the printback of commands on the display file indicates that the session has been completed.
	• When issued within the SPSS Manager (not available on all systems), FINISH terminates command processing and causes SPSS to query whether you want to continue working. If you answer **yes,** you can continue creating and editing files in both the Input Window and the Output Window; however, you can no longer run commands.

Example

```
TITLE  'A COMMAND FILE'.

DATA LIST FILE=RAWDATA /NAME 1-15(A) V1 TO V15 16-30.
LIST.
FINISH.
REPORT FORMAT=AUTO LIST /VARS=NAME V1 TO V10.
```

• FINISH causes SPSS to stop reading commands after LIST is executed. The REPORT command is not executed.

Example

```
SPSS> TITLE  'A PROMPTED SESSION'.

SPSS> DATA LIST FILE=RAWDATA /NAME 1-15(A) V1 TO V15 16-30.
SPSS> LIST.
SPSS> FINISH.
```

• FINISH terminates the prompted session.

FLIP

```
FLIP [[VARIABLES=] {ALL    }]
                  {varlist}

     [/NEWNAMES=variable]
```

Example:

```
FLIP VARIABLES=WEEK1 TO WEEK52 /NEWNAMES=DEPT.
```

Overview   SPSS requires a file structure in which the variables are the columns and observations (cases) are the rows. If a file is organized such that variables are in rows and observations are in columns, you need to use FLIP to reorganize it. FLIP transposes the rows and columns of the data on the SPSS active system file, so that what was in row 1, column 2 is now in row 2, column 1, and so forth.

Options   **Variable Subsets.** You can transpose specific variables (columns) from the original file. See the VARIABLES subcommand.

Variable Names. You can use the values of one of the variables from the original file as the variable names in the new file. See the NEWNAMES subcommand.

Basic Specification   The basic specification is the command keyword FLIP, which transposes all rows and columns. In addition, FLIP

- Assigns default variable names VAR001 to VARn to the transposed variables in the new file.
- Creates the new variable CASE_LBL, whose values are the variable names that existed before the transposition.
- Displays a list of variable names in the transposed file.

Subcommand Order   • VARIABLES must precede NEWNAMES.

Operations   • FLIP replaces the SPSS active system file with one in which the original rows and columns have been exchanged.

- FLIP discards any previous VARIABLE LABELS, VALUE LABELS, and WEIGHT settings. Values defined as user-missing in the original file are translated to system-missing (.) in the transposed file.
- FLIP obeys any SELECT IF, N, and SAMPLE commands in effect.
- FLIP does not obey the TEMPORARY command. Any transformations are permanent if followed by FLIP.
- String variables in the original file are assigned system-missing values (.) after transposition.
- Numeric variables are assigned a default format of F8.2 after transposition (with the exceptions of CASE_LBL and the variable specified on NEWNAMES).
- The variable CASE_LBL is created and added to the active system file each time FLIP is executed.
- If CASE_LBL already exists as the result of a previous FLIP, its current values are used as the names of variables in the new file (if NEWNAMES is not specified).

Example 1   The following is LIST output for a data file arranged in a typical spreadsheet format, with variables in rows and observations in columns:

```
A            B          C          D

INCOME       22.00      31.00      43.00
PRICE        34.00      29.00      50.00
YEAR       1970.00    1971.00    1972.00
```

The command

```
FLIP.
LIST.
```

transposes all variables on the file. The LIST output for the transposed file is as follows:

```
CASE_LBL    VAR001    VAR002    VAR003

A               .         .         .
B           22.00     34.00    1970.00
C           31.00     29.00    1971.00
D           43.00     50.00    1972.00
```

* The values for the new variable CASE_LBL are the variable names from the original file.
* Case A has system-missing values since variable A had the string values INCOME, PRICE, and YEAR.
* The names of the variables in the new file are VAR001, VAR002, and VAR003.

VARIABLES Subcommand

VARIABLES names one or more variables (columns) to be transposed. The specified variables become observations (rows) in the new active system file.

* The VARIABLES subcommand is optional. If it is not used, all variables are transposed.
* The actual keyword VARIABLES can be omitted.
* If the VARIABLES subcommand is used, variables not named are discarded.

Example 2

Using the original, untransposed file from Example 1, the command

```
FLIP VARIABLES=A TO C.
LIST.
```

transposes only variables A through C. The LIST output for the transposed file is as follows:

```
CASE_LBL    VAR001    VAR002    VAR003

A               .         .         .
B           22.00     34.00    1970.00
C           31.00     29.00    1971.00
```

* Series D is not transposed and is discarded from the active system file.

NEWNAMES Subcommand

NEWNAMES specifies a variable whose values are used as the new variable names.

* The NEWNAMES subcommand is optional. If it is not used, the new variable names are either VAR001 to VARn, or the values of CASE_LBL if it exists.
* Only one variable can be specified on NEWNAMES.
* The variable specified on NEWNAMES does not become an observation (case) on the new active system file, regardless of whether it is specified on the VARIABLES subcommand.
* If the variable specified is numeric, its values become a character string beginning with the letter "V."
* If the variable specified is a long string, only the first eight characters are used.
* Lowercase character values of a string variable are converted to uppercase, and any bad character values, such as blank spaces, are replaced with underscore (_) characters.
* If the variable's values are not unique, a numeric extension n is added to the end of a value after its first occurrence, with n increasing by 1 at each subsequent occurrence.

Example 3   Using the original, untransposed file from Example 1, the command

```
FLIP NEWNAMES=A.
LIST.
```

uses the values for variable A as the names for variables in the new file. The LIST output for the transposed file is as follows:

```
CASE_LBL    INCOME    PRICE      YEAR

B            22.00    34.00    1970.00
C            31.00    29.00    1971.00
D            43.00    50.00    1972.00
```

• Note that variable A does not become an observation in the new file.

The following command transposes this file back to a form resembling its original structure:

```
FLIP.
LIST.
```

The LIST output for the transposed file is as follows:

```
CASE_LBL       B          C          D

INCOME      22.00      31.00      43.00
PRICE       34.00      29.00      50.00
YEAR      1970.00    1971.00    1972.00
```

• Since the NEWNAMES subcommand is not used, the values of CASE_LBL from the previous FLIP (B, C, and D) are used as variable names in the new file.

• The values of for CASE_LBL now become INCOME, PRICE, and YEAR.

FORMATS

```
FORMATS varlist(format) [varlist...]
```

Example:
```
FORMATS SALARY (DOLLAR8) / HOURLY (DOLLAR7.2)/ RAISE BONUS(PCT2).
```

Overview

FORMATS changes variable print and write formats. Print and write formats are *output* formats in SPSS. Print formats control the forn in which values are displayed by a procedure or by the PRINT command; wrile formats control the form in which values are written by the WRITE command.

FORMATS changes a variable's print formats *and* write formats. See the PRINT FORMATS command for changing just the print format. See the WRITE FORMATS command for changing just the write format. See the DATA LIST command for assigning *input* formats during data definition.

Table 1 shows the output formats that can be assigned with FORMATS, PRINT FORMATS, and WRITE FORMATS. For a definition of formats A, F, COMMA, DOT, DOLLAR, and PCT, see Universals: Variable Formats. For a definition of all but the custom currency formats (CCw, CCw.d) from Table 1, see Appendix E. For a definition of the custom currency formats, see SET.

Basic Specification

- The basic specification is a variable list followed by the new format specification in parentheses. All the specified variables receive the new format.

Syntax Rules

- Only one format can be specified in the parentheses.

- To reference consecutive variables in the active system file, use keyword TO in the variable list.

- To assign different formats to different variables, use a slash to separate specifications for each different format.

- Format specifications on FORMATS are *output* formats. When specifying the width for the format type, enough positions must be allowed to include any punctuation characters such as decimal points, commas, dollar signs, or date and time delimiters. (This is different from assigning an *input* format on DATA LIST. SPSS automatically expands input formats to accommodate punctuation characters in the output.)

- A custom currency format (CCw, CCw.d) must first be defined on the SET command before it can be used on FORMATS.

- FORMATS *cannot* be used with string variables, because the declared length of a string variable cannot be changed. To effectively change the length of a string variable, declare a new variable of the desired length with the STRING command, then use COMPUTE to copy values from the existing string into the new string.

- To save the new print and write formats, the active file must be saved as a new system file with the SAVE or XSAVE commands. The new formats are used as dictionary formats in the new system file.

Table 1 shows the formats that can be assigned by FORMATS, PRINT FORMATS, or WRITE FORMATS. The first column of the table lists the FORTRAN-like specification. The column labeled PRINT indicates whether the format can be used to display values. The columns labeled Min w and Max w refer to the minimum and maximum widths allowed for the format type.

Table 1 Output data formats

Format type	PRINT	Min w	Max w	Max d	Result form
Numeric					
Fw, Fw.d	yes	1*	40	16	
COMMAw, COMMAw.d	yes	1*	40	16	
DOTw, DOTw.d	yes	1*	40	16	
DOLLARw, DOLLARw.d	yes	2*	40	16	
CCw, CCw.d	yes	2*	40	16	
PCTw, PCTw.d	yes	1*	40	16	
PIBHEXw	yes	2**	16**		
RBHEXw	yes	4**	16**		
Zw, Zw.d	yes	1	40	16	
IBw, IBw.d	no	1	8	16	
PIBw, PIBw.d	no	1	8	16	
Nw	yes	1	40		
Pw, Pw.d	no	1	16	16	
Ew, Ew.d	yes	6	40		
PKw, PKw.d	no	1	16	16	
RBw	no	2	8		
String					
Aw	yes	1	254		
AHEXw	yes	2**	510		
Date and time					**Result form**
DATEw	yes	9	40		dd-mmm-yy
		11			dd-mmm-yyyy
ADATEw	yes	8	40		mm/dd/yy
		10			mm/dd/yyyy
JDATEw	yes	5	40		yyddd
		7			yyyyddd
QYRw	yes	6	40		q Q yy
		8			q Q yyyy
MOYRw	yes	6	40		mmm yy
		8			mmm yyyy
WKYRw	yes	8	40		ww WK yy
		10			ww WK yyyy
WKDAYw	yes	2+	40		
MONTHw	yes	3+	40		
TIMEw	yes	5++	40		hh:mm
TIMEw.d	yes	10	40	16	hh:mm:ss.s
DTIMEw	yes	8++	40		dd hh:mm
DTIMEw.d	yes	13	40	16	dd hh:mm:ss.s
DATETIMEw	yes	17++	40		dd-mmm-yyyy hh:mm
DATETIMEw.d	yes	22	40	16	dd-mmm-yyyy hh:mm:ss.s

*Add number of decimals plus 1 if number of decimals is more than 0. Total width cannot exceed 40 characters.
**Must be a multiple of 2.
+As the field width is expanded, the output string is expanded until the entire name of the day or month is produced.
++Add 3 to display seconds.

Operations
- Unlike most transformations, which do not take effect until the data are read, FORMATS takes effect as soon as it is encountered in the command sequence. Thus, special attention should be paid to its position among commands. For more information, see Universals: Command Order.

- Variables not specified on FORMATS retain their current print and write formats in the active file. To see the current formats, use the DISPLAY command.

- The new formats are changed only in the active file and are in effect for the duration of the SPSS session or until changed again with a FORMATS, PRINT FORMATS, or WRITE FORMATS command. Formats in the original system file (if one exists) are not changed.

- When the transformation language is used to create a new numeric variable, the dictionary print and write formats are both F8.2 (or the format specified on the FORMAT subcommand of SET). The FORMATS command can be used to change the new variable's print and write formats.

- Default formats for string variables created using the SPSS transformation language are those specified on the STRING command that declares the variable. FORMATS cannot be used to change the format of a new string variable.

- If a data value exceeds its width specification, SPSS makes an attempt to produce some value nevertheless. It takes out punctuation characters, then it tries scientific notation, and finally, if there is still not enough space, it produces asterisks indicating that a value is present which cannot be displayed in the assigned width.

Example
```
FORMATS SALARY (DOLLAR8) /HOURLY (DOLLAR7.2)
        /RAISE BONUS (PCT2).
```

- The print and write formats for SALARY are changed to DOLLAR format with eight positions including the dollar sign and comma when appropriate. The value 11550 displays as $11,550. An eight-digit number would require a DOLLAR11 format specification: 8 characters for the digits, 2 characters for commas, and 1 character for the dollar sign.

- The print and write formats for HOURLY are changed to DOLLAR format with seven positions including the dollar sign, decimal point, and two decimal places. The number 115 displays as $115.00. If DOLLAR6.2 had been specified for HOURLY, the value 115 would display as $115.0. SPSS truncates the last 0 because the format width of 6 places is not wide enough to display the full value.

- The print and write formats for both RAISE and BONUS are changed to PCT format with two positions: one position for the percentage and one position for the percent sign. Since the format allows for only two positions in the displayed output, the value 9 displays as 9% and the value 10 displays as 10, the percent sign being truncated.

Example
```
COMPUTE V3=V1 + V2.
FORMATS V3 (F3.1).
```

- COMPUTE creates the new numeric variable V3. By default, V3 is assigned an F8.2 format (or the format defined on SET as the default for numeric variables).
- FORMATS changes both the print and write formats for V3 to F3.1.

Example
```
SET CCA='-/-.Dfl ..-'.
FORMATS COST (CCA14.2).
```

- SET defines a European currency format for the custom currency format type CCA.
- FORMATS assigns format CCA to variable COST. With the format defined for CCA on SET, the value 37419 displays as Dfl 37.419,00. See the SET command for more information on custom currency formats.

FREQUENCIES

```
FREQUENCIES [VARIABLES=]varlist[(min,max)] [varlist...]

[/FORMAT=[{CONDENSE}] [{NOTABLE }] [NOLABELS] [WRITE]
         {ONEPAGE }   {LIMIT(n)}

        [{DVALUE}] [DOUBLE] [NEWPAGE] [INDEX]]
         {AFREQ }
         {DFREQ }

[/MISSING=INCLUDE]

[/BARCHART=[MINIMUM(n)] [MAXIMUM(n)] [{FREQ(n)   }]]
                                     {PERCENT(n)}

[/HISTOGRAM=[MINIMUM(n)] [MAXIMUM(n)] [{FREQ(n)   }]
                                      {PERCENT(n)}

           [{NONORMAL}] [INCREMENT(n)]]
            {NORMAL  }

[/HBAR=same as HISTOGRAM]

[/NTILES=n]

[/PERCENTILES=value list]

[/STATISTICS=[DEFAULT] [MEAN] [STDDEV] [MINIMUM] [MAXIMUM]
     [SEMEAN] [VARIANCE] [SKEWNESS] [SESKEW] [RANGE] [MODE]
     [KURTOSIS] [SEKURT] [MEDIAN] [SUM] [ALL] [NONE]]
```

Example:

```
FREQUENCIES VAR=RACE /STATISTICS=ALL.
```

Overview

FREQUENCIES produces tables of frequency counts and percentages for the values of individual variables. FREQUENCIES has two principal applications: to obtain frequencies and statistics for categoric variables, and to obtain statistics and graphic output for continuous variables.

Options

Display Format. You can condense, expand, or suppress tables and alter the order of values within tables.

Statistical Display. Percentiles or ntiles are available for each numeric variable. The following statistics are also available: mean, median, mode, standard deviation, variance, skewness, kurtosis, and sum.

Plots. Histograms are available for numeric variables, and bar charts are available for numeric or string variables.

Basic Specification

• The basic specification is the VARIABLES subcommand and at least one variable name, which generates a frequency table.

Subcommand Order

• Subcommands can be named in any order.

Syntax Rules

• Multiple NTILES specifications generate separate percentile groupings. Repeat occurrences of the same percentiles are consolidated.
• BARCHART, HISTOGRAM, and HBAR are mutually exclusive. HBAR is used whenever any two of these subcommands are specified on the same FREQUENCIES command.

Operations
- Variables are tabulated in the order that they are mentioned on the VARIABLES subcommand. If a variable is mentioned more than once, it is tabulated more than once.
- If a requested ntile or percentile cannot be calculated, a period (.) is displayed.
- The display always uses narrow format regardless of the width defined on SET.
- FREQUENCIES operates in integer or general mode, depending on the VARIABLES specification.

General Mode
- FREQUENCIES runs in general mode if VARIABLES specifies a variable list, but no value ranges.
- FREQUENCIES tabulates numeric variables (with or without decimal values), short string variables, and the short string portion of long string variables.
- Keyword ALL on VARIABLES refers to all user-defined variables in the active system file.
- FREQUENCIES dynamically builds the table, setting up one cell for each unique value encountered in the data.

Integer Mode
- FREQUENCIES runs in integer mode if VARIABLES specifies a variable list and, in parentheses after each variable name, a value range to use for the table.
- Specified variables must be numeric. Numeric variables with decimal positions are truncated to their whole number value.
- FREQUENCIES uses the specified ranges for each variable and includes in the table only values within the range. Values outside the range are grouped into an out-of-range category and considered missing for calculation of percents and statistics.

General vs. Integer Mode
- Integer mode usually takes less computation time. (Computation time depends upon the range of values and the order in which values are read.)
- Integer mode requires less memory than does general mode, except when variables are sparsely distributed.
- In integer mode, the value range specification can eliminate extremely low or high values.
- Since integer mode truncates decimal positions, you can obtain grouped frequency tables for continuous variables without having to recode them to integers. On the other hand, general mode tabulates short strings and does not truncate nonintegers.

Limitations
- A maximum of 500 variables total per FREQUENCIES command.
- A maximum value range of 32,767 for a variable in integer mode.
- A maximum of 32,767 observed values over all variables.

Example
```
FREQUENCIES VAR=RACE /STATISTICS=ALL.
```
- FREQUENCIES requests a frequency table and all statistics for the categoric variable RACE.
- General mode is used because there is no range specified for RACE.

Example
```
FREQUENCIES STATISTICS=ALL /HISTOGRAM
/VARIABLES=SEX (1,2) TVHOURS (0,24) SCALE1 TO SCALE5 (1,7)
/FORMAT=NOTABLE.
```
- FREQUENCIES requests separate statistics and histograms for SEX, TV-HOURS, and all variables between and including SCALE1 and SCALE5.
- Integer mode is used because a value range is specified for each variable.
- FORMAT suppresses all the frequency tables, which are not useful for continuous variables.

VARIABLES **Subcommand**	VARIABLES names the variables to be tabulated and is the only required subcommand. The actual keyword VARIABLES may be omitted.

- The VARIABLES specification determines whether FREQUENCIES runs in integer or general mode. If value ranges are specified in parentheses after each variable name, FREQUENCIES runs in *integer* mode. If no value ranges are specified, FREQUENCIES runs in *general* mode. You cannot mix general and integer mode specifications.

FORMAT Subcommand

By default, FREQUENCIES displays as many single-spaced tables with complete labeling information as fit within the page length.

- The minimum specification is a single keyword to override one aspect of the default display.

Table Formats

CONDENSE *Condensed format.* Displays counts in three columns without value labels and with valid and cumulative percentages rounded to integers. Overrides ONEPAGE.

ONEPAGE *Conditional condensed format.* Uses condensed format for tables that would otherwise require more than one page.

NEWPAGE *Each table starts on a new page.*

NOLABELS *No value labels.*

DOUBLE *Double-space frequency tables.*

Table Order

The default table is ordered by ascending value (numeric variables) or in alphabetical order (string variables).

AFREQ *Sort categories in ascending order of frequency.* Ignored when HISTO-GRAM, HBAR, NTILES, or PERCENTILES are requested.

DFREQ *Sort categories in descending order of frequency.* Ignored when HISTO-GRAM, HBAR, NTILES, or PERCENTILES are requested.

DVALUE *Sort categories in descending order of values (numeric variables) or in reverse alphabetical order (string variables).* Ignored when HISTO-GRAM, HBAR, NTILES, or PERCENTILES are requested.

Table Suppression

LIMIT(n) *No frequency tables with more than* n *categories.* The number of missing and valid cases and requested statistics are displayed for suppressed tables.

NOTABLE *No frequency tables.* The number of missing and valid cases are displayed for suppressed tables. Overrides LIMIT.

Table Index

Keyword INDEX obtains both a positional index of frequency tables and an index arranged alphabetically by variable name.

INDEX *Index of tables.*

Writing Tables to a File

Keyword WRITE directs the FREQUENCIES display to a separate output file. WRITE can only be specified if a PROCEDURE OUTPUT command precedes the FREQUENCIES command.

WRITE *Direct display to another file.*

Example

```
PROCEDURE OUTPUT  OUTFILE=CODEBOOK.
FREQUENCIES  VARIABLES=ALL /FORMAT=ONEPAGE WRITE.
```

- PROCEDURE OUTPUT specifies CODEBOOK as the file to receive the frequency tables.
- FREQUENCIES uses the conditional condensed formats for the frequency tables and directs the frequency tables to the file CODEBOOK, specified on PROCEDURE OUTPUT.
- Frequency tables are not shown in the display file.

BARCHART Subcommand

BARCHART produces a bar chart for each variable named on the VARIABLES subcommand. By default, the horizontal axis for each bar chart is scaled in frequencies, and the interval width is determined by the largest frequency count for the variable being plotted. Bar charts are labeled with value labels or with the value if no value label is defined.

- The minimum specification is the keyword BARCHART, which generates default bar charts.
- BARCHART cannot be used with HISTOGRAM or HBAR. HBAR is used whenever any two of these subcommands appear on the same FREQUENCIES command.

MIN(n)   *Lower bound* below which values are not plotted.

MAX(n)   *Upper bound* above which values are not plotted.

PERCENT(n) *Horizontal axis scaled in percentages.* The *n* specifies the preferred maximum and is not required. With no *n* or a too-small *n*, FREQUENCIES chooses 5, 10, 25, 50, or 100, depending on the frequency count for the largest category.

FREQ(n)   *Horizontal axis scaled in frequencies,* where optional *n* is the maximum. With no *n* or a too-small *n*, FREQUENCIES chooses 10, 20, 50, 100, 200, 500, 1000, 2000, and so forth, depending on the largest category. This is the default.

Example

```
FREQUENCIES VAR=RACE /BARCHART.
```

- FREQUENCIES requests a frequency table and the default bar chart for variable RACE.

Example

```
FREQUENCIES VAR=V1 V2 /BAR=MAX(10).
```

- FREQUENCIES requests a frequency table and bar chart with values through 10 for each of variables V1 and V2.

HISTOGRAM Subcommand

HISTOGRAM displays a plot for each numeric variable named on the VARIABLES subcommand. By default, the horizontal axis of each histogram is scaled in frequencies and the interval width is determined by the largest frequency count of the variable being plotted.

- The minimum specification is the keyword HISTOGRAM, which generates default histograms.
- The HISTOGRAM subcommand on the SET command controls the character used to draw histograms.
- HISTOGRAM cannot be used with BARCHART or HBAR. HBAR is used whenever any two of these subcommands appear on the same FREQUENCIES command.

MIN(n)   *Lower bound* below which values are not plotted.

MAX(n)   *Upper bound* above which values are not plotted.

PERCENT(n)   *Horizontal axis scaled in percentages,* where optional *n* is the preferred maximum. With no *n* or a too-small *n*, FREQUENCIES chooses 5, 10, 25, 50, or 100, depending on the largest category.

FREQ(n)   *Horizontal axis scaled in frequencies,* where optional *n* is the scale. With no *n* or a too-small *n*, FREQUENCIES chooses 10, 20, 50, 100, 200, 500, 1000, 2000, and so forth, depending on the largest category. This is the default.

INCREMENT(n) *Interval width,* where *n* is the size of the interval. Overrides the default number of intervals on the vertical axis, which depends on the system page length. For a variable that ranges from 1 to 100, INCREMENT(2) produces 50 intervals with 2 values each.

NORMAL   *Superimpose a normal curve.* Based on all valid values for the variable, including values excluded by MIN and MAX.

Example   `FREQUENCIES VAR=V1 /HIST=NORMAL INCREMENT(4).`

• FREQUENCIES requests a histogram with a superimposed normal curve and an interval width of 4.

HBAR Subcommand

HBAR produces a plot for each numeric and string variable named on the VARIABLES subcommand. For numeric variables, HBAR produces a bar chart if the number of categories fits within the page length (see SET). Otherwise, HBAR produces a histogram. HBAR produces bar charts for short string variables and for the short-string portion of long string variables, regardless of the number of values.

   By default, the horizontal axis of each plot is scaled in frequencies and the interval is determined by the largest frequency count. All keyword specifications for HISTOGRAM and BARCHART work with HBAR.

PERCENTILES Subcommand

PERCENTILES displays the value below which the specified percentage of cases falls. There are no default percentiles.

Example   `FREQUENCIES VAR=V1 /PERCENTILES=10 25 33.3 66.7 75.`

• FREQUENCIES requests the values for percentiles 10, 25, 33.3, 66.7, and 75 for V1.

NTILES Subcommand

NTILES calculates the percentages that divide the distribution into the specified number of categories and displays the values below which the requested percentages of cases fall. There are no default ntiles for the NTILES subcommand.

• Multiple NTILES subcommands are allowed. Each NTILES subcommand generates separate percentiles. Repeat occurences of the same percentiles are consolidated.

Example   `FREQUENCIES VARIABLE=V1 /NTILES=4.`

• FREQUENCIES requests quartiles (percentiles 25, 50, and 75) for V1.

Example   `FREQUENCIES VARIABLE=V1 /NTILES=4 /NTILES=10.`

• The first NTILES subcommand requests percentiles 25, 50, and 75.

• The second NTILES subcommand requests percentiles 10 through 100 in increments of 10.

• The 50th percentile occurs in both specifications but is consolidated in the output; hence, it displays only once.

STATISTICS Subcommand

STATISTICS controls the display of statistics. By default, cases with missing values are excluded from the calculation of statistics.

• The minimum specification is the keyword STATISTICS, which generates the mean, standard deviation, minimum, and maximum (these are the DEFAULT statistics).

• In integer mode, only cases with values in the specified range are used in the computation of statistics.

The following can be specified on the STATISTICS subcommand:

MEAN   *Mean.*

SEMEAN   *Standard error of the mean.*

MEDIAN   *Median.* Ignored with AFREQ or DFREQ on the FORMAT subcommand.

MODE   *Mode.* If there is more than one mode, only the first mode is displayed.

STDDEV   *Standard deviation.*

VARIANCE	*Variance.*
SKEWNESS	*Skewness.*
SESKEW	*Standard error of the skewness statistic.*
KURTOSIS	*Kurtosis.*
SEKURT	*Standard error of the kurtosis statistic.*
RANGE	*Range.*
MINIMUM	*Minimum.*
MAXIMUM	*Maximum.*
SUM	*Sum.*
DEFAULT	*Mean, standard deviation, minimum, and maximum.*
ALL	*Display all available statistics.*
NONE	*No statistics.*

Example

```
FREQUENCIES VAR=AGE /STATS=MODE.
```

• STATISTICS requests only the mode of AGE.

Example

```
FREQUENCIES VAR=AGE /STATS=DEF MODE.
```

• STATISTICS requests the default statistics (mean, standard deviation, minimum, and maximum) plus the mode of AGE.

MISSING Subcommand

By default, both user- and system-missing values are labeled as missing in the table but are not included in the valid and cumulative percentages, in the calculation of descriptive statistics, or in bar charts and histograms.

INCLUDE *Include cases with user-missing values.* Cases with user-missing values will be included in the statistics and plots.

Annotated Example

For a complete example with output, see Examples following the Command Reference.

GET

```
GET FILE=file

[/KEEP={ALL     }] [/DROP=varlist]
        {varlist}

[/RENAME=(old varlist=new varlist)...]

[/MAP]
```

Example:
```
GET FILE=EMPL.
```

Overview

GET reads an SPSS system file that was created by the SAVE or XSAVE commands. A system file is in a format only SPSS can read and contains data plus a dictionary. The dictionary contains a name for each variable on the system file, plus any assigned variable and value labels, missing-value flags, and variable print and write formats. The dictionary also contains document text created with the DOCUMENTS command.

GET is used only for reading SPSS system files. See DATA LIST for defining variables and values in a raw data file. See MATRIX DATA for defining raw matrix materials. See FILE TYPE and REPEATING DATA for defining complex data files that cannot be defined with DATA LIST.

SPSS can also read data files created for other software applications. See IMPORT to read a *portable file* created with EXPORT in SPSS/PC+ or SPSS. See commands such as GET TRANSLATE, GET SCSS, GET SAS, GET BMDP, and GET OSIRIS for reading files created by other software programs. Your SPSS *Operations Guide* tells you the types of files you can read on your system (for example, dBASE, Lotus, or Multiplan files).

Options

Variable Subsets and Order. You can read a subset of variables and also reorder variables that are copied into the active system file. See DROP and KEEP subcommands.

Variable Names. You can rename variables as they are copied into the active system file.

Variable Map. To confirm any renaming, subsetting, or reordering, you can display the names of the variables copied into the active file alongside their corresponding names in the system file.

Basic Specification

• The basic specification is the FILE subcommand, which specifies the system file to be read. GET copies all variables from the system file into the active file. Variables in the active file are in the same order and have the same names as variables in the system file. Documentary text from the system file is copied into the dictionary of the active file.

Subcommand Order

• FILE must be specified first.
• KEEP, DROP, RENAME, and MAP can be used multiple times and in any order but must follow FILE.

Syntax Rules

• FILE is required and can be specified only once.
• KEEP, DROP, RENAME, and MAP may be used as many times as needed.
• Documentary text from the active file can be dropped from the system file with the DROP DOCUMENTS command.

Operations

• GET causes the dictionary of the system file to be read.
• If KEEP is not specified, variables in the active system file are in the same order as variables in the system file.

- A file saved with weighting in effect maintains the values of variable $WEIGHT. For a discussion of turning off weights, see WEIGHT.
- If KEEP is not used, the order of cases in the active system file is the same as their order in the system file. The values of $CASENUM are those from the raw data file, before any selecting (see SELECT IF) or sorting (see SORT).

Limitations

- GET cannot be used inside a DO IF structure.
- GET cannot be used inside a LOOP structure.

FILE Subcommand

FILE specifies the system file to be read. FILE is required and can only be specified once. FILE must be the first specification on GET.

DROP and KEEP Subcommands

DROP and KEEP copy a subset of variables into the active system file. DROP specifies the variables to drop from the active file; KEEP specifies the variables to keep on the active file.

- Variables may be specified in any order. The variable order on KEEP determines the variable order in the active file. Variable order on DROP does not affect the order of variables in the active file: the variables are copied in the same sequence in which they appear in the system file.
- Multiple DROP and KEEP subcommands are allowed.
- If a variable is referenced twice, only the first mention of the variable is recognized.

Reordering Variables

- The variable order on KEEP determines the variable order in the active file.
- Keyword ALL on KEEP refers to all remaining variables not previously specified. ALL must be the last specification on KEEP.

Example

```
GET FILE=HUBTEMP /DROP=DEPT79 TO DEPT84 SALARY79.
```

- The active system file is copied from system file HUBTEMP. All variables between and including DEPT79 and DEPT84, as well as SALARY79, are excluded from the active file. All other variables are copied into the active file.
- Variables in the active file are in the same order as the variables in the original system file.

Example

```
GET FILE=PRSNL /DROP=GRADE STORE  /KEEP=LNAME NAME TENURE JTENURE
ALL.
```

- DROP specifies that variables GRADE and STORE be dropped when file PRSNL is copied into the active system file.
- KEEP determines that LNAME, NAME, TENURE, and JTENURE are the first four variables in the active file, followed by all remaining variables not specified on DROP. Variables not specified on KEEP are copied into the active file in the same sequence in which they appear in the original system file.

RENAME Subcommand

RENAME changes the names of variables as they are copied into the active system file.

- Name changes can be specified in the form *old varname=new varname*. Multiple sets of variable specifications are allowed. Each set may be enclosed in optional parentheses.
- As an alternative to the above, name changes can be specified with a list of old variable names followed by an equals sign and a list of new variable names. The same number of variables must be specified on both lists. Keyword TO can be used in either or both lists to refer to consecutive variables. A single set of parentheses enclosing the entire specification is required for this method.
- Old variable names need not be specified according to their order in the system file.

• Name changes take place in one operation. Therefore, variable names can be exchanged between two variables.

• Variables cannot be renamed to scratch variables.

• Multiple RENAME subcommands are allowed.

Example   `GET FILE=EMPL88 /RENAME  AGE=AGE88 JOBCAT=JOBCAT88.`

• RENAME specifies two name changes for the active system file. AGE is renamed to AGE88, and JOBCAT is renamed to JOBCAT88.

Example   `GET FILE=EMPL88 /RENAME (AGE JOBCAT=AGE88 JOBCAT88).`

• The name changes are identical to those in the previous example. AGE is renamed to AGE88, and JOBCAT is renamed to JOBCAT88. The parentheses are required with this method.

MAP Subcommand

MAP displays a list of the variables in the active system file and their corresponding names in the system file.

• The only specification is keyword MAP. MAP has no additional specifications.

• Multiple MAP subcommands are allowed. Each MAP subcommand maps the results of subcommands that precede it, but not results of subcommands that follow it.

Example   `GET FILE=EMPL88 /RENAME=(AGE=AGE86) (JOBCAT=JOBCAT88)`
`/KEEP=LNAME NAME JOBCAT88 ALL /MAP.`

• MAP confirms that variable AGE is renamed to AGE86 and JOBCAT is renamed to JOBCAT88. MAP also confirms that the first three variables in the active file are LNAME, NAME, and JOBCAT88, and that all remaining variables from the system file are present in the active file.

GET BMDP

This command is not available on all operating systems.

```
GET BMDP FILE=file
```

```
[/SCAN={YES }] [/CODE=name]
        {ONLY}
```

```
[/CONTENT=name] [/LABEL=quoted string]
```

```
[/KEEP={ALL** }] [/DROP=varlist]
        {varlist}
```

```
[/RENAME=(old varlist=new varlist)...]
```

```
[/MAP]
```

**Default if the subcommand is omitted.

Example:

```
GET BMDP FILE=BMDPFIL3.
```

Overview

GET BMDP reads a save file from a BMDP data set. The specified save file from the data set becomes the SPSS active system file. BMDP variable names and missing values are automatically converted (if necessary) so they comply with SPSS conventions.

Options

Save Files. You can specify a particular save file within the data set to read. See the CONTENT, CODE, and LABEL subcommands.

Variable Subsets and Order. You can read a subset of variables and also reorder variables that are copied into the active file. See DROP and KEEP subcommands.

Variable Names. You can rename variables as they are copied into the active file.

Variable Map. To confirm any renaming, subsetting, or reordering, you can display the names of the variables copied into the SPSS active system file alongside their corresponding names in the BMDP save file.

Basic Specification

- The basic specification is the FILE subcommand, which specifies the BMDP data set. SPSS reads the first save file within the data set with the content field DATA. All variables from the BMDP save file are copied into the SPSS active system file. Variables in the active file are in the same order as variables in the save file. However, SPSS may have to rename BMDP variables so they conform to SPSS naming conventions (see BMDP to SPSS Data Conversion below).

Subcommand Order

- FILE must be first.
- If present, SCAN must immediately follow FILE.
- CONTENT, CODE, and LABEL may appear in any order but must follow FILE and SCAN.
- KEEP, DROP, RENAME, and MAP may appear multiple times and in any order but must follow all other subcommands.

Operations

- If KEEP is not specified, variables in the active file are in the same order as variables in the BMDP save file.
- SPSS makes assumptions about the record format and other characteristics of the BMDP data set based on the type of computer and operating system. This information is in the SPSS *Operations Guide* for your system.

Case Selection

- In a BMDP save file, each case includes an automatic variable USE, whose value determines whether the case is included in an analysis. Only cases in which USE has a positive, nonmissing value are included. GET BMDP retains all cases, and it retains the variable USE unless the KEEP or DROP subcommands indicate otherwise. SPSS can use the same case selection as BMDP if the SELECT IF command is used before an analysis, as in: SELECT IF USE > 0.

BMDP to SPSS Data Conversion

In most instances, GET BMDP is able to retrieve the information from save files that is to be stored into SPSS system files. SPSS makes the following conversions to force BMDP variable names to comply with SPSS conventions.

Variable Names

- Initial blanks and special characters are changed to @. $VAR, .VAR, /VAR, and VAR preceded by a blank all become @VAR (but see below about duplicate names).
- Internal blanks and special characters are changed to underscores. VAR ONE and VAR/ONE both become VAR_ONE.
- Parentheses are removed. X(1) becomes X1.
- Hash marks are added to SPSS reserved keywords. GT becomes GT#, and ALL becomes ALL#.
- If conversion using these rules produces duplicate names, SPSS creates names of the form V*n*, in which *n* is an integer.

Missing Values

- All three BMDP missing values (missing, lower than the minimum, and higher than the minimum) are converted to the SPSS system-missing value.

Print and Write Formats

- GET BMDP supplies print and write formats of F8.2 for all numeric variables and A4 for all string variables. FORMATS, PRINT FORMATS, and WRITE FORMATS in SPSS can be used to change these formats if they are inappropriate.
- SPSS recognizes as string variables only those identified by the LABEL clause of BMDP's VARIABLE paragraph. Other string variables might exist and not be detected. The REFORMAT command, originally designed for conversion of system files from earlier versions of SPSS, can be useful in this instance.

Limitations

- Although it is possible to read files with content other than DATA, such files are likely to be interpreted incorrectly. A certain amount of trial and error may be necessary to read and redefine such files.
- Information generated by the BMDP GROUPS paragraph is ignored.

FILE Subcommand

FILE specifies the BMDP data set. One or more BMDP save files can exist within a single BMDP data set. FILE specifies only the data set; unless the CODE, CONTENT, or LABEL subcommands are specified, SPSS reads the first save file within the specified data set with the content field DATA. FILE is required and must be the first specification on GET BMDP.

SCAN Subcommand

SCAN displays information about the save files within the BMDP data set. The information includes the content, code, and label fields that identify the BMDP save files. Code and label are specified by the user within BMDP; content is supplied by the BMDP program to identify the type of file (data, correlation matrix, and so on).

- When used, SCAN must immediately follow FILE.
- SCAN can specify one of two keywords: YES and ONLY. When YES is specified, the save file is read. When ONLY is specified, the save file is not read.

YES *Display the code, content, and label fields and other information from the save file. Also read the file.*

ONLY *Display the code, content, and label fields and other information from the save file. Do not read the file.*

Example

```
GET BMDP FILE=BMDPFIL3  /SCAN ONLY.
```

- FILE specifies the BMDPFIL3 data set.
- SCAN displays information about the save files within the data set. However, no files are read. Information about the save file can be used for making specifications on the CONTENT, CODE, or LABEL subcommands of another GET BMDP command.

CONTENT, CODE, and LABEL Subcommands

CONTENT, CODE, and LABEL specify a particular save file within a single data set. The specification for each can be a single word or a string enclosed in apostrophes.

- If CONTENT is not specified, SPSS assumes DATA content.
- If CODE or LABEL are not specified, SPSS reads the first save file with the specified CONTENT (or DATA by default).
- If CODE or LABEL are specified, SPSS reads the first file that matches all of the information provided.

Example

```
GET BMDP FILE=BMDPFIL /LABEL= 'OLD DATA'.
```

- SPSS reads the first save file in data set BMDPFIL with content DATA and label OLD DATA.

DROP and KEEP Subcommands

DROP and KEEP copy a subset of variables into the active system file. DROP specifies the variables not to copy into the active file; KEEP specifies the variables to copy into the active file.

- DROP and KEEP cannot precede the FILE, CONTENT, CODE, or LABEL subcommands.
- DROP and KEEP specifications must use SPSS variable names, not BMDP variable names (see BMDP to SPSS Data Conversion, above).
- Keyword TO can be used to specify a group of consecutive variables from the BMDP save file.
- Variables can be specified in any order. The variable order on KEEP determines the variable sequence in the active file. Variable order on DROP does not affect the order of variables in the active file: the variables are copied in the same sequence in which they appear in the BMDP save file.
- Multiple DROP and KEEP subcommands are allowed.
- If a variable is referenced twice, only the first mention of the variable is recognized.

Reordering Variables

- The variable order on KEEP determines the variable sequence in the active file.
- Keyword ALL on KEEP refers to all remaining variables not previously specified. ALL must be the last specification on KEEP.

Example

```
GET BMDP FILE=BMDPFIL /DROP=X1 TO X4, X9 /KEEP=X7 X6 ALL.
```

- GET BMDP reads the BMDP data set BMDPFIL; the first save file with content DATA is copied into the SPSS active system file. Assume that the save file contains variables X(1) to X(20). Note that DROP and KEEP use the SPSS variable names and not the BMDP variable names. (In SPSS, the parentheses are dropped from the variable name.)
- DROP excludes all variables between and including X1 and X4, as well as X9, from the active system file. All other variables are copied into the active system file.
- KEEP determines that X7 and X6 are the first two variables in the active system file, followed by all remaining variables not specified on DROP. Variables not specified on KEEP are copied into the active system file in the same sequence they appear in the original BMDP save file.

RENAME Subcommand

RENAME changes the names of variables as they are copied into the active system file.

- RENAME cannot precede the FILE, CONTENT, CODE, or LABEL subcommands.
- Name changes can be specified in the form *old varname=new varname*. Multiple sets of variable specifications are allowed. Each set can be enclosed in optional parentheses.

• As an alternative to the above, name changes can be specified with a list of old variable names followed by an equals sign and a list of new variable names. The same number of variables must be specified on both lists. A single set of parentheses enclosing the entire specification is required for this method.

• RENAME specifications must use SPSS variable names, not BMDP variable names (see BMDP to SPSS Data Conversion, above).

• Old variable names need not be specified according to their order in the BMDP save file.

• Name changes take place in one operation. Therefore, variable names can be exchanged between two variables.

• Variables cannot be renamed to scratch variables.

• Multiple RENAME subcommands are allowed.

Example
```
GET BMDP FILE= BMDPFIL4  /SCAN YES
  /KEEP = X1 X2 V1 V2
  /RENAME = (X1 X2 V1 V2 = X1_A X2_A X1_B X2_B).
```

• Assume the save file within data set BMDPFIL4 contains variables named X(1), X(2), X1, and X2 (and some others), in that order. SPSS converts the variable names X(1) and X(2) to X1 and X2. Then, because of duplication, it converts X1 and X2 to V1 and V2 (see BMDP to SPSS Data Conversion above). Note that the KEEP and RENAME specifications use the SPSS names.

• RENAME changes variable names X1 to X1_A, X2 to X2_A, V1 to X1_B, and V2 to X2_B. Because all the old variable names are listed to the left of the equals sign and all the new variable names to the right of the equals sign, parentheses are required to enclose the entire specification.

MAP Subcommand

MAP displays a list of the variables in the active system file and their corresponding names in the BMDP save file.

• MAP cannot precede the FILE, CONTENT, CODE, or LABEL subcommands.

• The only specification is keyword MAP. MAP has no additional specifications.

• Multiple MAP subcommands are allowed. Each MAP subcommand maps the results of subcommands that precede it, but not results of subcommands that follow it.

Example
```
GET BMDP FILE=BMDPFIL4  /SCAN YES
  /KEEP=X1 X2 V1 V2 ALL
  /RENAME=(X1 X2 V1 V2 = X1_A X2_A X1_B X2_B)
  /MAP.
```

• MAP confirms all the name changes. MAP also confirms that the first four variables in the active system file are X1_A, X2_A, X1_B, and X2_B, and that all remaining variables from the BMDP save file are present in the active system file.

GET OSIRIS

This command is not available on all operating systems.
```
GET OSIRIS DICTIONARY=file1 DATA=file2

    [/RENAME=(old varlist=new varlist)...]

    [/KEEP={ALL**   }] [/DROP=varlist]
           {varlist}

    [/MAP]
```

Example:
```
GET OSIRIS DATA=DATA48 DICTIONARY=DICT48.
```

Overview

GET OSIRIS generates an SPSS active system file from an OSIRIS data set. OSIRIS variable numbers are converted into SPSS variable names. Print and write formats are automatically assigned using SPSS conventions. Variable label information is read from the OSIRIS dictionary.

Options

Variable Subsets and Order. You can read a subset of variables and also reorder variables that are copied into the active system file. See the DROP and KEEP subcommands.

Variable Names. You can rename variables as they are copied into the active file.

Variable Map. To confirm any renaming, subsetting, or reordering, you can display the names of the variables copied into the active file alongside their corresponding names in the OSIRIS data set.

Basic Specification

• The basic specification uses two subcommands: DATA and DICTIONARY.
• DATA assigns a file for the OSIRIS data file.
• DICTIONARY assigns a file for the OSIRIS dictionary file.

The OSIRIS dictionary is converted into an SPSS active system file dictionary, and an SPSS tranformation program is generated to read cases in the OSIRIS data set. All variable numbers from the OSIRIS data set are copied into the SPSS active system file. OSIRIS variable numbers are converted to SPSS variable names (see OSIRIS to SPSS Data Conversion, below).

Subcommand Order

• DATA and DICTIONARY must precede all other subcommands.
• KEEP, DROP, RENAME, and MAP may each appear multiple times and in any order but must follow DATA and DICTIONARY.

Syntax Rules

• DATA and DICTIONARY specifications are not separated by a slash.
• KEEP, DROP, RENAME, and MAP specifications must be separated by a slash.

Operations

• If KEEP is not specified, variables in the active system file are in the same order as variables in the data set.
• There are three types of OSIRIS data sets: types 1, 3, and 5. SPSS can currently read only types 1 and 3. Type 1 data sets are the usual form for distribution; they are produced only by the OSIRIS system after many edit checks have been made. Type 3 data sets may be produced using ordinary text-editing software (or a card punch). Each data set consists of a fixed-format raw data file and a dictionary file containing data definitions associated with OSIRIS variables.
• Variable label information is read from the OSIRIS dictionary. Type 1 data sets may include a dictionary-codebook file containing value label information, which GET OSIRIS automatically converts into SPSS value labels. Missing-value specifications are read from the OSIRIS data set.

OSIRIS to SPSS Data Conversion	In most instances, GET OSIRIS is able to retrieve the information from OSIRIS data files that is to be stored into SPSS system files. SPSS makes the following conversions to force OSIRIS data sets to comply with SPSS conventions.
Variable Types	• Both SPSS and OSIRIS recognize two variable types, numeric and string. During the conversion process, OSIRIS numeric variables become SPSS numeric variables, and OSIRIS string variables become SPSS string variables of the same length.
Variable Names	• OSIRIS variable numbers refer to responses to single- or multiple-response survey questions. SPSS converts a multiple-response variable n with k possible responses to k variables named Mn.1 through M$n.k$. An SPSS variable name is limited to eight characters. Thus, with the form M$n.k$, if n has four digits, k can have no more than two, and if n has five digits, k can have only one. The form Mnk is used, without the decimal point, when n has five digits and k has two.
Variable Labels	• In OSIRIS, the term *variable name* has the same sense as the term *variable label* in SPSS. OSIRIS variable names are converted to SPSS variable labels of the same length.
Missing Values	• For missing values, OSIRIS allows single values or size limits to be specified. Single values, if specified, are used as missing values for the corresponding variables in SPSS.
	• An OSIRIS negative size limit x becomes the SPSS missing range (LO THRU x), and a positive size limit y becomes the SPSS missing range (y THRU HI).
	• Range-missing values are not used for string variables. No missing values are used for long string variables. Warnings are issued if missing values occur in violation of these rules.
Value Labels	• The dictionary codebook in an OSIRIS type 1 data set may include value label information. If so, this information will be associated with the corresponding SPSS variables using the same values. When converted, labels longer than 60 characters are truncated.
Print and Write Formats	• OSIRIS string variables with length l are given an A format with width l for print and write formats.
	• OSIRIS numeric variables are assigned one of three formats corresponding to the three forms of OSIRIS data values: numeric character, fixed-point binary, and floating-point binary.
	• Table 1 shows the assignment of numeric print and write formats. The width w and the number of decimal places d are taken from the OSIRIS data set.

Table 1 Print and write formats for numeric variables

OSIRIS data format	SPSS print format	SPSS write format
Numeric character	Fw.d	Fw.d
Fixed-point binary	Fw.d	IBw.d
Floating-point binary	Ew.d	RBw

Limitations	• Type 3 OSIRIS data sets may contain multiple logical records per case, and they may contain variable values that span logical records. GET OSIRIS can handle type 3 data sets when there is only one logical record per case.
	• GET OSIRIS can handle a logical record length of 80 with no variable values spanning different logical records.
	• Because SPSS treats OSIRIS multiple-response variables as separate variables, GET OSIRIS can handle a multiple-response variable that spans different logical records provided no corresponding individual SPSS variable spans different logical records.

DATA and DICTIONARY Subcommands

DATA and DICTIONARY together specify the OSIRIS data set. DATA assigns a file for the OSIRIS data file. DICTIONARY assigns a file for the OSIRIS dictionary file.

- DATA and DICTIONARY are required and must be the first specification on GET OSIRIS.
- A slash is not used to separate the DATA and DICTIONARY specifications. However, slashes are used to separate any other subcommands used on GET OSIRIS.

Example

```
GET OSIRIS DATA=DATA48 DICTIONARY=DICT48.
```

- DATA identifies DATA48 as the OSIRIS data file and DICTIONARY identifies DICT48 as the OSIRIS dictionary file.

DROP and KEEP Subcommands

DROP and KEEP copy a subset of variables into the active file. DROP specifies the variables not to copy into the active file; KEEP specifies the variables to copy into the active file.

- DROP and KEEP specifications must use SPSS variable names, not OSIRIS variable names (called variable numbers in OSIRIS; see OSIRIS to SPSS Data Conversion, above).
- Keyword TO can be used to specify a group of consecutive variables from the OSIRIS data set.
- Variables may be specified in any order. The variable order on KEEP determines the variable sequence in the active file. Variable order on DROP does not affect the order of variables in the active file: the variables are copied in the same sequence in which they appear in the OSIRIS data set.
- Multiple DROP and KEEP subcommands are allowed.
- If a variable is referenced twice, only the first mention of the variable is recognized.

Reordering Variables

- The variable order on KEEP determines the variable sequence in the active file.
- Keyword ALL on KEEP refers to all remaining variables not previously specified. ALL must be the last specification on KEEP.

Example

```
GET OSIRIS DATA=DATA48 DICTIONARY=DICT48
    /DROP=M5.1 TO M5.3 M5.9 /KEEP=M5.7 M5.6 ALL.
```

- DROP excludes all variables between and including M5.1 to M5.3, as well as M5.9, from the active system file. All other variables are copied into the active system file.
- KEEP determines that M5.7 and M5.6 are the first two variables in the active system file, followed by all remaining variables not specified on DROP. Variables not specified on KEEP are copied into the active system file in the same sequence in which they appear in the original OSIRIS data set.
- Note that DROP and KEEP use the SPSS variable names and not the OSIRIS variable numbers.

RENAME Subcommand

RENAME changes the names of variables as they are copied into the active system file.

- OSIRIS data sets contain both single- and multiple-response questions. By default, GET OSIRIS converts a single-response variable with the number n to the SPSS variable name Vn, and it converts a multiple-response variable n with k possible responses to k SPSS variable names: $Mn.1$, $Mn.2$, through $Mn.k$. RENAME can be used to change the default names assigned by GET OSIRIS. (See OSIRIS to SPSS Data Conversion, above, for more information on the differences between SPSS and OSIRIS conventions.)
- Name changes can be specified in the form *old varname=new varname*. Multiple sets of variable specifications are allowed. Each set may be enclosed in optional parentheses.

- As an alternative to the above, name changes can be specified with a list of old variable names followed by an equals sign and a list of new variable names. The same number of variables must be specified on both lists. A single set of parentheses enclosing the entire specification is required for this method.
- RENAME specifications must use SPSS variable names, not OSIRIS variable names.
- Old variable names need not be specified according to their order in the OSIRIS save file.
- Name changes take place in one operation. Therefore, variable names can be exchanged between two variables.
- Variables cannot be renamed to scratch variables.
- Multiple RENAME subcommands are allowed.

Example
```
GET OSIRIS DATA=DATA48 DICTIONARY=DICT48
   /DROP=M5.1 TO M5.3 M5.9 /KEEP=M5.7 M5.6 ALL
   /RENAME (M5.7 M5.6=CHOICE1 CHOICE2).
```

- RENAME changes variable name M5.7 to CHOICE1 and M5.6 to CHOICE2. Because all the old variable names are listed to the left of the equals sign and all the new variable names to the right of the equals sign, parentheses are required to enclose the entire specification.

MAP Subcommand

MAP prints a list of the variables in the active system file and their corresponding names in the OSIRIS data set.

- The only specification is keyword MAP. MAP has no additional specifications.
- Multiple MAP subcommands are allowed. Each MAP subcommand maps the results of subcommands that precede it but not results of subcommands that follow it.

Example
```
GET OSIRIS DATA=DATA48 DICTIONARY=DICT48
   /DROP=M5.1 TO M5.3 M5.9 /KEEP=M5.7 M5.6 ALL
   /RENAME (M5.7 M5.6=CHOICE1 CHOICE2)
   /MAP.
```

- MAP confirms all the name changes. MAP also confirms that the first two variables in the active system file are CHOICE1 and CHOICE2, and that all remaining variables from the OSIRIS data set are present in the active file.

GET SAS

This command is not available on all operating systems.

```
GET SAS DATA=ddname.membername [SASLIB=ddname]

[/KEEP={ALL**  }] [/DROP=varlist]
       {varlist}

[/RENAME=(old varlist=new varlist)...]

[/MAP]
```

Example:

```
GET SAS DATA=ELECT.Y1948.
```

Overview

GET SAS (available only on IBM CMS and OS systems) reads SAS data sets. In most instances, SAS data and data definition items can be retrieved, including the file label, variable and value labels, print and write formats, and missing values. If necessary, SAS variable names, print and write formats, and missing values are automatically converted so that they comply with SPSS conventions.

Options

Variable Labels and Formats. You can retrieve SAS labels and formats even when they are not stored in SPSS's default library for your operating system. See SUBLIB Subcommand.

Variable Subsets and Order. You can read a subset of variables and also reorder variables that are copied into the SPSS active system file. See DROP and KEEP subcommands.

Variable Names. You can rename variables as they are copied into the active system file.

Variable Map. To confirm any renaming, subsetting, or reordering, you can display the names of the variables copied into the active system file alongside their corresponding names in the SAS data set.

Basic Specification

• The basic specification is DATA followed by the name of the SAS data set. The name consists of two parts separated by a period (for the meaning of the parts see DATA Subcommand, below). The SAS data set is copied into the active system file and any necessary data conversions are effected (see SAS to SPSS Data Conversion, below).

Subcommand Order

• DATA must be the first specification.

• When used, SASLIB must immediately follow DATA.

• KEEP, DROP, RENAME, and MAP may each appear multiple times and in any order but must follow DATA and SASLIB.

Syntax Rules

• DATA and SASLIB specifications are not separated by a slash.

• KEEP, DROP, RENAME, and MAP specifications must be separated by a slash.

Operations

• If KEEP is not specified, variables in the active file are in the same order as variables in the SAS data set.

SAS to SPSS Data Conversion

In most instances, GET SAS is able to retrieve the information from SAS data sets that is to be stored into SPSS system files. SPSS makes the following conversions to force SAS data sets to comply with SPSS conventions.

File Label

• The file label for the SPSS file is obtained from the name specified on the LABEL option of the SAS DATA statement.

Variable Types
- Both SAS and SPSS allow two types of variables: numeric and character string. During conversion, SAS numeric variables become SPSS numeric variables, and SAS character string variables become SPSS character string variables of the same length.
- Values for SAS variables that can be identified in date format are converted to the number of seconds from October 15, 1582, to the given date. Similarly, values for any SAS variables that are clearly in date-time format are changed to the number of seconds from October 15, 1582, to the given date and time.

Missing Values
- SAS and SPSS treat missing values in basically different ways. In SPSS, the user can designate certain numbers or strings in the data as missing. In SAS, special values (like the SPSS system-missing value) indicate missing data items, and there is no way to tell what type of information was intended in the missing code and missing values fields. Since SAS has no user-defined missing values, all SAS missing codes are converted to SPSS system-missing values.

Print and Write Formats
- Formats are present in the SAS data set only if an INFORMAT or a FORMAT statement appeared in the DATA step that created the data set. The FORMAT statement gives the format to use on output, so if there is an equivalent printable format in SPSS, it will be used as the print format. Otherwise, SPSS attempts to use the INFORMAT. The INFORMAT, if present, is preferred for the SPSS write format. If an INFORMAT is not present, SPSS attempts to use the format on the FORMAT statement.
- If there are no SPSS equivalents for SAS formats, or if no format information exists, a default F8.2 format is used for numeric variables and an A format is used for character string variables. The only exceptions are date formats, which default to F14.0, and date-time formats, which have a default of F16.1.
- Table 1 shows the correspondence between SPSS and SAS formats.

Table 1 Output format correspondence

SPSS format	SAS format	Print	Write
Aw	$w	x	x
AHEXw	$HEXw	x	x
COMMAw.d	COMMAw.d	x	x
DOLLARw.d	DOLLARw.d	x	x
Fw.d	w.d	x	x
IBw.d	IBw.d		x
PIBHEXw	HEXw wa=16	x	x
Pw.d	PDw.d		x
PIBw.d	PIBw.d		x
PKw.d,PKw	n/a	n/a	n/a
RBw.d	RBw.d		x
RBHEX16	HEX16	x	x
Zw.d	ZDw.d		x
Ew.d	Ew.d	x	x

Variable Names
- Like SPSS, SAS allows variable names up to eight characters long, but the SAS naming conventions are somewhat different from those in SPSS. A SAS variable name must begin with a letter or an underscore. The underscore can be used within SPSS variable names but not at the beginning of a name. All leading underscores in SAS files are therefore changed to @ symbols.
- If an SPSS reserved keyword is used as a SAS variable name, SPSS appends the # symbol to the name and issues a warning message. The SPSS reserved keywords are ALL, AND, BY, GE, GT, LE, LT, NE, NOT, OR, TO, and WITH. A SAS variable named AND, for example, would be converted to AND#.

Variable Labels
- Variables mentioned on a LABEL statement in the SAS DATA step will have the corresponding label in SPSS.

Value Labels
• Two conditions must be met to obtain value label data from SAS data sets: SAS form value labels must have been stored into a SASLIB via the DDNAME = option on the PROC FORMAT statement; and a FORMAT statement must have appeared on the DATA step to associate the value labels with variables in the data set. If these conditions are met, SPSS attempts to read and convert the value labels. To be usable as an SPSS value label, a numeric format should have a FUZZ value equal to or smaller than the standard value assigned by SAS.

DATA Subcommand
DATA names the SAS data set to be used as input. DATA is required and must be the first specification on GET SAS.

• The only specification is the name of the SAS data set. The name consists of two parts separated by a period. The meaning of the parts depends on whether the operating system is in an IBM OS or IBM CMS environment.

• In an OS environment, the first part of the SAS data set name refers to the DDNAME in the JCL, and the second to the member name, or the internal name of the SAS file. If the DDNAME begins with TAPE, the SAS file is assumed to be in tape format. Other DDNAMES refer to SAS files in disk format.

• In a CMS environment, the first part of the data set name corresponds to the *file type* and the second part to the *file name.* If the file type begins with TAPE, the SAS file is expected to be in tape format. If a file in tape format resides on disk, it must have a *file mode* of 4, for example, A4. A FILEDEF command must be used to let SPSS know the SAS file is in tape format. Other file types correspond to SAS files in disk format.

Example
`GET SAS DATA=ELECT.Y1948.`

• If the environment is IBM OS, DATA specifies a disk-formatted SAS FILE whose DDNAME is ELECT and whose member name is Y1948.

• If the environment is IBM CMS, DATA specifies a SAS data set with file type ELECT and filename Y1948.

SASLIB Subcommand
SASLIB specifies the DDNAME for the library containing SAS formats. These formats may contain value labels for some or all of the variables.

• SASLIB can be omitted if value labels are not needed, if formats are stored in the STEPLIB, JOBLIB, or link libraries in an OS environment, or if formats are stored as TEXT files in CMS.

• When used, SASLIB must immediately follow DATA.

• A slash is not used to separate the DATA and SASLIB specifications. However, slashes are used to separate any other subcommands used on GET SAS.

Example
`GET SAS DATA=ELECT.Y1948 SASLIB=LABELS.`

• SASLIB indicates data formats are in the SAS library file LABELS.

DROP and KEEP Subcommands
DROP and KEEP copy a subset of variables into the active file. DROP specifies the variables not to copy into the active file; KEEP specifies the variables to copy into the active file.

• DROP and KEEP specifications must use SPSS variable names, not SAS variable names (see SAS to SPSS Data Conversion, above).

• Keyword TO can be used to specify a group of consecutive variables from the SAS data set.

• Variables may be specified in any order. The variable order on KEEP determines the variable sequence in the active file. Variable order on DROP does not affect the order of variables in the active system file: the variables are copied in the same sequence in which they appear in the SAS data set.

• Multiple DROP and KEEP subcommands are allowed.

• If a variable is referenced twice, only the first mention of the variable is recognized.

Reordering Variables
- The variable order on KEEP determines the variable sequence in the active file.
- Keyword ALL on KEEP refers to all remaining variables not previously specified. ALL must be the last specification on KEEP.

Example
```
GET SAS DATA=ELECT.Y1948
   /DROP=@V1 TO @V3 @V9 /KEEP=@V7 @V6 ALL.
```
- DROP excludes all variables between and including @V1 to @V3, as well as @V9, from the active file. All other variables are copied into the active file.
- KEEP determines that @V7 and @V6 are the first two variables in the active file, followed by all remaining variables not specified on DROP. Variables not specified on KEEP are copied into the active file in the same sequence in which they appear in the original SAS data set.
- Note that DROP and KEEP use the SPSS variable names and not the SAS variable names.

RENAME Subcommand

RENAME changes the names of variables as they are copied into the active system file.

- Name changes can be specified in the form *old varname=new varname.* Multiple sets of variable specifications are allowed. Each set may be enclosed in optional parentheses.
- As an alternative to the above, name changes can be specified with a list of old variable names followed by an equals sign and a list of new variable names. The same number of variables must be specified on both lists. A single set of parentheses enclosing the entire specification is required for this method.
- RENAME specifications must use SPSS variable names, not SAS variable names (see SAS to SPSS Data Conversion, above).
- Old variable names need not be specified according to their order in the SAS save file.
- Name changes take place in one operation; hence, variable names can be exchanged between two variables.
- Variables cannot be renamed to scratch variables.
- Multiple RENAME subcommands are allowed.

Example
```
GET SAS DATA=ELECT.Y1948
   /DROP=@V1 TO @V3 @V9 /KEEP=@V7 @V6 ALL
   /RENAME (@V7 @V6=CHOICE1 CHOICE2).
```
- RENAME changes variable name @V7 to CHOICE1 and @V6 to CHOICE2. Because all the old variable names are listed to the left of the equals sign and all the new variable names to the right of the equals sign, parentheses are required to enclose the entire specification.

MAP Subcommand

MAP prints a list of the variables in the active system file and their corresponding names in the SAS data set.

- The only specification is keyword MAP. MAP has no additional specifications.
- Multiple MAP subcommands are allowed. Each MAP subcommand maps the results of subcommands that precede it but not results of subcommands that follow it.

Example
```
GET SAS DATA=ELECT.Y1948
   /DROP=@V1 TO @V3 @V9 /KEEP=@V7 @V6 ALL
   /RENAME (@V7 @V6=CHOICE1 CHOICE2)
   /MAP.
```
- MAP confirms all the name changes. MAP also confirms that the first two variables in the active file are CHOICE1 and CHOICE2, and that all remaining variables from the SAS data set are present in the active file.

GET SCSS

This command is not available on all operating systems.

```
GET SCSS MASTERFILE=file [/WORKFILE=file]

                      {ALL**                   }
                      {varlist                 }
       [/VARIABLES={$varlist                 }]
                      {$ALL                     }
                      {(old varlist=new varlist)}
```

**Default if the subcommand is omitted.

Example:

```
GET SCSS MASTERFILE=MHUBIN  WORKFILE=WHUBIN.
```

Overview

GET SCSS reads an SCSS masterfile or a workfile/masterfile combination. If necessary, problem missing-value treatments from SCSS are recoded.

Options

Workfiles. You can specify a workfile to read with the masterfile. See the WORKFILE subcommand.

Variable Subsets, Order, and Names. You can read a subset of variables and reorder and/or rename variables that are copied into the SPSS active system file. See VARIABLES Subcommand.

Basic Specification

• The basic specification is the MASTERFILE subcommand, which specifies the SCSS masterfile to be read. The masterfile is copied into the active file.

Subcommand Order

• If both MASTERFILE and WORKFILE are specified, they can be used in either order.
• VARIABLES (when used) must be the last specification.

Operations

• In most instances, GET SCSS is able to retrieve the information from the SCSS masterfile and workfile. SPSS may have to recode data in the manner explained in the following sections.

Missing Values

• SPSS and SCSS handle missing values differently. First, SCSS allows more than three missing values. In addition, SCSS variables can have missing-value ranges that include valid values. Also, SCSS can use alphabetic ranges to declare missing values. Problem numeric values are recoded to the system-missing value and problem alphabetic values are recoded to blanks.
• In SCSS a value can be missing for some cases (via value revision) and not for other cases. SPSS considers such a value missing for all cases when the file is read using GET SCSS.
• A warning message is issued to indicate the action taken any time SPSS recodes a missing value.

Formats

• The print and write formats for numeric variables are based on the length of the values. Variables copied with original alphanumeric values have print and write formats of A1, A2, or A4 for variables with three or four characters. (Alphanumeric values cannot occur in a variable in a masterfile created using the SAVE SCSS command in SPSS but can occur in a masterfile defined directly in SCSS where the original values are alphanumeric but were revised as the masterfile was created.)

MASTERFILE Subcommand

MASTERFILE specifies the masterfile to be read. If the masterfile alone is specified, only masterfile information is copied.

• MASTERFILE is required and must precede VARIABLES (if used).

• If WORKFILE is not specified, revisions or additions kept on any of the workfiles that point to the specified masterfile are not available to SPSS.

Example   GET SCSS MASTERFILE=HUBIN.

• GET SCSS retrieves the SCSS masterfile HUBIN.

**WORKFILE
Subcommand**

WORKFILE specifies a workfile associated with the masterfile being read. If WORKFILE is specified, SPSS builds the active system file to reflect changes recorded in the workfile including labels, revisions to existing variables, and computed variables.

• MASTERFILE and WORKFILE can be used in either order. An optional slash can separate the MASTERFILE and WORKFILE subcommands.

• Both MASTERFILE and WORKFILE must precede VARIABLES.

• If the workfile alone is specified, SPSS tries to locate the masterfile but cannot always succeed (depending on the completeness of the specification in the workfile and on the operating system).

Example   GET SCSS WORKFILE=WHUBIN MASTERFILE=MHUBIN.

• WORKFILE specifies workfile WHUBIN, which stores changes made to the masterfile MHUBIN.

**VARIABLES
Subcommand**

VARIABLES limits the number of variables SPSS copies from the SCSS files. VARIABLES can also be used to determine the order of variables in the active file and to rename variables.

• VARIABLES must be the last specification on GET SCSS. VARIABLES can specify a variable list or keywords ALL or $ALL. ALL is the default if a workfile is specified. $ALL specifies the unrevised masterfile version of all of the variables.

• Variables are copied in the order specified on VARIABLES.

• Variable name THRU is allowed in SCSS but not SPSS, so it must be renamed.

Renaming Variables
• Name changes can be specified in the form *old varname=new varname*. The specification can be enclosed in optional parentheses.

• As an alternative to the above, name changes can be specified with a list of old variable names followed by an equals sign and a list of new variable names. The same number of variables must be specified on both lists. A single set of parentheses enclosing the entire specification is required for this method.

• Name changes take place in one operation. Therefore, variable names can be exchanged between two variables.

• Variables cannot be renamed to scratch variables.

Example   GET SCSS WORKFILE=WHUBIN MASTERFILE=MHUBIN
                 /VARIABLES=MOHIRED TO SEX, JOBCAT.

• Variables in the active file are limited to those between and including MO-HIRED to SEX, and also JOBCAT.

Example   GET SCSS WORKFILE=WHUBIN MASTERFILE=MHUBIN
                 /VARIABLES=MOHIRED TO SEX ($SEX=SEX$) JOBCAT.

• This example uses the dollar sign to tell SCSS to use the unrevised masterfile version of variable SEX. Since variable names beginning with dollar signs are not allowed in SPSS, the variable has to be renamed.

Example   GET SCSS WORKFILE=WHUBIN MASTERFILE=MHUBIN
                 /VARIABLES=(DEPT,SALARY,HOURLY=DEPT1,SALARY1,HOURLY1).

• Variable DEPT is renamed DEPT1, SALARY is renamed SALARY1, and HOURLY is renamed HOURLY1.

GET TRANSLATE

This command is not available on all operating systems.

```
GET TRANSLATE† FILE=file

[/TYPE={WK1}] [/FIELDNAMES]*
        {WKS}
        {WR1}  [/RANGE={name       }]*
        {WRK}          {start..stop}
        {SLK}          {start:stop }
        {DBF}


  [/KEEP={ALL    }] [/DROP=varlist]
        {varlist}
```

†Not available on all systems.
*Available only for spreadsheet files.

Keyword	Foreign file
WK1	1-2-3 Release 2.0
WKS	1-2-3 Release 1A
WR1	Symphony Release 2.0
WRK	Symphony Release 1.0
SLK	Multiplan (symbolic format only)
DBF	all dBase

Example:
```
GET TRANSLATE FILE='PROJECT.WKS'
 /FIELDNAMES
 /RANGE=D3..J279.
```

Overview

GET TRANSLATE creates an SPSS active system file from a foreign file. Supported formats are 1-2-3, Symphony, Multiplan, dBASE-II, dBASE-III, and dBASE-IV.

Options

Variable Subsets. You can use the DROP and KEEP subcommands to specify variables to omit or retain in the resulting active system file.

Spreadsheet Files. You can use the RANGE subcommand to translate a subset of cells from a spreadsheet file. You can use the FIELDNAMES subcommand to translate field names in the spreadsheet file to SPSS variable names.

Basic Specification

• The basic specification is FILE with a file specification enclosed in apostrophes.

• If the file extension for the file is not the default for the type of file you are getting, TYPE must also be specified.

Subcommand Order

• Subcommands can be named in any order.

Operations

• GET TRANSLATE replaces an existing active system file.

Spreadsheets

A spreadsheet file suitable for SPSS should be arranged so that each row represents a case and columns indicate variables.

• By default, the new active system file contains all rows and up to 256 columns from 1-2-3 or Symphony, or up to 255 columns from Multiplan files.

• By default, GET TRANSLATE uses the column letters as variable names in the active system file.

• The first row of a spreadsheet or specified range may contain field labels immediately followed by rows of data. These names can be transferred as SPSS variable names (see the FIELDNAMES subcommand).

• The current value of a formula is translated to the active system file.

• Blank, ERR, and NA values in 1-2-3 and Symphony are translated as system-missing in the SPSS active system file.

• Hidden columns and cells in 1-2-3 Release 2 and Symphony files are translated into the SPSS active system file.

- Column width and format type are transferred to the dictionary of the active system file.
- The format type is assigned from values in the first data row. By default, the first data row is row 1. If RANGE is specified, the first data row is the first row in the range. If FIELDNAMES is specified, the first data row follows immediately after the single row containing field names.
- If a cell in the first data row is empty, the variable is assigned the global default format from the spreadsheet.
- The formats from 1-2-3, Symphony, and Multiplan are translated by default as follows:

1-2-3/Symphony	Multiplan	SPSS
Fixed	Fixed	Number
	Integer	Number
Scientific	Exponent	Number
Currency	$ (dollar)	Dollar
,(comma)		Comma
General	General	Number
+/−	* (bargraph)	Number
Percent	Percent	Number
Date		Number
Time		Number
Text		Number
Label	Alpha	String

- If a string is encountered in a column with numeric format, the active system file contains the system-missing value.
- If a numeric value is encountered in a column with string format, the active system file contains a blank.
- Blank lines are translated as cases containing the system-missing value for numeric variables and blanks for string variables.
- 1-2-3 and Symphony date and time indicators (shown at the bottom of the screen) are not transferred from WKS, WK1, WRK, or WR1 files.

Databases   Database files are logically very similar to SPSS data files.

- By default, all fields and records from dBASE-II, dBASE-III, or dBASE-IV files are included in the SPSS active system file.
- Field names are automatically translated to SPSS variable names.
- If the FIELDNAMES subcommand is used with database files, it is ignored.
- Field names to be translated should comply with SPSS variable-naming conventions.
- Field names longer than eight characters are truncated.
- Field names must be unique in the first eight characters. If a field name is not unique, the field will be dropped.
- Colons used in dBASE-II field names are translated to underscores.
- Records in dBASE-II, dBASE-III, or dBASE-IV that have been marked for deletion but that have not actually been purged are included in the active system file. To differentiate these cases, GET TRANSLATE creates a new string variable D_R, which contains an asterisk for cases marked for deletion. Other cases contain a blank for D_R.
- Character, floating, and numeric fields are transferred directly to SPSS variables. Date and logical fields are converted into string variables. Memo fields are ignored. The following table shows how dBASE formats are translated to SPSS:

dBASE	SPSS
Character	String
Logical	String
Date	Number
Numeric	Number
Floating	Number
Memo	Ignored

Limitations   The maximum number of variables that can be translated into the SPSS active system file is determined by the maximum number of variables the foreign file can handle:

Foreign file	Maximum variables
1-2-3	256
Symphony	256
Multiplan	255
dBASE-IV	255
dBASE-III	128
dBASE-II	32

FILE Subcommand   FILE names the foreign file to read. The only specification is the name of the foreign file enclosed in apostrophes.

Example   `GET TRANSLATE FILE='PROJECT.WKS'.`

- GET TRANSLATE creates an active system file from the 1-2-3 Release 1.0 spreadsheet with the name PROJECT.WKS.
- The active file contains all rows and uses the column letters as variable names.
- The format for each variable is determined by the format of the value in the first row of each column.

TYPE Subcommand   TYPE indicates the format of a foreign file.

- TYPE can be omitted if the file extension named on FILE is the default for the type of file you are getting.
- The TYPE subcommand takes precedence over the file extension.
- You can create a Lotus format file in Multiplan and translate it to a SPSS active system file with TYPE=WKS.
- Available keywords on TYPE are

WK1   *1-2-3 Release 2.0.*

WKS   *1-2-3 Release 1A.*

WR1   *Symphony Release 2.0.*

WRK   *Symphony Release 1.0.*

SLK   *Multiplan (symbolic format).*

DBF   *All dBASE files.*

Example   `GET TRANSLATE FILE='PROJECT.OCT' /TYPE=SLK.`

- GET TRANSLATE creates an active system file from the Multiplan spreadsheet PROJECT.OCT.

FIELDNAMES Subcommand   FIELDNAMES translates spreadsheet field names into SPSS variable names.

- FIELDNAMES can be used with spreadsheets only. FIELDNAMES is ignored when used with database files.
- Each cell in the first row of the spreadsheet file or range must contain a field name. If a column does not contain a name, the column is dropped.
- Field names to be translated into SPSS should conform to the SPSS variable-naming conventions. They must be unique in the first eight characters and cannot have leading blanks.
- Variable names that exceed eight characters are truncated.
- If two or more columns in the spreadsheet have the same field name, only the first occurrence is translated to the active system file.
- Illegal characters in field names are changed to underscores in SPSS.
- If you use SPSS reserved words (ALL, AND, BY, EQ, GE, GT, LE, LT, NE, NOT, OR, TO, or WITH) as field names in a spreadsheet file, GET TRANS-LATE appends a dollar sign ($) to the variable name. For example, 1-2-3

columns named GE, GT, EQ, and BY are named GE$, GT$, EQ$, and BY$ in the SPSS active system file.

Example   `GET TRANSLATE FILE='MONTHLY.WRK' /FIELDNAMES.`

- GET TRANSLATE creates an active system file from a Symphony spreadsheet. The first row in the spreadsheet contains field names that are used as variable names in the active file.

RANGE Subcommand

RANGE translates a specified set of cells from a spreadsheet file.

- RANGE cannot be used for translating from database files.
- For 1-2-3 or Symphony, specify the beginning of the range with a column letter and row number, two periods, and the end of the range with a column letter and row number, as in A1..K14.
- For Multiplan spreadsheets, specify the beginning and ending cells of the range separated by a colon, as in R1C1:R14C11.
- You can also specify the range using range names supplied in Symphony, 1-2-3, or Multiplan.
- If you specify FIELDNAMES with RANGE, the first row of the range must contain field names.

Example   `GET TRANSLATE FILE='PROJECT.WKS' /FIELDNAMES /RANGE=D3..J279.`

- GET TRANSLATE creates an active system file from the 1-2-3 Release 1A file PROJECT.WKS.
- Variable names are assigned from the field names in the first row of the range, in this case row 3.
- Data from cells D4 through J279 are transferred to the active file.

DROP and KEEP Subcommands

Use DROP or KEEP to copy only a subset of variables into the active system file. DROP specifies a set of variables to exclude, and KEEP specifies a set of variables to retain.

- Specify a list of variables, column, or field names separated by commas or spaces.
- KEEP does not affect the order of variables in the resulting file. Variables are kept in their original order.
- If FIELDNAMES is specified when translating from a spreadsheet, the DROP and KEEP subcommands must refer to the field names, not the default column letters.
- If you specify both RANGE and KEEP, the resulting file contains only variables that are both within the range and specified on KEEP.
- If you specify both RANGE and DROP, the resulting file contains only variables within the range and excludes those mentioned on the DROP subcommand, even if they are within the range.

Example   `GET TRANSLATE FILE='ADDRESS.DBF' /DROP=PHONENO, ENTRY.`

- GET TRANSLATE creates an active system file from the dBASE file ADDRESS.DBF, omitting the fields named PHONENO and ENTRY.

Example   `GET TRANSLATE FILE='PROJECT.OCT' /TYPE=WK1 /FIELDNAMES`
`/KEEP=NETINC, REP, QUANTITY, REGION, MONTH, DAY, YEAR.`

- GET TRANSLATE creates an SPSS active system file from the 1-2-3 Release 2.0 file called PROJECT.OCT.
- Subcommand FIELDNAMES indicates that the first row of the spreadsheet contains field names, which will be translated into variable names in the SPSS active system file.
- Subcommand KEEP translates columns with the field names NETINC, REP, QUANTITY, REGION, MONTH, DAY, and YEAR to the SPSS active system file.

GRAPH

GRAPH is operational only on those machines where SPSS Graphics is installed.

```
GRAPH

    [/TITLE='line 1' ['line 2']]

    [/SUBTITLE='line']

    [/FOOTNOTE='line 1' ['line 2']]

    [/DRAW={FULL**}]
           {QUICK }
           {NO    }

    [/EXECUTE={MENU† }]
             {RETURN}
             {NO†   }

    [/GCMDFILE=file]  [/GDATA=file]  [/GOUT=file]

    [/ADEVICE=device]  [/GDEVICE=device]

    [/GMEMORY=integer [{K}]]
                      {M}

    [/BAR [{(SIMPLE)      }]={sumf(varlist) [sumf(varlist)]... }]
                            {sumf(var) BY var                  }
                            {countf BY var                     }

          {(COMPOSITIONAL)} ={sumf(varlist) [sumf(varlist)] ...}
                            {sumf(var) BY var                   }
                            {countf BY var                      }

          {(GROUPED)      } ={sumf(varlist) [sumf(varlist)] ... BY var}††
                            {sumf(var) BY var BY var               }
                            {countf BY var BY var                  }

          {(STACKED)      } ={sumf(varlist) [sumf(varlist)] ... BY var}††
                            {sumf(var) BY var BY var               }
                            {countf BY var BY var                  }

          {(RANGE)        } ={sumf(var) sumf(var) [sumf(var) sumf(var)] ... BY var}
                            {sumf(var) sumf(var) BY var BY var                    }

    [/PIE [(RADIAL)]={sumf(varlist) [sumf(varlist)] ...}]
                    {sumf(var) BY var                   }
                    {countf BY var                      }

    [/LINE [{(SIMPLE)    }]={sumf(var) BY var}]
                          {countf BY var     }

           {(MULTIPLE) } ={sumf(varlist) [sumf(varlist)] ... BY var}††
                         {sumf(var) BY var BY var               }
                         {countf BY var BY var                  }

           {(AREA)     } ={sumf(varlist) [sumf(varlist)] ... BY var}
                         {sumf(var) BY var BY var               }
                         {countf BY var [BY var]                }

           {(DIFFERENCE)} ={sumf(var) BY var BY dvar }
                          {sumf(var) sumf(var) BY var}
                          {countf BY var BY dvar      }
```

```
[/PYRAMID={sumf(var) sumf(var) [sumf(var) sumf(var)] ... BY var}]
          {sumf(varlist) [sumf(varlist)] ... BY var BY dvar   }
          {sumf(var) BY var BY dvar BY var                    }
          {countf BY var BY dvar [BY var]                     }

[/BLOCK={sumf(varlist) [sumf(varlist)] ... BY var}]
        {sumf(var) BY var BY var                  }
        {countf BY var [BY var]                   }

[/HISTOGRAM=var]

[/SCATTERPLOT={varlist WITH varlist [(PAIR)] [BY var [(NAME)]]}]
              {var WITH var [(PAIR)] [BY var] [BY var (NAME)] }

[/MAP [{(CHOROPLETH)}]=sumf(var) BY var]
       {(PRISM)     }

[/BOUNDARY={USSTATES}]
           {USCOUNTY}
           {CANADA  }
           {PROVINCE}
           {WORLD   }
           {EUROPE  }
           {'file'  }

[/REGION={DEFAULT}]
         {'file '}

[/TABLE={sumf(varlist) [sumf(varlist)] ... [BY var [BY var]]}]
        {sumf(sumvar) [BY var [BY var [BY var]]]             }
        {countf BY var [BY var [BY var]]                     }

[/CASEFILE= varlist [BY varlist]]
```

**Default if the subcommand is omitted.
†Default in some operating systems. See the SPSS *Operations Guide* for your system.
††There must be at least two summary variables in this subcommand, either aggregated by the same function as in MEAN(S1 S2) BY C, or aggregated by different summary functions as in MEAN(S1) SUM(S2) BY C.

Key to abbreviations:

var   variable
varlist   list of variables
dvar   dichotomous variable
sumf   summary function
countf   count function

The function VALUE(varlist) may be used in place of sumf(varlist) BY var.

Summary functions:

MINIMUM	Minimum
MAXIMUM	Maximum
N	Weighted N
SUM	Sum
CUSUM	Cumulative sum
MEAN	Mean
STDDEV	Standard deviation
VARIANCE	Variance
MEDIAN	Median
MODE	Mode
PTILE(x)	Xth percentile
PLT(x)	Percent less than x
PGT(x)	Percent greater than x
NLT(x)	Number less than x
NGT(x)	Number greater than x

PIN(x1,x2)	Percent between x1 & x2
NIN(x1,x2)	Number between x1 & x2
VALUE	Value by case. Use VALUE(varlist) in place of SUM(varlist) BY N where varlist is a variable list and N is the case number of each record.

Count functions:

COUNT	Count
PCT	Percent
CUPCT	Cumulative percent
FREQ	Frequency
CUFREQ	Cumulative frequency

Example:

```
SET ADEVICE = SUN
  /GDEVICE = SUNC.

GRAPH BAR = MEAN (MURDER) BY CITY
  /EXECUTE = RETURN.
```

Overview

GRAPH generates the instructions and data for producing a chart in SPSS Graphics. The chart can be a bar chart, pie chart, line chart, pyramid chart, block diagram, histogram, scatterplot, or map. SPSS can invoke the graphics system and cause the plot to be drawn directly; or you can instruct it to save the files, which you can later use in an SPSS Graphics session.

Options

Titles and Footnotes. You can specify a title, subtitle, and footnote for the chart.

GRAPH Execution. You can control whether GRAPH returns you to the SPSS session or leaves you in Graphics. See EXECUTE Subcommand.

Output File. You can specify a file to which SPSS Graphics sends the graph. After you leave Graphics, the file can then be used by a displayer, plotter, or terminal to draw the graph. (See GOUT Subcommand.)

The following options can be specified on the SET command or on GRAPH.

- **Graphics Display.** You can control whether Graphics draws the full graph or a simplified version of the graph (to save time). You can also suppress the drawing. (See DRAW Subcommand.)

- **Intermediate Files.** You can name the graphics command file and the graphics data file. (See GCMDFILE and GDATA subcommands.)

- **Data Device.** You can specify the terminal used to enter data onto the SPSS Graphics menu. (See ADEVICE Subcommand.)

- **Graphics Device.** You can specify the terminal, workstation, or printer on which the graph will be created. (See GDEVICE Subcommand.)

- **Memory.** You can set the amount of memory allocated to SPSS Graphics. (See GMEMORY Subcommand.)

Basic Specification

The basic specification is ADEVICE, GDEVICE, and a chart type subcommand.

- ADEVICE specifies the terminal used to enter data into the SPSS Graphics menu.

- GDEVICE specifies the terminal, plotter, or printer on which the graph will be created.

- The chart type subcommand specifies the type of chart to create. In most instances there must be at least one variable and one aggregating function on the chart type subcommand.

Subcommand Order

Subcommands can be named in any order.

Syntax Rules

- Only one chart type subcommand can be specified.

- If ADEVICE and GDEVICE are specified on the SET command, they can be omitted from the GRAPH command. Otherwise, they are required.

• If any subcommands are specified on GRAPH (including ADEVICE or GDEVICE), a chart type subcommand must also be specified. The command GRAPH by itself initiates a normal SPSS Graphics session.

• If the chart type is MAP, the REGION and BOUNDARY subcommands can be specified. If the chart type is not MAP, neither the REGION nor the BOUNDARY subcommand can be specified.

Settings on the SET Command

The following GRAPH subcommands can be specified on the SET command: ADEVICE, GDEVICE, DRAW, GCMDFILE, GDATA, and GMEMORY. When specified on SET, these subcommands apply to all GRAPH commands in the SPSS session. When specified on GRAPH, they apply only to the current GRAPH command. Settings specified on GRAPH override those specified on SET. To see the current settings, use SHOW.

Operations

• You must be able to run SPSS Graphics on your system to use the GRAPH command.

• GRAPH creates two intermediate files: an SPSS system file containing all the variables (aggregated and unaggregated) used in the chart, and an SPSS Graphics command file. SPSS Graphics uses those two files to create the final charts.

• Depending on the setting of the EXECUTE subcommand, GRAPH runs the newly created command file and leaves you in Graphics, runs the file and returns you to SPSS, or remains in SPSS but creates the files so you can later run the Graphics command file. The default for EXECUTE varies by operating system, and some operating systems allow only the last option. For more information, see the SPSS *Operations Guide* for your system.

• The system file created by GRAPH is a normal SPSS system file. You can load it into SPSS with the GET command or load it into SPSS Graphics with the menu selection: Create data set from SPSS-X system file.

• The Graphics command file is a text file that can be edited. To modify the command file after SPSS generates it, see the SPSS Graphics Rerun Facility in the *SPSS Graphics Coordinator's Notebook*.

• When SPSS Graphics runs the command file, it creates a table or casefile in SPSS Graphics. The filename always starts with the prefix XDE and ends with a number.

• Some operating systems may not allow SPSS to dynamically invoke SPSS Graphics. In those operating systems you must exit SPSS and invoke SPSS Graphics from the command prompt. This means that GRAPH cannot be used without subcommands and that EXECUTE=MENU is ignored. For more details, see the SPSS *Operations Guide* for your system.

• Value labels are passed to SPSS Graphics and used to label the appropriate values on the graph. If a value label exists for a value, that value is included in the system file built by GRAPH and is included in most types of charts even if that value is defined as missing or if no cases with that value occur in the data. You can omit categories using the edit data facility within SPSS Graphics.

• Variable labels for non-aggregated variables are passed to SPSS Graphics and used to label appropriate portions of the graph.

• Aggregated variable labels are constructed from the aggregating function name and the variable name. For instance, STDDEV(MURDER) would have the label "Standard deviation of MURDER."

• In most instances, the variables in the new system file have the same names they have in the original file. If there is a naming conflict GRAPH constructs a new variable name with two or three parts. The prefix comes from the aggregating function and the root from the original variable. The prefix and suffix are always separated by an underscore. For example, if the STDDEV function is applied to the existing variable MURDER, GRAPH creates a variable named SD_MURDE. If that doesn't uniquely identify the variable, a numerical suffix is added. If a variable with that name already exists, GRAPH creates a variable named SD_MUR01.

• GRAPH works the same whether it is executed within interactive SPSS or from within a command file that is executed by SPSS.

Limitations
- In some operating systems Graphics does not allow strings over eight characters long. In these operating systems, a long string on the GRAPH command generates an error. For more information, see the SPSS *Operations Guide* for your system.
- Up to 99 variables can be aggregated with GRAPH.

Example
```
SET ADEVICE = SUN
   /GDEVICE = SUNC.
GRAPH BAR = SUM (MURDER) BY CITY
   /EXECUTE = RETURN.
```

- The SET command specifies a Sun workstation as the alpha or menuing device and the Sun color workstation as the graphics display device.
- The BAR subcommand produces a simple bar chart showing the number of murders in each city.
- The EXECUTE subcommand tells SPSS what to do after the graph is finished. When the graph is drawn and the user presses RETURN, the system exits SPSS Graphics and returns to the SPSS session.

Example
```
GRAPH TABLE = MEAN (AGE) BY EYECOLOR.
```

- The TABLE subcommand creates an aggregated SPSS system file from which it generates an SPSS Graphics data set containing the summary variable "Mean of AGE" and the category variable "Eye color". The data could be used to create any kind of chart which can be made with a single summary variable and a single category variable.

Example
```
GRAPH MAP = MEAN (MURDER) BY COUNTY
   /BOUNDARY = USCOUNTY.
```

- The MAP subcommand generates a choropleth map of the murders that occurred in each county. COUNTY must identify the counties by geographic code. These codes are listed in Appendix A of the *SPSS Graphics* manual.
- The BOUNDARY subcommand tells Graphics that the outlines of the counties indicated by the COUNTY variable are contained in a file called USCOUNTY.

TITLE, SUBTITLE, and FOOTNOTE Subcommands

Subcommands TITLE, SUBTITLE, and FOOTNOTE specify lines of text placed at the top or bottom of the graph.

- One or two lines of text can be specified for TITLE or FOOTNOTE, one line of text for SUBTITLE.
- Each line of text must be enclosed in apostrophes or quotation marks. The maximum length of any line is 72 characters.
- Font sizes and weights are the defaults within SPSS Graphics for the various titling elements.
- The default title, subtitle, and footnote are all blank.

Example
```
GRAPH TITLE = 'Murder in Major U.S Cities'
   /SUBTITLE = 'per 100,000 people'
   /FOOTNOTE = 'The above data was reported on August 26, 1987'
   /BAR = SUM(MURDER) BY CITY.
```

Figure 1 Title and footnote options

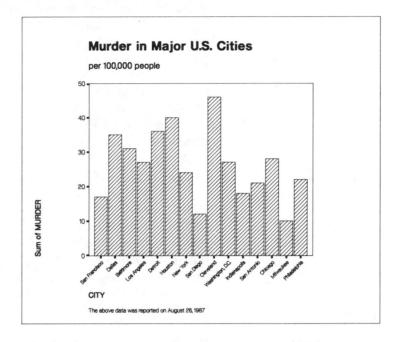

Basic Chart Specifications

Subcommands BAR, PIE, LINE, PYRAMID, BLOCK, HISTOGRAM, SCATTERPLOT, and MAP specify the type of chart to be graphed. Some of the chart types can be further qualified by a keyword in parentheses, as in

```
/BAR (STACKED) = SUM(SALARY) BY YEAR BY DEPT
```

Each subcommand (and qualifying keyword, if there is one) is followed by an equals sign and the specification for the data to be graphed.

Subcommands BAR, PIE, LINE, PYRAMID, and BLOCK define charts based upon a table of aggregated data. Subcommand TABLE takes any specification that is legal for those subcommands but does not identify a chart type. The specification contains at least one function and usually one or more variables that determine the groups within which the function is calculated, as in these examples:

```
/BAR = COUNT BY JOBCAT
/LINE = MEAN(SALES) BY MONTH BY TERRITRY
/PYRAMID = SUM(SALARY) BY JOBCAT BY SEX BY DEPT
/TABLE = MEAN(SALARY) BY JOBCAT BY DEPT
```

Subcommands HISTOGRAM and SCATTERPLOT define charts based upon a file of unaggregated cases. Subcommand CASEFILE builds a file of unaggregated cases which can be used within SPSS Graphics to generate histograms and scatterplots. The specification contains the name(s) of the variable(s) with no aggregating function, as in these examples:

```
/HISTOGRAM = BONUS
/SCATTERPLOT = SALARY WITH GRADE BY SEX
/CASEFILE = SALARY BONUS BENEFIT BY JOBCAT DEPT
```

Aggregation Functions

Two groups of functions can be used in specifying a chart: *summary functions,* and *count functions.*

Summary Functions

These functions are usually used with summary variables (variables which record continuous values, like age or expenses). To specify a summary function, put the name of one or more variables in parentheses after the name of the function, as in

```
/BAR = SUM(SALARY) BY DEPT
```

The summary functions are as follows:

MINIMUM	*Minimum value of the variable.*
MAXIMUM	*Maximum value of the variable.*
N	*Number of cases for which the variable has a non-missing value.*
SUM	*Sum of the values of the variable.*
CUSUM	*Sum of the summary variable, accumulated across values of the category variable.*
MEAN	*Mean.*
STDDEV	*Standard deviation.*
VARIANCE	*Variance.*
MEDIAN	*Median.*
MODE	*Mode.*
PTILE(x)	*Xth percentile value of the variable.* X must be greater than 0 and less than 100.
PLT(x)	*Percentage of cases for which the variable is less than x.*
PGT(x)	*Percent greater than x.*
NLT(x)	*Number less than x.*
NGT(x)	*Number greater than x.*
PIN(x1,x2)	*Percentage of cases for which the variable is greater than or equal to x1, and less than or equal to x2.* X1 must be no greater than x2.
NIN(x1,x2)	*Number of cases for which the variable is greater than or equal to x1, and less than or equal to x2.* X1 must be no greater than x2.

Multiple Summary Functions

Most chart type subcommands allow you to specify multiple summary functions, which can take several forms. The same function can be applied to a list of variables, as in

```
/BAR = SUM(SALARY BONUS BENEFIT) BY DEPT
```

This syntax is equivalent to

```
/BAR = SUM(SALARY) SUM(BONUS) SUM(BENEFIT) BY DEPT
```

Different functions can be applied to the same variable, as in

```
/BAR = MEAN(SALARY) MEDIAN(SALARY) BY DEPT
```

or different functions and variables can be combined, as in

```
/BAR(RANGE) = MIN(SALARY81) MAX(SALARY81)
  MIN(SALARY82) MAX(SALARY82) BY JOBCAT
```

The ways in which multiple summary functions contribute to the structure of various types of chart are illustrated in the discussions of specific chart types.

Count Functions

Count functions yield the count or percentage of valid cases with categories determined by one or more BY variables. For example:

```
/BAR = PCT BY REGION
```

In places where COUNT BY *variable* is expected, you can specify just a variable, as in

```
/BAR = DEPT
```

This is interpreted as COUNT BY DEPT, even though the function COUNT and the keyword BY are not explicitly specified.

The count functions are as follows:

COUNT	*Count of cases in each category.*
PCT	*Count of cases in each category expressed as a percentage of the whole.*
CUPCT	*Cumulative percentage.*
FREQ	*Frequency.* FREQ is the same as COUNT.
CUFREQ	*Cumulative frequency.*

The VALUE Function

The VALUE function yields the value of the specified variable for each case. VALUE(X) implies value of X by n, where n is a sequential number identifying each case. You can specify multiple variables, as in

    /BAR = VALUE(SALARY BONUS BENEFIT)

which gives the salary, bonus, and benefit for each employee. Note that no BY variable is expected.

Data and Conventions Used in the Examples

The examples of chart types (except those for maps) are based upon personnel data from a small (and fictitious) consulting company. The data include a number of summary (continuous) variables such as age, salary, benefits, and bonus. Where these occur in the examples, a continuous variable is appropriate. The data also include many category variables such as sex, race, EEO classification, grade (rank within the organization), and job category. Where these occur in the examples, a category variable is appropriate. Most of this information was collected for four years and saved in separate variables for each year. Thus there are four salary variables (SALARY79, SALARY80, SALARY81, and SALARY82), four variables for grade (GRADE79, etc.), and so on.

Within the following examples, *single function* refers to any one summary or count function and *multiple functions* refers to two or more summary functions as defined in Multiple Summary Functions (above). *BY variable* refers to the keyword BY followed by the name of a category variable. A BY variable divides the data into groups which are plotted separately.

BAR Subcommand

The BAR subcommand creates one of five bar charts. Keywords SIMPLE, GROUPED, STACKED, COMPOSITIONAL, and RANGE determine the kind of bar chart generated.

SIMPLE Keyword

Simple bar chart. A simple bar chart can be defined by a single function and a single BY variable or by multiple summary functions and no BY variable. It is the default if no qualifying keyword to the BAR subcommand is specified and the variables define a simple bar chart (Figures 2–4).

Figure 2 /BAR=MEAN(SALARY82) BY JOBCAT

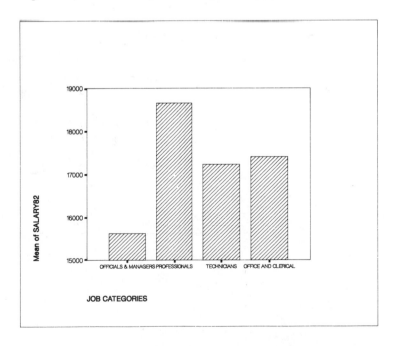

Figure 3 /BAR=COUNT BY JOBCAT

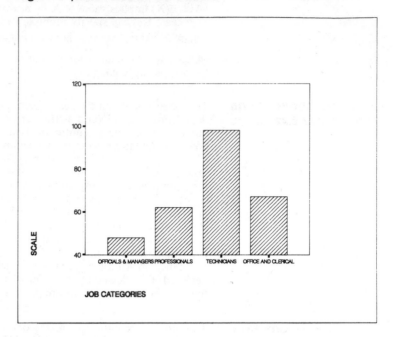

Figure 4 /BAR=MEAN(SALARY79 TO SALARY82)

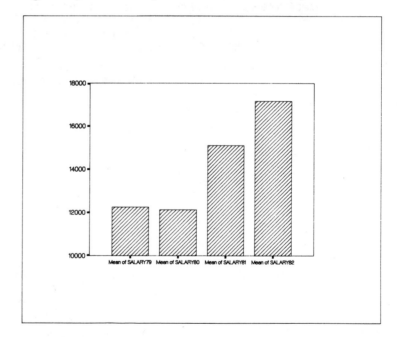

COMPOSITIONAL Keyword

Compositional bar chart. A compositional bar chart divides a single bar into segments stacked one on top of the other. The height of each segment represents the value of the category as a percentage of the whole. It can be defined by a single function and a single BY variable or by multiple summary functions and no BY variable (Figures 5 and 6).

Figure 5 /BAR (COMPOSITIONAL)=COUNT BY JOBCAT

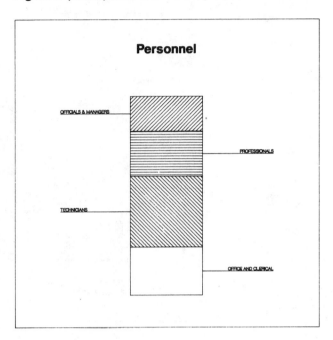

Figure 6 /BAR (COMPOSITIONAL)=SUM(SALARY82 BONUS82 BEN82)

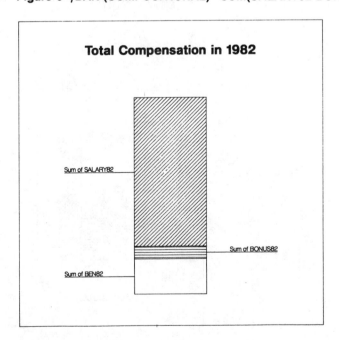

GROUPED Keyword

Grouped bar chart. A grouped bar chart is defined by a single function and two BY variables or by multiple functions and a single BY variable. It is the default if no qualifying keyword to the BAR subcommand is specified and the variables define a grouped bar chart (Figures 7 and 8).

Figure 7 /BAR=MEAN(SALARY82) BY JOBCAT BY SEX

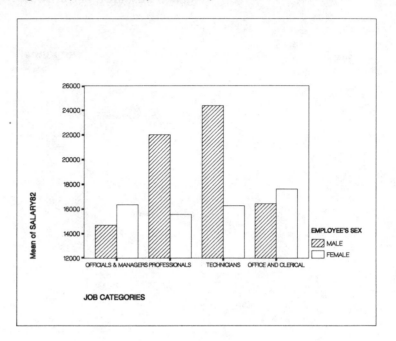

Figure 8 /BAR=MEAN(SALARY79 TO SALARY82) BY SEX

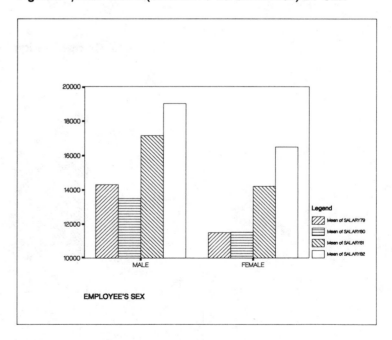

STACKED Keyword

Stacked bar chart. A stacked bar chart displays a series of bars, each divided into segments stacked one on top of the other. The height of each segment represents the value of the category. Like a grouped bar chart, it is defined by a single function and two BY variables or by multiple functions and a single BY variable (Figures 9 and 10).

Figure 9 /BAR(STACKED)=SUM(SALARY82) BY JOBCAT BY LOCATN82

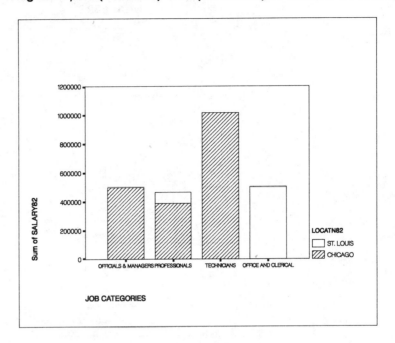

Figure 10 /BAR(STACKED)=SUM(SALARY82 BONUS82 BEN82) BY LOCATN82

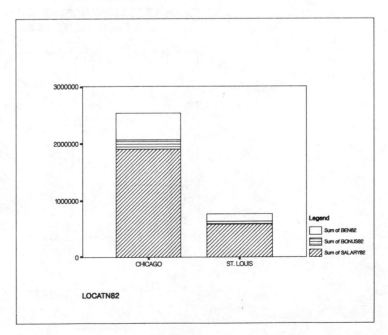

RANGE Keyword

Range bar chart. You can use this kind of chart to compare pairs of variables. A range bar chart displays a set of vertical bars floating above the base axis. The bottom of each bar represents the smaller value between the paired variables. The top represents the larger value. A simple range bar chart is defined by a pair of summary functions and a single BY variable (Figure 11).

Figure 11 /BAR(RANGE)=MIN(SALARY82) MAX(SALARY82) BY GRADE82

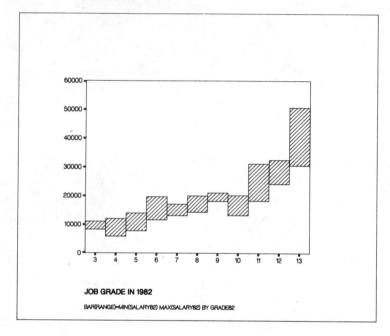

A grouped range bar chart is defined by a pair of summary functions and two BY variables, or by multiple pairs of summary functions (Figures 12 and 13).

Figure 12 /BAR(RANGE)=PTILE(25)(SALARY82) PTILE(75)(SALARY82) BY JOBCAT BY SEX

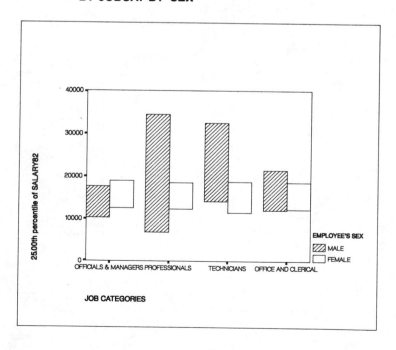

**Figure 13 /BAR(RANGE)=MIN(SALARY81) MAX(SALARY81)
MIN(SALARY82) MAX(SALARY82) BY JOBCAT**

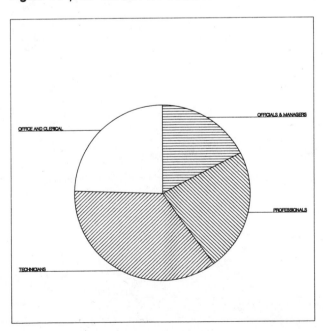

You cannot use count functions in range bar charts.

PIE Subcommand

The PIE subcommand creates one of two kinds of pie charts. With no qualifying keyword, PIE creates a normal pie chart. With the keyword RADIAL, PIE creates a radial pie chart.

Normal Pie Chart

A normal pie chart divides a circle into wedge-shaped sectors. The size of each sector indicates the value of the category relative to the whole. A pie chart can be defined by a single function and a single BY variable or by multiple summary functions and no BY variable (Figures 14 and 15).

Figure 14 /PIE=COUNT BY JOBCAT

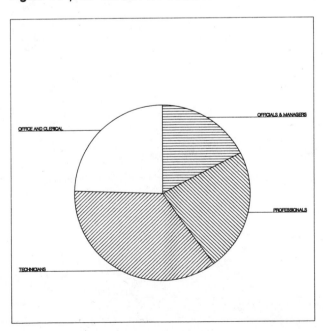

Figure 15 /PIE=SUM(SALARY82 BONUS82 BEN82)

Radial Pie Chart   A radial pie chart divides a circle into equal-angle sectors. The distance from the center of the circle to the edge of the sector indicates the value of the category. The specification is the same as for a normal pie chart (Figures 16 and 17).

Figure 16 /PIE(RADIAL)=COUNT BY GRADE82

Figure 17 /PIE(RADIAL)=MEAN(SALARY79 TO SALARY82)

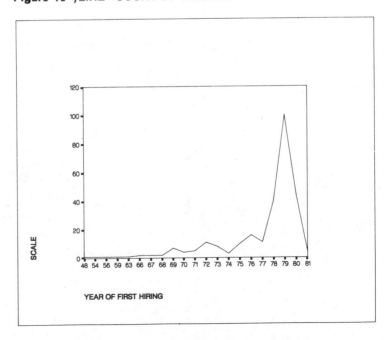

LINE Subcommand

The LINE subcommand creates one of four types of line charts. Keywords SIMPLE, MULTIPLE, AREA, and DIFFERENCE determine the type of line chart generated.

SIMPLE Keyword

Simple line chart. A simple line chart is defined by a single function and a single BY variable. It is the default if no qualifying keyword is specified and the data define a simple line (Figures 18 and 19).

Figure 18 /LINE=COUNT BY YRHIRED

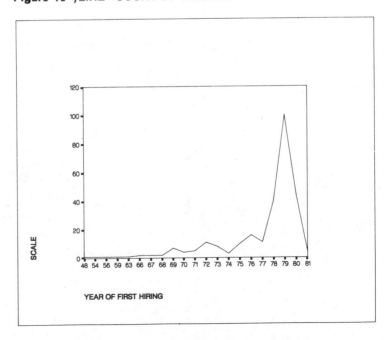

Figure 19 /LINE=PTILE(75)(SALARY82) BY GRADE82

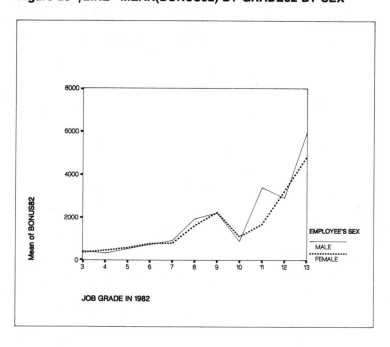

MULTIPLE Keyword

Multiple line chart. A multiple line chart is defined by a single function and two BY variables or by multiple functions and a single BY variable. It is the default if no qualifying keyword is specified and the data define a multiple line (Figures 20 and 21).

Figure 20 /LINE=MEAN(BONUS82) BY GRADE82 BY SEX

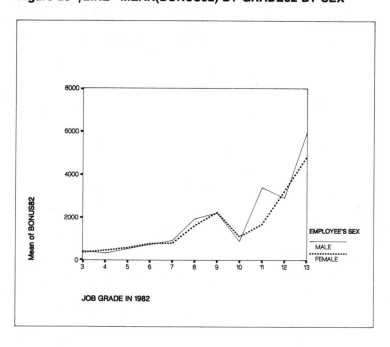

Figure 21   /LINE=MEAN(BONUS81 BONUS82) BY GRADE82

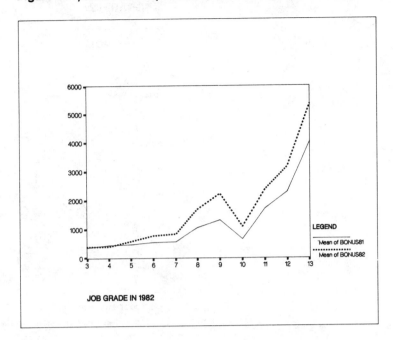

AREA   *Area line chart.* An area line chart fills the area beneath each line with a color or pattern. When multiple lines are specified, the second line is the sum of the first and second variables, the third line is the sum of the first, second, and third variables, and so on. The specification is the same as that for a simple or multiple line chart. Figures 22 and 23 show area line charts with multiple lines.

Figure 22   /LINE(AREA)=CUFREQ BY YRHIRED BY RACE

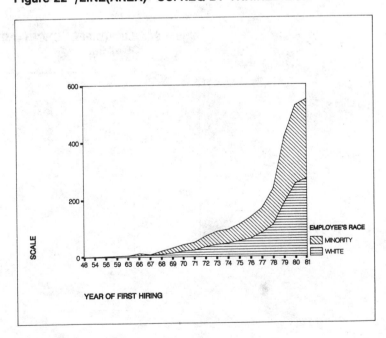

Figure 23 /LINE(AREA)=SUM(SALARY82 BONUS82 BEN82) BY
GRADE82

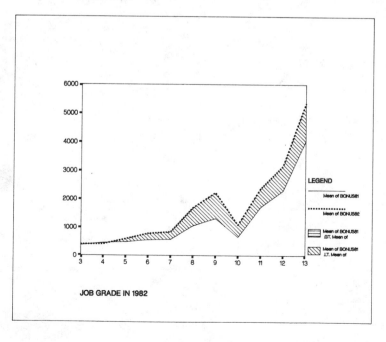

DIFFERENCE Keyword

Difference line chart. You can use this kind of chart to compare two variables or two categories of a single variable. A difference line chart fills the area between two lines with a color or pattern. The two lines represent either two variables or two values of a dichotomous variable. A difference line chart can be defined by two functions and a single BY variable (Figure 24) or by a single function, a BY variable, and a second BY variable which must have exactly two values (Figure 25).

Figure 24 /LINE(DIFFERENCE)=MEAN(BONUS81 BONUS82) BY
GRADE82

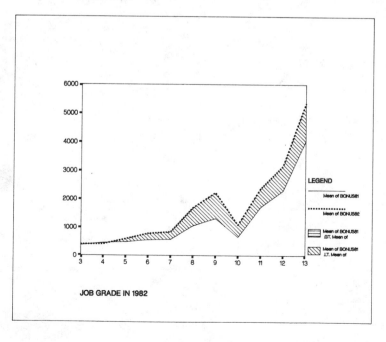

Figure 25   /LINE(DIFFERENCE)=COUNT BY YRHIRED BY SEX

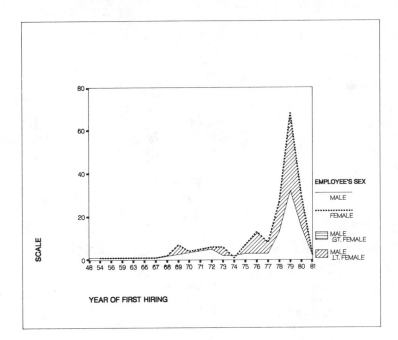

PYRAMID Subcommand

The PYRAMID subcommand produces a population pyramid. You can use a population pyramid to compare pairs of variables or values of a dichotomous variable. A population pyramid stacks a series of horizontal bars on either side of a vertical axis. The bars to the right represent one variable or one value of a dichotomous variable. The bars to the left represent the other variable or value. A simple population pyramid can be defined by a single function, a BY variable, and a second, dichotomous BY variable (Figure 26), or by a pair of functions and a single BY variable (Figure 27).

Figure 26   /PYRAMID=MEAN(BONUS82) BY GRADE82 BY SEX

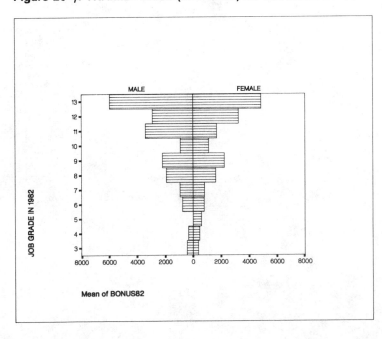

Figure 27 /PYRAMID=MEAN(BONUS81 BONUS82) BY GRADE82

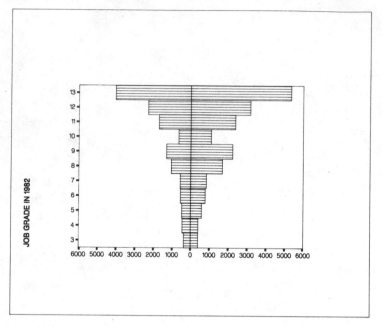

A stacked population pyramid can be defined by a single function, a BY variable, a second, dichotomous BY variable, and a third BY variable that divides each bar into a stack (Figure 28) or by multiple pairs of functions, a BY variable, and a second, dichotomous BY variable (Figure 29).

Figure 28 /PYRAMID=MEAN(SALARY82) BY EEO82 BY SEX BY RACE

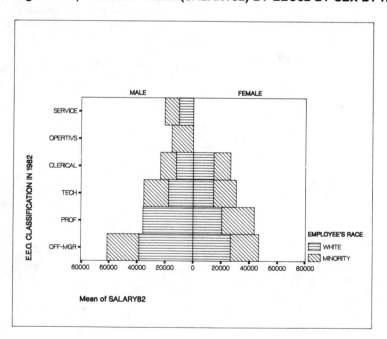

Figure 29   /PYRAMID=MEAN(SALARY82 BONUS82 BEN82) BY EEO82 BY SEX

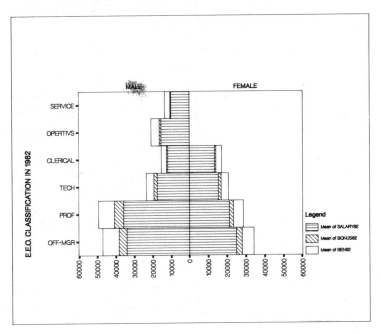

BLOCK Subcommand

The BLOCK subcommand produces a three-dimensional block diagram. It can be defined by a single function and two BY variables or by multiple functions and a single BY variable (Figures 30 and 31).

Figure 30   /BLOCK=COUNT BY JOBCAT BY SEX

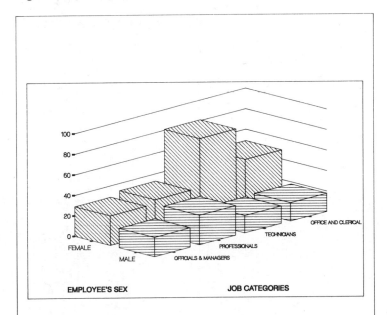

Figure 31 /BLOCK=SUM(SALARY79 TO SALARY82) BY JOBCAT

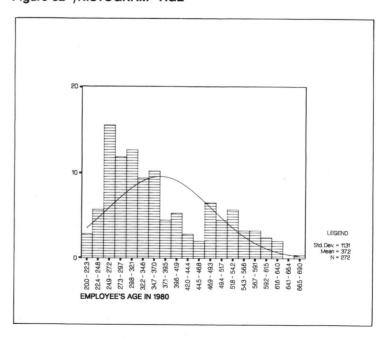

HISTOGRAM Subcommand

The HISTOGRAM subcommand creates a histogram. SPSS sends the values of the specified variable to SPSS GRAPHICS, which divides the values into several evenly spaced intervals and produces a bar chart showing the number of times the value for the variable falls within each interval. Because SPSS sends the actual values, you can adjust the intervals within the Graphics system. Only one variable can be specified (Figure 32).

Figure 32 /HISTOGRAM=AGE

**SCATTERPLOT
Subcommand**

The SCATTERPLOT subcommand produces one or more two-dimensional scatterplots. Multiple scatterplots are plotted within the same frame, and the axes are scaled to accommodate the minimum and maximum values across all variables.

Basic Scatterplot

A basic scatterplot is defined by two variables separated by the keyword WITH (Figure 33).

Figure 33   /SCATTERPLOT=BONUS82 WITH SALARY82

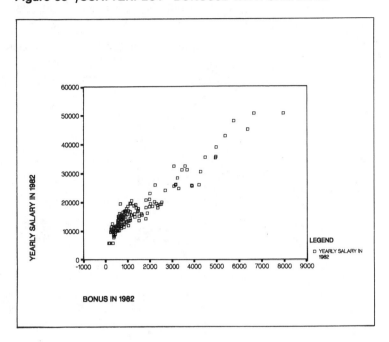

Control Scatterplot

Adding a BY variable produces a control scatterplot, in which the different values of the BY variable are indicated by different colors or plotting symbols (Figure 34).

Figure 34   /SCATTERPLOT=BONUS82 WITH SALARY82 BY SEX

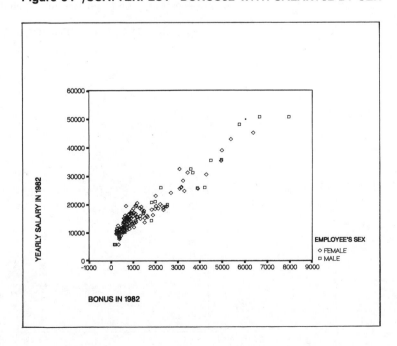

Overlay Scatterplot

Adding variables to either side of WITH produces multiple plots. All plots are drawn within the same frame and are differentiated by color or plotting symbol.

Keyword PAIR. By default, one scatterplot is drawn for each combination of variables on the left of WITH with variables on the right. Thus

```
/SCATTERPLOT=BONUS79 BONUS82 WITH SALARY79 SALARY82 (PAIR)
```

generates four overlaid plots. Keyword PAIR allows you to combine the first variable on the left of WITH with the first variable on the right, the second on the left with the second on the right, and so on. Specify PAIR within parentheses, as in Figure 35.

Figure 35 /SCATTERPLOT=BONUS79 BONUS82 WITH SALARY79 SALARY82 (PAIR)

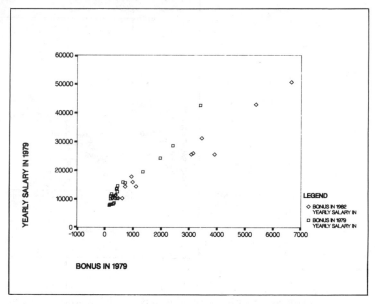

Name Plot

You can display the value label of an identifier variable at the plotting position for each case. Add BY *variable name* (NAME) to the end of any valid scatterplot specification. Figure 36 shows a simple scatterplot with a NAME variable (only cases with age 60 or greater are selected from the file.)

Figure 36 /SCATTERPLOT=BONUS82 WITH SALARY82 BY NAME (NAME)

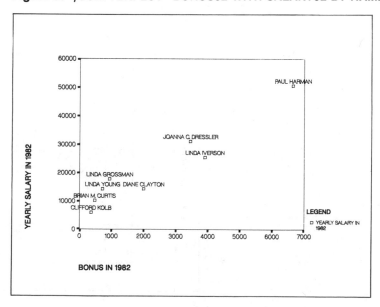

Figure 37 shows a plot with a control variable and a name variable.

**Figure 37   /SCATTERPLOT=BONUS82 WITH SALARY82 BY RACE BY
NAME (NAME)**

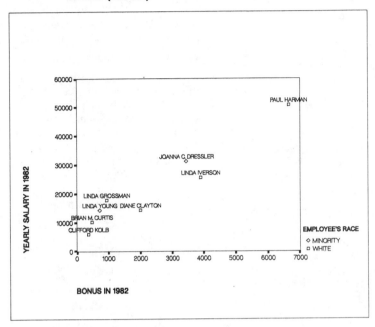

MAP Subcommand

The MAP subcommand creates one of two kinds of maps. Qualifying keywords CHOROPLETH and PRISM determine the type of map. If no keyword is specified, a choropleth map is produced.

Both types of map are defined by a single function and a single BY variable. The BY variable must be a category variable that contains valid geocodes for the mapped region. (A geocode is a numerical code which identifies map areas. For a list of valid geocodes, see the *SPSS Graphics* manual.)

CHOROPLETH

A choropleth map indicates values associated with map areas by the color or pattern with which the area is drawn.

PRISM

A prism map indicates values associated with map areas by the height of the area.

**BOUNDARY
Subcommand**

If the MAP subcommand is specified, you can also specify the boundary file (the file that contains the outlines of the areas to be mapped) with the BOUNDARY subcommand. If no boundary is specified, USSTATES is used. There are six boundary files included with SPSS Graphics.

USSTATES   *The United States of America by state.*

USCOUNTY   *The United States of America by county.*

CANADA   *Canada by census division.*

PROVINCE   *Canada by province.*

WORLD   *World by country.*

EUROPE   *Europe by division.*

REGION Subcommand

If the MAP subcommand is specified, you can also specify the region file (a file of aggregated areas associated with a boundary file) with the REGION subcommand. After the equals sign either specify DEFAULT or specify the name of a custom region file surrounded by apostrophes. (See the *SPSS Graphics* manual for an explanation of custom region files.) The following map boundary files have associated sets of default regions:

USSTATES *States are aggregated into census regions. (For example: Northeast, Mid-Atlantic, and East-Northcentral.)*

USCOUNTY *Counties are aggregated into individual states.*

CANADA *Census divisions are aggregated into provinces.*

WORLD *Countries are aggregated into continents.*

If you specify DEFAULT, you get one of the above region files, depending upon the boundary file you specified with the BOUNDARY subcommand.

If you specify a region file with the REGION subcommand, the geocodes in your data set must identify regions in the specified file, not areas in the boundary file. For example, the following subcommands produce the map in Figure 38:

```
/MAP = SUM(COAL) BY REGION
/BOUNDARY = USSTATES
/REGION = DEFAULT
```

Figure 38 A choropleth map

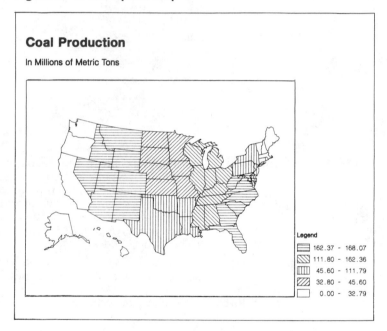

TABLE Subcommand

Use the TABLE subcommand to aggregate data for Graphics without specifying a chart. When in Graphics, you can use the aggregated data to generate whatever kind of chart is appropriate for the data you defined. The specification can be the same as that for any of the following chart types: BAR, LINE, PIE, PYRAMID, BLOCK, MAP.

CASEFILE subcommand

Use the CASEFILE subcommand to build a data file for histograms or scatterplots. Like TABLE, CASEFILE does not generate a chart. When in Graphics, you can use the data file to create a histogram or scatterplot. If you want a different kind of chart, pass the data to Graphics with the TABLE subcommand. The CASEFILE variable list consists of a list of variables optionally followed by the keyword BY and one or more category variables. For example,

```
/CASEFILE = SALARY BONUS BENEFIT BY SEX JOBCAT
```

is a valid CASEFILE subcommand.

DRAW Subcommand

The DRAW subcommand controls what happens when GRAPH invokes SPSS Graphics. There are three possible keywords: FULL, QUICK, and NO.

FULL   *When SPSS Graphics is invoked, a fully detailed graph is drawn.* If the EXECUTE option is MENU or RETURN, and no DRAW subcommand is specified, a full graph is drawn.

QUICK   *Executes a Quick Draw.* This uses the saved Quick Draw parameters in your AUTOLIB graphics library. By default this will substitute a stick font instead of filled Helios.

NO   *When SPSS Graphics is invoked, no graph is drawn.*

EXECUTE Subcommand

The EXECUTE subcommand controls what happens after GRAPH has constructed an SPSS Graphics command file. There are three possibilities: MENU, RETURN, and NO.

MENU   *GRAPH invokes SPSS Graphics, generates the requested graph, then leaves you in the SPSS Graphics menu system.* On most systems this is the default. When you quit from the SPSS Graphics menus, GRAPH returns you to the SPSS session.

RETURN   *GRAPH invokes SPSS Graphics, generates the requested graph, then returns to the SPSS session.*

NO   *GRAPH does not invoke SPSS Graphics.* To generate the graph, run SPSS Graphics. On the opening screen (the one that says "SPSS Graphics"), type &RERUN *filename,* where *filename* is the name of the command file generated by GRAPH. On a few systems the only possible option is NO, which is the default. For more information, see the SPSS *Operations Guide* for your system.

GCMDFILE Subcommand

The GCMDFILE subcommand names the command file generated by GRAPH. If no file is specified, the name is GRAPHCMD. When the file already exists it will be overwritten in most operating systems.

GDATA Subcommand

The GDATA subcommand names the SPSS system file generated by GRAPH. When GRAPH aggregates data for SPSS Graphics it creates new variables. These variables are stored in a new SPSS system file accessible either from Graphics or SPSS. If no name is specified, the data file is called GRAPHDAT. When the file already exists it will be overwritten in most operating systems.

GOUT Subcommand

The GOUT subcommand names an SPSS Graphics output file. This file contains the graphics device codes which tell a printer, plotter, or terminal what the graph looks like. When you send the output file to the appropriate device, you get the graph you specified. If you specify an output file, the Graphics output is sent to that file rather than directly to the specified graphics device.
Warning: If you specify an output file on the GOUT subcommand and that file already exists, the graphics output is directed to your screen. If the specified device is a printer or plotter file and your screen does not understand the language, this produces several pages of unintelligible characters on your screen before the Graphics menus reappear.

ADEVICE Subcommand

The ADEVICE subcommand names the alpha device used with SPSS Graphics. (The alpha device is the terminal you use to enter data on the SPSS Graphics menus. If you need to know what to call your terminal, invoke SPSS Graphics. When it asks you to specify the alpha device, press return. You get a list of all the possible SPSS Graphics alpha devices. You must specify the name of the device, not its number on the list.) You must specify the alpha device either on the GRAPH command or on a SET command preceding the GRAPH command.

GDEVICE Subcommand

The GDEVICE subcommand names the graphics device used with SPSS Graphics. (The graphics device is the terminal, plotter, or printer on which the graph is to be created.) If GDEVICE is a printer or plotter, and it is not directly attached to your terminal, remember to specify the output file with GOUT; otherwise, the printer code is sent to your screen.

GMEMORY Subcommand

The GMEMORY subcommand specifies how much memory GRAPH should allocate for SPSS Graphics to run in. Specify an integer followed by the keyword K for kilobytes, or M for megabytes. If you don't specify a keyword, kilobytes are assumed. If you don't specify a GMEMORY subcommand, Graphics allocates enough memory for most charts. GMEMORY does not work in some systems. For more information, see the SPSS *Operations Guide* for your system.

HELP

This command is not available on all operating systems.

```
{HELP} [ {topic    [subtopic   ] }] [SYNTAX]
{ ?  }   {command [subcommand] }
```

Example:

```
SPSS> HELP REGRESSION SYNTAX.
```

Overview

HELP (alias "?") provides online help during an SPSS-prompted session. The HELP command is not allowed in command files. Consult your SPSS *Operations Guide* for types of online help available on your system.

HELP messages describe the function, syntax, and operation of commands. HELP also gives information about files, command order, and subcommands for complex procedures.

Syntax Rules

- The minimum specification is simply the command keyword or a question mark, either of which obtains a listing of available HELP topics.
- From any HELP screen that offers subtopics, type the number corresponding to the subtopic and press return. Use the numeral keys to type the numbers, not the programmable function keys.
- To get help on specific commands, specify the command name on HELP.
- To get help on specific subcommands, specify the command and subcommand names on HELP.
- To get help on specific keywords, specify the command, subcommand, and keyword names on HELP.
- To see the syntax for any command, specify the command name and keyword SYNTAX on HELP.
- Help is available from any prompt. However, from the CONTINUE>, DATA>, DEFINE>, or HELP> prompts, help must be requested with the question mark; keyword HELP can only be used from the SPSS> prompt.
- Generally, three-character truncation of keywords on help requests is permitted. If truncation is not unique (for example, REP might be REPORT or REPEAT-ING DATA), at least a fourth character must be specified.
- On some computers, the minus (−) and plus (+) keys move through screens in the HELP system. On other computers, the directional arrow keys move among screens. For details on your computer, see your SPSS *Operations Manual* or the online documentation available with the keyword LOCAL on the INFO command. Alternatively, type HELP with no specifications within the prompt-ed session and choose the appropriate selection from the listing of available HELP topics.
- To exit the HELP system, press the Return (or Enter) key at any blank HELP> prompt.

Operations

- HELP is an operations command and is executed immediately.

Example

```
SPSS> HELP DESCRIPTIVES SYNTAX.
```

- The HELP command is issued at the SPSS> prompt and requests syntax for procedure DESCRIPTIVES.
- This request can only be specified from the SPSS> command prompt because it uses keyword HELP.

Example   CONTINUE> ? REPORT FORMAT AUTOMATIC

• A question mark is used to request help from a CONTINUE> prompt. Help is requested for keyword AUTOMATIC, available on REPORT's FORMAT subcommand.

• The request can be specified from any prompt because it uses the question mark (?) alias for HELP.

Example   CONTINUE> ? REG STA

• This command requests information on REGRESSION's STATISTICS subcommand.

• The request can be specified from any prompt because it uses the question mark (?) alias for HELP.

• The request takes advantage of spelling permitted by three-character truncation of keywords.

HILOGLINEAR

This command is included in the SPSS Advanced Statistics option.

```
HILOGLINEAR {varlist} (min,max) [varlist (min,max)...]
            {ALL    }

[/METHOD [= BACKWARD]]

[/MAXORDER = k]

[/CRITERIA = [CONVERGE({0.25})] [ITERATE({20})] [P({0.05})]
                      {n   }            {n }        {prob}

             [DELTA({0.5})] [MAXSTEPS({10})] [DEFAULT]]
                   {d  }             {n }

[/CWEIGHT = {varname }]
            {(matrix)}

[/PRINT = [DEFAULT]  [ASSOCIATION]
          [FREQ]     [RESID]
          [ESTIM]    [ALL]
          [NONE]]

[/PLOT = [DEFAULT]  [RESID]
         [NORMPROB] [NONE ]]

[/MISSING = {LISTWISE} [INCLUDE]]
            {DEFAULT }

[/DESIGN = effectname effectname*effectname ...]

[/DESIGN = ... ]
```

Example:

```
HILOGLINEAR V1(1,2) V2(1,2) V3(1,3) V4(1,3)
  /DESIGN=V1*V2*V3, V4.
```

Overview

HILOGLINEAR fits hierarchical log-linear models to multidimensional contingency tables using iterative proportional-fitting algorithms. HILOGLINEAR also estimates parameters for saturated models. These techniques are described in Everitt (1977), Bishop et al. (1975), and Goodman (1978). HILOGLINEAR is much more efficient for these models than the LOGLINEAR procedure because HILOGLINEAR uses an iterative proportional fitting algorithm.

Options

Design Specification. You can request automatic model selection using backward elimination with the METHOD subcommand. You can also specify any hierarchical design and request multiple designs using the DESIGN subcommand.

Design Control. You can control the criteria used in the iterative proportional-fitting and model-selection routines with CRITERIA. You can also limit the order of effects in the model with MAXORDER and specify structural zeros for cells in the tables you analyze with CWEIGHT.

Display and Plots. With PRINT, you can select the display for each design. For saturated models you can request tests for different orders of effects. You can request residuals plots or normal probability plots of residuals with PLOT.

Basic Specification

• The basic specification is a variable list with at least two variables followed by their minimum and maximum values. HILOGLINEAR estimates a saturated model for all variables in the analysis.

Subcommand Order

- The variable list must be specified first.
- Subcommands affecting a given DESIGN subcommand must appear before DESIGN. Otherwise, subcommands can appear in any order.
- MISSING can be placed anywhere after the variable list.

Syntax Rules

- DESIGN is optional. If DESIGN is omitted or DESIGN is not the last subcommand, a default saturated model is estimated.
- You can specify multiple PRINT, PLOT, CRITERIA, MAXORDER, and CWEIGHT subcommands. The last of each type specified is in effect for subsequent designs.
- PRINT, PLOT, CRITERIA, MAXORDER and CWEIGHT remain in effect until they are overridden by new subcommands.
- You can specify multiple METHOD subcommands, but each one affects only the next design.
- MISSING can be specified only once.

Operations

- HILOGLINEAR builds a contingency table using all variables on the variable list. The table contains a cell for each possible combination of values within the ranges specified for each of the variables.
- HILOGLINEAR assumes there is a category for every integer value in the range of each variable. Empty categories waste space and can cause computational problems. If there are empty categories, you should use the RECODE command to create consecutive integer values for categories.
- Cases with values outside the range specified for any variable are excluded.
- If the last subcommand is not a DESIGN subcommand, HILOGLINEAR displays a warning and generates the default model. This is the saturated model unless MAXORDER is specified. This model is in addition to any that are explicitly requested.
- If the model is not saturated (for example, when MAXORDER is less than the number of factors), only the goodness-of-fit and the observed and expected frequencies are given.
- The display uses the WIDTH defined on SET. If the defined width is less than 132, some portions of the display may be deleted.

Limitations

Procedure HILOGLINEAR cannot estimate all possible frequency models, and it produces limited output for unsaturated models.

- It can estimate only hierarchical log-linear models.
- It treats all table variables as nominal. (You can use LOGLINEAR to fit nonhierarchical models to tables involving variables that are ordinal.)
- It can produce parameter estimates for saturated models only (those with all possible main effect and interaction terms).
- It can estimate partial associations for saturated models only.
- It can handle tables with no more than 10 factors.

Example

```
HILOGLINEAR V1(1,2) V2(1,2) V3(1,3) V4(1,3)
   /DESIGN=V1*V2*V3, V4.
```

- HILOGLINEAR builds a $2 \times 2 \times 3 \times 3$ contingency table for analysis.
- DESIGN specifies the generating class for a hierarchical model. This model consists of main effects for all four variables, two-way interactions among V1, V2, and V3, and the three-way interaction term V1 by V2 by V3.

Variable List   The required variable list specifies the variables in the analysis. The variable list must precede all other subcommands.

- Variables must be numeric and have integer values. If a variable has a fractional value, the fractional portion is truncated.
- Keyword ALL can be used to refer to all user-defined variables in the active system file. If ALL is specified, all variables must have the same range.
- A range must be specified for each variable, with the minimum and maximum values separated by a comma and enclosed in parentheses.
- If the same range applies to several variables, the range can be specified once after the last variable to which it applies.

METHOD Subcommand   By default, HILOGLINEAR tests the model specified on the DESIGN subcommand (or the default model) and does not perform any model selection. All variables are entered and none are removed. Use METHOD to specify automatic model selection using backward elimination for the next design specified.

- You can specify METHOD alone or with keyword BACKWARD for an explicit specification.
- METHOD affects only the next design.

BACKWARD   *Backward elimination.* Perform backward elimination of terms in the model. All terms are entered. Those that do not meet the P criteria specified on the CRITERIA subcommand (or the default P) are removed one at a time.

MAXORDER Subcommand   MAXORDER controls the maximum order of terms in the model estimated for subsequent designs. If MAXORDER is specified, HILOGLINEAR tests a model only with terms of that order or less.

- MAXORDER specifies the highest-order term that will be considered from the next design. MAXORDER can thus be used to abbreviate computations for the BACKWARD method.
- If the integer on MAXORDER is less than the number of factors, parameter estimates and measures of partial association are not available. Only goodness-of-fit and the observed and expected frequencies are displayed.
- You can use MAXORDER with backward elimination to find the best model with terms of a certain order or less. This is computationally much more efficient than eliminating terms from the saturated model.

Example
```
HILOGLINEAR V1 V2 V3(1 2)
   /MAXORDER=2
   /DESIGN=V1 V2 V3.
   /DESIGN=V1*V2*V3
```

- HILOGLINEAR builds a 2 × 2 × 2 contingency table for V1, V2, and V3.
- MAXORDER has no effect on the first DESIGN subcommand, since the design requested considers only main effects.
- MAXORDER restricts the terms in the model specified on the second DESIGN subcommand to two-way interactions or less.

CRITERIA Subcommand   Use CRITERIA to change the values of constants in the iterative proportional-fitting and model-selection routines for subsequent designs.

- The default criteria are in effect if the CRITERIA subcommand is omitted (see below).
- You cannot specify the CRITERIA subcommand without any keywords.
- Specify each CRITERIA keyword followed by a criterion value in parentheses. Only those criteria specifically altered are changed.

- You can specify more than one keyword on CRITERIA, and they can be in any order.

DEFAULT *Reset parameters to their default values.* If you have specified criteria other than the defaults for a design, use this keyword to restore the defaults for a subsequent design.

CONVERGE(n) *Convergence criterion.* The default is 10^{-3} * the largest cell size, or .25, whichever is larger.

ITERATE(n) *Maximum number of iterations.* The default is 20.

P(n) *Probability for change in chi-square if term removed.* Specify the significance level. The default is .05.

MAXSTEPS(n) *Maximum number of steps for model selection.* The default is 10.

DELTA(d) *Cell delta value.* The value of delta is added to each cell frequency for the first iteration. It is left in the cells for saturated models only. The default value is .5. You can specify any decimal value between 0 and 1 for d. HILOGLINEAR does not display parameter estimates or the covariance matrix of parameter estimates if any zero cells (either structural or sampling) exist in the expected table after DELTA is added.

CWEIGHT Subcommand

CWEIGHT specifies cell weights for a model. CWEIGHT is typically used to specify structural zeros in the table. You can also use CWEIGHT to adjust tables to fit new margins.

- You can specify the name of a variable whose values are cell weights or provide a matrix of cell weights enclosed in parentheses.
- The variable named on CWEIGHT must be numeric.
- You must specify a weight for every cell in the contingency table, where the number of cells equals the product of the number of values of all variables.
- Cell weights are indexed by the values of the variables in the order in which they are·specified on the variable list. The index values of the rightmost variable change the most quickly.
- You can use the notation $n*cw$ to indicate that cell weight cw is repeated n times in the matrix.

Example
```
HILOGLINEAR V1(1,2) V2(1,2) V3(1,3)
  /CWEIGHT=CELLWGT
  /DESIGN V1*V2, V2*V3, V1*V3.
```

- This example uses the variable CELLWGT to assign cell weights for the table.

Example
```
HILOGLINEAR V4(1,3) V5(1,3)
  /CWEIGHT=(0 1 1  1 0 1  1 1 0)
  /DESIGN=V4, V5.

HILOGLINEAR V4(1,3) V5(1,3)
  /CWEIGHT=(0 3*1 0 3*1 0)
  /DESIGN=V4,V5.
```

- These two equivalent HILOGLINEAR commands set the diagonal cells in the model to structural zeros. This type of model is known as a quasi-independence model.
- Because both V4 and V5 have three values, weights must be specified for nine cells.
- The first HILOGLINEAR command specifies cell weights explicitly.
- The second HILOGLINEAR command uses the $n*cw$ notation to indicate that the cell weight is repeated.
- The first cell weight is applied to the cell in which V4 is 1 and V5 is 1; the second weight is applied to the cell in which V4 is 1 and V5 is 2, and so forth.

Example
```
TITLE 'AMERICAN BLADDER NUT SEPARABILITY  HARRIS(1910)'.
SUBTITLE 'AN INCOMPLETE RECTANGULAR TABLE'.
DATA LIST FREE / LOCULAR RADIAL FREQ.
WEIGHT BY FREQ.
BEGIN DATA
1 1 462
1 2 130
1 3 2
1 4 1
2 1 103
2 2 35
2 3 1
2 4 0
3 5 614
3 6 138
3 7 21
3 8 14
3 9 1
4 5 443
4 6 95
4 7 22
4 8 8
4 9 5
END DATA.
HILOGLINEAR LOCULAR (1,4) RADIAL (1,9)
   /CWEIGHT=(4*1 5*0   4*1 5*0   4*0 5*1   4*0 5*1)
   /DESIGN LOCULAR RADIAL.
```

- This example uses aggregated table data as input.
- The DATA LIST command defines three variables. The values of LOCULAR and RADIAL index the levels of those variables, so that each case defines a cell in the table. The values of FREQ are the cell frequencies.
- The WEIGHT command weights each case by the value of the variable FREQ. Since in this example each case reqresents a cell, the WEIGHT command assigns the frequencies for each cell.
- The BEGIN DATA and END DATA commands enclose the lines of data.
- The HILOGLINEAR variable list specifies two variables. LOCULAR has values 1, 2, 3, and 4. RADIAL has integer values 1 through 9.
- The CWEIGHT subcommand identifies a block rectangular pattern of cells that are logically empty. There is one weight specified for each cell of the 36-cell table.
- In this example the matrix form needs to be used in CWEIGHT, since the structural zeros do not appear in the actual data. (For example, there is no case corresponding to LOCULAR»1, RADIAL»5.)
- The DESIGN subcommand specifies main effects only for LOCULAR and RADIAL. Lack of fit for this model indicates an interaction of the two variables.
- Since there is no PRINT or PLOT subcommand, HILOGLINEAR produces the default output for an unsaturated model.

PRINT Subcommand

PRINT controls the display produced for the following designs.

- If PRINT is omitted or included with no specifications, the default display is produced.
- If any keywords are specified on PRINT, only output specifically requested is displayed.
- HILOGLINEAR displays Pearson and likelihood ratio chi-square goodness-of-fit tests for models. For saturated models, it also provides tests that the k-way effects and the k-way and higher-order effects are zero.
- Both adjusted and unadjusted degrees of freedom are displayed for tables with sampling or structural zeros. K-way and higher tests use the unadjusted degrees of freedom.
- The unadjusted degrees of freedom are not adjusted for zero cells, and estimate the upper bound of the true degrees of freedom. These are the same degrees of freedom you would get if all cells were filled.

• The adjusted degrees of freedom are calculated from the number of non-zero fitted cells minus the number of parameters that would be estimated if all cells were filled (i.e., unadjusted degrees of freedom minus the number of zero fitted cells). This estimate of degrees of freedom may be too low if some parameters do not exist because of zeros.

DEFAULT   *Default displays.* This option includes FREQ and RESID output for nonsaturated models, and FREQ, RESID, ESTIM, and ASSOCIATION output for saturated models. For saturated models, the observed and expected frequencies are equal, and the residuals are zeros.

FREQ   *Observed and expected cell frequencies.*

RESID   *Raw and standardized residuals.*

ESTIM   *Parameter estimates for a saturated model.*

ASSOCIATION   *Partial associations.* You can request partial associations of effects only when you specify a saturated model. This option is computationally expensive for tables with many factors.

ALL   *All available output.*

NONE   *Design information and goodness-of-fit statistics only.* Use of this option overrides all other specifications on PRINT.

PLOT Subcommand

Use PLOT to request residuals plots.

• If PLOT is included without specifications, standardized residuals and normal probability plots are produced.

• Plots use the box characters specified on the BOX subcommand of the SET command.

• No plots are displayed for saturated models.

• If PLOT is omitted, no plots are produced.

RESID   *Standardized residuals by observed and expected counts.*

NORMPLOT   *Normal probability plots of adjusted residuals.*

NONE   *No plots.* Specify NONE to suppress plots requested on a previous PLOT subcommand. This is the default if PLOT is omitted.

DEFAULT   *Default plots.* Includes RESID and NORMPLOT. This is the default when PLOT is specified without keywords.

ALL   *All available plots.*

DESIGN Subcommand

The default model is a saturated model that includes all variables in the variable list. A saturated model contains all main effects and interactions for those variables. Use DESIGN to specify a different generating class for the model. In a hierarchical model, higher-order interaction effects imply lower-order interaction and main effects. The highest-order effects to be estimated are the generating class.

• If DESIGN is omitted or included without specifications, the default model is estimated. When DESIGN is omitted, SPSS issues a warning message.

• To specify a design, list the highest-order terms, using variable names and asterisks (*) to indicate interaction effects.

• Higher-order interaction terms specified on DESIGN imply all lower-order interaction and main effect terms. V1*V2*V3 implies the three-way interaction V1 by V2 by V3, two-way interactions V1 by V2, V1 by V3, and V2 by V3, and main effects for V1, V2, and V3.

• One model is estimated for each DESIGN subcommand.

• If the last subcommand on HILOGLINEAR is not DESIGN, the default model will be estimated in addition to models explictly requested.

- Any PRINT, PLOT, CRITERIA, METHOD, and MAXORDER subcommands that apply to a DESIGN subcommand must appear before it.
- All variables named on DESIGN must be named or implied on the variable list.
- You can specify more than one DESIGN subcommand.

MISSING Subcommand

By default, a case with missing values for any variable named on the variable list is omitted from the analysis. Use MISSING to change the treatment of cases with user-missing values.

- MISSING can be named only once and can be placed anywhere following the variable list.
- MISSING cannot be used without specifications.
- A case with a system-missing value for any variable named on the variable list is always excluded from the analysis.

LISTWISE *Delete cases with missing values listwise.* This is the default if the subcommand is omitted. You can also request listwise deletion with keyword DEFAULT.

INCLUDE *Include user-missing values as valid.* Only cases with system-missing values are deleted.

Annotated Example

For a complete example with output, see Examples following the Command Reference.

References

Bishop, Y., S. Feinberg, and P. Holland. 1975. *Discrete multivariate analysis: Theory and practice.* Cambridge: MIT Press.

HOST

This command is not available on all operating systems.

```
HOST [system command]
```

Overview   HOST executes an operating-system command from within an SPSS prompted session, then returns to the session without having affected the SPSS session in progress. HOST is not available in windowed environments since a windowing system lets you change applications without using HOST.

SPSS cannot control actions taken by other software that you invoke through HOST and therefore cannot guarantee that any particular program will run safely.

Syntax Rules   • On some operating systems, an operating-system command must be specified after the keyword HOST. The system command should be in uppercase letters and cannot be continued onto another line.

• On those operating systems requiring a command terminator that is the same as the terminator required by SPSS, the terminator must be specified twice.

• Some operating systems allow the HOST command to be specified by itself, without a system command. Results of doing so differ depending upon the host system. For example, specifying "HOST" in IBM CMS puts the operating system into CMS subset; control is not returned to SPSS until the RETURN command is specified. To see how HOST works on your operating system, consult your SPSS *Operations Guide.*

Example   System commands used with HOST vary according to the host system. The IBM CMS system permits the following command:

```
SPSS> HOST LISTFILE.
```

• From the SPSS> prompt the CMS command LISTFILE is executed, which produces a list of files.

• Once the host command is completed, the SPSS session resumes without having been affected.

IF

```
IF [(]logical expression[)] target variable=expression
```

The following relational operators can be used in logical expressions:

Symbol	Definition	Symbol	Definition
EQ or =	Equal to	NE or a= or <>	Not equal to
LT or <	Less than	LE or <=	Less than or equal to
GT or >	Greater than	GE or >=	Greater than or equal to

The following logical operators can be used in logical expressions:

Symbol	Definition
AND or &	Both relations must be true
OR or | or ¦	Either relation can be true
NOT or ¬ or ~	Reverses the outcome of an expression

Example:
```
IF (AGE > 20 AND SEX = 1) GROUP=2.
```

Overview

IF conditionally executes a single COMPUTE-like transformation based upon logical conditions found in the data. The transformation can create a new variable or modify the values of an existing variable for each case in the active system file. You can create or modify the values of both numeric and string variables, though to create a new string variable you must first declare it on the STRING command.

IF has three components: a *logical expression* (see Universals: Logical Expressions) that sets up the logical criteria, a *target variable* (the one to be modified or created), and an *assignment expression*. The target variable's values are modified according to the assignment expression.

IF is most efficient when used to express a single, conditional, COMPUTE-like transformation. If you need multiple IF statements to define the condition, it is usually more efficient to use the RECODE command or a DO IF—END IF structure.

Basic Specification

• The basic specification is the logical expression, followed by a target variable, a required equals sign, and the assignment expression. The assignment is executed only if the logical expression is true.

Syntax Rules

• Logical expressions can be simple logical variables or relations, or they can be complex logical tests involving variables, constants, functions, relational operators, and logical operators. Both the logical expression and the assignment expression can use any of the numeric or string functions allowed in COMPUTE transformations (see COMPUTE and Universals: Functions).

• Parentheses can be used to enclose the logical expression. Parentheses can also be used within the logical expression to specify the order of operations. Extra blanks or parentheses may be used to make the expression easier to read.

• Blanks (not commas) must separate relational operators from expressions.

• A relation can include variables, constants, or more complicated arithmetic expressions. Relations cannot be abbreviated: (A EQ 2 OR A EQ 5) is valid, (A EQ 2 OR 5) is invalid.

• A relation cannot compare a string variable to a numeric value or variable, or vice versa. A relation cannot compare the result of the logical functions SYSMIS, MISSING, ANY, or RANGE to a number.

• String values used in expressions must be specified in quotes and must include any leading or trailing blanks. Lowercase letters are considered distinct from uppercase letters.

• String variables that are used as target variables must already exist. To declare a new string variable, first create the variable with the STRING command, then specify the new variable as the target variable on IF.

Operations

• Each IF command evaluates every case in the data. Compare IF with ELSE IF, which passes control for a case out of the DO IF—END IF structure as soon as a logical condition is met.

• The logical expression is evaluated as true, false, or missing. The assignment is executed only if the logical expression is true.

• If the logical expression is false or if one of the variables used in the logical expression is system- or user-missing, the assignment is not made. Existing target variables remain unchanged; new numeric variables retain their initial values.

Numeric Variables

• Numeric variables created with IF are initially set to the system-missing value. By default, they are assigned an F8.2 format.

• Logical expressions are evaluated in the following order: functions, followed by exponentiation, arithmetic operations, relations, and logical operators. When more than one logical operator is used, NOT is evaluated, then AND, then OR. You can change the order of operations using parentheses.

• Assignment expressions are evaluated in the following order: functions, then exponentiation, then arithmetic operators.

String Variables

• New string variables declared on IF are initially set to a blank value and are assigned the format specified on the STRING command that creates them.

• Logical expressions are evaluated in the following order: string functions, then relations, then logical operators. When more than one logical operator is used, NOT is evaluated, then AND, then OR. You can change the order of operations using parentheses.

• If the transformed value of a string variable exceeds the variable's defined format, the transformed value is truncated. If the transformed value is shorter than the format width defined for that variable, the string is right-padded with blanks to the length of the defined format.

Missing Values and Logical Operators

When two or more relations are joined by logical operators AND and OR, SPSS always returns a missing value if all of the relations in the expression are missing. However, if any one of the relations can be determined, SPSS interprets the expression as true or false according to the logical outcomes shown in Table 1. The asterisk flags expressions where SPSS can evaluate the outcome with incomplete information.

Table 1 Logical outcome

Expression	Outcome	Expression	Outcome
true AND true	= true	true OR true	= true
true AND false	= false	true OR false	= true
false AND false	= false	false OR false	= false
true AND missing	= missing	true OR missing	= true*
missing AND missing	= missing	missing OR missing	= missing
false AND missing	= false*	false OR missing	= missing

Example

    IF (AGE > 20 AND SEX = 1) GROUP=2.

• Numeric variable GROUP is set to 2 for cases where AGE is greater than 20 *and* SEX is equal to 1 (in other words, when the expression is true).

• When the expression is false or missing, the value of GROUP remains unchanged. If GROUP has not been previously defined, it contains the system-missing value.

Example   `IF (SEX EQ 'F') EEO=QUOTA+GAIN.`

- The logical expression tests string variable SEX for the value "F".
- When the expression is true (when SEX equals F), the value of numeric variable EEO is assigned the value of QUOTA plus GAIN. Both QUOTA and GAIN must be previously defined numeric variables.
- When the expression is false or missing (for example, if SEX equals f), the value of EEO remains unchanged. If EEO has not been previously defined, it contains the system-missing value.

Example   ```
COMPUTE V3=0.
IF ((V1-V2) LE 7)) V3=V1**2.
```

- COMPUTE assigns V3 the value 0.
- The logical expression tests whether V1 minus V2 is less than or equal to 7. If it is, the value of V3 is assigned the value of V1 squared. Otherwise, the value of V3 remains at 0.

**Example**     `IF (ABS(A-C) LT 100) INT=100.`

- IF tests whether the absolute value of variable A minus variable C is less than 100. If it is, INT is assigned the value 100. Otherwise, the value is unchanged or, if INT has not been previously defined, system-missing.

**Example**     `IF (MEAN(V1 TO V5) LE 7) INDEX=1.`

- If the mean of variables V1 through V5 is less than or equal to 7, value 1 is assigned to INDEX.

**Example**     ```
TITLE   'TEST FOR LISTWISE DELETION OF MISSING VALUES'.

DATA LIST / V1 TO V6 1-6.
STRING SELECT(A1).
COMPUTE SELECT='V'.
VECTOR V=V1 TO V6.

LOOP #I=1 TO 6.
IF MISSING(V(#I)) SELECT='M'.
END LOOP.

BEGIN DATA
123456
    56
1 3456
123456
123456
END DATA.

FREQUENCIES VAR=SELECT.
```

- STRING declares string variable SELECT with an A1 format and COMPUTE sets the value of SELECT equal to V.
- VECTOR defines vector V as the original variables V1 to V6. Variables on a single vector must be all numeric or all string variables. In this example, because vector V is used as an argument on the MISSING function of IF, the variables have to be numeric (MISSING is not available for string variables).
- The loop structure executes 6 times: once for each VECTOR element. If a value is missing for any element, SELECT is set equal to M. In effect, if any case has even a single missing value, SELECT is set to M.
- FREQUENCIES generates a frequency table for SELECT. The table gives a count of how many cases have missing values for at least one variable and how many cases have valid values for all variables. Commands in this example can be used to determine whether cases may have been dropped from an analysis

that uses listwise deletion of missing values. See COMPUTE for an example that counts the number of missing values per case.

- See DO IF for an alternative way to test for listwise deletion of missing values.

Example
```
COMPUTE #X=0.
IF #X=0 LNAME=UPCASE(LNAME).
IF DEPT='SALES' DIVISION='TRANSFERRED'.
```

- COMPUTE creates scratch variable #X and sets the value to 0 for every case.

- Since the condition for the first IF command is true for all cases, any values that are entered in lowercase letters for string variable LNAME are converted to uppercase letters.

- The logical expression on the second IF command tests whether DEPT equals "SALES." When the condition is true, the value for string variable DIVISION is changed to "TRANSFERRED" but is truncated if the format for DIVISION is not at least 11 columns wide. For any other value of DEPT, the value of DIVISION remains unchanged.

- Though there are two IF statements, each defines a separate and independent condition. The IF command is used rather than the DO IF—END IF structure because you want to test both conditions on every case rather than pass control for a case out of the structure as soon as the logical condition is met for the first IF.

Example
```
IF (STATE EQ 'IL' AND CITY EQ 13) COST=COST + .07 * COST.
```

- The logical expression tests whether STATE equals IL and CITY equals 13.

- If the logical expression is true, numeric variable COST is assigned the original value of COST plus 7% of the original value of COST (1.07 × COST).

- For any other value of STATE or CITY, the value of COST remains unchanged.

Example
```
STRING GROUP (A18).
IF (HIRED GE 1988) GROUP='HIRED AFTER MERGER'.
```

- STRING declares string variable GROUP and assigns it a width of 18 characters.

- When HIRED is greater than or equal to 1988, GROUP is assigned the value HIRED AFTER MERGER. When HIRED is less than 1988, GROUP is defined as an eighteen-column blank field.

Example
```
IF (RECV GT DUE OR (REVNUES GE EXPNS AND BALNCE GT 0))STATUS
    ='SOLVENT'.
```

- First, SPSS tests whether REVNUES is greater than or equal to EXPNS and whether BALNCE is greater than 0.

- Second, SPSS evaluates if RECV is greater than DUE.

- If either of these expressions is true, STATUS is assigned the value "SOL-VENT."

- If both expressions are false, STATUS remains unchanged.

- STATUS is a string variable in the active system file. Otherwise, it would have to be declared on a preceding STRING command.

IMPORT

```
IMPORT FILE=file

[/TYPE={COMM}]
       {TAPE}

[/KEEP={ALL** }] [/DROP=varlist]
       {varlist}

[/RENAME=(old varlist=new varlist)...]

[/MAP]
```

Example:

```
IMPORT FILE=NEWDATA /RENAME=(V1 TO V3=ID, SEX, AGE) /MAP.
```

Overview

IMPORT reads SPSS portable data files created with the EXPORT command in SPSS or SPSS/PC+. A portable file contains all of the data and dictionary information stored in the system file from which it was created. Portable files are used for transporting files between installations having different conversions of SPSS (such as for the PRIME, VAX, or HONEYWELL GCOS computers) or for transporting files between SPSS, SPSS/PC+, or other software using the same portable file format.

SPSS can also read data files created by other software programs. See commands such as GET SCSS, GET SAS, GET BMDP, and GET OSIRIS for reading files created by other statistical software packages. See your SPSS *Operations Guide* for the other types of files you can read on your system (for example, dBASE, Lotus, or Multiplan files).

Options

Format. You can define the format of the portable file as either magnetic- or communications-format data (see TYPE Subcommand). For more information on magnetic tapes and communications programs, see Methods of Transporting Portable Files in EXPORT.

Variables. You can read a subset of variables from the active system file, and you can rename variables. You can also produce a record of all variables and their names in the active file. See the DROP, KEEP, RENAME, and MAP subcommands.

Basic Specification

• The basic specification is the FILE subcommand with a file specification. All variables from the portable file are copied into the active system file with their original names, variable and value labels, missing-value flags, and print and write formats.

Subcommand Order

• Subcommands can be named in any order.

Operations

• The portable data file and dictionary become the SPSS active system file.

• A file saved with weighting in effect (using the WEIGHT command) automatically uses the case weights when the file is read.

Example

```
IMPORT FILE=NEWDATA /RENAME=(V1 TO V3=ID,SEX,AGE) /MAP.
```

• The active file is generated from the portable file NEWDATA.

• Variables V1, V2, and V3 are renamed ID, SEX, and AGE in the active file. Their names remain V1, V2, and V3 in the portable file. None of the other variables copied into the active file are renamed.

• MAP requests a display of the variables in the active file.

FILE Subcommand

FILE specifies the portable file. FILE is the only required subcommand on IMPORT.

TYPE Subcommand

TYPE defines the format of the portable file as either communications- or tape-formatted. TYPE can specify one of two keywords, COMM or TAPE. COMM is the default. (For more information on magnetic tapes and communications programs, see EXPORT.)

- TYPE=COMM specifies a communications-formatted file. This is the default.
- TYPE=TAPE specifies a tape-formatted file.
- All portable files from releases earlier than SPSS-X 2.1 are in tape format and may not be suitable for transmission by communications programs.

Example

```
IMPORT TYPE=TAPE /FILE=HUBOUT.
```

- File HUBOUT is read as a tape-formatted portable file.

DROP and KEEP Subcommands

DROP and KEEP read a subset of variables from the portable file.

- DROP excludes a variable or list of variables from the active file. All variables not named are included in the active file.
- KEEP includes a variable or list of variables in the active file. All variables not named are excluded.
- Variables can be specified on DROP and KEEP in any order.
- With the DROP subcommand, the order of variables in the active file is the same as their order in the portable file.
- With the KEEP subcommand, the order of variables in the active file is the order they are named on KEEP. Thus, KEEP can be used to reorder variables in the active file.
- Both DROP and KEEP can be used on the same IMPORT command, provided they do not name any of the same variables.
- Keyword TO can be used to specify a group of consecutive variables in the portable file.
- The portable file is not affected by DROP or KEEP.

Example

```
IMPORT FILE=NEWSUM /DROP=DEPT TO DIVISION.
```

- The active system file is generated from the portable file NEWSUM. Variables between and including DEPT and DIVISION in the portable file are excluded from the active file.
- All other variables are copied into the active file.

RENAME Subcommand

RENAME renames variables being read from the portable file. The renamed variables retain their variable and value labels, missing-value flags, and print formats from the portable file.

- To rename a variable, specify the name of the variable in the portable file, a required equals sign, and the new name.
- A variable list can be specified on both sides of the equals sign. The number of variables on both sides must be the same, and the entire specification must be enclosed in parentheses.
- Keyword TO can be used for both variable lists (see Universals: Variable-Naming Conventions).
- If a renamed variable is specified on a subsequent DROP or KEEP subcommand, the new variable name must be used on DROP or KEEP.

Example

```
IMPORT FILE=NEWSUM /DROP=DEPT TO DIVISION
  /RENAME=(NAME,WAGE=LNAME,SALARY).
```

- RENAME renames NAME and WAGE to LNAME and SALARY.
- LNAME and SALARY retain the variable and value labels, missing-value flags, and print formats assigned to NAME and WAGE.

MAP Subcommand

MAP displays any changes that have been specified by the RENAME, DROP, or KEEP subcommands. MAP displays only the changes specified on the subcommands that precede the MAP request.

- MAP can be specified as often as desired.
- When MAP is specified last, it produces a listing of the contents of the current active file.

Example

```
IMPORT FILE=NEWSUM /DROP=DEPT TO DIVISION /MAP
   /RENAME NAME=LNAME WAGE=SALARY /MAP.
```

- The first MAP subcommand produces a listing of the variables in the file after DROP has dropped the specified variables.
- RENAME renames NAME and WAGE.
- The second MAP subcommand shows the variables in the file after renaming. Since this is the last subcommand, the listing will show the variables that are currently in the active file.

INCLUDE

```
INCLUDE [FILE**]=file
```

Example:
```
INCLUDE FILE=GSSLABS.
```

Overview

INCLUDE includes a file of SPSS commands in an SPSS session. INCLUDE is especially useful for including a long series of data definition statements or transformations. Another use for INCLUDE is to set up a library of commonly used commands and include them in the command sequence as they are needed.

Using INCLUDE during a prompted session can save time and provide the advantage of running multiple commands together. Complex or repetitive commands can be stored in a file to be included, while simpler commands or commands unique to the current analysis are entered during the session (before and after the included file).

Basic Specification

• The only specification is the FILE subcommand, which specifies the file to include. When INCLUDE is executed, the commands in the specified file are processed.

Syntax Rules

• Commands in an included file must begin in column 1, and continuation lines for each command must be indented at least one column.

• A file of raw data can be used as an include file if the first line of the included file contains the BEGIN DATA command, and the last line contains the END DATA command. However, because the data are specified between BEGIN DATA and END DATA, they are limited to a maximum of 80 columns (the maximum may be fewer than 80 columns on some systems).

• As many INCLUDE commands as needed can be used in a session. However, a file cannot be included that is still open from a previous step.

• INCLUDE commands can be nested so that one set of included commands includes another set of commands. This nesting can go to five levels.

Operations

• If an included file contains a FINISH command, the SPSS session ends and no further commands are processed.

• If a journal file is created for the SPSS session, INCLUDE is copied to the journal file. Commands from the included file are also copied to the journal file but are treated like printed messages. Thus, INCLUDE can be executed from the journal file if the journal is later used as a command file. Commands from the included file are executed only once.

• For the affected IBM systems, the NUMBERED or UNNUMBERED setting in effect before the INCLUDE command is restored at the end of the included file. The original printback status is also restored when the end of the included file is reached.

FILE Subcommand

FILE identifies the file containing SPSS commands or inline data. FILE is the only specification on INCLUDE and is required.

Example

```
SPSS> TITLE 'A PROMPTED SESSION'.

SPSS> INCLUDE FILE=GSSLABS.
```

• INCLUDE includes file GSSLABS in the prompted session. When INCLUDE is executed, the commands in file GSSLABS are processed.

• The include file GSSLABS contains the following:

```
DATA LIST FILE=DATA52
  /RELIGION 5 OCCUPAT 7 SES 12 ETHNIC 15
   PARTY 19 VOTE48 33 VOTE52 41.
```

• The active system file is thus defined and ready for analysis.

INFO

```
INFO [OUTFILE = file]
     [OVERVIEW]
     [LOCAL]
     [ERRORS]
     [FACILITIES]
     [PROCEDURES]
     [ALL]
     [procedure name] [/procedure name...]
     [SINCE release number]
```

Example:

```
INFO LOCAL.
```

Overview

INFO makes available two kinds of online documentation: local and update.

Local Documentation

Local documentation concerns the environment in which SPSS is run. It includes some or all of the following, depending on the operating system:

- Commands or job control language for running SPSS.
- Conventions for referring to files. These include instructions on how your computer's operating system accesses or creates a particular file.
- Conventions for handling tapes and other input/output devices.
- Data formats. The formats SPSS reads and writes may differ from one computer and operating system to another.
- Default values for parameters controlled by the SET command. Many defaults for the parameters are set at the individual installation. The SHOW command displays the values that are in effect on a given run. Local documentation may contain more information on why one setting is preferred over another.
- Specific information about your computer and operating system or your individual installation.

Update Documentation

Update documentation includes changes to existing procedures and facilities made after publication of this manual, new procedures and facilities, and corrections to this manual. Update documentation can be requested for all available releases, or since a particular release of SPSS.

Syntax Rules

- The minimum specification is a single keyword or procedure name.
- Multiple keywords and/or procedure names are allowed on a single INFO command.
- Multiple procedure names must be separated by slashes.
- The order of specifications is unimportant and does not affect the order in which the documentation is printed.
- Three- or four-character truncation does *not* apply to INFO command specifications. Spell all keywords out in full. For procedure names, spell the first word out in full and subsequent words through at least the first three characters.

Operations

- By default, the INFO command produces update information only for the current release.
- Documentation for earlier releases may also be available, and that fact is indicated in the INFO overview.
- If overlapping sets of information are requested, only one copy is printed.
- If there is no available documentation for the requested information, only a copyright page is printed.
- If information is requested for an unrecognized topic, SPSS prints an error message.

• The characteristics of the output file produced by the INFO command may vary by computer type. As implemented at SPSS Inc., the file includes carriage control, with the maximum length of a page determined by the LENGTH subcommand on the SET command. A printer width of 132 characters is assumed for some examples, though the text is generally much narrower.

Limitations

SPSS requires more computer resources than most printing utilities. Your installation may therefore provide an alternative method for printing INFO documentation. In that case, the INFO command may simply provide instructions for using the preferred documentation facility.

Types of information

INFO has the following keywords for selecting the different types of available documentation:

OVERVIEW   *Overview of available documentation.* Includes a table of contents for the documentation available with INFO, along with information about documentation available in print.

LOCAL   *Local documentation,* as described above.

ERRORS   *List of known unfixed errors.* Lists the known unfixed errors in the current release of SPSS. Since ERRORS applies only to the current release, the SINCE keyword (described below) will have no effect with ERRORS.

FACILITIES   *Update information for SPSS facilities.* Covers all differences, except in procedures, between the system as documented in this manual and the system as installed on your computer— whether those differences result from updates to the system, revisions required for conversions to particular operating systems, or errors in this manual. Only updates for the most current release are printed, unless keyword SINCE is specified.

PROCEDURES   *Update information for procedures.* This includes full documentation for procedures new in the current release and update information for procedures that existed prior to the current release.

procedure(s)   *Documentation for the procedures named.* This is the same information as that printed by the PROCEDURES keyword, but limited to the procedure named. Separate procedure names with a slash.

ALL   *All available documentation.* ALL includes OVERVIEW, LOCAL, ERRORS, FACILITIES, and PROCEDURES.

Example

`INFO  OVERVIEW FACILITIES FREQUENCIES / CROSSTABS.`

• INFO produces an overview and documentation for any changes made to system facilities and to the FREQUENCIES and CROSSTABS procedures.

• Because keyword SINCE is not specified, INFO prints only documentation for the current release.

SINCE Keyword

Releases of SPSS are numbered by integers, with decimal digits indicating maintenance releases between major releases. The release number appears in the default heading for SPSS output. Each SPSS manual is identified in the preface by the number of the release it documents.

Keyword SINCE obtains information for earlier releases or limits the information to maintenance releases since the last major release.

• The minimum specification is keyword SINCE followed by a release number.

• SINCE is not inclusive—SINCE 3.0 does not include changes made to the system in Release 3.0.

- To identify a maintenance release, enter the exact number, with decimal, as in 3.1.
- Information for some earlier releases may not be available. For example, information for Release 2.2 and earlier releases is not available if INFO is run on SPSS Release 4.0.
- INFO contains only information since the latest published manual.

Example   `INFO  OVERVIEW FACILITIES FREQUENCIES / CROSSTABS SINCE 3.`

- INFO prints documentation for all changes to system facilities and procedures FREQUENCIES and CROSSTABS since Release 3.0.

OUTFILE Subcommand

OUTFILE sends INFO output to a separate file.

Example   `INFO OUTFILE=SPSSDOC ALL SINCE 3.`

- INFO creates a file of text that includes an overview, local documentation, changes, and new procedures since Release 3.0.
- The OUTFILE subcommand sends the documentation to file SPSSDOC.

INPUT PROGRAM—END INPUT PROGRAM

```
INPUT PROGRAM
commands to create or define cases
END INPUT PROGRAM
```

Example:

```
INPUT PROGRAM.
DATA LIST FILE=PRICES /YEAR 1-4 QUARTER 6 PRICE 8-12(2).

DO IF (YEAR GE 1881). /*STOP READING BEFORE 1881
END FILE.
END IF.
END INPUT PROGRAM.
```

Overview

The INPUT PROGRAM and END INPUT PROGRAM commands enclose data definition and transformation commands that build cases from input records. These commands establish flow of control with one or more DO IF or LOOP structures and usually include multiple DATA LIST commands. In addition, at least one of four utility commands is usually needed to complete definition of the input program: the END CASE or END FILE command, the REREAD command, or the REPEATING DATA command.

END CASE builds cases from the commands within the input program and passes them on to the next procedure.

END FILE terminates processing of a data file before the actual end of the file, or it defines the end of the file when the input program is used to create raw data.

REREAD rereads the current record using a different DATA LIST.

REPEATING DATA reads repeating groups of data from the same input record.
For more information, see the discussion for each command.

Input Programs

SPSS builds the active file dictionary as it encounters commands that create and define variables. At the same time, SPSS builds an *input program* that will construct the cases and an optional *transformation program* that will modify the cases prior to analysis or display. By the time SPSS encounters a procedure command that tells it to read the data, the active file dictionary is ready, and the programs that construct and modify the cases in the active file are built.

The internal input program is usually built from either a single DATA LIST command or from any of the commands that read or combine system files (for example GET, ADD FILES, MATCH FILES, UPDATE, etc.). The input program can also be built from the FILE TYPE—END FILE TYPE structure used to define nested, mixed, or grouped files. The third type of input program is specified with the INPUT PROGRAM—END INPUT PROGRAM commands.

With INPUT PROGRAM—END INPUT PROGRAM you can create your own input program to perform many different operations on raw data. You can use transformation commands to build cases. You can read nonrectangular files, concatenate raw data files, and build cases selectively. You can also create an active system file without reading any data at all.

Input programs are used to create a dictionary and data for an active file; they cannot be used to process SPSS system files. To process direct-access and keyed data files, use an input program and the conventions described in the SPSS *Operations Guide* for your system.

Input State

There are four program states in SPSS: the *initial state,* in which there is no active file dictionary; the *input state,* in which cases are created from the input file; the *transformation state,* in which cases are transformed; and the *procedure state,* in which procedures are executed. While these states are generally of no real importance to you, when specifying either FILE TYPE—END FILE TYPE or INPUT PROGRAM—END INPUT PROGRAM you must pay attention to which commands are allowed within the input state, which commands can appear only within the input state, and which are not allowed within the input state. See Appendix A for a discussion of the four program states, command precedence, and a table that describes what happens to each command when it is encountered in each of the four states.

Basic Specification

• The basic specification is INPUT PROGRAM, the commands used to create cases, and END INPUT PROGRAM. INPUT PROGRAM and END INPUT PROGRAM have no further specifications.

Operations

• The INPUT PROGRAM—END INPUT PROGRAM structure is a transformation and is executed when the data are read for the next procedure.

• INPUT PROGRAM clears the current active file to create a new active file.

Example

```
TITLE 'SELECT CASES WITH AN INPUT PROGRAM'.

INPUT PROGRAM.
DATA LIST FILE=PRICES /YEAR 1-4 QUARTER 6 PRICE 8-12(2).

DO IF (YEAR GE 1881). /*STOP READING BEFORE 1881

END FILE.
END IF.
END INPUT PROGRAM.

LIST.
```

• The input program is defined between the INPUT PROGRAM and END INPUT PROGRAM commands.

• This example assumes data records are entered chronologically by year. The DO IF—END IF structure specifies an end of file when the first record with a YEAR of 1881 or later is reached.

• LIST executes the input program and lists cases from the active file. The case for 1881 that caused the end of the file is not included in the active file generated by the input program.

• If you know the exact number of cases you want SPSS to create, you can use N OF CASES as an alternative to this input program to select the same records for the active system file. Another alternative is to use SELECT IF to select cases before 1881, but then SPSS would unnecessarily read the rest of the file.

Example

```
TITLE  'CREATE DATA WITHOUT ANY DATA INPUT'.

INPUT PROGRAM.
LOOP #I=1 TO 20.
COMPUTE AMOUNT=RND(UNIFORM(5000))/100.
END CASE.
END LOOP.
END FILE.
END INPUT PROGRAM.

LIST.
```

• This example creates 20 cases with a single variable AMOUNT, a uniformly distributed number between 0 and 5000, rounded to an integer and divided by 100 to provide a variable in dollars and cents.

• The END FILE command is required to terminate processing once the LOOP structure is complete.

Example

```
TITLE      'CREATE DATA WITHOUT ANY DATA INPUT'.
SUBTITLE   'RANDOM NUMBERS'.

INPUT PROGRAM.
+  LOOP #I = 1 TO 1000.
+     DO REPEAT RESPONSE = R1 TO R400.
+        COMPUTE RESPONSE = UNIFORM(1) > 0.5.
+     END REPEAT.
+     COMPUTE AVG = MEAN(R1 TO R400).
+     END CASE.
+  END LOOP.
+  END FILE.
END INPUT PROGRAM.

FREQUENCIES VARIABLE=AVG
  /FORMAT=CONDENSE
  /HISTOGRAM
  /STATISTICS=MEAN MEDIAN MODE STDDEV MIN MAX.
```

- The INPUT PROGRAM—END INPUT PROGRAM structure defines the bounds of an input program that builds cases from transformation commands.

- The LOOP—END LOOP structure specifies that the commands within the loop be executed 1000 times.

- The DO REPEAT—END REPEAT structure generates 400 variables, each with a 50% chance of being 0, and a 50% chance of being 1. This is accomplished by specifying a logical expression on COMPUTE that compares the values returned by UNIFORM to the value 0.5. Logical expressions are evaluated as false (0), true (1), or missing. Thus, each random number returned by UNIFORM that is 0.5 or less is evaluated as false and assigned the value 0, and each random number returned by UNIFORM that is greater than 0.5 is evaluated as true and assigned the value 1.

- The second COMPUTE creates variable AVG which, for each case, is the mean of R1 TO R400.

- END CASE builds a case with the variables created within each loop. Thus, the loop structure creates 1000 cases, each with 400 variables.

- END FILE signals the end of the data file generated by the input program.

- FREQUENCIES produces a condensed frequency table, histogram, and statistics for AVG. The histogram for AVG shows a normal distribution.

Example

```
SET FORMAT=F8.0.

INPUT PROGRAM.
LOOP I=1 TO 1000.
+ COMPUTE SCORE=EXP(NORMAL(1)).
+ END CASE.
END LOOP.
END FILE.
END INPUT PROGRAM.

FREQUENCIES VARIABLES=SCORE /FORMAT=NOTABLE /HISTOGRAM
  /PERCENTILES=1 10 20 30 40 50 60 70 80 90 99
  /STATISTICS=ALL.
```

- The input program creates 1000 cases with a single variable SCORE. Values for SCORE approximate a log-normal distribution.

Example
```
TITLE  'CONCATENATE THREE RAW DATA FILES'.

INPUT PROGRAM.
NUMERIC #EOF1 TO #EOF3. /*THESE WILL BE USED AS THE END= VARIABLES.

DO IF    #EOF1 NE 1.
+     DATA LIST  FILE=ONE END=#EOF1 NOTABLE /1 NAME 1-20(A)
              AGE 21-22 SEX 24(A).
ELSE IF    #EOF2 NE 1.
+     DATA LIST  FILE=TWO  END=#EOF2 NOTABLE / NAME 1-20(A)
              AGE 21-22 SEX 24(A).
ELSE IF  #EOF3 NE 1.
+       DATA LIST  FILE=THREE END=#EOF3 NOTABLE / NAME 1-20(A)
              AGE 25-26 SEX 29(A).
ELSE.
+       END FILE.
END IF.
END CASE.
END INPUT PROGRAM.

REPORT FORMAT AUTOMATIC LIST /VARS=NAME AGE SEX.
```

- The INPUT PROGRAM contains a DO IF—ELSE IF—END IF structure.
- Scratch variables are used on each END subcommand so the value will not be reinitialized to the system-missing value after each case is built.
- Three data files are read, two of which contain data in the same format. The third requires a slightly different format for the data items. All three DATA LIST commands are placed within the DO IF structure.
- END FILE is placed after the ELSE command to trigger end-of-file processing once all data records have been read.
- This application can also be handled by creating three separate SPSS system files and using ADD FILES to put them together. The advantage of using the END subcommand on DATA LIST is that additional files are not required to store the separate system files prior to performing the ADD FILES. In addition, the files remain raw data files: they are not converted to system files.

Example
```
*   READ EACH RECORD TWO CONSECUTIVE TIMES.  THE SECOND READING
      DEFINES DATA ACCORDING TO INFORMATION LEARNED ON THE FIRST.

INPUT PROGRAM.
DATA LIST FILE=CARPARTS/KIND 10-14 (A).

DO IF (KIND EQ 'FORD').
REREAD.
DATA LIST /PARTNO 1-2 PRICE 3-6 (DOLLAR,2) QUANTITY 7-9.
END CASE.

ELSE IF (KIND EQ 'CHEVY').
REREAD.
DATA LIST /PARTNO 1-2 PRICE 15-18 (DOLLAR,2) QUANTITY 19-21.
END CASE.
END IF.
END INPUT PROGRAM.
```

- The first DATA LIST defines variable KIND for testing in the DO IF and ELSE IF commands.
- REREAD tells SPSS to set the pointer back to the *current* record. The current record is the last record in multiple record DATA LIST specifications.
- END CASE is used with each DATA LIST within the input program to assure that each case that is read is passed on to the next command outside the input program.
- These data are stored in a mixed file, and can also be read with FILE TYPE MIXED.

Example

```
TITLE  'BUILD MULTIPLE CASES FROM EACH RECORD'.

INPUT PROGRAM.
DATA LIST FILE=VEHICLE/SEQNUM 2-4 NUMPERS 6-7 NUMVEH 9-10.
REPEATING DATA STARTS=12 /OCCURS=NUMVEH
   /DATA=MAKE 1-8 (A) MODEL 9 (A) NUMCYL 10.
END INPUT PROGRAM.
```

- DATA LIST defines variables for file VEHICLE.

- REPEATING DATA reads information from repeating groups and builds new cases. The repeating groups start in column 12. The number of repeating groups for each record (and therefore the number of cases built from each record) is specified by the value of variable NUMVEH.

Example

```
TITLE  'SKIP THE FIRST "N" RECORDS IN A FILE'.

INPUT PROGRAM.
NUMERIC         #INIT.            /* "Set" when initialization done
DO IF           NOT (#INIT).
+  LOOP         #I = 1 TO 5.
+     DATA LIST      NOTABLE/.    /* No data - just skip record
+  END LOOP.
+  COMPUTE      #INIT = 1.
END IF.
DATA LIST       NOTABLE/ X 1.
END INPUT PROGRAM.

BEGIN DATA
A                              /* The first 5 records are skipped
B
C
D
E
1
2
3
4
5
END DATA.
LIST.
```

- NUMERIC declares scratch variable #INIT. Once declared, #INIT can be used in the transformation language before it is created on COMPUTE.

- The DO IF structure is executed if #INIT exists but has no defined vaules. Thus, the structure is entered when #INIT is initialized. Because #INIT is a scratch variable, it is initialized only once: before any records are read.

- LOOP is executed five times. Within the LOOP, DATA LIST is specified without variable names, causing SPSS to read records in the data file without copying them into the active system file. Because the LOOP executes five times, SPSS reads five records. END LOOP terminates this loop.

- COMPUTE creates scratch variable #INIT and sets it equal to 1. Because #INIT is assigned for value 1 on all records, the DO IF structure will not be executed again.

- END IF terminates the DO IF structure.

- The second DATA LIST specifies numeric variable X, which is located in column 1 of each record. Because SPSS has already read five records, the first value for X that is copied into the active system file is read from record 6.

KEYED DATA LIST

This command is not available on all operating systems.

```
KEYED DATA LIST KEY=varname IN=varname

[FILE=file] [{TABLE  }]
            {NOTABLE}
```

Example:

```
FILE HANDLE EMPL/ file specifications.
KEYED DATA LIST FILE=EMPL KEY=#NXTCASE IN=#FOUND
        /YRHIRED 1-2 SEX 3 JOBCLASS 4.
```

Overview

KEYED DATA LIST reads raw data from two types of nonsequential files: direct access files, which provide direct access by a record number, and keyed files, which provide access by a record key. An example of a direct access file is a file of 50 records, each corresponding to one of the United States. If you know the relationship between the states and the record numbers, you can retrieve the data for any specific state. An example of a keyed file is a file containing a social security number and other information about a firm's employees. The social security number can be used to identify the records in the file.

Where permitted by the host system, SPSS can read a key-sequenced data set sequentially from a point that a key value controls (see POINT). SPSS can also read IBM VSAM (Virtual Storage Access Method) files. This discussion of KEYED DATA LIST is general. For more details on reading VSAM files under IBM OS, IBM CMS, and IBM DOS operating systems, see the pertinent SPSS *Operations Guide*. For more information on reading keyed files under other operating systems, access the online documentation available through the INFO command.

Direct Access Files

There are various types of direct access files. The SPSS concept of a direct access file, however, is very specific. The file must be one from which individual records can be selected according to their number. The records in a 100-record direct access file, for example, are numbered from 1 to 100.

Although the concept of record number applies to almost any file, not all files can be treated by SPSS as direct access files. In fact, some host environments provide no direct access capabilities at all, and others permit only a narrowly defined subset of all files to be treated as direct access.

Very few files turn out to be good candidates for direct access organization. In the case of an inventory file, for instance, the usual large gaps in the part numbering sequence would result in large amounts of wasted file space. Gaps are not a problem, however, if they are predictable. For instance, if you recognize that telephone area codes have first digits of 2 through 9, second digits of 0 or 1, and third digits of 0 through 9, you can transform an area code into a record number by using the following COMPUTE statement:

```
COMPUTE RECNUM = 20*(DIGIT1-2) + 10*DIGIT2 + DIGIT3 + 1.
```

where DIGIT1, DIGIT2, and DIGIT3 are variables corresponding to the respective digits in the area code, and RECNUM is the resulting record number. The record numbers would range from 1, for the nonexistent area code 200, through 160, for area code 919. The file would then have a manageable number of unused records.

Keyed Files

Of the many kinds of keyed files, the ones to which SPSS can provide access are generally known as *indexed sequential files*. A file of this kind is basically a sequential file in which the host system maintains an index so that the file may be processed either sequentially or selectively. In effect, such a file consists of an underlying data file that is accessed by way of a file of index entries. The file of index entries may, for example, contain the fact that data record 797 is associated with social security number 476-77-1359. Depending on the implementation, the underlying data may or may not be maintained in sequential order.

The key for each record in the file is generally composed of one or more pieces of information found within the record. An example of a complex key is a customer's last name and house number, plus the consonants in the street name, plus the zip code, plus a uniqueness digit in case there are duplicates. Regardless of the information contained in the key, SPSS treats it as a character string.

Some implementations have keyed files with more than one key associated with each record. That is, the records in a file can be identified according to different types of information. Although the primary key for a file normally must be unique, sometimes the secondary keys need not be. Thus, the records in an employee file might be identified by social security number and job classification.

Options

Data Source. You can specify the file on KEYED DATA LIST, or by default, read the last file that was specified on an SPSS input command, such as DATA LIST or REPEATING DATA.

Summary Table. You can display a table that summarizes the variable definitions.

Basic Specification

The basic specification requires two subcommands, KEY and IN, each of which specifies one variable. After all subcommands are specified, a slash followed by the variable definitions must be specified. Variable definitions are similar to those used with DATA LIST.

- KEY specifies the variable whose value will be used to read a record. For direct access files, the variable must be numeric; for keyed files, it must be a string variable.
- IN creates in the result file a logical variable that flags whether a record was successfully read.

Subcommand Order

- Subcommands can be named in any order.
- Variable definitions must follow all specified subcommands.

Syntax Rules

- Specifications for the variable definitions are the same as those described for DATA LIST. The only difference is that no slashes may appear within the definition of the variables (to denote multiple records) since only one record will be read.
- The FILE HANDLE command must be used to define file specifications for the nonsequential files read by KEYED DATA LIST.
- KEYED DATA LIST may appear in an input program, or it may be used as part of the transformation language to change an existing active file. The fact that it may appear in a transformation program sets it apart from all the other SPSS input commands, such as GET and DATA LIST, which create new active files when used.

Operations

- Variable definitions are interpreted the same as they are for the DATA LIST command. See DATA LIST for details.

Example

```
FILE HANDLE EMPL/ file specifications.
KEYED DATA LIST FILE=EMPL KEY=#NXTCASE IN=#FOUND
        /YRHIRED 1-2 SEX 3 JOBCLASS 4.
```

- FILE HANDLE defines the handle for the data file to be read by KEYED DATA LIST. The handle is specified on the FILE subcommand of KEYED DATA LIST.
- KEY on KEYED DATA LIST specifies the variable used as the access key. For a direct access file, the value of the variable must be between 1 and the number of records in the file. For a keyed file, the value must be a string.
- IN creates the logical scratch variable #FOUND, whose value will be 1 if the record is successfully read, or 0 if the record is not found.
- The variable definitions are the same as those used for DATA LIST.

Example

```
TITLE      'READING A DIRECT ACCESS FILE'.
SUBTITLE   'SAMPLE 1 OUT OF 25 RECORDS'.

FILE HANDLE      EMPL/ file specifications.
INPUT PROGRAM.
COMPUTE #INTRVL = TRUNC(UNIF(49))+1. /* Mean interval = 25
COMPUTE #NXTCASE = #NXTCASE+#INTRVL. /* Next record number
COMPUTE #EOF = #NXTCASE > 1000.      /* End of file check
DO IF   #EOF.
+ END FILE.
ELSE.
+ KEYED DATA LIST  FILE=EMPL, KEY=#NXTCASE, IN=#FOUND, NOTABLE
                   /YRHIRED 1-2 SEX 3 JOBCLASS 4.
+ DO IF       #FOUND.
+    END CASE.                       /* Return a case
+ ELSE.
+    PRINT / 'Oops. #NXTCASE=' #NXTCASE.
+ END IF.
END IF.
END INPUT PROGRAM.
EXECUTE.
```

- FILE HANDLE defines the handle for the data file to be read by the KEYED DATA LIST command. FILE HANDLE is required with KEYED DATA LIST. The record numbers for this example are generated by the SPSS transformation language; they are not based on data taken from another file.

- The INPUT PROGRAM and END INPUT PROGRAM commands begin and end the block of commands that build cases from the input file. Since the session generates cases, an input program is required.

- The first two COMPUTE statements determine the number of the next record to be selected. This is done in two steps. First, the integer portion is taken from the sum of 1 and a uniform pseudo random number between 1 and 49. The result is a mean interval of 25. Second, the variable #NXTCASE is added to this number to generate the next record number. This record number, #NXTCASE, will be used for the key variable on the KEYED DATA LIST command. The third COMPUTE creates a logical scratch variable, #EOF, that has a value of 0 if the record number is less than or equal to 1000, or 1 if the value of the record number is greater than 1000.

- The DO IF—END IF structure controls the building of cases. If the record number is out of range, #EOF equals 1, and the END FILE command tells SPSS to stop reading data and end the file. If the record number is within range, #EOF equals 0, and control passes to the next level of the DO IF—END IF structure.

- If the record number is within range, the record is read via KEYED DATA LIST using the value of #NXTCASE. A case is generated if the record exists (#FOUND equals 1).

- EXECUTE causes the transformations to be executed.

- This example illustrates the differences between a DATA LIST command, which always reads the next record in a file, and a KEYED DATA LIST command, which reads a record specified by a unit origin integer. The example also shows that the KEYED DATA LIST command depends on another command to generate the number of the record to be read.

Example

```
TITLE      'READING A KEYED FILE'.
SUBTITLE   'READ SELECTED RECORDS'.

FILE HANDLE STUDENTS/ file specifications.
FILE HANDLE COURSES/ file specifications.
GET FILE=STUDENTS/KEEP=AGE,SEX,COURSE.
STRING #KEY(A4).
COMPUTE #KEY = STRING(COURSE,N4). /* Create a string key
KEYED DATA LIST FILE=COURSES KEY=#KEY IN=#FOUND NOTABLE
     /PERIOD 13 CREDITS 16.
SELECT IF #FOUND.
LIST.
```

- The first FILE HANDLE references the SPSS system file that contains a course identification for each student. The course identification will be used as the key for selecting one record from a file of courses. The second FILE HANDLE references the file of courses.

- GET defines the data file to SPSS and selects the variables needed for the analysis.

- The STRING and COMPUTE commands transform the course identification from numeric to string for use as a key. For keyed files, the key variable must be a string.

- KEYED DATA LIST uses the value of the newly created string variable #KEY as the key to search the course file. If a record that matches the value of #KEY is found, #FOUND is set to 1; otherwise, it is set to 0. Note that KEYED DATA LIST appears outside an input program in this example.

- If the course file contains the requested record, #FOUND equals 1, and the case is selected via the SELECT IF command; otherwise, the case is dropped.

- LIST lists the values of the cases.

- This example shows how existing cases can be updated on the basis of information read from a keyed file.

- Whether this program represents an efficient solution to the problem at hand depends heavily on the percentage of the records in the course file that need to be accessed. If fewer than 10% of the course file records are read, the use of KEYED DATA LIST probably makes sense. As the percentage of the records that are read increases, a method more likely to be efficient is reading the entire course file and combining it with the student file via the MATCH command. There are no hard and fast rules for determining which method is more economical, but you should be aware that direct retrieval from a keyed file can be costly.

FILE Subcommand

FILE specifies the handle for the data file described by KEYED DATA LIST. The file handle must have a corresponding FILE HANDLE command (or, in the case of the IBM OS environment, a corresponding DD statement in the JCL).

- FILE is optional.

- If FILE is omitted, KEYED DATA LIST reads from the last file specified on an SPSS input command, such as DATA LIST or REPEATING DATA.

Example

```
FILE HANDLE EMPL/ file specifications.
KEYED DATA LIST FILE=EMPL KEY=#NXTCASE IN=#FOUND
        /YRHIRED 1-2 SEX 3 JOBCLASS 4.
```

- FILE HANDLE specifies EMPL as the file handle for the data. FILE on KEYED DATA LIST specifies handle EMPL.

KEY Subcommand

KEY specifies the variable whose value will be used as the direct access key. This variable must already exist as the result of a prior DATA LIST, KEYED DATA LIST, GET, or transformation command.

- KEY is required. Its only specification is a single variable. The variable can be a permanent variable or a scratch variable.

- For direct access files, the key variable must be numeric, and its value must be between 1 and the number of records in the file.

- For keyed files, the key variable must be a string variable. Where the keys on a file are numbers, such as social security numbers, the STRING function may be used to assign a value to the key variable. For example, something like the following might be required to get the value of a numeric key into exactly the same format as used on the file:

```
COMPUTE #KEY=STRING(123,IB4).
```

Example
```
TITLE  'A DIRECT ACCESS FILE'.

FILE HANDLE EMPL/ file specifications.
KEYED DATA LIST FILE=EMPL KEY=#NXTCASE IN=#FOUND
          /YRHIRED 1-2 SEX 3 JOBCLASS 4.
```

• KEY indicates that the value of the existing scratch variable #NXTCASE will be used as the key to reading each record.

• Because data are in a direct access file, #NXTCASE must be numeric, and its values must be between 1 and the number of records in the file.

Example
```
TITLE  'A KEYED FILE'.

FILE HANDLE STUDENTS/ file specifications.
FILE HANDLE COURSES/ file specifications.
GET FILE=STUDENTS/KEEP=AGE,SEX,COURSE.
STRING #KEY(A4).
COMPUTE #KEY = STRING(COURSE,N4). /* Create a string key
KEYED DATA LIST FILE=COURSES KEY=#KEY IN=#FOUND NOTABLE
     /PERIOD 13 CREDITS 16.
SELECT IF #FOUND.
LIST.
```

• The STRING and COMPUTE commands transform the course identification from numeric to string for use as a key. For keyed files, the key variable must be a string.

• KEYED DATA LIST uses the value of the newly created string variable #KEY as the key to search the course file. If a record that matches the value of #KEY is found, #FOUND is set to 1; otherwise, it is set to 0.

IN Subcommand

IN specifies a numeric variable whose value is set by the KEYED DATA LIST command according to whether or not the specified record is found. The value of the variable is 1 if the record is successfully read, or 0 if the record is not found.

• IN is required. Its only specification is a single numeric variable. The variable can be a permanent variable or a scratch variable.

Example
```
FILE HANDLE EMPL/ file specifications.
KEYED DATA LIST FILE=EMPL KEY=#NXTCASE IN=#FOUND
          /YRHIRED 1-2 SEX 3 JOBCLASS 4.
```

• IN creates the logical scratch variable #FOUND. The values of #FOUND will be 1 if the record indicated by the key value in #NXTCASE is found or 0 if the record does not exist. If the record does not exist, KEYED DATA LIST does no further processing and the values of the variables YRHIRED, SEX, and JOBCLASS do not change. If the record can be read, the values of the variables are updated.

TABLE and NOTABLE Subcommands

TABLE and NOTABLE determine whether SPSS displays a table that summarizes the variable definitions. TABLE, the default, displays the table. NOTABLE suppresses the table.

• TABLE and NOTABLE are optional and mutually exclusive.

• The only specification for TABLE or NOTABLE is the subcommand keyword. Neither subcommand has additional specifications.

Example
```
FILE HANDLE EMPL/ file specifications.
KEYED DATA LIST FILE=EMPL KEY=#NXTCASE IN=#FOUND NOTABLE
          /YRHIRED 1-2 SEX 3 JOBCLASS 4.
```

• NOTABLE suppresses the summary table.

LEAVE

```
LEAVE varlist
```

Example:
```
COMPUTE TSALARY=TSALARY+SALARY.
LEAVE TSALARY.
FORMAT TSALARY (DOLLAR8)/ SALARY (DOLLAR7).
EXECUTE.
```

Overview

LEAVE determines that a variable is left at its current value when SPSS reads the next case. Normally, SPSS reinitializes both numeric and string variables each time it prepares to read a new case. LEAVE is frequently used with COMPUTE to create a variable that is used to store an accumulating sum. LEAVE is also useful for spreading a variable's values across multiple cases when VECTOR is used within an INPUT PROGRAM to restructure a data file.

LEAVE can be used only with standard dictionary (permanent) variables. For information on using scratch variables, see Universals: Scratch Variables. Scratch variables are not reinitialized each time a new case is read, but they are not saved on the active system file and therefore cannot be used in procedures.

Basic Specification

- The basic specification is the variable(s) whose values are not to be reinitialized as each new case is read. Numeric variables named on LEAVE are initialized to 0 for the first case only, and string variables are initialized to blanks. The variables named on LEAVE are not reinitialized as new cases are read.

Syntax Rules

- Variables named on LEAVE must already exist and cannot be scratch variables.
- Multiple variables can be named. String and numeric variables can be specified on the same LEAVE command. Keyword TO can be used to reference a list of consecutive variables.

Operations

- LEAVE takes effect as soon as it is encountered in the command sequence, unlike most transformations, which do not take effect until the data are read.
- Numeric variables named on LEAVE are initialized to 0 for the first case only, and string variables are initialized to blanks.

Example

```
COMPUTE TSALARY=TSALARY+SALARY.
LEAVE TSALARY.
FORMAT TSALARY (DOLLAR8)/ SALARY (DOLLAR7).
```

- These commands keep a running total of salaries across all cases. SALARY is the variable containing the employee's salary, and TSALARY is the new variable containing the cumulative salaries for all previous cases.
- For the first case, TSALARY is initialized to 0 and TSALARY=0 + SALARY. For the rest of the cases, TSALARY stores the cumulative totals for SALARY.
- LEAVE follows COMPUTE because TSALARY must first be defined before it can be specified on LEAVE. If LEAVE were not specified for this computation, TSALARY would be initialized to system-missing for the first case. TSALARY would remain system-missing for all cases because its value would be missing for every computation.

Example
```
SORT CASES DEPT.
IF DEPT NE LAG(DEPT,1) TSALARY=0.      /*INITIALIZE FOR NEW DEPT
COMPUTE TSALARY=TSALARY+SALARY.        /*SUM SALARIES
LEAVE TSALARY.                         /*PREVENT INITIALIZATION EACH
CASE
FORMAT TSALARY (DOLLAR8)/ SALARY (DOLLAR7).
```

- These commands accumulate a sum across groups of department cases.

- SORT first sorts cases by the values of variable DEPT.

- IF specifies that if the value for DEPT on the current case is not equal to the value of DEPT on the previous case, set TSALARY equal to 0. Thus, TSALARY is reset to 0 each time the value of DEPT changes. (On the first case in the file, the logical expression on IF is missing. However, the desired effect is obtained because TSALARY is initialized to zero for the first case, independent of the IF statement.)

- LEAVE prevents TSALARY from being initialized for each case.

Example
```
TITLE       'RESTRUCTURING A DATA FILE'.
SUBTITLE    'CREATE A SEPARATE CASE FOR EACH BOOK ORDER'.

INPUT PROGRAM.
DATA LIST  /ORDER 1-4 #X1 TO #X22 (1X,11(F3.0,F2.0,1X)).

LEAVE ORDER.
VECTOR BOOKS=#X1 TO #X22.

LOOP #I=1 TO 21 BY 2  IF NOT SYSMIS(BOOKS(#I)).
- COMPUTE ISBN=BOOKS(#I).
- COMPUTE QUANTITY=BOOKS(#I+1).
- END CASE.
END LOOP.
END INPUT PROGRAM.
BEGIN DATA
1045 182 2 155 1 134 1 153 5
1046 155 3 153 5 163 1
1047 161 5 182 2 163 4 186 6
1048 186 2
1049 155 2 163 2 153 2 074 1 161 1
END DATA.

SORT CASES ISBN.
LIST
```

- Data are extracted from a file whose records store values for an invoice number, a series of book codes, and quantities of books ordered. Invoice 1045 is for nine books of four different titles: two copies of book 182, one copy each of 155 and 134, and five copies of book 153.

- The task is to break each individual book order into a record, preserving the order number on each new case. The easiest way to do so is to use the REPEATING DATA command. This example is effectively long hand for REPEATING DATA.

- INPUT PROGRAM and END INPUT PROGRAM begin and end the block of commands that build cases from the input file. They are required because the END CASE command is used to create multiple cases from single input records.

- DATA LIST specifies ORDER as a permanent variable and defines 22 scratch variables to hold as many alternating book numbers and quantities as will fit within 72 columns.

- LEAVE preserves the value of variable ORDER across the new cases to be generated. If LEAVE were not specified, each of the five values for ORDER would print on only one case. All other cases in the active system file would receive the system-missing value for ORDER.

- VECTOR sets up vector BOOKS with the original scratch variables as its elements. The first element is #X1, the second is #X2, and so forth.
- If the element for vector BOOKS is not system-missing, LOOP initiates the LOOP structure that moves through vector BOOKS picking off the book numbers and quantities. The indexing clause initiates the indexing variable #I at 1, to be increased by 2 to a maximum of 22.
- The first COMPUTE command sets variable ISBN equal to the element in vector BOOKS indexed by #I, which is the current book number. The second COMPUTE sets variable QUANTITY equal to the next element in vector BOOKS, which is the quantity associated with the book number now stored in variable ISBN.
- END CASE tells SPSS to write out a case with the current values of the three variables: ORDER, ISBN, and QUANTITY.
- END LOOP terminates the loop structure and control is returned to the LOOP command, where #I is increased by 2 and looping continues (until #I exceeds 21).

LIST

```
LIST [[VARIABLES=]{ALL**  }] [/FORMAT=[{WRAP**}] [{UNNUMBERED**}]]
                 {varlist}              {SINGLE}   {NUMBERED    }

[/CASES=[FROM {1**}] [TO {eof**}] [BY {1**}]]
              {n  }      {n    }      {n  }
```

Example:
```
LIST VARIABLES=V1 V2 /CASES=FROM 10 TO 100 BY 2.
```

Overview
LIST displays the values of variables for cases in the active system file. The variable display with LIST is similar to the variable display available with the PRINT command. However, LIST is a procedure and reads data, whereas PRINT is a transformation and requires a procedure (or the EXECUTE command) to execute it.

Options
Limiting the Cases Listed. You can specify a list of variables to be listed. See the VARIABLES subcommand.

Wrapping and Numbering. You can limit each case listing to a single line, and you can request that the case number be displayed for each listed case. See the FORMAT subcommand.

Case Sequences. You can limit the listing to a particular sequence of cases. See the CASES subcommand.

Basic Specification
• The basic specification is simply the command keyword, which displays the values for all variables in the active file.

Subcommand Order
• All subcommands are optional and can be named in any order.

Operations
• If VARIABLES is not specified, variables are listed in the order in which they appear in the active file.
• LIST does not display values for scratch or system variables.
• LIST uses dictionary print formats (see Universals: Formats). Alternative formats cannot be specified on LIST (as they can be on the PRINT and WRITE commands).
• The LIST display uses the width specified on SET.
• If a numeric value is longer than the format, SPSS first attempts to list the value by removing punctuation characters, then it uses scientific notation, and finally, if that fails, it prints asterisks (*).
• If a long string variable cannot be listed within the page width, it is truncated.
• Values of the variables listed for a case are always separated by at least one blank.
• System-missing values are listed as a period (.) for numeric variables and a blank for string variables.
• For case listings that fit on one line, the column width for each variable is determined by the length of the variable name or the format, whichever is greater. If the variable names do not fit on one line, they are printed vertically.
• If case listings require more than one line, they are wrapped. LIST displays a table illustrating the location of the variables in the listing and prints the name of the first variable in each line at the beginning of the line.
• Each execution of LIST begins at the top of a new page. If SPLIT FILE is in effect, each split also begins at the top of a new page.

Example	LIST.

- LIST by itself requests a display of the values for all variables in the active file. Cases wrap to multiple lines if all the values do not fit within the page width specified on the SET command. Case numbers are not displayed for the listed cases.

Example	LIST VARIABLES=V1 V2 /CASES=FROM 10 TO 100 BY 2.

- LIST produces a list of every second case for variables V1 and V2, starting with Case 10 and stopping at Case 100.

VARIABLES Subcommand

VARIABLES specifies the variables to be listed. Keyword VARIABLES may be omitted. The variables must already exist, and they cannot be scratch or system variables.

- If VARIABLES is used, only the specified variables are listed.
- Variables are listed in the order in which they are named.
- If a variable is named more than once, it is listed more than once.
- Keyword ALL (the default) can be used to request all variables. ALL can be used with a variable list.

ALL *List all user-defined variables.* Variables are listed in the order in which they appear in the active file. This is the default if VARIABLES is omitted.

Example	LIST VARIABLES=V15 V31 ALL.

- VARIABLES is used to list values for V15 and V31 before all other variables. Keyword ALL then requests that all variable values be listed.
- Values for V15 and V31 are also listed by ALL and are therefore listed twice. The advantage to using VARIABLES in this example is to list values for V15 and V31 in a more prominent position than they would otherwise be listed.

FORMAT Subcommand

FORMAT determines whether cases wrap if they cannot fit on a single line. FORMAT also determines whether the case number is displayed for each listed case. The default display uses more than one line per case (if necessary) and does not number cases.

- The minimum specification is a single keyword to override one of FORMAT's two defaults. The default that is not changed remains in effect.
- If SPLIT FILE is in effect for NUMBERED, numbering restarts at each split. To get sequential numbering regardless of splits, a variable can be set equal to the system variable $CASENUM and then named as the first variable on the VARIABLES subcommand. An appropriate format should be specified for the new variable before it is used on LIST.

One of the two keywords below can be used to control case wrapping.

WRAP *Wrap case listings if they do not fit on a single line.* Page width is determined by the SET command. This is the default.

SINGLE *Limit each case listing to one line.* If the variables requested do not fit on a single line, LIST is not executed.

One of the two keywords below can be used to control case numbering.

UNNUMBERED *Do not include the sequence number of each case in the listing.* This is the default.

NUMBERED *Include the sequence number of each case in the listing.* The sequence number is displayed to the left of the listed values.

CASES Subcommand   CASES limits the number and pattern of cases listed. By default, all cases in the active file are listed.

- Any or all of the keywords below can be used. Defaults that are not changed remain in effect.
- If LIST is preceded by a SAMPLE or SELECT IF command, case selections specified by CASES are taken from those cases that were selected by SAMPLE or SELECT IF.
- If SPLIT FILE is in effect, case selections specified by CASE are restarted for each split.

FROM n *The case number of the first case to be listed.* The default is 1.

TO n *Upper limit on the cases to be listed.* The default is the end of the active file. CASES 100 is interpreted as CASES TO 100.

BY n *Increment used to choose cases for listing.* The default is 1.

Example   `LIST CASES BY 3 /FORMAT=NUMBERED.`

- CASES requests that every third case be listed for all variables in the active file. Cases begin with the first case and list to the end of the file.
- FORMAT displays the case number of each listed case.

Example   `LIST CASES FROM 10 TO 20.`

- Cases from Case 10 through Case 20 are listed for all variables in the active file.

LOGISTIC REGRESSION

This command is included in the SPSS Advanced Statistics option.

```
LOGISTIC REGRESSION [VARIABLES=] dependent var [WITH ind. varlist]
                    [BY var [BY var] ... ]

[/CATEGORICAL= var1, var2, ... ]

                                      {DEVIATION [(refcat)]       }
                                      {SIMPLE [(refcat)]          }
                                      {DIFFERENCE                 }
[/CONTRAST (categorical var)={HELMERT                    }]
                                      {REPEATED                   }
                                      {POLYNOMIAL[({1,2,3...})]}
                                      {               {metric  }  }
                                      {SPECIAL (matrix)           }
                                      {INDICATOR [(refcat)]       }

[/METHOD={ENTER**         } [[ALL**                              }]
         {FSTEP [(({WALD**})]}  {varlist [varname BY varname]}
         {       {LR    }   }
         {BSTEP [(({WALD**})]}
         {       {LR    }   }

[/SELECT={ALL**                }]
         {varname relation value}

[/{NOORIGIN**}]
  {ORIGIN   }

[/ID = [variable]]

[/PRINT=[ALL] [SUMMARY] [CORR] [DEFAULT**] [ITER [(({1**})]]]
                                                   {n }

[/CRITERIA=[BCON ({0.001**})]]
                 {value }

           [ITERATE({20**})] [LCON({0.01**})]
                   {n  }           | {value }

           [PIN({0.05**})] [POUT({0.10**})] [EPS({.00000001**})]
               {value }         {value }         {value       }

[/CLASSPLOT]

[/MISSING={EXCLUDE **}]
          {INCLUDE   }

[/CASEWISE=[tempvarlist]  [OUTLIER({2**  })]]
                                  {value}

[/SAVE=tempvar[(newname)] tempvar[(newname)]...]

[/EXTERNAL]
```

**Default if the subcommand or keyword is omitted.

Temporary variables for logistic regression analysis are: PRED, PGROUP, RESID, DEV, LRESID, SRESID, ZRESID, LEVER, COOK, DFBETA.

Example:

```
LOGISTIC REGRESSION PROMOTED WITH AGE, JOBTIME, JOBRATE.
```

Overview

LOGISTIC REGRESSION regresses a dichotomous dependent variable on a set of independent variables (Aldrich & Nelson, 1984; Fox, 1984). Categorical independent variables can be replaced by sets of contrast variables, each set entering and leaving the model as a unit.

Options

Processing of Independent Variables. You can specify which of the independent variables are categorical in nature (the CATEGORICAL subcommand). Treatment of categorical independent variables is controlled by the CONTRAST subcommand. Five methods are available for entering independent variables into the model (the METHOD subcommand). Interaction terms can be entered into the model by using the keyword BY between variable names.

Selecting Cases. The SELECT subcommand defines subsets of cases to be used in estimating a model.

Regression Through the Origin. The inclusion or exclusion of a constant term from a model is determined by the ORIGIN or NOORIGIN subcommands.

Specifying Termination and Model-Building Criteria. The CRITERIA subcommand provides additional control over computations.

Adding New Variables to the Active System File. You can SAVE the residuals, predicted values, and diagnostics generated by LOGISTIC REGRESSION in the active system file.

Output. You can print optional output (see the PRINT subcommand), request analysis of residuals (see the CASEWISE subcommand), and specify a variable whose values or value labels identify cases (see the ID subcommand). You can request plots of the actual and predicted values for each case (see the CLASS-PLOT subcommand).

Basic Specification

- The basic specification after the procedure name is VARIABLES followed by the name of a single dichotomous dependent variable. Following the dependent variable, you can specify WITH and a list of independent variables. The list of independent variables is optional if the independent variables are listed on a METHOD subcommand. The keyword TO cannot be used in any variable list.

- The default output includes goodness-of-fit tests for the model and a classification table for the predicted and observed group memberships. The regression coefficient, standard error of the regression coefficient, Wald statistic and its significance level, and a multiple correlation coefficient adjusted for the number of parameters (Atkinson, 1980) are displayed for each variable in the equation.

Subcommand Order

- Subcommands can be named in any order.

- The ordering of METHOD subcommands determines the order in which models are estimated. Different sequences may result in different models.

Syntax Rules

- Only one dependent variable can be specified for each LOGISTIC REGRESSION.

- Any number of independent variables may be listed. The dependent variable may not appear on this list.

- The independent variable list is required if any of the METHOD subcommands are used without a variable list or if the METHOD subcommand is not used.

- If you specify keyword WITH on the VARIABLES subcommand, all independent variables must be listed.

- If keyword WITH is used on the VARIABLES subcommand, interaction terms do not have to be specified on the variable list, but the individual variables comprising the interactions must be listed.

- The minimum truncation for this command is LOGI REG.

Operations

- Multiple METHOD subcommands are allowed.

- Independent variables specified by CATEGORICAL are replaced by sets of contrast variables. In stepwise analyses, the set of contrast variables associated with a categorical variable is entered or removed from the model as a block.

- Independent variables are screened to detect and eliminate redundancies.

- If the linearly dependent variable is one of a set of contrast variables, the set will be reduced by the redundant variable or variables. A warning will be issued, and the reduced set will be used.

- For the forward stepwise method, redundancy checking is done when a variable is to be entered into the model.

- When backward stepwise or direct entry methods are requested, all variables for each method subcommand are checked for redundancy before that analysis begins.

Limitations
- The dependent variable must be dichotomous for each split-file group. Specifying a dependent variable with more or less than two non-missing values per split-file group will result in an error.

Example
`LOGISTIC REGRESSION PASS WITH GPA, MAT, GRE.`

- PASS is specified as the dependent variable.
- GPA, MAT, and GRE are specified as independent variables.
- LOGISTIC REGRESSION produces the default output for the logistic regression of PASS on GPA, MAT, and GRE.

VARIABLES Subcommand

VARIABLES specifies the dependent variable and, optionally, all independent variables in the model. The dependent variable appears first in the list and is separated from the independent variables by keyword WITH.

- One VARIABLES subcommand is allowed for each LOGISTIC REGRESSION procedure.
- The dependent variable must be dichotomous. That is, it must have exactly two values other than system-missing and user-missing values for each split file group.
- The dependent variable may be a string variable if its two values can be differentiated by their first eight characters.
- You can indicate an interaction term on the variable list by using keyword BY to separate the individual variables.
- If all METHOD subcommands are accompanied by independent variable lists, keyword WITH and the list of independent variables may be omitted.
- If keyword WITH is used, all independent variables must be specified. For interaction terms, only the individual variable names that make up the interaction (e.g., X1, X2) need to be specified; specifying the actual interaction term (e.g., X1 BY X2) on the VARIABLES subcommand is optional if you specify it on a METHOD subcommand.

Example
`LOGISTIC REGRESSION PROMOTED WITH AGE,JOBTIME,JOBRATE,`
`    AGE BY JOBTIME`

- PROMOTED is specified as the dependent variable.
- AGE, JOBTIME, JOBRATE, and the interaction AGE BY JOBTIME are specified as the independent variables.
- Since no METHOD is specified, all three single independent variables and the interaction are entered into the model.
- LOGISTIC REGRESSION produces the default output.

CATEGORICAL Subcommand

CATEGORICAL identifies independent variables that are nominal or ordinal. Variables that are declared to be categorical are automatically transformed to a set of contrast variables (see CONTRAST Subcommand). If a variable coded as 0-1 is declared as categorical, its coding scheme will be changed to deviation contrasts by default.

- Independent variables not specified on CATEGORICAL are assumed to be at least interval level.
- Variables specified on CATEGORICAL must also appear after WITH keyword on the VARIABLES subcommand. If there is no WITH keyword and list, variables specified on CATEGORICAL must also appear after the METHOD subcommand.
- Variables specified on CATEGORICAL are replaced by sets of contrast variables. If the categorical variable has N distinct values, there will be N-1 contrast variables generated. The set of contrast variables associated with a categorical variable are entered or removed from the model together.
- If any one of the variables in an interaction term is specified on CATEGORICAL, the interaction term is replaced by contrast variables.

- String variables may be specified on CATEGORICAL. Only the first eight characters of each value of a string variable are used in distinguishing between values. Thus, if two values of a string variable are identical for the first eight characters, the values are treated as though they were the same value.

Example
```
LOGISTIC REGRESSION PASS WITH GPA, GRE, MAT, CLASS, TEACHER
/CATEGORICAL = CLASS,TEACHER.
```

- The dichotomous dependent variable PASS is regressed on the interval-level independent variables GPA, GRE, and MAT and the categorical variables CLASS and TEACHER.

CONTRASTS Subcommand

CONTRASTS specifies the type of contrast used for categorical independent variables. The interpretation of the regression coefficients for categorical variables depends on the contrasts used. The default is DEVIATION. The categorical independent variable is specified in parentheses following CONTRASTS. The closing parenthesis is followed by one of the CONTRASTS keywords.

- If the categorical variable has N values, there will be N-1 rows in the contrast matrix. Each contrast matrix is treated as a set of independent variables in the analysis.
- Only one categorical independent variable can be specified per CONTRASTS subcommand, but multiple CONTRASTS subcommands can be specified.

The following contrast types are available. See Finn, 1974, and Kirk, 1982, for further information on a specific type.

DEVIATION(refcat) — *Deviations from the overall effect.* This is the default. The effect for each category of the independent variable except one is compared to the overall effect. Refcat is the category for which parameter estimates are not displayed (they must be calculated from the others). By default, refcat is the last category. To omit a category other than the last, specify the sequence number of the omitted category (which is not necessarily the same as its value) in parentheses after the DEVIATION keyword.

SIMPLE(refcat) — *Each category of the independent variable except the last is compared to the last category.* To use a category other than the last as the omitted reference category, specify its sequence number (which is not necessarily the same as its value) in parentheses following the keyword SIMPLE.

DIFFERENCE — *Difference or reverse Helmert contrasts.* The effects for each category of the independent variable except the first are compared to the mean effect of the previous categories.

HELMERT — *Helmert contrasts.* The effects for each category of the independent variable except the last is compared to the mean effects of subsequent categories.

POLYNOMIAL(metric) — *Polynomial contrasts.* The first degree of freedom contains the linear effect across the categories of the independent variable; the second contains the quadratic effect; and so on. By default, the categories are assumed to be equally spaced; unequal spacing can be specified by entering a metric consisting of one integer for each category of the independent variable in parentheses after the keyword POLYNOMIAL. For example, CONTRAST (STIMULUS) = POLYNOMIAL(1,2,4) indicates that the three levels of STIMULUS are actually in the proportion 1:2:4. The default metric is always $(1,2,...,k)$, where k categories are involved. Only the relative differences between the terms of the metric matter: (1,2,4) is the same metric as (2,3,5) or (20,30,50), because in each instance the difference between the second and third numbers is twice the difference between the first and second.

REPEATED *Comparison of adjacent categories.* Each category of the independent variable except the first is compared to the previous category.

SPECIAL(matrix) *A user-defined contrast.* After this keyword a matrix is entered in parentheses with k-1 rows and k columns (where k is the number of categories of the independent variable). The rows of the contrast matrix contain the special contrasts indicating the desired comparisons between categories. If the special contrasts are linear combinations of each other, LOGISTIC REGRESSION reports the linear dependency and stops processing. If k rows are entered, the first row is discarded and only the last k-1 rows are used as the contrast matrix in the analysis.

INDICATOR(refcat) *Indicator variables.* Contrasts indicate the presence or absence of category membership. By default, refcat is the last category (represented in the contrast matrix as a row of zeroes). To omit a category other than the last, specify the sequence number of the omitted category (which is not necessarily the same as its value) in parentheses after keyword INDICATOR.

Example
```
LOGISTIC REGRESSION PASS WITH GRE, CLASS
/CATEGORICAL = CLASS
/CONTRAST(CLASS)=HELMERT.
```

• A logistic regression analysis of the dependent variable PASS is performed on the interval-level independent variable GRE and the categorical independent variable CLASS.

• PASS is a dichotomous variable representing course pass/fail status and CLASS identifies whether a student is in one of three classrooms. A HELMERT type contrast is requested.

Example
```
LOGISTIC REGRESSION PASS WITH GRE, CLASS
/CATEGORICAL = CLASS
/CONTRAST(CLASS)=SPECIAL(2 -1 -1
                         0  1 -1).
```

• In this example, the comparisons are specified using keyword SPECIAL.

METHOD Subcommand

METHOD indicates how the independent variables enter the model. The specification is METHOD followed by a single method keyword. Keyword METHOD can be omitted. Optionally, specify the independent variables and interactions for which the method is to be used. Use keyword BY between variable names of an interaction term.

• If no variable list is specified or if keyword ALL is used, all the independent variables following keyword WITH in the VARIABLES subcommand are eligible for inclusion in the model.

• If no METHOD subcommand is specified, the default method is ENTER.

• Variables specified on CATEGORICAL are replaced by sets of contrast variables. The set of contrast variables associated with a categorical variable are entered or removed from the model together.

• Any number of METHOD subcommands can appear in a LOGISTIC REGRESSION procedure. METHOD subcommands are processed in the order in which they are specified. Each method starts with the results from the previous method. If BSTEP is used, all remaining eligible variables are entered at the first step. All variables are then eligible for entry and removal unless they have been excluded from the METHOD variable list.

• The beginning model for the first METHOD subcommand is either the constant variable (by default or if NOORIGIN is specified) or an empty model (if ORIGIN is specified).

The available METHOD keywords are

ENTER *Forced entry.* All variables are entered in a single step. This is the default.

FSTEP *Forward stepwise.* The independent variables specified in the variable list are tested for entry into the model one by one, based on the significance level of the score statistic. The variable with the smallest significance less than PIN is entered into the model. Additionally, variables that are already in the model at each step are tested for possible removal, based on either the significance of the WALD (default) or likelihood ratio (LR) criterion. The variable with the largest probability greater than the specified POUT value is removed and the model reestimated. Variables in the model are then again evaluated for removal. Once no more variables satisfy the removal criterion, variables not in the model are evaluated for entry.

BSTEP *Backward stepwise.* On the first step, all variables specified on the BSTEP variable list are entered into the model. The variable with the largest significance level greater than POUT for the Wald (default) or LR statistic is then removed. The model is reestimated without the variable, and again the variable with the largest significance level greater than POUT is removed. This continues until no more variables meet removal criteria. Variables not in the model are then considered for entry based on the PIN criteria. After each entry, variables are again considered for removal. Model building stops when no more variables meet entry and removal criteria, or when one variable meets poth PIN and POUT criteria.

- METHOD keywords FSTEP and BSTEP can be followed by an additional keyword in parentheses to indicate which statistic should be used to determine whether a variable is to be removed.

- Keyword WALD indicates that removal of a variable is based on the significance of the Wald statistic. This is the default.

- Keyword LR (likelihood ratio) indicates that the criterion for removal is the significance of the change in the log likelihood when the variable is removed from the model.

- If LR is specified, the model must be reestimated without each of the variables in the model. This can substantially increase computational time. However, the likelihood ratio statistic is better than the Wald statistic for deciding which variables are to be removed.

Example
```
LOGISTIC REGRESSION PROMOTED WITH
 AGE,JOBTIME,JOBRATE,RACE,SEX,AGENCY
 /CATEGORICAL RACE,SEX,AGENCY
 /METHOD ENTER AGE, JOBTIME
 /METHOD BSTEP (LR) RACE,SEX,JOBRATE,AGENCY.
```

- AGE, JOBTIME, JOBRATE, RACE, SEX, and AGENCY are specified as independent variables. RACE, SEX, and AGENCY are specified as categorical independent variables.

- The first METHOD subcommand enters AGE and JOBTIME into the model.

- Variables in the model at the termination of the first METHOD subcommand are included in the model at the beginning of the second METHOD subcommand.

- The second METHOD subcommand adds the variables SEX, RACE, JOBRATE, and AGENCY to the previous model.

- Backward stepwise logistic regression analysis is then done with only the variables in the BSTEP variable list tested for removal using the LR statistic.

- The procedure continues until all variables from the BSTEP variable list have been removed or the removal of a variable will not result in a decrease in the log likelihood with a probability larger than POUT.

SELECT Subcommand

By default, all cases on the active system file are considered for inclusion in LOGISTIC REGRESSION. Use the optional SELECT subcommand to include a subset of cases in the analysis.

- The specification is either a logical expression or keyword ALL. ALL is the default. The format is

```
/SELECT=varname relation value
```

- Variables named on VARIABLES, CATEGORICAL, or METHOD subcommands cannot appear on SELECT.
- In the logical expression on SELECT, the relation can be EQ, NE, LT, LE, GT, or GE. The variable must be numeric and the value can be any number.
- Only cases for which the logical expression on SELECT is true are included in calculations. All other cases, including those with missing values for the variable named on SELECT, are unselected.
- Diagnostic statistics and classification statistics are reported for both selected and unselected cases.
- Cases deleted from the active system file with the SELECT IF or SAMPLE commands are not included among either the selected or unselected cases.

Example

```
LOGISTIC REGRESSION VARIABLES=GRADE WITH GPA,TUCE,PSI
/SELECT SEX EQ 1 /CASEWISE=RESID.
```

- Only cases with the value 1 for SEX are included in the logistic regression analysis.
- Residual values generated by CASEWISE are displayed for both selected and unselected cases.

ORIGIN and NOORIGIN Subcommands

ORIGIN and NOORIGIN control whether or not the constant is included. NOORIGIN (the default) includes a constant term (intercept) in all equations. ORIGIN suppresses the constant term and requests regression through the origin. (NOCONST can be used as an alias for ORIGIN.)

- The only specification is either ORIGIN or NOORIGIN.
- ORIGIN or NOORIGIN can be specified only once per LOGISTIC REGRESSION procedure, and it affects all METHOD subcommands.

Example

```
LOGISTIC REGRESSION VARIABLES=PASS WITH GPA,GRE,MAT /ORIGIN.
```

- ORIGIN suppresses the automatic generation of a constant term.

ID Subcommand

ID specifies a variable whose values or value labels identify the casewise listing. By default, cases are labeled by their case number.

- The only specification is the name of a single variable that exists on the active system file.
- Only the first eight characters of a string variable are used to label cases.
- Only the first eight characters of the variable's value label are used to label cases. If the variable has no value labels, the values are used.

PRINT Subcommand

PRINT controls the display of optional output. The minimum specification is a single keyword. If PRINT is omitted, DEFAULT output (defined below) is displayed.

- The minimum specification is PRINT followed by a single keyword.
- If PRINT is used, only the requested output is displayed.

DEFAULT   *Classification tables and statistics for the variables in and not in the equation at each step.* Tables and statistics are displayed for each split file and METHOD subcommand.

SUMMARY   *Summary information.* Same output as DEFAULT, except that the output for each step is not displayed.

CORR   *Correlation matrix of parameter estimates for the variables in the model.*

ITER(value)   *Iterations at which parameter estimates are to be printed.* The value in parentheses controls the spacing of iteration reports. If the value is N, the parameter estimates are printed for every N^{th} iteration starting at 0. If a value is not supplied, intermediate estimates are printed at each iteration.

ALL   *All available output.*

Example

```
LOGISTIC REGRESSION VARIABLES=PASS WITH GPA,GRE,MAT
/METHOD FSTEP
/PRINT CORR SUMMARY ITER(2).
```

- A forward stepwise logistic regression analysis of PASS on GPA, GRE, and MAT is specified.

- PRINT CORR causes the correlation matrix of parameter estimates for the variables in the model to be displayed.

- SUMMARY suppresses the output display for each step. Results are displayed for the final model only.

- ITER specifies that parameter estimates are to be displayed at every second iteration.

CRITERIA Subcommand

The optional CRITERIA subcommand controls the statistical criteria used in building the logistic regression models. The way in which these criteria are used depends on the method specified on the METHOD subcommand. The default criteria are noted in the description of each keyword below. Iterations will stop if the criteria for BCON, LCON, or ITERATE are satisfied.

BCON(value)   *Change in parameter estimates to terminate iteration.* Iteration terminates when the parameters change by less than this value. The default is 0.001. To eliminate this criteria, specify a value of 0.

ITERATE   *Maximum number of iterations.* The default is 20.

LCON(value)   *Percent change in the log likelihood ratio for termination of iterations.* If the log likelihood decreases by less than this, iteration terminates. The default is 0.01%. To eliminate this criteria, specify a value of 0.

PIN(value)   *Probability of score statistic for variable entry.* The default is 0.05. The larger the specified probability, the easier it is for a variable to enter the model.

POUT(value)   *Probability of Wald or LR statistic to remove a variable.* The default is 0.1. The larger the specified probability, the easier it is for a variable to remain in the model.

EPS(value)   *Epsilon value used for redundancy checking.* The specified value must be less than or equal to 0.05 and greater than or equal to 10^{-12}. The default is 0.00000001. Larger values make it harder for variables to pass the redundancy check, i.e., they are more likely to be removed from the analysis.

Example

```
LOGISTIC REGRESSION PROMOTED WITH AGE,JOBTIME,RACE
/CATEGORICAL RACE
/METHOD BSTEP
/CRITERIA BCON(0.01) ITERATE(10) PIN(0.01) POUT(0.05).
```

- A backward stepwise logistic regression analysis is performed for the dependent variable PROMOTED and the independent variables AGE, JOBTIME, and RACE.

- CRITERIA alters four of the statistical criteria that control the building of a model.

- BCON specifies that if the change in the absolute value of all of the B estimates is less than 0.01, the iterative estimation process should stop. Larger values lower the number of iterations required. Notice that the ITER and LCON criteria remain unchanged and that if either of them is met before BCON, iterations will terminate. (LCON can be set to 0 if only BCON and ITER are to be used.)

- ITERATE specifies that the maximum number of iterations is 10.
- POUT requires that the probability of the statistic used to test whether a variable should remain in the model be smaller than 0.05. This is more stringent than the default value of 0.1.
- PIN requires that the probability of the score statistic used to test whether a variable should be included be smaller than 0.01. This makes it more difficult for variables to be included in the model than the default PIN value of 0.05.

CLASSPLOT Subcommand

The optional CLASSPLOT subcommand generates a classification plot of the actual and predicted values of the dichotomous dependent variable at each step.

- Keyword CLASSPLOT is the only specification.
- If CLASSPLOT is not specified, plots are not generated.

Example

```
LOGISTIC REGRESSION PROMOTED WITH JOBTIME RACE
  /CATEGORICAL RACE
  /CLASSPLOT.
```

- A logistic regression model is constructed for the dichotomous dependent variable PROMOTED and the independent variables JOBTIME and RACE.
- CLASSPLOT produces a classification plot for the dependent variable PROMOTED. The vertical axis of the plot is the frequency of the variable PROMOTED. The horizontal axis is the predicted probability of membership in the second of the two levels of PROMOTED.

CASEWISE Subcommand

CASEWISE produces a casewise listing of the values of the temporary variables created by LOGISTIC REGRESSION.

- The minimum specification is CASEWISE. This produces a listing of PRED, PGROUP, RESID, and ZRESID.

The following keywords are available for specifying temporary variables (see Fox, 1984). If a list of variable names is given, only those names are displayed.

PRED   *Predicted probability.* For each case, the predicted probability of having the second of the two values of the dichotomous dependent variable.

PGROUP   *Predicted group.* The group to which a case is assigned based on the predicted probability.

RESID   *Difference between observed and predicted probability.*

DEV   *Deviance values.* For each case, a log-likelihood-ratio statistic is computed which measures how well the model fits the data.

LRESID   *Logit residual.* Residual divided by the product of PRED and 1-PRED.

SRESID   *Studentized residual.*

ZRESID   *Normalized residual.* Residual divided by the square root of the product of PRED and 1-PRED.

LEVER   *Leverage value.* A measure of the relative influence of each observation on the model's fit.

COOK   *Analog of Cook's influence statistic.*

DFBETA   *Difference in beta.* The difference in the estimated coefficients for each independent variable if the case is omitted.

- The following keyword is available for restricting the cases to be printed, based on the absolute value of SRESID.

OUTLIER (value)   Cases with absolute values of SRESID greater than or equal to the specified value are displayed. If OUTLIER is specified with no value, cases with an absolute values of SRESID greater than or equal to 2 are displayed.

Example
```
LOGISTIC REGRESSION PROMOTED WITH JOBTIME, RACE, SEX
/CATEGORICAL SEX
/METHOD ENTER
/CASEWISE SRESID LEVER DFBETA.
```

- CASEWISE produces a casewise listing of the temporary variables SRESID, LEVER, and DFBETA. There will be four values of DFBETA, one corresponding to the constant and one corresponding to each of the independent variables in the model.

MISSING Subcommand

MISSING controls the processing of missing values. The default is EXCLUDE.

EXCLUDE   *Listwise deletion of all cases with missing values.* A case is omitted from the analysis if any of the variables specified in the procedure have user- or system-missing values for that case. If a case has a missing value on the dependent variable and nonmissing values on all independent variables, predicted values are calculated for that case.

INCLUDE   *Include user-missing values in the analysis.*

SAVE Subcommand

SAVE saves the temporary variables created by LOGISTIC REGRESSION. To specify variable names for the new variables, assign the new names in parentheses following each temporary variable name. If new variable names are not specified, LOGISTIC REGRESSION generates default names.

- Assigned variable names must be unique on the active system file. Scratch or system variable names cannot be used (that is, the variable names cannot begin with # or $).
- A temporary variable can only be saved once on the same SAVE subcommand.

Example
```
LOGISTIC REGRESSION PROMOTED WITH JOBTIME AGE
/SAVE PRED (PREDPRO) DFBETA (DF).
```

- A logistic regression analysis of PROMOTED on the independent variables JOBTIME and AGE is performed.
- SAVE adds four variables to the active system file: one variable named PREDPRO, containing the predicted value from the specified model for each case, and three variables named DF0, DF1, and DF2 containing, respectively, the DFBETA values for each case for the constant, the independent variables JOBTIME, and the independent variable AGE.

EXTERNAL Subcommand

EXTERNAL indicates that the data for each split file group should be held in an external scratch file during processing. This can help conserve memory resources when running complex analyses or analyses with large data sets.

- Keyword EXTERNAL is the only specification.
- Specifying EXTERNAL may result in slightly longer processing time.
- If EXTERNAL is not specified, all data is held internally and no scratch file is written.

Annotated Example

For a complete example with output, see Examples following the Command Reference.

References

Aldrich, J. H., and F. D. Nelson. 1984. *Linear probability, logit, and probit models.* Beverly Hills, California: Sage Publications.

Atkinson, A. C. 1980. A note on the generalized information criterion for choice of a model. *Biometrika* 67:413–418.

Bartolucci, A. A., and M. D. Fraser. 1977. Comparative step-up and composite tests for selecting prognostic indicators associated with survival. *Biometrics* 19:437-48.

Bock, R. Darrell. 1985. *Multivariate statistical methods in behaviorial research.* Mooresville, Indiana: Scientific Software, Inc.

Finn, J. D. 1974. *A general model for multivariate analysis.* New York: Holt, Rinehart & Winston.

Fox, J. 1984. *Linear statistical models and related methods: With applications to social research.* New York: John Wiley & Sons.

Kirk, R. E. 1982. *Experimental design.* 2d ed. Monterey, California: Brooks/Cole Publishing Company.

Lawless, J. F., and K. Singhal. 1978. Efficient screening of nonnormal regression models. *Biometrics* 34:318-26.

——. 1987. ISMOD: an all-subsets regression program for generalized linear models. *Computer Methods and Programs in Biomedicine* 24:117-24.

Neter, J., and W. Wasserman. 1974. *Applied linear statistical models: Regression, analysis of variance, and experimental designs.* Homewood, Illinois: Richard D. Irwin, Inc.

Rao, C. R. 1973. *Linear statistical inference and its applications.* 2d ed. New York: John Wiley & Sons.

Wald, A. 1943. Tests of statistical hypotheses concerning several parameters with applications to problems of estimation. *Transcripts of American Mathematical Society* 54:426-82.

LOGLINEAR

This command is included in the SPSS Advanced Statistics option.

```
LOGLINEAR varlist(min,max)...[BY] varlist(min,max)

             [WITH covariate varlist]

  [/CWEIGHT={varname }] [/CWEIGHT=(matrix)...]
           {(matrix)}

  [/GRESID={varlist }]  [/GRESID=(matrix)...]
          {(matrix)}

  [/PRINT={DEFAULT**}] [/NOPRINT={ESTIM** }]
          {FREQ**   }            {COR**   }
          {RESID**  }            {DESIGN**}
          {DESIGN   }            {RESID   }
          {ESTIM    }            {FREQ    }
          {COR      }            {DEFAULT }
          {ALL      }            {ALL     }
          {NONE     }


  [/PLOT={DEFAULT }]
         {RESID   }
         {NORMPROB}
         {NONE**  }


                       {DEVIATION [(refcat)]       }
                       {DIFFERENCE                  }
                       {HELMERT                     }
  [/CONTRAST (varname)={SIMPLE [(refcat)]           }]...[/CONTRAST...]
                       {REPEATED                    }
                       {POLYNOMIAL [({1,2,3,...})]  }
                       {            {metric    }    }
                       {[BASIS] SPECIAL(matrix)     }


  [/CRITERIA=[CONVERGE({0.001**})] [ITERATE({20**})] [DELTA({0.5**})]
                      {eps    }             {n  }           {d  }
             [DEFAULT]]


  [/MISSING={LISTWISE**} [INCLUDE]]
            {DEFAULT   }


  [/WIDTH={132}]
          { n }


  [/DESIGN=effect[(n)] effect[(n)]... effect BY effect...] [/DESIGN...]
```

**Default if the subcommand is omitted.

Example:

```
LOGLINEAR JOBSAT (1,2) ZODIAC (1,12) /DESIGN=JOBSAT.
```

Overview

LOGLINEAR is a general procedure for model fitting, hypothesis testing, and parameter estimation for any model that has categorical variables as its major components. As such, LOGLINEAR subsumes a variety of related techniques, including general models of multi-way contingency tables, logit models, logistic regression on categorical variables, and quasi-independence models.

LOGLINEAR models cell frequencies using the multinomial response model and produces maximum likelihood estimates of parameters by means of the Newton-Raphson algorithm (Haberman, 1978). HILOGLINEAR, which uses an iterative proportional fitting algorithm, is more efficient for hierarchical models, but it cannot produce parameter estimates for unsaturated models, does not permit specification of contrasts for parameters, and does not display a correlation matrix of the parameters.

Options

Model Specification. You can specify the model or models to be fit. See DESIGN Subcommand.

Cell Weights and Structural Zeros. You can specify cell weights, such as structural zeros, for the model. See CWEIGHT Subcommand.

Optional Displayed Output. You can control the types of display output. See PRINT and NOPRINT subcommands.

Optional Plots. You can produce plots of adjusted residuals against observed and expected counts, and normal and detrended normal plots. See PLOT Subcommand.

Linear Combinations. You can calculate linear combinations of observed cell frequencies, expected cell frequencies, and adjusted residuals. See GRESID Subcommand.

Contrasts. You can indicate the type of contrast desired for a factor. See CONTRAST Subcommand.

Criteria for Algorithm. You can control the values of algorithm-tuning parameters. See CRITERIA Subcommand.

Formatting Options. You can control the width of the display output. See WIDTH Subcommand.

Basic Specification

The basic specification is two or more variables that define the crosstabulation table. The minimum and maximum values for each variable must be specified in parentheses after the variable name.

By default, LOGLINEAR estimates the saturated model for a multi-dimensional table. Output includes the factors or effects, their levels, and any labels; observed and expected frequencies and percentages for each factor and code; residuals, standardized residuals, and adjusted residuals; two goodness-of-fit statistics (the likelihood ratio chi-square and Pearson's chi square); and estimates of the parameters with accompanying Z-values and 95% confidence intervals.

Subcommand Order

- The variables specification must come first.
- The subcommands that affect a DESIGN subcommand should be placed before the DESIGN subcommand.
- All subcommands can be used more than once and, with the exception of the DESIGN subcommand, are carried from model to model unless explicitly overridden.
- If DESIGN is not the last subcommand, LOGLINEAR generates the saturated model.

Example

```
LOGLINEAR JOBSAT (1,2) ZODIAC (1,12) /DESIGN=JOBSAT, ZODIAC.
```

- The variable list specifies two categorical variables JOBSAT and ZODIAC. JOBSAT has the values 1 and 2. ZODIAC has values 1 through 12.
- DESIGN specifies a model with only main effects.

Example

```
LOGLINEAR GSLEVEL (4,8) EDUC (1,4) SEX (1,2)
    /DESIGN=GSLEVEL EDUC SEX.
```

- GSLEVEL is a categorical variable with values 4, 5, 6, 7, and 8. EDUC is a categorical variable with values 1 through 4. SEX has two values: 1 and 2.
- DESIGN specifies a model with only main effects. SEX and EDUC are independent.

Example   `LOGLINEAR DPREF (2,3) RACE CAMP (1,2).`

- DPREF is a categorical variable with values 2 and 3. RACE and CAMP are categorical variables with values 1 and 2.
- This is a general log-linear model since no BY keyword appears. The design defaults to a saturated model in which all main effects and interaction effects are fitted.

Example   `LOGLINEAR GSLEVEL (4,8) BY EDUC (1,4) SEX (1,2)`
`           /DESIGN=GSLEVEL, GSLEVEL BY EDUC, GSLEVEL BY SEX.`

- Keyword BY in the variable list specifies a logit model in which GSLEVEL is the dependent variable, and EDUC and SEX are independent variables.
- DESIGN specifies a model that can be used to test that there is no joint effect of SEX and EDUC on GSLEVEL.

Variable List   The variable list specifies the variables to be included in the model. LOG-LINEAR analyzes two classes of variables: categorical and continuous. *Categorical variables* are used to define the cells of the table. *Continuous variables* can be used as cell covariates and can only be specified after the keyword WITH at the end of the list of categorical variables.

- The list of categorical variables must be first. Categorical variables must be numeric and integer.
- A range must be defined for each categorical variable by specifying, in parentheses after each variable name, the minimum and maximum values for that variable. Separate the two values with at least one space or comma.
- To specify the same range for a list of variables, specify the list of variables followed by a single range. The range applies to all variables in the list.
- To specify a logit model, use keyword BY. (See Logit Model, below.) A variable list without keyword BY generates a general log-linear model.
- Cases with values outside the specified range are excluded from the analysis. Noninteger values within the range are truncated for the purpose of building the table.

Logit Model
- To segregate independent variables from the dependent variable in a logit model, use keyword BY. The categorical variable preceding BY is the dependent variable; categorical variables following BY are the independent variables.
- Up to nine variables can be included as independent variables following keyword BY.
- A DESIGN subcommand should be used to request the desired logit model.
- LOGLINEAR displays an analysis of dispersion and two measures of association: entropy and concentration. These measures are discussed in Haberman (1982) and can be used to quantify the magnitude of association among the variables. Both are proportional reduction in error measures. The entropy statistic is analogous to Theil's entropy measure, while the concentration statistic is analogous to Goodman and Kruskal's tau-*b*. Both statistics measure the strength of association between the dependent variable and the predictor variable set.

Cell Covariates
- Continuous variables can be used as covariates. When used, the covariates must be specified after keyword WITH at the end of the list of categorical variables. Ranges are not specified for the continuous variables.
- A variable cannot be named as both a categorical variable and a cell covariate.
- To enter cell covariates into a model, the covariates must be specified on the DESIGN subcommand.
- Cell covariates are not applied on a case-by-case basis. The mean covariate value for a cell in the contingency table is applied to that cell.

Example
```
LOGLINEAR DPREF(2,3) RACE CAMP (1,2) WITH CONSTANT
    /DESIGN=DPREF RACE CAMP CONSTANT.
```

- Variable CONSTANT is a continuous variable specified as a cell covariate. Cell covariates must be specified after keyword WITH at the end of the variable list. No range is defined for cell covariates.

- To include the cell covariate in the model, variable CONSTANT is specified on DESIGN.

DESIGN Subcommand

DESIGN specifies the model or models to be fit. If DESIGN is omitted or used with no specifications, the saturated model is produced. The saturated model fits all main effects and all interaction effects.

- To specify more than one model, use more than one DESIGN subcommand. Each DESIGN specifies one model.

- To obtain simple effects models, name all the variables listed on the variables specification.

- To obtain interactions, use keyword BY to specify each interaction, as in: A BY B, C BY D. To obtain the single-degree-of-freedom partition of a specified contrast, specify the partition in parentheses following the factor (see the example below).

- To include cell covariates in the model, first identify them on the variable list by naming them after keyword WITH, then specify the variable name(s) on DESIGN.

- Interaction between a cell covariate and an independent variable is permitted; interaction between two cell covariates is not permitted. To obtain interactions between two cell covariates, use COMPUTE to create new interaction variables.

- To specify an *equiprobability model,* name a cell covariate that is actually a constant of 1.

Example
```
COMPUTE X=MONTH.
LOGLINEAR MONTH (1,12) WITH X
    /DESIGN X.
```

- The variable specification identifies MONTH as a categorical variable with values 1 through 12. Keyword WITH identifies X as a covariate.

- DESIGN tests the linear effect of MONTH.

Example
```
TITLE 'SPECIFYING MAIN EFFECTS MODELS'.

LOGLINEAR A(1,4) B(1,5)
    /DESIGN=A
    /DESIGN=A,B.
```

- The first DESIGN model tests the homogeneity of B-category probabilities; it fits the marginal frequencies on A, but assumes that membership in any of the categories of B is equiprobable.

- The second DESIGN model tests the independence of A and B. It fits the marginals on both A and B.

Example
```
TITLE 'SPECIFYING INTERACTIONS'.

LOGLINEAR A(1,4) B(1,5) C(1,3)
    /DESIGN=A,B,C, A BY B.
```

- This DESIGN consists of the A main effect, the B main effect, the C main effect, and the interaction of A and B.

Example
```
TITLE 'SINGLE-DEGREE-OF-FREEDOM PARTITIONS'.

LOGLINEAR A(1,4) BY B(1,5)
    /CONTRAST(B)=POLYNOMIAL
    /DESIGN=A,A BY B(1).
```

- B(1) refers to the first partition of B, which is the linear effect of B; this follows from the contrast specified on the CONTRAST subcommand.

Example
```
TITLE    'SPECIFYING CELL COVARIATES'.

COMPUTE DISTANCE=ABS(HUSED - WIFED).
COMPUTE CWT=1.
IF (HUSED EQ WIFED) CWT=0.

LOGLINEAR HUSED WIFED(1,4) WITH DISTANCE
   /CWEIGHT=CWT
   /DESIGN=HUSED WIFED DISTANCE.
```

- The continuous variable DISTANCE is identified as a cell covariate by specifying it after WITH on the variable list. The cell covariate is then included in the model by naming it on DESIGN.
- CWEIGHT specifies variable CWT, which imposes structural zeros on the diagonal.

Example
```
TITLE 'EQUIPROBABILITY MODEL'.

COMPUTE  X=1.
LOGLINEAR  MONTH(1,18) WITH X
   /DESIGN=X.
```

- This model tests whether the frequencies in the 18-cell table are equal by using a cell covariate that is a constant of 1.

CWEIGHT Subcommand

CWEIGHT specifies cell weights, such as structural zeros, for a model. By default, cell weights are equal to 1.

- The specification is either one numeric variable or a matrix of weights enclosed in parentheses.
- If a matrix of weights is specified, the matrix must contain the same number of elements as the product of the levels of the categorical variables. An asterisk can be used to signify repetitions of the same value.
- If weights are specified for a multiple-factor model, the index value of the rightmost factor increments most rapidly.
- If a numeric variable is specified, only one CWEIGHT subcommand can be used on LOGLINEAR. To use multiple cell weights on the same LOGLINEAR, specify all weights in matrix format. Each matrix must be specified on a separate CWEIGHT subcommand, and each CWEIGHT specification remains in effect until explicitly overridden with another CWEIGHT subcommand.
- CWEIGHT can be used to impose structural, or *a priori*, zeros on the model. This feature is useful in the analysis of symmetric tables.

Example
```
COMPUTE  CWT=1.
IF (HUSED EQ WIFED) CWT=0.
LOGLINEAR HUSED WIFED(1,4) WITH DISTANCE
   /CWEIGHT=CWT
   /DESIGN=HUSED WIFED DISTANCE.
```

- COMPUTE initially assigns CWT the value of 1 for all cases.
- IF assigns CWT the value 0 when HUSED equals WIFED.
- CWEIGHT imposes structural zeros on the diagonal of the symmetric crosstabulation table. Because a variable name is specified, only one CWEIGHT can be used.

Example
```
/CWEIGHT=(0 1 1 1 0 1 1 1 0 1 1 1)
/CWEIGHT=(0 3*1 0 3*1 0 3*1)
```

- These two matrix specifications are equivalent.

Example
```
LOGLINEAR  HUSED WIFED(1,4) WITH DISTANCE
   /CWEIGHT=(0, 4*1, 0, 4*1, 0, 4*1, 0)
   /DESIGN=HUSED WIFED DISTANCE
   /CWEIGHT=(16*1)
   /DESIGN=HUSED WIFED DISTANCE.
```

- The first CWEIGHT matrix specifies the same values as variable CWT provided in the first example. By using the matrix format on CWEIGHT rather than a variable name, a different CWEIGHT subcommand can be used for the second model.

GRESID Subcommand

GRESID (Generalized Residual) calculates linear combinations of observed cell frequencies, expected cell frequencies, and adjusted residuals.

- The specification is either a numeric variable or a matrix whose contents are coefficients of the desired linear combinations.

- If a matrix of coefficients is specified, the matrix must contain the same number of elements as the number of cells implied by the variables specification. An asterisk can be used to signify repetitions of the same value.

- Each GRESID subcommand specifies a single linear combination. Each matrix or variable must be specified on a separate GRESID subcommand. All GRESIDs specified are displayed for each design.

Example

```
/GRESID=(1 1 1 0 0 1 1 1)
/GRESID=(3*1,2*0,3*1)
```

- These two matrix specifications are equivalent.

Example

```
LOGLINEAR  MONTH(1,18) WITH Z
 /GRESID=(6*1,12*0)
 /GRESID=(6*0,6*1,6*0)
 /GRESID=(12*0,6*1)
 /DESIGN=Z.
```

- The first GRESID subcommand combines the first six months into a single effect. The second GRESID subcommand combines the second six months, and the third GRESID subcommand combines the last six months.

- For each effect, LOGLINEAR displays the observed and expected count, the residual, the standardized residual, and the adjusted residual.

PRINT and NOPRINT Subcommands

PRINT requests statistics that are not produced by default. NOPRINT suppresses the display of specified output.

- By default, LOGLINEAR displays the frequency table and residuals. The parameter estimates of the model are also displayed if DESIGN is not used. To turn off these defaults, use NOPRINT.

- Multiple PRINT and NOPRINT subcommands are permitted. The specifications are cumulative.

The following keywords can be used on both PRINT and NOPRINT.

FREQ   *Observed and expected cell frequencies and percentages.*   This is displayed by default.

RESID   *Raw, standardized, and adjusted residuals.*   This is displayed by default.

DESIGN   *The design matrix of the model, showing the basis matrix corresponding to the contrasts used.*

ESTIM   *The parameter estimates of the model.* If you do not specify a design on the DESIGN subcommand, LOGLINEAR generates a saturated model and displays the parameter estimates for the saturated model. LOGLINEAR does not display parameter estimates or correlation matrices of parameter estimates if any sampling zero cells exist in the expected table after DELTA is added. Parameter estimates and a correlation matrix are displayed when structural zeros are present.

COR   *The correlation matrix of the parameter estimates.*

ALL   *All available output.*

DEFAULT   *FREQ and RESID.* ESTIM is also displayed by default if the DESIGN subcommand is not used.

NONE   *The design information and goodness-of-fit statistics only.* This option overrides all other specifications on the PRINT subcommand. The NONE option applies only to the PRINT subcommand.

Example
```
LOGLINEAR A(1,2) B(1,2)
 /PRINT=ESTIM
 /NOPRINT=DEFAULT
 /DESIGN=A,B,A BY B
 /PRINT=ALL
 /DESIGN=A,B.
```

- The first design is the saturated model. Since it fits the data exactly, there is no need to see the frequencies and residuals. The parameter estimates are displayed by PRINT=ESTIM. The frequencies and residuals output is suppressed by NOPRINT=DEFAULT.

- The second design is the main effects model, which tests the hypothesis of no interaction. The second PRINT subcommand displays all available display output for this model.

PLOT Subcommand

PLOT produces optional plots. None are displayed by default. Multiple PLOT subcommands can be used; the specifications are cumulative.

RESID   *Plots of adjusted residuals against observed and expected counts.*

NORMPROB *Normal and detrended normal plots of the adjusted residuals.*

NONE   *No plots.*

DEFAULT   *RESID and NORMPROB.*

Example
```
LOGLINEAR  RESPONSE(1,2) BY TIME(1,4)
   /CONTRAST(TIME)=SPECIAL(4*1, 7 14 27 51, 8*1)
   /PLOT=DEFAULT
   /DESIGN=RESPONSE TIME(1) BY RESPONSE
   /PLOT=NONE
   /DESIGN.
```

- RESID and NORMPROB plots are displayed for the first design.

- No plots are displayed for the second design.

CONTRAST Subcommand

CONTRAST indicates the type of contrast desired for a factor, where a factor is any categorical dependent or independent variable. The default contrast is DEVIATION for each factor.

- The specification is CONTRAST followed by a variable name in parentheses, then the contrast.

- To specify a contrast for more than one factor, use a separate CONTRAST subcommand for each specified factor. Only one contrast can be in effect for each factor on each DESIGN.

- A contrast specification remains in effect for subsequent designs until explicitly overridden with another CONTRAST subcommand.

- In LOGLINEAR, contrasts do not have to sum to 0 or be orthogonal.

- The design matrix used for the contrasts can be displayed by specifying keyword DESIGN on the PRINT subcommand. However, this matrix is the basis matrix which is used to determine contrasts; it is not the contrast matrix itself.

- CONTRAST can be used for a multinomial logit model, in which the dependent variable has more than two categories.

- CONTRAST can be used for fitting linear logit models. Keyword BASIS is not appropriate for such models.

- In a logit model, CONTRAST is used to transform the independent variable into a metric variable. Again, keyword BASIS is not appropriate.

DEVIATION(refcat)   *Deviations from the overall effect.* DEVIATION is the default contrast if the CONTRAST subcommand is not used. Refcat is the category for which parameter estimates are not displayed (they are the negative of the sum of the others). By default, refcat is the last category of the variable.

DIFFERENCE	*Levels of a factor with the average effect of previous levels of a factor.* Also known as *reverse Helmert* contrasts.
HELMERT	*Levels of a factor with the average effect of subsequent levels of a factor.*
SIMPLE(refcat)	*Each level of a factor to the reference level.* By default, LOGLINEAR uses the last category of the factor variable as the reference category. Optionally, any level can be specified as the reference category enclosed in parentheses after keyword SIMPLE. The level, not the actual value, must be specified.
REPEATED	*Adjacent comparisons across levels of a factor.*
POLYNOMIAL(metric)	*Orthogonal polynomial contrasts.* The default is equal spacing. Optionally, the coefficients of the linear polynomial can be specified in parentheses, indicating the spacing between levels of the treatment measured by the given factor.
[BASIS]SPECIAL(matrix)	*User-defined contrast.* As many elements as the number of categories squared must be specified. If BASIS is specified before SPECIAL, a basis matrix is generated for the special contrast, which makes the coefficients of the contrast equal to the special matrix. Otherwise, the matrix specified is the basis matrix used to determine coefficients for the contrast matrix.

Example
```
LOGLINEAR  A(1,4) BY B(1,4)
 /CONTRAST(B)=POLYNOMIAL
 /DESIGN=A A BY B(1)
 /CONTRAST(B)=SIMPLE
 /DESIGN=A A BY B(1).
```

- The first CONTRAST subcommand requests polynomial contrasts of B for the first design.

- The second CONTRAST subcommand requests the SIMPLE contrast of B, with the last category (value 4) used as the reference category for the second DESIGN subcommand.

Example
```
TITLE 'MULTINOMIAL LOGIT MODEL'.

LOGLINEAR  PREF(1,5) BY RACE ORIGIN CAMP(1,2)
 /CONTRAST(PREF)=SPECIAL(5*1, 1 1 1 1 -4, 3 -1 -1 -1 0,
        0 1 1 -2 0, 0 1 -1 0 0).
```

- LOGLINEAR builds special contrasts among the five categories of the dependent variable. The variable PREF measures preference for training camps among Army recruits. For PREF, 1=stay, 2=move to north, 3=move to south, 4=move to unnamed camp, and 5=undecided.

- The four contrasts are (1) move or stay versus undecided; (2) stay versus move; (3) named camp versus unnamed; and (4) northern versus southern camp. Because these contrasts are orthogonal, SPECIAL and BASIS SPECIAL produce equivalent results. Use BASIS SPECIAL to obtain parameter estimates for nonorthogonal comparisons.

Example
```
TITLE 'CONTRASTS FOR A LINEAR LOGIT MODEL'.

LOGLINEAR RESPONSE(1,2) BY YEAR(0,20)
 /PRINT=DEFAULT ESTIM
 /CONTRAST(YEAR)=SPECIAL(21*1, -10, -9, -8, -7, -6, -5, -4,
                  -3, -2, -1, 0, 1, 2, 3, 4, 5, 6, 7,
                  8, 9, 10, 399*1)
 /DESIGN=RESPONSE RESPONSE BY YEAR(1).
```

• YEAR measures years of education and ranges from 0 to 20. Therefore, allowing for the constant effect, YEAR has 20 estimable parameters associated with it.

• The SPECIAL contrast specifies the constant—that is, 21*1—and the linear effect of YEAR—that is, −10 to 10. The other 399 1's fill out the 21*21 matrix.

Example
```
TITLE 'CONTRASTS FOR A LOGISTIC REGRESSION MODEL'.

LOGLINEAR RESPONSE(1,2) BY TIME(1,4)
  /CONTRAST(TIME) = SPECIAL(4*1, 7 14 27 51, 8*1)
  /PRINT=ALL /PLOT=DEFAULT
  /DESIGN=RESPONSE, TIME(1) BY RESPONSE.
```

• CONTRAST is used to transform the independent variable into a metric variable.

• TIME represents elapsed time in days. Therefore, the weights in the contrast represent the metric of the passage of time.

CRITERIA Subcommand

CRITERIA specifies the values of some constants in the Newton-Raphson algorithm. Defaults or specifications remain in effect until overridden with another CRITERIA subcommand.

CONVERGE(eps) *Convergence criterion.* Specify a value for the convergence criterion. The default is 0.001.

ITERATION(n) *Maximum number of iterations.* Specify the maximum number of iterations for the algorithm. The default number is 20.

DELTA(d) *Cell delta value.* The value of delta is added to each cell frequency for the first iteration. For saturated models, it remains in the cell. The default value is 0.5. LOGLINEAR does not display parameter estimates or correlation matrices of parameter estimates if any sampling zero cells exist in the expected table after DELTA is added. Parameter estimates and correlation matrices can be displayed in the presence of structural zeros.

DEFAULT *Default values are used.* DEFAULT can be used to reset the parameters to the default.

Example
```
LOGLINEAR  DPREF(2,3) BY RACE ORIGIN CAMP(1,2)
  /CRITERIA=ITERATION(50) CONVERGE(.0001).
```

• ITERATION increases the maximum number of iterations to 50.

• CONVERGE lowers the convergence criterion to 0.0001.

WIDTH Subcommand

WIDTH specifies the display width. The default display uses the width specified on SET.

• Only one width can be in effect at a time, and it controls all display.

• WIDTH can be placed anywhere after the variables specification.

• With narrow width settings, the frequency table displays fewer statistics and has fewer decimal places. In addition, observed and expected percentages are omitted.

Example
```
LOGLINEAR  DPREF(2,3) RACE CAMP(1,2)
  /WIDTH=72.
```

• WIDTH sets the display width to 72 columns.

MISSING Subcommand   MISSING controls missing values. LISTWISE is the default. If INCLUDE is specified, user-missing values must also be included in the value range specification.

LISTWISE   *Delete cases with missing values listwise.* Cases with missing values on any variable listed on the variables specification are deleted. This is the default, which can be made explicit by specifying keyword DEFAULT.

INCLUDE   *Include user-missing values as valid.*

Example
```
MISSING VALUES A(0).
LOGLINEAR A(0,2) B(1,2) /MISSING=INCLUDE
 /DESIGN=B.
```

• Even though 0 was specified as missing, it is treated as a non-missing category of A in this analysis.

Annotated Example   For a complete example with output, see Examples following the Command Reference.

References   Haberman, S. J. 1978. *Analysis of qualitative data.* Vol. I, Introductory topics. New York: Academic Press.

——. 1979. *Analysis of qualitative data.* Vol. II, New developments. New York: Academic Press.

LOOP—END LOOP

```
LOOP [varname=n TO m [BY {1**}]]  [IF [(]logical expression[)]]
                        {n  }

transformations

END LOOP [IF [(]logical expression[)]]
```

**Default if the subcommand is omitted.

Example:

```
SET MXLOOPS=10.     /*MAXIMUM NUMBER OF LOOPS ALLOWED
COMPUTE X=0.
LOOP.               /*LOOP WITH NO LIMIT OTHER THAN MXLOOPS
COMPUTE X=X+1.
END LOOP.
```

Example:

```
COMPUTE X=0.
LOOP #I=1 TO 5.     /*LOOP FIVE TIMES
COMPUTE X=X+1.
END LOOP.
```

Overview

The LOOP—END LOOP structure controls the execution of commands on a single case or on a single input record containing information on multiple cases. Commands specified within the loop are executed repeatedly until they reach a cutoff limit. The limit can be specified by an indexing clause on the LOOP command, an IF clause on the END LOOP command, or a BREAK command within the loop structure (see BREAK). In addition, an IF clause on the LOOP command can be used to control each iteration of the loop. The maximum number of loops allowed for any non-iterative loop structure is determined by the MXLOOPS subcommand on SET. The default MXLOOPS is 40.

Compare the loop structure with the DO IF—END IF structure: LOOP—END LOOP performs repeated transformations on the *same* case; DO IF—END IF transforms data on *subsets* of cases.

Also compare the loop structure with the DO REPEAT—END REPEAT structure, which replicates transformations on a specified set of variables. Generally, LOOP is more efficient than DO REPEAT. In addition, LOOP is more flexible because it allows conditional entry into the loop, conditional termination of the loop, and also allows nested loops. DO REPEAT, on the other hand, can replicate transformations for a set of variables that are not adjacent on the active system file. It also allows more flexibility in the set of replacement values it uses in the transformations (that is, the replacement values do not have to be consecutive and do not have to conform to an ordered pattern).

For information on defining a vector within a loop referencing a list of permanent or temporary variables to be used in other transformations, see VECTOR. For information on using END CASE within a loop to change the structure of a file, see END CASE.

Options

Missing Values. You can prevent cases with missing values on any of the variables used in the LOOP structure from entering the loop. See Missing Values, below.

Creating Data. A LOOP structure within an input program can be used to generate data. See Creating Data, below.

Defining Complex File Structures. A LOOP structure within an input program can be used to define complex files that cannot be handled by standard file definition facilities. See Complex File Structures, below.

Basic Specification
- The basic specification is LOOP and at least one transformation command. The structure must end with the END LOOP command. Commands within the loop are executed until the cutoff limit is reached.

Syntax Rules
- If both an indexing and an IF clause are used on LOOP, the indexing clause must be first.
- LOOP structures can be nested within other LOOP structures or within DO IF structures, and vice versa.

Operations
- The LOOP command defines the beginning of a LOOP structure, and the END LOOP command defines its end. Every LOOP structure must have both a LOOP and an END LOOP command.
- When specified within a LOOP structure, definition commands, such as MISSING VALUES and VARIABLE LABELS, and utility commands, such as SET and SHOW, are invoked once when they are encountered in the command file.

Example
```
SET MXLOOPS=10.
COMPUTE X=0.
LOOP. /*LOOP WITH NO LIMIT OTHER THAN MXLOOPS
COMPUTE X=X+1.
END LOOP.
```

- The SET MXLOOPS command limits the number of times the loop is executed to 10. The function of MXLOOPS is to prevent infinite loops when there is no iteration clause.
- The first COMPUTE command initializes the value of X to 0; otherwise, it would be initialized to system-missing.
- Within the LOOP structure, the first iteration for the first case sets the value of X to 0 plus 1. Control then returns to the LOOP command, and the value of X is set to 1 plus 1. After ten iterations, as specified in the SET command, the loop is terminated.

Example
```
COMPUTE X=0.
LOOP.
COMPUTE X=X+1.
END LOOP IF (X EQ 5).        /*LOOP UNTIL X IS 5
```

- Iterations continue until the logical expression on the END LOOP is true, which for every case is when X equals 5.
- This corresponds to the programming notion of DO UNTIL. The loop is always executed at least once.

Example
```
COMPUTE X=0.
LOOP IF (X LT 5).            /*LOOP WHILE X IS LESS THAN 5
COMPUTE X=X+1.
END LOOP.
```

- The IF clause is evaluated each trip through the structure, so looping stops once X equals 5.
- This corresponds to the programming notion of DO WHILE. The loop may be executed zero times.

Example
```
COMPUTE X=0.
LOOP IF (Y GT 10).          /*LOOP ONLY FOR CASES WITH Y GT 10
COMPUTE X=X+1.
END LOOP IF (X EQ 5).       /*LOOP UNTIL X IS 5
```

- Variable X will be 5 for cases with values greater than 10 for variable Y. Variable X is 0 for all other cases.

Indexing Clause for the LOOP Command

The indexing clause limits the number of loops by specifying the number of times SPSS should execute commands within the structure. The indexing clause is specified on the LOOP command and includes an indexing variable followed by initial and terminal values. SPSS sets the *indexing variable* to the *initial value* and increases it by the specified increment each time the loop is executed for a case. When the indexing variable reaches the specified *terminal value*, no further loops are executed. By default, SPSS increases the indexing variable by 1 for each iteration. Keyword BY overrides this increment.

- The indexing variable can have any valid variable name. Unless you specify a scratch variable, the indexing variable is treated as a permanent variable and is saved on the active system file. If the indexing variable is assigned the same name as an existing variable, the values of the existing variable are altered by the LOOP structure as it is executed, and the original values are lost.

- An indexing clause overrides the maximum number of loops specified by SET MXLOOPS.

- The initial and terminal values of the indexing clause can be numeric expressions. Noninteger and negative expressions are allowed.

- If the expression for the initial value is greater than the terminal value, no iterations of the loop are executed. #J=X TO Y is a zero-trip loop if X is 0 and Y is −1.

- If the expressions for the initial and terminal values are equal, the loop is executed once. #J=0 TO Y is a one-trip loop when Y is 0.

- SPSS protects the value of the iteration variable from modification with a loop. The process involves using a copy of the iteration variable to control execution of the loop and to update the value of the actual iteration variable each time the copy is updated. If the loop is exited via BREAK or a conditional clause on the END LOOP statement, the actual iteration variable is not updated. If the LOOP statement contains both an iteration clause and a conditional clause, the iteration clause is executed first, and the actual iteration variable will be updated regardless of which clause causes termination of the loop.

Example

```
COMPUTE X=0.
LOOP #I=1 TO 5.              /*LOOP FIVE TIMES
COMPUTE X=X+1.
END LOOP.
```

- Scratch variable #I (the indexing variable) is set to the initial value of 1 and increased by 1 each time the loop is executed for a case. When #I reaches the terminal value 5, no further loops are executed. Thus, the value of X will be 5 for every case.

Example

```
COMPUTE X=0.
LOOP #I=1 TO 5  IF (Y GT 10). /*LOOP TO X=5 ONLY FOR CASES Y GT 10
COMPUTE X=X+1.
END LOOP.
```

- Both an indexing and an IF clause are specified on LOOP. The indexing clause precedes the IF clause.

Example

```
COMPUTE X=0.
LOOP #I=1 TO Y.              /*LOOP TO THE VALUE OF Y
COMPUTE X=X+1.
END LOOP.
```

- The number of iterations for a case depends on the value of variable Y for the case. For a case with value 0 for variable Y, the loop is not executed and X is 0. For a case with value 1 for variable Y, the loop is executed once and X is 1.

Example

```
* REPLACE A CASE'S MISSING VALUES WITH THE MEAN OF ALL
  NON-MISSING VALUES FOR THAT CASE.

DATA LIST FREE /V1 V2 V3 V4 V5 V6 V7 V8.
MISSING VALUES V1 TO V8 (99).
COMPUTE MEANSUB=MEAN(V1 TO V8).

VECTOR V=V1 TO V8.
LOOP #I=1 TO 8.
+ DO IF  MISSING(V(#I)).
+ COMPUTE V(#I)=MEANSUB.
+ END IF.
END LOOP.

BEGIN DATA
1 99 2 3 5 6 7  8
2  3 4 5 6 7 8  9
2  3 5 5 6 7 8 99
END DATA.
LIST.
```

- The first COMPUTE calculates variable MEANSUB as the mean of all non-missing values on each case.
- VECTOR defines vector V with the original variables as its elements.
- The loop is executed for each variable in the data, and the COMPUTE within the loop is executed only for variables that have missing values. COMPUTE replaces the missing values with the value of MEANSUB.
- In the data, the missing value for variable V2 in the first case is set equal to MEANSUB's value on the first case. The missing value for variable V8 in the third case is set equal to MEANSUB's value on the third case.

Example

```
TITLE  'FACTORIAL ROUTINE'.

DATA LIST FREE / X.
BEGIN DATA
1 2 3 4 5 6 7
END DATA.

COMPUTE FACTOR=1.
LOOP #I=1 TO X.
COMPUTE FACTOR=FACTOR * #I.
END LOOP.
LIST.
```

- The LOOP structure computes FACTOR as the factorial value of X (X!).

Example

```
TITLE  'TEST FOR LISTWISE DELETION OF MISSING VALUES'.

DATA LIST / V1 TO V6 1-6.
STRING SELECT(A1).
COMPUTE SELECT='V'.
VECTOR V=V1 TO V6.

LOOP #I=1 TO 6.
IF MISSING(V(#I)) SELECT='M'.
END LOOP.

BEGIN DATA
123456
    56
1 3456
123456
123456
END DATA.

FREQUENCIES VAR=SELECT.
```

- STRING declares string variable SELECT with an A1 format and COMPUTE sets the value of SELECT equal to V.

- VECTOR defines vector V as the original variables V1 to V6. Variables on a single vector must be all numeric or all string variables. In this example, because vector V is used as an argument on the MISSING function of IF, the variables have to be numeric (MISSING is not available for string variables).
- The loop structure executes six times: once for each VECTOR element. If a value is missing for any element, SELECT is set equal to M. In effect, if any case has even a single missing value, SELECT is set to M.
- FREQUENCIES generates a frequency table for SELECT. The table gives a count of how many cases have missing values for at least one variable and how many cases have valid values for all variables. Commands in this example can be used to determine whether cases may have been dropped from an analysis that uses listwise deletion of missing values. For information on using the NMISS function to count the number of missing values in each case, see COMPUTE.

Example

```
TITLE    'DEMONSTRATE THE CYCLE OF NESTED LOOPS'.
SUBTITLE 'COMPUTE EVERY COMBINATION OF VALUES FOR EACH VARIABLE'.

INPUT PROGRAM.
-LOOP #I=1 TO 4.        /* LOOP TO NUMBER OF VALUES FOR I
+    LOOP #J=1 TO 3.        /* LOOP TO NUMBER OF VALUES FOR J
.        LOOP #K=1 TO 4.        /* LOOP TO NUMBER OF VALUES FOR K

.            COMPUTE I=#I.
.            COMPUTE J=#J.
.            COMPUTE K=#K.
.            END CASE.

.        END LOOP.
+    END LOOP.
-END LOOP.
END FILE.
END INPUT PROGRAM.
LIST.
```

- The first loop iterates four times. The first iteration sets the indexing variable #I equal to 1 and then passes control to the second loop. #I remains 1 until the second loop has completed all of its iterations.
- The second loop is executed four times, iterating three times for each value of #I. The first iteration sets the Indexing variable #J equal to 1 and then passes control to the third loop. #J remains 1 until the third loop has completed all of its iterations.
- The third loop results in 48 iterations ($4 \times 3 \times 4$). The first iteration sets #K equal to 1. The COMPUTE statements set the variables I, J, and K each to 1, and END CASE creates a case. The third loop iterates a second time, setting #K equal to 2. Variables I, J, and K are then computed with the respective values 1, 1, 2, and a second case is created. The third loop's third and fourth iterations result in cases with I, J, and K respective values of 1, 1, 3 and 1, 1, 4. After the fourth iteration within the third loop, control passes back to the second loop.
- The second loop executes again. #I remains 1, while #J increases to 2, and control returns to the third loop. The third loop completes its iterations, resulting in four more cases with I=1, J=2, and K increasing from 1 to 4. This cycle repeats, resulting in cases with I=1, J=3, and K increasing from 1 to 4. Since the second loop has completed three iterations, control passes back to the first loop, and the entire cycle is repeated for the next increment of #I.
- Once the first loop completes four iterations, control passes out of the looping structures to END FILE. END FILE defines the resulting cases as a data file, the input program terminates, and the LIST command is executed.
- This example does not require a LEAVE command because the iteration variables are #I, #J, and #K. If the iteration variables were I, J, and K, LEAVE would be required for I and J.

Example   TITLE   'MODIFY THE LOOP ITERATION VARIABLE'.

```
INPUT PROGRAM.
PRINT SPACE    2.
LOOP           A = 1 TO 3.                      /*Simple iteration
+   PRINT         /'A WITHIN LOOP: ' A(F1).
+   COMPUTE       A = 0.
END LOOP
PRINT          /'A AFTER LOOP:   ' A(F1).

NUMERIC        #B.
LOOP           B = 1 TO 3.                      /*Iteration + UNTIL
+   PRINT         /'B WITHIN LOOP: ' B(F1).
+   COMPUTE       B = 0.
+   COMPUTE       #B = #B+1.
END LOOP       IF #B = 3.
PRINT          /'B AFTER LOOP:   ' B(F1).

NUMERIC        #C.
LOOP           C = 1 TO 3 IF #C NE 3.   /*Iteration + WHILE
+   PRINT         /'C WITHIN LOOP: ' C(F1).
+   COMPUTE       C = 0.
+   COMPUTE       #C = #C+1.
END LOOP.
PRINT          /'C AFTER LOOP:   ' C(F1).

NUMERIC        #D.
LOOP           D = 1 TO 3.                      /*Iteration + BREAK
+   PRINT         /'D WITHIN LOOP: ' D(F1).
+   COMPUTE       D = 0.
+   COMPUTE       #D = #D+1.
+   DO IF         #D = 3.
+      BREAK.
+   END IF.
END LOOP.
PRINT          /'D AFTER LOOP:   ' D(F1).

LOOP           E = 3 TO 1.                      /*Zero trip iteration
+   PRINT         /'E WITHIN LOOP: ' E(F1).
+   COMPUTE       E = 0.
END LOOP.
PRINT          /'E AFTER LOOP:   ' E(F1).
END FILE.
END INPUT PROGRAM.
EXECUTE.
```

- If a loop is exited via BREAK or a conditional clause on the END LOOP statement, the iteration variable is not updated.
- If the LOOP statement contains both an iteration clause and a conditional clause, the iteration clause is executed first, and the actual iteration variable will be updated regardless of which clause causes termination of the loop.
- Figure 1 shows the output from this example.

Figure 1   Modify the loop iteration variable

```
A WITHIN LOOP: 1
A WITHIN LOOP: 2
A WITHIN LOOP: 3
A AFTER LOOP:  4
B WITHIN LOOP: 1
B WITHIN LOOP: 2
B WITHIN LOOP: 3
B AFTER LOOP:  0
C WITHIN LOOP: 1
C WITHIN LOOP: 2
C WITHIN LOOP: 3
C AFTER LOOP:  4
D WITHIN LOOP: 1
D WITHIN LOOP: 2
D WITHIN LOOP: 3
D AFTER LOOP:  0
E AFTER LOOP:  3
```

BY Keyword   By default, SPSS increases the indexing variable by 1 for each iteration. Keyword BY overrides this increment.

- The *increment value* can be a numeric expression and can therefore be noninteger or negative. Zero causes a warning and results in a zero-trip loop.
- If the initial value is greater than the terminal value and the increment is positive, the loop is never entered. #I=1 TO 0 BY 2 is a zero-trip loop.
- If the initial value is less than the terminal value and the increment is negative, the loop is never entered. #I=1 TO 2 BY −1 is a zero-trip loop.

Example

```
LOOP #I=2 TO 10 BY 2.          /*LOOP FIVE TIMES BY 2'S
COMPUTE X=X+1.
END LOOP.
```

- Scratch variable #I starts at 2 and increases by 2 for each of five iterations until it equals 10 for the last iteration. Order is unimportant: 2 BY 2 TO 10 is equivalent to 2 TO 10 BY 2.

Example

```
COMPUTE X=0.
LOOP #I=1 TO Y BY Z.           /*LOOP TO Y INCREMENTING BY Z
COMPUTE X=X+1.
END LOOP.
```

- The loop is executed once for a case with Y equal to 2 and Z equal to 2, because #I is 3 after one loop. The loop is executed twice if Y is 3 and Z is 2.

Example

```
TITLE     'RESTRUCTURING A DATA FILE'.
SUBTITLE  'CREATE A SEPARATE CASE FOR EACH BOOK ORDER'.

INPUT PROGRAM.
DATA LIST  /ORDER 1-4 #X1 TO #X22 (1X,11(F3.0,F2.0,1X)).

LEAVE ORDER.
VECTOR BOOKS=#X1 TO #X22.

LOOP #I=1 TO 21 BY 2  IF NOT SYSMIS(BOOKS(#I)).
- COMPUTE ISBN=BOOKS(#I).
- COMPUTE QUANTITY=BOOKS(#I+1).
- END CASE.
END LOOP.
END INPUT PROGRAM.
BEGIN DATA
1045 182 2 155 1 134 1 153 5
1046 155 3 153 5 163 1
1047 161 5 182 2 163 4 186 6
1048 186 2
1049 155 2 163 2 153 2 074 1 161 1
END DATA.

SORT CASES ISBN.
DO IF $CASENUM EQ 1.
- PRINT EJECT /'Order ISBN Quantity'.
- PRINT SPACE.
END IF.

FORMATS ISBN (F3)/ QUANTITY (F2).
PRINT /' ' ORDER ' ' ISBN '  ' QUANTITY.

EXECUTE.
```

- Data are extracted from a file whose records store values for an invoice number, a series of book codes, and quantities of books ordered. Invoice 1045 is for nine books of four different titles: two copies of book 182, one copy each of 155 and 134, and five copies of book 153.
- The task is to break each individual book order into a record, preserving the order number on each new case. The easiest way to do so is to use the REPEATING DATA command. This example is, in effect, longhand for REPEATING DATA.

• INPUT PROGRAM and END INPUT PROGRAM begin and end the block of commands that build cases from the input file. They are required because the END CASE command is used to create multiple cases from single input records.

• DATA LIST specifies ORDER as a permanent variable and defines 22 scratch variables to hold as many alternating book numbers and quantities as will fit within 72 columns. In the format specification, the first element skips 1 space after the value for variable ORDER. The 11 is a repetition factor that repeats the parenthesized format that follows it 11 times: once for each book number and quantity pair. The specified format is F3.0 for book numbers, F2.0 for the quantities, and the element 1X skips 1 column after each quantity value.

• LEAVE preserves the value of variable ORDER across the new cases to be generated.

• VECTOR sets up vector BOOKS with the original scratch variables as its elements. The first element is #X1, the second is #X2, and so forth.

• If the element for vector BOOKS is not system-missing, LOOP initiates the LOOP structure that moves through vector BOOKS picking off the book numbers and quantities. The indexing clause initiates the indexing variable #I at 1, to be increased by 2 to a maximum of 22.

• The first COMPUTE command sets variable ISBN equal to the element in vector BOOKS indexed by #I, which is the current book number. The second COMPUTE sets variable QUANTITY equal to the next element in vector BOOKS, which is the quantity associated with the book number now stored in variable ISBN.

• END CASE tells SPSS to write out a case with the current values of the three variables: ORDER, ISBN, and QUANTITY.

• END LOOP terminates the loop structure and control is returned to the LOOP command, where #I is increased by 2 and looping continues (until #I exceeds 21).

• SORT CASES sorts the new cases by book number in preparation for displaying.

• The DO IF structure encloses a PRINT EJECT command and a PRINT SPACE command to set up titles for the displayed output.

• PRINT FORMATS establishes dictionary print formats for new variables ISBN and QUANTITY (see Figure 2).

• EXECUTE is shown here as the procedure that processes the cases for displaying; any procedure will do.

Figure 2 PRINT output showing new cases

```
Order ISBN Quantity

1049   74    1
1045  134    1
1045  153    5
1046  153    5
1049  153    2
1045  155    1
1046  155    3
1049  155    2
1047  161    5
1049  161    1
1046  163    1
1047  163    4
1049  163    2
1045  182    2
1047  182    2
1047  186    6
1048  186    2
```

Example

```
TITLE  'EFFECT REPEATING DATA'.

INPUT PROGRAM.
DATA LIST       NOTABLE/ ORDER 1-4(N) #BKINFO 6-71(A).
LEAVE ORDER.
LOOP            #I = 1 TO 66 BY 6 IF SUBSTR(#BKINFO,#I,6) a= ''.
+  REREAD          COLUMN = #I+5.
+  DATA LIST       NOTABLE/ ISBN 1-3(N) QUANTITY 4-5.
+  END CASE.
END LOOP.
END INPUT PROGRAM.
SORT CASES      BY ISBN ORDER.
BEGIN DATA
1045 182 2 155 1 134 1 153 5
1046 155 3 153 5 163 1
1047 161 5 182 2 163 4 186 6
1048 186 2
1049 155 2 163 2 153 2 074 1 161 1
END DATA.

DO IF           $CASENUM = 1.
+  PRINT EJECT    /'Order' 1  'ISBN' 7  'Quantity' 13.
END IF.
PRINT           /ORDER 2-5(N) ISBN 8-10(N) QUANTITY 13-17.
EXECUTE.
```

- Using the book order data from the previous example, this example shows a different approach to restructuring a file. As with the previous example, this example uses LOOP to effect a REPEATING DATA command.
- DATA LIST specifies scratch variable #BKINFO as a string variable (format A) to allow blanks in the data.
- LOOP is executed if the SUBSTR function returns anything other than a blank or null value. SUBSTR returns a six-character substring of #BKINFO, beginning with the character in the position specified by the value of the indexing variable #I. As specified on the indexing clause, #I begins with a value of 1 and is increased by 6 for each execution of LOOP, up to a maximum #I value of 61 (because $1+10\times6=61$).

Missing Values

- If SPSS encounters a case with a missing value for the initial, terminal, or increment expressions in an indexing clause, or if the conditional expression on the LOOP command returns missing, a zero-trip loop results and control is passed to the first command after the END LOOP command.
- If a case has a missing value for the conditional expression on an END LOOP command, the loop is terminated after the first iteration.
- To prevent cases with missing values on any of the variables used in the LOOP structure from ever entering the loop, use the IF clause on the LOOP command.

Example

```
COMPUTE X=0.
LOOP #I=1 TO Z  IF (Y GT 10). /*LOOP TO X=Z FOR CASES Y GT 10
COMPUTE X=X+1.
END LOOP.
```

- The value of X remains at 0 for cases with a missing value for Y or a missing value for Z (or if Z is less than 1).

Example

```
MISSING VALUES X(5).
COMPUTE X=0.
LOOP.
COMPUTE X=X+1.
END LOOP IF (X GE 10). /*LOOP UNTIL X IS AT LEAST 10 OR MISSING
```

- Looping is terminated when the value of X reaches 5, because 5 is the missing value for X, and the logical expression on the END LOOP command returns a missing value. The value of X is 5 for every case.

Example
```
COMPUTE X=0.
LOOP IF NOT MISSING(Y).        /*LOOP ONLY WHEN Y ISN'T MISSING
COMPUTE X=X+Y.
END LOOP IF (X GE 10).         /*LOOP UNTIL X IS AT LEAST 10
```

- Variable X is 0 for cases with a missing value for Y, since the loop is never entered.

Creating Data

A LOOP structure and an END CASE command within an INPUT PROGRAM can be used to create data without any data input. An END FILE command must be used outside the loop (but within the input program) to terminate processing.

Example
```
INPUT PROGRAM.
LOOP #I=1 TO 20.
COMPUTE AMOUNT=RND(UNIFORM(5000))/100.
END CASE.
END LOOP.
END FILE.
END INPUT PROGRAM.

PRINT FORMATS AMOUNT (DOLLAR6.2).
PRINT /AMOUNT.
EXECUTE.
```

- This example creates 20 cases with a single variable AMOUNT, a uniformly distributed number between 0 and 5000, rounded to an integer and divided by 100 to provide a variable in dollars and cents.

- The END FILE command is required to terminate processing once the LOOP structure is complete.

Example
```
TITLE  'CREATE VAR THAT APPROXIMATES A LOG-NORMAL DISTRIBUTION'.

SET FORMAT=F8.0.

INPUT PROGRAM.
LOOP I=1 TO 1000.
+ COMPUTE SCORE=EXP(NORMAL(1)).
+ END CASE.
END LOOP.
END FILE.
END INPUT PROGRAM.

FREQUENCIES VARIABLES=SCORE /FORMAT=NOTABLE /HISTOGRAM
  /PERCENTILES=1 10 20 30 40 50 60 70 80 90 99
  /STATISTICS=ALL.
```

- The input program creates 1000 cases with a single variable SCORE. Values for SCORE approximate a log-normal distribution.

Complex File Structures

Some file structures may require looping on a DATA LIST command in order to spread information from one or more header records to individual records.

Example   TITLE 'READ A COMPLEX FILE STRUCTURE'.

```
INPUT PROGRAM.
DATA LIST   /#RECS 1 HEAD1 HEAD2 3-4(A).    /*READ HEADER INFO
LEAVE  HEAD1 HEAD2.

LOOP  #I=1 TO #RECS.
DATA LIST   /INDIV 1-2(1).                   /*READ INDIVIDUAL INFO
PRINT  /#RECS HEAD1 HEAD2 INDIV.
END CASE.                                    /*CREATE COMBINED CASE
END LOOP.
END INPUT PROGRAM.
BEGIN DATA
1 AC
91
2 CC
35
43
0 XX
1 BA
34
3 BB
42
96
37
END DATA.
EXECUTE.
```

- DATA are from a file with header records that indicate how many individual records follow. The 1 in the first column of the first header record (AC), says that only one individual record (91) follows. The 2 in the first column of the second header record (CC) says that two individual records (35 and 43) follow. The next header record has no individual records, indicated by the 0 in column 1, and so on.

- The first DATA LIST reads the expected number of individual records for each header record into temporary variable #RECS. #RECS is then used as the terminal value in the LOOP command to read the correct number of individual records using the second DATA LIST.

- Variables HEAD1 and HEAD2 are the information in columns 3 and 4, respectively, in the header records. The LEAVE command retains HEAD1 and HEAD2 so that this information can be spread to the individual records.

- Variable INDIV is the information from the individual record. INDIV is then combined with #RECS, HEAD1, and HEAD2 to create the new case. Notice in the output from the PRINT command in Figure 3 that no case is created for the header record with 0 as #RECS.

- END CASE passes each case out of the input program to the LIST command.

Figure 3 Printed information for individual records

```
1 A C 9.1
2 C C 3.5
2 C C 4.3
1 B A 3.4
3 B B 4.2
3 B B 9.6
3 B B 3.7
```

Macro Facility

```
DEFINE macro name ( [{argument name=} {!TOKENS (n)                          }] )
                     {!POSITIONAL= } {!CHAREND ('char')                     }
                                     {!ENCLOSE ('startsym','endsym')}
                                     {!CMDEND                               }
```

```
[!DEFAULT (default string)] [!NOEXPAND]
```

```
[/{argument name=} ...] ] )
  {!POSITIONAL= }
```

```
macro body
!ENDDEFINE
```

SET command controls:
```
PRESERVE
RESTORE
```

Assignment:
```
!LET
```

Conditional processing:
```
!IF (expression) !THEN statements
   [!ELSE statements]
!IFEND
```

Looping constructs:
```
!DO !varname=start !TO finish [BY step]
   statements  [!BREAK]
!DOEND
```

```
!DO !varname !IN (list)
   statements  [!BREAK]
!DOEND
```

Macro directives:
```
!OFFEXPAND
!ONEXPAND
```

String manipulation functions:
```
!LENGTH (string)
!CONCAT (string1,string2)
!SUBSTR (string,from,[length])
!INDEX (string1,string2)
!HEAD (string)
!TAIL (string)
!QUOTE (string)
!UNQUOTE (string)
!UPCASE (string)
!BLANKS (n)
!NULL
!EVAL (string)
```

Example:
```
DEFINE sesvars ().
  age sex educ religion.
!ENDDEFINE.
```

Overview

The macro facility builds blocks of SPSS syntax elements and controls the execution of those blocks. In effect, it allows you to create your own SPSS commands out of existing ones.

A macro can be useful in several different contexts. For example, a macro can be used to

- Issue a series of the same or similar commands repeatedly, using looping constructs rather than redundant specifications.
- Group sets of variables.
- Produce output from several SPSS procedures with a single command.
- Create complex input programs, procedure specifications, or whole sessions that can then be executed.

There are two stages to using a macro: the macro definition and the macro call. In the *macro definition* you specify any part of a valid SPSS command and give it a name. In the *macro call* you include the name of the macro as part of the command sequence. When SPSS encounters the macro name, it performs macro expansion.

Note: In the examples of macro definition throughout this reference, the macro name, body, and arguments are shown in lower case for readability. However, macro keywords, which are always preceded by an exclamation point, are shown in upper case.

Options

Macro Arguments. You can declare and use arguments in the macro definition and then assign specific values to these arguments in the macro call. You can define defaults for the arguments, and indicate whether an argument should be expanded when the macro is called.

Macro Directives. You can turn macro expansion on and off.

String Manipulation Functions. You can process one or more character strings and produce either a new character string or a character representation of a numeric result.

Conditional Processing. You can build IF constructs, as well as looping constructs.

Macro Variables. You can directly assign values to macro variables.

Basic Specification

The basic specification is both the macro definition and the macro call.

Macro Definition. All macros must start with the SPSS DEFINE command and end with the macro !ENDDEFINE command. These commands identify the beginning and end of a macro definition and are used to separate the macro definition from the rest of the command sequence.

- Immediately after DEFINE, specify the macro name. All macros must have a name. The name is used in the macro call to refer to the macro. Macro names follow the usual SPSS naming conventions In addition, macro names can begin with an exclamation point (!). Starting a name with an ! assures that the names do not conflict with the other text or variables in the session.
- Immediately after the macro name, specify, in parentheses, an optional argument definition. This specification indicates the arguments that will be read when the macro is called. If you do not want to include arguments, specify just the parentheses; *the parentheses are required, whether or not they enclose an argument.*
- Next specify the body of the macro. The macro body can include SPSS commands, parts of SPSS commands, or macro statements (macro directives, string manipulation statements, or conditional processing statements).
- At the end of the macro body, specify the !ENDDEFINE command.

The Macro Call. The second step in using the macro facility is to invoke the macro with a macro call.

- To call a macro, specify the macro name and any necessary arguments. If there are no arguments, only the macro name is required.

Operations
- When macros are used in a prompted session, the SPSS> prompt changes to DEFINE> between the DEFINE and !ENDDEFINE commands.
- When SPSS reads the macro definition, it translates into upper case all text not enclosed in quotation marks. This is done at the time the macro definition is read. It does not apply to macro arguments when the macro is called. Arguments are read in upper and lower case.
- The macro facility does not build and execute commands; rather, it expands strings in a process called *macro expansion*. A macro call initiates macro expansion. After the strings are expanded, the commands (or parts of commands) that contain the expanded strings are executed as part of the SPSS command sequence. Whether the macro is a partial command, a full command, or a series of commands, if there are elements on the macro call that are not used in the macro expansion, SPSS still reads those elements. If the elements specify legal SPSS syntax (relative to the final statement on the macro definition) they are used as part of the session. If the elements do not specify legal SPSS syntax (relative to the final statement on the macro definition) SPSS generates either a warning or an error message, depending on the nature of the syntax problem.

Limitations
- The BEGIN DATA/END DATA commands are not allowed within a macro.
- The DEFINE command is not allowed within a macro.

Example
```
TITLE     'A MACRO WITHOUT ARGUMENTS'.
SUBTITLE  'SPECIFY A GROUP OF VARIABLES'.

DEFINE sesvars ().
   age sex educ religion.
!ENDDEFINE.

FREQUENCIES VARIABLES=sesvars.
```
- The macro name is SESVARS. Because the parentheses are empty, SESVARS has no arguments. The macro body defines four variables: AGE, SEX, EDUC, and RELIGION.
- The macro call is specified on FREQUENCIES. When the call is executed, SESVARS is expanded into variables AGE, SEX, EDUC, and RELIGION.
- After the macro expansion, FREQUENCIES is executed.

Example
```
TITLE     'A MACRO WITHOUT ARGUMENTS'.
SUBTITLE  'REPEAT A SEQUENCE OF COMMANDS'.

1  DATA LIST FILE = MAC4D /GROUP 1    REACTIME 3-5 ACCURACY 7-9.
2  VALUE LABELS GROUP      1'normal'
3                          2'learning disabled'.
4  COMMENT macro definition.
5  DEFINE check ().
6  split file by group.
7  frequencies variables = reactime accuracy
8     /histogram.
9  descriptives reactime accuracy.
10 list.
11 split file off.
12 regression variables = group reactime accuracy
13    /dependent = accuracy
14    /enter
15    /scatterplot (reactime, accuracy).
16 !ENDDEFINE.
17
18 CHECK.
19
20 COMPUTE REACTIME = SQRT (REACTIME).
21 COMPUTE ACCURACY = SQRT (ACCURACY).
22
23 CHECK.
24
25 COMPUTE REACTIME = lg10 (REACTIME * REACTIME).
26 COMPUTE ACCURACY = lg10 (ACCURACY * ACCURACY).
27
28 CHECK.
```

- The name of the macro is CHECK. The empty parentheses indicate there are no arguments to the macro.
- The macro body (lines 6–15) contains the command sequence to be repeated, SPLIT FILE BY GROUP, FREQUENCIES, DESCRIPTIVES, SPLIT FILE OFF, and REGRESSION. !ENDDEFINE indicates the end of the macro definition.
- The macro is called three times, in lines 18, 23 and 28. Every time CHECK is encountered, it is replaced with the command sequence SPLIT FILE, FREQUENCIES, DESCRIPTIVES, LIST, and REGRESSION. The command sequence using the macro facility is identical to the command sequence in which the specified commands are explicitly stated three separate times.

Example
```
TITLE  'A MACRO WITH AN ARGUMENT'.

DEFINE myfreq (vars = !CHAREND(/)).
frequencies variables = !vars
  /format = notable
  /hbar = normal
  /statistics = default skewness kurtosis.
!ENDDEFINE.

MYFREQ VARS = AGE SEX EDUC RELIGION /.
```

- Four variables are the *argument* to the macro MYFREQ. When SPSS expands the MYFREQ macro, it substitutes the argument, AGE, SEX, EDUC, and RELIGION, for !vars, and executes the resulting commands.

Macros with Arguments

The macro facility allows *arguments* in the macro definition. The arguments can be assigned specific values in the macro call. There are two types of arguments: keyword and positional. *Keyword arguments* are assigned names in the macro definition; in the macro call, they are identified by name. *Positional arguments* are declared after keyword !POSITIONAL in the macro definition; in the macro call, they are identified by their relative position within the macro definition.

- There is no limit to the number of arguments that can be specified in a macro.
- All arguments must be separated with slashes.
- If both keyword and positional arguments are specified in the same definition, the positional arguments must be defined, used in the macro body, and invoked in the macro call before the keyword arguments.

Example
```
TITLE  'A KEYWORD ARGUMENT'.

DEFINE macname (arg1 = !TOKENS(1)).
frequencies variables = !arg1.
!ENDDEFINE.

MACNAME   ARG1 = V1.
```

- The macro definition defines MACNAME as the macro name and ARG1 as the argument. ARG1 is a keyword argument and can be assigned any value in the macro call.
- The macro call MACNAME causes the macro to be expanded. The argument is identified by its name, ARG1 and assigned the value V1. V1 is substituted for ARG1 wherever !ARG1 appears in the macro body. The macro body in this example is the FREQUENCIES command.

Example
```
TITLE  'A POSITIONAL ARGUMENT'.

DEFINE macname (!POSITIONAL !TOKENS(1)
                /!POSITIONAL !TOKENS(2)).
frequencies variables = !1 !2.
!ENDDEFINE.

MACNAME V1 V2 V3.
```

- The macro definition defines MACNAME as the macro name with two positional arguments. The first argument has 1 token and the second argument has 2 tokens. The tokens can be assigned any values in the macro call.

• The macro call MACNAME causes the macro to be expanded. The arguments are identified by their positions. V1 is substituted for !1 wherever !1 appears in the macro body. V2 and V3 are substituted for !2 wherever !2 appears in the macro body. The macro body in this example is the FREQUENCIES command.

Keyword Arguments

Keyword arguments are called with user-defined keywords that can be specified in any order. In the macro body, the argument name is preceded by an exclamation point. On the macro, the argument is specified without the exclamation point.

• Keyword argument definitions contain the argument name, an equals sign, and the !TOKENS, !ENCLOSE, !CHAREND, or !CMDEND keyword.
• Argument names are limited to seven characters and cannot match the character portion of a macro keyword. For example, DEFINE is not a valid argument name.
• The keyword !POSITIONAL cannot be used in keyword argument definitions.
• Keyword arguments do not have to be called in the order they were defined.

Example
```
DATA LIST FILE=MAC / V1 1-2 V2 4-5 V3 7-8.
COMMENT macro definition.
DEFINE macdef2 (arg1 = !TOKENS(1)
               /arg2 = !TOKENS(1)
               /arg3 = !TOKENS(1)).
frequencies  variables = !arg1 !arg2 !arg3.
!ENDDEFINE.
COMMENT macro call.
MACDEF2 ARG1=V1  ARG2=V2   ARG3=V3.
MACDEF2 ARG3=V3  ARG1=V1   ARG2=V2.
```

• Three arguments are defined: ARG1, ARG2, and ARG3. In the first macro call, ARG1 is assigned the value V1, ARG2 is assigned the value V2, and ARG3 is assigned the value V3.

• The second macro call yields the same results as the first one. With keyword arguments, you do not need to call the arguments in the order they were defined.

Positional Arguments

Positional arguments must be declared in the order they will be specified on the macro call. The first positional argument defined in a macro is referred to by !1 in the macro body, the second positional argument defined is referred to by !2, and so on. Similarly, the value of the first argument in the macro call is assigned to !1, the second argument is assigned to !2, and so on.

• Positional arguments can be collectively referred to in the macro body by specifying !*. The !* convention concatenates arguments, separating individual arguments with a blank.

Example
```
DATA LIST FILE=MAC / V1 1-2 V2 4-5 V3 7-8.
COMMENT macro definition.
DEFINE macdef (!POS !TOKENS(1).
              /!POS !TOKENS(1).
              /!POS !TOKENS(1)).
frequencies variables = !1 !2 !3.
!ENDDEFINE.
COMMENT macro call.
MACDEF  V1   V2   V3.
MACDEF  V3   V1   V2.
```

• Three positional arguments with one token each are defined. The first positional argument is referenced by !1 in the FREQUENCIES command. Similarly, the second and third positional arguments are referenced by !2 and !3.
• When the macro is expanded for the first call, the first positional argument (!1) is assigned the value V1, the second positional argument (!2) is assigned the value V2, and the third positional argument (!3) is assigned the value V3.
• When the macro is expanded for the second call, the first positional argument is assigned the value var3, the second positional argument is assigned the value var1, and the third positional argument is assigned the value var2.

Example   DEFINE macdef (!POS !TOKENS(3)).
                 frequencies variables = !1.
                 !ENDDEFINE.

                 MACDEF V1   V2   V3.

- The macro definition is a shorthand way of defining the macro shown in the previous example. It assigns the three tokens to one argument instead of three.

Example   DEFINE macdef (!POS !TOKENS(1)
                             /!POS !TOKENS(1)
                             /!POS !TOKENS(1)).
                 frequencies variables = !*.
                 !ENDDEFINE.

                 MACDEF V1   V2   V3.

- This is a third alternative for achieving the macro expansion shown in the previous two examples. It specifies three arguments but then joins them all together on one FREQUENCIES command using the symbol !*.

Assigning Tokens to Arguments

In addition to argument type, the argument declaration must include a keyword that indicates which tokens following the macro name are associated with each argument. A *token* is a character or a group of characters that has a predefined function in a specified context.

- Any SPSS keyword, variable name, or delimiter (a slash, a comma, etc.) is a valid token.
- The arguments for a given macro can use a combination of the token keywords.

!TOKENS (n)   *Assign the next* n *tokens to the argument.* n can be any positive integer. !TOKENS allows you to specify exactly how many tokens are desired. This mechanism allows for access to individual tokens or groups of tokens.

!CHAREND ('char')   *Assign all tokens up to the specified character to the argument.* The character must be a one-character string specified in apostrophes and enclosed in parentheses. !CHAREND allows you to specify the character that will end the argument assignment. This is useful when the number of assigned tokens is arbitrary or not known in advance.

!ENCLOSE ('char','char')   *Assign all tokens between the indicated characters to the argument.* The starting and ending characters can be any special one-character strings enclosed in apostrophes. The two strings must also be separated by a comma and the entire specification enclosed in parentheses. !ENCLOSE allows you to group multiple tokens within a specified pair of symbols. This is useful when the number of tokens to be assigned to an argument is indeterminate, or when the use of an ending character is not directly possible.

!CMDEND   *Assign to the argument all the remaining text on the macro call, up to the start of the next command.* !CMDEND is useful for changing the defaults on an existing SPSS command. Since !CMDEND reads up to the next command, only the last argument in the argument list can be specified with the !CMDEND keyword. If !CMDEND is not the final argument, the arguments following !CMDEND are read as text.

Example

```
TITLE  'KEYWORD !TOKENS'.

DEFINE macname (!POSITIONAL !TOKENS (3)).
      macro body
!ENDDEFINE.

MACNAME ABC DEFG HI.
```

- The three tokens following MACNAME (ABC, DEFG, and HI) are assigned to the positional argument !1 in the macro body.

Example

```
1  TITLE  'USING !TOKENS'.
2
3  COMMENT macro definition.
4  DEFINE earnrep (varrep = !TOKENS (1)).
5  sort cases by !varrep.
6  report variables = earnings
7    /break = !varrep
8    /summary = mean.
9  !ENDDEFINE.
10 COMMENT call the macro three times.
11 EARNREP VARREP= SALESMAN.
12 EARNREP VARREP = REGION.
13 EARNREP VARREP = MONTH.
```

- This macro runs a REPORT command three times, each time with a different break variable. Without the macro facility, this session involves a good deal of redundant code.

- In this example, the macro name is EARNREP.

- There is one keyword argument, VARREP, which takes one token.

- In the first macro call (line 11), the argument SALESMAN is substituted for !VARREP when the macro is expanded. Similarly, REGION and MONTH are substituted for !VARREP when the macro is expanded in the second and third calls (lines 12 and 13).

Example

```
TITLE  'KEYWORD !CHAREND'.

DEFINE macname (!POSITIONAL !CHAREND ('/')
                /!POSITIONAL !TOKENS(2)).
frequencies variables = !1.
correlations variables= !2.
!ENDDEFINE.

MACNAME A B C D / E F.
```

- When the macro is called, all tokens up to the slash (A, B, C, and D) are assigned to the positional argument !1. E and F are assigned to the positional argument !2.

Example

```
TITLE  'KEYWORD !CHAREND'.

DEFINE macname (!POSITIONAL !CHAREND ('/')).
frequencies variables = !1.
!ENDDEFINE.

MACNAME A B C D / E F.
```

- Though E and F are not part of the positional argument and not used in the macro expansion, SPSS still reads them as text and interprets them in relation to where the macro definition ends.

- In this example, macro definition ends after the expanded variable list. E and F are names of variables. Adding variables to a variable list is valid SPSS syntax. Thus, E and F are added to the variable list and FREQUENCIES is executed. Frequency tables are generated for A, B, C, D, E, and F. You must be aware that macro *expands* strings, it does not write and execute commands. If there are elements on the macro call that are not used in the expansion, SPSS still reads those elements and applies them to the session. See the next example for a similar situation.

Example   TITLE 'KEYWORD !ENCLOSE'.

```
DEFINE macname (!POSITIONAL !ENCLOSE('(',')')).
frequencies variables = !1
  /statistics = default skewness.
!ENDDEFINE.

MACNAME (A B C) D E.
```

- When the macro is called, the three tokens enclosed in parentheses, A, B, and C, are assigned to the positional argument !1 in the macro body. Note that the starting and ending character can differ on !ENCLOSE.

- As with the previous example, after macro expansion is complete, SPSS reads the remaining characters on the macro call as text. In this instance, the macro definition ends with keyword SKEWNESS on the STATISTICS subcommand. Adding variable names to the STATISTICS subcommand is invalid SPSS syntax. SPSS therefore generates a warning message, but is still able to execute the frequencies command. Frequency tables and the specified statistics are generated for variables A, B, and C. See Operations, above, for an explanation of how the macro facility operates.

Example   TITLE 'KEYWORD !CMDEND'.

```
DEFINE macname (!POSITIONAL !tokens(2)
                /!POSITIONAL !CMDEND).
frequencies variables = !1.
correlations variables= !2.
!ENDDEFINE.

MACNAME A B C D E.
```

- When the macro is called, the first two tokens following MACNAME (A and B) are assigned to the positional argument !1. C, D, and E are assigned to the positional argument !2. Compare this result with the next example, which declares the arguments in the reverse order.

Example   TITLE 'INCORRECT ORDER FOR !CMDEND'.

```
DEFINE macname  (!POSITIONAL !CMDEND
                /!POSITIONAL !tokens(2)).
frequencies variables = !1.
correlations variables= !2.
!ENDDEFINE.

MACNAME A B C D E.
```

- When the macro is called, all five tokens, A, B, C, D, and E, are assigned to the first positional argument. The variable list for CORRELATIONS is empty, causing SPSS to generate an error message. Compare this result with the previous example, which declares the arguments in the correct order.

Example   TITLE   'USING !CMDEND'.
                SUBTITLE 'CHANGING DEFAULTS ON A COMMAND'.

```
DEFINE myfreq (!POSITIONAL !CMDEND ).
frequencies !1
    /statistics=default skewness  /* modify default statistics.
!ENDDEFINE.
MYFREQ VAR = A B /HIST.
```

- The macro MYFREQ contains specific options from the FREQUENCIES command. When the macro is called, MYFREQ is expanded to perform a FREQUENCIES analysis on variables A and B. The analysis produces a histogram, all default statistics, plus the skewness statistic.

| **Example** | ```
TITLE     'KEYWORD ARGUMENTS'.
SUBTITLE  'USING A COMBINATION OF TOKEN KEYWORDS'.

DATA LIST FREE / A B C D E.
DEFINE macdef3 (arg1 = !TOKENS(1)
               /arg2 = !ENCLOSE ('(',')')
               /arg3 = !CHAREND('%')).
frequencies variables = !arg1  !arg2 !arg3.
!ENDDEFINE.
MACDEF3 ARG1 = A  ARG2=(B C)  ARG3=DE %.
``` |

- Because ARG1 is declared with the !TOKENS keyword, the value for ARG1 is simply specified as A. ARG2 is specified in parentheses, as indicated in the !ENCLOSE declaration. The value for ARG3 is followed by a percent sign, as indicated in the !CHAREND declaration.

Defining Defaults

The optional !DEFAULT keyword in the macro definition establishes default settings for arguments.

!DEFAULT *Default argument.* After !DEFAULT, specify the value you want to use as a default for that argument. A default can be specified for each argument.

| **Example** | ```
DEFINE macdef (arg1 = !DEFAULT (v1) !TOKENS(1)
              /arg2 = !TOKENS(1)
              /arg3 = !TOKENS(1)).
frequencies variables = !arg1 !arg2 !arg3.
!ENDDEFINE.

MACDEF ARG2=V2  ARG3=V3.
``` |

- V1 is defined as the default value for argument ARG1. Since ARG1 is not specified on the macro call, it is set to V1.
- If !DEFAULT (v1) were not specified, the value of ARG1 would be set to a null string.

Controlling Expansion

The optional !NOEXPAND keyword indicates that an argument should not be expanded when the macro is called.

!NOEXPAND *Do not expand the specified argument.* !NOEXPAND applies to one individual argument and is useful only with imbedded macros (that is, a macro that calls another macro).

Macro Directives

Two directives, !ONEXPAND and !OFFEXPAND, determine whether macro expansion is on or off. !ONEXPAND activates macro expansion and !OFFEXPAND stops macro expansion. Within a macro definition, all symbols between !OFFEXPAND and !ONEXPAND will not be expanded. Use these functions outside macro definition to prevent unwanted macro expansion.

!ONEXPAND *Turn macro expansion on.*

!OFFEXPAND *Turn macro expansion off.* !OFFEXPAND is effective only when SET MEXPAND is ON (the default).

String Manipulation Functions

String manipulation functions process one or more character strings and produce either a new character string or a character representation of a numeric result.

- Since the macro processor is a character handling facility, the concept of number does not exist; therefore, any result that is returned is treated as a character string.

- The arguments to string manipulation functions can be strings, variables, or even other macro calls.
- Within string manipulation functions, the macro facility expects strings either to be single tokens, such as ABC, or to be delimited by apostrophes or quotation marks, as in 'A B C'. See Table 1 for a set of expressions and their results.

Table 1 Expressions and results

Expression	Result
!UPCASE(abc)	ABC
!UPCASE('abc')	ABC
!UPCASE(a b c)	error
!UPCASE('a b c')	A B C
!UPCASE(a/b/c)	error
!UPCASE('a/b/c')	A/B/C
!UPCASE(!CONCAT(a,b,c))	ABC
!UPCASE(!CONCAT('a','b','c'))	ABC
!UPCASE(!CONCAT(a, b, c))	ABC
!UPCASE(!CONCAT('a ','b ','c '))	A B C
!UPCASE(!CONCAT('a,b,c'))	A,B,C
!QUOTE(abc)	ABC
!QUOTE('abc')	abc
!QUOTE('Bill''s')	Bill''s
!QUOTE("Bill's")	Bill''s
!QUOTE(Bill's)	error
!QUOTE(!UNQUOTE('Bill''s'))	Bill''s

!LENGTH (str)	*Return the length of the specified string.* The result is character representation of the string length. The argument string in the function call can also be a macro argument or another function call. If an argument is used in place of a string and it is set to null, this function will return 0. For example, !LENGTH(abcdef) returns 6. If the string had been specified with apostrophes around it, each apostrophe would add 1 to the length, so that !LENGTH ('abcdef') would be 8.
!CONCAT(str,str)	*Return a string that is the concatenation of the strings.* !CONCAT(abc,def) returns abcdef.
!SUBSTR (str,from,L)	*Return a substring of the specified string.* The substring starts at the position marked *from* and continues for the specified length. If length is not specified, substring begins at *from* and ends at the end of the input string. For example, !SUBSTR (abcdef, 3, 2) returns cd.
!INDEX (haystack,needle)	*Return the position of the first occurrence of the needle in the haystack.* If the needle is not found in the haystack, the function returns 0. !INDEX (abcdef,def) returns 4.
!HEAD (str)	*Return the first token within a string.* The input string is not changed. !HEAD ('a b c') returns a.
!TAIL (str)	*Return all tokens except the head token.* The input string is not changed. !TAIL('a b c') returns b c.

!QUOTE (str)	*Put apostrophes around the argument.* !QUOTE replicates any imbedded apostrophe. !QUOTE(abc) returns 'abc'. Assuming !1 equals Bill's, !QUOTE(!1) returns 'Bill''s'.
!UNQUOTE (str)	*Remove quotes and apostrophes from the enclosed string.* Assuming that !1 equals 'abc', !UNQUOTE(!1) is abc. Internal paired quotes are unpaired; if !1 equals 'Bill''s', then !UNQUOTE(!1) is Bill's. !UNQUOTE(!QUOTE(anything)) is anything.
!UPCASE	*Convert all lowercase characters in the argument to uppercase.* !UPCASE('abc def') returns ABC DEF.
!BLANKS (n)	*Generate a string containing the specified number of blanks.* The *n* specification must be a positive integer. !BLANKS(5) returns a string of 5 blank spaces. Unless the blanks are quoted, they cannot be processed, since macro compresses blanks.
!NULL	*Generate a string of length 0.* This can help determine whether an argument was ever assigned a value, as in !IF (!1 !EQ !NULL) !THEN . . . .
!EVAL	*Scan the argument for possible macro calls.* During macro definition, an argument to a function or an operand in an expression is not scanned for possible macro calls unless the !EVAL function is used. It returns a string that is the expansion of its argument. For example, if MAC1 is a macro, then !EVAL(MAC1) returns the expansion of MAC1. If MAC1 is not a macro, !EVAL(MAC1) returns MAC1.

SET Subcommands for Use with Macro

Four subcommands on the SET command were designed for use with the macro facility.

MPRINT   *Controls whether SPSS includes in your display file the command list after macro expansion.* The specification for MPRINT is YES or NO (alias ON or OFF). The default at the start of an SPSS session is NO. The MPRINT subcommand is independent of the PRINTBACK command.

MEXPAND   *Controls whether macro expansion will occur.* MEXPAND is on, by default, unless it is set off. Specifying SET MEXPAND OFF prevents macro expansion. Specifying SET MEXPAND ON reestablishes macro expansion. YES and NO can be used in place of ON and OFF.

MNEST   *Controls the normal maximum nesting level for macros.* The default number of levels that can be nested is 50. The maximum number of levels is dependent on storage capacity.

MITERATE   *Controls the maximum loop traversals permitted in macro expansions.* The default number of traversals is 1000.

Restoring SET Specifications

The PRESERVE and RESTORE commands bring more flexibility and control over SET command parameters. PRESERVE and RESTORE are available generally within SPSS but are especially useful in macros.

• The settings of all SET subcommands—those set explicitly and those set by default (except MEXPAND)—are saved with PRESERVE. PRESERVE has no further specifications.

• With RESTORE, all SET subcommands, those explicitly specified on SET and those set by default (except MEXPAND) are changed to what they were when the PRESERVE command was executed. RESTORE has no further specifications.

• PRESERVE...RESTORE sequences can be nested up to five levels.

PRESERVE   *Store the current SET specifications at this point in the SPSS session.*

RESTORE   *Restore the SET specifications to what they were when PRESERVE was encountered.*

Example

```
TITLE  'TWO NESTED LEVELS OF PRESERVE AND RESTORE'.

DEFINE macdef ().
preserve.
set format F5.3.
descriptives v1 v2.
+ preserve.
set format F3.0 blanks=999.
descriptives v3 v4.
+ restore.
descriptives v5 v6.
restore.
!ENDDEFINE.
```

• The first PRESERVE command saves all the current SET conditions. If none have been specified, the default settings are saved.

• Next, the format is set to F5.3 and descriptive statistics on V1 and V2 are obtained.

• The second PRESERVE command saves the F5.3 format setting and all other settings in effect.

• The second SET command changes the format to F3.0 and BLANKS (which defaulted to SYSMIS) are now set to 999. Descriptive statistics are then obtained for V3 and V4.

• The last RESTORE restores the settings in effect at the first PRESERVE.

Conditional Processing

The !IF construct specifies conditions for processing and reserves four keywords within the macro processor: !IF, !IFEND, !THEN, and !ELSE. !IF, !THEN, and !IFEND are all required. !ELSE is optional.

• If the result of the expression is true, the statements following the !THEN statement are executed. If the result of the expression is false, the statements following !ELSE are executed (if any were specified). Otherwise, the program continues.

• Valid operators for the expressions include !EQ, !NE, !GT, !LT, !GE, and !LE, or =, a=, >, <, >=, <=, a, &, and |. !OR, !NOT, and !AND are also allowed. Valid conditional processing and looping constructs are interpreted after parameter substitution and function execution.

• !IF statements can be nested whenever necessary. Parentheses are permitted to specify the order of evaluation of logical expresssions. The default precedence is the same as in transformations: !NOT has precedence over !AND, which has precedence over !OR.

Syntax

```
!IF (expression) !THEN statements
                 [!ELSE statements ]
!IFEND
```

Looping Constructs

Looping constructs accomplish repetitive tasks. Loops can be nested to whatever depth is required, but loops cannot be crossed. The macro facility has two looping constructs: the index loop (DO loop) and the list processing loop (DO IN loop).

Index Loop

• !var must be a variable name that begins with an exclamation point. It is used as an index in the loop.

• Start, finish, and step must be numbers or expressions that evaluate to numbers.

- The loop begins at the value specified for start and continues until it reaches the value specified for finish (unless a !BREAK statement is encountered). The step is optional and can be used to specify a subset of the iterations. If start is set to 1, finish to 10, and by to 3, the DO loop will be executed four times with the index variable assigned values 1, 4, 7, and 10.

- The statements can be any valid SPSS statements or macro commands. !DOEND specifies the end of the loop. !BREAK is an optional specification. It can be used in conjunction with conditional processing to cause the loop to be exited.

Syntax
```
!DO !var = start !TO finish [ !BY step ]
    statements
!BREAK
!DOEND
```

Example
```
DEFINE MACDEF (arg1 = !TOKENS(1)
              /arg2 = !TOKENS(1)).
!DO !i = !ARG1 !TO !ARG2.
frequencies variables = !CONCAT(var,!i).
!DOEND.
!ENDDEFINE.
MACDEF ARG1 = 1 ARG2 = 3.
```

- The variable I is initially assigned the value 1 (ARG1). ARG1 is incremented until it equals 3, at which point the DO loop ends.

- The loop concatenates VAR and I value 1, VAR and I value 2, and finally VAR and I value 3 on its three iterations. The result of this loop is that FREQUENCIES receives three variables, VAR1, VAR2, and VAR3.

List Processing Loop
- The !DO and !DOEND statements begin and end the loop, and !BREAK allows an exit from the loop.

- A list is specified for the !IN function and the variable !var will be set to each of the members in the list.

- The list can be any expression, although it is usually a string. Only one list can be specified in each list processing loop.

Syntax
```
!DO !var !IN (list)
    statements
!BREAK
!DOEND
```

Example
```
DEFINE macdef (!POS !CHAREND('/') ).
!DO !i !IN ( !1).
frequencies variables = !i.
!DOEND.
!ENDDEFINE.
MACDEF VAR1 VAR2 VAR3  /.
```

- The macro call assigns three variables, VAR1, VAR2, and VAR3, to the positional argument !1. Thus, the list processing loop completes three iterations.

- In the first iteration, I is set to value VAR1. In the second and third iterations, I is set to VAR2 and VAR3, respectively. Thus, FREQUENCIES receives VAR1, VAR2, and VAR3 as variables.

Example
```
DEFINE earnrep (!POS !CHAREND('/') ).
!DO !i !IN ( !1).
sort cases by !i.
report var = earnings
  /break = !i
  /summary = mean.
!DOEND.
!ENDDEFINE.
MACDEF SALESMAN REGION MONTH /.
```

- The positional argument !1 is assigned the three variables, salesman, region, and month. When the list processing loop is executed, the index argument I is set to each of the variables in succession. The macro creates three reports.

Direct Assignment of Macro Variables

The macro command !LET assigns values to macro variables.

- !var is a macro variable and the expression must either be a single term or be enclosed in parentheses.
- !var cannot be one of the reserved macro keywords, and it cannot be the name of one of the arguments within the macro definition. Thus, !LET cannot be used to change the value of an argument.
- !var can be a new variable or one previously assigned by a !DO command or another !LET command.

Syntax

```
!LET !var = expression
```

Example

```
!LET !A = 1.
!LET !B = !CONCAT(ABC,!SUBSTR(!1,3,1),DEF).
!LET !C = (!2 a= !NULL).
```

- The first !LET sets !A equal to 1.
- The second !LET sets !B equal to ABC followed by 1 character taken from the 3rd position of !1 followed by DEF.
- The last !LET evaluates as 0 (false) if !2 is a null string or as 1 (true) if !2 is not a null string.

MANOVA: Overview

This command is included in the SPSS Advanced Statistics option.

```
MANOVA dependent varlist [BY factor list (min,max)
        [factor list...] [WITH covariate list]]


[/WSFACTORS=name (levels) name...]


[/TRANSFORM [(varlist [/varlist])]=[ORTHONORM] [{CONTRAST}]]
        [{DEVIATIONS (refcat) }]                     {BASIS    }
         {DIFFERENCE           }
         {HELMERT               }
         {SIMPLE (refcat)       }
         {REPEATED              }
         {POLYNOMIAL [(metric)] }
         {SPECIAL (matrix)      }


[/WSDESIGN=effect effect...]


[/MEASURE=newname newname...]


[/RENAME={newname} {newname}...]
         {*      } {*      }
[/MISSING=[LISTWISE] [INCLUDE]]


[/{PRINT  }= [CELLINFO ([MEANS] [SSCP] [COV] [COR] [ALL])]]
  {NOPRINT}

    [HOMOGENEITY ([BARTLETT] [COCHRAN] [BOXM] [ALL])]

    [DESIGN ([ONEWAY] [OVERALL] [DECOMP] [BIAS] [SOLUTION]
            [REDUNDANCY] [COLLINEARITY] [ALL])]

    [ERROR ([SSCP] [COV] [COR] [STDDEV] [ALL])]

    [SIGNIF ([MULTIV] [EIGEN] [DIMENR] [UNIV] [HYPOTH]
            [AVERF] [AVONLY] [HF] [GG] [EFSIZE]
            [SINGLEDF] [BRIEF] [STEPDOWN] [ALL] [NONE])]

    [PARAMETERS ([ESTIM] [ORTHO] [COR] [NEGSUM] [ALL])]
                [EFSIZE] [OPTIMAL]]

    [TRANSFORM]

[/PLOT=[CELLPLOTS] [STEMLEAF] [ZCORR] [NORMAL] [BOXPLOTS]]
      [ALL]


[/PCOMPS [COR] [NCOMP(n)] [MINEIGEN(eigencut)]
        [COV] [ROTATE(rottype)] [ALL]]


[/DISCRIM [RAW] [STAN] [ESTIM] [COR] [ALL]
        [ROTATE(rottype)] [ALPHA({.25})]]
                                 { a }

[/OMEANS [VARIABLES(varlist)] [TABLES ({factor name    })]]
                                       {factor BY factor}
                                       {CONSTANT        }
[/PMEANS [VARIABLES(varlist)] [TABLES ({factor name    })]]
                                       {factor BY factor}
        [PLOT]                         {CONSTANT        }


[/RESIDUALS [CASEWISE] [PLOT]]
[/METHOD=[MODELTYPE ({MEANS       })]
                    {OBSERVATIONS}

    [ESTIMATION ({QR      } {NOLASTRES} {NOBALANCED} {CONSTANT  })]
                {CHOLESKY} {LASTRES  } {BALANCED  } {NOCONSTANT}


    [SSTYPE ({UNIQUE    })]]
            {SEQUENTIAL}
```

```
[/MATRIX=[IN({file})]  [OUT({file})]]
             { *   }        { *   }


[/ANALYSIS [({CONDITIONAL  })]=dependent varlist
             {UNCONDITIONAL}   [WITH covariate varlist]
                                [/dependent varlist...]]


[/PARTITION (factorname)[=({1,1...  })]]
                            {df,df...}


                             {DEVIATION [(refcat)]   }
                             {SIMPLE [(refcat)]       }
                             {DIFFERENCE              }
[/CONTRAST (factorname)={HELMERT                 }]
                             {REPEATED                }
                             {POLYNOMIAL[({1,2,3...})]}
                             {           {metric  }   }
                             {SPECIAL (matrix)        }


        {WITHIN            }     {W }
[/ERROR={RESIDUAL          } or {R }]
        {WITHIN + RESIDUAL}     {WR}
        {n                 }


[/POWER=[T({.05})]  [F({.05})]  [{APPROXIMATE}]]
          { a}       { a}        {EXACT      }


[/CINTERVAL=[{INDIVIDUAL}][({.95}) ]] [UNIVARIATE ({BONFER })]
             {JOINT     }   { a}                  {SCHEFFE}

             [MULTIVARIATE  ({ROY     })]]
                             {PILLAI  }
                             {BONFER  }
                             {HOTELLING}
                             {WILKS   }


          {[CONSTANT...]                                              }
          {[effect effect...]                                         }
          {[CONTIN (varlist)...]                                      }
          {[effects BY effects...]                                    }
[/DESIGN={[effects {WITHIN} effects...]                          }]
          {        {W    }                                           }
          {[effect + effect...]                                       }
          {[factor (level)... [WITHIN factor (partition)...]]          }
          {[MUPLUS...]                                                }
          {[MWITHIN...]                                               }
          {[{terms-to-be-tested} {AGAINST} {WITHIN  }    {W }]}
          {{term=n            } {VS     } {RESIDUAL} or {R }}
          {                                  {WR      }    {RW}}
          {                                  {n       }         }
```

Example 1: Analysis of Variance

```
MANOVA RESULT BY TREATMNT(1,4) GROUP(1,2).
```

Example 2: Analysis of Covariance

```
MANOVA RESULT BY TREATMNT(1,4) GROUP(1,2) WITH RAINFALL.
```

Example 3: Repeated-Measures Analysis

```
MANOVA SCORE1 TO SCORE4 BY CLASS(1,2)
  /WSFACTORS=MONTH(4).
```

Example 4: Parallelism Test with Crossed Factors

```
MANOVA YIELD BY PLOT(1,4) TYPEFERT(1,3) WITH FERT
  /ANALYSIS YIELD
  /METHOD SSTYPE(SEQUENTIAL)
  /DESIGN FERT, PLOT, TYPEFERT,
  FERT BY PLOT + FERT BY TYPEFERT
  + FERT BY PLOT BY TYPEFERT.
```

Overview   MANOVA (multivariate analysis of variance) is a generalized procedure for analysis of variance and covariance. You can use MANOVA to analyze a wide variety of univariate and multivariate designs, including analysis of repeated measures. MANOVA is not restricted to multivariate analysis of variance. Some univariate designs, such as those involving mixed models, partitioned effects, nested factors, or factor-by-covariate interactions, can be analyzed in SPSS only by this procedure.

To simplify the presentation, reference material on MANOVA is divided into three sections: *univariate* designs with one dependent variable; *multivariate* designs with several interrelated dependent variables; and *repeated-measures* designs in which the dependent variables represent the same types of measurements taken at more than one time.

If you are unfamiliar with the models, assumptions, and statistics used in MANOVA, consult the *SPSS Advanced Statistics User's Guide.*

The full syntax diagram for MANOVA is presented here. The MANOVA sections that follow include partial syntax diagrams showing the subcommands and specifications discussed in that section. Individually, those diagrams are incomplete. Subcommands listed for univariate designs are available for any analysis, and subcommands listed for multivariate designs can be used in any multivariate analysis, including repeated measures.

MANOVA was designed and programmed by Philip Burns of Northwestern University.

Annotated Example   For a complete example with output, see Examples following the Command Reference.

References   Bacon, L. 1980. Unpublished data.

Bancroft, T. A. 1968. *Topics in intermediate statistical methods.* Ames: Iowa State Univ. Press.

Bock, R. D. 1975. *Multivariate statistical methods in behavioral research.* New York: McGraw-Hill.

Burns, P. R. 1984. *SPSS-6000 MANOVA update manual.* Chicago: Vogelback Computing Center.

Cochran, W. G., and G. M. Cox. 1957. *Experimental design.* 2d ed. New York: John Wiley & Sons.

Cohen, J. 1977. *Statistical power analysis for the behavioral sciences.* New York: Academic Press.

Cooley, W. W., and P. R. Lohnes. 1971. *Multivariate data analysis.* New York: John Wiley & Sons.

Davies, O. L. 1954. *Design and analysis of industrial experiments.* New York: Hafner.

Elashoff, J. . 1981. Data for the panel session in software for repeated measures analysis of variance. *Proceedings of the Statistical Computing Section.* American Statistical Association.

Everitt, B. S. 1978. *Graphical techniques for multivariate data.* New York: North-Holland.

Finn, J. D. 1974. *A general model for multivariate analysis.* New York: Holt, Rinehart & Winston.

Fisher, R. A. 1936. The use of multiple measurements in taxonomic problems. *Annals of Eugenics.* 7:179-88.

Green, P. 1977. *Analyzing multivariate data.* New York: John Wiley & Sons.

Hays, W. L. 1973. *Statistics for the social sciences.* New York: Holt, Rinehart & Winston.

——. 1981. *Statistics for the social sciences.* 3d ed. New York: Holt, Rinehart & Winston.

Heck, D. L. Charts of some upper percentage points of the distribution of the largest characteristic root. *Annals of Mathematical Statistics* 31:625-642.

Hicks, C. R. 1973. *Fundamental concepts in the design of experiments.* 2d ed. New York: Holt, Rinehart & Winston.

Huberty, C. J. 1972. Multivariate indices of strength of association. *Multivariate Behavioral Research* 7:523-26.

Huynh, H., and G. K. Mandevill. 1979. Validity conditions in repeated measures designs.

Morrison, D. F. 1976. *Multivariate statistical methods*. 2d ed. New York: McGraw-Hill.

Mudholkar, G. S., Y. P. Chaubey, and Ching-Choung Lin. 1976. Some approximations for the noncentral-F distribution. *Technometrics* 18:351-58.

Muller, K. E. & B. L. Peterson. 1984. Practical methods for computing power in testing the multivariate general linear hypothesis. *Computational Statistics & Data Analysis* 2:143-58.

Norusis, M. J. 1985. *SPSS advanced statistics guide*. Chicago: SPSS Inc.

___. 1986. *SPSS/PC+ advanced statistics*. Chicago: SPSS Inc.

Norusis, M. J., and SPSS Inc. 1989. *SPSS advanced statistics user's guide*. Chicago: SPSS Inc.

Pillai, K. C. S. 1967. Upper percentage points of the largest root of a matrix in multivariate analysis. *Biometrika* 54:189-93.

Rao, C. R. 1973. *Linear statistical inference and its applications*. 2d ed. New York: John Wiley & Sons.

Roy, J., and R. E. Bargmann. 1958. Tests of multiple independence and the associated confidence bounds. *Annals of Mathematical Statistics* 29:491-503.

Searle, S. R. 1971. *Linear models*. New York: John Wiley & Sons.

Snedecor, G. W., and W. G. Cochran. 1967. *Statistical methods*. 6th ed. Ames: Iowa State Univ. Press.

Timm, N. H. 1975. *Multivariate analysis with applications in education and psychology*. Monterey, California: Brooks/Cole.

Tukey, J. W. 1977. *Exploratory data analysis*. Addison-Wesley.

Winer, B. J. 1971. *Statistical principles in experimental design*. 2d ed. New York: McGraw-Hill.

MANOVA: Univariate

This command is included in the SPSS Advanced Statistics option.

```
MANOVA dependent var [BY factor list (min,max) [factor list...]

                     [WITH covariate list]   ]

    [/MISSING=[LISTWISE] [INCLUDE] ]

                 {[CELLINFO ([MEANS**] [SSCP] [COV] [COR] [ALL])]        }
                 {                                                         }
                 {[HOMOGENEITY ([BARTLETT**] [COCHRAN**] [ALL])]          }    ]
                 {                                                         }
    [/{PRINT  }={[DESIGN ([ONEWAY] [OVERALL**] [DECOMP] [BIAS] [SOLUTION])]}
      {NOPRINT}  {        [REDUNDANCY] [COLLINEARITY]                      }
                 {                                                         }
                 {[PARAMETERS ([ESTIM**] [ORTHO] [COR] [NEGSUM] [ALL])]   }
                 {                                                         }
                 {[SIGNIF(SINGLEDF)]                                       }
                 {                                                         }
                 {[ERROR(STDDEV)]                                          }

    [/PLOT=[CELLPLOTS] [STEMLEAF] [NORMAL] [BOXPLOTS] [ALL] ]

    [/OMEANS[=[VARIABLES(varlist)] [TABLES ({factor name    })]]]]
                                           {factor BY factor}
                                           {CONSTANT        }

    [/PMEANS[=[VARIABLES(varlist)] [TABLES ({factor name    })]]]]
                                           {factor BY factor}
             [PLOT]                        {CONSTANT        }

    [/RESIDUALS=[CASEWISE**] [PLOT] ]

    [/METHOD=[MODELTYPE ({MEANS       })]
                        {OBSERVATIONS}

             [ESTIMATION ({QR      } {NOLASTRES} {NOBALANCED} {CONSTANT  })]
                         {CHOLESKY} {LASTRES  } {BALANCED  } {NOCONSTANT}

             [SSTYPE ({UNIQUE    })]]
                     {SEQUENTIAL}

    [/MATRIX=[IN({file})]  [OUT({file})]]
                {*   }         {*   }

    [/ANALYSIS=dependent var [WITH covariate list]]

    [/PARTITION (factorname)[=({1,1...  })]]]
                              {df,df...}

                                 {DEVIATION [(refcat)]           }
                                 {SIMPLE [(refcat)]              }
                                 {DIFFERENCE                     }
    [/CONTRAST (factorname)={HELMERT                        }]
                                 {REPEATED                       }
                                 {POLYNOMIAL[({1,2,3...})]       }
                                 {           {metric  }          }
                                 {SPECIAL (matrix)               }

           {WITHIN            }   {W }
    [/ERROR={RESIDUAL         } or {R }]
           {WITHIN + RESIDUAL}   {WR}
           {n                }

    [/POWER=[T({.05})] [F({.05})] [{APPROXIMATE}]]
               { a}      { a}      {EXACT      }

    [/CINTERVAL=[{INDIVIDUAL}][({.95}) ]] [UNIVARIATE ({BONFER })]
                {JOINT     }   { a}                   {SCHEFFE}

           {[CONSTANT...]          }
           {[effect effect...]     }
           {[POOL (varlist)...]    }
           {[effects BY effects...]}

    [/DESIGN={[effects {WITHIN} effects...]                        }]
             {         {W     }                                    }
             {[effect + effect...]                                 }
             {[factor (level)... [WITHIN factor (partition)...]]   }
             {[CONPLUS...]                                         }
             {[MWITHIN...]                                         }
             {[{term-to-be-tested} {AGAINST} {WITHIN  }   {W }]    }
             {{term=n            } {VS     } {RESIDUAL} or {R }     }
             {                              {WR      }    {RW}     }
             {                              {n       }             }
```

**Defaults if subcommands are entered without specifications.

Example:
```
MANOVA YIELD BY SEED(1,4) FERT(1,3) WITH RAIN
  /PRINT=CELLINFO(MEANS COV) PARAMETERS(ESTIM)
  /DESIGN.
```

Overview

MANOVA is the most powerful of the analysis-of-variance procedures in SPSS and can be used for both univariate and multivariate designs. Only MANOVA allows you to

- Specify nesting of effects.
- Specify individual error terms for effects in mixed model analyses.
- Estimate covariate-by-factor interactions to test the assumption of homogeneity of regression lines.
- Obtain parameter estimates for a variety of contrast types, including irregularly-spaced polynomial contrasts with multiple factors.
- Test user-specified special contrasts with multiple factors.
- Partition effects in models.
- Pool effects in models.

This section describes the use of MANOVA for univariate analyses. However, the subcommands described here can be used in any type of analysis with MANOVA. For additional subcommands used in those types of analysis, see MANOVA: Multivariate, and MANOVA: Repeated Measures. If you are unfamiliar with the models, assumptions, and statistics used in MANOVA, consult the *SPSS Advanced Statistics User's Guide.*

Options

Design Specification. You can specify which terms to include in the design. This allows you to estimate a model other than the full factorial model, incorporate factor-by-covariate interactions, indicate nesting of effects, and indicate specific error terms for each effect in mixed models.

Contrast Types. You can specify contrasts other than the default deviation contrasts.

Parameter Estimation. You can request parameter estimates for the model. You can also control the manner in which the model is estimated by requesting the observations model rather than the cell-means model, by specifying sequential decomposition of the sums of squares, and by choosing among alternative methods of parameter estimation.

Optional Output. You can choose from a wide variety of optional output. Output appropriate to univariate designs includes cell means, design or other matrices, parameter estimates, tests for homogeneity of variance across cells, tables of observed and/or predicted means, and various plots useful in checking assumptions. In addition, you can request observed power values based on fixed-effect assumptions, and you can request simultaneous confidence intervals for each parameter estimate and regression coefficient.

Matrix Materials. You can write matrices of intermediate results to a matrix system file, and you can read such matrices in performing further analyses.

Basic Specification

- The basic specification is a variable list identifying the dependent variable, the factors (if any), and the covariates (if any).
- By default, MANOVA uses a full factorial model, which includes all main effects and all possible interactions among factors. By default, estimation is performed using the cell-means model and UNIQUE (regression-type) sums of squares, adjusting each effect for all other effects in the model. By default, factors are tested using *deviation* contrasts to determine if their categories differ significantly from the mean.

Subcommand Order

- The variable list must be first.
- Remaining subcommands can be used in any order.
- If the last subcommand is not a DESIGN specification, MANOVA generates a full factorial model.

Syntax Rules
- Most subcommands include specifications, which can be separated by spaces or commas. Some of these specifications, in turn, have parenthetical subspecifications.
- For many analyses, the MANOVA variable list and the DESIGN subcommand are the only specifications needed. If a full factorial design is desired, DESIGN can be omitted.
- DESIGN triggers the estimation of a specific model. An analysis of one model is produced for each DESIGN subcommand.
- All other subcommands apply only to designs that follow them. If you do not enter a DESIGN subcommand or if you enter any subcommand after the last DESIGN subcommand, MANOVA will use a full factorial model for the last DESIGN.
- Unless replaced, MANOVA subcommands other than DESIGN remain in effect for all subsequent models.
- MISSING can be specified only once.
- The following keywords cannot be used as factor names: BY, CONSTANT, WITHIN, W, MUPLUS, AGAINST, VS, MWITHIN, or POOL.

Limitations
- Memory requirements depend primarily on the number of cells in the design. For the default saturated model, this equals the product of the number of levels or categories in each factor.
- MANOVA does not calculate covariate-by-covariate interaction terms. You must calculate these using the COMPUTE statement before invoking MANOVA.

Example
```
MANOVA YIELD BY SEED(1,4) FERT(1,3) WITH RAINFALL
  /PRINT=CELLINFO(MEANS) PARAMETERS(ESTIM)
  /DESIGN.
```
- YIELD is the dependent variable; SEED (with values 1, 2, 3, and 4) and FERT (with values 1, 2, and 3) are factors; RAINFALL is a covariate.
- The means of the dependent variable for each cell are requested with PRINT = CELLINFO(MEANS).
- The parameter estimates have been requested with PRINT = PARAMETERS(ESTIM).
- The default design, a full factorial model, will be estimated. This statement could have been omitted, or could have been specified in full as DESIGN = SEED, FERT, SEED BY FERT.

MANOVA Variable List

The variable list specifies all variables that will be used in any subsequent analyses.

- The dependent variable must be the first specification on MANOVA.
- By default, MANOVA treats a list of dependent variables as jointly dependent, implying a multivariate design. However, you can change the role of a variable or its inclusion status in the analysis with the ANALYSIS specification.
- The names of the factors follow the dependent variable. Use the keyword BY to separate the dependent variable from the factors.
- Factors must have adjacent integer values, and you must supply the minimum and maximum values in parentheses after the factor name(s).
- If several factors have the same value range, you can specify a list of factors followed by a single value range in parentheses.
- Certain one-cell designs, such as univariate and multivariate regression analysis, canonical correlation, and one-sample Hotelling's T^2, do not require a factor specification. To perform these analyses, omit keyword BY and the factor list.

- Enter the covariates, if any, following the factors and their ranges. Use keyword WITH to separate covariates from factors (if any) and the dependent variable.
- MANOVA will remove the linear effect of the covariates from your dependent variable before performing analysis of variance.

Example   `MANOVA DEPENDNT BY FACTOR1 (1,3) FACTOR2, FACTOR3 (1,2).`

- In this example three factors are specified.
- FACTOR1 has values 1, 2, and 3, while FACTOR2 and FACTOR3 have values 1 and 2.

DESIGN Subcommand

DESIGN specifies the effects included in a specific model. It must be the last subcommand entered for any model.

The cells in a design are defined by all of the possible combinations of levels of the factors in that design. The number of cells equals the product of the number of levels of all the factors. A design is *balanced* if each cell contains the same number of cases. MANOVA can analyze both balanced and unbalanced designs.

- Specify a list of terms to be included in the model, separated by spaces or commas.
- The default design, which can be specified with the DESIGN subcommand, is a saturated model containing all main effects and all orders of factor-by-factor interaction.
- If DESIGN is omitted, or if any other subcommand is entered after the last DESIGN subcommand, a default (saturated) design is estimated.
- To include a term for the main effect of a factor, enter the name of the factor on the DESIGN statement.
- To include a term for an interaction between factors, specify FACT1 BY FACT2, where FACT1 and FACT2 are the names of the factors involved in the interaction.
- Terms are entered into the model in the order in which you list them on DESIGN. If you have specified METHOD = SSTYPE(SEQUENTIAL) to partition the sums of squares in a hierarchical fashion, this order may affect the significance tests.
- You can specify other types of terms in the model, as described in the following sections.

Example
```
MANOVA Y BY A(1,2) B(1,2) C(1,3)
  /DESIGN
  /DESIGN A, B, C
  /DESIGN A, B, C, A BY B, A BY C.
```

- The first DESIGN produces the default full factorial design, with all main effects and interactions for factors A, B, and C.
- The second DESIGN produces an analysis with main effects only for A, B, and C.
- The third DESIGN produces an analysis with main effects and the interactions between A and the other two factors. The interaction between B and C is not in the design, nor is the interaction between all three factors.

Example
```
MANOVA Y BY A(1,3) WITH X
  /DESIGN.
```

- The linear effect of the covariate X is removed from the dependent variable Y before any other effects are estimated.
- The default full factorial design in this case is simply the factor A.

Nesting Effects (WITHIN Keyword)

The effects of a factor are nested within those of another factor if the levels of the nested factor are substantively different within each level of the second factor. In the example at the beginning of this section, the two factors were type of seed (SEED) and type of fertilizer (FERT). If different fertilizers were used for each type of seed, the effects of FERT would be nested within the effects of SEED.

- Indicate a nested effect with keyword WITHIN; for example, FERT WITHIN SEED. WITHIN can be abbreviated to W (FERT W SEED).
- An effect can be nested within an interaction term, for example, FERT WITHIN SEED BY PLOT. Here the levels of FERT are considered distinct for each combination of levels of SEED and PLOT.

Simple Effects (WITHIN Keyword)

- A factor can be nested within one specific level of another factor by indicating the level in parentheses. The term FERT WITHIN SEED(2) allows you to estimate simple effects or the effect of FERT within only the second level of SEED.
- Simple effects can be obtained for higher order interactions as well.

```
FERT WITHIN PLOT(1) WITHIN SEED(2)
```

will give the simple effect of FERT withn the second SEED level of the first PLOT level.

MWITHIN Keyword

A term of the form MWITHIN factor (level) tests whether the dependent variable is zero within the specified level of the factor.

- MWITHIN is followed by the name of a factor and, in parentheses, the number of one of its levels.
- The level is indicated by ordinal position, not value. If you have specified TIME(3,6) on the MANOVA variable list, the term MWITHIN TIME(1) refers to the first level of TIME, which is the level associated with the value 3.

Pooled Effects

Different effects can be pooled for the purpose of significance testing.

- To pool effects, connect them with a plus sign, for example, FERT + FERT BY SEED. A single test will be made for the combined effect of FERT and the FERT by SEED interaction.
- Keyword BY is evaluated before effects are pooled together. Syntactically, A + B BY C is evaluated as A + (B BY C). Parentheses are not allowed in this context. To get the equivalent of (A + B) BY C, specify A BY C + B BY C.

MUPLUS Keyword

If a term is preceded by keyword MUPLUS, the constant term (MU) in the model is combined with that term. The normal use of this specification is to obtain parameter estimates that represent weighted mean for the levels of some factor. For example, the term MUPLUS SEED represents the constant, or overall mean, plus the effect for each level of SEED. The significance of such effects is usually uninteresting, but the parameter estimates represent the weighted means for each level of SEED, adjusted for any covariates in the model.

- MUPLUS cannot appear more than once on a given DESIGN subcommand.
- MUPLUS (factor) is the only way to get standard errors for the predicted mean for each level of that factor. The predicted mean itself can be obtained with the PMEANS subcommand.
- Parameter estimates are not displayed by default; you must explicitly request them on the PRINT subcommand.
- You can obtain the unweighted mean by specifying the full factorial model, excluding those terms contained by an effect, and prefixing the effect whose mean is to be found by MUPLUS.
- You can use the OMEANS and PMEANS subcommands to display marginal and adjusted means. However, only by using the MUPLUS approach can you obtain the standard errors of the marginal means.

Partitioned Effects

To identify individual degrees of freedom or partitions of the degrees of freedom associated with an effect, enter a number in parentheses on DESIGN.

- If you specify PARTITION, the number refers to a partition.
- If you do not use PARTITION, the number refers to a single degree of freedom associated with the effect. For example, if SEED is a factor with four levels, you can treat its three degrees of freedom as independent effects by naming them SEED(1), SEED(2), and SEED(3) on the DESIGN subcommand.
- The number in parentheses always refers to an individual level for a factor if that

factor follows keyword WITHIN or MWITHIN, regardless of how or whether you have partitioned the degrees of freedom.

- Partitions can include more than one degree of freedom provided that you use the PARTITION subcommand. If the first partition of SEED includes two degrees of freedom, the term SEED(1) on a DESIGN subcommand tests both degrees of freedom.

- A factor has one less degree of freedom than it has levels or values.

Effects of Continuous Variables

Usually you name factors but not covariates on the DESIGN subcommand. The linear effects of covariates are removed from the dependent variable before the design is tested. However, the design can include variables measured at the interval level and originally named as covariates or as additional dependent variables.

- Continuous variables on a DESIGN subcommand must be named as dependents or covariates on the MANOVA variable list.

- Before you can name a continuous variable on a DESIGN subcommand, you must supply an ANALYSIS subcommand that does *not* name the variable. This excludes it from the analysis as a dependent variable or covariate and makes it eligible for inclusion on DESIGN.

- More than one continuous variable can be pooled into a single effect (provided that they are all excluded on an ANALYSIS subcommand) with keyword POOL(varlist). For a single continuous variable, POOL(VAR) is equivalent to VAR.

- The TO convention in the variable list for POOL refers to the order of continuous variables (dependent variables and covariates) on the original MANOVA variable list, which is not necessarily their order on the active system file. This is the only allowable use of keyword TO on a DESIGN subcommand.

- You can specify interaction terms between factors and continuous variables. If FAC is a factor and COV is a covariate that has been omitted from an ANALYSIS subcommand, FAC BY COV is a valid term on a DESIGN statement.

- You cannot specify an interaction between two continuous variables. Use the COMPUTE command to create a variable representing the interaction prior to MANOVA.

Example

This example tests whether the regression line of the dependent variable Y on the two variables X1 and X2 has the same slope across all the categories of the factors AGE and TREATMNT.

```
MANOVA Y BY AGE(1,5) TREATMNT(1,3) WITH X1, X2
   /ANALYSIS = Y
   /METHOD = SSTYPE(SEQUENTIAL)
   /DESIGN = POOL(X1,X2),
             AGE, TREATMNT, AGE BY TREATMNT,
             POOL(X1,X2) BY AGE + POOL(X1,X2) BY TREATMNT
               + POOL(X1,X2) BY AGE BY TREATMNT.
```

- ANALYSIS excludes X1 and X2 from the standard treatment of covariates, so that they can be used in the design.

- METHOD requests a sequential (or hierarchical) decomposition of the sums of squares.

- DESIGN includes five terms. POOL(X1,X2), the overall regression of the dependent variable on X1 and X2, is entered first, followed by the two factors and their interaction.

- The last term is the test for equal regressions. It consists of three factor-by-continuous-variable interactions pooled together. POOL(X1,X2) BY AGE is the interaction between AGE and the combined effect of the continuous variables X1 and X2. It is combined with similar interactions between TREATMNT and the continuous variables and between the AGE BY TREATMNT interaction and the continuous variables.

- If the last term is not statistically significant, there is no evidence that the regression of Y on X1 and X2 is different across any combination of the categories of AGE and TREATMNT.

Error Terms for Individual Effects

The "error" sum of squares against which terms in the design are tested is specified on the ERROR subcommand. For any particular term on a DESIGN subcommand, you can specify a different error term to be used in the analysis of variance. To do so, name the term followed by keyword VS (or AGAINST) and the error term keyword.

- To test a term against only the within-cells sum of squares, specify the term followed by VS WITHIN on the DESIGN subcommand. For example, GROUP VS WITHIN tests the effect of the factor GROUP against only the within-cells sum of squares. For most analyses this is the default error term.

- To test a term against only the residual sum of squares (the sum of squares for all terms not included in your DESIGN), specify the term followed by VS RESIDUAL.

- To test against the combined within-cells and residual sums of squares, specify the term followed by VS WITHIN+RESIDUAL.

- To test against any other sum of squares in the analysis of variance, include a term corresponding to the desired sum of squares in the design and assign it to a number between 1 and 10. You can then test against the number of the error term. It is often convenient to test against the term before you define it. This is perfectly acceptable, so long as you define the error term on the same DESIGN subcommand.

Example

```
MANOVA DEP BY A, B, C (1,3)
   /DESIGN=A VS 1,
          B WITHIN A = 1 VS 2,
          C WITHIN B WITHIN A = 2 VS WITHIN.
```

- In this example the factors A, B, and C are completely nested; levels of C occur within levels of B, which occur within levels of A. Each factor is tested against everything within it.

- A, the outermost factor, is tested against the B WITHIN A sum of squares, to see if it contributes anything beyond the effects of B within each of its levels. The B WITHIN A sum of squares is defined as error term number 1.

- B nested within A, in turn, is tested against error term number 2, which is defined as the C WITHIN B WITHIN A sum of squares.

- Finally, C nested within B nested within A is tested against the within-cells sum of squares.

User-defined error terms are specified by simply inserting = n after a term. Keywords used in building a design term, such as BY or WITHIN, are evaluated first. For example, error term number 2 in the above example consists of the entire term C WITHIN B WITHIN A. An error-term *number,* but not an error-term *definition,* can follow keyword VS.

CONSTANT Keyword

By default, the constant term is included as the first term in the model.

- If you have specified NOCONSTANT on the METHOD subcommand, a constant term will not be included in any design unless you request it with the CONSTANT keyword on DESIGN.

- You can specify an error term for the constant.

- A factor named CONSTANT will not be recognized on the DESIGN subcommand.

ERROR Subcommand

ERROR allows you to specify or change the error term used to test all effects for which you do not explicitly specify an error term on DESIGN. ERROR affects all terms in all subsequent designs, except terms for which you explicitly provide an error term.

WITHIN

Terms in the model are tested against the within-cell sum of squares. Can be abbreviated to W. This is the default unless there is no variance within cells or unless the observations model is used (see the MODELTYPE parameter under METHOD Subcommand).

RESIDUAL	*Terms in the model are tested against the residual sum of squares.* Can be abbreviated to R. This includes all terms not named on the DESIGN statement.
WITHIN+RESIDUAL	*Terms are tested against the pooled within-cells and residual sum of squares.* Can be abbreviated to WR or RW. This is the default for designs processed using the observations model.
ERROR NUMBER	*Terms are tested against a numbered error term.* The error term must be defined on each DESIGN subcommand (for a discussion of error terms, see DESIGN Subcommand).

- If you specify ERROR=WITHIN+RESIDUAL and one of the components does not exist, MANOVA uses the other component alone.
- If you specify your own error term by number, you must define a term with that number on each DESIGN subcommand. If a design does not have an error term with the specified number, MANOVA does not carry out significance tests. It will, however, display hypothesis sums of squares and, if requested, parameter estimates.

Example
```
MANOVA DEP BY A(1,2) B(1,4)
  /ERROR = 1
  /DESIGN = A, B, A BY B = 1 VS WITHIN
  /DESIGN = A, B.
```

- ERROR defines error term 1 as the default error term.
- In the first design, A by B is defined as error term 1 and is therefore used to test the A and B effects. The A by B effect itself is explicitly tested against the within-cells error.
- In the second design, no term is defined as error term 1, so no significance tests are carried out. Hypothesis sums of squares are displayed for A and B.

CONTRAST Subcommand

Use CONTRAST to specify the type of contrast desired among the levels of a factor. For a factor with k levels or values, the contrast type determines the meaning of its $(k-1)$ degrees of freedom.

- Specify the factor name in parentheses following the subcommand CONTRAST.
- You can specify only one factor per CONTRAST subcommand, but you can enter multiple CONTRAST subcommands.
- After closing the parentheses, enter an equals sign followed by one of the CONTRAST keywords.
- To obtain significance levels for individual degrees of freedom for the specified contrast, enter the factor name followed by a number in parentheses on the DESIGN subcommand. The number refers to a partition of the factor's degrees of freedom. If you do not use the PARTITION subcommand, each degree of freedom is a distinct partition.
- Parameter estimates for specified CONTRASTS are not displayed by default. To obtain them, use PRINT PARAM(EST).

Example
```
MANOVA DEP BY FAC(1,5)
  /CONTRAST(FAC)=DIFFERENCE
  /PRINT=PARAM(ESTIM)
  /DESIGN=FAC(1) FAC(2) FAC(3) FAC(4).
```

- The factor FAC has five categories and therefore four degrees of freedom.
- CONTRAST requests DIFFERENCE contrasts, which compare each level (except the first) with the mean of the previous levels.
- Each of the four degrees of freedom is tested individually on the DESIGN subcommand.
- Parameter estimates for each degree of freedom will be displayed.

Orthogonal contrasts are particularly useful. In a balanced design, contrasts are orthogonal if the sum of the coefficients in each contrast row is 0 and if, for any pair of contrast rows, the products of corresponding coefficients sum to 0. Difference, Helmert, and polynomial contrasts always meet these criteria in balanced designs.

The available contrast types are:

DEVIATION   *Deviations from the grand mean.* This is the default. Each level of the factor except one is compared to the grand mean. One category (by default the last) must be omitted so that the effects will be independent of one another. To omit a category other than the last, specify the number of the omitted category (which is not necessarily the same as its value) in parentheses after keyword DEVIATION. For example,

```
MANOVA A BY B(2,4)
  /CONTRAST(B)=DEVIATION(1).
```

omits the first category, in which B has the value 2. Deviation contrasts are not orthogonal.

DIFFERENCE   *Difference or reverse Helmert contrasts.* Each level of the factor except the first is compared to the mean of the previous levels. In a balanced design, difference contrasts are orthogonal.

HELMERT   *Helmert contrasts.* Each level of the factor except the last is compared to the mean of subsequent levels. In a balanced design, Helmert contrasts are orthogonal.

SIMPLE   *Each level of the factor except the last is compared to the last level.* To use a category other than the last as the omitted reference category, specify its number (which is not necessarily the same as its value) in parentheses following keyword SIMPLE. For example,

```
MANOVA A BY B(2,4)
  /CONTRAST(B)=SIMPLE(1).
```

compares the other levels to the first level of B, in which B has the value 2. Simple contrasts are not orthogonal.

POLYNOMIAL   *Polynomial contrasts.* The first degree of freedom contains the linear effect across the levels of the factor; the second contains the quadratic effect; and so on. In a balanced design, polynomial contrasts are orthogonal. By default, the levels are assumed to be equally spaced; you can specify unequal spacing by entering a metric consisting of one integer for each level of the factor in parentheses after keyword POLYNOMIAL. For example, CONTRAST(STIMULUS) = POLYNOMIAL(1,2,4) indicates that the three levels of STIMULUS are actually in the proportion 1:2:4. The default metric is always $(1,2,...,k)$, where k variables are involved. Only the relative differences between the terms of the metric matter $(1,2,4)$ is the same metric as $(2,3,5)$ or $(20,30,50)$, because in each instance the difference between the second and third numbers is twice the difference between the first and second.

REPEATED   *Comparison of adjacent levels.* Each level of the factor except the first is compared to the previous level. Repeated contrasts are not orthogonal.

SPECIAL   *A user-defined contrast.* After this keyword enter a square matrix in parentheses with as many rows and columns as there are levels in the factor. The first row represents the mean effect of the factor and is generally a vector of 1's. It represents a set of weights indicating how to collapse over the categories of this factor in estimating parameters for other factors. The other rows of the contrast matrix contain the special contrasts indicating the desired comparisons between levels of the factor. If the special contrasts are linear combinations of each other, MANOVA reports the linear dependency and stops processing.

PARTITION Subcommand

PARTITION subdivides the degrees of freedom associated with a factor. This permits you to test the significance of the effect of a specific contrast or group of contrasts of the factor instead of the overall effect of all contrasts of the factor.

- Specify the factor name in parentheses following the PARTITION subcommand.
- After closing the parentheses, you can enter an equals sign followed by a parenthetical list of integers indicating the degrees of freedom for each partition or subdivision.
- If you omit the list specifying degrees of freedom, MANOVA partitions the factor into single degrees of freedom.
- Each value in the partition list must be a positive integer and the sum of the values cannot exceed the degrees of freedom for the factor.
- The degrees of freedom available for a factor are one less than the number of levels of the factor.
- The meaning of each degree of freedom depends upon the contrast type for the factor. For example, with deviation contrasts (the default), each degree of freedom represents the deviation of the dependent variable in one level of the factor from its grand mean over all levels. With polynomial contrasts, the degrees of freedom represent the linear effect, the quadratic effect, and so on.
- If your list does not account for all the degrees of freedom, MANOVA adds one final partition containing the remaining degrees of freedom.
- You can use a repetition factor of the form $n*$ to specify a series of partitions with the same number of degrees of freedom. PARTITION(TREATMNT) = (3*2,1) builds three partitions with two degrees of freedom, each followed by a fourth partition with a single degree of freedom. If any degrees of freedom remain, they will be placed in a fifth partition.
- Include the effect of a specific partition of a factor in your design with a number in parentheses on the DESIGN subcommand (see example below).
- If you want the default single-degree-of-freedom partition, you can omit the PARTITION subcommand and simply enter the appropriate term on the DESIGN subcommand.

Example

```
MANOVA OUTCOME BY TREATMNT(1,12)
   /PARTITION(TREATMNT) = (3,2,6)
   /DESIGN TREATMNT(2).
```

- The factor TREATMNT has 12 categories, hence 11 degrees of freedom.
- PARTITION divides the effect of TREATMNT into three partitions, containing respectively 3, 2, and 6 degrees of freedom. The specification (3,2) would have produced the same division, since MANOVA would have supplied a final partition to contain the remaining six degrees of freedom.
- DESIGN specifies a model in which only the second partition of TREATMNT is tested. This partition contains the fourth and fifth degrees of freedom.
- Since the default contrast type is DEVIATION (see CONTRAST Subcommand), this second partition represents the deviation of the fourth and fifth levels of TREATMNT from the grand mean.

ANALYSIS Subcommand

ANALYSIS allows you to work with a subset of the continuous variables (dependent variable and covariates) you have named on the MANOVA variable list. In univariate analysis of variance, you can use ANALYSIS to allow factor-by-covariate interaction terms in your model (see DESIGN Subcommand). You can also use it to switch the roles of the dependent variable and a covariate.

- In general, ANALYSIS gives you complete control over which continuous variables are to be dependent variables, which are to be covariates, and which are to be neither.
- ANALYSIS specifications are like the MANOVA variables specification except that factors are not named. Enter the dependent variable and, if there are covariates, keyword WITH and the covariates.

- Only variables listed as dependent variables or covariates on the MANOVA variable specification can be entered on an ANALYSIS subcommand.
- In a univariate analysis of variance, the most important use of ANALYSIS is to omit covariates altogether from the analysis list, thereby making them available for inclusion on DESIGN (see following example and examples in DESIGN Subcommand).
- For more information on ANALYSIS, refer to MANOVA: Multivariate.

Example
```
MANOVA DEP BY FACTOR(1,3) WITH COV
  /ANALYSIS DEP
  /DESIGN FACTOR, COV, FACTOR BY COV.
```

- COV, a continuous variable, is included on the MANOVA variable list as a covariate.
- COV is not mentioned on ANALYSIS so it will not be included in the model as a dependent variable or covariate. It can, therefore, be explicitly included on the DESIGN subcommand.
- DESIGN includes the main effects of FACTOR and COV, and the FACTOR by COV interaction.

PRINT and NOPRINT Subcommands

Use PRINT and NOPRINT to control the display of optional output. (Additional output can be obtained on the PCOMPS, DISCRIM, OMEANS, PMEANS, PLOT, and RESIDUALS subcommands.) PRINT specifications appropriate for univariate MANOVA are described below. For information on PRINT specifications appropriate for other MANOVA models, see MANOVA: Multivariate, and MANOVA: Repeated Measures.

- Specifications on PRINT remain in effect for all subsequent designs.
- Some PRINT output, such as CELLINFO, applies to the entire MANOVA procedure and is displayed only once.
- You can turn off optional output that you request on PRINT by entering a NOPRINT subcommand with the specifications originally used on the PRINT subcommand.
- Some optional output greatly increases the processing time. Request only the output you want to see.

CELLINFO   *Basic information about each cell in the design.*

PARAMETERS   *Parameter estimates.*

HOMOGENEITY *Tests for homogeneity of variance.*

DESIGN   *Design information.*

ERROR   *Error standard deviations* (in univariate analysis).

CELLINFO Keyword

Use the CELLINFO keyword on PRINT to request any of the following:

- Enclose CELLINFO specifications in parentheses after the CELLINFO keyword.
- Since output from CELLINFO is displayed once before the analysis of any particular design, specify CELLINFO only once.

MEANS   *Cell means, standard deviations, and counts for the dependent variable and covariates.* Confidence intervals for the cell means are displayed if you have set width wide.

SSCP   *Within-cell sum-of-squares and cross-products matrices for the dependent variable and covariates.*

COV   *Within-cell variance-covariance matrices for the dependent variable and covariates.*

COR   *Within-cell correlation matrices, with standard deviations on the diagonal, for the dependent variable and covariates.*

ALL   *MEANS, SSCP, COV, COR.*

- When you specify SSCP, COV, or COR, the cells are numbered for identification, beginning with Cell 1.
- The levels vary most rapidly for the factor named last on the MANOVA variables specification.
- Empty cells are neither displayed nor numbered.
- A table showing the levels of each factor corresponding to each cell number is displayed at the beginning of MANOVA output.

Example
```
MANOVA DEP BY A(1,4) B(1,2) WITH COV
    /PRINT=CELLINFO(MEANS COV)
    /DESIGN.
```

- For each combination of levels of A and B, MANOVA displays separately the means and standard deviations of DEP and COV. Beginning with Cell 1, it will then display the variance-covariance matrix of DEP and COV within each non-empty cell.
- A table of cell numbers will be displayed to show the factor levels corresponding to each cell.
- Keyword COV, as a parameter of CELLINFO, is not confused with variable COV.

PARAMETERS Keyword   Keyword PARAMETERS displays information relating to the estimated size of the effects in the model.

- Specify any of the following in parentheses on PARAMETERS.
- There is no default specification for PARAMETERS.

ESTIM   *The estimated parameters themselves, along with their standard errors,* t *tests, and confidence intervals.* Only nonredundant parameters are displayed.

NEGSUM   *The negative of the sum of parameters for each effect.* For DEVIATION main effects this equals the parameter for the omitted (redundant) contrast. NEGSUM is displayed along with the parameter estimates.

ORTHO   *The orthogonal estimates of parameters used to produce the sums of squares.*

COR   *Covariances and correlations among the parameter estimates.*

EFSIZE   *The effect size values.*

OPTIMAL   *Optimal Scheffé contrast coefficients.*

ALL   *ESTIM, ORTHO, COR, NEGSUM, EFSIZE, and OPTIMAL.*

SIGNIF Keyword   The SIGNIF keyword requests special significance tests, most of which apply to multivariate designs (see MANOVA: Multivariate). The following specification is useful in univariate applications of MANOVA:

SINGLEDF   *Significance tests for the single degree of freedom making up each effect for ANOVA tables in univariate designs.* When orthogonal contrasts are being applied, these degrees of freedom correspond to the degrees of freedom in the contrast. This output is therefore particularly useful for orthogonal contrasts. You can always see the exact linear combinations being tested by requesting the solution matrix with PRINT = DESIGN(SOLUTION).

Example
```
MANOVA DEP BY FAC(1,5)
    /CONTRAST(FAC)=POLY
    /PRINT=SIGNIF(SINGLEDF) DESIGN(SOLUTION)
    /DESIGN.
```

- POLYNOMIAL contrasts are applied to FAC, testing the linear, quadratic, cubic, and quartic components of its five levels. POLYNOMIAL contrasts are orthogonal in balanced designs.

- The SINGLEDF specification on PRINT=SIGNIF requests significance tests for each of these four components.
- The SOLUTION matrix is also requested to verify the linear combinations tested with SIGNIF(SINGLEDF).

HOMOGENEITY Keyword

The HOMOGENEITY keyword requests tests for the homogeneity of variance of the dependent variable and covariates across the cells of the design. Enter one or more of the following specifications in parentheses:

BARTLETT   *Bartlett-Box* F *test.*

COCHRAN   *Cochran's* C.

DESIGN Keyword

You can request the following by entering one or more of the specifications in parentheses following keyword DESIGN. See Bock (1975) for discussion of these matrices.

ONEWAY   *The one-way basis matrix (not the contrast matrix) for each factor.*

OVERALL   *The overall reduced-model basis (design) matrix (not the contrast matrix).*

DECOMP   *The QR/CHOLESKY decomposition of the design.*

BIAS   *Contamination coefficients displaying the bias present in the design.*

SOLUTION   *Coefficients of the linear combinations of the cell means used in significance testing.* These are not the coefficients used in estimating parameters, unless the parameters are orthogonal.

REDUNDANCY   *Exact linear combinations of parameters which form a redundancy.* This keyword only displays a table if QR (the default) is the estimation method.

COLLINEARITY   *Collinearity diagnostics for design matrices.* These diagnostics include the singular values of decomposition, condition indices corresponding to each singular value, and the proportion of variance of the corresponding parameter accounted for by each principal component. For greatest accuracy, use the QR method of estimation whenever you request collinearity diagnostics.

ALL   *All DESIGN options.*

- The DECOMP and BIAS matrices can provide valuable information on the confounding of the effects and the estimability of the chosen contrasts. If two effects are confounded, the entry corresponding to them in the BIAS matrix will be nonzero; if they are orthogonal, the entry will be zero. This is particularly useful in designs with unpatterned empty cells.
- The SOLUTION matrix shows the exact linear combination of cell means used to test effects and can be useful in interpreting those tests.

ERROR Keyword

Generally, keyword ERROR on PRINT produces error matrices. In univariate analyses, the only valid specification for ERROR is STDDEV.

STDDEV   *The error standard deviation.* Normally this is the within-cells standard deviation of the dependent variable. If you specify multiple error terms on DESIGN (a mixed model), this specification will display the standard deviation of each.

OMEANS Subcommand

OMEANS (observed means) displays tables of the means of continuous variables for levels or combinations of levels of the factors.

- Use keywords VARIABLES and TABLES to indicate which observed means you want to display.
- With no specifications, the OMEANS subcommand is equivalent to PRINT = CELLINFO(MEANS).

- OMEANS displays confidence intervals for the cell means if you have SET WIDTH=132.

- Since output from OMEANS is displayed once before the analysis of any particular design, this subcommand should be specified only once.

VARIABLES *Continuous variables for which you want means.* Specify the variables in parentheses after keyword VARIABLES. You can request means for the dependent variable or any covariates. If you omit the VARIABLES keyword, observed means are displayed for the dependent variable and all covariates. If you enter keyword VARIABLES, you must also enter keyword TABLES, discussed below.

TABLES *Factors for which you want the observed means displayed.* List in parentheses the factors, or combinations of factors, separated with BY. Observed means are displayed for each level, or combination of levels, of the factors named (see example, below). Both weighted means (based on all cases) and unweighted means (where all cells are weighted equally regardless of the number of cases they contain) are displayed. If you enter keyword CONSTANT, the grand mean is displayed.

Example
```
MANOVA DEP BY A(1,3) B(1,2)
  /OMEANS=TABLES(A,B)
  /DESIGN.
```

- Since there is no VARIABLES specification on the OMEANS subcommand, observed means are displayed for all continuous variables. DEP is the only dependent variable here, and there are no covariates.

- The TABLES specification on the OMEANS subcommand requests tables of observed means for each of the three categories of A (collapsing over B) and for both categories of B (collapsing over A).

- MANOVA displays both weighted means, in which all cases count equally, and unweighted means, in which all cells count equally.

PMEANS Subcommand

PMEANS (predicted means) displays a table of the predicted cell means of the dependent variable, both adjusted for the effect of covariates in the cell and unadjusted for covariates. For comparison, it also displays the observed cell means.

- Output from PMEANS can be computationally expensive.

- PMEANS without any additional specifications displays a table showing for each cell the observed mean of the dependent variable, the predicted mean adjusted for the effect of covariates in that cell (ADJ. MEAN), the predicted mean unadjusted for covariates (EST. MEAN), and the raw and standardized residuals from the estimated means.

- Cells are numbered in output from PMEANS, so that the levels vary most rapidly on the factor named last in the MANOVA variables specification (as in output from PRINT=CELLINFO). A table showing the levels of each factor corresponding to each cell number is displayed at the beginning of the MANOVA output.

- Predicted means are suppressed if the last term is being calculated by subtraction because of METHOD = ESTIM(LASTRES).

- Predicted means are also suppressed for any design in which the MUPLUS keyword appears.

- Covariates are not predicted.

- If the WSFACTORS and WSDESIGN subcommands are used to do a repeated measures design, PMEANS displays the means of the orthonormalized variables. If the TRANSFORM subcommand is used for non-repeated measures designs, PMEANS uses the scale of the transformed variables.

- In designs with covariates and multiple error terms, use the ERROR subcommand to designate which error terms's regression coefficients are to be used in calculating the standardized residuals.

The following keywords are available to modify the output of the PMEANS subcommand:

VARIABLES *The dependent variables for which you want tables of predicted means.* Used in multivariate MANOVA. If you enter the VARIABLES keyword, you must also enter the TABLES keyword.

TABLES *Additional tables showing adjusted predicted means for specified factors or combinations of factors.* Enter the names of factors or combinations of factors in parentheses after this keyword. For each factor or combination, MANOVA displays the predicted means (adjusted for covariates) collapsed over all other factors.

PLOT *A plot of the predicted means for each cell.*

Example
```
MANOVA DEP BY A(1,4) B(1,3)
  /PMEANS TABLES(A, B, A BY B)
  /DESIGN = A, B.
```

- PMEANS displays the default table of observed and predicted means (adjusted for covariates, and unadjusted) for DEP and raw and standardized residuals in each of the twelve cells in the model.

- The TABLES specification on PMEANS displays tables of predicted means for A (collapsing over B), for B (collapsing over A), and all combinations of A and B.

- Since A and B are the only factors in the model, the means for A by B in the TABLES specification come from every cell in the model. They are identical to the adjusted predicted means in the default PMEANS table, which always includes all nonempty cells.

- Predicted means for A by B can be requested in the TABLES specification, even though the A by B effect is not in the design.

Example
```
MANOVA DEP BY A B C(1,3)
  /PMEANS
  /ERROR=1
  /DESIGN A, B WITHIN A = 1, C VS W.
```

- Two error terms are used in this design: the B within A sum of squares, which is defined as error term 1 (to test the A effect), and the usual within-cells sum of squares (to test B within A itself as well as the C effect).

- To use B within A as the error term for standardized residuals, the PMEANS subcommand requires an error specification on the ERROR subcommand. If the ERROR subcommand is omitted, MANOVA uses the within-cells error term.

- Since there is no TABLES keyword on the PMEANS subcommand, the default table of predicted means for each cell is produced.

PLOT Subcommand

MANOVA can display a variety of plots useful in checking the assumptions needed in the analysis. Plots are produced only once in the MANOVA procedure, regardless of how many DESIGN subcommands you enter. Use the following keywords on the PLOT subcommand to request plots:

CELLPLOTS *Cell statistics, including a plot of cell means vs. cell variances, a plot of cell means vs. cell standard deviations, and a histogram of cell means.* Plots are produced for each continuous variable (dependent or covariate) named on the MANOVA variable list. The first two plots aid in detecting heteroscedasticity (nonhomogeneous variances) and in determining an appropriate data transformation if one is needed. The third plot gives distributional information for the cell means.

BOXPLOTS *Boxplots.* Plots are displayed for each continuous variable (dependent or covariate) named on the MANOVA variable list. Boxplots provide a simple graphical means of comparing the cells in terms of mean location and spread. The data must be stored in memory for these plots; if there is not enough memory, boxplots are not produced and a warning message is issued.

NORMAL *Normal and detrended normal plots.* Plots are produced for each continuous variable (dependent or covariate) named on the MANOVA variable list. MANOVA ranks the scores and then plots the ranks against the expected normal deviate, or detrended expected normal deviate, for that rank. These plots aid in detecting non-normality and outlying observations. All data must be held in memory to compute ranks. If not enough memory is available, MANOVA displays a warning and skips the plots.

STEMLEAF *A stem-and-leaf display.* Plots are produced for each continuous variable (dependent or covariate) named on the MANOVA variable list. This display details the distribution of each continuous variable as a whole, not for each cell. The plots are not produced if there is insufficient memory.

• ZCORR, an additional plot available on the PLOT subcommand, is described in MANOVA: Multivariate.

• You can request other plots on the PMEANS and RESIDUALS subcommands.

RESIDUALS Subcommand

Use RESIDUALS to display and plot casewise values and residuals for your models.

• Use the ERROR subcommand to specify the error term to be used to standardize the residuals if one other than the default error term is produced.

• If a designated error term does not exist for a given design, no predicted values or residuals are calculated.

• If you specify RESIDUALS without any specifications, CASEWISE output is displayed.

The following keywords are available.

CASEWISE *A case-by-case listing of the observed, predicted, residual, and standardized residual values for each dependent variable.*

PLOT *A plot of observed values, predicted values, and case numbers vs. the standardized residuals, plus normal and detrended normal probability plots for the standardized residuals (five plots in all).*

METHOD Subcommand

Use METHOD to control computational aspects of your MANOVA analysis. You can specify any or all of three keywords:

SSTYPE *The method of partitioning sums of squares.*

MODELTYPE *The model for parameter estimation.*

ESTIMATION *How parameters are to be estimated.*

SSTYPE Keyword

MANOVA offers two different methods of partitioning the sums of squares. Specify either one in parentheses following keyword SSTYPE.

UNIQUE *Regression approach.* Each term is corrected for every other term in the model. With this approach, sums of squares for various components of the model do not add up to the total sum of squares unless the design is balanced. SSTYPE(UNIQUE) is the default.

SEQUENTIAL *Hierarchical decomposition of the sums of squares.* Each term is adjusted only for the terms that precede it in the DESIGN statement. This is an orthogonal decomposition, and the sums of squares in the model add up to the total sum of squares.

MODELTYPE Keyword

This keyword specifies the model for parameter estimation. You can specify either of the following in parentheses after the keyword MODELTYPE:

MEANS *The cell means model.* This model uses cell means for estimations. It requires significantly less processing time and is the default unless you specify continuous variables on the DESIGN subcommand.

OBSERVATIONS	*The observations model.* This model uses each individual observation for estimations. It is the more costly model and is used by default when you specify one or more continuous variables on the DESIGN subcommand.

ESTIMATION Keyword   Four different aspects of parameter estimation are controlled by keyword ESTIMATION. You can enter one choice from each of the following pairs of alternatives in parentheses after ESTIMATION. In each case, the default is listed first.

QR **CHOLESKY**	QR uses Householder transformations to effect a QR (orthogonal) decomposition of the design matrix. This method bypasses the normal equations and the inaccuracies that can result from creating the cross-products matrix, and it generally results in extremely accurate parameter estimates. The CHOLESKY method is computationally less expensive but sometimes less accurate.
NOBALANCED **BALANCED**	By default, MANOVA assumes that your design is not balanced. If you are analyzing a balanced, orthogonal design, specifying the BALANCED keyword can result in substantial savings in processing time. Use BALANCED only if 1) all cell sizes are equal; 2) you are using the cell-means model; and 3) the contrast type for each factor is orthogonal. If you specify balanced processing but your design does not conform to these requirements, MANOVA reverts to the more general unbalanced processing mode. If you have specified METHOD = ESTIMATION(BALANCED), you can revert to unbalanced estimation in a later design with METHOD = ESTIMATION(NOBALANCED).
NOLASTRES **LASTRES**	By default MANOVA explicitly calculates all effects in the design. You can sometimes save processing time by suppressing the calculation of the last effect in the model with the LASTRES keyword. Do this only if 1) you have specified SSTYPE (SEQUENTIAL) in a METHOD subcommand; 2) you do not want parameter estimates for the last effect in the model (you can get a significance test for this effect); and 3) the last effect in the model does not contain any continuous variables. With LASTRES, the sum of squares for the last effect in the DESIGN statement is calculated as the residual sum of squares, by subtraction from the total sum of squares. This is particularly economical when the last effect is a high-order interaction term, a common situation. If you have specified LASTRES, you can revert to normal direct estimation with METHOD = ESTIMATION(NOLASTRES).
CONSTANT **NOCONSTANT**	CONSTANT requests that all models include a constant (grand mean) term, even if none is explicitly specified on the DESIGN subcommand. NOCONSTANT excludes constant terms from models that do not include keyword CONSTANT on the DESIGN subcommand. If you have specified ESTIMATION (NOCONSTANT), you can revert to the default on later models by entering ESTIMATION(CONSTANT).

Example

```
MANOVA DEP BY A B C (1,4)
  /METHOD=SSTYPE(SEQUENTIAL) ESTIMATION(CHOLESKY BALANCED
LASTRES)
  /DESIGN
  /METHOD=ESTIMATION(NOLASTRES)
  /PRINT=PARAM(ESTIM)
  /DESIGN=A, B, C, A BY B, A BY C, B BY C.
```

- For the first design, a fully saturated model, the METHOD options are chosen to reduce processing costs as much as possible.
- If the conditions detailed above are not met, LASTRES will be turned off automatically by MANOVA.
- Parameter estimates are not requested for the first design, so it does not matter that estimates for the last effect are unavailable.
- The second METHOD turns off LASTRES so that in subsequent designs all terms are estimated directly. Other parameters from the first METHOD remain in effect.
- PRINT requests parameter estimates for subsequent designs.
- The second DESIGN omits the third-order interaction. If no METHOD subcommand had been entered to restore NOLASTRES, the final term (B by C) would have been estimated by subtraction and its parameter estimates would not have been displayed.

POWER Subcommand

POWER requests observed power values based on fixed-effect assumptions for all univariate and multivariate F tests and t-tests. Both approximate and exact power values can be computed, though exact multivariate power is displayed only when there is one hypothesis degree of freedom.

- Specify the appropriate keywords after the POWER subcommand, along with the type of test (either F or t), and the significance level at which the power is to be calculated.
- If POWER is specified by itself, with no keywords, MANOVA calculates the observed power of all F tests at 0.05 significance level.
- For univariate F tests and t-tests, MANOVA computes a measure of the effect size based on partial eta-squared which is an overestimate of the actual effect size. However, it is a consistent measure of effect size and is applicable to all F tests and t-tests. For a discussion of effect size measures, see Cohen (1977) or Hays (1981).

$$\text{partial eta-squared} = dfh*F/(dfh*F+dfe)$$

APPROXIMATE *Approximate power values.* This is the default. Approximate power values for univariate tests are derived from an Edgeworth-type normal approximation to the non-central beta distribution. Approximate values are normally accurate to three decimal places, and are much cheaper to compute than exact values.

EXACT *Exact power values.* Exact power values for univariate tests are computed from the non-central incomplete beta distribution. Exact multivariate power values will be displayed only if there is one hypothesis degree of freedom.

F(a) *Alpha level at which the power is to be calculated for* F *tests.* The default is 0.05. To change the default, specify a decimal number between 0 and 1 in parentheses after F. The numbers 0 and 1 themselves are not allowed.

T(a) *Alpha level at which the power is to be calculated for t-tests.* The default is 0.05. To change the default, specify a decimal number between 0 and 1 in parentheses after T. The numbers 0 and 1 themselves are not allowed.

CINTERVAL Subcommand

CINTERVAL requests simultaneous confidence intervals for each parameter estimate and regression coefficient. Both univariate (Scheffé and Bonferroni) and multivariate (Roy, Pillai, Bonferroni, Hotelling, and Wilks) confidence intervals are available. You can request either joint or individual univariate and multivariate confidence intervals, and also vary the confidence level. You can request only one type of confidence interval per design.

• Specify the CINTERVAL subcommand followed by the appropriate keywords.

• Without any specifications, CINTERVAL will automatically display individual-univariate confidence intervals at the 0.95 level.

• MANOVA provides either individual or joint confidence intervals at any desired confidence level. You can compute joint confidence intervals using either Scheffé or Bonferroni intervals. Scheffé intervals are based on all possible contrasts, while Bonferroni intervals are based on the number of contrasts actually made. For a large number of contrasts, Bonferroni intervals will be larger than Scheffé. Timm (1975) provides a good discussion of which intervals are best for certain situations. Both Scheffé and Bonferroni intervals are computed separately for each term in the design.

• To obtain joint intervals within each dependent variable, rather than across all dependent variables, request univariate Scheffé or Bonferroni intervals.

INDIVIDUAL(a)   *Individual confidence intervals, and the confidence level desired.* The default is 0.95. To change the default, specify any decimal number between 0 and 1 in parentheses after INDIVIDUAL. When individual intervals are requested, BONFER and SCHEFFE will have no effect.

JOINT(a)   *Joint confidence intervals, and the confidence level desired.* The default is 0.95. To change the default, specify any decimal number between 0 and 1 in parentheses after JOINT.

UNIVARIATE(type)   *Univariate confidence interval, and its type.* Specify either SCHEFFE for Scheffé intervals or BONFER for Bonferroni intervals in parentheses after UNIVARIATE. The default specification is SCHEFFE.

MISSING Subcommand

By default, cases with missing values for any of the variables on the MANOVA variable list are excluded from the analysis. The MISSING subcommand allows you to include cases with user-missing values.

• The same missing-value treatment is used to process all designs in a single execution of MANOVA.

• If you enter more than one MISSING subcommand, the last one entered will be in effect for the entire procedure, including designs specified before the MISSING subcommand.

• Pairwise deletion of missing data is not available in MANOVA.

• Keywords INCLUDE and EXCLUDE are mutually exclusive; however, each can be specified with LISTWISE.

LISTWISE   *Cases with missing values for any variable named on the MANOVA variable list are excluded from the analysis.* This is the default.

INCLUDE   *User-missing values are treated as valid.* For factors, you must include the missing-value codes within the range specified on the MANOVA variable list. It may be necessary to recode these values so that they will be adjacent to the other factor values. System-missing values cannot be included in the analysis.

EXCLUDE   *Exclude both user-missing and system-missing values.*

MATRIX Subcommand

MATRIX reads and writes SPSS matrix system files. It writes correlation type matrices that can be read by subsequent MANOVA procedures.

• Either IN or OUT is required to specify the matrix file in parentheses. When both IN and OUT are used on the same MANOVA procedure, they can be specified on separate MATRIX subcommands, or both on the same subcommand.

- The matrix materials include the N, mean, and standard deviation. Documents from the original file will not be included in the matrix file and will not be present if the matrix file becomes the active system file.
- MATRIX=IN cannot be used in place of GET or DATA LIST to begin a new SPSS command file. MATRIX is a subcommand on MANOVA, and MANOVA cannot run before an active system file is defined. To begin a new command file and immediately read a matrix, first GET the matrix file, then specify IN(*) on MATRIX.
- Records in the matrix system file read by MANOVA can be in any order, with the following exceptions: the order of split file groups cannot be violated; all CORR vectors must appear contiguously within each split file group.
- When MANOVA reads matrix materials, it ignores the record containing the total number of cases. In addition, it skips unrecognized records. (MANOVA does not issue a warning when it skips records.)

OUT *Write a matrix system file.* Specify either a file or an asterisk, and enclose the specification in parentheses. If you specify a file, the file is stored on disk and can be retrieved at any time. If you specify an asterisk (*), the matrix system file replaces the active system file but is not stored on disk unless you use SAVE or XSAVE. You can use an empty set of parentheses in place of the asterisk in parentheses.

IN *Read a matrix system file.* If the matrix system file *is not* the current active system file, specify a file in parentheses. If the matrix system file *is* the current active system file, specify an asterisk (*) in parentheses. You can use an empty set of parentheses in place of the asterisk in parentheses.

Format of the Matrix System File

The matrix system file includes two special variables created by SPSS: ROWTYPE_ and VARNAME_. Variable ROWTYPE_ is a short string variable having values N, MEAN, CORR (for Pearson correlation coefficient) and STDDEV.

- Variable VARNAME_ is a short string variable whose values are the names of the variables and covariates used to form the correlation matrix. When ROWTYPE_ is CORR, VARNAME_ gives the variable associated with that row of the correlation matrix.
- Between ROWTYPE_ and VARNAME_ is the factor variable(s) (if any) defined in the BY portion of the MANOVA variable list. (Factor variables receive the system-missing value on vectors that represent pooled values.)
- Remaining variables are the variables used to form the correlation matrix.

Split Files and Variable Order

- When split-file processing is in effect, the first variables in the matrix system file will be the split variables, followed by ROWTYPE_, the factor variable(s), VARNAME_, then the variables used to form the correlation matrix.
- A full set of matrix materials is written for each subgroup defined by the split variable(s).
- A split variable cannot have the same variable name as any other variable written to the matrix system file.
- If a split file is in effect when a matrix is written, the same split file must be in effect when that matrix is read into another procedure.

Additional Statistics

In addition to the CORR values, MANOVA always includes with the matrix materials:

- The total weighted number of cases used to compute each correlation coefficient.
- A vector of N's for each cell in the data.
- A vector of MEAN's for each cell in the data.
- A vector of pooled standard deviations STDDEV. This is the square root of the within-cells mean square error for each variable.

Example
```
GET FILE IRIS.
MANOVA SEPALLEN SEPALWID PETALLEN PETALWID BY TYPE(1,3)
    /MATRIX=OUT(*).
LIST.
```

- MANOVA reads raw data from file IRIS and writes one set of matrix materials to the file MANMTX.
- The active system file is still the file IRIS. Subsequent commands are executed on file IRIS.

Example
```
GET FILE IRIS.
MANOVA SEPALLEN SEPALWID PETALLEN PETALWID BY TYPE(1,3)
    /MATRIX=OUT(*).
LIST.
```

- MANOVA writes the same matrix as in the example above. However, the matrix system file replaces the active system file. The LIST command is executed on the matrix file, not on the file IRIS.

Example
```
GET FILE=PRSNNL.
FREQUENCIES VARIABLE=AGE.

MANOVA SEPALLEN SEPALWID PETALLEN PETALWID BY TYPE(1,3)
    /MATRIX=IN(MANMTX).
```

- This example assumes that you want to perform a frequencies analysis on file PRSNNL and then use MANOVA to read a different file. The file you want to read is an existing matrix system file.
- MATRIX=IN specifies a file because the current active system file is PRSNNL. MATRIX=IN must therefore specify the file from which the matrix materials will be read.
- MANMTX does not replace PRSNNL as the active system file.

Example
```
GET FILE=MANMTX.
MANOVA SEPALLEN SEPALWID PETALLEN PETALWID BY TYPE(1,3)
    /MATRIX=IN(*).
```

- This example assumes that you are starting a new session and want to read an existing matrix system file. GET retrieves the matrix system file MANMTX.
- MATRIX=IN specifies an asterisk because the current active system file is the matrix system file MANMTX. MATRIX=IN must therefore specify the active system file as the file from which the matrix materials will be read.
- If the GET command is omitted, SPSS issues an error message.
- If MATRIX=IN(MANMTX) is specified, SPSS issues an error message.

Annotated Example
For a complete example with output, see Examples following the Command Reference.

MANOVA: Multivariate

This command is included in the SPSS Advanced Statistics option.

```
MANOVA dependent varlist [BY factor list (min,max) [factor list...]

                                [WITH covariate varlist]]

[/TRANSFORM [(varlist [/varlist])]=[ORTHONORM] [{DEVIATIONS (refcat)  }]]
                                                {DIFFERENCE           }
                                  [{CONTRAST}]  {HELMERT              }
                                  [{BASIS   }]  {SIMPLE (refcat)      }
                                                {REPEATED             }
                                                {POLYNOMIAL [(metric)]}
                                                {SPECIAL (matrix)     }

[/RENAME={newname} {newname}...]
         {*      } {*      }

        {[HOMOGENEITY ([BOXM**])]                                       }
        {                                                               }
[/{PRINT  }={[ERROR ([SSCP] [COV**] [COR**] [STDDEV])]                  }]
  {NOPRINT}  {[SIGNIF [(([MULTIV] [EIGEN] [DIMENR] [UNIV] [HYPOTH]      }
        {            [STEPDOWN] [{AVERF }] [BRIEF] [SINGLEDF])]         }
        {                       {AVONLY}                               }
        {            [HF] [GG] [EFSIZE]                                 }
        {                                                               }
        {[TRANSFORM]                                                    }

[/PCOMPS=[COR**] [NCOMP(n)] [MINEIGEN(eigencut)] ]
         [COV] [ROTATE(rottype)]

[/PLOT=[ZCORR]]

[/DISCRIM[=[RAW**] [STAN**] [ESTIM**] [COR**] [ALL]]]
           [ROTATE(rottype)] [ALPHA(alpha)]

[/ANALYSIS [({CONDITIONAL  })]=dependent varlist ]
            {UNCONDITIONAL}

                              [WITH covariate varlist]

                              [/dependent varlist...]

[/POWER=[T({.05})] [F({.05})] [{APPROXIMATE}]]
          { a}      { a}       {EXACT      }

[/CINTERVAL=[MULTIVARIATE  ({ROY      })]]
                           {PILLAI   }
                           {BONFER   }
                           {HOTELLING}
                           {WILKS    }
```

**Defaults if subcommands are entered without specifications. In repeated measures, SIGNIF(AVERF) is printed by default instead of SIGNIF(UNIV).

Example:

```
MANOVA SCORE1 TO SCORE4 BY METHOD(1,3).
```

Overview

This section discusses the subcommands that are used in multivariate analysis of variance and covariance designs with several interrelated dependent variables. It does not contain information on all the subcommands you will need to specify the design. For subcommands not covered here, see MANOVA: Univariate.

Basic Specification

• Multivariate syntax for MANOVA is identical to univariate syntax, except that two or more dependent variables are named before keyword BY in the MANOVA variables specification.

Syntax Rules

- Several subcommands are available in multivariate analysis that do not apply to univariate analysis. Additional keywords for some subcommands are also available.
- If you enter one of the multivariate specifications in a univariate analysis, MANOVA will ignore it.

MANOVA Variable List

The basic syntax for the MANOVA variables specification in multivariate designs is

```
MANOVA dependent varlist BY factors(range) WITH covariates
```

- Multivariate MANOVA calculates statistical tests that are valid for analyses of dependent variables that are correlated with one another.
- If the dependent variables are uncorrelated, univariate significance tests (also available in MANOVA) have greater statistical power.

ANALYSIS Subcommand

ANALYSIS is discussed in MANOVA: Univariate as a means of obtaining factor-by-covariate interaction terms. In multivariate analyses it is considerably more useful.

- ANALYSIS specifies a subset of the continuous variables (dependent variables and covariates) listed on the MANOVA variable list and completely redefines which variables are dependent and which are covariates.
- All variables named on an ANALYSIS subcommand must have been named on the MANOVA variable list. It does not matter whether they were named as dependent variables or as covariates.
- Factors cannot be named on an ANALYSIS subcommand.
- After keyword ANALYSIS, specify the names of one or more dependent variables and, optionally, keyword WITH followed by one or more covariates.
- An ANALYSIS specification remains in effect for all designs until you enter another ANALYSIS subcommand.
- Continuous variables named on the MANOVA variable list but omitted from the ANALYSIS subcommand currently in effect can be specified on the DESIGN subcommmand.
- You can use an ANALYSIS subcommand to request analyses of several groups of variables, provided that the groups do not overlap. Separate the groups of variables with slashes and enclose the entire ANALYSIS specification in parentheses.

When you specify multiple analyses on a single subcommand, you can specify keyword CONDITIONAL in parentheses after the subcommand but before the equals sign.

- If you specify CONDITIONAL on an ANALYSIS subcommand, the variables in an analysis group will be used as covariates in subsequent analysis groups.
- The default is to process each list of variables separately, without regard to other lists. Keyword UNCONDITIONAL can be used to explicitly request this treatment.
- CONDITIONAL analysis is not carried over from one ANALYSIS subcommand to another.
- You can specify a final covariate list outside the parentheses. These covariates apply to every list within the parentheses, regardless of whether you specify CONDITIONAL or UNCONDITIONAL. The variables in this global covariate list must not be specified in the individual lists.

Example
```
MANOVA A B C BY FAC(1,4) WITH D, E
    /ANALYSIS = (A, B / C / D WITH E)
    /DESIGN.
```

- The first analysis uses A and B as dependent variables and uses no covariates.
- The second analysis uses C as a dependent variable and uses no covariates.
- The third analysis uses D as the dependent variable and uses E as a covariate.

Example   You can share one or more covariates among all the ANALYSIS groups by factoring them out from the parentheses, as in the following:
```
MANOVA A, B, C, D, E BY FAC(1,4) WITH F G
    /ANALYSIS = (A, B / C / D WITH E) WITH F G
    /DESIGN.
```

- The first analysis uses A and B, with F and G as covariates.
- The second analysis uses C, with F and G as covariates.
- The third analysis uses D, with E, F, and G as covariates.
- Factoring out F and G is the only way to use them as covariates in all three analyses, since no variable can be named more than once on an ANALYSIS subcommand.

Example
```
MANOVA A B C BY FAC(1,3)
    /ANALYSIS(CONDITIONAL) = (A WITH B / C)
    /DESIGN.
```

- In the first analysis, A is the dependent variable, B is a covariate, and C is not used.
- In the second analysis, C is the dependent variable, and both A and B are covariates.

TRANSFORM Subcommand

TRANSFORM performs linear transformations of some or all of the continuous variables (dependent variables and covariates).

- Transformations apply to all subsequent designs unless replaced by another TRANSFORM subcommand.
- TRANSFORM subcommands are not cumulative. Only the transformation specified most recently is in effect at any time. You can restore the original variables in later designs by requesting TRANSFORM=SPECIAL with an identity matrix.
- You should not use TRANSFORM when you use the WSFACTORS subcommand to request repeated measures analysis; a transformation is automatically performed in repeated measures analysis (see MANOVA: Repeated Measures).
- Transformations are in effect for the duration of the MANOVA procedure only. After the procedure is complete, the original variables remain in the active system file.
- The transformation matrix is not displayed by default. Use PRINT= TRANSFORM to see the matrix generated by the TRANSFORM subcommand.
- If you do not use the RENAME subcommand with TRANSFORM, the continuous variables listed in the MANOVA variables specification are renamed temporarily (for the duration of the procedure) as T1, T2, etc. Explicit use of RENAME is recommended.
- Subsequent references to transformed variables should use the new names. The only exception is when you supply a VARIABLES specification on the OMEANS subcommand after using TRANSFORM. In this case, specify the original names. OMEANS displays observed means of original variables.

Specifications on TRANSFORM include an optional list of variables to be transformed; optional keywords to describe how to generate a transformation matrix from the specified contrasts; and a required keyword specifying the transformation contrasts.

Variable Lists	• By default MANOVA applies the transformation you request to all continuous variables (dependent variables and covariates) together.
	• You can enter a variable list in parentheses following the TRANSFORM keyword; if you do, only the listed variables are transformed.
	• You can enter multiple variable lists, separated by slashes, within a single set of parentheses. Each list must have the same number of variables, and the lists must not overlap. The transformation is applied separately to the variables in each list.
	• In designs with covariates it is usually inappropriate to transform them together with the dependent variables. Transform only the dependent variables, or, in some designs, apply the same transformation to the dependent variables and the covariates.
Optional Keywords	• You can enter the optional keywords CONTRAST, BASIS, and ORTHONORM following the TRANSFORM subcommand, the variable list(s) (if any), and an equals sign. CONTRAST and BASIS are alternatives; ORTHONORM can be requested along with either CONTRAST or BASIS.
	• By default, the transformation matrix is generated directly from the contrast matrix of the given type (see CONTRAST Subcommand in MANOVA: Univariate). You can request this method explicitly with keyword CONTRAST.
	• If you enter keyword BASIS, the transformation matrix is generated from the one-way basis matrix corresponding to the specified contrast. This only makes a difference if the transformation contrasts are not orthogonal.
	• Keyword ORTHONORM requests that the transformation matrix be orthonormalized by rows before use. MANOVA eliminates redundant rows. Orthonormalization is not done by default.
	• ORTHONORM is independent of the CONTRAST/BASIS choice; you can enter it before or after either of those keywords.
Transformation Methods	To indicate the type of transformation contrasts you want, you must enter one of the keywords listed below on the TRANSFORM subcommand. There is no default.
	• The transformation keyword (and its specifications, if any) must follow all other specifications on the TRANSFORM subcommand.
	Note that these are identical to the keywords available for the CONTRAST subcommand (see MANOVA: Univariate). However, in univariate designs, they are applied to the different levels of a factor. Here they are applied to the continuous variables in the analysis. This reflects the fact that the different dependent variables in a multivariate MANOVA setup can often be thought of as corresponding to different levels of some factor.
DEVIATION	*Deviations from the mean of the variables being transformed.* The first transformed variable is the mean of all variables in the transformation. Other transformed variables represent deviations of individual variables from the mean. One of the original variables (by default the last) is omitted as redundant. To omit a variable other than the last, specify the number of the variable to be omitted in parentheses after the DEVIATION keyword. For example, TRANSFORM (A B C) = DEVIATION(1) omits A and creates variables representing the mean, the deviation of B from the mean, and the deviation of C from the mean. A deviation transformation is not orthogonal.
DIFFERENCE	*Difference or reverse Helmert transformation.* The first transformed variable is the mean of the original variables. Each of the original variables except the first is then transformed by subtracting the mean of those (original) variables that precede it. A difference transformation is orthogonal.
HELMERT	*Helmert transformation.* The first transformed variable is the mean of the original variables. Each of the original variables except the last is then transformed by subtracting the mean of

those (original) variables that follow it. A Helmert transformation is orthogonal.

SIMPLE   *Each original variable, except the last, is compared to the last of the original variables.* To use a variable other than the last as the omitted reference variable, specify its number in parentheses following keyword SIMPLE. For example, TRANSFORM(A B C) = SIMPLE(2) specifies the second variable, B, as the reference variable. The three transformed variables represent the mean of A, B, and C; the difference between A and B; and the difference between C and B. A simple transformation is not orthogonal.

POLYNOMIAL   *Orthogonal polynomial transformation.* The first transformed variable represents the mean of the original variables. Other transformed variables represent the linear, quadratic, and higher-degree components. By default, values of the original variables are assumed to represent equally spaced points. You can specify unequal spacing by entering a metric consisting of one integer for each variable in parentheses after keyword POLYNOMIAL. For example, TRANSFORM(RESP1 RESP2 RESP3) = POLYNO-MIAL(1,2,4) might indicate that three response variables correspond to levels of some stimulus that are in the proportion 1:2:4. The default metric is always $(1,2,...,k)$, where k variables are involved. Only the relative differences between the terms of the metric matter: (1,2,4) is the same metric as (2,3,5) or (20,30,50), because in each instance the difference between the second and third numbers is twice the difference between the first and second.

REPEATED   *Comparison of adjacent variables.* The first transformed variable is the mean of the original variables. Each additional transformed variable is the difference between one of the original variables and the original variable that followed it. Such transformed variables are often called *difference scores.* A repeated transformation is not orthogonal.

SPECIAL   *A user-defined transformation.* After keyword SPECIAL, enter a square matrix in parentheses with as many rows and columns as there are variables to transform. MANOVA multiplies this matrix by the vector of original variables to obtain the transformed variables (see examples below).

Example
```
MANOVA X1 TO X3 BY A(1,4)
   /TRANSFORM(X1 X2 X3) = SPECIAL( 1  1 -1,
                                    2  0  1,
                                    1  0 -1 )
   /DESIGN.
```

- The given matrix will be multiplied by the three continuous variables (considered as a column vector) to yield the transformed variables. The first transformed variable will therefore equal X1 + X2 − X3, the second will equal 2X1 + X3, and the third will equal X1 − X3.

- The variable list is optional in this example, since all three interval-level variables are transformed.

- You do not need to enter the matrix one row at a time, as shown here. TRANSFORM = SPECIAL(1 1 −1 2 0 1 1 0 −1) is fully equivalent.

- You can specify a repetition factor, followed by an asterisk, to indicate multiple consecutive elements of a SPECIAL transformation matrix. TRANSFORM = SPECIAL (2*1 −1 2 0 2*1 0 −1) is equivalent to the above matrix.

Example
```
MANOVA X1 TO X3, Y1 TO Y3 BY A(1,4)
   /TRANSFORM(X1 X2 X3/Y1 Y2 Y3) = SPECIAL( 1  1 -1
                                             2  0  1
                                             1  0 -1 )
   /DESIGN.
```

- Here the same transformation shown in the previous example is applied to X1, X2, X3 and also to Y1, Y2, Y3.

RENAME Subcommand

Use RENAME to assign new names to transformed variables. Renaming variables after a transformation is strongly recommended. If you transform but do not rename the variables, the names T1, T2, ..., Tn are used as names for the transformed variables.

- Follow RENAME with a list of new variable names.
- You must enter a new name for each dependent variable and covariate on the MANOVA variables specification.
- Enter the new names in the order the original variables appeared in the MANOVA variables specification.
- To retain the original name for one or more of the interval variables, you can either enter an asterisk or reenter the old name as the new name.
- References to dependent variables and covariates on subcommands following RENAME must use the new names. The original names will not be recognized within the MANOVA procedure. The only exception is the OMEANS subcommand, which displays observed means of the original (untransformed) variables. Use the original names on OMEANS.
- The new names exist only during the MANOVA procedure that created them. They do not remain in the active system file after the procedure is complete.

Example

```
MANOVA A, B, C, V4, V5 BY TREATMNT(1,3)
   /TRANSFORM(A, B, C) = REPEATED
   /RENAME = MEANABC, AMINUSB, BMINUSC, *, *
   /DESIGN.
```

- The REPEATED transformation produces three transformed variables, which are then assigned mnemonic names MEANABC, AMINUSB, and BMINUSC.
- V4 and V5 retain their original names.

Example

```
MANOVA WT1, WT2, WT3, WT4 BY TREATMNT(1,3) WITH COV
   /TRANSFORM (WT1 TO WT4) = POLYNOMIAL
   /RENAME = MEAN, LINEAR, QUAD, CUBIC, *
   /ANALYSIS = MEAN, LINEAR, QUAD WITH COV
   /DESIGN.
```

- After the polynomial transformation of the four WT variables, RENAME assigns appropriate names to the various trends.
- Even though only four variables were transformed, RENAME applies to all five continuous variables. An asterisk is required to retain the original name for COV.
- The ANALYSIS subcommand following RENAME refers to the interval variables by their new names.

PRINT and NOPRINT Subcommands

All of the PRINT specifications described in MANOVA: Univariate are available in multivariate analyses. The following additional output can also be requested. To suppress any optional output, specify the appropriate keyword on NOPRINT.

ERROR   *Error matrices.* Three types of matrices are available.

SIGNIF   *Significance tests.*

TRANSFORM   *Transformation matrix.* It is available if you have transformed the dependent variables with the TRANSFORM subcommand.

HOMOGENEITY *A test for multivariate homogeneity of variance, BOXM, is available.*

ERROR Keyword

In multivariate analysis, error terms consist of entire matrices, not single values. You can display any of the following error matrices on a PRINT subcommand by requesting them in parentheses following keyword ERROR. If you enter PRINT=ERROR without further specifications, COV and COR are displayed.

SSCP *Error sums-of-squares and cross-products matrix.*

COV   *Error variance-covariance matrix.*

COR   *Error correlation matrix with standard deviations on the diagonal.* This also displays the determinant of the matrix and Bartlett's test of sphericity, a test of whether the error correlation matrix is significantly different from an identity matrix.

SIGNIF Keyword   You can request any of the optional output listed below by entering the appropriate specification in parentheses after the SIGNIF keyword on the PRINT subcommand. Further specifications for SIGNIF are described in MANOVA: Repeated Measures.

- By default, MANOVA displays the display corresponding to MULTIV and UNIV for a multivariate analysis not involving repeated measures.
- If you enter any specification for SIGNIF on the PRINT subcommand, the default output is suppressed and MANOVA displays only what you have explicitly requested.

MULTIV   *Multivariate* F *tests for group differences.* This is displayed by default.

EIGEN   *Eigenvalues of the $S_h S_e^{-1}$ matrix.* This matrix is the product of the hypothesis sums-of-squares and cross-products (SSCP) matrix and the inverse of the error SSCP matrix.

DIMENR   *A dimension-reduction analysis.*

UNIV   *Univariate* F *tests.* This is displayed by default, except in repeated measures analysis. If the dependent variables are uncorrelated, univariate tests have greater statistical power.

HYPOTH   *The hypothesis SSCP matrix.*

STEPDOWN   *Roy-Bargmann stepdown* F *tests.*

BRIEF   *Abbreviated multivariate output.* This is similar to a univariate analysis of variance table but with Wilks' multivariate F approximation (lambda) replacing the univariate F. BRIEF overrides any of the SIGNIF specifications listed above.

The SINGLEDF keyword described in MANOVA: Univariate, does not apply to analysis of variance tables in multivariate designs, except for the averaged F tests described in MANOVA: Repeated Measures.

TRANSFORM Keyword   PRINT = TRANSFORM displays the transposed transformation matrix in use for each subsequent design. This matrix is helpful in interpreting a multivariate analysis in which you have transformed the interval-level variables with either TRANSFORM or WSFACTORS.

- The matrix displayed by this option is the *transpose* of the transformation matrix.
- Original variables correspond to the rows of the matrix, and transformed variables to the columns.
- A transformed variable is a linear combination of the original variables, using the coefficients displayed in the column corresponding to that transformed variable.

HOMOGENEITY Keyword   In addition to the BARTLETT and COCHRAN specifications described in MANOVA: Univariate, the following test for homogeneity is available for multivariate analyses:

BOXM   *Box's* M *statistic.*

PLOT Subcommand   In addition to the plots described in MANOVA: Univariate, the following is available for multivariate analyses:

ZCORR   *A half-normal plot of the within-cells correlations among the dependent variables.* MANOVA first transforms the correlations using Fisher's Z transformation. If errors for the dependent variables are uncorrelated, the plotted points should lie close to a straight line.

PCOMPS Subcommand

PCOMPS requests a principal components analysis of each error sum-of-squares and cross-product matrix in a multivariate analysis. You can display the principal components of the error correlation matrix, the error variance-covariance matrix, or both. These principal components are corrected for differences due to the factors and covariates in the MANOVA analysis. They tend to be more useful than principal components extracted from the raw correlation or covariance matrix when there are significant group differences between the levels of the factors or when a significant amount of error variance is accounted for by the covariates. You can specify any of the keywords listed below on PCOMPS.

- You must specify either COR or COV (or both). Otherwise, MANOVA will not produce any principal components.

COR   *Principal components analysis of the error correlation matrix.*

COV   *Principal components analysis of the error variance-covariance matrix.*

ROTATE   *Rotate the principal components solution.* By default, no rotation is performed. Specify a rotation type (either VARIMAX, EQUA-MAX, QUARTIMAX, or NOROTATE) in parentheses after keyword ROTATE. Specify PCOMPS = ROTATE (NOROTATE) to cancel a rotation specified for a previous design.

NCOMP(n)   *The number of principal components to rotate.* Specify a number in parentheses. The default is the number of dependent variables.

MINEIGEN(n) *The minimum eigenvalue for principal component extraction.* Specify a cutoff value in parentheses. Components with eigenvalues below the cutoff will not be retained in the solution. The default is 0: all components (or the number specified on NCOMP) are extracted.

ALL   *COR, COV, and ROTATE.*

- Both NCOMP and MINEIGEN limit the number of components that are rotated.

- If the number specified on NCOMP is less than two, two components are rotated (provided that at least two components have eigenvalues greater than any value specified on MINEIGEN).

- Principal components analysis is computationally expensive if the number of dependent variables is large.

DISCRIM Subcommand

DISCRIM produces a canonical discriminant analysis for each effect in a design. (For covariates, DISCRIM produces a canonical correlation analysis.) These analyses aid in the interpretation of multivariate effects. You can request the following statistics by entering the appropriate keywords after the subcommand DISCRIM:

RAW   *Raw discriminant function coefficients.*

STAN   *Standardized discriminant function coefficients.*

ESTIM   *Effect estimates in discriminant function space.*

COR   *Correlations between the dependent variables and the canonical variables defined by the discriminant functions.*

ROTATE *Rotation of the matrix of correlations between dependent and canonical variables.* Specify VARIMAX, EQUAMAX, or QUARTIMAX in parentheses after this keyword.

ALPHA   *Set the significance level required before a canonical variable is extracted.* The default is 0.25. To change the default, specify a decimal number between 0 and 1 in parentheses after ALPHA.

ALL   *RAW, STAN, ESTIM, COR and ROTATE.*

- The correlations between dependent variables and canonical discriminant functions are not rotated unless at least two discriminant functions are significant at the level defined by ALPHA.

• If you set ALPHA to 1.0, all discriminant functions are reported (and rotated, if you so request).

• If you set ALPHA to 0, no discriminant functions are reported.

POWER Subcommand

The following specifications are available for POWER in multivariate analysis. For applications of POWER in univariate analysis, see MANOVA: Univariate.

• Exact multivariate power is only available when there is one hypothesis degree of freedom. In this case, all the multivariate criteria have identical power, which can be found from the non-central F distribution. For all other cases, approximate power values for Pillai's Trace, Hotelling's Trace, and Wilks' Lambda are obtained using the methods given by Muller & Peterson (1984). These approximate power estimates have been found to be accurate to about two digits. For information on the multivariate generalizations of power and effect size, see Muller & Peterson (1984), Green (1977), and Huberty (1972).

APPROXIMATE   *Approximate power values.* This is the default. Approximate power values for multivariate tests are derived from procedures presented by Muller & Peterson (1984). Approximate values are normally accurate to three decimal places and are much cheaper to compute than exact values.

EXACT   *Exact power values.* Exact power values for multivariate tests are computed from the non-central F distribution. Exact multivariate power values will be displayed only if there is one hypothesis degree of freedom.

CINTERVAL Subcommand

In addition to the specifications described in MANOVA: Univariate, keyword MULTIVARIATE is available for multivariate analysis.

• The Wilks, Pillai and Hotelling intervals are computed by approximating the percentage points with percentage points of the F distribution. These approximate confidence intervals are thought to match exact intervals well across a wide range of alpha levels especially for large sample sizes (Burns, 1984). Use of these intervals, however, has not been widely investigated.

• For Roy intervals, an approximation given by Pillai (1967) is used. This approximation is accurate for upper percentage points (0.95 to 1), but it is not as good for lower percentage points. Thus, for Roy intervals the user is restricted to the range 0.95 to 1.

• Bonferroni intervals, based on the Student's t distribution, are also available.

• To obtain multivariate intervals separately for each parameter, choose individual multivariate intervals. For individual multivariate confidence intervals, the hypothesis degree of freedom is set to 1, in which case Hotelling, Pillai, Wilks and Roy intervals will be identical and equivalent to those computed from percentage points of Hotelling's T-squared distribution. Individual Bonferroni intervals will differ and, for a small number of dependent variables, will generally be shorter.

MULTIVARIATE(type)   *Multivariate confidence interval, and its type.* In parentheses after MULTIVARIATE, specify ROY for Roy's largest root, PILLAI for Pillai's trace, BONFER for Bonferroni intervals, HOTELLING for Hotelling's trace, or WILKS for Wilks' Lambda. The default specification is ROY.

Annotated Example

For a complete example with output, see Examples following the Command Reference.

MANOVA: Repeated Measures

This command is included in the SPSS Advanced Statistics option.

```
MANOVA dependent varlist [BY factor list (min,max)
        [factor list...] [WITH covariate list]]

    /WSFACTORS=name (levels) [name...]

    [/RENAME=newname newname...]

    [/MEASURE=newname newname...]

    [/WSDESIGN=effect effect...]

    [/{PRINT  }=[SIGNIF({AVERF }) (MULTIV) (HF)] ]
      {NOPRINT}          {AVONLY}  (GG)  (EFSIZE)
```

Overview

This section discusses the subcommands that are used in repeated measures designs on MANOVA, in which the dependent variables represent measurements of the same variable (or variables) at different times. This section does not contain information on all subcommands you will need to specify the design. For some subcommands not covered here, such as DESIGN and PRINT, see MANOVA: Univariate. For information on optional output and the multivariate significance tests available, see MANOVA: Multivariate.

- In a simple repeated-measures analysis, all dependent variables represent different measurements of the same variable for different values (or levels) of a *within-subjects factor*. Between-subjects factors and covariates can also be included in the model, just as in analyses not involving repeated measures.

- A within-subjects factor is simply a factor that distinguishes measurements made on the same subject or case, rather than distinguishing different subjects or cases.

- MANOVA permits more complex analyses, in which the dependent variables represent levels of two or more within-subjects factors.

- MANOVA also permits analyses in which the dependent variables represent measurements of several variables for the different levels of the within-subjects factors. These are known as *doubly multivariate* designs.

- A repeated-measures analysis includes a within-subjects design describing the model to be tested with the within-subjects factors, as well as the usual between-subjects design describing the effects to be tested with between-subjects factors. The default for both types of design is a full factorial model.

- MANOVA always performs an orthonormal transformation of the dependent variables in a repeated-measures analysis. By default, MANOVA renames them as T1, T2, and so forth.

Basic Specification

- The basic specification is a variable list followed by the WSFACTORS subcommand.

- By default, MANOVA performs special repeated-measures processing. Default output includes SIGNIF(AVERF) but not SIGNIF(UNIV). In addition, for any within-subjects effect involving more than one transformed variable, the Mauchly test of sphericity is displayed to test the assumption that the covariance matrix of the transformed variables is constant on the diagonal and 0 off the diagonal. The Greenhouse-Geiser epsilon and the Huynh-Feldt epsilon are also displayed for use in correcting the significance tests in the event that the assumption of sphericity is violated. These tests are discussed in the *SPSS Advanced Statistics User's Guide*.

Subcommand Order   • The list of dependent variables, factors, and covariates must be first.

• WSFACTORS must be the first subcommand used after the variable list.

Syntax Rules   • The WSFACTORS (within-subject factors), WSDESIGN (within-subjects design), and MEASURE subcommands are used only in repeated-measures analysis.

• WSFACTORS is required for any repeated-measures analysis. A default WSDESIGN consisting of all main effects and interactions among within-subjects factors is used if you do not enter a WSDESIGN subcommand. The MEASURE subcommand is used for doubly multivariate designs, in which the dependent variables represent repeated measurements of more than one variable.

• WSFACTORS automatically triggers special repeated-measures analysis and implies a full factorial within-subjects design (unless you specify the WSDESIGN subcommand).

• Do not use the TRANSFORM subcommand with the WSFACTORS subcommand, since WSFACTORS automatically causes an orthonormal transformation of the dependent variables.

• WSFACTORS determines how the dependent variables on the MANOVA variable list will be interpreted.

• The number of cells in the within-subjects design is the product of the number of levels for each within-subjects factor.

• The number of dependent variables on the MANOVA variable list must be a multiple of the number of cells in the within-subjects design. If there are six cells in the within-subjects design, each group of six dependent variables represents a single variable that has been measured in each of the six cells.

• Normally, the number of dependent variables should equal the number of cells in the within-subjects design multiplied by the number of variables named on the MEASURE subcommand (if one is used). If you have more groups of dependent variables than are accounted for by the MEASURE subcommand, MANOVA will choose variable names to label the output, which may therefore be difficult to interpret.

• If you use covariates in a repeated-measures analysis, there must be one covariate for each cell in the within-subjects design. Normally the covariates should be identical copies of one another (you can create these with the COMPUTE command).

Example
```
MANOVA Y1 TO Y4 BY GROUP(1,2)
  /WSFACTORS=YEAR(4)
  /CONTRAST(YEAR)=POLYNOMIAL
  /RENAME=CONST, LINEAR, QUAD, CUBIC
  /PRINT=TRANSFORM PARAM(ESTIM)
  /WSDESIGN=YEAR
  /DESIGN=GROUP.
```

• WSFACTORS immediately follows the MANOVA variable list and specifies a repeated-measures analysis in which the four dependent variables represent a single variable measured at four levels of the within-subjects factor. The within-subjects factor is called YEAR for the duration of the MANOVA procedure.

• CONTRAST requests polynomial contrasts for the levels of YEAR. Since the four variables Y1, Y2, Y3, Y4 in the active system file represent the four levels of YEAR, the effect is to perform an orthonormal polynomial transformation of these variables.

• RENAME assigns names to the dependent variables to reflect the transformation.

• PRINT requests that the transformation matrix and the parameter estimates be displayed.

- WSDESIGN specifies a within-subjects design that includes only the effect of the YEAR within-subjects factor. Since YEAR is the only within-subjects factor specified, this is the default design and WSDESIGN could have been omitted.
- DESIGN specifies a between-subjects design that includes only the effect of the GROUP between-subjects factor. This subcommand could have been omitted.

Example

```
COMPUTE SES1 = SES.
COMPUTE SES2 = SES.
COMPUTE SES3 = SES.
COMPUTE SES4 = SES.
MANOVA SCORE1 TO SCORE4 BY METHOD(1,2) WITH SES1 TO SES4
  /WSFACTORS=SEMESTER(4)
  /CONTRAST(SEMESTER)=DIFFERENCE
  /RENAME=MEAN,DIF2 TO DIF4,*,*,*,*.
```

- The four dependent variables represent a score measured four times (corresponding to the four levels of SEMESTER).
- The four COMPUTE commands create four copies of the constant covariate SES so that there will be one covariate for each of the within-subjects cells.
- RENAME supplies names for the difference transformation of the within-subjects factor SEMESTER. Since the MANOVA variable specification includes eight continuous variables, eight names are specified. The four asterisks indicate that the existing names are kept for the covariates.
- Covariates are transformed in the same way as the dependent variables. However, since these covariates are identical, the orthonormal transformation does not affect them.

WSFACTORS Subcommand

WSFACTORS names the within-subjects factors and specifies the number of levels for each.

- For repeated-measures designs, WSFACTORS must be the first subcommand after the MANOVA variable list.
- Only one WSFACTORS subcommand is permitted per execution of MANOVA.
- Names for the within-subjects factors are specified on the WSFACTORS subcommand. Factor names must not duplicate any of the dependent variables, factors, or covariates named on the MANOVA variable list.
- If there is more than one within-subjects factor, they must be named in the order corresponding to the order of the dependent variables on the MANOVA variable list. MANOVA varies the levels of the last-named WSFACTOR most rapidly when assigning dependent variables to within-subjects cells (see example below).
- Levels of the factors must be represented in the data by the dependent variables named on the MANOVA variable list.
- Enter a number in parentheses after each factor to indicate how many levels the factor has. If two or more adjacent factors have the same number of levels, you can enter the number of levels in parentheses after all of them.
- You enter only the number of levels for WSFACTORs, not a range of values.

Example

```
MANOVA X1Y1 X1Y2 X2Y1 X2Y2 X3Y1 X3Y2 BY TREATMNT(1,5) GROUP(1,2)
  /WSFACTORS=X(3) Y(2)
  /DESIGN.
```

- The MANOVA variable list names six dependent variables and two between-subjects factors, TREATMNT and GROUP.
- WSFACTORS identifies two within-subjects factors whose levels distinguish the six dependent variables. X has three levels and Y has two. Thus, there are 3 * 2 = 6 cells in the within-subjects design, corresponding to the six dependent variables.
- Variable X1Y1 corresponds to levels 1,1 of the two WSFACTORS; variable X1Y2 corresponds to levels 1,2; X2Y1 to levels 2,1; and so on up to X3Y2, which corresponds to levels 3,2. The first within-subjects factor named, X,

varies most slowly, and the last within-subjects factor named, Y, varies most rapidly in the list of dependent variables.

- Since there is no WSDESIGN subcommand, the within-subjects design will include all main effects and interactions: X, Y, and X by Y.
- Likewise, the between-subjects design includes all main effects and interactions: TREATMNT, GROUP, TREATMNT by GROUP.
- In addition, repeated-measures analysis always includes interactions between the within-subjects factors and the between-subjects factors. There are three such interactions for each of the three within-subjects effects.

WSDESIGN Subcommand

WSDESIGN specifies the design for within-subjects factors. Its specifications are like those of the DESIGN subcommand, but it uses the within-subjects factors rather than the between-subjects factors.

- The default WSDESIGN is a full factorial design, which includes all main effects and all interactions for within-subjects factors. The default is in effect whenever a design is processed without a preceding WSDESIGN or when the preceding WSDESIGN subcommand has no specifications.
- A WSDESIGN specification can include main effects for WS factors, factor-BY-factor interactions among WS factors, nested terms (term WITHIN term) involving WS factors and their interactions, terms using keyword MWITHIN, and combinations of the above pooled together with the plus sign.
- A WSDESIGN specification cannot include between-subjects factors or terms based on them, interval-level variables, keywords MUPLUS or CONSTANT, or error-term definitions or references.
- The WSDESIGN specification applies to all subsequent between-subjects designs until another WSDESIGN subcommand is encountered.

Example

```
MANOVA JANLO,JANHI,FEBLO,FEBHI,MARLO,MARHI BY SEX(1,2)
    /WSFACTORS MONTH(3) STIMULUS(2)
    /WSDESIGN MONTH, STIMULUS
    /DESIGN SEX
    /WSDESIGN.
```

- There are six dependent variables, corresponding to three months and two different levels of stimulus.
- The dependent variables are named on the MANOVA variable list in such an order that the level of stimulus varies more rapidly than the month. Thus, STIMULUS is named last on the WSFACTORS subcommand.
- The first WSDESIGN subcommand specifies only the main effects for within-subjects factors. There is no MONTH by STIMULUS interaction term.
- The second WSDESIGN subcommand has no specifications and therefore invokes the default within-subjects design, which includes the main effects and their interaction.
- Since the last subcommand is not DESIGN, MANOVA generates a full factorial design at the end. In this example there is only one between-subjects factor, SEX, so the last design is identical to the one specified by DESIGN =SEX. The last design, however, will include the MONTH BY STIMULUS within-subjects interaction. It will automatically include the interaction between SEX and MONTH BY STIMULUS; you do not need to specify (and indeed cannot specify) such interactions between elements of the within-subjects and the between-subjects designs.

PRINT Subcommand

The following additional specifications on PRINT are useful in repeated-measures analysis.

- SIGNIF (AVERF) and SIGNIF (AVONLY) are mutually exclusive.
- When you request repeated-measures analysis with the WSFACTORS subcommand, the default display includes SIGNIF(AVERF) but does not include the usual SIGNIF(UNIV).

- The averaged *F* tests are appropriate in repeated measures because the dependent variables that are averaged actually represent contrasts of the WSFACTOR variables. When the analysis is not doubly multivariate, as discussed below, you can specify PRINT = SIGNIF (AVERF UNIV) to obtain significance tests for each degree of freedom, just as in univariate MANOVA.

SIGNIF(AVERF)   *An averaged* F *test for use with repeated measures.* This is the default display in repeated measures analysis. The averaged *F* test in the multivariate setup for repeated measures is equivalent to the univariate (or split-plot or mixed-model) approach to repeated measures.

SIGNIF(AVONLY)   *Only the averaged* F *test* for repeated measures. AVONLY produces the same output as AVERF and suppresses all other PRINT=SIGNIF output.

SIGNIF(HF)   *The Huynh-Feldt corrected significance values for averaged univariate* F *tests.*

SIGNIF(GG)   *The Greenhouse-Geisser corrected significance values for averaged univariate* F *tests.*

SIGNIF(EFSIZE)   *The effect size for the univariate* F *and* t *tests.*

MEASURE Subcommand

In a doubly multivariate analysis, the dependent variables represent multiple variables measured under the different levels of the within-subjects factors. Use MEASURE to assign names to the variables that you have measured for the different levels of within-subjects factors.

- Specify a list of one or more variable names to be used in labeling the multivariate pooled results.

- The number of dependent variables on the DESIGN subcommand should equal the product of the number of cells in the within-subjects design and the number of names on MEASURE.

- If you do not enter a MEASURE subcommand and there are more dependent variables than cells in the within-subjects design, MANOVA assigns names (normally MEAS.1, MEAS.2, etc.) to the different measures.

- All of the dependent variables corresponding to each measure should be listed together and ordered so that the within-subjects factor named last on the WSFACTORS subcommand varies most rapidly.

Example
```
MANOVA TEMP1 TO TEMP6, WEIGHT1 TO WEIGHT6 BY GROUP(1,2)
   /WSFACTORS=DAY(3) AMPM(2)
   /MEASURE=TEMP WEIGHT
   /WSDESIGN=DAY, AMPM, DAY BY AMPM
   /PRINT=SIGNIF(HYPOTH AVERF)
   /DESIGN.
```

- There are twelve dependent variables: six temperatures and six weights, corresponding to morning and afternoon measurements on three days.

- WSFACTORS identifies the two factors (DAY and AMPM) that distinguish the temperature and weight measurements for each subject. These factors define six within-subjects cells.

- MEASURE indicates that the first group of six dependent variables correspond to TEMP and the second group of six dependent variables correspond to WEIGHT.

- These labels, TEMP and WEIGHT, are used on the output requested by PRINT = SIGNIF (HYPOTH AVERF).

- WSDESIGN requests a full factorial within-subjects model. Since this is the default, WSDESIGN could have been omitted.

CONTRAST Subcommand for WSFACTORS

The levels of a within-subjects factor are represented by different dependent variables. Therefore, contrasts between levels of such a factor compare these dependent variables. Specifying the type of contrast amounts to specifying a transformation to be performed on the dependent variables.

- An orthonormal transformation is automatically performed on the dependent variables in a repeated-measures analysis.

- To specify the type of orthonormal transformation, use the CONTRAST subcommand for the within-subjects factors.

- Regardless of the contrast type you specify, the transformation matrix is orthonormalized before use.

- If you do not specify a contrast type for within-subjects factors, the default contrast type (deviation) is orthonormalized and used to form a transformation matrix. Parameter estimates based on this transformation are not particularly suited to repeated-measures analysis. The contrast types that are intrinsically orthogonal are recommended for within-subjects factors if you wish to examine each degree-of-freedom test. These are difference, Helmert, and polynomial. AVERF tests are identical no matter what contrast was specified.

- To perform non-orthogonal contrasts, you must use the TRANSFORM subcommand instead of CONTRAST (the TRANSFORM subcommand is discussed in MANOVA: Multivariate).

- When you implicitly request a transformation of the dependent variables with CONTRAST for within-subjects factors, the same transformation is applied to any covariates in the analysis. There must be as many covariates as dependent variables. Normally the covariates are identical copies of one another, in which case the orthonormal transformation does not have any effect.

- You can display the transpose of the transformation matrix generated by your within-subjects contrast by using keyword TRANSFORM on the PRINT subcommand.

Example
```
MANOVA SCORE1 SCORE2 SCORE3 BY GROUP(1,4)
   /WSFACTORS=ROUND(3)
   /CONTRAST(ROUND)=DIFFERENCE
   /CONTRAST(GROUP)=DEVIATION
   /PRINT=TRANSFORM PARAM(ESTIM).
```

- This analysis has one between-subjects factor, GROUP, with levels 1, 2, 3, and 4, and one within-subjects factor, ROUND, with three levels that are represented by the three dependent variables.

- The first CONTRAST subcommand specifies difference contrasts for ROUND, the within-subjects factor.

- There is no WSDESIGN subcommand, so a default full factorial within-subjects design is assumed. This could also have been specified as WSDESIGN =ROUND, or simply WSDESIGN.

- The second CONTRAST subcommand specifies deviation contrasts for GROUP, the between-subjects factor. This subcommand could have been omitted since deviation contrasts are the default.

- PRINT requests the display of the transformation matrix generated by the within-subjects contrast and the parameter estimates for the model.

- There is no DESIGN subcommand, so a default full factorial between-subjects design is assumed. This could also have been specified as DESIGN = GROUP, or simply DESIGN.

Example
```
COMPUTE COV2=COV.
COMPUTE COV3=COV.
COMPUTE COV4=COV.
MANOVA DEP1 DEP2 DEP3 DEP4 BY FAC(1,2) WITH COV COV2 COV3 COV4
   /WSFACTOR=MONTH(4)
   /CONTRAST(MONTH)=POLYNOMIAL
   /RENAME=CONST,LINEAR,QUAD, CUBIC,*,*,*,*
   /PRINT=TRANSFORM PARAM(ESTIM)
   /DESIGN.
```

- Since there are four dependent variables, four copies of the covariate are needed. Three COMPUTE commands create the extra copies.
- The MANOVA variable list names four dependent variables representing the levels of the within-subjects factor MONTH, a single between-subjects factor with two categories, and the four copies of the covariate.
- CONTRAST specifies an orthonormalized polynomial transformation of the dependent variables. This transformation will also be applied, separately, to the covariates.
- PRINT requests the display of the transformation matrix and the parameter estimates.

RENAME Subcommand

Since any repeated-measures analysis involves a transformation of the dependent variables, it is always a good idea to rename the dependent variables. Choose appropriate names depending on the type of contrast specified for within-subjects factors. This is easier to do if you are using one of the orthogonal contrasts; the most reliable way to assign new names is to inspect the transformation matrix.

Example

```
MANOVA LOW1 LOW2 LOW3 HI1 HI2 HI3
  /WSFACTORS=LEVEL(2) TRIAL(3)
  /CONTRAST(TRIAL)=DIFFERENCE
  /RENAME=CONST LEVELDIF TRIAL2 TRIAL3 HITRIAL2 HITRIAL3
  /PRINT=TRANSFORM
  /DESIGN.
```

- This analysis has two within-subjects factors and no between-subjects factors.
- Difference contrasts are requested for TRIAL, which has three levels.
- Since all orthonormal contrasts are equivalent for a factor with two levels, there is no point in specifying a contrast type for LEVEL.
- New names are assigned to the transformed variables based on the transformation matrix, which was displayed in a previous trial. These names correspond to the meaning of the transformed variables: the mean or constant, the average difference between levels, the average effect of Trial 2 compared to 1, the average effect of Trial 3 compared to 1 and 2; and the two interactions between LEVEL and TRIAL.

Transformation matrix

	CONST	LEVELDIF	TRIAL2	TRIAL3	HITRIAL2	HITRIAL3
LOW1	0.408	0.408	−0.500	−0.289	−0.500	−0.289
LOW2	0.408	0.408	0.500	−0.289	0.500	−0.289
LOW3	0.408	0.408	0.000	0.577	0.000	0.577
HI1	0.408	−0.408	−0.500	−0.289	0.500	0.289
HI2	0.408	−0.408	0.500	−0.289	−0.500	0.289
HI3	0.408	−0.408	0.000	0.577	0.000	−0.577

PARTITION Subcommand

The PARTITION subcommand also applies to factors named on WSFACTORS. (See PARTITION Subcommand on page 371.)

Annotated Example

For a complete example with output, see Examples following the Command Reference.

MATCH FILES

```
MATCH FILES {FILE  }={file}
            {TABLE }  {*   }

[/RENAME=(old varlist=new varlist)...]

[/IN=varname]

[/{FILE  }=...]
  {TABLE }

[/BY varlist]

[/MAP]

[/KEEP={ALL**   }]  [/DROP=varlist]
       {varlist}

[/FIRST=varname]  [/LAST=varname]
```

**Default if the subcommand is omitted.

Example:

```
MATCH FILES FILE=PART1 /FILE=PART2 /FILE=*.
```

Overview

MATCH FILES combines two to fifty SPSS system files. MATCH FILES can make *parallel* or *nonparallel* matches between different files or perform *table lookups*. Parallel matches combine files sequentially by case. Nonparallel matches combine files according to the values of one or more key variables. In a table lookup, MATCH FILES reads (or looks up) information in one file that it then tranfers to another file (a case file).

MATCH FILES works with SPSS system files created with the SAVE or XSAVE commands. MATCH FILES can also be used to add variables from a raw data file to an existing SPSS system file. MATCH FILES combines files to produce a new active system file. Statistical procedures following MATCH FILES use this combined file unless you replace it by building another active system file. You must use the SAVE or XSAVE commands if you want to write the combined file to disk as an SPSS system file.

In general, MATCH FILES combines files containing the same cases but different variables. See ADD FILES for combining files containing the same variables but different cases. Also, see UPDATE for updating existing SPSS system files. MATCH FILES is often used with the AGGREGATE command to add variables with summary measures (sum, mean, etc.) to the data. One example is given below. For more examples, see AGGREGATE.

Options

Variable Selection. You can choose which variables from each input file are retained on the new active file. See DROP and KEEP subcommands.

Variable Names. You can rename variables on each input file before combining the files. This permits you to combine variables that are the same but whose names differ on different input files or to distinguish different variables whose names are the same on different input files. See RENAME Subcommand.

Variable Flag. You can create a variable that indicates whether a case came from the input file named on the preceding FILE subcommand. (See IN Subcommand.) You can also create a variable that flags the first or last case of a group of cases with the same value on the BY variable. (See FIRST and LAST subcommands.)

Variable Map. You can request a map showing all the variables on the new active file, their order, and the input file(s) from which they came. See MAP Subcommand.

Basic Specification

The basic specification is two or more FILE subcommands, each of which specifies a file to be matched. In addition, BY is required to match nonparallel files; both BY and TABLE are required to match table-lookup files.

- BY specifies the key variable(s) for the file match.
- TABLE specifies the table-lookup file.

All variables from all input files are included in the new active file unless DROP or KEEP is specified.

Subcommand Order

- RENAME and IN must immediately follow the FILE subcommand to which they apply.
- BY must follow the FILE subcommands and any associated RENAME and IN subcommands.
- FIRST and LAST must be used after all TABLE and FILE subcommands and their associated RENAME and IN subcommands.
- MAP, DROP, and KEEP must be placed after all FILE and RENAME subcommands.

Syntax Rules

- An asterisk can be specified on FILE or TABLE to denote the active system file.
- RENAME applies only to variables in the file named on the immediately preceding FILE or TABLE subcommand. RENAME can be repeated after each FILE or TABLE subcommand.
- IN can be used only for a nonparallel match or for a table lookup. (Thus, IN can be used only if BY is specified.)
- BY can be specified only once. However, multiple variables can be specified on BY. When BY is used, all files must be sorted in ascending order by the key variable(s) named on BY.
- MAP can be repeated as often as desired.

Operations

- MATCH FILES causes all input files named on FILE or TABLE to be read and builds a new active system file that replaces the active system file created earlier in the session.
- The new active system file contains complete dictionary information copied from the input files, including variable names, labels, print and write formats, and missing-value indicators. The new file also contains the documents from each of the input files unless DROP DOCUMENTS is used to drop the document text.
- MATCH FILES copies all variables in order from the first input file, then all variables in order from the second input file, and so on. Variables that are not common among all files receive the system-missing value for cases that do not contain those variables.
- The new active system file contains all cases that are in any of the input files named on FILE subcommands.
- Cases that are absent from one of the input files will be assigned missing values for variables that exist only in that file.
- If BY is not used, SPSS performs a parallel or sequential match, combining the first case from each file, then the second case from each file, and so on, without regard to any identifying values that may be present.
- BY specifies that cases should be combined according to a common value on one or more key variables present in all input files. All input files must be sorted in ascending order of the key variables.
- If the current active file is named as an input file, any N and SAMPLE commands that have been specified are applied to that file before the input files are matched.

Limitations
- Maximum 50 files total can be combined on one MATCH FILES command.
- Maximum 1 BY subcommand. However, BY can specify multiple variables.
- The TEMPORARY command cannot be in effect for any active system file that is used as an input file.
- MAP cannot be used for a match of more than 12 files.

Example

```
MATCH FILES FILE=PART1 /FILE=PART2 /FILE=*.
```

- MATCH FILES combines three files (the active system file and two SPSS system files) in a parallel (or sequential) match. Cases are combined according to their order in each file.
- The new active file contains as many cases as are in the largest of the three input files.
- If the same variable name is used in more than one input file, data are taken from the file listed first: PART1, then PART2, and then the active system file.

Example

```
GET FILE=HUBEMPL /KEEP=LOCATN DEPT HOURLY RAISE SEX.

AGGREGATE OUTFILE=AGGFILE /BREAK=LOCATN DEPT
   /AVGHOUR AVGRAISE=MEAN(HOURLY RAISE).

SORT CASES BY LOCATN DEPT.
MATCH FILES  TABLE=AGGFILE /FILE=* /BY LOCATN DEPT
   /KEEP AVGHOUR AVGRAISE LOCATN DEPT SEX HOURLY RAISE /MAP.

COMPUTE HOURDIF=HOURLY/AVGHOUR.
COMPUTE RAISEDIF=RAISE/AVGRAISE.
LIST.
```

- GET reads the HUBEMPL system file and keeps a subset of variables.
- AGGREGATE creates a file aggregated by LOCATN and DEPT with the two new variables AVGHOUR and AVGRAISE, indicating the means by location and department for HOURLY and RAISE. The aggregated file is saved as the system file AGGFILE.
- SORT CASES sorts the active system file in ascending order by the same variables used as AGGREGATE break variables: LOCATN and DEPT.
- MATCH FILES specifies a table-lookup match with the AGGFILE system file as the table file and the sorted active file as the case file.
- BY indicates that the keys for the match are the same variables used on SORT CASES: LOCATN and DEPT.
- KEEP specifies the subset and order of variables to be retained on the resulting file.
- MAP provides a listing of the variables in the resulting file and the two input files.
- The COMPUTE commands calculate the ratios of each employee's hourly wage and raise to the department averages for wage and raise. The results are stored in variables HOURDIF and RAISEDIF.
- LIST displays the resulting file.

FILE Subcommand

FILE identifies each input file (except a table file) to be combined. At least one FILE subcommand is required on MATCH FILES. A separate FILE subcommand must be used to specify each input file.

- An asterisk on FILE refers to the current active file.
- The order in which files are named on FILE determines the order of variables in the new active file. In addition, the order in which files are named determines which input file is used as the source for variables that can be taken from more than one input file (they are taken from the file named first).
- If the files have unequal numbers of observations, cases are generated from the longer file. System-missing values are assigned for variables unique to the shorter file.

Raw Data Files Variables from a raw data file can be added to an existing system file. To do so, DATA LIST must be used to define the data file as the active system file. MATCH FILES can then combine the active file with the system file.

Example
```
DATA LIST FILE=GASDATA/1 OZONE 10-12 CO 20-22 SULFUR 30-32.

VARIABLE LABELS OZONE 'LEVEL OF OZONE'
   CO 'LEVEL OF CARBON MONOXIDE'
   SULFUR 'LEVEL OF SULFUR DIOXIDE'.

MATCH FILES  FILE=PARTICLE /FILE=*.

SAVE  OUTFILE=POLLUTE.
```

- File PARTICLE is a previously saved SPSS system file, and GASDATA is the data obtained from a device measuring gases.
- The GASDATA file is defined on the DATA LIST command and variable labels are assigned on the VARIABLE LABELS command.
- FILE=* on MATCH FILES specifies the active system file, which is now the gas data. FILE=PARTICLE specifies the PARTICLE system file.
- SAVE saves the new active system file as an SPSS system file with the filename POLLUTE.

TABLE Subcommand

TABLE specifies a table-lookup file. A table file contributes variables, not cases, to the new active file. FILE must be used to specify the file(s) that supply the cases. A separate FILE subcommand must be used to specify each case file. A separate TABLE subcommand must be used to specify each lookup file.

- The BY subcommand is required when TABLE is used.
- All specified files must be sorted by the key variable(s), in ascending order. If necessary, use SORT CASES before MATCH FILES.
- A table file cannot contain duplicate cases (cases for which the key variable(s) named on BY have identical values).
- Variables from a table file are added to all of the cases from other file(s) which match on the key variable(s).
- An asterisk on TABLE refers to the current active file.
- Unmatched cases are assigned system-missing values (in numeric variables) or blanks (in string variables) for variables from the files that do not contain a match.
- An entry in a table file not matched with an entry in a case file is ignored.

Example
```
MATCH FILES FILE=* /TABLE=MASTER /BY EMP_ID.
```

- MATCH FILES combines variables from the system file MASTER to the current file, matching cases by the variable EMP_ID.
- No new cases are added to the current file as a result of the table lookup.
- Cases whose value for EMP_ID is not included in the table MASTER are assigned system-missing values for variables taken from the table.

RENAME Subcommand

RENAME renames variables on the input files *before* they are processed by MATCH FILES. RENAME must follow the FILE subcommand that contains the variables that will be renamed.

- RENAME applies only to the immediately preceding FILE or TABLE subcommand. To rename variables from more than one input file, enter a RENAME subcommand after each FILE or TABLE subcommand.
- Specifications for RENAME consist of a left parenthesis, a list of old variable names, an equals sign, a list of new variable names, and a right parenthesis. The two variable lists must have the same number of variables. If only one variable is renamed, the parentheses are optional.

- More than one such specification can be entered on a single RENAME subcommand, each enclosed in parentheses.
- RENAME takes effect immediately. Any KEEP and DROP subcommands entered prior to a RENAME must use the old names, while KEEP and DROP subcommands entered after a RENAME must use the new names.
- All specifications within a single set of parentheses take effect simultaneously: the specification RENAME (A,B = B,A) is legal and swaps the names of the two variables.
- You can use RENAME to correct a situation where a key variable has different names on different input files. Since BY must be entered last, it always uses the new name of a key variable.
- Variables cannot be renamed to scratch variables.
- Input system files are not changed on disk; only the copy of the file being combined is affected.

Example

```
MATCH FILES FILE=UPDATE /RENAME=(NEWPHONE, NEWID = PHONE, ID)
/FILE=MASTER /BY ID.
```

- MATCH FILES matches a master system file (MASTER) with an update system file (UPDATE).
- Two variables on UPDATE are renamed prior to the match. NEWPHONE is renamed PHONE to combine it with variable PHONE on the master file. NEWID is renamed ID so that it will have the same name as the identification variable in the master file and can be used on the BY subcommand.
- The BY subcommand ensures that only cases with the same ID are matched.

BY Subcommand

BY specifies one or more identification or key variables that determine which cases are to be combined. When BY is specified, cases from one file are matched only with cases from other files having the same values for the key variables. BY is required unless all input files are to be matched sequentially according to the order of cases.

- BY must follow the FILE subcommands and any associated RENAME and IN subcommands.
- BY must specify the names of one or more *key variables.* The key variables must be present in all input files. The key variables can be string variables (long strings are allowed).
- All input files must be sorted by the key variable(s), in ascending order. If necessary, use SORT CASES before MATCH FILES.
- Missing values on key variables are handled like any other values.
- Unmatched cases are assigned system-missing values (in numeric variables) or blanks (in string variables) for variables from the files that do not contain a match.

Duplicate Cases

Duplicate cases have the same values for the key variable(s) named on the BY subcommand. If no BY subcommand is specified, the question of duplicate cases does not arise.

- Duplicate cases are permitted in any input files except table files.
- When there is no table file, the first case in each file from a group of duplicates is matched with the first matching case (if any) from the other files; the second duplicate case is matched with a second matching duplicate, if any, and so on. In effect, a parallel (sequential) match is performed within groups of duplicate cases. Unmatched cases are assigned system-missing values (in numeric variables) or blanks (in string variables) for the variables from the absent files.
- When a table file is specified, data from the table file are added to all cases in the other files with matching values for the BY variable(s).
- SPSS displays a warning if it encounters duplicate keys in one or more of the files being matched.

Common Variables	Variables with the same name on two or more of the files being matched are called common variables. For the values of common variables, MATCH FILES automatically uses the values from the first file named in which a case exists for that variable.

- MATCH FILES uses the dictionary information from the first file containing value labels, missing values, or a variable label for the common variable. If the first file has no such information, MATCH FILES checks the second file, and so on, seeking dictionary information.

- The first file with a common variable must contain the appropriate dictionary information; otherwise, the value of the common variable can come from one file while the dictionary information can come from another.

DROP and KEEP Subcommands

DROP and KEEP are used to include only a subset of variables on the new active system file. DROP specifies a set of variables to exclude, and KEEP specifies a set of variables to retain. These subcommands apply only to the resulting file and must follow all FILE and RENAME subcommands.

- DROP and KEEP must specify one or more variables. If RENAME is used to rename variables, specify the new names on DROP and KEEP.

- Keyword ALL can be specified on KEEP. ALL must be the last specification on KEEP, and it refers to all variables not previously named on KEEP.

- DROP cannot be used with variables created by IN, FIRST, or LAST subcommands.

- KEEP can be used to change the order of variables in the resulting file. MATCH FILES first copies the variables in order from the first file, then copies the variables in order from the second file, and so on. With KEEP, variables are kept in the order they are listed on the subcommand. If a variable is named more than once on KEEP, only the first mention of the variable is in effect; all subsequent references to that variable name are ignored.

Example

```
MATCH FILES FILE=PARTICLE /RENAME=(PARTIC=POLLUTE1)
   /FILE=GAS /RENAME=(OZONE TO SULFUR=POLLUTE2 TO POLLUTE4)
   /DROP=POLLUTE4.
```

- The renamed variable POLLUTE4 is dropped from the resulting file. DROP is specified after all the FILE and RENAME subcommands, and it refers to the dropped variable by its new name.

IN Subcommand

IN creates a flag variable on the resulting file that indicates whether a case came from the input file named on the preceding FILE subcommand. IN applies only to the file specified on the immediately preceding FILE subcommand.

- IN has only one specification, the name of the flag variable.

- The variable created by IN has the value 1 for every case that came from the associated input file, or the value 0 if the case came from a different input file.

- Variables created by IN are automatically attached to end of the resulting file and cannot be dropped. If FIRST or LAST are used, the variable created by IN precedes the variable(s) created by FIRST or LAST.

Example

```
MATCH FILES  FILE=WEEK10 /FILE=WEEK11 /IN=INWEEK11 /BY=EMPID.
```

- IN creates the variable INWEEK11, which has the value 1 for all cases in the resulting file that had values in the input file WEEK11 and the value 0 for those cases that were not in file WEEK11.

Example

```
MATCH FILES  FILE=WEEK10 /FILE=WEEK11 /IN=INWEEK11 /BY=EMPID.
SELECT IF  (NOT INWEEK11).
```

- The variable created by IN is used to screen partially missing cases for subsequent analyses.

- SELECT IF selects only the cases in the resulting file for which there are no matching cases in file WEEK11.

- Since IN variables have either the value 1 or 0, they can be used in logical expressions where 1=true and 0=false.

FIRST and LAST
Subcommands

FIRST and LAST create logical variables that flag the first or last case of a group of cases with the same value on the BY variables. FIRST and LAST must be placed after all TABLE and FILE subcommands and their associated RENAME and IN subcommands.

• FIRST and LAST have only one specification, the name of the flag variable.

• FIRST creates a variable with the value 1 for the first case of each group and the value 0 for all other cases.

• LAST creates a variable with the value 1 for the last case of each group and the value 0 for all other cases.

• Variables created by FIRST and LAST are automatically attached to the end of the resulting file and cannot be dropped.

• If one file has several cases with a single value on a key variable(s), FIRST or LAST can be used to create a variable that flags the first or last case of the group.

Example

```
MATCH FILES   TABLE=HOUSE /FILE=PERSONS
/BY=HOUSEID /FIRST=HEAD.
```

• The variable HEAD contains the value 1 for the first person in each household and the value 0 for all other persons. Assuming that the person file is sorted with the head of household as the first case for each household, variable HEAD identifies the case for the head of household.

Example

```
TITLE  'USING MATCH FILES WITH ONLY ONE FILE'.

*      THIS EXAMPLE FLAGS THE FIRST OF SEVERAL CASES WITH
       THE SAME VALUE ON A KEY VARIABLE.

MATCH FILES  FILE=PERSONS /BY HOUSEID /FIRST=HEAD.
SELECT IF  (HEAD EQ 1).
CROSSTABS  JOBCAT BY SEX.
```

• MATCH FILES replaces the GET command and reads the system file PERSONS. BY and FIRST identify the key variable (HOUSEID) and create the variable HEAD with the value 1 for the first case in each household and value 0 for all other cases.

• SELECT IF selects only the cases with value 1 for HEAD, and the CROSSTABS procedure is run on these cases.

MAP Subcommand

MAP produces a map showing which variables are in the new active system file and from what file or files they may be taken. Variables are listed in the order in which they appear in the new active file. MAP has no specifications and must be placed after all FILE and RENAME subcommands.

• Multiple MAP subcommands can be used. Each MAP shows the current status of the active system file and reflects only the subcommands that precede the MAP subcommand.

• To obtain a map of the new active file in its final state, specify MAP last.

• If a variable is renamed, its original name is shown in the source file and its new name appears in the resulting file. Variables created by IN, FIRST, and LAST are not included in the map since they are automatically attached to end of the file and cannot be dropped.

• MAP can be used with the EDIT command to obtain a map of what the resulting file will look like, without actually reading the data and executing the match.

• MAP cannot be used for a match of more than 12 files; the display page is not wide enough.

MATRIX—END MATRIX

This command is included in the SPSS Advanced Statistics option. It is not available on all operating systems.

```
MATRIX
matrix-language statements
END MATRIX
```

The following matrix-language statements can be used in a matrix program:

BREAK	ELSE IF	MSAVE
CALL	END IF	PRINT
COMPUTE	END LOOP	READ
DISPLAY	GET	RELEASE
DO IF	LOOP	SAVE
ELSE	MGET	WRITE

The following functions can be used in matrix-language statements:

ABS	Absolute values of matrix elements
ALL	Test if all elements are positive
ANY	Test if any element is positive
ARSIN	Arc sines of matrix elements
ARTAN	Arc tangents of matrix elements
BLOCK	Create block diagonal matrix
CDFNORM	Cumulative normal distribution function
CHICDF	Cumulative chi-squared distribution function
CHOL	Cholesky decomposition
CMAX	Column maxima
CMIN	Column minima
COS	Cosines of matrix elements
CSSQ	Column sums of squares
CSUM	Column sums
DESIGN	Create design matrix
DET	Determinant
DIAG	Diagonal of matrix
EOF	Check end of file
EVAL	Eigenvalues of symmetric matrix
EXP	Exponentials of matrix elements
FCDF	Cumulative F distribution function
GINV	Generalized inverse
GSCH	Gram Schmidt orthonormal basis
IDENT	Create identity matrix
INV	Inverse
KRONEKER	Kroneker product of two matrices
LG10	Logarithms to base 10 of matrix elements
LN	Logarithms to base e of matrix elements
MAGIC	Create magic square
MAKE	Create a matrix with all elements equal
MDIAG	Create a matrix with the given diagonal
MMAX	Maximum element in matrix
MMIN	Minimum element in matrix
MOD	Remainders after division
MSSQ	Matrix sum of squares
MSUM	Matrix sum
NCOL	Number of columns
NROW	Number of rows
RANK	Matrix rank
RESHAPE	Change shape of matrix
RMAX	Row maxima
RMIN	Row minima
RND	Round off matrix elements to nearest integer
RNKORDER	Rank elements in matrix averaging ties
RSSQ	Row sums of squares
RSUM	Row sums
SIN	Sines of matrix elements

SOLVE	Solve systems of linear equations
SQRT	Square roots of matrix elements
SSCP	Sums of squares and cross products
SVAL	Singular values
SWEEP	Perform sweep transformation
T	(Synonym for TRANSPOS)
TCDF	Cumulative normal t-distribution function
TRACE	Calculate trace (sum of diagonal elements)
TRANSPOS	Transposition of matrix
TRUNC	Truncation of matrix elements to integer
UNIFORM	Create matrix of uniform random numbers

Example:

```
MATRIX.
READ A /FILE=MATRDATA /SIZE={6,6} /FIELD=1 TO 60.
CALL EIGEN(A,EIGENVEC,EIGENVAL).
LOOP J=1 TO NROW(EIGENVAL).
+ DO IF (EIGENVAL(J) > 1.0).
+   PRINT EIGENVAL(J) / TITLE="Eigenvalue:" /SPACE=3.
+   PRINT T(EIGENVEC(:,J)) / TITLE="Eigenvector:" /SPACE=1.
+ END IF.
END LOOP.
END MATRIX.
```

Overview

The MATRIX and END MATRIX commands enclose statements that are executed by the SPSS MATRIX processor. Such MATRIX programs enable you to write your own statistical routines using the compact language of matrix algebra. MATRIX programs can include mathematical calculations, control structures, display of results, reading and writing matrices as character files or SPSS system files.

As discussed below, a MATRIX program is for the most part independent of the rest of the SPSS session, although it can read and write SPSS system files, including the active system file.

This reference section does not attempt to explain the rules of matrix algebra. Many textbooks, such as Hadley (1961) and O'Nan (1971) teach the application of matrix methods to statistics.

The SPSS MATRIX procedure was originally developed at the Madison Academic Computing Center, University of Wisconsin.

Terminology

A variable within a MATRIX program represents a *matrix,* which is simply a set of values arranged in a rectangular array of rows and columns.

- An $n \times m$ matrix (read "n by m") is one that has n rows and m columns. The integers n and m are the *dimensions* of the matrix. An n $\times$ m matrix contains n $\times$ m *elements,* or data values.

- An $n \times 1$ matrix is sometimes called a *column vector,* and a $1 \times n$ matrix is sometimes called a *row vector.* A vector is a special case of a matrix.

- A 1×1 matrix, containing a single data value, is often called a *scalar.* A scalar is also a special case of a matrix.

- An *index* to a matrix or vector is an integer that identifies a specific row or column. Indices normally appear in printed works as subscripts, A_{31}, but are specified in the MATRIX language within parentheses, A(3,1). The row index for a matrix precedes the column index.

- The *main diagonal* of a matrix consists of the elements whose row index equals their column index. It begins at the top left corner of the matrix; in a square matrix it runs to the bottom right corner.

- The *transpose* of a matrix is the matrix with rows and columns interchanged. The transpose of an $m \times n$ matrix is an $n \times m$ matrix.

- A *symmetric matrix* is a square matrix that is unchanged by flipping it about the main diagonal. That is, the element in row i, column j, equals the element in row j, column i. A symmetric matrix equals its transpose.

Matrices are always rectangular, although it is possible to read or write symmetric matrices in triangular form. Vectors and scalars are considered degenerate rectangles.

• It is an error to try to create a matrix whose rows have different numbers of elements.

No processing over different cases is performed within a MATRIX program unless you specify it yourself, using the control structures of the MATRIX language. Unlike ordinary SPSS variables, MATRIX variables do not have distinct values for different cases. A matrix is a single entity.

Vectors in MATRIX processing should not be confused with the vectors temporarily created by the VECTOR command in SPSS. The latter are shorthand for a list of SPSS variables, and like all ordinary SPSS variables are unavailable during MATRIX processing.

MATRIX Variables

A MATRIX variable is created by a MATRIX statement that assigns a value to a variable name.

• A MATRIX variable name follows the same rules as an ordinary SPSS variable name.

• The names of MATRIX functions and procedures cannot be used as variable names within a MATRIX program. (In particular, the letter T cannot be used as a variable name, since T is an alias for the TRANSPOS function.)

• The COMPUTE, READ, GET, MGET, and CALL statements create matrices. An index variable named on a LOOP statement creates a scalar and assigns a value to it.

• A variable name can be redefined within a MATRIX program without regard to the dimensions of the matrix it represents. The same name can represent scalars, vectors, and full matrices at different points in the MATRIX program.

• MATRIX does not include any special processing for missing data. When reading a data matrix from an SPSS system file, you must therefore specify whether missing data are to be accepted as valid or excluded from the matrix.

String Variables in MATRIX

MATRIX variables can contain short string data. Support for string variables is limited, however:

• MATRIX will attempt to carry out calculations with string variables if you so request. The results will not be meaningful.

• You must specify a format (such as "A8") when you display a matrix that contains string data.

Syntax of the MATRIX Language

A MATRIX program consists of *statements*. MATRIX statements must appear in a MATRIX program, between the MATRIX and END MATRIX commands. They are analogous to SPSS commands, and follow the rules of the SPSS command language regarding the abbreviation of keywords; the equivalence of upper and lower case; the use of spaces, commas, and equal signs; and the splitting of statements across multiple lines. However, commas are *required* to separate arguments to MATRIX functions and procedures and to separate variable names on the RELEASE statement.

MATRIX statements are composed of the following elements:

• Keywords, such as the names of MATRIX statements.

• Variable names.

• Explicitly written matrices, which are enclosed within braces ({}).

• Arithmetic and logical operators.

• Matrix functions.

• Punctuation. Commas and semicolons are used to delimit the elements of explicitly written matrices. Braces enclose explicitly written matrices. Parentheses enclose, and commas separate, matrix indexes and arguments to matrix functions. Finally, the SPSS command terminator serves as a statement terminator within a MATRIX program.

Comments in Matrix Programs. Within a MATRIX program, you can enter comments in any of the forms recognized by SPSS: on lines beginning with the COMMENT command; on lines beginning with an asterisk; or between the characters /* and the characters */ on a command line.

Matrix Notation in SPSS

To write a matrix explicitly:

• Enclose the matrix within braces.
• Separate the elements of each row by commas.
• Separate the rows by semicolons.

Thus	{1,2,3;4,5,6}	represents	1 2 3 4 5 6
	{1,2;3,4;5,6}	represents	1 2 3 4 5 6

{1,2,3} is a row vector, while {1;2;3} is a column vector.

• A scalar can be written without the braces: {3} is equivalent to 3.

String elements must be enclosed in either apostrophes or quotation marks, as is generally true in the SPSS command language.

Matrix Construction

Several notational shortcuts simplify the construction of matrices.

Consecutive integers. You can use a colon to indicate a range of consecutive integers. The vector {1,2,3,4,5,6} can be written {1:6}.

Incremented ranges of integers. Use a second colon followed by the increment. The matrix {1,3,5,7;2,5,8,11} can be written {1:7:2;2:11:3}. The first row is 1:7:2, indicating the integers from 1 to 7 incrementing by 2, and the second row is 2:11:3, indicating the integers from 2 to 11 incrementing by 3.

• You must use integers when specifying a range in either of these ways. Numbers with fractional parts are truncated to integers.

Extraction of an element. Use parentheses to write an **index,** which is the way that you extract a single element from a vector or matrix. If V is a vector and M is a matrix, then $V(2)$ is the second element of V and $M(2,3)$ is is the element in row 2, column 3 of M.

The index used to extract an element of a vector must be an integer or (equivalently) a scalar matrix with an integer value. Similarly, the two indexes used to extract an element of a matrix must be integers or scalar matrices. However, you can use a vector as an index when extracting vectors from matrices or from other vectors. In the following examples, suppose that A is a 5 × 4 matrix containing these data:

$$A = \begin{matrix} 11 & 12 & 13 & 14 \\ 21 & 22 & 23 & 24 \\ 31 & 32 & 33 & 34 \\ 41 & 42 & 43 & 44 \\ 51 & 52 & 53 & 54 \end{matrix}$$

Extraction of a vector from a matrix or from another vector. The index can be a vector or an expression representing a vector. Thus A(2,1:4) is the elements in row 2, columns 1 through 4, namely the row vector {21,22,23,24}. A(1:5:2,1) is the elements in rows 1, 3, and 5—1 through 5 incrementing by 2—and column 1, namely the column vector {11;31;51}.

Extraction of an entire row or column vector from a matrix. In the important special case where an entire row or column is to be extracted, use a colon by itself as the index. A(4,:) is the entire 4th row of A, and A(:,I) is the I-th column of A, provided that I is a scalar with an integer value between 1 and 4.

Extraction of a matrix from another matrix. This is done with two indexes that evaluate as vectors. For example, A(1:2,1:3) is the matrix {11,12,13;21,22,23}, and A(:,2:4) is A with the first column removed.

The index expressions can be composed of other matrices. For example, if R is the vector {1,5} and C is the vector {1,3,4}, A(R,C) is the submatrix formed by the intersection of rows 1 and 5 with columns 1, 3, and 4, namely {11,13,14;51,53,54}.

• The distinction between row vectors and column vectors does not matter when they are used as indexes in this way; R and C could equally well have been defined as column vectors.

Construction of a matrix from other matrices. If the column vector V has n rows and matrix M has the dimensions $n \times m$, you can form an $n \times m+1$ matrix by writing {M,V}. In fact, you can paste together any number of matrices and vectors this way, separating row expressions by semicolons and components of row expressions by commas. All of the components of each row expression must have the same number of actual rows, and all of the row expressions must have the same number of actual columns.

• The distinction between row vectors and column vectors must be observed carefully when constructing matrices in this way, so that the components will fit together properly.

Example   Suppose that

```
CORNER = 11  12       COL3PART = 13    ROW3 = 31  32  33
         21  22                   23
```

```
                                         11  12  13
Then {CORNER, COL3PART; ROW3} constructs  21  22  23
                                         31  32  33
```

Several of the MATRIX functions are also useful in constructing matrices; see in particular the MAKE, UNIFORM, and IDENT functions.

Matrix Calculations: Conformable Matrices

Many operations with matrices make sense only if the matrices involved have "suitable" dimensions. Most often, this means that they should be the same size, with the same number of rows and the same number of columns. Matrices that are the right size for an operation are said to be **conformable.** If you attempt to do something in a MATRIX program with a matrix that is not conformable for that operation—a matrix that has the wrong dimensions—you will receive an error message, and the operation will not be performed. An important exception, where one of the matrices is a scalar, is discussed below.

Requirements for carrying out MATRIX operations include:

• Matrix addition and subtraction require that the two matrices be the same size.
• The relational and logical operations described below require that the two matrices be the same size.
• Matrix multiplication requires that the number of columns of the first matrix equal the number of rows of the second matrix.
• Raising a matrix to a power can only be done if the matrix is square. This includes the important operation of *inverting* a matrix, where the power is -1.

Conformability requirements for matrix functions are noted in Matrix Functions in the COMPUTE statement, below.

Operations Involving Scalars. When you combine a matrix with a scalar in an operation that requires two matrices of the same size, the scalar is treated as a matrix of the correct size in order to carry out the operation. This internal scalar expansion is performed for the following operations:

• Addition and subtraction.
• Elementwise multiplication, division, and exponentiation. Note that multiplying a matrix elementwise by an expanded scalar is equivalent to ordinary scalar multiplication: each element of the matrix is multiplied by the scalar.
• All relational and logical operators.

Matrix Calculations: Arithmetic Operators

You can add, subtract, multiply, or exponentiate matrices according to the rules of matrix algebra; or you can perform elementwise arithmetic, in which you multiply, divide, or exponentiate each element of a matrix separately.

- Use these operators only with numeric matrices. The results are undefined when they are used with string matrices.

The arithmetic operators are listed below.

Unary -   *Sign reversal.* A minus sign placed in front of a matrix reverses the sign of each element. (The unary + is also accepted, but has no effect.)

+   *Matrix addition.* Corresponding elements of the two matrices are added. The matrices must have the same dimensions, or one must be a scalar.

–   *Matrix subtraction.* Corresponding elements of the two matrices are subtracted. The matrices must have the same dimensions, or one must be a scalar.

*   *Multiplication.* There are two cases. First, *scalar multiplication:* if either of the matrices is a scalar, then each element of the other matrix is multiplied by that scalar. Second, *matrix multiplication:* if A is an $m \times n$ matrix and B is an $n \times p$ matrix, then $A*B$ is an $m \times p$ matrix in which the element in row i, column k, is equal to $\Sigma_{j=1}^{n} A(i,j) \times B(j,k)$.

/   *Division.* The division operator performs elementwise division (described below). True matrix division, the inverse operation of matrix multiplication, is accomplished by taking the INV function (square matrices) or the GINV function (rectangular matrices) of the denominator, and multiplying.

**   *Matrix exponentiation.* A matrix can be raised only to an integer power. The matrix, which must be square, is multiplied by itself as many times as the absolute value of the exponent. If the exponent is negative, the result is then inverted.

&*   *Elementwise multiplication.* Each element of the matrix is multiplied by the corresponding element of the second matrix. The matrices must have the same dimensions, or one must be a scalar.

&/   *Elementwise division.* Each element of the matrix is divided by the corresponding element of the second matrix. The matrices must have the same dimensions, or one must be a scalar.

&**   *Elementwise exponentiation.* Each element of the first matrix is raised to the power of the corresponding element of the second matrix. The matrices must have the same dimensions, or one must be a scalar.

:   *Sequential integers.* This operator creates a vector of consecutive integers from the value preceding the operator to the value following it. You can specify an optional increment following a second colon. See Matrix Construction, above, for the principal use of this operator.

Matrix Comparisons: Relational and Logical Operators

The relational and logical operators of the matrix language compare two matrices, element by element. The matrices must either be of the same dimensions, or one must be a scalar. The result is a matrix of the same size as the (expanded) operands and containing either 1 or 0 in each element, corresponding to the values *true* and *false*.

- Use these operators only with numeric matrices. The results are undefined when they are used with string matrices.
- The symbolic and alphabetic forms of these operators are equivalent.

The relational operators are:

>, GT   *Greater than.* (An element of the result matrix is true if the corresponding element of the first matrix is greater than the corresponding element of the second matrix.)

<, LT	*Less than.*	
<>, NE, ¬=	*Not equal to.*	
<=, LE	*Less than or equal to.*	
>=, GE	*Greater than or equal to.*	
=, EQ	*Equal to.*	

Logical operators combine two matrices, normally two matrices containing values of 1 (true) or 0 (false). When used with other numerical matrices, they treat all positive values as true, and all negative and zero values as false. The logical operators are:

NOT *Reverses the truth of the matrix that follows it.* Positive elements yield 0, and negative or zero elements yield 1.

AND *Both must be true.* The matrix A AND B is 1 where the corresponding elements of A and B are both positive, and 0 elsewhere.

OR *Either must be true.* The matrix A OR B is 1 where the corresponding element of either A or B is positive, and 0 where both elements are negative or zero.

XOR *Either must be true, but not both.* The matrix A XOR B is 1 where one, but not both, of the corresponding elements of A and B is positive, and 0 where both are positive or neither is positive.

Precedence of Operators

Parentheses can be used to control the order in which complex expressions are evaluated. When the order of evaluation is not specified by parentheses, operations listed highest in Table 1 are carried out first. Operations of equal precedence are performed left to right.

Table 1 Precedence of operators

```
+ -                        (Unary)
:
** &**
*   &*   &/
+ -                        (Addition and Subtraction)
> < >= <= = <> ¬=
NOT
AND
OR XOR
```

Examples

```
COMPUTE A = {1,2,3;4,5,6}.
COMPUTE B = A + 4.
COMPUTE C = A &** 2.
COMPUTE D = 2 &** A.
COMPUTE E = A < 5.
COMPUTE F = (C &/ 2) < B.
```

The result of these COMPUTE statements is:

$$A = \begin{matrix} 1 & 2 & 3 \\ 4 & 5 & 6 \end{matrix} \qquad B = \begin{matrix} 5 & 6 & 7 \\ 8 & 9 & 10 \end{matrix} \qquad C = \begin{matrix} 1 & 4 & 9 \\ 16 & 25 & 36 \end{matrix}$$

$$D = \begin{matrix} 2 & 4 & 8 \\ 16 & 32 & 64 \end{matrix} \qquad E = \begin{matrix} 1 & 1 & 1 \\ 1 & 0 & 0 \end{matrix} \qquad F = \begin{matrix} 1 & 1 & 1 \\ 0 & 0 & 0 \end{matrix}$$

MATRIX and Other SPSS Commands

A MATRIX program is a single procedure within an SPSS session.

• No active system file is needed to run a MATRIX program. If one exists, it is ignored during MATRIX processing unless you specifically reference it (with an asterisk) on the GET, SAVE, MGET, or MSAVE statements.

• Variables defined in the SPSS active system file are unavailable during MATRIX processing, except with the GET or MGET statements.

• MATRIX variables are unavailable after the END MATRIX command, unless you use SAVE or MSAVE to write them to the active system file.

MATRIX Statements

Table 2 lists all the statements that are accepted within a MATRIX program. Most of them have the same name as an analogous SPSS command, and perform an exactly analogous function. Use only these statements between the MATRIX and END MATRIX commands. Any command not recognized as a valid MATRIX statement will be rejected by the MATRIX processor.

Table 2   Valid MATRIX statements

BREAK	ELSE IF	MSAVE
CALL	END IF	PRINT
COMPUTE	END LOOP	READ
DISPLAY	GET	RELEASE
DO IF	LOOP	SAVE
ELSE	MGET	WRITE

Exchanging Data with SPSS System Files

MATRIX programs can read and write SPSS system files.

• The GET and SAVE statements read and write ordinary (case-oriented) SPSS system files, treating each case as a row of a matrix and each ordinary variable as a column.

• The MGET and MSAVE statements read and write matrix-format SPSS system files, respecting the structure defined by SPSS when it creates a matrix system file.

These statements are discussed below.

Special Considerations for Using the Active System File

You can use the GET statement to read a case-oriented active system file into a MATRIX variable. The result is a rectangular data matrix in which cases have become rows, and variables have become columns. Special circumstances can affect the processing of this data matrix.

Split-file Processing.   After a SPLIT FILE command in SPSS, a MATRIX program will read one split-file group with each execution of a GET statement. This enables you to process the subgroups separately within the MATRIX program.

• *For commands run within a prompted session,* a MATRIX program cannot GET the active system file when split-file processing is in effect.

Case Selection.   When a subset of cases is selected for processing, as the result of a SELECT IF, SAMPLE, or N OF CASES command, only the selected cases will be read by the GET statement in MATRIX.

Temporary Transformations.   The entire MATRIX program is treated as a single procedure by the SPSS central system. Temporary transformations—those preceded by the TEMPORARY command—entered immediately before a MATRIX program are in effect throughout that program (even if you GET the active system file repeatedly), and are no longer in effect at the end of the MATRIX program.

Case Weighting.   Case weighting in an SPSS system file is ignored when the file is read into a MATRIX program.

MATRIX in a Prompted Session

When you run the MATRIX procedure in a prompted session, each MATRIX statement is executed as soon as it is entered. (Statements within a LOOP or DO IF structure are executed as soon as all such structures are closed.)

The MATRIX processor issues its own prompts in a prompted session. The normal MATRIX prompt is:

```
MATRIX>
```

When a LOOP structure is open, the prompt changes to LOOP>, and when a DO IF structure is open, the prompt changes to DO IF>. If several structures are open, the prompt for the innermost structure is displayed. The continuation prompt during matrix processing remains the same:

```
CONTINUE>
```

If you do not terminate a MATRIX statement during a prompted session, this prompt reminds you to do so. The SPSS command terminator (by default a period or a blank line) is required to terminate MATRIX statements during a prompted session.

MATRIX Command

The MATRIX command, when encountered in an SPSS session, invokes the MATRIX processor, which reads MATRIX statements until the END MATRIX or FINISH command is encountered.

- MATRIX is a procedure and cannot be entered inside a transformation structure such as DO IF or LOOP.
- The MATRIX procedure does not require an active system file.
- Comments are removed before subsequent lines are passed to the MATRIX processor.
- Macros are expanded before subsequent lines are passed to the MATRIX processor.
- During a prompted session, the command prompt changes to

  MATRIX>

  after the MATRIX command is entered.

END MATRIX Command

The END MATRIX command terminates matrix processing and returns control to the SPSS Command Processor.

- The contents of MATRIX variables are lost after an END MATRIX command.
- The active system file, if any, becomes available again after an END MATRIX command.
- During a prompted session, the command prompt changes back to

  SPSS>

  after the END MATRIX command is entered.

COMPUTE Statement

The COMPUTE statement carries out most of the calculations in the MATRIX program. It closely resembles the COMPUTE command in the SPSS transformation language.

- The basic specification is the target variable, an equals sign, and the assignment expression. Values of the target variable are calculated according to the specification on the assignment expression.
- The target variable must be named first, and the equals sign is required. Only one target variable is allowed per COMPUTE command.
- The target variable can be a single element or an entire matrix. It cannot be an expression (including expressions such as M(1,:) or M(1:3,4) that extract portions of a matrix).
- Matrix functions must specify at least one argument enclosed in parentheses. If an expression has two or more arguments, each argument must be separated by a comma. For a complete discussion of the functions and their arguments, see Matrix Functions, below.

String Values in COMPUTE. MATRIX variables, unlike those in the SPSS transformation language, are not checked for data type (numeric or string) when you use them in a COMPUTE statement.

- Numerical calculations with matrices containing string values will produce meaningless results.
- One or more elements of a matrix can be set equal to string constants by enclosing the string constants in apostrophes or quotation marks on a COMPUTE statement.

- String values can be copied from one matrix to another with the COMPUTE statement.
- There is no way to display a matrix that contains both numeric and string values, if you compute one for some reason.

Example.

```
COMPUTE LABELS={"Observe", "Predict", "Error"}.
PRINT LABELS /FORMAT=A7.
```

Arithmetic Operations

The expression on a COMPUTE statement can be formed from matrix constants and variables, combined with the arithmetic, relational, and logical operators discussed above. Matrix constructions, as discussed above, and the matrix functions discussed below are also allowed.

Examples.

```
COMPUTE PI = 3.14159265.
COMPUTE RSQ = R * R.
COMPUTE FLAGS = EIGENVAL >= 1.
COMPUTE ESTIM = {OBS, PRED, ERR}.
```

- The first statement computes a scalar. Note that the braces are optional on a scalar constant.
- The second statement computes the square of the matrix R. R can be any square matrix, including a scalar.
- The third statement computes a vector named FLAGS which has the same dimension as the existing vector EIGENVAL. Each element of FLAGS equals 1 if the corresponding element of EIGENVAL is greater than or equal to 1, and 0 if the corresponding element is less than 1.
- The fourth statement constructs a matrix ESTIM by concatenating the three vectors or matrices OBS, PRED, and ERR. The component matrices must have the same number of rows.

MATRIX Functions

The following functions are available in the matrix language. Except where noted, each takes one or more numeric matrices as arguments and returns a matrix value as its result. The arguments must be enclosed in parentheses, and multiple arguments must be separated by commas.

- In the list below, matrix arguments are represented by names beginning with M. Unless otherwise noted, these arguments can be vectors or scalars. Arguments that must be vectors are represented by names beginning with V, and arguments that must be scalars are represented by names beginning with S.

ABS(M)	*Absolute value.* Takes a single argument. Returns a matrix having the same dimensions as the argument, containing the absolute values of its elements.
ALL(M)	*Test for all elements nonzero.* Takes a single argument. Returns a scalar: 1 if all elements of the argument are nonzero, and 0 if any element is zero.
ANY(M)	*Test for any element nonzero.* Takes a single argument. Returns a scalar: 1 if any element of the argument is nonzero, and 0 if all elements are zero.
ARSIN(M)	*Inverse sine.* Takes a single argument, whose elements must be between −1 and +1. Returns a matrix having the same dimensions as the argument, containing the inverse sines (arc sines) of its elements. The results are in radians, and are in the range from $-\pi/2$ to $+\pi/2$.
ARTAN(M)	*Inverse tangent.* Takes a single argument. Returns a matrix having the same dimensions as the argument, containing the inverse tangents (arc tangents) of its elements, in radians. (To convert radians to degrees, multiply by $180/\pi$, which you can compute as 45/ARTAN(1).) For example

```
COMPUTE DEGREES = ARTAN(M) * 45/ARTAN(1).
```

BLOCK(M1,M2,...)   *Create a block diagonal matrix.* Takes any number of arguments. Returns a matrix with as many rows as the sum of the rows in all the arguments, and as many columns as the sum of the columns in all the arguments, with the argument matrices down the diagonal and zeros elsewhere. For example

```
If   A = 1 1 1    B = 2 2    C = 3 3 3    D = 4 4 4
         1 1 1        2 2        3 3 3
                                 3 3 3
                                 3 3 3
```

```
then BLOCK(A,B,C,D) =  1 1 1 0 0 0 0 0 0 0 0
                       1 1 1 0 0 0 0 0 0 0 0
                       0 0 0 2 2 0 0 0 0 0 0
                       0 0 0 2 2 0 0 0 0 0 0
                       0 0 0 0 0 3 3 3 0 0 0
                       0 0 0 0 0 3 3 3 0 0 0
                       0 0 0 0 0 3 3 3 0 0 0
                       0 0 0 0 0 3 3 3 0 0 0
                       0 0 0 0 0 0 0 0 4 4 4
```

CDFNORM(M)   *Standard normal cumulative distribution function of elements.* Takes a single argument. Returns a matrix having the same dimensions as the argument, containing the values of the cumulative normal distribution function for each of its elements. If an element of the argument is x, the corresponding element of the result is a number between 0 and 1, giving the proportion of a normal distribution that is less than x. Thus CDFNORM({-1.96,0,1.96}) is approximately {.025,.5,.975}.

CHICDF(M,S)   *Chi-square cumulative distribution function of elements.* Takes two arguments, a matrix of chi-square values and a scalar giving the degrees of freedom (which must be positive). Returns a matrix having the same dimensions as the first argument, containing the values of the cumulative chi-square distribution function for each of its elements. If an element of the first argument is x and the second argument is S, then the corresponding element of the result is a number between 0 and 1, giving the proportion of a chi-square distribution with S degrees of freedom that is less than x. If x is not positive, the result is 0.

CHOL(M)   *Cholesky decomposition.* Takes a single argument, which must be a symmetric positive-definite matrix (a square matrix, symmetric about the main diagonal, with positive eigenvalues). Returns a matrix having the same dimensions as the argument. If M is a symmetric positive-definite matrix and $B=CHOL(M)$, then $T(B)*B=M$, where T is the transpose function defined below.

CMAX(M)   *Column maxima.* Takes a single argument. Returns a matrix having one row and the same number of columns as the argument. Each column of the result contains the maximum value of the corresponding column of the argument.

CMIN(M)   *Column minima.* Takes a single argument. Returns a matrix having one row and the same number of columns as the argument. Each column of the result contains the minimum value of the corresponding column of the argument.

COS(M)   *Cosines.* Takes a single argument. Returns a matrix having the same dimensions as the argument, containing the cosines of the elements of the argument. Elements of the argument matrix are assumed to be measured in radians. (To convert degrees to radians, multiply by $\pi/180$, which you can compute as ARTAN(1)/45.) For example

```
COMPUTE COSINES = COS(DEGREES * ARTAN(1)/45).
```

CSSQ(M)   *Column sums of squares.* Takes a single argument. Returns a matrix having one row and the same number of columns as the argument. Each column of the result contains the sum of the squared values of the elements in the corresponding column of the argument.

CSUM(M)   *Column sums.* Takes a single argument. Returns a row vector with the same number of columns as the argument. Each column of the result contains the sum of the elements in the corresponding column of the argument.

DESIGN(M)   *Main effects design matrix from the columns of a matrix.* Takes a single argument. Returns a matrix having the same number of rows as the argument, and as many columns as the sum of the numbers of unique values in each column of the argument. Constant columns in the argument are skipped with a warning message. The result contains 1 in the row(s) where the value in question occurs in the argument. For example

$$
\text{If } A = \begin{array}{ccc} 1 & 2 & 8 \\ 1 & 3 & 8 \\ 2 & 6 & 5 \\ 3 & 3 & 8 \\ 3 & 6 & 5 \end{array} \quad \text{then DESIGN(A)} = \begin{array}{cccccccc} 1 & 0 & 0 & 1 & 0 & 0 & 1 & 0 \\ 1 & 0 & 0 & 0 & 1 & 0 & 1 & 0 \\ 0 & 1 & 0 & 0 & 0 & 1 & 0 & 1 \\ 0 & 0 & 1 & 0 & 1 & 0 & 1 & 0 \\ 0 & 0 & 1 & 0 & 0 & 1 & 0 & 1 \end{array}
$$

The first three columns of the result correspond to the three distinct values 1, 2, and 3 in the first column of A; the fourth through sixth columns of the result correspond to the three distinct values 2, 3, and 6 in the second column of A; and the last two columns of the result correspond to the two distinct values 8 and 5 in the third column of A.

DET(M)   *Determinant.* Takes a single argument, which must be a square matrix. Returns a scalar, the determinant of the argument.

DIAG(M)   *Diagonal of a matrix.* Takes a single argument. Returns a column vector with as many rows as the minimum of the number of rows and the number of columns in the argument. The *i*th element of the result is the value in row *i*, column *i* of the argument.

EOF(file)   *End of file indicator,* normally used after a READ statement. Takes a single argument, which must either be a file name in apostrophes or quotation marks, or a file handle defined on a FILE HANDLE command that preceded the MATRIX program. Returns a scalar equal to 1 if the last attempt to read that file encountered the last record in the file, and equal to 0 if the last attempt did not encounter the last record in the file. Calling the EOF function causes a REREAD specification on the READ statement to be ignored on the next attempt to read the file.

EVAL(M)   *Eigenvalues of a symmetric matrix.* Takes a single argument, which must be a symmetric matrix. Returns a column vector with the same number of rows as the argument, containing the eigenvalues of the argument in decreasing numerical order.

EXP(M)   *Exponentials of matrix elements.* Takes a single argument. Returns a matrix having the same dimensions as the argument, in which each element equals *e* raised to the power of the corresponding element in the argument matrix.

FCDF(M,S1,S2)

Cumulative F *distribution function of elements.* Takes three arguments, a matrix of *F* values and two scalars giving the degrees of freedom (which must be positive). Returns a matrix having the same dimensions as the first argument *M,* containing the values of the cumulative *F* distribution function for each of its elements. If an element of the first argument is *x* and the second and third arguments are *S1* and *S2,* then the corresponding element of the result is a number between 0 and 1, giving the proportion of an *F* distribution with *S1* and *S2* degrees of freedom that is less than *x.* If *x* is not positive, the result is 0.

GINV(M)

Generalized Moore-Penrose inverse of a matrix. Takes a single argument. Returns a matrix with the same dimensions as the transpose of the argument. If *A* is the generalized inverse of a matrix *M,* then $M*A*M=M$. Thus if *M* is an $m \times n$ matrix, then $M*A$ is an $m \times m$ identity matrix, and $A*M$ is an $n \times n$ identity matrix.

GSCH(M)

Gram-Schmidt orthonormal basis for the space spanned by the column vectors of a matrix. Takes a single argument, in which there must be as many linearly independent columns as there are rows. (That is, the rank of the argument must equal the number of rows.) Returns a square matrix with as many rows as the argument. The columns of the result form a basis for the space spanned by the columns of the argument.

IDENT(S1 [,S2])

Create an identity matrix. Takes either one or two arguments, which must be scalars. Returns a matrix with as many rows as the first argument and as many columns as the second argument, if any. If the second argument is omitted, the result is a square matrix. Elements on the main diagonal of the result equal 1, and all other elements equal 0.

INV(M)

Inverse of a matrix. Takes a single argument, which must be square and nonsingular (that is, its determinant must not be 0). Returns a square matrix having the same dimensions as the argument. If *A* is the inverse of *M,* then $M*A=A*M=I$, the identity matrix.

KRONEKER(M1,M2)

Kroneker product of two matrices. Takes two arguments. Returns a matrix whose row dimension is the product of the row dimensions of the arguments, and whose column dimension is the product of the column dimensions of the arguments. The Kroneker product of two matrices *A* and *B* takes the form of an array of scalar products:

```
A(1,1)*B  A(1,2)*B  ...A(1,N)*B
A(2,1)*B  A(2,2)*B  ...A(2,N)*B
  ...
A(M,1)*B  A(M,2)*B  ...A(M,N)*B
```

LG10(M)

Base 10 logarithms of the elements. Takes a single argument, all of whose elements must be positive. Returns a matrix having the same dimensions as the argument, in which each element is the logarithm to base 10 of the corresponding element of the argument.

LN(M)

Natural logarithms of the elements. Takes a single argument, all of whose elements must be positive. Returns a matrix having the same dimensions as the argument, in which each element is the logarithm to base *e* of the corresponding element of the argument.

MAGIC(S)   *Magic square.* Takes a single scalar, which must be 3 or larger, as an argument. Returns a square matrix with S rows and S columns, containing the integers from 1 through S^2. All the row sums and all the column sums are equal in the result matrix. (The result matrix is only one of several possible magic squares.)

MAKE(S1,S2,S3)   *Create a matrix all of whose elements equal a specified value.* Takes three scalars as arguments. Returns an $S1 \times S2$ matrix, all of whose elements equal $S3$.

MDIAG(V)   *Create a square matrix with a specified main diagonal.* Takes a single vector as an argument. Returns a square matrix with as many rows and columns as the dimension of the vector. The elements of the vector appear on the main diagonal of the matrix, and the other matrix elements are all 0.

MMAX(M)   *Maximum element in a matrix.* Takes a single argument. Returns a scalar equal to the numerically largest element in the argument M.

MMIN(M)   *Minimum element in a matrix.* Takes a single argument. Returns a scalar equal to the numerically smallest element in the argument M.

MOD(M,S)   *Remainders after division by a scalar.* Takes two arguments, a matrix and a scalar (which must not be 0). Returns a matrix having the same dimensions as M, each of whose elements is the remainder after the corresponding element of M is divided by S. The sign of each element of the result is the same as the sign of the corresponding element of the matrix argument M.

MSSQ(M)   *Matrix sum of squares.* Takes a single argument. Returns a scalar that equals the sum of the squared values of all the elements in the argument.

MSUM(M)   *Matrix sum.* Takes a single argument. Returns a scalar that equals the sum of all the elements in the argument.

NCOL(M)   *Number of columns in a matrix.* Takes a single argument. Returns a scalar that equals the number of columns in the argument.

NROW(M)   *Number of rows in a matrix.* Takes a single argument. Returns a scalar that equals the number of rows in the argument.

RANK(M)   *Rank of a matrix.* Takes a single argument. Returns a scalar that equals the number of linearly independent rows or columns in the argument.

RESHAPE(M,S1,S2) *Matrix of different dimensions.* Takes three arguments, a matrix and two scalars, whose product must equal the number of elements in the matrix. Returns a matrix whose dimensions are given by the scalar arguments. For example, if M is any matrix with exactly 50 elements, then RESHAPE(M, 5, 10) is a matrix with 5 rows and 10 columns. Elements are assigned to the reshaped matrix in order by row.

RMAX(M)   *Row maxima.* Takes a single argument. Returns a column vector with the same number of rows as the argument. Each row of the result contains the maximum value of the corresponding row of the argument.

RMIN(M)   *Row minima.* Takes a single argument. Returns a column vector with the same number of rows as the argument. Each row of the result contains the minimum value of the corresponding row of the argument.

RND(M) *Elements rounded to the nearest integers.* Takes a single argument. Returns a matrix having the same dimensions as the argument. Each element of the result equals the corresponding element of the argument rounded to an integer.

RNKORDER(M) *Ranking of matrix elements in ascending order.* Takes a single argument. Returns a matrix having the same dimensions as the argument *M*. The smallest element of the argument corresponds to a result element of 1, and the largest element of the argument to a result element equal to the number of elements, except that ties (equal elements in *M*) are resolved by assigning a rank equal to the arithmetic mean of the applicable ranks. For example

$$\text{If } M = \begin{array}{rrr} -1 & -21.7 & 8 \\ 0 & 3.91 & -21.7 \\ 8 & 9 & 10 \end{array} \text{ then RNKORDER}(M) = \begin{array}{rrr} 3 & 1.5 & 6.5 \\ 4 & 5 & 1.5 \\ 6.5 & 8 & 9 \end{array}$$

RSSQ(M) *Row sums of squares.* Takes a single argument. Returns a column vector having the same number of rows as the argument. Each row of the result contains the sum of the squared values of the elements in the corresponding row of the argument.

RSUM(M) *Row sums.* Takes a single argument. Returns a column vector having the same number of rows as the argument. Each row of the result contains the sum of the elements in the corresponding row of the argument.

SIN(M) *Sines.* Takes a single argument. Returns a matrix having the same dimensions as the argument, containing the sines of the elements of the argument. Elements of the argument matrix are assumed to be measured in radians. (To convert degrees to radians, multiply by $\pi/180$, which you can compute as ARTAN(1) / 45.) For example

```
COMPUTE SINES = SIN(DEGREES * ARTAN(1)/45).
```

SOLVE(M1,M2) *Solution of systems of linear equations.* Takes two arguments, the first of which must be square and nonsingular (its determinant must be nonzero), and the second of which must have the same number of rows as the first. Returns a matrix with the same dimensions as the second argument. If A*X=B, then X=SOLVE(A, B). In effect, this function sets its result equal to INV(M1)*M2, where *M1* and *M2* are the arguments .

SQRT(M) *Square roots of elements.* Takes a single argument, whose elements must not be negative. Returns a matrix having the same dimensions as the arguments, whose elements are the positive square roots of the corresponding elements of the argument.

SSCP(M) *Sums of squares and cross products.* Takes a single argument. Returns a square matrix having as many rows (and columns) as the argument has columns. SSCP(M) equals *T(M)*M*, where *T* is the transpose function defined below.

SVAL(M) *Singular values of a matrix.* Takes a single argument. Returns a column vector containing as many rows as the minimum of the numbers of rows and columns in the argument, containing the singular values of the argument in decreasing numerical order. The singular values of a matrix *M* are the square roots of the eigenvalues of *T(M)*M*, where *T* is the transpose function discussed below.

SWEEP(M,S)   *Sweep transformation of a matrix.* Takes two arguments, a matrix and a scalar, which must be less than or equal to both the number of rows and the number of columns of the matrix. (In other words, the pivot element of the matrix, which is *M(S,S),* the element on the main diagonal indexed by the scalar, must exist.) Returns a matrix of the same dimensions as *M,* whose elements are computed as follows:

```
If M(k,k) is not zero and A = SWEEP(M,k), then

A(k,k) = 1 / M(k,k)
A(i,k) = -M(i,k) / M(k,k)   for i not equal to k
A(k,j) =  M(k,j) / M(k,k)   for j not equal to k
A(i,j) = (M(k,k)*M(i,j)-M(i,k)*M(k,j))/M(k,k)
                            for i,j not equal to k

If M(k,k) equals zero and A = SWEEP(M,k), then

A(i,k) = A(k,i) = 0   for all i
A(i,j) = M(i,j)  for i,j not equal to k
```

TCDF(M,S)   *Cumulative* t *distribution function of elements.* Takes two arguments, a matrix of *t* values and a scalar giving the degrees of freedom (which must be positive). Returns a matrix having the same dimensions as *M,* containing the values of the cumulative *t* distribution function for each of its elements. If an element of the first argument is *x* and the second argument is *S,* then the corresponding element of the result is a number between 0 and 1, giving the proportion of a *t* distribution with *S* degrees of freedom that is less than *x.*

TRACE(M)   *Sum of the main diagonal elements.* Takes a single argument. Returns a scalar, which equals the sum of the elements on the main diagonal of the argument.

TRANSPOS(M)   *Short form:* T. *Transpose of the matrix.* Takes a single argument. Returns the transpose of the argument. The two forms TRANSPOS(M) and T(M) are equivalent.

TRUNC(M)   *Truncation of elements to integers.* Takes a single argument. Returns a matrix having the same dimensions as the argument, whose elements equal the corresponding elements of the argument truncated to integers.

UNIFORM(S1,S2)   *Uniformly distributed pseudo-random numbers between 0 and 1.* Takes two scalars as arguments. Returns a matrix with the number of rows specified by the first argument and the number of columns specified by the second argument, containing pseudo-random numbers uniformly distributed between 0 and 1.

The CALL Statement

Closely related to the MATRIX functions are the MATRIX procedures, which are invoked with the CALL statement. Procedures accept arguments just as functions do, in parentheses and separated by commas, and return their result in one or more of the arguments as noted in the individual descriptions below. They are implemented as procedures rather than as functions so that they can return more than one value, or (in the case of SETDIAG) so that they can modify a matrix without making a copy of it.

EIGEN(M,name1,name2)   *Eigenvectors and eigenvalues of a symmetric matrix.* Takes three arguments: a symmetric matrix and two valid variable names to which the results are assigned. If *M* is a symmetric matrix, then the statement *CALL EIGEN(M, A, B)* will assign to *A* a matrix having the same dimensions as *M*, containing the eigenvectors of *M* as its columns, and will assign to *B* a column vector having as many rows as *M*, containing the eigenvalues of *M* in descending numerical order. The eigenvectors in *A* are ordered to correspond with the eigenvalues in *B*: thus the first column corresponds to the largest eigenvalue, the second to the second largest, and so on.

SETDIAG(M,V) — *Set the main diagonal of a matrix.* Takes two arguments, a matrix and a vector. Elements on the main diagonal of *M* are set equal to the corresponding elements of *V*. If *V* is a scalar, all the diagonal elements are set equal to that scalar. Otherwise, if *V* has fewer elements than the main diagonal of *M*, remaining elements on the main diagonal are unchanged. If *V* has more elements than are needed, the extra elements are not used. See also the MDIAG matrix function.

SVD(M,name1,name2,name3) — *Singular value decomposition of a matrix.* Takes four arguments: a matrix and three valid variable names to which the results are assigned. If *M* is a matrix, then the statement *CALL SVD(M,U,Q,V)* will assign to *Q* a diagonal matrix of the same dimensions as *M*, and to *U* and *V* unitary matrices (matrices whose inverses equal their transposes) of appropriate dimensions, such that $M = U*Q*T(V)$, where *T* is the transpose function defined above. The singular values of *M* are in the main diagonal of *Q*.

The PRINT Statement

The PRINT statement displays matrices or matrix expressions. Its syntax is:

```
PRINT [matrix expression]

    [/FORMAT="format descriptor"]

    [/TITLE="title"]

    [/SPACE=[{NEWPAGE}]
            {lines  }

    [{/RLABELS=list of quoted names}]
     {/RNAMES=vector of names      }

    [{/CLABELS=list of quoted names}]
     {/CNAMES=vector of names      }
```

Matrix expression is a single MATRIX variable name or a matrix expression to be displayed. If present, it must precede any of the other specifications of the PRINT statement.

• If no matrix name or expression appears on a PRINT statement, no data will be displayed. The /TITLE and /SPACE specifications will be honored, however.

• Any matrix expression other than a single matrix name, a matrix raised to a power, or a matrix function (with its arguments in parentheses) should be enclosed in parentheses. *PRINT A* or *PRINT INV(A)* or even *PRINT B**DET(T(C)*D)* is legal, but *PRINT A+B* must be written as *PRINT (A+B)*.

• Constant expressions are allowed. (A MATRIX program can consist entirely of PRINT statements, with no MATRIX variables defined.)

FORMAT lets you specify a single format descriptor for display of the matrix data.

- All matrix elements are displayed with the same format.
- You can use any printable numeric format (for numeric matrices) or string format (for string matrices) as defined in FORMATS.
- The MATRIX processor will choose a suitable numeric format if you omit the FORMAT specification, but a string format such as A8 is essential when displaying a matrix containing string data.
- String values exceeding the width of a string format are truncated.
- See The Scaling Factor in PRINT Displays, below, for default formatting of matrices containing large or small values.

TITLE lets you specify a title for the matrix displayed. The title must be enclosed in quotation marks or apostrophes. If it exceeds the maximum display width, it is truncated. The slash preceding TITLE is required, even if the title specification is the only thing on the PRINT statement. If you omit the TITLE specification, the matrix name or expression from the PRINT statement is used as a default title.

SPACE lets you control output spacing before the title and data are displayed. The NEWPAGE keyword requests a page eject before printing. The lines specification lets you indicate a (positive) number of lines to skip before displaying the title. The slash preceding SPACE is required, even if the space specification is the only thing on the PRINT statement.

RLABELS lets you supply row labels for the matrix. The labels must be separated by commas. They may be individually enclosed in quotation marks or apostrophes, and must be so enclosed if they contain imbedded commas or if you wish to preserve lowercase letters. If too many names are supplied, the extras are ignored. If not enough names are supplied, the last rows remain unlabeled.

RNAMES lets you supply the name of a vector or a vector expression containing row labels for the matrix. Either a row vector or a column vector can be used, but the vector must contain string data. If too many names are supplied, the extras are ignored. If not enough names are supplied, the last rows remain unlabeled.

CLABELS lets you supply column labels for the matrix. The labels must be separated by commas. They may be individually enclosed in quotation marks or apostrophes, and must be so enclosed if they contain imbedded commas or if you wish to preserve lowercase letters. If too many names are supplied, the extras are ignored. If not enough names are supplied, the last columns remain unlabeled.

CNAMES lets you supply the name of a vector or a vector expression containing column labels for the matrix. Either a row vector or a column vector can be used, but the vector must contain string data. If too many names are supplied, the extras are ignored. If not enough names are supplied, the last columns remain unlabeled.

The Scaling Factor in PRINT Displays

When a matrix contains very large or very small numbers, it may be necessary to use scientific notation to display the data. If you do not specify a display format, the MATRIX processor chooses a power-of-ten multiplier that will allow the largest value to be displayed, and displays this multiplier on a heading line before the data. The multiplier is not repeated for each element in the matrix. The displayed values, multiplied by the power of ten that is indicated in the heading, equal the actual values (possibly rounded).

- Values that are very small, relative to the multiplier, are displayed as zero.
- If you explicitly specify a scientific-notation format (/FORMAT=E$w.d$), each matrix element is displayed using that format. This permits you to display very large and very small numbers in the same matrix without losing precision.

Example.

```
COMPUTE M = {.0000000001357, 2.468, 3690000000}.
PRINT M /TITLE "Default format".
PRINT M /FORMAT "E13" /TITLE "Explicit exponential format".
```

```
Default format
  10 ** 9   X
    .000000000    .000000002   3.690000000

Explicit exponential format
  1.3570000E-10 2.4680000E+00 3.6900000E+09
```

- The default format uses the same multiplier, 10^9 in this case, for each element of the matrix. This results in the first element being displayed as 0, and the second being rounded to one significant digit.
- An explicitly-specified exponential format allows each element to be displayed with full precision.

MATRIX Control Structures

The matrix language includes two structures that allow you to alter the flow of control within a MATRIX program.

- The DO IF statement tests a logical expression to determine whether one or more subsequent MATRIX statements should be executed.
- The LOOP statement defines the beginning of a block of MATRIX statements that should be executed repeatedly, until a termination criterion is satisfied or a BREAK statement is executed.

These statements closely resemble the DO IF and LOOP commands in the SPSS transformation language. In particular, these structures can be nested within one another as deeply as the available memory allows.

DO IF Structures

A DO IF structure in a MATRIX program begins with the DO IF statement and ends with the END IF statement. It can contain one or more ELSE IF statements, and it can contain a single ELSE statement. These statements affect the flow of control exactly as the analogous commands affect an SPSS transformation program, except that missing-value considerations do not arise in a MATRIX program.

- The DO IF statement marks the beginning of the structure and the END IF statement marks its end.
- The ELSE IF statement is optional and can be repeated as many times as desired within the structure.
- The ELSE statement is optional. It can be used only once and must follow any ELSE IF statements.
- The END IF statement must follow any ELSE IF or ELSE statements.
- The DO IF and ELSE IF statements must contain a logical expression, normally one involving the relational operators EQ, GT, and so on, or their symbolic equivalents. However, the matrix language allows any expression that evaluates to a scalar to be used as the logical expression. Scalars greater than 0 are considered true, and scalars less than or equal to zero are considered false.

A DO IF structure affects the flow of control within a matrix program as follows:

- If the logical expression on the DO IF statement is true, the statements immediately following the DO IF are executed up to the next ELSE IF or ELSE in the structure. Control then passes to the first statement following the END IF for that structure.
- If the expression on the DO IF statement is false, control passes to the first ELSE IF, where the logical expression is evaluated. If this expression is true, statements following the ELSE IF are executed up to the next ELSE IF or ELSE statement, and control passes to the first statement following the END IF for that structure.
- If the expressions on the DO IF and the first ELSE IF statements are both false, control passes to the next ELSE IF, where that logical expression is evaluated. If none of the expressions are true on any of the ELSE IF statements, statements following the ELSE statement are executed and control falls out of the structure.
- If none of the expressions on the DO IF statement or the ELSE IF statements are true and there is no ELSE statement, then a case falls through the entire structure with no change.

LOOP Structures

A LOOP structure in a MATRIX program begins with the LOOP statement and ends with the END LOOP statement. Statements between LOOP and END LOOP are executed repeatedly until one of the following three conditions is met:

1   A logical expression on an IF clause of the LOOP or END LOOP statement is evaluated as false.

2   An index variable used on the LOOP statement passes beyond its terminal value.

3   A BREAK statement is executed within the loop structure (but outside of any nested loop structures).

LOOP Statement. The LOOP statement itself has the form

```
LOOP [index variable=
          initial value TO terminal value [BY increment]]
     [IF (logical expression)]
```

Both the index clause and the IF clause are optional. If both are present, the index clause must appear first. An index clause on a LOOP statement takes the form

```
index-variable = initial-value TO terminal-value [BY increment]
```

Here *index-variable must be a valid MATRIX variable name. Initial-value, terminal-value,* and (if present) *increment* must be scalars or MATRIX expressions evaluating to scalars. If they are not integers, they are truncated to integers before use. If BY and the increment are absent, an increment of 1 is used.

An index clause on a LOOP statement creates the scalar whose name appears as index-variable on the index clause, and assigns it a value of initial-value. Each time through the loop the scalar is incremented by increment and tested against the terminal-value. When it is greater than terminal-value (for positive increments) or less than terminal-value (for negative increments), control passes to the statement after the END LOOP statement.

An IF clause on a LOOP statement takes the form

```
IF (logical expression)
```

The logical expression is evaluated before each iteration of the loop structure. If it is false, the loop terminates and control passes to the statement after END LOOP. As in the DO IF structure, the logical expression is actually evaluated as a scalar, with positive values being treated as true and zero or negative values as false.

END LOOP Statement. The END LOOP statement marks the end of the loop structure. It has the form:

```
END LOOP [IF (logical expression)]
```

When an IF clause is present on an END LOOP statement, the logical expression is evaluated after each iteration of the loop structure. If it is true, the loop terminates and control passes to the statement following the END LOOP statement.

BREAK Statement. The BREAK statement within a loop structure transfers control immediately to the statement following the (next) END LOOP statement. It is normally placed within a DO IF structure inside the LOOP structure:

```
LOOP LOCATION = 1 TO NROW(VEC).
+   DO IF (VEC(LOCATION) = TARGET).
+      BREAK.
+   END IF
END LOOP.
```

• This loop searches for the (first) location of a specific value TARGET in a vector VEC.

• The DO IF statement checks whether the vector element indexed by LOCATION equals the target.

• If so, the BREAK statement transfers control out of the loop, leaving LOCATION as the index of TARGET in VEC.

The READ Statement: Reading Character Data

The READ statement reads data into a matrix or sub-matrix from a character-format file, that is, a file containing ordinary numbers or words in readable form. The file can contain values in freefield or fixed column format. The data can appear in any of the field formats supported by DATA LIST. More than one matrix can be read from a single input record, by rereading the record.

The format for the READ statement is:

```
READ  variable reference

    [/FILE = file reference]

     /FIELD = startcol TO endcol [BY width]

    [/SIZE = size expression]

    [/MODE = {RECTANGULAR}]
             {SYMMETRIC  }

    [/REREAD]

    [/FORMAT = format descriptor]
```

Variable-reference Specification

The *variable reference* on the READ statement is a MATRIX variable name, with or without indexes. If it is simply a variable name, READ creates that MATRIX variable.

• You must specify its size with the SIZE specification.
• The matrix need not exist when READ is executed.
• If the matrix already exists, it is replaced by the matrix read from the file.

On the other hand, if *variable reference* is an indexed name such as M(:,I), the MATRIX variable named must already exist.

• You can define any submatrix with indexes. (To define an entire existing matrix, specify *M(:,:)*.)
• Since the indexes along with the size of the existing matrix completely specify the size of the submatrix, you can omit the SIZE specification. If you include a SIZE specification, however, its value must match the size of the specified submatrix.

FILE Specification

The *file reference* following the keyword FILE designates the character file containing the data. It can be an actual filename in apostrophes or quotation marks, or a file handle defined on a FILE HANDLE command that preceded the MATRIX program.

• The filename or handle must specify an existing file containing character data, not an SPSS system file or a specially formatted file of another kind such as a spreadsheet file.

The FILE specification is required on the first READ statement in a MATRIX program (first in order of appearance, not necessarily in order of execution). If you omit the FILE specification from a later READ statement, the statement uses the last file (in order of appearance) named on a READ statement in the same MATRIX program.

FIELD Specification

The FIELD specification specifies which positions of a fixed-format record contain the data for matrix elements.

• The FIELD specification is required. Its form is:
```
FIELD = startcol TO endcol [BY width]
```
• *Startcol* is the number of the leftmost column of the area.
• *Endcol* is the number of the rightmost column of the area.

Both *startcol* and *endcol* are required, and both must be constants. For example,

```
FIELD = 9 TO 72
```

specifies that values to be read appear between columns 9 and 72 (inclusive) of each input record.

- The BY clause, if present, indicates that each value appears within a fixed set of columns on the input record; that is, one value is separated from the next by its column position rather than by a space or comma. *Width* is the width of the area designated for each value. For example,

```
FIELD = 1 TO 80 BY 10
```

indicates that there are eight possible values per record and that one will appear between columns 1 and 10 (inclusive), another between columns 11 and 20, and so on up to columns 71-80. The value in the BY clause must evenly divide the length of the field. That is, *endcol* − *startcol* + 1 must be a multiple of *width*.

You can use the FORMAT specification (see below) to supply the same information as the BY clause. If you omit the BY clause from the FIELD specification and you omit the FORMAT specification, READ assumes that values are separated by blanks or commas within the designated field.

SIZE Specification

The SIZE specification is a matrix expression that, when evaluated, specifies the size of the matrix to be read.

- The expression should evaluate to a two-element row or column vector. The first element designates the number of rows in the matrix to be read; the second gives the number of columns.
- Values of the SIZE specification are truncated to integers if necessary.
- The *size expression* may be a constant, like {5;5}, or a MATRIX variable name, like READSIZE, or any valid expression, such as INFO(1,:) or {4,6}.
- If you use a scalar as the size expression, a column vector containing that number of rows is read. Thus SIZE=1 reads a scalar, and SIZE=3 reads a 3 × 1 column vector.

You must include a SIZE specification whenever you name an entire matrix (rather than a submatrix) in the READ statement. If you specify a submatrix, the SIZE specification is optional; but if it is included, it must agree with the size of the specified submatrix.

MODE Specification

If you specify MODE = SYMMETRIC, the READ statement actually reads only matrix elements on and below the main diagonal, setting the elements above the diagonal equal to the corresponding symmetric elements below the diagonal.

- The MATRIX processor first checks that the number of rows and the number of columns are the same.
- Each row is read beginning on a new record, although it may span more than one record. Only a single value is read from the first record; two values are read from the second record; and so on.

MODE = RECTANGULAR indicates the matrix is completely represented in the file. Each row begins on a new record and all entries in that row are present on that and (possibly) succeeding records.

- If you omit the MODE specification, the default is MODE = RECTANGULAR.

REREAD Specification

The REREAD specification indicates that the current READ statement should begin reading with the last record read by a previous READ statement.

- REREAD has no further specifications.
- REREAD cannot be used on the first READ statement to read from a file.
- If you omit REREAD, the first record read by the current READ statement is the record following the last record read by the previous READ statement.

- If the end of the file is encountered during a READ operation (that is, some elements could be read, but not enough to satisfy the SIZE value), a warning message is displayed, and the contents of the unread elements of the matrix are unpredictable.

- The REREAD specification is ignored on the (first) READ statement following a call to the EOF function for the same file.

FORMAT Specification

Use the FORMAT specification to specify how the MATRIX processor should interpret the input data. *Format descriptor* can be any valid SPSS data format descriptor, such as F6, E12.2, or A6, or it can be just a type code, for example, F, E, or A. (See FORMATS for valid format descriptors.)

- If you omit the FORMAT specification, FORMAT=F is assumed.

- You can specify the width of fixed-size data fields either with a FORMAT specification or with a BY clause in a FIELD specification. You can include it in both places only if you specify the same value.

- If you do not include either a FORMAT or a FIELD width specification, READ expects values separated by blanks or commas.

- If the format descriptor starts with a digit, such as 10F8, it must be enclosed in apostrophes or quotation marks.

- Only one format descriptor can be specified. A specification such as FORMAT = '5F2.0 3F3.0 F2.0' is invalid.

The WRITE Statement: Writing Character Data

The WRITE statement writes the value of a matrix expression to a named external file. The format of the WRITE statement is:

```
WRITE   matrix expression

   [/OUTFILE = file reference]

    /FIELD = startcol TO endcol [BY width]

   [/MODE = {RECTANGULAR}]
           {TRIANGULAR }

   [/HOLD]

   [/FORMAT = format descriptor]
```

Matrix-expression Specification

The WRITE statement writes the elements of a single matrix expression to a file. The *matrix expression* is any MATRIX language expression which evaluates to the value(s) to be written.

- Any matrix expression other than a single matrix name, a matrix raised to a power, or a matrix function (with its arguments in parentheses) should be enclosed in parentheses. *WRITE A* or *WRITE INV(A)* or even *WRITE B**DET(T(C)*D)* is legal, but *WRITE A+B* must be written as *WRITE (A+B)*.

OUTFILE Specification

The *file reference* following the keyword OUTFILE designates the character file containing to which the matrix expression should be written. It can be an actual filename in apostrophes or quotation marks, or a file handle defined on a FILE HANDLE command that preceded the MATRIX program. The filename or file handle must specify a valid file specification.

- The OUTFILE specification is required on the first WRITE statement in a MATRIX program (first in order of appearance, not necessarily in order of execution).

- If you omit the OUTFILE specification from a later WRITE statement, the statement uses the last file (in order of appearance) named on a WRITE statement in the same MATRIX program.

FIELD Specification

The FIELD specification specifies the positions of a fixed-format record to which the data should be written.

• The FIELD specification is required.

Its form is:

```
FIELD = startcol TO endcol [BY width]
```

• *Startcol* is the number of the leftmost column of the area.

• *Endcol* is the number of the rightmost column of the area.

Both *startcol* and *endcol* are required, and both must be constants. For example,

```
FIELD = 9 TO 72
```

specifies that values should be written between columns 9 and 72 (inclusive) of each output record.

• The BY clause, if present, indicates how many characters should be allocated to the output value of a single matrix element. The value *width* is the width of the area designated for each value. For example,

```
FIELD = 1 TO 80 BY 10
```

indicates that up to eight values should be written per record, and that one should go between columns 1 and 10 (inclusive), another between columns 11 and 20, and so on up to columns 71-80. The value in the BY clause must evenly divide the length of the field. That is, *endcol* − *startcol* + 1 must be a multiple of *width*.

You can use the FORMAT specification (see below) to supply the same information as the BY clause. If you omit the BY clause from the FIELD specification and you omit the FORMAT specification, WRITE uses free format, separating matrix elements by single blank spaces.

MODE Specification

MODE = TRIANGULAR indicates that only the lower triangular entries (and the main diagonal) are to be written to the file. This mode may save file space.

• Each row begins a new record and may span more than one record.

• A matrix written this way may be read with MODE = SYMMETRIC.

• A matrix written with MODE = TRIANGULAR must be square, but it need not be symmetric. If it is not, values in the upper triangle are not written.

MODE = RECTANGULAR indicates that the entire matrix is to be written. Each row starts a new record, and all the values in that row are present in that and (possibly) subsequent records.

• If the MODE specification is omitted, MODE = RECTANGULAR is assumed.

HOLD Specification

The HOLD specification causes the last line written by the current WRITE statement to be held so that the next WRITE to that file will write on the same line. Use HOLD to write more than one matrix on a line.

FORMAT Specification

Use the FORMAT specification to indicate how the internal (binary) values of matrix elements should be converted to character format for output.

• The *format descriptor* is any valid SPSS data format description, such as F6, E12.2, or A6, or just a format type code, like F, E, or A. It specifies how the written data are encoded and, if a width is specified, how wide the fields containing the data are. (See FORMATS for valid format descriptors.)

• If you omit the FORMAT specification, FORMAT=F is assumed.

• The data field widths may be specified either here or after BY in the FIELD specification. You may specify the width in both places only if you give the same value.

• An additional way of specifying the width is to supply a repetition factor without a width (for example, 10F, 5COMMA, or 3E). The field width is then calculated by dividing the width of the whole output area on the FIELD specification by the repetition factor. A format descriptor starting with a digit (for the repetition factor) must be enclosed in quotes.

- If the field width is not specified in any of these ways, then the freefield format is used: matrix values are written separated by one blank, and each value occupies as many positions as necessary to avoid the loss of precision.

- Each row of the matrix is written starting with a new output record.

- Only one format descriptor can be specified. A specification such as FORMAT= '5F2.0 3F3.0 F2.0' is invalid.

The GET Statement: Reading SPSS System Files

Use the GET statement to read an SPSS system file, which can be the active system file. GET has the form:

```
GET variable reference

    [/FILE = {file reference}]
            {*             }

    [/VARIABLES = variable list]

    [/NAMES = names vector]

    [/MISSING = {ACCEPT}]
               {OMIT  }
               {value }

    [/SYSMIS = {OMIT }]
              {value}
```

Variable-reference Specification

The *variable reference* on the GET statement is a MATRIX variable name, with or without indexes. If it is simply a variable name, GET creates that MATRIX variable. Its size is determined by the amount of data read from the system file. The matrix need not exist when READ is executed. If the matrix already exists, it is replaced by the matrix read from the system file.

On the other hand, if *variable reference* is an indexed name such as M(:,I), the MATRIX variable named must already exist. The indexes along with the size of the existing matrix specify completely the size of the submatrix, which must agree with the dimensions of the data read from the system file.

FILE Specification

Use the FILE specification to designate the file containing the SPSS system file to be read. Use an asterisk, or simply omit the FILE specification, to designate the current active system file.

- The *file reference* can be either a filename enclosed in apostrophes or quotation marks, or a file handle defined on a FILE HANDLE command that preceded the MATRIX program.

- If you omit the FILE specification, the current active system file is used.

- *For command files executed through your operating system:* If a SPLIT FILE command preceded the MATRIX program, then a GET statement that references the SPSS active system file will read a single split-file group of cases.

- *For commands run within SPSS:* A GET statement that references the active system file is not allowed in a MATRIX program that follows a SPLIT FILE command.

VARIABLES Specification

Use the VARIABLES specification to specify a list of variable names to be read from the SPSS system file.

- The *variable list* is entered much the same as in other SPSS procedures except that commas must separate variable names.

- The *variable list* can consist of the keyword ALL to get all the variables in the SPSS system file.

- If the VARIABLES specification is omitted, all variables are included by default.

- All variables read from the system file should be numeric. If a string variable is specified, a warning message is issued and the string variable is skipped.

Example.

```
GET M /VARIABLES = AGE, RESIDE, INCOME TO HEALTH.
```

- The variables AGE, RESIDE, and INCOME TO HEALTH from the SPSS active system file will form the columns of the matrix M.
- As the example shows, you can use the TO convention in the VARIABLES specification.

NAMES Specification The optional NAMES specification gives a vector name as a location to store the variable names from the system file.

- If you omit the NAMES specification, the variable names are not available to the MATRIX procedure.
- In place of a vector name, you can use a matrix expression that evaluates to a vector, such as $A(N+1,:)$.

MISSING Specification Use the MISSING specification to indicate how missing values declared for the system file should be handled.

- The MISSING specification is required if the system file contains missing values for any variable being read.
- If you omit the MISSING specification and a missing value is encountered for a variable being read, the MATRIX procedure will display an error message and not execute the GET statement.

The following keywords are accepted on the MISSING specification. There is no default.

ACCEPT *Specifies that a value is to be accepted for entry even though it may be designated as a user-missing value.* The system missing value is never accepted for entry. (See SYSMIS Specification, below.)

OMIT *Skips an entire observation when a variable with a missing value is encountered.*

value *Recodes all missing values encountered (including the system missing value) to the specified value.* The replacement value can be any numeric constant, since GET accepts only numeric variables.

SYSMIS Specification Use the SYSMIS specification to indicate how system-missing values should be handled when you have specified MISSING=ACCEPT.

- The SYSMIS specification is ignored unless MISSING=ACCEPT is specified.
- If you omit the SYSMIS specification but specify MISSING=ACCEPT, and a system-missing value is encountered for a variable being read, the MATRIX procedure will display an error message and not execute the GET statement.

The following keywords are accepted on the SYSMIS specification. There is no default.

OMIT *Skips an entire observation when a variable with a system-missing value is encountered.*

value *Recodes all system-missing values encountered to the specified value.* The replacement value can be any numeric constant.

Example.

```
GET SCORES
   /VARIABLES = TEST1,TEST2,TEST3
   /NAMES = VARNAMES
   /MISSING = ACCEPT
   /SYSMIS = -1.0.
```

- A matrix named SCORES is read from the SPSS active system file.

- The variables TEST1, TEST2, and TEST3 form the columns of the matrix, while the cases in the active system file form the rows.

- A vector named VARNAMES is created whose three elements contain the variable names TEST1, TEST2, and TEST3.

- User-missing values defined in the active system file are accepted into the matrix SCORES.

- System-missing values in the active system file are converted to the value −1 in the matrix SCORES.

The SAVE Statement: Writing SPSS System Files

Use the SAVE statement to write matrices to an SPSS system file, or to create or replace the current SPSS active system file. The statement has the form:

```
SAVE matrix expression

[/OUTFILE = {file reference}]
            {*             }

[/VARIABLES = variable list]

[/NAMES = names vector]

[/STRINGS = variable list]
```

Matrix-expression Specification

The SAVE statement writes the elements of a single matrix expression to an SPSS system file. The rows of the matrix expression become cases, and the columns become variables. The *matrix expression* following the keyword SAVE is any matrix language expression that evaluates to the value(s) to be written as a system file.

- Any matrix expression other than a single matrix name, a matrix raised to a power, or a matrix function (with its arguments in parentheses) should be enclosed in parentheses. *SAVE A* or *SAVE INV(A)* or even *SAVE B**DET(T(C)*D)* is legal, but *SAVE A+B* must be written as *SAVE (A+B)*.

OUTFILE Specification

The *file reference* following the keyword OUTFILE designates the SPSS system file to which the matrix expression should be written. It can be an asterisk, an actual filename in apostrophes or quotation marks, or a file handle defined on a FILE HANDLE command that preceded the MATRIX program. The filename or handle must specify a valid file specification.

- To save a matrix expression as the active system file (replacing any active system file created before the matrix program), specify OUTFILE=*. If there is no active system file, one will be created; if there is one, it will be replaced with the saved matrix.

- The OUTFILE specification is required on the first SAVE statement in a MATRIX program (first in order of appearance, not necessarily in order of execution). If you omit the OUTFILE specification from a later SAVE statement, the statement uses the last file (in order of appearance) named on a SAVE statement in the same MATRIX program.

- If more than one SAVE statement writes to the active system file in a single MATRIX program, the dictionary of the new active system file is written on the basis of the information given by the first such SAVE. All the subsequently saved matrices are appended to the new active system file as additional cases. If the number of columns differs, an error occurs.

- *For command files executed through your operating system:* The SAVE statement creates a new system file at the end of the MATRIX program's execution, so any attempt to GET the system file obtains the original system file, if any.

- *For commands run within SPSS:* SAVE creates a new system file immediately, but the file remains open, so you cannot GET it until after the END MATRIX statement.

VARIABLES Specification You can provide variable names for the system file with the VARIABLES specification. The *variable list* is a list of valid SPSS variable names separated by commas. You can use the TO convention, as shown below.

• You can also use the NAMES specification, discussed below, to provide variable names.

Example.
```
SAVE {A,B,X,Y} /OUTFILE=*
  /VARIABLES = A,B,X1 TO X50,Y1,Y2.
```

• The matrix expression on the SAVE statement constructs a matrix from two column vectors A and B, and two matrices X and Y. All four MATRIX variables must have the same number of rows so that this matrix construction will be valid.

• The VARIABLES specification provides descriptive names so that the SPSS variable names in the new active system file will resemble the names used in the MATRIX program.

NAMES Specification As an alternative to the explicit list in the VARIABLES specification, you can specify a name list with a matrix expression that evaluates to a vector containing character strings. The elements of this vector are used as names for the variables.

• The NAMES specification on SAVE is designed to complement the NAMES specification on the GET statement. Names extracted from a system file can be used in a new system file by specifying the same vector name on both NAMES specifications.

• If you specify both VARIABLES and NAMES, a warning message is displayed and the VARIABLES specification is used.

• If you omit both the VARIABLES and NAMES specifications, or if you do not specify names for all columns of the matrix, the MATRIX procedure creates default names. The names have the form COLn, where *n* is the column number.

STRINGS Specification The STRINGS specification lets you provide the names of variables that contain short-string data, rather than numeric data.

• By default, all variables are assumed to be numeric.

• The *variable-list* specification following STRINGS consists of a list of SPSS variable names separated by commas. The names must be among those used by SAVE.

The MGET Statement: Reading SPSS Matrix System Files Use MGET to read an SPSS matrix-format system file. MGET puts the data it reads into separate MATRIX variables. It also names these new variables automatically. MGET has the form:

```
MGET [ [/] FILE = file reference]

    [/TYPE = {COV    }]
            {CORR   }
            {MEAN   }
            {STDDEV }
            {N      }
            {COUNT  }
```

Since MGET assigns names to the matrices that it reads, you do not provide a matrix name on the MGET statement.

FILE Specification The *file reference* designates an SPSS matrix-format system file to read. (See MATRIX DATA for a discussion of matrix-format system files.) To designate the current active system file (if it is a matrix-format system file), use an asterisk, or simply omit the FILE specification.

- The *file reference* can be either a filename enclosed in apostrophes or quotation marks, or a file handle defined on a FILE HANDLE command that preceded the MATRIX program.

- If you omit the FILE specification, the current active system file is used.

TYPE Specification

The TYPE specification lets you select the rowtype(s) to read.

- By default, records of all rowtypes are read.

- If the matrix-format system file does not contain rows of the requested type, an error occurs.

Valid keywords on the TYPE specification are:

COV   *A matrix of covariances.*
CORR   *A matrix of correlation coefficients.*
MEAN   *A vector of means.*
STDDEV *A vector of standard deviations.*
N   *A vector of numbers of cases.*
COUNT *A vector of counts.*

Names of MATRIX Variables from MGET

The MGET statement automatically creates MATRIX variable names for the matrices that it reads. The first two characters of the name identify the row type:

CV *A covariance matrix (rowtype COV).*
CR *A correlation matrix (rowtype CORR).*
MN *A vector of means (rowtype MEAN).*
SD *A vector of standard deviations (rowtype STDDEV).*
NC *A vector of numbers of cases (rowtype N).*
CN *A vector of counts (rowtype COUNT).*

If there are no cells and no SPLIT FILE groups, these two characters constitute the name. Otherwise, characters 3–5 of the variable name identify the cell number or the split-group number. If there are both cells and split groups, characters 3–5 identify the cell, and characters 6–8 identify the split group.

- Cell identifiers consists of the letter *F* and a two-digit cell number.

- Split-group identifiers consist of the letter *S* and a two-digit split-group number.

After the name is constructed as described above, any leading zeros are removed from the cell number and the split-group number.

- The maximum number of split-file groups that can be read is 99.

- The maximum number of cells that can be read is 99.

Examples of the variable names that MGET constructs are CRF12S21, CVF2S1, MNF3, SDS2, NC, CNF2S99.

- All new variables created by MGET are reported to a user.

- If a MATRIX variable already exists with the same name that MGET chose for a new variable, the new variable is not created, and a warning is issued. (The RELEASE statement can be used to get rid of a variable. A COMPUTE statement followed by RELEASE can be used to change the name of an existing MATRIX variable.)

- The same matrix-format SPSS system file can be read more than once.

- MGET ignores the SPLIT FILE command in SPSS when reading the active system file. It does honor the split-file groups that were in effect when the matrix-format system file was created, as noted above.

The MSAVE Statement: Writing SPSS Matrix System Files

The MSAVE statement writes matrix expressions to an SPSS matrix-format system file that can be used as matrix input to other SPSS procedures. (See MATRIX DATA for discussion of matrix-format system files.)

- Only one matrix-format system file can be saved in a single MATRIX program.
- Each MSAVE statement writes records of a single rowtype. Therefore several MSAVE statements will normally be required to write a complete matrix-format system file.
- Most specifications are retained from one MSAVE statement to the next, so that it is not necessary to repeat the same specifications on a series of MSAVE statements. The exception is the FACTOR specification, as noted below.

Example. If the MATRIX variables *M, S,* and *C* have been calculated to contain, respectively, vectors of means and standard deviations and a matrix of correlation coefficients, then the following sequence of MATRIX statements will create an SPSS matrix-format system file suitable for use in a procedure such as FACTOR.

```
MSAVE M /TYPE=MEAN /OUTFILE=CORRMAT /VARIABLES=V1 TO V8.
MSAVE S /TYPE STDDEV.
MSAVE MAKE(1,8,24) /TYPE N.
MSAVE C /TYPE CORR.
```

- The first MSAVE statement saves *M* as a vector of means. This statement specifies OUTFILE, a previously defined file handle, and VARIABLES, a list of variable names to be used in the SPSS system file.
- The second MSAVE statement saves *S* as a vector of standard deviations. Note that the OUTFILE and VARIABLES specifications do not have to be repeated.
- The third MSAVE statement saves a vector of case counts. The MATRIX function MAKE constructs an 8-element vector with values equal to the case count (24 in this example).
- The last MSAVE statement saves *C,* a 8×8 matrix, as the correlation matrix.

An MSAVE statement has the form:

```
MSAVE matrix expression

        /TYPE = {COV   }
                {CORR  }
                {MEAN  }
                {STDDEV}
                {N     }
                {COUNT }


        [/OUTFILE = {file reference}]
                    {*             }


        [/VARIABLES = variable list]


        [/SNAMES = variable list]


        [/SPLIT = split vector]


        [/FNAMES = variable list]


        [/FACTOR = factor vector]
```

Matrix-expression Specification

An MSAVE statement writes the elements of a single matrix expression to an SPSS matrix-format system file as a logical record of the type specified by TYPE (below). The *matrix expression* following the keyword SAVE is any MATRIX language expression that evaluates to the value(s) to be written to the matrix-format system file.

- Any matrix expression other than a single matrix name, a matrix raised to a power, or a matrix function (with its arguments in parentheses) should be enclosed in parentheses. Thus MSAVE N * WT must be written MSAVE (N * WT).

TYPE Specification

The TYPE specification lets you select the rowtype to write.

- Only a single rowtype can be written by any one MSAVE statement.

Valid keywords on the TYPE specification are:

COV   *A matrix of covariances.*

CORR   *A matrix of correlation coefficients.*

MEAN   *A vector of means.*

STDDEV   *A vector of standard deviations.*

N   *A vector of numbers of cases.*

COUNT   *A vector of counts.*

OUTFILE Specification

The *file reference* following the keyword OUTFILE designates the SPSS matrix-format system file containing to which the matrix expression should be written. It can be an asterisk, an actual filename in apostrophes or quotation marks, or a file handle defined on a FILE HANDLE command that preceded the MATRIX program. The filename or handle must specify a valid file specification.

• To save a matrix expression as the active system file (replacing any active system file created before the matrix program), specify OUTFILE=*.

• The OUTFILE specification is required on the first MSAVE statement in a MATRIX program.

• Since only one matrix-format system file can be written in a single MATRIX program, any OUTFILE specification on the second and later MSAVE statements in a MATRIX program must specify the same destination as that named on the first MSAVE statement.

VARIABLES Specification

You can provide variable names for the system file with the VARIABLES specification. The *variable list* is a list of valid SPSS variable names separated by commas. You can use the TO convention, as shown above.

• The VARIABLES specification names only the data variables in the matrix. Split-file variables and grouping or factor variables are named on the SNAMES and FNAMES specifications.

• The names in the VARIABLES specification become the values of the special variable named VARNAME_ in the matrix-format system file, for rowtypes of CORR and COV.

• You cannot specify the reserved names ROWTYPE_ and VARNAME_ on the VARIABLES specification.

• If you omit the VARIABLES specification, the default names COL1, COL2, ..., are used.

FNAMES Specification

To write an SPSS matrix-format system file with factor or group codes, you can use the FNAMES specification to provide variable names for the grouping or factor variables. (You also use the FACTOR specification, described below.)

• The *variable list* following the keyword FNAMES is a list of valid SPSS variable names, separated by commas.

• If you omit the FNAMES specification, the default names FAC1, FAC2, ..., are used.

FACTOR specification

To write an SPSS matrix-format system file with factor or group codes, you must use the FACTOR specification to provide a row matrix containing the values of each of the factors or group variables for the matrix expression being written by the current MSAVE statement.

• The *factor vector* must have the same number of columns as there are factors in the matrix system file being written. You can use a scalar when the groups are defined by a single variable. For example, FACTOR=1 indicates that the matrix data being written are for the value 1 of the factor variable.

• The values of the *factor vector* are written to the matrix-format system file as values of the factors in the file.

• To create a complete matrix-format system file with factors, you must execute an MSAVE statement for every combination of values of the factors or grouping variables, in other words for every group. (If split-file variables are also present, you must execute an MSAVE statement for every combination of factor codes within every combination of values of the split-file variables.)

Example.
```
MSAVE M11 /TYPE=MEAN /OUTFILE=CORRMAT /VARIABLES=V1 TO V8
   /FNAMES=SEX, GROUP /FACTOR={1,1}.
MSAVE S11 /TYPE STDDEV.
MSAVE MAKE(1,8,N(1,1)) /TYPE N.
MSAVE C11 /TYPE CORR.
MSAVE M12 /TYPE=MEAN /FACTOR={1,2}.
MSAVE S12 /TYPE STDDEV.
MSAVE MAKE(1,8,N(1,2)) /TYPE N.
MSAVE C12 /TYPE CORR.
MSAVE M21 /TYPE=MEAN /FACTOR={2,1}.
MSAVE S21 /TYPE STDDEV.
MSAVE MAKE(1,8,N(2,1)) /TYPE N.
MSAVE C21 /TYPE CORR.
MSAVE M22 /TYPE=MEAN /FACTOR={2,2}.
MSAVE S22 /TYPE STDDEV.
MSAVE MAKE(1,8,N(2,2)) /TYPE N.
MSAVE C22 /TYPE CORR.
```

• The first four MSAVE statements provide data for a group defined by the variables SEX and GROUP, with both factors having the value 1.

• The second, third, and fourth groups of four MSAVE statements provide the corresponding data for the other groups, in which SEX and GROUP respectively equal 1 and 2, 2 and 1, 2 and 2.

• Within each group of MSAVE statements, a suitable number-of-cases vector is created with the MATRIX function MAKE.

SNAMES Specification

To write an SPSS matrix-format system file with split-file groups, you can use the SNAMES specification to provide variable names for the split-file variables. (You also use the SPLIT specification, described below.)

• The *variable list* following the keyword SNAMES is a list of valid SPSS variable names, separated by commas.

• If you omit the SNAMES specification, the default names SPL1, SPL2, ..., are used.

SPLIT Specification

To write an SPSS matrix-format system file with split-file groups, you must use the SPLIT specification to provide a row matrix containing the values of each of the split-file variables for the matrix expression being written by the current MSAVE statement.

• The *split vector* must have the same number of columns as there are split-file variables in the matrix system file being written. You can use a scalar when there is only one split-file variable. For example, SPLIT=3 indicates that the matrix data being written are for the value 3 of the split-file variable.

• The values of the *split vector* are written to the matrix-format system file as values of the split-file variable(s).

• To create a complete matrix-format system file with split-file variables, you must execute the MSAVE statements for every combination of values of the split-file variables. (If factor variables are present, you must execute MSAVE statements for every combination of factor codes within every combination of values of the split-file variables.)

The DISPLAY Statement

The DISPLAY statement provides information on the MATRIX variables currently defined in a MATRIX program, and on usage of internal memory by the MATRIX processor. Its format is:

```
DISPLAY [{DICTIONARY}]
        {STATUS    }
```

DICTIONARY *A display showing, for each MATRIX variable currently defined, its name and its row and column dimensions.*

STATUS *A display showing the status and size of internal tables.* This display is intended as a debugging aid when writing large MATRIX programs that approach the memory limitations of your system.

If you enter the DISPLAY statement with no specifications, both DICTIONARY and STATUS information are displayed.

The RELEASE Statement

Use the RELEASE statement to release the work areas in memory assigned to MATRIX variables, after those variables are no longer needed. Its format is:

```
RELEASE variable list
```

- The *variable-list* is a list of currently defined matrix variable names, which must be separated by commas.

- The RELEASE statement discards the contents of the named matrix variables. Releasing a large matrix when it is no longer needed makes memory available for additional MATRIX variables.

- All MATRIX variables are released when the END MATRIX statement is encountered.

Macros Using the Matrix Language

Macro expansion (see MACRO) occurs before command lines are passed to the MATRIX processor. Therefore,

- Previously defined macro names can be used within a matrix program. If the macro name expands to one or more valid MATRIX statements, the MATRIX processor will execute those statements.

- Similarly, you can define an entire MATRIX program, including the MATRIX and END MATRIX commands, as a macro.

- You cannot define a macro within a MATRIX program, since MACRO is not a valid MATRIX statement.

Annotated Example

For a complete example with output, see Examples following the Command Reference.

References

Hadley, G. 1961. *Linear algebra.* Reading, Mass.: Addison-Wesley.
O'Nan, Michael. 1971. *Linear algebra.* New York: Harcourt Brace Jovanovich.

MATRIX DATA

```
MATRIX DATA VARIABLES=varlist    [/FILE= {INLINE**}]
                                         {file    }

[/FORMAT= [{LIST**}]   [{LOWER**}]   [{DIAGONAL**}]]
          {FREE  }     {UPPER  }     {NODIAGONAL}
                       {FULL   }

[/SPLIT= varlist]    [/FACTORS= varlist]

[/CELLS= number of cells]    [/N= sample size]

[/CONTENTS= [CORR**]   [COV]   [MAT]   [MSE]   [DFE]   [MEAN]

          [SD]   [PROX]   [STDDEV]   [N_SCALAR]   [N_VECTOR]   [N]

          [N_MATRIX]   [COUNT]]
```

**Default if the subcommand is omitted.

Example:
```
MATRIX DATA VARIABLES=ROWTYPE_ SAVINGS POP15 POP75 INCOME
GROWTH.
BEGIN DATA
MEAN 9.6710 35.0896 2.2930 1106.7784 3.7576
STDDEV 4.4804 9.1517 1.2907 990.8511 2.8699
N 50 50 50 50 50
CORR 1
CORR -.4555 1
CORR .3165 -.9085 1
CORR .2203 -.7562 .7870 1
CORR .3048 -.0478 .0253 -.1295  1
END DATA.
```

Overview

MATRIX DATA reads raw matrix materials and converts them to a matrix system file that can be read by SPSS procedures that handle matrix materials, such as FACTOR, REGRESSION, etc. The data can include various vector statistics (for example, means and standard deviations) as well as matrices.

MATRIX DATA is similar to a DATA LIST command: it defines variable names and their order in a raw data file. However, MATRIX DATA can read only data that conform to the general format of SPSS matrices.

Matrix Files

Like the matrix system files created by procedures, the file that MATRIX DATA defines contains the following variables in the indicated order. If the variables are in a different order in the raw data file, MATRIX DATA rearranges them automatically in the active system file.

- *Split-file variables.* These optional variables define the split files. There can be up to eight split variables, and they must have numeric values. Split-file variables will appear in the order in which they are specified on SPLIT.

- *ROWTYPE_.* ROWTYPE_ is a string variable with A8 format. Its values define the data type for each record. For example, it might identify a row of values as means, standard deviations, or correlation coefficients. Every matrix in SPSS has a ROWTYPE_ variable.

- *Factors.* There can be any number of factors. They occur only if the data include within-cell information, such as the within-cell means. The factors have the system-missing value on records that define pooled information. Factor variables appear in the order in which they are specified on FACTORS.

- *VARNAME_.* This is a string variable with A8 format. Its values correspond to the variables named on VARIABLES. Values for VARNAME_ are blank for records that define vector information, such as the mean and standard deviation. Every matrix in SPSS has a VARNAME_ variable. You never enter values for VARNAME_. MATRIX DATA automatically generates VARNAME_ and its values.

- *Continuous variables.* These are the variables to which the aggregated data pertain. There can be any number of them. Continuous variables appear in the order in which they are specified on VARIABLES.

Options	**Data Files.** You can define both inline data and data from an external file. **Data Format.** You can enter data in both LIST and FREE format. Matrices can be entered in upper or lower triangular format, with or without diagonal values. Matrices can also be entered in full rectangular format. **Variable Types.** You can enter split-file and factor variables. In addition, you can identify record types by including ROWTYPE_ values in the data, or defining ROWTYPE_ values on MATRIX DATA.

Basic Specification

The basic specification is VARIABLES and a list of variables. Additional specifications are required if the following are not true:

- *Data are inline.* If data are not inline, FILE is required to specify the data file.
- *Data are in lower-triangle format with diagonal values included.* If data are in any other format, FORMAT is required.
- *Data contain nothing but matrix coefficients.* If data contain other values, such as the mean and standard deviation, either variable ROWTYPE_ must be specified on VARIABLES and ROWTYPE_ values must be included in the data, or CONTENTS must be used to describe the data.
- *There are no split-file variables.* If the data include split-file variables, SPLIT is required.

Subcommand Order

- SPLIT and FACTORS, when used, must follow VARIABLES. Remaining subcommands can be used in any order.

Syntax Rules

- No commands can be specified between MATRIX DATA and BEGIN DATA— not even a VARIABLE LABELS or FORMATS command. Data transformations cannot be used until after MATRIX DATA is executed.
- Specifications on most MATRIX DATA subcommands depend on whether ROWTYPE_ is explicitly specified or implied on VARIABLES. Table 1 summarizes the status of each MATRIX DATA subcommand in relation to the ROWTYPE_ specification.
- MATRIX DATA does not allow format specifications for the matrix materials. The procedure assigns the formats shown in Table 2. To change data formats (or perform other transformations), execute MATRIX DATA and then assign new formats with the FORMATS, PRINT FORMATS, or WRITE FORMATS commands.

Format of the Raw Matrix Data File

- If LIST is in effect on the FORMAT subcommand, each scalar, vector, or row of a matrix begins on a new record, and the data are entered in freefield format, using blanks and commas as separators. Unlike LIST format with DATA LIST, a vector or row of the matrix can be continued on multiple records. The continuation records do not have a value for ROWTYPE_.
- ROWTYPE_ values can be enclosed in apostrophes or quotes.
- The order of the variables in the input data file must match the order in which they are specified on VARIABLES. However, this order does not have to correspond to the order of variables in the resulting SPSS matrix system file.
- The way records are entered for pooled vectors or matrices when factors are present depends upon whether ROWTYPE_ is explicit or implicit on the VARIABLES subcommand. For an explanation, see FACTOR Subcommand.
- MATRIX DATA recognizes plus and minus signs as field separators when they are not preceded by the letter "D" or the letter "E." This allows MATRIX DATA to read scientific notation and to read correlation matrices written by FORTRAN in F10.8 format. A plus sign preceded by a "D" or "E" is read as part of the number in scientific notation. A plus sign that is not preceded by a "D" or "E" is interpreted as a field separator.

Table 1 Subcommands in relation to ROWTYPE_

Subcommand	ROWTYPE_ implicit on VARIABLES	ROWTYPE_ explicit on VARIABLES
FILE	Defaults to INLINE	Defaults to INLINE
VARIABLES	Required	Required
FORMAT	Defaults to LOWER DIAG	Defaults to LOWER DIAG
SPLIT	Required if split files*	Required if split files
FACTORS	Required if factors	Required if factors
CELLS	Required if factors	Inapplicable
CONTENTS	Defaults to CORR	Optional
N	Optional	Optional

*If the data do not contain values for the split-file variables, this subcommand can specify a single variable that is not specified on the VARIABLES subcommand.

Table 2 Print and write formats for matrix variables

Variable type	Format
ROWTYPE_, VARNAME_	A8
Split-file variables	F4.0
Factors	F4.0
Continuous variables	F10.4

Operations

- MATRIX DATA defines and writes data in one step.
- MATRIX DATA clears the current active system file to create a new active system file.
- If ROWTYPE_ is not specified on VARIABLES, and if CONTENTS is not used, MATRIX DATA infers record types and issues warning messages to alert you to its major assumptions.
- With default format, data values, including the diagonal values, must be in the lower triangle of the matrix. If MATRIX DATA encounters values in the upper triangle, it issues a series of warnings stating that it will ignore extraneous text on the records.
- With default format, if any matrix rows span records in the data file, and if values are entered in the upper triangle, MATRIX DATA cannot form the matrix properly. If data contain values in the upper triangle, use the FORMAT subcommand.

Example

```
MATRIX DATA
     VARIABLES=ROWTYPE_ SAVINGS POP15 POP75 INCOME GROWTH.
BEGIN DATA
MEAN 9.6710 35.0896 2.2930 1106.7784 3.7576
STDDEV 4.4804 9.1517 1.2907 990.8511 2.8699
N 50 50 50 50 50
CORR 1
CORR -.4555 1
CORR .3165 -.9085 1
CORR .2203 -.7562 .7870 1
CORR .3048 -.0478 .0253 -.1295  1
END DATA.
```

- Variable ROWTYPE_ is specified on VARIABLES. ROWTYPE_ values are included in the data.
- No other specifications are required to define records.

Example
```
TITLE 'MATRIX DATA WITH PROCEDURE DISCRIMINANT'.

MATRIX DATA VARIABLES=WORLD ROWTYPE_ FOOD APPL SERVICE RENT
  /FACTOR=WORLD.
BEGIN DATA
1 N        25 25 25 25
1 MEAN     76.64 77.32 81.52 101.40
2 N        7 7 7 7
2 MEAN     76.1428571 85.2857143 60.8571429 249.571429
3 N        13 13 13 13
3 MEAN     55.5384615 76 63.4615385 86.3076923
. SD       16.4634139 22.5509310 16.8086768 77.1085326
. CORR     1
. CORR     .1425366 1
. CORR     .5644693 .2762615 1
. CORR     .2133413 -.0499003  .0417468 1
END DATA.

DISCRIMINANT GROUPS=WORLD(1,3)
  /VARIABLES=FOOD APPL SERVICE RENT  /METHOD=WILKS /
MATRIX=IN(*).
```

- Procedure DISCRIMINANT reads the MEAN, COUNT (unweighted N), and N (weighted N) for each cell in the data, as well as pooled values for STDDEV and CORR. If COUNT=N, only N need be supplied. MATRIX DATA is used to generate an active system file that DISCRIMINANT can read.

- ROWTYPE_ is explicit on VARIABLES to identify record types. Though CONTENTS and CELLS could be used to identify record types and distinguish between within-cell data and pooled values, it is usually easier to specify ROWTYPE_ on VARIABLES and enter the ROWTYPE_ values in the data.

- Because factors are present in the data, the continuous variables (FOOD, APPL, SERVICE, and RENT) must be specified last on VARIABLES and also last in the data.

- The FACTOR subcommand identifies WORLD as the factor variable.

- BEGIN DATA immediately follows MATRIX DATA.

- N and MEAN values for each cell are entered in the data.

- ROWTYPE_ values for the pooled records are SD and COR. MATRIX DATA assigns the values STDDEV and CORR to the corresponding vectors in the matrix.

- Records with pooled information have the system-missing value (.) for the factors.

- Procedure DISCRIMINANT reads the data matrix. An asterisk (*) is specified as the input file on the MATRIX subcommand because the data are in the active system file.

Example
```
TITLE  'MATRIX DATA WITH PROCEDURE REGRESSION'.

MATRIX DATA VARIABLES=SAVINGS POP15 POP75 INCOME GROWTH
  /CONTENTS=MEAN SD N CORR /FORMAT=UPPER NODIAGONAL.
BEGIN DATA
9.6710 35.0896 2.2930 1106.7784 3.7576
4.4804 9.1517 1.2908 990.8511 2.8699
50 50 50 50 50
-.4555 .3165 .2203 .3048
-.9085 -.7562 -.0478
 .7870 .0253
-.1295
END DATA.

REGRESSION MATRIX=IN(*) /VARIABLES=SAVINGS TO GROWTH
  /DEP=SAVINGS /ENTER.
```

- REGRESSION reads and writes matrices that always contain the mean, standard deviation, N, and Pearson correlation coefficients. Data in this example do not have ROWTYPE_ values, and the correlation values are from the upper triangle of the matrix without the diagonal values. MATRIX DATA is used to generate a matrix that REGRESSION can read.

- ROWTYPE_ is not specified on VARIABLES because its values are not included in the data.
- Because there are no ROWTYPE_ values, CONTENTS is required to define the record types and also the order of the records in the file.
- By default, MATRIX DATA reads values from the lower triangle of the matrix, including the diagonal values. FORMAT is required in this instance to indicate that the data are in the upper triangle and do not include diagonal values.
- BEGIN DATA immediately follows the MATRIX DATA command.
- Procedure REGRESSION reads the data matrix. An asterisk (*) is specified as the input file on the MATRIX subcommand because the data are in the active system file. Since there is a single vector of N's in the data, missing values are handled LISTWISE (the default for REGRESSION).

Example

```
TITLE  'MATRIX DATA WITH PROCEDURE ONEWAY'.

MATRIX DATA VARIABLES=EDUC ROWTYPE_ WELL /FACTOR=EDUC.
BEGIN DATA
1 N 65
2 N 95
3 N 181
4 N 82
5 N 40
6 N 37
1 MEAN 2.6462
2 MEAN 2.7737
3 MEAN 4.1796
4 MEAN 4.5610
5 MEAN 4.6625
6 MEAN 5.2297
. MSE 6.2699
. DFE 494
END DATA.

ONEWAY WELL BY EDUC(1,6) /MATRIX=IN(*)
```

- One of the two types of matrices that procedure ONEWAY reads includes a vector of frequencies for each factor level, a vector of means for each factor level, a record containing the pooled variance (within-group mean square error), and the degrees of freedom for the MSE. MATRIX DATA is used to generate an active system file containing this type of matrix data for procedure ONEWAY.
- ROWTYPE_ is explicit on VARIABLES and identifies record types.
- Because factors are present in the data, the continuous variables (WELL) must be specified last on VARIABLES and last in the data.
- The FACTOR subcommand identifies EDUC as the factor variable.
- MSE is entered in the data as the ROWTYPE_ value for the vector of square pooled standard deviations.
- DFE is entered in the data as the ROWTYPE_ value for the vector of degrees of freedom.
- Records with pooled information have the system-missing value (.) for the factors.

**VARIABLES
Subcommand**

VARIABLES specifies the names of the variables in the data and the order in which they occur. VARIABLES is required on all MATRIX DATA specifications. There is no limit to the number of variables that can be specified.

Continuous variables are all that must be specified on VARIABLES when either of two conditions is met:

1   The data contain only correlation coefficients. There can be no additional information—such as the mean and standard deviation—and no factor information or split-file variables. MATRIX DATA assigns the record type CORR to all records.

2   CONTENTS is used to define all record types. The data can then contain information such as the mean and standard deviation, but no factor information or split-file variables. MATRIX DATA assigns the record types defined on the CONTENTS subcommand.

If neither of these two conditions is met in the data, VARIABLES requires some combination of the following (in addition to the continuous variables), depending on the nature of the data:

- Variable ROWTYPE_. If ROWTYPE_ is named on VARIABLES, the continuous variables must be the last variables specified on the subcommand.

- Split-file variables. If split-file variables are present, they must also be specified on SPLIT.

- Factor variables. If factor variables are present, they must also be specified on FACTORS.

VARNAME_ Variable
- VARNAME_ cannot be named on the VARIABLES subcommand. VARNAME_ has special meaning in matrix files. The MATRIX DATA command always generates variable VARNAME_ automatically. VARNAME_ can never be specified anywhere on MATRIX DATA, and its values can never be specified in the data.

ROWTYPE_ Variable
- ROWTYPE_ is a string variable with A8 format. Its values define the data types. All matrices in SPSS contain a ROWTYPE_ variable.

- If ROWTYPE_ is explicitly specified on VARIABLES and its values entered in the data, MATRIX DATA is primarily used to define the names and order of the variables in the raw data file.

- ROWTYPE_ can be specified anywhere on VARIABLES. However, if factor variables are present, ROWTYPE_ must precede the continuous variables.

- Valid ROWTYPE_ values in the data are: CORR, COV, MAT, MSE, DFE, MEAN, STDDEV (or SD), N_VECTOR (or N), N_SCALAR, N_MATRIX, COUNT, or PROX. For definitions of these values, see CONTENTS Subcommand. Three-character abbreviations for these values are permitted. These values can also be enclosed in quotes or apostrophes.

- If ROWTYPE_ is not explicitly specified on VARIABLES, MATRIX DATA must precisely define the data. In particular, CONTENTS must be used to define the order in which the records occur within the file. MATRIX DATA strictly adheres to those specifications. A data-entry error, especially skipping a record, can cause the procedure to assign the wrong values to the wrong records.

Example
```
TITLE     'ROWTYPE_ IS EXPLICIT ON VARIABLES'.

MATRIX DATA
     VARIABLES=ROWTYPE_ SAVINGS POP15 POP75 INCOME GROWTH.
BEGIN DATA
MEAN 9.6710 35.0896 2.2930 1106.7784 3.7576
STDDEV 4.4804 9.1517 1.2907 990.8511 2.8699
N 50 50 50 50 50
CORR 1
CORR -.4555 1
CORR .3165 -.9085 1
CORR .2203 -.7562 .7870 1
CORR .3048 -.0478 .0253 -.1295  1
END DATA.
```

- ROWTYPE_ is specified on VARIABLES. ROWTYPE_ values in the data identify each record type.

- Note that VARNAME_ is not specified on VARIABLES, and its values are not entered in the data.

Example   TITLE   'ROWTYPE_ IS EXPLICIT ON VARIABLES'.

```
MATRIX DATA
    VARIABLES=ROWTYPE_ SAVINGS POP15 POP75 INCOME GROWTH.
BEGIN DATA
'MEAN     ' 9.6710 35.0896 2.2930 1106.7784 3.7576
'SD       ' 4.4804 9.1517 1.2907 990.8511 2.8699
'N        ' 50 50 50 50 50
"CORR     " 1
"CORR     " -.4555 1
"CORR     " .3165 -.9085 1
"CORR     " .2203 -.7562 .7870 1
"CORR     " .3048 -.0478 .0253 -.1295 1
END DATA.
```

- ROWTYPE_ values of mean, standard deviation, N, and Pearson correlation coefficient are abbreviated and enclosed in apostrophes or quotations.

Example   TITLE   'ROWTYPE_ IS IMPLICIT ON VARIABLES'.

```
MATRIX DATA VARIABLES=SAVINGS POP15 POP75 INCOME GROWTH
   /CONTENTS=MEAN SD N CORR.
BEGIN DATA
9.6710 35.0896 2.2930 1106.7784 3.7576
4.4804 9.1517 1.2907 990.8511 2.8699
50 50 50 50 50
 1
-.4555 1
 .3165 -.9085 1
 .2203 -.7562 .7870 1
 .3048 -.0478 .0253 -.1295 1
END DATA.
```

- ROWTYPE_ is not specified on VARIABLES, and its values are not included in the data.

- CONTENTS is required to define the record types and the order of the records in the file.

FILE Subcommand

FILE specifies the file containing the data. The default specification is INLINE, which indicates that the data are included within the command sequence between the BEGIN DATA and END DATA commands. If data are in an external file, FILE must specify the file. If FILE is omitted, data must be inline.

Example   `MATRIX DATA FILE=RAWMTX /VARIABLES=varlist.`

- FILE indicates data are in the file RAWMTX.

FORMAT Subcommand

FORMAT indicates how the matrix data are formatted. It applies only to matrix values in the data, not to vector values, such as the mean and standard deviation. The format specifications include

- The data-entry format for the data. By default, data are assumed to be in LIST format.
- The matrix shape. By default, the matrix is assumed to be a lower triangle.
- Whether or not the data include diagonal values. By default, the matrix is assumed to include diagonal values.

FORMAT can specify up to three keywords: one to specify the data-entry format, one to specify matrix shape, and one to specify whether the data include diagonal values. The minimum specification is a single keyword. The other default settings remain in effect unless explicitly overridden.

Data-Entry Format   FORMAT has two keywords that specify the data-entry format:

LIST   *Each scalar, vector, and matrix row must begin on a new record.* A vector or row of the matrix may be continued on multiple records. This is the default.

FREE   *Record boundaries are of no consequence.* Any item can begin in the middle of a record.

Matrix Shape   FORMAT has three keywords that specify the matrix shape. Note that with either of the triangular shapes, no values—not even missing indicators—are entered for the implied values in the matrix.

LOWER   *Read data values from the lower triangle.* This is the default.

UPPER   *Read data values from the upper triangle.*

FULL   *Read the full square matrix of data values.* FULL cannot be specified with NODIAGONAL.

Diagonal Values   FORMAT has two keywords that refer to the diagonal values:

DIAGONAL   *Data include the diagonal values.* This is the default.

NODIAGONAL   *Data do not include diagonal values.* The diagonal value is set to the system-missing value for all matrices except the correlation matrices. For correlation matrices, the diagonal value is set to 1. NODIAGONAL cannot be specified with FULL.

Table 3 shows how data might be entered for each combination of FORMAT settings that govern matrix shape and diagonal values. Notice that with UPPER NODIAGONAL and LOWER NODIAGONAL, you do not enter the matrix row that has blank values for the continuous variables. If you enter that row, MATRIX DATA cannot properly form the matrix.

Table 3 Various FORMAT settings

FULL				UPPER DIAGONAL				UPPER NODIAGONAL				LOWER DIAGONAL				LOWER NODIAGONAL			
MEAN	5	4	3	MEAN	5	4	3	MEAN	5	4	3	MEAN	5	4	3	MEAN	5	4	3
SD	3	2	1	SD	3	2	1	SD	3	2	1	SD	3	2	1	SD	3	2	1
N	9	9	9	N	9	9	9	N	9	9	9	N	9	9	9	N	9	9	9
CORR	1	.6	.7	CORR	1	.6	.7	CORR		.6	.7	CORR	1			CORR	.6		
CORR	.6	1	.8	CORR		1	.8	CORR			.8	CORR	.6	1		CORR	.7	.8	
CORR	.7	.8	1	CORR			1					CORR	.7	.8	1				

Example
```
MATRIX DATA VARIABLES=ROWTYPE_ V1 TO V3
    /FORMAT=UPPER NODIAGONAL.
BEGIN DATA
MEAN 5 4 3
SD 3 2 1
N 9 9 9
CORR .6 .7
CORR .8
END DATA.
LIST.
```

• FORMAT specifies the upper-triangle format with no diagonal values. The default LIST is in effect for the data-entry format.

Example
```
MATRIX DATA VARIABLES=ROWTYPE_ V1 TO V3
             /FORMAT=UPPER NODIAGONAL.
BEGIN DATA
MEAN 5 4 3
SD 3 2 1
N 9 9 9
CORR .6 .7
CORR .8
END DATA.
LIST.
```

- This example is identical to the previous example. It shows that data do not have to be aligned in columns. Data throughout this chapter are aligned in columns to emphasize the matrix format.

SPLIT Subcommand

SPLIT specifies the variables whose values define the split files. SPLIT must follow the VARIABLES subcommand.

- SPLIT can specify a subset of up to eight of the variables named on VARIABLES. All split variables must be numeric. Keyword TO can be used to imply variables in the order in which they are named on VARIABLES.

- A separate data matrix must be entered in the data for each value of each split variable. MATRIX DATA generates a complete set of matrix materials for each value of each split variable.

- If the data contain neither ROWTYPE_ nor split-file information, SPLIT can specify a single split-file variable that does not appear on the VARIABLES subcommand. MATRIX DATA assigns values 1, 2, 3, etc., to the split variable until end of data is encountered and generates a complete set of matrix materials for each set of matrix materials in the data.

Example
```
MATRIX DATA  VARIABLES=S1 ROWTYPE_ V1 TO V3 /SPLIT=S1.
BEGIN DATA
0 MEAN    5   4   3
0 SD      1   2   3
0 N       9   9   9
0 CORR    1
0 CORR    .6  1
0 CORR    .7  .8  1
1 MEAN    9   8   7
1 SD      5   6   7
1 N       9   9   9
1 CORR    1
1 CORR    .4  1
1 CORR    .3  .2  1
END DATA.
LIST.
```

- Split variable S1 has two values: 0 and 1. Two separate matrices are entered in the data, one for each value S1.

- S1 must be specified on both VARIABLES and SPLIT.

Example
```
MATRIX DATA VARIABLES=V1 TO V3 /CONTENTS=MEAN SD N CORR
     /SPLIT=SPL.
BEGIN DATA
5   4   3
1   2   3
9   9   9
1
.6  1
.7  .8  1
9   8   7
5   6   7
9   9   9
1
.4  1
.3  .2  1
END DATA.
LIST.
```

- Split variable SPL is not specified on VARIABLES, and values for SPL are not included in the data.
- Two sets of matrix materials are present in the data. MATRIX DATA therefore assigns values 1 and 2 to variable SPL, and generates two matrices in the matrix system file.

FACTORS Subcommand

FACTORS specifies the variables whose values define the cells represented by the within-cell data. FACTORS must follow the VARIABLES subcommand.

- FACTORS must specify a subset of the variables named on the VARIABLES subcommand. Keyword TO can be used to imply variables in the order in which they are named on VARIABLES.
- The way pooled information is entered when factors are present depends upon whether ROWTYPE_ is explicit or implicit on VARIABLES.

ROWTYPE_ Explicit

- If ROWTYPE_ is explicit on VARIABLES and its values are included in the data, MATRIX DATA uses missing values to determine whether the data represent within-cell information or pooled information, since the values of ROWTYPE_ are ambiguous.
- On records that represent pooled information, decimal points must be used to enter missing values for the factors.

ROWTYPE_ Implicit

- If ROWTYPE_ is not specified on VARIABLES and its values are not in the data, enter data values only for the factor records representing within-cell information. Enter nothing for the factor records that represent pooled information.
- CELLS must be specified to indicate the number of within-cells records.
- CONTENTS must be specified to indicate which record types have within-cell data.

Example

```
TITLE 'ROWTYPE_ EXPLICIT'.

MATRIX DATA VARIABLES=ROWTYPE_ F1 F2  VAR1 TO VAR3
   /FACTORS=F1 F2.
BEGIN DATA
MEAN 1 1  1  2  3
SD   1 1  5  4  3
N    1 1  9  9  9
MEAN 1 2  4  5  6
SD   1 2  6  5  4
N    1 2  9  9  9
MEAN 2 1  7  8  9
SD   2 1  7  6  5
N    2 1  9  9  9
MEAN 2 2  9  8  7
SD   2 2  8  7  6
N    2 2  9  9  9
CORR . . .1
CORR . . .6  1
CORR . . .7 .8  1
END DATA.
```

- ROWTYPE_ is explicitly specified on VARIABLES.
- Factor variables must be specified on both VARIABLES and FACTOR.
- Decimal points in the data represent missing values for the CORR factor values.

Example   ```
TITLE 'ROWTYPE_ IMPLICIT'.

MATRIX DATA VARIABLES=Fl F2 VAR1 TO VAR3
   /FACTORS=Fl F2 /CONTENTS=(MEAN SD N) CORR /CELLS=4.
BEGIN DATA
1 1 1   2   3
1 1 5   4   3
1 1 9   9   9
1 2 4   5   6
1 2 6   5   4
1 2 9   9   9
2 1 7   8   9
2 1 7   6   5
2 1 9   9   9
2 2 9   8   7
2 2 8   7   6
2 2 9   9   9
      1
     .6 1
     .7 .8 1
END DATA.
```

- ROWTYPE_ is not specified on VARIABLES.
- Nothing is entered for the CORR factor values because the records define pooled information.
- CELLS is required because there are factors present without an explicit ROWTYPE_ specification.
- CONTENTS is required to define the record types and to differentiate between the within-cell and pooled types.

## CELLS Subcommand

CELLS specifies the number of within-cell records in the data. The only valid specification for CELLS is a single integer, which indicates the number of sets of within-cell information that MATRIX DATA must read.

- CELLS is required when there are factors in the data but ROWTYPE_ is not explicitly specified on VARIABLES.
- If CELLS is used when ROWTYPE_ is specified on VARIABLES, MATRIX DATA issues a warning and ignores the CELLS subcommand.

**Example**    ```
MATRIX DATA VARIABLES=Fl VAR1 TO VAR3 /FACTORS=Fl /CELLS=2
   /CONTENTS=(MEAN SD N) CORR.
BEGIN DATA
1  5   4   3
1  3   2   1
1  9   9   9
2  8   7   6
2  6   7   8
2  9   9   9
   1
  .6  1
  .7 .8  1
END DATA.
```

- CELLS=2 because the factor variable F1 has two values (1 and 2) and there are therefore two sets of within-cell information.
- If there were two factor variables, F1 and F2, and each had two values, 1 and 2, CELLS would equal 4 to account for the four possible factor combinations (assuming all 4 combinations are present in the data).

CONTENTS
Subcommand

CONTENTS defines the record types when ROWTYPE_ is not included in the data. Each different type of record in the data is indicated by a keyword. The minimum specification is a single keyword. The default is CORR.

- CONTENTS is required to define record types and record order whenever ROWTYPE_ is not specified on VARIABLES and its values are not in the data. The only exception to this rule is the rare situation in which all data values represent pooled correlation records and there are no factors. In this case, MATRIX DATA reads the data values and assigns the default ROWTYPE_ of CORR to all records.

- The order in which keywords are specified on CONTENTS must correspond to the order in which the records appear in the data. If the keywords on CONTENTS are in the wrong order, MATRIX DATA will incorrectly assign values to the records.

CORR	*Matrix of correlation coefficients.* This is the default. If ROWTYPE_ is not specified on the VARIABLES subcommand and you omit the CONTENTS subcommand, MATRIX DATA assigns the ROWTYPE_ value CORR to all matrix rows.
COV	*Matrix of covariance coefficients.*
MAT	*Generic square matrix.*
MSE	*Vector of mean squared errors.*
DFE	*Vector of degrees of freedom.*
MEAN	*Vector of means.*
STDDEV	*Vector of standard deviations.* SD is a synonym for STDDEV. If SD is specified, MATRIX DATA assigns the ROWTYPE_ value STDDEV to the record.
N_VECTOR	*Vector of counts.* MATRIX DATA assigns ROWTYPE_ value N to the record. N is a synonym for N_VECTOR.
N_SCALAR	*Count.* Scalars are a shorthand mechanism for representing vectors in which all elements have the same value. This would be the case for a vector of N's calculated using listwise deletion of missing values. Enter N_SCALAR as the ROWTYPE_ value in the data and then the N_SCALAR value for the first continuous variable only. MATRIX DATA assigns the ROWTYPE_ value N to the record, and copies the specified N_SCALAR value across all the continuous variables.
N_MATRIX	*Square matrix of counts.* Enter N_MATRIX as the ROWTYPE_ value for each row of counts in the data. MATRIX DATA assigns ROWTYPE_ value N to each of those rows.
COUNT	*Count vector accepted by procedure DISCRIMINANT.* This contains unweighted N's.
PROX	*Matrix produced by PROXIMITIES.* Any proximity matrix that can be used with PROXIMITIES or CLUSTER. A value label of SIMILARITY or DISSIMILARITY should be specified for PROX as well. This is done by using the VALUE LABELS command after END DATA.

Example

```
MATRIX DATA VARIABLES=V1 TO V3 /CONTENTS=MEAN SD N_SCALAR CORR.
BEGIN DATA
   5   4   3
   3   2   1
   9
   1
  .6   1
  .7  .8   1
END DATA.
LIST.
```

Example

```
MATRIX DATA VARIABLES=V1 TO V3 /CONTENTS=PROX.
BEGIN DATA
data records
END DATA.
VALUE LABELS ROWTYPE_ 'PROX' 'DISSIMILARITY'.
```

- ROWTYPE_ is not specified on VARIABLES, and ROWTYPE_ values are not in the data. CONTENTS is therefore required to identify record types.
- CONTENTS indicates that the matrix records are in the following order: mean, standard deviation, N, and correlation coefficients.
- Notice that the N_SCALAR value is entered for the first continuous variable only.

Within-Cells Record Definition

When factors are present and ROWTYPE_ is not specified, CONTENTS distinguishes between keywords that identify within-cell information and keywords that identify pooled information by enclosing the within-cell keywords in parentheses. For information on specifying factors when ROWTYPE_ is explicit, see FACTOR Subcommand.

There are two methods for using the parentheses on CONTENTS, depending on how the data are organized:

1 Enclose multiple-cell keywords together within a single set of parentheses if their associated records appear collectively for each set of factor values.

2 Enclose a cell keyword within its own parentheses if its associated records are grouped together across factor values.

Example

```
MATRIX DATA VARIABLES=F1 VAR1 TO VAR3 /FACTORS=F1 /CELLS=2
  /CONTENTS=(MEAN SD N) CORR.
```

- MEAN, SD, and N contain within-cells information and are therefore specified within parentheses. CORR is outside the parentheses because it identifies pooled records.
- CELLS is required because there is a factor specified and ROWTYPE_ is implicit on VARIABLES.

Example

```
MATRIX DATA VARIABLES=F1 VAR1 TO VAR3 /FACTORS=F1 /CELLS=2
  /CONTENTS=(MEAN SD N) CORR.
BEGIN DATA
1   5   4   3
1   3   2   1
1   9   9   9
2   4   5   6
2   6   5   4
2   9   9   9
    1
   .6   1
   .7  .8   1
END DATA.
```

- Parentheses on the CONTENTS keywords indicate that data include the mean, the standard deviation, and N for F1 value 1, followed by the mean, standard deviation, and N for F1 value 2.

Example

```
MATRIX DATA VARIABLES=F1 VAR1 TO VAR3 /FACTORS=F1 /CELLS=2
  /CONTENTS=(MEAN) (SD) (N) CORR.
BEGIN DATA
1   5   4   3
2   4   5   6
1   3   2   1
2   6   5   4
1   9   9   9
2   9   9   9
    1
   .6   1
   .7  .8   1
END DATA.
```

- Parentheses on the CONTENTS keywords indicate that the data include the means for all the cells, followed by the standard deviations for all the cells, followed by the N values for all the cells.

Example

```
MATRIX DATA VARIABLES=F1 VAR1 TO VAR3 /FACTORS=F1 /CELLS=2
        /CONTENTS=(MEAN SD) (N) CORR.
BEGIN DATA
1  5  4  3
1  3  2  1
2  4  5  6
2  6  5  4
1  9  9  9
2  9  9  9
   1
   .6  1
   .7 .8  1
END DATA.
```

- Parentheses on the CONTENTS keywords indicate that the data include the mean and standard deviation for F1 value 1, followed by the mean and standard deviation for F1 value 2, followed by the N values for all the cells.

Optional Specification with ROWTYPE_ Explicit

When ROWTYPE_ is explicitly named on VARIABLES, MATRIX DATA uses ROWTYPE_ values to determine record types.

- When ROWTYPE_ is explicitly named on VARIABLES, CONTENTS can be used for informational purposes. However, ROWTYPE_ values in the data still determine record types.

- If MATRIX DATA reads values for ROWTYPE_ that are not specified on CONTENTS, it issues a warning to point out the discrepancy.

- Missing values for the factors must be entered as decimal points, even though CONTENTS is specified (see FACTOR).

Example

```
MATRIX DATA VARIABLES=ROWTYPE_ F1 F2 VAR1 TO VAR3
        /FACTORS=F1 F2 /CONTENTS=(MEAN SD N) CORR.
BEGIN DATA
MEAN 1 1  1  2  3
SD   1 1  5  4  3
N    1 1  9  9  9
MEAN 1 2  4  5  6
SD   1 2  6  5  4
N    1 2  9  9  9
CORR . .  1
CORR . . .6  1
CORR . . .7 .8  1
END DATA.
```

- ROWTYPE_ is explicit on VARIABLES. MATRIX DATA therefore uses ROWTYPE_ values in the data to identify record types.

- Because ROWTYPE_ is specified on VARIABLES, CONTENTS is optional. However, CONTENTS is specified for informational purposes. This is most useful when data are in an external file and the ROWTYPE_ values cannot be seen in the data.

- Note that missing values for the factors must still be entered as decimal points, even though CONTENTS is specified.

N Subcommand

N specifies the population N when the data do not include it. The only valid specification is an integer, which indicates the population N.

- MATRIX DATA generates one record for each split file with a ROWTYPE_ of N, and it uses the specified N value for each continuous variable.

Example
```
MATRIX DATA VARIABLES=V1 TO V3 /CONTENTS=MEAN SD CORR
  /N=99.
BEGIN DATA
 5   4   3
 3   4   5
 1
.6   1
.7  .8   1
END DATA.
```

• MATRIX DATA uses 99 as the N value for all continuous variables.

MCONVERT

```
MCONVERT [[/MATRIX=] [IN({*   })] [OUT({*   })]]
                         {file}        {file}
         [{/REPLACE}]
          {/APPEND }
```

Example:

```
MCONVERT MATRIX=OUT(CORMTX) /APPEND.
```

Overview MCONVERT converts covariance matrix materials to correlation matrix materials, or vice versa. For MCONVERT to convert a correlation matrix, data must contain CORR values (Pearson correlation coefficients) and a vector of standard deviations (STDDEV). For MCONVERT to convert a covariance matrix, only COV values are required in the data.

Defaults By default, MCONVERT reads the original matrix from the active system file and then replaces it with the converted matrix.

Tailoring **Matrix Files.** MCONVERT can read matrix materials from an external matrix system file, and it can write converted matrix materials to an external file.

Matrix Materials. MCONVERT can either write the converted matrix alone to the output file, or it can append the converted matrix to the end of the original matrix and write both to the output file.

Syntax Rules
- The minimum specification is the command keyword.
- Files specified on the IN and OUT keywords of the MATRIX subcommand must be enclosed in parentheses.
- Keywords IN and OUT cannot specify the same external file.
- The APPEND and REPLACE subcommands cannot be specified on the same MCONVERT command.

Operations
- If the data are covariance matrix materials, MCONVERT converts them to a correlation matrix plus a vector of standard deviations.
- If the data are a correlation matrix and vector of standard deviations, MCONVERT converts them to a covariance matrix.
- If there are multiple CORR or COV matrices (i.e., one for each factor or one for each split variable), each will be converted to a separate matrix, preserving the values of any factor or split variables.
- All cases with ROWTYPE_ values other than CORR or COV, such as MEAN, N, and STDDEV, are always copied into the resulting system file.

Limitations
- MCONVERT cannot read raw matrix values. If your data are raw values, use the MATRIX DATA command to convert the raw matrix materials to a matrix system file.
- Split variables (if any) must occur first in the file that MCONVERT reads, followed by variable ROWTYPE_, the grouping variables (if any), and variable VARNAME_. All variables following VARNAME_ are the variables for which a matrix will be read and created.
- The total number of split variables plus grouping variables cannot exceed eight.

Example
```
MATRIX DATA VARIABLES=ROWTYPE_ SAVINGS POP15 POP75 INCOME GROWTH
   /FORMAT=FULL.
BEGIN DATA
COV     20.0740459  -18.678638    1.8304990   978.181242 3.9190106
COV    -18.678638     83.7541100 -10.731666  -6856.9888  -1.2561071
COV      1.8304990   -10.731666    1.6660908 1006.52742    .0937992
COV    978.181242   -6856.9888    1006.52742 981785.907 -368.18652
COV      3.9190106    -1.2561071     .0937992 -368.18652  8.2361574
END DATA.
MCONVERT.
FACTOR MATRIX IN(COR=*).
```

- MATRIX DATA defines the variables in the file and creates an active system file of matrix materials.
- Because record type (COV) values are in the data, ROWTYPE_ is specified on the VARIABLES subcommand.
- The FORMAT subcommand indicates that data are in full square format.
- MCONVERT converts the covariance matrix to a correlation matrix plus a vector of standard deviations. By default, the converted matrix is written to the active system file.
- FACTOR reads the correlation matrix from the active system file and performs factor analysis.

MATRIX Subcommand

The MATRIX subcommand specifies the file for the matrix materials. MATRIX has two keywords, IN and OUT, which specify the matrix file in parentheses. Keywords IN and OUT each have two specifications:

(*)   *Active system file.* Both keywords IN and OUT use an asterisk to refer to the active system file. IN(*) instructs MCONVERT to read the matrix from the active system file; OUT(*) instructs MCONVERT to write the matrix to the active system file. This is the default for both IN and OUT.

(file)   *External matrix system file.* Both keywords IN and OUT can refer to an external file by specifying the file in parentheses.

- The minimum specification is the MATRIX subcommand with one keyword and, in parentheses, a file specification. The actual keyword MATRIX is optional.
- IN specifies the file that MCONVERT reads. OUT specifies the file that MCONVERT writes. IN and OUT cannot specify the same external file.
- By default, MATRIX reads the original matrix from the active system file, then replaces that matrix with the converted matrix.
- MATRIX=IN cannot be used in place of GET or DATA LIST. To begin a new command file or session and immediately read a matrix, first GET the matrix file and then use MCONVERT.

Example
```
GET FILE=COVMTX.
MCONVERT MATRIX=OUT(CORMTX).
```

- By default, MCONVERT reads the original matrix from the active system file (COVMTX). IN(*) can be specified to make the default explicit.
- Keyword OUT on MATRIX writes the converted matrix to file CORMTX.

REPLACE Subcommand

By default, MCONVERT replaces the original matrix with the converted matrix and writes only the converted matrix to the output file. The REPLACE subcommand makes the default explicit.

- The only specification is the keyword REPLACE.
- REPLACE cannot be used with APPEND.

APPEND Subcommand   APPEND appends the converted matrix to the end of the original matrix.

- The only specification is the keyword APPEND.
- If there are multiple sets of matrix materials in the file that MCONVERT reads, each converted matrix is appended to the end of its original matrix.
- MCONVERT writes both the original and the converted matrices to the output file.
- APPEND cannot be used with REPLACE.

Example   `MCONVERT MATRIX=OUT(COVMTX) /APPEND.`

- MCONVERT reads matrix materials from the active system file.
- The APPEND subcommand appends each converted matrix to the end of its original matrix.
- Both the original and the converted matrix materials are written to file COVMTX.

MEANS

General mode:
```
MEANS [TABLES=]{varlist} BY varlist [BY...] [/varlist...]
              {ALL     }


   [/MISSING={TABLE**  }]
            {INCLUDE  }
            {DEPENDENT}


   [/FORMAT={LABELS**  }  {NAMES**}  {VALUES**}  {TABLE**}]
           {NOLABELS  }  {NONAMES}  {NOVALUES}  {TREE   }
           {NOCATLABS}


   [/CELLS=[DEFAULT**]  [MEAN**   ]  [ALL]]
           [COUNT**  ]  [STDDEV** ]
           [SUM      ]  [VARIANCE]


   [/STATISTICS=[ANOVA] [LINEARITY] [ALL] [NONE] ]
```

Integer mode:
```
MEANS VARIABLES=varlist({min,max         }) [varlist...]
                       {LOWEST,HIGHEST}


   /{TABLES     }={varlist} BY varlist [BY...] [/varlist...]
    {CROSSBREAK} {ALL     }


   [/MISSING={TABLE**  }]
            {INCLUDE  }
            {DEPENDENT}


   [/FORMAT={LABELS**  }  {NAMES**}  {VALUES**}]
           {NOLABELS  }  {NONAMES}  {NOVALUES}
           {NOCATLABS}


   [/CELLS=[DEFAULT**]  [MEAN**   ]  [ALL]]
           [COUNT**  ]  [STDDEV** ]
           [SUM      ]  [VARIANCE]


   [/STATISTICS=[ANOVA] [LINEARITY] [ALL] [NONE] ]
```
**Default if the subcommand is omitted.

Example:
```
MEANS TABLES=V1 TO V5 BY GROUP
  /FORMAT=NONAMES
  /STATISTICS=ANOVA.
```

Overview MEANS (alias BREAKDOWN) displays means, standard deviations, and group counts for a dependent variable within groups defined by one or more independent variables. This operation is similar to crosstabulation, where each mean and standard deviation summarizes the distribution of a complete row or column of a contingency table. Other SPSS procedures that display univariate statistics are FREQUENCIES and DESCRIPTIVES.

Options **Methods for Building Tables.** MEANS operates in two different modes: general and integer. *General mode* operates via the TABLES subcommand and requires fewer specifications. It also offers an optional tree format for output. *Integer mode* operates via the TABLES and VARIABLES subcommands and requires that you specify the minimum and maximum values for the variables. This mode builds tables more efficiently.

Cell Information. By default, MEANS displays means, standard deviations, and cell counts for a dependent variable across groups defined by one or more independent variables. Optionally, you can also display sums and variances. See CELLS Subcommand.

Additional Statistics. In addition to the statistics displayed for groups, you can obtain a one-way analysis of variance and test of linearity. See STATISTICS Subcommand.

Formatting Options. You can request a tree format with general mode and suppress labels and values in either mode (see FORMAT Subcommand). With integer mode you can obtain a crosstabular format (see CROSSBREAK Subcommand).

Basic Specification

The basic specification is TABLES with a table list.

- The minimum table list specifies a dependent variable, keyword BY, and an independent variable. Keyword TABLES can be omitted in general mode. If keyword TABLES is used, it must be followed by an equals sign.

- By default, MEANS displays means, standard deviations, and number of cases. The default table is labeled with the variable name and label of the dependent and independent variables. Groups are labeled with the variable name, variable label, values, and value labels of the independent variables.

Subcommand Order

- If keyword TABLES is omitted, the table list must be first.

- If keyword TABLES is explicitly used, subcommands can be specified in any order. The exception is in integer mode, where VARIABLES must precede TABLES.

Operations

- MEANS displays requested univariate statistics for the population as a whole and for each value of the first independent variable defined for the table in addition to statistics for groups.

- If an independent variable is a long string, only the short-string portion is used to identify groups in the analysis. Use the REPORT procedure to break down variables by long strings.

- Specifying a string variable as a dependent variable on any table list stops execution of the MEANS procedure.

Specifications for MEANS subcommands depend on whether *general mode* or *integer mode* is used to build tables, and whether CROSSBREAK tables are requested. Each of the three methods has advantages and disadvantages in computational efficiency, statistics, and additional options.

- General mode permits alphanumeric or noninteger control variables with no range specifications. It also provides the optional tree format.

- Integer mode builds breakdown tables more quickly. However, it requires more space if the matrix of control variables has many empty cells. By specifying the appropriate bounds, you can eliminate outliers for the dependent variable or select a subset of the values of the control variables.

- The CROSSBREAK subcommand displays tables of two or more control variables in a crosstabular format and displays statistics for each of two variables controlling for the other. The optional analysis-of-variance table and test of linearity are not available for CROSSBREAK.

Narrow Output

If the width is set to 80 columns and the requested tables require more room, the command is not executed (the exception is the CROSSBREAK format, where tables will wrap if they don't fit in the specified width). To display 80-column output, you must limit the number of output columns by specifying only 3 of the 5 cell statistics, by suppressing value labels, or by suppressing variable names and category labels, etc. To display sums and variances in addition to the default cell statistics, the width should be set to at least 96 columns.

Limitations   The following limitations apply to MEANS in general mode:

- Maximum 200 variables total per MEANS command.
- Maximum 250 tables.
- Maximum 6 dimensions per table.
- Maximum 30 table lists per MEANS command.
- Maximum 200 value labels displayed on any single table.

The following limitations apply to MEANS in integer mode:

- Maximum 100 variables named or implied on VARIABLES.
- Maximum 100 variables named or implied on TABLES.
- Maximum 100 tables.
- Maximum 6 dimensions per table.
- Maximum 30 table lists per MEANS command.
- Maximum 200 nonempty rows and columns in a CROSSBREAK table.

Example
```
MEANS TABLES=V1 TO V5 BY GROUP
  /FORMAT=NONAMES
  /STATISTICS=ANOVA.
```

- TABLES specifies that V1 through V5 are the dependent variables. GROUP is the independent variable.
- Assuming that variables V2, V3, and V4 lie between between V1 and V5 on the active system file, five tables are produced: V1 by GROUP, V2 by GROUP, V3 by GROUP, and so on.
- FORMAT suppresses the display of variable name GROUP.
- STATISTICS requests one-way analysis-of-variance tables of V1 through V5 by GROUP.

Example
```
MEANS VARA BY VARB BY VARC/V1 V2 BY V3 V4 BY V5.
```

- This command contains two TABLES subcommands that omit the optional TABLES keyword.
- The first table list requests one table. Statistics are produced for VARA within groups defined by each combination of values of VARB and VARC.
- The second table list requests four tables: V1 by V3 by V5; V1 by V4 by V5; V2 by V3 by V5; and V2 by V4 by V5.

TABLES Subcommand   Use TABLES with MEANS in both general and integer mode.

General Mode   TABLES specifies a table list. Keyword TABLES may be omitted.

- The dependent variable is named first and must be numeric. The independent variables follow the BY keyword and can be numeric or string.
- More than one dependent variable can be specified in a table list. More than one independent variable can be specified in each dimension of a table list.
- Each use of keyword BY in a table list adds a dimension to the tables requested and introduces a new order of control among the independent variables.
- A table is built for each dependent variable by each combination of independent variables across dimensions.
- Each combination of values of the independent variables defined for a table defines a group.

- The order in which independent variables are displayed is the same as the order in which they are named. The values of the first independent variable defined for the table appear in the left-most column of the table and change most slowly in the definition of groups. Although the MEANS table list is the same as the tables list in the CROSSTABS procedure, in CROSSTABS the values of the first variable in the table change most quickly.
- Keyword ALL in each dimension refers to all user-defined variables.
- You can specify multiple TABLES subcommands on a single MEANS command. The slash between the subcommands is required; the keyword is not.

Integer Mode

To run MEANS in integer mode, the values of all the independent variables must be integers. Two subcommands are required. VARIABLES specifies all the variables to be used in the MEANS procedure and the minimum and maximum values for building tables. TABLES specifies the table lists. Repeated VARIABLES and TABLES subcommands are allowed.

- TABLES has the same syntax in integer mode as it has in general mode. However, there is one important difference between the table requests in integer mode and the table requests in general mode. In integer mode, the order of variables implied on TABLES is established by the order in which variables are named or implied on VARIABLES. In general mode, the order of variables implied on TABLES is established by their order in the active system file.
- You can use multiple TABLES subcommands or name multiple table lists separated by slashes on one TABLES subcommand.
- Variables named on TABLES must have been previously named or implied on VARIABLES.
- Integer mode can produce more tables in a given amount of core storage space than general mode, and the processing is faster. In integer mode, you define the dimensions of the table with the independent variables, rather than having SPSS calculate the dimensions based on values encountered in your data. In addition, integer mode has an alternate CROSSBREAK display format.

VARIABLES Subcommand

VARIABLES identifies variables to be included on TABLES. Specify the lowest and highest values in parentheses after each variable. These values must be integers.

- To specify the same range for multiple variables, specify a variable list followed by the defined range.
- Explicit numeric bounds must be specified as integers. For example, (0,HI) excludes nonnegative values.
- Explicit ranges do not have to be specified for dependent variables because they are usually continuous and are not assumed to be integers. However, you must provide bounds. Use keywords LOWEST (or LO) and HIGHEST (or HI) for dependent variables. You can also use explicit bounds to eliminate outliers from the calculation of the summary statistics.
- Keywords LOWEST, LO, HIGHEST, HI cannot be used with independent variables.
- Variables may appear in any order. However, variable order on VARIABLES affects their implied order on the TABLES.
- MEANS allocates tables according to the specified bounds. One cell is allocated for each possible combination of values of the control variables for a requested table before the data are read. Thus, it is inefficient to specify more generous bounds than the control variables actually have. If the table is sparse because the control variables do not have values falling throughout the range specified, consider using the general mode or recoding the control variables. If, on the other hand, values of control variables fall outside the specified range, cases with these values are considered missing and are not used in the computation of the table.

Example
```
MEANS  VARIABLES=DEPT81(1,4) EE081(1,9) RAISE81(LO,HI)
  /TABLES=RAISE81 BY DEPT81 BY EE081.
```
- Dependent variable RAISE88 has a range from the lowest to the highest value.
- Independent variables cannot use keywords HI or LO. Thus, DEPT88 has an explicit range of 1 to 4, and EEO81 has an explicit range of 1 to 9.

CROSSBREAK Subcommand

CROSSBREAK displays tables in a crosstabular form. CROSSBREAK can be used only in integer mode, and it is used in place of the TABLES subcommand.

- CROSSBREAK syntax is identical to TABLES syntax. As with TABLES, repeated CROSSBREAK subcommands are allowed. However, CROSS-BREAK and TABLES subcommands cannot be mixed.
- Tables displayed in crossbreak form resemble CROSSTABS tables, but their contents are considerably different. The cells contain means, counts, and standard deviations for the dependent variable. The first independent variable defines the rows and the second independent variable defines the columns.
- The CROSSBREAK format is especially suited to breakdowns with two control variables.
- CROSSBREAK displays separate subtables for each combination of values when you specify three or more dimensions.

CELLS Subcommand

By default, MEANS displays the means, standard deviations, and cell counts in each cell. Use CELLS to modify cell information.

- If CELLS is specified without keywords, MEANS displays ALL cell information.
- If CELLS is specified with a keyword or keywords, MEANS displays only the requested information.

DEFAULT	*Display the means, standard deviations, and cell counts in each cell. This is the default if CELLS is omitted.*
MEAN	*Display cell means.*
STDDEV	*Display cell standard deviations.*
COUNT	*Display cell frequencies.*
SUM	*Display cell sums.*
VARIANCE	*Display variances.*
ALL	*Display the means, counts, standard deviations, sums, and variances in each cell. This is the default if CELLS is specified without keywords.*

STATISTICS Subcommand

MEANS automatically computes means, standard deviations, and counts for subpopulations. Optionally, you can obtain a one-way analysis of variance for each table as well as a test of linearity. STATISTICS computes additional statistics.

- Statistics requested on STATISTICS are computed in addition to the statistics displayed in each cell of the table.
- If STATISTICS is specified without keywords, MEANS computes ANOVA.
- STATISTICS is not available if CROSSBREAK is used.
- If a two-way or higher-order breakdown is specified, the second and subsequent dimensions are ignored in the analysis of variance table. To obtain a two-way and higher analysis of variance, use procedure ANOVA or MANOVA. Procedure ONEWAY calculates a one-way analysis of variance with multiple comparison tests.

ANOVA	*Analysis of variance.* ANOVA displays a standard analysis of variance table and calculates *ETA* and *ETA²*. This is the default if STATISTICS is specified without keywords.

LINEARITY   *Test of linearity.* LINEARITY calculates the sums of squares, degrees of freedom, and mean square associated with linear and nonlinear components, as well as the F ratio, Pearson's r, and r^2. ANOVA must be requested to obtain LINEARITY. LINEARITY is ignored if the control variable is a short string.

ALL   *Both ANOVA and LINEARITY.*

NONE   *No additional statistics.* This is the default if STATISTICS is omitted.

Example
```
MEANS TABLES=INCOME BY SEX BY RACE
  /STATISTICS=ANOVA.
```

• MEANS produces a breakdown of INCOME by RACE within SEX but computes an analysis of variance only for INCOME by SEX.

MISSING Subcommand

By default, MEANS deletes cases with missing values on a tablewide basis. A case missing on any of the variables specified for a table is not used. Every case contained in a table will have a complete set of nonmissing values for all variables in that table. When you separate table requests with a slash, missing values are handled separately for each list. Use MISSING to control missing values.

TABLE   *Delete cases with missing values on a tablewide basis.* This is the default.

INCLUDE   *Include user-missing values.* Handles user-missing values as if they were not missing.

DEPENDENT   *Exclude user-missing values for dependent variables only.* DEPENDENT treats user-missing values as valid for all independent variables.

FORMAT Subcommand

By default, MEANS displays variable and value labels and the names and values of independent variables. All tables display in report format. Use FORMAT to control table formats.

LABELS   *Display both variable and value labels for each table.* This is the default if FORMAT is omitted.

NOLABELS   *Suppress variable and value labels.*

NOCATLABS   *Suppress value (category) labels.*

NAMES   *Display the names of independent variables.* This is the default if FORMAT is omitted.

NONAMES   *Suppress names of independent variables.*

VALUES   *Display the values of independent variables.* This is the default if FORMAT is omitted.

NOVALUES   *Suppress values of independent variables.* This is useful when there are category labels.

TABLE   *Display each table in report format.* This is the default if FORMAT is omitted.

TREE   *Display each table in tree format.* This option is available for general mode only. The individual cells of the MEANS table are displayed as blocks.

Annotated Example

For a complete example with output, see Examples following the Command Reference.

MISSING VALUES

```
MISSING VALUES {varlist(value list) [[/]varlist ...]}
               {ALL(value)                            }
```

Numeric Value List Keywords:

LO, LOWEST, HI, HIGHEST, THRU   &2

Example:

```
MISSING VALUES V1 (8,9) V2 V3 (0) V4 ('X') V5 TO V9 ('    ').
```

Overview

MISSING VALUES declares values for numeric and short string variables as user-missing. These values can then be treated specially in data transformations, statistical calculations, and case selection. By default, user-missing values are treated the same as the system-missing values. System-missing values are assigned automatically when no legal value can be assigned, as when input data for a numeric field are blank or when an illegal calculation is requested.

Basic Specification

• The basic specification is a single variable followed by the user-missing value(s) in parentheses. Each specified value for the variable is treated as user-missing for any analysis.

Syntax Rules

• Each variable can have a maximum of three individual user-missing values. A space or comma must separate each value. See Specifying Ranges of Missing Values, below.

• The same value(s) can be declared as missing for more than one variable by specifying a variable list followed by the value(s) in parentheses.

• Different values can be declared as missing for different variables by specifying separate variable lists for each value. An optional slash can be used to separate specifications.

• The missing-value specification must correspond to the variable type (numeric or string).

• Variable lists must have either all numeric or all string variables.

• Missing values cannot be assigned to long strings or scratch variables.

• Missing values for short string variables must be enclosed in apostrophes or quotation marks (see Universals: Strings). The value specifications must include any leading or trailing blanks.

• A variable list followed by an empty value specification (an empty set of parentheses) deletes any missing-value declarations for those variables.

• Keyword ALL can be used to refer to all user-defined variables in the active system file, provided the variables are either all numeric or all string. If ALL is used to delete all existing missing-value flags by specifying empty parentheses (), variables in the active system file can be both numeric and string.

• More than one MISSING VALUES command can be specified per session.

Operations

• MISSING VALUES takes effect as soon as it is encountered in the command sequence, unlike most transformations, which do not take effect until the data are read. Thus, special attention should be paid to its position among commands. See Universals: Command Order for more information.

• If a variable is mentioned more than once on one or more MISSING VALUES commands before a procedure, only the last specification is used.

• Missing-value specifications can be changed between procedures. New declarations replace previous ones.

- Missing-value declarations are saved in system files (see SAVE) and portable files (see EXPORT).
- If a value specified for a string variable is shorter than the variable, the specified value is right-padded without warning. If the value specified is longer than the variable, the specified value is truncated without warning. SPSS cannot read more characters in the value than have been defined for the string variable.

Example   `MISSING VALUES V1 (8,9) V2 V3 (0) V4 ('X') V5 TO V9 ('    ').`

- Values 8 and 9 are declared missing for numeric variable V1.
- Value 0 is missing for numeric variables V2 and V3.
- Value X is missing for string variable V4.
- Blanks are declared missing for the variables between and including V5 and V9. All these variables must be string variables four columns wide.

Example   `MISSING VALUES V1 ().`

- Any previously declared missing values for V1 are deleted by the empty value specification.

Example   `MISSING VALUES ALL (9).`

- Value 9 is declared missing for all variables in the active system file; the variables must all be numeric.
- All previous missing value declarations are overridden. Value 9 becomes the only user-missing value for all variables.

Example   `MISSING VALUES ALL ().`

- All previously declared missing values for all variables in the active system file are deleted. Thus, there are no longer any user-missing values in the active system file.
- Variables in the active system file can be both numeric and string variables.

Specifying Ranges of Missing Values

A range of values can be specified as missing for numeric variables but not for string variables.

- Keyword THRU indicates an inclusive list of values. Values must be separated from THRU by at least one blank space.
- Keywords HIGHEST and LOWEST with THRU indicate the highest and lowest values of a variable. HIGHEST and LOWEST can be abbreviated to HI and LO.
- Only one THRU specification can be used for each variable list. Each THRU specification can be combined with one additional missing value. A maximum of three values can be specified (one value or keyword on each side of THRU, plus one additional value).

Example   `MISSING VALUES V1 (LOWEST THRU 0).`

- All negative values and 0 are missing for variable V1.

Example   `MISSING VALUES V1 (0 THRU 1.5).`

- Values 0 through (and including) 1.5 are missing.

Example   `MISSING VALUES V1 (LO THRU 0, 999).`

- All negative values, 0, and 999 are missing for variable V1.
- The maximum number of missing values (three) is specified: LO, 0, and 999.

MULT RESPONSE

```
MULT RESPONSE†

{/GROUPS=groupname['label'](itemlist ({value1,value2}))  }
                                     {value         }
      ...[groupname...]

{/VARIABLES=itemlist(min,max)  [itemlist...]            }

{/FREQUENCIES=itemlist                                  }

{/TABLES=itemlist BY itemlist... [BY itemlist] [(PAIRED)]}
      [/itemlist BY...]

[/MISSING=[{TABLE**}] [INCLUDE]]
          {MDGROUP}
          {MRGROUP}

[/FORMAT={LABELS**}  {TABLE** }  [DOUBLE]]
         {NOLABELS}  {CONDENSE}
                     {ONEPAGE }

[/BASE={CASES**  }]
       {RESPONSES}

[/CELLS=[COUNT**] [ROW    ]  [ALL]]
                  [COLUMN]
                  [TOTAL ]
```

† A minimum of two subcommands must be used; at least one from the pair GROUPS or VARIATIONS, and at least one from the pair FREQUENCIES or TABLES.
**Default if the subcommand is omitted.

Example:
```
MULT RESPONSE  GROUPS=MAGS (TIME TO STONE (2))
   /FREQUENCIES=MAGS.
```

Overview

Procedure MULT RESPONSE displays frequencies and optional percentages for multiple-response items in univariate tables and multivariate crosstabulations.

Another procedure that analyzes multiple-response items is TABLES, which has most, but not all, of the functionality of MULT RESPONSE. TABLES has special formatting capabilities that make it useful for preparing presentations.

Multiple-response items are questions that can have more than one value for an individual case. For example, the respondent may have been asked to circle all answers that apply in a list of magazines read within the last month. When you enter the data for an SPSS file, you can create a variable for each possible response and code one of two values, such as 1 for no and 2 for yes; this is the multiple-dichotomy method. Or, you can estimate the maximum number of possible answers from a respondent, create that number of variables, and enter a code for each answer, such as 1 for *Time*, 2 for *Newsweek*, and 3 for *PC Week*. If an individual did not give that many answers, the extra variables are given a missing-value code. This is the multiple-response method of coding answers.

To analyze the data entered by either method, you combine SPSS variables into groups. The specific technique for grouping variables depends on whether you have defined multiple-dichotomy variables or multiple-response variables. When you create a multiple-dichotomy group, each of the component variables having at least one "yes" value becomes a category of the group variable. When you create a multiple-response group, each value becomes a category and SPSS calculates the frequency for a particular value by adding the frequencies of all component variables having that value. Both multiple-dichotomy and multiple-response groups can be crosstabulated with other variables in MULT RESPONSE.

Options

You can specify percentaging, formatting, and missing-value options and create stub and banner tables.

Cell Counts and Percentages

By default, crosstabulations include only counts and no percentages. You can request row, column, and total table percentages. Optionally, you can also base percentages on responses instead of respondents.

Formatting Options

You can suppress the display of value labels, print tables on an 8-1/2-by-11-inch page, and request condensed-format frequency tables.

Basic Specification

MULT RESPONSE operates via major and optional subcommands. The major subcommands (GROUPS, VARIABLES, FREQUENCIES, and TABLES) define or specify the groups and variables that will be included in the analysis and determine the type of table display used for the tabulation.

The basic specification requires at least two of the four major subcommands: either the GROUPS subcommand to define one or more groups or the VARIABLES subcommand to specify existing SPSS variables, and either the FREQUENCIES or TABLES subcommand to request tables.

- GROUPS names groups of multiple-response items to be analyzed and determines how the variables will be combined.
- VARIABLES identifies all individual SPSS variables to be analyzed.
- FREQUENCIES requests frequency tables for items identified by the GROUPS and VARIABLES subcommands.
- TABLES requests the crosstabulation of items identified by the GROUPS and VARIABLES subcommands.

Subcommand Order

- The major subcommands must be used in the following order: GROUPS, VARIABLES, FREQUENCIES, TABLES.
- All major subcommands must precede all optional subcommands. Optional subcommands can be used in any order.

Operations

- MULT RESPONSE produces frequency tables and crosstabulations of groups and existing SPSS variables.
- Totally empty categories are not displayed in either frequency or crosstabular tables.
- If you define a multiple-response group with a very wide range, the tables require substantial amounts of workspace. If the component variables are sparsely distributed, you might consider recoding them to minimize the workspace required.
- You may wish to use MULT RESPONSE to produce only crosstabulations of existing SPSS variables in order to take advantage of its special formatting options. In that case, the GROUPS subcommand is not required and the VARIABLES subcommand becomes the first subcommand.
- With appropriate data transformations, you can create tables with more than one variable in each dimension. You can do this with the COUNT command.

Limitations

- One set of subcommands per MULT RESPONSE command.
- The component variables must have integer values. Non-integer values are truncated.
- Maximum 100 existing SPSS variables named or implied by GROUPS and VARIABLES together.
- Maximum 20 groups defined on GROUPS.
- Maximum 32,767 categories for a multiple-response group or an individual variable.
- Maximum 10 tables lists on TABLES.
- Maximum 5 dimensions per table.

- Maximum 100 groups and existing SPSS variables named or implied on FREQUENCIES and TABLES together.
- Maximum 200 nonempty rows in a single table.
- Maximum 200 nonempty columns in a single table.
- MULT RESPONSE stores category labels in workspace. If there is insufficient space to store the labels after the tables are built, the labels are not displayed.

GROUPS Subcommand

GROUPS defines both multiple-dichotomy and multiple-response groups. Specify a name for the group (with an optional label), followed by a list of the component variables in the group and the value(s) to be used in the tabulation. Enclose the variable list in parentheses, and enclose the values in an inner set of parentheses following the last variable in the list.

Multiple-Dichotomy Groups

To define a multiple-dichotomy group, specify only one tabulating value (the value "yes") following the variable list. Each component variable becomes a value of the group variable, and the number of cases that have the tabulating value becomes the frequency. However, if no case has the tabulating value for a given component variable, that variable does not appear in the tabulation.

Multiple-Response Groups

To define a multiple-response group, specify two values following the variable list. These are the minimum and maximum values that define the inclusive range for the variables in the group. The group variable takes on the same range of values as the component variables. The frequencies for these values are tabulated across all the component variables in the list.

- You can use any valid SPSS variable name for the group. The group name should be unique; however, you may reuse an existing group name on another MULT RESPONSE command. The group variable must not have the same name as an existing SPSS variable specified on the same MULT RESPONSE command.
- The group names and labels exist only during the execution of MULT RESPONSE and disappear once MULT RESPONSE has been executed. Reference to any of the group names in another procedure results in errors.
- For a multiple-dichotomy group, the category labels come from the variable labels defined for the component variables.
- For a multiple-response group, the category labels come from the value labels attached to the first variable in the group. If categories are missing for the first variable but are present for other variables in the group, you must define value labels for the missing categories. One way to define the extra value labels is to use the ADD VALUE LABELS command, listing the first variable and the extra value labels.

Example

```
MULT RESPONSE  GROUPS=MAGS "MAGAZINES READ" (TIME TO STONE (2))
     /FREQUENCIES=MAGS.
```

- The GROUPS subcommand creates MAGS, a multiple-dichotomy group which is tabulated from all the variables between and including TIME and STONE that have the value 2 indicating yes (read the magazine).
- The group label, MAGAZINES READ, is optional and can be up to 40 characters in length, including imbedded blanks. For compatibility with other types of SPSS labels, apostrophes are used to delimit the label, but they are not required.
- The number of cases of each magazine that have the value 2 becomes the frequency for that magazine, to be displayed in the FREQUENCIES table.

Example

```
MULT RESPONSE  GROUPS=PROBS "PERCEIVED NATIONAL PROBLEMS"
   (PROB1 TO PROB3 (1,9))
     /FREQUENCIES=PROBS.
```

- The GROUPS subcommand creates the multiple-response group PROBS using as component variables the existing SPSS variables between and including PROB1 and PROB3 and tabulates values 1 through 9.
- The frequency for a given value is the number of cases that have that value in any of the variables PROB1 to PROB3.

VARIABLES Subcommand

VARIABLES follows GROUPS (when used) and specifies existing SPSS variables used in frequency tables and crosstabulations. Each variable is followed by parentheses enclosing a minimum and a maximum value, which indicate the range of values to be used to allocate cells for tables that use the variable.

- To provide the same minimum and maximum for each of a set of variables, specify a variable list followed by a range specification.
- You can specify any numeric variable with VARIABLES, but noninteger values are truncated.
- The items named by GROUPS can be used in frequency tables and crosstabulations, but you must name them again with VARIABLES, along with a range for the values. You do not have to respecify the items in the groups if they will not be used as individual variables in any tables.

Example

```
MULT RESPONSE  GROUPS=MAGS 'MAGAZINES READ' (TIME TO STONE (2))
  /VARIABLES SEX(1,2) EDUC(1,3)
  /FREQUENCIES=MAGS SEX EDUC.
```

- The VARIABLES subcommand names variables SEX and EDUC so that they can be used in a frequencies table.

Example

```
MULT RESPONSE  GROUPS=MAGS 'MAGAZINES READ' (TIME TO STONE (2))
  /VARIABLES=EDUC (1,3) TIME (1,2).
  /TABLES=MAGS BY EDUC TIME.
```

- The variable TIME is used as an item in a group and also in a table.

FREQUENCIES Subcommand

FREQUENCIES requests frequency tables for groups and individual variables. A frequency table by default contains the count for each value, as well as the percentage of responses and the percentage of cases. For another method of producing frequency tables for individual variables, see the FREQUENCIES procedure.

- All groups must be created by GROUPS, and all individual variables to be tabulated must be named on VARIABLES.
- You can use keyword TO to imply a set of adjacent items of the same type only (group or individual), whose order is determined by the order in which they were named on either GROUPS or VARIABLES.

Example

```
MULT RESPONSE  GROUPS=MAGS 'MAGAZINES READ' (TIME TO STONE (2))
  /FREQUENCIES=MAGS.
```

- The FREQUENCIES subcommand requests a frequency table for a multiple-dichotomy group, tabulating the frequencies for the "2" responses of the component variables included in the multiple-dichotomy group MAGS.

Example

```
MULT RESPONSE
  GROUPS=MAGS 'MAGAZINES READ' (TIME TO STONE (2))
  PROBS 'PERCEIVED NATIONAL PROBLEMS' (PROB1 TO PROB3 (1,9))
  MEMS 'SOCIAL ORGANIZATION MEMBERSHIPS' (VFW AMLEG ELKS (1))
  /VARIABLES SEX(1,2) EDUC(1,3)
  /FREQUENCIES=MAGS TO MEMS SEX EDUC.
```

- The FREQUENCIES subcommand requests frequency tables for MAGS, PROBS, MEMS, SEX, and EDUC.
- You cannot specify MAGS TO EDUC because SEX and EDUC are individual variables, while MAGS, PROBS, and MEMS are group variables.

TABLES Subcommand

TABLES follows the FREQUENCIES subcommand (when used). It names the crosstabulations to be produced by MULT RESPONSE. Both individual variables and group items can be tabulated together.

- The first item list defines the rows of the tables; the next item list (following BY) defines the columns of the tables. Subsequent item lists define controls producing subtables. Use keyword BY to separate the dimensions. You can specify up to five dimensions for a table.

- To produce more than one table, name one or more items for each dimension of the tables. Use keyword TO to imply a set of adjacent variables of the same type only (group items or individual variables).
- The value labels for the columns display on three lines with eight characters per line. To avoid splitting words, reverse the row and column variables, or redefine the variable or value labels (depending on whether the variables are dichotomy variables or multiple-response variables).

Example
```
MULT RESPONSE  GROUPS=MAGS 'MAGAZINES READ' (TIME TO STONE (2))
  /VARIABLES=EDUC (1,3)/TABLES=EDUC BY MAGS.
```

- The TABLES subcommand requests a crosstabulation of the variable EDUC by the multiple-dichotomy group MAGS.

Example
```
MULT RESPONSE  GROUPS=MAGS 'MAGAZINES READ' (TIME TO STONE (2))
  MEMS 'SOCIAL ORGANIZATION MEMBERSHIPS' (VFW AMLEG ELKS (1))
  /VARIABLES EDUC (1,3)/TABLES=MEMS MAGS BY EDUC.
```

- The TABLES subcommand specifies two crosstabulations—MEMS with EDUC and MAGS with EDUC.

Example
```
MULT RESPONSE  GROUPS=MAGS 'MAGAZINES READ' (TIME TO STONE (2))
  /VARIABLES SEX (1,2) EDUC (1,3)
  /TABLES=MAGS BY EDUC SEX/EDUC BY SEX/MAGS BY EDUC BY SEX.
```

- The TABLES subcommand uses slashes to separate three tables lists. It produces two tables from the first tables list (MAGS with EDUC and MAGS with SEX) and one table from the second tables list (EDUC with SEX). The third tables list produces separate tables for each sex (MAGS with EDUC for male and for female).

Example
```
MULT RESPONSE  GROUPS=MAGS 'MAGAZINES READ' (TIME TO STONE (2))
  PROBS 'NATIONAL PROBLEMS MENTIONED' (PROB1 TO PROB3 (1,9))
  /TABLES=MAGS BY PROBS.
```

- The TABLES subcommand requests a crosstabulation of the multiple-dichotomy group MAGS with the multiple-response group PROBS.

PAIRED Keyword
For multiple-response groups, PAIRED pairs the first variable in the first group with the first variable in the second group, the second variable in the first group with the second variable in the second group, and so on. When MULT RESPONSE crosstabulates two groups without PAIRED (the default), it tabulates all component variables of the first group with all component variables of the second group, pooling the responses so that some responses can be counted more than once. Use keyword PAIRED in parentheses on the TABLES subcommand following the last variable named for a specific tables list.

- When you request paired crosstabulations, the order of the component variables on the GROUPS subcommand determines the construction of the table.
- In a paired table request, although the tables can contain individual variables and multiple-dichotomy groups, only items within multiple-response groups are paired.
- The paired option also applies to a multiple-response group used as a controlling variable in a three-way or higher-order table.
- Paired tables are identified in the output by the label **PAIRED GROUP** in the table header.
- Percentages in paired tables are always based upon responses rather than cases.

Example
```
MULT RESPONSE  GROUPS=PSEX 'SEX OF CHILD' (P1SEX P2SEX P3SEX(1,2))
  /PAGE 'AGE OF ONSET OF PREGNANCY' (P1AGE P2AGE P3AGE (1,4))
  /TABLES=PSEX BY PAGE (PAIRED).
```

- The (PAIRED) keyword produces a paired crosstabulation of PSEX by PAGE, which is a combination of the tables P1SEX with P1AGE, P2SEX with P2AGE, and P3SEX with P3AGE.

Example
```
MULT RESPONSE  GROUPS=PSEX 'SEX OF CHILD' (P1SEX P2SEX P3SEX(1,2))
  PAGE 'AGE OF ONSET OF PREGNANCY' (P1AGE P2AGE P3AGE (1,4))
  /VARIABLES=EDUC (1,3)
  /TABLES=PSEX BY PAGE BY EDUC (PAIRED).
```

• The TABLES subcommand pairs only PSEX with PAGE, since EDUC is an individual variable, not a multiple-response group.

CELLS Subcommand

By default, MULT RESPONSE displays cell counts but no cell percentages in the crosstabulation tables. CELLS requests percentages for crosstabulations. You can specify CELLS alone or with one or more keywords. CELLS alone requests ALL available cell percentages. If you specify one or more keywords on CELLS, MULT RESPONSE displays cell counts plus the percentage(s) you request. The count cannot be eliminated from the table cells.

COUNT	*Display cell counts.* This is the default if you omit the CELLS subcommand.
ROW	*Display row percentages.*
COLUMN	*Display column percentages.*
TOTAL	*Display two-way table total percentages.*
ALL	*Display cell counts, row percentages, column percentages, and two-way table total percentages.* This is the default if you specify the CELLS subcommand alone, with no keywords.

Example
```
MULT RESPONSE  GROUPS=MAGS 'MAGAZINES READ' (TIME TO STONE (2))
   /VARIABLES=SEX (1,2) (EDUC (1,3)
   /TABLES=MAGS BY EDUC SEX
   /CELLS=ROW COLUMN.
```

• The CELLS subcommand requests row and column percentages in addition to counts.

BASE Subcommand

BASE lets you obtain cell percentages based on responses rather than respondents. Specify only one of the BASE subcommand's two keywords:

CASES	*Base cell percentages on cases.* This is the default if you omit the BASE subcommand. You cannot use this specification for paired tables.
RESPONSES	*Base cell percentages on responses.* This is the default if you request paired tables, and it cannot be overridden.

Example
```
MULT RESPONSE  GROUPS=PROBS 'NATIONAL PROBLEMS MENTIONED'
   (PROB1 TO PROB3 (1,9))/VARIABLES=EDUC (1,3)
   /TABLES=EDUC BY PROBS
   /CELLS=ROW COLUMN
   /BASE=RESPONSES.
```

• The BASE subcommand requests table marginals and cell percentages based on responses.

MISSING Subcommand

MISSING controls missing values. Its minimum specification is a single keyword. The default keyword is TABLE.

• By default, MULT RESPONSE deletes cases with missing values on a table-by-table basis for both individual variables and groups. Also, values falling outside the specified range are not tabulated and are included in the missing category. Therefore, specifying a range that excludes missing values is equivalent to the default treatment of missing values.

• By default, a case is considered missing for a multiple-dichotomy group if none of its component variables contains the tabulating value. Keyword MDGROUP overrides the default and specifies listwise deletion for multiple-dichotomy groups.

• By default, a case is considered missing for a multiple-response group if none of its components has valid values falling within the tabulating range. Thus, cases with missing or excluded values on some (but not all) of the components of a group are included in tabulations of the group variable. Keyword MRGROUP overrides the default and specifies listwise deletion for multiple-response groups.

• You can use INCLUDE with MDGROUP or MRGROUP. This combination includes cases that would otherwise be excluded for having a user-missing value. The user-missing value is tabulated and must be included in the range specification.

The MISSING subcommand has the following keywords:

TABLE   *Exclude missing values.* Missing values are excluded on a table-by-table basis for both component variables and groups. This is the default if you omit the MISSING subcommand.

INCLUDE   *Include user-missing values.* User-missing values are included in tables if they are encompassed by the range specification on the GROUPS or VARIABLES subcommands.

MDGROUP *Exclude missing values listwise for multiple-dichotomy groups.* Cases missing on any component dichotomy variable are excluded from the tabulation of the multiple-dichotomy group.

MRGROUP *Exclude missing values listwise for multiple-response groups.* Cases missing on any component variable are excluded from the tabulation of the multiple-response group.

Example

```
MULT RESPONSE  GROUPS=FINANCL 'FINANCIAL PROBLEMS MENTIONED'
   (FINPROB1 TO FINPROB3 (1,3))
   SOCIAL 'SOCIAL PROBLEMS MENTIONED'
   (SOCPROB1 TO SOCPROB4 (4,9))
   /VARIABLES=EDUC (1,3)
   /TABLES=EDUC BY FINANCL SOCIAL
   /MISSING=MRGROUP.
```

• The MISSING subcommand indicates that a case will be excluded from counts in the first table if any of the variables in the group FINPROB1 to FINPROB3 has a value outside the range 1 to 3. In the second table, a case is excluded if any of the variables in the group SOCPROB1 to SOCPROB4 has a value outside the range 4 to 9.

FORMAT Subcommand

The FORMAT subcommand controls table formats. Its minimum specification is a single keyword.

• By default, MULT RESPONSE displays the value labels defined for variables in frequency and crosstabulation tables. It displays the frequency tables with up to ten column categories across a page. For frequencies tables, MULT RESPONSE uses more than one page to display frequencies with more than 20 categories.

The labels are controlled by two keywords:

LABELS   *Display value labels in frequency and crosstabulation tables.* This is the default.

NOLABELS *Suppress value labels in frequency and crosstabulation tables for multiple-response variables and individual variables.* You cannot suppress the display of variable labels used as value labels for multiple-dichotomy groups.

The following keywords apply to the format of frequencies tables:

DOUBLE   *Use double spacing for frequency tables.* By default MULT RESPONSE uses single spacing.

TABLE   *Display frequencies tables with up to ten column categories across a page.* This is the default if you omit the FORMAT subcommand.

CONDENSE *Display a condensed-format frequency table.* CONDENSE displays frequency tables in a three-column condensed format for all multiple-response groups and individual variables. Labels are suppressed. This option does not apply to multiple-dichotomy groups.

ONEPAGE *Display a conditional condensed-format frequency table.* Frequency tables display in a three-column condensed format if the multiple-response group or individual variable has more than 20 categories. Items with fewer categories display in the default format. This option does not apply to multiple-dichotomy groups.

Example
```
MULT RESPONSE  GROUPS=PROBS 'NATIONAL PROBLEMS MENTIONED'
   (PROB1 TO PROB3 (1,9))/VARIABLES=EDUC (1,3)
   /FREQUENCIES=EDUC PROBS
   /FORMAT=CONDENSE.
```

• The /FORMAT subcommand specifies condensed format, which eliminates category labels and displays the categories in three parallel sets of columns, each set containing one or more rows of categories (rather than displaying in one set of columns aligned vertically down the page).

Annotated Example

For a complete example with output, see Examples following the Command Reference.

N OF CASES

```
N OF CASES n
```

Example:
```
N OF CASES 100.
```

Overview   N OF CASES (alias N) limits the number of cases in the active system file to the first *n* cases.

Basic Specification   • The basic specification is N OF CASES followed by at least one space and a positive integer. Cases in the active system file are limited to the number specified by the integer.

Syntax   • To limit the number of cases analyzed by all procedures in the session, place N OF CASES before the first command in the session that causes the data to be read (for a list of these commands, see Universals: Command Order). In these applications, any subsequent N OF CASES command specifying a greater number of cases will be ignored.

• To limit the number of cases for the next procedure only, use N OF CASES after the first command that causes the data to be read and immediately before the procedure to which it applies. Assuming that there are no transformation commands between N OF CASES and the procedure to which it applies, this placement causes N OF CASES to be in effect for that one procedure only. If there are intervening transformation commands, the N OF CASES becomes permanent and is in effect for the rest of the session.

Operations   • N OF CASES takes effect as soon as it is encountered in the command sequence, unlike most transformations, which do not take effect until the data are read. Thus, special attention should be paid to its position among commands. For more information, see Universals: Command Order.

• If N OF CASES specifies more cases than can actually be built, SPSS obtains as many cases as possible.

• N controls the building of cases, not the reading of individual data records.

• If N OF CASES is used with SAMPLE or SELECT IF, SPSS reads as many records as required to build the specified *n*. It makes no difference whether the N OF CASES precedes or follows the SAMPLE or SELECT IF.

Example
```
GET FILE=CITY.
N 100.
```

• N OF CASES limits the number of cases on the active system file to the first 100 cases. Cases are limited for all subsequent analysis.

Example
```
DATA LIST FILE=PRSNNL / NAME 1-20 (A) AGE 22-23 SALARY 25-30.
N 25.
SELECT IF (SALARY GT 20000).
LIST.
```

• DATA LIST defines variables from file PRSNNL.

• N OF CASES limits the active system file to 25 cases after cases have been selected by SELECT IF. Cases are limited for all subsequent analyses.

• SELECT IF selects only cases in which SALARY is greater than $20,000.

• LIST produces a listing of the 25 (or fewer) cases in the active system file.

Example
```
DATA LIST FILE=PRSNNL / NAME 1-20 (A) AGE 22-23 SALARY 25-30 DEPT
32.
LIST.
N 25.
FREQUENCIES VAR=SALARY.
N 50.
FREQUENCIES VAR=AGE.
REPORT FORMAT=AUTO /VARS=NAME AGE SALARY /BREAK=DEPT /
SUMMARY=MEAN.
```

- Each N OF CASES command is temporary because it comes after the first command in the session that causes the data to be read (LIST), and because no transformation commands intervene between N OF CASES and the procedure to which it applies.
- The first frequency table is based on 25 cases. The second frequency table is based on 50 cases. The report is based on all cases from file PRSNNL.

NLR

This command is included in the SPSS Advanced Statistics option.

```
MODEL PROGRAM parameter=value [parameter=value ...]
transformation commands

[DERIVATIVES
 transformation commands]
```

Procedure CNLR (Constrained NonLinear Regression):

```
[CONSTRAINED FUNCTIONS
 transformation commands]

CNLR depvar WITH varlist

 [/FILE=file]    [/OUTFILE=file]

 [/PRED=varname]

 [/SAVE [PRED] [RESID[(varname)]] [DERIVATIVES] [LOSS]]

 [/CRITERIA=[ITER n] [MITER n] [CKDER {0.5**}]
                                     {n    }

        [ISTEP {1Ep20**}] [FPR n] [LFTOL n]
               {n      }

        [LSTOL n] [STEP {2**}] [NFTOL n]
                        {n  }

        [FTOL n] [OPTOL n] [CRSHTOL {.01**}]]]
                                    {n    }

 [/BOUNDS=expression, expression, ...]

 [/LOSS=varname]

 [/BOOTSTRAP [=n]]
```

Procedure NLR (NonLinear Regression):

```
NLR depvar WITH varlist

 [/FILE=file]    [/OUTFILE=file]

 [/PRED=varname]

 [/SAVE [PRED] [RESID [(varname)] [DERIVATIVES]]

 [/CRITERIA=[ITER {100**}] [CKDER {0.5**}]
                  {n   }          {n   }

    [SSCON {1E-8**}] [PCON {1E-8**}] [RCON {1E-8**}]]
           {n    }         {n    }          {n    }
```

**Default if subcommand is omitted.

Example:

```
MODEL PROGRAM A=.5 B=1.6.
COMPUTE PRED=A*SPEED**B.
DERIVATIVES.
COMPUTE D.A=SPEED**B.
COMPUTE D.B=A*LN(SPEED)*SPEED**B.
NLR STOP WITH SPEED.
```

Overview
Nonlinear regression is used to estimate parameter values and regression statistics for models that are not linear in their parameters. SPSS has two procedures for estimating nonlinear equations. CNLR (Constrained NonLinear Regression) uses a sequential quadratic programming algorithm and can be used for both constrained and unconstrained problems. NLR (NonLinear Regression) uses a Levenberg-Marquardt algorithm and can only be used for unconstrained problems.

CNLR is more general. It allows linear and nonlinear constraints on any combination of parameters. It will estimate parameters by minimizing any smooth loss function (objective function), and can optionally compute bootstrap estimates of parameter standard errors and correlations. The individual bootstrap parameter estimates can optionally be saved in a separate system file.

Both programs estimate the values of the parameters for the model and, optionally, compute and save predicted values, residuals, and derivatives. Final parameter estimates can be saved in a system file and used in subsequent analyses.

CNLR and NLR use much of the same syntax. Some of the following sections discuss features common to both procedures; in these sections, the notation [C]NLR means that either the CNLR or NLR procedure can be specified. Sections that apply only to CNLR or only to NLR are clearly identified.

Options
The Model. You can use any number of transformation commands to define complex models. See MODEL PROGRAM.

Derivatives. You can use any number of transformation commands to supply derivatives. See DERIVATIVES.

Predicted Values, Residuals, and Derivatives. You can add predicted values, residuals, and derivatives to the active system file. See SAVE Subcommand.

Parameter Estimates. You can save final parametes estimates on a system file (see OUTFILE Subcommand) and use them in subsequent analyses (see FILE Subcommand).

Iterations. You can control the iteration process used in the regression. See CRITERIA Subcommand.

Additional CNLR Controls. For CNLR, you can impose linear and nonlinear constraints on the parameters (see BOUNDS), specify a loss function for CNLR to minimize (see LOSS Subcommand), and provide bootstrap estimates of the parameter standard errors, confidence intervals, and correlations (see BOOTSTRAP Subcommand).

Basic Specification
The basic specification requires three commands: MODEL PROGRAM, COMPUTE (or any other computational transformation command), and either CNLR or NLR.

• The MODEL PROGRAM command assigns initial values to the parameters and signifies the beginning of the model program.

• The COMPUTE command generates a new variable to define the model. If you name this variable PRED, it simplifies the [C]NLR specification. If you use any other name for this variable, the PRED subcommand on [C]NLR is required.

• The [C]NLR command provides the regression specifications. The minimum specification is the dependent variable followed by keyword WITH and the independent variable(s).

For each iteration, the residual sum of squares and estimated values of the model parameters are displayed. Statistics generated include regression and residual sums of squares and mean squares, corrected and uncorrected total sums of squares, R squared, parameter estimates with their asymptotic standard errors and 95% confidence intervals, and an asymptotic correlation matrix of the parameter estimates.

Command Order
- The MODEL PROGRAM command must precede the [C]NLR command and be followed by one or more transformation commands. The transformations in the MODEL PROGRAM block must follow any permanent transformations in a program because the SPSS system variables created by the MODEL PROGRAM transformations do not become a part of the active system file.
- The optional DERIVATIVES command (when used) must follow the model program. DERIVATIVES is followed by its own set of transformation commands, each of which calculates a derivative for one of the parameters. DERIVATIVES and its transformation statements must precede the [C]NLR command.
- The optional CONSTRAINED FUNCTION command (when used) must immediately precede the CNLR command. CONSTRAINED FUNCTION cannot be used with the NLR command. For information on nonlinear constraints, see BOUNDS Subcommand.
- The [C]NLR command must follow the block of transformations for the model program, the derivatives program (when specified), and the constrained function (when specified).
- Subcommands on [C]NLR can be named in any order.

Syntax Rules
- The FILE, OUTFILE, PRED, and SAVE subcommands work the same for both CNLR and NLR.
- The CRITERIA subcommand is used by both CNLR and NLR; however, different iteration criteria are used in CNLR and NLR. Keywords for CRITERIA are thus documented separately for CNLR and NLR.
- The BOUNDS, LOSS, and BOOTSTRAP subcommands can be used only with CNLR. They cannot be used with NLR.

Operations
- By default, the predicted values, residuals, and derivatives are created as temporary variables by the model, and derivatives programs are not saved permanently. To save these variables, use the SAVE subcommand.

Weighting Cases
- If case weighting is in effect, [C]NLR uses case weights when calculating the residual sum of squares and derivatives. However, the degrees of freedom in the ANOVA table are always based on unweighted cases.
- When the model program is first invoked for each case, the weight variable's value is set equal to its value in the active system file. The model program may recalculate that value. For example, to effect a robust estimation, the model program may recalculate the weight variable value as an inverse function of the residual magnitude. [C]NLR uses the weight variable's value after the model program executes.

Cautions
- The selection of good initial values for the parameters in the model program is very important to the operation of [C]NLR. The selection of poor initial values can result in no solution, a local rather than a general solution, or a physically impossible solution.

Missing Values

Cases with missing values for any of the dependent or independent variables named on the [C]NLR command are excluded.
- Predicted values, but not residuals, can be calculated for cases with missing values on the dependent variable.
- [C]NLR ignores cases that have missing, negative, or zero weights. The procedure displays a warning message if it encounters any negative or zero weights at any time during its execution.

- If a variable used in the model program or the derivatives program is omitted from the independent variable list on the [C]NLR command, the predicted value and some or all of the derivatives may be missing for every case. If this happens, SPSS generates an error message.

Example

```
MODEL PROGRAM A=.5 B=1.6.
COMPUTE PRED=A*SPEED**B.
DERIVATIVES.
COMPUTE D.A=SPEED**B.
COMPUTE D.B=A*LN(SPEED)*SPEED**B.
NLR STOP WITH SPEED.
```

- MODEL PROGRAM assigns values to the model parameters A and B.

- COMPUTE generates the variable PRED that is used to define the nonlinear model using parameters A and B and the variable SPEED from the active system file. Because this variable is named PRED, the PRED subcommand is not required on NLR.

- DERIVATIVES indicates that calculations for derivatives are being supplied.

- The two COMPUTE statements in the DERIVATIVES transformations list calculate the derivatives for the parameters A and B. If either one had been omitted, NLR would have calculated it numerically.

- NLR declares the dependent variable, STOP, and one independent variable, SPEED, from the active system file.

MODEL PROGRAM Command

The MODEL PROGRAM command assigns initial values to the parameters and signifies the beginning of the model program. The statements immediately following the MODEL PROGRAM command are SPSS transformation commands that specify the nonlinear equation chosen to model the data. There is no default model.

- The MODEL PROGRAM command is required and must precede the [C]NLR command.

- The MODEL PROGRAM command and each associated transformation must begin in Column 1.

- MODEL PROGRAM must specify the name of each parameter in the model program. Parameters can be assigned any acceptable SPSS variable name. However, if you intend to write the final parameter estimates to a file with the OUTFILE subcommand on [C]NLR, the model program cannot create new variables named SSE or NCASES (see OUTFILE Subcommand).

- Each parameter must be individually named on the MODEL PROGRAM command. Keyword TO is not allowed.

- Each parameter in the model program must be assigned a value. The value can be specified on the MODEL PROGRAM command, or it can be read from an existing system file. To read parameter values from a system file, use the FILE subcommand on [C]NLR.

- Zero should be avoided as an initial value, since it provides no information on the scale of the parameters. This is especially true for CNLR.

- The MODEL PROGRAM command must be followed by one or more transformation commands, including at least one command that uses the parameters and the independent variables (or preceding transformations of these) to calculate the predicted value of the dependent variable. This predicted value defines the nonlinear model. There is no default model.

- The equation specified by the transformation command(s) in the model program is used to calculate predicted values for the dependent variable, based on the parameter estimates and the values of the independent variables. By default, the program assumes that the variable name PRED is assigned to the result of the transformation. If you use a different variable name for the predicted values, supply the name on the PRED subcommand of [C]NLR.

- Variable labels can be assigned to the predicted values variable and its print and write formats can be changed in the MODEL PROGRAM transformation commands. Missing values, however, should not be specified.

- The MODEL PROGRAM block of transformation statements can contain any kind of computational command (such as COMPUTE, IF, DO IF, LOOP, END LOOP, END IF, RECODE, or COUNT) in the transformation language. It can also contain output commands (WRITE, PRINT, or XSAVE). It cannot contain input commands (such as DATA LIST, GET, MATCH FILES, or ADD FILES).

- Transformations in the model program are used only by [C]NLR, and do not affect the active system file.

Example
```
MODEL PROGRAM A=10 B=1 C=5 D=1.
COMPUTE PRED= A*exp(B*X) + C*exp(D*X).
```

- The MODEL PROGRAM command assigns starting values to the four parameters A, B, C, and D.

- COMPUTE defines the model to be fit as the sum of two exponentials.

DERIVATIVES Command

The optional DERIVATIVES command supplies some or all of the derivatives of the model. DERIVATIVES is followed by a block of transformation statements for computing the derivatives. The derivatives command must follow the model program but precede the [C]NLR command.

If the DERIVATIVES command is not used, [C]NLR numerically estimates derivatives for all the parameters. Providing derivatives reduces computational time and, in some situations, may result in a better solution.

- The DERIVATIVES command and each associated transformation must begin in Column 1.

- DERIVATIVES signals the beginning of the derivatives program. DERIVATIVES has no further specifications but must be followed by the set of transformation statements that calculates the derivatives.

- The set of transformation statements can contain any kind of computational command (such as COMPUTE, IF, DO IF, LOOP, END LOOP, END IF, RECODE, or COUNT) in the transformation language. It can also contain output commands (WRITE, PRINT, or XSAVE). It cannot contain input commands (such as DATA LIST, GET, MATCH FILES, or ADD FILES).

- To name the derivatives, specify the prefix "D." before each parameter name. For example, the derivative name for the parameter PARM1 must be D.PARM1.

- Once a derivative has been calculated by a transformation, the variable for that derivative can be used in subsequent transformations.

- You do not need to supply all of the derivatives. Those that are not supplied will be estimated by the program. During the first iteration of the nonlinear estimation procedure, derivatives calculated in the derivatives program are compared with numerically calculated derivatives. This serves as a check on the supplied values (see CRITERIA Subcommand).

- Transformations in the DERIVATIVES command are used by [C]NLR only and do not affect the active system file.

Example
```
DERIVATIVES.
COMPUTE D.A = exp (B * X).
COMPUTE D.B = A * exp (B * X) * X.
COMPUTE D.C = exp (D * X).
COMPUTE D.D = C * exp (D * X) * X.
```

• The derivatives program specifies derivatives for the sum of two exponentials model described by the following equation:

$$Y = Ae^{Bx} + Ce^{Dx}$$

Example
```
DERIVATIVES.
COMPUTE D.A = exp (B * X).
COMPUTE D.B = A * X * D.A.
COMPUTE D.C = exp (D * X).
COMPUTE D.D = C* X * D.C.
```

• This is an alternative way to express the same derivatives program specified in the previous example.

Constrained Functions Program

The optional CONSTRAINED FUNCTIONS command followed by transformation commands specifies nonlinear constraints. CONSTRAINED FUNCTIONS is specified after the model program and the derivatives program (when used). It can only be used with, and must precede, the CNLR command. For more information, see BOUNDS Subcommand.

Example
```
MODEL PROGRAM A=5 B=.3.
COMPUTE PRED = ...
CONSTRAINED FUNCTION.
COMPUTE CF=A-EXP(B).
CNLR Y WITH X, Z
   /BOUNDS CF s 0.
```

CNLR/NLR Command

Either the CNLR or the NLR command is required to specify the dependent and independent variables for the nonlinear regression.

• For either CNLR or NLR, the minimum specification is a dependent variable followed by keyword WITH and a list of independent variables.

• For the dependent variable, only a single numeric variable can be specified. This variable must be in the active system file and cannot be a variable generated by either the model or derivatives program.

• The list of independent variables is required and must include every variable from the active system file used in the transformation commands associated with the MODEL PROGRAM and DERIVATIVES commands. Keyword TO can be used in specifying this list.

OUTFILE Subcommand

OUTFILE stores final parameter estimates for use on a subsequent [C]NLR command. The only specification on OUTFILE is the target system file. Some or all of the values from this system file can be read into a subsequent [C]NLR procedure with the FILE subcommand.

The system file created by OUTFILE stores the following variables:

• All the split-file variables (OUTFILE writes one case of values for each split-file group in the active system file). The labels, formats, and missing values of the split-file variables and the parameters are those defined for them previous to their use in the [C]NLR procedure.

• All the parameters named on the MODEL PROGRAM command.

• The sum of squared residuals (named SSE). The SSE variable has no labels or missing values. The print and write format for SSE is F10.8.

• The number of cases on which the analysis was based (named NCASES). The NCASES variable has no labels or missing values. The print and write format for NCASES is F8.0.

When OUTFILE is used, the model program cannot create variables named SSE or NCASES.

Example
```
MODEL PROGRAM A=.5 B=1.6.
COMPUTE PRED=A*SPEED**B.
NLR STOP WITH SPEED /OUTFILE=PARAM.
```

• OUTFILE generates a system file containing one case for four variables: A and B, SSE, and NCASES.

FILE Subcommand

FILE reads starting values for the parameters from a system file created by an OUTFILE subcommand from a previous [C]NLR procedure. When starting values are read from a file, they do not have to be specified on the MODEL PROGRAM command. Rather, the MODEL PROGRAM command simply names the parameters that correspond to the parameters in the system file.

• The only specification on FILE is the system file that contains the starting values.

• Some new parameters may be specified for the model on the MODEL PROGRAM while others are read from the designated system file.

• The parameters do not have to be named on MODEL PROGRAM in the order they occur in the system file. Moreover, only a partial list of the variables contained in the file need be named.

• If a starting value for a parameter is specified on MODEL PROGRAM and also in the file specified on the FILE subcommand, the value from the MODEL PROGRAM command is used.

• If split-file processing is in effect, the starting values for the first subfile are taken from the first case of the parameter system file. Subfiles are matched with cases in order until the starting value file runs out of cases; all subsequent subfiles use the starting values for the last case.

• To read starting values from a system file and then replace those system file values with the final results from [C]NLR, specify the same file on the FILE and OUTFILE subcommands. The input file is read completely before anything is written on the output file.

Example
```
MODEL PROGRAM A B C=1 D=3.
COMPUTE PRED=A*SPEED**B + C*SPEED**D.
NLR STOP WITH SPEED /FILE=PARAM /OUTFILE=PARAM.
```

• MODEL PROGRAM names four of the parameters used to calculate PRED but assigns values to only C and D. The values of A and B are read from the existing system file PARAM.

• After NLR computes the final estimates of the four parameters, OUTFILE writes over the old input file. If in addition to these new final estimates the former starting values of A and B are still desired, different system files can be specified on the FILE and OUTFILE subcommands.

PRED Subcommand

PRED identifies the predicted values variable for [C]NLR.

• The only specification is a variable name, which must be identical to the variable name used to calculate predicted values in the model program.

• If the transformation statement in the model program names the predicted values variable PRED, the PRED subcommand can be omitted on [C]NLR. If the transformation statement uses any other name for the predicted values variable, the PRED subcommand is required. The predicted variable is not saved on the active system file unless the SAVE subcommand is used.

Example
```
MODEL PROGRAM A=.5 B=1.6.
COMPUTE PSTOP=A*SPEED**B.
NLR STOP WITH SPEED /PRED=PSTOP.
```

- COMPUTE in the model program creates a variable named PSTOP to temporarily store the predicted values for the dependent variable STOP.
- PRED identifies PSTOP as the model to be used for the NLR procedure.

SAVE Subcommand

SAVE is used to save the temporary variables for the predicted values, residuals, and derivatives created by the model program and derivatives program.

- The minimum specification is a single keyword.
- The names of the saved variables cannot already exist on the active file, except as temporary variable names (names of variables created after the TEMPORARY or MODEL PROGRAM commands). If a naming conflict exists, the variables are not created.

The following keywords are available and can be used in any combination. Although the keywords may be specified in any order on SAVE, the new variables are always appended to the active file in the order in which these keywords are presented:

PRED *Save the predicted values.* The variable's name, label, and formats are those specified for it (or assigned by default) in the model program.

RESID [(varname)] *Save the residuals variable.* If no varname is specified, the name of this variable is the same as the specification used for this keyword. For example, if RESID is abbreviated to RES, the variable name is RES. Optionally, specify an alternative name in parentheses for the variable. The residuals variable has the same print and write format as the predicted variable created by the model program. It has no variable label and no values defined as missing. It is system-missing for any case in which either the dependent variable is missing or the predicted value cannot be computed.

DERIVATIVES *Save the derivative variables.* The derivative variable names are created by adding the prefix D. to the first six characters of the parameter names. Derivative variables use the print and write formats of the predicted variable and have no value labels or defined missing values. Derivative variables are saved in the same order as the parameters named on the MODEL PROGRAM command. Derivatives are saved for all parameters, whether or not the derivative was supplied in the derivatives program.

LOSS *Save the user-specified loss function variable.* This specification is available only if the LOSS subcommand has also been specified. LOSS is only available with CNLR.

Asymptotic standard errors of predicted values and residuals, and special residuals used for outlier detection and influential case analysis are not provided by the [C]NLR procedure. However, for a squared loss function, the asymptotically correct values for all these statistics can be calculated using the SAVE subcommand with [C]NLR and then using the REGRESSION procedure. In REGRESSION, the dependent variable is still the same, and derivatives of the model parameters are used as independent variables. Casewise plots, standard errors of prediction, partial regression plots, and other diagnostics of the regression are valid for the nonlinear model.

Example
```
MODEL PROGRAM A=.5 B=1.6.
COMPUTE PSTOP=A*SPEED**B.
NLR STOP WITH SPEED /PRED=PSTOP
  /SAVE=RESID(RSTOP) DERIVATIVES PRED.
REGRESSION VARIABLES=STOP D.A D.B /ORIGIN
  /DEPENDENT=STOP /ENTER D.A D.B /RESIDUALS.
```

- Keyword RESID on SAVE creates the residuals variable RSTOP.

- Keyword DERIVATIVES on SAVE creates the derivative variables D.A and D.B.

- Since the PRED subcommand is used to identify PSTOP as the predicted variable in the nonlinear model, keyword PRED on SAVE adds the variable PSTOP to the active system file.

- Thus, SAVE adds four new variables to the active system file, PSTOP, RSTOP, D.A, and D.B, in that order.

- The subcommand RESIDUALS for REGRESSION produces the default analysis of residuals.

CRITERIA Subcommand

CRITERIA controls the values of the cutoff points used to stop the iterative calculations in [C]NLR.

- The minimum specification is a criteria keyword and an appropriate value. The value can be specified in parentheses, after an equals sign, or after a space or comma.

- Multiple keywords can be specified in any order. Defaults are in effect for keywords not specified.

Keywords available for CRITERIA differ between CNLR and NLR. The following sections discuss the keywords available for each separately.

Iteration Criteria for CNLR

The CNLR procedure uses NPSOL (Version 4.03) Fortran Package for Nonlinear Programming (Gill et al., 1986). The CRITERIA subcommand of CNLR gives the control features of NPSOL. The following section summarizes the NPSOL documentation.

CNLR uses a sequential quadratic programming algorithm, with a quadratic programming subproblem to determine the search direction. If constraints or bounds are specified, the first step is to find a point that is feasible with respect to those constraints. Each major iteration sets up a quadratic program to find the search direction, p. Minor iterations are used to solve this subprogram. Then, the major iteration determines a steplength α by a linesearch, and the function is evaluated at the new point. An optimal solution is found when the optimality tolerance criterion is met.

The CRITERIA subcommand has the following keywords when used with CNLR:

ITER n
: *Maximum number of major iterations.* Specify any positive integer for n. The default is $\max(50,3(p+m_L)+10m_N)$, where p is the number of parameters, m_L is the number of linear constraints, and m_N is the number of nonlinear constraints. If the search for a solution stops because this limit is exceeded, CNLR issues a warning message.

MINORITERATION n
: *Maximum number of minor iterations.* Specify any positive integer. This is the number of minor iterations allowed within each major iteration. The default is $\max(50,3(n+m_L+m_N))$.

CKDER n
: *Critical value for derivative checking.* Specify a number between 0 and 1 for n. The default is 0.5. Specify 0 to disable this criterion.

On the first iteration, CNLR always checks any derivatives calculated on the derivatives program by comparing them with numerically calculated derivatives. For each comparison, it computes an agreement score. A score of 1 indicates agreement to machine precision; a score of 0 indicates definite disagreement. If a score is less than 1, either an incorrect derivative was supplied or there are numerical problems in estimating the derivative. The lower the score, the more likely it is that the supplied derivatives are incorrect. Highly correlated parameters may cause disagreement even when a correct derivative is supplied. Be sure to check the derivatives if the agreement score is not 1.

During the first iteration, CNLR checks each derivative score. If any score is below 1, it begins displaying a table to show the worst (lowest) score for each derivative. If any score is below the critical value, the program stops.

CRSHTOL n   *Crash tolerance.* CRSHTOL *n* is used to determine if initial values are within their specified bounds. A constraint of the form a'X *l* is considered a valid part of the working set if |a'X − *l*| *CRSHTOL (1+|l|)*. Specify any value between 0 and 1. The default value is 0.01.

STEPLIMIT n   *Step limit.* The step limit can prevent very early steps from going too far from good initial estimates. This bound prevents CNLR from making a change in the length of the parameter vector of more than a factor of STEPLIMIT in the CNLR algorithm. Specify any positive value. The default value is 2.

FTOLERANCE n *Feasibility tolerance.* This is the maximum absolute difference allowed for both linear and nonlinear constraints for a solution to be considered feasible. Specify any value greater than 0. The default value is the square root of your machine's epsilon.

LFTOLERANCE n *Linear feasibility tolerance.* If specified, this overrides FTOLERANCE for linear constraints and bounds. Specify any value greater than 0. The default value is the square root of your machine's epsilon.

NFTOLERANCE n *Nonlinear feasible tolerance.* If specified, this overrides FTOLERANCE for nonlinear constraints. Specify any value greater than 0. The default value is the square root of your machine's epsilon.

LSTOLERANCE n *Line search tolerance.* This value must be between 0 and 1 (but not including 1), and controls the accuracy required of the line search that forms the innermost search loop. The default value, 0.9, specifies an inaccurate search. This is appropriate for many problems, particularly if nonlinear constraints are involved. A smaller positive value, corresponding to a more accurate line search, may give better performance if there are no nonlinear constraints, all (or most) derivatives are supplied in the derivatives program, and the data fit in memory.

OPTOLERANCE n *Optimality tolerance.* If an iteration point is a feasible point, and the next step will not produce a relative change in either the parameter vector or the objective function of more than the square root of OPTOLERANCE, an optimal solution has been found. OPTOLERANCE can also be thought of as the number of significant digits in the objective function at the solution. For example, if OPTOLERANCE=10^{-6}, the objective function should have approximately six significant digits accuracy. Specify any number between the FPRECISION value and 1. The default value for OPTOLERANCE is epsilon $**0.8$.

FPRECISION n   *Function precision.* This is a measure of the accuracy with which the objective function can be measured. It acts as a relative precision when the function is large, and an absolute precision when the function is small. For example, if the objective function is larger than 1, and six significant digits are desired, FPRECISION should be $1E-6$. If, however, the objective function is of the order 0.001, FPRECISION should be $1E-9$ to get six digits of accuracy. Specify any number between 0 and 1. The choice of FPRECISION can be very complicated for a badly scaled problem. Chapter 8 of Gill et al. (1981) gives some scaling suggestions. The default value is epsilon $**0.9$.

ISTEP n   *Infinite step size.* This value is the magnitude of the change in parameters that is defined as infinite. That is, if the change in the parameters at a step is greater than ISTEP, the problem is considered unbounded, and estimation stops. Specify any positive number. The default value is $1E+20$.

Iteration Criteria for NLR   The NLR procedure uses an adaptation of subroutine LMSTR from the MINPACK package by Garbow et al. Since the NLR algorithm differs substantially from CNLR, the CRITERIA subcommand for NLR has a different set of keywords.

The NLR procedure uses the Levenberg-Marquardt method for computing parameter estimates. At each iteration, NLR evaluates the estimates against a set of control criteria. The iterative calculations continue until one of five cutoff points is met, at which point the iterations stop and the reason for stopping is displayed.

The CRITERIA subcommand has the following keywords when used with NLR:

ITER n   *Maximum number of iterations allowed.* Specify any positive integer for *n*. The default is 100 iterations per parameter. If the search for a solution stops because this limit is exceeded, NLR issues a warning message.

SSCON n   *Convergence criterion for the sum of squares.* Specify any nonnegative number for *n*. The default is $1E-8$. If successive iterations fail to reduce the sum of squares by this proportion, the procedure stops. Specify 0 to disable this criterion.

PCON n   *Convergence criterion for the parameter values.* Specify any nonnegative number for *n*. The default is $1E-8$. If successive iterations fail to change any of the parameter values by this proportion, the procedure stops. Specify 0 to disable this criterion.

RCON n   *Convergence criterion for the correlation between the residuals and the derivatives.* Specify any nonnegative number for *n*. The default is $1E-8$. If the largest value for the correlation between the residuals and the derivatives becomes this small, the procedure stops because it lacks the information it needs to estimate a direction for its next move. This criterion is often referred to as a gradient convergence criterion. Specify 0 to disable this criterion.

CKDER n   *Critical value for derivative checking.* Specify a number between 0 and 1 for n; the default is 0.5. Specify 0 to disable this criterion.

On the first iteration, NLR always checks any derivatives calculated on the derivatives program by comparing them with numerically calculated derivatives. For each comparison, it computes an agreement score. A score of 1 indicates agreement to machine precision; a score of 0 indicates definite disagreement. If a score is less than 1, either an incorrect derivative was supplied or there are numerical problems in estimating the derivative. The lower the score, the more likely it is that the supplied derivatives are incorrect. Highly correlated parameters may cause disagreement even when a correct derivative is supplied. Be sure to check the derivatives if the agreement score is not 1.

During the first iteration, NLR checks each derivative score. If any score is below 1, it begins displaying a table to show the worst (lowest) score for each derivative. If any score is below the critical value, the program stops.

Example

```
MODEL PROGRAM A=.5 B=1.6.
COMPUTE PRED=A*SPEED**B.
NLR STOP WITH SPEED /CRITERIA=ITER(80) SSCON=.000001.
```

- CRITERIA changes two of the five iteration cutoff values, ITER and SSCON, and leaves the remaining three, PCON, RCON, or CKDER, at their default values.

BOUNDS Subcommand

The BOUNDS subcommand can be used to specify both linear and nonlinear constraints. It can be used only with CNLR; it cannot be used with NLR.

Simple Bounds and Linear Constraints

BOUNDS can be used to impose bounds on parameter values. These bounds can involve either single parameters or a linear combination of parameters and can be either equalities or inequalities.

- All bounds are specified on the same BOUNDS subcommand and are separated by semicolons.
- The only variables allowed on BOUNDS are parameter variables (those that were specified in the model program).
- When a parameter is multiplied by a constant, the constant must be specified first.
- Only multiplication, addition, and subtraction can be used. All the relational operators can be used, and they can be specified as either a symbol or the two-letter abbreviation (for example, EQ or =). When two relational operators are used (as in the third bound in the example below) they must both be in the same direction.

Example

```
/BOUNDS 5 > A;
       B > 9;
      .01 < 2*A + C < 1;
    D + 2*E = 10
```

- BOUNDS imposes bounds on the parameters A, B, C, and D. Specifications for each parameter are separated by a semicolon.

Nonlinear Constraints

Nonlinear constraints on the parameters can also be specified. The constrained function must be calculated and stored in a variable by a CONSTRAINED FUNCTION program, directly preceding the CNLR command. The constraint is then specified on the BOUNDS subcommand as bounds on that variable.

In general, nonlinear bounds will not be obeyed until an optimal solution has been found. This is different from simple and linear bounds, which are satisfied at each iteration. The constrained functions must be smooth near the solution.

Example

```
MODEL PROGRAM A=5 B=.3.
COMPUTE PRED = ...
CONSTRAINED FUNCTION.
COMPUTE DIFF=A-10**B.
CNLR Y WITH X, Z
   /BOUNDS DIFF s 0.
```

- The constrained function is calculated by a CONSTRAINED FUNCTION program and stored in variable DIFF. The CONSTRAINED FUNCTION command immediately precedes CNLR.

- BOUNDS imposes bounds on variable DIFF.

- CONSTRAINED FUNCTION variables and parameters named in the MODEL PROGRAM command cannot be combined in the same BOUNDS expression. For example, you cannot specify (DIFF = A) > 0 on the BOUNDS subcommand.

LOSS Subcommand

LOSS specifies a loss function for CNLR to minimize. By default, CNLR minimizes the sum of squared residuals. LOSS can be used only with CNLR; it cannot be used with NLR.

- The loss function must first be computed in the model program. LOSS is then used to specify the name of the computed variable.

- The minimizing algorithm may fail if it is given a loss function that is not smooth, such as the absolute value of residuals.

- If derivatives are supplied, the derivative of each parameter must be computed with respect to the loss function, rather than the predicted value. The easiest way to do this is in two steps: first compute derivatives of the model, and then compute derivatives of the loss function with respect to the model and multiply by the model derivatives.

- When LOSS is used, the usual summary statistics are not computed. Standard errors, confidence intervals, and correlations of the parameters are available only if the BOOTSTRAP subcommand is specified.

Example

```
MODEL PROGRAM  A=1 B=1.
COMPUTE PRED=EXP(A+B*T)/(1+EXP(A+B*T)).
COMPUTE LOSS=-W*(Y*LN(PRED)+(1-Y)*LN(1-PRED)).

DERIVATIVES.
COMPUTE D.A=PRED/(1+EXP(A+B*T)).
COMPUTE D.B=T*PRED/(1+EXP(A+B*T)).
COMPUTE D.A=(-W*(Y/PRED - (1-Y)/(1-PRED)) * D.A).
COMPUTE D.B=(-W*(Y/PRED - (1-Y)/(1-PRED)) * D.B).

CNLR Y WITH T W /LOSS=LOSS.
```

- The second COMPUTE command in the model program computes the loss functions and stores its values in variable LOSS. Variable LOSS is then specified on the LOSS subcommand.

- Because derivatives are supplied, the derivative of each parameter is computed with respect to the loss function, rather than the predicted value.

BOOTSTRAP Subcommand

BOOTSTRAP provides bootstrap estimates of the parameter standard errors, confidence intervals, and correlations. BOOTSTRAP can be used only with CNLR; it cannot be used with NLR.

Bootstrapping is a way of estimating the standard error of a statistic using repeated samples from the original data set. This is done by sampling with replacement to get many samples of the same size as the original data set.

- The minimum specification is the subcommand keyword. Optionally, specify the number of samples to use for generating bootstrap results.

- By default, BOOTSTRAP generates bootstrap results based on $10*p*(p+1)/2$ samples, where p is the number of parameters. That is, 10 samples are drawn for each statistic (standard error or correlation) to be calculated.

- When BOOTSTRAP is used, the nonlinear equation is estimated for each sample. The standard error of each parameter estimate is then calculated as the standard deviation of the bootstrapped estimates. Parameter values from the original data are used as starting values for each bootstrap sample. Even so, bootstrapping is computationally expensive.

- If the OUTFILE subcommand is specified, a case is written to the output file for each bootstrap sample. The first case in the file will be the actual parameter estimates, followed by the bootstrap samples. After the first case is eliminated (using SELECT IF), other SPSS procedures (such as FREQUENCIES) can be used to examine the bootstrap distribution.

Example

```
MODEL PROGRAM A=.5 B=1.6.
COMPUTE PSTOP=A*SPEED**B.
CNLR STOP WITH SPEED /BOOTSTRAP /OUTFILE=PARAM.
GET FILE=PARAM.
LIST.
SELECT IF (SAMPLE > 1).
FREQUENCIES A B /FORMAT=NOTABLE /HISTOGRAM.
```

- CNLR generates the bootstrap standard errors, confidence intervals, and parameter correlation matrix. OUTFILE saves the bootstrap estimates in the file PARAM.

- GET retrieves the system file PARAM.

- LIST lists the different sample estimates along with the original estimate. The NCASES variable in the listing (see the OUTFILE subcommand) refers to the number of distinct cases in the sample, since cases are duplicated in each bootstrap sample.

- FREQUENCIES generates histograms of the bootstrapped parameter estimates.

Annotated Example

For a complete example with output, see Examples following the Command Reference.

References

Draper, N., and H. Smith. 1981. *Applied regression analysis.* 2d ed. New York: John Wiley & Sons.

Gill, P. E., W. M. Murray, and M. H. Wright. 1981. *Practical optimization.* London: Academic Press.

Gill, P. E., W. M. Murray, M. A. Saunders, and M. H. Wright. 1984. Procedures for optimization problems with a mixture of bounds and general linear constraints. *ACM Transactions on Mathematical Software* 10 (3): 282-96.

——. 1986. *User's guide for NPSOL (version 4.0): A fortran package for nonlinear programming.* Technical Report SOL 86-2, Department of Operations Research, Stanford University.

Hinds, M. A., and G. A. Milliken. 1982. Statistical methods to use nonlinear models to compare silage treatments. Unpublished paper.

Kvalseth, T. O. 1985. Cautionary note about R squared. *American Statistical Association* 39 (4): 279-85.

NONPAR CORR

```
NONPAR CORR [VARIABLES=] varlist [WITH varlist] [/varlist...]

[/PRINT={ONETAIL**}  {SIG**}  {SPEARMAN**}]
         {TWOTAIL  }  {NOSIG}  {KENDALL   }
                               {BOTH      }


[/SAMPLE]

[/MISSING={PAIRWISE**} [INCLUDE]]
          {LISTWISE  }

[/FORMAT={MATRIX**}]
         {SERIAL  }

[/MATRIX=OUT({*   })]
             {file}
```

**Default if the subcommand is omitted.

Example:

```
NONPAR CORR VARIABLES=PRESTIGE SPPRES PAPRES16 DEGREE PADEG
MADEG.
```

Overview

NONPAR CORR computes two rank-order correlation coefficients, Spearman's rho and Kendall's tau-b, with their significance levels. You can obtain either or both coefficients. When you use NONPAR CORR, SPSS automatically computes the ranks and stores the cases in memory. Therefore, memory required is directly proportional to the number of cases being analyzed.

Options

Coefficients and Significance Levels. By default, NONPAR CORR computes Spearman coefficients. Below each coefficient it displays both the number of cases and the one-tailed significance level. Optionally, you can request a two-tailed test, suppress the number of cases and significance level for each coefficient, compute only the Kendall coefficients, or compute both Spearman and Kendall coefficients. See PRINT Subcommand.

Random Sampling. You can request a random sample of cases when there is not enough space to store all the cases. See SAMPLE Subcommand.

Formatting Options. By default, NONPAR CORR displays correlations in matrix format. You can also display them in serial format. See FORMAT Subcommand.

Matrix Output. You can write matrix materials to a system file. The matrix materials include the number of cases used to compute each coefficient and either the Spearman or Kendall coefficients for each variable, whichever is requested. These materials can be read by other SPSS procedures. See MATRIX Subcommand.

Basic Specification

- The basic specification is VARIABLES and a list of numeric variables. The actual keyword VARIABLES can be omitted. By default, Spearman correlation coefficients are calculated.

Subcommand Order

- VARIABLES must be first.
- Remaining subcommands can be used in any order.

Operations
- NONPAR CORR produces one or more matrices of correlation coefficients. For each coefficient, NONPAR CORR displays the number of cases used and the significance level.
- Depending on how the variable list is specified, NONPAR CORR displays either a lower-triangular or a rectangular matrix (see VARIABLES Subcommand).
- If all cases have a missing value for a given pair of variables, or if they all have the same value for a variable, the coefficient cannot be computed. If a correlation cannot be computed, NONPAR CORR displays a decimal point.
- If both Spearman and Kendall coefficients are requested and MATRIX is used to write matrix materials to a system file, only Spearman's coefficient will be written with the matrix materials.

Limitations
- Maximum 25 variable lists.
- Maximum 100 variables total per NONPAR CORR command.

Example
```
NONPAR CORR VARIABLES=PRESTIGE SPPRES PAPRES16 DEGREE PADEG
MADEG.
```
- NONPAR CORR produces a triangular matrix. The correlation of a variable with itself (the diagonal) and redundant coefficients are not displayed.
- By default, Spearman correlation coefficients are calculated. The number of cases upon which the correlations are based and the one-tailed significance level are displayed for each correlation.

VARIABLES Subcommand
VARIABLES specifies the variable list. The keyword VARIABLES is optional. If keyword VARIABLES is explicitly used, an equals sign must precede the variable list.

- All variables must be numeric.
- If a simple variable list is specified, NONPAR CORR displays the correlations of each variable with every other variable in the list in a lower-triangular matrix.
- To obtain a rectangular matrix, specify two variable lists separated by keyword WITH. NONPAR CORR displays a rectangular matrix of variables in the first list correlated with variables in the second list.
- To write a correlation matrix to a matrix system file, specify a simple variable list on VARIABLES, and use the MATRIX subcommand. Keyword WITH cannot be used when the MATRIX subcommand is used.
- To request more than one matrix, use a slash to separate the specifications for each of the requested matrices.

Example
```
NONPAR CORR VARS=PRESTIGE SPPRES PAPRES16 WITH DEGREE PADEG
MADEG.
```
- Nine correlations are calculated. The variables listed before keyword WITH define the rows of the matrix, and those listed after keyword WITH define the columns.
- Unless a variable is in both lists, there are no identity coefficients in the matrix.

Example
```
NONPAR CORR VARIABLES=SPPRES PAPRES16 PRESTIGE
                     /SATCITY WITH SATHOBBY SATFAM.
```
- NONPAR CORR produces two correlation matrices. The first matrix contains three coefficients in triangular form. The second matrix is rectangular and contains two coefficients.

PRINT Subcommand	Use PRINT to request the Kendall correlation coefficient or both Spearman and Kendall coefficients. PRINT can also be used to switch to a two-tailed test and to suppress the display of the number of cases and significance level.

- By default, NONPAR CORR displays Spearman correlation coefficients. Below each coefficient it displays the number of cases and the significance level. The significance level is based on a one-tailed test.
- Both the Spearman and the Kendall coefficients are based on ranks.
- If keyword WITH is used in a variable list, the display will be a rectangular matrix with the number of cases suppressed and asterisks indicating significance levels.
- If both FORMAT=SERIAL and PRINT=NOSIG are specified, only FORMAT=SERIAL is in effect.

SPEARMAN *Spearman's rho.* Only Spearman coefficients are displayed. This is the default.

KENDALL *Kendall's tau-*b. Only Kendall coefficients are displayed.

BOTH *Kendall and Spearman coefficients.* Both coefficients are displayed. If MATRIX is used to write the correlation matrix to a system file, only Spearman's coefficient will be written with the matrix materials.

SIG *Display the number of cases and significance level.* This is the default.

NOSIG *Suppress the display of the number of cases and significance level.* An asterisk (*) following a coefficient indicates significance at the 0.01 level or less. Two asterisks (**) following a coefficient indicate significance at the 0.001 level or less.

ONETAIL *One-tailed test of significance.* This test is appropriate when the direction of the relationship between a pair of variables can be specified in advance of the analysis. This is the default.

TWOTAIL *Two-tailed test of significance.* This test is appropriate when the direction of the relationship cannot be determined in advance, as is often the case in exploratory data analysis.

SAMPLE Subcommand	NONPAR CORR must store cases in memory to build matrices. SAMPLE selects a random sample of cases when computer resources are insufficient to store all the cases.

- To request a random sample, simply specify the subcommand. SAMPLE has no additional specifications.

MISSING Subcommand	MISSING controls missing-value treatments.

- By default, NONPAR CORR deletes cases with missing values on a pair-by-pair basis. A case missing on one or both of the pair of variables for a specific correlation coefficient is not used for that coefficient. Because each coefficient is based on all cases that have valid codes on that particular pair of variables, the maximum information available is used in every calculation. This also results in a set of coefficients based on a varying number of cases.

PAIRWISE *Exclude missing values pairwise.* Cases missing for one or both of a pair of variables for a specific correlation coefficient are excluded from the analysis. This is the default.

LISTWISE *Exclude missing values listwise.* Cases missing on any variable named in a list are excluded from all analyses. Each variable list on a command is evaluated separately. If multiple variable lists are specified, a case missing for one matrix might be used in another matrix. This option decreases the amount of memory required and significantly decreases computational time.

INCLUDE *Include user-missing values.* User-missing values are treated as if they are not missing.

FORMAT Subcommand

FORMAT controls the format of the correlation matrix.

MATRIX *Display correlations in matrix format.* This is the default.

SERIAL *Display correlations in serial string format.* Coefficients from the first row of the matrix are displayed first, followed by coefficients from the second row, and so on for all of the rows in the matrix. Each coefficient is identified with the name of the variables for which it was calculated. The number of cases and significance level are displayed below the correlation, just as they are in matrix format.

MATRIX Subcommand

MATRIX writes matrix materials to a system file. The matrix materials always include the number of cases used to compute each coefficient, and either the Spearman (RHO) or the Kendall (TAUB) correlation coefficient for each variable, whichever is requested.

• The remaining variables in the file are the variables used to form the correlation matrix.

Split Files and Variable Order

• When split-file processing is in effect, the first variables in the matrix system file will be the split variables, followed by ROWTYPE_, VARNAME_, and the variables used to form the correlation matrix.

• A full set of matrix materials is written for each split-file group defined by the split variable(s).

• A split variable cannot have the same variable name as any other variable written to the matrix system file.

• If split-file processing is in effect when a matrix is written, the same split file must be in effect when that matrix is read by any procedure.

Additional Statistics

• NONPAR CORR always includes with the matrix materials the number of cases used to compute each coefficient. This information immediately precedes the correlation matrix in the output file.

• You cannot write both Spearman's and Kendall's coefficients to the same matrix system file. To obtain a matrix of both Spearman's and Kendall's coefficients, specify separate NONPAR CORR commands for each coefficient and define different matrix system outfiles for each command.

• If PRINT=BOTH is in effect, NONPAR CORR displays a matrix in the listing file for both coefficients but writes only the Spearman coefficients to the matrix system file.

• NONPAR CORR can write matrix materials for a simple variable list but not for variable lists containing keyword WITH. If more than one variable list is specified, only the last variable list that does not use keyword WITH is written to the matrix system file.

• Keyword OUT specifies the file to which the matrix is written. Specify the matrix file in parentheses.

• To use the RHO or TAUB matrix as a correlation matrix for another procedure, the RECODE command must be used to change the ROWTYPE_ value RHO or TAUB to CORR.

- Documents from the original file will not be included in the matrix file and will not be present if the matrix file becomes the active system file.

OUT *Write a matrix system file.* Specify either a file or an asterisk, and enclose the specification in parentheses. If you specify a file, the file is stored on disk and can be retrieved at any time. If you specify an asterisk (*), the matrix system file replaces the active system file but is not stored on disk unless you use SAVE or XSAVE.

Format of the Matrix System File

- The matrix system file has two special variables created by SPSS: ROWTYPE_ and VARNAME_. Variable ROWTYPE_ is a short string variable with values N and RHO (for Spearman's correlation coefficient). If you specify Kendall's coefficient, the values are N and TAUB. The next variable, VARNAME_, is a short string variable whose values are the names of the variables used to form the correlation matrix. When ROWTYPE_ is RHO (or TAUB), VARNAME_ gives the variable associated with that row of the correlation matrix.

Missing Values

- With PAIRWISE treatment of missing values (the default), the matrix of N's used to compute each coefficient is included with the matrix materials.
- With LISTWISE or INCLUDE treatments, a single N used to calculate all coefficients is included with the matrix materials.

Example

```
GET FILE GSS80 /KEEP PRESTIGE SPPRES PAPRES16 DEGREE PADEG
MADEG.
NONPAR CORR VARIABLES=PRESTIGE TO MADEG
  /MATRIX OUT(NPMAT).
```

- NONPAR CORR reads raw data from file GSS80 and writes one set of correlation matrix materials to the file NPMAT.
- The active system file is still the file GSS80. Subsequent commands are executed on file GSS80.

Example

```
GET FILE GSS80 /KEEP PRESTIGE SPPRES PAPRES16 DEGREE PADEG
MADEG.
NONPAR CORR VARIABLES=PRESTIGE TO MADEG
  /MATRIX OUT(*).
LIST
DISPLAY DICTIONARY
```

- NONPAR CORR writes the same matrix as in the example above. However, the matrix system file replaces the active system file. The LIST and DISPLAY commands are executed on the matrix file, not on the file GSS80.

Example

```
NONPAR CORR VARIABLES=PRESTIGE SPPRES PAPRES16 DEGREE PADEG
MADEG
       /PRESTIGE TO DEGREE /PRESTIGE WITH DEGREE
  /MATRIX OUT(NPMAT).
```

- Only the matrix for PRESTIGE TO DEGREE is written to the matrix system file because it is the last variable list that does not use keyword WITH.

Annotated Example

For a complete example with output, see Examples following the Command Reference.

NPAR TESTS

```
NPAR TESTS [CHISQUARE=varlist[(lo,hi)]/]
            [/EXPECTED={EQUAL        }]
                       {f1,f2,...fn}

[/K-S({UNIFORM[,lo,hi]})=varlist]
      {NORMAL[,m,sd] }
      {POISSON[,m]   }

[/RUNS({MEAN  })=varlist]
       {MEDIAN}
       {MODE  }
       {value }

[/BINOMIAL[({.5})]=varlist[({v1,v2})]]
           { p}            {value}

[/MCNEMAR=varlist [WITH varlist [(PAIRED)]]]

[/SIGN=varlist [WITH varlist [(PAIRED)]]]

[/WILCOXON=varlist [WITH varlist [(PAIRED)]]]

[/COCHRAN=varlist]

[/FRIEDMAN=varlist]

[/KENDALL=varlist]

[/MEDIAN[(value)]=varlist BY var (v1,v2)]

[/M-W=varlist BY var (v1,v2)]

[/K-S=varlist BY var (v1,v2)]

[/W-W=varlist BY var (v1,v2)]

[/MOSES[(n)]=varlist BY var (v1,v2)]

[/K-W=varlist BY var (v1,v2)]

[/MISSING={ANALYSIS**}  [INCLUDE]]
          {LISTWISE  }

[/SAMPLE]

[/STATISTICS=[DESCRIPTIVES]  [QUARTILES] [ALL]]
```
**Default if the subcommand is omitted.

Example:

```
NPAR TESTS K-S(UNIFORM)=V1 /K-S(NORMAL,0,1)=V2.
```

Overview   NPAR TESTS is a collection of nonparametric tests that make minimal assumptions about the underlying distribution of data. All of these tests are described in Siegel (1956). In addition to the nonparametric tests available in NPAR TESTS, the *k*-sample chi-square and Fisher's exact test are available in procedure CROSSTABS.

The tests available in NPAR TESTS can be grouped into three broad categories based on how the data are organized: one-sample tests, related-samples tests, and independent-samples tests. A one-sample test analyzes one variable. A test for related samples compares two or more variables for the same set of cases. An independent-samples test analyzes one variable grouped by categories of another variable. The one-sample tests available in procedure NPAR TESTS are

- BINOMIAL.
- CHISQUARE.
- K-S (Kolmogorov-Smirnov).
- RUNS.

Tests for two related samples are

- MCNEMAR.
- SIGN.
- WILCOXON.

Tests for *k* related samples are

- COCHRAN.
- FRIEDMAN.
- KENDALL.

Tests for two independent samples are

- M-W (Mann-Whitney).
- K-S (Kolmogorov-Smirnov).
- W-W (Wald-Wolfowitz).
- MOSES.

Tests for *k* independent samples are

- K-W (Kruskal-Wallis).
- MEDIAN.

Tests are described below in alphabetical order.

Options   **Statistical Display.** In addition to the tests, you can request univariate statistics, quartiles, and counts for all variables named on the command. You can also control the pairing of variables in two-related-samples tests.

Random Sampling. NPAR TESTS must store cases in memory for tests that use ranks. You can use random sampling when there is not enough space to store all cases.

Basic Specification   • The basic specification is a single test subcommand and its arguments.

Subcommand Order   • Subcommands can be used in any order.

Syntax Rules
- Each test subcommand specifies a test and a list of variables to be tested. Some tests require additional specifications. CHISQUARE has an optional subcommand.
- The STATISTICS, SAMPLE, and MISSING subcommands are optional. Each can be specified only once per NPAR TESTS command.
- You can request any or all tests, and you can specify a test subcommand more than once on a single NPAR TESTS command.
- Keyword ALL in any variable list refers to all user-defined variables in the active system file.
- Keyword WITH controls pairing of variables in two-related-samples tests.
- Keyword BY introduces the grouping variable in two- and k-independent-samples tests.
- Keyword PAIRED on the MCNEMAR, SIGN, and WILCOXON tests can be used with keyword WITH to obtain sequential pairing of variables for two related samples.

Operations
- The display always uses narrow format.
- Specifying a string variable on any subcommand will stop execution of NPAR TESTS.
- When ALL is used, requests for tests of variables with themselves are ignored and a warning is displayed.

Limitations
- Maximum 100 subcommands.
- Maximum 500 variables total per NPAR TESTS command.
- Maximum 200 values for subcommand CHISQUARE.

BINOMIAL Subcommand

```
NPAR TESTS BINOMIAL [({.5})]=varlist[({value,value})]
                       {p }              {value      }
```

BINOMIAL tests whether the observed distribution of a dichotomous variable is the same as that expected from a specified binomial distribution. By default, each variable named is assumed to have only two values, and the distribution of each variable named is compared to a binomial distribution with p (the proportion of cases expected in the first category) equal to 0.5. The default display includes the number of valid cases in each group, the test proportion, and the two-tailed probability of the observed proportion.

Syntax
- The minimum specification is a list of variables to be tested.
- To change the default 0.5 test proportion, specify a value in parentheses immediately after keyword BINOMIAL.
- A single value in parentheses following the variable list is used as a cutting point. Cases with values equal to or less than the cutting point form the first category; the remaining cases form the second.
- If two values appear in parentheses after the variable list, cases with values equal to the first value form the first category, and cases with values equal to the second value form the second category.
- If no values are specified, the variables must be dichotomous.

Operations
- The proportion observed in the first category is compared to the test proportion. The probability of the observed proportion occurring given the test proportion and a binomial distribution is then computed.
- If the test proportion is the default (0.5), a two-tailed probability is displayed. For any other test proportion, a one-tailed probability is displayed. The

direction of the one-tailed test depends on the observed proportion in the first category. If the observed proportion is more than the test proportion, the significance of observing that many or more in the first category is reported. If the observed proportion is less than the test proportion, the one-tailed significance is of observing that many or fewer in the first category. That is, the test is always done in the observed direction.

• A test statistic is calculated for each variable.

Example   `NPAR TESTS BINOMIAL(.667)=V1(0,1).`

• If more than .667 of the cases have the value 0, this will give the probability of observing that many or more 0's in a binomial distribution with probability .667. If fewer than .667 of the cases are 0, the test will be of observing that many or fewer, again with probability .667.

CHISQUARE Subcommand

```
NPAR TESTS CHISQUARE=varlist [(lo,hi)]
                               [/EXPECTED={EQUAL**     }]
                                          '{f1,f2,... fn}
```

The CHISQUARE (alias CHI-SQUARE) one-sample test tabulates a variable into categories and computes a chi-square statistic based on the differences between observed and expected frequencies. By default, equal frequencies are expected in each category. The display includes the frequency distribution, expected frequencies, residuals, chi-square, degrees of freedom, and probability.

Syntax   • The minimum specification is a list of variables to be tested.

• Optionally, you can specify a value range in parentheses following the variable list.

• You can also specify expected proportions with the EXPECTED subcommand.

• If you use the EXPECTED subcommand to specify unequal expected frequencies, you must specify a value greater than 0 for each observed category of the variable or the keyword EQUAL.

• The expected frequencies are specified in ascending order of category value.

• You can use the notation $n*f$ to indicate that frequency f is expected for n consecutive categories.

• Specifying keyword EQUAL on the EXPECTED subcommand has the same effect as omitting the EXPECTED subcommand.

• EXPECTED applies to all variables named on the CHISQUARE subcommand.

• Use multiple CHISQUARE and EXPECTED subcommands to specify different expected proportions for variables.

• You can request CHISQUARE with its alias CHI-SQUARE.

Operations   • If no range is specified for the variables to be tested, each distinct value encountered defines a category.

• If a range is specified, integer-valued categories are established for each value within the range. Noninteger values are truncated before classification. Cases with values outside the specified range are excluded.

• EXPECTED values are interpreted as proportions, not absolute values. Values are summed, and then each value is divided by the total to calculate the proportion of cases expected in the corresponding category.

• A test statistic is calculated for each variable named.

Example   `NPAR TESTS CHISQUARE=V1 (1,5) /EXPECTED= 12, 3*16, 18.`

• This example requests the chi-square test for values 1 through 5 of variable V1.

• The observed frequencies for variable V1 are compared with the hypothetical distribution of 12/78 occurrences of value 1; 16/78 occurrences each of values 2, 3, and 4; and 18/78 occurrences of value 5.

**COCHRAN
Subcommand**

```
NPAR TESTS COCHRAN=varlist
```

COCHRAN calculates Cochran's Q, which tests whether the distribution of values of k related dichotomous variables is the same for all the variables. The display shows the frequency distribution for each variable, degrees of freedom, and probability.

Syntax
- The minimum specification is a list of two variables.
- Variables must be dichotomous and must be coded with the same two values.

Operations
- An $n \times k$ contingency table (cases vs. variable) is constructed for dichotomous variables and the proportions for each variable are computed.
- Cochran's Q statistic has approximately a chi-square distribution.
- A single test comparing all variables is performed.

Example
```
NPAR TESTS COCHRAN=RV1 TO RV3.
```

- This example tests whether the distribution of values 0 and 1 for RV1, RV2, and RV3 is the same.

**FRIEDMAN
Subcommand**

```
NPAR TESTS FRIEDMAN=varlist
```

FRIEDMAN tests whether k related samples have been drawn from the same population. The display shows the mean rank for each variable, number of valid cases, chi-square, degrees of freedom, and probability.

Syntax
- The minimum specification is a list of two variables.
- Variables should be at least at the ordinal level of measurement.

Operations
- The values of k variables are ranked from 1 to k for each case and the mean rank is calculated for each variable over all cases.
- The test statistic has approximately a chi-square distribution.
- A single test statistic comparing all variables is calculated.

Example
```
NPAR TESTS FRIEDMAN=V1 V2 V3
  /STATISTICS=DESCRIPTIVES.
```

- This example tests variables V1, V2, and V3, and requests univariate statistics for all three.

**K-S Subcommand
(One Sample)**

```
NPAR TESTS K-S({NORMAL [mean,stddev]})=varlist
              {POISSON [mean]       }
              {UNIFORM [min,max]    }
```

The K-S (alias KOLMOGOROV-SMIRNOV) one-sample test compares the cumulative distribution function for a variable with a uniform, normal, or Poisson distribution and tests whether the distributions are homogeneous. The parameters of the test distribution can be specified; the defaults are the observed parameters. The display shows the number of valid cases, parameters of the test distribution, most-extreme absolute, positive, and negative differences, K-S Z, and two-tailed probability for each variable.

Syntax
- The minimum specification is a distribution keyword and a list of variables. The distribution keywords are

NORMAL *Normal distribution.* Default parameters are the observed mean and standard deviation.

POISSON *Poisson distribution.* The default parameter is the observed mean.

UNIFORM *Uniform distribution.* Default parameters are the observed minimum and maximum values.

- The distribution keyword and its optional parameters must be enclosed within parentheses.
- The distribution keyword must be separated from its parameters by blanks or commas.
- You can request K-S with its alias KOLMOGOROV-SMIRNOV.

Operations
- The Kolmogorov-Smirnov Z is computed from the largest difference in absolute value between the observed and test distribution functions.
- The K-S probability levels assume that the test distribution is specified entirely in advance. The distribution of the test statistic and resulting probabilities change when the parameters of the test distribution are estimated from the sample. No correction is made.
- For a mean of 100,000 or larger, a normal approximation to the Poisson distribution is used.
- A test statistic is calculated for each variable.

Example   `NPAR TESTS K-S(UNIFORM)=Vl /K-S(NORMAL,0,1)=V2.`
- The first K-S subcommand compares the distribution of V1 with a uniform distribution that has the same range as V1.
- The second K-S subcommand compares the distribution of V2 with a normal distribution with a mean of 0 and a standard deviation of 1.

K-S Subcommand (Two Sample)

`NPAR TESTS K-S=varlist BY variable(valuel,value2)`

K-S (alias KOLMOGOROV-SMIRNOV) tests whether the distribution of a variable is the same in two independent samples defined by a grouping variable. The test is sensitive to any difference in median, dispersion, skewness, and so forth, between the two distributions. The display shows the count in each group, the largest absolute, positive, and negative differences between the two groups, K-S Z, and the two-tailed probability for each variable.

Syntax
- The minimum specification is a test variable, the keyword BY, a grouping variable, and a pair of values in parentheses.
- The test variable should be at least at the ordinal level of measurement.
- Cases with the first value form one group and cases with the second value form the other. The order in which values are specified determines which difference is the largest positive and which is the largest negative.
- You can request K-S with its alias KOLMOGOROV-SMIRNOV.

Operations
- The observed cumulative distributions for both groups are computed, as are the maximum positive, negative, and absolute differences.
- Cases with values other than those specified for the grouping variable are excluded.
- A test statistic is calculated for each variable named before BY.

Example   `NPAR TESTS K-S=Vl V2 BY V3(0,1).`
- This example specifies two tests. The first compares the distribution of V1 for cases with value 0 for V3 with the distribution of V1 for cases with value 1 for V3.
- A parallel test is calculated for V2.

K-W Subcommand

`NPAR TESTS K-W=varlist BY variable(valuel,value2)`

K-W (alias KRUSKAL-WALLIS) tests whether k independent samples defined by a grouping variable are from the same population. The display shows the number of valid cases, mean rank of the variable in each group, chi-square, probability, and chi-square and probability after correcting for ties.

Syntax	• The minimum specification is a test variable, the keyword BY, a grouping variable, and a pair of values in parentheses.
	• Every value in the range defined by the pair of values forms a group.
	• You can request K-W with its alias KRUSKAL-WALLIS.
Operations	• Cases from the k groups are ranked in a single series, and the rank sum for each group is computed.
	• Kruskal-Wallis H has approximately a chi-square distribution.
	• Cases with values other than those specified for the grouping variable are excluded.
	• A test statistic is calculated for each variable named before BY.
Example	`NPAR TESTS K-W=V1 BY V2(0,4).`
	• This example tests V1 for groups defined by values 0 through 4 of V2.

KENDALL Subcommand

`NPAR TESTS KENDALL=varlist`

KENDALL tests whether k related samples are from the same population. W is a measure of agreement among judges or raters where each case is one judge's rating of several entities (variables). The display includes the mean rank for each variable, valid count, W, chi-square, degrees of freedom, and probability.

Syntax	• The minimum specification is a list of two variables.
Operations	• The values of the k variables are ranked from 1 to k for each case and the mean rank is calculated for each variable over all cases.
	• Kendall's W and a corresponding chi-square statistic are calculated, correcting for ties.
	• W ranges between 0 (no agreement) and 1 (complete agreement).
	• A single test statistic is calculated for all variables.
Example	```
	DATA LIST /V1 TO V5 1-10
	BEGIN DATA
	2 5 4 5 1
	3 3 4 5 3
	3 4 4 6 2
	2 4 3 6 2
	END DATA.
	NPAR TESTS KENDALL=ALL.
	``
	• This example tests four judges (cases) on five entities (variables V1 through V5).

M-W Subcommand

`NPAR TESTS M-W=varlist BY variable(value1,value2)`

M-W (alias MANN-WHITNEY) compares two independent samples defined by a grouping variable on a single test variable. The test statistic uses the rank of each case to test whether the groups are drawn from the same population. The display shows the mean rank of the variable within each group, the valid count for each group, the Mann-Whitney U, Wilcoxon W (the rank sum of the smaller group), the two-tailed probability of U (or W), the Z statistic, and the two-tailed probability of Z corrected for ties.

Syntax	• The minimum specification is a test variable, the keyword BY, a grouping variable, and a pair of values in parentheses.
	• Cases with the first value form one group and cases with the second value form the other. Order is unimportant.
	• You can request M-W with its alias MANN-WHITNEY.
Operations	• Cases are ranked in order of increasing size, and test statistic U—the number of times a score from Group 1 precedes a score from Group 2—is computed.
	• For fewer than than 30 cases, an exact significance level is computed.

• For more than 30 cases, *U* is transformed into a normally distributed *Z* statistic.
• Cases with values other than those specified for the grouping variable are excluded.
• A test statistic is calculated for each variable named before BY.

Example   NPAR TESTS M-W=V1 BY V2(1,2).

• This example tests V1 based on the two groups defined by values 1 and 2 of V2.

MCNEMAR Subcommand

NPAR TESTS MCNEMAR=varlist [WITH varlist [(PAIRED)]]

MCNEMAR tests whether the changes in proportions are the same for pairs of dichotomous variables. The display shows the 2 × 2 contingency table, number of valid cases, and two-tailed probability for each pair of variables.

Syntax
• The minimum specification is a list of two variables.
• Variables must be dichotomous and must have the same two values.
• Without keyword WITH, each variable pair in the list is tested.
• With keyword WITH, each variable before WITH is tested with each variable following WITH.
• With (PAIRED) and WITH, the first variable before WITH is paired with the first variable after WITH, the second variable before WITH with the second variable after WITH, and so on.
• With (PAIRED) and WITH, the number of variables specified before and after WITH must be the same. (PAIRED) must be specified after the second variable list.
• (PAIRED) cannot be specified without WITH.

Operations
• A 2 × 2 table is constructed for each pair of dichotomous variables and a chi-square statistic is computed for cases having different values for the two variables.
• If fewer than 25 cases change values from the first variable to the second variable, the binomial distribution is used to compute the probability.

Example   NPAR TESTS MCNEMAR=V1 V2 V3.

• This example performs the MCNEMAR test on variable pairs V1 and V2, V1 and V3, and V2 and V3.

MEDIAN Subcommand

NPAR TESTS MEDIAN [(value)]=varlist BY variable(value1,value2)

MEDIAN determines if *k* independent samples have been drawn from populations with the same median. The independent samples are defined by a grouping variable. For each variable, the display shows a table of the number of cases greater than and less than or equal to the median in each category of the grouping variable, the median, chi-square, degrees of freedom, and probability. By default, the median tested is calculated from all cases included in the test.

Syntax
• The minimum specification is a single test variable, the keyword BY, a grouping variable, and two values in parentheses.
• If the first grouping value is less than the second, every value in the range defined by the pair of values forms a group and a *k*-sample test is performed.
• If the first value is greater than the second, two groups are formed using the two values and a two-sample test is performed.
• To override the default median, specify a median value in parentheses following the MEDIAN subcommand keyword.

Operations
• A 2 × *k* contingency table is constructed with counts of the number of cases greater than the median and less than or equal to the median for the *k* groups.
• For more than 30 cases, a chi-square statistic is computed.

- For 30 or fewer cases, Fisher's exact procedure (one-tailed) is used instead of chi-square.
- For a two-sample test, cases with values other than the two specified are excluded.
- A test statistic is calculated for each variable named before BY.

Example
```
NPAR TESTS MEDIAN(8.4)=V1 BY V2(1,2) /MEDIAN=V1 BY V2(1,2)
    /MEDIAN=V1 BY V3(1,4) /MEDIAN=V1 BY V3(4,1).
```

- The first two MEDIAN subcommands test variable V1 grouped by values 1 and 2 of variable V2. The first test specifies a median of 8.4 and the second uses the observed median.
- The third MEDIAN subcommand requests a four-samples test, dividing the sample into four groups based on values 1, 2, 3, and 4 of variable V3.
- The last MEDIAN subcommand requests a two-samples test, grouping cases based on values 1 and 4 of V3 and ignoring all other cases.

MOSES Subcommand

```
NPAR TESTS MOSES[(n)]=varlist BY variable(value1,value2)
```

The MOSES test of extreme reactions tests whether the range of an ordinal variable is the same in a control group and a comparison group defined by a grouping variable. For each variable tested, the display includes the count in the two groups, the number of outliers removed, the span of the control group before and after outliers are removed, and the one-tailed probability of the span with and without outliers. By default, 5% of the cases are trimmed from each end of the range of the control group to remove outliers.

Syntax
- The minimum specification is a test variable, the keyword BY, a grouping variable, and two values in parentheses.
- The test variable must be at least at the ordinal level of measurement.
- The first value of the grouping variable defines the control group, and the second value defines the comparison group.
- You can override the default 5% of cases to be trimmed from each end of the control group by specifying a value in parentheses following the subcommand keyword MOSES. This value represents an actual number of cases, not a percentage.

Operations
- Scores from the groups are arranged in a single ascending sequence.
- The span of the control group is computed as the number of cases in the sequence containing the lowest and highest control score.
- No adjustments are made for tied cases.
- Cases with values other than those specified for the grouping variable are excluded.
- A test statistic is calculated for each variable named before BY.

Example
```
NPAR TESTS MOSES=V1 BY V3(0,1) /MOSES=V1 BY V3(1,0).
```

- The first MOSES subcommand tests V1 using value 0 of V3 to define the control group and value 1 for the experimental group. The second MOSES subcommand reverses the experimental and control groups.

RUNS Subcommand

```
NPAR TESTS RUNS({MEAN  })=varlist
               {MEDIAN}
               {MODE  }
               {value }
```

RUNS tests whether the sequence of values of a dichotomized variable is random. The display includes the test value (cutting point used to dichotomize the variable tested), number of runs, number of cases below the cutting point, number of cases equal to or greater than the cutting point, and test statistic Z with its one-tailed probability.

Syntax
- The minimum specification is a cutting point in parentheses followed by a test variable.
- The cutting point can be specified by an exact value or one of the keywords MEAN, MEDIAN, or MODE.

Operations
- All variables tested are treated as dichotomous: values less than the cutting point form one category, and values equal to or greater than the cutting point form the other category.
- A test statistic is calculated for each variable named.

Example
```
NPAR TESTS RUNS(MEDIAN)=V2 /RUNS(24.5)=V2 /RUNS(1)=V3.
```
- This example performs three runs tests. The first two test variable V2, first using the median and then using 24.5 as the cutting point.
- The third test is for variable V3, with value 1 specified as the cutting point.

SIGN Subcommand

```
NPAR TESTS SIGN=varlist [WITH varlist [(PAIRED)] ]
```

SIGN tests whether the distribution of two paired variables in a two-related-samples test is the same. The display includes the number of positive differences, number of negative differences, number of ties, and the two-tailed binomial probability.

Syntax
- The minimum specification is a list of two variables.
- Variables should be at least at the ordinal level of measurement.
- Without keyword WITH, each variable in the list is paired with every other variable in the list.
- With keyword WITH, each variable before WITH is paired with each variable after WITH.
- With (PAIRED) and WITH, the first variable before WITH is paired with the first variable after WITH, the second variable before WITH with the second variable after WITH, and so on.
- With (PAIRED) and WITH, the number of variables specified before and after WITH must be the same. (PAIRED) must be specified after the second variable list.
- (PAIRED) cannot be specified without WITH.

Operations
- The positive and negative differences between the pair of variables are counted. Ties are ignored.
- The probability is taken from the binomial distribution if 25 or fewer differences are observed. Otherwise, the probability comes from the Z distribution.
- Under the null hypothesis for large sample sizes, Z is approximately normally distributed with a mean of 0 and a variance of 1.

Example
```
NPAR TESTS SIGN=N1,M1 WITH N2,M2 (PAIRED).
```
- In this example, N1 is tested with N2, and M1 is tested with M2.

W-W Subcommand

```
NPAR TESTS W-W=varlist BY variable(value1,value2)
```

W-W (alias WALD-WOLFOWITZ) tests whether the distribution of a variable is the same in two independent samples. A runs test is performed with group membership as the criterion. The display includes the number of valid cases in each group, the number of runs, Z, and the one-tailed probability of Z. If ties are present, the minimum and maximum number of ties possible, their Z statistics, and one-tailed probabilities are displayed.

Syntax
- The minimum specification is a single test variable, the keyword BY, a grouping variable, and two values in parentheses.
- Cases with the first value form one group and cases with the second value form the other. Order is unimportant.
- You can request W-W with its alias WALD-WOLFOWITZ.

Operations
- Cases are combined from both groups and ranked from lowest to highest.
- A runs test is performed using group membership as the criterion.
- For ties involving cases from both groups, both the minimum and maximum number of runs possible are calculated.
- For a sample size of 30 or less, the exact one-tailed probability is calculated.
- For a sample size greater than 30, the normal approximation is used.
- Cases with values other than those specified for the grouping variable are excluded.
- Test statistics are calculated for each variable named before BY.

Example
```
NPAR TESTS W-W=V1 BY V3(0,1).
```
- This example ranks cases from lowest to highest based on their values for V1. A runs test on the group variable is done.

WILCOXON Subcommand

```
NPAR TESTS WILCOXON=varlist [WITH varlist [(PAIRED)] ]
```

WILCOXON tests the hypothesis that there are no differences between two paired populations of ordered-metric scores. The test takes into account the magnitude of the differences between two paired variables. The display includes the number of positive and negative differences and their respective means, the number of ties, the valid count, Z, and the probability of Z.

Syntax
- The minimum specification is a list of two variables.
- Without keyword WITH, each variable is paired with every other variable in the list.
- With keyword WITH, each variable before WITH is paired with each variable after WITH.
- With (PAIRED) and WITH, the first variable before WITH is paired with the first variable after WITH, the second variable before WITH with the second variable after WITH, and so on.
- With (PAIRED) and WITH, the number of variables specified before and after WITH must be the same. (PAIRED) must be specified after the second variable list.
- (PAIRED) cannot be specified without WITH.

Operations
- The differences between the pair of variables are counted, the absolute differences ranked, the positive and negative ranks summed, and the test statistic Z computed from the positive and negative rank sums.
- Under the null hypothesis for large sample sizes, Z is approximately normally distributed with a mean of 0 and a variance of 1.

Example
```
NPAR TESTS WILCOXON=A B WITH C D (PAIRED).
```
- This example pairs A and C, B and D. It does not pair A with D, B with C, as is the case without (PAIRED).

STATISTICS Subcommand

In addition to the statistics provided for each test, you can also obtain two types of summary statistics for variables named on each of the subcommands. Use STATISTICS to request the following:

DESCRIPTIVES *Univariate statistics.* Displays the mean, maximum, minimum, standard deviation, and number of nonmissing cases for each variable named on the combined subcommands.

QUARTILES *Quartiles and number of cases.* Displays values corresponding to the 25th, 50th, and 75th percentiles for each variable named on the combined subcommands.

ALL *All statistics available on NPAR TESTS.*

MISSING Subcommand   By default, cases with missing values are deleted on a test-by-test basis. For subcommands specifying several tests, each test is evaluated separately.

ANALYSIS   *Exclude missing values on a test-by-test basis.* This is the default.

LISTWISE   *Exclude missing values listwise.* Cases missing on any variable named on any subcommand are excluded from all analyses.

INCLUDE   *Include user-missing values.* User-missing values are treated as if they were not missing.

ANALYSIS and LISTWISE are mutually exclusive; however, each can be specified with INCLUDE.

SAMPLE Subcommand   NPAR TESTS must store cases in memory. You may not have sufficient computer resources to store all the cases to produce the tests requested. SAMPLE allows you to select a random sample of cases when there is not enough space to store all the cases. SAMPLE has no additional specifications.

Because sampling would invalidate a runs test, this option is ignored when the RUNS subcommand is used.

Annotated Example   For a complete example with output, see Examples following the Command Reference.

References   Siegel, S. 1956 *Nonparametric statistics for the behavioral sciences.* New York: McGraw-Hill.

NUMBERED, UNNUMBERED

{NUMBERED   }
{UNNUMBERED }

Overview

NUMBERED and UNNUMBERED are IBM-specific commands. Usually IBM systems reserve columns 73–80 of each input line for line numbers. NUMBERED reserves columns 73–80 for those line numbers; UNNUMBERED indicates that the columns are not reserved for numbers. The default may vary by installation. Use the SHOW command to see the default for your installation.

Basic Specification

• The only specification is either NUMBERED or UNNUMBERED. NUMBERED instructs SPSS to check only the first 72 columns for data. UNNUMBERED instructs SPSS to check all 80 columns for data.

Operations

• If NUMBERED is in effect and data extend beyond Column 72, SPSS issues a warning message.
• NUMBERED and UNNUMBERED column settings apply only to inline data; they do not apply to data in an external file.

Example

UNNUMBERED.

• SPSS checks up to 80 columns of each input line for data.

NUMERIC

```
NUMERIC varlist[(format)] [/varlist...]
```

Example:

```
NUMERIC V1 V2 (F4.0) / V3 (F1.0).
```

Overview
NUMERIC declares new numeric variables that can be referred to in the transformation language before they are created. Commands such as COMPUTE, IF, RECODE, and COUNT can be used to create the new numeric variables.

Basic Specification
- The basic specification is the name of the new variable(s). Optionally specify a FORTRAN-like format in parentheses. If no format is specified, the default F8.2 format is used. Variables named on NUMERIC can then be used in the transformation language.

Syntax Rules
- Keyword TO can be used to declare multiple numeric variables. The specified format applies to each variable named and implied by the TO construction.
- To declare variables with different formats, separate each format group with a slash.
- NUMERIC, specified within an INPUT PROGRAM, can be used to predetermine the order of numeric variables in the dictionary of the active system file. When used for this purpose, NUMERIC must precede DATA LIST in the INPUT PROGRAM.

Operations
- NUMERIC takes effect as soon as it is encountered in the command sequence, unlike most transformations, which do not take effect until the data are read. Thus, special attention should be paid to its position among commands. For more information, see Universals: Command Order.
- If no format is specified for the variable(s), the default F8.2 format (or whatever default is specified on SET) is used. Formats are used as both the PRINT FORMAT and WRITE FORMAT.
- Permanent or temporary variables are initialized to the system-missing value. Scratch variables are initialized to 0.
- Variables named on NUMERIC are added to the active system file in the order in which they are specified on NUMERIC. Regardless of the order in which they are used in the transformation language, the order of the variables in the active system file remains the order specified on NUMERIC.

Example
```
NUMERIC V1 V2 (F4.0) / V3 (F1.0).
```
- NUMERIC declares variables V1 and V2 with F4.0 formats, and variable V3 with F1.0 format.

Example
```
NUMERIC V1 TO V6 (F3.1) / V7 V10 (F6.2).
```
- NUMERIC declares variables V1 through V6, each with format F3.1, and variables V7 and V10, each with format F6.2.

Example
```
NUMERIC SCALE85 IMPACT85 SCALE86 IMPACT86 SCALE87 IMPACT87
        SCALE88 IMPACT88.
```
- Variables SCALE85 TO IMPACT88 are added to the active system file in the order specified on NUMERIC. Regardless of the order in which they are used in the transformation language, the order of the variables in the active system file remains the order specified on NUMERIC.

Example   TITLE 'PREDETERMINE VARIABLE ORDER'.

```
INPUT PROGRAM.
STRING CITY (A24).
NUMERIC POP81 TO POP83 (F9)/ REV81 TO REV83(F10).
DATA LIST FILE=POPDATA RECORDS=3
  /1 POP81 22-30 REV81 31-40
  /2 POP82 22-30 REV82 31-40
  /3 POP83 22-30 REV83 31-40
  /4 CITY 1-24(A).
END INPUT PROGRAM.
```

- STRING and NUMERIC are specified within an INPUT PROGRAM to predetermine variable order in the active system file. Though data in the file are in a different order, the active system file dictionary uses the order specified on STRING and NUMERIC. Thus, CITY is the first variable in the dictionary, followed by POP81, POP82, POP83, REV81, REV82, and REV83.

- Formats should be specified for the variables on NUMERIC. Otherwise, SPSS takes the default numeric format (F8.2) from the NUMERIC command for the dictionary format, even though it will use the format on DATA LIST to read the data (that is, the dictionary uses the first formats it encounters, even though DATA LIST may use different formats to read cases).

ONEWAY

```
ONEWAY  varlist BY varname(min,max)

[/POLYNOMIAL=n]  [/CONTRAST=coefficient list] [/CONTRAST=... ]

[/RANGES={LSD          }({0.05 }) ] [/RANGES=...]
         {DUNCAN       } {alpha}
         {SNK          }
         {TUKEYB       }
         {TUKEY        }
         {MODLSD       }
         {SCHEFFE      }
         {ranges values}

[/HARMONIC={NONE** or PAIR}]
           {ALL           }

[/FORMAT={NOLABELS**}]
         {LABELS    }

[/STATISTICS=[NONE        **]]
             [DESCRIPTIVES]
             [EFFECTS     ]
             [HOMOGENEITY ]
             [ALL         ]

[/MISSING={ANALYSIS**}  [{EXCLUDE**}]]
          {LISTWISE  }  [{INCLUDE  }

[/MATRIX =[IN({*    })] [OUT({*    })]]]
             {file}        {file}
```

**Default if the subcommand is omitted.

Example:

```
ONEWAY V1 BY V2(1,4).
```

Overview   ONEWAY produces a one-way analysis of variance for an interval-level dependent variable by one numeric independent variable that defines the groups for the analysis. Other SPSS procedures that perform analysis of variance are MEANS, ANOVA, and MANOVA (see the *SPSS Advanced Statistics User's Guide)*. Some tests not included in the other procedures are available as options in ONEWAY.

Options   **Trends, Contrasts, and Ranges.** You can partition the between-groups sums of squares into linear, quadratic, cubic, and higher-order trend components (see POLYNOMIAL Subcommand). You can specify up to 10 contrasts to be tested with the t statistic (see CONTRAST Subcommand). You can also specify seven different range tests for comparisons of all possible pairs of group means, or multiple comparisons (see RANGES Subcommand).

Display Format. You can label groups with the value labels of the independent variable. See FORMAT Subcommand.

Statistical Display. In addition to the default display, you can obtain means, standard deviations, and other descriptive statistics for each group (see STATISTICS Subcommand). Fixed- and random-effects statistics as well as several tests for homogeneity of variance are also available. The harmonic mean of all group sizes can be used as the sample size for each group in range tests (see HARMONIC Subcommand).

Writing and Reading Matrices. You can write means, standard deviations, and category frequencies to a matrix system file that can be used in subsequent ONEWAY commands. You can also read matrix materials consisting of means, category frequencies, pooled variance, and degrees of freedom for the pooled variance. See MATRIX Subcommand.

Basic Specification   • The basic specification is a dependent variable, keyword BY, an independent variable, and, in parentheses, the minimum and maximum values of the independent variable. ONEWAY produces a labeled table for each dependent variable by the independent variable. The table contains the between- and within-groups sums of squares, mean squares, and degrees of freedom. The F ratio and the probability of F for the test are displayed.

Subcommand Order

- The variable list must be first.
- Subcommands can be used in any order.

Operations

- Noninteger values for the independent variable are truncated.
- Cases with values outside the range specified for the independent variable are omitted from the analysis.
- ONEWAY does not execute if a string variable is specified as an independent or dependent variable.
- The display uses the width defined on SET.

Limitations

- Maximum 100 dependent variables and 1 independent variable.
- An unlimited number of categories for the independent variable. However, contrasts and range tests are not performed if the actual number of nonempty categories exceeds 50.
- Only 1 POLYNOMIAL subcommand.
- Maximum 10 CONTRAST subcommands and 10 RANGES subcommands.
- Any alpha values between 0 and 1 are permitted for the LSD, MODLSD, and SCHEFFE range tests. SNK, TUKEY, and TUKEYB use an alpha value of 0.05, regardless of what is specified. DUNCAN uses an alpha value of 0.01 if the alpha specified is less than 0.05; 0.05 if the alpha specified is greater than or equal to 0.05 but less than 0.10; 0.10 if the alpha specified is greater than or equal to 0.10; or 0.05 if no alpha is specified.

Example

ONEWAY V1 BY V2(1,4).

- ONEWAY names V1 as the dependent variable and V2 as the independent variable with a minimum value of 1 and a maximum value of 4.

Analysis Design

A ONEWAY analysis list consists of a dependent variable list, keyword BY, and an independent (grouping) variable with its minimum and maximum values.

- Only one analysis list is allowed, and it must be specified before any of the optional subcommands.
- All variables named must be numeric.
- The minimum and maximum values of the independent variable must be separated by a comma or a space and enclosed in parentheses. These values must be integers,

POLYNOMIAL Subcommand

POLYNOMIAL partitions the between-groups sums of squares into linear, cubic, quadratic, or higher-order trend components. The display is an expanded analysis-of-variance table that provides the degrees of freedom, sums of squares, mean square, F, and probability of F for each partition.

- The value specified on POLYNOMIAL denotes the highest-degree polynomial to be used.
- The polynomial value must be a positive integer less than or equal to 5 and less than the number of groups. If the polynomial specified is greater than the number of groups, the highest-degree polynomial possible is assumed.
- ONEWAY computes the sums of squares for each order polynomial from weighted polynomial contrasts, using the group code as the metric. These contrasts are orthogonal.

- With unbalanced designs and equal spacing between groups, ONEWAY also computes sums of squares using the unweighted polynomial contrasts. These contrasts are not orthogonal.
- The deviation sums of squares are always calculated from the weighted sums of squares (Speed, 1976).
- Only one POLYNOMIAL subcommand can be specified per ONEWAY command. If more than one is used, only the last one specified is in effect.

Example
```
ONEWAY WELL BY EDUC6 (1,6)
   /POLYNOMIAL=2.
```

- ONEWAY requests an analysis of variance of WELL by EDUC6 with second-order (quadratic) polynomial contrasts.

CONTRAST Subcommand

Use CONTRAST to specify a priori contrasts to be tested by the t statistic. Contrasts are specified as a vector of coefficients, where each coefficient corresponds to a category of the independent variable. The display for each contrast list is the value of the contrast, the standard error of the contrast, the t statistic, the degrees of freedom for t, and the two-tailed probability of t. Both pooled- and separate-variance estimates are displayed.

- A contrast must be specified or implied for every group in the range specified for the independent variable, even if the group is empty. If the number of contrast values is less than the number of groups, contrast values of 0 are assumed for the remaining groups.
- Only one set of contrast coefficients can be specified per CONTRAST subcommand. Additional contrasts on a single CONTRAST subcommand are ignored.
- The notation $n*c$ can be used to indicate that coefficient c is repeated n times.
- Coefficients are assigned to empty and nonempty groups defined by ascending integer values of the independent variable.
- Trailing coefficients of 0 do not need to be expressed.
- A warning is issued when sets of contrasts do not sum to 0. The program will still give an estimate of this contrast.

Example
```
ONEWAY V1 BY V2(1,4)
   /CONTRAST = -1 -1 1 1
   /CONTRAST = -1 0 0 1
   /CONTRAST = -1 0 .5 .5.
```

- The first CONTRAST subcommand contrasts the combination of the first two groups with the combination of the last two groups.
- The second CONTRAST subcommand contrasts the first group with the last group.
- The third CONTRAST subcommand contrasts the first group with the combination of the third and fourth groups.

Example
```
ONEWAY V1 BY V2(1,4)
   /CONTRAST = -1 1 2*0
   /CONTRAST = -1 1 0 0
   /CONTRAST = -1 1.
```

- All three CONTRAST subcommands specify the the same contrast coefficients for a four-group analysis. The first group is contrasted with the second group in all three cases.
- The first CONTRAST uses the $n*c$ notation and the last CONTRAST omits the trailing zero coefficients.

RANGES Subcommand

Each RANGES subcommand specifies one of seven different tests for multiple comparisons between means. The RANGES display always includes multiple comparisons between all groups. Nonempty group means are sorted in ascending order, with asterisks indicating significantly different groups. In addition, homogeneous subsets are calculated for balanced designs, and for all designs when HARMONIC=ALL. The means of the groups included within a subset are not significantly different.

• By default, the range tests use sample sizes of the two groups being compared. This is equivalent to using the harmonic mean of the sample size of the two groups being compared. You can use the HARMONIC subcommand to change this default.

• The default alpha for all tests is 0.05. For some tests, you can specify a different alpha.

LSD(p)	*Least-significant difference.* Alpha can be specified between 0 and 1. The default is 0.05.
DUNCAN(p)	*Multiple range test.* Alpha can be specified as 0.01, 0.05, and 0.10 only. The default is 0.05. DUNCAN uses 0.01 if the alpha specified is less than 0.05; 0.05 if the alpha specified is greater than or equal to 0.05 but less than 0.10; 0.10 if the alpha specified is greater than or equal to 0.10; and 0.05 if no alpha is specified.
SNK	*Student-Newman-Keuls.* Alpha is 0.05.
BTUKEY	*Tukey's alternate procedure.* Alpha is 0.05.
TUKEY	*Honestly significant difference.* Alpha is 0.05.
MODLSD(p)	*Modified LSD.* Alpha can be specified between 0 and 1. The default is 0.05. Keyword LSDMOD is an alias for MODLSD.
SCHEFFE(p)	*Scheffé's test.* Alpha can be specified between 0 and 1. The default is 0.05.

Alternatively, you can use any other type of range by specifying range values:

• Specify the range values separated by commas or blanks.

• Up to $k-1$ range values can be specified in ascending order, where k is the number of groups and where the range value times the standard error of the combined subset is the critical value.

• If less than $k-1$ values are specified, the last value specified is used for the remaining range values.

• The notation $n*r$ can be used to indicate that the range r is repeated n times.

• To use a single critical value for all subsets, specify one range value.

Example
```
ONEWAY WELL BY EDUC6 (1,6)
   /RANGES=SNK
   /RANGES=SCHEFFE (.01).
```

• ONEWAY requests two different range tests. The first uses the Student-Newman-Keuls test and the second uses Scheffé's test with an alpha of 0.01.

Example
```
ONEWAY WELL BY EDUC (1,6)
   /RANGES=2.81, 3.34, 3.65, 3.88, 4.05.
```

• RANGES specifies five range values.

HARMONIC Subcommand

HARMONIC determines the sample size estimate to be used when the N's are not equal in all groups. Either only the sample sizes in the two groups being compared are used, or an average sample size of all groups is used.

• HARMONIC=NONE is the default, which uses the harmonic mean of the sizes of just the two groups being compared.

• To use the harmonic mean of *all* group sizes, specify keyword ALL.

• If ALL is used, ONEWAY calculates homogeneous subsets for SCHEFFE, TUKEY, TUKEYB, and LSDMOD tests on unbalanced designs.

• Specify only one keyword on HARMONIC.

NONE	*Harmonic mean of the sizes of the two groups being compared.* Keyword PAIR can be used as an alias for NONE. This is the default.
ALL	*Harmonic mean of all group sizes as sample sizes for range tests.* If the harmonic mean is used for unbalanced designs, ONEWAY determines homogeneous subsets for all range tests.

FORMAT Subcommand   The default display identifies groups as GRP1, GRP2, and so forth. Use FORMAT to identify the groups by their value labels.

NOLABELS   *Suppress value labels.* This is the default.

LABELS   *Use value labels for group labels.* Use the first eight characters from the value labels of the independent variable as group labels.

STATISTICS Subcommand   By default, ONEWAY displays the between- and within-groups sums of squares, mean squares, degrees of freedom, the F ratio, and the probability of F for the test. It also calculates any statistics specified on the CONTRASTS and RANGES subcommands. Use STATISTICS to obtain additional statistics.

NONE   *No optional statistics.* This is the default.

DESCRIPTIVES   *Group descriptive statistics.* DESCRIPTIVES displays the number of cases, mean, standard deviation, standard error, minimum, maximum, and 95% confidence interval for each dependent variable for each group.

EFFECTS   *Fixed- and random-effects statistics.* EFFECTS displays the standard deviation, standard error, and 95% confidence interval for the fixed-effects model, and the standard error, 95% confidence interval, and estimate of between-component variance for the random-effects model.

HOMOGENEITY   *Homogeneity-of-variance tests.* HOMOGENEITY displays Cochran's C, the Bartlett-Box F, and Hartley's F max.

ALL   *All statistics available for ONEWAY.*

MISSING Subcommand   MISSING controls missing values.

- By default, cases with missing values on either the independent or dependent variable are excluded from the test. The default keywords are ANALYSIS and EXCLUDE.
- Keywords ANALYSIS and LISTWISE are mutually exclusive. Each can be used with INCLUDE or EXCLUDE.

ANALYSIS   *Exclude missing values on a pair-by-pair basis.* A case missing on either the dependent variable or grouping variable for a given analysis is not used for that analysis. Also, a case outside the range specified for the grouping variable is not used. This is the default.

EXCLUDE   *Exclude cases with user-missing values.* This is the default.

LISTWISE   *Exclude missing values listwise.* Cases missing on any variable named are excluded from all analyses.

INCLUDE   *Include user-missing values.* User-missing values are treated as valid values.

MATRIX Subcommand   MATRIX reads and writes SPSS matrix system files. It writes means, standard deviations, and frequencies to a matrix system file that can be used by subsequent ONEWAY procedures. In addition, MATRIX reads means, frequencies, pooled variance, and degrees of freedom for the pooled variance.

- Either IN or OUT is required to specify the matrix file in parentheses. When both IN and OUT are used on the same ONEWAY procedure, they can be specified on separate MATRIX subcommands, or both on the same subcommand.
- MATRIX recognizes keyword NONE (the default). Use MATRIX=NONE to explicitly indicate that the data are not matrix materials.
- If IN and OUT are specified on separate MATRIX subcommands, ONEWAY issues a warning indicating that, should a conflict arise in the specifications, only the last MATRIX subcommand will be executed.
- Documents from the original file are not included in the matrix file and will not be present if the matrix file becomes the active system file.

- MATRIX=IN cannot be used in place of GET or DATA LIST to begin a new SPSS command file. MATRIX is a subcommand on ONEWAY, and ONEWAY cannot run before an active system file is defined.

- To begin a new command file and immediately read a matrix, first GET the matrix file, then specify IN(*) on MATRIX. Alternatively, ONEWAY can read a matrix written to the active system file by another procedure.

- The dependent variables named on ONEWAY may be a subset of the dependent variables in the matrix system file.

Procedure ONEWAY reads two types of matrices. The first type includes:

- A vector of frequencies for each factor level.
- A vector of means for each factor level.
- A vector of standard deviations.

The second type includes:

- A vector of frequencies for each factor level.
- A vector of means for each factor level.
- A record containing the pooled variance (within-group mean square error).
- The degrees of freedom for the MSE.

OUT   *Write a matrix system file.* Specify either a file or an asterisk, and enclose the specification in parentheses. If you specify a file, the file is stored on disk and can be retrieved at any time. If you specify an asterisk (*), the matrix system file replaces the active system file but is not stored on disk unless you use SAVE or XSAVE.

IN   *Read a matrix system file.* If the matrix system file *is not* the current active system file, specify a file in parentheses. If the matrix system file *is* the current active system file, specify an asterisk (*) in parentheses.

Format of the Matrix System File
- The matrix system file includes two special variables created by SPSS: ROWTYPE_ and VARNAME_. Variable ROWTYPE_ is a short string variable having values MEAN, STDDEV, and N. VARNAME_ is a short string variable that never has values for procedure ONEWAY. VARNAME_ is included with the matrix materials, so ONEWAY's matrix output can be read by procedures that expect to read a VARNAME_ variable.

- Between variables ROWTYPE_ and VARNAME in the file is the independent variable.

- The remaining variable(s) in the matrix file is the dependent variable(s).

Split Files and Variable Order
- When split-file processing is in effect, the first variables in the matrix system file will be the split variables, followed by ROWTYPE_, the independent variable, VARNAME_, and the dependent variable(s).

- A full set of matrix materials is written for each split-file group defined by the split variable(s).

- A split variable cannot have the same variable name as any other variable written to the matrix system file.

- If split-file processing is in effect when a matrix is written, the same split file must be in effect when that matrix is read by any procedure.

- Generally, matrix rows, independent variables, and dependent variables can be in any order in the matrix system file read by keyword IN. However, all split-file variables must precede variable ROWTYPE_, and all split-group rows must be contiguous. ONEWAY ignores unrecognized ROWTYPE_ values.

Additional Statistics
- ONEWAY writes only one type of matrix: a matrix with the mean, standard deviation, and number of cases for each factor level.

- ONEWAY can read the matrices it writes, and it can also read matrix materials that include the means, category frequencies, pooled variance, and degrees of freedom for the pooled variance. The pooled variance has a ROWTYPE_ value MSE, and the pooled variance has the ROWTYPE_ value DFE.

Missing Values
- Missing value treatment affects the values written to a matrix system file. When reading a matrix system file, be sure to specify a missing value treatment on ONEWAY that is compatible with the treatment used to generate the matrix materials.

Example
```
GET FILE=GSS80.
ONEWAY  WELL BY EDUC6(1,6)
 /MATRIX=OUT(ONEMTX).
```

- ONEWAY reads raw data from file GSS80 and writes one set of matrix materials to the file ONEMTX.
- The active system file is still file GSS80. Subsequent commands are executed on file GSS80.

Example
```
GET FILE=GSS80.
ONEWAY  WELL BY EDUC6(1,6)
 /MATRIX=OUT(*).
LIST
```

- ONEWAY writes the same matrix as in the example above. However, the matrix system file replaces the active system file. The LIST command is executed on the matrix file, not on file GSS80.

Example
```
GET FILE=PRSNNL.
FREQUENCIES VARIABLE=AGE.

ONEWAY  WELL BY EDUC6(1,6)
 /MATRIX=IN(ONEMTX).
```

- This example assumes that you want to perform a frequencies analysis on file PRSNNL and then use ONEWAY to read a different file. The file you want to read is an existing matrix system file.
- MATRIX=IN specifies a file because the current active system file is PRSNNL. MATRIX=IN must therefore specify the file from which the matrix materials will be read.
- ONEMTX does not replace PRSNNL as the active system file.

Example
```
GET FILE=ONEMTX.
ONEWAY  WELL BY EDUC6(1,6)
 /MATRIX=IN(*).
```

- This example assumes that you are starting a new session and want to read an existing matrix system file. GET retrieves the matrix system file ONEMTX.
- MATRIX=IN specifies an asterisk because the current active system file is the matrix system file ONEMTX. MATRIX=IN must therefore specify the active system file as the file from which the matrix materials will be read.
- If the GET command is omitted, SPSS issues an error message.
- If MATRIX=IN(ONEMTX) is specified, SPSS issues an error message, since ONEMTX is already open.

Example
```
MATRIX DATA VARIABLES=EDUC ROWTYPE_ WELL /FACTOR=EDUC.
BEGIN DATA
1 N 65
2 N 95
3 N 181
4 N 82
5 N 40
6 N 37
1 MEAN 2.6462
2 MEAN 2.7737
3 MEAN 4.1796
4 MEAN 4.5610
5 MEAN 4.6625
6 MEAN 5.2297
. MSE 6.2699
. DFE 494
END DATA.
LIST.
ONEWAY WELL BY EDUC(1,6) /MATRIX=IN(*) /RANGES=DUNCAN.
```

- MATRIX DATA reads raw matrix data and creates an active system file that, for each factor in the data, contains a vector of frequencies and a vector of means. The active system file also includes one record each for the pooled variance and the degrees of freedom for the MSE.
- LIST displays the matrix materials that are on the active file.
- ONEWAY reads the data matrix. An asterisk (*) is specified as the IN file on MATRIX because the data are in the active system file.
- A Duncan Multiple Range test is performed.

Annotated Example For a complete example with output, see Examples following the Command Reference.

References Speed, M. F. 1976. Response curves in the one way classification with unequal numbers of observations per cell. *Proceedings of the Statistical Computing Section.* American Statistical Association,

PARTIAL CORR

```
PARTIAL CORR [VARIABLES=] varlist [WITH varlist]
    BY control list (levels) [/varlist...]

[/SIGNIFICANCE={ONETAIL**}]
               {TWOTAIL  }

[/STATISTICS=[NONE**] [CORR] [DESCRIPTIVES] [BADCORR] [ALL]]

[/FORMAT={MATRIX** }]
         {SERIAL   }
         {CONDENSED}

[/MISSING={LISTWISE**}  [{EXCLUDE**}]]
          {ANALYSIS  }  {INCLUDE  }

[/MATRIX=[NONE**] [IN({*   })] [OUT({*   })]]
                     {file}        {file}
```

**Default if the subcommand is omitted.

Example:

```
PARTIAL CORR VARIABLES=PUBTRANS MECHANIC BUSDRVER BY NETPURSE
(1).
```

Overview

PARTIAL CORR produces partial correlation coefficients that describe the relationship between two variables while adjusting for the effects of one or more additional variables. PARTIAL CORR calculates a matrix of Pearson product-moment correlations. It can also read the zero-order correlation matrix as input. Other procedures producing zero-order correlation matrices that can be read by PARTIAL CORR include CORRELATIONS, REGRESSION, DISCRIMINANT, and FACTOR.

Options

Significance Levels. By default, the significance level for each partial correlation coefficient is based on a one-tailed test. Optionally, you can request that the significance level be calculated using a two-tailed test. See SIGNIFICANCE Subcommand.

Optional Statistics. In addition to the partial correlation coefficient, degrees of freedom, and significance level, you can obtain the mean, standard deviation, and number of nonmissing cases for each variable, and zero-order correlation coefficients for each pair of variables. See STATISTICS Subcommand.

Formatting Options. You can print more rows and columns of coefficients than the default allows and suppress the degrees of freedom and significance level for each coefficient. You can also print only the nonredundant coefficients. See FORMAT Subcommand.

Matrix Input and Output. You can read and write zero-order correlation matrices. See MATRIX Subcommand.

Basic Specification

• The basic specification is a VARIABLES subcommand that supplies a variable list to be correlated, one or more control variables following the keyword BY, and a list of order values in parentheses. The order values define the level of control. PARTIAL CORR calculates the partial correlation of each variable with every other variable on the correlation variable list.

Subcommand Order

• Subcommands can be used in any order.

Syntax Rules

• If VARIABLES is the first subcommand used on PARTIAL CORR, keyword VARIABLES may be omitted.

• If VARIABLES is not the first subcommand specified on PARTIAL CORR, the equals sign is required.

Operations
- PARTIAL CORR produces one matrix of partial correlation coefficients for each of up to five order values. For each coefficient, PARTIAL CORR prints the degrees of freedom and the significance level.

Limitations
- Maximum 25 requests on a single PARTIAL CORR command. Each request must contain a correlation list, a control list and order values.
- Maximum 400 variables total can be named or implied per PARTIAL CORR command.
- Maximum 100 control variables.
- Maximum 5 different order values per single list. The largest order value that can appear is 100.

Example

```
PARTIAL CORR VARIABLES=PUBTRANS MECHANIC BUSDRVER BY NETPURSE
   (1).
```

- PARTIAL CORR produces a square matrix containing three unique first-order partial correlations: PUBTRANS correlated with MECHANIC, controlling for NETPURSE; PUBTRANS with BUSDRVER, controlling for NETPURSE; and MECHANIC with BUSDRVER, controlling for NETPURSE.
- The 1 in parentheses indicates a first-order partial correlation.

VARIABLES Subcommand

VARIABLES requires three types of information:

- A *correlation list* of one or more pairs of variables for which partial correlations are desired. This list does not include the control variables.
- A *control list* of one or more variables that will be used as controls for the variables in the correlation list.
- One or more *order values* indicating the order of partials desired from the correlation and control list.

Correlation List

The correlation list specifies pairs of variables to be correlated while controlling for the variable(s) in the control list.

- To request a square or lower-triangular matrix, specify a simple list of variables. This obtains the partial correlation of each variable with every other variable in the list.
- To request a rectangular matrix, specify a variable list followed by keyword WITH and a second variable list. This obtains the partial correlation of specific variable pairs. The first variable list defines the rows of the matrix, and the second list defines the columns.

Control List and Order Values

The control list names the variables to be used as controls for each pair of variables specified by the correlation list.

- The control list precedes the order values that specify the exact partials to be computed.
- The order value must be specified, even if only one control variable is specified. Order values must be integers between 1 and the number of control variables.
- The correlation between a pair of variables is referred to as a zero-order correlation. Controlling for one variable produces a first-order partial correlation, controlling for two variables produces a second-order partial, and so on.
- The number of control variables determines the orders that can be requested, while the order value(s) indicate the partial correlation matrix or matrices to be printed.
- One partial is produced for every unique combination of control variables which add up to the order value.
- To specify multiple sets of partials on one PARTIAL CORR command, specify multiple order values within a single set of parentheses. Up to five order values can be specified. Separate each value with at least one space or comma.

Specifying Multiple Analyses

To specify multiple analyses, use multiple VARIABLES subcommands, or a slash (/) to separate each set of specifications on one VARIABLES subcommand.

- PARTIAL CORR computes the zero-order correlation matrix for each analysis list separately.
- Depending upon the distribution of missing values in the variables, different sets of cases may be used for different analysis lists despite variables common to them.

Example
```
PARTIAL CORR RENT FOOD PUBTRANS WITH TEACHER MANAGER
  BY NET SALRY(1).
```

- PARTIAL CORR produces a rectangular matrix. Variables RENT, FOOD, and PUBTRANS form the matrix rows, and variables TEACHER and MANAGER form the columns.
- Keyword VARIABLES is omitted. This is allowed because the variable list is the first specification on PARTIAL CORR.

Example
```
PARTIAL CORR  RENT WITH TEACHER BY NETSALRY, NETPRICE (1).
PARTIAL CORR  RENT WITH TEACHER BY NETSALRY, NETPRICE (2).
PARTIAL CORR  RENT WITH TEACHER BY NETSALRY, NETPRICE (1,2).

PARTIAL CORR  RENT FOOD PUBTRANS BY NETSALRY NETPURSE NETPRICE
  (1,3).
```

- The first PARTIAL CORR produces two first-order partials: RENT with TEACHER, controlling for NETSALRY; and RENT with TEACHER, controlling for NETPRICE.
- The second PARTIAL CORR produces one second-order partial of RENT with TEACHER, controlling simultaneously for NETSALRY and NETPRICE.
- The third PARTIAL CORR uses one command to specify both sets of partials specified by the previous two commands.
- The fourth PARTIAL CORR produces both first-order and third-order partial correlations.

Example
```
PARTIAL CORR  RENT FOOD WITH TEACHER BY NETSALRY NETPRICE (1,2)
  /WCLOTHES MCLOTHES BY NETPRICE (1).
```

- PARTIAL CORR produces three matrices for the first correlation list, control list, and order values.
- The second correlation list, control list, and order value produce one matrix.

SIGNIFICANCE Subcommand

SIGNIFICANCE determines whether the significance level is based on a one-tailed or two-tailed test.

- By default, the significance level is based on a one-tailed test. This is appropriate when the direction of the relationship between a pair of variables can be specified in advance of the analysis.
- When the direction of the relationship cannot be determined in advance, a two-tailed test is appropriate.

ONETAIL *One-tailed test of significance.* This is the default.

TWOTAIL *Two-tailed test of significance.*

STATISTICS Subcommand

The partial correlation coefficient, degrees of freedom, and significance level are automatically printed on PARTIAL CORR. Use STATISTICS to obtain additional statistics.

- When omitted, STATISTICS defaults to NONE, for no additional statistics.
- When used, STATISTICS calculates only the additional statistics you request.
- If both CORR and BADCORR are requested, CORR takes precedence over BADCORR and the zero-order correlations are printed.

NONE *No additional statistics.* This is the default.

CORR *Zero-order correlations with degrees of freedom and significance level.*

DESCRIPTIVES *Mean, standard deviation, and number of nonmissing cases. Descriptive statistics are not available with matrix input.*

BADCORR	*Zero-order correlation coefficients if (and only if) any of the zero-order correlations are noncomputable.* Noncomputable coefficients are printed as a period (.).
ALL	*All additional statistics available with PARTIAL CORR.*

FORMAT Subcommand

FORMAT determines page format. Its default keyword is MATRIX, which requires four print lines per matrix row and displays the degrees of freedom and the significance level. The default output also prints redundant coefficients.

• Keyword CONDENSED requires only one print line per matrix row and suppresses the degrees of freedom and significance.

• Keyword SERIAL prints only the nonredundant coefficients. They are displayed in serial string format with the coefficients from the first row of the matrix printed first, followed by all the unique coefficients from the second row and so on for all the rows of the matrix.

• If both CONDENSED and SERIAL are specified, only SERIAL is in effect.

• A single star (*) following a coefficient indicates significance at the 0.01 level or less. Two stars (**) following a coefficient indicate significance at the 0.001 level or less.

MATRIX	*Print the degrees of freedom and significance level in matrix format.* This is the default.
CONDENSED	*Suppress the printing of the degrees of freedom and significance level.*
SERIAL	*Print only the nonredundant coefficients in serial string format.*

MISSING Subcommand

MISSING controls missing values. By default, MISSING deletes cases with missing values on a LISTWISE basis. A case missing on any of the variables listed, including the set of control variables, is not used. User-missing values are excluded from the analysis.

• When multiple analysis lists are specified, missing values are handled separately for each analysis list.

• When pairwise deletion is in effect, the degrees of freedom for a particular partial coefficient are based on the smallest number of cases used in the calculation of any of the simple correlations.

• LISTWISE and ANALYSIS are mutually exclusive. Each, however, can be used with either INCLUDE or EXCLUDE.

LISTWISE	*Exclude missing values listwise.* Cases missing on any of the variables listed, including the set of control variables, are not used in the calculation of zero-order correlation coefficients. This is the default.
ANALYSIS	*Exclude missing values on a pair-by-pair basis.* Cases missing on one or both of a pair of variables are not used in the calculation of zero-order correlation coefficients.
EXCLUDE	*Exclude user-missing values.* User-missing values are excluded from the analysis. This is the default.
INCLUDE	*Include user-missing values.* User-missing values are included in the analysis.

MATRIX Subcommand

MATRIX reads and writes SPSS matrix system files. The matrix materials that PARTIAL CORR writes can be used by subsequent PARTIAL CORR procedures, or by other SPSS procedures that read correlation type matrices (see the table of matrix types in Universals: Defining Matrices).

• Either IN or OUT is required to specify the matrix file in parentheses. When both IN and OUT are used on the same PARTIAL CORR procedure, they can be specified on separate MATRIX subcommands, or both on the same subcommand.

• In addition to the Pearson correlation coefficients, the matrix materials PARTIAL CORR writes include the mean, standard deviation, and number of cases used to compute each coefficient. However, if PARTIAL CORR reads matrix data for its input and then writes matrix materials based on that data, the outfile matrix will not include means and standard deviations with the matrix materials.

- PARTIAL CORR writes a full square matrix for the analysis specified on the first VARIABLES subcommand (or first variable list if keyword VARIABLES is omitted). The matrix materials include all the variables specified on the first VARIABLES subcommand, including those specified after keywords WITH (when used) and BY. No matrix is written for subsequent variable lists.

- Documents from the original file are not included in the matrix file and are not present if the matrix file becomes the active system file.

- When the matrix materials are read from a file other than the active system file, both the active system file and the matrix system file specified by the keyword IN on PARTIAL CORR must contain all the variables referenced by the VARIABLES subcommand(s) on PARTIAL CORR.

- MATRIX=IN cannot be used in place of GET or DATA LIST to begin a new SPSS command file. MATRIX is a subcommand on PARTIAL CORR and PARTIAL CORR cannot run before an active system file is defined.

- To begin a new command file and immediately read a matrix, first GET the matrix file, and then specify IN(*) on MATRIX.

- PARTIAL CORR can read a matrix written to the active system file by another procedure.

- With matrix input, SPSS reads variable names, variable and value labels, and print and write formats from the dictionary of the matrix system file.

OUT   *Write the (zero-order) correlation matrix to a system file.* Specify either a file or an asterisk, and enclose the specification in parentheses. If you specify a file, the file is stored on disk and can be retrieved at any time. If you specify an asterisk (*), the matrix system file replaces the active system file but is not stored on disk unless you use SAVE or XSAVE.

IN   *Read a matrix system file.* Both the active system file and the matrix file must contain all the variables referenced by the VARIABLES subcommand(s) on PARTIAL CORR. If the matrix system file *is not* the current active system file, specify a file in parentheses. If the matrix system file *is* the current active system file, specify an asterisk (*) in parentheses.

Format of the Matrix System File

- The matrix system file includes two special variables created by SPSS: ROWTYPE_ and VARNAME_. Variable ROWTYPE_ is a short string variable with values N, MEAN, STDDEV, and CORR (for Pearson's correlation coefficient). Variable VARNAME_ is a short string variable whose values are the names of the variables used to form the correlation matrix. When ROWTYPE_ is CORR, VARNAME_ gives the variable associated with that row of the correlation matrix.

- The remaining variables in the file are the variables used to form the correlation matrix.

Split Files and Variable Order

- When split-file processing is in effect, the first variables in the matrix system file will be the split variables, followed by ROWTYPE_, VARNAME_, and the variables used to form the correlation matrix.

- A full set of matrix materials is written for each split-file group defined by the split variable(s).

- A split variable cannot have the same variable name as any other variable written to the matrix system file.

- If split-file processing is in effect when a matrix is written, the same split file must be in effect when that matrix is read by any procedure.

Additional Statistics

- PARTIAL CORR always includes with the matrix materials the mean, standard deviation, and number of cases used to compute each coefficient. This information immediately precedes the correlation matrix in the output file.

Missing Values

- With pairwise treatment of missing values (the treatment of the default keyword ANALYSIS), the matrix of N's used to compute each coefficient is included with the matrix materials.

- With LISTWISE treatment, a single N used to calculate all coefficients is included with the matrix materials.
- When reading a matrix system file, be sure to specify a missing value treatment on PARTIAL CORR that is compatible with the treatment used to generate the matrix materials.

Example
```
GET FILE=CITY.
PARTIAL CORR VARIABLES=BUSDRVER MECHANIC ENGINEER TEACHER COOK BY
   NETSALRY(1)
   /MATRIX=OUT(PTMTX).
```

- PARTIAL CORR reads raw data from file CITY and writes one set of matrix materials to file PTMTX.
- The active system file is still the file CITY. Subsequent commands are executed on file CITY.

Example
```
GET FILE=CITY.
PARTIAL CORR VARIABLES=BUSDRVER MECHANIC ENGINEER TEACHER COOK BY
   NETSALRY(1)
   /MATRIX=OUT(*).
LIST
```

- PARTIAL CORR writes the same matrix as in the example above. However, the matrix system file replaces the active system file. The LIST command is executed on the matrix file, not on the file CITY.

Example
```
GET FILE=PRSNNL.
FREQUENCIES VARIABLE=AGE.

PARTIAL CORR VARIABLES=BUSDRVER MECHANIC ENGINEER TEACHER COOK BY
   NETSALRY(1)
   /MATRIX=IN(CORMTX).
```

- This example assumes that you want to perform a frequencies analysis on file PRSNNL and then use PARTIAL CORR to read a different file. The file you want to read is an existing matrix system file.
- MATRIX=IN specifies a file because the current active system file is PRSNNL. MATRIX=IN must therefore specify the file from which the matrix materials will be read. Both the active system file and the CORMTX file must contain all the variables referenced by the VARIABLES subcommand(s) on PARTIAL CORR.
- CORMTX does not replace PRSNNL as the active system file.

Example
```
GET FILE=CORMTX.
PARTIAL CORR VARIABLES=BUSDRVER MECHANIC ENGINEER TEACHER COOK BY
   NETSALRY(1)
   /MATRIX=IN(*).
```

- This example assumes that you are starting a new session and want to read an existing matrix system file. GET retrieves the matrix system file CORMTX.
- MATRIX=IN specifies an asterisk because the current active system file is the matrix system file CORMTX. MATRIX=IN must therefore specify the active system file as the file from which the matrix materials will be read.
- If the GET command is omitted, SPSS issues an error message.
- If MATRIX=IN(CORMTX) is specified, SPSS issues an error message.

Example
```
GET FILE=CITY.
REGRESSION MATRIX=OUT(*) /VARIABLES=NETPURSE PUBTRANS MECHANIC
   BUSDRVER
   /DEPENDENT=NETPURSE /ENTER.
PARTIAL CORR  PUBTRANS MECHANIC BUSDRVER BY NETPURSE(1)
   / MATRIX=IN(*).
```

- GET defines the data to SPSS and selects the variables needed for the analysis.
- REGRESSION computes correlations among the specified variables. The MATRIX=OUT(*) specification writes a matrix system file and replaces the active system file with the matrix system file.
- The MATRIX=IN(*) specification on PARTIAL CORR reads the matrix materials that REGRESSION has written to the active system file.

Annotated Example   For a complete example with output, see Examples following the Command Reference.

PLOT

```
PLOT [HSIZE = {80**}] [/VSIZE = {40**}]
             {n   }             {n   }

[/CUTPOINT = {EVERY(({1**}))}]
             {      {n  }   }
             {value list    }

[/SYMBOLS = {ALPHANUMERIC**                          }]
            {NUMERIC                                 }
            {'symbols'[,'overplot symbols']          }
            {X'hexsymbs'[,'overplot hexsymbs']       }
            {DEFAULT                                 }

[/MISSING = [{PLOTWISE**}] [INCLUDE]]
             {LISTWISE  }

[/FORMAT = {DEFAULT**        }]
           {CONTOUR[(({10}))]}
           {         {n }    }
           {OVERLAY          }
           {REGRESSION       }

[/TITLE = 'title']

[/HORIZONTAL = ['title'] [STANDARDIZE] [REFERENCE(value list)]
               [MIN(min)] [MAX(max)] [UNIFORM]]

[/VERTICAL = ['title'] [STANDARDIZE] [REFERENCE(value list)]
             [MIN(min)] [MAX(max)] [UNIFORM]]

/PLOT = {varlist} WITH varlist [(PAIR)] [BY varname] [;varlist...]
        {ALL     }

[/PLOT=...]
```

** Default if the subcommand is omitted.

Example:

```
PLOT FORMAT=OVERLAY /SYMBOLS='MD' /VSIZE=12 /HSIZE=60
  /TITLE='Marriage and Divorce Rates'
  /VERTICAL='Rates per 1000 population'
  /HORIZONTAL='Year' REFERENCE (1918, 1945) MIN (1880) MAX (2000)
  /PLOT=MARRATE DIVRATE WITH YEAR.
```

Overview

PLOT produces two-dimensional line-printer plots, including simple bivariate scatterplots, scatterplots with a control variable, contour plots, and overlay plots. You can also request bivariate regression statistics. You can choose from a variety of options for plot symbols, and you can add reference lines. You have control over size, labeling, and scaling of each axis, and for a series of plots, you can constrain the axes to be uniform.

Options

Types of Plots. You can introduce a control variable for bivariate scatterplots or request regression plots with or without a control variable, contour plots, or overlay plots. See FORMAT Subcommand.

Plot Tailoring. You can specify a title for the plot (see TITLE Subcommand). You can scale and label the horizontal and vertical axes, request reference lines, and plot standardized variables (see the VERTICAL and HORIZONTAL subcommands). You can control the plot size (see the HSIZE and VSIZE subcommands), and you can specify plotting symbols and the frequency they represent (see the SYMBOL and CUTPOINT subcommands).

Basic Specification

• The basic specification is a PLOT subcommand that names the variable(s) for the vertical (Y) axis, keyword WITH, and the variable(s) for the horizontal (X) axis. By default, PLOT produces separate bivariate scatterplots for all combinations formed by each variable on the left side of WITH with each variable on the right.

Subcommand Order

- PLOT must be the last subcommand specified.
- Remaining subcommands can be used in any order.

Syntax Rules

- The PLOT subcommand can be specified more than once.
- Subcommands MISSING, VSIZE, HSIZE, CUTPOINT, and SYMBOLS apply to all plots requested and can be specified only once. They must be entered before the final PLOT subcommand.
- Subcommands HORIZONTAL, VERTICAL, FORMAT, and TITLE can be specified more than once and apply only to the following PLOT subcommand.

Operations

- The default plot frame size depends on the page size specified on SET. HSIZE and VSIZE override the default plot size.
- A longer page length can produce longer default plots within the same width. A wider page does not produce a wider default plot unless the page length is changed accordingly.

Limitations

There are no limitations on the number of plots requested or on the number of variables specified on a PLOT command. The following limitations apply to the optional subcommands:

- Maximum 60 characters for a title specified on TITLE.
- Maximum 36 symbols per SYMBOLS subcommand.
- Maximum 35 cutpoints per CUTPOINT subcommand.
- Maximum 10 reference points on each HORIZONTAL or VERTICAL subcommand.
- Maximum 40 characters per label on each HORIZONTAL or VERTICAL subcommand.

Example

```
PLOT FORMAT=OVERLAY /SYMBOLS='MD' /VSIZE=12 /HSIZE=60
   /TITLE='Marriage and Divorce Rates'
   /VERTICAL='Rates per 1000 population'
   /HORIZONTAL='Year' REFERENCE (1918, 1945) MIN (1900) MAX
   (1983)
   /PLOT=MARRATE DIVRATE WITH YEAR.
```

- This example produces an overlay plot of marriage and divorce rates by year.
- SYMBOLS selects the symbols M and D, respectively, for the two plots.
- VSIZE and HSIZE limit the vertical and horizontal axes to 12 lines and 60 columns, respectively.
- TITLE specifies a plot title, and VERTICAL provides a title for the vertical axis.
- HORIZONTAL provides a title for the horizontal axis. REFERENCE, MIN, and MAX provide reference lines at values 1918 and 1945 and minimum and maximum scale values on the horizontal axis.

PLOT Subcommand

The PLOT subcommand names the variables to be plotted on each axis. The PLOT subcommand can also name a control or contour variable.

- PLOT is the only required subcommand.
- Multiple PLOT subcommands are allowed.
- No other subcommands can follow the last PLOT subcommand.
- Each plot list first specifies a list of variables to be plotted on the vertical axis, then keyword WITH, and then a list of variables to be plotted on the horizontal axis.
- By default, PLOT creates separate plots for each combination of variables listed on the left side of WITH, with variables on the right.

- Use semicolons to separate multiple plot lists on a single PLOT subcommand.
- Keyword ALL can be used to refer to all user-defined variables.
- To specify a control or contour variable, use keyword BY followed by a variable name.
- Only one control variable can be specified on any plot list.
- If a control variable is specified, PLOT uses the first character of the control variable's value label as the plot symbol. If value labels have not been specified, the first character of the value is used. The symbol $ indicates that more than one control value occurs in that display position.

You can also request special pairing of variables with the following keyword:

(PAIR) *Plot corresponding pairs of variables.* The first variable before WITH is plotted against the first variable after WITH, and so on.

Example
```
PLOT PLOT=MARRATE WITH YEAR AGE;
          BIRTHS DEATHS WITH INCOME1 INCOME2 (PAIR);
          DIVRATE WITH AGE BY YEAR.
```

- This PLOT subcommand contains three plot lists. The first requests a plot of MARRATE with YEAR and of MARRATE with AGE.
- The second uses the keyword (PAIR) to request two plots: BIRTHS with INCOME1 and DEATHS with INCOME2.
- The third requests a plot of DIVRATE with AGE using YEAR as a control variable. The value labels for YEAR will be used to obtain plotting characters in this control plot.

FORMAT Subcommand

FORMAT controls the type of plot produced.

- FORMAT can be specified only once before each PLOT subcommand and applies only to plots requested on that PLOT subcommand.
- If FORMAT is not used or keyword DEFAULT is specified, bivariate scatterplots are displayed.
- Only one keyword can be specified on each FORMAT subcommand.

DEFAULT *Bivariate scatterplot.* When there is no control variable on the plot list, each symbol represents the case count at that plot position. When a control variable is specified, each symbol represents the first character of the value label of the control variable.

OVERLAY *Overlay plots.* All bivariate plots on the next PLOT subcommand appear in one plot frame. PLOT selects a unique symbol for each plot to be overlaid, plus a symbol to represent multiple plot points in one display position.

CONTOUR(n) *Contour plot with* n *levels.* Contour plots use a continuous variable as the control variable and *n* successive symbols to represent lowest to highest levels of the variable. Specify the control variable after BY on the PLOT subcommand. This variable is recoded into *n* equal-width intervals. If the levels specification is omitted, the default of 10 is used; the maximum is 35. When more than one level of the contour variable occurs at the same plot position, PLOT displays the value of the highest level.

REGRESSION *Regression of vertical-axis variable on horizontal-axis variable.* The regression-line intercepts on each axis are marked with the letter R. When there is no control variable, each symbol represents the frequency of cases at that plot position. If a control variable is specified, regression statistics are pooled over all categories and each symbol represents the first character of the value labels of the control variable.

Plot Symbols

A wide range of alphabetical, numeric, and hexadecimal characters are available for use as PLOT symbols. Two subcommands control the display of symbols: the SYMBOLS subcommand controls the choice of plot symbols, and the CUT-

POINT subcommand controls the frequencies represented by a symbol. SYM-BOLS and CUTPOINT can each be specified only once and apply to all plots requested in a PLOT command. If you have more than one FORMAT subcommand within a PLOT command, the meaning of the plotting symbols can vary. The operation of SYMBOLS and CUTPOINT for each FORMAT specification is summarized below.

- *DEFAULT or REGRESSION plot, no control.* Each symbol represents the frequency of cases. Controlled by SYMBOLS and CUTPOINT.
- *DEFAULT or REGRESSION plot, control.* Each symbol represents one value of the control variable. SYMBOLS and CUTPOINT do not apply. The plot symbol is the first character of the control variable's value label or the first character of the actual value if no VALUE LABELS have been declared; the uniqueness of these symbols is not checked.
- *OVERLAY.* Each symbol represents one of the overlaid plots. SYMBOLS is applicable; CUTPOINT is not.
- *CONTOUR.* Each symbol represents one level of the contour variable. SYM-BOLS is applicable; CUTPOINT is not.

CUTPOINT Subcommand

By default, each frequency in a frequency plot is represented by a different plot symbol, and successive plotting symbols represent an interval width of 1. Use the CUTPOINT subcommand to alter the categories represented by plot symbols for bivariate and regression plots.

- CUTPOINT can be specified only once and applies to all frequency plots on the PLOT command.
- If CUTPOINT is omitted, the default interval of width 1 is in effect.
- Only one specification can be given on CUTPOINT.

EVERY(n) *Frequency intervals of width* n. Each plot symbol represents the specified frequency interval. The default is an interval width of 1. If SYMBOLS is used as well as EVERY, the last symbol specified will represent all frequencies greater than those for the next-to-last symbol.

(value list) *Each value defines a cutpoint.* Successive plot symbols are assigned to each cutpoint. Up to 35 cutpoints can be specified. Specify values separated by blanks or commas. The number of cutpoints is one less than the number of intervals.

Example

```
PLOT CUTPOINT=EVERY(2) /PLOT=Y WITH X.
PLOT CUTPOINT=(5,10,20) /PLOT=Y WITH X.
```

- In the first PLOT command, 1 or 2 cases on a display position are represented by a 1; 3 or 4 cases by a 2, and so forth.
- In the second PLOT command, 1 to 5 cases on a display position are represented by a 1; 6 to 10 cases by a 2; 11 to 20 cases by a 3; and 21 or more cases by a 4.

SYMBOLS Subcommand

SYMBOLS defines the plotting symbols for bivariate scatterplots and bivariate regression, overlay, and contour plots. Successive symbols represent increasing frequencies in scatterplots or regression plots, successive subplots in overlay plots, and successive intervals in contour plots.

- SYMBOLS can be specified only once and applies to all plots requested except control plots.
- If the subcommand is omitted, the default alphanumeric symbol set is used.
- If SYMBOLS is specified, a table defining the plotting symbols is displayed.

ALPHANUMERIC *Alphanumeric plotting symbols.* Includes the characters 1 through 9, A through Z, and *. Thirty-six or more cases at a position are represented by a *. This is the default.

NUMERIC *Numeric plotting symbols.* Includes the characters 1 through 9 and *. Ten or more cases at a plot position are represented by a *.

'symbols'[,'ovprnt'] *List of plot symbols.* Up to 36 symbols can be specified. Symbols are specified without any intervening blanks or commas. Optionally, you can specify a second list of overprinting symbols separated from the first list by a comma or space. The overprinting symbols can be either hexadecimal representations (preceded by an X) or keyboard characters.

X'hexsym'[,'ovprnt'] *List of hexadecimal plot symbols.* Indicate hexadecimal symbols by specifying X before the hexadecimal representation list enclosed in apostrophes. Optionally, you can specify a second list of overprinting symbols separated from the first list by a comma or space. The overprinting symbols can be either hexadecimal representations or keyboard characters.

Example
```
PLOT CUTPOINTS=EVERY(5)/SYMBOLS='.+O',' X'
    /PLOT=Y BY X.
```

- This example uses a period (.) to represent 5 or fewer cases at one point, a plus sign (+) to represent 6 to 10 cases at the same position, and a symbol overprinting O and X to represent 11 or more cases at one position. Note the leading blanks in the list of overprint symbols.

VSIZE and HSIZE Subcommands

Use VSIZE and HSIZE respectively to specify the vertical and horizontal frame size for the plot.

- VSIZE and HSIZE can each be used only once per PLOT command and apply to all plots requested.
- The default size of a plot depends on the current page size. With a typical computer page width of 132 horizontal print positions and a typical page length (vertically) of 59 lines, the default width is 80 positions and the default length is 40 lines.
- VSIZE and HSIZE each use a single integer as their only specification.
- VSIZE and HSIZE values do not include display lines for the plot frame itself or for auxiliary information such as titles, axis scale numbers, regression statistics, or symbol table.
- The size specified on HSIZE must be at least 15 positions less than the size specified on the SET WIDTH command (or its default). Thus, if SET WIDTH=80, the largest horizontal size you can request (and the default) is 65.
- If VSIZE is greater than the length specified on SET LENGTH, VSIZE will override the length, but the symbol table and other information normally printed below a plot will appear on the following page. To ensure that this information will print on the same page, the length on SET LENGTH should be at least 20 lines longer than VSIZE.

VERTICAL and HORIZONTAL Subcommands

VERTICAL and HORIZONTAL control labeling and scaling for the vertical and horizontal axes, respectively.

- VERTICAL and HORIZONTAL can each be specified once before each PLOT subcommand.
- VERTICAL and HORIZONTAL apply only to plots requested by the next PLOT subcommand.
- If VERTICAL and HORIZONTAL are omitted, all defaults are in effect. If VERTICAL and HORIZONTAL are included, only those defaults explicitly altered are changed.

The following keywords are available for both VERTICAL and HORIZONTAL:

'label' *Label for axis.* The label can contain up to 40 characters. A label that will not fit in the plot frame is truncated. The default is the variable label or the variable name if no variable label has been declared.

MIN (n) *Minimum axis value.* If you specify a minimum value greater than the observed minimum value, some points

	will not be included in the plot. The default is the minimum observed value.
MAX (n)	*Maximum axis value.* If you specify a maximum value greater than the observed maximum value, some points will not be included in the plot. The default is the maximum observed value.
UNIFORM	*Uniform values on axis.* All plots on the PLOT subcommand will have the same value scale on the axis. A uniform scale is implied when both MIN and MAX are specified. If UNIFORM is specified, PLOT determines the minimum and maximum observed values across all variables on the PLOT subcommand.
REFERENCE(values)	*Values at which reference lines will be drawn.* Specify the values separated by blanks or commas. The default is no reference lines.
STANDARDIZE	*Standardize variables on the axes.* Standardized variables are useful for overlay plots of variables with different scales. The default is to plot observed values.

TITLE Subcommand

Use the TITLE subcommand to label plots.

- TITLE can be specified once before each PLOT subcommand.
- TITLE applies to all plots named on the next PLOT subcommand.
- The default title is either the names of the variables in a bivariate plot or the type of plot requested on FORMAT.
- The title can be up to 60 characters long.
- The rules for specifying titles follow the usual conventions for strings (see Universals: Strings).
- The title is truncated if it exceeds the width specified on the HSIZE subcommand.

MISSING Subcommand

MISSING controls the handling of cases with missing values.

- MISSING can be specified only once on each PLOT command and applies to all plots.
- By default, cases with system-missing or user-missing values for any variables in a plot are omitted from that plot.
- Keywords LISTWISE and PLOTWISE (the default) are alternatives. Either one may also be specified with INCLUDE.

PLOTWISE	*Delete cases with missing values plotwise.* This is the default. Cases with missing values for any variable in a plot are not included in that plot. In overlay plots, PLOTWISE applies separately to each overlaid plot in the frame, not to the full list specified on the PLOT subcommand.
LISTWISE	*Delete cases with missing values listwise.* Cases with missing values for any variable named on the PLOT subcommand are deleted from all plots specified on that PLOT subcommand.
INCLUDE	*Include cases with user-missing values.* Only cases with system-missing values are excluded according to the missing-value treatment specified (PLOTWISE, LISTWISE, or the default).

Annotated Example

For a complete example with output, see Examples following the Command Reference.

POINT

This command is not available on all operating systems.

```
POINT KEY=varname [FILE=file]
```

Example:

```
FILE HANDLE DRIVERS/ file specifications.
POINT FILE=DRIVERS /KEY=#FRSTAGE.
```

Overview

POINT establishes, in a *keyed file,* the location at which sequential access to the file begins (or resumes). A keyed file is a file that provides access to information by a record *key.* An example of a keyed file is a file containing a social security number and other information about a firm's employees. The social security number can be used to identify the records in the file.

Where permitted by the host system, POINT prepares for reading the key-sequenced data set sequentially from a point that the key value controls. SPSS data selection commands can then be used to limit the file to the portion you wish to analyze. A DATA LIST command is used to read the data. To read keyed files (and also direct access files), see the KEYED DATA LIST command.

The following discussion of POINT is general. Refer to your SPSS *Operations Guide* for a discussion of reading keyed files on your operating systems.

Keyed Files

Of the many kinds of keyed files, the ones to which SPSS can provide access are generally known as *indexed sequential files.* A file of this kind is basically a sequential file in which the host system maintains an index so that the file may be processed either sequentially or selectively. In effect, such a file consists of an underlying data file that is accessed by way of a file of index entries. The file of index entries may, for example, contain the fact that data record 797 is associated with social security number 476-77-1359. Depending on the implementation, the underlying data may or may not be maintained in sequential order.

The key for each record in the file generally comprises one or more pieces of information found within the record. An example of a complex key is a customer's last name and house number, plus the consonants in the street name, plus the zip code, plus a uniqueness digit in case there are duplicates. Regardless of the information contained in the key, SPSS treats it as a character string.

Some implementations have keyed files with more than one key associated with each record. That is, the records in a file can be identified according to different types of information. Although the primary key for a file normally must be unique, sometimes the secondary keys need not be. Thus, the records in an employee file might be identified by social security number and job classification.

Basic Specification

The basic specification is the KEY subcommand and a string variable. The value of the string variable is used as the file key for determining where sequential retrieval (via DATA LIST) begins or resumes.

Subcommand Order

• Subcommands can be named in any order.

• Each POINT command must precede its corresponding DATA LIST command.

Syntax Rules

• POINT can be used more than once to change the order of retrieval during processing.

• The FILE HANDLE command must be used to define file specifications for the nonsequential files read by POINT.

• POINT must appear in an input program. POINT, therefore, cannot be used to add cases to an existing file.

Operations

• The next DATA LIST command executed after the POINT command (for the same file) will read a record whose key value is at least as great as that of the specified key. To prevent an infinite loop, in which the same record is read again and again, either the contents of the key variable must change from case to case or provision must be made to execute the POINT command only once.

- POINT provides no feedback on whether the file contains a record that exactly matches the specified key. Only by examining the contents of the record read via the subsequent DATA LIST command can a missing-record condition be detected.

- If the file contains a record whose key exactly matches the value of the KEY variable, the next execution of DATA LIST will read that record, the second execution of DATA LIST will read the next record, and so on. If an exact match is not found, the results depend on the operating system being used. For example, in IBM implementations, reading will begin or resume at the record that has the next higher key. Also in IBM implementations, if the key variable's value is a string that is shorter than the file's key, the key variable's value is logically extended with the lowest character in the collating sequence. For example, if the value of the key variable is the single letter M, retrieval would begin or resume at the first record that had a key (regardless of length) beginning with the letter M or a character higher in the collating sequence.

Example

```
FILE HANDLE DRIVERS/ file specifications.
POINT FILE=DRIVERS /KEY=#FRSTAGE.
```

- FILE HANDLE defines the handle for the data file to be read by POINT. The handle is specified on the FILE subcommand of POINT.

- KEY on POINT specifies the variable used as the access key. The variable must be a string variable, and it must already exist as the result of a prior DATA LIST, KEYED DATA LIST, or transformation command.

Example

```
TITLE      'A KEYED FILE'.
SUBTITLE   'SELECT A SUBSET OR RECORDS'.

FILE HANDLE      DRIVERS/ file specifications.
INPUT PROGRAM.
STRING           #FRSTAGE(A2).
DO IF            #FRSTAGE = ' '.     /* First case check
+  COMPUTE       #FRSTAGE = '26'.    /* Initial key
+  POINT         FILE=DRIVERS /KEY=#FRSTAGE.
END IF.
DATA LIST        FILE=DRIVERS NOTABLE/
                 AGE 19-20(A) SEX 21(A) TICKETS 12-13.
DO IF            AGE > '30'.         /* We want 26 through 30
+  END FILE.
END IF.
END INPUT PROGRAM.
LIST.
```

- This example illustrates how to execute POINT for only the first case. The file contains information about traffic violations, and it uses the individual's age as the key. Ages between 26 and 30 are selected.

- FILE HANDLE specifies the file handle DRIVERS.

- The INPUT PROGRAM and END INPUT PROGRAM commands begin and end the block of commands that build cases. POINT must appear in an input program.

- STRING declares the string variable #FRSTAGE, whose value will be used as the key on the POINT command. Since string variables are initialized as blanks, this value can be used as a first case check.

- The first DO IF—END IF structure is executed only if no records have been read, when #FRSTAGE is equal to its initialized value. If the value of #FRSTAGE is equal to a blank, the COMPUTE statement resets #FRSTAGE to the value of the initial key. This value is set to 26 because only the ages from 26 to 30 are to be selected.

- POINT is executed only during the generation of the first case, and it causes the first execution of DATA LIST to read a record whose key is at least 26.

- DATA LIST reads the variables AGE, SEX, and TICKETS from the file DRIVERS.

- The second DO IF—END IF structure executes an END FILE command as soon as a record is read that contains a driver's age greater than 30.

- There are three things to notice about this example. First, the POINT command is part of an input program, as is required. Second, the actual reading of data from the keyed file is accomplished with DATA LIST rather than a direct access input command. Third, any feedback about the key of the record read is obtained from the contents of the record.

FILE Subcommand

FILE specifies the handle for the data file described by POINT. The file handle must have a corresponding FILE HANDLE command (or, in the case of the IBM OS environment, a corresponding DD statement in the JCL).

- FILE is optional.
- If FILE is omitted, POINT reads from the last file specified on an SPSS input command, such as DATA LIST.

Example

```
FILE HANDLE DRIVERS/ file specifications.
POINT FILE=DRIVERS /KEY=#NXTCASE.
```

- FILE HANDLE specifies DRIVERS as the file handle for the data. FILE on POINT specifies handle DRIVERS.

KEY Subcommand

KEY specifies the variable whose value will be used as the file key for determining where sequential retrieval (via DATA LIST) will begin or resume. This variable must be a string variable, and it must already exist as the result of a prior DATA LIST, KEYED DATA LIST, or transformation command.

- KEY is required. Its only specification is a single variable. The variable can be a permanent variable or a scratch variable.
- Where the keys on a file are inherently numbers, such as social security numbers, the STRING function may be used to assign a value to the key variable.

Example

```
FILE HANDLE DRIVERS/ file specifications.
POINT FILE=DRIVERS /KEY=#NXTCASE.
```

- KEY indicates that the value of the existing scratch variable #FRSTAGE will be used as the key to reading each record.
- Variable #FRSTAGE must be an existing string variable.

PRESERVE

PRESERVE

Overview

PRESERVE preserves current SET specifications that can later be restored by the RESTORE command. PRESERVE and RESTORE are especially useful when using the SPSS macro facility. PRESERVE ... RESTORE sequences can be nested up to five levels.

Basic Specification

• The only specification is the command keyword. PRESERVE has no additional specifications.

Example

```
GET FILE=PRSNNL.
FREQUENCIES VAR=DIVISION /STATISTICS=ALL.
PRESERVE.
SET XSORT=NO WIDTH=90 UNDEFINED=NOWARN BLANKS=000 CASE=UPLOW.
SORT CASES BY DIVISION.
REPORT FORMAT=AUTO LIST /VARS=LNAME FNAME DEPT SOCSEC SALARY
   /BREAK=DIVISION /SUMMARY=MEAN.
RESTORE.
```

• GET reads the SPSS system file PRSNNL.

• FREQUENCIES requests a frequency table and all statistics for variable DIVISION.

• PRESERVE stores all current SET specifications.

• SET changes several subcommand settings.

• SORT sorts cases in preparation for a report. Because SET XSORT=NO, the SPSS sort program is not used to sort cases; another sort program must be available.

• REPORT requests a report organized by variable DIVISION.

• RESTORE restores all the SET specifications that were in effect before PRESERVE was specified.

PRINT

```
PRINT [OUTFILE=file] [RECORDS={1}] [{NOTABLE}]
                              {n}   {TABLE  }


     /{1    }  varlist [[{col location [(format)]}] [varlist...]
      {rec #}            {(format list)         }
                         {*                     }


     [/{2    }...]
       {rec #}
```

Example:
```
PRINT / MOHIRED YRHIRED DEPT SALARY NAME.
EXECUTE.
```

Overview

PRINT displays the values of variables for each case in the data. PRINT is designed to be simple enough for a quick check on reading and transforming data and yet flexible enough for formatting simple reports.

The variable display with PRINT is similar to the variable display available with the LIST command. However, LIST is a procedure and reads data, whereas PRINT is a transformation and requires a procedure (or the EXECUTE command) to execute it. Similar to the REPORT command, PRINT can specify column headings, column locations, and print formats for variables. If you use PRINT with PRINT EJECT, you can control page breaks between cases and display the column headings at the top of every page of the displayed output. However, REPORT is a much more comprehensive formatting tool for writing reports.

Options

Display Formats. You can specify formats for the numeric variables you want displayed. String variables can display only with their dictionary formats. See Specifying Formats, below.

Strings. You can include strings with the variable specifications. The strings can label values or create extra space between values. Strings can also be used to display column headings that identify the displayed variables. See Using Strings, below.

Multiple Lines per Case. You can display variables on more than one line for each case. See RECORD Subcommand.

Output File. You can direct the displayed output to a target file. See OUTFILE Subcommand.

Summary Table. You can display a table that summarizes the variable formats. See TABLE Subcommand.

Subcommand Order

• Subcommands can be named in any order. However, all subcommands must be used before the slash that precedes the first variable list.

Basic Specification

• The basic specification is a slash followed by a variable list. The values for all the variables on the list are printed in the display file.

Syntax Rules

• A slash must precede the variable specifications. The first slash begins definition of the first (and possibly only) line per case of the PRINT display.

• Specified variables must already exist, but they can be numeric, string, scratch, temporary, or system variables.

• Keyword ALL can be used to display the values of all the variables in the active system file.

Operations

• PRINT executes once for each case constructed from the data file.

• If PRINT is not followed by a procedure command that causes the data to be read, SPSS does nothing. To execute the PRINT command anyway, use the EXECUTE command.

- PRINT uses the dictionary print formats assigned when the variables are defined on DATA LIST, PRINT FORMATS, or FORMATS, or assigned when the variables are created with transformation commands.

- Values in the display file display with a blank space between them. However, a format specified for a variable suppresses the blank space for that variable's values.

- Values are printed in the display file as the data are read. The displayed variables appear before the output of the first procedure.

- If more variables are specified than can be displayed in 132 columns or within the width specified with the WIDTH subcommand of SET, the line is wrapped. The wrapped line begins in the second column of the next line. (The first column of the listing file is reserved for carriage control.)

- User-missing values are displayed like any other value for a variable specified on PRINT.

- System-missing values are represented by a period.

- Because PRINT is a transformation, the results of a PRINT command can be intermixed with casewise procedure output. Procedures that produce individual case listings (REPORT and LIST) should not be used immediately after PRINT. At the least, an intervening EXECUTE command should be specified.

Limitations

- Lines of output on PRINT cannot exceed 132 characters (if WIDTH is set to the maximum). Lines over 132 characters are continued on the next line.

Example

```
PRINT   / MOHIRED YRHIRED DEPT SALARY NAME.
FREQUENCIES VARIABLES=DEPT.
```

- PRINT displays values for each variable on the variable list. The FREQUEN-CIES procedure executes PRINT.

- All variables display with their dictionary formats. One blank space separates the values of each variable.

Example

```
PRINT /ALL.
EXECUTE.
```

- PRINT displays values for all the variables in the active system file. The EXECUTE command executes PRINT.

Specifying Formats

You can specify formats for some or all of the numeric variables you want displayed. For a string variable, a specified format must have a width that is equivalent to that of the dictionary format.

- A format specification following a list of variables applies to all the variables in the list. An asterisk within the list can be used to prevent the specified format from applying to variables that precede the asterisk in the list.

- Format specifications can be either column-style or FORTRAN-style. Printable numeric formats are F, COMMA, DOLLAR, CC, DOT, N, E, PCT, PIBHEX, RBHEX, Z, and the date and time formats. Printable string formats are A and AHEX. See your SPSS *Operations Guide* for a complete table of output format types.

- Format specifications are in effect only for the output of the PRINT command. They do not change the dictionary print formats.

- When a format is specified, the automatic blank following the variables in the display file is suppressed. To specify a blank between variables in the display file, use a literal, or specify blank columns in the format, or use an X or T format element in the PRINT specifications. The automatic blank following the variable is preserved for variables that display with the default format as the result of an asterisk specification.

Example

```
PRINT / TENURE (F2.0) ' ' MOHIRED YRHIRED DEPT *
        SALARY85 TO SALARY88 (4(DOLLAR8,1X)) NAME.
EXECUTE.
```

- Format F2.0 is specified for TENURE. A blank between apostrophes is specified as a string after TENURE because the automatic blank following the variable is suppressed by the format specification.

- MOHIRED, YRHIRED, and DEPT display with default formats because the asterisk prevents them from receiving the DOLLAR8 format specified for SALARY85 TO SALARY88. The automatic blank that displays after a value in the display file is preserved for MOHIRED, YRHIRED, and DEPT, but the blank is suppressed for SALARY85 TO SALARY88 by the format specification. The element 1X is therefore specified with DOLLAR8 to add one blank after each value of SALARY85 to SALARY88.

- NAME displays with the default dictionary format.

Using Strings

You can include strings with the variable specifications on the PRINT command. Strings must be enclosed in apostrophes or quotation marks.

- If a format is specified for a variable list, the format is interrupted by a specified string. Thus, the string has the same effect within a variable list as an asterisk.

- Strings can be used to create column headings that identify the displayed variables. The PRINT command that specifies the column headings must be used within a DO IF—END IF structure. If you want to specify a page ejection so the column headings begin a new page in the display file, use a PRINT EJECT command rather than a PRINT command to specify the headings. See the PRINT EJECT command for controlling page ejections for the displayed variables.

Example
```
PRINT / NAME 'HIRED=' MOHIRED(F2) '/' YRHIRED
            ' SALARY=' SALARY (DOLLAR8).
EXECUTE.
```

- Three strings are specified. The strings 'HIRED=' and 'SALARY=' label the values being displayed. The string '/' inserts a slash between the month hired (MOHIRED) and the year hired (YRHIRED) to create a composite hiring date.

- The F2 format is supplied for variable MOHIRED in order to suppress the blank that would follow it if the dictionary format were used.

- NAME and YRHIRED display with default formats. The string 'HIRED=' prevents the F2 format from applying to NAME; the string ' SALARY=' prevents the DOLLAR8 format from applying to YRHIRED.

Example
```
DO IF $CASENUM EQ 1.
PRINT /'   NAME ' 1 'DEPT' 25 'HIRED' 30 '   SALARY' 35.
END IF.
PRINT / NAME DEPT *
          MOHIRED 30-31 '/' YRHIRED *
          SALARY 35-42(DOLLAR).
EXECUTE.
```

- Values are displayed with column headings that identify the variables. Since PRINT is executed once for each case in the data, the PRINT command that displays the column headings must be used within the DO IF—END IF structure.

- The first PRINT command specifies strings, only. The strings will be used as column headings for the variables. The DO IF $CASENUM EQ 1 causes the PRINT command that defines the column heads to be executed only once, as the first case is processed. END IF closes the structure.

- The second PRINT command specifies the variables to be displayed. It is executed once for each case in the data. To align the column headings with the list of values, formats are specified for the displayed variables rather than relying on the defaults. In this example, the T format element could be used to align the variables and the column headings. For example, specifying MOHIRED (T30,F2) begins the display of the values for the variable MOHIRED in column 30 in order to line up the composite hiring date under the title HIRED.

- The asterisk after DEPT prevents the format specified for MOHIRED from also applying to NAME and DEPT. The asterisk after YRHIRED prevents the format specified for SALARY from also applying to YRHIRED.

RECORDS Subcommand

RECORDS indicates the total number of lines displayed per case. The number specified on RECORDS is informational only. A slash within the variable list is the specification that actually causes variables to display on a new line. Each new line is requested by another slash in the variable list.

- RECORD must be used before the slash that precedes the first variable list.
- The only specification on RECORDS is an integer to indicate the number of records for displayed output. If the number does not agree with the actual number of records specified by slashes in the variable list, SPSS issues a warning and ignores the specification on RECORDS.
- RECORDS is informational and may be omitted from the specification. The slashes alone cause values to display on new lines.
- Specifications for each line of output must begin with a slash in the variable list. Optionally, an integer can follow the slash, indicating on which line the values are to be displayed. The integer is informational. It cannot be used to rearrange the order of records in the display file. If the integer does not agree with the actual record number determined by the slashes in the variable list, the integer is ignored.
- A slash that is not followed by a variable list generates a blank line in the display file.

Example

```
PRINT RECORDS=3 /EMPLOYID NAME DEPT
                /EMPLOYID TENURE SALARY
                /.
EXECUTE.
```

- PRINT displays the values of an individual's name and department on one line, tenure and salary on the next line, the employee identification number on both lines, followed by a completely blank third line. In effect, two lines display for each case, and cases in the display file are separated by a blank line.

Example

```
PRINT RECORDS=3 /1 EMPLOYID NAME DEPT
                /2 EMPLOYID TENURE SALARY
                /3.
EXECUTE.
```

- This command is equivalent to the command in the preceding example.

Example

```
PRINT / EMPLOYID NAME DEPT / EMPLOYID TENURE SALARY /.
EXECUTE.
```

- This command is equivalent to the commands in both preceding examples.

OUTFILE Subcommand

OUTFILE specifies the target file for the output from the PRINT command. By default, the PRINT command sends the results to the display file.

- OUTFILE must be used before the slash that precedes the first variable list.
- The output from PRINT cannot be longer than 132 characters, even if the external file is defined with a longer record length.

Example

```
PRINT OUTFILE=PRINTOUT
   /1 EMPLOYID DEPT SALARY /2 NAME.
EXECUTE.
```

- OUTFILE specifies PRINTOUT as the file that receives the displayed variable list.

TABLE Subcommand

TABLE requests a format table in the display file showing how the variable information is formatted. NOTABLE is the default.

- TABLE must be used before the slash that precedes the first variable list.

Example

```
PRINT TABLE /1 EMPLOYID DEPT SALARY /2  NAME.
EXECUTE.
```

- TABLE requests a summary table describing the PRINT specifications. The table is printed in the display file.

PRINT EJECT

```
PRINT EJECT [OUTFILE=file] [RECORDS={1}] [{NOTABLE}]
                                    {n}   {TABLE  }


  /{1    } varlist [[{col location [(format)]}]] [varlist...]
   {rec #}           {(format list)           }
                     {*                       }


  [/{2    }...]
    {rec #}
```

Example:
```
DO IF $CASENUM EQ 1.
PRINT EJECT /'   NAME ' 1 'DEPT' 25 'HIRED' 30 '  SALARY' 35.
END IF.
PRINT / NAME DEPT *
        MOHIRED(T30,F2) '/' YRHIRED *
        SALARY (T35,DOLLAR8).
EXECUTE.
```

Overview

PRINT EJECT displays specified information at the top of a new page of an output or display file. PRINT EJECT causes a page ejection each time it is executed. If PRINT EJECT is not used in a DO IF—END IF structure, it is executed for each case in the data and displays the values each time on a separate page.

PRINT EJECT is designed to be used with the PRINT command to insert titles and column headings above the values displayed by PRINT. PRINT can also generate titles and headings, but PRINT cannot be used to control page ejections. PRINT never causes a page ejection. PRINT EJECT causes a page ejection each time it is executed, and it always displays information on the top line of the new page.

PRINT EJECT and PRINT can be used for writing simple reports. However, the REPORT command is a much more comprehensive formatting tool for writing reports.

Options

The options available for PRINT EJECT are identical to those available for PRINT:

- You can specify formats for the numeric variables you want displayed. For PRINT EJECT, it is common to use column-style formats to specify column locations for strings. The strings would be those used for titles and column headings.
- You can include strings with the variable specifications. For PRINT EJECT, the strings are usually used as titles or column headings.
- You can display variables on more than one line for each case.
- You can direct the displayed output to a target file.
- You can display a table that summarizes the variable formats.

All of these features are documented in detail for the PRINT command and work identically for PRINT EJECT. Refer to PRINT for additional information on any of the above options.

Basic Specification

- The basic specification is a slash followed by a variable list and/or a list of string specifications that will be used as column headings or titles. The values for each variable or string on the list are printed on the top line of a new page in the display file. Because PRINT EJECT causes a page ejection each time it is executed, it should be used within a DO IF—END IF structure to control execution.

Operations

PRINT EJECT executes once for each case constructed from the data file.

- If PRINT EJECT is not followed by a procedure command that causes the data to be read, SPSS does nothing. To execute the PRINT EJECT command anyway, use the EXECUTE command.

- If PRINT EJECT is not used in a DO IF—END IF structure, it is executed for each case in the data and displays the values each time on a separate page.
- PRINT EJECT uses the dictionary print formats assigned when the variables are defined on DATA LIST, PRINT FORMATS, or FORMATS, or assigned when the variables are created with transformation commands.
- Values in the display file print with a blank space between them. However, a format specified for a variable suppresses the blank space for that variable's values.
- Values are printed in the display file as the data are read. The displayed variables appear before the output of the first procedure.
- If more variables are specified than can be displayed in 132 columns or within the width specified with the WIDTH subcommand of SET, the line is wrapped. The wrapped line begins in the second column of the next line. (The first column of the listing file is reserved for carriage control.)

Limitations
- User-missing values are displayed like any other value for a variable specified on PRINT EJECT.
- System-missing values are represented by a period.
- Lines of output on PRINT EJECT cannot exceed 132 characters (if WIDTH is set to the maximum). Lines over 132 characters are continued on the next line.

Example
```
DO IF $CASENUM EQ 1.
PRINT EJECT /'    NAME ' 1 'DEPT' 25 'HIRED' 30 '   SALARY' 35.
END IF.
PRINT / NAME DEPT *
        MOHIRED(T30,F2) '/' YRHIRED *
        SALARY (T35,DOLLAR8).
EXECUTE.
```

- DO IF—END IF controls the PRINT EJECT command, allowing it to be executed only once, when the system variable $CASENUM is equal to 1 (the value assigned to the first case in the file). If there are multiple pages of case listings, the column headings display on the first page only. See the next example for controlling page ejections that print the column headings at the top of every new page of the output.
- A PRINT command could have been used in place of the PRINT EJECT command to generate the column headings. With PRINT, the printed values in the display file would begin immediately after the command printback. PRINT EJECT causes a page ejection, and the column headings begin a new page in the display file.

Example
```
DO IF MOD($CASENUM,50) = 1.
PRINT EJECT OUTFILE=OUT /'    NAME ' 1 'DEPT' 25 'HIRED' 30 '
  SALARY' 35.
END IF.
PRINT OUTFILE=OUT / NAME DEPT *
        MOHIRED 30-31 '/' YRHIRED *
        SALARY 35-42(DOLLAR).
EXECUTE.
```

- DO IF specifies that the headings will be displayed if MOD (remainder; see COMPUTE) of $CASENUM divided by 50 equals 1.
- PRINT EJECT specifies strings for the column headings. PRINT EJECT causes a page ejection each time it executes, and it displays the headings at the top of the new page. PRINT could be used to specify the headings, but PRINT would not cause a page ejection, and the headings would simply display after every 50th line.
- Both PRINT EJECT and PRINT specify the same file for the displayed output. If the FILE subcommands on PRINT EJECT and PRINT do not specify the same file, the column headings and the displayed values will be in different files.

PRINT FORMATS

```
PRINT FORMATS varlist(format) [varlist...]
```

Example:
```
PRINT FORMATS SALARY (DOLLAR8) / HOURLY (DOLLAR7.2)
 / RAISE BONUS (PCT2).
```

Overview

PRINT FORMATS changes variable print formats. Print formats are output formats in SPSS and control the form in which values are displayed by a procedure or by the PRINT command.

PRINT FORMATS changes a variable's print format only. See the WRITE FORMATS command for changing the write format. See the FORMATS command for changing both the print and write formats with a single specification. See the DATA LIST command for assigning input formats during data definition.

A table of output formats that can be assigned with PRINT FORMATS, WRITE FORMATS, or FORMATS is shown with the reference documentation for the FORMATS command. See that table for a list of available print formats.

Basic Specification

- The basic specification is a variable list followed by the new format specification in parentheses. All the specified variables receive the new format.

Syntax Rules

- Only one format can be specified in the parentheses.
- Different formats can be assigned to different variables by using a slash to separate specifications for each different format.
- Format specifications on PRINT FORMATS are *output* formats. When specifying the width for the format type, enough positions must be allowed to include any punctuation characters such as decimal points, commas, dollar signs, or date and time delimiters. (This is different from assigning an *input* format on DATA LIST. SPSS automatically expands input formats to accommodate punctuation characters in the output.)
- A custom currency format (CCw, CCw.d) must first be defined on the SET command before it can be used on PRINT FORMATS.
- PRINT FORMATS cannot be used with string variables because the declared length of a string variable cannot be changed. To effectively change the length of a string variable, declare a new variable of the desired length with the STRING command, then use COMPUTE to copy values from the existing string into the new string.
- To save the new print formats, the active system file must be saved as a new system file with the SAVE or XSAVE commands. The new print formats are used as dictionary formats in the new system file.

Operations

- PRINT FORMATS takes effect as soon as it is encountered in the command sequence, unlike most transformations, which do not take effect until the data are read. Thus, special attention should be paid to its position among commands. For more information, see Universals: Command Order.
- Variables not specified on PRINT FORMATS retain their current print formats in the active system file. To see the current formats, use the DISPLAY command.
- The new print formats are changed in the active system file only and are in effect for the duration of the SPSS session or until changed again with a PRINT FORMATS or FORMATS command. If GET was used to create the active system file, formats in the original system file are not changed.
- When the transformation language is used to create a new numeric variable, the dictionary print and write formats are both F8.2 (or the format specified on the FORMAT subcommand of SET). The PRINT FORMATS command can be used to change the new variable's print format.
- Default formats for string variables created using the SPSS transformation language are those specified on the STRING command that declares the

variable. PRINT FORMATS cannot be used to change the print format of a new string variable.

- If a data value exceeds its width specification, SPSS makes an attempt to produce some value nevertheless. It takes out punctuation characters, then it tries scientific notation, and only then, if there is still not enough space, it produces asterisks indicating that a value is present which cannot be printed in the assigned width.

Example

```
PRINT FORMATS SALARY (DOLLAR8) / HOURLY (DOLLAR7.2)
    / RAISE BONUS (PCT2).
```

- The print format for SALARY is changed to DOLLAR format with eight positions including the dollar sign and comma when appropriate. The value 11550 prints as $11,550. An eight-digit number would require a DOLLAR11 format specification: eight characters for digits, two characters for commas, and one character for the dollar sign.

- The print format for HOURLY is changed to DOLLAR format with seven positions including the dollar sign, decimal point, and two decimal places. The number 115 prints as $115.00. If DOLLAR6.2 had been specified for HOURLY, the value 115 would print as $115.0. SPSS truncates the last 0 because the format width of six places is not wide enough to print the full value.

- The print format for both RAISE and BONUS is changed to PCT format with two positions: one position for the percentage and one position for the percent sign. The value 9 prints as 9%. The value 10 prints as 10 because the percent sign is truncated: the format allows for only two positions in the printed output.

Example

```
COMPUTE V3=V1 + V2.
PRINT FORMATS V3 (F3.1).
```

- COMPUTE creates the new numeric variable V3. By default, V3 is assigned an F8.2 format.

- PRINT FORMATS changes the print format for V3 to F3.1.

Example

```
SET CCA='-/-.Dfl ..-'.
PRINT FORMATS COST (CCA14.2).
```

- SET defines a European currency format for the custom currency format type CCA.

- PRINT FORMATS assigns the print format CCA to variable COST. With the format defined for CCA on SET, the value 37419 prints as Dfl'37.419,00. See the SET command for more information on custom currency formats.

PRINT SPACE

```
PRINT SPACE [OUTFILE=file] [numeric expression]
```

Example:

```
PRINT / NAME DEPT82 *
        MOHIRED(T30,F2) '/' YRHIRED *
        SALARY82 (T35,DOLLAR8).
PRINT SPACE.
EXECUTE.
```

Overview

PRINT SPACE displays blank lines in an output file. PRINT SPACE is useful with a PRINT or WRITE command for entering blank lines in displayed output. Because PRINT SPACE displays a blank space each time it is executed, it is often used in a DO IF—END IF structure.

Basic Specification

• PRINT SPACE with no specifications prints one blank line in the display file.

Syntax Rules

• To specify the number of blank lines to display, specify a numeric expression after PRINT SPACE. The expression can be an integer or a complex expression. By default, PRINT SPACE displays one blank line.

• OUTFILE specifies the output file. The default is the display file. OUTFILE must specify the same file specified on the PRINT or WRITE command that is used with PRINT SPACE.

Operations

• PRINT SPACE executes once for each case constructed from the data file.

• If PRINT SPACE is not used in a DO IF—END IF structure, it is executed for each case in the data and displays a blank line after every case.

Example

```
PRINT / NAME DEPT82 *
        MOHIRED(T30,F2) '/' YRHIRED *
        SALARY82 (T35,DOLLAR8).
PRINT SPACE.
EXECUTE.
```

• PRINT SPACE displays one blank line each time it is executed. Because PRINT SPACE is not used in a DO IF—END IF structure, it is executed once for each case. In effect, the displayed output is double-spaced.

Example

```
NUMERIC #LINE.
DO IF MOD(#LINE,5) = 0.
PRINT SPACE 2.
END IF.
COMPUTE #LINE=#LINE + 1.
PRINT / NAME DEPT *
        MOHIRED 30-31 '/' YRHIRED *
        SALARY 35-42(DOLLAR).
EXECUTE.
```

• DO IF specifies that PRINT SPACE will be displayed if MOD (remainder; see COMPUTE) of $CASENUM divided by 5 equals 1.

• PRINT SPACE specifies two blank lines each time it executes. Thus, cases display in groups of five with two blank spaces between each group.

Example

```
TITLE  'PRINTING ADDRESSES ON LABELS'.

DATA LIST FILE=ADDRESS/RECORD 1-40 (A).   /*READ A RECORD
COMPUTE #LINES=#LINES+1.             /*BUMP COUNTER AND PRINT
WRITE OUTFILE=LABELS /RECORD.

DO IF RECORD EQ ' '.                 /*BLANK BETWEEN ADDRESSES
+   PRINT SPACE OUTFILE=LABELS 8 - #LINES.  /*EXTRA BLANK #LINES
+   COMPUTE #LINES=0.
END IF.

EXECUTE.
```

- PRINT SPACE uses a complex expression for specifying the number of blank lines to display. Data contain a variable number of input records for each name and address that must be printed in a fixed number of lines for mailing labels. The goal is to know when the last line for each address has been printed, how many lines have printed, and therefore how many blank records must be printed in order for the next address to fit on the next label. The example assumes that there is already one blank line between each address on input and that you want to print eight lines per label.

- Variable #LINES is the key to this example. #LINES is intialized to 0 as a scratch variable. Then it is incremented for each record written. When SPSS encounters a blank line (RECORD EQ ' '), PRINT SPACE prints a number of blank lines equal to 8 minus the number already printed, and #LINES is then reset to 0.

- OUTFILE on PRINT SPACE specifies the same file specified by OUTFILE on WRITE.

PROBIT

This command is included in the SPSS Advanced Statistics option.

```
PROBIT response count varname OF observation count varname

        WITH varlist [BY varname(min,max)]

[/MISSING={LISTWISE**}] [/MODEL={PROBIT**}] [/LOG[={10**  }]]
          {INCLUDE }             {LOGIT }            {2.718*}
          {DEFAULT }             {BOTH  }            {base  }
                                                     {NONE  }


[/CRITERIA=[CONVERGE({0.001**})][ITERATE({20**})][P({0.15**})]]
                     {eps    }            {n  }    {p      }


[/NATRES[=c]]

[/PRINT=[ALL] [CI**] [FREQ**] [RMP**] [PARALL] [NONE] [DEFAULT]]
```

**Default if the subcommand is omitted.
*Default if the subcommand is included and the specification omitted.

Example:
```
PROBIT  R OF N BY ROOT(1,2) WITH X
  /MODEL = BOTH.
```

Overview

PROBIT can be used to estimate the effects of one or more independent variables on a dichotomous dependent variable (such as dead or alive, employed or unemployed, product purchased or not). The program is designed for dose-response analyses and related models, but PROBIT can also estimate logistic regression models.

Options

Specifying the Model. You can specify a PROBIT or LOGIT response model, or both, for the observed response proportions. See MODEL Subcommand.

Transform Predictors. You can specify the base of the log transformation applied to all predictors. You can also request no log transformation of the predictors. See LOG Subcommand.

Natural Response Rates. You can instruct PROBIT to estimate the natural response rate (threshold) of the model, or you can supply a known natural response rate to be used in the solution. See NATRES Subcommand.

Algorithm Control Parameters. You can specify values of algorithm control parameters such as the limit on iterations. See CRITERIA Subcommand.

Statistics. By default PROBIT calculates frequencies, fiducial confidence intervals, and the relative median potency. It also produces a plot of the observed probits or logits against the values of a single independent variable. Optionally, you can obtain a test of the parallelism of regression lines for different levels of the grouping variable. You can suppress any or all of these statistics. See PRINT Subcommand.

Basic Specification

- The basic specification is the response count variable, keyword OF, the observation count variable, keyword WITH, and at least one independent variable. PROBIT calculates maximum likelihood estimates for the parameters of the requested response model. The procedure automatically displays estimates of the regression coefficient and intercept terms, their standard errors, a covariance matrix of parameter estimates, and a Pearson chi-square goodness-of-fit test of the model.

Subcommand Order

- The variable specification must be first.
- Subcommands can be named in any order.

Syntax Rules
- The variables must include a response count, an observation count, and at least one predictor. A categorical grouping variable is optional.
- All subcommands are optional and each can appear only once.
- Generally, data should not be entered for individual observations. PROBIT expects predictor values, response counts, and total number of observations as the input case.
- If the data are available only in case-by-case form, first use AGGREGATE to compute the required response and observation counts.

Operations
- The transformed response variable is predicted as a linear function of other variables.
- PROBIT always adds 5 to the intercept to make the new values uniformly positive (or nearly so), as in Finney (1971).
- PROBIT always divides the logit by 2 (and adds 5 to the intercept) to produce values similar to those derived from the probit transformation.
- If individual cases are entered in the data, PROBIT skips the plot of transformed response proportions and predictor values.
- If individual cases are entered, the degrees of freedom for the chi-square goodness-of-fit statistic are based on the individual cases.

Limitations
- Only one prediction model can be tested in a single PROBIT procedure, although both probit and logit response models can be requested for that prediction.
- Confidence limits, the plot of transformed response proportions and predictor values, and computation of relative median potency are necessarily limited to single-predictor models.

Example
```
PROBIT  R OF N BY ROOT(1,2) WITH X
   /MODEL = BOTH.
```
- This example specifies that both the probit and logit response models be applied to the response frequency R, given N total observations and the predictor X.
- By default the predictor is log transformed.

Example
To produce collapsed input cases procedure AGGREGATE can be used. For the dose-response model analyzed above, the data recorded for each subject can be summarized by cases representing all subjects who received the same preparation at the same dose.

```
TITLE  'AGGREGATING CASE-BY-CASE DATA'.

DATA LIST FREE/PREPARTN DOSE RESPONSE.
BEGIN DATA
     1.00    1.50      .00
     ...
     4.00   20.00     1.00
END DATA.
AGGREGATE OUTFILE=*
  /BREAK=PREPARTN DOSE
  /SUBJECTS=N(RESPONSE)
  /NRESP=SUM(RESPONSE).
PROBIT NRESP OF SUBJECTS BY PREPARTN(1,4) WITH DOSE.
```
- AGGREGATE computes summary cases for observations having the same values for the group and predictor variables, PREPARTN and DOSE.
- The number of cases having a nonmissing response is recorded in the aggregated variable SUBJECTS.
- Because RESPONSE is coded as 0 for no response and 1 for a response, the SUM of the values gives the number of observations with a response.
- PROBIT requests a default analysis.
- The parameter estimates for this analysis are the same as those calculated for individual cases in the example above. The chi-square test, however, is based on the number of dosages.

Example `TITLE  'USING DATA IN CASE-BY-CASE FORM'.`

`DATA LIST FREE / PREPARTN DOSE RESPONSE.`
`BEGIN DATA`
`1 1.5 0`
`   ...`
`4 20.0 1`
`END DATA.`
`COMPUTE SUBJECT = 1.`
`PROBIT RESPONSE OF SUBJECT BY PREPARTN(1,4) WITH DOSE.`

- This dose-response model (from Finney, 1971) illustrates case-by-case analysis. A researcher tests four different preparations at varying doses and observes whether each subject responds. The data are individually recorded for each subject, with 1 indicating a response and 0 indicating no response. The number of observations is always 1 and is stored in variable SUBJECT.
- PROBIT warns that the data are in case-by-case form and that the plot is therefore skipped.
- Degrees of freedom for the goodness-of-fit test are based on individual cases, not dosage groups.
- PROBIT displays predicted and observed frequencies for all individual input cases unless the output is suppressed on PRINT.

Variable Specification

The PROBIT variable specification identifies the variables for response count, observation count, groups, and predictors. The variable specification is required.

- The variable specification must be first. The specification shows the response count variable, followed by keyword OF, then the observation count variable.
- If the value of the response count variable exceeds that of the observation count variable, a procedure error occurs and PROBIT is not executed.
- One or more continuous predictors must be specified following keyword WITH. The number of predictors is limited only by available workspace.
- To specify a categorical grouping variable, name the variable after keyword BY, and, in parentheses after the variable name, specify a range to indicate the minimum and maximum values. Each integer value in the specified range defines a group. Only one variable can be specified; it must be numeric and can contain only integer values.
- Cases with values for the grouping variable that are outside the specified range are excluded from the analysis.
- Keywords BY and WITH can appear in either order. However, both must follow the response and observation count variables.
- OF is not a reserved word and can be used as a variable name.

Example `PROBIT R OF N WITH X.`

- The number of observations having the measured response appears in variable R, and the total number of observations is in N. The predictor is X.

Example `PROBIT  R OF N BY ROOT(1,2) WITH X.`
`PROBIT  R OF N WITH X BY ROOT(1,2).`

- Because BY and WITH can be used in either order, these two commands are equivalent. Each command specifies X as a continuous variable and ROOT as a categorical grouping variable used to predict response rates.
- Groups are identified by the levels of variable ROOT, which may be 1 or 2.
- For each combination of predictor and grouping variables, the variable R contains the number of observations with the response of interest, and N contains the total number of observations.

MODEL Subcommand

MODEL specifies the form of the dichotomous response model.

The response models can be thought of as transformations (T) of response rates, which are proportions or probabilities (p). The transformations, whether logit or probit, add 5 to make the new values uniformly positive (or nearly so), as in Finney (1971). For the probit response model, the program uses

$$T(p) = PROBIT(p) + 5$$

A probit is the inverse of the cumulative standard normal distribution function. Thus, for any proportion, the probit transformation returns the value below which that proportion of standard normal deviates is found. Hence:

$T(0.025) = PROBIT(0.025) + 5 = -1.96 + 5 = 3.04$
$T(0.400) = PROBIT(0.400) + 5 = -0.25 + 5 = 4.75$
$T(0.500) = PROBIT(0.500) + 5 = 0.00 + 5 = 5.00$
$T(0.950) = PROBIT(0.950) + 5 = 1.64 + 5 = 6.64$

A logit is simply the natural log of the odds ratio, $p/(1 - p)$. In the PROBIT procedure, the response function is given as

$$T(p) = \log_e(p/(1-p))/2 + 5$$

The simple logit is scaled by 2 to produce values similar to those derived from the probit transformation. Hence:

$T(0.025) = LOGIT(0.025)/2 + 5 = -1.83 + 5 = 3.17$
$T(0.400) = LOGIT(0.400)/2 + 5 = -0.20 + 5 = 4.80$
$T(0.500) = LOGIT(0.500)/2 + 5 = 0.00 + 5 = 5.00$
$T(0.950) = LOGIT(0.950)/2 + 5 = 1.47 + 5 = 6.47$

- If subgroups and multiple predictor variables are defined, PROBIT estimates a separate intercept (a_i) for each subgroup and a regression coefficient (b_j) for each predictor.

PROBIT *Probit response model.* This is the default.

LOGIT *Logit response model.*

BOTH *Both probit and logit response models.* PROBIT displays all the output for the logit model followed by the output for the probit model.

LOG Subcommand

LOG specifies the base of the logarithmic transformation of the predictor variables or suppresses the default log transformation.

- LOG applies to all predictors.
- To transform only selected predictors, use COMPUTE commands before the PROBIT procedure. Then specify NONE on LOG.
- If LOG is omitted, a logarithm base of 10 is used.
- If LOG is used without a specification, a logarithm base of 2.718 is used.

10 *Logarithm base of 10.* This is the default if the LOG subcommand is omitted.

2.718 *The natural logarithmic base, e.* This is the default if LOG is specified without an explicit base.

base *Logarithm base other than defaults.* To specify any other base, indicate its numeric value following the equals sign on LOG.

NONE *No transformation of the predictors.*

Example
```
PROBIT R OF N BY ROOT (1,2) WITH X
  /LOG = 2.
```

- LOG specifies a base 2 logarithmic transformation.

CRITERIA Subcommand

Use CRITERIA to specify the values of PROBIT algorithm-control parameters. Specify any or all of the keywords below. Defaults remain in effect for parameters that are not changed.

CONVERGE(eps) *Criterion for convergence of predicted values.* Specify the cutoff value of the convergence criterion for the iterative estimation algorithm. The default value is 0.001.

ITERATE(n) *Iteration limit.* Specify the maximum number of iterations. The default is 20.

P(p) *Heterogeneity criterion probability.* Specify the cutoff value for the significance of the goodness-of-fit test. The default is 0.15. The cutoff value determines whether a heterogeneity factor is included in calculations of confidence levels for effective levels of a predictor. If the significance of chi-square is greater than the cutoff, the heterogeneity factor is not included.

NATRES Subcommand

Use NATRES in either of two ways: to instruct PROBIT to estimate the natural (or threshold) response rate of the model, or to supply a known natural response rate to be used in the solution.

- To instruct PROBIT to estimate the natural response rate of the model, a control level must be provided. Indicate the control level by giving a 0 value to any of the predictor variables.
- To supply a known natural response rate as a constraint on the model solution, specify a constant on NATRES. The value of the constant must be between 0 and 1 but cannot be equal to 0 or 1.

Example
```
DATA LIST FREE / SOLUTION DOSE NOBSN NRESP.
BEGIN DATA
1   5 100 20
1  10  80 30
1   0 100 10
    ...
END DATA.
PROBIT NRESP OF NOBSN BY SOLUTION(1,4) WITH DOSE
   /NATRES.
```

- This example reads four variables and requests a default analysis with an estimate of the natural response rate.
- The predictor variable, DOSE, has a value of 0 for the third case.
- The response count (10) and the observation count (100) for this case establish the initial estimate of the control level for the analysis.

Example
```
DATA LIST FREE / SOLUTION DOSE NOBSN NRESP.
BEGIN DATA
1   5 100 20
1  10  80 30
    ...
END DATA.
PROBIT NRESP OF NOBSN BY SOLUTION(1,4) WITH DOSE
   /NATRES = 0.10.
```

- This example reads four variables and requests an analysis in which the natural response rate is set to 0.10. No control level is included in the data.

PRINT Subcommand

Use PRINT to control the statistics calculated by PROBIT.

- By default, FREQ, CI, and RMP are calculated.
- If PRINT is used, the requested statistics are calculated in addition to the plot and parameter estimates.

DEFAULT   *FREQ, CI, and RMP.* This is the default.

ALL   *All available output.* This is the same as requesting FREQ, CI, RMP, and PARALL.

FREQ   *Frequencies.* Display a table of observed and predicted frequencies with their residual values. If observations are entered on a case-by-case basis, this listing can be quite lengthy.

CI   *Fiducial confidence intervals.* Print Finney's (1971) fiducial confidence intervals for the levels of the predictor needed to produce each proportion of responses. PROBIT displays this default output for single-predictor models only. If a categorical grouping variable is specified, PROBIT produces a table of confidence intervals for each group. If the Pearson chi-square goodness-of-fit test is significant ($p < 0.15$ by default), PROBIT uses a heterogeneity factor to calculate the limits.

RMP   *Relative median potency.* Display the relative median potency (RMP) of each pair of groups defined by the grouping variable. PROBIT displays this default output for single-predictor models only. For any pair of groups, the RMP is the ratio of the *stimulus tolerances* in those groups. Stimulus tolerance is the value of the predictor necessary to produce a 50% response rate. If the derived model for one predictor and two groups estimates that a predictor value of 21 produces a 50% response rate in the first group, and a predictor value of 15 produces a 50% response rate in the second group, the relative median potency would be $21/15 = 1.40$. In biological assay analyses, RMP measures the comparative strength of preparations.

PARALL *Parallelism test.* Produce a test of the parallelism of regression lines for different levels of the grouping variable. This test displays a chi-square value and its associated probability. It requires an additional pass through the data and thus additional processing time.

NONE *No conditional displayed output.* This option can be used to override any other specification on the PRINT subcommand for PROBIT. With NONE, only the unconditional output is displayed: the PROBIT case and model information, the PROBIT plot (for a single-predictor model), and the parameter estimates and covariances for the PROBIT model.

MISSING Subcommand

MISSING controls the missing-value treatment. Cases containing system-missing values for any variable in the analysis are always deleted. In the output, PROBIT indicates how many cases it rejected because of missing data. This information is displayed with the *DATA information* that prints at the beginning of the output.

LISTWISE *Delete cases with missing values listwise.* PROBIT deletes cases having a missing value for any variable. This is the default, and you can make it explicit by using the keyword DEFAULT.

INCLUDE *Include user-missing values.* PROBIT treats user-missing values as valid.

Annotated Example

For a complete example with output, see Examples following the Command Reference.

PROCEDURE OUTPUT

```
PROCEDURE OUTPUT OUTFILE=file
```

Example:
```
PROCEDURE OUTPUT OUTFILE=CELLDATA.
CROSSTABS VARIABLES=FEAR SEX (1,2)
    /TABLES=FEAR BY SEX
    /WRITE=ALL.
```

Overview PROCEDURE OUTPUT is used to specify output files for cell totals from the CROSSTABS procedure, and to display files from the FREQUENCIES procedure or life table records from the SURVIVAL procedure. PROCEDURE OUTPUT has no other applications.

Basic Specification • The only specification is OUTFILE and the output file. PROCEDURE OUTPUT must precede the command to which it applies.

Example
```
PROCEDURE OUTPUT OUTFILE=CELLDATA.
CROSSTABS VARIABLES=FEAR SEX (1,2)
    /TABLES=FEAR BY SEX
    /WRITE=ALL.
```

• PROCEDURE OUTPUT precedes CROSSTABS and specifes CELLDATA as the file to receive the cell totals.

• The WRITE subcommand on CROSSTABS is required for writing cell records to an output file.

Example
```
PROCEDURE OUTPUT OUTFILE=CODEBOOK.
FREQUENCIES VARIABLES=ALL
    /FORMAT=ONEPAGE WRITE.
```

• PROCEDURE OUTPUT precedes FREQUENCIES and specifes CODEBOOK as the file to receive the frequency displays.

• The WRITE keyword on the FORMAT subcommand of FREQUENCIES is required for writing the display to an output file.

Example
```
PROCEDURE OUTPUT OUTFILE=SURVTBL.
SURVIVAL  TABLES=ONSSURV,RECSURV BY TREATMNT(1,3)
    /STATUS = RECURSIT(1,9) FOR RECSURV
    /STATUS = STATUS(3,4) FOR ONSSURV
    /INTERVAL=THRU 50 BY 5 THRU 100 BY 10/PLOTS/COMPARE
    /CALCULATE=CONDITIONAL PAIRWISE
    /WRITE=TABLES.
```

• PROCEDURE OUTPUT precedes SURVIVAL and specifes SURVTBL as the file to receive the survival tables.

• The WRITE subcommand on SURVIVAL is required for writing survival tables to an output file.

PROXIMITIES

```
PROXIMITIES  varlist

[/STANDARDIZE=[{VARIABLE}] [{NONE** }] ]
                {CASE    }   {Z     }
                             {SD    }
                             {RANGE }
                             {MAX   }
                             {MEAN  }
                             {RESCALE}


[/VIEW={CASE**  } ]
       {VARIABLE}


[/MEASURE=[{NONE        }] [ABSOLUTE] [REVERSE] [RESCALE]]
           {EUCLID**    }
           {SEUCLID     }
           {COSINE      }
           {CORR        }
           {BLOCK       }
           {CHEBYCHEV   }
           {POWER(p,r)  }
           {MINKOWSKI(p)}
           {CHISQ       }
           {PH2         }
           {RR[(p[,np])]}
           {SM[(p[,np])]}
           {JACCARD[(p[,np])]}
           {DICE[(p[,np])]}
           {SS1[(p[,np])]}
           {RT[(p[,np])]}
           {SS2[(p[,np])]}
           {K1[(p[,np])]}
           {SS3[(p[,np])]}
           {K2[(p[,np])]}
           {SS4[(p[,np])]}
           {HAMANN[(p[,np])]}
           {OCHIAI[(p[,np])]}
           {SS5[(p[,np])]}
           {PHI[(p[,np])]}
           {LAMBDA[(p[,np])]}
           {D[(p[,np])]}
           {Y[(p[,np])]}
           {Q[(p[,np])]}
           {BEUCLID[(p[,np])]}
           {SIZE[(p[,np])]}
           {PATTERN[(p[,np])]}
           {BSEUCLID[(p[,np])]}
           {BSHAPE[(p[,np])]}
           {DISPER[(p[,np])]}
           {VARIANCE[(p[,np])]}
           {BLWMN[(p[,np])]}


[/PRINT [={PROXIMITIES**}] ]
          {NONE         }


[/ID=varname ]


[/MISSING={LISTWISE**} ]
          {INCLUDE   }


[/MATRIX=[IN({file})] [OUT({file})]]
             {*   }        {*   }
```

**Default if the subcommand is omitted.

Example:

```
PROXIMITIES A B C.
```

Overview

PROXIMITIES computes measures of similarity, dissimilarity, or distance, providing a variety of different measures. It computes the measures between pairs of cases or pairs of variables for moderate-sized data sets (see Limitations, below). Output from PROXIMITIES can be used as input matrices for procedure ALSCAL, CLUSTER, or FACTOR. To learn more about proximity matrices and their uses, consult Anderberg (1973) and Romesburg (1984).

Options

Standardizing Data. You can standardize the values for each variable or each case by any of several different methods. See STANDARDIZE Subcommand.

Proximity Measures. PROXIMITIES can compute many similarity, dissimilarity, and distance measures. (Similarity measures increase with greater similarity; dissimilarity and distance measures decrease.) PROXIMITIES can compute measures for continuous data, frequency count data, and binary data. Only one measure can be requested in any one PROXIMITIES procedure. See MEASURE Subcommand.

Printed Output. You can have PROXIMITIES print a computed matrix (see PRINT Subcommand). By default, PROXIMITIES identifies cases by sequence number. Optionally you can specify a string variable that contains an identifier for each case. See ID Subcommand.

File Output and Input. You can write a computed distance matrix to an SPSS system file. In this way, you can pass a matrix computed by PROXIMITIES to procedure CLUSTER, ALSCAL, or FACTOR. In addition, you can read a similarity, dissimilarity, or distance matrix from the matrix input file. This option lets you rescale or transform existing proximity matrices. See MATRIX Subcommand.

Basic Specification

- The basic specification is a variable list, which obtains the default measure of the Euclidean distances between cases based on the values of each specified variable.

Subcommand Order

- The variable list must be first.
- Subcommands can be named in any order.

Limitations

- Storage requirements increase rapidly with the number of cases and the number of items (cases or variables) for which PROXIMITIES computes coefficients. PROXIMITIES keeps the raw data for the current split-file group in memory. You may not be able to compute a proximity matrix for more than 150 cases and a small number of variables in an 80K-byte workspace.
- PROXIMITIES ignores case weights when computing coefficients.

Example

PROXIMITIES A B C.

- PROXIMITIES computes Euclidean distances between cases based on the values of variables A, B, and C.

Variable Specification

The variable list must be first and can be used in three distinct ways:

- It can identify the variables for computing proximities between cases.
- It can identify the variables for computing proximities between variables.
- If the data are matrix materials, the variable list can be omitted. This is true only for matrix input.

STANDARDIZE Subcommand

Use STANDARDIZE to standardize data values for either cases or variables before computing proximities. One of two options can be specified to control the direction of standardization:

VARIABLE *Standardize the values for each variable.* This is the default.

CASE *Standardize the values within each case.*

Several standardization methods are available. These allow you to equalize selected properties of the values. Only one standardization method can be specified; all methods can be used with either VARIABLE or CASE.

- If STANDARDIZE is omitted, proximities are computed using the original values (keyword NONE is the default).
- If STANDARDIZE is used without specifications, proximities are computed using Z scores (keyword Z is the default).

NONE   *Do not standardize.* Compute proximities using the original values. This is the default if STANDARDIZE is omitted.

Z   *Standardize values to Z scores, having 0 mean and unit standard deviation.* PROXIMITIES subtracts the mean from each value for the variable or case being standardized and then divides by the standard deviation of the values. If a standard deviation is 0, PROXIMITIES sets all values for the case or variable to 0. This is the default if STANDARDIZE is used without specifications.

RANGE   *Standardize values to unit range.* PROXIMITIES divides each value for the variable or case being standardized by the range of the values. If the range is 0, PROXIMITIES leaves all values unchanged.

RESCALE   *Standardize values to a range of 0 to 1.* From each value for the variable or case being standardized, PROXIMITIES subtracts the minimum value and then divides by the range. If a range is 0, PROXIMITIES sets all values for the case or variable to 0.50.

MAX   *Standardize values to a maximum magnitude of 1.* PROXIMITIES divides each value for the variable or case being standardized by the maximum of the values. If the maximum of a set of values is 0, PROXIMITIES uses an alternate process to produce a comparable standardization: it divides by the absolute magnitude of the smallest value and adds 1.

MEAN   *Standardize values to unit mean.* PROXIMITIES divides each value for the variable or case being standardized by the mean of the values. If a mean is 0, PROXIMITIES adds 1 to all values for the case or variable to produce a mean of 1.

SD   *Standardize values to unit standard deviation.* PROXIMITIES divides each value for the variable or case being standardized by the standard deviation of the values. PROXIMITIES does not change the values if their standard deviation is 0.

Example

```
PROXIMITIES A B C
  /STANDARDIZE=CASE RANGE.
```

- Values are standardized within each case, and the values are standardized to unit ranges.

VIEW Subcommand

Use VIEW to indicate whether to compute proximities between cases or between variables.

CASE   *Compute proximity values between cases.* This is the default.

VARIABLE   *Compute proximity values between variables.*

MEASURE Subcommand

MEASURE specifies the similarity, dissimilarity, or distance measure that PROXIMITIES computes. Three transformations are available with any of these measures:

ABSOLUTE   *Take the absolute values of the proximities.* Use ABSOLUTE where the sign of the values indicates the direction of the relations (as with correlation coefficients), but only the magnitude of the relations is of interest.

REVERSE   *Transform similarity values into dissimilarities, or vice versa.* Use this specification to reverse the ordering of the proximities by negating the values.

RESCALE   *Rescale the proximity values to a range of 0 to 1.* RESCALE standardizes the proximities by first subtracting the value of the smallest and then dividing by the range. You would not usually use RESCALE with measures that are already standardized on meaningful scales, as are correlations, cosines, and many binary coefficients.

- If more than one transformation is specified, PROXIMITIES does them in the order listed above: first ABSOLUTE, then REVERSE, then RESCALE.

PROXIMITIES can compute any one of a number of measures between items. You can choose among measures for continuous data, frequency count data, or binary data (available keywords for each of these types of measures are defined in the sections below). In addition, keyword NONE specifies that no measure is to be computed.

NONE *Do not compute proximity measures.* Use NONE only if you input an existing proximity matrix using the IN keyword on the MATRIX subcommand. Doing this lets you apply the ABSOLUTE, REVERSE, and/or RESCALE transformations to an existing matrix of proximity values.

- Only one measure can be specified. However, each measure can be specified with any of the transformations ABSOLUTE, REVERSE, or RESCALE.
- Each entry in the proximity matrix that PROXIMITIES computes represents a pair of items. The items can be either cases or variables, whichever is specified on the VIEW subcommand.
- When the items are cases, the computation for each pair of cases involves pairs of values for specified variables.
- When the items are variables, the computation for each pair of variables involves pairs of values for the variables across all the cases.

Example
```
PROXIMITIES A B C
   /MEASURE=EUCLID REVERSE.
```

- MEASURE specifies a EUCLID measure and a REVERSE transformation.

Measures for Continuous Data

To obtain proximities for continuous data, use any one of the following on MEASURE:

EUCLID *Euclidean distance.* This is the default specification for MEASURE. The distance between two items, x and y, is the square root of the sum of the squared differences between the values for the items.

$$EUCLID(x,y) = \sqrt{\Sigma_i(x_i - y_i)^2}$$

SEUCLID *Squared Euclidean distance.* The distance between two items is the sum of the squared differences between the values for the items.

$$SEUCLID(x,y) = \Sigma_i(x_i - y_i)^2$$

CORRELATION *Correlation between vectors of values.* This is a pattern similarity measure.

$$CORRELATION(x,y) = \frac{\Sigma_i(Z_{xi}Z_{yi})}{N-1}$$

where Z_{xi} is the (standardized) Z-score value of x for the *i*th case or variable, and N is the number of cases or variables.

COSINE *Cosine of vectors of values.* This is a pattern similarity measure.

$$COSINE(x,y) = \frac{\Sigma_i(x_iy_i)}{\sqrt{(\Sigma_i x_i^2)(\Sigma_i y_i^2)}}$$

CHEBYCHEV *Chebychev distance metric.* The distance between two items is the maximum absolute difference between the values for the items.

$$CHEBYCHEV(x,y) = max_i|x_i - y_i|$$

BLOCK *City-block, or Manhattan, distance.* The distance between two items is the sum of the absolute differences between the values for the items.

$$BLOCK(x,y) = \Sigma_i |x_i - y_i|$$

MINKOWSKI(p) *Distance in an absolute Minkowski power metric.* The distance between two items is the *p*th root of the sum of the absolute differences to the *p*th power between the values for the items. Appropriate selection of the integer parameter *p* yields Euclidean and many other distance metrics.

$$MINKOWSKI(x,y) = (\Sigma_i |x_i - y_i|^p)^{1/p}$$

POWER(p,r) *Distances in an absolute power metric.* The distance between two items is the *r*th root of the sum of the absolute differences to the *p*th power between the values for the items. Appropriate selection of integer parameters *p* and *r* yields Euclidean, squared Euclidean, Minkowski, city-block, and many other distance metrics.

$$POWER(x,y) = (\Sigma_i |x_i - y_i|^p)^{1/r}$$

Measures for Frequency Count Data

To obtain proximities for frequency count data, use either of the following on MEASURE:

CHISQ *Chi-square test of equality for two sets of frequencies.* The magnitude of this similarity measure depends on the total frequencies of the two cases or variables whose proximity is computed. Expected values are from the model of independence of cases (or variables), x and y.

$$CHISQ(x,y) = \sqrt{\frac{\Sigma_i(x_i - E(x_i))^2}{E(x_i)} + \frac{\Sigma_i(y_i - E(y_i))^2}{E(y_i)}}$$

PH2 *Phi-squared between sets of frequencies.* This is the CHISQ measure normalized by the square root of the combined frequency. Therefore, its value does not depend on the total frequencies of the two cases or variables whose proximity is computed.

$$PH2(x,y) = \sqrt{\frac{\frac{\Sigma_i(x_i - E(x_i))^2}{E(x_i)} + \frac{\Sigma_i(y_i - E(y_i))^2}{E(y_i)}}{N}}$$

Measures for Binary Data

Different binary measures emphasize different aspects of the relation between sets of binary values. However, all the measures are specified in the same way. Each measure has two optional integer-valued parameters, *p* (present) and *np* (not present).

• If both parameters are specified, PROXIMITIES uses the value of the first as an indicator that a characteristic is present and the value of the second as an indicator that a characteristic is absent. PROXIMITIES skips all other values.

• If only the first parameter is specified, PROXIMITIES uses that value to indicate presence and all other values to indicate absence.

• If no parameters are specified, PROXIMITIES assumes that 1 indicates presence and 0 indicates absence.

Using the indicators for presence and absence within each item (case or variable), PROXIMITIES constructs a 2×2 contingency table for each pair of items in turn. It uses this table to compute a proximity measure for the pair.

	Item 2 characteristics	
	Present	Absent
Item 1 characteristics		
Present	a	b
Absent	c	d

PROXIMITIES computes all binary measures from the values of a, b, c, and d. These values are tallies across variables (when the items are cases) or tallies across cases (when the items are variables). For example, if variables V, W, X, Y, Z have values 0, 1, 1, 0, 1 for case 1 and values 0, 1, 1, 0, 0 for case 2 (where 1 indicates presence and 0 indicates absence), the contingency table is

	Case 2 characteristics	
	Present	Absent
Case 1 characteristics		
Present	2	1
Absent	0	2

The available binary measures include matching coefficients, conditional probabilities, predictability measures, and others.

Matching Coefficients. Table 1 shows a classification scheme for the PROXIMITIES matching coefficients. In this scheme, *matches* are joint presences (value a in the contingency table) or joint absences (value d). *Nonmatches* are equal in number to value b plus value c. Matches and nonmatches may be weighted equally or not. The three coefficients JACCARD, DICE, and SS2 are related monotonically; SM, SS1, and RT also are related monotonically. All the coefficients in Table 1 are similarity measures, and all except two (K1 and SS3) range from 0 to 1. (K1 and SS3 have a minimum value of 0 and no upper limit.)

Table 1   Binary matching coefficients in PROXIMITIES

	Joint absences excluded from numerator	Joint absences included in numerator
All matches included in denominator		
Equal weight for matches and nonmatches	RR	SM
Double weight for matches		SS1
Double weight for nonmatches		RT
Joint absences excluded from denominator		
Equal weight for matches and nonmatches	JACCARD	
Double weight for matches	DICE	
Double weight for nonmatches	SS2	
All matches excluded from denominator		
Equal weight for matches and nonmatches	K1	SS3

RR[(p[,np])]   *Russell and Rao similarity measure.* This is the binary dot product.

$$RR(x,y) = \frac{a}{a + b + c + d}$$

SM[(p[,np])]   *Simple matching similarity measure.* This is the ratio of the number of matches to the total number of characteristics.

$$SM(x,y) = \frac{a + d}{a + b + c + d}$$

JACCARD[(p[,np])]   *Jaccard similarity measure.* This is also known as the *similarity ratio.*

$$JACCARD(x,y) = \frac{a}{a + b + c}$$

DICE[(p[,np])]   *Dice (or Czekanowski, or Sorenson) similarity measure.*

$$DICE(x,y) = \frac{2a}{2a + b + c}$$

SS1[(p[,np])]   *Sokal and Sneath similarity measure 1.*

$$SS1(x,y) = \frac{2(a + d)}{2(a + d) + b + c}$$

RT[(p[,np])]   *Rogers and Tanimoto similarity measure.*

$$RT(x,y) = \frac{a + d}{a + d + 2(b + c)}$$

SS2[(p[,np])]   *Sokal and Sneath similarity measure 2.*

$$SS2(x,y) = \frac{a}{a + 2(b + c)}$$

K1[(p[,np])]   *Kulczynski similarity measure 1.* This measure has a minimum value of 0 and no upper limit. It is undefined when there are no nonmatches (b=0 and c=0). Therefore, PROXIMITIES assigns an artificial upper limit of 10,000 to K1 when it is undefined or exceeds this value.

$$K1(x,y) = \frac{a}{b + c}$$

SS3[(p[,np])]   *Sokal and Sneath similarity measure 3.* This measure also has a minimum value of 0, has no upper limit, and is undefined when there are no nonmatches (b=0 and c=0). As with K1, PROXIMITIES assigns an artificial upper limit of 10,000 to SS3 when it is undefined or exceeds this value.

$$SS3(x,y) = \frac{a + d}{b + c}$$

Conditional Probabilities.
The following binary measures yield values that can be interpreted in terms of conditional probability. All three are similarity measures.

K2[(p[,np])]   *Kulczynski similarity measure 2.* This yields the average conditional probability that a characteristic is present in one item given that the characteristic is present in the other item. The measure is an average over both items acting as predictors. It has a range of 0 to 1.

$$K2(x,y) = \frac{a/(a + b) + a/(a + c)}{2}$$

SS4[(p[,np])]   *Sokal and Sneath similarity measure 4.* This yields the conditional probability that a characteristic of one item is in the same state (presence or absence) as the characteristic of the other item. The measure is an average over both items acting as predictors. It has a range of 0 to 1.

$$SS4(x,y) = \frac{a/(a + b) + a/(a + c) + d/(b + d) + d/(c + d)}{4}$$

HAMANN[(p[,np])]   *Hamann similarity measure.* This measure gives the probability that a characteristic has the same state in both items (present in both or absent from both) minus the probability that a characteristic has different states in the two items (present in one and absent from the other). HAMANN has a range of -1 to $+1$ and is monotonically related to SM, SS1, and RT.

$$HAMANN(x,y) = \frac{(a + d) - (b + c)}{a + b + c + d}$$

Predictability Measures. The following four binary measures assess the association between items as the predictability of one given the other. All four measures yield similarities.

LAMBDA[(p[,np])]   *Goodman and Kruskal lambda (similarity).* This coefficient assesses the predictability of the state of a characteristic on one item (presence or absence) given the state on the other item. Specifically, lambda measures the proportional reduction in error using one item to predict the other when the directions of prediction are of equal importance. Lambda has a range of 0 to 1.
$t_1 = max(a,b) + max(c,d) + max(a,c) + max(b,d)$
$t_2 = max(a + c, b + d) + max(a + d, c + d)$

$$LAMBDA(x,y) = \frac{t_1 - t_2}{2(a + b + c + d) - t_2}$$

D[(p[,np])]   *Anderberg's D (similarity).* This coefficient assesses the predictability of the state of a characteristic on one item (presence or absence) given the state on the other. D measures the actual reduction in the error probability when one item is used to predict the other. The range of D is 0 to 1.
$t_1 = max(a,b) + max(c,d) + max(a,c) + max(b,d)$
$t_2 = max(a + c, b + d) + max(a + d, c + d)$

$$D(x,y) = \frac{t_1 - t_2}{2(a + b + c + d)}$$

Y[(p[,np])]   *Yule's Y coefficient of colligation (similarity).* This is a function of the cross ratio for a 2×2 table. It has a range of -1 to $+1$.

$$Y(x,y) = \frac{\sqrt{ad} - \sqrt{bc}}{\sqrt{ad} + \sqrt{bc}}$$

Q[(p[,np])]   *Yule's Q (similarity).* This is the 2×2 version of Goodman and Kruskal's ordinal measure *gamma*. Like Yule's Y, Q is a function of the cross ratio for a 2×2 table and has a range of -1 to $+1$.

$$Q(x,y) = \frac{ad - bc}{ad + bc}$$

Other Binary Measures. The remaining binary measures available in PROXIMITIES are either binary equivalents of association measures for continuous variables or measures of special properties of the relation between items.

OCHIAI[(p[,np])]   *Ochiai similarity measure.* This is the binary form of the cosine. It has a range of 0 to 1 and is a similarity measure.

$$\text{OCHIAI}(x,y) = \sqrt{\frac{a}{a+b} \cdot \frac{a}{a+c}}$$

SS5[(p[,np])]   *Sokal and Sneath similarity measure 5.* This is a similarity measure. Its range is 0 to 1.

$$\text{SS5}(x,y) = \frac{ad}{\sqrt{(a+b)(a+c)(b+d)(c+d)}}$$

PHI[(p[,np])]   *Fourfold point correlation (similarity).* This is the binary form of the Pearson product-moment correlation coefficient. Phi is a similarity measure, and its range is 0 to 1.

$$\text{PHI}(x,y) = \frac{ad-bc}{\sqrt{(a+b)(a+c)(b+d)(c+d)}}$$

BEUCLID[(p[,np])]   *Binary Euclidean distance.* This is a distance measure. Its minimum value is 0, and it has no upper limit.

$$\text{BEUCLID}(x,y) = \sqrt{b+c}$$

BSEUCLID[(p[,np])]   *Binary squared Euclidean distance.* This is also a distance measure. Its minimum value is 0, and it has no upper limit.

$$\text{BSEUCLID}(x,y) = b + c$$

SIZE[(p[,np])]   *Size difference.* This is a dissimilarity measure with a minimum value of 0 and no upper limit.

$$\text{SIZE}(x,y) = \frac{(b-c)^2}{(a+b+c+d)^2}$$

PATTERN[(p[,np])]   *Pattern difference.* This is also a dissimilarity measure. Its range is 0 to 1.

$$\text{PATTERN}(x,y) = \frac{bc}{(a+b+c+d)^2}$$

BSHAPE[(p[,np])]   *Binary shape difference.* This dissimilarity measure has no upper or lower limit.

$$\text{BSHAPE}(x,y) = \frac{(a+b+c+d)(b+c)-(b-c)^2}{(a+b+c+d)^2}$$

DISPER[(p[,np])]   *Dispersion similarity measure.* This similarity measure has a range of -1 to $+1$.

$$\text{DISPER}(x,y) = \frac{ad-bc}{(a+b+c+d)^2}$$

VARIANCE[(p[,np])]   *Variance dissimilarity measure.* This dissimilarity measure has a minimum value of 0 and no upper limit.

$$\text{VARIANCE}(x,y) = \frac{b+c}{4(a+b+c+d)}$$

BLWMN[(p[,np])]   *Binary Lance-and-Williams nonmetric dissimilarity measure.* Also known as the Bray-Curtis nonmetric coefficient, this dissimilarity measure has a range of 0 to 1.

$$BLWMN(x,y) = \frac{b + c}{2a + b + c}$$

Example   PROXIMITIES A B C
    /MEASURE=RR(1,2).

- MEASURE tells PROXIMITIES to compute Russell and Rao coefficients from data in which 1 indicates the presence of a characteristic and 2 indicates the absence of a characteristic. Other values are ignored.

Example   PROXIMITIES A B C
    /MEASURE=SM(2).

- MEASURE tells PROXIMITIES to compute simple matching coefficients from data in which 2 indicates presence and all other values indicate absence.

PRINT Subcommand

PROXIMITIES always prints the name of the measure it computes and the number of cases. Use PRINT to control printing of the proximity matrix.

- By default, the proximity matrix is printed. The default keyword is PROXIMITIES.
- NONE suppresses the printing of the proximity matrix.
- If PRINT is specified without a keyword, the default PROXIMITIES is used.

PROXIMITIES   *Print the matrix of the proximities between items.* This is the default. The matrix may have been either read or computed. When the number of cases or variables is large, this specification produces a large volume of output and uses significant CPU time.

NONE   *Do not print the matrix of proximities.*

ID Subcommand

By default, PROXIMITIES identifies cases by case number alone. Use ID to specify an identifying string variable for cases. Any string variable in the active system file can be named as the identifier. PROXIMITIES uses the values of this variable to identify cases in procedure output.

MISSING Subcommand

By default, PROXIMITIES deletes missing values listwise and excludes user-missing values from the analysis. Use MISSING to change or to make explicit the treatment of cases with missing values.

LISTWISE   *Delete cases with missing values listwise.* This is the default.

INCLUDE   *Include user-missing values as valid.* This option deletes listwise only those cases with system-missing values.

MATRIX Subcommand

MATRIX reads and writes SPSS matrix system files. It writes proximity type matrices that can be used by PROXIMITIES or other procedures (see the table of matrix types in Universals: Matrix System Files). Procedures CLUSTER and ALSCAL can read a proximity matrix directly. Procedure FACTOR can read a correlation matrix written by PROXIMITIES, but RECODE must first be used to change the ROWTYPE_ value PROX to a ROWTYPE_ value CORR. Also, if using a proximity matrix in FACTOR, the ID subcommand on PROXIMITIES cannot be used.

- Either IN or OUT is required to specify the matrix file in parentheses. When both IN and OUT are used on the same PROXIMITIES command, they can be specified on separate MATRIX subcommands, or both on the same subcommand.

Matrix Output
- If VIEW=VARIABLE, the variables in the new file will have the names and labels of the original variables. If VIEW=CASE (the default), the names of the variables in the new file will be CASE1, CASE2...CASEn, where *n* is the number of cases in the file or in the largest split-file group. The new file will preserve the names and values of any split-file variables in effect.

- Documents from the original file will not be included in the matrix file and will not be present if the matrix file becomes the active system file.

- With a large number of variables, the display file for the matrix system file wraps and the matrix format is difficult to read. Nonetheless, the matrix values are accurate and can be used as matrix input values.

Matrix Input
- MATRIX=IN cannot be used in place of GET or DATA LIST to begin a new SPSS command file. MATRIX is a subcommand on PROXIMITIES, and PROXIMITIES cannot run before an active system file is defined.

- To begin a new session and immediately read a matrix, first GET the matrix file, then specify IN(*) on MATRIX.

- PROXIMITIES can read a matrix written to the active system file by a previous PROXIMITIES procedure.

- SPSS reads variable names, variable and value labels, and print and write formats from the dictionary of the matrix system file.

- When reading matrix input, the variable list on PROXIMITIES may be omitted.

- When the variable list is omitted, all variables in the matrix system file are used in the analysis.

- When a variable list is specified, the specified variables may be a subset of the variables resident in the matrix file.

- The order among rows and variables in the input matrix file is unimportant, so long as values for split file variables precede values for ROWTYPE_.

- PROXIMITIES ignores unrecognized ROWTYPE_ values. In addition, it ignores variables present in the matrix file that are not specified (or used by default) on the PROXIMITIES variable list.

OUT *Write a matrix system file.* Specify either a file or an asterisk, and enclose the specification in parentheses. If you specify a file, the file is stored on disk and can be retrieved at any time. If you specify an asterisk (*), the matrix system file replaces the active system file but is not stored on disk unless you use SAVE or XSAVE.

IN *Read a matrix system file.* If the matrix system file *is not* the current active system file, specify a file in parentheses. If the matrix system file *is* the current active system file, specify an asterisk (*) in parentheses.

Format of the Matrix System File
- The matrix system file includes two special variables created by SPSS: ROWTYPE_ and VARNAME_. Variable ROWTYPE_ is a short string variable having values PROX, for proximity measure. PROX is assigned value labels containing the distance measure used to create the matrix; it is also assigned a SIMILARITY or DISSIMILARITY keyword. Variable VARNAME_ is a short string variable whose values are the case numbers of the ID variable.

- If reading in a matrix created with MATRIX DATA, you should supply a value label for PROX of either SIMILARITY or DISSIMILARITY so the matrix is correctly identified. If you do not supply a label, CLUSTER assumes DISSIMILARITY.

- The matrix file includes the identifying string variable named on the ID subcommand (when used). This variable is used to identify cases. Up to 20 characters can be displayed for the identifying variable; ID variables longer than 20 characters are truncated. The identifying variable is present only when VIEW=CASE (the default) and the ID subcommand is used.

- The remaining variables in the matrix file are the variables used to form the matrix.

Split Files and Variable Order
- When split-file processing is in effect, the first variables in the matrix system file will be the split variables, followed by ROWTYPE_, the case identifier variable (if VIEW=CASE and the ID subcommand is used), VARNAME_, and the variable(s) which make up the matrix.

- A full set of matrix materials is written for each split-file group defined by the split variable(s).

- A split variable cannot have the same variable name as any other variable written to the matrix system file.

- If split-file processing is in effect when a matrix is written, the same split file must be in effect when that matrix is read by any procedure.

Additional Statistics

- PROXIMITIES writes a variety of proximity type matrices. Each has ROWTYPE_ values of PROX. PROXIMITIES neither reads nor writes additional statistics with its matrix materials.

Example

```
PROXIMITIES  V1 TO V20
   /MATRIX=OUT(DISTOUT).
```

- PROXIMITIES produces a default Euclidean distance matrix for cases by using variables V1 through V20 and saves the matrix in the SPSS file DISTOUT.

- The names of the variables on this file will be CASE1, CASE2...CASEn.

Example

```
GET FILE=CRIME.
PROXIMITIES MURDER TO MOTOR
   /ID=CITY
   /MEASURE=EUCLID
   /MATRIX=OUT(PROXMTX).
```

- PROXIMITIES reads raw data from file CRIME and writes one set of matrix materials to file PROXMTX.

- The active system file is still the file CRIME. Subsequent commands are executed on file CRIME.

Example

```
GET FILE=CRIME.
PROXIMITIES MURDER TO MOTOR
   /ID=CITY
   /MEASURE=EUCLID
   /MATRIX=OUT(*).
LIST.
DISPLAY DICTIONARY.
```

- PROXIMITIES writes the same matrix as in the example above. However, the matrix system file replaces the active system file. The LIST and DISPLAY commands are executed on the matrix file, not on the file CRIME.

Example

```
GET FILE PRSNNL.
FREQUENCIES VARIABLE=AGE.

PROXIMITIES CASE1 TO CASE8
   /ID=CITY
   /MATRIX=IN(PROXMTX).
```

- This example assumes that you want to perform a frequencies analysis on file PRSNNL, then use PROXIMITIES to read a different file. The file you want to read is an existing matrix system file.

- MATRIX=IN specifies a file because the current active system file is PRSNNL. MATRIX=IN must therefore specify the file from which the matrix materials will be read.

- PROXMTX does not replace PRSNNL as the active system file.

Example

```
GET FILE PROXMTX.
PROXIMITIES CASE1 TO CASE8
   /ID=CITY
   /MATRIX=IN(*).
```

- This example assumes that you are starting a new session and want to read an existing matrix system file. GET retrieves the matrix system file PROXMTX.

- MATRIX=IN specifies an asterisk because the current active system file is the matrix system file PROXMTX. MATRIX=IN must therefore specify the active system file as the file from which the matrix materials will be read.

- If the GET command is omitted, SPSS issues an error message.

- If MATRIX=IN(PROXMTX) is specified, SPSS issues an error message.

Example

```
GET FILE=CRIME.
PROXIMITIES MURDER TO MOTOR
   /ID=CITY
   /MATRIX=OUT(*).
PROXIMITIES
   /MATRIX=IN(*)
   /STANDARDIZE.
```

- GET defines the data to SPSS.

- The first PROXIMITIES command specifies variables for the analysis and reads the raw data from file CRIME. ID specifies CITY as the case-identifying variable. MATRIX determines that the resulting matrix is written to the active system file.

- The variable list is omitted on the second PROXIMITIES command. This is permitted because the presence of the MATRIX subcommand indicates data are matrix materials. The specification on MATRIX indicates that data are resident in the active system file.

- The slash preceding the MATRIX subcommand on the second PROXIMITIES is required because there is an implied variable list present. Without the slash, PROXIMITIES would attempt to interpret MATRIX as a variable name rather than a subcommand name.

Example   In this example, PROXIMITIES and FACTOR are used for a *Q*-factor analysis, in which factors account for variance shared among observations rather than among variables. Procedure FACTOR does not perform *Q*-factor analysis without some preliminary transformation such as that provided by PROXIMITIES. Because the number of cases exceeds the number of variables, the model is not of full rank and FACTOR will print a warning. This is a common occurrence when inputting case-by-case matrices from PROXIMITIES to FACTOR.

```
TITLE 'Recoding a PROXIMITIES matrix for procedure FACTOR'.

GET FILE=CRIME.
PROXIMITIES    MURDER TO MOTOR
  /MEASURE=CORR
  /MATRIX=OUT(*).

RECODE ROWTYPE_ ('PROX' = 'CORR').

FACTOR MATRIX IN(COR=*).
```

- GET defines the data to SPSS.

- PROXIMITIES specifies variables for the analysis. Because the matrix materials will be used in procedure FACTOR, the ID subcommand is not specified.

- The MEASURE subcommand selects correlation as the similarity measure for computing proximities.

- The MATRIX subcommand on PROXIMITIES writes the correlation matrix materials to the active system file.

- RECODE recodes ROWTYPE_ values from PROX to CORR so procedure FACTOR can read the matrix.

- When FACTOR reads matrix materials, it reads all the variables in the file. The MATRIX subcommand on FACTOR indicates that the matrix is a correlation matrix, and data are in the active system file.

Annotated Example   For a complete example with output, see Examples following the Command Reference.

QUICK CLUSTER

```
QUICK CLUSTER {varlist}
             {ALL     }

[/MISSING=[{LISTWISE**}] [INCLUDE]]
           {PAIRWISE  }
           {DEFAULT   }

[/FILE=file]

[/INITIAL=(value list)]

[/CRITERIA=[CLUSTER({2**})] [NOINITIAL] [NOUPDATE]]
                    {k  }

[/PRINT=[INITIAL**] [CLUSTER] [ID(varname)] [DISTANCE] [ANOVA]

        [NONE]]

[/OUTFILE=file]

[/SAVE=[CLUSTER(varname)] [DISTANCE(varname)]]
```

** Default if the subcommand is omitted.

Example:
```
QUICK CLUSTER V1 TO V4
  /CRITERIA=CLUSTERS(4)
  /SAVE=CLUSTER(GROUP).
```

Overview

When the desired number of clusters is known, QUICK CLUSTER groups cases efficiently into clusters. It is not as flexible as CLUSTER, but it uses considerably less processing time and memory, especially when the number of cases is large.

Options

Algorithm Specifications. You can specify what the number of clusters will be, how to select initial cluster centers, and whether to update the centers. See CRITERIA Subcommand.

Initial Cluster Centers. By default, QUICK CLUSTER chooses the initial cluster centers, but it can read initial cluster centers from a system file instead (see FILE Subcommand). Alternatively, you can provide initial centers within the program itself (see INITIAL Subcommand).

Optional Printed Output. You can print the cluster membership of each case with the distance of each case from its classification cluster center. You can also choose to print the distances between the final cluster centers as well as a univariate analysis of variance between clusters for each clustering variable. See PRINT Subcommand.

Saving Results. You can write the final cluster centers to a system file (see OUTFILE Subcommand). In addition, you can save the cluster membership of each case in the SPSS active system file, and you can also save in the active system file the distance from each case to its classification cluster center. See SAVE subcommand.

Basic Specification

• The basic specification is a list of variables. QUICK CLUSTER produces clusters by finding cluster centers based on the values of the cluster variables and by assigning cases to the centers that are nearest.

Subcommand Order

• The variable list must be first.
• Subcommands can be named in any order.

Operations

The procedure involves three steps. First, QUICK CLUSTER selects initial cluster centers. A center is an estimate of the average value of each clustering variable for the cases in a cluster. (A center includes one value for each variable.) By default, QUICK CLUSTER selects k cases with well-separated, nonmissing values as initial centers, where k is the number of clusters you request. This selection provides a good starting point for the next two steps of the algorithm. If CRITERIA=NOINITIAL, QUICK CLUSTER selects the first k cases without missing values as initial cluster centers. The NOINITIAL option followed by the remaining steps of the default QUICK CLUSTER algorithm makes QUICK CLUSTER equivalent to MacQueen's k-means clustering method.

The second step of the algorithm updates the values of the initial cluster centers to derive the classification cluster centers. (This step can be eliminated to cluster a very large number of cases, as explained below.) Measuring by squared Euclidean distance, QUICK CLUSTER assigns each case in turn to the nearest cluster center. When a case is assigned, the procedure updates the center to a mean for the cases that are thus far in the cluster. As cases are processed, the centers migrate to concentrations of observations.

The third and final step of the algorithm reassigns each case to the nearest of the updated (classification) cluster centers, yielding the final clusters. The final cluster centers result from the variable means for the cases in the final clusters.

- The cluster solution depends on the order of cases in the file: if the order changes, the cluster solution changes. To minimize the discrepancy, run QUICK CLUSTER until the solution stabilizes. This might require multiple runs. Use the OUTFILE subcommand to save final centers on one run, and use the FILE subcommand on the next run to use those final centers as initial centers.

- By default, initial cluster centers are formed by choosing one case (with valid data for the clustering variables) for each cluster requested. These centers are chosen to be well separated from one another, so this initial selection requires a pass through the data.

- Variables measured on different scales should be standardized prior to their use in QUICK CLUSTER. Otherwise, the scale on which different variables are measured will affect the distances used in forming clusters.

Extremely Large Numbers of Cases

When there are a great many cases, directly clustering them all may be impractical. Instead, you can cluster a sample of the cases and then use the cluster solution for the sample to classify the very large group of cases. This requires two uses of QUICK CLUSTER (see the example below).

- The first use of QUICK CLUSTER involves all three steps of the QUICK CLUSTER algorithm, and thus three passes through the data for the selected sample. QUICK CLUSTER obtains a cluster solution for this sample of the cases and must use OUTFILE to save the final cluster centers to a system file.

- The second use of QUICK CLUSTER involves only the third step and thus only one pass through the very large data set. QUICK CLUSTER must use FILE to define the final cluster centers from the first analysis as the initial cluster centers for the second analysis. You can specify NOUPDATE on the CRITERIA subcommand so QUICK CLUSTER will directly assign each case to the cluster with the nearest center.

Example

```
QUICK CLUSTER V1 TO V4
   /CRITERIA=CLUSTERS(4)
   /SAVE=CLUSTER(GROUP).
```

- This example clusters cases based on their values for all variables between and including V1 and V4 on the active system file.

- Four clusters, rather than the default two, will be formed.

- Initial cluster centers will be chosen by the default method, by finding four widely spaced cases.

- The four final cluster centers are saved in variable GROUP on the active system file. GROUP has integer values from 1 to 4 indicating the cluster to which each case belongs.

Variable List   The variable list identifies the variables on which cases are to be clustered.

- The variable list is required and must be the first specification on QUICK CLUSTER.
- You can use keyword ALL to refer to all user-defined variables on the active system file.
- QUICK CLUSTER uses squared Euclidean distance, which equally weights all clustering variables. If the variables are measured in units that are not comparable, the procedure gives more weight to variables with large variances. However, you can standardize the variables before clustering by using procedure DESCRIPTIVES.

CRITERIA Subcommand   Use CRITERIA to specify the number of clusters desired or to control the options for the clustering algorithm. You can use any or all of the following keywords:

CLUSTER(k)   *Number of clusters.* QUICK CLUSTER assigns cases to *k* clusters. The default is two clusters.

NOINITIAL   *No initial cluster center selection.* This keyword specifies that as initial centers, QUICK CLUSTER uses the first *k* cases without missing values, where *k* is the number of clusters specified on the CLUSTER keyword. If you do not use NOINITIAL, QUICK CLUSTER selects as initial centers *k* cases without missing values, and—at the expense of greater processing time—the selection process guarantees that the cases are well separated.

NOUPDATE   *No updating of cluster centers.* This option produces a very quick clustering, but the results are not as good as those from the default procedure. You should choose this option when you use QUICK CLUSTER to classify cases on the basis of a previous clustering.

Initial Cluster Centers   Initial cluster centers can be set either by entering them in your procedure specifications (see INITIAL Subcommand), or by reading them from a system file (see FILE Subcommand).

INITIAL Subcommand   Use INITIAL to set the initial cluster centers. One value for each clustering variable must be included for as many clusters as you request.

Example
```
QUICK CLUSTER  A B C D
  /CRITERIA = CLUSTER(3)
  /INITIAL = (13 24  1  8
               7 12  5  9
              10 18 17 16).
```

- This example specifies four clustering variables and requests three clusters. Thus, twelve values are supplied.
- In this example, the initial center of the first cluster has a value of 13 for variable A, 24 for variable B, 1 for C, and 8 for D.

FILE Subcommand   Use FILE to obtain initial cluster centers from a system file.

Example
```
QUICK CLUSTER  A B C D
  /FILE=INIT
  /CRITERIA = CLUSTER(3).
```

- In this example, the initial cluster centers are read from file INIT. The four clustering variables are A, B, C, and D. QUICK CLUSTER assigns the cases to three clusters.

PRINT Subcommand   QUICK CLUSTER always displays the initial cluster centers, the updated centers used to classify cases (classification cluster centers), the mean values of the cases in each cluster (final cluster centers), and the number of cases in each cluster. Use PRINT to request additional output.

• Some PRINT options will markedly increase the volume of output or the processing time required for large cluster problems.

INITIAL   *Initial cluster centers.* The initial cluster centers print by default, whether they are read from a file, specified in the program, or selected from input cases in the first phase of the clustering process. When SPLIT FILES is in effect, the initial cluster center for each split file is printed, followed by the cluster results for each subfile.

CLUSTER   *Cluster membership for each case.* Each case displays an identifying number or value, the number of the cluster to which it was assigned, and its distance from the center of that cluster. This output is extensive when you process a large number of cases.

ID(varname)   *Case identification in output.* SPSS will use the value of the variable named to identify cases in output. By default, cases are identified by their sequential numbers in the active system file.

DISTANCE   *Pairwise distances between all final cluster centers.* When a very large number of clusters is requested, this output can consume a great deal of processing time.

ANOVA   *Descriptive univariate F tests for the clustering variables.* Since cases are assigned to clusters so as to maximize differences between the clusters, it is not legitimate to interpret the *F* tests as tests of the null hypothesis that there are no differences between clusters. The tests are descriptive only. Cases are systematically assigned to clusters to maximize differences on the clustering variables. Statistics after clustering are also available through procedure DISCRIMINANT or MANOVA.

NONE   *Unconditional output.* Keyword NONE can be used on PRINT for QUICK CLUSTER to print only the unconditional output: classification and final cluster centers and the number of cases in each cluster. If other specifications are used with NONE on PRINT, the others are ignored.

Example

```
QUICK CLUSTER A B C D E
  /CRITERIA=CLUSTERS(6)
  /PRINT=CLUSTER ID(CASEID) DISTANCE.
```

• Six clusters are formed on the basis of the five variables A, B, C, D, and E.

• Cluster membership and distance from cluster center are displayed for each case in the file.

• Cases are identified by the values of the variable CASEID.

• Distances between all cluster centers are printed.

Saving Results

You can save different clustering results on a system file (see OUTFILE Subcommand) or on the active system file (see SAVE Subcommand).

OUTFILE Subcommand

Use OUTFILE to save the final cluster centers on a system file. You can later use these final cluster centers as initial cluster centers for a different sample of cases that use the same variables. You can also cluster the final cluster centers themselves to obtain clusters of clusters.

Example

```
QUICK CLUSTER A B C D
  /CRITERIA = CLUSTER(3)
  /OUTFILE = QC1.
```

• QUICK CLUSTER writes the cluster centers to file QC1.

SAVE Subcommand

Use SAVE to save results of the cluster analysis as new variables on the active system file.

CLUSTER(varname)   *The cluster number of each case.* Specify a variable name in parentheses. The value of this variable will be set to an integer from 1 to the number of clusters.

DISTANCE(varname)   *The distance of each case from its cluster center.* Specify a variable name in parentheses. For each case, the value of this variable will be the distance of that case from its cluster center.

Example

```
QUICK CLUSTER A B C D
    /CRITERIA=CLUSTERS(6)
    /SAVE=CLUSTER(CLUSNUM) DISTANCE(DISTCNTR).
```

- Six clusters of cases are formed on the basis of variables A, B, C, and D.
- The variable CLUSNUM will be set to an integer between 1 and 6 to indicate cluster membership for each case.
- The variable DISTCNTR will be set to the Euclidean distance between a case and the center of the cluster to which it is assigned.

MISSING Subcommand

MISSING controls the treatment of cases with missing values.

- LISTWISE, PAIRWISE, and DEFAULT are mutually exclusive. Each, however, can be used with INCLUDE.

LISTWISE   *Delete cases with missing values listwise.* A case with a missing value on any of the clustering variables is deleted from the analysis and will not be assigned to a cluster. This is the default.

PAIRWISE   *Assign each case to the nearest cluster on the basis of the clustering variables for which the case has nonmissing values.* Cases are deleted if they have missing values on all clustering variables.

INCLUDE   *Treat user-missing values as valid.*

DEFAULT   *Same as LISTWISE.*

Annotated Example

For a complete example with output, see Examples following the Command Reference.

RANK

```
RANK [VARIABLES=] varlist [(({A**}))] [BY varlist]
                            {D  }

[/TIES={MEAN**  }]
       {LOW     }
       {HIGH    }
       {CONDENSE}

[/FRACTION={BLOM**}]
           {TUKEY }
           {VW    }
           {RANKIT}

[/PRINT={YES**}]
        {NO   }

[/MISSING={EXCLUDE**}]
          {INCLUDE  }
```

(The following rank function subcommands can each be specified once.)

```
[/RANK**] [/NTILES(k)] [/NORMAL] [/PERCENT]
[/RFRACTION] [/PROPORTION] [/N] [/SAVAGE]
```

(INTO can be used with any rank function subcommand.)

```
[INTO rankvarlist]
```

**Default if the subcommand is omitted.

Example:

```
RANK VARIABLES=SALARY JOBTIME.
```

Overview

RANK produces new variables containing ranks, normal scores, and Savage and related scores, for numeric variables.

Options

Methods. You can rank variables in ascending or descending order (see VARIABLES Subcommand). You can compute different functions of ranks and also name the new rank function variables (see RANK Function Subcommands). You can specify the method for handling ties (see TIES Subcommand). You can determine how the proportion estimate is computed for the rank functions NORMAL and PROPORTIONAL (see FRACTION Subcommand).

Output. You can suppress display of the summary table that lists variables ranked with their associated new variables in the active system file. See PRINT Subcommand.

Basic Specification

The basic specification is VARIABLES and at least one variable from the active system file.

- By default, RANK displays a summary table that includes a list of ranked variables and each new variable in the active system file into which computed ranks have been stored.

- The default ranking function is RANK. Direction is ascending. Missing values are excluded. Ties are handled by assigning the mean rank to tied values.

Subcommand Order

- VARIABLES must be first.
- Remaining subcommands can be named in any order.

Operations

- RANK does not change the way the active system file is sorted.
- If new variable names are not specified with the INTO keyword on the ranking function subcommand, RANK creates default names. (See INTO keyword.)
- RANK automatically assigns variable labels to the new variables. The labels identify the source variables. For example, the label for a new variable with the default name RSALARY is "RANK of SALARY."

Limitations
- String variables cannot be specified on RANK. AUTORECODE can be used to order string variables.

Example

`RANK VARIABLES=SALARY JOBTIME.`

- RANK ranks SALARY and JOBTIME into two new variables in the active file, RSALARY and RJOBTIME.

VARIABLES Subcommand

VARIABLES specifies the variables to be ranked. Keyword VARIABLES can be omitted.

- VARIABLES is required and must be the first specification on RANK. The minimum specification is a single numeric variable. To rank more than one variable, specify a variable list.
- Optionally, after the variable list specify the direction for ranking. Specify (A) for ascending or (D) for descending ranks. (A) is the default. The (A) or (D) applies to all preceding variables in the list.
- To rank some variables in ascending order and others in descending order, use both (A) and (D) in the same variable list.
- To organize rankings into subgroups, specify keyword BY followed by the variable whose values determine the subgroups. The active system file does not have to be sorted by the BY variable.

Example

`RANK VARIABLES=MURDERS ROBBERY (D).`

- RANK ranks MURDERS and ROBBERY into two new variables on the active system file: RMURDERS AND RROBBERY.
- (D) specifies descending order of rank (largest value gets smallest rank). The (D) applies to both MURDERS and ROBBERY.

Example

`RANK VARIABLES=MURDERS (D) ROBBERY (A) BY ETHNIC.`

- MURDERS is ranked in descending order, ROBBERY is ranked in ascending order.
- Ranks are computed within each group defined by ETHNIC. The active system file does not have to be sorted by ETHNIC.

RANK Function Subcommands

The optional rank function subcommands specify different functions of ranks. RANK is the default rank function.

- Any combination of RANK function subcommands can be specified for a RANK procedure, but each RANK function can be specified only once.
- Each RANK function subcommand must be preceded by a slash.
- The RANK functions assign default names to the new RANK variables, unless keyword INTO is used (see keyword INTO).

RANK *Simple rank.* Value equals rank. Rank can either be ascending or descending. (See VARIABLES Subcommand.) Rank values can be affected by the keyword specified on the TIES subcommand.

RFRACTION *Fractional ranks.* Value equals rank divided by the sum of the weights of the non-missing cases. For TIES=HIGH, fractional rank values are an empirical cumulative distribution.

NORMAL *Normal scores* (Lehmann, 1975). The new variable contains the inverse of the standard normal cumulative distribution of the proportion estimate defined by FRACTION. The default is FRACTION=BLOM. (See FRACTION Subcommand.)

PERCENT *Fractional rank as a percent.* The new variable contains fractional ranks multiplied by 100.

PROPORTION *Proportion estimates.* The estimation method is specified by FRACTION. The default is FRACTION=BLOM. (See FRACTION Subcommand.)

N *Sum of case weights.* The new variable is a constant.

SAVAGE	*Savage score.* The new variable contains Savage (exponential) scores (Lehmann 1975).
NTILES(k)	*Percentile groups.* The new variable contains values from 1 to k. Each group value is the integer that is equal to or less than y_i where $y_i = 1 + R_i k/(w+1)$ and where R_i is the rank of the ith case of the variable being ranked, k is the number of groups specified on the NTILES subcommand, and w is the sum of the case weights. Group values can be affected by the keyword specified on TIES. (See TIES Subcommand.) There is no default value for k, the number of groups generated.

INTO Keyword

INTO specifies variable names for the new variable(s) added to the active system file. INTO can be used with any of the RANK function subcommands. If INTO is not specified on a RANK function, RANK creates default names for the new variables according to the following rules:

- The first letter of the ranking function is added to the first seven characters of the original variable name.

- If some of the resulting names are not unique (in the dictionary of the active system file or in an INTO new variable list), the non-unique variables are named XXXnnn. XXX represents the first three characters of the ranking function and nnn is a three-digit number starting with 001 and being increased by one for each variable. If the ranking function is N, XXX is reduced to N.

- If some of the names resulting from the first and second step are not unique, the non-unique variables are named RNKXXnn. XX is the first two characters of the ranking function and nn is a two-digit number starting with 01 and being increased by one for each variable.

- If it is not possible to generate unique names, an error results.

Example

```
RANK VARIABLES=SALARY
 /NORMAL INTO SALNORM
 /SAVAGE INTO SALSAV
 /NTILES(4) INTO SALQUART.
```

- RANK generates three new variables from the variable SALARY.

- NORMAL produces the new variable SALNORM. SALNORM contains normal scores for SALARY computed with the default formula BLOM.

- SAVAGE produces the new variable SALSAV. SALSAV contains Savage scores for SALARY.

- NTILES(4) produces the new variable SALQUART. SALQUART contains the value 1, 2, 3, or 4 to represent one of the four percentile groups of salary.

TIES Subcommand

TIES determines the way tied values are handled. The default method is MEAN.

MEAN	*Mean rank applied to tied values.*
LOW	*Lowest rank applied to tied values.*
HIGH	*Highest rank applied to tied values.*
CONDENSE	*Consecutive ranks with ties sharing a value.* Distinct values of the ranked variable are assigned consecutive ranks in the new variable. Ties share their value. The next untied value is assigned the value consecutive to the value assigned the ties.

Example

```
RANK VARIABLES=BURGLARY /RANK INTO RMEAN /TIES=MEAN.
RANK VARIABLES=BURGLARY /RANK INTO RCONDS /TIES=CONDENSE.
RANK VARIABLES=BURGLARY /RANK INTO RHIGH /TIES=HIGH.
RANK VARIABLES=BURGLARY /RANK INTO RLOW /TIES=LOW.
```

- The values of BURGLARY and the results of these four procedures are shown below.

COMMUNITY	BURGLARY	RMEAN	RCONDS	RHIGH	RLOW
1	0	3	1	5	1
2	0	3	1	5	1
3	0	3	1	5	1
4	0	3	1	5	1
5	0	3	1	5	1
6	1	6.5	2	7	6
7	1	6.5	2	7	6
8	3	8	3	8	8

FRACTION Subcommand

FRACTION specifies the way to compute a proportion estimate P for the NORMAL and PROPORTION rank functions. This optional subcommand can be used only with function subcommands NORMAL or PROPORTION. With other rank function subcommands, FRACTION is ignored and a warning message is displayed. The default is BLOM.

- Only one formula can be specified for each RANK procedure. If more than one is specified, an error results. In the following formulas, r is the rank and w is the sum of case weights.

BLOM Blom's transformation, defined by the formula $(r - 3/8) / (w + 1/4)$. (See Blom, 1958.)

RANKIT Uses the formula $(r - 1/2) / w$. (See Chambers et al., 1983.)

TUKEY Tukey's transformation, defined by the formula $(r - 1/3) / (w + 1/3)$. (See Tukey, 1962.)

VW Van der Waerden's transformation, defined by the formula $r / (w + 1)$. (See Lehmann, 1975.)

Example
```
RANK VARIABLES=MORTGAGE VALUE /FRACTION=BLOM
   /NORMAL INTO MORTNORM VALNORM.
```

- RANK generates new variables MORTNORM and VALNORM. MORTNORM contains normal scores for MORTGAGE, and ETHNNORM contains normal scores for VALUE.

PRINT Subcommand

PRINT determines whether the summary tables are displayed with the output. The default is YES.

YES *Display summary table.*

NO *Do not display summary table.*

MISSING Subcommand

MISSING controls the treatment of cases with user-missing values. The default is EXCLUDE.

INCLUDE *Include all user-missing values.*

EXCLUDE *Exclude all missing values.*

Example
```
MISSING VALUE SALARY (0).
RANK VARIABLES=SALARY /RANK INTO SALRANK /MISSING=INCLUDE.
```

- RANK generates the new variable SALRANK.
- MISSING=INCLUDE causes user-missing value 0 to be included in the ranking process.

Annotated Example

For a complete example with output, see Examples following the Command Reference.

References

Blom, G. 1958. *Statistical estimates and transformed beta variables.* New York: John Wiley & Sons.

Chambers, J. M., W. S. Cleveland, B. Kleiner, and P. A. Tukey. 1983. *Graphical methods for data analysis.* Belmont, California: Wadsworth International Group; Boston: Duxbury Press.

Fisher, R. A. 1973. *Statistical methods for research workers.* 14th ed. New York: Hafner Publishing Company.

Frigge, M., D. C. Hoaglin, and B. Iglewicz. 1987. Some implementations of the boxplot. In *Computer science and statistics proceedings of the 19th symposium on the interface,* R. M. Heiberger and M. Martin, eds. Alexandria, Virginia: American Statistical Association.

Lehmann, E. L. 1975. *Nonparametrics: statistical methods based on ranks.* San Francisco: Holden-Day.

Tukey, J. W. 1962. The future of data analysis. *Annals of Mathematical Statistics* 33:22.

RECODE

For numeric variables:
```
RECODE varlist (value list=value)...(value list=value)
       [INTO varlist] [/varlist...]
```

Input Keywords:
LO, LOWEST, HI, HIGHEST, THRU, MISSING, SYSMIS, ELSE

Output Keywords:
COPY, SYSMIS

For string variables:
```
RECODE varlist [('string',['string'...]='string')]
       [INTO varlist] [/varlist...]
```

Input Keywords:
CONVERT, ELSE

Output Keyword:
COPY

Examples:
```
RECODE V1 TO V3 (0=1) (1=0) (2,3=-1) (9=9) (ELSE=SYSMIS).

RECODE STRNGVAR ('A','B','C'='A')('D','E','F'='B')(ELSE=' ').
```

Overview

RECODE changes the coding scheme of an existing variable. RECODE can be executed on a value-by-value basis or for a range of values. Where it can be used, RECODE is much more efficient than the series of IF commands that produce the same transformation.

With RECODE, you must specify the new codes for all recoded values. See AUTORECODE to automatically generate a coding scheme of consecutive integers for the values of both string and numeric variables.

Options

Recoded Variables. RECODE can change, rearrange, or consolidate the values of an existing variable, or it can generate a target variable as a recoded version of its source variable.

Variable Type. RECODE can recode a string variable into a new numeric variable for more efficient processing. RECODE can also recode a numeric variable into a new string variable to provide more descriptive values.

Basic Specification

The basic specification is a variable name and, within parentheses, the original value(s) followed by a required equals sign and a recoded value. RECODE changes the value(s) on the left of the equals sign into the single value on the right of the equals sign.

Syntax Rules

- The variable(s) to be recoded must already exist and must precede all value specifications.
- Value specifications are enclosed in parentheses. The original values must appear to the left of an equals sign, and a single recoded value must appear to the right of the equals sign.
- Multiple values can be consolidated into a single recoded value by specifying, to the left of the equals sign, a list of values separated by blanks or commas. Only one recoded value per set of original values is allowed.
- Multiple sets of value specifications are permitted; each set must be enclosed in a separate set of parentheses. Each set of parentheses can result in only one recoded value.

- Original values that are not mentioned remain unchanged, unless the ELSE keyword is used. ELSE refers to all original values not previously mentioned.
- COPY replicates original values without recoding them.
- INTO is required to recode a string variable into a numeric variable or a numeric variable into a string variable.
- Multiple variables can be recoded together by specifying a variable list before the value specifications. When a variable list precedes the value specifications, each variable in the list is recoded identically.
- A single RECODE command can execute multiple recode transformations. Each transformation's variable and value specifications must be separated by a slash.

Numeric Variables

- THRU specifies a value range, inclusive of specified end values.
- LOWEST and HIGHEST (LO and HI) specify the lowest and highest values encountered in the data. LOWEST and HIGHEST include user-missing values, but do not include the system-missing value.
- ELSE includes all original values not already specified, including the system-missing value. ELSE should be the last specification for the variable.
- MISSING specifies user- and system-missing values for recoding. MISSING is an original specification only.
- SYSMIS specifies the system-missing value and can be used as both an original and recoded value.

String Variables

- Both short and long string variables can be recoded.
- Values must be enclosed in apostrophes or quotation marks.
- Blanks are significant characters.
- Original and recoded values must be specified according to the format width of their source or target variables (see Universals: Strings).

Operations

- Recode value specifications are scanned left-to-right.
- A value is recoded only once per RECODE command.
- Invalid syntax stops processing of the RECODE command and cancels any recoding of variables named on the command.

Numeric Variables

- Blank fields for numeric variables are handled according to the SET BLANKS specification prior to recoding.
- When you recode a value that was previously defined as user-missing on the MISSING VALUE command, the recoded value is not missing but is the new, recoded value.

String Variables

- If the original or recoded value is shorter than the format width defined for that variable, the string is right-padded with blanks to the length of the variable being recoded.
- If the original or recoded value is longer than the format width defined for that variable, SPSS generates an error.

Limitations

- You can recode (and count using the COUNT command) approximately 400 values prior to a data pass.
- Invalid specifications on a RECODE command that result in errors stop all processing of that RECODE command.

Example

```
RECODE V1 TO V3 (0=1) (1=0) (2,3=-1) (9=9) (ELSE=SYSMIS)
  /QVAR(1 THRU 5=1)(6 THRU 10=2)(11 THRU HI=3)(ELSE=0).
```

- Values for the list of numeric variables between and including V1 and V3 are changed: original values 0 and   1 are switched respectively to 1 and 0, 2 and 3 become −1, 9 remains 9, and any other value is changed to the system-missing value.
- Values for variable QVAR are also changed: original values 1 through 5 become 1, 6 through 10 become 2, 11 through the highest value become 3, and any other value, including system-missing, becomes 0.

Example   RECODE STRNGVAR ('A','B','C'='A')('D','E','F'='B')(ELSE=' ').
                 RECODE PET ('IGUANA', 'SNAKE ' = 'WILD ').

- Values A, B, and C are changed to value A. Values D, E, and F are changed to value B. All other values are changed to a blank.
- Values IGUANA and SNAKE are changed to value WILD. The variable PET has a format width of six characters. Thus, values SNAKE and WILD include trailing blanks to total six characters.
- Note that each string value is enclosed within apostrophes.

INTO Keyword   INTO specifies a target variable to receive recoded values from a source variable. Source variables remain unchanged after the recode.

- INTO must follow all the parenthetic value recodes specified for the source variable(s).
- The number of target variables must equal the number of source variables.

Numeric Variables • Target variables can be existing or new variables. For existing variables, cases with values not mentioned in the recode specification are not changed. For new variables, cases with values not mentioned in the recode specification are assigned the system-missing value.

- New numeric variables have default print and write formats of F8.2 or the format specified on SET.

Example   RECODE AGE (MISSING=9) (18 THRU HI=1) (0 THRU 18=0) INTO VOTER.

- The recoded AGE values are stored in target variable VOTER, leaving AGE unchanged.

Example   RECODE V1 TO V3 (0=1) (1=0) (2=−1) INTO DEFENSE WELFARE HEALTH.

- V1 through V3 are recoded into DEFENSE, WELFARE, and HEALTH. V1 through V3 remain unchanged.

String Variables • Target variables must already exist. To declare a new variable, first create the variable with the STRING command, then specify the new variable as the target variable on RECODE.

- The recoded string cannot be longer than the defined width for the target variable.
- If the recoded string is shorter than the defined width of the target variable, the string is right-padded with blanks to the length of the target variable.
- Multiple target variables are allowed. The target variables must all be the same length, though they needn't be the same length as the source variables.
- If the source and target variables have different lengths, the criterion for the length of the original values is the format width defined for the source variable; the criterion for the length of the recoded values is the format width defined for the target variable.

Example   STRING STATE1 (A2).
                 RECODE STATE ('IO'='IA') (ELSE=COPY) INTO STATE1.

- STRING declares variable STATE1 so it can be used on RECODE.
- RECODE specifies STATE as the source variable and STATE1 as the target variable. Keywords ELSE and COPY are used to copy the other state codes over unchanged. Variables STATE and STATE1 are identical except for cases with original value IO.

Example   RECODE SEX ('M'=1) ('F'=2) INTO NSEX.

- RECODE recodes string variable SEX into numeric variable NSEX. Any value other than M or F becomes system-missing.
- SPSS can process a large number of cases more efficiently with the numeric variable NSEX than it can with the string variable SEX.

CONVERT Keyword CONVERT recodes the string representation of numbers to their numeric representation.

- If keyword CONVERT precedes the specified recodes, cases with numbers are recoded immediately and blanks are recoded to the system-missing value, even if you specifically recode blanks into a value.
- To recode blanks into a value other than system missing, you must place a recode specification for blanks *before* the keyword CONVERT.
- SPSS converts numbers as if the variable were being re-read using the F format.
- If SPSS encounters a field that cannot be converted, it scans the remaining recode specifications.
- If a code cannot be converted and there is no specific recode specification for that code, the target variable will be system-missing.

Example   `RECODE #JOB (CONVERT) ('-'=11) ('&'=12) INTO JOB.`

- RECODE first recodes all numbers in string variable #JOB to numbers for target variable JOB.
- RECODE then specifically recodes the minus sign (the "eleven" punch) to 11 and the ampersand (or "twelve" punch in EBCDIC) to 12. Keyword CONVERT is specified first as an efficiency measure to recode cases with numbers immediately. Blanks are recoded to the system-missing value.

Example   `RECODE #JOB (' '=-99) (CONVERT) ('-'=11) ('&'=12) INTO JOB.`

- The result is the same as in the above example, except that blanks will be changed to −99 in JOB.

RECORD TYPE

For FILE TYPE MIXED
```
RECORD TYPE {value list} [SKIP]
            {OTHER     }
```

For FILE TYPE GROUPED
```
RECORD TYPE {value list} [SKIP] [CASE=col loc]
            {OTHER     }
```

```
[DUPLICATE={WARN  }] [MISSING={WARN  } ]
           {NOWARN}           {NOWARN}
```

For FILE TYPE NESTED
```
RECORD TYPE {value list} [SKIP] [CASE=col loc]
            {OTHER     }
```

```
[SPREAD={YES}] [MISSING={WARN  }]
        {NO }           {NOWARN}
```

Example:
```
FILE TYPE   MIXED RECORD=RECID 1-2.
RECORD TYPE 23.
DATA LIST    /SEX 5 AGE 6-7 DOSAGE 8-10 RESULT 12.
END FILE TYPE.

BEGIN DATA
21   145010 1
22   257200 2
25   235    250  2
35   167              300      3
24   125150 1
23   272075 1
21   149050 2
25   134    035  3
30   138              300      3
32   229              500      3
END DATA.
```

Overview

RECORD TYPE is used with DATA LIST within a FILE TYPE—END FILE TYPE structure to define complex data files. The types of files include mixed files, grouped files, and nested files. *Mixed files* contain several types of records that define different types of cases; hierarchical or *nested files* contain several types of records with a defined relationship among the record types; and *grouped files* contain several records for each case with some records missing or duplicated or out of order. See FILE TYPE for more complete information. A fourth type of complex file, files with *repeating groups* of information, can be read with the REPEATING DATA command. (REPEATING DATA can also be used to read MIXED files and the lowest level of NESTED files.)

Within each type of complex file are varying types of records. One set of RECORD TYPE and DATA LIST commands is used to define each type of record in the data. The specifications available for RECORD TYPE vary according to whether MIXED, GROUPED, or NESTED is specified for FILE TYPE.

Basic Specification

The basic specification is the value(s) of the record type variable defined on the RECORD subcommand of FILE TYPE.

• RECORD TYPE must be followed by a DATA LIST command defining the variables for the specified records, unless SKIP is used.

• Separate associated RECORD TYPE and DATA LIST commands must be used for each defined record type.

The resulting file, the active system file, is always a rectangular file, regardless of the structure of the original data file.

Syntax Rules
- A list of values can be specified if a set of different record types has the same variable definitions. Each value must be separated by a space or comma. String values must be enclosed in apostrophes or quotation marks.
- For MIXED files, each DATA LIST can name variables with the same variable name, since each record type defines a separate case. For GROUPED and NESTED files, the variable names on each DATA LIST must be unique since a case is built by combining all record types together onto a single record.
- For MIXED files, if the record types have different variables or if they have the same variables recorded in different locations, separate RECORD TYPE and DATA LIST commands are required for each record type.
- For MIXED files, if the same variable is defined for more than one record type, the format type and length of the variable should be defined the same on all DATA LIST commands. SPSS refers to the first DATA LIST command that defines a variable for the print and write formats to be included in the dictionary of the active system file.
- For NESTED files, the order of the RECORD TYPE commands defines the hierarchical structure of the file. The first RECORD TYPE defines the highest-level record type, the next RECORD TYPE defines the next highest-level record, and so forth. The last RECORD TYPE command defines a case in the active system file.

Operations
- If a record type is defined on more than one RECORD TYPE command, SPSS uses the DATA LIST for the first occurrence and ignores all others.
- For NESTED files, the first record in the file should be the type specified on the first RECORD TYPE command—the highest-level record of the hierarchy. If the first record in the file is not the highest-level type, SPSS skips all records until it encounters a record of the highest-level type. If the MISSING or DUPLI-CATE subcommands have been specified on the FILE TYPE command, these records may produce warning messages but will not be used to build a case on the active system file.

Example

```
TITLE      'A MIXED FILE'.
SUBTITLE   'READING ONLY ONE RECORD TYPE'.

FILE TYPE   MIXED RECORD=RECID 1-2.
RECORD TYPE 23.
DATA LIST    /SEX 5 AGE 6-7 DOSAGE 8-10 RESULT 12.
END FILE TYPE.

BEGIN DATA
21   145010 1
22   257200 2
25   235   250  2
35   167             300      3
24   125150 1
23   272075 1
21   149050 2
25   134   035  3
30   138             300      3
32   229             500      3
END DATA.
```

- FILE TYPE begins the file definition for this mixed file and END FILE TYPE indicates the end of the definitions. FILE TYPE specifies a MIXED file type. Data are in the command file. The record identification variable RECID is located in columns 1 and 2.
- RECORD TYPE specifies that only records with value 23 for variable RECID are copied onto the active system file. All other records are skipped.
- DATA LIST defines variables on only those records with the value 23 for variable RECID.

Example
```
TITLE      'A MIXED FILE'.
SUBTITLE   'READING MULTIPLE RECORD TYPES'.

FILE TYPE  MIXED FILE=TREATMNT RECORD=RECID 1-2.
RECORD TYPE 21,22,23,24.
DATA LIST    /SEX 5 AGE 6-7 DOSAGE 8-10 RESULT 12.
RECORD TYPE 25.
DATA LIST    /SEX 5 AGE 6-7 DOSAGE 10-12 RESULT 15.
END FILE TYPE.
```

- Data are the same as in the previous example. This time they are read from an external file.

- The variable DOSAGE is read from columns 8-10 on record types 21, 22, 23, and 24 and from columns 10-12 on record type 25. RESULT is read from column 12 on record types 21, 22, 23, and 24 and from column 15 on record type 25.

- The active system file contains the values for all variables defined on the DATA LIST commands for record types 21 through 25. All other record types are skipped.

Example
```
TITLE      'A NESTED FILE'.
SUBTITLE   'ACCIDENT RECORDS'.

FILE TYPE NESTED RECORD=6 CASE=ACCID 1-4.
RECORD TYPE 1.
DATA LIST    /ACC_ID 9-11 WEATHER 12-13 STATE 15-16 (A)
             DATE 18-24 (A).
RECORD TYPE 2.
DATA LIST /STYLE 11 MAKE 13 OLD 14 LICENSE 15-16 (A)
             INSURNCE 18-21(A).
RECORD TYPE 3.
DATA LIST /PSNGR_NO 11 AGE 13-14 SEX 16 (A) INJURY 18
             SEAT 20-21 (A) COST 23-24.

END FILE TYPE.

BEGIN DATA
0001 1   322 1 IL 3/13/88   /* Type 1:  accident record
0001 2     1 44MI 134M      /* Type 2:    vehicle record
0001 3     1 34 M 1 FR   3  /* Type 3:    person record
0001 2     2 16IL 322F      /*            vehicle record
0001 3     1 22 F 1 FR  11  /*            person record
0001 3     2 35 M 1 FR   5  /*            person record
0001 3     3 59 M 1 BK   7  /*            person record
0001 2     3 21IN 146M      /*            vehicle record
0001 3     1 46 M 0 FR   0  /*            person record
END DATA.
```

- FILE TYPE identifies the file as a nested file type. The record identifier, located in column 6, is not assigned a variable name. The default scratch variable name ####RECD is therefore used. The case identification variable ACCID is located in columns 1-4.

- Because there are three record types, there are three RECORD TYPE commands. For each RECORD TYPE there is a DATA LIST to define variables for records with the corresponding record type. The order of the RECORD TYPE commands defines the hierarchical structure of the file.

- END FILE TYPE signals the end of file definition.

- SPSS builds a case for each type 3 record (each person in the file). There can be only one type 1 and one type 2 record for each type 3 record: each person can be in only one vehicle, and each vehicle can be in only one accident.

OTHER Keyword
OTHER specifies all record types that have not been mentioned on previous RECORD TYPE commands.

- OTHER can be specified only on the last RECORD TYPE command in the file definition.

- OTHER may be used with SKIP to skip all undefined record types.
- For NESTED files, OTHER can be used only with SKIP. Neither can be used separately.
- If WILD=WARN is specified on the FILE TYPE command, OTHER cannot be specified on the RECORD TYPE command.

Example
```
TITLE  'A MIXED FILE'.

FILE TYPE  MIXED FILE=TREATMNT RECORD=RECID 1-2.
RECORD TYPE 21,22,23,24.
DATA LIST    /SEX 5 AGE 6-7 DOSAGE 8-10 RESULT 12.
RECORD TYPE 25.
DATA LIST    /SEX 5 AGE 6-7 DOSAGE 10-12 RESULT 15.
RECORD TYPE OTHER.
DATA LIST    /SEX 5 AGE 6-7 DOSAGE 18-20 RESULT 25.
END FILE TYPE.
```

- The first two RECORD TYPE commands specify record types 21-25. All other record types are specified by the third RECORD TYPE.

Example
```
TITLE  'A NESTED FILE'.

FILE TYPE NESTED FILE=ACCIDENT RECORD=#RECID 6 CASE=ACCID 1-4.
RECORD TYPE 1.          /*ACCIDENT RECORD
DATA LIST    /WEATHER 12-13.
RECORD TYPE 2.          /*VEHICLE RECORD
DATA LIST /STYLE 16.
RECORD TYPE OTHER SKIP.
END FILE TYPE.
```

- Because data are in a nested file, OTHER can be used only with SKIP.
- The third RECORD TYPE specifies OTHER SKIP. Type 2 records are therefore the lowest-level records on the active system file. SPSS builds one case for each vehicle record. The person records are skipped.

SKIP Subcommand

SKIP tells SPSS to skip all records of the type listed on its associated RECORD TYPE command.

- To skip only selected record types, specify the values for the types you want to skip, then specify SKIP.
- By default for MIXED file types, SPSS skips all records that are not specified on one of the RECORD TYPE commands.
- By default for GROUPED file types, SPSS issues a warning message for all record types not defined on a RECORD TYPE command.
- For NESTED files, SKIP can be used only with OTHER. Neither can be used separately.

Example
```
FILE TYPE GROUPED FILE=HUBDATA RECORD=#RECID 80 CASE=ID 1-5
                              WILD=NOWARN.
RECORD TYPE 1.
DATA LIST    /MOHIRED YRHIRED 12-15 DEPT79 TO DEPT82 SEX 16-20.
RECORD TYPE OTHER SKIP.
END FILE TYPE.
```

- SPSS reads variables from type 1 records and skips all other type.
- WILD=NOWARN on the FILE TYPE command suppresses the warning messages that SPSS prints by default for undefined record types. Keyword OTHER cannot be used when the default WILD=WARN specification is in effect.

Example
```
FILE TYPE GROUPED FILE=HUBDATA RECORD=#RECID 80 CASE=ID 1-5.
RECORD TYPE 1.
DATA LIST    /MOHIRED YRHIRED 12-15 DEPT79 TO DEPT82 SEX 16-20.
RECORD TYPE 2,3 SKIP.
END FILE TYPE.
```

- Record type 1 is defined for each case, and record types 2 and 3 are skipped.
- WILD=WARN, the default on FILE TYPE GROUPED, is in effect. SPSS therefore issues a warning message for any record types it encounters other than types 1, 2, and 3. Even though record types 2 and 3 are skipped, no warning message is printed for them because they are explicitly specified on a RECORD TYPE command.

CASE Subcommand   CASE specifies the column location(s) of the case identification variable when the variable is not in the location defined by the CASE subcommand on FILE TYPE.

- CASE on RECORD TYPE applies only to those records specified by that RECORD TYPE command. The identifier for all other defined record types must be in the location specified by CASE on FILE TYPE, or in the location specified by CASE on another RECORD TYPE.

- CASE can be used for NESTED and GROUPED file types only. CASE cannot be used for MIXED file types.

- CASE can be used on RECORD TYPE only if a CASE subcommand is specified on FILE TYPE.

- The format type of the case identification variable must be the same on all records. Thus, if the case identification variable is defined as a string on FILE TYPE, it cannot be defined as a numeric variable on RECORD TYPE, and vice versa.

Example
```
TITLE      'A GROUPED FILE'.
SUBTITLE   'SPECIFYING CASE ON THE RECORD TYPE COMMAND'.

FILE TYPE GROUPED FILE=HUBDATA RECORD=#RECID 80 CASE=ID 1-5.
RECORD TYPE 1.
DATA LIST    /MOHIRED YRHIRED 12-15 DEPT79 TO DEPT82 SEX 16-20.
RECORD TYPE 2.
DATA LIST    /SALARY79 TO SALARY82 6-25 HOURLY81 HOURLY82 40-53(2)
             PROMO81 72  AGE 54-55 RAISE82 66-70.
RECORD TYPE 3  CASE=75-79.
DATA LIST    /JOBCAT 6 NAME 25-48 (A).
END FILE TYPE.
```

- CASE on FILE TYPE indicates that the case identification variable is located in columns 1–5. Columns 1–5 apply only to record types 1 and 2 because the CASE subcommand on the third RECORD TYPE command overrides the case setting for type 3 records. For type 3 records, the case identification variable is located in columns 75–79.

MISSING Subcommand   MISSING determines whether SPSS issues a warning when it encounters a missing record type for a case. Regardless of whether SPSS issues the warning, it builds the case in the active system file with system-missing values for the variables defined on the missing record. MISSING is optional for GROUPED and NESTED files. MISSING cannot be used with MIXED files.

- The only specification is a single keyword. NOWARN is the default for NESTED files. WARN is the default for GROUPED files.

- For GROUPED files, SPSS checks whether there is a record for each case identification number. For NESTED files, SPSS verifies that each defined case includes one record of each type.

- MISSING on RECORD TYPE applies only to those records specified by that RECORD TYPE command. The treatment of missing records for all other defined record types is determined by the FILE TYPE command, or by the MISSING specification on another RECORD TYPE.

NOWARN   *Do not issue a warning message when a missing record type is encountered for a case.* This is the default for NESTED files.

WARN   *Issue a warning message when a missing record type is encountered for a case.* This is the default for GROUPED files.

Example
```
FILE TYPE GROUPED FILE=HUBDATA RECORD=#RECID 80 CASE=ID 1-5.
RECORD TYPE 1.
DATA LIST    /MOHIRED YRHIRED 12-15 DEPT79 TO DEPT82 SEX 16-20.
RECORD TYPE 2  MISSING=NOWARN.
DATA LIST    /SALARY79 TO SALARY82 6-25 HOURLY81 HOURLY82 40-53
(2)
             PROMO81 72 AGE 54-55 RAISE82 66-70.
RECORD TYPE 3.
DATA LIST    /JOBCAT 6 NAME 25-48 (A).
END FILE TYPE.
```

• MISSING is not specified on FILE TYPE. Therefore the default MISSING=WARN is in effect for all record types.

• MISSING=NOWARN is specified on the second RECORD TYPE, overriding the FILE TYPE setting for type 2 records only. WARN is still in effect for type 1 and type 3 records.

DUPLICATE Subcommand

DUPLICATE determines whether SPSS prints a warning message when it encounters more than one record of each type for a single case. DUPLICATE on RECORD TYPE can be used for GROUPED files only. DUPLICATE cannot be used for MIXED or NESTED files.

• The only specification is a single keyword. WARN is the default.

• DUPLICATE on RECORD TYPE applies only to those records specified by that RECORD TYPE command. The treatment of duplicate records for all other defined record types is determined by the FILE TYPE command, or by the DUPLICATE specification on another RECORD TYPE.

• Regardless of the specification on DUPLICATE, duplicate records are not included in the active system file. Only the last record from a set of duplicates is included in the active system file.

WARN   *Issue a warning message.* SPSS prints a warning message and the first 80 characters of the last record of the duplicate set of record types. This is the default.

NOWARN   *Do not issue a warning message.* SPSS simply skips all duplicate record types when building each case and does not print warning messages.

Example

```
TITLE      'A GROUPED FILE'.
SUBTITLE   'SPECIFYING DUPLICATE ON THE RECORD TYPE COMMAND'.

FILE TYPE GROUPED FILE=HUBDATA RECORD=#RECID 80 CASE=ID 1-5.
RECORD TYPE 1.
DATA LIST   /MOHIRED YRHIRED 12-15 DEPT79 TO DEPT82 SEX 16-20.
RECORD TYPE 2  DUPLICATE=NOWARN.
DATA LIST   /SALARY79 TO SALARY82 6-25 HOURLY81 HOURLY82 40-53
(2)
              PROMO81 72  AGE 54-55 RAISE82 66-70.
RECORD TYPE 3.
DATA LIST   /JOBCAT 6 NAME 25-48 (A).
END FILE TYPE.
```

• DUPLICATE is not specified on FILE TYPE. Therefore the default DUPLICATE=WARN is in effect for all record types.

• DUPLICATE=NOWARN is specified on the second RECORD TYPE, overriding the FILE TYPE setting for type 2 records only. WARN is still in effect for type 1 and type 3 records.

SPREAD Subcommand

SPREAD determines whether the values for variables defined for a record type are spread to all the built cases related to that record. SPREAD can be used for NESTED files only. SPREAD cannot be used for MIXED or GROUPED files.

• The only specification is a single keyword. YES is the default.

• SPREAD on RECORD TYPE applies only to those records specified by that RECORD TYPE command. The default YES is in effect for all other defined record types.

YES   *Spread the values in this record type to all cases.* This is the default.

NO   *Spread the values in this record type only to the first case built from the set of records related to this record type.* All other cases built from the same record are assigned the system-missing value for the variables defined on the record type.

Example   TITLE   'A NESTED FILE'.

```
FILE TYPE NESTED RECORD=#RECID 6 CASE=ACCID 1-4.
RECORD TYPE 1.
DATA LIST    /ACC_NO 9-11 WEATHER 12-13 STATE 15-16 (A)
              DATE 18-24(A).
RECORD TYPE 2   SPREAD=NO.
DATA LIST /STYLE 11 MAKE 13 OLD 14 LICENSE 15-16 (A)
           INSURNCE 18-21(A).
RECORD TYPE 3.
DATA LIST /PSNGR_NO 11 AGE 13-14 SEX 16 (A) INJURY 18 SEAT 20-21(A)
           COST 23-24.
END FILE TYPE.

BEGIN DATA
0001 1   322 1 IL 3/13/88   /* Type 1:  accident record
0001 2     1 44MI 134M      /* Type 2:   vehicle record
0001 3     1 34 M 1 FR   3  /* Type 3:     person record
0001 2     2 16IL 322F      /*             vehicle record
0001 3     1 22 F 1 FR  11  /*              person record
0001 3     2 35 M 1 FR   5  /*              person record
0001 3     3 59 M 1 BK   7  /*              person record
0001 2     3 21IN 146M      /*             vehicle record
0001 3     1 46 M 0 FR   0  /*              person record
END DATA.
```

- The first vehicle record has one related person record and the values for STYLE, MAKE, OLD, LICENSE, and INSURNCE are spread to the case built for the person record.

- The second vehicle record has three related person records, and the values for STYLE, MAKE, OLD, LICENSE, and INSURNCE are spread only to the case built from the first person record. The other two persons have the system-missing values for STYLE, MAKE, OLD, LICENSE, and INSURNCE.

- The third vehicle record has one related person record, and the values for type 2 records are spread to that case.

REFORMAT

```
REFORMAT  {ALPHA  } = varlist [/...]
          {NUMERIC}
```

Example:

```
REFORMAT ALPHA=STATE /NUMERIC=HOUR1 TO HOUR6.
```

Overview

REFORMAT converts BMDP files to files with SPSS formats. It also converts files from very old versions of SPSS to files with the current SPSS formats. REFORMAT changes the print formats, write formats, and missing-value specifications for variables from alphanumeric to numeric, or from numeric to alphanumeric. The ALPHA subcommand declares variables as string variables. The NUMERIC subcommand declares variables as numeric variables.

Basic Specification

- The basic specification is ALPHA and a list of variables, or NUMERIC and a list of variables. If both ALPHA and NUMERIC are specified, they must be separated by a slash. REFORMAT converts the variables to SPSS formats.

Syntax Rules

- To declare new format lengths or a different number of decimal places for numeric variables, use the PRINT FORMATS, WRITE FORMATS, or FORMATS commands. Format lengths and decimal places cannot be specified on REFORMAT.

- To declare new format lengths for string variables, use the STRING and COMPUTE commands to perform data transformations. Format lengths cannot be specified on REFORMAT.

- The SAVE or XSAVE commands can be used to save the reformatted variables in an SPSS system file. This avoids the trouble of having to REFORMAT the variable formats each time the SPSS or BMDP data set is used.

Operations

- REFORMAT always assigns the print and write format F8.2 (or the format specified using the SET command) to variables specified after the NUMERIC keyword, and format A4 to variables specified after the ALPHA keyword. Missing-value specifications for variables named with both ALPHA and NUMERIC are also changed to conform to the new formats.

Example

```
TITLE  'CONVERT AN OLD SPSS FILE TO A CURRENT SPSS SYSTEM FILE'.

GET FILE R9FILE.
REFORMAT ALPHA=STATE /NUMERIC=HOUR1 TO HOUR6.
STRING XSTATE (A2) /NAME1 TO NAME6 (A15).
COMPUTE XSTATE=STATE.
FORMATS HOUR1 TO HOUR6 (F2.0).
SAVE OUTFILE=NEWFILE /DROP=STATE
    /RENAME=(XSTATE=STATE).
```

- GET accesses the old SPSS system file.

- REFORMAT converts variable STATE to a string variable with an A4 format. REFORMAT also converts variables HOUR1 TO HOUR6 to numeric variables with F8.2 formats.

- STRING declares XSTATE as a string variable with two positions.

- COMPUTE transfers the information from the old system-file variable STATE to the string variable XSTATE.

- FORMATS changes the F8.2 formats for HOUR1 TO HOUR6 to F2.0 formats.

- SAVE saves a new SPSS system file. The DROP subcommand drops the old SPSS system-file variable STATE, which has an inappropriate format. RENAME renames the new SPSS string variable XSTATE to the original variable name STATE.

REGRESSION

```
REGRESSION [MATRIX=[IN({file})]  [OUT({file})])]]
                       {*   }         {*   }

[/VARIABLES={varlist      }]
            {(COLLECT)**}
            {ALL          }

[/DESCRIPTIVES=[DEFAULTS] [MEAN] [STDDEV] [CORR] [COV]
               [VARIANCE] [XPROD] [SIG] [N] [BADCORR]
               [ALL] [NONE**]]

[/SELECT={varname relation value}

[/MISSING=[{LISTWISE**      }] [INCLUDE]]
           {PAIRWISE        }
           {MEANSUBSTITUTION}

[/WIDTH={132**}]
        {n   }

[/REGWGT=varname]

[/STATISTICS=[DEFAULTS**] [R**] [COEFF**] [ANOVA**] [OUTS**]
             [ZPP] [LABEL] [CHA] [CI] [F] [BCOV] [SES] [LINE]
             [HISTORY] [XTX] [COLLIN] [END] [TOL] [SELECTION] [ALL]]

[/CRITERIA=[DEFAULTS**] [TOLERANCE({0.0001**})]] [MAXSTEPS(n)]
                                  {value    }

        [PIN({0.05**})] [POUT({0.10**})]
             {value }         {value }

        [FIN({3.84 })] [FOUT({2.71 })]
             {value}         {value}

        [CIN({ 95**})]]]
             {value}

[/{NOORIGIN**}]
  {ORIGIN   }

/DEPENDENT=varlist

[/METHOD=]{STEPWISE [varlist]        } [...] [/...]
          {FORWARD [varlist]         }
          {BACKWARD [varlist]        }
          {ENTER [varlist]           }
          {REMOVE varlist            }
          {TEST(varlist)(varlist)...}
```

**Default if the subcommand is omitted.

Example:

```
REGRESSION VARIABLES=POP15,POP75,INCOME,GROWTH,SAVINGS
 /DEPENDENT=SAVINGS
 /METHOD=ENTER POP15,POP75,INCOME
 /METHOD=ENTER GROWTH.
```

Overview REGRESSION calculates multiple regression equations and associated statistics and plots. REGRESSION also calculates collinearity diagnostics, predicted values, residuals, measures of fit and influence, and several statistics based on these (see REGRESSION: Residuals).

Options The options for procedure REGRESSION can be grouped into logically related operations or specifications.

Global-Control Subcommands. These optional subcommands can be named only once and apply to the entire REGRESSION command. DESCRIPTIVES requests descriptive statistics on the variables in the analysis. SELECT estimates the model based on a subset of cases. REGWGT specifies a weight variable for estimating weighted least-squares models. MISSING specifies the treatment of cases with missing values. MATRIX reads and writes SPSS matrix system files.

Equation-Control Subcommands. These optional subcommands control the calculation and display statistics for each equation. STATISTICS controls the statistics displayed, CRITERIA specifies the criteria used by the variable selection method, and ORIGIN specifies whether regression is through the origin.

Display Format. The WIDTH subcommand controls the width of the display for REGRESSION only. It applies to all output from the REGRESSION command.

Analysis of Residuals, Fit, and Influence. The optional subcommands that analyze and plot residuals, and (optionally) add new variables to the active system file containing predicted values, residuals, measures of fit and influence, or related information, are described in REGRESSION: Residuals. These subcommands apply to the final equation, after processing is complete for all METHOD subcommands for a dependent variable.

Basic Specification

The basic specification is DEPENDENT, which initiates the equation(s) and defines at least one dependent variable, and METHOD, which specifies the method to be used in selecting independent variables.

- By default, all variables named on DEPENDENT and METHOD are used in the analysis.

- For each block of variables selected, the default display includes summary statistics for the goodness of fit of the model (including R^2 and analysis of variance), coefficients and related statistics for variables in the equation, and statistics for the variables not yet in the equation.

- By default, all cases in the active system file with valid values for all the selected variables are used to compute the correlation matrix on which the regression equations are based. The default equations include a constant (intercept).

Subcommand Order

The standard subcommand order for REGRESSION is:

```
REGRESSION MATRIX=...
        / VARIABLES=...
        / DESCRIPTIVES=...
        / SELECT=...
        / MISSING=...
        / WIDTH=...
        / REGWGT=...
```

```
                    Equation Block(s)

        / STATISTICS=...
        / CRITERIA=...
        / ORIGIN
        / NOORIGIN
        / DEPENDENT=...

                        Method Block(s)

            / METHOD=...
            [ /METHOD...]...

        / RESIDUALS=...
        / SAVE=...
        / CASEWISE=...
        / SCATTERPLOT=...
        / PARTIALPLOT=...
```

- Subcommands listed outside the boxes apply to the all analyses performed by the REGRESSION command. Subcommands listed in the equation block apply to all methods used in estimating that equation.

- When used, MATRIX must be first.

- A REGRESSION command can include multiple equation blocks, and each equation block can contain multiple METHOD subcommands. These methods are applied, one after the other, to the estimation of the equation.
- The STATISTICS, CRITERIA, and ORIGIN/NOORIGIN subcommands must precede the DEPENDENT subcommand for the equation to which they apply.
- The RESIDUALS, CASEWISE, SCATTERPLOT, SAVE, and PARTIALPLOT subcommands must follow the last METHOD subcommand in an equation block and apply only to the final equation after all METHOD subcommands have been processed.

Syntax Rules

- VARIABLES can be used only once and must be specified before the DEPENDENT and METHOD subcommands. If omitted, VARIABLES defaults to (COLLECT).
- A DEPENDENT subcommand must be followed immediately by one or more METHOD subcommands.
- CRITERIA, STATISTICS, and ORIGIN subcommands remain in effect for all subsequent equations, until replaced.
- More than one DEPENDENT variable can be listed. An equation is estimated for each variable listed on a DEPENDENT subcommand.
- If no variable list is specified on METHOD, all variables named on VARIABLES but not on DEPENDENT will be considered for selection.

Operations

- REGRESSION calculates a correlation matrix that includes all variables named on VARIABLES. All equations requested on the REGRESSION command are calculated from the same correlation matrix.
- The MISSING, DESCRIPTIVES, and SELECT subcommands control the calculation of the correlation matrix and associated displays.
- Multiple METHOD subcommands operate, in sequence, on the equations defined by the preceding DEPENDENT subcommand.
- Only independent variables that pass the tolerance criterion are candidates for entry (see CRITERIA Subcommand).
- If the width set is less than 132, some statistics requested may not be displayed. The WIDTH subcommand within REGRESSION makes it possible to increase the display width and obtain all the statistics available.

Limitations

- There are no programmed limitations beyond global system limitations.

Example

```
REGRESSION VARIABLES=POP15,POP75,INCOME,GROWTH,SAVINGS
/DEPENDENT=SAVINGS
/METHOD=ENTER POP15,POP75,INCOME
/METHOD=ENTER GROWTH.
```

- VARIABLES requests that a correlation matrix of variables POP15 to SAVINGS be calculated for use by REGRESSION.
- DEPENDENT defines a single equation, with SAVINGS as the dependent variable.
- The first METHOD subcommand requests that POP15, POP75, and INCOME be entered into the equation.
- The second METHOD subcommand requests that GROWTH be added to the equation containing POP15 to INCOME.

VARIABLES Subcommand

VARIABLES names all the variables to be used in the analysis with either a variable list or a keyword.

- The minimum specification is a list of two variables or the keyword ALL or (COLLECT). (COLLECT) is the default.
- There cannot be more than one VARIABLES subcommand, and it must precede any DEPENDENT or METHOD subcommands.

• You can name any user-defined variable in the active system file to refer to consecutive variables in the active system file.

• The order of variables in the correlation matrix constructed by REGRESSION is the same as their order on VARIABLES.

• If you omit the VARIABLES subcommand or explicitly specify the default (COLLECT), the order of variables in the correlation matrix is the order in which they are first listed on the DEPENDENT and METHOD subcommands.

You can specify either of the following keywords instead of a variable list:

ALL *Include all user-defined variables in the active system file.*

(COLLECT) *Include all variables named on the DEPENDENT and METHOD subcommands.* If (COLLECT) is used, the METHOD subcommands must have variable lists.

Example
```
REGRESSION VARIABLES=(COLLECT)
 /DEPENDENT=SAVINGS
 /METHOD=STEP POP15 POP75 INCOME
 /METHOD=ENTER GROWTH
 /DEPENDENT=GROWTH
 /METHOD=ENTER INCOME.
```

• (COLLECT) requests that the correlation matrix include SAVINGS, POP15, POP75, INCOME, and GROWTH. Since (COLLECT) is the default, the VARIABLES subcommand could have been omitted in this example.

• The first DEPENDENT subcommand defines a single equation in which SAVINGS is the dependent variable.

• The first METHOD subcommand requests that the block of variables POP15, POP75, and INCOME be considered for inclusion using a stepwise procedure.

• The second METHOD subcommand specifies that variable GROWTH be added to the equation.

• A second DEPENDENT subcommand requests an equation in which GROWTH is the dependent variable.

• INCOME is entered into this equation.

DEPENDENT Subcommand

The required DEPENDENT subcommand specifies a list of variables and requests that an equation be built for each.

• The minimum specification is a single variable. There is no default variable list.

• More than one DEPENDENT subcommand can be specified. Each must be followed by at least one METHOD subcommand.

• Keyword TO on a DEPENDENT subcommand refers to the order in which variables are named on the VARIABLES subcommand. If VARIABLES= (COLLECT), TO refers to the order of variables in the active system file.

• If DEPENDENT names more than one variable, an equation is built for each using the same independent variable(s) and methods.

METHOD Subcommand

The required METHOD subcommand specifies a variable selection method and names a block of variables to be evaluated using that method.

• The minimum specification is a method keyword and, for some methods, a list of variables. Keyword METHOD itself can be omitted.

• The default variable list for methods FORWARD, BACKWARD, STEPWISE, and ENTER consists of all variables named on VARIABLES that are not named on the preceding DEPENDENT subcommand.

• There is no default variable list for the REMOVE and TEST methods.

• If VARIABLES=(COLLECT), you must name the variables.

• Keyword TO in a variable block named on METHOD refers to the order in which variables are named on the VARIABLES subcommand. If VARIABLES= (COLLECT), TO refers to the order of variables in the active system file.

• At least one METHOD subcommand must follow each DEPENDENT subcommand.

• When more than one METHOD subcommand is specified for a single DEPENDENT subcommand, each METHOD subcommand is applied to the equation which resulted from the previous METHOD subcommands.

The available stepwise methods are

BACKWARD [varlist] *Backward elimination.* Variables in the block are considered for removal. At each step, the variable with the largest probability-of-F value is removed, provided that the value is larger than POUT (see CRITERIA Subcommand). If no variables are in the equation when BACKWARD is specified, the independent variables are first entered.

FORWARD [varlist] *Forward entry.* Variables in the block are added to the equation one at a time. At each step, the variable not in the equation with the smallest probability of F is entered if the value is smaller than PIN (see CRITERIA Subcommand).

STEPWISE [varlist] *Stepwise selection.* If there are independent variables already in the equation, the variable with the largest probability of F is removed if this value is larger than POUT. The equation is recomputed omitting the removed variable and the evaluation process is repeated until no more independent variables can be removed. Then, the independent variable not in the equation with the smallest probability of F is entered if this value is smaller than PIN. Then all variables in the equation are again examined for removal. This process continues until no variables in the equation can be removed and no variables not in the equation are eligible for entry, or until the maximum number of steps has been reached (see CRITERIA Subcommand).

The methods that enter or remove the entire variable block in a single step are

ENTER [varlist] *Forced entry.* All variables in the block are entered in a single step in order of decreasing tolerance. If the order in which variables are entered is important, use multiple METHOD=ENTER subcommands.

REMOVE varlist *Forced removal.* All variables are removed in a single step. REMOVE requires a variable list.

TEST (varlist) (varlist) *Calculate R^2 change and its test of significance for sets of independent variables.* This method first adds all variables named on the METHOD=TEST subcommand to the current equation. It then removes in turn each subset from the equation and displays requested statistics. Specify test subsets in parentheses. A variable can be used in more than one subset, and each subset can include any number of variables. Variables named on TEST remain in the equation when the METHOD is completed.

Example
```
REGRESSION VARIABLES=POP15 TO GROWTH, SAVINGS
 /DEPENDENT=SAVINGS
 /METHOD=STEPWISE
 /METHOD=ENTER.
```

• STEPWISE applies the stepwise procedure to variables POP15 to GROWTH.

• All variables not in the equation when the STEPWISE method is complete will be forced into the equation with ENTER.

Example
```
REGRESSION VARIABLES=(COLLECT)
 /DEPENDENT=SAVINGS
 /METHOD=TEST(MEASURE3 TO MEASURE9)(MEASURE3,INCOME)
 /METHOD=ENTER GROWTH.
```

• The VARIABLES=(COLLECT) specification assembles a correlation matrix that includes all variables named on the DEPENDENT and METHOD subcommands. MEASURE3 to MEASURE9 refers to all variables between and including MEASURE3 and MEASURE9 in the active system file.

- REGRESSION first builds the full equation of all the variables named on the first METHOD subcommand: SAVINGS regressed on MEASURE3 TO MEASURE9 and INCOME. For each set of test variables, the R^2 change, F, probability, sums of squares, and degrees of freedom are displayed.
- GROWTH is added to the equation by the second METHOD subcommand. Variables MEASURE3 to MEASURE9 and INCOME are still in the equation when this subcommand is executed.

STATISTICS Subcommand

STATISTICS controls the display of statistics for the equation and for the independent variables.

- If STATISTICS is omitted or if it is specified with no keywords, R, ANOVA, COEFF, and OUTS are displayed (see below).
- If any statistics are specified on STATISTICS, only those statistics specifically requested are displayed.
- A STATISTICS subcommand affects any equations that are subsequently defined and remains in effect until overridden by another STATISTICS subcommand.
- A STATISTICS subcommand cannot be placed between the DEPENDENT and METHOD subcommands.
- If the width is set to less than 132, some requested statistics may not be displayed.

Global Statistics

DEFAULTS *R, ANOVA, COEFF, and OUTS.* These are displayed if STATISTICS is omitted or if it is specified without keywords.

ALL *Display all statistics except F, LINE, and END.*

Equation Statistics

R *Multiple R.* Keyword *R* includes R^2, adjusted R^2, and standard error of the estimate.

ANOVA *Analysis of variance table.* ANOVA includes regression and residual sum of squares, mean square, *F*, and probability of *F*.

CHA *Change in* R^2. CHA includes the change in R^2 between steps, *F* at the end of each step and its probability, and *F* for the equation and its probability. For stepwise methods (BACKWARD, FORWARD, and STEPWISE), these statistics are displayed at the end of each step. For other methods, the statistics are displayed for the variable block.

BCOV *Variance-covariance matrix for unstandardized regression coefficients.* Matrix has covariances below the diagonal, correlations above the diagonal, and variances on the diagonal.

XTX *Swept correlation matrix.*

COLLIN *Collinearity diagnostics.* COLLIN includes the variance inflation factors (VIF), the eigenvalues of the scaled and uncentered cross-products matrix, condition indices, and variance-decomposition proportions (Belsley et al., 1980).

SELECTION *Aids to selecting set of regressors.* SELECTION includes Akaike information criterion (AIC), Ameniya's prediction criterion (PC), Mallow's conditional mean squared error of prediction criterion (Cp), and Schwarz Bayesian criterion (SBC) (Judge et al., 1980).

Statistics for the Independent Variables

COEFF *Regression coefficients.* COEFF includes regression coefficients (B), standard errors of the coefficients, standardized regression coefficients (beta), *t*, and two-tailed probability of *t*.

OUTS *Statistics for variables not yet in the equation that have been named on METHOD subcommands for the equation.* OUTS displays beta, *t*, two-tailed probability of *t*, and minimum tolerance of the variable if it were the only variable entered next.

ZPP *Zero-order, part, and partial correlation.*

CI *95% confidence interval for the unstandardized regression coefficient.*

SES *Approximate standard error of the standardized regression coefficients.* (Meyer & Younger, 1976.)

TOL *Tolerance.* TOL displays tolerance for variables in the equation and, for variables not in the equation, the tolerance each variable would have if it were the only variable entered next.

F *F value for B and its probability.* This is displayed instead of the *t* value.

Step Summary Statistics The full summary line displayed by keywords LINE, END, and HISTORY includes R, R^2, adjusted R^2, F, probability of F, R^2 change, F of the change, probability of R^2 change, and statistics on variables added or removed. For stepwise methods (BACKWARD, FORWARD, and STEPWISE), the statistics refer to each step. For other methods (ENTER, REMOVE, and TEST), the statistics refer to the entire variable block. If other statistics are requested, the summary line may not be produced for a block that does not entail steps.

LINE *Display a single summary line for each step for stepwise methods only.* LINE does not affect direct methods. The default or requested statistics are displayed at the end of each method block for all methods.

END *Display the same summary line produced by LINE after each step for stepwise methods and after each variable block for other methods.* For TEST, the summary line is displayed only if the equation changes. Other default or requested statistics are displayed at the completion of the last METHOD subcommand for the equation.

HISTORY *Display a final summary report.* HISTORY can be requested in addition to LINE or END. For stepwise methods, the report includes a summary line for each step. For ENTER and REMOVE, the report includes a summary line for each method; for TEST, the summary line is displayed only if the equation changes. If HISTORY is the only statistic requested, COEFF is displayed for the final equation.

CRITERIA Subcommand

CRITERIA controls the statistical criteria used in building the regression equations. The way in which these criteria are used depends on the method specified on METHOD. The default criteria are noted in the description of each CRITERIA keyword below.

• The minimum specification is a criterion keyword and its arguments, if any.

• If CRITERIA is omitted or included with no specifications, the default criteria are in effect.

• A CRITERIA subcommand affects any subsequent DEPENDENT and METHOD subcommands and remains in effect until overridden by another CRITERIA subcommand.

• CRITERIA cannot be placed between the DEPENDENT subcommand and its METHOD subcommands.

Tolerance and Minimum Tolerance Criteria Variables must pass both tolerance and minimum tolerance tests in order to enter and remain in a regression equation. Tolerance is the proportion of the variance of a variable in the equation that is not accounted for by other independent variables in the equation. The minimum tolerance of a variable not in the equation is the smallest tolerance any variable already in the equation would have if the variable being considered were included in the analysis.

If a variable passes the tolerance criteria, it is eligible for inclusion based on the method in effect.

Criteria for Variable Selection The ENTER, REMOVE, and TEST methods use only the TOLERANCE criterion.

• BACKWARD removes variables according to the probability of *F*-to-remove (keyword POUT). Specify FOUT to use *F*-to-remove instead.

• FORWARD enters variables according to the probability of *F*-to-enter (keyword PIN). Specify FIN to use *F*-to-enter instead.

• STEPWISE uses both PIN and POUT (or FIN and FOUT) as criteria. If the criterion for entry (PIN or FIN) is less stringent than the criterion for removal (POUT or FOUT), the same variable can cycle in and out until the maximum number of steps is reached. Therefore, if PIN is larger than POUT or FIN is smaller than FOUT, REGRESSION adjusts POUT or FOUT and issues a warning.

DEFAULTS	*PIN(0.05), POUT(0.10), and TOLERANCE(0.0001).* These are the defaults if CRITERIA is omitted. If criteria have been changed, keyword DEFAULTS restores these defaults.
PIN(value)	*Probability of* F-*to-enter.* The default value is 0.05. Either PIN or FIN can be used. If more than one is used, the last mentioned is in effect.
FIN(value)	F-*to-enter.* If no value is specified, the value is 3.84. Either PIN or FIN can be used. If more than one is used, the last mentioned is in effect.
POUT(value)	*Probability of* F-*to-remove.* The default value is 0.10. Either POUT or FOUT can be used. If more than one is used, the last mentioned is in effect.
FOUT(value)	F-*to-remove.* If no value is specified, the value defaults to 2.71. Either POUT or FOUT can be used. If more than one is used, the last mentioned is in effect.
TOLERANCE(value)	*Tolerance.* The default value is 0.0001. If the tolerance chosen is very low, REGRESSION issues a warning.
MAXSTEPS(n)	*Maximum number of steps.* The value of MAXSTEPS is the sum of the maximum number of steps over each method for the equation. The default values are BACKWARD or FORWARD methods: the number of variables meeting PIN/POUT or FIN/FOUT criteria. STEPWISE method: twice the number of independent variables.

Confidence Intervals

CIN(value) *Reset the value of the percent for confidence intervals.* The default is 95%. This sets the percentage interval used in the computation of the temporary variable types MCIN and ICIN. See the Operations section in REGRESSION: Residuals.

Example

```
REGRESSION VARIABLES=POP15 TO GROWTH, SAVINGS
 /CRITERIA=PIN(.1) POUT(.15)
 /DEPENDENT=SAVINGS
 /METHOD=FORWARD
 /CRITERIA=DEFAULTS
 /DEPENDENT=SAVINGS
 /METHOD=STEPWISE.
```

• The first CRITERIA subcommand relaxes the default criteria for entry and removal while the FORWARD method is used. Note that the specified PIN is less than POUT.

• The second CRITERIA subcommand reestablishes the defaults for the second equation.

ORIGIN and NOORIGIN Subcommands

ORIGIN and NOORIGIN control whether or not the constant is suppressed. By default, the constant is included in the model.

• The specification is either the ORIGIN or NOORIGIN subcommand.

• ORIGIN and NOORIGIN must be specified before the DEPENDENT and METHOD subcommands they modify.

• ORIGIN requests regression through the origin. The constant term is suppressed.

• Once specified, ORIGIN remains in effect until NOORIGIN is requested.

• If you specify ORIGIN, statistics requested on the DESCRIPTIVES subcommand are computed as if the mean were 0.

• ORIGIN/NOORIGIN determines the way the correlation matrix is built. These keywords cannot be used to reverse their effect if reading matrix materials. In fact, whichever keyword is specified on the REGRESSION command that writes matrix materials to a system file must also be used in any subsequent procedure that reads that matrix file.

Example
```
REGRESSION VAR=(COL)
 /DEP=HOMICIDE
 /METHOD=ENTER POVPCT
 /ORIGIN
 /DEP=HOMICIDE
 /METHOD=ENTER POVPCT
 /NOORIGIN
 /DEP=POVPCT
 /METHOD=ENTER SOUTHPCT.
```

- The subcommand VAR=(COL) builds a correlation matrix that includes HOMICIDE, POVPCT, and SOUTHPCT.
- The REGRESSION command requests three equations. The first regresses HOMICIDE on POVPCT and includes a constant term because the default (NOORIGIN) is in effect. The second regresses HOMICIDE on POVPCT and suppresses the constant (ORIGIN). The third regresses POVPCT on SOUTHPCT and includes a constant term because NOORIGIN has been specified.

REGWGT Subcommand

The only specification on REGWGT is the name of the variable containing the weights to be used in estimating a weighted least-squares model. With REGWGT the default display is the usual REGRESSION display.

- REGWGT is a global subcommand.
- If more than one REGWGT subcommand is specified on a REGRESSION procedure, only the last one is executed.
- REGWGT can be used with MATRIX OUT, but REGWGT cannot be used with MATRIX IN.
- Residuals saved from equations using the REGWGT command are not weighted. To obtain weighted residuals, residuals created with SAVE should be multiplied by the square root of the weighting variable in a COMPUTE statement.
- REGWGT is in effect for all equations and determines how the correlation matrix is built. Thus, if REGWGT is specified on a REGRESSION procedure that writes matrix materials to a system file, subsequent REGRESSION procedures using that file also will be automatically weighted.

Example
```
REGRESSION VARIABLES=GRADE GPA STARTLEV TREATMNT
 /DEPENDENT=GRADE
 /METHOD=ENTER
 /SAVE PRED(P).
COMPUTE WEIGHT=1/(P*(1-P)).
REGRESSION VAR=GRADE GPA STARTLEV TREATMNT
 /REGWGT=WEIGHT.
 /DEP=GRADE
 /METHOD=ENTER
```

- VARIABLES builds a correlation matrix that includes GRADE, GPA, STARTLEV, and TREATMNT.
- DEPENDENT identifies GRADE as the dependent variable.
- METHOD regresses GRADE on GPA, STARTLEV, and TREATMNT.
- SAVE adds the predicted values from the regression equation to the active system file as the variable P (see REGRESSION: Residuals).
- COMPUTE creates the variable WEIGHT as a transformation of P.
- The second REGRESSION procedure performs a weighted regression analysis on the same set of variables using WEIGHT as the weighting variable.

Example
```
REGRESSION VAR=GRADE GPA STARTLEV TREATMNT
 /REGWGT=WEIGHT
 /DEP=GRADE
 /METHOD=ENTER
 /SAVE RESID(RGRADE).
COMPUTE WRGRADE=RGRADE * SQRT(WEIGHT).
```

- This example illustrates the use of COMPUTE with SAVE to weight the residuals.
- REGRESSION performs a weighted regression analysis of GRADE on GPA, STARTLEV, and TREATMNT, using WEIGHT as the weighting variable.

- SAVE saves the residuals as RGRADE (see REGRESSION: Residuals). These residuals are not weighted.
- COMPUTE computes weighted residuals as WRGRADE in the active system file.

DESCRIPTIVES Subcommand

By default, descriptive statistics are not displayed. Use DESCRIPTIVES to request the display of correlations and descriptive statistics.

- The minimum specification is simply the subcommand keyword, which obtains MEAN, STDDEV, and CORR.
- If DESCRIPTIVES is used with keywords, only those statistics specifically requested are displayed.
- Descriptive statistics are displayed only once for all variables named or implied on VARIABLES.
- Descriptive statistics are based on all valid cases for each variable if PAIRWISE or MEANSUBSTITUTION has been specified on MISSING. Otherwise, only cases included in the computation of the correlation matrix are included in the calculation of the descriptive statistics.
- If regression through the origin has been requested (subcommand ORIGIN), statistics are computed as if the mean were 0.

NONE	*Turn off all descriptive statistics. This is the default if the subcommand is omitted.*
DEFAULTS	*MEAN, STDDEV, and CORR. This is the same as using DESCRIPTIVES without specifications.*
MEAN	*Variable means.*
STDDEV	*Variable standard deviations.*
VARIANCE	*Variable variances.*
CORR	*Correlation matrix.*
SIG	*One-tailed probabilities of the correlation coefficients.*
BADCORR	*Display the correlation matrix only if some coefficients cannot be computed.*
COV	*Covariance matrix.*
XPROD	*Cross-product deviations from the mean.*
N	*Numbers of cases used to compute correlation coefficients.*
ALL	*Display all descriptive statistics.*

Example
```
REGRESSION DESCRIPTIVES=DEFAULTS SIG COV
  /VARIABLES=AGE,FEMALE,YRS_JOB,STARTPAY,SALARY
  /DEPENDENT=SALARY
  /METHOD=ENTER STARTPAY
  /METHOD=ENTER YRS_JOB.
```

- The variable means, variable standard deviations, correlation matrix, one-tailed probabilities of the correlation coefficients, and covariance matrix are displayed.
- Statistics are displayed for all variables named on VARIABLES, even though only variables SALARY, STARTPAY, and YRS_JOB are used to build the equations.
- STARTPAY is entered into the equation by the first METHOD subcommand. YRS_JOB is entered by the second METHOD subcommand.

SELECT Subcommand

By default, all cases in the active system file are considered for inclusion on REGRESSION. Use SELECT to include a subset of cases in the correlation matrix and resulting regression statistics.

- The minimum specification is a logical expression or the keyword ALL (the default if the subcommand is omitted).
- Do not include the variable named on SELECT on the VARIABLES subcommand.

- The logical expression on SELECT is of the form

  ```
  /SELECT=varname relation value
  ```

  where the relation can be EQ, NE, LT, LE, GT, or GE.
- Only cases for which the logical expression on SELECT is true are included in the calculation of the correlation matrix and regression statistics. All other cases, including those with missing values for the variable named on SELECT, are not included in the computations.
- By default, residuals and predicted values are calculated and reported separately for both selected and unselected cases (see REGRESSION: Residuals).
- Cases deleted from the active system file with the SELECT IF, a temporary SELECT IF, or SAMPLE commands are not passed to REGRESSION. Such cases are not reviewed by the SELECT subcommand and are not included among either the selected or unselected cases.
- Do not use a variable from a temporary transformation as a selection variable. If you use a variable created from a temporary transformation (with IF and COMPUTE statements), the variable will disappear when the data are read a second time. The file will be read more than once if you request residuals processing. If the selection variable is the result of a temporary recode specification, the value of the variable will change when the file is read a second time.
- The display of the values of the variable named on SELECT is controlled by that variable's format (see DATA LIST).

Example

```
REGRESSION SELECT SEX EQ 'M'
 /VARIABLES=AGE,STARTPAY,YRS_JOB,SALARY
 /DEPENDENT=SALARY
 /METHOD=STEP
 /RESIDUALS=NORMPROB.
```

- Only cases with the value M for SEX are included in the correlation matrix calculated by REGRESSION.
- Separate normal probability plots are displayed for cases with SEX equal to M and for other cases (see REGRESSION: Residuals).

MATRIX Subcommand

MATRIX reads and writes SPSS matrix system files. It can read files written by previous REGRESSION procedures or files written by other procedures such as CORRELATIONS. Either the IN or OUT keyword is required with MATRIX.

- When used, MATRIX must be the first subcommand specified in a REGRESSION procedure.
- A REGRESSION analysis that performs residual analysis, RESIDUALS, CASEWISE, SCATTERPLOT, PARTIALPLOT, or SAVE, cannot read or write a matrix system file.
- If matrices are to be used for building multiple regression models, some passing through the origin and some not, separate REGRESSION procedures must be used for those models with ORIGIN and those models with NOORIGIN.

OUT(filename) *Write a matrix system file to the designated filename.* Specifying * overwrites the active system file.

IN(filename) *Read a matrix system file from the designated file.* Specifying * reads the active system file.

Format of the Matrix System File

- The file has two special variables created by SPSS: ROWTYPE_ and VARNAME_. Variable ROWTYPE_ is a short string variable having values MEAN, STDDEV, N, and CORR (for Pearson correlation coefficient). Variable VARNAME_ is a short string variable whose values are the names of the variables used to form the correlation matrix. When ROWTYPE_ is CORR, VARNAME_ gives the variable associated with that row of the correlation matrix.
- The remaining variables in the file are the variables used to form the correlation matrix.

• To suppress the constant term when ORIGIN is used in the analysis, value OCORR (rather than value CORR) is written to the matrix system file. OCORR indicates that the regression passes through the origin.

Split Files and Variable Order

• When split variables are present in a matrix system file, they occur first in the file, followed by ROWTYPE_, VARNAME_, and the variables used to form the correlation matrix.

• A full set of matrix materials is written for each subgroup defined by the split variable(s).

• A split variable cannot have the same variable name as any other variable written to the matrix system file.

• If a split file is in effect when a matrix is written, the same split file must be in effect when that matrix is read by any procedure.

Additional Statistics

• REGRESSION always includes with the matrix materials the mean, standard deviation, and number of cases used to compute each coefficient. This information immediately precedes the correlation matrix in the output file.

Missing Values

• With PAIRWISE treatment of missing values, the matrix of N's used to compute each coefficient is included with the matrix materials.

• With LISTWISE treatment (the default) or MEANSUBSTITUTION, a single N used to calculate all coefficients is included in the matrix system file.

Example

```
REGRESSION MATRIX IN(PAY_DATA) OUT(*)
/VARIABLES=AGE,STARTPAY,YRS_JOB,SALARY
/DEPENDENT=SALARY
/METHOD=STEP.
```

• MATRIX IN reads the SPSS matrix system file PAY_DATA.

• A stepwise regression analysis of SALARY is performed on AGE, STARTPAY, and YRS_JOB.

• MATRIX OUT replaces the active system file with the matrix system file that was previously stored in the PAY_DATA file.

MISSING Subcommand

By default, a case that has a user- or system-missing value for any variable named or implied on VARIABLES is omitted from the computation of the correlation matrix on which all analyses are based. Use MISSING to change the treatment of cases with missing values.

• The minimum specification is a keyword specifying a missing-value treatment.

The available keywords are

LISTWISE *Delete cases with missing values listwise.* Only cases with valid values on all variables named on the current VARIABLES subcommand are used. If INCLUDE is also specified, only cases with system-missing values are deleted listwise. LISTWISE is the default if the MISSING subcommand is omitted.

PAIRWISE *Delete cases with missing values pairwise.* Each correlation coefficient is computed using cases with complete data for the pair of variables correlated. If INCLUDE is also specified, only cases with system-missing values are deleted pairwise.

MEANSUBSTITUTION *Replace missing values with the variable mean.* All cases are included and the substitutions are treated as valid observations. If INCLUDE is also specified, user-missing values are included in the computation of the means.

INCLUDE *Include cases with user-missing values.* All user-missing values are treated as valid values. This keyword can be specified along with the methods LISTWISE, PAIRWISE, or MEANSUBSTITUTION.

Example
```
REGRESSION  VARIABLES=POP15,POP75,INCOME,GROWTH,SAVINGS
  /DEPENDENT=SAVINGS
  /METHOD=STEP
  /MISSING=MEANSUBSTITUTION.
```

- Missing values are replaced with the means of the variables when the correlation matrix is calculated.

WIDTH Subcommand

WIDTH controls the width of the display within the REGRESSION procedure.

- The minimum specification is an integer between 72 and 132.
- The default display uses the width specified on SET. The width specified on the WIDTH subcommand within REGRESSION overrides the width on SET for the REGRESSION display only.
- The WIDTH subcommand can appear anywhere.
- If more than one WIDTH subcommand is included, the last WIDTH specified will be in effect for the display.
- If the width is less than 132, some statistics may not be displayed.

Annotated Example

For a complete example with output, see Examples following the Command Reference.

References

Belsley, D. A., E. Kuh, and R. E. Welsch. 1980. *Regression diagnostics: Identifying influential data and sources of collinearity.* New York: John Wiley & Sons.

Berk, K. N. 1977. Tolerance and condition in regression computation. *Journal of the American Statistical Association* 72:863-66.

Judge, G. G., W. E. Griffiths, R. C. Hill, H. Lutkepohl, and T. C. Lee. 1980. *The theory and practice of econometrics.* 2d ed. New York: John Wiley & Sons.

Meyer, L. S., and M. S. Younger. 1976. Estimation of standardized coefficients. *Journal of the American Statistical Association* 71:154-57.

REGRESSION: Residuals

```
REGRESSION  VARIABLES=varlist/ DEPENDENT=varname/ METHOD=method
  [/RESIDUALS=[DEFAULTS] [DURBIN]

       [OUTLIERS({ZRESID      })] [ID (varname)]
                {tempvarlist}

       [NORMPROB({ZRESID     })] [HISTOGRAM({ZRESID      })]
                {tempvarlist}              {tempvarlist}

       [SIZE({SMALL})] [{SEPARATE}]]
             {LARGE}    {POOLED }

  [/CASEWISE=[DEFAULTS] [{OUTLIERS({3     })}]
                        {          {value} }
                        {ALL             }

            [PLOT({ZRESID })]  [{DEPENDENT PRED RESID}]]
                  {tempvar}     {tempvarlist          }

  [/SCATTERPLOT=(varname,*tempvarname)... [SIZE({SMALL})]]
                                               {LARGE}

  [/PARTIALPLOT=[{ALL               }] [SIZE({SMALL})]]
                {varname,varname,...}        {LARGE}

  [/SAVE=tempvar[(newname)] [tempvar[(newname)]... ] [FITS]]
```

Temporary residual variables are:

```
PRED ADJPRED SRESID MAHAL RESID ZPRED SDRESID
COOK DRESID ZRESID SEPRED LEVER
DFBETA SDBETA DFFIT SDFFIT COVRATIO MCIN ICIN
```

SAVE FITS saves:

```
DFFIT, SDFIT, DFBETA, SDBETA, COVRATIO
```

Example:

```
REGRESSION VARIABLES=SAVINGS INCOME POP15 POP75
  /WIDTH=132
  /DEPENDENT=SAVINGS
  /METHOD=ENTER
  /RESIDUALS
  /CASEWISE
  /SCATTERPLOT (*ZRESID *ZPRED)
  /PARTIALPLOT
  /SAVE ZRESID(STDRES) ZPRED(STDPRED).
```

Overview

REGRESSION automatically calculates predicted values, residuals, measures of fit and influence, and several statistics based on these.

Options

The distribution of these statistics can be examined and outliers can be identified. The temporary variables are available for analysis within REGRESSION by means of casewise plots, scatterplots, histograms, normal probability plots, and partial plots of the variables. In addition, any of the residuals subcommands can be specified to obtain descriptive statistics for the predicted values, residuals, and their standardized versions. Any of the temporary variables can be added to the active system file with the SAVE subcommand.

Basic Specification

• All residuals analysis subcommands are optional but most have active defaults that can be requested by including the subcommand without any further specifications. These active defaults are described in the discussion of each subcommand below.

Subcommand Order • The optional residuals subcommands RESIDUALS, CASEWISE, SCATTER-PLOT, and PARTIALPLOT must follow the last METHOD subcommand for an equation.

• If there is more than one dependent variable, residual analysis can be requested for each.

• Residuals subcommands can be specified in any order.

Operations • The residuals subcommands follow the last METHOD subcommand of any equation for which residuals analysis is requested. Statistics are based on this final equation.

• Residuals subcommands affect only the equation they follow.

• The temporary variables PRED, RESID, ZPRED, and ZRESID are calculated and descriptive statistics are printed for these variables whenever any residuals subcommand is specified. Referring to any of the other temporary variables causes additional temporary variables to be calculated.

• Predicted values and statistics based on predicted values are calculated for every observation that has valid values for all variables in the equation.

• Residuals and statistics based on residuals are calculated for all observations that have a valid predicted value and a valid value for the dependent variable.

• The missing-values option therefore affects the calculation of residuals and predicted values.

• The amount of information displayed in a casewise plot is limited by the display width (see REGRESSION).

• The widest page allows a maximum of eight variables in a casewise plot.

• No residuals or predictors are generated for cases deleted from the active system file with the SELECT IF, a temporary SELECT IF, or SAMPLE commands.

• All variables are standardized before plotting. If the unstandardized version of a variable is requested, the standardized version is plotted.

• The residuals subcommands cannot be specified if matrix input is used.

• For each analysis, REGRESSION can calculate several types of temporary variables:

PRED	*Unstandardized predicted values.*
RESID	*Unstandardized residuals.*
DRESID	*Deleted residuals.*
ADJPRED	*Adjusted predicted values.*
ZPRED	*Standardized predicted values.*
ZRESID	*Standardized residuals.*
SRESID	*Studentized residuals.*
SDRESID	*Studentized deleted residuals.* (See Hoaglin & Welsch, 1978.)
SEPRED	*Standard errors of the predicted values.*
MAHAL	*Mahalanobis' distances.*
COOK	*Cook's distances.* (See Cook, 1977.)
LEVER	*Centered leverage values.* (See Velleman & Welsch, 1981.)
DFBETA	*DFBETA.* This is the change in the regression coefficient that results from the deletion of the *i*th case. (See Belsley et al., 1980.) A DFBETA value is computed for each case for each regression coefficient generated in a model.
SDBETA	*Standardized DFBETA.* (See Belsley et al., 1980.) An SDBETA value is computed for each case for each regression coefficient generated in a model.
DFFIT	*DFFIT.* The change in the predicted value when the *i*th case is deleted. (See Belsley et al., 1980.)
SDFIT	*Standardized DFFIT.* (See Belsley et al., 1980.)

COVRATIO	*COVRATIO.* Ratio of the determinant of the covariance matrix with the ith case deleted to the determinant of the covariance matrix with all cases included. (See Belsley et al., 1980.)
MCIN	*Lower and upper bounds for the prediction interval of the mean predicted response.* (See Dillon & Goldstein, 1984.) A lowerbound LMCIN and an upperbound UMCIN are generated. The default confidence interval is 95%. The interval may be reset with the CIN subcommand.
ICIN	*Lower and upper bounds for the prediction interval for a single observation.* (See Dillon & Goldstein, 1984.) A lowerbound LICIN and an upperbound UICIN are generated. The default confidence interval is 95%. The interval may be reset with the CIN subcommand.

Limitations

• There are no programmed limitations beyond global system limitations.

Example

```
REGRESSION VARIABLES=SAVINGS INCOME POP15 POP75
  /WIDTH=132
  /DEPENDENT=SAVINGS
  /METHOD=ENTER
  /RESIDUALS
  /CASEWISE
  /SCATTERPLOT (*ZRESID *ZPRED)
  /PARTIALPLOT
  /SAVE ZRESID(STDRES) ZPRED(STDPRED).
```

• REGRESSION requests a single equation in which SAVINGS is the dependent variable and INCOME, POP15, and POP75 are independent variables.

• RESIDUALS requests the default residuals output.

• Because residuals processing has been requested, statistics for predicted values, residuals, and standardized versions of predicted values and residuals are displayed.

• CASEWISE requests a default casewise plot of ZRESID of cases for which the absolute value of ZRESID is greater than 3. Values of the dependent variable, predicted value, and residual are listed for each case.

• SCATTERPLOT requests a small plot of the standardized predicted value and the standardized residual.

• PARTIALPLOT requests small partial residual plots for all of the independent variables.

• SAVE requests that the standardized residual and the standardized predicted value be added to the active system file as new variables named STDRES and STDPRED.

RESIDUALS Subcommand

RESIDUALS controls the display and labeling of summary information on outliers as well as the display of the Durbin-Watson statistic and histograms and normal probability plots for the temporary variables.

• RESIDUALS without specifications displays a histogram of the standardized residuals, a normal probability plot of the standardized residuals, the values of $CASENUM and ZRESID for the ten cases with the largest absolute value of ZRESID, and the Durbin-Watson test statistic. The default SIZE of both plots is LARGE when no specifications are given.

• If any keyword specifications are given for RESIDUALS, only the displays requested are produced.

DEFAULTS	*SIZE(LARGE), DURBIN, NORMPROB(ZRESID), HISTOGRAM(ZRESID), OUTLIERS(ZRESID).* These are the defaults if RESIDUALS is used without specifications.
SIZE(plotsize)	*Plot sizes.* The plot size can be SMALL or LARGE. The default is large plots if the display width is at least 121 (see REGRESSION) and the page length is at least 58

(see SET). Four small histograms or normal probability plots can be displayed on a single page if the width is 132 (see REGRESSION) and the page length is 59.

HISTOGRAM(tempvars) *Histogram of the standardized temporary variable or variables.* The default is ZRESID. The other temporary variables for which histograms are available are PRED, RESID, ZPRED, DRESID, ADJPRED, SRESID, and SDRESID. The specification of any temporary variable other than these will result in an error.

NORMPROB(tempvars) *Normal probability (P-P) plot of standardized values.* The default is ZRESID. The other temporary variables available for normal probability plots are PRED, RESID, ZPRED, DRESID, ADJPRED, SRESID, and SDRESID. The specification of any temporary variable other than these will result in an error.

OUTLIERS(tempvars) *The ten cases with the largest absolute values of the specified temporary variables.* The default is ZRESID. The listing includes the value of $CASENUM and of the temporary variables for the ten cases. The other temporary variables available for OUTLIERS are RESID, SRESID, SDRESID, DRESID, MAHAL, and COOK. The specification of any temporary variable other than these will result in an error.

DURBIN *Durbin-Watson test statistic.*

ID(varname) *The case identifier on outlier plots.* Any variable on the active system file can be named. ID also labels the list of cases produced by CASEWISE.

POOLED *Display pooled plots and statistics using all cases in the active file when the SELECT subcommand is in effect* (see REGRESSION). The alternative to POOLED is the default keyword SEPARATE, which requests separate reporting of residuals statistics and plots for selected and unselected cases.

Example   /RESID=DEFAULT ID(SVAR)

- DEFAULT produces the default residuals statistics: Durbin-Watson statistic, a normal probability plot and histogram of ZRESID, and an outlier listing for ZRESID.
- Descriptive statistics for ZRESID, RESID, PRED, and ZPRED are automatically displayed.
- ID(SVAR) names SVAR the case identifier on outlier plots. If the CASEWISE subcommand is also included, SVAR is used to label cases in the casewise plot.

CASEWISE Subcommand

CASEWISE requests a casewise plot of residuals. On it you specify a temporary residual variable for casewise plotting (PLOT) and control the selection of cases for plotting (OUTLIERS or ALL). CASEWISE can also be used to specify variables to be listed for each case next to the plot.

- CASEWISE without specifications displays a casewise plot of ZRESID for cases for which the absolute value of ZRESID is at least 3. By default, the values of the case sequence number, DEPENDENT, PRED, and RESID are listed next to the plot entry for each case. To label each point with a case identifier, use the ID keyword on the RESIDUALS subcommand.
- Only those defaults specifically altered are changed.

DEFAULTS *OUTLIERS(3), PLOT(ZRESID), DEPENDENT, PRED, and RESID.* These are the defaults if CASEWISE is used without specifications.

OUTLIERS(value) *Plot only cases for which the absolute standardized value of the plotted variable is at least as large as the value given.* The default value is 3. The alternative to a casewise plot of outliers is a plot of all cases (keyword ALL). Keyword OUTLIERS is ignored if keyword ALL is also present.

ALL   *Include all cases in the casewise plot.* ALL is the alternative to keyword OUTLIERS.

PLOT(tempvar)   *Plot the standardized values of the temporary variable in the casewise plot.* The default temporary variable is ZRESID. Other variables that can be plotted are RESID, DRESID, SRESID, and SDRESID. The specification of any temporary variable other than these will result in an error.

temp varlist   *Display the values of these variables for each case next to its casewise plot entry.* The default variables are DEPENDENT (the dependent variable), PRED, and RESID. Any of the other temporary variables can be also named. If an ID variable is specified on RESIDUALS, the ID variable is also listed if the width is sufficient.

Example   `/CASEWISE=DEFAULT ALL SRE MAH COOK SDR`

- This example requests a casewise plot of the standardized residuals for all cases.
- The dependent variable and the temporary variables PRED, RESID, SRESID, MAHAL, COOK, and SDRESID are also listed for all cases.

SCATTERPLOT Subcommand

SCATTERPLOT names pairs of variables for scatterplots and controls the size of the plots.

- The minimum specification for SCATTERPLOT is a pair of variables in parentheses.
- There are no default specifications for SCATTERPLOT.
- The first variable named in each set of parentheses is plotted along the vertical axis, and the second variable is plotted along the horizontal axis.
- Specify as many pairs of variables in parentheses as you want.
- Plotting symbols are used to represent multiple points occurring at the same print position.
- Specify the temporary variable names with a asterisk prefix to distinguish temporary from user-defined variables.
- All scatterplots are standardized. That is, specifying *RESID is the same as specifying *ZRESID, and *PRED is the same as *ZPRED.

(varname,varname)   *Plot the variables specified.* Available temporary variables are PRED, RESID, ZPRED, ZRESID, DRESID, ADJPRED, SRESID, SDRESID, along with any variable on VARIABLES. The specification of any temporary variable other than these will result in an error.

SIZE(plotsize)   *Plot sizes.* The plot size can be either SMALL or LARGE. The default is always small. Four small scatterplots can be displayed on a single page if the width is at least 121 (see REGRESSION) and the page length is at least 58 (see SET).

Example   `/SCATTERPLOT (*RES,*PRE)(*RES,SAVINGS)`

- This example specifies two scatterplots: residuals against predicted values and residuals against the values of the variable SAVINGS.

PARTIALPLOT Subcommand

Use PARTIALPLOT to request partial residual plots and to control the size of the plots. Partial residual plots are scatterplots of the residuals of the dependent variable and an independent variable when both of these variables are regressed on the rest of the independent variables.

- If PARTIALPLOT is included without specifications, a partial residual plot is produced for every independent variable in the equation.
- All plots are standardized.

- Plots are displayed in descending order of the standard errors of the regression coefficients.

varlist *List of variables to be plotted.* Any variable entered into the equation can be named. At least two independent variables must be in the equation for partial residual plots to be produced. The default is every independent variable in the equation. You can request the default with keyword ALL.

SIZE(plotsize) *Plot sizes.* The plotsize can be either SMALL or LARGE. The default is always small. Four small partial plots can be displayed on a single page if the width is at least 121 (see REGRESSION) and the page length is at least 58 (see SET).

Example
```
REGRESSION VARS=PLOT15 TO SAVINGS
  /DEP=SAVINGS
  /METH=ENTER
  /RESID=DEFAULTS
  /PARTIAL.
```

- A partial residual plot is produced for every independent variable in the equation.

SAVE Subcommand

Use SAVE to add new variables to the active system file containing one or more temporary residual or fit variables.

- Specifications for SAVE consist of one or more of the temporary variable types (see Operations, above), each optionally followed by a new variable name in parentheses.
- New variable names must be unique.
- If temporary variable types are specified without new variable names, the procedure generates a stem corresponding to a shortened form of the temporary variable name with a suffix to identify its creation sequence.
- If you specify DFBETA or SDBETA on the SAVE subcommand, the number of new variables saved is equal to the total number of variables in the equation.

FITS *Save all influence statistics.* Save DFFIT, SDFIT, DFBETA, SDBETA, and COVRATIO. You cannot specify new variable names when using this keyword. Default names will be generated.

Example `/SAVE=PRED(PREDVAL) RESID(RESIDUAL) COOK(CDISTANC)`

- This subcommand adds three variables to the end of the file: PREDVAL, containing the unstandardized predicted value for the case, RESIDUAL, containing the unstandardized residual for the case, and CDISTANC, containing Cook's distance for the case.

Example `/SAVE=PRED RESID`

- This subcommand adds two variables, named PRE_1 and RES_1, to the end of the file.

Example
```
REGRESSION DEPENDENT=Y
  /METHOD=ENTER X1 X2
  /SAVE DFBETA(DFBVAR).
```

- The SAVE subcommand will create and save three new variables with the names DFBVAR0, DFBVAR1, and DFBVAR2.

Example
```
REGRESSION VARIABLES=SAVINGS INCOME POP15 POP75 GROWTH
  /DEPENDENT=SAVINGS
  /METHOD=ENTER INCOME POP15 POP75
  /SAVE=PRED(PREDV) SDBETA(BETA) ICIN.
```

- The SAVE subcommand adds seven variables to the end of the file: PREDV, containing the unstandardized predicted value for the case; BETA0, the standardized DFBETA for the intercept; BETA1, BETA2, and BETA3, the standardized DFBETA's for the three independent variables in the model; LICL_1, the lower bound for the prediction interval for an individual case; and UICL_1, the upper bound for the prediction interval for an individual case.

Annotated Example   For a complete example with output, see Examples following the Command Reference.

References

Belsley, D. A., E. Kuh, and R. E. Welsch. 1980. *Regression diagnostics: Identifying influential data and sources of collinearity.* New York: John Wiley & Sons.

Cook, R. D. 1977. Detection of influential observations in linear regression. *Technometrics* 19:15–18.

Dillon, W. R., and M. Goldstein. 1984. *Multivariate analysis: Methods and applications.* New York: John Wiley & Sons.

Hoaglin, D. C., and R. E. Welsch. 1978. The hat matrix in regression and ANOVA. *American Statistician* 32:17–22.

Velleman, P. F., and R. E. Welsch. 1981. Efficient computing of regression diagnostics. *American Statistician* 35:234–42.

RELIABILITY

```
RELIABILITY VARIABLES={varlist}
                      {ALL    }

[/SCALE(scalename)=varlist [/SCALE... ]]

[/MODEL={ALPHA        }] [/VARIABLES...]
        {SPLIT[(n)]   }
        {GUTTMAN      }
        {PARALLEL     }
        {STRICTPARALLEL}

[/STATISTICS=[DESCRIPTIVE] [SCALE     ] [{ANOVA   }] [ALL]]
             [COV        ] [TUKEY     ] {FRIEDMAN}
             [CORR       ] [HOTELLING ] {COCHRAN }

[/SUMMARY=[MEANS   ] [COV ] [TOTAL]]
          [VARIANCE] [CORR] [ALL  ]

[/METHOD=COV]

[/FORMAT={LABELS**}]
         {NOLABELS}

[/MISSING={EXCLUDE**}]
          {INCLUDE  }

[/MATRIX =[IN({*   })] [OUT({*   })] [NOPRINT]]
             {file}         {file}
```

**Default if the subcommand is omitted.

Example:
```
RELIABILITY  VARIABLES=SCORE1 TO SCORE10
   /SCALE (OVERALL) = ALL
   /MODEL = ALPHA
   /SUMMARY = MEANS TOTAL.
```

Overview   RELIABILITY estimates reliability statistics for the components of multiple-item additive scales. It uses any of five models for reliability analysis and offers a great variety of statistical displays. RELIABILITY can also be used to perform a repeated measures design analysis of variance, a two-way factorial analysis of variance with one observation per cell, Tukey's test for additivity, Hotelling's T^2 test for equality of means in repeated measures designs, and Friedman's two-way analysis of variance on ranks. For more complex repeated measures designs, see MANOVA.

Options   **Model Type.** You can specify any of five models.

Statistical Display. Available statistics include descriptive statistics, correlation and covariance matrices, a repeated-measures analysis-of-variance table, Hotelling's T^2, Tukey's test for additivity, Friedman's chi-square for the analysis of ranked data, and Cochran's Q.

Computational Method. You can force RELIABILITY to use the covariance method, even when you are not requesting any output that requires it.

Matrix Materials. You can read data in the form of cases or correlation matrices. In addition, you can write correlation-type matrix materials to a system file.

Basic Specification   • The basic specification is VARIABLES and a variable list. By default, RELIABILITY displays the number of cases, number of items, and Cronbach's α. Whenever possible, it uses an algorithm that does not require the calculation of the covariance matrix.

Subcommand Order   • VARIABLES must be first.
• Remaining subcommands can be named in any order.

Operations
- STATISTICS and SUMMARY are cumulative. If you enter them more than once, all requested statistics are produced for each scale.
- If you request output that is not available for your model or for your data, RELIABILITY ignores the request.
- RELIABILITY uses an economical algorithm whenever possible but calculates a covariance matrix when necessary (see METHOD Subcommand).

Limitations
- Maximum 10 VARIABLES subcommands.
- Maximum 50 SCALE subcommands.
- Maximum 500 variables referenced on the combined VARIABLES subcommands. Each mention of a variable counts one toward this limit.
- Maximum 500 variables referenced on one SCALE subcommand.
- Maximum 1,000 variables referenced on the combined SCALE subcommands. Each mention of a variable counts one toward this limit.
- If insufficient workspace is available to handle multiple VARIABLES subcommands, RELIABILITY deletes them in the reverse order in which they were specified until the allocated workspace is sufficient.

Example
```
RELIABILITY  VARIABLES=SCORE1 TO SCORE10
    /SCALE (OVERALL) = ALL
    /SCALE (ODD) = SCORE1 SCORE3 SCORE5 SCORE7 SCORE9
    /SUMMARY = MEANS TOTAL.
```
- This example analyzes two additive scales composed of the variables (or items) from SCORE1 to SCORE10.
- One scale (labeled **OVERALL** in the display output) is composed of all ten items. Another (labeled **ODD**) is composed of every other item.
- Summary statistics are displayed for each scale, showing item means and the relation of each item to the total scale.

Example
```
RELIABILITY  VARIABLES=SCORE1 TO SCORE10.
```
- One scale (labeled ALL in the display output) is composed of all ten items.
- Because there is no SUMMARY subcommand, no summary statistics are displayed.

VARIABLES Subcommand

VARIABLES specifies the variables to be used in the analysis. Only numeric variables can be used.

- VARIABLES is required and must be specified first.
- You can use keyword ALL to refer to all user-defined variables in the active system file.
- You can specify VARIABLES more than once in a single RELIABILITY command. Each VARIABLES subcommand builds a covariance matrix and vector of means. Cases with missing values are deleted from the computation of the matrix.

SCALE Subcommand

SCALE defines a scale for analysis, providing a name for the scale, and specifying its component variables. If SCALE is omitted, all variables named on VARIABLES are used, and the name for the scale is ALL. If SCALE is used, specify:

- A name for the scale, in parentheses. The name can be a maximum of eight characters and can use only the letters A to Z and the numbers 0 to 9. This name is used only to label the output from RELIABILITY. RELIABILITY does not add any new variables to the active system file. If the analysis is satisfactory, use COMPUTE to create a new variable containing the sum of the component items.
- A list of variables to be used as components for the additive scale. Use keyword ALL to refer to all variables named on the preceding VARIABLES subcommand.

RELIABILITY analyzes the scale formed by adding the component variables.

- Variables named on SCALE must have been named on the previous VARIABLES subcommand.
- To analyze different groups of the component variables, specify SCALE more than once following a VARIABLES subcommand.

Example
```
RELIABILITY VARIABLES = ITEM1 TO ITEM20
  /SCALE (A) = ITEM1 TO ITEM10
  /SCALE (B) = ITEM1 ITEM3 ITEM5 ITEM16 TO ITEM20
  /SCALE (C) = ALL.
```

- This command analyzes three different scales: scale A has 10 items, scale B has 8 items, and scale C has 20 items.

MODEL Subcommand

MODEL specifies the type of reliability analysis for the scale on the preceding SCALE subcommand. If you do not specify MODEL, ALPHA is the default. Available models are:

ALPHA
Cronbach's α. *Standardized item* α *is also displayed if* METHOD=COV. *This is the default.*

SPLIT
Split-half coefficients. By default, the first half of the items is compared with the last half of the items (with the odd item, if any, going to the first half). You can specify a number in parentheses to override this default division, indicating how many items should be in the second half. For example, MODEL SPLIT (6) takes the last six variables for the second half, with all others in the first half.

GUTTMAN
Guttman's lower bounds for true reliability.

PARALLEL
Maximum-likelihood reliability estimate under parallel assumptions. This model assumes that items have the same variance, but not necessarily the same mean.

STRICTPARALLEL
Maximum-likelihood reliability estimate under strictly parallel assumptions. This model assumes that items have the same means, the same true score variances over a set of objects being measured, and the same error variance over replications.

STATISTICS Subcommand

STATISTICS displays optional statistics. There are no default statistics. After STATISTICS, you can specify one or more of the following:

DESCRIPTIVES *Item means and standard deviations.*

COVARIANCES *Inter-item variance-covariance matrix.*

CORRELATIONS *Inter-item correlation matrix.*

SCALE *Scale mean(s) and scale variance(s).*

TUKEY
Tukey's test for additivity. This helps determine whether a transformation of the items in your scale is needed to reduce non-additivity. The test displays an estimate of the power to which the items should be raised in order to be additive.

HOTELLING
Hotelling's T^2. This is a test for equality of means among the items.

ANOVA *Repeated-measures analysis of variance table.*

FRIEDMAN
Friedman's chi-square and Kendall's coefficient of concordance. These apply to ranked data. You must request ANOVA in addition to FRIEDMAN; the Friedman chi-square appears in place of the usual *F* test.

COCHRAN
Cochran's Q. This applies when all of the items are dichotomies. You must request ANOVA in addition to COCHRAN; the *Q* statistic appears in place of the usual *F* test.

ALL *All applicable statistics.*

The STATISTICS subcommand is cumulative. If you enter it more than once, all statistics that you request are produced for each scale.

SUMMARY Subcommand

SUMMARY displays summary statistics for each individual item in the scale. After SUMMARY, you can specify one or more of the following:

MEANS
Statistics on item means. The average, minimum, maximum, range, ratio of maximum to minimum, and variance of the item means.

VARIANCE
Statistics on item variances. Same statistics as for MEANS.

COVARIANCES
Statistics on item covariances. Same statistics as for MEANS.

CORRELATIONS
Statistics on item correlations. Same statistics as for MEANS.

TOTAL
Statistics comparing each individual item to the scale composed of the other items. Includes the scale mean, variance, and Cronbach's α without the item, and the correlation between the item and the scale without it.

ALL
All applicable summary statistics.

The SUMMARY subcommand is cumulative. If you enter it more than once, all statistics that you request are produced for each scale.

METHOD Subcommand

Two computational methods are available with the RELIABILITY procedure. The space-saver method does not require the calculation of a covariance matrix and is used whenever possible. RELIABILITY does compute the covariance matrix for all variables on each VARIABLES subcommand if any of the following is true:

- You specify a model other than ALPHA or SPLIT.
- You request COV, CORR, FRIEDMAN, or HOTELLING on the STATISTICS subcommand.
- You request anything other than TOTAL on the SUMMARY subcommand.
- You write the matrix to a matrix system file, using MATRIX=OUT(file).

Even if none of these conditions applies, you can force RELIABILITY to use the covariance matrix with the METHOD subcommand. Only a single specification applies:

COVARIANCE
Calculate and use the covariance matrix, even if it is not needed.

FORMAT Subcommand

By default, RELIABILITY displays the variable label of each variable in the scale before reporting on the analysis. FORMAT lets you suppress this initial display of variable names and labels. Specify one of the following after FORMAT:

LABELS
Display names and labels for all items before the analysis. This is the default.

NOLABELS
Do not display names and labels.

MISSING Subcommand

RELIABILITY deletes cases from analysis if they have a missing value for any variable named on the current VARIABLES subcommand. By default, both system-missing and user-missing values are excluded. Use MISSING to control deletion of missing data. Specify one of the following after MISSING:

EXCLUDE
Exclude user-missing as well as system-missing values. This is the default.

INCLUDE
Treat user-missing values as valid, excluding only system-missing values.

MATRIX Subcommand

MATRIX reads and writes SPSS matrix system files. It writes correlation-type matrices and includes the N's, means, and standard deviations with the matrix materials. These matrix materials can be used by RELIABILITY or other procedures (see the table of matrix types in Universals: Matrix System Files).

- Either IN or OUT is required to specify the matrix file in parentheses. When both IN and OUT are used on the same RELIABILITY procedure, they can be specified on separate MATRIX subcommands, or both on the same subcommand.

- If both IN and OUT are used on the same RELIABILITY command and there are one or more grouping variables, these variables are treated as if they were split variables. Values of the grouping variables are passed on to the output matrix.

Matrix Output

- RELIABILITY writes only correlation-type matrices and includes the number of cases, mean, and standard deviation with the matrix materials.

- Documents from the original file will not be included in the matrix file and will not be present if the matrix file becomes the active system file.

- RELIABILITY displays the scale analyses when it writes matrix materials. If you don't want the scale analyses to display, specify keyword NOPRINT on MATRIX.

Matrix Input

- RELIABILITY can read a matrix written to the active system file by a previous RELIABILITY command or by another procedure. The matrix input file must have records of type N, MEAN, STDDEV, and CORR for each split-file group.

- SPSS reads variable names, variable and value labels, and print and write formats from the dictionary of the matrix system file.

- MATRIX=IN cannot be used in place of GET or DATA LIST to begin a new SPSS command file. MATRIX is a subcommand on RELIABILITY, and RELIABILITY cannot run before an active system file is defined.

- To begin a new command file and immediately read a matrix, first GET the matrix file, then specify IN(*) on MATRIX.

OUT *Write a matrix system file.* Specify either a file or an asterisk, and enclose the specification in parentheses. If you specify a file, the file is stored on disk and can be retrieved at any time. If you specify an asterisk (*), the matrix system file replaces the active system file but is not stored on disk unless you use SAVE or XSAVE.

IN *Read a matrix system file.* If the matrix system file *is not* the current active system file, specify a file in parentheses. If the matrix system file *is* the current active system file, specify an asterisk (*) in parentheses.

Format of the Matrix System File

- The matrix system file includes two special variables created by SPSS: ROWTYPE_ and VARNAME_. Variable ROWTYPE_ is a short string variable having values N, MEAN, STDDEV, and CORR. Variable VARNAME_ is a short string variable whose values are the names of the variables used to form the correlation matrix. When ROWTYPE_ is CORR, VARNAME_ gives the variable associated with that row of the correlation matrix.

- The remaining variables in the matrix file are the variables used to form the correlation matrix.

Split Files and Variable Order

- When split-file processing is in effect, the first variables in the matrix system file will be the split variables, followed by ROWTYPE_, VARNAME_, and the dependent variable(s).

- If grouping variables are in the matrix input file (for example, if you are reading matrix materials written by a procedure such as DISCRIMINANT), their values display between ROWTYPE_ and VARNAME_. However, though grouping variables are displayed among the matrix variables, they are treated like split-file variables and do not affect computations.

- A full set of matrix materials is written for each split-file group defined by the split variable(s).

- A split variable cannot have the same variable name as any other variable written to the matrix system file.

- If split-file processing is in effect when a matrix is written, the same split file must be in effect when that matrix is read by any procedure.

Additional Statistics

- RELIABILITY writes only correlation-type matrices that include the number of cases, mean, and standard deviation for each split-file group. An input matrix must have all these records in order for RELIABILITY to read the matrix materials.

Missing Values

- Missing-value treatment affects the values written to a matrix system file. When reading a matrix system file, be sure to specify a missing-value treatment on RELIABILITY that is compatible with the treatment used to generate the matrix materials.

Example

```
DATA LIST / TIME1 TO TIME5 1-10.
BEGIN DATA
 0 0 0 0 0
 0 0 1 1 0
 0 0 1 1 1
 0 1 1 1 1
 0 0 0 0 1
 0 1 0 1 1
 0 0 1 1 1
 1 0 0 1 1
 1 1 1 1 1
 1 1 1 1 1
END DATA.
RELIABILITY  VARIABLES=TIME1 TO TIME5
   /MATRIX=OUT(RELMTX).
LIST.
```

- RELIABILITY reads raw data from the active system file and writes one set of matrix materials to file RELMTX.

- The active system file is still the file defined by DATA LIST. Subsequent commands are executed on the file defined by DATA LIST.

Example

```
DATA LIST  / TIME1 TO TIME5 1-10.
BEGIN DATA
 0 0 0 0 0
 0 0 1 1 0
 0 0 1 1 1
 0 1 1 1 1
 0 0 0 0 1
 0 1 0 1 1
 0 0 1 1 1
 1 0 0 1 1
 1 1 1 1 1
 1 1 1 1 1
END DATA.
RELIABILITY  VARIABLES=TIME1 TO TIME5
   /MATRIX=OUT(*) NOPRINT.
LIST.
```

- RELIABILITY writes the same matrix as in the example above. However, the matrix system file replaces the active system file. The LIST command is executed on the matrix file, not on the file defined by DATA LIST.

- Because NOPRINT is specified on MATRIX, the scale analyses are not displayed with matrix output.

Example

```
GET FILE=RELMTX.
RELIABILITY VARIABLES=ALL
   /MATRIX=IN(*).
```

- This example assumes that you are starting a new session and want to read an existing matrix system file. GET retrieves the matrix system file RELMTX.

- MATRIX=IN specifies an asterisk because the current active system file is the matrix system file RELMTX. MATRIX=IN must therefore specify the active system file as the file from which the matrix materials will be read.

- If the GET command is omitted, SPSS issues an error message.

- If MATRIX=IN(RELMTX) is specified, SPSS issues an error message.

Example

```
GET FILE=PRSNNL.
FREQUENCIES VARIABLE=AGE.

RELIABILITY VARIABLES=ALL
   /MATRIX=IN(RELMTX).
```

- This example assumes that you want to perform a frequencies analysis on file PRSNNL and then use RELIABILITY to read a different file. The file you want to read is an existing matrix system file. In order for this to work, the analysis variables named in RELMTX must also exist in PRSNNL.

- RELMTX must have records of type N, MEAN, STDDEV, and CORR for each split-file group.
- RELMTX does not replace PRSNNL as the active system file.

Example

```
GET FILE=RAWDATA.
CORRELATIONS VARIABLES=V1 TO V5
  /MATRIX=OUT(*).
RELIABILITY VARIABLES=V1 TO V5
  /MATRIX=IN(*).
```

- RELIABILITY uses matrix input from procedure CORRELATIONS. An asterisk is used to specify the active file for both the matrix output from CORRELATIONS and the matrix input for RELIABILITY.

Annotated Example

For a complete example with output, see Examples following the Command Reference.

RENAME VARIABLES

```
RENAME VARIABLES {(varname=varname)  [(varname ...)]}
                 {(varlist=varlist)                }
```

Example:
```
RENAME VARIABLES (JOBCAT=TITLE).
```

Overview

RENAME VARIABLES changes the names of variables in the active system file while preserving their original order, values, variable labels, value labels, missing values, and print and write formats. It is especially useful for renaming variables that have been generated and named by an SPSS statistical procedure, such as the Z-score transformation variables generated by the DESCRIPTIVES command.

Basic Specification

• The basic specification is in the form *old varname=new varname.* The equals sign is required. Multiple sets of variable specifications are allowed. Each set may be enclosed in optional parentheses.

Syntax Rules

• Name changes can be specified with a list of old variable names followed by a required equals sign and a list of new variable names. The same number of variables must be specified on both lists.

• Keyword TO can be used in either or both variable lists to refer to consecutive variables. A single set of parentheses enclosing the entire specification is required for this method.

• Old variable names need not be specified according to their order in the active system file.

• Name changes take place in one operation. Therefore, variable names can be exchanged between two variables.

• Multiple RENAME VARIABLES commands are allowed.

Limitations

• RENAME VARIABLES cannot follow either a TEMPORARY or a MODEL PARAMETERS command.

Example

```
RENAME VARIABLES (JOBCAT=TITLE).
```

• RENAME VARIABLES changes variable name JOBCAT to TITLE. The parentheses are optional.

Example

```
RENAME VARIABLES (MOHIRED=MOSTART) (YRHIRED=YRSTART).
RENAME VARIABLES (MOHIRED YRHIRED=MOSTART YRSTART).
```

• In each example, MOHIRED is renamed to MOSTART and YRHIRED is renamed to YRSTART. The parentheses are optional in the first example but required in the second.

Example

```
RENAME VARIABLES (A=B) (B=A).
```

• Variable names are exchanged between two variables: A is renamed to B, and B is renamed to A. This is possible because name changes take place in one operation.

REPEATING DATA

```
REPEATING DATA [FILE=file] /STARTS=beg pos[-end pos]
   /OCCURS={value  }
           {varname}

[/LENGTH={value  }] [/CONTINUED[=beg pos[-end pos]]]
         {varname}

[/ID={col loc}=varname] [/{TABLE  }]
     {format }           {NOTABLE}

   /DATA=data list specifications
```

Example:

```
INPUT PROGRAM.
DATA LIST / SEQNUM 2-4 NUMPERS 6-7 NUMVEH 9-10.
REPEATING DATA STARTS=12 /OCCURS=NUMVEH
 /DATA=MAKE 1-8 (A) MODEL 9 (A) NUMCYL 10.
END INPUT PROGRAM.

BEGIN DATA
1001 02 02 FORD    T8PONTIAC C6
1002 04 01 CHEVY   C4
1003 02 03 CADILAC C8FORD    T6VW     C4
END DATA.
LIST.
```

Overview

REPEATING DATA reads input cases whose records contain repeating groups of data. For each repeating group, REPEATING DATA builds one output case in the active system file. In effect, REPEATING DATA generates a LEAVE command that references all previously defined variables.

All the repeating groups in the data must contain the same type of information, though the number of groups on each input case may vary. Information common to the repeating groups on a single input case can be recorded once for that case and then spread to each resulting output case. In this respect, a file with a repeating data structure is like a hierarchical file with both levels of information recorded on a single record rather than on separate record types. For information on reading hierarchical files, see FILE TYPE.

REPEATING DATA must be used within an INPUT PROGRAM structure, or within a FILE TYPE structure with MIXED or NESTED data. In an INPUT PROGRAM structure, REPEATING DATA must be preceded by a DATA LIST command. In a FILE TYPE structure, the DATA LIST command may not be necessary. DATA LIST is used to define those variables on each input case that are spread to each resulting output case; REPEATING DATA is used to define the variables within the repeating groups.

Input Programs

When session commands are submitted for execution, SPSS builds a dictionary for the active system file as it encounters commands that create and define variables. At the same time, SPSS builds an *input program* that constructs cases and an optional *transformation program* that modifies cases prior to analysis or display. By the time SPSS encounters a procedure command that tells it to read the data, the dictionary of the active system file is ready and the programs that construct and modify the active system file cases are built. See the discussion of system file dictionaries in Universals. Applications that make up the transformation program are discussed under the individual command name.

The input program is usually built from either a single DATA LIST command or any of the commands that read or combine system files (for example GET, MATCH FILES, and ADD FILES). The input program can also be specified with the INPUT PROGRAM and END INPUT PROGRAM commands. The third type of input program is built from the FILE TYPE— END FILE TYPE structure used to define nested or mixed files.

REPEATING DATA can only be used in an input program explicitly specified with the INPUT PROGRAM—END INPUT PROGRAM commands, or in a FILE TYPE—END FILE TYPE structure for MIXED or NESTED file types. REPEATING DATA cannot be used with FILE TYPE GROUPED.

Options   **Length of Repeating Groups.** If you do not want to read all the data columns in each repeating group, or if the length of the repeating groups varies across input cases, you can specify a length for repeating groups. See LENGTH Subcommand.

Continuation Records. You can read data when the repeating groups for each input case are continued on successive records (see CONTINUED Subcommand). You can also compare the value of an identification variable across records of the same input case (see ID Subcommand).

Summary Tables. You can suppress the display of the summary table that lists the names, locations, and format types of the variables specified on the DATA subcommand. See the TABLE and NOTABLE subcommands.

Basic Specification   The basic specification requires three subcommands: STARTS, OCCURS, and DATA.

- STARTS specifies the beginning position of the repeating data segments. Optionally when there are continuation records, STARTS can specify the ending position of the last repeating group on the first record of each input case.
- OCCURS specifies the number of repeating groups on each input case. OCCURS can specify a number if the number of repeating groups is the same on all input cases. Otherwise, OCCURS should specify the name of a previously defined variable whose value for each input case indicates the number of repeating groups on that case.
- DATA specifies a variable name, location within the repeating segment, and format type for each variable to be read from the repeated groups.

Subcommand Order   - DATA must be the last subcommand specified on REPEATING DATA.
- Remaining subcommands can be named in any order.

Syntax Rules   - REPEATING DATA can be used only within an INPUT PROGRAM structure, or within a FILE TYPE structure with MIXED or NESTED data. DATA LIST, REPEATING DATA, and any transformation commands used to build the output cases must be placed within the INPUT PROGRAM or FILE TYPE structure. Transformations that apply to the built cases, however, should be placed after the END INPUT PROGRAM or END FILE TYPE command.
- LENGTH must be used if the last variable specified on the DATA subcommand is not read from the last position of each repeating group, or if the length of the repeating groups varies across input cases.
- CONTINUED must be used if repeating groups for each input case are continued on successive records.
- Because the REPEATING DATA command creates cases, the DATA LIST command used with REPEATING DATA must define all fixed-format data for the records, even if the fixed-format data follow the repeating data. (Repeating groups are usually recorded at the end of records rather than within them, but you may encounter the problem in data structures such as IBM SMF and RMF records.) The following sequence might help in extreme cases:

```
DATA LIST ...
REREAD  COLUMNS= ...
DATA LIST ...
REPEATING DATA ...
```

Operations   - Fixed-location data specified on any DATA LIST are spread to each output case built on the active system file.
- If LENGTH is not specified, SPSS uses the default length, which is determined from specifications on the DATA subcommand. For more information on the default length, see LENGTH Subcommand.

Cases Generated   - Barring a data error on the ID variable or the variable specifying the starting or ending column, the number of output cases generated will be as specified by OCCURS. Physical record length or whether fields are non-blank have nothing to do with the number of cases generated. If the parameter specified for OCCURS is non-positive or missing, no cases are generated.

Records Read
- If CONTINUED is not specified, all repeating groups are read from the first record of each input case, regardless of the length of that record. Thus, continuation records cannot be read unless CONTINUED is used.

- If CONTINUED is specified, the first continuation record is read when the first record for the input case is exhausted. Exhaustion for the first record is detected when the next repeating group would extend past the end of the record. The ending column for the first record is defined on STARTS. If the ending column is not specified on STARTS, the host system's record length is used. For inline data, the record length is always 80. For data stored in a file, the record length is generally whatever was specified on the FILE HANDLE command, and shorter records are extended with blanks when they are read. For IBM implementations, the physical record length is available and is used.

- Subsequent continuation records are read when the current continuation record is exhausted. Exhaustion of the current continuation record is detected when the next repeating group would extend past the end of the record. The ending column for continuation records is defined on CONTINUED. If the ending column is not specified on CONTINUED, the host system's record length is used. For inline data, the record length is always 80. For data stored in a file, the record length is generally whatever was specified on the FILE HANDLE command, and shorter records are extended with blanks when they are read. For IBM implementations, the physical record length is available and is used.

Reading Past End of Record
- If CONTINUED is not specified, all the repeating groups are read from the first record of each input case, regardless of the length of that record. If a given field extends past the end of the actual record, the action taken depends on the type of data item being read:

  For string data being read under "A" format, the data record is considered to be extended logically with blanks. If the entire field lies past the end of the record, the result value will be all blanks.

  For numeric data, a warning is issued and the result value receives the system-missing value.

- If CONTINUED is specified, the ending column specified on either STARTS or CONTINUED can force the processing of data fields which lie beyond the end of the actual record. The result is as outlined above: string variables receive blanks as values and numeric variables receive the system-missing value.

Example

```
TITLE      'BUILD A FILE WITH EACH CASE REPRESENTING ONE VEHICLE'.
SUBTITLE   'SPREAD INFORMATION ABOUT THE HOUSEHOLD TO EACH CASE'.

INPUT PROGRAM.
DATA LIST / SEQNUM 2-4 NUMPERS 6-7 NUMVEH 9-10.
REPEATING DATA STARTS=12 /OCCURS=NUMVEH
 /DATA=MAKE 1-8 (A) MODEL 9 (A) NUMCYL 10.
END INPUT PROGRAM.

BEGIN DATA
1001 02 02 FORD      T8PONTIAC C6
1002 04 01 CHEVY     C4
1003 02 03 CADILAC C8FORD      T6VW       C4
END DATA.
LIST.
```

- Data are extracted from a file representing household records. Each input case is recorded on a single record; there are no continuation records.

- Total number of persons living in the house and number of vehicles owned by the household is recorded on each record. Each record also includes a repeating group of information about each vehicle: the make of vehicle, model, and number of cylinders. The first field of numbers (columns 1–4) for each record is an identification number unique to each record. The next two fields of numbers are number of persons in household and number of vehicles. The remaining portion of the record contains the repeated groups—one for each vehicle.

- INPUT PROGRAM indicates the beginning of the data definition commands, and END INPUT PROGRAM indicates the end of the data definition program.

- DATA LIST reads the variables from the household portion of the record. All fixed-format variables are defined on DATA LIST.

- REPEATING DATA reads the information from the repeating groups and builds the new output cases. Repeating groups start in column 12. The number of repeating groups for each input case is given by the value of variable NUMVEH. Three variables are defined for each repeating group: MAKE, MODEL, and NUMCYL.

- The first record in the data contains information on two vehicles producing two output cases on the active system file. One output case is built from the second record which contains information on one vehicle, and three output cases are built from the third record. The values of the fixed-format variables defined on DATA LIST are spread to every case built on the active system file. Six cases result, as shown in Figure 1.

Figure 1 Output cases built with REPEATING DATA

SEQNUM	NUMPERS	NUMVEH	MAKE	MODEL	NUMCYL
1	2	2	FORD	T	8
1	2	2	PONTIAC	C	6
2	4	1	CHEVY	C	4
3	2	3	CADILAC	C	8
3	2	3	FORD	T	6
3	2	3	VW	C	4

```
NUMBER OF CASES READ =        6    NUMBER OF CASES LISTED =        6
```

Example

```
TITLE    'READ ONLY TYPE 003 RECORDS'.
SUBTITLE 'USE REPEATING DATA WITH FILE TYPE MIXED'.

FILE TYPE   MIXED RECORD=#SEQNUM 2-4.
RECORD TYPE 003.
REPEATING DATA STARTS=12 /OCCURS=3
 /DATA=MAKE 1-8(A) MODEL 9(A) NUMCYL 10.
END FILE.
END FILE TYPE.

BEGIN DATA
1001 02 02 FORD    T8PONTIAC C6
1002 04 01 CHEVY    C4
1003 02 03 CADILAC C8FORD    T6VW      C4
END DATA.
LIST.
```

- Data are the same as in the previous example. However, the task in this example is to read only records with the value 003 for variable #SEQNUM.

- For this application, REPEATING DATA is used within a FILE TYPE structure, which specifies a MIXED file type. The record identification variable #SEQNUM is located in columns 2–4.

- RECORD TYPE determines that only records with value 003 for #SEQNUM are copied onto the active system file. All other records are skipped.

- REPEATING DATA indicates that the repeating groups start in column 12. The OCCURS subcommand indicates there are 3 repeating groups on each input case, and the DATA subcommand specifies variable names, column locations, and formats for the repeating groups.

- None of the information on the input cases is spread to the resulting output cases. Thus, the DATA LIST command is not required in this example. However, if there were multiple input cases with the value 003 for #SEQNUM and they did not all have 3 repeating groups, DATA LIST would be required to define a variable whose value for each input case indicated the number of repeating groups for that case. That variable could then be specified on the OCCURS subcommand.

Example
```
TITLE  'CREATE A DATA SET OF CHILD RECORDS'.

INPUT PROGRAM.
DATA LIST / PARENTID 1 DATE 3-6 NCHILD 8.
REPEATING DATA STARTS=9 /OCCURS=NCHILD
 /DATA=BIRTHDAY 2-5 VACDATE 7-10.
END INPUT PROGRAM.

COMPUTE AGE=DATE - BIRTHDAY.
COMPUTE VACAGE=VACDATE - BIRTHDAY.

DO IF PARENTID NE LAG(PARENTID,1) OR $CASENUM EQ 1.
COMPUTE CHILD=1.
ELSE.
COMPUTE CHILD=LAG(CHILD,1)+1.
END IF.
FORMAT AGE VACAGE CHILD (F2).

BEGIN DATA
1 1987 2 1981 1983 1982 1984
2 1988 1 1979 1984
3 1988 3 1978 1981 1981 1986 1983 1986
4 1988 1 1984 1987
END DATA.
LIST.
```

- Data are from a file that tracks information on parents within a school district. Each input case is recorded on a single record; there are no continuation records.

- Each record identifies the parents by a number and indicates how many children they have. Each record also identifies the years of birth and vaccination for each child.

- REPEATING DATA indicates that the repeating groups begin in column 9. The value of NCHILD indicates how many repeating groups there are for each record. The data in the repeating groups are defined as birth and vaccination days.

- The first two COMPUTE commands compute an age for each child, and also each child's age at vaccination. These transformation commands are specified outside the INPUT PROGRAM structure.

- Because the repeating groups do not have descriptive values, the DO IF structure computes variable CHILD to distinguish between the first-born child, second-born child, etc. The value for CHILD will be 1 for the first-born, 2 for the second-born, and so forth. The resulting output cases are shown in Figure 2.

Figure 2 Output cases built with REPEATING DATA

```
PARENTID DATE NCHILD BIRTHDAY VACDATE AGE VACAGE CHILD

       1   1987    2     1981     1983    6    2      1
       1   1987    2     1982     1984    5    2      2
       2   1988    1     1979     1984    9    5      1
       3   1988    3     1978     1981   10    3      1
       3   1988    3     1981     1986    7    5      2
       3   1988    3     1983     1986    5    3      3
       4   1988    1     1984     1987    4    3      1


NUMBER OF CASES READ =      7    NUMBER OF CASES LISTED =      7
```

STARTS Subcommand

STARTS indicates the beginning location of the repeating data segment of the first record of each input case. STARTS is required and can specify either a number or a variable name.

- If the repeating groups on the first record of each input case begin in the same position, STARTS should specify a column number.

- If the repeating groups on the first record of each input case do not begin in the same position, STARTS should specify the name of a previously defined variable. The variable's value for each input case must indicate the beginning location of the repeating segment of the first record. The specified variable can be one defined on DATA LIST or one created by transformation commands that precede REPEATING DATA.

- STARTS must always specify a beginning position for repeating groups. When repeating groups are continued on multiple records for each input case, STARTS may also have to specify an ending position. An ending position is required when data on the first record of each input case are not as long as the operating system's logical record length. The ending position applies only to the first record of each input case.

- If the ending position is required but not supplied, SPSS generates output cases with system-missing values for the variables specified on the DATA subcommand. In many instances, this will mean that SPSS misreads all data after the first or second record in the data file (see CONTINUED Subcommand).

- If STARTS specifies a variable for the ending position and the variable has undefined or missing values for an input case, SPSS displays a warning message and builds no output cases from that input case. If the variable specified as the ending position on STARTS has a value that is less than the value specified for the starting position, SPSS issues a warning and builds output cases only from the continuation record(s) on the input case; it does not build cases from the first record of the input case.

- Specifications for the beginning position and the ending position must be separated by a dash. The ending position can be specified with a number or a variable name. The values of the variable used to define the ending position must be valid values and must be larger than the starting value.

Example
```
TITLE  'REPEATING GROUPS IN THE SAME LOCATION'.

INPUT PROGRAM.
DATA LIST FILE=VEHICLE / SEQNUM 2-4 NUMPERS 6-7 NUMVEH 9-10.
REPEATING DATA STARTS=12 /OCCURS=NUMVEH
/DATA=MAKE 1-8 (A) MODEL 9 (A) NUMCYL 10.
END INPUT PROGRAM.
```

- STARTS specifies column number 12. The repeating groups must therefore be in column 12 for the first record of each input case.

Example
```
TITLE  'REPEATING GROUPS IN VARYING LOCATIONS'.

INPUT PROGRAM.
DATA LIST FILE=VEHICLE / SEQNUM 2-4 NUMPERS 6-7 NUMVEH 9-10.
+    DO IF    (SEQNUM LE 100).
+    COMPUTE FIRST=12.
+    ELSE IF
+    COMPUTE FIRST=15.
+    END IF.
REPEATING DATA STARTS=FIRST /OCCURS=NUMVEH
/DATA=MAKE 1-8 (A) MODEL 9 (A) NUMCYL 10.
END INPUT PROGRAM.
```

- This example assumes that each input case is recorded on a single record and that there are no continuation records.

- Repeating groups in the data begin in column 12 for all records with sequence numbers 1 through 100 and in column 15 for all records with sequence numbers greater than 100.

- The sequence number is defined as variable SEQNUM on the DATA LIST command for each record. The DO IF—END IF structure and the COMPUTE commands create the variable FIRST with the value 12 for records with sequence numbers through 100 and the value 15 for records with sequence numbers greater than 100.

- Variable FIRST is specified on the STARTS subcommand. The value for FIRST then indicates the beginning position of the repeating data groups for each record.

OCCURS Subcommand

OCCURS specifies the number of repeating groups on each input case. OCCURS is required and can specify a number if the number of groups is the same on all input cases or a variable if the number of groups varies across input cases. The variable must be defined on a DATA LIST command or created with the transformation commands.

• If the number of repeating groups is the same for each input case, or if you want to read the same number of repeating groups from each input case, OCCURS should specify a number. Otherwise OCCURS should specify a variable whose value for each input case indicates the number of repeating groups on that case.

Example

```
INPUT PROGRAM.
DATA LIST / SEQNUM 2-4 NUMPERS 6-7 NUMVEH 9-10.
REPEATING DATA STARTS=12 /OCCURS=NUMVEH
 /DATA=MAKE 1-8 (A) MODEL 9 (A) NUMCYL 10.
END INPUT PROGRAM.

BEGIN DATA
1001 02 02 FORD    T8PONTIAC C6
1002 04 01 CHEVY   C4
1003 02 03 CADILAC C8FORD    T6VW      C4
END DATA.
LIST.
```

• Data for each input case are recorded on a single record; there are no continuation records.

• The value on variable NUMVEH from columns 9 and 10 indicates the number of repeating groups for each record. One output case is built on the active system file for each occurrence of a repeating group.

• In the data NUMVEH has the value 2 on the first record, 1 on the second record, and 3 on the third. Thus, six cases are built from these records. If the value of NUMVEH is 0, no cases are built from that record.

Example

```
TITLE    'LIMIT THE NUMBER OF REPEATING GROUPS'.
SUBTITLE 'READ ONLY THE FIRST REPEATING GROUP FROM EACH
RECORD'.

INPUT PROGRAM.
DATA LIST FILE=VEHICLE / SEQNUM 2-4 NUMPERS 6-7 NUMVEH 9-10.
REPEATING DATA STARTS=12 /OCCURS=1
 /DATA=MAKE 1-8 (A) MODEL 9 (A) NUMCYL 10.
END INPUT PROGRAM.
```

• One output case is built from the first repeating group on each input case regardless of the total number of repeating groups actually recorded on each input case.

DATA Subcommand

DATA specifies a variable name, location within each repeating segment, and format type for each variable to be read from the repeating groups. DATA is required and must be the last subcommand on REPEATING DATA.

• The specifications for DATA are the same as for the DATA LIST command. The specified location of the variables on DATA is their location within each repeating group—*not* the location within the record.

• Any input format type available with the DATA LIST command can be specified on the DATA subcommand. Also the FORTRAN-like format specifications as well as the column-format specifications can be used.

• If LENGTH is not specified, the default length is in effect for each repeating data group. For information on how the default length is determined, see LENGTH Subcommand.

Example

```
TITLE  'READ ALL THE VARIABLES RECORDED FOR EACH VEHICLE'.

INPUT PROGRAM.
DATA LIST FILE=VEHICLE / SEQNUM 2-4 NUMPERS 6-7 NUMVEH 9-10.
REPEATING DATA STARTS=12 /OCCURS=NUMVEH
 /DATA=MAKE 1-8 (A) MODEL 9 (A) NUMCYL 10.
END INPUT PROGRAM.
LIST.
```

• Variable MAKE is a string variable read from positions 1 through 8 of each repeating group; MODEL is a single-character string variable read from position 9; and NUMCYL is a one-digit numeric variable read from position 10. DATA defines a total length of 10 for each repeating group.

• Variables SEQNUM, NUMPERS, and NUMVEH, defined on the DATA LIST command for each input case, are spread to each output case built from the repeating groups.

FILE Subcommand

REPEATING DATA must be used with a DATA LIST, FILE TYPE NESTED, or FILE TYPE MIXED command. By default, REPEATING DATA reads the file specified on the DATA LIST or FILE TYPE command. The FILE subcommand on REPEATING DATA explicitly specifies the name of the file.

• FILE must specify the same file as its associated DATA LIST or FILE TYPE command.

Example

```
TITLE  'EXPLICITLY SPECIFY THE DATA FILE'.

INPUT PROGRAM.
DATA LIST FILE=VEHICLE / SEQNUM 2-4 NUMPERS 6-7 NUMVEH 9-10.
REPEATING DATA FILE=VEHICLE /STARTS=12 /OCCURS=NUMVEH
 /DATA=MAKE 1-8 (A) MODEL 9 (A) NUMCYL 10.
END INPUT PROGRAM.
```

• FILE on REPEATING DATA specifically identifies the file.

LENGTH Subcommand

LENGTH specifies the length of each repeating data group. The default length for each repeating group is determined as the number of columns between the beginning column for repeating groups and the ending column for the last variable specified on DATA. (For the first record of each input case, STARTS specifies the beginning column for repeating groups. For continuation records, repeating groups are read from column 1 by default, or from the column specified on CONTINUED.)

• The specification for LENGTH can be a number or the name of a previously defined variable.

• LENGTH must be used if the last variable specified on the DATA subcommand is not read from the last position of each repeating group, or if the length of the repeating groups varies across input cases.

• If the length of the repeating groups varies across input cases, the specification must be a variable whose value for each input case is the length of the repeating groups on that case. The variable can be one specified on DATA LIST or a variable created with transformation commands.

• If the value of the variable specified on LENGTH is an undefined or missing value, SPSS displays a warning message and builds only one output case for that input case.

Example

```
TITLE  'READ ONLY THE VARIABLE MAKE FOR EACH VEHICLE'.
```

```
* THE DATA CONTAIN TWO VALUES THAT ARE NOT SPECIFIED ON THE
  DATA SUBCOMMAND.  THE FIRST VALUE IS IN POSITION 9 OF THE
  REPEATING GROUPS, AND THE SECOND IS IN POSITION 10 OF THE
  REPEATING GROUPS.

INPUT PROGRAM.
DATA LIST FILE=VEHICLE / SEQNUM 2-4 NUMPERS 6-7 NUMVEH 9-10.
REPEATING DATA STARTS=12 /OCCURS=NUMVEH /LENGTH=10
 /DATA=MAKE 1-8 (A).
END INPUT PROGRAM.
```

• LENGTH indicates that each repeating group is ten positions long. LENGTH is required because the DATA subcommand does not specify MODEL (position 9) or NUMCYL (position 10) from the repeating groups. (The DATA subcommand shown in preceding examples specifies both variables MODEL and NUMCYL.) MAKE is not read from the last position of each repeating group, so LENGTH must be used to indicate the full length of each group.

• DATA specifies that MAKE is to be read from positions 1 through 8 of each repeating group. Thus, positions 9 and 10 of each repeating group are skipped.

CONTINUED Subcommand

CONTINUED indicates that the repeating groups are continued onto more than one record for each input case.

• Each repeating group must be fully recorded on a single record: a repeating group cannot be split across records.

- If CONTINUED is specified without beginning and ending positions, SPSS assumes that the repeating groups begin in column 1 of continuation records and searches for repeating groups by scanning to the end of the record or to the value specified by OCCURS. See Operations, above.
- If the repeating groups on continuation records do not begin in column 1, CONTINUED must specify the column in which the repeating groups begin for all continuation records.
- If data on the first record of each input case are not as long as the operating system's logical record length, the STARTS subcommand must indicate an ending position for the records. The ending position on STARTS applies only to the first record of each input case.
- If data on the continuation records are not as long as the operating system's logical record length, the CONTINUED subcommand must indicate an ending position for the continuation records. The ending position on CONTINUED applies to all continuation records.

Example

```
* THIS EXAMPLE ASSUMES THE COMPUTER'S LOGICAL RECORD LENGTH IS
    80.

INPUT PROGRAM.
DATA LIST / ORDERID 1-5 NITEMS 7-8.
REPEATING DATA STARTS=10 /OCCURS=NITEMS /CONTINUED=7
 /DATA=ITEM 1-9 (A) QUANTITY 11-13 PRICE (DOLLAR7.2,1X).
END INPUT PROGRAM.

BEGIN DATA
10020 07 01-923-89 001   25.99 02-899-56 100 101.99 03-574-54 064
61.29
10020 04-780-32 025   13.95 05-756-90 005   56.75 06-323-47 003
23.74
10020 07-350-95 014   11.46
20030 04 01-781-43 010   10.97 02-236-54 075 105.95 03-655-83 054
22.99
20030 04-569-38 015   75.00
END DATA.
LIST.
```

- Data are extracted from a mail-order file. Each input case represents one complete order. The data show two complete orders that are recorded on a total of five records.
- The order number is recorded in columns 1 through 5 of each record. The first three records contain information for order 10020; the next two records contain information for order 20030. The second field of numbers on the first record of each order indicates the total number of items ordered. The repeating groups begin in column 10 of the first record of each order and in column 7 of continuation records. Each repeating data group represents information on one item ordered and contains three variables—the item inventory number, the quantity ordered, and the price of the item.
- DATA LIST defines variables ORDERID and NITEMS on the first record of each input case.
- STARTS on REPEATING DATA indicates that the repeating groups on the first record of each input case begin in column 10.
- OCCURS indicates that the total number of repeating groups for each input case is the value of NITEMS.
- CONTINUED must be used because the repeating groups can be continued onto successive records on each input case. CONTINUED must specify a beginning position because the repeating groups on the continuation records begin in column 7 rather than in column 1.
- DATA defines variables ITEM, QUANTITY, and PRICE for each repeating data group. ITEM and QUANTITY define 13 columns, PRICE defines 7 columns of data followed by 1 blank column. The length of the repeating groups is therefore defined as 21 columns. The output cases resulting from this example are shown in Figure 3.

Figure 3 Cases generated by REPEATING DATA

```
ORDERID NITEMS ITEM        QUANTITY      PRICE

 10020     7   01-923-89        1       $25.99
 10020     7   02-899-56      100      $101.99
 10020     7   03-574-54       64       $61.29
 10020     7   04-780-32       25       $13.95
 10020     7   05-756-90        5       $56.75
 10020     7   06-323-47        3       $23.74
 10020     7   07-350-95       14       $11.46
 20030     4   01-781-43       10       $10.97
 20030     4   02-236-54       75      $105.95
 20030     4   03-655-83       54       $22.99
 20030     4   04-569-38       15       $75.00

NUMBER OF CASES READ =     11    NUMBER OF CASES LISTED =      11
```

Example

```
TITLE  'SPECIFYING AN END POSITION ON THE STARTS SUBCOMMAND'.

* THIS EXAMPLE ASSUMES THE COMPUTER'S LOGICAL RECORD LENGTH IS
80.

INPUT PROGRAM.
DATA LIST / ORDERID 1-5 NITEMS 7-8.
REPEATING DATA STARTS=10-55 /OCCURS=NITEMS /CONTINUED=7
 /DATA=ITEM 1-9 (A) QUANTITY 11-13 PRICE (DOLLAR7.2,1X).
END INPUT PROGRAM.

BEGIN DATA
10020 07 01-923-89 001  25.99 02-899-56 100 101.99
10020 03-574-54 064  61.29 04-780-32 025   13.95 05-756-90 005
56.75
10020 06-323-47 003  23.74 07-350-95 014  11.46
20030 04 01-781-43 010   10.97 02-236-54 075 105.95
20030 03-655-83 054  22.99 04-569-38 015  75.00
END DATA.
LIST.
```

- Data are the same as in the previous example; however, records are entered differently. The first record for each input case stores only two repeating groups.
- DATA LIST defines columns 1 through 9 for variables ORDERID and NITEMS. Column 9 is left blank. DATA defines each repeating group as 21 columns wide. The record length for the first record of each input case is therefore 51 columns: 21 columns for each of two repeating groups, plus the eight columns defined on DATA LIST, plus Column 9, which is blank. The operating system's logical record length is 80, enough room for one more repeating group on the first record of each input case. STARTS must therefore specify an ending position that does not provide enough columns for another repeating group; otherwise, SPSS will create an output case with missing values for the variables specified on DATA.
- STARTS indicates that SPSS is to scan only the first 55 positions of the first record of each input case looking for repeating data groups. It will scan all columns of continuation records until the value specified on the OCCURS subcommand is reached.

Example

```
TITLE  'SPECIFYING AN END POSITION ON THE CONTINUED SUBCOMMAND'.

* THIS EXAMPLE ASSUMES THE COMPUTER'S LOGICAL RECORD LENGTH IS
   80.

INPUT PROGRAM.
DATA LIST / ORDERID 1-5 NITEMS 7-8.
REPEATING DATA STARTS=10-55 /OCCURS=NITEMS /CONTINUED=7-55
 /DATA=ITEM 1-9 (A) QUANTITY 11-13 PRICE (DOLLAR7.2,1X).
END INPUT PROGRAM.

BEGIN DATA
10020 07 01-923-89 001  25.99 02-899-56 100 101.99
10020 03-574-54 064  61.29 04-780-32 025   13.95
10020 05-756-90 005  56.75 06-323-47 003   23.74
10020 07-350-95 014  11.46
20030 04 01-781-43 010   10.97 89-236-54 075 105.95
20030 03-655-83 054  22.99 04-569-38 015  75.00
END DATA.
LIST.
```

- Again, data are the same as in the previous two examples, but records are entered differently. The first record for each input case again stores only two repeating groups. However, the continuation records in these data also store only two repeating groups.
- The operating system's logical record length is 80, leaving room for more repeating groups on all records.
- STARTS indicates that SPSS is to scan only the first 55 positions of the first record of each input case looking for repeating data groups.
- CONTINUED indicates that SPSS is to scan only the first 55 positions of all continuation records.

ID Subcommand

ID compares the value of an identification variable across records of the same input case. ID can only be used when CONTINUED is specified. The identification variable must be defined on a DATA LIST command and must be recorded on all records in the file.

- The ID subcommand has two specifications: the location of the variable on the continuation records and the name of the variable (as specified on the DATA LIST command). The specifications must be separated from each other by an equals sign. The format type and format length must be the same as that specified as for the variable defined on the first record.
- If the values of the ID variable are not equal for all records of a single input case, SPSS displays an error message and stops reading data.

Example

```
INPUT PROGRAM.
DATA LIST / ORDERID 1-5 NITEMS 7-8.
REPEATING DATA STARTS=10-50 /OCCURS=NITEMS
 /CONTINUED=7 /ID=1-5=ORDERID
 /DATA=ITEM 1-9 (A) QUANTITY 11-13 PRICE 15-20 (2).
END INPUT PROGRAM.

BEGIN DATA
10020 04 45-923-89 001  25.9923-899-56 100 101.99
10020 63-780-32 025  13.9554-756-90 005  56.75
20030 03 45-781-43 010  10.9789-236-54 075 105.95
20030 32-569-38 015  75.00
END DATA.
LIST.
```

- The order number in the data is recorded in positions 1–5 of each record.
- ORDERID is defined on the DATA LIST command as a five-digit integer variable. The first specification on the ID subcommand must therefore specify a five-digit integer variable. Only the location of the identification number can be different on continuation records.

NOTABLE Subcommand

By default, SPSS displays a summary table for all variables defined on the DATA subcommand. The summary table lists the names, locations, and format types of the variables. The format of the summary table is identical to the summary table displayed by the DATA LIST command. TABLE explicitly specifies the default table. NOTABLE suppresses the table.

Example

```
TITLE   'SUPPRESS THE SUMMARY TABLE'.

INPUT PROGRAM.
DATA LIST FILE=VEHICLE / SEQNUM 2-4 NUMPERS 6-7 NUMVEH 9-10.
REPEATING DATA STARTS=12 /OCCURS=NUMVEH /NOTABLE
 /DATA=MAKE 1-8 (A) MODEL 9 (A) NUMCYL 10.
END INPUT PROGRAM.
```

- NOTABLE suppresses the display of the summary table.

REPORT

```
REPORT

[/FORMAT=[{MANUAL   }] [{NOLIST    }] [ALIGN({LEFT  })]
          {AUTOMATIC}    {LIST[(n)]}          {CENTER}
                                             {RIGHT }

        [TSPACE({1})] [CHDSPACE({1})] [FTSPACE({1 })]
               {n}             {n}            {n}

        [SUMSPACE({1})] [COLSPACE({4})] [BRKSPACE({ 1 })]
                 {n}             {n}             {  n }
                                                {-1†}

        [LENGTH({1,length})] [MARGINS({1,width})]
               {n,n     }            {n,n    }
               {*,*     }            {*,*    }

        [CHALIGN({TOP     })] [UNDERSCORE({OFF})]
                {BOTTOM†}                {ON†}

        [PAGE1({1})] [MISSING {"."}]]
              {n}            {'s'}

[/OUTFILE=file]

[/STRING=stringname (varname[(width)] [(BLANK)] ['literal...'])

/VARIABLES=varname ({VALUE}) [+ varname({VALUE})] ['col head']
                   {LABEL}              {LABEL}
                   {DUMMY}              {DUMMY}
    [(option list)]

where option list can contain any of the following:
    width   OFFSET({0      })  {LEFT  }
                  {n      }  {CENTER}
                  {CENTER†}  {RIGHT }

[/MISSING={VAR           }]
          {NONE          }
          {LIST(varlist{1})}
                       {n}

[    /TITLE='line1''line2'...][    /FOOTNOTE='line1''line2'...]
          or                              or
[/TITLE=LEFT 'line1''line2'...][/FOOTNOTE=LEFT 'line1''line2'...]
[      CENTER 'line1''line2'...][      CENTER 'line1''line2'...]
[      RIGHT 'line1''line2'...][      RIGHT 'line1''line2'...]

        [)PAGE]   [)DATE]   [)var]

[/BREAK=varlist [(TOTAL)] ['col head'] [(option list)]]

where option list can contain any of the following:
    width   {VALUE }   {NOTOTAL}   SKIP({1})   PAGE[(RESET)]
            {LABEL†}   {TOTAL  }        {n}

    OFFSET({0      })  UNDERSCORE[(varlist)]  {LEFT  } {NONAME}
          {n      }                          {CENTER} {NAME  }
          {CENTER†}                          {RIGHT }

[/SUMMARY=function...['summary title'][(break col #1)]

        [SKIP({0})]]
              {n}

or

[/SUMMARY=PREVIOUS[({1})]]]
                   {n}

where function is

aggregate [(varname[({PLAIN })][(d)][varname...])]
                    {DOLLAR}
                    {COMMA }

or

composite(agg(varname)...)[(report col[({PLAIN })][(d)])]]
                                       {DOLLAR}
                                       {COMMA }
```

†Default if FORMAT=AUTOMATIC.

Aggregate functions:

VALIDN	VARIANCE	PLT(n)
SUM	KURTOSIS	PIN(min,max)
MIN	SKEWNESS	FREQUENCY(min,max)
MAX	MEDIAN(min,max)	PERCENT(min,max)
MEAN	MODE(min,max)	
STDDEV	PGT(n)	

Composite functions:
DIVIDE(agg(varname) agg(varname)[factor]
PCT(agg(varname) agg(varname)
SUBTRACT(agg(varname) agg(varname)
ADD(agg(varname) agg(varname)...)[factor]
GREAT(agg(varname) agg(varname)...)
LEAST(agg(varname) agg(varname)...)
AVERAGE(agg(varname) agg(varname)...)
MULTIPLY(agg(varname) agg(varname)...)[factor]

Example:
```
REPORT FORMAT=LIST
   /VARIABLES=PRODUCT (LABEL) ' ' 'Retail' 'Products'
             SALES 'Annual' 'Sales' '1981'
   /BREAK=DEPT 'Department' (LABEL)
   /SUMMARY=VALIDN (PRODUCT) MEAN (SALES).
```

Overview

REPORT produces both case listings and summary statistics and gives you considerable control over the appearance of the output. REPORT calculates all the univariate statistics available in DESCRIPTIVES and the statistics and subpopulation means available in MEANS. In addition, REPORT calculates statistics not directly available in any other SPSS procedure, such as computations involving aggregated statistics.

REPORT provides complete report format defaults or lets you customize column widths, titles, footnotes, spacing, and other elements. Because REPORT is so flexible and the output has so many components, it is often efficient to preview report output using a small number of cases until you find the format that best meets your needs.

Defaults

A listing report without subgroup classification requires FORMAT and VARIABLES. A listing report with subgroup classification requires FORMAT, VARIABLES, and BREAK. A report with summary statistics requires VARIABLES, BREAK, and SUMMARY.

By default, column heads use variable labels, or variable names if no variable labels have been specified.

By default, cases with user-missing values are excluded from the calculation of report statistics, and missing-value indicators are ignored for variables named on BREAK.

Column Widths

Default column widths are determined by REPORT, using the maximum of the following for each variable:

• The widest print format in the column, whether it is a variable print format or a summary print format.

• The width of any temporary variable defined with the STRING subcommand.

• The length of the longest title line in the heading, if a column heading is assigned.

• The length of the variable's longest value label, if you specify (LABEL). (If MANUAL is in effect, REPORT uses the length of the variable's longest label, up to a maximum of 20 characters.)

Intercolumn Spacing

Intercolumn spacing adjusts automatically, using a minimum of one and a maximum of four spaces between columns.

Automatic Fit

When the above criteria for column width result in a report that is too wide for the report margins, FORMAT=AUTOMATIC shrinks the report. AUTOMATIC performs the following two steps sequentially, stopping as soon as the report fits within the margins:

1   FORMAT=AUTOMATIC reduces intercolumn spacing incrementally until it reaches a minimum intercolumn space of 1. It will never reduce it to 0.

2 As a last resort, AUTOMATIC shortens widths for strings specified on the STRING subcommand. It begins with the longest string if that string is at least 15 characters wide. It shortens the column width for that string as much as needed (up to 40% of its length), wrapping the string within the new width. If necessary it repeats the step, using different defined strings. It will not shorten the column width of the same string twice.

REPORT does not implement the automatic fit criteria unless FORMAT = AUTOMATIC.

Many default settings depend on whether FORMAT=AUTOMATIC or MANUAL. Table 1, below, shows the defaults according to both specifications.

Table 1 Keyword default settings

Subcommand	Keyword	Default for Automatic	Default for Manual
FORMAT	ALIGN	left	left
	BRKSPACE		
	summary report	1	1
	listing report	-1	1
	CHALIGN	bottom	top
	CHDSPACE	1	1
	COLSPACE	4	4
	FTSPACE	1	1
	LENGTH	1,system length	1,system length
	LIST|NOLIST	NOLIST	NOLIST
	MARGINS	1,system length	1,system length
	MISSING	.	.
	PAGE1	1	1
	SUMSPACE	1	1
	TSPACE	1	1
	UNDERSCORE	on	off
VARIABLES	LABEL|VALUE|DUMMY	VALUE	VALUE
	LEFT|CENTER|RIGHT	CENTER	RIGHT for numbers LEFT for strings
	OFFSET	CENTER	0
BREAK	LABEL|VALUE	LABEL	VALUE
	LEFT|CENTER|RIGHT	CENTER	RIGHT for numbers LEFT for strings
	NAME|NONAME	NONAME	NONAME
	OFFSET	CENTER	0
	PAGE	off	off
	SKIP	1	1
	TOTAL|NOTOTAL	NOTOTAL	NOTOTAL
	UNDERSCORE	off	off
SUMMARY	PREVIOUS	1	1
	SKIP	0	0

Options **Display Format.** REPORT provides full report format defaults and offers you optional control over page length, vertical spacing, margin and column widths, page titles, footnotes, and labels for statistics. The maximum width and length of the report are controlled by specifications on the SET command.

FORMAT controls how the report is laid out on a page and whether case listings are displayed. VARIABLES names the report variables used to compute statistics and controls the titles, width, and contents of report columns. BREAK specifies the variables that define groups and controls the titles, width, and contents of break columns. SUMMARY specifies statistics and controls the titles and spacing of summary lines. TITLE and FOOTNOTE control the specification and placement of multiple-line titles and footnotes. STRING concatenates variables to create temporary variables that can be referenced on VARIABLES or BREAK.

Report Output. You can direct reports to a separate listing file other than the listing file used for the rest of the output from your session. See OUTFILE Subcommand.

Statistical Display. The statistical display is controlled by the SUMMARY subcommand. Statistics can be calculated for each category of a break variable and for the group as a whole. Available statistics include mean, variance, standard deviation, skewness, kurtosis, sum, minimum and maximum value, mode, median, and percentages. Composite functions perform arithmetic operations using two or more summary statistics calculated on single variables.

Missing Values. You can override the default to include user-missing values in report statistics and listings with the MISSING subcommand. You can also use FORMAT to define a missing-value symbol to represent missing data.

Basic Specification

The basic specification depends on whether you want a listing report or a summary report.

Listing Reports. FORMAT=LIST is required, as is VARIABLES with a variable list. Case listings are displayed for each variable named on VARIABLES. There are no break groups or summary statistics unless BREAK and SUMMARY are specified.

Summary Reports. VARIABLES, BREAK, and SUMMARY are required. The report is organized according to the values of the variable named on BREAK; the variable named on BREAK must be named on a preceding SORT CASES command. Specified statistics are displayed for each break group.

Subcommand Order

Though VARIABLES is the only subcommand required on every REPORT, the following order must be observed among subcommands when they are used:

- FORMAT must precede all other subcommands.
- VARIABLES must precede BREAK.
- OUTFILE must precede BREAK.
- Each SUMMARY must immediately follow its associated BREAK. Multiple SUMMARY subcommands associated with the same BREAK must be specified consecutively.
- TITLE and FOOTNOTE can appear anywhere after FORMAT except between BREAK and SUMMARY.
- MISSING must follow VARIABLES and precede the first BREAK.
- STRING must precede VARIABLES.

Syntax Rules

- Only one each of the FORMAT, STRING, VARIABLES, and MISSING subcommands is allowed.
- To obtain multiple break groups, use multiple BREAK subcommands.
- To obtain multiple summaries for a break level, specify multiple SUMMARY subcommands for the associated BREAK.
- Keywords on REPORT subcommands have default specifications that are in effect if the keyword is not specified. Specify keywords only when you wish to change a default.
- Keywords are enclosed in parentheses if the subcommand takes variable names as arguments.

Operations

- REPORT processes cases sequentially. When the value of a break variable changes, REPORT displays a statistical summary for cases processed since the last set of summary statistics was displayed.
- The file must be sorted in order on the break variable or variables.
- The maximum width and page length of the report are the width and page length specified on the SET command.

- If the column is not wide enough to display numeric values, REPORT first rounds decimal digits, then converts to scientific notation if possible, and then displays asterisks. String variables that are wider than the column are truncated.
- The format used to display values in case listings is controlled by the dictionary format of the variable. Each statistical function in REPORT has a default format.

Limitations
- Maximum 500 variables per VARIABLES subcommand. Maximum 10 dummy variables per VARIABLES subcommand.
- Maximum 20 MODE and MEDIAN requests per SUMMARY subcommand.
- Maximum 20 PGT, PLT, and PIN requests per SUMMARY subcommand.
- Maximum 50 strings per STRING subcommand.
- The length of titles and footnotes cannot exceed the report width.
- The length of string variables created on STRING cannot exceed the page width.
- There is no fixed limit on the number of BREAK and SUMMARY subcommands. However, the page width limits the number of variables displayed and thereby limits the number of break variables.
- The maximum width of a displayed report is 255 characters.
- The number of report variables that can be specified depends upon the width of the report, the width of the variable columns, and the number of BREAK subcommands.
- Neither FREQUENCY nor PERCENT can be named with other statistics on a single SUMMARY subcommand. For both functions, however, you can specify up to 20 variables. In addition, neither FREQUENCY nor PERCENT can be named more than once per subcommand.
- Workspace is required to store all labeling information, frequency counts (if summaries request FREQUENCY, PERCENT, MEDIAN or MODE), strings, and computed summary statistics.
- Memory requirements significantly increase if FREQUENCY, PERCENT, MEDIAN or MODE is requested with variables having a wide range of values. The amount of workspace required is $20 + 8*(max - min + 1)$ bytes per variable per function per break.
- If TOTAL is in effect, workspace requirements are almost doubled.
- Memory requirements also increase if value labels are displayed for variables with many value labels. The amount of workspace required is $4 + 24*n$ labels per variable.
- If the same range is used for different statistics for the same variable, only one set of cells is collected. For example, FREQUENCY(1,100)(VARA) PERCENT(1,100)(VARA) requires only 820 bytes.
- There should be enough workspace in 5000 bytes for a report of moderate size with a few strings, titles, and footnotes, two break levels, and simple descriptive statistics.

Example
```
SORT CASES BY DEPT.
REPORT FORMAT=LIST
   /VARIABLES=PRODUCT (LABEL) ' ' 'Retail' 'Products'
           SALES 'Annual' 'Sales' '1981'
   /BREAK=DEPT 'Department' (LABEL)
   /SUMMARY=VALIDN (PRODUCT) MEAN (SALES) 'No.Sold,Mean Sales'.
```

- This report is a listing of products and sales by department. A summary of the total number of products sold and the average sales by department is also produced.
- Cases are first sorted by DEPT to ensure that cases are appropriately grouped for the calculation of statistics.

- FORMAT requests a report that includes a listing of cases within each break group.
- VARIABLES specifies PRODUCT and SALES as the report variables and requests that the value labels identifying products be displayed. Three-line column headings are provided for each report column. The first line of the column head is blank for the variable PRODUCT.
- BREAK identifies DEPT as the break variable and provides a one-line column title for the break column. (LABEL) specifies that the value label be displayed instead of the value itself.
- SUMMARY requests the calculation of the valid number of cases for PRODUCT and the mean of SALES for each value of DEPT. A title is provided for the summary line to override the default title, VALIDN.

FORMAT Subcommand

```
FORMAT=[AUTOMATIC|MANUAL]   [NOLIST|LIST[(n)]]
       [PAGE(n)]   [LENGTH(t,b)]   [MARGINS(l,r)]
       [ALIGN(LEFT|CENTER|RIGHT)]   [COLSPACE(n)]
       [CHALIGN(TOP|BOTTOM)]   [UNDERSCORE(ON|OFF)]
       [TSPACE(n)]   [CHDSPACE(n)]   [BRKSPACE(n)]
       [SUMSPACE(n)]   [FTSPACE(n)]   [MISSING 's']
```

FORMAT controls the overall width and length of the report and vertical spacing.

- Keyword specifications and their arguments can be named in any order.

The following can be specified on FORMAT:

AUTOMATIC
MANUAL
The default settings. AUTOMATIC facilitates report design as follows: displays labels for break variables, centers all data, centers column headings but left-justifies column headings if value labels or string values exceed the width of the longest word in the heading, bottom-aligns and underscores column headings, extends column widths to accommodate the longest word in a variable label or the variable's longest value label, shrinks a report that is too wide for its margins. MANUAL does the following: displays values for break variables, right-justifies numeric values and their column headings, left-justifies value labels and string values and their column headings, top-aligns and does not underscore column headings, extends column widths to accommodate the variable's longest value label (but not the longest word in the variable label) up to a width of 20, generates an error message when a report is too wide for its margins. MANUAL is the default.

NOLIST
LIST[(n)]
Listing of individual cases. List the values of all variables named on VARIABLES for each case. The optional *n* inserts a blank line after each *n* cases; the default is not to insert a blank line. Values for cases are listed using the default formats for the variables. The default is the alternative NOLIST, which requests that no case listing be produced.

PAGE(n)
The number for the first page of the report. The default is 1.

LENGTH(t,b)
The top and bottom lines of the report. The value for the bottom line cannot be greater than the system page length. The system page length is controlled by SET. By default, the top of the report begins at line 1, and the bottom of the report is the last line of the system page length. You can use an asterisk to indicate a default value.

MARGINS(l,r)
The columns for the left and right margins. By default, the left margin is display column 1 and the right margin is the rightmost display column of the system page width, which is controlled by the SET WIDTH command. The right column cannot be beyond the width specified on SET. You can use an asterisk to indicate a default value.

ALIGN	*The report's placement relative to its margins.* The specification is either (LEFT), (CENTER), or (RIGHT). (LEFT) left justifies the report. (CENTER) centers the report between its margins. (RIGHT) right justifies the report. The default is (LEFT).
COLSPACE(n)	*The number of spaces between each column.* The default is the lesser either of 4 or the result obtained by first subtracting the combined column widths of the break and report variables from the REPORT margins and then dividing the difference by the number of columns minus one. When AUTOMATIC is in effect, REPORT overrides the specified column spacing if necessary to fit the report between its margins.
CHALIGN	*Alignment of column headings.* The specification is either (TOP) or (BOTTOM). (TOP) aligns all column headings with the first, or top, line of multi-line headings. (BOTTOM) aligns headings with the last, or bottom, line of multi-line headings. When AUTO-MATIC is in effect, the default is (BOTTOM); when MANUAL is in effect, the default is (TOP).
UNDERSCORE	*Heading underscores.* The specification is either (ON) or (OFF). (ON) underscores the bottom line of each column heading for the full width of the column. (OFF) suppresses the underscore. When AUTOMATIC is in effect, the default is (ON); when MANUAL is in effect, the default is (OFF).
TSPACE(n)	*The number of blank lines between the report title and the column heads.* The default is 1.
CHDSPACE(n)	*The number of blank lines beneath the longest column head.* The default is 1.
BRKSPACE(n)	*The number of blank lines between the break head and the next line.* The next line is a case if LIST is in effect or the first summary line if NOLIST is in effect. BRKSPACE(-1) places the first summary statistic or the first case listing on the same line as the break value. When a summary line is placed on the same line as the break value, the summary title is suppressed. When AUTO-MATIC is in effect, the default is -1; when MANUAL is in effect, it is 1.
SUMSPACE(n)	*The number of blank lines between the last summary line at the lower break and the first summary line at the higher break when they break simultaneously.* SUMSPACE also controls spacing between the last case listed and the first summary line if LIST is in effect. The default is 1.
FTSPACE(n)	*The minimum number of blank lines between the last listing on the page and the footnote.* The default is 1.
MISSING 's'	*Missing-value symbol.* The symbol can be only one character and is used to represent both system- and user-missing values. The default is a period (.).

Example   `FORMAT=AUTOMATIC LIST MARGINS(1,60) LENGTH(5,30) MISSING ('*')`

• FORMAT requests a case listing, defines a new page size smaller than the system page size, and specifies an asterisk as the missing-value symbol.

Page Layout   Figure 1 displays the complete page layout and subcommand specifications used to control the basic structure of the report.

Figure 1 Page layout for REPORT

```
——————————————————————————— top of page ———————————————————————————
                        ****************** TITLE ******************       ◄——— LENGTH
                                                                         ◄——— TSPACE

BREAK HEAD              BREAK HEAD            COLUMN   COLUMN   COLUMN   COLUMN
                                             HEAD     HEAD     HEAD     HEAD
                                             [VAR]    [VAR]    [VAR]    [VAR]
                                                                         ◄——— CHDSPACE
BREAK A VALUE 1        BREAK B VALUE 1                                    ◄——— BRKSPACE
                                             VALUE    VALUE    VALUE    VALUE
                                             VALUE    VALUE    VALUE    VALUE
                                                                         ◄——— LIST
                                             VALUE    VALUE    VALUE    VALUE
                                             VALUE    VALUE    VALUE    VALUE
                                                                         ◄——— SUMSPACE
                       SUMMARY TITLE         AGG.     AGG.     AGG.     AGG.
                                                                         ◄——— SKIP with SUMMARY
                       SUMMARY TITLE         AGG.     AGG.     AGG.     AGG.
                                                                         ◄——— SKIP with BREAK
                       BREAK B VALUE 2                                    ◄——— BRKSPACE
                                             VALUE    VALUE    VALUE    VALUE
                                             VALUE    VALUE    VALUE    VALUE
                                                                         ◄——— LIST
                                             VALUE    VALUE    VALUE    VALUE
                                             VALUE    VALUE    VALUE    VALUE
                                                                         ◄——— SUMSPACE
                       SUMMARY TITLE         AGG.     AGG.     AGG.     AGG. ◄——— stats for B=2, A=1

                       SUMMARY TITLE         AGG.     AGG.     AGG.
                                                                         ◄——— SUMSPACE
SUMMARY TITLE                                AGG.     AGG.     AGG.     AGG. ◄——— stats for A=1

SUMMARY TITLE                                AGG.     AGG.     AGG.     AGG.
                                                                         ◄——— SKIP with BREAK
BREAK A VALUE 2        BREAK B VALUE 1                                    ◄——— BRKSPACE
                                             VALUE    VALUE    VALUE    VALUE
                                             VALUE    VALUE    VALUE    VALUE
                                                                         ◄——— LIST
                                             VALUE    VALUE    VALUE    VALUE
                                             VALUE    VALUE    VALUE    VALUE
                                                                         ◄——— SUMSPACE
                       SUMMARY TITLE         AGG.     AGG.     AGG.     AGG.
                                                                         ◄——— SKIP
                       SUMMARY TITLE         AGG.     AGG.     AGG.     AGG.
                                                                         ◄——— SKIP with BREAK
                       BREAK B VALUE 2                                    ◄——— BRKSPACE
                                             VALUE    VALUE    VALUE    VALUE
                                             VALUE    VALUE    VALUE    VALUE
                                                                         ◄——— LIST
                                             VALUE    VALUE    VALUE    VALUE
                                             VALUE    VALUE    VALUE    VALUE

                       SUMMARY TITLE         AGG.     AGG.     AGG.     AGG.

                       SUMMARY TITLE         AGG.     AGG.     AGG.     AGG.
                                                                         ◄——— SUMSPACE
SUMMARY TITLE                                AGG.     AGG.     AGG.     AGG.

SUMMARY TITLE                                AGG.     AGG.     AGG.     AGG.
                                                                         ◄——— FTSPACE
                        **************** FOOTNOTE ****************        ◄——— LENGTH
——————————————————————————— bottom of page ———————————————————————————
|                                                                              |
left margin                                                          right margin
```

OUTFILE Subcommand

OUTFILE allows you to direct the report to a separate listing file other than the listing file used for the rest of the output from your session. You can later print this file without having to delete the extraneous material that would be present in the listing file.

- OUTFILE must follow FORMAT and must precede BREAK.
- To append multiple reports to the same listing file, name the same file on the OUTFILE subcommand of each separate report.

Example
```
REPORT FORMAT=AUTOMATIC LIST
   /OUTFILE=PRSNLRPT
   /VARIABLES=LNAME AGE TENURE JTENURE SALARY
   /BREAK=DIVISION
   /SUMMARY=MEAN.
REPORT FORMAT=AUTOMATIC
   /OUTFILE=PRSNLRPT
   /VARIABLES=LNAME AGE TENURE JTENURE SALARY
   /BREAK=DIVISION
   /SUMMARY=MEAN
   /SUMMARY=MIN
   /SUMMARY=MAX.
```

• Both a listing report and a summary report are written to file PRSNLRPT.

VARIABLES Subcommand

```
/VARIABLES=var|var TO var [(VALUE|LABEL|DUMMY)] ['col head']
            [(LEFT|CENTER|RIGHT)] [(width)]
            [(OFFSET(n|CENTER))] [varname...]
```

The required VARIABLES subcommand names the variables to be listed and summarized in the report. Optionally, you can use VARIABLES to control column titles, column widths, and the contents of report columns.

• The minimum VARIABLES specification is a list of variables. These are the report variables. The number of variables that can be named is limited by the system page width.

• Each report variable defines a report column. Each report column can be thought of as having the name of the variable that defines it.

• Variables are assigned to columns in the order in which they are named on VARIABLES.

• The value of the variable or an aggregate statistic calculated on the variable is displayed in that variable's report column.

• When FORMAT=LIST, variables can be stacked in a single column by linking them with + signs on the VARIABLES subcommand. If no column heading is specified, REPORT uses the default heading from the first variable on the list. Only values from the first variable in the stacked list are used to calculate summaries.

• Optional specifications can be given in any order following the variable name to which they apply.

• Optional specifications apply only to the immediately preceding variable or list of variables implied by the TO keyword.

• Variables named on BREAK can also be named on VARIABLES.

The following options can be specified:

(VALUE)
(LABEL)
(DUMMY)
Contents of the report column assigned to the variable. If no specification is given, the keyword (VALUE) is in effect. (VALUE) specifies that values of the variable be displayed in the column. The alternative keyword (LABEL) displays value labels if value labels are defined; otherwise, it displays values. (VALUE) and (LABEL) have no effect unless LIST has been specified on the FORMAT subcommand.

(DUMMY) defines a report column for a variable that does not exist in the active system file. Such dummy variables are used to control spacing or to reserve space for statistics computed upon other variables. Do not name an existing SPSS variable as a dummy variable.

When AUTOMATIC is in effect, value labels or string values are centered in the column based on the length of the longest string or label; numeric values are centered based on the width of the widest value or summary format. When MANUAL is in effect, value labels or string values are left-justified in the column; numeric values are right-justified.

'column title'
Title used for the report column assigned to the variable. Specify multiple-line titles by enclosing each line in a set of apostrophes or quotes, using the conventions for strings (see Universals: Strings).

Separate the specifications for title lines with at least one blank.

If no column title is specified, the default column title is the variable label or, if no variable label has been specified, the variable name.

Default column titles wrap for as many lines as are required to display the entire label. If AUTOMATIC is in effect, user-specified column titles appear exactly as specified, even if the column width must be extended. If MANUAL is in effect, user-specified titles wrap to fit within the column width.

(LEFT)
(CENTER)
(RIGHT)

Alignment of the column heading. If AUTOMATIC is in effect, column headings are centered within their columns; if value labels or string values exceed the width of the longest word in the heading, the heading is left-justified. If MANUAL is in effect, column headings are left-justified for value labels or string values and right-justified for numeric values.

(width)

Width for the report column. If no width is specified for a variable, REPORT determines a default width using the criteria described under Defaults, above. If you specify a width that is not wide enough to display numeric values, REPORT first rounds decimal digits, then converts to scientific notation if possible, and then displays asterisks. Value labels or string values that exceed the width are truncated.

(OFFSET)

Adjust the position of the report column contents. The specification is either (*n*) or (CENTER). (OFFSET(*n*)) indicates the number of spaces to offset. Contents are offset from the left for value labels or string values, and from the right for numeric values. (OFFSET(CENTER)) centers contents within the center of the column. If AUTOMATIC is in effect, the default is CENTER. (However, entering a number on OFFSET offsets the contents from the justified position, not from the center.) If MANUAL is in effect, the default is 0.

Example
```
/VARIABLES=V1 TO V3(LABEL) (15)
   V4 V5 (LABEL)(OFFSET (2))(10)
   SEP1 (DUMMY) (2) ''
   V6 'Results using' "Lieben's Method" 'of Calculation'
```

- The variables from V1 through V3 have report columns with a width of 15 each. Values are listed in the case listing. Value labels are displayed for these variables in the case listing.

- Variable V4 has a report column with the default width. Values are listed in the case listing.

- Value labels are displayed for variable V5. The column has a width of 10 columns. Column contents are offset two spaces from the left.

- SEP1 is a dummy variable. The column width is two, and there is at least one space column on each side of SEP1. Thus, there are at least four blanks between the columns for V5 and V6. SEP1 is given a null title to override the default column title SEP1.

- V6 is given a three-line title. Its column has the default width, and values are listed in the case listing.

STRING Subcommand

```
/STRING=stringname (varname [(width)] [(BLANK)] ['literal'])

      [stringname...]
```

STRING concatenates variables and user-specified strings into temporary string variables that exist only within REPORT.

- The minimum specification is a name for the string variable followed by a variable name or a user-specified string enclosed in parentheses.

- The name assigned to the string variable must be unique.

- Any combination of string variables, numeric variables, and user-specified strings can be used enclosed in parentheses to define the string.

• Keyword TO cannot be used within the parentheses to imply a variable list.

• More than one string variable can be defined on STRING.

• If a variable within the parentheses has a missing value, the string has a system-missing value, and the missing-value symbol is used for that value in case listings.

• A string variable defined in REPORT cannot exceed the system page width.

• String variables defined on STRING can be used on VARIABLES or BREAK.

The following options can be specified:

(width) *Column width within the string of the preceding variable.* The default width is the dictionary width of the variable.

If the width specified is less than required by the value, asterisks are displayed for numeric values, and string values are truncated on the right. If the width exceeds the width of a value, values of numeric variables are padded with zeros on the left and values of string variables are padded with blanks on the right.

The maximum width for numeric variables within the string definition is 16. The maximum width for a string variable is the system page width.

(BLANK) *Left-pad values of the preceding numeric variable with blanks.* If the specification is omitted, the default is to left-pad values of numeric variables with zeros. If a numeric variable has a DOLLAR or COMMA format, it is automatically left-padded with blanks.

'literal' *A user-specified string.* Any combination of characters can be specified within apostrophes or quotes.

Example
```
/STRING=JOB1(AVAR VARN)
        JOB2(AVAR(2) VARN(3))
        JOB3(AVAR(2) VARN(BLANK) (4))
```

• STRING defines three string variables to be used within the report.

• Assume that AVAR is a string variable read from a four-column field using keyword FIXED on DATA LIST and that VARN is a computed numeric variable with the default format of eight columns with two implied decimal places.

• If a case has the value 'KJ ' for AVAR and the value 241 for VARN, JOB1 displays the value KJ 00241.00, JOB2 the value KJ241, and JOB3 the value KJ 241.

Example
```
/STRING=SOCSEC(S1 '-' S2 '-' S3)
```

• STRING concatenates the three variables S1, S2, and S3, which each contain a portion of the social security number.

• Hyphens are inserted between the portions when the values of SOCSEC are displayed.

• This example assumes that the variables S1, S2, and S3 were read from three-column, two-column, and four-column fields respectively, using the keyword FIXED on DATA LIST. These variables have format widths of three, two, and four columns, and are not left-padded with zeros.

BREAK Subcommand

```
/BREAK= varlist [(VALUE|LABEL)] ['col title']
        [(LEFT|CENTER|RIGHT)] [(width)] [(OFFSET(n|CENTER))]
        [(UNDERSCORE[(varlist)])] [(NOTOTAL|TOTAL)]
        [(NONAME|NAME)] [(SKIP(n))|(PAGE[(RESET)])]
```

BREAK specifies the variables that define the subgroups for the report display, or specifies summary totals for reports with no subgroups. BREAK also allows you to control the titles, width, and contents of break columns and to begin a new page for each level of the break variable.

• A break occurs when any one of the break variables named on BREAK changes value. Cases must be presorted by the values of all BREAK variables on all BREAK subcommands.

- To obtain summary totals without any break levels, use the keyword (TOTAL) on BREAK without listing any variables. (TOTAL) must be specified on the first BREAK subcommand.
- Optional specifications can be given in any order following the last variable named.
- To obtain multiple break levels, use multiple BREAK subcommands.
- Missing-value specifications are ignored for variables named on BREAK. There is one break category for system-missing values and one for user-missing values. The values are displayed using the missing-value symbol controlled by FORMAT.
- The BREAK subcommand must precede the SUMMARY subcommand that defines the summary line for the break.
- A break column is reserved for each BREAK subcommand.
- If more than one variable is specified on a BREAK subcommand, a single break column is used. The value or value label for each variable is displayed on a separate line, in the order in which the variables are named on BREAK. The first variable named changes most slowly. The default column width is the longest of the default widths for any of the break variables.
- Optional specifications apply to all variables in the break column and to the break column as a whole.

The following can be specified on BREAK:

(VALUE) *Contents of the break column.* (VALUE) specifies that values of
(LABEL) the break variables be displayed in the column. The alternative keyword (LABEL) displays value labels if value labels have been defined; otherwise, it displays values. The value is displayed only once for each break change and is not repeated at the top of the page in a multiple-page break group. When AUTOMATIC is in effect, the default is (LABEL); when MANUAL is in effect, it is (VALUE).

When AUTOMATIC is in effect, value labels and string values are centered in the column based on the length of the longest string or label; numeric values are centered based on the width of the widest value or summary format. When MANUAL is in effect, value labels and string values are left-justified in the column; numeric values are right-justified.

'column head' *Title used for the break column.* Specify multiple-line titles by enclosing each line in a set of apostrophes or quotes, following the conventions for strings (see Universals: Strings). Separate the specifications for title lines with at least one blank.

The default title is the variable label of the break variable or the variable name if no label has been defined. If the break column is defined by more than one variable, the label or name of the first variable is used.

Default column titles wrap for as many lines as are required to display the entire label. User-specified column titles appear exactly as specified, even if the column width must be extended.

(LEFT) *Alignment of the column heading.* When AUTOMATIC is in
(CENTER) effect, column headings are centered within their columns.
(RIGHT) However, if value labels or string values exceed the width of the longest word in the heading, the heading is left-justified. When MANUAL is in effect, column headings are left-justified for value labels or string values, and right-justified for numeric values.

(width) *Column width for the break column.* If no width is specified for a variable, REPORT determines a default width using the criteria described under Defaults, above. If you specify a width that is not wide enough to display numeric values, REPORT first rounds decimal digits, then converts to scientific notation

	if possible, and then displays asterisks. Value labels or string values that exceed the width are truncated.
(OFFSET)	*Adjust the position of the break column contents.* The specification is either (*n*) or (CENTER). (OFFSET(*n*)) indicates the number of spaces to offset. Contents are offset from the left for value labels or string values, and from the right for numeric values. (OFFSET(CENTER)) centers contents within the center of the column. If AUTOMATIC is in effect, the default is CENTER. (However, entering a number on OFFSET offsets the contents from the justified position, not from the center.) If MANUAL is in effect, the default is 0.
(UNDERSCORE)	*Underscores before summary statistics.* The keyword UNDERSCORE underscores columns of the case listing produced by FORMAT LIST, before displaying summary statistics. You can optionally specify the names of one or more report variables after UNDERSCORE. If so, only those specified are underscored.
(TOTAL) **(NOTOTAL)**	*(TOTAL) calculates summary statistics specified on the next SUMMARY subcommand for all the cases on the report.* (TOTAL) must be specified on the first BREAK subcommand. (NOTOTAL) is the default and displays summary statistics only for each break.
(SKIP) **(PAGE)**	*The vertical spacing between the last summary line for a break and the next break.* The specification is either (*n*) or (PAGE). If (SKIP(*n*)) is specified, each break begins following *n* blank lines. The default is 1. If (PAGE) is specified, each break begins on a new page. If (RESET) is specified on (PAGE), the page counter resets to the PAGE1 setting on the FORMAT subcommand every time the break value changes for the specified variable. (PAGE(RESET)) is not allowed on listing reports with no break levels.
(NAME) **(NONAME)**	*Display the name of the break variable alongside each value or value label of the break variable.* (NAME) requires 10 spaces (the maximum eight-character length of SPSS variable names plus two parentheses) in addition to the space needed to display break values or value labels. (NAME) is ignored if the break-column width is insufficient. If the default keyword (NONAME) is specified, the name of the break variable is omitted.

Example

```
SORT DIVISION BRANCH DEPT.
REPORT FORMAT=AUTOMATIC MARGINS (1,70) BRKSPACE(-1)

  /VARIABLES=SPACE(DUMMY) ' ' (4)
   SALES 'Annual' 'Sales' '1981' (15) (OFFSET(2))
   EXPENSES 'Annual' 'Expenses' '1981' (15)(OFFSET(2))


  /BREAK=DIVISION
         BRANCH (10) (TOTAL) (OFFSET(1))
  /SUMMARY=MEAN

  /BREAK=DEPT 'Department' (10)
  /SUMMARY=MEAN.
```

- This example creates a report that breaks on three variables. BRANCH breaks within values of DIVISION, and DEPT breaks within values of BRANCH.

- FORMAT sets margins to a maximum of 70 columns and requests that the summary line be displayed on the same report line as the break values. Because LIST is not specified on FORMAT, only summary statistics are displayed.

- VARIABLES defines three report columns, each occupied by a report variable: SPACE, SALES, and EXPENSES.

- The variable SPACE is a dummy variable that exists only within REPORT. It has a null title and a width of 4. It is used as a space holder to separate the break columns from the report columns.

- SALES is given a three-line title and a width of 15. The values of SALES are offset two spaces from the right.

- EXPENSES is the third report variable and has the same width and offset specifications as SALES.

- The leftmost column in the report is reserved for the first two break variables, DIVISION and BRANCH. The break column has a width of 10, and the value labels are offset one space from the left. Any value label more than nine characters long is truncated. The default column title is used. (TOTAL) requests that the BRANCH summary line be displayed when all values of DIVISION and BRANCH have been cycled through, that is, at the end of the report.

- The summary line for the first BREAK consists of the mean of each report variable displayed in its own report column. This line is displayed each time the value of DIVISION or BRANCH changes.

- The third break variable, DEPT, occupies the second column from the left in the report. The break column has a width of 10 and has a one-line title. The first ten characters of the value labels are displayed in the break column.

- The second SUMMARY displays the mean for each report variable when the value of DEPT changes.

SUMMARY Subcommand

```
/SUMMARY={function...['summary title'][(break col #)] [SKIP(n)]}
         {PREVIOUS[(n)]                                        }
```

where function is

```
aggregate [(varname[(d)][(PLAIN|DOLLAR|COMMA)][varname...]))]
```

or

```
composite(agg(varname)...)[(report col[(d)][(PLAIN|DOLLAR|COMMA)])])]
```

SUMMARY calculates a wide range of aggregate and composite statistics.

- SUMMARY must be specified if LIST is not specified on FORMAT.

- Each SUMMARY subcommand following a BREAK subcommand specifies a new summary line.

- The minimum specification is an aggregate function or a composite function and its arguments. This must be the first specification on SUMMARY.

- The default format can be altered for any function. Format specifications in an aggregate modify only the immediately preceding result.

- The default location of the summary title is the column of the break variable to which the summary applies.

- When more than one function is named on SUMMARY, the default summary title is that of the function named first.

- Both the title and the default column location of the title can be altered.

- SUMMARY subcommands apply only to the preceding BREAK subcommand. If there is no SUMMARY subcommand after a BREAK subcommand, no statistics are displayed for that break level.

- To use the summary specifications from a previous BREAK subcommand for the current BREAK subcommand, specify keyword PREVIOUS on SUMMARY.

- More than one function can be specified on SUMMARY as long as you do not attempt to place two results in the same column.

- Multiple summary statistics requested on one SUMMARY subcommand are all displayed on the same summary report line.

- To insert blank lines between summaries when more than one summary line is requested for a break, use keyword SKIP.

- To place results of more than one function in the same report column, use multiple SUMMARY subcommands

- An implicit or explicit attempt to place the result of two or more functions in the same report column stops execution of REPORT.

• Summary lines can combine any composite functions and aggregate functions (except FREQUENCY and PERCENT).

Aggregate Functions Use the aggregate functions to request descriptive statistics on report variables.

• If no variable names are given as arguments to an aggregate function, the statistic is calculated for all variables named on VARIABLES, that is, for all report variables.

• To request an aggregate function for a subset of the report variables, specify the list of report variables in parentheses after the function keyword.

• All variables specified on an aggregate function must have been named on VARIABLES.

• Keyword TO cannot be used to specify a list of variables for an aggregate function.

• The result of an aggregate function is always displayed in the report column reserved for the variable on which the function was calculated.

• To use several aggregate functions on the same report variable, specify multiple SUMMARY subcommands. The results are displayed on different summary lines.

• The aggregate functions FREQUENCY and PERCENT have special display formats and cannot be placed on the same summary line with other aggregate or composite functions.

• Aggregate functions use only cases with valid values.

The following aggregate functions are available:

VALIDN	*Valid number of cases.* This is the only function that operates on string variables.
SUM	*Sum of values.*
MIN	*Minimum value encountered.*
MAX	*Maximum value encountered.*
MEAN	*Mean.*
STDDEV	*Standard deviation.* Aliases are SD and STDEV.
VARIANCE	*Variance.*
KURTOSIS	*Kurtosis.*
SKEWNESS	*Skewness.*
MEDIAN(min,max)	*Median value for values within the range.* MEDIAN sets up integer-valued bins for counting all values in the specified range. Noninteger values are truncated when the median is calculated.
MODE(min,max)	*Modal value for values within the range.* MODE sets up integer-valued bins for counting all values in the specified range. Noninteger values are truncated when the mode is calculated.
PGT(n)	*Percentage of cases with values greater than specified value.* An alias is PCGT.
PLT(n)	*Percentage of cases with values less than specified value.* An alias is PCLT.
PIN(min,max)	*Percentage of cases within the inclusive value range specified.* An alias is PCIN.
FREQUENCY(min,max)	*Frequency counts for values within the inclusive range.* FREQUENCY sets up integer-valued bins for counting all values in the specified range. Noninteger values are truncated when the frequency is computed. FREQUENCY cannot be mixed with other aggregate statistics on a summary line.
PERCENT(min,max)	*Percentages for values within the inclusive range.* PERCENT sets up integer-valued bins for counting all values

in the specified range. Noninteger values are truncated when the frequency is computed. PERCENT cannot be mixed with other aggregate statistics on a summary line.

Example
```
SORT CASES BY BVAR AVAR.
REPORT FORMAT=AUTOMATIC LIST /VARIABLES=XVAR YVAR ZVAR

  /BREAK=BVAR
    /SUMMARY=SUM
    /SUMMARY=MEAN (XVAR YVAR ZVAR)
    /SUMMARY=VALIDN(XVAR)

  /BREAK=AVAR
    /SUMMARY=PREVIOUS.
```

- FORMAT requests a case listing, and VARIABLES establishes a report column for variables XVAR, YVAR, and ZVAR. The report columns have default widths and titles.

- Both break variables, BVAR and AVAR, have default widths and titles.

- Every time the value of BVAR changes, three summary lines are displayed. The first line contains the sums for variables XVAR, YVAR, and ZVAR. The second line contains the means of all three variables. The third line displays the number of valid cases for XVAR in the report column for XVAR.

- Every time the value of AVAR changes within each value of BVAR, the three summary lines requested for BVAR are displayed. These summary lines are based on cases with the current value of BVAR that also have the current value of AVAR.

Example
```
SORT CASES BY DEPT.
REPORT FORMAT=AUTOMATIC
  /VARIABLES=WAGE BONUS TENURE
  /BREAK=DEPT (23)
  /SUM=SUM(WAGE BONUS) MEAN(TENURE) 'Sum Income: Mean Tenure'.
```

- SUMMARY defines a summary line consisting of the sums of WAGE and BONUS and the mean of TENURE. The result of each aggregate function is displayed in the report column of the variable on which the function is calculated.

- A title is assigned to the summary line. A width of 23 is defined for the break column to accommodate the right-justified summary-line title.

Composite Functions   Use composite functions to obtain statistics based on aggregated statistics, to place a summary statistic in a column other than that of the report variable on which it was calculated, or to manipulate variables not named on VARIABLES.

- Composite functions can be computed upon constants and any variable in the active system file.

- The following aggregate functions can also be arguments to composite functions: VALIDN, SUM, MIN, MAX, MEAN, STDEV, VARIANCE, KURTOSIS, and SKEWNESS. When used within composite functions, aggregate functions can have only one variable as an argument.

- A composite function and its arguments cannot be separated from each other by other SUMMARY specifications.

- By default, the results of a composite function are placed in the report column of the first variable named on the composite function that is also named on VARIABLES.

- The result of a composite function can be placed in any report column, including columns of dummy or string variables, by specifying a target column. To specify a target column, enclose the variable name of a report column in parentheses after the composite function and its arguments.

- The format for the result of a composite function can be specified in parentheses after the name of the column location and within the parentheses that enclose the column-location specification.

The following composite functions are available:

DIVIDE(agg() agg() [factor])	*Divide the first argument by the second and multiply by the optional factor.*
MULTIPLY(agg() ... agg())	*Multiply the arguments.*
PCT(agg() agg())	*Percentage of the first argument over the second.*
SUBTRACT(agg()agg())	*Subtract the second argument from the first argument.*
ADD(agg() ... agg())	*Add the arguments.*
GREAT(agg() ... agg())	*Give the maximum of the arguments.*
LEAST(agg() ... agg())	*Give the minimum of the arguments.*
AVERAGE(agg() ... agg())	*Give the average of the arguments.*

Example

```
SORT CASES BY DEPT.
REPORT FORMAT=AUTOMATIC BRKSPACE(-1)
  /VARIABLES=WAGE BONUS SPACE1 (DUMMY) '' BNFT1 BNFT2 SPACE2
    (DUMMY)''
  /BREAK=DEPT
    /SUMMARY=MEAN(WAGE BONUS BNFT1 BNFT2)
        ADD(VALIDN(WAGE)) (SPACE2)

    /SUMMARY=ADD(SUM(WAGE) SUM(BONUS))
        ADD(SUM(BNFT1) SUM(BNFT2)) 'Totals' SKIP(1)

    /SUMMARY=DIVIDE(MEAN(WAGE) MEAN(BONUS)) (SPACE1 (COMMA)(2))
        DIVIDE(MEAN(BNFT1) MEAN(BNFT2)) (SPACE2 (COMMA)(2))
        'Ratios'
        SKIP(1).
```

- VARIABLES defines six report columns. The columns called WAGE, BONUS, BNFT1, and BNFT2 contain aggregate statistics based on those variables. The variables SPACE1 and SPACE2 are dummy variables that are created for use as space holders; each is given a blank title to suppress the default column head.

- The first SUMMARY computes the means of the variables WAGE, BONUS, BNFT1, and BNFT2. Because BRKSPACE=−1, this summary line will be placed on the same report line as the break value and will have no summary title. The means are displayed in the report column for each variable. SUMMARY also computes the valid number of cases for WAGE inside a composite function and places the result in SPACE2 column.

- The second SUMMARY adds the sum of WAGE to the sum of BONUS. Since no location is specified, the result is displayed in the WAGE column. In addition, the sum of BNFT1 is added to the sum of BNFT2, and the result is placed in the BNFT1 column. One line is skipped before the summary line requested by this SUMMARY subcommand is displayed.

- The third summary line divides the mean of WAGE by the mean of BONUS and places the result in SPACE1. The ratio of the mean of BNFT1 to the mean of BNFT2 is displayed in the SPACE2 column. Because locations are specified, formats can also be given. The results are displayed with commas and two decimal places. One line is skipped before the summary line requested by this SUMMARY subcommand is displayed.

Summary Titles

The default titles for summary lines are listed below:

Keyword	Title
VALIDN	N
VARIANCE	Variance
SUM	Sum
MEAN	Mean
STDDEV	StdDev
MIN	Minimum
MAX	Maximum
SKEWNESS	Skewness
KURTOSIS	Kurtosis
PGT(n)	>n

Keyword	Title
PLT(n)	<n
PIN(n1,n2)	In n1 to n2
FREQUENCY(min,max)	Total
PERCENT(min,max)	Total
MEDIAN(min,max)	Median
MODE(min,max)	Mode

- You can specify a summary title enclosed in apostrophes or quotes, following the conventions for strings (see Universals: Strings).
- The summary title must be specified after the first function and its arguments. It cannot separate any function from its arguments.
- A summary title can be only one line long.
- A summary title wider than the break column extends into the next break column to the right. If the title is wider than all of the available break columns, it is truncated.
- Only one summary title applies per summary line. If more than one is specified, the last is used.
- The summary title is left- or right-justified depending upon whether the break title is left- or right-justified.
- The default location for the summary title is the column of the BREAK variable to which the summary applies.
- With multiple breaks, you can override the default placement of the title by specifying, in parentheses following the title, the break-column number in which you want the summary title to be displayed.
- In a report with no break levels, REPORT displays the summary title above the summary line at the left margin.

Summary Print Formats

All functions have default formats that are used to display results (see Table 2). You can override these defaults by specifying a format keyword and/or the number of decimal places.

- A format specification must be enclosed in parentheses.
- For aggregate functions, one or both format specifications are placed after the variable name, within the parentheses that enclose the variable name. The variable must be explicitly named as an argument.
- For composite functions, one or both format specifications are placed after the variable name of the column location, within the parentheses that enclose the variable name. The column location must be explicitly specified.
- If the report column is wide enough, SUM, MEAN, STDDEV, MIN, MAX, MEDIAN, and MODE use DOLLAR or COMMA format, if a DOLLAR or COMMA format has been declared for the variable on either the FORMATS or PRINT FORMATS command.
- If the column is not wide enough to display the decimal digits for a given function, REPORT displays fewer decimal places. If the column is not wide enough to display the integer portion of the number, REPORT adopts scientific notation and then displays asterisks.
- An exact value of 0 is displayed with one 0 to the left of the decimal point and as many 0 digits to the right as specified by the format. A number less than 1 in absolute value is displayed without a 0 to the left of the decimal point, except with DOLLAR and COMMA formats.

The following format keywords are available:

(DOLLAR) *Display the value using DOLLAR format.*

(COMMA) *Display the value using COMMA format.*

(PLAIN) *Override DOLLAR or COMMA dictionary formats. PLAIN is the default for all functions except MEAN, STDDEV, MIN, MAX, MEDIAN, and MODE. For these functions, the default is the dictionary format.*

Example   `/SUMMARY=MEAN(INCOME (DOLLAR)(2))`
`                 ADD(SUM(INCOME)SUM(WEALTH) (WEALTH(DOLLAR)(2))`

- SUMMARY displays the mean of INCOME with dollär format and two decimal places. The format can be specified because INCOME is specified as an argument to the MEAN function. The result is displayed in the INCOME column.

- The sums of INCOME and WEALTH are added, and the result is displayed with dollar format and two decimal places. The format can be specified because an explicit location is given for the results of ADD. The result is displayed in the WEALTH column.

Table 2 Default print formats for functions

Function	Width	Decimal places
VALIDN	5	0
SUM	Dictionary print format + 2	Dictionary print format
MEAN	Dictionary print format	Dictionary print format
STDDEV	Dictionary print format	Dictionary print format
VARIANCE	Dictionary print format	Dictionary print format
MIN	Dictionary print format	Dictionary print format
MAX	Dictionary print format	Dictionary print format
SKEWNESS	5	2
KURTOSIS	5	2
PGT	6	1
PLT	6	1
PIN	6	1
MEDIAN	Dictionary print format	Dictionary print format
MODE	Dictionary print format	Dictionary print format
PERCENT	6	1
FREQUENCY	5	0
DIVIDE	Dictionary print format	0
PCT	6	2
SUBTRACT	Dictionary print format	0
ADD	Dictionary print format	0
GREAT	Dictionary print format	0
LEAST	Dictionary print format	0
AVERAGE	Dictionary print format	0
MULTIPLY	Dictionary print format	0

Other SUMMARY Keywords

Spacing between multiple summary lines for a single break and references to previously defined summary lines are controlled by the following keywords:

SKIP(n)   *Blank lines before the summary line.* SKIP is not enclosed in parentheses. The default is 0. SKIP on the first SUMMARY subcommand for a BREAK skips the specified lines after skipping the number of lines specified for BRKSPACE on FORMAT.

PREVIOUS(n)   *Use the SUMMARY subcommands for the nth BREAK.* If no specification is given in parentheses, PREVIOUS points to the set of SUMMARY subcommands for the previous BREAK. If an integer specification is given, the SUMMARY subcommands from the nth BREAK are used.

No other specification can be used on SUMMARY with PREVIOUS. For a multiple-break report for which you want the same sets of summaries, specify SUMMARY subcommands for the higher BREAK subcommand and keyword PREVIOUS for lower breaks.

TITLE and FOOTNOTE Subcommands

```
/TITLE ='title' (centered head)
/FOOTNOTE='title' (centered foot)
```

or

```
/TITLE=[LEFT 'title' (left-justified head)]
     [CENTER 'title' (centered head)]
       [RIGHT 'title' (right-justified head)]
/FOOTNOTE=[LEFT 'title' (left-justified foot)]
        [CENTER 'title' (centered foot)]
          [RIGHT 'title' (right-justified foot)]

        [)PAGE]   [)DATE]   [)var]
```

- TITLE and FOOTNOTE are optional and can be placed anywhere after FORMAT except among the BREAK and SUMMARY subcommands.
- The default REPORT title is the title specified on the TITLE command. If there is no TITLE command specified in your SPSS session, the default REPORT title is the first line of the SPSS header.
- A title or footnote is specified by providing a string in apostrophes or quotes on TITLE or FOOTNOTE.
- If the title or footnote is more than one line, enclose each line in apostrophes or quotes and separate the specifications for each line by at least one blank.
- The positional keywords LEFT, CENTER, and RIGHT can each be specified only once.
- Titles are displayed beginning in the first line of the system page.
- Footnotes end in the last line of the system page.
- Centered titles and footnotes are centered within the report page width.
- Titles and footnotes are repeated on each page of a multiple-page report.
- If the total width requested for the combined titles or footnotes for a line exceeds the page width, REPORT generates an error message.

Three keywords can be used in a title or footnote.

)PAGE   *Display the page number right-justified in a five-character field.*

)DATE   *Display the current date in the form* dd/mmm/yy, *right-justified in a nine-character field.*

)var   *Display this variable's value label in this relative position.* If you specify a variable that has no value label, the value itself will display, formatted according to its print format. You cannot specify a scratch or system variable, nor can you specify a variable you create with the STRING subcommand. In addition, you cannot use variables named DATE or PAGE in the *)var* argument because they will only display the current date or a page number. If you want to use a variable named DATE or PAGE, change the variable's name with the RENAME VARIABLES command before you use it in the *)var* argument.

Each variable you specify with *)var* must be one you've defined in the active system file, though it does not need to be a variable you've included as a column on your report. One label or value from each variable specified in a *)var* argument displays on every page of the report. The label displayed for each varies from page to page and is chosen from cases determined as follows:

- If a new page starts with a case listing, REPORT takes the value label from the first case listed.
- If a new page starts with a BREAK line, REPORT takes the value label from the first case of the new break group.
- If a new page starts with a summary line, REPORT takes the value label from the last case of the break group being summarized.

Example	`/TITLE=LEFT 'Personnel Report' 'Prepared on )DATE'` `      RIGHT 'Page: )PAGE'`

- TITLE specifies two lines for a left-justified title, and one line for a right-justified title. These titles are displayed at the top of each page of the report.
- The second line of the left-justified title contains the date on which the report was processed.
- The right-justified title displays the page number following the string "Page:".

MISSING Subcommand

`/MISSING=VAR|NONE|LIST [([varlist][n])]`

MISSING controls the handling of cases with missing values. By default, cases with missing values are included in case listings but are excluded from the calculation of functions on a function-by-function basis.

- MISSING specifications apply to variables named on VARIABLES and SUMMARY as well as to strings created with the STRING subcommand.
- The character used to indicate missing values is controlled by the FORMAT subcommand.

VAR *Missing values are treated separately for each variable.* Missing values are displayed in case listings but are not included in summary statistics. This is the default.

NONE *User-missing value indicators are ignored.* This applies to all variables named on VARIABLES.

LIST[([varlist][n])] *Eliminates any case with the specified number of missing values among the specified list of variables.* If no *n* is specified, the default is 1. If no variables are specified, all variables named on VARIABLES are assumed.

Example `/MISSING= LIST (XVAR,YVAR,ZVAR 2)`

- Any case with a missing value for two or more of the variables XVAR, YVAR, and ZVAR is omitted from the report.

Annotated Example

For a complete example with output, see Examples following the Command Reference.

REREAD

```
REREAD [COLUMN=expression]
```

Example:

```
INPUT PROGRAM.
DATA LIST /KIND 10-14 (A).

DO IF (KIND EQ 'FORD').
REREAD.
DATA LIST /PARTNO 1-2 PRICE 3-6 (DOLLAR,2) QUANTITY 7-9.
END CASE.

ELSE IF (KIND EQ 'CHEVY').
REREAD.
DATA LIST /PARTNO 1-2 PRICE 15-18 (DOLLAR,2) QUANTITY 19-21.
END CASE.
END IF.
END INPUT PROGRAM.
BEGIN DATA
111295100FORD
11        CHEVY 295015
END DATA.
LIST.
```

Overview

REREAD, available only within an INPUT PROGRAM structure, instructs SPSS to read the same record again—usually to define data in light of information gleaned from a previous reading of the record. REREAD is usually used within a conditional structure, such as DO IF—END IF, and is followed by a DATA LIST command. When it receives control for a case, REREAD places the pointer back to column 1 for the current case and begins reading data as defined by the DATA LIST which follows.

Options

Beginning Column. You can specify a beginning column number for REREAD if the pointer is placed in a column other than column 1.

Basic Specification

• The basic specification is the command keyword, REREAD. SPSS rereads the current case according to the data definitions specified on the DATA LIST that follows REREAD.

Syntax Rules

• REREAD is available only within an INPUT PROGRAM structure.

• Multiple REREAD commands can be used within the input program. Each must be followed by an associated DATA LIST command. Multiple REREAD commands executed without an intervening DATA LIST will not have a cumulative effect. All but the first are ignored, except that the starting column comes from the last REREAD specified.

Operations

• When it receives control for a case, REREAD places the pointer back to column 1 for the current case and begins reading data as defined by the DATA LIST which follows. If the COLUMN subcommand is specified, the pointer begins reading in the specified column rather than in column 1.

• REREAD can be used to read part of a record in fixed-field format and the remainder of the record in LIST format. An attempt to mix FIXED and FREE formats, however, yields unpredictable results.

Example
```
INPUT PROGRAM.
DATA LIST /PARTNO 1-2 KIND 10-14 (A).

DO IF (KIND EQ 'FORD').
REREAD.
DATA LIST /PRICE 3-6 (DOLLAR,2) QUANTITY 7-9.
END CASE.

ELSE IF (KIND EQ 'CHEVY').
REREAD.
DATA LIST /PRICE 15-18 (DOLLAR,2) QUANTITY 19-21.
END CASE.
END IF.
END INPUT PROGRAM.

BEGIN DATA
111295100FORD       CHAPMAN AUTO SALES
121199005VW     MIDWEST VOLKSWAGEN SALES
11 395025FORD       BETTER USED CARS
11        CHEVY 195005    HUFFMAN SALES & SERVICE
11        VW    595020    MIDWEST VOLKSWAGEN SALES
11        CHEVY 295015    SAM'S AUTO REPAIR
12        CHEVY 210 20    LONGFELLOW CHEVROLET
 9555032 VW             HYDE PARK IMPORTS
END DATA.
LIST.
```

• Data are extracted from an inventory of automobile parts. The automobile part number always appears in columns 1 and 2, and the automobile manufacturer always appears in columns 10 through 14. Otherwise, the location of other information such as the price and quantity depends on both the part number and the type of automobile.

• The first DATA LIST extracts the part number and the type of automobile.

• Depending on the information from the first DATA LIST, the records are reread using one or another format, pulling the price, quantity, and buyer from different places.

• The two END CASE commands limit the active system file to only those cases with Part 11 and automobile type Ford or Chevrolet. Without the END CASE commands, cases would be created on the active system file for other part numbers and automobile types with missing values for price, quantity, and buyer.

• The results of the LIST command are shown in Figure 1.

Figure 1 Listed information for Part 11

```
PARTNO KIND   PRICE QUANTITY
   11   FORD  $12.95     100
   11   FORD   $3.95      25
   11   CHEVY  $1.95       5
   11   CHEVY  $2.95      15
```

COLUMN Subcommand

COLUMN specifies the beginning column for the REREAD command if the pointer should be placed in a column other than column 1. You can specify a numeric expression for the column.

Example
```
INPUT PROGRAM.
DATA LIST /KIND 10-14 (A).
COMPUTE #COL=1.
IF (KIND EQ 'CHEVY') #COL=13.

DO IF (KIND EQ 'CHEVY' OR KIND EQ 'FORD').
REREAD COLUMN #COL.
DATA LIST /PRICE 3-6 (DOLLAR,2) QUANTITY 7-9.
END CASE.
END IF.
END INPUT PROGRAM.
BEGIN DATA
111295100FORD        CHAPMAN AUTO SALES
121199005VW      MIDWEST VOLKSWAGEN SALES
11 395025FORD        BETTER USED CARS
11        CHEVY 195005      HUFFMAN SALES & SERVICE
11        VW     595020      MIDWEST VOLKSWAGEN SALES
11        CHEVY 295015      SAM'S AUTO REPAIR
12        CHEVY 210 20      LONGFELLOW CHEVROLET
 9555032 VW              HYDE PARK IMPORTS
END DATA.
LIST.
```

- Data are the same as in the previous example. Suppose you do not want to read the part number from the parts file. Notice that price and quantity for Chevrolets are 12 columns away from price and quantity for Fords. Therefore, you could apply the same DATA LIST to both types of automobiles.

- Scratch variable #COL is set to 13 for Chevrolets and left at 1 for all other automobiles. Thus, for Fords, the DATA LIST begins in column 1 and variable PRICE is read from columns 3 through 6. When the record is a Chevrolet, the DATA LIST begins in column 13, forcing variable PRICE to be read from columns 15 through 18 (15 is 3, 16 is 4, and so forth).

Example
```
TITLE  'REREAD USED WITH BOTH FIXED AND LIST INPUT'.

INPUT PROGRAM.
DATA LIST      NOTABLE FIXED/ A 1-14(A). /*Read the fixed
portion
REREAD         COLUMN = 15.
DATA LIST      LIST/ X Y Z.            /*Read the list format
portion
END INPUT PROGRAM.

*   THE VALUE 1 ON THE FIRST RECORD IS IN COLUMN 15.

LIST.
BEGIN DATA
FIRST RECORD  1 2 3 -1 -2 -3
NUMBER 2      4 5
THE THIRD     6 7 8
#4
FIFTH AND LAST9 10 11
END DATA.
```

- Columns 1 through 14 are read in FIXED format. REREAD then resets the pointer to column 15. Thus, beginning in column 15, values are read in LIST format.

- The second DATA LIST specifies only three variables. Thus, the values -1, -2, and -3 on the first record are not read.

- SPSS generates a warning in response to the missing value on record number 2, and a second warning for the three missing values on record #4.

- Notice that on the fifth and last record there is no delimiter between the value LAST and the value 9. Nonetheless, REREAD makes it possible to read the 9 in LIST format.

Example

```
TITLE   "MULTIPLE REREAD'S ON THE SAME RECORD".

INPUT PROGRAM.
DATA LIST        NOTABLE/ CDIMAGE 1-20(A).
REREAD           COLUMN = 6.  /* A, C, and E are in column 6
REREAD           COLUMN = 11. /* B, D, and F are in column 11
DATA LIST        NOTABLE/ INFO 1(A).
END INPUT PROGRAM.
LIST.
BEGIN DATA
1    A    B
2    C    D
3    E    F
END DATA.
```

• Multiple REREAD's are used without an intervening DATA LIST. Thus, the starting column comes from the last REREAD specified and the pointer is reset to column 11.

• Figure 2 shows the results from the LIST command.

Figure 2 Listed information after multiple REREAD commands

```
CDIMAGE              INFO

1    A    B           B
2    C    D           D
3    E    F           F
```

RESTORE

```
RESTORE
```

Overview   RESTORE restores SET specifications that were preserved by a previous PRESERVE command. RESTORE and PRESERVE are especially useful when using the SPSS macro facility. PRESERVE ... RESTORE sequences can be nested up to five levels.

Basic Specification   • The only specification is the command keyword. RESTORE has no additional specifications.

Example
```
GET FILE=PRSNNL.
FREQUENCIES VAR=DIVISION /STATISTICS=ALL.
PRESERVE.
SET XSORT=NO WIDTH=90 UNDEFINED=NOWARN BLANKS=000 CASE=UPLOW.
SORT CASES BY DIVISION.
REPORT FORMAT=AUTO LIST /VARS=LNAME FNAME DEPT SOCSEC SALARY
    /BREAK=DIVISION /SUMMARY=MEAN.
RESTORE.
```

• GET reads the SPSS system file PRSNNL.

• FREQUENCIES requests a frequency table and all statistics for variable DIVISION.

• PRESERVE stores all current SET specifications.

• SET changes several subcommand settings.

• SORT sorts cases in preparation for a report. Because SET XSORT=NO, the SPSS sort program is not used to sort cases; another sort program must be available.

• REPORT requests a report organized by variable DIVISION.

• RESTORE restores all the SET specifications that were in effect before PRESERVE was specified.

SAMPLE

```
SAMPLE {percentage}
       {n FROM m  }
```

Example:
```
SAMPLE .25.
```

Overview

SAMPLE permanently draws a random sample of cases for processing in all subsequent procedures. For a temporary sample, precede SAMPLE with a TEMPORARY command.

Basic Specification

The basic specification is either a decimal value between 0 and 1, or the sample size followed by keyword FROM and the size of the active system file.

- To select an approximate percentage of cases, specify a decimal value between 0 and 1.
- To select an exact-sized random sample, specify a positive integer value less than the file size, followed by keyword FROM and the file size.

Operations

- SAMPLE is a permanent transformation.
- Sampling is based on a pseudo random-number generator that depends on a seed value established by SPSS. The first time a random number series is needed, SPSS uses the seed value established by the SEED subcommand of the SET command. Since this number defaults to a fixed integer, a SAMPLE command of the *n* FROM *m* type generates the identical sample each time a session is rerun. To generate a different sample each time, use the SET command to reset SEED to a different value for each run.
- If sampling is done by the *n* FROM *m* method and the TEMPORARY command is used, successive samples will not be the same because the seed value changes each time a random number series is needed in a session.
- A proportional sample (a sample based on a decimal value) usually does not produce the exact proportion specified.
- If the number (*n*) following FROM is less than the actual file size, the sample is drawn only from the first *n* cases.
- If the number following FROM is greater than the actual file size, SPSS samples an equivalent proportion of cases from the active system file (see example below).
- If SAMPLE follows SELECT IF, it samples only cases selected by SELECT IF.
- If SAMPLE precedes SELECT IF, cases are selected from the sample.
- If more than one SAMPLE is specified in a session, each acts upon the sample selected by the preceding SAMPLE command.
- If N OF CASES is used with SAMPLE, SPSS reads as many records as required to build the specified *n*. It makes no difference whether the N OF CASES precedes or follows the SAMPLE.

Limitations   SAMPLE (and also SELECT IF and WEIGHT) cannot be placed in an input program defined by the FILE TYPE—END FILE TYPE structure or by the INPUT PROGRAM—END INPUT PROGRAM structure. It can be placed nearly anywhere following these commands in a transformation program. See Appendix A for a discussion of the program states in SPSS and the placement of commands.

Example   SAMPLE .25.

• This command samples approximately 25% of the cases in the active system file.

Example   SAMPLE 500 FROM 3420.

• In this example, the active system file must have 3420 cases or more to obtain a random sample of exactly 500 cases.

• If the file contains fewer than 3420 cases, proportionally fewer cases are sampled.

• If the file contains more than 3420 cases, a random sample of 500 cases is drawn from the first 3420 cases.

Example   SAMPLE .50.
DESCRIPTIVES   SALARY85 TO SALARY88.
SAMPLE .50.
DESCRIPTIVES   SALARY85 TO SALARY88.

• In this example, the first DESCRIPTIVES command computes statistics for approximately 50% of the cases, and the second DESCRIPTIVES command computes statistics for approximately 50% of those cases, or 25% of the original cases.

Example   DO IF SEX EQ 'M'.
SAMPLE 1846 FROM 8000.
END IF.

• SAMPLE is placed inside a DO IF—END IF structure to sample substrata differentially. Assume that this is a survey of 10,000 people in which 80% of the sample is male, while the known universe is 48% male. To obtain a sample that corresponds to the known universe and that maximizes the size of the sample, 1846 of the 8000 (48/52*2000) males and all of females must be sampled. The DO IF structure is used to restrict the sampling process to the males.

SAVE

```
SAVE OUTFILE=file

[/KEEP={ALL     }] [/DROP=varlist]
        {varlist}

[/RENAME=(old varlist=new varlist)...]

[/MAP] [/{COMPRESSED  }]
         {UNCOMPRESSED}
```

Example:
```
SAVE OUTFILE=EMPL /RENAME=(AGE=AGE86) (JOBCAT=JOBCAT88).
```

Overview

SAVE produces an SPSS system file. The system file includes all data and a data dictionary with variable and value labels (if specified), missing-value flags, and print formats for each variable. The principal advantage of SAVE over XSAVE is that SAVE causes data to be read; XSAVE is not executed until data are read for the next procedure. With SAVE, the sole purpose of the SPSS session can be to create a new system file.

Options

Variable Subsets and Order. You can save a subset of variables and also reorder variables that are copied to the system file. See the DROP and KEEP subcommands.

Variable Names. You can rename variables as they are copied to the system file.

Variable Map. To confirm any renaming, subsetting, or reordering, you can display the names of the variables saved in the system file alongside their corresponding names in the active system file.

System File. You can specify that the system file be written in a compressed or uncompressed form.

Basic Specification

• The basic specification is the OUTFILE subcommand, which specifies the output system file. The placement of SAVE relative to other commands determines what is saved in the system file. New variables created by transformations and procedures previous to the SAVE command are included in the new system file, and variables altered by transformations are saved in their modified form. Results of any temporary transformations immediately preceding the SAVE command are included in the system file; scratch variables are not. Documentary text from the active system file is saved in the dictionary of the system file.

Subcommand Order

• Subcommands may be used in any order.

Syntax Rules

• OUTFILE is required and can be specified only once. If OUTFILE is specified more than once, only the last OUTFILE specification is in effect.

• KEEP, DROP, RENAME, and MAP can be used multiple times each and in any order.

• Only one of the subcommands COMPRESSED or UNCOMPRESSED can be specified per SAVE command.

• Documentary text can be dropped from the active system file with the DROP DOCUMENTS command.

Operations
- SAVE is executed immediately and causes the data to read. Compare with XSAVE, which is a transformation and is not executed until data are read for the next procedure.
- The system file dictionary is arranged in the same order as the active system file.
- System files are binary files designed to be read and written by SPSS only. System files can be edited only with the UPDATE command. See also the MATCH FILES and ADD FILES commands for joining system files.
- The active system file remains available for SPSS transformations and procedures after the system file is created.
- SAVE processes the dictionary first and displays a message that indicates how many *variables* will be saved. Once the data are written, SAVE indicates how many *cases* were saved. If the second message does not appear, the file was probably not completely written.

Limitations
- SAVE does not save scratch variables.

Example
```
GET FILE=HUBEMPL.
SAVE OUTFILE=EMPL88 /RENAME=(AGE=AGE88) (JOBCAT=JOBCAT88).
```
- The GET command retrieves the system file HUBEMPL.
- The OUTFILE subcommand on SAVE specifies EMPL88 as the output system file. The original system file HUBEMPL is not changed.
- The RENAME subcommand renames variable AGE to AGE88 and variable JOBCAT to JOBCAT88.
- SAVE causes the data to be read.

Example
```
GET FILE=HUBEMPL.
TEMPORARY.
RECODE DEPT85 TO DEPT88 (1,2=1) (3,4=2) (ELSE=9).
VALUE LABELS DEPT85 TO DEPT88 1 'MANAGEMENT' 2 'OPERATIONS'
9 'UNKNOWN'.
SAVE OUTFILE=HUBTEMP.
CROSSTABS DEPT85 TO DEPT88 BY JOBCAT.
```
- The GET command retrieves the system file HUBEMPL.
- The TEMP subcommand indicates that the following transformations (RECODE and VALUE LABELS) are in effect only for the next command that reads the data (SAVE).
- The RECODE command recodes values for all variables between and including DEPT85 and DEPT88 on the active file.
- The VALUE LABELS command specifies new labels for the recoded values.
- The OUTFILE subcommand on SAVE specifies HUBTEMP as the output system file. HUBTEMP will include the recoded values for DEPT85 to DEPT88 and the new value labels.
- The CROSSTABS command crosstabulates DEPT85 to DEPT88 with JOBCAT. Since the RECODE and VALUE LABELS commands were temporary, the CROSSTABS output does not reflect the recoding and new labels.
- If SAVE is replaced with XSAVE, data are read only once and both the saved system file and the CROSSTABS output will reflect the temporary recoding and labeling of the department variables.

OUTFILE Subcommand

OUTFILE specifies the output system file. OUTFILE is required and can be specified only once. If OUTFILE is specified more than once, only the last OUTFILE specification is in effect.

DROP and KEEP Subcommands

DROP and KEEP save a subset of variables. DROP specifies the variables not to save in the new system file; KEEP specifies the variables to save in the new system file.

- Variables may be specified in any order. The variable order on KEEP determines their sequence in the system file. Variable order on DROP does not affect the order of variables in the system file: the variables are saved in the same sequence they appear in the active system file.
- Multiple DROP and KEEP subcommands are allowed.
- If a variable is referenced twice, only the first mention of the variable is recognized.

Reordering Variables

- The variable order on KEEP determines variable order in the output system file. New variables created by transformations or procedures are added to the end of the active system file. KEEP can save these variables in a different order.
- Keyword ALL on KEEP refers to all remaining variables not previously specified. ALL must be the last specification on KEEP.

Example

```
SAVE OUTFILE=HUBTEMP /DROP=DEPT79 TO DEPT84 SALARY79.
```

- The system file is saved as file HUBTEMP. All variables between and including DEPT79 and DEPT84, as well as SALARY79, are excluded from the system file. All other variables are saved in the system file.

Example

```
GET FILE=PRSNL.
COMPUTE   TENURE=(12-CMONTH +(12*(88-CYEAR)))/12.
COMPUTE   JTENURE=(12-JMONTH +(12*(88-JYEAR)))/12.
VARIABLE LABELS   TENURE 'Tenure in Company'
                  JTENURE 'Tenure in Grade'.
SAVE OUTFILE=PRSNL88 /DROP=GRADE STORE.
 /KEEP=LNAME NAME TENURE JTENURE ALL.
```

- Variables TENURE and JTENURE are created by COMPUTE commands and assigned variable labels by the VARIABLE LABELS command. TENURE and JTENURE are added to the end of the active system file.
- DROP specifies that variables GRADE and STORE be dropped when file PRSNL88 is generated. KEEP determines that LNAME, NAME, TENURE, and JTENURE are the first four variables in file PRSNL88, followed by all remaining variables not specified on DROP. Variables not specified on KEEP are saved on PRSNL88 in the same sequence they appear in the original file.

RENAME Subcommand

RENAME changes the names of variables as they are copied into the system file.

- Name changes can be specified in the form *old varname=new varname*. Multiple sets of variable specifications are allowed. Each set may be enclosed in optional parentheses.
- As an alternative to the above, name changes can be specified with a list of old variable names followed by an equals sign and a list of new variable names. The same number of variables must be specified on both lists. Keyword TO can be used in either or both lists to refer to consecutive variables. A single set of parentheses enclosing the entire specification is required for this method.
- Old variable names need not be specified according to their order in the active system file.
- Name changes take place in one operation. Therefore, variable names can be exchanged between two variables.
- Multiple RENAME subcommands are allowed.

Example   `SAVE OUTFILE=EMPL88 /RENAME  AGE=AGE88 JOBCAT=JOBCAT88.`

- RENAME specifies two name changes for file EMPL88: AGE is renamed to AGE88, and JOBCAT is renamed to JOBCAT88.

Example   `SAVE OUTFILE=EMPL88 /RENAME (AGE JOBCAT=AGE88 JOBCAT88).`

- The name changes are identical to those in the previous example: AGE is renamed to AGE88, and JOBCAT is renamed to JOBCAT88. The parentheses are required with this method.

MAP Subcommand

MAP displays a list of the variables in the system file and their corresponding names in the active system file.

- The only specification is keyword MAP. MAP has no additional specifications.
- Multiple MAP subcommands are allowed. Each MAP subcommand maps the results of subcommands that precede it, but not results of subcommands that follow it.

Example
```
GET FILE=HUBEMPL.
SAVE OUTFILE=EMPL88 /RENAME=(AGE=AGE86) (JOBCAT=JOBCAT88)
/KEEP=LNAME NAME JOBCAT88 ALL /MAP.
```

- MAP confirms that variable AGE is renamed to AGE86 and JOBCAT is renamed to JOBCAT88. MAP also confirms that the first three variables in file EMPL88 are LNAME, NAME, and JOBCAT88, and that all remaining variables from the active system file are present in file EMPL88.

COMPRESSED Subcommand

COMPRESSED tells SPSS to save the system file in compressed form. In a compressed file, small integers (from -99 to 155) are stored in one byte, instead of the usual eight bytes.

- The only specification is keyword COMPRESSED. COMPRESSED has no additional specifications.
- Compressed system files occupy less disk space than do uncompressed system files.
- Compressed system files take longer to read than do uncompressed system files.
- No additional specification is required on the GET command to read a compressed system file.
- Only one of the subcommands COMPRESSED or UNCOMPRESSED can be specified per SAVE command. COMPRESSED is usually the default, though UNCOMPRESSED may be the default at some installations.

UNCOMPRESSED Subcommand

UNCOMPRESSED tells SPSS to save the system file in uncompressed form.

- The only specification is keyword UNCOMPRESSED. UNCOMPRESSED has no additional specifications.
- Uncompressed system files are quicker to read than are compressed system files.
- Uncompressed system files occupy more disk space than do compressed system files.
- No additional specification is required on the GET command to read an uncompressed system file.
- Only one of the subcommands COMPRESSED or UNCOMPRESSED can be specified per SAVE command. COMPRESSED is usually the default, though UNCOMPRESSED may be the default at some installations.

SAVE SCSS

This command is not available on all operating systems.

```
SAVE SCSS OUTFILE=file

[/KEEP={ALL     }] [/DROP=varlist]
       {varlist}

[/RENAME=(old varlist=new varlist)...]
```

Example:

```
SAVE SCSS OUTFILE=HUBOUT.
```

Overview

SAVE SCSS saves the SPSS active system file as an SCSS master file.

See SAVE and XSAVE for saving SPSS systems files. See SAVE TRANS-LATE for saving foreign files, such as Lotus, dBASE, and Multiplan files. See EXPORT for saving files in a format that can be read by other software programs.

Options

Variable Subsets. You can specify a subset of variables to copy to the SCSS master file. See the DROP and KEEP subcommands.

Variable Names. You can rename variables that are copied into the SCSS master file. See RENAME Subcommand.

Basic Specification

• The basic specification is OUTFILE and the name of the SCSS master file.

Subcommand Order

• OUTFILE must be first.

• Remaining subcommands can be named in any order.

Operations

• SAVE SCSS saves all dictionary information from the active system file, plus the data in their form at the point SAVE SCSS is encountered. This includes all permanent transformations and any temporary transformations made just prior to the SAVE SCSS command.

• SCSS does not support string variables, and they are not saved. SPSS informs you which variables were not saved.

• The system-missing value for each numeric variable is recoded, usually to the variable's highest value plus one. A variable-by-variable listing in SPSS output shows the missing value selected for each variable.

• In converting from double precision in SPSS to single precision in SCSS, numeric values are usually truncated (SPSS actually does a mixed-mode assignment which may result in rounding in some operating-system environments). If alphanumeric or extreme values are encountered for numeric variables when the data are read, those variables are dropped in the master file and their names displayed in the SAVE SCSS output.

• SCSS has reserved keywords that are not reserved in SPSS, so variables with the names AGAINST, ON, SPSS, and SPSS0001 will not be saved. These SPSS variables can be renamed using the RENAME subcommand.

Example

```
SAVE SCSS OUTFILE=HUBOUT
 /DROP=DEPT79 TO DEPT81, SALARY79 TO SALARY81, HOURLY81
 /RENAME=(SALARY82,HOURLY82,PROMO81=SALARY,HOURLY,PROMO).
```

- The SCSS master file HUBOUT is created. DROP specifies variables not to be copied into the master file. RENAME drops the year indicator from each of the specified variables.

OUTFILE Subcommand

OUTFILE is required and must be first. It specifies the master file to be saved.

DROP and KEEP Subcommands

DROP and KEEP specify a list of variables to be dropped or kept in the master file.

- DROP and KEEP affect only the master file, not the SPSS active system file.
- KEEP can be used to control the order in which variables are written into the SCSS master file. Variables are written in the order named on KEEP. If a subset of variables is followed by the keyword ALL, the variables specifically named are saved in the order specified; remaining variables are saved according to their order on the SPSS active system file.

RENAME Subcommand

RENAME renames variables saved on the SCSS master file. Variables that have been renamed retain their variable and value labels.

- Specify, in parentheses, *old names = new names*. The same number of variables must be specified on each side of the equals sign.
- Alternatively, rename variables one at a time. Parentheses are optional with this method.
- Renaming variables with SAVE SCSS does not rename them on the SPSS active system file. However, if RENAME precedes DROP or KEEP, refer to variables by their new names on DROP or KEEP.

SAVE TRANSLATE

This command is not available on all operating systems.

```
SAVE TRANSLATE† OUTFILE=file

[/TYPE={WK1}]  [/FIELDNAMES]*
       {WKS}
       {WR1}
       {WRK}
       {SLK}
       {DB2}
       {DB3}
       {DB4}

[/KEEP={ALL     }]  [/DROP=varlist]
       {varlist}
```

†Not available on all systems.

*Available only for spreadsheet files.

Keyword	Foreign file
WK1	1-2-3 Release 2.0
WKS	1-2-3 Release 1A
WR1	Symphony Release 2.0
WRK	Symphony Release 1.0
SLK	Multiplan (symbolic format only)
DB2	dBASE-II
DB3	dBASE-III
DB4	dBASE-IV

Example:

```
SAVE TRANSLATE OUTFILE='SALESREP.SLK'
 /KEEP=SALES, UNITS, MONTHS, PRICE1 TO PRICE20
 /FIELDNAMES.
```

Overview

SAVE TRANSLATE translates the SPSS active system file into a foreign file. Supported formats are 1-2-3, Symphony, Multiplan, dBASE-II, dBASE-III, and dBASE-IV.

Options

Variable Subsets. You can use the DROP and KEEP subcommands to specify variables to omit or retain in the resulting file.

Spreadsheet Files. You can use the FIELDNAMES subcommand to translate SPSS variable names to field names.

Basic Specification

- The basic specification is OUTFILE with a file specification in apostrophes.
- TYPE, with a keyword to indicate the type of dBASE file, is also required to save dBASE database files.

Subcommand Order

- Subcommands can be named in any order.

Operations

- After SAVE TRANSLATE is executed, the active system file remains available for SPSS transformations and procedures.
- User-missing values are transferred as the actual values.
- If the SPSS active system file contains more variables than the foreign file can receive, SAVE TRANSLATE writes the maximum number of variables the foreign file can receive.

Spreadsheets

Variables in the active system file become columns, and cases become rows in the spreadsheet file.

- If you specify FIELDNAMES, variable names become the first row and indicate field names.

• String variable values are left-justified, and numeric variable values are right-justified.

• The resulting spreadsheet file is given the range name of SPSS.

• System-missing values are translated to NA in spreadsheet files.

• SPSS formats are translated as follows:

SPSS	1-2-3/Symphony	Multiplan
Number	Fixed	Fixed
Comma	Comma	Fixed
Dollar	Currency	$ (dollar)
String	Label	Alpha

Databases Variables in the active system file become fields, and cases become records in the database file.

• Characters that are allowed in SPSS variable names (but are not allowed in dBASE field names) are translated to colons in dBASE-II and underscores in dBASE-III and dBASE-IV.

• SPSS numeric variables containing the system-missing value are translated to **** in dBASE III and dBASE-IV, or 0 (zero) for dBASE II.

• The width and precision of numeric variables that are translated are derived from the SPSS Print Format; the number of total characters for the number is taken from the width of the print format, and the number of digits to the right of the decimal point is taken from the decimals in the print format. Use the PRINT FORMATS command (if necessary) to adjust the width and precision prior to using SAVE TRANSLATE. Values that cannot be converted to the given width and precision are converted to missing values (all asterisks in dBASE) upon translation.

• SPSS variable formats are translated to dBASE formats as follows:

SPSS	dBASE
Number	Numeric
String	Character
Dollar	Numeric
Comma	Numeric

Limitations • Maximum 2048 cases can be translated to 1-2-3 Release 1A, maximum 8192 cases to 1-2-3 Release 2.0 or Symphony files, and maximum 4095 cases to Multiplan files.

• Maximum 65,535 cases and 32 variables can be translated to a dBASE-II file; maximum 1 billion cases to dBASE-III or dBASE-IV files (subject to disk space availability) and 128 variables (dBASE-III) or 255 variables (dBASE-IV).

OUTFILE Subcommand OUTFILE assigns a name to the file to be saved. The only specification is the name of the foreign file enclosed in apostrophes.

Example `SAVE TRANSLATE OUTFILE='STAFF.DBF'/TYPE=DB3.`

• SAVE TRANSLATE creates a dBASE-III file called STAFF.DBF. The TYPE subcommand is required to specify the type of dBASE file to save.

TYPE Subcommand TYPE indicates the format of a foreign file.

• TYPE can be omitted for translating to spreadsheet files if the file extension named on OUTFILE is the default for the type of file you are saving.

• TYPE with keyword DB2, DB3, or DB4 is required for translating the SPSS active system file into a dBASE file.

• TYPE takes precedence over the file extension.

- Available keywords on TYPE are

WK1 *1-2-3 Release 2.0.*

WKS *1-2-3 Release 1A.*

WR1 *Symphony Release 2.0.*

WRK *Symphony Release 1.0.*

SLK *Multiplan (symbolic format).*

DB2 *dBASE-II.* Specify DB2 on TYPE when translating to a dBASE-II file.

DB3 *dBASE-III.* Specify DB3 on TYPE when translating to a dBASE-III or dBASE-III PLUS file.

DB4 *dBASE-IV.* Specify DB4 on TYPE when translating to a dBASE-IV file.

Example   `SAVE TRANSLATE OUTFILE='PROJECT.OCT' /TYPE=SLK.`

- SAVE TRANSLATE translates the SPSS active system file into the Multiplan spreadsheet PROJECT.OCT.

**FIELDNAMES
Subcommand**

FIELDNAMES translates SPSS variable names into field names in the spreadsheet.

- FIELDNAMES can be used with spreadsheets only. FIELDNAMES is ignored when used with database files.
- SPSS variable names are transferred to the first row of the spreadsheet file.

Example   `SAVE TRANSLATE OUTFILE='STAFF.WRK' /FIELDNAMES.`

- SAVE TRANSLATE creates a Symphony spreadsheet file containing all variables from the SPSS active system file. The variable names are transferred to the Symphony file.

**DROP and KEEP
Subcommands**

Use DROP or KEEP to include only a subset of variables in the resulting file. DROP specifies a set of variables to exclude, and KEEP specifies a set of variables to retain.

- Specify a list of variable, column, or field names separated by commas or spaces.
- KEEP does not affect the order of variables in the resulting file. Variables are kept in their original order.

Example   `SAVE TRANSLATE OUTFILE='ADDRESS.DBF' /TYPE=DB4 /DROP=PHONENO, EN-`
`TRY.`

- SAVE TRANSLATE creates a dBASE-IV file named ADDRESS.DBF, dropping the SPSS variables PHONENO and ENTRY.

SELECT IF

```
SELECT IF [(]logical expression[)]
```

The following relational operators can be used in logical expressions:

Symbol	Definition	Symbol	Definition
EQ or =	Equal to	NE or ã= or <>	Not equal to
LT or <	Less than	LE or <=	Less than or equal to
GT or >	Greater than	GE or >=	Greater than or equal to

The following logical operators can be used in logical expressions:

Symbol	Definition
AND or &	Both relations must be true
OR or | or ¦	Either relation can be true
NOT or ã or ~	Reverses the outcome of an expression

Example:
```
SELECT IF (SEX EQ 'MALE').
SELECT IF (V1 GE V2).
SELECT IF (SYSMIS(V1)).
```

Overview

SELECT IF permanently selects cases for analysis based upon logical conditions found in the data. These conditions are specified in a *logical expression*. The logical expression can contain relational operators, logical operators, arithmetic operations, and any functions allowed in COMPUTE transformations (see COMPUTE; Universals: Logical Expressions; and Universals: Functions). For temporary case selection, precede SELECT IF with a TEMPORARY command.

Syntax Rules

- Parentheses may be used to make the logical expression easier to read. Parentheses may also be used to specify the order of evaluation.
- Each relational operator must be preceded and followed by a variable name or an expression. Abbreviated syntax such as (AGE GE 18 AND LE 65) is not allowed.
- At least one relation or function must be included in the logical expression.
- A relation includes a variable name, a relational operator, and a value or variable.

Operations

- SELECT IF permanently selects cases.
- The logical expression is evaluated as true, false, or missing.
- If a logical expression is true, the case is selected; if it is false or missing, the case is not selected.
- Multiple SELECT IF commands issued prior to a procedure command must all be true for a case to be selected.
- SELECT IF should be placed before other transformations for efficiency considerations.
- Logical expressions are evaluated in the following order: first, numeric functions, then exponentiation, then arithmetic operators, then relational operators, and, finally, logical operators.
- Use parentheses to change the order of evaluation.
- If N OF CASES is used with SELECT IF, SPSS reads as many records as required to build the specified *n*. It makes no difference whether the N OF CASES precedes or follows the SELECT IF.

Missing Values
- If the logic of the expression is indeterminate because of missing values, the case is not selected. In a simple relational expression, the logic is indeterminate if the expression on either side of the relational operator is missing.
- If a compound expression is used in which relations are joined by the logical operator OR, the case is selected if either relation is true, even if the other is missing.
- To select cases with missing values for the variables within the expression, use the missing-value functions described in Universals: Functions.
- To include cases with values that have been declared user-missing along with other cases, use the VALUE function.
- System variable $CASENUM is the sequence number of the case in the active system file. It is established for each case after the case has been selected. Although it is syntactically correct to use $CASENUM on SELECT IF, it does not produce the expected results. To select a set of cases based on their sequence in a file, create your own sequence variable with the transformation language prior to selecting (see the example below).

Limitations   SELECT IF (and also SAMPLE and WEIGHT) cannot be placed in an input program defined by the FILE TYPE—END FILE TYPE structure or by the INPUT PROGRAM—END INPUT PROGRAM structure. It can be placed nearly anywhere following these commands in a transformation program. See Appendix A for a discussion of the program states in SPSS and the placement of commands.

Example   `SELECT IF (SEX EQ 'MALE').`
- All subsequent procedures will use only cases in which the value of SEX is equal to MALE.
- Since upper and lower case are different in comparisons of string variables, cases for which SEX equals 'male' are not selected.

Example   `SELECT IF (INCOME GT 75000 OR INCOME LE 10000).`
- The logical expression tests whether a case has a value greater than 75,000 or less than 10,000. If either relation is true, the case is used in subsequent analyses. Notice that the variable name INCOME is repeated before the second relational operator.

Example   `SELECT IF (V1 GE V2).`
- This example selects cases where variable V1 is greater than or equal to V2. If either V1 or V2 is missing, the logic of the expression is indeterminate and the case is not selected.

Example   `SELECT IF (SEX = 'F' & INCOME <= 10000).`
- The logical expression tests whether string variable SEX is equal to F and if numeric variable INCOME is less than or equal to 10,000. Cases that meet both conditions are included in subsequent analyses.

Example   `SELECT IF (SYSMIS(V1)).`
- The logical expression tests whether V1 is equal to the system-missing value. If the value of V1 is system-missing, the case is selected for subsequent analyses.

Example   `SELECT IF (VALUE(V1) GT 0).`

- Cases are selected if V1 is greater than 0, even if the value of V1 has been declared user-missing.

`SELECT IF (V1 GT 0).`

- In this example cases are not selected if V1 is user-missing, even if its value is greater than 0.

Example   `SELECT IF (RECEIV GT DUE AND (REVNUS GE EXPNS OR BALNCE GT 0)).`

- By default, AND is executed before OR. This expression uses parentheses to change the order of evaluation.

- First, SPSS tests whether variable REVNUS is greater than or equal to variable EXPNS, or variable BALNCE has a value greater than 0. Second, SPSS tests whether RECEIV is greater than DUE.

- Without the parentheses, SPSS would first test whether RECEIV is greater than DUE and REVNUS is greater than or equal to EXPNS. Second, SPSS would test whether BALNCE is greater than 0.

Example   `SELECT IF ((V1-15) LE (V2*(-0.001))).`

- The logical expression compares whether V1 minus 15 is less than or equal to V2 multiplied by −0.001. If the expression is true, the case is selected for subsequent analyses.

Example   `SELECT IF ((YRMODA(88,13,0) - YRMODA(YVAR,MVAR,DVAR)) LE 30).`

- The logical expression subtracts the number of days representing the date YVAR (year), MVAR (month), and DVAR (day) from the number of days representing the last day in 1988. If the difference is less than or equal to 30, the case is selected for subsequent analyses.

Example
```
TITLE 'CREATING A SEQUENCE NUMBER'
COMPUTE  #CASESEQ=#CASESEQ+1.
SELECT IF (MOD(#CASESEQ,2)=0).
```

- This example computes a scratch variable, #CASESEQ, containing the sequence numbers for each case, and it selects every other case beginning with the second.

- It is important that the sequence number variable (#CASESEQ in this example) be a scratch variable so that it is not reinitialized for every case. (See LEAVE for an alternative.)

Example
```
DO IF  SEX EQ 'M'.
+    SELECT IF PRESTIGE GT 50.
ELSE IF  SEX EQ 'F'.
+    SELECT IF PRESTIGE GT 45.
END IF.
```

- The SELECT IF commands within the DO IF structure select males with prestige scores above 50 and females with prestige scores above 45.

- In this example, the optional plus sign in column 1 indents the SELECT IF commands for readability.

SET

```
SET [BLANKS={SYSMIS}]  [BOX={'-I+[++++++++]'}]  [CASE={UPPER}]
           {value }        {X'hexstring '}          {UPLOW}

    [CCA={"-,,,"      }]  [CCB={"-,,,"      }]  [CCC={"-,,,"      }]
         {'format-spec'}       {'format-spec'}       {'format-spec'}

    [CCD={"-,,,"      }]  [CCE={"-,,,"      }]
         {'format-spec'}       {'format-spec'}

    [COMPRESSION={ON }]  [ENDCMD={'.'     }]  [ERRORS={LISTING }]
                 {OFF}           {'string'}           {TERMINAL}
                                                      {BOTH    }
                                                      {NONE    }

    [FORMAT={F8.2}]  [HEADER={YES}]  [JOURNAL=[{ON }] [file]]
            {Fw.d}           {NO }            {OFF}

    [LENGTH={59  }]  [MESSAGES={LISTING }]  [MEXPAND={ON }]
            {n   }             {TERMINAL}            {OFF}
            {NONE}             {BOTH    }
                              {NONE    }

    [MITERATE={1000}]  [MNEST={50}]  [MPRINT={ON }]
              {n   }          {n }          {OFF}

    [MXERRS={40}]  [MXLOOPS={40}]  [MXWARNS={80 }]
            {n }            {n }            {n  }

    [NULLINE={YES}]  [PRINTBACK={LISTING }]  [RESULTS={LISTING }]
             {NO }             {TERMINAL}             {TERMINAL}
                              {BOTH    }             {BOTH†   }
                              {NONE    }             {NONE    }

    [SCRIPTTAB={'@'      }]  [SEED={2000000}]
               {'character'}         {n      }

    [TBFONT={'1234'    }]  [TB1={'-I[++++++++'}]  [TB2={'          '}]
            {X'hexstring'}        {X'hexstring' }        {X'hexstring'}

    [UNDEFINED={WARN  }]  [WIDTH={132}]  [XSORT={YES}]
               {NOWARN}          {80† }          {NO }
                                {n   }
```

Settings for generating square plots in SPSS Categories:

```
SET [CPI={10}]  [LPI={6}]
         {n }          {n}
```

Settings for the GRAPH command

```
SET [ADEVICE=device]  [/DRAW={FULL**}]  [/GCMDFILE=file]
                             {QUICK }
                             {NO    }

    [/GDATA=file]  [/GDEVICE=device]  [/GMEMORY=integer[{K}]]
                                                        {M}
```

Defaults may differ by installation.
†Default in a prompted session.

Example:

```
SET BLANKS=0/UNDEFINED=NOWARN/MXWARNS=200.
```

Overview

SET changes SPSS running options. To see the current running options, use the SHOW command. Use the PRESERVE command to save the current SET conditions so that you can return to them later in the session with the RESTORE command. PRESERVE and RESTORE are especially useful with the macro facility.

This chapter discusses the SET subcommands common to most systems. Refer to your SPSS *Operations Guide* to see if there are additional SET subcommands for your operating system.

Options   **Blanks and Undefined Input Data.** You can specify the value that SPSS should use any time it encounters a completely blank field for a numeric-format item. You can also turn off the warning message that SPSS issues when it encounters a completely blank field for a numeric variable.

Maximum Errors and Loops. You can raise or lower the default number of 40 maximum errors and of 80 maximum warnings allowed in an SPSS session before processing discontinues. In addition, you can raise or lower the default maximum of 40 loops SPSS allows for loops defined on a LOOP—END LOOP structure.

Output Destination. You can send error messages, resource utilization messages, command printback, and SPSS command results to your terminal, a listing file, both, or neither.

Output Form and Layout. You can change the length and width of output, determine whether output sent to the display file is printed in upper or mixed case, and also whether command printback and headers are included in the display file. You can change the default F8.2 print and write formats used for numeric variables. In addition, you can specify the characters used to draw grids in procedures such as CROSSTABS, MULT RESPONSE, and TABLES, or the characters used to draw histograms or bar charts in procedures such as FREQUENCIES and REGRESSION.

Custom Currency Formats. You can customize currency formats for your own applications. For example, you can display currency as French francs rather than American dollars.

Samples and Random Numbers. You can change the initial seed value to a particular number or have SPSS select a random number.

Sorting Data. You can decide which sort program to use: the one built into SPSS or the default sort program on your system.

Scratch File Compression. You can specify whether scratch files are kept in compressed or uncompressed form.

Command Terminators and Journal Files. You can change the default command terminator from a period to a character of your choice. You can specify either that a blank line be ignored or taken as a command terminator during a prompted session. In addition, you can determine whether SPSS keeps a journal of the commands entered during an SPSS session.

Macro Displays. You can control the process of macro expansion, the maximum number of loop traversals, and nesting levels. You can also control display of the variables, commands, and parameters that a macro uses.

SET and the TABLES Procedure. You can define the characters used for line drawings by the TABLES procedure.

SET and the Categories Option. For procedures in the SPSS Categories option (an add-on option to SPSS), all two-dimensional plots require that the scale of the vertical axis be identical to that of the horizontal axis (that is, that the plots be square). You can define the number of characters per inch and the number of lines per inch used to scale those plots.

SET and the GRAPH Procedure. You can define the type of graph to be drawn by SPSS Graphics and also the name of the command, data, and output files generated. In addition, you can name the alpha and graphics device used with GRAPH and specify the amount of memory to be allocated for SPSS Graphics.

Basic Specification   • The basic specification is at least one subcommand and setting. The setting is in effect until it is changed, or the session is ended.

Subcommand Order   • Subcommands can be named in any order.

Syntax Rules   • Subcommands must be separated by at least one space or slash.

• Only one keyword or argument can be specified for each subcommand.

- SET can be used more than once in the command sequence.
- Each time SET is entered, only the named specifications are affected. All others remain at their previous settings or the default.
- YES is accepted as an alias for keyword ON.
- NO is accepted as an alias for keyword OFF.

Example   `SET BLANKS=0/UNDEFINED=NOWARN/MXWARNS=200.`

- BLANKS=0 specifies 0 as the value SPSS should display whenever it encounters a completely blank field for a numeric variable.
- UNDEFINED=NOWARN suppresses the message that displays whenever SPSS encounters anything other than a number or a blank as the value for a numeric-format item.
- MXWARNS=200 specifies that an SPSS session can generate a maximum of 200 warnings before the session is terminated for generating too many warnings. The default is 40.

Treatment of Numeric Blanks

By default, SPSS translates entirely blank fields read with a numeric format to the system-missing value. Use BLANKS to specify some other value. If SPSS encounters anything other than a number or a blank as the value for a numeric-format item, it issues a warning. Use UNDEFINED to suppress the message.

- BLANKS controls only the translation of numeric fields.
- If a blank field is read with a non-numeric format, the resulting value is a blank.
- The BLANKS specification controls all numeric-variable blanks. You cannot have different specifications for different variables.
- BLANKS must be specified before data are read, since blanks in numeric fields are converted to system-missing as they are read.
- When UNDEFINE=WARN, the message is displayed for each conversion of an alphanumeric symbol to the system-missing value.
- Suppressing the warning message does not stop the counting of warnings toward the maximum allowed before session termination. To control the number of conversions of undefined data permitted within a session, use the MXWARNS subcommand.
- UNDEFINED does not allow you to recode alphanumeric values to numbers. To accomplish that, define the variable as alphanumeric and then recode it into a numeric variable.

BLANKS   *Blanks for numeric fields.* Specify any number. Blanks are translated to this number. The number is not automatically defined as missing. The default, however, is the system-missing value.

UNDEFINED   *Warning message for undefined data.* Specify WARN or NOWARN. NOWARN suppresses the message. WARN is the default.

Example   `SET BLANKS=-1 /UNDEFINED=NOWARN.`

- BLANKS translates all numeric-variable blanks to the value −1.
- UNDEFINED suppresses the warning message that displays when SPSS encounters anything other than a number or a blank as the value for a numeric variable.

Maximum Errors and Loops

You can raise or lower the maximum number of warnings and the maximum number of errors SPSS allows when processing command files before it discontinues processing. In addition, you can raise or lower the maximum number of loops SPSS allows for loops defined on a LOOP—END LOOP structure.

• When you run SPSS in prompted mode, each command is executed immediately. Any error or message relative to the command displays upon execution. The MXERRS and MXWARNS settings are therefore ignored when you run SPSS from prompts.

MXERRS *Maximum number of errors permitted before session is terminated.* Specify a number. The default is 40. Errors counted are those that cause SPSS to disregard the command on which the error occurred but to continue processing. This setting applies only to command files submitted for execution through the operating system.

MXWARNS *Maximum number of warnings and errors permitted, collectively, before session is terminated.* Specify a number. The default is 80. All errors are included with warnings in the count toward the MXWARNS limit. Notes are not. This setting applies only to command files submitted for execution through the operating system.

MXLOOPS *Maximum executions of a loop on a single case.* Specify a number. The default is 40. The LOOP and END LOOP commands execute a set of transformation and data definition commands repeatedly for a single case or input record. Without an indexing clause, it is possible to set up a loop such that the conditions for ending it are never met. To cut short such infinite loops, SPSS counts the number of times a loop is executed on each case and terminates the loop when a limit is reached.

Example   `SET MXERRS=5 /MXWARNS=200 /MXLOOPS=10.`

• MXERRS determines that a maximum of 5 errors can occur before an SPSS session is terminated.

• MXWARNS determines that a maximum of 200 warnings can be issued before an SPSS session is terminated.

• MXLOOPS determines that a loop can be executed a maximum of 10 times before processing of SPSS commands is terminated.

Routing Output

You can route error messages, resource utilization messages (for example, the banner and session summaries that display in SPSS output), command printback, and SPSS command results separately. Default routes vary by operating system and also according to whether command files are executed through the operating system or run within SPSS; typical defaults are shown in Table 1.

Table 1 Defaults for ERRORS, MESSAGES, PRINTBACK, and RESULTS

Subcommand	Run through operating system	Run in SPSS
ERRORS	Both	Both
MESSAGES	Listing	Listing
PRINTBACK	Listing	Listing
RESULTS	Listing	Both

• To direct output to the listing file only, use keyword LISTING.

• To direct output to the terminal only, use keyword TERMINAL. Page headers are not routed to the terminal with the rest of the output.

• To direct output to both the terminal and the listing file, use keyword BOTH. Synonyms for BOTH are YES and ON.

• To suppress the display of the output, use keyword NONE. Synonyms for NONE are NO and OFF.

The following subcommands on SET route SPSS output. Each can specify any one of the keywords LISTING, TERMINAL, BOTH, or NONE.

ERRORS   *Error messages.*

MESSAGES   *Resource utilization messages.* These include the summaries at the end of a command run: for example, the amounts of memory used by a command or the amount of time it required to run.

PRINTBACK   *Echoing of SPSS commands read from a file.*

RESULTS   *Results generated by SPSS commands.*

Example   SET ERRORS=BOTH MESSAGES=NONE PRINTBACK=LISTING
RESULTS=TERMINAL.

• Error messages are directed to both the terminal and the listing file.

• Resource utilization messages are suppressed.

• Command printback is directed only to the listing file.

• SPSS command results are directed only to the terminal.

Output Form and Layout

You can control the page length and width for the display file, and the print and write formats for numeric variables created by transformation commands. You can also control whether lowercase letters in labels and error messages are translated to uppercase in the display file and whether your commands are printed back along with other output from your SPSS commands. You can control the box-drawing characters displayed in procedures like CROSSTABS and MULT RESPONSE and the character used to draw histograms or bar charts in procedures such as FREQUENCIES and REGRESSION. In addition, SET has subcommands that determine whether headings print at the beginning of every page in the display, and whether macro expansion command lines are included in the command printback.

LENGTH   *The maximum page length for output.* Initially, the length is set to 59 lines. Specify any length from 40 to 999,999 lines. The length includes the lines from the first printed line on the page to the last that can be printed. The printer you use most likely includes a margin at the top; that margin is not included in the length used by SPSS. The default of 59 lines allows for a 1/2-inch margin at the top and bottom of an 11-inch page printed with 6 lines per inch, or an 8 1/2-inch page printed with 8 lines per inch.

If a long page length is specified, SPSS continues to give page ejects and titles at the start of each procedure and at logical points in the display, such as between crosstabulation tables. To suppress page ejects altogether, use keyword NONE. SPSS will then continue to insert titles at logical points in the display, but the display does not jump to the top of the page when a title is inserted.

WIDTH   *The maximum width of the display file.* Specify any number of characters from 80 through 132. The specified width does not include the carriage control character. All procedures can fit the output to an 80-column page. The default width is 132 for command files executed through your operating system and 80 for commands run within SPSS.

FORMAT   *The default print and write formats for numeric variables created by transformation commands or read in with the default format on a DATA LIST command specifying LIST or FREE formatted data.* The specification must be a simple F format, as in FORMAT=F3.0 The default is F8.2.

The format established by the FORMAT subcommand applies to all numeric variables created by transformation commands and to numeric variables read on a DATA LIST command with LIST or FREE specified, unless the format is specified. You can use the PRINT FORMATS, WRITE FORMATS, and FORMATS commands to specify the print and write formats for individual variables. Note that the actual value maintained on the active system file and saved in a permanent system file is not affected by the print or write format.

CASE *Case for letters in the display file.* SPSS accepts variable labels and value labels in upper and lower case and maintains the case distinction on system files. However, the system may translate these labels to upper case before sending them to the display file, depending on the default at your installation. To have them displayed in the case in which they were entered, use the CASE subcommand.

To set the case to all upper case, specify SET CASE=UPPER. Use the SHOW command to display your installation's default. Error messages will appear in upper and lower case if CASE=UPLOW is set, otherwise in upper case only.

Command printback is not affected by the case established by SET CASE. Commands are printed back in the case in which they were entered. The same is true of titles. The reason for this is that commands and titles must be entered as part of the command file, and it is assumed they will be entered in the case appropriate for the device that will print the output. Labels, however, may come from a system file, and it is handy to have a mechanism within SPSS for translating these before printing.

Lowercase letters within string variables are not translated to uppercase. Thus, the results of PRINT and WRITE are not translated even if they are directed to the display file.

BLOCK *The character used for drawing bar charts.* The default is an asterisk. Specify any single character, either as a quoted string or a hexadecimal string (a quoted string containing hexadecimal digits preceded by the character X). For example, to use a pound sign as the character, specify SET BLOCK='#', or SET BLOCK=X'7B'.

HISTOGRAM *The character used for drawing histograms.* The default is an asterisk. Specify any single character, either as a quoted string or a hexadecimal string (a quoted string containing hexadecimal digits preceded by the character X). For example, to use a pound sign as the character, specify SET HISTOGRAM='#', or SET HIST-OGRAM=X'7B'.

HEADER *Specifies whether output includes headings.* The HEADER subcommand applies to both default headings and those specified on the TITLE and SUBTITLE commands.

The specification on HEADER is either YES or NO (alias ON or OFF). YES is the default. HEADER=NO suppresses the heading.

When HEADER=NO, all general SPSS headings in the output, including pagination, are replaced by a single blank line. Some procedure-specific headers like those generated by FREQUEN-CIES, REPORT, and TABLES will still be displayed.

BOX *The characters used to draw grids in procedures such as CROSS-TABS, MULT RESPONSE, and TABLES.* Other procedures, like FACTOR and REGRESSION, may also use these characters in plots and other displays. The specification is either a 3- or an 11-character quoted string in which the characters represent, respectively:

```
1 the horizontal line
2 the vertical line
3 middle (cross)
4 lower-left corner
5 upper-left corner
6 lower-right corner
7 upper-right corner
8 left T
9 right T
10 top T
11 bottom T
```

If the characters are specified as hexadecimal pairs, specify an X before the quoted string (see the example below). The default settings may have been altered by your local installation to take advantage of characters available on your printer, such as the long dash and vertical bar. To see the current settings, use the SHOW command.

Currently, only TABLES uses all eleven characters (see SET and the TABLES Procedure, below). All other procedures use only the first three characters, where the third character defines all other intersections. Any characters specified in the fourth through eleventh positions will be ignored by all procedures except TABLES. (If you specify only three characters for TABLES, the same character is used for all nine intersections. See the example below.)

Example

```
DATA LIST FREE FILE=PRSNNL / COMPANY (A10) NAME (A20) AGE.
SET LENGTH=50 /WIDTH=80 /CASE=UPLOW /PRINTBACK=NO /HEADER=NO /
FORMAT=F2.0.
FREQUENCIES VAR=AGE.
```

• DATA LIST defines variables for file PRSNNL.

• SET sets a page length of 50 lines and a page width of 80 characters for output. Variable labels, value labels, and error messages will print in the display file in upper- and lowercase letters. The display file will not contain command printback or headers. The format for the numeric variable AGE is F2.0.

• FREQUENCIES produces a frequency table for variable AGE.

Example

```
SET BOX '-I+++++++++'.
SET BOX X'60C94E4E4E4E4E4E4E4E4E'.
```

• In IBM conversions, these two settings are equivalent. Each is the default setting for box-drawing characters.

Example

```
SET BOX '-I*'.
SET BOX '-I*********'.
```

• Each specification produces output that uses the dash character for horizontal lines, the capital I for vertical lines, and the asterisk for intersections.

Custom Currency Formats

You can specify up to five custom currency formats for your own applications, using the subcommands CCA, CCB, CCC, CCD, and CCE. Each custom currency subcommand defines one custom format and includes four specifications: a negative prefix, a prefix, a suffix, and a negative suffix.

• The four specifications are separated by either periods or commas, whichever you do not want SPSS to use as a decimal point in the printed format.

• Each currency specification must always contain three commas or three periods. All other specifications are optional.

• Use blanks in the specification only where you want blanks in the formatted numbers.

• A specification cannot exceed 16 characters (excluding the apostrophes).

• Custom currency formats cannot be specified on the DATA LIST command. Use them only on output commands such as FORMATS, WRITE FORMATS, PRINT FORMATS, WRITE, and PRINT.

Example

```
TITLE  'THE DOLLAR FORMAT SHOWN AS A CUSTOM CURRENCY FORMAT'.
SET CCA='-,$,,'.
```

• A minus sign (−) precedes the first comma; therefore, the minus sign is the negative prefix.

• A dollar sign is specified for the prefix.

• There are no suffixes.

• The commas used as separators indicate that SPSS should use a period for a decimal point in numbers assigned the CCA format.

Example   `SET CCA='(,,,-)'  CCB=',,%,'  CCC='(,$,,)'  CCD='-/-.Dfl ..-'.`
                 `FORMATS VARA(CCA9.0)/ VARB(CCB6.1)/ VARC(CCC8.0)/ VARD(CCD14.2).`

• SET defines four custom currency formats. Table 2 summarizes the currency specifications.
• FORMATS assigns these formats to specific variables.

Table 2 Custom currency examples

	CCA	CCB	CCC	CCD
negative prefix	(	none	(	-/-
prefix	none	none	$	Dfl
suffix	none	%	none	none
negative suffix	-)	none	)	-
separator	,	,	,	
sample positive number	23,456	13.7%	$352	Dfl 37.419,00
sample negative number	(19,423-)	13.7%	($189)	-/-Dfl 135,19-

Samples and Random Numbers

The pseudo random-number generator that SPSS uses in selecting random samples or in creating uniform or normal distributions of random numbers begins with a *seed,* a large integer. Starting with the same seed, the system will repeatedly produce the same sequence of numbers and will select the same sample from a given data file. You can set the seed yourself with the SEED subcommand.

• At the start of each session, the seed is set by SPSS to a value that may vary or may be fixed, depending on the implementation.
• The argument can be any integer, preferably a large one but less than 2,000,000,000, which approaches the limit on some machines.
• The command sets the seed for the next time the random number generator is called. Thus, you can reset it following each procedure command in the command sequence if you want to repeat the same random distribution. To replicate samples across sessions or procedures, specify the same seed each time.
• In the absence of the SEED subcommand, SPSS will not reset the seed, so all distributions and samples during the session will be different.
• The random number seed can be changed any number of times within a session.

SEED   *The random number seed.* Specify a positive integer.

Example   `SET SEED=987654321.`

• The random number seed is set to the value 987,654,321.

Sorting Data

XSORT determines which sort program is used: the one built into SPSS, or the default sort program on your system. The specification is either YES or NO (alias ON or OFF).

• To use the SPSS sort program, specify XSORT=YES.
• To use another sort program, specify XSORT=NO.
• The default sort program used by SPSS is determined by your SPSS coordinator. To see whether XSORT is the default at your site, use the SHOW command.
• Because XSORT does not compress intermediate work files, it may need more scratch disk space than some other sort programs.

XSORT   *The sort program used to sort data.* Use XSORT if your installation does not have a sort program that works with SPSS, or if your installation provides another sort program you want to use instead of XSORT.

Scratch File Compression

COMPRESSION determines whether scratch files during an SPSS session are in compressed or uncompressed form.

- A compressed scratch file occupies less space on disk than does an uncompressed scratch file.
- A compressed scratch file requires more processing resources than does an uncompressed scratch file.
- The command takes effect the next time a scratch file is written and stays in effect until SET COMPRESSION is specified again or until the end of the session.

COMPRESSION   *Compression of the scratch file.* Specify ON or OFF (alias YES or NO). COMPRESS=ON causes SPSS to compress scratch files. With COMPRESS=OFF scratch files are not compressed. The default varies by installation. Use SHOW to see the default at your site.

Example   `SET COMPRESS=ON.`

- Scratch files for this session will be compressed.

Command Terminators and Journal Files

Use the ENDCMD and NULLINE subcommands to control command termination. Use the JOURNAL subcommand to control journaling.

- When commands are run within SPSS, every command must end with a command terminator. By default, the terminator is a period, but you can change it with ENDCMD. When commands are run within SPSS, each line is considered part of the current command until the command terminator is reached.
- During a prompted session, when NULLINE is ON (the default), a completely empty input line is accepted as an alternative command terminator. If you SET NULLINE OFF, you must enter the character specified for ENDCMD.
- The ENDCMD specification can be any character.
- Do not specify a command terminator that is the last character in any of your variable names, nor a character with special syntactic meaning in SPSS (such as a slash). Such specifications will often result in syntactic ambiguity.
- Journal files created when commands are entered within SPSS are erased at the beginning of each SPSS session. If you want to preserve the contents of a journal file, assign it a name with SET JOURNAL at the beginning of the session that creates the file. If SPSS assigns the default name to the file, use the RENAME command (or its equivalent) on your operating system to rename the file before beginning another SPSS session.
- If you use multiple journal files, you should not start with one file, go to another file, and then return to the first file. SPSS will not append new information to the first file. It will write over the previous contents.

ENDCMD   *The command terminator.* Specify a character in apostrophes. The default is a period.

NULLINE   *Empty lines as an alternative command terminator* (prompted sessions, only). Specify ON or OFF. The default is NULLINE=ON.

JOURNAL   *Journaling during an SPSS session.* The specification is either ON, OFF (alias YES or NO), or a file. The default name of the journal file depends on the file-naming convention at your site. SET JOURNAL OFF during the session turns off the command log. Use SHOW to determine whether journaling is on or off.

Example   `SPSS> SET ENDCMD="!" / NULLINE=OFF.`

- This example shows a prompted session. The command terminator is set to an exclamation point. A blank line will not be accepted as a command terminator.

Example   SET JOURNAL MYLOG.
                GET FILE=HUBDATA.
                SET JOURNAL OFF.
                LIST.
                SET JOURNAL ON.
                FREQUENCIES VARIABLES=ALL.

- The first SET command opens the journal file MYLOG. The actual file specifications depend on your operating system.
- The GET command is copied into the journal file. The SET command then turns the journal off. The LIST command is not copied into the journal file but is executed in the command file. The second SET command turns the journal on again, and the FREQUENCIES command is copied into the journal file.

Macro Displays

You can control the process of macro expansion, the maximum number of loop traversals, and nesting levels. You can also control display of the variables, commands, and parameters that macro uses.

MEXPAND   *Controls whether macro expansion will occur.* The specification is either ON or OFF (alias YES or NO). MEXPAND is ON by default. Specifying SET MEXPAND OFF will prevent macro expansion. Specifying SET MEXPAND ON will reestablish macro expansion.

MITERATE *Controls the maximum loop traversals permitted in macro expansions.* The specification on MITERATE is a positive integer. The default number of traversals is 1000.

MNEST   *Controls the maximum nesting level for macros.* The specification on MNEST is a positive integer. The default number of levels that can be nested is 50.

MPRINT   *Controls whether the display file includes the command list after macro expansion.* The specification is either ON or OFF (alias YES or NO). If MPRINT=ON, the expanded command list is printed. If MPRINT is not included or if you specify MPRINT=OFF, the expanded command list is not printed. The MPRINT command can be used only in conjuction with the MACRO command and is independent of the PRINTBACK command.

SET and the TABLES Procedure

Three subcommands on SET and SHOW apply only to the TABLES procedure. The TB1 and TB2 subcommands define the characters used for line drawing. The TBFONT subcommand defines the font codes used by a Xerox 9700 laser printer. These subcommands produce exactly the same results as BOXCHARS and FONTCHARS within the TABLES procedure but allow you to define these parameters only once, rather than each time you invoke the TABLES command.

TBFONTS   *Sets the default TABLES font characters.* The parameter is either a 4-character string or an 8-digit hexadecimal string beginning with the character X and followed by a quoted string of hexadecimal pairs, in which the characters represent, respectively:

              1   LIGHT ROMAN used for line drawing and general text
              2   LIGHT ITALIC
              3   BOLD ROMAN
              4   BOLD ITALIC

TB1   *Sets the box characters.* TB1 has the same specifications as the BOX subcommand: the characters are specified as either a 3- or 11-character string, and correspond, in order, to the horizontal line, the vertical line, and the nine intersections: middle (cross), lower-left corner, upper-left corner, lower-right corner, upper-right corner, left T, right T, top T, and bottom T. You can specify the characters as a quoted string of hexadecimal pairs preceded by the letter X. The third character will be printed for all nine intersections if only three characters are specified.

TB2   *Specifies characters that overprint the characters defined in SET TB1.* This can be especially useful for printers that do not have T characters (where a vertical and horizontal line meet), so that two corners can be overprinted to form a T. The parameters are the same as for TB1.

Example

```
SET WIDTH=80.
SET TB1 '-I------II--'.
SET TB2 '  I        '.
TABLES   PTITLE = 'CENSUS TRACT SUMMARIES FROM STF3A'
         /FTOTAL = T1 'TOTAL'
         /OBSERVATION = T3.1   T6.1   T9.1   T10.1
         /TABLE = T3.1 + T6.1 + T9.1 + T10.1 BY TRACT + T1
         /TTITLE = 'KENWOOD SUMMARIES (SELECTED TRACTS)'
         /STATISTICS = SUM.
```

- SET TB1 defines dashes for horizontal lines and the capital I for vertical lines; SET TB2 specifies a vertical line to overprint the third character in the first string to form a T.

SET and the Categories Option

Two subcommands on SET and SHOW apply only to procedures available with the SPSS Categories option. The subcommands (CPI and LPI) set the scale of the vertical and horizontal axis of all two-dimensional plots generated by procedures ANACOR, HOMALS, PRINCALS, and OVERALS. The default settings for CPI and LPI produce square plots on most printers. If they do not produce square plots on your printer, consult the manual that came with your printer to see the appropriate settings.

CPI   *Sets the number of characters per inch used to scale the horizontal axis.* Specify a real number. The default is 10.

LPI   *Sets the number of lines per inch used to scale the vertical axis.* Specify a real number. The default is 6.

CPI and LPI are only used to set the scale of the axes; they cannot be used to change the plot's size. To re-size the plot, use SET LENGTH or SET WIDTH.

SET and the GRAPH Procedure

Several subcommands on SET and SHOW apply only to the GRAPH procedure. The settings can be overridden on GRAPH (GRAPH is an add-on option for SPSS and is not available on all systems).

ADEVICE   *Names the alpha device used with Graphics.* The alpha device is the terminal used to enter data on the SPSS Graphics menus. See the GRAPH command for more information.

DRAW   *Determines whether a full or quick graph is drawn.* Keywords are FULL, QUICK, and NO.

FULL draws a fully detailed graph. If the EXECUTE option (see the GRAPH command) is MENU or RETURN, and no DRAW subcommand is specified on GRAPH, a full graph is drawn.

QUICK draws a quick graph. Quick graphs substitute lines of text with boxes that have X's drawn through them. The boxes show the position of text but not the content.

NO suppresses the drawing of the graph.

GCMDFILE *Names the command file generated by GRAPH.* The default name is GRAPHCMD.

GDATA *Names the Graphics data file generated by GRAPH.* When GRAPH aggregates data for SPSS Graphics it creates new variables. These variables are stored in a new SPSS system file accessible either from Graphics or SPSS. The default name of the data file is GRAPHDAT.

GDEVICE *Names the graphics device used with SPSS Graphics.* The graphics device is the terminal, workstation, or printer used to create the graph. If GDEVICE is a printer or plotter, remember to specify the output file with GOUT; otherwise the printer codes are sent to your screen.

GMEMORY *Specifies the amount of memory to allocate for SPSS Graphics.* Specify an integer followed by the keyword K for kilobytes (the default), or M for megabytes. GMEMORY may not work in some operating systems; consult your *Operations Guide* to see whether it works on your system.

SHOW

SHOW [**ALL**] [BLANKS] [BLKSIZE] [BOX] [BUFNO] [CASE] [CCA] [CCB]

[CCC] [CCD] [CCE] [COMPRESSION] [ENDCMD] [FORMAT] [HEADER]

[JOURNAL] [LENGTH] [MEXPAND] [MITERATE] [MNEST] [MPRINT]
[MXERRS]

[MXLOOPS] [MXWARNS] [N] [NULLINE] [NUMBERED] [PRINTBACK]

[SCOMPRESSION] [SCRIPTTAB] [SEED] [SYSMIS] [TBFONTS] [TB1]

[TB2] [UNDEFINED] [WEIGHT] [WIDTH] [XSORT] [$VARS]

Settings for procedures in the SPSS Categories option:

[CPI] [LPI]

Settings for the GRAPH command†

[/ADEVICE] [/DRAW] [/GCMDFILE] [/GDATA] [/GDEVICE] [/GMEMORY]

†Available only on systems with SPSS Graphics installed.

Overview

SHOW displays current running options, most of which can be changed with the SET command.

This chapter documents the SHOW subcommands common to most systems. To see if there are additional subcommands for your operating system, consult your SPSS *Operations Guide*.

Basic Specification

• The basic specification is simply the command keyword, which displays ALL current settings.

Subcommand Order

• Subcommands can be named in any order.

Operations

• SHOW can be used more than once in the command sequence. Each time SHOW is entered, only the named specifications are displayed.

Example

SHOW BLANKS /UNDEFINED /MXWARNS.

• BLANKS shows the value to which a completely blank field for a numeric variable is translated.

• UNDEFINED shows whether a message displays whenever SPSS encounters anything other than a number or a blank as the value for a numeric-format item.

• MXWARNS shows the maximum number of warnings allowed before a session is terminated for generating too many warnings.

Subcommands

The following alphabetical list shows the available subcommands.

BLANKS
Value to which blanks read in numeric format should be translated. The default is the system-missing value.

BLKSIZE
Default block length used for scratch data files and SPSS system files. The setting may vary by installation. BLKSIZE can be specified for SHOW only; it cannot be changed with SET.

BOX
Characters used to draw boxes. Both character and hexadecimal representations are given when SHOW is specified. The default is set by the installation.

BLOCK
Character used to draw bar charts. Both character and hexadecimal representations are given when SHOW is specified. The default is an asterisk.

HISTOGRAM
Character used to draw histograms. Both character and hexadecimal representations are given when SHOW is specified. The default is an asterisk.

BUFFNO	*The default number of buffers used for all files managed by the SPSS I/O subsystem.* The setting may vary by installation. BUFFNO can be specified for SHOW only; it cannot be changed with SET.
CASE	*Case for display of labels and error messages.* Specifications are UPPER (the default) and UPLOW. The default may vary by installation.
CC	*Custom currency formats.* CC shows the current custom currency formats that have been defined for any of the subcommands CCA, CCB, CCC, CCD, and CCE.
COMPRESSION	*Compression of scratch files.* The specification is either ON or OFF (alias YES or NO). The default is set by the installation.
ENDCMD	*Command terminator for SPSS commands.* The specification can be any single character. The default is a period (.).
ERRORS	*Directs error messages.* The specifications are BOTH (the default; alias YES or ON), LISTING, TERMINAL, or NONE (alias NO or OFF).
FORMAT	*Default print and write formats for numeric variables created by transformations.* The specification can be any F format. The default setting is F8.2.
HEADER	*Headings for output.* The specification is either YES or NO (alias ON or OFF). The default is YES.
JOURNAL	*Journal file during an SPSS session.* The specification is either ON or OFF (alias YES or NO). The default varies by installation.
LENGTH	*Page length for output.* The default is 59.
MESSAGES	*Directs resource utilization messages.* The specifications are LISTING (the default), TERMINAL, BOTH (alias YES or ON), or NONE (alias NO or OFF).
MEXPAND	*Macro expansion.* The specification is either ON or OFF (alias YES or NO). The default is ON.
MITERATE	*Maximum loop traversals permitted in macro expansions.* The default is 1000.
MNEST	*Maximum nesting level for macros.* The default is 50.
MPRINT	*Inclusion of macro expansion command list in the display file.* The specification is either ON and OFF (alias YES or NO). OFF is the default.
MXERRS	*Maximum number of errors permitted before session is terminated.* The default is 40. This setting applies only to command files submitted for execution through the operating system.
MXLOOPS	*Maximum executions of a loop on a single case.* The default is 40.
MXWARNS	*Maximum number of warnings and errors permitted, collectively, before session is terminated.* The default is 80. This setting applies only to command files submitted for execution through the operating system.
N	*Unweighted number of cases in the active system file.* N can be specified for SHOW only; it cannot be changed with SET. N displays UNKNOWN if no active system file has been created yet.
NULLINE	*Null line command terminator for prompted sessions.* The specification is YES or NO (alias ON or OFF). The default is YES.
NUMBERED	*The current status of the switch set by the NUMBERED and UNNUMBERED commands.* The default may vary by installation. NUMBERED can be specified for SHOW only; it cannot be changed with SET.

PRINTBACK	*Directs command printback from commands used in SPSS.* The specifications are LISTING (the default), TERMINAL, BOTH (alias YES or ON), or NONE (alias NO or OFF).
RESULTS	*Directs the output of statistical procedures.* Specifications are LISTING (the default when command files are submitted through the operating system), BOTH (alias YES or ON; the default when commands are run within SPSS), TERMINAL, or NONE (alias NO or OFF).
SCOMPRESSION	*Default setting for compression of SPSS system files.* This setting can be overridden by the COMPRESSED or UN-COMPRESSED subcommands on the SAVE or XSAVE commands. The default setting may vary by installation. SCOMPRESSION can be specified for SHOW only; it cannot be changed with SET.
SEED	*Seed for the random-number generator.* The default is 2,000,000 but may vary by machine.
SYSMIS	*The system-missing value.* SYSMIS can be specified for SHOW only; it cannot be changed with SET.
TBFONTS	*Font characters for the TABLES procedure.* Both character and hexadecimal representations are given when SHOW is specified. The default is set by the installation.
TB1	*Box characters for the TABLES procedure.* Both character and hexadecimal representations are given when SHOW is specified. The default is set by the installation.
TB2	*Box overprint characters for the TABLES procedure.* Both character and hexadecimal representations are given when SHOW is specified. The default is set by the installation.
UNDEFINED	*Warning message for undefined data.* Specifications are WARN (the default) and NOWARN. NOWARN suppresses messages but does not alter the count of warnings toward the MXWARNS total.
WEIGHT	*The name of the variable used to weight cases.* WEIGHT can be specified for SHOW only; it cannot be changed with SET.
WIDTH	*Maximum page width for the display file.* The default is 132 columns.
XSORT	*The sort program used to sort data.* The specification is either YES (alias ON) for *use SPSS sort* or NO (alias OFF) for *use another sort program*. The default is set by the individual installation.
$VARS	*Values of system variables.* $VARS can be specified for SHOW only; it cannot be changed with SET.
ALL	*Display all settings. This is the default.* ALL can be specified for SHOW only.

The following subcommands affect procedures available with the SPSS Categories option only:

CPI   *The number of characters per inch used to scale the horizontal axis in two-dimensional plots.*

LPI   *The number of lines per inch used to scale the vertical axis in two-dimensional plots.*

The following subcommands apply only to graphs drawn by the SPSS Graphics option:

ADEVICE   *Name of the alpha device used with Graphics.* The alpha device is the terminal used to enter data on the SPSS Graphics menus.

DRAW   *The type of graph (full or quick) drawn by SPSS Graphics.*

GCMDFILE   *Name of the command file generated by GRAPH.* The default name is GRAPHCMD.

GDATA   *Name of the Graphics data file generated by GRAPH.* The default name is GRAPHDAT.

GDEVICE   *Name of the graphics device used with SPSS Graphics.* The graphics device is the terminal, workstation, or printer used to create the graph.

GMEMORY   *The amount of memory allocated for SPSS Graphics.*

SORT CASES

```
SORT CASES [BY] varlist[({A})] [varlist...]
                        {D}
```

Example:
```
SORT CASES BY DIVISION (A) STORE (D).
```

Overview
SORT CASES reorders the sequence of cases in the active system file based on the values of one or more variables.

Options
You can sort cases in ascending or descending order, or use combinations of ascending and descending order for different variables.

Basic Specification
- The basic specification is a list of variables that are used as sort keys. Cases are sorted in ascending order for each variable, starting with the first variable named. For each subsequent variable, cases are sorted in ascending order within categories of previously named variables.

Syntax Rules
- Variables can be numeric or string, but they cannot be scratch, system, or temporary variables.
- Keyword BY is optional.
- You can explicitly request the default sort order (ascending) by specifying (A) or (UP) after the variable name.
- To sort cases in descending order, specify (D) or (DOWN).
- An order specification (A or D) applies to all variables to its left and to the right of a previous order specification. Thus, if you combine ascending and descending order on the same specification, you may need to specify the default (A) explicitly.

Operations
- SORT CASES begins by sorting the file according to the first variable named. For subsequent variables, cases are sorted within categories of previously named variables.
- The sort sequence of string variables depends on the character set in use at your installation. With EBCDIC character sets, most special characters are sorted first, followed by lowercase alphabetic characters, uppercase alphabetic characters, and, finally, numbers. The order is almost exactly reversed with ASCII character sets. Numbers are sorted first, followed by uppercase alphabetic characters and lowercase alphabetic characters. In addition, special characters are sorted between the other character types. Consult documentation available via the INFO command for information on the character set in use at your installation and the exact sort sequence.

SORT CASES with other Procedures
- Since REPORT processes cases in the active system file sequentially and reports summary statistics when the value of the break variable or variables changes, the file should be grouped by break variable or variables. The SORT CASES command is the most direct means of reorganizing a file for REPORT. Specify the SORT CASES command before the REPORT command, and list the break variables in the same order on each.

- AGGREGATE assumes that cases are sorted on the break variable or variables. You do not have to use SORT CASES prior to running AGGREGATE, as the procedure does its own sorting.
- You can use SORT CASES in conjunction with the BY keyword in ADD FILES to interleave cases with the same variables but from different files.
- Cases must be sorted in the same order for all files you combine using MATCH FILES.
- With UPDATE, cases must be sorted in ascending order on the key variable or variables in both the master file and all transaction files.
- The PRINT command is not an executable command and must be followed by a procedure or EXECUTE. Thus, to use the PRINT command to check the results of a SORT CASES command, you must specify EXECUTE.

Example   `SORT CASES BY DIVISION (A) STORE (D).`

- Cases are sorted in ascending order of variable DIVISION.
- Cases are further sorted in descending order of STORE within categories of DIVISION.

Example   `SORT DIVISION STORE (A) AGE (D).`

- Cases are sorted in ascending order of DIVISION.
- Cases are further sorted in ascending order of STORE within values of DIVISION. Specification A applies to both DIVISION and STORE.
- Cases are further sorted in descending order of AGE within values of STORE and DIVISION.
- This example takes advantage of the ability to omit keyword BY.

Example   ```
SORT CASES BY EDUC SEX.
REPORT VARS=SCORE1 TO SCORE5
  /BREAK=EDUC
  /SUMMARY= MEAN
  /BREAK=SEX
  /SUMMARY=MEAN.
```

- Each variable named on a BREAK subcommand in REPORT is first named on SORT CASES.
- Variables are named on SORT CASES in the order in which they will be used on REPORT.
```

SPLIT FILE

```
SPLIT FILE {BY varlist}
           {OFF      }
```

Example:

```
SORT CASES BY SEX.
SPLIT FILE BY SEX.
FREQUENCIES VARS=INCOME /STATISTICS=MEDIAN.
```

Overview

SPLIT FILE splits the active system file into subgroups that can be analyzed separately by SPSS. These subgroups or splits are sets of adjacent cases on the file that have the same values for the specified (split) variable(s). When the file is split, each value of each split variable is considered a break group. Cases within a break group must be grouped together in the active system file. If cases in the file are not grouped according to the values of the split variable(s), the SORT CASES command must precede SPLIT FILE to sort cases in the proper order.

Basic Specification

- The basic specification is keyword BY followed by the variable or variables that control split-file processing. The only additional SPLIT FILE specification is keyword OFF, which turns off split-file processing.

Syntax Rules

- SPLIT FILE can specify both numeric and string variables. This includes long string variables and variables created by temporary transformations. It does not include scratch or system variables.

- SPLIT FILE is in effect for all procedures in a session unless you limit it with a TEMPORARY command, turn it off, or override it with a new SPLIT FILE or SORT CASES command.

Operations

- Unlike most transformations, which do not take effect until the data are read, SPLIT FILE takes effect as soon as it is encountered in the command sequence. Thus, special attention should be paid to its position among commands. For more information, see Universals: Command Order.

- SPLIT FILE creates a new subgroup each time it reads a change in the value of any split variable. The file is processed sequentially. A change or break in values on any one of the split variables signals the end of one break group and the beginning of the next.

- If SPLIT FILE is in effect when a procedure writes matrix materials, SPSS writes one set of matrix materials for every split. If a procedure reads a file that contains multiple sets of matrix materials, the procedure automatically detects the presence of multiple sets.

- If SPLIT FILE names any variable that was defined by the NUMERIC command, SPSS prints page headings indicating the split-file grouping.

Limitations

- SPLIT FILE can specify or imply up to eight variables.

- Scratch variables and system variables cannot be used with SPLIT FILE.

- AGGREGATE ignores the SPLIT FILE command. To split files using AGGREGATE, name the variable(s) used to split the file as break variables ahead of any other break variables. AGGREGATE still produces one file, but the aggregated cases are in the same order as the splits.

Example

```
SORT CASES BY SEX.
SPLIT FILE BY SEX.
FREQUENCIES VARS=INCOME /STATISTICS=MEDIAN.
```

- SORT CASES arranges cases in the file according to the values of variable SEX.

- SPLIT FILE splits the file according to the values for each case for variable SEX, causing FREQUENCIES to generate separate median income tables for men and women.

Example
```
SORT CASES BY SEX.
TEMPORARY.
SPLIT FILE BY SEX.
FREQUENCIES VARS=INCOME /STATISTICS=MEDIAN.
FREQUENCIES VARS=INCOME /STATISTICS=MEDIAN.
```

- Because of the placement of the TEMPORARY command, SPLIT FILE applies to the first procedure only. Thus, the first FREQUENCIES procedure generates separate median income tables for men and women. The second FREQUENCIES procedure generates one median income table that includes both sexes.

Example
```
SORT CASES BY SEX.
SPLIT FILE BY SEX.
FREQUENCIES VARS=INCOME /STATISTICS=MEDIAN.
SPLIT FILE OFF.
FREQUENCIES VARS=INCOME /STATISTICS=MEDIAN.
```

- SPLIT FILE applies to the first procedure only because it is turned off after the first FREQUENCIES procedure. This set of commands produces the same results as the example above.

Example
```
SORT CASES BY SEX RACE.
SPLIT FILE BY SEX.
FREQUENCIES VARS=INCOME /STATISTICS=MEDIAN.
SPLIT FILE BY SEX RACE.
FREQUENCIES VARS=INCOME /STATISTICS=MEDIAN.
```

- SPLIT FILE BY SEX RACE, the second SPLIT command, turns off the SPLIT FILE BY SEX command and splits the file by sex and race. This split is in effect for the second FREQUENCIES procedure.

Example
```
SORT CASES BY SEX.
SPLIT FILE BY SEX.
FREQUENCIES VAR=JOBCAT.
SORT CASES BY JOBCAT.
REPORT FORMAT=AUTO /VARS=NAME AGE WAGES /BREAK=JOBCAT /SUM=MEAN.
```

- FREQUENCIES generates separate job category tables for men and women.
- The second SORT CASES command overrides the SPLIT FILE command, and REPORT generates a single report, organized by the values of variable JOBCAT. (Compare these results to the next example.)

Example
```
SORT CASES BY SEX JOBCAT.
SPLIT FILE BY SEX.
FREQUENCIES VAR=JOBCAT.
REPORT FORMAT=AUTO /VARS=NAME AGE WAGES /BREAK=JOBCAT /SUM=MEAN.
```

- The file is sorted by variable SEX, then each subgroup of SEX is sorted by the values of variable JOBCAT.
- The FREQUENCIES procedure is unaffected by the sort on variable JOBCAT.
- The REPORT procedure generates two reports, one for each value of SEX. Each report is organized by the values of variable JOBCAT.

STRING

```
STRING varlist (An) [/varlist...]
```

Example:

```
STRING STATE1 (A2).
RECODE STATE ('IO'='IA') (ELSE=COPY) INTO STATE1.
```

Overview

STRING declares new string variables that may be used as target variables in data transformations. The length of each string variable is fixed by the format given when it is declared and cannot be changed.

Basic Specification

• The basic specification is the name of the new variable(s) and, in parentheses, the variable format.

Syntax Rules

• If keyword TO is used to declare multiple string variables, the specified format applies to each variable named and implied by the TO construction.

• To declare variables with different formats, separate each format group with a slash.

• STRING, specified within an INPUT PROGRAM, can be used to predetermine the order of string variables in the dictionary of the active system file. When used for this purpose, STRING must precede DATA LIST in the INPUT PROGRAM.

Operations

• Unlike most transformations, which do not take effect until the data are read, STRING takes effect as soon as it is encountered in the Thus, special attention should command sequence. be paid to its position among commands. For more information, see Universals: Command Order.

• New string variables are initialized as blanks unless the LEAVE command is used.

• All implementations of SPSS allow the A format. Other valid string formats may be available at some installations. Also, the definition of a long string depends on the operating system. Keyword LOCAL on the INFO command provides documentation for your operating system.

• Variables named on STRING are added to the active system file in the order in which they are specified on STRING. Regardless of the order in which they are used in the transformation language, the order of the variables in the active system file remains as specified on STRING.

Limitations

• The length of a string variable is fixed by the format given when it is declared and cannot be changed. To change the length, declare a new variable with the desired length.

• STRING cannot be used to redefine an existing variable.

• String variables cannot have zero length (format A0).

Example   STRING STATE1 (A2).
                RECODE STATE ('IO'='IA') (ELSE=COPY) INTO STATE1.

- STRING declares variable STATE1 with an A2 format.
- RECODE specifies STATE as the source variable and STATE1 as the target variable. Keywords ELSE and COPY are used to copy the other state codes unchanged. Variables STATE and STATE1 are identical except that STATE has cases with the original value IO and STATE1 has corresponding cases with the corrected value IA.

Example   STRING V1 TO V6 (A8) / V7 V10 (A16).

- STRING declares variables V1 through V6, each with an A8 format, and variables V7 and V10, each with an A16 format.

Example   TITLE 'PREDETERMINE VARIABLE ORDER IN THE DICTIONARY'

                INPUT PROGRAM.
                STRING CITY (A24).
                NUMERIC POP81 TO POP83 (F9)/ REV81 TO REV83(F10).
                DATA LIST FILE=POPDATA RECORDS=3
                  /1 POP81 22-30 REV81 31-40
                  /2 POP82 22-30 REV82 31-40
                  /3 POP83 22-30 REV83 31-40
                  /4 CITY 1-24(A).
                END INPUT PROGRAM.

- STRING and NUMERIC are specified within an INPUT PROGRAM to predetermine variable order in the active system file. Though data in the file are in a different order, the dictionary of the active system file uses the order specified on STRING and NUMERIC. Thus, CITY is the first variable in the dictionary, followed by POP81, POP82, POP83, REV81, REV82, and REV83.
- Formats should be specified for the variables on NUMERIC. Otherwise, SPSS takes the default numeric format (F8.2) from the NUMERIC command for the dictionary format, even though it will use the format on the DATA LIST to read the data (that is, the dictionary of the active system file uses the first formats it encounters, even though DATA LIST may use different formats to read cases).

SUBTITLE

```
SUBTITLE [']text[']
```

Example:

```
SUBTITLE "Children's Training Shoes Only".
```

Overview

SUBTITLE inserts a left-justified subtitle on the second line from the top of each page of the display file. The default subtitle contains the installation name and information about the hardware and operating system.

Basic Specification

- The only specification is the subtitle itself.

Syntax Rules

- The subtitle can include any characters. To specify a blank subtitle, enclose a blank between apostrophes.
- The subtitle can be up to 60 characters long. Subtitles longer than 60 characters are truncated.
- A subtitle may be enclosed within either apostrophes or quotation marks (see Universals: Strings). This allows you to include quotation marks and apostrophes in the subtitle.
- If the subtitle is enclosed in apostrophes, double apostrophes within the string will display as single apostrophes and quotation marks are valid characters; if the subtitle is enclosed in quotation marks, double quotation marks will display as single quotation marks and apostrophes are valid characters.
- More than one SUBTITLE command is allowed in a single session.
- A subtitle cannot be placed between a procedure command and BEGIN DATA when data are inline, or within the data records.

Operations

- Each SUBTITLE command overrides the previous one and takes effect on the next display page.
- SUBTITLE is independent of TITLE and can be changed separately.
- The HEADER subcommand on the SET command determines whether any heading (default or specified) displays. Be sure that HEADER=YES (the default) when you specify a subtitle.

Example

```
TITLE 'Running Shoe Study from Runner''s World Data'.
SUBTITLE "Children's Training Shoes Only".
```

- The title is enclosed in apostrophes, so the apostrophe in *Runner's* must be specified as a double apostrophe.
- The subtitle is enclosed in quotations, so the apostrophe in *Children's* is a valid character.

Example

```
TITLE 'Running Shoe Study from Runner''s World Data'.
SUBTITLE ' '.
```

- This subtitle is specified as a blank. This effectively suppresses the default subtitle because the subtitle displays as a blank line.

SURVIVAL

This command is included in the SPSS Advanced Statistics option.

```
SURVIVAL TABLES=survival varlist [BY independent varlist
(min,max)...]

                    [BY control varlist (min,max)...]

  /INTERVALS=THRU n BY a [THRU m BY b ...]

  /STATUS=status variable({min,max}) FOR {ALL             }
                         {value   }      {survival varlist}
  [/STATUS=...]

  [/PLOTS({ALL**    })={ALL**            } BY {ALL**               }
          {LOGSURV  }   {survival varlist}   {independent varlist}
          {SURVIVAL}
          {HAZARD   }   BY {ALL**         }]
          {DENSITY  }      {control varlist}


  [/PRINT={TABLE**}]
          {NOTABLE}


  [/COMPARE={ALL**            } BY {ALL**               }
            {survival varlist}    {independent varlist}

            BY {ALL**         }]
               {control varlist}


  [/CALCULATE=[{EXACT**     }] [PAIRWISE] [COMPARE]]
               {CONDITIONAL}
               {APPROXIMATE}


  [/MISSING={GROUPWISE**}  [INCLUDE]]
            {LISTWISE   }


  [/WRITE[={NONE**}]]]
          {TABLES}
          {BOTH  }
```

**Default if the subcommand is omitted.

Example:

```
SURVIVAL TABLES=MOSFREE BY TREATMNT(1,3)
  /STATUS = PRISON (1) FOR MOSFREE
  /INTERVAL=THRU 24 BY 3.
```

Overview
SURVIVAL produces life tables, plots, and related statistics for examining the length of time between two events (Berkson & Gage, 1950). Cases can be classified into groups and separate analyses and comparisons obtained for the groups. The time interval between two dates can be calculated with the SPSS date and time conversion functions (for example, CTIME.DAYS or YRMODA).

Options
Life Tables. You can list the variables to be used in the analysis, including any control variables (see TABLES Subcommand). You can also suppress printing of the life tables in the output (see PRINT Subcommand).

Intervals. SURVIVAL reports the percentage alive at various times after the initial event. You can select the time points for reporting with the INTERVALS subcommand.

Survival Status. To determine whether the terminal event has occurred for a particular observation, SURVIVAL checks the value of a status variable. See STATUS Subcommand.

Plots. You can plot the survival functions for all cases or separately for various subgroups. See PLOTS Subcommand.

Comparisons. When control variables are listed on TABLES, you can compare groups based on the Lee & Desu (1972) *D* statistic (see COMPARE Subcommand). Pairwise comparisons are available, as are approximate comparisons for aggregated data (see CALCULATE Subcommand).

Writing a File. You can write the life tables, including the labeling information, to a file for use with other programs, or with a graphics device that produces high-quality graphics. See WRITE Subcommand.

Basic Specification

The basic specification requires three subcommands: TABLES, INTERVALS, and STATUS.

- TABLES: Identify at least one survival variable from the active system file. Optionally, use keyword BY to specify control variables.
- INTERVALS: To divide the time period into equal intervals, specify THRU followed by a constant which defines the termination point for the analysis. Then specify BY and a constant which defines the length of each interval.
- STATUS: For each variable, name a variable that indicates whether the terminal event occurred. In parentheses after the variable name, specify the value(s) that indicate that the terminal event occurred.

The basic specification prints one or more life tables, depending on the number of survival and control variables specified.

Subcommand Order

- TABLES must be first.
- Remaining subcommands can be named in any order.

Limitations

- Maximum 20 survival variables.
- Maximum 100 control variables on the first- and second-order control variable lists combined.
- Maximum 20 THRU . . . BY . . . specifications on INTERVALS.
- Maximum 35 values can appear on a plot.

Example

```
SURVIVAL TABLES=MOSFREE BY TREATMNT(1,3)
   /STATUS = PRISON (1) FOR MOSFREE
   /INTERVALS = THRU 24 BY 3.
```

- Survival analysis is used to examine the length of time between release from prison and return to prison for prisoners in three treatment programs. The variable MOSFREE is the length of time in months to reentry. The variable TREATMNT indicates the treatment group for each case.
- A value of 1 on the STATUS variable PRISON indicates a terminal outcome. That is, cases coded as 1 have returned to prison. Cases with other nonnegative values for PRISON have not returned. Such cases are called *censored* since we don't know their final outcome.
- Life tables are produced for each of the three subgroups. INTERVALS specifies that the survival experience be described every three months for the first two years.

Example

The data in this example are from a study of 647 cancer patients. The variables are

- TREATMNT—the type of treatment received.
- ONSETMO, ONSETYR—month and year cancer was discovered.
- RECURSIT—indicates whether a recurrence took place.

- RECURMO, RECURYR—month and year of recurrence.
- OUTCOME—status of patient at end of study: alive or dead.
- DEATHMO, DEATHYR—month and year of death, or, for those who are still presumed alive, the date of last contact.

Using these date variables and the YRMODA function, the number of months from onset to recurrence and from onset to death or last contact are calculated. These new variables become the survival variables with TREATMNT as the single control variable. The SPSS commands are

```
SET WIDTH=132.
DATA LIST  FILE = SURVDATA/ 1 TREATMNT 15 ONSETMO 19-20
            ONSETYR 21-22 RECURSIT 48 RECURMO 49-50 RECURYR 51-52
            OUTCOME 56 DEATHMO 57-58 DEATHYR 59-60.
COMMENT  TRANSFORM ALL DATES TO DAYS FROM AN ARBITARY TIME
         POINT.
COMPUTE  ONSDATE=YRMODA(ONSETYR,ONSETMO,15).
COMPUTE  RECDATE=YRMODA(RECURYR,RECURMO,15).
COMPUTE  DEATHDT=YRMODA(DEATHYR,DEATHMO,15).

COMMENT  NOW COMPUTE ELAPSED TIME IN MONTHS FROM DIAGNOSIS TO
         LAST CONTACT OR DEATH.
COMPUTE  ONSSURV = (DEATHDT-ONSDATE)/30.

COMMENT   COMPUTE TIME TO RECURRENCE.
IF   RECURSIT EQ 0 RECSURV = ONSSURV.
IF   RECURSIT NE 0 RECSURV = (RECDATE-ONSDATE)/30.

VARIABLE LABELS   TREATMNT 'PATIENT TREATMENT'
            ONSSURV 'MONTHS FROM ONSET TO DEATH'
            RECSURV 'MONTHS FROM ONSET TO RECURRENCE'.
VALUE LABELS   TREATMNT 1 'TREATMENT A' 2 'TREATMENT B'
            3 'TREATMENT C'.
SURVIVAL  TABLES = ONSSURV,RECSURV BY TREATMNT(1,3)
  /STATUS = RECURSIT(1,9) FOR RECSURV
  /STATUS = OUTCOME(3,4) FOR ONSSURV
  /INTERVALS = THRU 50 BY 5 THRU 100 BY 10
  /PLOTS /COMPARE /CALCULATE=CONDITIONAL PAIRWISE.
```

- The SET command sets the page width to 132.
- The onset, recurrence, and death dates are transformed to days from a starting date using the YRMODA function in the COMPUTE command. The constant 15 is used as the day argument for YRMODA since only month and year were recorded, not the actual day.
- ONSSURV, the first survival variable, is the number of months between the date of death (or survival) and the date the cancer was discovered (ONSDATE). The number of days between the two events is divided by 30 to convert it from days to months.
- RECSURV, the second survival variable, is calculated conditionally using the IF command. For cases with RECURSIT values of 0, indicating no recurrence took place, the length of time to recurrence is equal to the length of time from diagnosis to last contact or death.
- The TABLES subcommand in SURVIVAL specifies two survival variables, ONSSURV and RECSURV, and one control variable, TREATMNT.
- The status variable for RECSURV is RECURSIT, with codes 1 THRU 9 indicating that the termination event, recurrence, took place. OUTCOME is the status variable for ONSSURV with codes 3 and 4 indicating death.
- The INTERVALS subcommand requests reporting at five-month intervals for the first 50 months, and at ten-month intervals for the remaining 50 months.
- The default plots are requested using PLOTS.
- COMPARE with no specifications requests comparisons for all variables.
- Keyword CONDITIONAL on the CALCULATE subcommand requests approximate comparisons if memory is insufficient for exact comparisons. Keyword PAIRWISE requests that all pairs of treatments be compared.

TABLES Subcommand

TABLES identifies the survival variables and control variables to be included in the analysis.

- The minimum specification is one or more survival variables.
- To specify one or more first-order control variables, use keyword BY followed by the control variable(s).
- Separate life tables are generated for each combination of values of the first order and second order controls.
- Each control variable must be followed by a value range in parentheses. These values must be integers separated by a comma or a blank. Noninteger values in the data are truncated and the case is assigned to a subgroup based on the integer portion of its value on the variable. To specify only one value for a control variable, use the same value for the minimum and maximum.
- Use a second BY keyword to separate first- and second-order control variable lists. As with first-order control variables, second-order control variables must be followed by a value range in parentheses.
- To generate life tables for all cases combined, as well as for control variables, use COMPUTE to create a variable that has the same value for all cases. With this variable as a control, tables for the entire set of cases, as well as for the control variables, will be produced.

Example

```
SURVIVAL TABLES = MOSFREE BY TREATMNT(1,3) BY RACE(1,2)
         /STATUS = PRISON(1)
         /INTERVAL=THRU 24 BY 3.
```

- MOSFREE is the survival variable, and TREATMNT is the first-order control variable. The second BY defines RACE as a second-order control group having a value of 1 or 2.
- Keyword FOR is omitted on STATUS, since it applies to all survival variables on the TABLES subcommand (in this case, just MOSFREE).
- Six life tables are produced, one for each pair of values for the two control variables. Each is accompanied by its respective median survival time.

INTERVALS Subcommand

INTERVALS determines the period of time to be examined and how the time will be grouped for the analysis. Only one INTERVALS subcommand can be used in a SURVIVAL command. The interval specifications apply to all the survival variables listed on TABLES.

- Specify THRU, the final value, BY, and the grouping increment. SURVIVAL always uses 0 as the starting point for the first interval. You do not specify the 0. The INTERVALS specification must begin with keyword THRU.
- The final interval includes any observations that exceed the range specified with keyword THRU.
- The grouping increment, which follows keyword BY, is in the same units as the survival variable.
- The period to be examined can be divided into intervals of varying lengths by repeating the THRU and BY keywords. The period must be divided in ascending order. If the time period is not a multiple of the increment, the endpoint of the period is adjusted upward to the next even multiple of the BY value.
- When the period is divided into intervals of varying lengths by repeating the THRU and BY specifications, the adjustment of one period to produce even intervals changes the starting point of subsequent periods. If the upward adjustment of one period completely overlaps the next period, no adjustment is made and the procedure terminates with an error.

Example

```
SURVIVAL TABLES = MOSFREE BY TREATMNT(1,3)
         /STATUS = PRISON(1) FOR MOSFREE
         /INTERVALS=THRU 12 BY 1 THRU 24 BY 3.
```

- MOSFREE (months free) is the survival variable, and TREATMNT is the first-order control variable. A terminal event for MOSFREE is coded with a value of 1 for PRISON.

- INTERVALS produces life tables computed from 0 to 12 months at one-month intervals and from 13 to 24 months at three-month intervals.

Example

```
/INTERVALS = THRU 50 BY 6
```

- The value following BY (6) does not divide evenly into the period to which it applies (50). Thus, the endpoint of the period is adjusted upward to the next even multiple of the BY value, resulting in a period of 54 with 9 intervals of 6 units each.

Example

```
/INTERVALS = THRU 50 BY 6 THRU 100 BY 10 THRU 200 BY 20
```

- The period is divided into intervals of varying lengths by repeating the THRU and BY specifications. The adjustment of one period to produce even intervals changes the starting point of subsequent periods. Thus, the INTERVALS specification is automatically readjusted to result in a first period through 54 by 6, a second period through 104 by 10, and a third period through 204 by 20.

STATUS Subcommand

To determine whether the terminal event has occurred for a particular observation, SURVIVAL checks the value of a status variable. STATUS lists the status variable associated with each survival variable and the codes which indicate that a terminal event occurred.

- Specify a status variable followed by a value range enclosed in parentheses. The value range identifies the codes that indicate that the terminal event has taken place. All cases with non-negative times that do not have a code in the value range are classified as censored cases, which are cases for whom the terminal event has not yet occurred. If the status variable does not apply to all the survival variables, specify FOR and the name of the survival variable(s) to which the status variable applies.

- Each survival variable on TABLES must have an associated status variable identified by a STATUS subcommand.

- Only one status variable can be listed on each STATUS subcommand. To specify multiple status variables, use multiple STATUS subcommands.

- If FOR is omitted on the STATUS specification, the status variable specification applies to all of the survival variables not named on another STATUS subcommand.

- If more than one STATUS subcommand omits keyword FOR, the final STATUS subcommand without FOR applies to all survival variables not specified by FOR in other STATUS subcommands. No warning is printed.

Example

```
SURVIVAL  ONSSURV BY TREATMNT (1,3)
   /INTERVALS = THRU 50 BY 5, THRU 100 BY 10
   /STATUS= OUTCOME (3,4) FOR ONSSURV.
```

- STATUS specifies that a code of 3 or 4 on OUTCOME means that the terminal event for the survival variable ONSSURV occurred.

Example

```
SURVIVAL TABLES = NOARREST MOSFREE BY TREATMNT(1,3)
   /STATUS = ARREST (1) FOR NOARREST
   /STATUS = PRISON (1)
   /INTERVAL=THRU 24 BY 3.
```

- STATUS defines the terminal event for NOARREST as a value of 1 for ARREST. Any other value for ARREST is considered censored.

- The second STATUS subcommand defines the value of 1 for PRISON as the terminal event. Keyword FOR is omitted. Thus, the status variable specification applies to MOSFREE, which is the only survival variable not named on another STATUS subcommand.

- Separate life tables are produced for each of the survival variables for each of the three values of TREATMNT.

PLOTS Subcommand

PLOTS produces plots of the cumulative survival distribution, the hazard function, and the probability density function. PLOTS can only plot the survival functions generated by the TABLES subcommand; PLOTS cannot eliminate control variables.

- The minimum specification, the subcommand PLOT, produces all available plots for each survival variable. Points on each plot are identified by values of the first-order control variables. If second-order controls are used, a separate plot is generated for every value of the second-order control variables.

- To request specific plots, specify, in parentheses following PLOTS, any combination of the keywords defined below.

- Optionally, generate plots for only a subset of the requested life tables. Use the same syntax as used on TABLES for specifying survival and control variables, omitting the value ranges. Each survival variable named on PLOTS must have as many control levels as were specified for that variable on TABLES; however, only one control variable need be specified for each level. If a required control level is omitted on the PLOTS specification, the default BY ALL is used for that level. Keyword ALL can be used to refer to an entire set of survival or control variables.

- To determine the number of plots that will be produced, multiply the number of functions plotted by the number of survival variables times the number of first-order controls times the number of distinct values represented in all of the second-order controls.

ALL   *Plot all available functions.* ALL is the default if PLOTS is used without specifications.

LOGSURV   *Plot the cumulative survival distribution on a logarithmic scale.*

SURVIVAL   *Plot the cumulative survival distribution on a linear scale.*

HAZARD   *Plot the hazard function.*

DENSITY   *Plot the density function.*

Example

```
SURVIVAL TABLES = NOARREST MOSFREE BY TREATMNT(1,3)
  /STATUS = ARREST (1) FOR NOARREST
  /STATUS = PRISON (1) FOR MOSFREE
  /INTERVALS = THRU 24 BY 3
  /PLOTS (SURVIVAL,HAZARD) = MOSFREE.
```

- NOARREST with status variable ARREST and MOSFREE with status variable PRISON are the survival variables, and TREATMNT, the first-order control variable.

- Separate life tables are produced for each of the survival variables for each of the three values of TREATMNT.

- PLOTS produces plots of the cumulative survival distribution and the hazard rate for MOSFREE for the three values of TREATMNT, even though TREATMNT is not included on the PLOTS specification. Since plots are requested only for the survival variable MOSFREE, no plots are generated for variable NOARREST.

PRINT Subcommand

By default, SURVIVAL prints life tables. PRINT can be used to suppress the printing of the life tables.

TABLE   *Print the life tables.* This is the default.

NOTABLE   *Suppress the printing of the life tables.* Only plots and comparisons are printed. The WRITE subcommand, used to write the life tables to a file, can be used when NOTABLES is in effect.

Example

```
SURVIVAL TABLES = MOSFREE BY TREATMNT(1,3)
  /STATUS = PRISON (1) FOR MOSFREE
  /INTERVALS = THRU 24 BY 3
  /PLOTS (ALL)
  /PRINT = NOTABLE.
```

- MOSFREE with status variable PRISON is the survival variable, and TREATMNT, the first-order control variable.

- PLOTS produces all four available function plots for MOSFREE, controlling for the three categories of TREATMNT.

- PRINT NOTABLE suppresses the printing of life tables.

COMPARE Subcommand

COMPARE compares the survival experience of subgroups defined by the control variables. At least one first-order control variable is required for calculating comparisons.

- The minimum specification, the subcommand keyword, produces comparisons using the TABLES variable list.
- Alternatively, specify the survival and control variables for the comparisons. Use the same syntax as used on TABLES for specifying survival and control variables, omitting the value ranges. Only variables that appear on TABLES can be listed on COMPARE, and their role as survival, first-order, and second-order control variables cannot be altered. Keyword TO can be used to refer to a group of variables and keyword ALL can be used to refer to an entire set of survival or control variables.
- By default, COMPARE calculates exact comparisons between subgroups. Use the CALCULATE subcommand to obtain pairwise comparisons or approximate comparisons.

Example

```
SURVIVAL TABLES = MOSFREE BY TREATMNT(1,3)
  /STATUS = PRISON (1) FOR MOSFREE
  /INTERVAL = THRU 24 BY 3
  /COMPARE.
```

- MOSFREE is the survival variable, and TREATMNT, the first-order control variable. Life tables are produced for each of the values of TREATMNT.
- COMPARE computes a test statistic, degrees of freedom, and observed significance level for the hypothesis that the three survival curves based on the values of TREATMNT are identical. (See Lee & Desu, 1972.)

Example

```
SURVIVAL TABLES=ONSSURV,RECSURV BY TREATMNT(1,3)
  /STATUS = RECURSIT(1,9) FOR RECSURV
  /STATUS = STATUS(3,4) FOR ONSSURV
  /INTERVAL=THRU 50 BY 5 THRU 100 BY 10
  /COMPARE=ONSSURV BY TREATMNT.
```

- COMPARE requests a comparison of ONSSURV by TREATMNT. No comparison is made of RECSURV by TREATMNT.

CALCULATE Subcommand

CALCULATE controls the comparisons of survival for subgroups specified on the COMPARE subcommand. If CALCULATE is specified, the COMPARE subcommand must also be specified.

- The minimum specification is a single keyword. EXACT is the default.
- Only one of the keywords EXACT, APPROXIMATE, and CONDITIONAL can be selected. If APPROXIMATE is used with either EXACT or CONDITIONAL, APPROXIMATE is in effect. If EXACT is used with CONDITIONAL, CONDITIONAL is in effect.
- PAIRWISE and COMPARE can be used for EXACT, APPROXIMATE, or CONDITIONAL comparisons.
- If CALCULATE is used without the COMPARE subcommand, CALCULATE is ignored. However, if CALCULATE=COMPARE is specified and the COMPARE subcommand is omitted, SPSS generates an error message.
- Data can be entered into SURVIVAL for each individual case or aggregated for all cases in an interval. The way in which data are entered affect the way in which the statistic for comparing groups can be calculated. With individual data, you can obtain exact comparisons based on the survival experience of each observation. While this method is the most accurate, it requires that all of the data be in memory simultaneously. Thus, exact comparisons may be impractical for large samples. There are also situations in which individual data are not available and data aggregated by interval must be used. See Entering Aggregated Data, below.

EXACT *Calculate exact comparisons.* This is the default.

APPROXIMATE *Calculate approximate comparisons only.* Approximate comparisons are appropriate for aggregated data. The approximate comparison approach assumes that all events occur at the midpoint of the interval. Under EXACT comparisons, some of these midpoint ties can be resolved. However, if interval widths are not too great, the difference between EXACT and APPROXIMATE comparisons should be small.

CONDITIONAL *Calculate approximate comparisons if memory is insufficient.* Approximate comparisons are produced only if there is insufficient memory available for exact comparisons.

PAIRWISE *Perform pairwise comparisons.* Comparisons of all pairs of values of the first-order control variable are produced along with the overall comparison.

COMPARE *Produce comparisons only.* Survival tables specified on TABLES are not computed and requests for plots are ignored. This allows all available workspace to be used for comparisons. The WRITE subcommand cannot be used when this specification is in effect.

Examples
```
SURVIVAL TABLES = MOSFREE BY TREATMNT(1,3)
  /STATUS = PRISON (1) FOR MOSFREE
  /INTERVAL = THRU 24 BY 3
  /COMPARE /CALCULATE = PAIRWISE.
```

- MOSFREE with status PRISON is the survival variable, and TREATMNT, the first-order control variable. Life tables are produced for each of the values of TREATMNT.

- CALCULATE=PAIRWISE computes test statistics, degrees of freedom, and observed significance levels for each pair of values of TREATMNT, as well as for an overall comparison of survival across all three TREATMNT subgroups. Hence TREATMNT group 1 is compared with TREATMNT group 2, group 1 with group 3, and group 2 with group 3. All comparisons are exact comparisons.

Example
```
SURVIVAL TABLES = MOSFREE BY TREATMNT(1,3)
  /STATUS = PRISON (1) FOR MOSFREE
  /INTERVAL = THRU 24 BY 3
  /COMPARE /CALCULATE = APPROXIMATE COMPARE.
```

- CALCULATE=APPROXIMATE computes the *D* statistic, degrees of freedom, and probability for the overall comparison of survival across all three TREATMNT subgroups using the approximate method.

- Because keyword COMPARE is specified on CALCULATE, survival tables are not computed.

Entering Aggregated Data

When aggregated survival information is available, the number of censored and uncensored cases at each time point must be entered. Two records are entered for each interval, one for censored cases and one for uncensored cases. The number of cases included on each record is used as the weight factor. If control variables are used, there must be a pair of records (one for censored and one for uncensored cases) for each value of the control variable in each interval. These records must contain the value of the control variable and the number of cases that belong in the particular category as well as values for survival time and status.

Example
```
DATA LIST  / SURVEVAR 1-2 STATVAR 4 SEX 6 COUNT 8.
VALUE LABELS  STATVAR 1 'DECEASED' 2 'ALIVE'
                /SEX 1 'FEMALE' 2 'MALE'.
BEGIN DATA
 1 1 1 6
 1 1 1 1
 1 2 2 2
 1 1 2 1
 2 2 1 1
 2 1 1 2
 2 2 2 1
 2 1 2 3
   ...
END DATA.
WEIGHT  COUNT.
SURVIVAL  TABLES = SURVEVAR BY SEX (1,2)
  /INTERVALS = THRU 10 BY 1
  /STATUS = STATVAR (1) FOR SURVEVAR.
```

- This example reads aggregated data and performs a SURVIVAL analysis when a control variable with two values is used.
- The first data record has a code of 1 on the status variable STATVAR, indicating it is an uncensored case, and a code of 1 on SEX, the control variable. The number of cases for this interval is 6, the value of the variable COUNT. Intervals with weights of 0 do not have to be included.
- COUNT is not used in SURVIVAL but is the weight variable. In this example, each interval requires four records to provide all the data for each SURVEVAR interval.

MISSING Subcommand

MISSING controls missing value treatments. The default is GROUPWISE, which excludes cases with missing values on a variable from any calculation involving that variable.

- Negative values on the survival variables are automatically treated as missing data. In addition, cases outside the value range on a control variable are excluded.
- GROUPWISE and LISTWISE are mutually exclusive. However, each can be used with INCLUDE.

GROUPWISE *Exclude missing values groupwise.* Cases with missing values on a variable are excluded from any calculation involving that variable. This is the default.

LISTWISE *Exclude missing values listwise.* Cases missing on any variables named on TABLES are excluded from the analysis.

INCLUDE *Include missing values.* User-missing values are included in the analysis.

WRITE Subcommand

WRITE writes data in the survival tables to a procedure file. This file can be used for further analyses or to produce graphics displays.

- The only specification is a single keyword. WRITE without a specification is equivalent to WRITE=TABLES.
- When WRITE is used, a PROCEDURE OUTPUT command must precede the SURVIVAL command. The OUTFILE subcommand on PROCEDURE OUTPUT must specify the output file.

NONE *Do not produce a procedure file.* This is the default when WRITE is omitted.

TABLES *Write out survival table data records.* All survival table statistics are written to a file.

BOTH *Write out survival table data and label records.* Variable names, variable labels, and value labels are written out along with the survival table statistics.

Format
WRITE writes five types of records to a procedure file. Keyword TABLES writes record types 30, 31, and 40. Keyword BOTH writes record types 10, 20, 30, 31, and 40. Record type 10, produced only by keyword BOTH, is formatted as follows:

Columns	Content	Format
1–2	Record type (10)	F2.0
3–7	Table number	F5.0
8–15	Name of survival variable	A8
15–55	Variable label of survival variable	A40
56	Number of BY's (0, 1, or 2)	F1.0
57–60	Number of rows in current survival table	F4.0

The number (0, 1, or 2) in column 56 specifies the number of orders of control variables (none, first-order, or first- and second-order controls) that have been applied to the life table. Columns 57–60 specify the number of rows in the life table. This number is the number of intervals in the analysis that show subjects entering; intervals in which no subjects enter are not noted in the life tables. One type 10 record is produced for each life table.

Record type 20, also produced by keyword BOTH, is formatted as follows:

Columns	Content	Format
1–2	Record type (20)	F2.0
3–7	Table number	F5.0
8–15	Name of control variable	A8
16–55	Variable label of control variable	A40
56–60	Value of control variable	F5.0
61–80	Value label for this value	A20

One type 20 record is produced for each control variable on each life table. If only first-order controls have been placed on the survival analysis, one type 20 record will be produced for each table; if second-order controls have also been applied, two type 20 records will be produced per table.

Record type 30, and its continuation 31, produced by both keywords TABLES and BOTH, are formatted as follows:

Columns	Content	Format
1–2	Record type (30)	F2.0
3–7	Table number	F5.0
8–13	Beginning of interval	F6.2
14–21	Number entering interval	F8.2
22–29	Number withdrawn in interval	F8.2
30–37	Number exposed to risk	F8.2
38–45	Number of terminal events	F8.2

Columns	Content	Format
1–2	Record type (31)	F2.0
3–7	Table number	F5.0
8–15	Proportion terminating	F8.6
16–23	Proportion surviving	F8.6
24–31	Cumulative proportion surviving	F8.6
32–38	Probability density	F8.6
40–47	Hazard rate	F8.6
48–54	S.E. of cumulative proportion surviving	F7.4
55–61	S.E. of probability density	F7.4
62–68	S.E. of hazard rate	F7.4

Each pair of type 30 and 31 records contains the information from one line of the life table. As many type 30 and 31 record pairs are output for a table as it has lines (this number is noted in columns 57–60 of the type 10 record for the table).

Record type 40, produced by both keywords TABLES and BOTH, is formatted as follows:

Columns	Content	Format
1–2	Record type (40)	F2.0

Type 40 records indicate the completion of the series of records for one life table.

Record Order The SURVIVAL output file contains records for each of the life tables specified on the TABLES subcommand. All records for a given table are produced together in sequence.

The records for the life tables are produced in the same order as the tables themselves. All life tables for the first survival variable are written first. The values of the first- and second-order control variables rotate, with the values of the first-order controls changing most rapidly.

Example
```
PROCEDURE OUTPUT OUTFILE = SURVTBL.
SURVIVAL TABLES = MOSFREE BY TREATMNT(1,3)
    /STATUS = PRISON (1) FOR MOSFREE
    /INTERVAL = THRU 24 BY 3
    /WRITE = BOTH.
```

• SURVIVAL performs an analysis of MOSFREE with PRISON as the variable determining termination status. WRITE and the keyword BOTH generate a procedure file called SURVTBL, containing both life tables, variable names and labels, and value labels, stored as record types 10, 20, 30, 31, and 40.

Annotated Example

For a complete example with output, see Examples following the Command Reference.

References

Berkson, J., and R. Gage. 1950. Calculation of survival rates for cancer. *Proceedings of the Mayo Clinic* 25:270.

Lee, E., and M. Desu. 1972. A computer program for comparing *k* samples with right-censored data. *Computer Programs in Biomedicine* 2:315-21.

TEMPORARY

TEMPORARY

Example:

```
SORT CASES BY SEX.
TEMPORARY.
SPLIT FILE BY SEX.
FREQUENCIES VARS=INCOME /STATISTICS=MEDIAN.
FREQUENCIES VARS=INCOME /STATISTICS=MEDIAN.
```

Overview

TEMPORARY signals the beginning of temporary transformations that are in effect only for the next procedure. New numeric or string variables created after the TEMPORARY command are *temporary variables*. Any modifications made to existing variables after the TEMPORARY command are also temporary.

TEMPORARY makes it convenient to perform separate analyses on subgroups in the data and then repeat the analysis for the file as a whole. TEMPORARY also makes it convenient to transform data for one analysis but prevent those transformations from affecting subsequent analyses.

TEMPORARY can be used with the following commands:

- Transformation commands COMPUTE, RECODE, IF, and COUNT, and the DO REPEAT utility.
- The LOOP and DO IF control structures.
- Print and write commands PRINT, PRINT EJECT, PRINT SPACE, and WRITE.
- Format declarations PRINT FORMATS, WRITE FORMATS, and FORMATS.
- Data selection commands SELECT IF, SAMPLE, and WEIGHT.
- Variable declarations NUMERIC, STRING, and VECTOR.
- Labeling commands VARIABLE LABELS and VALUE LABELS, and the MISSING VALUES command.
- SPLIT FILE.
- XSAVE. (TEMPORARY followed by SAVE turns the temporary transformations off, whereas TEMPORARY followed by XSAVE leaves the temporary transformations in effect for the next procedure.)
- All procedure commands.

Basic Specification

The only specification is the keyword TEMPORARY. TEMPORARY has no additional specifications.

Limitations

- Once TEMPORARY is specified, you cannot refer to previously existing scratch variables.
- TEMPORARY cannot be used with SORT CASES, MATCH FILES, ADD FILES, or COMPUTE with a LAG function. If any of these commands follows TEMPORARY in the command sequence, there must be an intervening procedure to first execute the TEMPORARY command.
- TEMPORARY cannot be used within the DO IF—END IF or LOOP—END LOOP structures.

Example
```
SORT CASES BY SEX.
TEMPORARY.
SPLIT FILE BY SEX.
FREQUENCIES VARS=INCOME /STATISTICS=MEDIAN.
FREQUENCIES VARS=INCOME /STATISTICS=MEDIAN.
```

- SPLIT FILE applies to the first FREQUENCIES procedure, which generates separate median income tables for men and women.

- SPLIT FILE is no longer in effect for the second FREQUENCIES procedure, which generates a single median income table that includes both men and women.

Example
```
DATA LIST FILE=HUBDATA RECORDS=3
  /1 #MOBIRTH #DABIRTH #YRBIRTH 6-11 DEPT88 19.
COMPUTE AGE=($JDATE - YRMODA(#YRBIRTH,#MOBIRTH,#DABIRTH))/ 365.25.
VARIABLE LABELS AGE 'EMPLOYEE''S AGE'
             DEPT88 'DEPARTMENT CODE IN 1988'.

TEMPORARY.
RECODE AGE (LO THRU 20=1)(20 THRU 25=2)(25 THRU 30=3)
           (30 THRU 35=4)(35 THRU 40=5)(40 THRU 45=6)
           (45 THRU 50=7)(50 THRU 55=8)(55 THRU 60=9)
           (60 THRU 65=10)(65 THRU HI=11).
VARIABLE LABELS AGE 'EMPLOYEE AGE CATEGORIES'.
VALUE LABELS AGE 1 'Up to 20' 2 '20 to 25' 3 '25 to 30'
             4 '30 to 35' 5 '35 to 40' 6 '40 to 45'
             7 '45 to 50' 8 '50 to 55' 9 '55 to 60'
            10 '60 to 65' 11 '65 and older'.

FREQUENCIES VARIABLES=AGE.
MEANS AGE BY DEPT88.
```

- COMPUTE creates variable AGE from the dates in the data.

- FREQUENCIES uses the temporary version of variable AGE with temporary variable and value labels.

- MEANS uses the unrecoded values of AGE and the permanent variable label.

Example
```
GET FILE=HUBEMPL.
TEMPORARY.
RECODE DEPT85 TO DEPT88 (1,2=1) (3,4=2) (ELSE=9).
VALUE LABELS DEPT85 TO DEPT88 1 'MANAGEMENT' 2 'OPERATIONS'
  3 'UNKNOWN'.
XSAVE OUTFILE=HUBTEMP.
CROSSTABS DEPT85 TO DEPT88 BY JOBCAT.
```

- Both the saved system file and the CROSSTABS output will reflect the temporary recoding and labeling of the department variables.

- If XSAVE is replaced with SAVE, the data are read twice instead of just once, and the CROSSTABS output does not reflect the recoding.

TITLE

```
TITLE [']text[']
```

Example:

```
TITLE "Running Shoe Study from Runner's World Data".
```

Overview

TITLE inserts a left-justified title on the top line of each page of the display file. The default header for SPSS output includes the date, a title, and the page number. The default title indicates the version of the system being used.

Basic Specification

- The only specification is the title itself.

Syntax Rules

- The title can include any characters. To specify a blank title, enclose a blank between apostrophes.
- The title can be up to 60 characters long. Subtitles longer than 60 characters are truncated.
- A title may be enclosed within either apostrophes or quotation marks (see Universals: Strings). This allows you to include quotation marks and apostrophes in the title.
- If the title is enclosed in apostrophes, double apostrophes within the string will display as single apostrophes and quotation marks are valid characters; if the title is enclosed in quotation marks, double quotation marks will display as single quotation marks and apostrophes are valid characters.
- More than one TITLE command is allowed in a single session.
- A title cannot be placed between a procedure command and BEGIN DATA when data are inline, or within the data records.

Operations

- Only the title portion of the heading changes. The date and page number still display.
- Each TITLE command overrides the previous one and takes effect on the next display page.
- TITLE is independent of SUBTITLE and can be changed separately.
- The HEADER subcommand on the SET command determines whether any heading (default or specified) displays. Be sure that HEADER=YES (the default) when you specify a title.

Example

```
TITLE "Running Shoe Study from Runner's World Data".
SUBTITLE 'Children''s Training Shoes Only'.
```

- The title is enclosed in quotations, so the apostrophe in *Runner's* is a valid character.
- The subtitle is enclosed in apostrophes, so the apostrophe in *Children's* must be specified as a double apostrophe.

Example

```
TITLE ' '.
SUBTITLE ' '.
```

- The title and subtitle are specified as blanks. This effectively suppresses the default header because the title and subtitle display as blank lines. However, the date and page number still display.

T-TEST

Independent samples:

```
T-TEST GROUPS=varname ({1,2**      }) /VARIABLES=varlist
                       {value      }
                       {value,value}


[/MISSING={ANALYSIS**}   [INCLUDE]]
         {LISTWISE  }


[/FORMAT={LABELS**}]
        {NOLABELS}
```

Paired samples:

```
T-TEST PAIRS=varlist [WITH varlist [(PAIRED)]] [/varlist ...]


[/MISSING={ANALYSIS**}   [INCLUDE]]
         {LISTWISE  }


[/FORMAT={LABELS**}]
        {NOLABELS}
```

**Default if the subcommand is omitted.

Examples:

```
T-TEST GROUPS=WORLD(1,3) /VARIABLES=NTCPRI NTCSAL NTCPUR.

T-TEST PAIRS=TEACHER CONSTRUC MANAGER.
```

Overview

T-TEST compares sample means by calculating Student's t and displays the two-tailed probability of the difference between the means. Statistics are available for either independent samples (different groups of cases) or paired samples (different variables). Other procedures that compare group means are ANOVA, ONEWAY, and MANOVA.

Options

Display Format. You can suppress the display of variable labels. See the FORMAT subcommand.

Statistical Display. You can control which variables are paired in paired-samples tests. (See keyword PAIRED on the PAIRS subcommand.) There are no optional statistics. All statistics available are displayed by default.

Basic Specification

The basic specification depends on whether you want an independent-samples test or a paired-samples test. In either instance, in addition to Student's t, degrees of freedom, and two-tailed probabilities, T-TEST produces the mean, standard deviation, standard error, and count for each group or variable.

Independent-Samples Test. This test requires the GROUPS and VARIABLES subcommands. Both pooled- and separate-variance estimates are calculated, along with the F value used to test homogeneity of variance and its probability. The two-tailed probability is displayed for the t value.

Paired-Samples Test. This test requires the PAIRS subcommand. The default output includes the difference between the means, the two-tailed probability level for a test of the difference, the correlation coefficient for the two variables, and the two-tailed probability level for a test of the coefficient.

- To request both independent- and paired-samples tests, specify GROUPS, VARIABLES, and PAIRS.

Subcommand Order • Subcommands can be named in any order.

Operations • If a GROUPS variable is a long string, only the short-string portion is used to identify groups in the analysis.

• Probability levels are two-tailed. To obtain the one-tailed probability, divide the two-tailed probability by 2.

• The T-TEST display can be modified with SET WIDTH. For more information, see FORMAT Subcommand.

• The BOX subcommand controls the characters used in the table display (see SET).

Limitations • A maximum of 1 GROUPS and 1 VARIABLES subcommand per T-TEST command. Otherwise, T-TEST is constrained only by the amount of work space available on your computer.

Example T—TEST GROUPS=WORLD(1,3) /VARIABLES=NTCPRI NTCSAL NTCPUR.

• This independent-samples example compares the means of the two groups defined by WORLD for variables NTCPRIN, NTCSAL, and NTCPUR.

Example T—TEST PAIRS=TEACHER CONSTRUC MANAGER.

• This paired-samples example compares the means of TEACHER with CON-STRUC, TEACHER with MANAGER, and CONSTRUC with MANAGER.

GROUPS and VARIABLES Subcommands

Independent samples t-tests are requested with the GROUPS and VARIABLES subcommands. GROUPS names a variable used to group cases. VARIABLES names the dependent variable(s).

• GROUPS can name only one variable, which can be numeric or string.

• VARIABLES can name multiple variables, all of which must be numeric.

Any one of three methods can be used to define the two groups for the variable named on GROUPS:

• A single GROUPS value in parentheses groups all cases with a code equal to or greater than the value into one group and the remaining cases into the other group.

• Two GROUPS values in parentheses include cases with the first value in one group and cases with the second value in the other group. Cases with other values are excluded.

• If no GROUPS values are specified, (1,2) is assumed for numeric variables. Values must be specified for string variables.

PAIRS Subcommand

Use PAIRS to request paired-samples tests.

• The minimum specification for a paired-samples test is PAIRS with a single analysis list. Only numeric variables can be named on the analysis list. The minimum analysis list is two variables.

• To obtain multiple analysis lists, use multiple PAIRS subcommands, each separated by a slash. Keyword PAIRS is required only for the first analysis list; a slash can be used to separate each additional analysis list.

• An analysis list without keyword WITH compares each variable with every other variable.

• An analysis list with keyword WITH compares every variable to the left of WITH with every variable to the right of WITH. WITH can be used with (PAIRED) to obtain special pairing.

(PAIRED)   *Special pairing for paired-samples test.* (PAIRED) must be used with the keyword WITH. The first variable before WITH is compared to the first variable after WITH, the second variable before WITH is compared to the second variable after WITH, and so forth. The same number of variables should be specified before and after WITH; unmatched variables are ignored and generate a warning message. (PAIRED) generates an error message if keyword WITH is not specified on PAIRS.

Example
```
T-TEST   PAIRS=TEACHER CONSTRUC MANAGER.
T-TEST   PAIRS=TEACHER MANAGER WITH CONSTRUC ENGINEER.
T-TEST   PAIRS=TEACHER MANAGER WITH CONSTRUC ENGINEER (PAIRED).
```

• The first T-TEST compares TEACHER with CONSTRUC, TEACHER with MANAGER, and CONSTRUC with MANAGER.

• The second T-TEST compares TEACHER with CONSTRUC, TEACHER with ENGINEER, MANAGER with CONSTRUC, and MANAGER with ENGINEER. TEACHER is not compared with MANAGER, and CONSTRUC is not compared with ENGINEER.

• The third T-TEST compares TEACHER with CONSTRUC and MANAGER with ENGINEER.

Example
```
T-TEST   PAIRS=WCLOTHES MCLOTHES / NTCPRI WITH NTCPUR NTCSAL.
```

• Two paired analysis lists are specified on PAIRS.

FORMAT Subcommand

By default, T-TEST prints variable labels. To suppress variable labels, specify NOLABELS on FORMAT.

• You can further modify the T-TEST output by using the SET WIDTH command to restrict output to a width of 80 characters.

LABELS   *Print variable labels.* This is the default.

NOLABELS   *Suppress variable labels.*

Example
```
GET FILE=CITY.
SET WIDTH 80.
T-TEST   PAIRS=WCLOTHES MCLOTHES
  /FORMAT=NOLABELS.
```

• SET WIDTH limits the output width to 80 characters.

• FORMAT suppresses variable labels.

MISSING Subcommand

MISSING controls the treatment of missing values. The default keyword is ANALYSIS.

• For independent-samples tests, cases missing on either the grouping variable or the analysis variable are, by default, excluded from the analysis of that variable.

• For paired-samples tests, a case missing on either of the variables in a given pair is, by dafault, excluded from the analysis of that pair.

• ANALYSIS and LISTWISE are mutually exclusive; however, each can be specified with INCLUDE.

ANALYSIS   *Delete cases with missing values on an analysis-by-analysis basis.* This is the default.

LISTWISE   *Exclude missing values listwise.* A case missing for any variable specified on either GROUPS or VARIABLES is excluded from any independent sample analysis. A case missing for any variable specified on PAIRS is excluded from any paired sample analysis.

INCLUDE   *Include user-missing values.* User-missing values are included in the analysis.

Annotated Example

For a complete example with output, see Examples following the Command Reference.

UPDATE

```
UPDATE FILE={Master File}
             {*          }

      [/RENAME=(old varlist=new varlist)...]

      [/IN=varname]

      /FILE={Transaction File1}
            {*                 }

      [/FILE=Transaction File2]

      /BY Key Variables

      [/MAP]

      [/KEEP={ALL**   }] [/DROP=varlist]
             {varlist}
```

**Default if the subcommand is omitted.

Example:

```
UPDATE FILE=MAILIST /FILE=NEWLIST /BY=ID.
```

Overview

UPDATE replaces values in a master file with updated values recorded in one or more files called *transaction files*. Cases in the master file and transaction file are matched according to a key variable.

UPDATE works with SPSS system files created with the SAVE or XSAVE commands. UPDATE can also use raw data in the active file to update values in the master file. UPDATE replaces values by creating a new active system file. Statistical procedures following UPDATE use this updated file unless you replace it by building another active system file. You must use the SAVE or XSAVE commands if you want to write the updated file to disk as a system file.

In general, UPDATE is designed to update values of existing variables on existing cases. See MATCH FILES for adding new variables to a system file. See ADD FILES for adding new cases to a system file.

Options

Variable Selection. You can choose which variables from each input file are retained in the new active system file.

Variable Names. You can rename variables on each input file before combining the files. This permits you to combine variables that are the same but whose names differ on different input files or to distinguish different variables whose names are the same on different input files.

Variable Flag. You can create a variable that indicates whether a case came from the input file named on the preceding FILE subcommand.

Variable Map. You can request a map showing all the variables in the new active system file, their order, and the input file(s) from which they came.

Basic Specification

The basic specification is two or more FILE subcommands and a BY subcommand.

• The first FILE must specify the master file. All other FILE subcommands identify the transaction file(s).
• BY specifies the key variable(s).

All files must be sorted in ascending order by the key variable(s) on BY. All variables from all input files are included in the new active system file, unless DROP or KEEP is specified.

Subcommand Order
- The master file must be specified first.
- BY must follow the FILE subcommands and any associated RENAME and IN subcommands.
- RENAME and IN must immediately follow the FILE subcommand to which they apply.
- MAP, DROP, and KEEP must be placed after all FILE and RENAME subcommands.

Syntax Rules
- An asterisk can be specified on FILE to indicate the active system file.
- BY can be specified only once. However, multiple variables can be specified on BY. All files must be sorted in ascending order by the key variable(s) on BY.
- Duplicate values for the key variable(s) are not permitted in the master file.
- RENAME applies only to variables in the file named on the immediately preceding FILE subcommand. RENAME can be repeated after each FILE subcommand.
- MAP can be repeated as often as desired.

Operations
- UPDATE causes all input files named on FILE to be read and builds a new active system file that replaces any active system file created earlier in the session. The result file is built when the data are read by one of the procedure commands or the EXECUTE, SAVE, or SORT CASES commands.
- The result file contains complete dictionary information copied from the input files, including variable names, labels, print and write formats, and missing-value indicators. The result file also contains the documents from each of the input files, unless the DROP DOCUMENTS command is used to drop the document text from the result file.
- UPDATE copies all variables in order from the master file, then all variables in order from the first transaction file, then all variables in order from the second transaction file, and so on. Variables that are not common to all files receive the system-missing value for cases that do not contain those variables.
- When the transaction and master files contain a common variable, cases in the new file take on values for that variable from the transaction file. If more than one transaction file is specified, the value comes from the last transaction file with a nonmissing value for that variable.
- Missing or blank values in the transaction files are not used to update values in the master file.
- When UPDATE encounters duplicate keys within the same transaction file or over several files, it applies each transaction sequentially to that case to produce one case per key value in the result file. If more than one transaction file is specified, the value for a variable comes from the last transaction file with a nonmissing value for that variable.
- When UPDATE encounters cases or nonmissing variables in the transaction files that are not in the master file, the new cases or variables are added to the master file. The value of the key variable determines where a new case resides in the result file.
- If the active system file is named as an input file, any N and SAMPLE commands that have been specified are applied to the active system file before files are combined.

Limitations
- Maximum 1 BY subcommand. However, BY can specify multiple variables.
- The TEMPORARY command cannot be in effect for any active system file that is used as an input file.

Example
```
UPDATE FILE=MAILIST /FILE=NEWLIST /BY=ID.
```

- MAILIST is defined as the master file. NEWLIST is the transaction file. ID is the key variable.
- Both MAILIST and NEWLIST must be sorted in ascending order by ID.
- If NEWLIST has cases or nonmissing variables that are not in MAILIST, the new cases or variables are added to the result file.

Example
```
SORT CASES BY LOCATN DEPT.
UPDATE  FILE=MASTER /FILE=* /BY LOCATN DEPT
   /KEEP AVGHOUR AVGRAISE LOCATN DEPT SEX HOURLY RAISE /MAP.
SAVE OUTFILE=PRSNNL.
```

- SORT CASES sorts the active system file in ascending order by the variables to be named as key variables on UPDATE.
- UPDATE specifies MASTER as the master file and the sorted active file as the transaction file. File MASTER must also be sorted by LOCATN and DEPT.
- BY indicates that the keys for identifying cases are the same variables used on SORT CASES: LOCATN and DEPT.
- KEEP specifies the subset and order of variables to be retained in the result file.
- MAP provides a listing of the variables in the result file and the two input files.
- SAVE saves the result file as a new SPSS system file.

FILE Subcommand

FILE identifies each input file. At least one FILE subcommand is required on UPDATE to specify the master file. A separate FILE subcommand must be used to specify each transaction file.

- The first FILE subcommand must specify the master file.
- An asterisk on FILE refers to the current active system file.
- All files must be sorted in ascending order according to the variable(s) specified on BY.
- When the transaction and master files contain a common variable, cases in the new file take on values for that variable from the transaction file. If more than one transaction file is specified, the value comes from the last transaction file with a nonmissing value for that variable.
- Missing or blank values in the transaction files are not used to update values in the master file.
- While duplicate values on the key variables are not allowed in master files, transaction files can and often do contain cases with duplicate keys. When UPDATE encounters duplicate keys within the same transaction file or over several files, it applies each transaction sequentially to that case to produce one case per key value in the result file. If more than one transaction file is specified, the value for a variable comes from the last transaction file with a nonmissing value for that variable.
- When UPDATE encounters cases or nonmissing variables in the transaction files that are not in the master file, the new cases or variables are added to the master file. The value of the key variable determines where a new case resides in the result file.

Raw Data Files

Cases from a raw data file can be used to update the master file. To do so, DATA LIST must be used to define the data file as the transaction file. UPDATE can then use the active system file to update the master file.

Example   `DATA LIST / ID 1-3 NAME 5-17 (A) ADDRESS 19-28 (A) ZIP 30-34.`

`BEGIN DATA`
`033              872 ONEIDA`
`041 BEVERLY JONES`
`...`
`078              14 OAK`
`043                          80618`
`END DATA.`

`SORT CASES BY ID.`

`UPDATE FILE=MAILIST1 /RENAME=(STREET=ADDRESS) /FILE=* /BY=ID`
`              /MAP.`

`SAVE OUTFILE=MAILIST2.`

- DATA LIST defines variables in the transaction file, which will be used to update values in the master file.
- The BEGIN DATA—END DATA commands indicate lines of data for the variables in the active system file. These values will be added to the master file.
- SORT CASES sorts cases in the transaction file in ascending order on the key variable, ID. Cases in the master file were previously sorted in this manner.
- UPDATE replaces values in the system file with values in the active system file. The first FILE subcommand refers to the master file, MAILIST1. The RENAME subcommand instructs SPSS to rename the variable STREET to ADDRESS on file MAILIST1.
- The second FILE subcommand refers to the active system file (*) defined on DATA LIST.
- BY indicates that values in MAILIST1 and the active system file are to be matched by the key variable, ID.
- MAP requests a map of the result file.
- SAVE saves the result file into the system file MAILIST2.

BY Subcommand   BY specifies one or more identification, or key, variables that are used to match cases between files. BY must follow the FILE subcommands and any associated RENAME and IN subcommands.

- BY must specify the names of one or more key variables. The key variables must be present in all input files and have the same names in all input files. The key variables may be string variables (long strings are allowed).
- All input files must be sorted by the key variable(s), in ascending order. If necessary, use SORT CASES before UPDATE.
- Missing values on key variables are handled like any other values.
- While duplicate values on the key variables are not allowed in master files, transaction files can and often do contain cases with duplicate keys.
- When UPDATE encounters cases or nonmissing variables in the transaction files that are not in the master file, the new cases or variables are added to the master file. The value of the key variable determines where a new case resides in the result file.

RENAME Subcommand   RENAME renames variables in the input files before they are processed by UPDATE. RENAME must follow the FILE subcommand that contains the variables that will be renamed.

- RENAME applies only to the immediately preceding FILE subcommand. To rename variables from more than one input file, enter a RENAME subcommand after each FILE subcommand that has variables to rename.
- Specifications for RENAME consist of a left parenthesis, a list of old variable names, an equals sign, a list of new variable names, and a right parenthesis. The two variable lists must have the same number of variables. If only one variable is renamed, the parentheses are optional.
- More than one such specification can be entered on a single RENAME subcommand, each enclosed in parentheses.
- RENAME takes effect immediately. Any KEEP and DROP subcommands entered prior to a RENAME must use the old names, while KEEP and DROP subcommands entered after a RENAME must use the new names.
- All specifications within a single set of parentheses take effect simultaneously: the specification RENAME (A,B = B,A) is legal and swaps the names of the two variables.
- You can use RENAME to correct a situation where a key variable has different names on different input files. Since BY must be entered last, it always uses the new name of a key variable.
- Variables cannot be renamed to scratch variables.
- Input system files are not changed on disk; only the copy of the file being combined is affected.

Example
```
UPDATE FILE=MASTER /FILE=CLIENTS
  /RENAME=(TEL_NO, ID_NO = PHONE, ID)
  /BY ID.
```

- UPDATE updates the master phone list by using current information from file CLIENTS.
- Two variables on CLIENTS are renamed prior to the match. TEL_NO is renamed PHONE to match the name used for phone numbers in the master file. ID_NO is renamed ID so that it will have the same name as the identification variable in the master file and can be used on the BY subcommand.
- All of the old variable names are listed before the equals sign, and all of the new variable names are listed in the same order, after the equals sign.
- The BY subcommand ensures that cases are matched according to client ID numbers.

DROP and KEEP Subcommands

DROP and KEEP are used to include only a subset of variables on the new active system file. DROP specifies a set of variables to exclude, and KEEP specifies a set of variables to retain. These subcommands apply only to the result file and must follow all FILE and RENAME subcommands.

- DROP and KEEP must specify one or more variables. Keyword TO can be used to refer to consecutive variables. If RENAME is used to rename variables, specify the new names on DROP and KEEP.
- Keyword ALL can be specified on KEEP. ALL must be the last specification on KEEP, and it refers to all variables not previously named on KEEP.
- DROP cannot be used with variables created by the IN subcommand.
- KEEP can be used to change the order of variables in the result file. With KEEP, variables are kept in the order in which they are listed on the subcommand. If a variable is named more than once on KEEP, only the first mention of the variable is in effect; all subsequent references to that variable name are ignored.

Example

```
UPDATE FILE=MAILIST /FILE=NEWLIST /RENAME=(STREET=ADDRESS)
                    /BY ID
         /KEEP=NAME ADDRESS CITY STATE ZIP ID.
```

• KEEP specifies the variables to keep in the result file. The variables are stored in the order specified on KEEP.

IN Subcommand

IN creates a flag variable in the result file that indicates whether a case came from the input file named in the preceding FILE subcommand. IN applies only to the file specified on the immediately preceding FILE subcommand.

• IN has only one specification, the name of the flag variable.

• The variable created by IN has the value 1 for every case that came from the associated input file, or the value 0 if the case came from a different input file.

• Variables created by IN are automatically attached to the end of the result file and cannot be dropped.

Example

```
UPDATE  FILE=WEEK10 /FILE=WEEK11 /IN=INWEEK11 /BY=EMPID.
```

• IN creates the variable INWEEK11, which has the value 1 for all cases in the result file that came from the input file WEEK11 and the value 0 for those cases that were not in file WEEK11.

MAP Subcommand

MAP produces a map showing which variables are in the new active system file and from what file or files they may be taken. Variables are listed in the order in which they exist in the result file. MAP has no specifications and must be placed after all FILE and RENAME subcommands.

• Multiple MAP subcommands can be used. Each MAP shows the current status of the active system file and reflects only the subcommands that precede the MAP subcommand.

• To obtain a map of the new active system file in its final state, specify MAP last.

• If a variable is renamed, its original name is shown in the source file and its new name appears in the result file. Variables created by IN, FIRST, and LAST are not included in the map since they are automatically attached to the end of the file and cannot be dropped.

• MAP can be used with the EDIT command to obtain a map of what the result file will look like without actually reading the data and executing the match.

VALUE LABELS

```
VALUE LABELS varlist value 'label' value 'label'...
  [/varlist...]
```

Example:

```
VALUE LABELS JOBGRADE 'P' 'Parttime Employee'
  'C' 'Customer Support'.
```

Overview

VALUE LABELS assigns new value labels or alters existing value labels, deleting all existing value labels for the specified variable(s). Compare to ADD VALUE LABELS, which adds new value labels or alters existing value labels without deleting existing labels when it does so.

Basic Specification

- The basic specification is a variable name and the individual values with the associated labels.

Syntax Rules

- Labels can be added to any previously defined variable. It is not necessary to enter value labels for all of a variable's values.
- Each value label must be enclosed in apostrophes or quotation marks.
- To enter an apostrophe as part of a label, enclose the label in quotation marks or enter a double apostrophe.
- Value labels cannot exceed 60 characters and can contain any characters, including blanks.
- The same labels can be assigned to the values of different variables by specifying a list of variable names. For string variables, the variables must be of equal length.
- Multiple sets of variable names and value labels can be specified on one VALUE LABELS command as long as each set is separated by slashes.
- To continue a label from one command line to the next, precede the continuation of the label with a plus (+) sign. Each string segment of the label must be enclosed in apostrophes or quotes. To insert a blank between the strings, the blank must be included in the label specification.
- To maintain compatibility with earlier releases of SPSS, the value can be enclosed in parentheses, and the label does not need to be enclosed in apostrophes. If you use this syntax, the slash separating the sets of value labels is required, and slashes or parentheses cannot be included in the label.

Operations

- VALUE LABELS takes effect as soon as it is encountered in the command sequence, unlike most transformations, which do not take effect until the data are read. Thus, special attention should be paid to its position among commands. See Universals: Command Order.
- The value labels are automatically displayed on the output from many procedures and are stored in the dictionary of the active system file.
- VALUE LABELS can be used for variables that have no previously assigned value labels.
- Labels added to values delete all labels previously assigned to other values of the specified variable(s).
- In the specification, if a value is specified that is longer than the format of the associated variable, SPSS will be unable to read the full value and may not be able to associate the value labels correctly. This occurs even though the values named on VALUE LABELS and the actual values agree.
- If the value specifications for string variables are shorter than the variable being labeled, the value specifications are right-padded without warning.

Limitations

- Each value label can be up to 60 characters long, although most procedures display only 20 characters.

- Some procedures display fewer than 20 characters in labels.
- The TABLES procedure (available in SPSS Tables) will display all 60 characters of a label.

Example

```
VALUE LABELS V1 TO V3 1 'Officials & Managers'
                      6 'Service Workers'
            /V4 'N' 'New Employee'.
```

- Labels are assigned to the values 1 and 6 of the variables between and including V1 and V3 in the active system file.
- Following the required slash, a label for value N of V4 is specified. N is a string value and must be enclosed in apostrophes or quotes.
- If labels exist for values 1 and 6 on V1 TO V3 and value N on V4, they are changed in the dictionary of the active system file. If labels do not exist for these values, new labels are added to the dictionary.
- Existing labels for values other than 1 and 6 on V1 TO V3 and value N on V4 are deleted.

Example

```
VALUE LABELS  OFFICE88 1 "EMPLOYEE'S OFFICE ASSIGNMENT PRIOR"
      + " TO 1988".
```

- The label for OFFICE88 is the result of concatenating two strings with the plus sign. To be included in the label, the blank between PRIOR and TO must be included in the first or second string.

String Value Labels

- Both the values and the labels for short string variables must be enclosed in apostrophes or quotation marks. Labels cannot be added to the values of long string variables.
- The values of a short string variable cannot be longer than the format of the associated variable.
- When assigning labels to a set of string variables, the variables must be of equal length.

Example

```
DATA LIST / CITY 1-8(A) STATE 10-12(A).
VALUE LABELS  STATE 'TEX' "TEXAS" 'TEN' "TENNESSEE"
                    'MIN' "MINNESOTA".

BEGIN DATA
AUSTIN    TEX
MEMPHIS   TEN
ST. PAUL MIN
END DATA.
FREQUENCIES VARIABLES=STATE.
```

- The DATA LIST command defines the formats of the variables in the file—CITY is eight characters wide and STATE is three characters.
- The VALUE LABELS command assigns labels to three values of variable STATE. Each value and each label is specified in either apostrophes or quotation marks.
- The format for variable STATE must be at least three characters wide, because values TEX, TEN, and MIN are three characters. If the actual format for STATE were 10-11 (two characters) instead of 10-12, SPSS would issue a warning stating that a value named on VALUE LABELS has more characters than the string variable it labels. Note that this would occur even though the values named on VALUE LABELS and the values after BEGIN DATA agree, because the controlling format is on the DATA LIST command.

Example

```
VALUE LABELS=STATE REGION 'U' "UNKNOWN".
```

- Label UNKNOWN is assigned to value U for both STATE and REGION.
- STATE and REGION must be string variables of equal length. If STATE and REGION have unequal lengths, a separate specification must be made for each, as in

```
VALUE LABELS STATE 'U' "UNKNOWN" / REGION 'U' "UNKNOWN".
```

VARIABLE LABELS

```
VARIABLE LABELS varname 'label' [/varname...]
```
Example:
```
VARIABLE LABELS YRHIRED 'YEAR OF FIRST HIRING'.
```

Overview

VARIABLE LABELS assigns a descriptive label to a variable.

Basic Specification

- The basic specification is a variable name and the associated label in apostrophes or quotes.

Syntax Rules

- Labels can be added to any previously defined variable. It is not necessary to enter labels for all variables in the active system file.
- Each variable label must be enclosed in apostrophes or quotation marks.
- To enter an apostrophe as part of a label, enclose the label in quotation marks or enter a double apostrophe.
- Variable labels cannot exceed 120 characters and can contain any characters including blanks.
- Multiple variables can be assigned labels on a single VARIABLE LABELS command. Only one label can be assigned to each variable, and each label can apply to only one variable.
- To continue a label from one command line to the next, precede the continuation of the label with a plus (+) sign. Each string segment of the label must be enclosed in apostrophes or quotes. To insert a blank between the strings, the blank must be included in the label specification.
- To maintain compatibility with earlier releases of SPSS, the command VAR LABELS is accepted and the label does not need to be enclosed in apostrophes. If you don't use quotes or apostrophes, the variable name must be separated from the label by at least one blank space or comma, and each variable and its label must be separated from the next variable and its label by a slash. The variable label specified in this manner cannot contain slashes and cannot begin with a quotation mark or an apostrophe.

Operations

- VARIABLE LABELS takes effect as soon as it is encountered in the command sequence, unlike most transformations, which do not take effect until the data are read. Thus, special attention should be paid to its position among commands. See Universals: Command Order.
- The variable labels are automatically displayed in the output from many procedures and are stored in the dictionary of the active system file.
- VARIABLE LABELS can be used for variables that have no previously assigned variable labels. If a variable has a previously assigned variable label, the new label replaces the old label.

Limitations

- Each value label can be up to 120 characters long, although most procedures print fewer than the 120 characters.

Example

```
VARIABLE LABELS  YRHIRED 'YEAR OF FIRST HIRING'
   DEPT88 'DEPARTMENT OF EMPLOYMENT IN 1988'
   SALARY88 'YEARLY SALARY IN 1988'
   JOBCAT 'JOB CATEGORIES'.
```

- Variable labels are assigned to the variables YRHIRED, DEPT88, SALARY88, and JOBCAT.

Example

```
VARIABLE LABELS  OLDSAL "EMPLOYEE'S GROSS SALARY PRIOR"
   + " TO 1988".
```

- The label for OLDSAL is the result of concatenating two strings with the plus sign. The blank between PRIOR and TO must be included in the first or second string to be included in the label.

VECTOR

```
VECTOR {vector name=varlist       } [/vector name...]
       {vector name(n [format])   }
```

Example:
```
VECTOR V=V1 TO V6.

STRING SELECT(A1).
COMPUTE SELECT='V'.

LOOP #I=1 TO 6.
IF MISSING(V(#I)) SELECT='M'.
END LOOP.
```

Overview

VECTOR defines a vector of new variables or associates a vector name with a collection of existing variables. A vector is a collection of variables that can be referenced with an index. The vector can reference either string or numeric variables, and the variables can be permanent or temporary.

For each variable in the reference list, VECTOR generates an element. Element names are formed by adding a subscript in parentheses to the end of the vector name. For example, if vector AGES has three elements, the elements are AGES(1), AGES(2), and AGES(3). Though the VECTOR command has other uses within the transformation language, its power is most fully exploited in conjunction with LOOP structures because the indexing variable on LOOP can be used to reference successive vector elements.

Options

File Structures. VECTOR, used with the END CASE command, can be used to restructure data files. You can build a single case from several cases or, conversely, you can build several cases from a single case. See the examples below.

Short Form Vectors. VECTOR can be used to create, simultaneously, a list of new variables and the vector that refers to them. VECTOR in the short form can be used to establish the dictionary order of a group of variables before they are defined on a DATA LIST command. See VECTOR: Short Form, below.

Basic Specification

- The basic specification is VECTOR, a vector name, a required equals sign, and the list of variables that the vector references. The TO convention must be used to specify the variable list.

- For the short form of VECTOR, the basic specification is VECTOR, an alphabetic prefix and, in parentheses, the number of variables to be created.

Syntax Rules

- Multiple vectors can be created on the same command by using a slash to separate each set of specifications.

- Variables specified on VECTOR must already be defined (unless the short form of VECTOR is used to create variables; see VECTOR: Short Form, below).

- The TO convention must be used to specify the variable list. Thus, variables specified must be consecutive and must be from the same dictionary, permanent or scratch.

- A single vector must be composed entirely of numeric variables or entirely of string variables. The string variables must be of the same length.

- A scalar, a vector, and a function can all have the same name, for example MINI. The scalar is always identified by the lack of a left parenthesis following the name. Where a vector has the same name as a function (or the abbreviation of a function), the vector name takes precedence. (See the example for VECTOR: Short Form.)

- Vector element names can never appear without a subscript in parentheses.

Operations

- VECTOR takes effect as soon as it is encountered in the command sequence, unlike most transformations, which do not take effect until the data are read. Thus, special attention should be paid to its position among commands. See Universals: Command Order.

- VECTOR is in effect only until the first procedure that follows it. The vector must be redeclared to be reused between procedures.

Limitations
- Vectors can be used in transformations but not in procedures.

Example
```
TITLE  'TEST FOR LISTWISE DELETION OF MISSING VALUES'.

DATA LIST / V1 TO V6 1-6.
STRING SELECT(A1).
COMPUTE SELECT='V'.
VECTOR V=V1 TO V6.

LOOP #I=1 TO 6.
IF MISSING(V(#I)) SELECT='M'.
END LOOP.

BEGIN DATA
123456
      56
1 3456
123456
123456
END DATA.

FREQUENCIES VAR=SELECT.
```

- STRING declares string variable SELECT with an A1 format and COMPUTE sets the initial value of SELECT equal to V.
- VECTOR defines vector V as the original variables V1 to V6. Variables on a single vector must be all numeric or all string variables. In this example, because vector V is used as an argument on the MISSING function of IF, the variables have to be numeric (MISSING is not available for string variables).
- The loop structure executes 6 times: once for each VECTOR element. If a value is missing for any element, SELECT is set equal to M. In effect, if any case has even a single missing value, SELECT is set to M.
- FREQUENCIES generates a frequency table for SELECT. The table gives a count of how many cases have missing values for at least one variable, and how many cases have valid values for all variables. Commands in this example can be used to determine whether cases may have been dropped from an analysis that uses listwise deletion of missing values. For information on using the NMISS function to count the number of missing values in each case, see COMPUTE.

Example
```
* REPLACE A CASE'S MISSING VALUES WITH THE MEAN OF ALL
  NON-MISSING VALUES FOR THAT CASE.

DATA LIST FREE /V1 V2 V3 V4 V5 V6 V7 V8.
MISSING VALUES V1 TO V8 (99).
COMPUTE MEANSUB=MEAN(V1 TO V8).

VECTOR V=V1 TO V8.

LOOP #I=1 TO 8.
+ DO IF  MISSING(V(#I)).
+ COMPUTE V(#I)=MEANSUB.
+ END IF.
END LOOP.

BEGIN DATA
1 99 2 3 5 6 7  8
2 3 4 5 6 7 8  9
2 3 5 5 6 7 8 99
END DATA.
LIST.
```

- The first COMPUTE calculates variable MEANSUB as the mean of all non-missing values in each case.
- VECTOR defines vector V with the original variables as its elements.
- The loop is executed for each variable in the data, and the COMPUTE within the loop is executed only for variables that have missing values. COMPUTE replaces the missing values with the value of MEANSUB.
- In the data, the missing value for variable V2 in the first case is set equal to MEANSUB's value in the first case. The missing value for variable V8 in the third case is set equal to MEANSUB's value in the third case.

Example

```
TITLE      'RESTRUCTURING A DATA FILE'.
SUBTITLE   'MAKE EACH DATA ITEM INTO A SINGLE CASE'.

INPUT PROGRAM.
DATA LIST /#X1 TO #X3 (3(F1,1X)).

VECTOR V=#X1 TO #X3.

LOOP #I=1 TO 3.
- COMPUTE X=V(#I).
- END CASE.
END LOOP.
END INPUT PROGRAM.

BEGIN DATA
2 1 1
3 5 1
END DATA.
FORMAT X(F1.0).
PRINT / X.
EXECUTE.
```

- INPUT PROGRAM and END INPUT PROGRAM begin and end the block of commands that build cases from the input file. They are required because the END CASE command is used to create multiple cases from single input records.
- DATA LIST defines three variables for the data. In the format specification, the first 3 is a repetition factor that repeats the format that follows it in parentheses three times: once for each variable. The specified format is F1, and the element 1X skips one column.
- VECTOR creates vector V with the original scratch variables as its three elements. The indexing expression on the LOOP command increments variable #I three times to control the number of iterations per input case and to provide the index for vector V.
- COMPUTE sets X equal to each of the scratch variables. END CASE tells SPSS to build a case. Thus, the first loop for the first case sets X equal to the first element of vector V. Since V(1) references #X1, and #X1 is 2, the value of X is 2. END CASE then builds the case. The END LOOP returns control to the LOOP command since the indexing is not complete. SPSS then sets X to #X2, which is 1, and builds the second case. The third iteration sets X equal to #X3, which is also 1, builds the third case, and terminates the loop. At this point, control is returned to the DATA LIST for the next input case. The six new cases are therefore:

```
2
1
1
3
5
1
```

Example

```
TITLE       'RESTRUCTURING A DATA FILE'.
SUBTITLE    'CREATE A SEPARATE CASE FOR EACH BOOK ORDER'.

INPUT PROGRAM.
DATA LIST   /ORDER 1-4 #X1 TO #X22 (1X,11(F3.0,F2.0,1X)).

LEAVE ORDER.
VECTOR BOOKS=#X1 TO #X22.

LOOP #I=1 TO 21 BY 2   IF NOT SYSMIS(BOOKS(#I)).
- COMPUTE ISBN=BOOKS(#I).
- COMPUTE QUANTITY=BOOKS(#I+1).
- END CASE.
END LOOP.
END INPUT PROGRAM.
BEGIN DATA
1045 182 2 155 1 134 1 153 5
1046 155 3 153 5 163 1
1047 161 5 182 2 163 4 186 6
1048 186 2
1049 155 2 163 2 153 2 074 1 161 1
END DATA.

SORT CASES ISBN.

DO IF $CASENUM EQ 1.
- PRINT EJECT /'Order ISBN Quantity'.
- PRINT SPACE.
END IF.

FORMATS ISBN (F3)/ QUANTITY (F2).
PRINT /' ' ORDER ' ' ISBN '   ' QUANTITY.

EXECUTE.
```

- Data are extracted from a file whose records store values for an invoice number, a series of book codes, and quantities of books ordered. Invoice 1045 is for nine books of four different titles: two copies of book 182, one copy each of 155 and 134, and five copies of book 153.

- The task is to break each individual book order into a record, preserving the order number on each new case. The easiest way to do so is to use the REPEATING DATA command. This example is, in effect, longhand for REPEATING DATA.

- INPUT PROGRAM and END INPUT PROGRAM begin and end the block of commands that build cases from the input file. They are required because the END CASE command is used to create multiple cases from single input records.

- DATA LIST specifies ORDER as a permanent variable and defines 22 scratch variables to hold as many alternating book numbers and quantities as will fit in 72 columns. In the format specification, the first element skips one space after the value for variable ORDER. The 11 is a repetition factor that repeats the parenthesized format that follows it eleven times: once for each book number and quantity pair. The specified format is F3.0 for book numbers, F2.0 for the quantities, and the element 1X skips one column after each quantity value.

- LEAVE preserves the value of variable ORDER across the new cases to be generated.

- VECTOR sets up vector BOOKS with the original scratch variables as its elements. The first element is #X1, the second is #X2, and so forth.

- If the element for vector BOOKS is not system-missing, LOOP initiates the LOOP structure that moves through vector BOOKS picking off the book numbers and quantities. The indexing clause initiates the indexing variable #I at 1, to be increased by 2 to a maximum of 21. It will terminate at 21 but is not executed if the element in vector BOOKS is missing.

- The first COMPUTE command sets variable ISBN equal to the element in vector BOOKS indexed by #I, which is the current book number. The second COMPUTE sets variable QUANTITY equal to the next element in vector BOOKS, which is the quantity associated with the book number now stored in variable ISBN.

- END CASE tells SPSS to write out a case with the current values of the three variables: ORDER, ISBN, and QUANTITY.
- END LOOP terminates the loop structure and control is returned to the LOOP command, where #I is increased by 2 and looping continues (until #I exceeds 21).
- SORT CASES sorts the new cases by book number in preparation for display.
- The DO IF structure encloses a PRINT EJECT command and a PRINT SPACE command to set up titles for the displayed output.
- PRINT FORMATS establishes dictionary print formats for new variables ISBN and QUANTITY. See the output from the PRINT command.
- EXECUTE is shown here as the procedure that processes the cases for display; any procedure will do.

PRINT output showing new cases

```
Order ISBN Quantity

1049   74   1
1045  134   1
1045  153   5
1046  153   5
1049  153   2
1045  155   1
1046  155   3
1049  155   2
1047  161   5
1049  161   1
1046  163   1
1047  163   4
1049  163   2
1045  182   2
1047  182   2
1047  186   6
1048  186   2
```

VECTOR: Short Form

VECTOR can be used to create simultaneously a list of new variables and the vector that refers to them. The short form of VECTOR specifies a prefix of alphanumeric characters followed, in parentheses, by the number of variables to be created.

- The new variable names must not conflict with existing variables. They are created according to the rules for scratch variables if the prefix is given a # character, or otherwise according to the rules for permanent and temporary variables.
- More than one vector of the same length can be created by naming two or more prefixes before the length specification.
- By default, variables created with the VECTOR receive F8.2 formats. Alternative formats for the variables can be specified by including the format specification with the length specification within the parentheses. The format and length, which can be specified in either order, must be separated by at least one space or comma. If multiple vectors are created, the assigned format applies to all of them unless you specify otherwise.

Example   `VECTOR #WORK(10).`

- SPSS creates vector #WORK, which references ten scratch variables: #WORK1, #WORK2, and so on, through #WORK10. Thus, element #WORK(5) of the vector is variable #WORK5.

Example   `VECTOR X,Y(5).`

- VECTOR creates vectors X and Y defining new variables X1 through X5 and Y1 through Y5, respectively.

Example   `VECTOR X(6,A5).`

- VECTOR assigns an A5 format to variables X1 through X6, making them string variables with a width of 5.

Example   `VECTOR X,Y(A5,6) Z(3,F2).`

- VECTOR assigns A5 formats to variables X1 to X6 and Y1 to Y6, and F2 formats to variables Z1 to Z3. Notice that it doesn't matter whether the format or the length is specified first within the parentheses.

Example   `TITLE'PREDETERMINE VARIABLE ORDER WITH THE SHORT FORM OF VECTOR'.`

```
INPUT PROGRAM.
VECTOR X Y (4,F1).
DATA LIST / X4 Y4 X3 Y3 X2 Y2 X1 Y1 1-8.
END INPUT PROGRAM.

PRINT /X1 TO X4  Y1 TO Y4.
BEGIN DATA
49382716
49382716
49382716
END DATA.
```

- The short form of VECTOR is used to establish the dictionary order of a group of variables before they are defined on a DATA LIST command. To predetermine variable order, both VECTOR and DATA LIST must be enclosed within INPUT PROGRAM and END INPUT PROGRAM commands.

- Variables X1, X2, X3, and X4, and Y1, Y2, Y3, and Y4 can be referenced using the TO convention even though they are interspersed and read from the input record in the reverse order.

- Default formats of F8.2 display for all the variables. Though SPSS reads the variables with the F1 format specified on DATA LIST, it writes the variables with F8.2 format because VECTOR determines the output format. A more general method for predetermining the variable order is to use NUMERIC (or STRING, if the variables are string variables) instead of VECTOR before the DATA LIST. The advantage of using NUMERIC or STRING is that you can assign mnemonic names to the variables rather than names that all have the same prefix and differ only in their numeric suffixes.

Example   `TITLE 'NAME CONFLICTS'.`

```
INPUT PROGRAM.
NUMERIC MIN MINI_A MINI_B MINIM(F2).
COMPUTE MINI_A = MINI(2).   /*MINI is function MINIMUM, abbrev.
VECTOR MINI(3,F2).
DO REPEAT I = 1 TO 3.
+  COMPUT MINI(I) = -I.
END REPEAT.
COMPUTE MIN = MIN(1).        /*MIN is function MINIMUM, abbrev.
COMPUTE MINI_B = MINI(2).    /*MINI now references vector MINI
COMPUTE MINIM = MINIM(3).    /*MINIM is function MINIMUM, abbrev.
END CASE.
END FILE.
END INPUT PROGRAM.

LIST.
```

- In this example, there are name conflicts between the scalars (the variables named on NUMERIC), the vectors (named on VECTOR), and the statistical function MINIMUM.

- A name that is not followed by a left parenthesis is treated as a scalar. A conflict between a vector name and a function name is resolved by giving the vector precedence.

VECTOR Outside a LOOP Structure

VECTOR is most commonly associated with the LOOP structure, since the index variable for LOOP can be used as the subscript. However, the subscript can come from elsewhere, including from the data.

Example

```
TITLE  'CREATE A SINGLE CASE FOR EACH OF STUDENTS 1, 2, AND 3'.
DATA LIST /STUDENT 1 SCORE 3-4 TESTNUM 6.
BEGIN DATA
1 10 1
1 20 2
1 30 3
1 40 4
2 15 2
2 25 3
3 40 1
3 55 3
3 60 4
END DATA.

VECTOR RESULT(4).
COMPUTE RESULT(TESTNUM)=SCORE.

AGGREGATE OUTFILE=*/BREAK=STUDENT
        /RESULT1 TO RESULT4=MAX(RESULT1 TO RESULT4).

PRINT FORMATS RESULT1 TO RESULT4 (F2.0).
PRINT /STUDENT RESULT1 TO RESULT4.
EXECUTE.
```

- Data are from scores on tests recorded in separate cases along with a student identification number and a test number. In this example, there are four possible tests for three students. Not all students took every test.
- Vector RESULT creates variables RESULT1 through RESULT4, and COMPUTE assigns SCORE values to these variables, depending on the value of TESTNUM.
- Aggregating by variable STUDENT creates new cases as shown by the results of the second PRINT command (see Figure 1). The MAX function in AGGREGATE returns the maximum value across cases with the same value for STUDENT.

Figure 1 PRINT output after aggregating

```
1 10 20 30 40
2  . 15 25  .
3 40  . 55 60
```

WEIGHT

```
WEIGHT {BY varname}
       {OFF      }
```

Example:

```
WEIGHT BY V1.
FREQUENCIES VAR=V2.
```

Overview   WEIGHT weights cases differentially for analysis. WEIGHT can be used to apply weights for obtaining population estimates when you have a sample from a population for which some substratum has been over- or undersampled. WEIGHT can also be used to weight a sample up to population size for reporting purposes. Or WEIGHT can be used to replicate an example from a table or other aggregated data as shown for the CROSSTABS procedure. With WEIGHT, you can arithmetically alter the sample size or its distribution.

Basic Specification   The basic specification is keyword BY followed by the name of the weight variable. Cases are weighted according to the values of the specified variable.

Syntax Rules
- Only one numeric variable can be specified. The variable can be a weighting factor already precoded when the data file was prepared, or it can be computed with the transformation language.
- WEIGHT OFF turns weighting off. You cannot weight the file by a variable named OFF.

Operations
- WEIGHT takes effect as soon as it is encountered in the command sequence, unlike most transformations, which do not take effect until the data are read. Thus, special attention should be paid to its position among commands. See Universals: Command Order.
- Weighting is permanent during a session unless it is preceded by a TEMPORARY command, changed, or turned off with the WEIGHT OFF specification.
- Each WEIGHT command overrides the previous one.
- WEIGHT tells SPSS to use the value of the specified variable to arithmetically replicate cases for subsequent procedures.
- Weight values do not need to be integer.
- Cases are not physically replicated.
- System-missing, user-missing, and negative values for the weighting variable are treated as 0 in the computation of weights.
- A file saved when weighting is in effect maintains the weighting.
- If the weighted number of cases exceeds the sample size, tests of significance are inflated; if it is smaller, they are deflated.

How Procedures Use Weights
- SPSS does not physically replicate cases when weighting is in effect. Rather, it arithmetically replicates them. For example, if you use CROSSTABS, the counts in the cells are actually the sums of the case weights. CROSSTABS then rounds cell counts when displaying the tables.
- Most procedures can handle noninteger weights. Two, NONPAR CORR and NPAR TESTS, cannot. An alternative weighting scheme is used for these procedures. In this scheme, a case is replicated as many times as the integer portion of the weight indicates. The fractional portion of the weight represents the probability that the case will be weighted to the next integer. For example, a case with a weight of 2.3 has a 30% probability of being weighted to 3. To do this, SPSS compares a random number generated by SPSS for each case with the fractional portion of the weight. If the random number is smaller than the proportion, the case is weighted up. Since, by default, the seed value used to generate the random number is the same across sessions, you can replicate a session. If you specify a different seed value using the SEED subcommand on the SET command, cases are weighted differently for those procedures requiring integer weights.

Limitations   WEIGHT (and also SAMPLE and SELECT IF) cannot be placed in an input program defined by the FILE TYPE—END FILE TYPE structure or by the INPUT PROGRAM—END INPUT PROGRAM structure. It can be placed nearly anywhere following these commands in a transformation program. See Appendix A for a discussion of the program states in SPSS and the placement of commands.

Example
```
WEIGHT BY V1.
FREQ VAR=V2.
```

- The frequency counts for the values of variable V2 will be weighted (multiplied) by the values of variable V1.

Example
```
COMPUTE WVAR=1.
IF (GROUP EQ 1) WVAR=.5.
WEIGHT BY WVAR.
```

- Variable WVAR is initialized to 1 with the COMPUTE command. The value of WVAR is changed to 0.5 with the IF command for cases where GROUP equals 1.
- Subsequent procedures will use a case base in which cases from Group 1 count only half as much as other cases.

Example
```
GET FILE CITY.
WEIGHT BY POP87.
DESCRIPTIVES  ALL.
WEIGHT BY POP88.
DESCRIPTIVES  ALL.
```

- The first DESCRIPTIVES command computes summary statistics based on cases weighted by POP87, and the second DESCRIPTIVES command computes summary statistics based on cases weighted by POP88.

WRITE

```
WRITE [OUTFILE=file] [RECORDS={1}] [{NOTABLE}]
                              {n}    {TABLE  }

  /{1    } varlist [{col location [(format)]}] [varlist...]
   {rec #}          {(format list)           }
                    {*                        }


  [/{2    }...]
    {rec #}
```

Example:
```
WRITE OUTFILE=PRSNNL / MOHIRED YRHIRED DEPT SALARY NAME.
EXECUTE.
```

Overview

WRITE writes case values to a file so that they can be read by other software. For information on printing case values in a format designed for people to read, see PRINT.

Options

Display Formats. You can specify formats for the numeric variables you want written. String variables can only be written with their dictionary formats. See Specifying Formats, below.

Strings. You can include strings with the variable specifications. The strings can label values or create extra space between values. See Using Strings, below.

Multiple Lines per Case. You can write variables on more than one line for each case. See RECORD Subcommand, below.

Output File. You can direct the written output to a target file. See OUTFILE Subcommand, below.

Summary Table. You can display a table that summarizes the variable formats. See TABLE Subcommand, below.

Subcommand Order

• Subcommands can be named in any order. However, all subcommands must be used before the slash that precedes the first variable list.

Basic Specification

• The basic specification is a slash followed by a variable list. The values for all the variables on the list are written to the display file.

Syntax Rules

• A slash must precede the variable specifications. The first slash begins definition of the first (and possibly only) line per case of the WRITE display.

• Specified variables must already exist, but they can be numeric, string, scratch, temporary, or system variables.

• Keyword ALL can be used to write the values of all the variables in the active system file.

Operations

• WRITE executes once for each case constructed from the data file.

• WRITE uses the dictionary write formats assigned when the variables are defined on a DATA LIST command, on a WRITE FORMATS, or FORMATS command, or assigned when the variables are created with transformation commands.

• Values are written on the display file as the data are read.

• Lines longer than 132 columns can be written. However, if the record width of the lines to be written exceeds the default output width or the width specified with the WIDTH subcommand of SET, SPSS issues an error message and terminates processing.

- There are no carriage control characters in the output file.
- User-missing values are written like any other value for a variable specified on WRITE. System-missing values are represented by blanks.
- Because WRITE is a transformation, the results of a WRITE command can be intermixed with casewise procedure output. Procedures that produce individual case listings (REPORT and LIST) should not be used immediately after WRITE. At the least, an intervening EXECUTE command should be specified.
- If you are going across machines, you should take into account that some data types cannot be read on another machine. Seek advice at your local installation.
- If long records are less convenient than multiple records per case with shorter record lengths, you can take advantage of the ability to write out a case identifier and to insert a literal as a record identification number. The software at the other end might then be able to check for missing record numbers should something happen to the data in transit.

Example
```
WRITE OUTFILE=PRSNNL / MOHIRED YRHIRED DEPT SALARY NAME.
FREQUENCIES VARIABLES=DEPT.
```

- WRITE writes values for each variable on the variable list to file PRSNNL. The FREQUENCIES procedure executes WRITE.
- All variables are written with their dictionary formats.

Example
```
WRITE OUTFILE=PRSNNL /ALL.
EXECUTE.
```

- WRITE writes values for all the variables on the active system file to file PRSNNL. The EXECUTE command executes WRITE.

Specifying Formats

You can specify formats for some or all of the *numeric* variables you want to write. For a string variable, a specified format must have a width that is equivalent to that of the dictionary format.

- A format specification following a list of variables applies to all the variables in the list. An asterisk within the list can be used to prevent the specified format from applying to variables that precede the asterisk in the list.
- Format specifications can be either column-style or FORTRAN-style. Numeric formats that can be used are F, COMMA, DOLLAR, CC, DOT, N, E, PCT, PIBHEX, RBHEX, Z, and the date and time formats. String formats that can be used are A and AHEX. In addition, write formats in IBM/OS can be IB, PIB, P, PK, and RB. See your SPSS *Operations Guide* for a complete table of output format types.
- Format specifications are in effect only for the output of the WRITE command. They do not change the dictionary write formats.
- To specify a blank between variables in the output file, use a literal, specify blank columns in the format, or use an X or T format element in the WRITE specifications.

Example
```
WRITE OUTFILE=PRSNNL / TENURE (F2.0) ' ' MOHIRED YRHIRED DEPT *
      SALARY85 TO SALARY88 (4(DOLLAR8,1X)) NAME.
EXECUTE.
```

- Format F2.0 is specified for TENURE. A blank between apostrophes is specified as a string after TENURE to separate values of TENURE from those of MOHIRED.
- MOHIRED, YRHIRED, and DEPT are written with default formats because the asterisk prevents them from receiving the DOLLAR8 format specified for SALARY85 TO SALARY88. The element 1X is specified with DOLLAR8 to add one blank after each value of SALARY85 to SALARY88.

• NAME is written with the default dictionary format.

Using Strings

You can include strings with the variable specifications on the WRITE command. Strings must be enclosed in apostrophes or quotation marks.

• If a format is specified for a variable list, the format is interrupted by a specified string. Thus, the string has the same effect within a variable list as an asterisk.

Example

```
WRITE OUTFILE=PRSNNL
  /EMPLOYID '1' MOHIRED YRHIRED SEX AGE JOBCAT NAME
  /EMPLOYID '2' DEPT86 TO DEPT88 SALARY86 TO SALARY88.
EXECUTE.
```

• Strings are used to assign the constant 1 to record 1 of each case, and 2 to record 2 to provide record identifiers in addition to the case identifier EMPLOYID.

RECORDS Subcommand

RECORDS indicates the total number of lines written per case. The number specified on RECORDS is informational only. A slash within the variable list is the specification that actually causes variables to write on a new line. Each new line is requested by another slash in the variable list.

• RECORD must be used before the slash that precedes the first variable list.

• The only specification on RECORDS is an integer to indicate the number of records for written output. If the number does not agree with the actual number of records specified by slashes in the variable list, SPSS issues a warning and ignores the specification on RECORDS.

• RECORDS is informational and may be omitted from the specification. The slashes alone cause values to be written on new lines.

• Specifications for each line of output must begin with a slash in the variable list. Optionally, an integer can follow the slash, indicating on which line the values are to be written. The integer is informational. It cannot be used to rearrange the order of records in the display file. If the integer does not agree with the actual record number determined by the slashes in the variable list, the integer is ignored.

• A slash that is not followed by a variable list generates a blank line in the written file.

Example

```
WRITE OUTFILE=PRSNNL RECORDS=2
  /EMPLOYID NAME DEPT
  /EMPLOYID TENURE SALARY.
EXECUTE.
```

• WRITE displays the values of an individual's name and department on one line, tenure and salary on the next line, the employee identification number on both lines.

Example

```
WRITE OUTFILE=PRSNNL RECORDS=2
  /1 EMPLOYID NAME DEPT
  /2 EMPLOYID TENURE SALARY.
EXECUTE.
```

• This command is equivalent to the command in the preceding example.

Example

```
WRITE OUTFILE=PRSNNL / EMPLOYID NAME DEPT
  / EMPLOYID TENURE SALARY.
EXECUTE.
```

• This command is equivalent to the commands in both preceding examples.

OUTFILE Subcommand   OUTFILE specifies the target file for the output from the WRITE command. By default, the WRITE command sends the results to the display file.

- OUTFILE must be used before the slash that precedes the first variable list.
- The output from WRITE can exceed 132 characters.

Example
```
WRITE OUTFILE=WRITEOUT
    /1 EMPLOYID DEPT SALARY /2 NAME.
EXECUTE.
```

- OUTFILE specifies WRITEOUT as the file that receives the written variable list.

TABLE Subcommand   TABLE requests a format table on the display file showing how the variable information is formatted. NOTABLE is the default.

- TABLE must be used before the slash that precedes the first variable list.

Example
```
WRITE OUTFILE=PRSNNL TABLE /1 EMPLOYID DEPT SALARY /2  NAME.
EXECUTE.
```

- TABLE requests a summary table describing the WRITE specifications. The table is displayed on the display file.

WRITE FORMATS

```
WRITE FORMATS varlist (format) [varlist...]
```

Example:

```
WRITE FORMATS SALARY (DOLLAR8)
            / HOURLY (DOLLAR7.2)
            / RAISE BONUS (PCT2).
```

Overview

WRITE FORMATS changes variable write formats. Write formats are *output* formats in SPSS and control the form in which values are written by the WRITE command.

WRITE FORMATS changes a variable's write format only. See the PRINT FORMATS command for changing the print format. See the FORMATS command for changing both the write and print formats with a single specification. See the DATA LIST command for assigning input formats during data definition.

A table of output formats that can be assigned with WRITE FORMATS, PRINT FORMATS, or FORMATS is shown with the reference documentation for the FORMATS command. Refer to that table for a list of available write formats.

Basic Specification

- The basic specification is a variable list followed by the new format specification in parentheses. All the specified variables receive the new format.

Syntax Rules

- Only one format can be specified in the parentheses.
- Different formats can be assigned to different variables by using a slash to separate specifications for each different format.
- Format specifications on WRITE FORMATS are output formats. When specifying the width for the format type, enough positions must be allowed to include any punctuation characters such as decimal points, commas, dollar signs, or date and time delimiters. (This is different from assigning an *input* format on DATA LIST. SPSS automatically expands input formats to accommodate punctuation characters in the output.)
- A custom currency format (CCw, CCw.d) must first be defined on the SET command before it can be used on WRITE FORMATS.
- WRITE FORMATS cannot be used with string variables because the declared length of a string variable cannot be changed. To change the length of a string variable, declare a new variable of the desired length with the STRING command and then use COMPUTE to copy values from the existing string into the new string.
- To save the new write formats, the active system file must be saved as a new system file with the SAVE or XSAVE commands. The new write formats are used as dictionary formats in the new system file.

Operations

- WRITE FORMATS takes effect as soon as it is encountered in the command sequence, unlike most transformations, which do not take effect until the data are read. Thus, special attention should be paid to its position among commands. See Universals: Command Order.
- Variables not specified on WRITE FORMATS retain their current write formats in the active system file. To see the current formats, use the DISPLAY command.
- The new write formats are changed in the active system file only, and they are in effect for the duration of the SPSS session or until changed again with a WRITE FORMATS or FORMATS command. If GET was used to create the active system file, formats in the original system file are not changed.
- When the transformation language is used to create a new numeric variable, the dictionary write and print formats are both F8.2 (or the format specified on the FORMAT subcommand of SET). The WRITE FORMATS command can be used to change the new variable's write format.

- Default formats for string variables created using the SPSS transformation language are those specified on the STRING command that declares the variable. WRITE FORMATS cannot be used to change the write format of a new string variable.
- If a data value exceeds its width specification, SPSS makes an attempt to produce some value nevertheless. It takes out punctuation characters, then it tries scientific notation, and, if there is still not enough space, it produces asterisks indicating that a value is present that cannot be written in the assigned width.

Example
```
WRITE FORMATS SALARY (DOLLAR8)
            / HOURLY (DOLLAR7.2)
            / RAISE BONUS (PCT2).
```

- The write format for SALARY is changed to DOLLAR format with eight positions including, when appropriate, the dollar sign and comma. An eight-digit number would require a DOLLAR11 format specification: 8 characters for the digits, 2 characters for commas, and 1 character for the dollar sign.
- The write format for HOURLY is changed to DOLLAR format with seven positions, including the dollar sign, decimal point, and two decimal places.
- The write format for both RAISE and BONUS is changed to PCT format with two positions: one for the percentage and one for the percent sign.

Example
```
COMPUTE V3=V1 + V2.
WRITE FORMATS V3 (F3.1).
```

- COMPUTE creates the new numeric variable V3. By default, V3 is assigned an F8.2 format.
- WRITE FORMATS changes the write format for V3 to F3.1.

Example
```
SET CCA='-/-.Dfl ..-'.
WRITE FORMATS COST (CCA14.2).
```

- SET defines a European currency format for the custom currency format type CCA.
- WRITE FORMATS assigns the write format CCA to variable COST. See the SET command for more information on custom currency formats.

XSAVE

```
XSAVE OUTFILE=file

[/KEEP={ALL    }] [/DROP=varlist]
       {varlist}

[/RENAME=(old varlist=new varlist)...]

[/MAP] [/{COMPRESSED  }]
         {UNCOMPRESSED}
```

Example:

```
XSAVE OUTFILE=EMPL /RENAME=(AGE=AGE86) (JOBCAT=JOBCAT88).
MEANS RAISE88 BY DEPT88.
```

Overview　XSAVE produces an SPSS system file. The system file includes all data and a data dictionary with variable and value labels (if specified), missing-value flags, and print formats for each variable. The principal advantage of XSAVE over SAVE is that it can reduce processing time. XSAVE is not executed until data are read for the next procedure, consolidating two data passes into one; SAVE is executed by itself.

Options　**Variable Subsets and Order.** You can save a subset of variables and also reorder variables that are copied to the system file. See the DROP and KEEP subcommands.

Variable names. You can rename variables as they are copied to the system file.

Variable map. To confirm any renaming, subsetting, or reordering, you can display the names of the variables saved in the system file alongside their corresponding names in the active system file.

System file. You can specify that the system file be written in a compressed or uncompressed form.

Basic Specification　• The basic specification is the OUTFILE subcommand, which specifies the output system file. The placement of XSAVE relative to other commands determines what is saved in the system file. New variables created by transformations and procedures preceding the XSAVE command are included in the new system file, and variables altered by transformations are saved in their modified form. Results of any temporary transformations immediately preceding the XSAVE command are included in the system file; scratch variables are not. Documentary text from the active system file is saved in the system file dictionary.

Subcommand Order　• Subcommands can be used in any order.

Syntax Rules　• OUTFILE is required and can be specified only once. If OUTFILE is specified more than once, only the last OUTFILE specification is in effect.
　• KEEP, DROP, RENAME, and MAP can be used multiple times each and in any order.
　• Only one of the subcommands COMPRESSED or UNCOMPRESSED can be specified per XSAVE command.
　• Documentary text can be dropped from the active system file with the DROP DOCUMENTS command.

Operations　• XSAVE is a transformation command and is executed when the data are read for the next procedure. Compare with SAVE, which is a procedure and reads data.
　• The system file dictionary is arranged in the same order as the active system file.

- System files are binary files designed to be read and written by SPSS only. System files can be edited with the UPDATE command only. See also the MATCH FILES and ADD FILES commands for joining system files.
- The active system file remains available for SPSS transformations and procedures after the system file is created.
- XSAVE processes the dictionary first and displays a message that indicates how many variables will be saved. Once the data are written, XSAVE indicates how many cases were saved. If the second message does not appear, the file was probably not completely written.

Limitations

- A maximum of 10 XSAVE commands are allowed in a session.
- XSAVE does not save scratch variables.
- XSAVE cannot appear with a DO REPEAT-END REPEAT structure.
- Multiple XSAVE commands writing to the same file are not permitted.

Example

```
GET FILE=HUBEMPL.
XSAVE OUTFILE=EMPL88 /RENAME=(AGE=AGE86) (JOBCAT=JOBCAT88).
MEANS RAISE88 BY DEPT88.
```

- OUTFILE specifies EMPL88 as the output system file. Variable AGE is renamed to AGE86, and variable JOBCAT is renamed to JOBCAT88.
- XSAVE is not executed until SPSS reads the data for procedure MEANS. With a single data pass, SPSS saves file EMPL88 and generates a MEANS table.
- After MEANS executes, file HUBEMPL is still the active system file. Variables AGE and JOBCAT retain their original names in the active system file.

Example

```
GET FILE=HUBEMPL.
TEMPORARY.
RECODE DEPT85 TO DEPT88 (1,2=1) (3,4=2) (ELSE=9).
VALUE LABELS DEPT85 TO DEPT88 1 'MANAGEMENT' 2 'OPERATIONS'
   3 'UNKNOWN'.
XSAVE OUTFILE=HUBTEMP.
CROSSTABS DEPT85 TO DEPT88 BY JOBCAT.
```

- Both the saved system file and the CROSSTABS output will reflect the temporary recoding and labeling of the department variables.
- If XSAVE is replaced with SAVE, the data are read twice instead of just once, and the CROSSTABS output does not reflect the recoding.

OUTFILE Subcommand

OUTFILE specifies the output system file. OUTFILE is required and can be specified only once. If OUTFILE is specified more than once, only the last OUTFILE specification takes effect.

DROP and KEEP Subcommands

DROP and KEEP save a subset of variables. DROP specifies the variables not to save in the new system file; KEEP specifies the variables to save in the new system file.

- Variables can be specified in any order. The variable order on KEEP determines their sequence in the system file. Variable order on DROP does not affect the order of variables in the system file: the variables are saved in the same sequence they appear in the active system file.
- Multiple DROP and KEEP subcommands are allowed.
- If a variable is referenced twice, only the first mention of the variable is recognized.

Reordering Variables

- The variable order on KEEP determines their sequence in the output system file. New variables created by transformations or procedures are added to the end of the active system file. KEEP can save these variables in a different order.
- Keyword ALL on KEEP refers to all remaining variables not previously specified. ALL must be the last specification on KEEP.

Example
```
XSAVE OUTFILE=HUBTEMP /DROP=DEPT79 TO DEPT84 SALARY79.
CROSSTABS DEPT85 TO DEPT88 BY JOBCAT.
```

- The system file is saved as file HUBTEMP. All variables between and including DEPT79 and DEPT84, as well as SALARY79, are excluded from the system file. All other variables are saved in the system file.

Example
```
GET FILE=PRSNL.
COMPUTE  TENURE=(12-CMONTH +(12*(88-CYEAR)))/12.
COMPUTE  JTENURE=(12-JMONTH +(12*(88-JYEAR)))/12.
VARIABLE LABELS   TENURE 'Tenure in Company'
                  JTENURE 'Tenure in Grade'.
XSAVE OUTFILE=PRSNL88 /DROP=GRADE STORE
 /KEEP=LNAME NAME TENURE JTENURE ALL.
REPORT FORMAT=AUTO /VARS=AGE TENURE JTENURE SALARY
 /BREAK=DIVISION /SUMMARY=MEAN.
```

- Variables TENURE and JTENURE are created by COMPUTE commands and assigned variable labels by the VARIABLE LABELS command. TENURE and JTENURE are added to the end of the active system file.

- DROP specifies that variables GRADE and STORE be dropped when file PRSNL88 is generated. KEEP determines that LNAME, NAME, TENURE, and JTENURE are the first four variables in file PRSNL88, followed by all remaining variables not specified on DROP. Variables not specified on KEEP are saved on PRSNL88 in the same sequence they appear in the original file.

RENAME Subcommand

RENAME changes the names of variables as they are copied into the system file.

- Name changes can be specified in the form *old varname=new varname*. Multiple sets of variable specifications are allowed. Each set can be enclosed in optional parentheses.

- As an alternative to the above, name changes can be specified with a list of old variable names followed by an equals sign and a list of new variable names. The same number of variables must be specified on both lists. Keyword TO can be used in either or both lists to refer to consecutive variables. A single set of parentheses enclosing the entire specification is required for this method.

- Old variable names need not be specified according to their order in the active system file.

- Name changes take place in one operation. Therefore, variable names can be exchanged between two variables.

- Multiple RENAME subcommands are allowed.

Example
```
XSAVE OUTFILE=EMPL88 /RENAME  AGE=AGE88 JOBCAT=JOBCAT88.
CROSSTABS DEPT85 TO DEPT88 BY JOBCAT.
```

- RENAME specifies two name changes for file EMPL88: AGE is renamed to AGE88, and JOBCAT is renamed to JOBCAT88.

Example
```
XSAVE OUTFILE=EMPL88 /RENAME (AGE JOBCAT=AGE88 JOBCAT88).
CROSSTABS DEPT85 TO DEPT88 BY JOBCAT.
```

- The name changes are identical to those in the previous example: AGE is renamed to AGE88, and JOBCAT is renamed to JOBCAT88. The parentheses are required with this method.

MAP Subcommand

MAP displays a list of the variables in the system file and their corresponding names in the active system file.

- The only specification is keyword MAP. MAP has no additional specifications.

- Multiple MAP subcommands are allowed. Each MAP subcommand maps the results of subcommands that precede it, but not results of subcommands that follow it.

Example
```
GET FILE=HUBEMPL.
XSAVE OUTFILE=EMPL88 /RENAME=(AGE=AGE86) (JOBCAT=JOBCAT88)
   /KEEP=LNAME NAME JOBCAT88 ALL /MAP.
MEANS RAISE88 BY DEPT88.
```

- MAP confirms that variable AGE is renamed to AGE86 and JOBCAT is renamed to JOBCAT88. MAP also confirms that the first three variables in file EMPL88 are LNAME NAME and JOBCAT88, and that all remaining variables from the active system file are present in file EMPL88.

COMPRESSED Subcommand

COMPRESSED tells SPSS to save the system file in compressed form. In a compressed file, small integers (from -99 to 155) are stored in one byte, instead of the usual eight bytes.

- The only specification is keyword COMPRESSED. COMPRESSED has no additional specifications.
- Compressed system files occupy less disk space than do uncompressed system files.
- Compressed system files take longer to read than do uncompressed system files.
- No additional specification is required on the GET command to read a compressed system file.
- Only one of the subcommands COMPRESSED or UNCOMPRESSED can be specified per XSAVE command. COMPRESSED is usually the default, though UNCOMPRESSED may be the default at some installations.

UNCOMPRESSED Subcommand

UNCOMPRESSED tells SPSS to save the system file in uncompressed form.

- The only specification is keyword UNCOMPRESSED. UNCOMPRESSED has no additional specifications.
- Uncompressed system files are quicker to read than are compressed system files.
- Uncompressed system files occupy more disk space than do compressed system files.
- No additional specification is required on the GET command to read an uncompressed system file.
- Only one of the subcommands COMPRESSED or UNCOMPRESSED can be specified per XSAVE command. COMPRESSED is usually the default, though UNCOMPRESSED may be the default at some installations.

Examples

Examples

The following examples illustrate two different applications of procedure ALSCAL.

Example 1 This example shows how ALSCAL performs classical nonmetric multidimensional scaling to uncover the dimensions on which Americans perceived 12 major presidential candidates for the 1968 election. Prior to the election, people were asked to rate the presidential hopefuls on a "Feeling Thermometer." The responses were then correlated, and the correlations were used as the input to ALSCAL. (Although distance measures are usually used in multidimensional scaling, correlation can be considered a proximity measure.) Since the input matrix was symmetric, all values above the diagonal were ignored. Data for this example come from the *Survey Research Center 1968 American National Election Study*, made available by the Inter-University Consortium for Political Research. The data have also been analyzed by Weisberg & Rusk (1970). The SPSS commands for the present analysis are

```
TITLE 'PERCEPTIONS OF 1968 PRESIDENTIAL CANDIDATES'.
SET WIDTH = 80.
UNNUMBERED. /* required only for some IBM operating systems
DATA LIST
  / WALLACE HUMPHREY NIXON MCCARTHY REAGAN ROCKFLLR JOHNSON
    ROMNEY KENNEDY MUSKIE AGNEW LEMAY 1-84.
BEGIN DATA
 1.000                                                                  WALLACE
-0.312  1.000                                                           HUMPHREY
-0.038 -0.179  1.000                                                    NIXON
-0.139  0.245  0.077  1.000                                             MCCARTHY
 0.197 -0.192  0.415  0.089  1.000                                      REAGAN
-0.140  0.163  0.122  0.329  0.189  1.000                               ROCKEFELLER
-0.226  0.702 -0.088  0.129 -0.105  0.150  1.000                        JOHNSON
-0.062  0.171  0.239  0.328  0.297  0.322  0.243  1.000                 ROMNEY
-0.219  0.526 -0.130  0.356 -0.108  0.228  0.467  0.259  1.000          KENNEDY
-0.260  0.579 -0.102  0.292 -0.077  0.272  0.459  0.236  0.429  1.000   MUSKIE
 0.122 -0.100  0.598  0.116  0.439  0.126 -0.034  0.336 -0.009 -0.028  1.000          AGNEW
 0.683 -0.206  0.113 -0.033  0.275 -0.040 -0.084  0.096 -0.091 -0.159  0.295  1.000   LEMAY
END DATA

ALSCAL VARIABLES = WALLACE TO LEMAY
  / LEVEL = ORDINAL (SIMILAR)
  / PLOT
  / PRINT = HEADER
  / CRITERIA = CUTOFF(-1.000).
```

- The DATA LIST command reads 12 variables in fixed format. The data are inline. ALSCAL uses only the values in the lower triangle of a symmetric matrix. Therefore, values above the diagonal are not entered.
- The VARIABLES subcommand following the ALSCAL command specifies the variables to be scaled.
- The LEVEL subcommand indicates that the input data are at the ordinal level of measurement. The SIMILAR specification indicates that ALSCAL should treat the input data as similarities rather than dissimilarities.

- The PLOT subcommand requests the default plots, which in this case are a plot of the stimulus coordinates, scatterplots of the linear and nonlinear fits between the data and the model, and a plot of the data transformation.
- The PRINT subcommand specifies that the printed output should include a header, defining the data, model, output, and algorithmic options in effect for the analysis.
- The CUTOFF option on the CRITERIA subcommand indicates that values less than or equal to -1.000 are to be treated as missing.

Figure 1 lists the ALSCAL procedure options in effect for the analysis.

Figure 1 ALSCAL header information

```
ALSCAL PROCEDURE OPTIONS

DATA OPTIONS—

NUMBER OF ROWS (OBSERVATIONS/MATRIX).    12
NUMBER OF COLUMNS (VARIABLES) . . .      12
NUMBER OF MATRICES   . . . . . . .       1
MEASUREMENT LEVEL  . . . . . . . .       ORDINAL
DATA MATRIX SHAPE . . . . . . . .        SYMMETRIC
TYPE  . . . . . . . . . . . . .          SIMILARITY
APPROACH TO TIES  . . . . . . . .        LEAVE TIED
CONDITIONALITY . . . . . . . . .         MATRIX
DATA CUTOFF AT . . . . . . . . .         -1.000000

MODEL OPTIONS—

MODEL . . . . . . . . . . . . .          EUCLID
MAXIMUM DIMENSIONALITY  . . . . .         2
MINIMUM DIMENSIONALITY  . . . . .         2
NEGATIVE WEIGHTS  . . . . . . .          NOT PERMITTED

OUTPUT OPTIONS—

JOB OPTION HEADER . . . . . . .          PRINTED
DATA MATRICES . . . . . . . . .          NOT PRINTED
CONFIGURATIONS AND TRANSFORMATIONS .     PLOTTED
OUTPUT DATASET . . . . . . . .           NOT CREATED
INITIAL STIMULUS COORDINATES  . . . .
                                         COMPUTED

ALGORITHMIC OPTIONS—

MAXIMUM ITERATIONS  . . . . . .          30
CONVERGENCE CRITERION . . . . .          0.00100
MINIMUM S-STRESS  . . . . . . .          0.00500
MISSING DATA ESTIMATED BY  . . . .
                                         ULBOUNDS
TIESTORE . . . . . . . . . . .           66
```

Figure 2 shows the iteration history for a two-dimensional solution. After five iterations, the improvement in S-STRESS is so small (0.00085) that the analysis stops, printing the message that the amount of improvement is less than the minimum permitted. ALSCAL then prints two goodness-of-fit measures, Kruskal's STRESS formula 1 (0.063) and the squared correlation coefficient (RSQ=0.982). Results in this case show a nearly perfect fit between the data and the solution.

Figure 2 Iteration history and goodness-of-fit measures

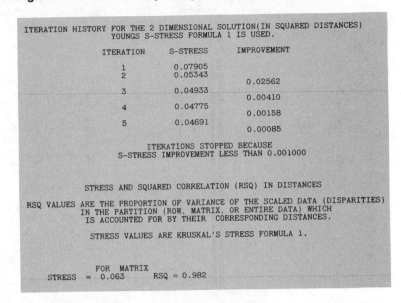

Figure 3 shows the derived configuration in two dimensions in printed form. ALSCAL assigns a stimulus number, stimulus name, plot symbol, and a pair of coordinates to each variable in the analysis.

Figure 3 Printed configuration

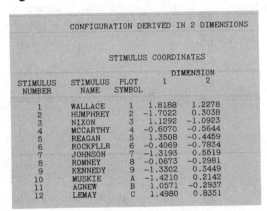

Figure 4 is a plot of the derived stimulus coordinates. Labels for the points are the plot symbols listed in Figure 3. Investigators are free to interpret the configuration in ways that they find meaningful.

Figure 4 Plot of the stimulus coordinates

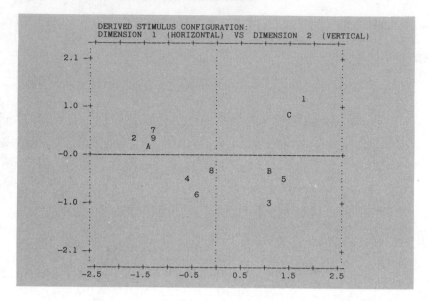

Figure 5 is a scatterplot of the linear fit between the distances in the stimulus space and the transformed data, or disparities. The plot in this case is nearly a straight line, with little scatter, indicating a close fit between the model and the input data.

Figure 5 Plot of the linear fit

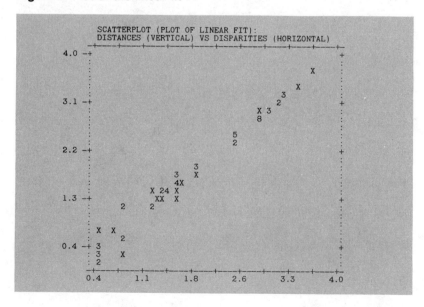

Figure 6 is a plot of the computed distances versus the actual observations (proximity values). Since the data are similarities, the distances should diminish (and they do) as the degree of similarity increases.

Figure 6 Plot of the nonlinear fit

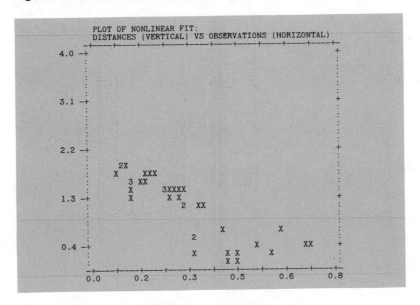

Figure 7 shows the relationship between the disparities (using Kruskal's least-squares monotonic transformation) and the actual proximities.

Figure 7 Plot of the data transformation

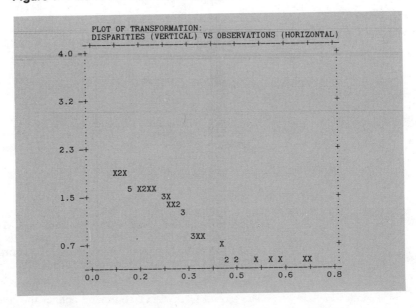

Example 2   This example demonstrates nonmetric external asymmetric scaling using an SPSS file containing initial configuration coordinates and weights. In this case, the START file contains stimulus configuration coordinates, subject weights, and stimulus weights. ALSCAL will use only the stimulus coordinates and subject weights. The SPSS commands used to produce the results are

```
SET WIDTH=80.
DATA LIST / DIM1 1-3 DIM2 4-6 TYPE_ 9-16(A).

BEGIN DATA
 2   2   CONFIG
 2   1   CONFIG
-1   2   CONFIG
 1  -2   CONFIG
-3  -3   CONFIG
 0  -1   CONFIG
 0   0   CONFIG
.6  .7   SUBJWGHT
.9  .4   SUBJWGHT
.7  .7   SUBJWGHT
.9  .2   SUBJWGHT
1.0 .2   SUBJWGHT
.6   1   STIMWGHT
.3  .9   STIMWGHT
.8  .7   STIMWGHT
.5  .5   STIMWGHT
.2  .5   STIMWGHT
.7  .5   STIMWGHT
.6  .9   STIMWGHT
END DATA.

SAVE OUTFILE = START.

DATA LIST / A1 TO A7 1-70.

BEGIN DATA
        0.000   3.000   5.196  12.083  16.583   9.434   6.633
        2.449   0.000   3.000   7.416  11.000   5.292   3.162
        5.745   5.196   0.000   8.124  10.392   5.196   3.000
        7.071   5.385   5.916   0.000   5.916   2.236   3.742

        . . .

        9.327   9.000   0.000   9.487  11.489   5.745   3.873
        7.348   5.745   7.141   0.000   9.950   3.000   4.243
       12.247  11.091   7.746   7.141   0.000   6.245   7.348
        7.937   6.928   4.583   3.464   9.644   0.000   1.732
END DATA

ALSCAL VARIABLES = A1 TO A7
 / SHAPE = ASYMMETR
 / LEVEL = ORDINAL
 / MODEL = AINDS
 / FILE = START
         CONFIG(FIXED)
         STIMWGHT(INITIAL)
 / PRINT = HEADER
 / PLOT.
```

- The first DATA LIST reads in three variables: DIM1, DIM2, and TYPE_. The data are inline. Variables DIM1 and DIM2 correspond to the first two ALSCAL dimensions; TYPE_ identifies the input values as stimulus coordinates (CONFIG), subject weights (SUBJWGHT), and stimulus weights (STIMWGHT).

- The SAVE command stores the configurations in an SPSS system file called START.

- The second DATA LIST command defines the column locations of the variables for the proximity matrix. Only part of the proximity data are shown.

- The VARIABLES subcommand following the ALSCAL command specifies seven variables to be scaled.
- The SHAPE subcommand defines the form of the proximity matrix as ASYMMETRIC.
- The LEVEL subcommand indicates that the proximity data are at the ordinal level of measurement. Since the SIMILAR option is not used, ALSCAL treats the proximity data as dissimilarities.
- The MODEL subcommand specifies the asymmetric individual differences Euclidean distance model (AINDS).
- The FILE subcommand defines the SPSS file containing the initial configuration and weights. The CONFIG (FIXED) and SUBJWGHT (INITIAL) options indicate that fixed stimulus coordinates and initial subject weights are to be read from the file START. ALSCAL will skip over TYPE_ values labeled STIMWGHT.
- The PRINT subcommand specifies that the printed output should include a header, defining the options in effect for the analysis.
- The PLOT subcommand requests default plots. In this case, ALSCAL will produce plots of the derived stimulus configuration, derived stimulus weights, and derived subject weights, as well as a scatterplot of the linear fit between the data and the model.

Figures 8 through 13 show portions of the display output. Figure 8 displays the options in effect for the analysis. The section on output options shows that ALSCAL computed initial subject weights (the default for MODEL=AINDS) and printed stimulus coordinates and stimulus weights.

Figure 8 ALSCAL header information

```
ALSCAL PROCEDURE OPTIONS

DATA OPTIONS-

NUMBER OF ROWS (OBSERVATIONS/MATRIX).       7
NUMBER OF COLUMNS (VARIABLES) . . .         7
NUMBER OF MATRICES . . . . . . . .          5
MEASUREMENT LEVEL . . . . . . . .           ORDINAL
DATA MATRIX SHAPE . . . . . . . .           ASYMMETRIC
TYPE . . . . . . . . . . . . . .            DISSIMILARITY
APPROACH TO TIES . . . . . . . .            LEAVE TIED
CONDITIONALITY . . . . . . . . .            MATRIX
DATA CUTOFF AT . . . . . . . . .            0.0

MODEL OPTIONS-

MODEL . . . . . . . . . . . . .             AINDS
MAXIMUM DIMENSIONALITY . . . . . .          2
MINIMUM DIMENSIONALITY . . . . .            2
NEGATIVE WEIGHTS . . . . . . . .            NOT PERMITTED

OUTPUT OPTIONS-

JOB OPTION HEADER . . . . . . . .           PRINTED
DATA MATRICES . . . . . . . . .             NOT PRINTED
CONFIGURATIONS AND TRANSFORMATIONS  .       PLOTTED
OUTPUT DATASET . . . . . . . . .            NOT CREATED
INITIAL STIMULUS COORDINATES . . .
                                            READ, PRINTED AND FIXED
INITIAL SUBJECT WEIGHTS . . . . .
                                            COMPUTED
INITIAL STIMULUS WEIGHTS  . . . .
                                            READ AND PRINTED

ALGORITHMIC OPTIONS-

MAXIMUM ITERATIONS  . . . . . . .           30
CONVERGENCE CRITERION  . . . . .            0.00100
MINIMUM S-STRESS  . . . . . . .             0.00500
MISSING DATA ESTIMATED BY . . . .
                                            ULBOUNDS
TIESTORE . . . . . . . . . . . .            245
```

Figure 9 shows the initial stimulus coordinates and initial stimulus weights in two dimensions as read from the START file. The remaining figures show the derived stimulus coordinates, subject weights, stimulus weights, and the flattened subject weights.

Figure 9 Initial stimulus coordinates and weights

```
ALSCAL will read initial and/or fixed values from file with handle START
  Label:
    Created 24 JAN 85 15:04:54        3 Variables

                    INITIAL CONFIGURATION


                  INITIAL STIMULUS SPACE

                                 DIMENSION
STIMULUS    STIMULUS      1          2

  NUMBER      NAME
     1        A1        2.0000     2.0000
     2        A2        2.0000     1.0000
     3        A3       -1.0000     2.0000
     4        A4        1.0000    -2.0000
     5        A5       -3.0000    -3.0000
     6        A6        0.0       -1.0000
     7        A7        0.0        0.0

                 INITIAL STIMULUS WEIGHTS
                           DIMENSION
STIMULUS    NAME        1          2
     1        A1        0.6000     1.0000
     2        A2        0.3000     0.9000
     3        A3        0.8000     0.7000
     4        A4        0.5000     0.5000
     5        A5        0.2000     0.5000
     6        A6        0.7000     0.5000
     7        A7        0.6000     0.9000
```

Figure 10 Derived stimulus coordinates

```
            CONFIGURATION DERIVED IN 2 DIMENSIONS


                    STIMULUS COORDINATES

                                    DIMENSION
STIMULUS    STIMULUS   PLOT     1          2
 NUMBER       NAME    SYMBOL

    1         A1        1      1.1315     1.1859
    2         A2        2      1.1315     0.6325
    3         A3        3     -0.6963     1.1859
    4         A4        4      0.5222    -1.0277
    5         A5        5     -1.9149    -1.5811
    6         A6        6     -0.0870    -0.4743
    7         A7        7     -0.0870     0.0791
```

Figure 11 Subject weights

```
                      SUBJECT WEIGHTS

                                    DIMENSION
 SUBJECT    PLOT    WEIRD-       1          2
 NUMBER    SYMBOL    NESS

    1         1     0.4636    0.5316     0.8421
    2         2     0.0612    0.8385     0.5406
    3         3     0.3764    0.5982     0.7966
    4         4     0.4321    0.9460     0.3211
    5         5     0.5476    0.9665     0.2546

OVERALL IMPORTANCE
OF EACH DIMENSION:            0.6345     0.3608
```

Figure 12 Stimulus weights

```
                    STIMULUS WEIGHTS

                              DIMENSION
   STIMULUS   STIMULUS   PLOT      1        2
    NUMBER      NAME    SYMBOL
       1         A1        1     0.5970   1.3672
       2         A2        2     0.2890   1.0440
       3         A3        3     0.8208   0.5820
       4         A4        4     0.5134   0.4177
       5         A5        5     0.2964   0.3747
       6         A6        6     0.8455   0.4088
       7         A7        7     0.6480   0.7666
```

Figure 13 Flattened subject weights

```
              FLATTENED SUBJECT WEIGHTS

                        VARIABLE
   SUBJECT    PLOT         1
   NUMBER    SYMBOL
      1         1       -1.2614
      2         2        0.0958
      3         3       -1.0041
      4         4        0.9469
      5         5        1.2227
```

ANOVA

The example illustrating the use of ANOVA is a three-way analysis of variance with one covariate. The data are 500 cases from the 1980 General Social Survey. The variables are

- PRESTIGE—the respondent's occupational prestige scale score. PRESTIGE is the dependent variable.
- EDUC—the respondent's education in years.
- RACE—the respondent's race, coded 1=WHITE, 2=BLACK, and 3=OTHER.
- SEX—the respondent's sex, coded 1=MALE and 2=FEMALE.
- REGION—The respondent's residence, coded as one of nine regions.

The task is twofold: determine the degree to which the American occupational structure differs across race, sex, and region; and measure the effect of the respondent's educational level, since education might prove to be a concomitant influence. The SPSS commands are

```
GET  FILE=GSS80 /KEEP PRESTIGE EDUC RACE SEX REGION.
ANOVA VARIABLES=PRESTIGE BY REGION(1,9) SEX,RACE(1,2) WITH EDUC
  /STATISTICS=REG
  /METHOD=HIERARCHICAL.
```

- The GET command defines the data to SPSS and selects the variables needed for the analysis.
- The ANOVA command names PRESTIGE as the dependent variable; REGION, SEX, and RACE as the factors; and EDUC as the covariate. The minimum and maximum values for REGION are 1 and 9, and the minimum and maximum values for both SEX and RACE are 1 and 2. Since variable RACE actually has values 1, 2, and 3, cases with value 3 are eliminated from the model.
- The STATISTICS subcommand requests the regression coefficient for the covariate EDUC.
- The METHOD subcommand requests the hierarchical approach for decomposing sums of squares. The covariate EDUC is assessed first to establish statistical control; then the effect of REGION is assessed, followed by the effect of SEX adjusted for REGION, followed by the effect of RACE adjusted for REGION and SEX. Finally, each of the interaction effects is assessed.

The ANOVA output from this example includes the following standard items of information:

Source of Variation   All interactions are printed by default. In this example, the sources of variation are the covariate, the main effects, the three two-way interactions, the three-way interaction, plus the explained, residual, and total variation.

Sum of Squares   The sum of squares associated with each effect is in part a function of the analysis of variance method chosen. In this example, the *hierarchical approach* was requested.

Degrees of Freedom (DF)   The degrees of freedom associated with each effect.

Mean Square   The sum of squares divided by the degrees of freedom.

F and Significance of F   The F statistic and the significance level of the F statistic for each effect.

Finally, SPSS prints the number of cases processed as well as the number of missing cases. By default, cases with missing values on any of the variables named are excluded from the analysis. In this example, 43 cases (8.6 percent of the data) are excluded due to missing values or values out of range for the RACE variable.

Analysis of variance output

```
          PRESTIGE  RESP'S OCCUPATIONAL PRESTIGE SCORE
     by   REGION    REGION OF INTERVIEW
          SEX
          RACE
     with EDUC      HIGHEST YEAR SCHOOL  COMPLETED


                            Sum of              Mean            Sig
Source of Variation         Squares     DF      Square     F    of F

Covariates                  23715.522    1    23715.522  191.701 .000
   EDUC                     23715.522    1    23715.522  191.701 .000

Main Effects                 2708.380   10      270.838    2.189 .018
   REGION                    1260.552    8      157.569    1.274 .255
   SEX                         22.413    1       22.413     .181 .671
   RACE                      1425.415    1     1425.415   11.522 .001

2-Way Interactions           3144.833   17      184.990    1.495 .092
   REGION    SEX             1349.220    8      168.653    1.363 .211
   REGION    RACE            1138.839    8      142.355    1.151 .328
   SEX       RACE             534.154    1      534.154    4.318 .038

3-Way Interactions           1663.399    6      277.233    2.241 .039
   REGION    SEX      RACE    1663.399    6      277.233    2.241 .039

Explained                   31232.135   34      918.592    7.425 .000

Residual                    52205.957  422      123.711

Total                       83438.092  456      182.978



Covariate   Raw Regression Coefficient

EDUC          2.331


500 cases were processed.
43 cases (8.6 pct) were missing.
```

AUTORECODE

Example 1   Because the TABLES procedure truncates string variables to eight characters, AUTORECODE is extremely useful if you want the whole values to appear in your table. For example, consider the string variable COMPANY, which contains the names of various hypothetical cat food companies. First you can use the AUTORECODE command to recode COMPANY into a numeric variable called RCOMPANY. Figure 1 shows the correspondence table from the PRINT subcommand for the original variable and the new variable. Then you can use the recoded new variable, RCOMPANY, in the TABLES procedure to produce a table of sales figures for each cat food company, similar to the one in Figure 2. Here the variable RCOMPANY is used in the banner. Note that the name of each company was not truncated, and that the entire name of each company was used in the TABLE. The commands that produced this table are shown below.

```
DATA LIST / COMPANY 1-21 (a) SALES 24-28.
BEGIN DATA
CATFOOD JOY             10000
OLD FASHIONED CATFOOD   11200
BOSTON CATFOOD          20800
RICHARD'S CATFOODS      11500
CHICAGO CATFOODS, INC.  12300
NEW YORK CATFOOD         9700
PRIME CATFOOD           10900
CHOICE CATFOOD          14600
rest of data here
END DATA.
AUTORECODE VARIABLES = COMPANY
  /INTO = RCOMPANY
  /PRINT.
TABLES     TABLE = SALES BY RCOMPANY
  /TTITLE = 'CATFOOD SALES BY COMPANY'.
```

Figure 1 PRINT subcommand output

```
                COMPANY   RCOMPANY
                Old Value New Value  Value Label

BOSTON CATFOOD                  1    BOSTON CATFOOD
CATFOOD JOY                     2    CATFOOD JOY
CHICAGO CATFOODS, INC           3    CHICAGO CATFOODS, INC
CHOICE CATFOOD                  4    CHOICE CATFOOD
NEW YORK CATFOOD                5    NEW YORK CATFOOD
OLD FASHIONED CATFOOD           6    OLD FASHIONED CATFOOD
PRIME CATFOOD                   7    PRIME CATFOOD
RICHARD'S CATFOODS              8    RICHARD'S CATFOODS
```

Figure 2 TABLES output with recoded variable

CATFOOD SALES BY COMPANY

	RCOMPANY							
	BOSTON CATFOOD	CATFOOD JOY	CHICAGO CATFOODS, INC	CHOICE CATFOOD	NEW YORK CATFOOD	OLD FASHIONED CATFOOD	PRIME CATFOOD	RICHARD'S CATFOODS
SALES								
9700					1			
10000		1			1			
10700							1	
10900								
11000		1						
11200						1		1
11500					1			
11600								
12300			1					1
12500			1					
12600				1				
12700							1	
12900						1		
13200								
13300			2					1
13400				1				
13800		1						
14100				1				
14600						1		
14700							1	
15900								
16800	2					1		
17200				1				
17600								1
18300					1			
19100								
20800	1							
21300	1							
22500		1						

Example 2   In statistical procedures, empty cells can reduce performance and increase memory requirements. This means that if factor variables contains empty categories, you should recode the variables into consecutive values. For example, if factor REGION has only five nonempty categories, represented by the numeric codes 1, 4, 6, 14 and 20, this problem would require 4429 bytes of memory:

```
ANOVA Y BY REGION (1,20).
```

In contrast, the amount of memory required by ANOVA if the variable is recoded into a new variable called RREGION, with consecutive values 1, 2, 3, 4, and 5, is 449 bytes.

```
ANOVA Y BY RREGION (1,5).
```

Figure 3 shows the correspondence table between the original variable and the new variable. The command that created this new variable is shown below. The original value labels are preserved with new values.

```
AUTORECODE VARIABLES=region
  /INTO=rregion
  /PRINT.
```

Figure 3   PRINT subcommand output

```
REGION    RREGION
Old Value New Value  Value Label

        1         1  northeast
        4         2  midwest
        6         3  northwest
       14         4  southeast
       20         5  southwest
```

Example 3   Since MANOVA requires consecutive integer values for factor levels, you need to recode noninteger values for factors into consecutive integers. In addition, if you have a wide value range for a factor, and most of the categories are empty, you must recode the variable to consecutive values. The AUTORECODE command allows you to recode these variables automatically, thus avoiding several RECODE specifications. For example, you could recode the six-value alphanumeric variable RELIGION, with values 'CATH', 'PROT', 'JEW', 'NONE', 'OTHER', and ' ' to numeric values 1, 2, 3, 4, 5, 6 and store the recoded values into a new variable called NRELIG. This new variable could then be used as a factor in MANOVA, as in:

```
DATA LIST / RELIGION 1-8 (A).
MISSING VALUES RELIGION ('  ').
BEGIN DATA
CATHOLIC
PROTEST
JEWISH
NONE
OTHER
END DATA.

AUTORECODE VARIABLES=RELIGION
  /INTO=NRELIG
  /PRINT.
MANOVA Y BY NRELIG(1,5).
```

Figure 4 shows the correspondence table from PRINT between the old and new variables. The value ' ' on both RELIGION and NRELIG is marked with an M to indicate it is missing. It is recoded to the largest value, 6, on NRELIG.

Figure 4 PRINT subcommand output

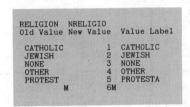

```
RELIGION  NRELIGIO
Old Value New Value  Value Label

  CATHOLIC        1   CATHOLIC
  JEWISH          2   JEWISH
  NONE            3   NONE
  OTHER           4   OTHER
  PROTEST         5   PROTESTA
          M       6M
```

CLUSTER

This example is a hierarchical cluster analysis of 25 cities according to data from the 1982 *Information Please Almanac*. The cities were the most populous in the United States in 1980. The clustering variables are:

- CHURCHES—number of churches.
- PARKS—number of parks. In some instances, a city has a missing-value code of 9999 for this variable because only total acreage rather than number of parks was available.
- PHONES—number of telephones.
- TVS—number of television sets.
- RADIOST—number of radio stations.
- TVST—number of television stations.
- POP80—city population in 1980.
- TAXRATE—property tax rate.

The aim is to cluster the cities into groups that are relatively homogeneous with respect to these variables. However, cities differ on most of the variables simply as a function of population. Therefore, most are rescaled to yield more comparable, per capita values. The SPSS commands follow, and printed and plotted output is shown in the figures cited below.

```
SET WIDTH=80.

DATA LIST  FILE=CITYDATA  RECORDS=3
  /1 CITY 6-18(A) POP80 53-60
  /2 CHURCHES 10-13 PARKS 14-17 PHONES 18-25 TVS 26-32
     RADIOST 33-35 TVST 36-38 TAXRATE 52-57(2).

MISSING VALUES PARKS (9999).
DO REPEAT X=CHURCHES PARKS PHONES TVS RADIOST TVST.
COMPUTE X=X/POP80.
END REPEAT.

CLUSTER CHURCHES TO TAXRATE
  /METHOD=BAVERAGE(CLUSMEM)
  /ID=CITY
  /PRINT=DISTANCE CLUSTER(3,5) SCHEDULE
  /PLOT=VICICLE HICICLE DENDROGRAM
  /SAVE=CLUSTER(3).
```

- The SET WIDTH command restricts printed output to a maximum of 80 columns.
- The DATA LIST command reads the necessary data.
- The DO REPEAT and COMPUTE commands divide six variables by city population, yielding per capita values for the number of churches, parks, and other measures.

- The CLUSTER variable specification names seven variables with the TO convention.
- The METHOD subcommand specifies the method of average linkage between groups. It also gives the rootname CLUSMEM to cluster membership variables created for this method.
- The ID subcommand specifies that the values of variable CITY will identify the cases.
- The measure for the clustering will be squared Euclidean distance, the default.
- The PRINT subcommand requests the computed distances between the cases, the cluster to which each case belongs for the three-, four-, and five-cluster solutions (see Figure 1), and the cluster agglomeration schedule (see Figure 2).
- The PLOT subcommand requests the cluster solution as a vertical icicle plot (see Figure 3), as a horizontal icicle plot (see Figure 4), and as a dendrogram (see Figure 5).
- The SAVE subcommand saves the cluster membership of the individual cases in the three-cluster solution as a new variable on the active system file. CLUSTER assigns this variable the name CLUSMEM3, deriving the name from the rootname CLUSMEM specified on the METHOD subcommand and from the three-cluster solution requested.

Figure 1 Cluster membership of cases

```
* * * * * * H I E R A R C H I C A L   C L U S T E R   A N A L Y S I S * * * * * *


Cluster Membership of Cases using Average Linkage (Between Groups)

                                   Number of Clusters

       Label          Case    5    4    3

       Baltimore         1     1    1    1
       Chicago           2     2    2    2
       Cleveland         3     1    1    1
       Columbus          4     3    1    1
       Dallas            5     4    3    3
       Denver            6     4    3    3
       Detroit           7     3    1    1
       Houston           8     4    3    3
       Indianapolis      9     5    4    2
       Jacksonville     10     4    3    3
       Los Angeles      11     4    3    3
       Memphis          12     3    1    1
       Nashville        13     1    1    1
       New Orleans      14     2    2    2
       New York         15     2    2    2
       Philadelphia     16     1    1    1
       Phoenix          17     4    3    3
       San Diego        18     3    1    1
       San Francisco    19     3    1    1
       San Jose         20     4    3    3
       Seattle          21     4    3    3
       Washington       22     4    3    3
```

Figure 2 Agglomeration schedule

```
* * * * * * H I E R A R C H I C A L   C L U S T E R   A N A L Y S I S * * * * * *


Agglomeration Schedule using Average Linkage (Between Groups)

                Clusters    Combined                   Stage Cluster 1st Appears    Next
     Stage    Cluster 1    Cluster 2    Coefficient    Cluster 1    Cluster 2      Stage

        1           5          20         .213571          0            0            8
        2          17          22         .261159          0            0            6
        3           4          18         .292620          0            0           11
        4           8          21         .656814          0            0            8
        5           3          13        3.067433          0            0           14
        6          10          17        3.173483          0            2           16
        7           1          16        5.655860          0            0           14
        8           5           8        8.083633          1            4           12
        9           7          12       13.270877          0            0           11
       10          14          15       16.843185          0            0           13
       11           4           7       33.221954          3            9           15
       12           5          11       38.605591          8            0           17
       13           2          14       48.604095          0           10           19
       14           1           3       73.268372          7            5           18
       15           4          19       88.134521         11            0           18
       16           6          10       97.164627          0            6           17
       17           5           6      250.892181         12           16           20
       18           1           4      651.010742         14           15           20
       19           2           9     1026.891846         13            0           21
       20           1           5     1710.032959         18           17           21
       21           1           2     5559.281250         20           19            0
```

Figure 3 A vertical icicle plot

```
* * * * * * H I E R A R C H I C A L   C L U S T E R   A N A L Y S I S * * * * * *

Vertical Icicle Plot using Average Linkage (Between Groups)

  (Down) Number of Clusters  (Across) Case Label and number

        I   N   N   C   W   P   J   D   L   S   H   S   D   S   M   D   S   C   N   C   P   B
        n   e   e   h   a   h   a   e   o   e   o   a   a   a   e   e   a   o   a   l   h   a
        d   w   w   i   s   o   c   n   s   a   u   n   n   n   m   t   n   l   s   e   i   l
        i       w   c   h   e   k   s       t   s   l       F   p   r   D   u   h   v   l   t
        a   Y   O   a   e   n   v   o   A   t   o   J   a   r   h   o   i   m   v   e   a   i
        n   o   r   g   s   i   x   r   n   l   n   o   l   a   i   i   e   b   i   l   d   m
        a   r   l   o   t   x       v   g   e   s   s   s   n   s   t   g   u   l   l   e   o
        p   k   e       o       i   i   e   s       e       c   t   e   o   s   l   a   l   r
        o       a       n       l   l   l   c       n       i       u       e   e   n   p   e
        l       n       s       l   l   e   o       s       s       s       g       d   h   e
        i       s       o       e   e   s           e       c           g               i
        s                                                   o                           a
```

```
        1   1       2   1   1       1   2       2   1   1           1           1       1
        9   5   4   2   7   0   6   1   1   8   0   5   9   2   7   8   4   3   3   6   1
     1 +XXXXXXXXXXXXXXXXXXXXXXXXXXXXXXXXXXXXXXXXXXXXXXXXXXXXXXXXXXXXXXX
     2 +XXXXXXXXXX   XXXXXXXXXXXXXXXXXXXXXXXXXXXXXXXXXXXXXXXXXXXXXXXXXXX
     3 +XXXXXXXXXX   XXXXXXXXXXXXXXXXXXXXXXXXXXX   XXXXXXXXXXXXXXXXXXXXXX
     4 +X   XXXXXX   XXXXXXXXXXXXXXXXXXXXXXXXXXX   XXXXXXXXXXXXXXXXXXXXXX
     5 +X   XXXXXX   XXXXXXXXXXXXXXXXXXXXXXXXXXX   XXXXXXXXXXXX   XXXXXXXX
     6 +X   XXXXXX   XXXXXXXXXX   XXXXXXXXXXXXXX   XXXXXXXXXXXX   XXXXXXXX
     7 +X   XXXXXX   XXXXXXX   X   XXXXXXXXXXXXXX   X   XXXXXXXXXX   XXXXXXXX
     8 +X   XXXXXX   XXXXXXX   X   XXXXXXXXXXXXXX   X   XXXXXXXXXX   XXXXXXXX
     9 +X   XXXXXX   XXXXXXX   X   XXXXXXXXXXXXXX   X   XXXXXXXXXX   XXXX   XXXX
    10 +X   XXXX   X   XXXXXXX   X   XXXXXXXXXXXXXX   X   XXXXXXXXXX   XXXX   XXXX
    11 +X   XXXX   X   XXXXXXX   X   X   XXXXXXXXXX   X   XXXXXXXXXX   XXXX   XXXX
    12 +X   XXXX   X   XXXXXXX   X   X   XXXXXXXXXX   X   XXXX   XXXX   XXXX   XXXX
    13 +X   X   X   X   XXXXXXX   X   X   XXXXXXXXXX   X   XXXX   XXXX   XXXX   XXXX
    14 +X   X   X   X   XXXXXXX   X   X   XXXXXXXXXX   X   X   X   XXXX   XXXX   XXXX
    15 +X   X   X   X   XXXXXXX   X   X   XXXX   XXXX   X   X   X   XXXX   XXXX   XXXX
    16 +X   X   X   X   XXXXXXX   X   X   XXXX   XXXX   X   X   X   XXXX   XXXX   X   X
    17 +X   X   X   X   XXXX   X   X   X   XXXX   XXXX   X   X   X   XXXX   XXXX   X   X
    18 +X   X   X   X   XXXX   X   X   X   XXXX   XXXX   X   X   X   XXXX   X   X   X   X
    19 +X   X   X   X   XXXX   X   X   X   X   X   XXXX   X   X   X   XXXX   X   X   X   X
    20 +X   X   X   X   XXXX   X   X   X   X   X   XXXX   X   X   X   X   X   X   X   X   X
    21 +X   X   X   X   X   X   X   X   X   X   X   XXXX   X   X   X   X   X   X   X   X   X
```

Figure 4 A horizontal icicle plot

```
* * * * * H I E R A R C H I C A L   C L U S T E R   A N A L Y S I S * * * * * *

Horizontal Icicle Plot Using Average Linkage (Between Groups)

                          Number of Clusters

                              111111111122
           C A S E         12345678901234567891
         Label        Seq  ++++++++++++++++++++++

         Indianapolis   9  XXXXXXXXXXXXXXXXXXXXX
                           XXX
                           XXX
         New York      15  XXXXXXXXXXXXXXXXXXXXX
                           XXXXXXXXXXX
                           XXXXXXXXXXX
         New Orleans   14  XXXXXXXXXXXXXXXXXXXXX
                           XXXXXXXX
                           XXXXXXXX
         Chicago        2  XXXXXXXXXXXXXXXXXXXXX
                           X
                           X
         Washington    22  XXXXXXXXXXXXXXXXXXXXX
                           XXXXXXXXXXXXXXXXXXXX
                           XXXXXXXXXXXXXXXXXXXX
         Phoenix       17  XXXXXXXXXXXXXXXXXXXXX
                           XXXXXXXXXXXXXXX
                           XXXXXXXXXXXXXXX
         Jacksonville  10  XXXXXXXXXXXXXXXXXXXXX
                           XXXXX
                           XXXXX
         Denver         6  XXXXXXXXXXXXXXXXXXXXX
                           XXXX
                           XXXX
         Los Angeles   11  XXXXXXXXXXXXXXXXXXXXX
                           XXXXXXXXX
                           XXXXXXXXX
         Seattle       21  XXXXXXXXXXXXXXXXXXXXX
                           XXXXXXXXXXXXXXX
                           XXXXXXXXXXXXXXX
         Houston        8  XXXXXXXXXXXXXXXXXXXXX
                           XXXXXXXXXXXXXX
                           XXXXXXXXXXXXXX
         San Jose      20  XXXXXXXXXXXXXXXXXXXXX
                           XXXXXXXXXXXXXXXX
                           XXXXXXXXXXXXXXXX
         Dallas         5  XXXXXXXXXXXXXXXXXXXXX
                           XX
                           XX
         San Francisco 19  XXXXXXXXXXXXXXXXXXXXX
                           XXXXXXX
                           XXXXXXX
         Memphis       12  XXXXXXXXXXXXXXXXXXXXX
                           XXXXXXXXXXXXX
                           XXXXXXXXXXXXX
         Detroit        7  XXXXXXXXXXXXXXXXXXXXX
                           XXXXXXXXXXX
                           XXXXXXXXXXX
         San Diego     18  XXXXXXXXXXXXXXXXXXXXX
                           XXXXXXXXXXXXXXXX
                           XXXXXXXXXXXXXXXX
         Columbus       4  XXXXXXXXXXXXXXXXXXXXX
                           XXXX
                           XXXX
         Nashville     13  XXXXXXXXXXXXXXXXXXXXX
                           XXXXXXXXXXXXXXX
                           XXXXXXXXXXXXXXX
         Cleveland      3  XXXXXXXXXXXXXXXXXXXXX
                           XXXXXXX
                           XXXXXXX
         Philadelphia  16  XXXXXXXXXXXXXXXXXXXXX
                           XXXXXXXXXXXXX
                           XXXXXXXXXXXXX
         Baltimore      1  XXXXXXXXXXXXXXXXXXXXX
```

Figure 5 A dendrogram

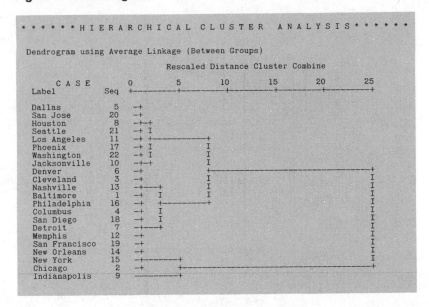

```
* * * * * * H I E R A R C H I C A L   C L U S T E R   A N A L Y S I S * * * * * *

Dendrogram using Average Linkage (Between Groups)

                            Rescaled Distance Cluster Combine

        C A S E            0         5        10        15        20        25
   Label          Seq      +---------+---------+---------+---------+---------+

   Dallas          5      -+
   San Jose       20      -+
   Houston         8      -+-+
   Seattle        21      -+ I
   Los Angeles    11      -+ +---------+
   Phoenix        17      -+ I         I
   Washington     22      -+ I         I
   Jacksonville   10      -+-+         I
   Denver          6      -+           +-----------------------------------+
   Cleveland       3      -+           I                                   I
   Nashville      13      -+---+       I                                   I
   Baltimore       1      -+   I       I                                   I
   Philadelphia   16      -+   +-------+                                   I
   Columbus        4      -+   I                                           I
   San Diego      18      -+   I                                           I
   Detroit         7      -+---+                                           I
   Memphis        12      -+                                               I
   San Francisco  19      -+                                               I
   New Orleans    14      -+                                               I
   New York       15      -+-------+                                       I
   Chicago         2      -+       +---------------------------------------+
   Indianapolis    9      ---------+
```

CORRELATIONS

This example analyzes 1979 prices and earnings in 45 cities around the world, compiled by the Union Bank of Switzerland. The variables are

- FOOD—the average net cost of 39 different food and beverage items in the city, expressed as a percentage above or below that of Zurich, where Zurich equals 100%.

- RENT—the average gross monthly rent in the city, expressed as a percentage above or below that of Zurich, where Zurich equals 100%.

- SERVICE—the average cost of 28 different goods and services in the city, expressed as a percentage above or below that of Zurich, where Zurich equals 100%.

- PUBTRANS—the average cost of a three-mile taxi ride within city limits, expressed as a percentage above or below that of Zurich, where Zurich equals 100%.

- TEACHER, COOK, ENGINEER, MECHANIC, BUS—the average gross annual earnings of primary-grade teachers in public schools, cooks, electrical engineers, automobile mechanics, and municipal bus drivers, working from 5 to 10 years in their respective occupations. Each of these variables is expressed as a percentage above or below those of Zurich, where Zurich equals 100%.

In this example, we determine the degree to which variation in the costs of goods and services in a city is related to variation in earnings in several occupations. We use CORRELATIONS to compute correlations between the average costs of various goods and services and the average gross earnings in five different occupations. The SPSS commands are

```
GET  FILE=CITY.
CORRELATIONS VARIABLES=FOOD RENT PUBTRANS TEACHER COOK ENGINEER/
        SERVICE PUBTRANS WITH MECHANIC BUS
  /STATISTICS=ALL
  /FORMAT=SERIAL.
```

- The GET command defines the data to SPSS and selects the variables needed for analysis.
- The CORRELATIONS command requests two correlation matrices. The first variable list produces correlation coefficients for each variable with every other variable. However, the redundant coefficients will be suppressed by the FORMAT subcommand. The second variable list produces four coefficients, pairing SERVICE with MECHANIC and BUS, and PUBTRANS with MECHANIC and BUS (see Figure 2).
- The STATISTICS subcommand requests the mean, standard deviation, and number of nonmissing cases for each variable, and the cross-product deviations and covariance for each pair of variables. The statistics for all the variable lists precede all the correlation matrices (see Figure 1).
- The FORMAT subcommand suppresses redundant coefficients in both correlation matrices. Because SERIAL format is specified, the default PRINT=NOSIG for the correlation matrix is overridden and PRINT=SIG is used.

Figure 1 Pearson correlation statistics

Variable	Cases	Mean	Std Dev
FOOD	45	70.4667	18.7442
RENT	45	120.0889	94.2250
PUBTRANS	45	48.1111	24.8141
TEACHER	44	38.3182	25.1819
COOK	44	64.6591	30.2785
ENGINEER	44	60.0455	26.1747
SERVICE	45	73.0889	19.0070
MECHANIC	44	50.7045	30.7462
BUS	43	42.9535	27.3652

Variables		Cases	Cross-Prod Dev	Variance-Covar	Variables		Cases	Cross-Prod Dev	Variance-Covar
FOOD	RENT	45	20191.1333	458.8894	FOOD	PUBTRANS	45	11865.6667	269.6742
FOOD	TEACHER	44	11227.9545	261.1152	FOOD	COOK	44	9561.0000	222.3488
FOOD	ENGINEER	44	10103.0000	234.9535	RENT	PUBTRANS	45	-1139.4444	-25.8965
RENT	TEACHER	44	-2566.6364	-59.6892	RENT	COOK	44	17747.2500	412.7267
RENT	ENGINEER	44	26927.5000	626.2209	PUBTRANS	TEACHER	44	18637.7727	433.4366
PUBTRANS	COOK	44	19434.2727	451.9598	PUBTRANS	ENGINEER	44	17630.3636	410.0085
TEACHER	COOK	43	20326.3023	483.9596	TEACHER	ENGINEER	43	18627.4884	443.5116
COOK	ENGINEER	44	25566.6818	594.5740					
SERVICE	MECHANIC	44	12034.8636	279.8805	SERVICE	BUS	43	12806.0233	304.9053
PUBTRANS	MECHANIC	44	23897.6364	555.7590	PUBTRANS	BUS	43	21561.6744	513.3732

Figure 2 Pearson correlation matrices

Variable Pair			Variable Pair			Variable Pair			Variable Pair			Variable Pair			Variable Pair		
FOOD with RENT	.2598 N(45) Sig .085		FOOD with PUBTRANS	.5798 N(45) Sig .000		FOOD with TEACHER	.5469 N(44) Sig .000		FOOD with COOK	.3945 N(44) Sig .008		FOOD with ENGINEER	.4823 N(44) Sig .001		RENT with PUBTRANS	-.0111 N(45) Sig .942	
RENT with TEACHER	-.0249 N(44) Sig .873		RENT with COOK	.1440 N(44) Sig .351		RENT with ENGINEER	.2528 N(44) Sig .098		PUBTRANS with TEACHER	.6858 N(44) Sig .000		PUBTRANS with COOK	.6058 N(44) Sig .000		PUBTRANS with ENGINEER	.6358 N(44) Sig .000	
TEACHER with COOK	.6215 N(43) Sig .000		TEACHER with ENGINEER	.6573 N(43) Sig .000		COOK with ENGINEER	.7502 N(44) Sig .000										
SERVICE with MECHANIC	.4842 N(44) Sig .001		SERVICE with BUS	.5868 N(43) Sig .000		PUBTRANS with MECHANIC	.7336 N(44) Sig .000		PUBTRANS with BUS	.7802 N(43) Sig .000							

Sig is 2-tailed, "." is printed if a coefficient cannot be computed.

CROSSTABS   The example illustrating CROSSTABS analyzes a 500-case sample from the 1980 General Social Survey. The variables are AGE, the respondent's age recoded to four categories, and DRUNK, the response to the question, Did you ever drink too much? This task examines how respondents in different age groups answer a question on alcohol-drinking habits. The following SPSS commands produce a crosstabulation of these two numeric variables and display several summary statistics:

```
GET FILE GSS80.
TEMPORARY.
RECODE  AGE (LOW THRU 29=1) (29 THRU 40=2) (40 THRU 58=3)
   (58 THRU HI=4)/ DRUNK (MISSING=8).
VARIABLE LABELS  AGE 'AGE IN FOUR CATEGORIES'.
VALUE LABELS  AGE 1 'YOUNGESTQUARTER' 4 'OLDEST  QUARTER'
   /DRUNK 1 'YES' 2 'NO' 8 "DON'T DRINK/NA".
CROSSTABS  VARIABLES=DRUNK (1,8) AGE (1,4)/ TABLES=DRUNK BY AGE
   /CELLS=COLUMN TOTAL
   /MISSING=REPORT
   /STATISTICS=CHISQ LAMBDA BTAU CTAU GAMMA D.
```

- The GET command defines the data to SPSS.

- The TEMPORARY command determines that the transformations are temporary.

- The RECODE command redefines the variable AGE into four categories and recodes all missing values for the variable DRUNK to one missing value.

- The VARIABLE LABELS command defines a new variable label for AGE, and the VALUE LABELS command defines value labels for AGE and DRUNK. The value labels for AGE are formatted to display appropriate labels for a column variable. Note that the label YOUNGESTQUARTER has no blanks between the words and the label OLDEST QUARTER has two blanks separating the words (see FORMAT Subcommand).

- The CROSSTABS command uses integer mode to set up the table. The VARIABLES subcommand specifies the variables and their minimum and maximum values, including the missing values that will be displayed. The TABLES subcommand specifies variable DRUNK as the row variable and AGE as the column variable.

- The CELLS subcommand requests row and column percents.

- The MISSING subcommand reports missing values in the table but does not include them in calculating percentages and statistics.

- The STATISTICS subcommand requests chi-square, lambda, Kendall's tau-*b*, Kendall's tau-*c*, gamma, and Somers' *d*. Although the table reports missing cases, they are not included in the calculation of statistics.

Output from the CROSSTABS command

```
DRUNK  EVER DRINK TOO MUCH  by  AGE  AGE IN FOUR CATEGORIES

                   AGE                                      Page 1 of 1
            Col Pct I
            Tot Pct IYOUNGEST                    OLDEST
                    IQUARTER                     QUARTER    Row
                    I     1 I     2 I     3 I     4 I Total
DRUNK       --------+-------+-------+-------+-------+
              1  I  57.9 I  34.7 I  37.9 I  18.8 I   147
   YES           I  16.2 I   8.6 I   9.4 I   4.2 I  38.5
            --------+-------+-------+-------+-------+
              2  I  42.1 I  65.3 I  62.1 I  81.2 I   235
   NO            I  11.8 I  16.2 I  15.4 I  18.1 I  61.5
            --------+-------+-------+-------+-------+
              8  I       I       I       I       I   118
DON'T DRINK/NA   I       I       I       I       I    .0
            --------+-------+-------+-------+-------+
         Column     107     95      95      85     382
         Total     28.0    24.9    24.9    22.3   100.0

      Chi-Square                Value          DF         Significance
  ---------------              --------       ----        ------------

  Pearson                      31.57228         3            .00000
  Likelihood Ratio             32.49027         3            .00000
  Mantel-Haenszel              26.54495         1            .00000

  Minimum Expected Frequency -   32.709

                                                          Approximate
      Statistic                Value       ASE1   T-value  Significance
  ---------------              --------    ----   -------  ------------


  Lambda :
     symmetric                 .09716     .04043  2.34152
     with DRUNK    dependent   .11565     .06617  1.64929
     with AGE      dependent   .08727     .03709  2.26282
  Goodman & Kruskal Tau :
     with DRUNK    dependent   .08265     .02707            .00000 *2
     with AGE      dependent   .02808     .00970            .00000 *2


  Kendall's Tau-b              .24165     .04394  5.46443
  Kendall's Tau-c              .28768     .05265  5.46443
  Gamma                        .39632     .06875  5.46443
  Somers' D :
     symmetric                 .23546     .04281  5.46443
     with DRUNK    dependent   .19222     .03519  5.46443
     with AGE      dependent   .30381     .05511  5.46443

  *2 Based on chi-square approximation

  Number of Missing Observations:  118
```

DESCRIPTIVES

This example analyzes 1979 prices and earnings in 45 cities around the world, compiled by the Union Bank of Switzerland. The variables are

- NTCPUR—the city's net purchasing power level, calculated as the ratio of labor expended (measured in number of working hours) to the cost of more than 100 goods and services, weighted by consumer habits. NTCPUR is expressed as a percentage above or below that of Zurich, where Zurich equals 100%.
- FOOD—the average net cost of 39 different food and beverage items in the city, expressed as a percentage above or below that of Zurich, where Zurich equals 100%.
- RENT—the average gross monthly rent in the city, expressed as a percentage above or below that of Zurich, where Zurich equals 100%.
- APPL—the average cost of six different household appliances, expressed as a percentage above or below that of Zurich, where Zurich equals 100%.
- SERVICE—the average cost of 28 different goods and services in the city, expressed as a percentage above or below that of Zurich, where Zurich equals 100%.

- WCLOTHES—the cost of medium-priced women's clothes, expressed as a percentage above or below that of Zurich, where Zurich equals 100%.
- MCLOTHES—the cost of medium-priced men's clothes, expressed as a percentage above or below that of Zurich, where Zurich equals 100%.
- CLOTHES—the average cost of medium-priced women's and men's clothes, expressed as a percentage above or below that of Zurich, where Zurich equals 100%.

In this example, we obtain univariate summary statistics about purchasing power and the costs of various goods and services in cities and generate standardized variables for the costs of men's and women's clothes. The SPSS commands are

```
GET  FILE=CITY/KEEP NTCPUR TO SERVICE.
COMPUTE  CLOTHES=(WCLOTHES + MCLOTHES)/2.
VAR LABELS  CLOTHES, AVERAGE COST OF W AND M CLOTHES.
DESCRIPTIVES VARIABLES=NTCPUR, FOOD, RENT TO SERVICE,
    WCLOTHES (ZWWEAR), MCLOTHES (ZMWEAR), CLOTHES (ZCLOTHES)
   /STATISTICS=VARIANCE DEFAULT
   /MISSING=LISTWISE.
```

- The GET command defines the data to SPSS and selects the variables needed for analysis.
- The COMPUTE command creates the variable CLOTHES by adding the values for WCLOTHES and MCLOTHES and dividing by 2.
- The VAR LABELS command assigns a label to the new variable CLOTHES.
- The DESCRIPTIVES command requests statistics for all the variables listed and computes Z scores for variables WCLOTHES, MCLOTHES, and CLOTHES. The new standardized variables are named ZWWEAR, ZMWEAR, and ZCLOTHES.
- The STATISTICS subcommand requests the variance plus the default statistics (mean, standard deviation, minimum, and maximum) for each variable.
- The MISSING subcommand specifies listwise deletion of user-missing values. A case missing on any variable specified on the DESCRIPTIVES command is excluded from the computation of statistics for all variables.
- Since no formatting option is specified, DESCRIPTIVES displays the statistics and variable labels for each variable on one line and can use more than 80 columns.

Output from DESCRIPTIVES

```
Number of valid observations (listwise) =        44.00


Variable     Mean    Std Dev   Variance   Minimum   Maximum   Label

NTCPUR       58.70    28.81     829.79        10       110    NET PURCHASING LEVEL
FOOD         71.00    18.61     346.42        40       130    AVG FOOD PRICES
RENT        121.75    94.65    8957.77        27       440    NORMAL RENT
APPL         78.70    22.23     494.03        54       165    PRICE FOR APPLIANCES
SERVICE      73.68    18.80     353.48        42       113    PRICE FOR SERVICES
WCLOTHES     81.20    30.36     921.70        21       174    MEDIUM PRICE FOR WOMEN'S CLOTHING
MCLOTHES     87.86    25.91     671.10        22       147    MEDIUM PRICE FOR MEN'S CLOTHING
CLOTHES      84.53    26.75     715.50     21.50    160.50    AVERAGE COST OF W AND M CLOTHES


The following Z-score variables have been saved on your active file:


From         To                                                          Weighted
Variable     Z-Score    Label                                            Valid N
--------     -------    -----                                            --------

WCLOTHES     ZWWEAR     Zscore:  MEDIUM PRICE FOR WOMEN'S CLOTHI               44
MCLOTHES     ZMWEAR     Zscore:  MEDIUM PRICE FOR MEN'S CLOTHING              44
CLOTHES      ZCLOTHES   Zscore:  AVERAGE COST OF W AND M CLOTHES             44
```

DISCRIMINANT

This example analyzes 1979 prices and earnings in 45 cities around the world, compiled by the Union Bank of Switzerland. The variables are

- FOOD—the average net cost of 39 different food and beverage items in the city, expressed as a percentage above or below that of Zurich, where Zurich equals 100%.
- SERVICE—the average cost of 28 different goods and services in the city, expressed as a percentage above or below that of Zurich, where Zurich equals 100%.
- BUS, MECHANIC, CONSTRUC, COOK, MANAGER, FSALES—the average gross annual earnings of municipal bus drivers, automobile mechanics, construction workers, cooks, managers, and female sales workers, working from five to ten years in their respective occupations. Each of these variables is expressed as a percentage above or below those of Zurich, where Zurich equals 100%.
- WORLD—economic development status of the country in which the city is located, divided into three groups: economically advanced nations, such as the United States and most European nations; nations that are members of the Organization for Petroleum Exporting Countries (OPEC); and nations that are economically underdeveloped. The groups are labeled 1ST WORLD, PETRO WORLD, and 3RD WORLD, respectively.

There are two objectives to this analysis. First, we discriminate between cities in different categories by examining their wage and price structures. Secondly, we predict a city's economic class category from coefficients calculated using wages and prices as predictors. The SPSS commands are

```
GET FILE UNIONBK.
DISCRIMINANT GROUPS=WORLD(1,3)
 /VARIABLES=FOOD SERVICE BUS MECHANIC CONSTRUC COOK MANAGER FSALES
 /PRIORS=SIZE/SAVE = CLASS=PRDCLAS SCORES=DISCSCR
 /STATISTICS=RAW TABLE.
SAVE OUTFILE=NEWUNION.
```

- The GET command defines the data to SPSS from the system file UNIONBK.
- The DISCRIMINANT command requests a three-group discriminant analysis. The variables FOOD, SERVICE, BUS, MECHANIC, CONSTRUC, COOK, MANAGER, and FSALES are used as discriminating variables during the analysis phase. During the classification phase, prior probabilities are equal to the size of the known groups (see Figure 1). Three variables are saved on the active system file: the predicted group for each of the classified cases (variable PRDCLAS) and the two discriminant scores (variables DISCSCR1 and DISCSCR2). The saved variables are shown in Figure 2.
- The STATISTICS subcommand requests display of the unstandardized discriminant functions and the classification results table (see Figure 3).
- The SAVE command saves the SPSS system file NEWUNION, which contains the three variables PRDCLAS, DISCSCR1, and DISCSCR2.

Figure 1 Prior probabilities

```
PRIOR PROBABILITIES

  GROUP     PRIOR      LABEL

      1    0.58140    1ST WORLD
      2    0.13953    PETRO WORLD
      3    0.27907    3RD WORLD

  TOTAL   1.00000
```

Figure 2 The saved variables

```
FOLLOWING VARIABLES HAVE BEEN CREATED:
   NAME          LABEL

   _____       _____

   PRDCLAS  ---  PREDICTED GROUP FOR ANALYSIS     1
   DISCSCR1 ---  FUNCTION   1 FOR ANALYSIS        1
   DISCSCR2 ---  FUNCTION   2 FOR ANALYSIS        1
```

Figure 3 Discriminant coefficients and classification results

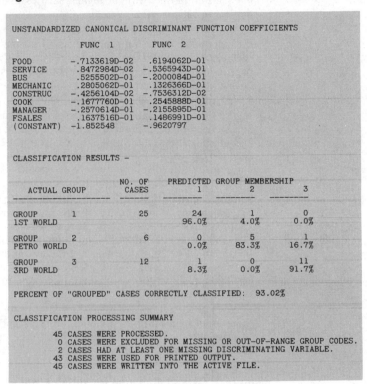

```
UNSTANDARDIZED CANONICAL DISCRIMINANT FUNCTION COEFFICIENTS

                 FUNC  1         FUNC  2
FOOD         -.7133619D-02    .6194062D-01
SERVICE       .8472984D-02   -.5365943D-01
BUS           .5255502D-01   -.2000084D-01
MECHANIC      .2805062D-01    .1326366D-01
CONSTRUC     -.4256104D-02   -.7536312D-02
COOK         -.1677760D-01    .2545888D-01
MANAGER      -.2570614D-01   -.2155895D-01
FSALES        .1637516D-01    .1486991D-01
(CONSTANT)  -1.852548        -.9620797


CLASSIFICATION RESULTS -


                         NO. OF    PREDICTED GROUP MEMBERSHIP
     ACTUAL GROUP        CASES       1         2         3
   _____     _____   _____   _____   _____

GROUP        1            25         24        1         0
1ST WORLD                          96.0%     4.0%      0.0%

GROUP        2             6          0        5         1
PETRO WORLD                         0.0%     83.3%     16.7%

GROUP        3            12          1        0         11
3RD WORLD                           8.3%     0.0%      91.7%

PERCENT OF "GROUPED" CASES CORRECTLY CLASSIFIED:  93.02%

CLASSIFICATION PROCESSING SUMMARY

     45 CASES WERE PROCESSED.
      0 CASES WERE EXCLUDED FOR MISSING OR OUT-OF-RANGE GROUP CODES.
      2 CASES HAD AT LEAST ONE MISSING DISCRIMINATING VARIABLE.
     43 CASES WERE USED FOR PRINTED OUTPUT.
     45 CASES WERE WRITTEN INTO THE ACTIVE FILE.
```

EXAMINE

This example uses EXAMINE to compare salaries and bonuses among male and female bank employees. The variables are:

- SALNOW—Current salary for each employee.

- JOBCAT—Job category for each employee. The value labels for variable JOBCAT are:

  1 Clerical Staff
  2 Office Trainee
  3 Security Officer
  4 College Trainee
  5 Exempt Employee
  6 MBA Trainee
  7 Technical Staff

- SEX—Employee sex. The value labels for variable SEX in the data are 0 Male, and 1 Female.

The SPSS commands for the analysis are:

```
GET FILE=BANK.
EXAMINE VARIABLES = SALNOW BY JOBCAT
  /STATISTICS=ALL /PLOT=BOXPLOT /ID=SEX.
```

- GET reads an existing SPSS system file, which defines the variables for the session.
- EXAMINE specifies one dependent variable (SALNOW) and one independent variable (JOBCAT). The STATISTICS subcommand specifies all statistics available on EXAMINE. The PLOT subcommand specifies boxplots. EXAMINE will print the statistics and plots for all employee salaries, then separate statistics and boxplots for salaries within each job category. The ID subcommand specifies that extreme values and outliers in the salary ranges will be identified according to employee sex.
- Figure 1 shows the statistics for overall salaries. The extreme values indicate that the five bank employees with the highest salaries all are male, and the five employees with the lowest salaries all are female.
- Figure 2 shows the boxplot for overall salaries. Again, from the plot you can see that the extreme values and higher outliers all are males. The only two female outliers are very close to the whisker of the box. Figure 3 shows the footnote that prints on the page following the boxplot. The footnote explains that the multiple occurrences of the outlier at the salary range of about $24,000 (this outlier is indicated by **note 1** in the plot) represent 1 male and 1 female employee.
- Figure 4 shows the statistics for three of the job categories: clerical staff, office trainees, and security officers. Comparing mean, median, and 5% trim values for clerical staff and office trainees, you can see there is very little difference in the salaries offered by each job category. Among clerical staff, the highest salaries are mixed between males and females; the lowest salaries are all females. Among office trainees, all the highest salaries are paid to men, and all the lowest salaries to women.
- Among security officers, all the highest and all the lowest salaries are paid to males, suggesting that all the security officers might be males. (This might prompt you to run a CROSSTABS of JOBCAT by SEX to see the distribution of males and females in each job category.) Notice the small inter-quartile range ($480) for security officers. Because the $47,700 range in salary values imposes a broad scale on the vertical axis, an inter-quartile range of only $480 causes the boxplot that prints for security officers (value 3 along the horizontal axis) to collapse into one spot. All you can see are the lower corners of the box.
- Looking at the number of cases in each job category (see Figure 5), you can see that there are a high number of clerical workers and office trainees, a small number of security officers, college trainees, and exempt employees, and very few MBA trainees and technical staff members.

Figure 1 Overall statistics for variable SALNOW

```
     SALNOW     CURRENT SALARY

Valid cases:        474.0  Missing cases:       .0   Percent missing:      .0

Mean      13767.83  Std Err   313.7244  Min     6300.000  Skewness    2.1246
Median    11550.00  Variance  46652514  Max    54000.00   S E Skew     .1122
5% Trim   12982.08  Std Dev   6830.265  Range  47700.00   Kurtosis    5.3778
                                        IQR    5265.000   S E Kurt     .2238

                          Extreme Values

    5   Highest    SEX                  5   Lowest    SEX

        54000      Male                     6300      Female
        44250      Male                     6360      Female
        41500      Male                     6480      Female
        41400      Male                     6540      Female
        40000      Male                     6600      Female
```

Figure 2 Boxplots for overall salaries

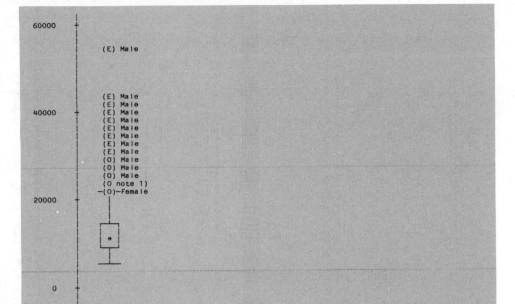

Figure 3 Footnote on the first page following the boxplots

```
Boxplot footnotes denote the following:
  1)    Female, Male
```

Figure 4 Salary statistics broken down by job category

```
      SALNOW     CURRENT SALARY
By  JOBCAT    1         Clerical Staff

Valid cases:        227.0  Missing cases:        .0  Percent missing:      .0


Mean       11134.82  Std Err    212.1638  Min       6300.000  Skewness    1.2922
Median     10500.00  Variance   10218056  Max       26750.00  S E Skew     .1615
5% Trim    10903.13  Std Dev    3196.569  Range     20450.00  Kurtosis    2.7254
                                          IQR       3660.000  S E Kurt     .3217

                               Extreme Values
                               ------- ------

   5     Highest    SEX                   5   Lowest     SEX

        26750       Male                     6300       Female
        21600       Female                   6360       Female
        21060       Male                     6480       Female
        20400       Female                   6540       Female
        20220       Male                     6600       Female


      SALNOW     CURRENT SALARY
By  JOBCAT    2         Office Trainee

Valid cases:        136.0  Missing cases:        .0  Percent missing:      .0


Mean       11136.41  Std Err    234.3188  Min       7260.000  Skewness    3.5272
Median     10950.00  Variance   7467119   Max       32000.00  S E Skew     .2078
5% Trim    10913.92  Std Dev    2732.603  Range     24740.00  Kurtosis   24.2175
                                          IQR       3075.000  S E Kurt     .4127

                               Extreme Values
                               ------- ------

   5     Highest    SEX                   5   Lowest     SEX

        32000       Male                     7260       Female
        17364       Male                     7680       Female
        16800       Male                     7860       Female
        15960       Male                     8040       Female
        15660       Male                     8160       Female


      SALNOW     CURRENT SALARY
By  JOBCAT    3         Security Officer

Valid cases:         27.0  Missing cases:        .0  Percent missing:      .0


Mean       12375.56  Std Err    162.7832  Min       9720.000  Skewness    -.3680
Median     12300.00  Variance   715456.4  Max       14100.00  S E Skew     .4479
5% Trim    12403.09  Std Dev    845.8466  Range     4380.000  Kurtosis    3.6515
                                          IQR       480.0000  S E Kurt     .8721

                               Extreme Values
                               ------- ------

   5     Highest    SEX                   5   Lowest     SEX

        14100       Male                     9720       Male
        13800       Male                     11400      Male
        13500       Male                     11820      Male
        12780       Male                     12000      Male
        12480       Male                     12120      Male
```

Figure 5 Salary boxplots broken down by job category

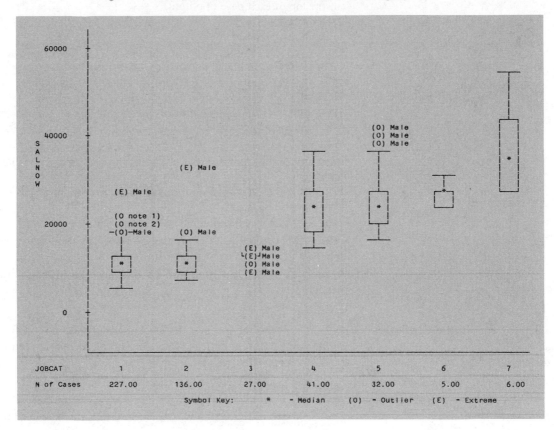

FACTOR In this example, six abortion items are used from a 500-case sample of the 1980 General Social Survey. Respondents indicate whether they favor or oppose abortion in the following contexts:

- ABHLTH—if the woman's health is seriously endangered.
- ABRAPE—if the woman is pregnant as a result of rape.
- ABDEFECT—if there is a strong chance of a serious defect in the child.
- ABPOOR—if the woman has a low income and cannot afford more children.
- ABSINGLE—if the woman is not married and doesn't want the child.
- ABNOMORE—if the woman is married and wants no more children.

The SPSS commands are

```
TITLE  'FACTOR ANALYSIS OF ABORTION ITEMS'.
GET  FILE GSS80/KEEP ABDEFECT TO ABSINGLE.
COMMENT  RECODE THE ITEMS SO THAT 1 IS FAVOR AND 0 IS OPPOSE.
RECODE  ABDEFECT TO ABSINGLE(1=1)(2=0).
MISSING VALUES  ABDEFECT TO ABSINGLE(7 THRU 9).
VALUE LABELS  ABDEFECT TO ABSINGLE
 0 'NO' 1 'YES' 7 'NAP' 8 'DK' 9 'NA'.
FACTOR  VARIABLES=ABDEFECT TO ABSINGLE
 /MISSING=MEANSUB
 /WIDTH=100
 /FORMAT=SORT BLANK(.3)
 /PLOT=ROTATION(1 2)
 /EXTRACTION=ML
 /ROTATION=OBLIMIN
 /SAVE REG (ALL FSULS).
```

- The TITLE command puts the title, FACTOR ANALYSIS OF ABORTION ITEMS, at the top of each page of output.
- The GET command accesses the data file and keeps only those variables that will be used in this factor analysis.
- The RECODE, MISSING VALUES, and VALUE LABELS commands redefine the abortion items and label the redefined responses for this analysis.
- The FACTOR command specifies variables ABDEFECT to ABSINGLE for the analysis.
- The MISSING subcommand forces mean substitution for missing data.
- The WIDTH subcommand limits the width of the output to 100 columns.
- The FORMAT subcommand displays the factor loadings in descending order of magnitude and suppresses the display of factor loadings less than 0.3 (see Figures 3 and 4).
- The EXTRACTION subcommand specifies maximum likelihood as the method of extraction.
- The ROTATION subcommand specifies an oblimin rotation.
- The SAVE subcommand computes all possible factor scores using the regression method.

Portions of the output produced by this set of commands appear in Figures 1 through 5.

Initial Statistics

Figure 1 contains the initial statistics that are produced by default. Initial statistics are the initial communalities, eigenvalues of the correlation matrix, and percentage of variance explained.

Figure 1   Initial statistics

```
ANALYSIS NUMBER  1  REPLACEMENT OF MISSING VALUES WITH THE MEAN


EXTRACTION  1  FOR ANALYSIS  1, MAXIMUM LIKELIHOOD (ML)


INITIAL STATISTICS:


VARIABLE      COMMUNALITY  *  FACTOR   EIGENVALUE   PCT OF VAR   CUM PCT
                           *
ABDEFECT        .44988     *    1       3.38153        56.4        56.4
ABNOMORE        .66747     *    2       1.19287        19.9        76.2
ABHLTH          .35555     *    3        .50823         8.5        84.7
ABPOOR          .66600     *    4        .40867         6.8        91.5
ABRAPE          .39760     *    5        .28847         4.8        96.3
ABSINGLE        .60394     *    6        .22024         3.7       100.0
```

Extraction Statistics

Figure 2 contains the extraction statistics that are produced by default. Extraction statistics are the communalities, eigenvalues, and unrotated factor loadings. Note the effect of sorting and blanking produced by the FORMAT subcommand.

Figure 2 Extraction statistics

```
FACTOR MATRIX:

                FACTOR  1    FACTOR  2

ABNOMORE         .86202
ABPOOR           .86070
ABSINGLE         .81336
ABDEFECT         .57319        .56773
ABRAPE           .56086        .42732

ABHLTH           .45491        .52697


FINAL STATISTICS:

VARIABLE      COMMUNALITY  *  FACTOR   EIGENVALUE   PCT OF VAR   CUM PCT
                           *
ABDEFECT         .65086    *     1      2.99548       49.9        49.9
ABNOMORE         .78498    *     2       .87734       14.6        64.5
ABHLTH           .48464    *
ABPOOR           .77461    *
ABRAPE           .49717    *
ABSINGLE         .68057    *
```

Rotation Statistics

Figure 3 contains the rotation statistics that are produced by default if the model is rotated. They are the rotated factor pattern and structure matrices (since this is an oblimin rotation), the factor transformation matrix, and the factor correlation matrix. (The Oblimin rotation will give a Factor correlation matrix, since it is an oblique rotation.)

Figure 3 Rotation statistics

```
OBLIMIN   ROTATION  1  FOR EXTRACTION  1  IN ANALYSIS  1 - KAISER NORMALIZATION.

   OBLIMIN CONVERGED IN    4 ITERATIONS.

PATTERN MATRIX:

                FACTOR  1    FACTOR  2

ABNOMORE         .89941
ABPOOR           .88066
ABSINGLE         .80192

ABDEFECT                       .80526
ABHLTH                         .72830
ABRAPE                         .63824


STRUCTURE MATRIX:

                FACTOR  1    FACTOR  2

ABNOMORE         .88574        .46625
ABPOOR           .88012        .48004
ABSINGLE         .82426        .47892

ABDEFECT         .44259        .80676
ABRAPE           .45973        .69893
ABHLTH           .33537        .69419


FACTOR CORRELATION MATRIX:

                FACTOR  1    FACTOR  2

FACTOR  1       1.00000
FACTOR  2        .54622       1.00000
```

Factor Plot   Figure 4 contains the plot of variables in the rotated factor space. Although the rotation is oblimin, the plot axes are orthogonal. Since variable 1 overlaps with variable 3 and variable 2 overlaps with variable 4, they do not appear on the plot.

Figure 4 Factor plot

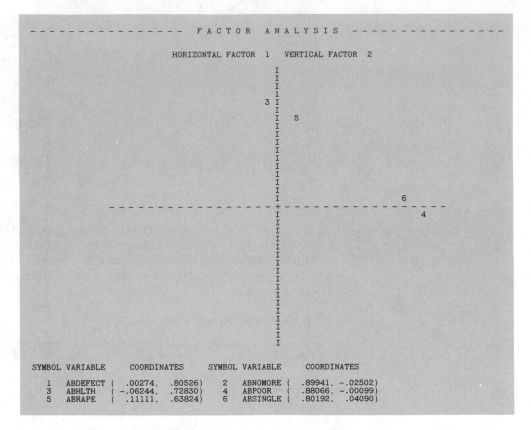

Saved Factor Scores   Figure 5 contains the information for the factor scores that are saved as new variables in the active system file as a result of the SAVE subcommand.

Figure 5 Saved factor scores

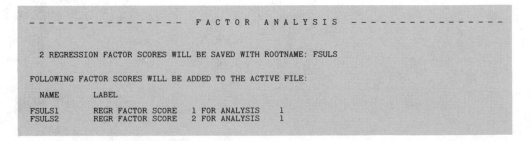

FREQUENCIES The following example demonstrates the use of FREQUENCIES to do some preliminary checks on a newly defined file. The file is based on employment data from Hubbard Consultants Inc. Variables include date employee was hired, employee's department, salary, job category, name, age, and sex, as well as salary increases from 1980 to 1982. The SPSS commands are

```
FILE TYPE  GROUPED FILE=HUBDATA RECORD=#RECID 80 CASE=ID 1-4.

RECORD TYPE 1.
DATA LIST   /MOHIRED YRHIRED 12-15 DEPT79 TO DEPT82 SEX 16-20.

RECORD TYPE 2.
DATA LIST   /SALARY79 TO SALARY82 6-25
             AGE 54-55 RAISE80 TO RAISE82 56-70.

RECORD TYPE 3.
DATA LIST   /JOBCAT 6 EMPNAME 25-48 (A).

END FILE TYPE.

MISSING VALUES  DEPT79 TO SALARY82 AGE (0)
                RAISE80 TO RAISE82 (-999) JOBCAT (9).

VARIABLE LABELS  SALARY79 'SALARY IN 1979'
                 SALARY80 'SALARY IN 1980'
                 SALARY81 'SALARY IN 1981'
                 SALARY82 'SALARY IN 1982'
                 JOBCAT 'JOB CATEGORIES'.
VALUE LABELS  SEX 1 'MALE' 2 'FEMALE'/
              JOBCAT 1 'OFFICIALS & MANAGERS' 2 'PROFESSIONALS'
              3 'TECHNICIANS' 4 'OFFICE & CLERICAL' 5 'CRAFTSMEN'
              6 'SERVICE WORKERS'.

FREQUENCIES  VARIABLES=SALARY79 TO SALARY82 SEX AGE JOBCAT
 /FORMAT=LIMIT(10) /STATISTICS=DEFAULT MEDIAN.
```

- Since there are three records per case, FILE TYPE GROUPED is used to check for duplicate or missing records.
- MISSING VALUES, VARIABLE LABELS, and VALUE LABELS complete the file definition.
- FREQUENCIES displays frequency tables for variables having 10 or fewer categories and statistics for all the variables named. The default statistics are the mean, standard deviation, minimum, and maximum.

FREQUENCIES display

```
SALARY79   SALARY IN 1979


Mean       12247.323      Median     10140.000      Std dev    6665.182
Minimum     6337.000      Maximum    45500.000


Valid cases     158    Missing cases   117

- - - - - - - - - - - - - - - - - - - - - - - - - - - - - - - - -

SALARY80   SALARY IN 1980


Mean       12123.725      Median     10400.000      Std dev    6316.356
Minimum     5720.000      Maximum    48100.000


Valid cases     273    Missing cases     2

- - - - - - - - - - - - - - - - - - - - - - - - - - - - - - - - -

SALARY81   SALARY IN 1981


Mean       15096.212      Median     12359.500      Std dev    8074.387
Minimum     7605.000      Maximum    52000.000


Valid cases     160    Missing cases   115

- - - - - - - - - - - - - - - - - - - - - - - - - - - - - - - - -

SALARY82   SALARY IN 1982


Mean       17161.552      Median     15132.000      Std dev    8695.734
Minimum     5830.000      Maximum    50700.000


Valid cases     145    Missing cases   130

- - - - - - - - - - - - - - - - - - - - - - - - - - - - - - - - -

SEX


                                                     Valid      Cum
Value Label                   Value  Frequency  Percent  Percent  Percent

MALE                             1        83      30.2     30.2     30.2
FEMALE                           2       192      69.8     69.8    100.0
                                      -------   ------   ------
                             Total      275     100.0    100.0

Mean        1.698      Median      2.000      Std dev      .460
Minimum     1.000      Maximum     2.000


Valid cases     275    Missing cases     0

- - - - - - - - - - - - - - - - - - - - - - - - - - - - - - - - -

AGE


Mean       37.158      Median     34.000      Std dev    11.335
Minimum    20.000      Maximum    69.000


Valid cases     272    Missing cases     3


- - - - - - - - - - - - - - - - - - - - - - - - - - - - - - - - -

JOBCAT    JOB CATEGORIES


                                                     Valid      Cum
Value Label                   Value  Frequency  Percent  Percent  Percent

OFFICIALS & MANAGERS             1        48      17.5     17.5     17.5
PROFESSIONALS                    2        62      22.5     22.5     40.0
TECHNICIANS                      3        98      35.6     35.6     75.6
OFFICE & CLERICAL                4        67      24.4     24.4    100.0
                                      -------   ------   ------
                             Total      275     100.0    100.0

Mean        2.669      Median      3.000      Std dev     1.030
Minimum     1.000      Maximum     4.000


Valid cases     275    Missing cases     0
```

HILOGLINEAR

HILOGLINEAR can efficiently model a variety of complete and incomplete frequency table models. Many hierarchical models for real data are collected as examples in *Discrete Multivariate Analysis* (Bishop et al., 1975). The following two examples from that book illustrate the use of HILOGLINEAR.

Example 1

This example illustrates a saturated model and backward elimination. In a market research study of laundry detergent preferences, consumers prefer either BRAND M or BRAND X detergent. The study considers three additional variables: water softness, previous use of BRAND M, and washing temperature. SPSS commands for analyzing the data are:

```
TITLE 'DETERGENT PREFERENCES (RIES & SMITH, 1963)'.
SET WIDTH = 80.
DATA LIST FREE / WATSOFT BRANDPRF PREVUSE TEMP FREQ.
VARIABLE LABELS WATSOFT  'Water Softness'
                BRANDPRF 'Brand Preference'
                PREVUSE  'Previous Use of Brand M'
                TEMP     'Water Temperature'
                FREQ     'Number in Condition'.
VALUE LABELS WATSOFT 1 'Soft' 2 'Medium' 3 'Hard'
             /BRANDPRF 1 'Brand X' 2 'Brand M'
             /PREVUSE 1 'Yes' 2 'No'
             /TEMP 1 'High' 2 'Low'.
BEGIN DATA
1 1 1 1 19
1 1 1 2 57
...
3 2 2 1 30
3 2 2 2 42
END DATA.
WEIGHT BY FREQ.
HILOGLINEAR WATSOFT (1,3) BRANDPRF PREVUSE TEMP (1,2)
   /PRINT = ALL
   /PLOT = DEFAULT
   /METHOD = BACKWARD
   /DESIGN.
```

- The TITLE command assigns a title, and SET WIDTH limits the page width.

- The DATA LIST command defines five variables, and the VARIABLE LABELS and VALUE LABELS commands assign labels to the variables and values.

- The WEIGHT command weights the observations by FREQ, the variable containing the number of observations for each combination of values.

- HILOGLINEAR specifies four variables. The variable WATSOFT has three levels and each of the other three variables has two.

- The PRINT subcommand requests all available output: observed, expected, and residual values; parameter estimates; and measures of partial association for effects.

- The PLOT subcommand requests the default plots: the normal and detrended normal probability plots and the plots of residuals against observed and expected values.

- The METHOD subcommand requests a search of the "best" model through backward elimination of terms from the specified model.

- The DESIGN subcommand successively eliminates terms from the default saturated model.

The HILOGLINEAR output begins with case and model information (see Figure 1). HILOGLINEAR then shows the results of the iterative proportional fitting algorithm (see Figure 2). For saturated models, the procedure should converge on the first iteration. If a model fails to converge, HILOGLINEAR displays a message and the values for the parameters at that point.

Figure 1 Default case and model information

```
DATA    Information

        24 unweighted cases accepted.
         0 cases rejected because of out-of-range factor values.
         0 cases rejected because of missing data.
      1008 weighted cases will be used in the analysis.


FACTOR Information

      Factor  Level  Label
      WATSOFT    3   Water Softness
      BRANDPRF   2   Brand Preference
      PREVUSE    2   Previous Use of Brand M
      TEMP       2   Water Temperature
```

Figure 2 Results of iterative fit for DESIGN

```
DESIGN 1 has generating class

      WATSOFT*BRANDPRF*PREVUSE*TEMP

The Iterative Proportional Fit algorithm converged at iteration 1.
The maximum difference between observed and fitted marginal totals is     .000
and the convergence criterion is     .250
```

HILOGLINEAR also displays the observed and expected frequencies for the saturated model. Saturated models perfectly account for data in a frequency table. Therefore the observed and expected frequencies are the same, and the residuals are zeros.

Figures 3 through 5 show additional default output. Figure 6 shows the output produced by the ASSOCIATION keyword (implied by keyword ALL). Figure 7 shows the parameter estimates.

Figure 3 Goodness-of-fit test for saturated model

```
Goodness-of-fit test statistics

      Likelihood ratio chi square =     .00000   DF = 0  P = 1.000
                Pearson chi square =     .00000   DF = 0  P = 1.000
```

Figure 4 Tests for order of saturated model

```
Tests that K-way and higher order effects are zero.

       K    DF   L.R. Chisq   Prob   Pearson Chisq   Prob   Iteration

       4     2        .738   .6916           .738   .6915      NA
       3     9       9.846   .3631          9.871   .3611      NA
       2    18      42.926   .0008         43.902   .0006      NA
       1    23     118.626   .0000        115.714   .0000       0
```

Figure 5 Tests for effects of each order

```
Tests that K-way effects are zero.
       K    DF   L.R. Chisq    Prob  Pearson Chisq    Prob   Iteration
       1     5       75.701   .0000         71.812   .0000          0
       2     9       33.079   .0001         34.032   .0001          0
       3     7        9.109   .2449          9.133   .2433          0
       4     2         .738   .6916           .738   .6915          0
```

Example 2 The second example relates two botanical measures of fruits from *Staphylea trifolia* (the American bladdernut). The two measures are locular composition (number of locules in the ovary and odd or even number of ovules) and radial symmetry (standard deviation of numbers of ovules in locules). Certain values of these measures cannot appear in combination, thus producing an incomplete frequency table. HILOGLINEAR tests the quasi-independence of the measures— that is, whether locular composition and radial symmetry are related apart from the mutual exclusivity of certain combinations.

```
TITLE 'FRUIT OF STAPHYLEA TRIFOLIA  (HARRIS, 1910)'.
SET WIDTH = 80.
DATA LIST FREE / LOCULAR RADIAL FREQ.
VARIABLE LABELS LOCULAR  'Locular Composition'
                RADIAL   'Coefficient Radial Asymmetry'
                FREQ     'Number in Condition'.
VALUE LABELS LOCULAR 1 '3 Even' 2 '0 Even' 3 '2 Even' 4 '1 Even'
             /RADIAL 1 '0.00' 2 '0.94' 3 '1.63' 4 '1.89'
                     5 '0.47' 6 '0.82' 7 '1.25' 8 '1.41'
                     9 '1.70'.
BEGIN DATA
1 1 462
1 2 130
1 3 2
1 4 1
2 1 103
2 2 35
2 3 1
2 4 0
3 5 614
3 6 138
3 7 21
3 8 14
3 9 1
4 5 443
4 6 95
4 7 22
4 8 8
4 9 5
END DATA.
WEIGHT BY FREQ.
HILOGLINEAR LOCULAR (1,4) RADIAL (1,9)
   /CWEIGHT = ( 4*1 5*0
                4*1 5*0
                4*0 5*1
                4*0 5*1 )
   /DESIGN LOCULAR RADIAL.
```

- DATA LIST and VARIABLE LABELS define and assign labels to three variables: a measure of locular composition, a measure of radial symmetry, and the number of nuts having that combination of values.

- The WEIGHT command weights the observations by FREQ, the variable containing the number of nuts with each combination of ratings.

- HILOGLINEAR specifies two variables: LOCULAR with four categories, and RADIAL with nine.

- The CWEIGHT subcommand identifies a pattern of cells that are logically empty.

- The DESIGN subcommand specifies main effects only for LOCULAR and RADIAL. Lack of fit for this model indicates an interaction of the two variables.
- Since there is no PRINT or PLOT subcommand, HILOGLINEAR produces default output for an unsaturated model.

Figures 6 and 7 show the display output for the quasi-independence model.

Figure 6 Observed and expected frequencies for incomplete table

```
Observed, Expected Frequencies and Residuals.
        Factor          Code        OBS count  EXP count  Residual  Std Resid

     LOCULAR         3 Even
       RADIAL        0.00          462.0      458.0      4.00       .19
       RADIAL        0.94          130.0      133.8     -3.75      -.32
       RADIAL        1.63            2.0        2.4      -.43      -.28
       RADIAL        1.89            1.0         .8       .19       .21
       RADIAL        0.47             .0         .0       .00       .00
       RADIAL        0.82             .0         .0       .00       .00
       RADIAL        1.25             .0         .0       .00       .00
       RADIAL        1.41             .0         .0       .00       .00
       RADIAL        1.70             .0         .0       .00       .00

     LOCULAR         0 Even
       RADIAL        0.00          103.0      107.0     -4.00      -.39
       RADIAL        0.94           35.0       31.2      3.75       .67
       RADIAL        1.63            1.0         .6       .43       .57
       RADIAL        1.89             .0         .2      -.19      -.44
       RADIAL        0.47             .0         .0       .00       .00
       RADIAL        0.82             .0         .0       .00       .00
       RADIAL        1.25             .0         .0       .00       .00
       RADIAL        1.41             .0         .0       .00       .00
       RADIAL        1.70             .0         .0       .00       .00

     LOCULAR         2 Even
       RADIAL        0.00             .0         .0       .00       .00
       RADIAL        0.94             .0         .0       .00       .00
       RADIAL        1.63             .0         .0       .00       .00
       RADIAL        1.89             .0         .0       .00       .00
       RADIAL        0.47          614.0      612.0      2.01       .08
       RADIAL        0.82          138.0      134.9      3.10       .27
       RADIAL        1.25           21.0       24.9     -3.90      -.78
       RADIAL        1.41           14.0       12.7      1.26       .35
       RADIAL        1.70            1.0        3.5     -2.47     -1.33

     LOCULAR         1 Even
       RADIAL        0.00             .0         .0       .00       .00
       RADIAL        0.94             .0         .0       .00       .00
       RADIAL        1.63             .0         .0       .00       .00
       RADIAL        1.89             .0         .0       .00       .00
       RADIAL        0.47          443.0      445.0     -2.01      -.10
       RADIAL        0.82           95.0       98.1     -3.10      -.31
       RADIAL        1.25           22.0       18.1      3.90       .92
       RADIAL        1.41            8.0        9.3     -1.26      -.41
       RADIAL        1.70            5.0        2.5      2.47      1.56
```

Figure 7 Goodness-of-fit test for quasi-independence

```
Goodness-of-fit test statistics
    Likelihood ratio chi square =    7.74676  DF (UNADJUSTED) = 24  P = .999
                                              DF (ADJUSTED)   =  6  P = .257
              Pearson chi square =    7.49360  DF (UNADJUSTED) = 24  P = .999
                                              DF (ADJUSTED)   =  6  P = .278
```

LOGISTIC REGRESSION

This example illustrates the use of logistic regression to predict students' grades in a class. The data are from Sage paperback #45 (Aldrich & Nelson, 1984). The variables are

- GPA — entering grade point average.
- TUCE — score on the pretest.
- PSI — teaching method, coded as 0 if the traditional method was used and 1 if the new PSI method was used.

- GRADE — coded as 1 if the student received an A, 0 otherwise. This is the dependent variable.
- INITIAL — student's initials used for identification purposes.

The SPSS commands are:

```
SET WIDTH 80.
TITLE    'A DICHOTOMOUS DEPENDENT VARIABLE'.
SUBTITLE 'LOGISTIC REGRESSION'.
* THE DATA COME FROM THE SAGE PAPERBACK #45 BY ALDRICH AND NELSON.
DATA LIST FILE=ALDNEL
  / GPA 1-4(2) TUCE 6-7 PSI 9 GRADE 11 INITIAL 13-14(A).
VARIABLES LABELS
 GPA 'ENTERING GRADE POINT AVERAGE'
 TUCE 'PRETEST SCORE'
 PSI 'TEACHING METHOD'
 GRADE 'FINAL GRADE'.
VALUE LABELS PSI 1 'PSI USED' 0 'OTHER    METHOD'
 /GRADE 1 'A' 0 'NOT A'.
COMPUTE ID=$CASENUM.
LOGISTIC REGRESSION GRADE WITH GPA TUCE PSI /CLASSPLOT
  /METHOD=ENTER GPA /METHOD=FSTEP(LR) TUCE PSI
  /PRINT=ITER(2) /ID=INITIAL
  /CASEWISE=PGROUP PRED RESID /SAVE=DFBETA.
PLOT PLOT DFB1_1 WITH ID BY GRADE.
```

- The DATA LIST command defines the variables. The VALUE LABELS and VARIABLE LABELS commands provide additional descriptive information for the variables.
- The COMPUTE command creates a sequential case number which is an additional identifier for each case. It will be used for plots.
- The LOGISTIC REGRESSION command identifies GRADE as the dependent variable and GPA, TUCE, and PSI as the independent variables. The CATEGORICAL subcommand is not used for the variable PSI since PSI is already an indicator (0,1) variable.
- The PRINT subcommand requests that parameter estimates be printed at every second iteration. By default intermediate estimates are not displayed.
- The ID subcommand instructs that the casewise plot be labeled with the values of the variable INITIAL.
- The first METHOD subcommand enters the GPA variable into an equation which already contains the constant. (The constant can be suppressed with the ORIGIN subcommand.) Figure 1 contains the output when GPA is entered into the model.
- The second METHOD subcommand requests forward stepwise variable selection using the likelihood ratio as the criterion for variable removal. Only the variables TUCE and PSI are eligible for entry and removal. The variable GPA is already in the model and cannot be removed during the stepwise algorithm since it is not included in the list of variables for FSTEP. If the variable list for FSTEP is not given, all independent variables are eligible for entry and removal.
- Figure 2 shows statistics for variables in the equation and those not in the equation when PSI is selected for entry into the model. It also shows the log likelihood for the model if PSI were removed. The message at the bottom of Figure 2 indicates that no additional variables meet the default entry and removal p-values, so model building terminates.
- The CLASSPLOT subcommand requests a plot of the estimated probabilities of receiving an A. Cases are identified on the plot by the first letter of the value label for the dependent variable. The plot when PSI is entered into the model containing the constant and GPA is shown in Figure 3.
- The SAVE subcommand requests that the change in coefficients when a case is eliminated from the analysis be saved. Three new variables named by default DFB0_1 to DFB2_1 are saved. The first variable corresponds to the constant, the second to GPA, and the third to PSI. Output from this step is shown in Figure 4.
- The CASEWISE subcommand requests the casewise plot shown in Figure 5. The variables PGroup (the predicted group membership), Pred (the predicted probability

of receiving an A), and Resid (the difference between the observed probability and that predicted by the model) are listed for all of the cases. Cases are identified by their value of INITIAL. Misclassified cases are marked with asterisks.

- The PLOT command requests a plot of the change in the coefficient for GPA when each case is removed from the analysis against the sequence number for each case. This plot is shown in Figure 6. Note the large change for the last case. (Each point is identified by the group to which it belongs.)

Figure 1

```
Beginning Block Number  1.  Method: Enter

Variable(s) Entered on Step Number
1..      GPA        ENTERING GRADE POINT AVERAGE

Estimation terminated at iteration number 4 because
Log Likelihood decreased by less than 0.01%.

                Iteration History:

Iteration   Log Likelihood      Constant        GPA
       1       -16.534755     -7.0342695    2.0561065
       3       -16.208908     -9.6927129    2.8369989

                      Chi-Square    df  Significance
-2 Log Likelihood       32.418     30     .3484
Model Chi-Square         8.766      1     .0031
Improvement              8.766      1     .0031
Goodness of Fit         39.815     30     .1085

Classification Table for GRADE
                     Predicted
                 NOT A      A      Percent Correct
                  N I      A
Observed        +-------+-------+
   NOT A    N  I   18  I    3  I   85.71%
                +-------+-------+
   A        A  I    5  I    6  I   54.55%
                +-------+-------+
                           Overall  75.00%

------------------------ Variables in the Equation ------------------------

Variable         B        S.E.      Wald    df     Sig      R     Exp(B)

GPA           2.8401     1.1270    6.3507    1    .0117   .3250  17.1168
Constant     -9.7032     3.6711    6.9861    1    .0082
```

Figure 2

```
------------------------ Variables in the Equation ------------------------
Variable         B        S.E.      Wald    df     Sig      R     Exp(B)

GPA           3.0631     1.2228    6.2751    1    .0122   .3631  21.3948
PSI           2.3376     1.0408    5.0449    1    .0247   .3065  10.3565
Constant    -11.6007     4.2127    7.5830    1    .0059
--------------- Variables not in the Equation ---------------
Residual Chi Square     .459 with         1 df     Sig =  .4980

Variable        Score    df     Sig      R

TUCE           .4592     1    .4980   .0000

--------------- Model if Term Removed ---------------

Term       Log                           Significance
Removed    Likelihood   -2 Log LR   df   of Log LR

PSI         -16.209       6.165      1       .0130

No variables can be removed.

No variables can be added.
```

Figure 3

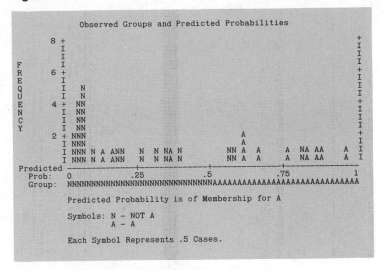

```
                Observed Groups and Predicted Probabilities

        8 +                                                              +
          I                                                              I
          I                                                              I
F         I                                                              I
R       6 +                                                              +
E         I                                                              I
Q         I   N                                                          I
U         I   N                                                          I
E       4 +  NN                                                          +
N         I  NN                                                          I
C         I  NN                                                          I
Y         I  NN                                                          I
          I  NN                              A                           I
        2 + NNN                              A                           +
          I NNN                              A                           I
          I NNN N A ANN   N  N NA N      NN  A  A    A  NA AA    A I      I
          I NNN N A ANN   N  N NA N      NN  A  A    A  NA AA    A I      I
Predicted ---------+---------+---------+---------+---------
    Prob:  0        .25       .5        .75        1
   Group:  NNNNNNNNNNNNNNNNNNNNNNNNNNNNNNAAAAAAAAAAAAAAAAAAAAAAAAAAAAAA

                Predicted Probability is of Membership for A

                Symbols: N - NOT A
                         A - A

                Each Symbol Represents .5 Cases.
```

Figure 4

```
3 new variables have been created.
   Name           Contents

   DFB0_1       Dfbeta for the constant
   DFB1_1       Dfbeta for GPA
   DFB2_1       Dfbeta for PSI
```

Figure 5

ID	Observed GRADE	PGroup	Pred	Resid
am	S N	N	.0307	−.0307
cd	S N	N	.0602	−.0602
ez	S N	N	.1746	−.1746
rt	S N	N	.0656	−.0656
mk	S A	A	.6574	.3426
or	S N	N	.0552	−.0552
fs	S N	N	.0412	−.0412
rn	S N	N	.0568	−.0568
an	S N	N	.0895	−.0895
ds	S A	A	.6003	.3997
kb	S N	N	.0281	−.0281
rp	S N	N	.1929	−.1929
bz	S N	N	.3396	−.3396
ak	S A **	N	.1659	.8341
cl	S N	N	.3126	−.3126
ws	S N	N	.0389	−.0389
ms	S N	N	.0400	−.0400
dh	S N	N	.0506	−.0506
ae	S N **	A	.5730	−.5730
pp	S A	A	.6026	.3974
nn	S N	N	.0496	−.0496
oy	S A	A	.8612	.1388
ap	S N	N	.3988	−.3988
fu	S N **	A	.8159	−.8159
hk	S A	A	.8293	.1707
rt	S A **	N	.3556	.6444
mz	S A	A	.7542	.2458
gg	S N	N	.2527	−.2527
hi	S A	A	.8718	.1282
ln	S A	A	.9521	.0479
dp	S N **	A	.5579	−.5579
ss	S A **	N	.1254	.8746

```
S=Selected U=Unselected cases
** = Misclassified cases
```

Figure 6

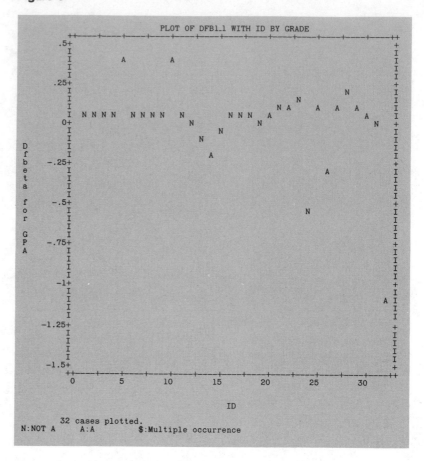

LOGLINEAR

LOGLINEAR   You can use LOGLINEAR to analyze many types of designs for categorical variables. Combinations of variables specifications, CWEIGHT, CONTRAST, GRESID, and DESIGN subcommands can produce general log-linear models, logit models, quasi-independence models, logistic regressions on category variables, and others. The following examples, although not exhaustive, demonstrate many of the types of models you can analyze. Most of these examples have been obtained from books and articles on the analysis of categorical data. The examples use the WEIGHT command to replicate the published tables.

Example 1: Logit Model   The logit model is a special case of the general log-linear model in which one or more variables are treated as dependent, and the rest are used as independent variables. Typically, logit models use dichotomous variables. This example uses dichotomous variables to analyze data from *The American Soldier* (Stouffer et al.,

1948). The researchers interviewed soldiers in training camps. The variables used in this example are

- PREF—preference for training camps, where 1=stay in the same camp, 2=move to a northern camp, 3=move to a southern camp, 4=move—but undecided about location, and 5=undecided.
- RACE—race of soldier, where 1=black and 2=white.
- ORIGIN, CAMP—geographic origin and geographic location of camp, where 1=north and 2=south.
- FREQ—actual cell count obtained from the published table.

In this example, we transform the preference variable into the dichotomy north vs. south. Typically, the first step in fitting a logit model is to use a saturated model and remove nonsignificant effects. This example fits only the significant effects in the interest of parsimony. The SPSS commands are

```
TITLE 'Stouffer''s American Soldier'.
DATA LIST LIST / RACE   ORIGIN  CAMP  PREF   FREQ.
WEIGHT BY FREQ.
VARIABLE LABELS RACE 'RACE OF RESPONDENT'
 ORIGIN 'GEOGRAPHICAL ORIGIN'
 CAMP 'PRESENT CAMP'
 PREF 'PREFENCE FOR LOCATION'.
VALUE LABELS RACE 1 'BLACK' 2 'WHITE'
 /ORIGIN 1 'NORTH' 2 'SOUTH'
 /CAMP 1 'NORTH' 2 'SOUTH'
 /PREF 1 'STAY' 2 'GO NORTH' 3 'GO SOUTH'
  4 'MOVE UNDECIDED' 5 'UNDECIDED'.

COMMENT COLLAPSE CATEGORIES INTO A DICHOTOMY.
DO IF (CAMP EQ 1).
+   RECODE PREF(1=2)(3=3)(ELSE=0) INTO DPREF.
+   ELSE.
+   RECODE PREF(1=3)(2=2)(ELSE=0) INTO DPREF.
END IF.

VARIABLE LABELS DPREF 'PREFERENCE FOR LOCATION'.
VALUE LABELS DPREF 2 'NORTH' 3 'SOUTH'.
BEGIN DATA
1 1 1 1 196
1 1 1 2 191
1 1 1 3  36
1 1 1 4  41
1 1 1 5  52
2 2 2 1 481
  ...
2 2 2 2  91
2 2 2 3 389
2 2 2 4  91
2 2 2 5  91
END DATA.

LOGLINEAR DPREF(2,3) BY RACE ORIGIN CAMP(1,2)
   /PRINT=DEFAULT ESTIM
   /DESIGN=DPREF, DPREF BY RACE, DPREF BY ORIGIN, DPREF BY CAMP,
    DPREF BY ORIGIN BY CAMP.
```

- The DATA LIST command reads the data with a LIST format. The LIST format is a freefield format with each case beginning on a new record.
- Variable FREQ is the actual cell count obtained from the published table. The WEIGHT command weights each case (which represents a cell) back to the sample size.
- The transformations inside the DO IF—END IF structure transform the five category preference variables into a dichotomy.

- The LOGLINEAR command specifies one design. The DESIGN subcommand specifies the dependent variable, as well as interactions involving the dependent variable. Note that this design is not the saturated model. When you specify a logit model with the keyword BY and do not use a DESIGN subcommand, LOGLINEAR implicitly includes all the effects and interactions of independent factors. See Haberman (1979) for more details.
- The PRINT subcommand prints the frequencies and residuals table as well as the estimates for the parameters.

Figures 1 and 2 contain portions of the display for this example. Figure 1 shows the final model fit. The chi-square statistics show a good fit, and all of the adjusted residuals are less than 1.

Figure 2 shows the parameter estimates for the final model. To obtain regression-like coefficients multiply the estimates by 2 (see Haberman, 1978). Use these coefficients to obtain log-odds coefficients; use their anti-log to translate the model into odds rather than log odds. Table 1 shows the model coefficients.

Table 1 Model coefficients

Effect	Coefficient	Coefficient*2	Antilog
DPREF	0.135	0.270	1.311
DPREF BY RACE	0.186	0.371	1.450
DPREF BY ORIGIN	0.620	1.239	3.452
DPREF BY CAMP	0.379	0.759	2.136
DPREF BY ORIGIN BY CAMP	−0.074	−0.149	0.862

The regression-like model implied by the coefficients is

$$\ln(F_{ijk1}/F_{ijk2}) = B + B(A)_i + B(B)_j + B(C)_k + B(BC)_{jk}$$

where F is an expected frequency, and

B equals	0.270
$B(A)_i$ equals	0.371 for i = 1
	−0.371 for i = 2
$B(B)_j$ equals	1.239 for j = 1
	−1.239 for j = 2
$B(C)_k$ equals	0.759 for k = 1
	−0.759 for k = 2
$B(BC)_{jk}$ equals	−0.149 for j = k
	0.149 for j ne k.

To evaluate the model in terms of odds rather than log odds, use an analogous multiplicative model, with the antilogs shown in Table 1 as coefficients. That is,

$$(F_{ijk}1/F_{ijk2}) = T * T(A)_i * T(B)_j * T(C)_k * T(BC)_{jk}$$

where

T equals	1.311
$T(A)_i$ equals	1.450 for i = 1
	1/1.450 for i = 2
$T(B)_j$ equals	3.452 for j = 1
	1/3.452 for j = 2
$T(C)_k$ equals	2.136 for k = 1
	1/2.136 for k = 2
$T(BC)_{jk}$ equals	0.862 for j = k
	1/1.862 for j ne k.

For example, consider someone whose race is black, who is originally from the north, and who is presently located in a northern camp. For this individual, $i=j=k=1$ because of the coding of the variable indicated at the beginning of this example. This person's observed odds of preferring northern versus southern camp location is 10.75 (91.49/8.51) from Figure 1. The expected odds given the model is 12.072 (92.35/7.65) from Figure 1. The model decomposes these expected odds into components

$$12.072 = (1.311)(1.450)(3.452)(2.136)(0.862)$$

where the effects are interpretable.

- 1.311 is the mean or overall effect.
- 1.450 is the race effect indicating the net effect of being black versus white on preference of camp location. Other things equal, blacks prefer northern camp locations by 1.450 to 1.
- 3.452 is the net effect of region of origin on present preference. Other things equal, someone originally from the north prefers a northern camp location by 3.452 to 1.
- 2.136 is the net effect of present location on camp preference. Other things equal, someone presently located in the north states a northern preference over twice as often as they state a southern preference.
- 0.862 is the interaction effect between region of origin and present camp location. The effect is negative; this means that the effect of being a northerner in a northern camp is less positive than is indicated by combining the main effect of being a northerner with the main effect of being in a northern camp.

Figure 1 Model fit

```
Observed, Expected Frequencies and Residuals
      Factor          Code        OBS. count & PCT.   EXP. count & PCT.   Residual    Std. Resid.   Adj. Resid.


DPREF           NORTH
  RACE          BLACK
    ORIGIN        NORTH
      CAMP          NORTH         387.00 (91.49)      390.64 (92.35)      -3.6431       -.1843        -.7714
      CAMP          SOUTH         876.00 (77.80)      879.35 (78.09)      -3.3479       -.1129        -.4178
    ORIGIN        SOUTH
      CAMP          NORTH         383.00 (58.65)      376.80 (57.70)       6.2000        .3194         .9994
      CAMP          SOUTH         381.00 (18.20)      380.21 (18.17)        .7909        .0406         .1131
  RACE          WHITE
    ORIGIN        NORTH
      CAMP          NORTH         955.00 (85.50)      951.36 (85.17)       3.6431        .1181         .7714
      CAMP          SOUTH         874.00 (63.15)      870.65 (62.91)       3.3479        .1135         .4178
    ORIGIN        SOUTH
      CAMP          NORTH         104.00 (37.14)      110.20 (39.36)      -6.2000       -.5906        -.9994
      CAMP          SOUTH          91.00 ( 9.47)       91.79 ( 9.55)       -.7909       -.0825        -.1131

DPREF           SOUTH
  RACE          BLACK
    ORIGIN        NORTH
      CAMP          NORTH          36.00 ( 8.51)       32.36 ( 7.65)       3.6431        .6405         .7714
      CAMP          SOUTH         250.00 (22.20)      246.65 (21.91)       3.3479        .2132         .4178
    ORIGIN        SOUTH
      CAMP          NORTH         270.00 (41.35)      276.20 (42.30)      -6.2000       -.3731        -.9994
      CAMP          SOUTH        1712.00 (81.80)     1712.79 (81.83)       -.7909       -.0191        -.1131
  RACE          WHITE
    ORIGIN        NORTH
      CAMP          NORTH         162.00 (14.50)      165.64 (14.83)      -3.6431       -.2831        -.7714
      CAMP          SOUTH         510.00 (36.85)      513.35 (37.09)      -3.3479       -.1478        -.4178
    ORIGIN        SOUTH
      CAMP          NORTH         176.00 (62.86)      169.80 (60.64)       6.2000        .4758         .9994
      CAMP          SOUTH         870.00 (90.53)      869.21 (90.45)        .7909        .0268         .1131


Goodness-of-Fit test statistics

    Likelihood Ratio Chi Square =    1.44756    DF = 3   P =  .694
              Pearson Chi Square =    1.45707    DF = 3   P =  .692
```

Figure 2 Parameter estimates

```
Estimates for Parameters
  DPREF

    Parameter        Coeff.        Std. Err.       Z-Value       Lower 95 CI     Upper 95 CI
        1        .1352217166         .01518         8.90608         .10546          .16498
  DPREF BY RACE

    Parameter        Coeff.        Std. Err.       Z-Value       Lower 95 CI     Upper 95 CI
        2        .1857281674         .01557        11.93145         .15522          .21624
  DPREF BY ORIGIN

    Parameter        Coeff.        Std. Err.       Z-Value       Lower 95 CI     Upper 95 CI
        3        .6195921388         .01687        36.72886         .58653          .65266
  DPREF BY CAMP

    Parameter        Coeff.        Std. Err.       Z-Value       Lower 95 CI     Upper 95 CI
        4        .3794390119         .01534        24.73658         .34937          .40950
  DPREF BY ORIGIN BY CAMP

    Parameter        Coeff.        Std. Err.       Z-Value       Lower 95 CI     Upper 95 CI
        5       -.0744977447         .01521        -4.89942        -.10430         -.04470
```

Example 2: A General Log-linear Model

The general log-linear model has all dependent variables. This example uses the same data analyzed as the logit model in the first example. The general log-linear model treats all variables as jointly dependent. The following LOGLINEAR command is used to request this model:

```
LOGLINEAR DPREF(2,3) RACE ORIGIN CAMP(1,2)
  /PRINT=DEFAULT ESTIM
  /DESIGN=DPREF, RACE, ORIGIN, CAMP,
    DPREF BY RACE, DPREF BY ORIGIN, DPREF BY CAMP,
    RACE BY CAMP, RACE BY ORIGIN, ORIGIN BY CAMP,
    RACE BY ORIGIN BY CAMP,
    DPREF BY ORIGIN BY CAMP.
```

The LOGLINEAR command for the general log-linear model does not use the keyword BY. The DESIGN subcommand uses all the variables as main effects or as part of an interaction term. Compare this with the logit model shown in the first example, which uses the dependent variable and interactions involving the dependent variable.

Figures 3 and 4 are the display produced by this example. Figure 3 shows that expected frequencies are identical to the logit model in the first example (Figure 1). However, observed and expected cell percentages differ. In the logit model, cell percentages sum to 100 across categories of the dependent variable within each combination of independent variable values. In other words, cell percentages in the logit model are comparable to row or column percentages in crosstabulation. In the general model, they sum to 100 across all categories and are comparable to total percentages in a crosstabulation.

Figure 3   Log-linear model fit for Example 2

```
Observed, Expected Frequencies and Residuals
       Factor          Code         OBS. count & PCT.   EXP. count & PCT.   Residual   Std. Resid.   Adj. Resid.


  DPREF          NORTH
    RACE           BLACK
      ORIGIN         NORTH
        CAMP           NORTH         387.00 (  4.82)     390.64 (  4.86)     -3.6431      -.1843        -.7714
        CAMP           SOUTH         876.00 (10.90)      879.35 (10.94)      -3.3479      -.1129        -.4178
      ORIGIN         SOUTH
        CAMP           NORTH         383.00 (  4.77)     376.80 (  4.69)      6.2000       .3194         .9994
        CAMP           SOUTH         381.00 (  4.74)     380.21 (  4.73)       .7909       .0406         .1131
    RACE           WHITE
      ORIGIN         NORTH
        CAMP           NORTH         955.00 (11.88)      951.36 (11.84)       3.6431       .1181         .7714
        CAMP           SOUTH         874.00 (10.87)      870.65 (10.83)       3.3479       .1135         .4178
      ORIGIN         SOUTH
        CAMP           NORTH         104.00 (  1.29)     110.20 (  1.37)     -6.2000      -.5906        -.9994
        CAMP           SOUTH          91.00 (  1.13)      91.79 (  1.14)      -.7909      -.0825        -.1131

  DPREF          SOUTH
    RACE           BLACK
      ORIGIN         NORTH
        CAMP           NORTH          36.00 (   .45)      32.36 (   .40)      3.6431       .6405         .7714
        CAMP           SOUTH         250.00 (  3.11)     246.65 (  3.07)      3.3479       .2132         .4178
      ORIGIN         SOUTH
        CAMP           NORTH         270.00 (  3.36)     276.20 (  3.44)     -6.2000      -.3731        -.9994
        CAMP           SOUTH        1712.00 (21.30)     1712.79 (21.31)      -.7909      -.0191        -.1131
    RACE           WHITE
      ORIGIN         NORTH
        CAMP           NORTH         162.00 (  2.02)     165.64 (  2.06)     -3.6431      -.2831        -.7714
        CAMP           SOUTH         510.00 (  6.35)     513.35 (  6.39)     -3.3479      -.1478        -.4178
      ORIGIN         SOUTH
        CAMP           NORTH         176.00 (  2.19)     169.80 (  2.11)      6.2000       .4758         .9994
        CAMP           SOUTH         870.00 (10.82)     869.21 (10.82)       .7909       .0268         .1131

  - - - - - - - - - - - - - - - - - - - - - - - - - - - - - - - - - - - - - - - - - - - - - - - - - - - - - -


  Goodness-of-Fit test statistics

     Likelihood Ratio Chi Square =    1.44756    DF = 3   P =  .694
                Pearson Chi Square =   1.45707    DF = 3   P =  .692
```

Figure 4 Parameter estimates for Example 2

```
Estimates for Parameters
 DPREF

   Parameter        Coeff.       Std. Err.      Z-Value     Lower 95 CI    Upper 95 CI
       1          .1352217166      .01518       8.90608        .10546         .16498
 RACE

   Parameter        Coeff.       Std. Err.      Z-Value     Lower 95 CI    Upper 95 CI
       2          .0355803941      .01363       2.61113        .00887         .06229
 ORIGIN

   Parameter        Coeff.       Std. Err.      Z-Value     Lower 95 CI    Upper 95 CI
       3          .0403904261      .01614       2.50201        .00875         .07203
 CAMP

   Parameter        Coeff.       Std. Err.      Z-Value     Lower 95 CI    Upper 95 CI
       4         -.4480592813      .01614     -27.76919       -.47968        -.41643
 DPREF BY RACE

   Parameter        Coeff.       Std. Err.      Z-Value     Lower 95 CI    Upper 95 CI
       5          .1857281674      .01557      11.93145        .15522         .21624
 DPREF BY ORIGIN

   Parameter        Coeff.       Std. Err.      Z-Value     Lower 95 CI    Upper 95 CI
       6          .6195921388      .01687      36.72886        .58653         .65266
 DPREF BY CAMP

   Parameter        Coeff.       Std. Err.      Z-Value     Lower 95 CI    Upper 95 CI
       7          .3794390119      .01534      24.73658        .34937         .40950
 RACE BY CAMP

   Parameter        Coeff.       Std. Err.      Z-Value     Lower 95 CI    Upper 95 CI
       8         -.1364780340      .01413      -9.65595       -.16418        -.10878
 RACE BY ORIGIN

   Parameter        Coeff.       Std. Err.      Z-Value     Lower 95 CI    Upper 95 CI
       9         -.4413477997      .01591     -27.73754       -.47253        -.41016
 ORIGIN BY CAMP

   Parameter        Coeff.       Std. Err.      Z-Value     Lower 95 CI    Upper 95 CI
      10         -.0375668525      .01632      -2.30190       -.06955        -.00558
 RACE BY ORIGIN BY CAMP

   Parameter        Coeff.       Std. Err.      Z-Value     Lower 95 CI    Upper 95 CI
      11         -.0885302170      .01359      -6.51497       -.11516        -.06190
 DPREF BY ORIGIN BY CAMP

   Parameter        Coeff.       Std. Err.      Z-Value     Lower 95 CI    Upper 95 CI
      12         -.0744977447      .01521      -4.89942       -.10430        -.04470
```

Compare Figure 4 with Figure 2 in the first example. Note that identical results are produced for effects in common in the two models.

Example 3: A Multinomial Logit Model

The first two examples analyze Stouffer's data with "preference for location" transformed into a dichotomy. Example 3 uses the original five-category preference variable to demonstrate the multinomial logit model. This example uses orthogonal special contrasts to make desired comparisons among the categories of the dependent variable. The LOGLINEAR command is as follows:

```
LOGLINEAR PREF(1,5) BY RACE ORIGIN CAMP(1,2)
  /PRINT=DEFAULT ESTIM
  /CONTRAST(PREF)=SPECIAL(5*1,1 1 1 1 -4,3 -1 -1 -1 0,
    0 1 1 -2 0,0 1 -1 0 0)
  /DESIGN=PREF, PREF BY RACE, PREF BY ORIGIN, PREF BY CAMP,
    PREF BY RACE BY ORIGIN, PREF BY RACE BY CAMP,
    PREF BY ORIGIN BY CAMP, PREF BY RACE BY ORIGIN BY CAMP.
```

Figure 5 is the display of the parameter estimates for Example 3. This example fits the saturated model. If no DESIGN subcommand had been specified, the saturated model would have also included effects that are redundant when a logit model is specified. Parameter estimates for a multinomial model can be more interpretable when you specify special contrasts as in this example. The CONTRAST subcommand contrasts the movers and stayers vs. the undecided, the movers vs. the stayers, the decided vs. the undecided, and northern vs. southern camps.

Figure 5 Parameter estimates for Example 3

```
Estimates for Parameters
PREF

Parameter        Coeff.        Std. Err.      Z-Value      Lower 95 CI    Upper 95 CI

    1         .1234825883        .00807        15.29520        .10766         .13931
    2         .0724662120        .00826         8.77654        .05628         .08865
    3         .2043174993        .01408        14.51506        .17673         .23191
    4         .1282571558        .02068         6.20092        .08772         .16880

PREF BY RACE

Parameter        Coeff.        Std. Err.      Z-Value      Lower 95 CI    Upper 95 CI

    5        -.0051416644        .00807         -.63687       -.02097         .01068
    6        -.0063669961        .00826         -.77112       -.02255         .00982
    7         .0062485789        .01408          .44391       -.02134         .03384
    8         .0960361288        .02068         4.64311        .05550         .13658

PREF BY ORIGIN

Parameter        Coeff.        Std. Err.      Z-Value      Lower 95 CI    Upper 95 CI

    9        -.0021584482        .00807         -.26736       -.01798         .01367
   10        -.0586990400        .00826        -7.10917       -.07488        -.04252
   11        -.0025353715        .01408         -.18012       -.03012         .02505
   12         .6555140380        .02068        31.69248        .61497         .69605

PREF BY CAMP

Parameter        Coeff.        Std. Err.      Z-Value      Lower 95 CI    Upper 95 CI

   13        -.0191848042        .00807        -2.37633       -.03501        -.00336
   14         .0320805342        .00826         3.88534        .01590         .04826
   15         .0038808442        .01408          .27570       -.02371         .03147
   16        -.0156364228        .02068         -.75598       -.05618         .02490

PREF BY RACE BY ORIGIN

Parameter        Coeff.        Std. Err.      Z-Value      Lower 95 CI    Upper 95 CI

   17        -.0033156723        .00807         -.41070       -.01914         .01251
   18        -.0237329647        .00826        -2.87435       -.03992        -.00755
   19         .0611636379        .01408         4.34517        .03357         .08875
   20        -.0516750973        .02068        -2.49836       -.09221        -.01114

PREF BY RACE BY CAMP

Parameter        Coeff.        Std. Err.      Z-Value      Lower 95 CI    Upper 95 CI

   21         .0030208725        .00807          .37418       -.01280         .01884
   22         .1027873616        .00826        12.44880        .08660         .11897
   23        -.0189810333        .01408        -1.34845       -.04657         .00861
   24         .0076967580        .02068          .37212       -.03284         .04824

PREF BY ORIGIN BY CAMP

Parameter        Coeff.        Std. Err.      Z-Value      Lower 95 CI    Upper 95 CI

   25         .0049220965        .00807          .60968       -.01090         .02075
   26         .1316990028        .00826        15.95036        .11552         .14788
   27        -.0090552616        .01408         -.64330       -.03664         .01853
   28        -.0320161528        .02068        -1.54790       -.07256         .00852

PREF BY RACE BY ORIGIN BY CAMP

Parameter        Coeff.        Std. Err.      Z-Value      Lower 95 CI    Upper 95 CI

   29        -.0008598058        .00807         -.10650       -.01668         .01496
   30         .0217737066        .00826         2.63706        .00559         .03796
   31        -.0115700249        .01408         -.82195       -.03916         .01602
   32         .0406113662        .02068         1.96346        .00007         .08115
```

Example 4: Frequency Table Models

You can use LOGLINEAR to analyze one-dimensional frequency tables by means of chi-square-based analysis. Example 4 uses data on the recall of stressful events over time (Haberman, 1978). Each case in the published table is one recall of a stressful event, and the measure is the length of time in months since the event occurred. The example tests two separate models: the equiprobability model and the log-linear time-trend model. The following SPSS commands are used:

```
DATA LIST LIST / MONTH  WT.
COMPUTE X=1.
COMPUTE Z=MONTH.
WEIGHT BY WT.
BEGIN DATA
 1 15  1 0
 2 11  1 0
 3 14  1 0
  ...
16  1  0 1
17  1  0 1
18  4  0 1
END DATA.

LOGLINEAR MONTH(1,18) WITH X Z
 /PRINT = ALL
 /*USE GRESID TO TEST COMBINATIONS OF THE OBSERVED FREQUENCIES
 /*NOTE:   THE THREE EFFECTS ARE EARLY, MIDDLE, AND LATE
 /GRESID =(6*1,12*0)
 /GRESID=(6*0,6*1,6*0)
 /GRESID=(12*0,6*1)
 /*MODEL 1:  THE EQUIPROBABILITY MODEL
 /DESIGN = X
 /*MODEL 2:  THE LOG-LINEAR TIME-TREND MODEL
 /DESIGN = Z.
```

- The DATA LIST command reads two variables: MONTH, scaled from 1 to 18; and WT, which contains the frequencies. It uses the LIST format.

- COMPUTE X=1 computes a vector of 1s.

- The second COMPUTE computes an index vector ranging from 1 to 18.

- The WEIGHT command is used to replicate the original file.

- The LOGLINEAR command names MONTH as the dependent variable and the two index variables as covariates.

- The GRESID subcommands request three linear combinations of the data: the first six, the middle six, and the last six observations, respectively, are combined. Generalized residual contrasts produce some of the statistics already seen: the observed count, the expected count, the residual, the standardized residual, and the adjusted residual.

- DESIGN=X tests the equiprobability model. This model assumes that the probability of dating an event in a particular past month is constant for all months. The covariate is a constant for this type of model.

- DESIGN=Z fits a log-linear time-trend model. The log of the cell probabilities is a linear function of the time before the interview. The index variable reflects the time period being studied for this type of model.

Figure 6 shows the frequencies and residuals for the equiprobability model. The expected counts and expected percentages are constant across all cells in the equiprobability model.

Figure 6 The equiprobability model fit for Example 4

```
Observed, Expected Frequencies and Residuals
     Factor           Code         OBS. count & PCT.    EXP. count & PCT.     Residual    Std. Resid.    Adj. Resid.
  MONTH                1            15.00  (10.20)        8.17  ( 5.56)         6.8333       2.3912         2.4605
  MONTH                2            11.00  ( 7.48)        8.17  ( 5.56)         2.8333        .9915         1.0202
  MONTH                3            14.00  ( 9.52)        8.17  ( 5.56)         5.8333       2.0412         2.1004
  MONTH                4            17.00  (11.56)        8.17  ( 5.56)         8.8333       3.0910         3.1806
  MONTH                5             5.00  ( 3.40)        8.17  ( 5.56)        -3.1667      -1.1081        -1.1402
  MONTH                6            11.00  ( 7.48)        8.17  ( 5.56)         2.8333        .9915         1.0202
  MONTH                7            10.00  ( 6.80)        8.17  ( 5.56)         1.8333        .6415          .6601
  MONTH                8             4.00  ( 2.72)        8.17  ( 5.56)        -4.1667      -1.4580        -1.5003
  MONTH                9             8.00  ( 5.44)        8.17  ( 5.56)         -.1667       -.0583         -.0600
  MONTH               10            10.00  ( 6.80)        8.17  ( 5.56)         1.8333        .6415          .6601
  MONTH               11             7.00  ( 4.76)        8.17  ( 5.56)        -1.1667       -.4082         -.4201
  MONTH               12             9.00  ( 6.12)        8.17  ( 5.56)          .8333        .2916          .3001
  MONTH               13            11.00  ( 7.48)        8.17  ( 5.56)         2.8333        .9915         1.0202
  MONTH               14             3.00  ( 2.04)        8.17  ( 5.56)        -5.1667      -1.8080        -1.8604
  MONTH               15             6.00  ( 4.08)        8.17  ( 5.56)        -2.1667       -.7582         -.7802
  MONTH               16             1.00  (  .68)        8.17  ( 5.56)        -7.1667      -2.5078        -2.5805
  MONTH               17             1.00  (  .68)        8.17  ( 5.56)        -7.1667      -2.5078        -2.5805
  MONTH               18             4.00  ( 2.72)        8.17  ( 5.56)        -4.1667      -1.4580        -1.5003

 - - - - - - - - - - - - - - - - - - - - - - - - - - - - - - - - - - - - - - - - - - - - - - - - - - - - - - - - - - - - -

Goodness-of-Fit test statistics

    Likelihood Ratio Chi Square =     50.84270     DF = 17   P =  .000
              Pearson Chi Square =     45.36735     DF = 17   P =  .000
```

Figure 7 is the display produced by the GRESID subcommands for the equiprobability model. The model systematically underpredicts the early scores and overpredicts the late scores in a way which cannot be ignored: the adjusted residuals are greater than 4 in magnitude in these two instances.

Figure 7 Generalized residuals for the equiprobability model for Example 4

```
Generalized Residual
      Contrast                              OBS. count    EXP. count    Residual    Std. Resid.    Adj. Resid.
         1                                     73.0         49.00        24.0000       3.4286        4.1991
         2                                     48.0         49.00        -1.0000       -.1429        -.1750
         3                                     26.0         49.00       -23.0000      -3.2857       -4.0242
```

Figure 8 shows the fit under the time-trend model. The expected counts come much closer to the observed counts using this model. With the exception of Month 13, the adjusted residuals are all under 2 in magnitude.

Figure 8 The time-trend model fit for Example 4

```
Observed, Expected Frequencies and Residuals
     Factor           Code         OBS. count & PCT.    EXP. count & PCT.     Residual    Std. Resid.    Adj. Resid.
  MONTH                1            15.00  (10.20)       15.17  (10.32)         -.1711       -.0439         -.0516
  MONTH                2            11.00  ( 7.48)       13.95  ( 9.49)        -2.9520       -.7903         -.8873
  MONTH                3            14.00  ( 9.52)       12.83  ( 8.73)         1.1692        .3264          .3551
  MONTH                4            17.00  (11.56)       11.80  ( 8.03)         5.2002       1.5138         1.6111
  MONTH                5             5.00  ( 3.40)       10.85  ( 7.38)        -5.8516      -1.7763        -1.8625
  MONTH                6            11.00  ( 7.48)        9.98  ( 6.79)         1.0204        .3230          .3355
  MONTH                7            10.00  ( 6.80)        9.18  ( 6.24)          .8223        .2714          .2804
  MONTH                8             4.00  ( 2.72)        8.44  ( 5.74)        -4.4402      -1.5284        -1.5751
  MONTH                9             8.00  ( 5.44)        7.76  ( 5.28)          .2380        .0854          .0881
  MONTH               10            10.00  ( 6.80)        7.14  ( 4.86)         2.8617       1.0711         1.1065
  MONTH               11             7.00  ( 4.76)        6.56  ( 4.47)          .4353        .1699          .1762
  MONTH               12             9.00  ( 6.12)        6.04  ( 4.11)         2.9629       1.2059         1.2560
  MONTH               13            11.00  ( 7.48)        5.55  ( 3.78)         5.4480       2.3121         2.4214
  MONTH               14             3.00  ( 2.04)        5.11  ( 3.47)        -2.1059       -.9320         -.9818
  MONTH               15             6.00  ( 4.08)        4.70  ( 3.19)         1.3044        .6020          .6381
  MONTH               16             1.00  (  .68)        4.32  ( 2.94)        -3.3183      -1.5968        -1.7032
  MONTH               17             1.00  (  .68)        3.97  ( 2.70)        -2.9713      -1.4910        -1.6003
  MONTH               18             4.00  ( 2.72)        3.65  ( 2.48)          .3479        .1820          .1965

 - - - - - - - - - - - - - - - - - - - - - - - - - - - - - - - - - - - - - - - - - - - - - - - - - - - - - - - - - - - - -

Goodness-of-Fit test statistics

    Likelihood Ratio Chi Square =     24.57038     DF = 16   P =  .078
              Pearson Chi Square =     22.71450     DF = 16   P =  .122
```

Figure 9 shows the output from the GRESID specifications for the time-trend model. In this model, the early, middle, and late contrasts now conform more closely to the observed frequencies than in the equiprobability model.

Figure 9 Generalized residuals for the time-trend model for Example 4

```
Generalized Residual
    Contrast                        OBS. count   EXP. count   Residual   Std. Resid.   Adj. Resid.
         1                             73.0        49.00       24.0000      3.4286        4.1991
         2                             48.0        49.00       -1.0000      -.1429        -.1750
         3                             26.0        49.00      -23.0000     -3.2857       -4.0242
```

Example 5: A Linear Logit Model

Example 5 is a linear logit model with one predictor. The level of education in years is used to predict the attitude of men toward women staying at home rather than working (Haberman, 1982). This variable is dichotomous. The SPSS commands are as follows:

```
DATA LIST LIST /YEAR RESPONSE WT.
WEIGHT BY WT.
VALUE LABELS RESPONSE 1 'AGREE' 2 'DISAGREE'.
BEGIN DATA
 0 1    4
 0 2    2
   ...
20 1    3
20 2   20
END DATA.
LOGLINEAR RESPONSE(1,2) BY YEAR(0,20)
 /PRINT=DEFAULT ESTIM
 /CONTRAST(YEAR)=SPECIAL(21*1, -10, -9, -8, -7, -6, -5, -4,
                   -3, -2, -1, 0, 1, 2, 3, 4, 5, 6, 7,
                   8, 9, 10, 399*1 )
 /DESIGN=RESPONSE RESPONSE BY YEAR(1).
```

- The DATA LIST command reads YEAR, RESPONSE, and WT, which is the frequency for each cell.
- The WEIGHT command weights the table to the original sample size.
- The variables specification on the LOGLINEAR command uses the keyword BY to define a logit model.
- The CONTRAST subcommand specifies a special contrast. The full design matrix is a 21*21 matrix. The first effect fit is the constant effect, so the special contrast begins with 21 1s. The second effect is the linear effect, parameterized as years of education minus 10. Higher order effects are not of interest, so 1s are used to fill out the matrix.
- The DESIGN subcommand fits the RESPONSE effect and the RESPONSE by linear-YEAR effect.

Figure 10 shows the linear logit fit. The chi-square statistics are all nonsignificant, and the largest adjusted residual is 1.99. Figure 11 shows the analysis of dispersion and the two measures of association. The two statistics indicate that there is about a 10% reduction in errors of classification on the response variable with knowledge of years of education. Figure 12 is the parameter estimates for the model.

Figure 10 Linear logit model fit for Example 5

```
Observed, Expected Frequencies and Residuals

      Factor            Code        OBS. count & PCT.    EXP. count & PCT.    Residual    Std. Resid.    Adj. Resid.

RESPONSE        AGREE
  YEAR            0          4.00 (66.67)         5.34 (89.07)       -1.3444       -.5815        -1.7884
  YEAR            1          2.00 (99.99)         1.73 (86.58)        .2684        .2040          .5599
  YEAR            2          4.00 (99.99)         3.34 (83.62)        .6552        .3583          .8948
  YEAR            3          6.00 (66.67)         7.21 (80.16)       -1.2141       -.4520        -1.0385
  YEAR            4          5.00 (50.00)         7.62 (76.17)       -2.6171       -.9483        -1.9887
  YEAR            5         13.00 (65.00)        14.33 (71.67)       -1.3336       -.3523         -.6901
  YEAR            6         25.00 (73.53)        22.67 (66.69)        2.3266        .4886          .8993
  YEAR            7         27.00 (64.29)        25.75 (61.30)        1.2533        .2470          .4212
  YEAR            8         75.00 (60.48)        68.98 (55.63)        6.0243        .7254         1.2564
  YEAR            9         29.00 (50.00)        28.88 (49.80)        .1167         .0217          .0320
  YEAR           10         32.00 (41.56)        33.86 (43.98)       -1.8627       -.3201         -.4469
  YEAR           11         36.00 (37.89)        36.40 (38.32)        -.4014       -.0665         -.0886
  YEAR           12        115.00 (31.94)       118.65 (32.96)       -3.6453       -.3347         -.4957
  YEAR           13         31.00 (30.69)        28.29 (28.01)        2.7138        .5103          .6348
  YEAR           14         28.00 (26.17)        25.19 (23.54)        2.8145        .5608          .6885
  YEAR           15          9.00 (28.13)         6.27 (19.59)        2.7317       1.0911         1.2470
  YEAR           16         15.00 (12.00)        20.20 (16.16)       -5.2023      -1.1574        -1.4309
  YEAR           17          3.00 ( 9.38)         4.24 (13.24)       -1.2355       -.6003         -.6659
  YEAR           18          1.00 ( 3.45)         3.12 (10.77)       -2.1237      -1.2016        -1.3136
  YEAR           19          2.00 (13.33)         1.31 ( 8.72)        .6920        .6051          .6443
  YEAR           20          3.00 (13.04)         1.62 ( 7.03)        1.3835       1.0881         1.1594

RESPONSE        DISAGREE
  YEAR            0          2.00 (33.33)          .66 (10.93)        1.3444       1.6603         1.7884
  YEAR            1           .00 (  .00)          .27 (13.42)        -.2684       -.5181         -.5599
  YEAR            2           .00 (  .00)          .66 (16.38)        -.6552       -.8095         -.8948
  YEAR            3          3.00 (33.33)         1.79 (19.84)        1.2141        .9085         1.0385
  YEAR            4          5.00 (50.00)         2.38 (23.83)        2.6171       1.6954         1.9887
  YEAR            5          7.00 (35.00)         5.67 (28.33)        1.3336        .5603          .6901
  YEAR            6          9.00 (26.47)        11.33 (33.31)       -2.3266       -.6913         -.8993
  YEAR            7         15.00 (35.71)        16.25 (38.70)       -1.2533       -.3109         -.4212
  YEAR            8         49.00 (39.52)        55.02 (44.37)       -6.0243       -.8121        -1.2564
  YEAR            9         29.00 (50.00)        29.12 (50.20)        -.1167       -.0216         -.0320
  YEAR           10         45.00 (58.44)        43.14 (56.02)        1.8627        .2836          .4469
  YEAR           11         59.00 (62.11)        58.60 (61.68)        .4014         .0524          .0886
  YEAR           12        245.00 (68.06)       241.35 (67.04)        3.6453        .2346          .4957
  YEAR           13         70.00 (69.31)        72.71 (71.99)       -2.7138       -.3182         -.6348
  YEAR           14         79.00 (73.83)        81.81 (76.46)       -2.8145       -.3112         -.6885
  YEAR           15         23.00 (71.88)        25.73 (80.41)       -2.7317       -.5385        -1.2470
  YEAR           16        110.00 (88.00)       104.80 (83.84)        5.2023        .5082         1.4309
  YEAR           17         29.00 (90.63)        27.76 (86.76)        1.2355        .2345          .6659
  YEAR           18         28.00 (96.55)        25.88 (89.23)        2.1237        .4175         1.3136
  YEAR           19         13.00 (86.67)        13.69 (91.28)        -.6920       -.1870         -.6443
  YEAR           20         20.00 (86.96)        21.38 (92.97)       -1.3835       -.2992        -1.1594
- - - - - - - - - - - - - - - - - - - - - - - - - - - - - - - - - - - - - - - - - - - - - - - - -

Goodness-of-Fit test statistics

     Likelihood Ratio Chi Square =    18.94502    DF = 19   P =  .460
              Pearson Chi Square =    19.40725    DF = 19   P =  .431
```

Figure 11 Linear logit model analysis of dispersion for Example 5

```
Analysis of Dispersion
                                        Dispersion
    Source of Variation       Entropy   Concentration    DF

       Due to Model           81.988       72.577
       Due to Residual       767.922      526.044
       Total                 849.911      598.621       1304
```

Figure 12 Linear logit model parameter estimates for Example 5

```
Estimates for Parameters
  RESPONSE

  Parameter      Coeff.       Std. Err.      Z-Value    Lower 95 CI    Upper 95 CI

       1      -.1210376490      .03334      -3.63002      -.18639        -.05568

  RESPONSE BY YEAR(1)

  Parameter      Coeff.       Std. Err.      Z-Value    Lower 95 CI    Upper 95 CI

       2      -.1170135446      .01009     -11.59226      -.13680        -.09723
```

You could get the same results by first calculating a variable equal to YEAR−10 and then specifying this new variable as a covariate on the LOGLINEAR command, as in:

```
COMPUTE X=YEAR-10.
LOGLINEAR RESPONSE(1,2) BY YEAR (0,20) WITH X
  /PRINT=DEFAULT ESTIM
  /DESIGN=RESPONSE RESPONSE BY X.
```

Using this approach, you do not need to specify the CONTRAST subcommand on the LOGLINEAR command.

Example 6: Logistic Regression On Category Variables

In the logistic regression model, a dichotomous dependent variable is predicted by one or more independent variables. In LOGLINEAR, the independent variables must be categorical, and one must be measured at the interval level of measurement.

Example 6 is a logistic regression in which a contrast is used to transform the categorical independent variable into a metric variable. The data for this example is taken from Dixon (1979). At a specified time, measured in number of days, a number of objects are tested and the number of failures are recorded. In this example, time is a metric variable, not merely an evenly spaced ordinal variable. RESPONSE is the dependent variable, and TIME is the independent variable. WT defines the number of observations in each cell. The following SPSS commands are used:

```
TITLE 'A LOGISTIC REGRESSION EXAMPLE FROM BMDP(1979) P.517.1'.
DATA LIST LIST/ RESPONSE TIME WT.
VALUE LABELS RESPONSE 1 'SUCCESS' 2 'FAILURE'.
IF (WT = 0) WT = .00001.
WEIGHT BY WT.
BEGIN DATA
1 1  55
2 1   0
1 2 155
2 2   2
1 3 152
2 3   7
1 4  13
2 4   3
END DATA.

LOGLINEAR RESPONSE(1,2) BY TIME(1,4)
  /CONTRAST(TIME) = SPECIAL(4*1, 7 14 27 51, 8*1)
  /PRINT = ALL/PLOT = DEFAULT
  /DESIGN = RESPONSE, TIME(1) BY RESPONSE.
```

• Since the log of 0 is undefined, sampling zeros (not structural zeros) should always be changed to some small positive number in log-linear analysis. Many corrections have been suggested, such as adding 0.5 to each cell or using pseudo-Bayes estimates (Bishop et al., 1975; Goodman, 1971). In this example, the IF command changes sampling zeros to 0.00001.

• The BY keyword in the variables specification on LOGLINEAR indicates a logit model.

• The PRINT subcommand requests all printed materials, and the PLOT subcommand requests the default plots.

• The SPECIAL contrast on the CONTRAST subcommand specifies the metric of time. The constant effect is specified first, followed by the linear effect in the metric of time: 7, 14, 27, 51. Since no higher order effect is of interest, the matrix is filled out with 1s.

• The DESIGN subcommand fits RESPONSE and RESPONSE by linear-TIME.

Figure 13 shows the design matrix for the model. Figure 14 shows the logistic regression fit. Overall, the fit is good. Both chi-square statistics are nonsignificant, and all adjusted residuals are well under 2 in magnitude. Figure 15 shows the estimated parameters and the correlation matrix of parameter estimates. As in logit models, you can multiply the two parameter values by 2 to obtain the constant and the regression coefficient for the logistic model. Finally, Figure 16 shows the normal and detrended normal plots of the residuals against their expected values produced by the NORMPROB default keyword. The plots show the characteristic S-curve shape associated with logistic regression.

Figure 13 Model design for Example 6

```
Correspondence Between Effects and Columns of Design/Model 1

    Starting  Ending
    Column    Column    Effect Name

       1         1      RESPONSE
       2         2      TIME(1) BY RESPONSE


- - - - - - - - - - - - - - - - - - - - - - - - - - - - - - - - - - - - - - -


Design Matrix

1-RESPONSE  2-TIME

Factor                               Parameter

   1   2              1         2

   1   1          1.00000    7.00000
   1   2          1.00000   14.00000
   1   3          1.00000   27.00000
   1   4          1.00000   51.00000
   2   1         -1.00000   -7.00000
   2   2         -1.00000  -14.00000
   2   3         -1.00000  -27.00000
   2   4         -1.00000  -51.00000
```

Figure 14 Model fit for Example 6

```
Observed, Expected Frequencies and Residuals

    Factor          Code      OBS. count & PCT.   EXP. count & PCT.   Residual   Std. Resid.   Adj. Resid.


RESPONSE    SUCCESS
   TIME                1       55.00 (100.0)       54.57 (99.22)       .4271      .0578         .7103
   TIME                2      155.00 (98.73)      154.87 (98.64)       .1322      .0106         .1226
   TIME                3      152.00 (95.60)      152.99 (96.22)      -.9867     -.0798        -.6085
   TIME                4       13.00 (81.25)       12.57 (78.58)       .4275      .1206         .6964

RESPONSE    FAILURE
   TIME                1         .00 (  .00)         .43 (  .78)      -.4271     -.6535        -.7103
   TIME                2        2.00 ( 1.27)        2.13 ( 1.36)      -.1322     -.0905        -.1226
   TIME                3        7.00 ( 4.40)        6.01 ( 3.78)       .9867      .4024         .6085
   TIME                4        3.00 (18.75)        3.43 (21.42)      -.4275     -.2309        -.6964


- - - - - - - - - - - - - - - - - - - - - - - - - - - - - - - - - - - - - - -


Goodness-of-Fit test statistics

    Likelihood Ratio Chi Square =    1.09592    DF = 2   P =  .578
              Pearson Chi Square =     .67485    DF = 2   P =  .714
```

Figure 15 Estimated parameters for Example 6

```
Estimates for Parameters
 RESPONSE

   Parameter        Coeff.         Std. Err.        Z-Value       Lower 95 CI      Upper 95 CI
       1         2.7075864999          .36377         7.44312         1.99460          3.42058
 TIME(1) BY RESPONSE

   Parameter        Coeff.         Std. Err.        Z-Value       Lower 95 CI      Upper 95 CI
       2        -.0403479334          .01118        -3.60955         -.06226          -.01844

- - - - - - - - - - - - - - - - - - - - - - - - - - - - - - - - - - - - - - - - - - - - - - - - - - -


 Covariance(below) and Correlation(above) Matrices of Parameter Estimates
 Parameter                                 Parameter

                     1          2

       1          .13233     -.91014
       2         -.00370      .00012
```

Figure 16 Plot of adjusted residuals for Example 6

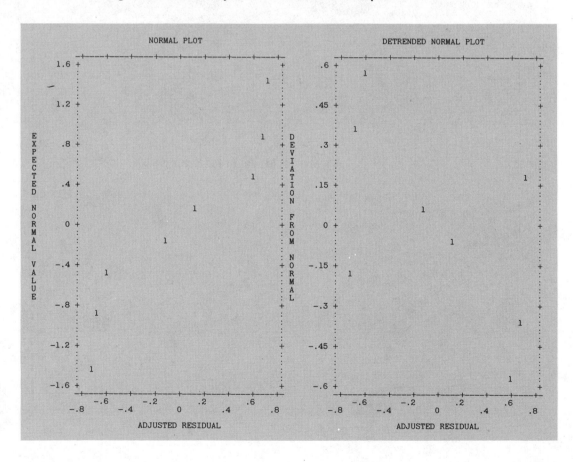

If the metric of the time measure is recorded on your data, you can specify the metric variable as a cell covariate and not specify the CONTRAST subcommand, as in:

```
DATA LIST LIST/RESPONSE TIME X WT.
IF (WT = 0) WT = .00001.
WEIGHT BY WT.
BEGIN DATA
1 1 7 55
2 1 7 0
1 2 14 155
2 2 14 2
1 3 27 152
2 3 27 7
1 4 51 13
2 4 51 3
END DATA.
LOGLINEAR RESPONSE (1,2) BY TIME(1,4) WITH X
  /PRINT=ALL/PLOT=DEFAULT
  /DESIGN=RESPONSE, X BY RESPONSE.
```

This approach can easily be extended to two or more independent variables with the metric values of the independent variables recorded in separate variables and specified as covariates on the LOGLINEAR variables specification and DESIGN subcommand.

Example 7: Multinomial Response Models

Example 7 illustrates the use of the CONTRAST subcommand and single-degree-of-freedom partitions to analyze a 4×6 crosstabulation table. The multinomial response models fit are generalizations of the logit model in the first example.

This example models the relationship between two variables— mental health status (MENTHLTH) by parental socioeconomic status (SES) (Haberman, 1979). MENTHLTH is scaled from 1 to 4 corresponding to Well and Impaired poles. SES is scaled from 1 to 6 corresponding to High and Low poles. The SPSS commands are

```
DATA LIST LIST /MENTHLTH SES WT.
VARIABLE LABELS MENTHLTH 'MENTAL HEALTH CATEGORY'
              SES 'PARENTAL SE STATUS'.
VALUE LABELS MENTHLTH 1 'WELL'  2 'MILD'  3 'MODERATE' 4 'IMPAIRED'
 /SES 1 'A--HIGH' 2 'B' 3 'C' 4 'D' 5 'E' 6 'F--LOW'.
WEIGHT BY WT.
BEGIN DATA
1 1  64 7
1 2  57 4
1 3  57 3
1 4  72 8
1 5  36 9
1 6  21 5
...
4 1  46 7
4 2  40 5
4 3  60 6
4 4  94 8
4 5  78 9
4 6  71 9

END DATA.

LOGLINEAR MENTHLTH(1,4) BY SES(1,6)
 /CONTRAST(MENTHLTH) = POLYNOMIAL
 /CONTRAST(SES) = POLYNOMIAL
 /PRINT = DEFAULT ESTIM
 /*MODEL 1:   THE MODEL OF COLUMN HOMOGENEITY
 /DESIGN=MENTHLTH
 /*MODEL 2:   THE SIMULTANEOUS LINEAR LOGIT MODEL
 /DESIGN = MENTHLTH, MENTHLTH BY SES(1)
 /*MODEL 3:   THE MODEL OF LINEAR BY LINEAR INTERACTION
 /DESIGN = MENTHLTH, MENTHLTH(1) BY SES(1)
 /*MODEL 4:   A MODEL FOR KNOWN ROW SCORES AND UNKNOWN COLUMN SCORES
 /DESIGN = MENTHLTH, MENTHLTH(1) BY SES.
```

- The BY keyword in the variables specification indicates a logit model.
- The CONTRAST subcommands specify polynomial contrasts for MENTHLTH and SES. The polynomial contrast is often useful in the analysis of polytomous variables.
- The PRINT subcommand requests the DEFAULT (keywords FREQ and RESID) and ESTIM to display output for all models.
- In Model 1, only the dependent variable appears on the DESIGN subcommand. This model is termed the model for column homogeneity because it fits the same expected cell percentage to all frequencies of a given column. Model 1 fits three parameters associated with the MENTHLTH effect and assumes no association between MENTHLTH and SES.
- Model 2 is termed the simultaneous linear logit model. It fits three parameters for the MENTHLTH effect, plus three parameters for the MENTHLTH by linear-SES interaction. That is, each dependent-variable logit is a linear function of the parents' socioeconomic score.
- Model 3 is the model of the linear-by-linear interaction. It fits four parameters—three for MENTHLTH and one for the linear-by-linear interaction of MENTHLTH and SES. Model 3 is the most parsimonious model accounting for association between MENTHLTH and SES.
- Model 4 is a model for known row scores and unknown column scores. Scores are given for the independent variable categories, but scores for the categories of the dependent variable are unknown. "Unknown" means that no scale for the dependent variable is assumed. The model fits three parameters for the MENTHLTH effect and five for the MENTHLTH-linear by SES interaction. Model 4 stands somewhat apart from Models 2 and 3 but appears here for the sake of completeness.

Figure 17 shows the Model 1 fit. The goodness-of-fit statistics show lack of fit of this model.

Figure 17 Model 1 fit for Example 7

```
Observed, Expected Frequencies and Residuals

       Factor          Code        OBS. count & PCT.    EXP. count & PCT.     Residual    Std. Resid.    Adj. Resid.

MENTHLTH      WELL
  SES         A--HIGH              64.00 (24.43)        48.45 (18.49)        15.5458       2.2333        2.6956
  SES         B                    57.00 (23.27)        45.31 (18.49)        11.6898       1.7366        2.0835
  SES         C                    57.00 (19.86)        53.08 (18.49)         3.9223        .5384         .6557
  SES         D                    72.00 (18.75)        71.02 (18.49)          .9831        .1167         .1474
  SES         E                    36.00 (13.58)        49.01 (18.49)       -13.0090      -1.8583       -2.2453
  SES         F--LOW               21.00 ( 9.68)        40.13 (18.49)       -19.1319      -3.0200       -3.5879

MENTHLTH      MILD
  SES         A--HIGH              94.00 (35.88)        95.01 (36.27)        -1.0145       -.1041        -.1421
  SES         B                    94.00 (38.37)        88.85 (36.27)         5.1506        .5464         .7413
  SES         C                   105.00 (36.59)       104.08 (36.27)         .9193        .0901         .1241
  SES         D                   141.00 (36.72)       139.26 (36.27)         1.7422        .1476         .2109
  SES         E                    97.00 (36.60)        96.10 (36.27)          .8976        .0916         .1251
  SES         F--LOW               71.00 (32.72)        78.70 (36.27)        -7.6952       -.8675       -1.1654

MENTHLTH      MODERATE
  SES         A--HIGH              58.00 (22.14)        57.13 (21.81)          .8651        .1144         .1410
  SES         B                    54.00 (22.04)        53.43 (21.81)          .5723        .0783         .0959
  SES         C                    65.00 (22.65)        62.59 (21.81)         2.4133        .3050         .3793
  SES         D                    77.00 (20.05)        83.74 (21.81)        -6.7398       -.7365        -.9500
  SES         E                    54.00 (20.38)        57.79 (21.81)        -3.7892       -.4984        -.6149
  SES         F--LOW               54.00 (24.88)        47.32 (21.81)         6.6783        .9708        1.1775

MENTHLTH      IMPAIRED
  SES         A--HIGH              46.00 (17.56)        61.40 (23.43)       -15.3964      -1.9649       -2.4470
  SES         B                    40.00 (16.33)        57.41 (23.43)       -17.4127      -2.2981       -2.8446
  SES         C                    60.00 (20.91)        67.25 (23.43)        -7.2548       -.8846       -1.1116
  SES         D                    94.00 (24.48)        89.99 (23.43)         4.0145        .4232         .5516
  SES         E                    78.00 (29.43)        62.10 (23.43)        15.9006       2.0178        2.5155
  SES         F--LOW               71.00 (32.72)        50.85 (23.43)        20.1488       2.8255        3.4634

- - - - - - - - - - - - - - - - - - - - - - - - - - - - - - - - - - - - - - - - - - - - - - - - - - - -

Goodness-of-Fit test statistics

     Likelihood Ratio Chi Square =   47.41785    DF = 15   P =  .000
               Pearson Chi Square =   45.98526    DF = 15   P =  .000
```

Figure 18 shows the Model 2 fit. The goodness-of-fit statistics indicate good fit, and the adjusted residuals are all less than 2 in magnitude.

Figure 18 Model 2 fit for Example 7

```
Observed, Expected Frequencies and Residuals
      Factor          Code         OBS. count & PCT.   EXP. count & PCT.    Residual   Std. Resid.   Adj. Resid.

MENTHLTH       WELL
   SES            A---HIGH          64.00 (24.43)       68.57 (26.17)       -4.5659       -.5514        -.9982
   SES            B                 57.00 (23.27)       55.68 (22.73)        1.3160        .1764         .2345
   SES            C                 57.00 (19.86)       56.11 (19.55)         .8943        .1194         .1475
   SES            D                 72.00 (18.75)       63.94 (16.65)        8.0551       1.0073        1.2970
   SES            E                 36.00 (13.58)       37.23 (14.05)       -1.2278       -.2012        -.2600
   SES            F---LOW           21.00 ( 9.68)       25.47 (11.74)       -4.4717       -.8860       -1.2001

MENTHLTH       MILD
   SES            A---HIGH          94.00 (35.88)       96.92 (36.99)       -2.9192       -.2965        -.5489
   SES            B                 94.00 (38.37)       91.00 (37.14)        2.9996        .3144         .4651
   SES            C                105.00 (36.59)      106.01 (36.94)       -1.0063       -.0977        -.1368
   SES            D                141.00 (36.72)      139.68 (36.38)        1.3176        .1115         .1625
   SES            E                 97.00 (36.60)       94.02 (35.48)        2.9814        .3075         .4584
   SES            F---LOW           71.00 (32.72)       74.37 (34.27)       -3.3731       -.3911        -.6501

MENTHLTH       MODERATE
   SES            A---HIGH          58.00 (22.14)       55.70 (21.26)        2.2967        .3077         .5053
   SES            B                 54.00 (22.04)       53.27 (21.74)         .7302        .1000         .1327
   SES            C                 65.00 (22.65)       63.20 (22.02)        1.7973        .2261         .2847
   SES            D                 77.00 (20.05)       84.82 (22.09)       -7.8228       -.8494       -1.1176
   SES            E                 54.00 (20.38)       58.15 (21.94)       -4.1502       -.5442        -.7379
   SES            F---LOW           54.00 (24.88)       46.85 (21.59)        7.1489       1.0444        1.5913

MENTHLTH       IMPAIRED
   SES            A---HIGH          46.00 (17.56)       40.81 (15.58)        5.1885        .8122        1.2173
   SES            B                 40.00 (16.33)       45.05 (18.39)       -5.0458       -.7518        -.9794
   SES            C                 60.00 (20.91)       61.69 (21.49)       -1.6853       -.2146        -.2711
   SES            D                 94.00 (24.48)       95.55 (24.88)       -1.5499       -.1586        -.2115
   SES            E                 78.00 (29.43)       75.60 (28.53)        2.3967        .2756         .3903
   SES            F---LOW           71.00 (32.72)       70.30 (32.40)         .6959        .0830         .1421


Goodness-of-Fit test statistics

      Likelihood Ratio Chi Square =    6.28076    DF = 12   P =  .901
             Pearson Chi Square =      6.28911    DF = 12   P =  .901
```

Figure 19 shows the Model 3 fit. Model 3 fits the data, and since Model 3 is simpler it is preferable to Model 2. Figure 20 shows the parameter estimates for Model 3.

Figure 19 Model 3 fit for Example 7

```
Observed, Expected Frequencies and Residuals

      Factor           Code          OBS. count & PCT.   EXP. count & PCT.   Residual   Std. Resid.   Adj. Resid.

  MENTHLTH          WELL
    SES             A---HIGH          64.00 (24.43)       65.29 (24.92)      -1.2908      -.1598        -.2304
    SES             B                 57.00 (23.27)       54.21 (22.13)       2.7865       .3784         .4850
    SES             C                 57.00 (19.86)       55.91 (19.48)       1.0917       .1460         .1802
    SES             D                 72.00 (18.75)       65.28 (17.00)       6.7234       .8322        1.0473
    SES             E                 36.00 (13.58)       38.96 (14.70)      -2.9616      -.4745        -.5793
    SES             F---LOW           21.00 ( 9.68)       27.35 (12.60)      -6.3491     -1.2141       -1.4999

  MENTHLTH          MILD
    SES             A---HIGH          94.00 (35.88)      104.42 (39.86)     -10.4234     -1.0200       -1.4673
    SES             B                 94.00 (38.37)       94.94 (38.75)       -.9375      -.0962        -.1350
    SES             C                105.00 (36.59)      107.20 (37.35)      -2.1991      -.2124        -.2967
    SES             D                141.00 (36.72)      137.04 (35.69)       3.9569       .3380         .4807
    SES             E                 97.00 (36.60)       89.56 (33.80)       7.4385       .7860        1.0640
    SES             F---LOW           71.00 (32.72)       68.84 (31.72)       2.1645       .2609         .3509

  MENTHLTH          MODERATE
    SES             A---HIGH          58.00 (22.14)       50.15 (19.14)       7.8546      1.1092        1.3647
    SES             B                 54.00 (22.04)       49.92 (20.37)       4.0821       .5778         .7022
    SES             C                 65.00 (22.65)       61.72 (21.50)       3.2845       .4181         .5185
    SES             D                 77.00 (20.05)       86.39 (22.50)      -9.3863     -1.0099       -1.3171
    SES             E                 54.00 (20.38)       61.81 (23.33)      -7.8150      -.9940       -1.2521
    SES             F---LOW           54.00 (24.88)       52.02 (23.97)       1.9801       .2745         .3421

  MENTHLTH          IMPAIRED
    SES             A---HIGH          46.00 (17.56)       42.14 (16.08)       3.8597       .5946         .8101
    SES             B                 40.00 (16.33)       45.93 (18.75)      -5.9312      -.8752       -1.0996
    SES             C                 60.00 (20.91)       62.18 (21.66)      -2.1771      -.2761        -.3454
    SES             D                 94.00 (24.48)       95.29 (24.82)      -1.2940      -.1326        -.1766
    SES             E                 78.00 (29.43)       74.66 (28.17)       3.3381       .3863         .5292
    SES             F---LOW           71.00 (32.72)       68.80 (31.70)       2.2045       .2658         .3994

- - - - - - - - - - - - - - - - - - - - - - - - - - - - - - - - - - - - - - - - - - - - - - - - - - - -

  Goodness-of-Fit test statistics

     Likelihood Ratio Chi Square =     9.89512     DF = 14   P =  .770
             Pearson Chi Square =     9.73185     DF = 14   P =  .782
```

Figure 20 Model 3 parameter estimates for Example 7

```
Estimates for Parameters

 MENTHLTH

 Parameter         Coeff.        Std. Err.      Z-Value      Lower 95 CI     Upper 95 CI

         1      .0492160727        .05392        .91272        -.05647          .15490
         2     -.3217618318        .05109      -6.29802        -.42190         -.22163
         3      .3941588489        .04777       8.25112         .30053          .48779

 MENTHLTH(1) BY SES(1)

 Parameter         Coeff.        Std. Err.      Z-Value      Lower 95 CI     Upper 95 CI

         4      .8482955490        .14037       6.04331         .57317         1.12342
```

Finally, Figure 21 shows the Model 4 fit.

Figure 21 Model 4 fit for Example 7

```
Observed, Expected Frequencies and Residuals

     Factor           Code          OBS. count & PCT.   EXP. count & PCT.    Residual    Std. Resid.   Adj. Resid.


  MENTHLTH         WELL
  SES              A--HIGH          64.00 (24.43)       60.15 (22.96)        3.8488        .4963         .8867
  SES              B                57.00 (23.27)       57.26 (23.37)        -.2596       -.0343        -.0613
  SES              C                57.00 (19.86)       56.43 (19.66)         .5650        .0752         .1285
  SES              D                72.00 (18.75)       69.86 (18.19)        2.1389        .2559         .4423
  SES              E                36.00 (13.58)       38.52 (14.53)       -2.5159       -.4054        -.6281
  SES              F--LOW           21.00 ( 9.68)       24.78 (11.42)       -3.7773       -.7588       -1.0953

  MENTHLTH         MILD
  SES              A--HIGH          94.00 (35.88)      102.54 (39.14)       -8.5431       -.8437       -1.2335
  SES              B                94.00 (38.37)       96.31 (39.31)       -2.3059       -.2350        -.3410
  SES              C               105.00 (36.59)      107.58 (37.48)       -2.5776       -.2485        -.3684
  SES              D               141.00 (36.72)      140.38 (36.56)        .6185        .0522         .0805
  SES              E                97.00 (36.60)       89.22 (33.67)        7.7829        .8240        1.2233
  SES              F--LOW           71.00 (32.72)       65.97 (30.40)        5.0252        .6187         .9149

  MENTHLTH         MODERATE
  SES              A--HIGH          58.00 (22.14)       52.46 (20.02)        5.5397        .7648         .9781
  SES              B                54.00 (22.04)       48.61 (19.84)        5.3907        .7732         .9837
  SES              C                65.00 (22.65)       61.54 (21.44)        3.4601        .4411         .5687
  SES              D                77.00 (20.05)       84.65 (22.05)       -7.6538       -.8319       -1.1133
  SES              E                54.00 (20.38)       62.02 (23.40)       -8.0181      -1.0181       -1.3021
  SES              F--LOW           54.00 (24.88)       52.72 (24.29)        1.2815        .1765         .2213

  MENTHLTH         IMPAIRED
  SES              A--HIGH          46.00 (17.56)       46.85 (17.88)        -.8454       -.1235        -.2297
  SES              B                40.00 (16.33)       42.83 (17.48)       -2.8251       -.4317        -.7925
  SES              C                60.00 (20.91)       61.45 (21.41)       -1.4475       -.1847        -.3692
  SES              D                94.00 (24.48)       89.10 (23.20)        4.8964        .5187        1.1104
  SES              E                78.00 (29.43)       75.25 (28.40)        2.7511        .3171         .7058
  SES              F--LOW           71.00 (32.72)       73.53 (33.88)       -2.5294       -.2950        -.7011

-  -  -  -  -  -  -  -  -  -  -  -  -  -  -  -  -  -  -  -  -  -  -  -  -  -  -  -  -  -  -  -  -  -  -  -


  Goodness-of-Fit test statistics

      Likelihood Ratio Chi Square =     6.82933     DF = 10   P =   .741
             Pearson Chi Square =     6.78143     DF = 10   P =   .746
```

Example 8: A Distance Model

Example 8 demonstrates the use of the CWEIGHT subcommand to impose zeros on the diagonal of a symmetric table and the use of a covariate to fit a model with a distance function. Distance models are used for ordered symmetric tables. Example 8 models the relationship between husband's education level (HUSED) and wife's education level (WIFED) (Haberman, 1979). HUSED and WIFED are ordinal variables with four levels. The original table has one empty cell. There is no woman with a graduate degree whose husband has less than a high-school education. To avoid degree-of-freedom problems, this cell is set to a small number in the table. The SPSS commands are

```
TITLE 'HABERMAN''S DISTANCE MODEL, PAGE 500'.
DATA LIST  LIST/ HUSED WIFED WT.
VARIABLE LABELS   HUSED 'HUSBAND''S EDUCATION'
                  WIFED 'WIFE''S EDUCATION'.
VALUE LABELS  HUSED WIFED 1 '< HS' 2 'HS OR JC'
   3 'COLLEGE' 4 'GRAD DEG'.
WEIGHT  BY WT.
COMPUTE  DISTANCE=ABS(HUSED - WIFED).
COMPUTE  CWT=1.
IF (HUSED EQ WIFED) CWT=0.
BEGIN DATA
1 1 259
1 2 123
1 3   2
1 4   0.1
2 1  82
2 2 370
2 3  30
2 4   7
3 1   5
3 2  59
3 3  34
3 4   4
4 1   2
4 2  41
4 3  29
4 4   8
END DATA.

LOGLINEAR  HUSED WIFED(1,4) WITH DISTANCE
  /CWEIGHT=CWT/PRINT DEF ESTIM
  /DESIGN=HUSED WIFED DISTANCE.
```

- The DATA LIST command defines HUSED, WIFED, and WT, which is the frequency count for each cell.
- The WEIGHT command weights the table to the original sample size.
- The first COMPUTE command computes the distance function, which is the absolute distance between husband's and wife's education.
- The second COMPUTE and the IF command create the variable CWT. CWT is set to 0 for the cases in the diagonal cells of the table and to 1 for all other cases.
- The variables specification on the LOGLINEAR command defines a general log-linear model with the distance function as a covariate.
- The CWEIGHT subcommand specifies the variable CWT, which imposes zeros on the diagonal.
- The DESIGN subcommand names the main effects and the covariate. Note that it is not a saturated model.

Figure 22 contains the fit and parameter estimates for the model.

Figure 22 Display for Example 8

```
Observed, Expected Frequencies and Residuals
      Factor          Code        OBS. count & PCT.    EXP. count & PCT.    Residual   Std. Resid.   Adj. Resid.

   HUSED           < HS
     WIFED           < HS             .00 (  .00)          .00 (  .00)      .0000        .0000         .0000
     WIFED           HS OR JC      123.00 (32.02)       121.97 (31.76)     1.0255        .0929         .7573
     WIFED           COLLEGE          2.00 (  .52)         2.71 (  .70)    -.7054       -.4289        -.5375
     WIFED           GRAD DEG          .10 (  .03)          .42 (  .11)    -.3201       -.4939        -.5183

   HUSED           HS OR JC
     WIFED           < HS            82.00 (21.35)        83.03 (21.62)    -1.0255      -.1125        -.7573
     WIFED           HS OR JC          .00 (  .00)          .00 (  .00)     .0000        .0000         .0000
     WIFED           COLLEGE         30.00 ( 7.81)        31.14 ( 8.11)    -1.1391      -.2041        -.6068
     WIFED           GRAD DEG         7.00 ( 1.82)         4.84 ( 1.26)     2.1646       .9844        1.4648

   HUSED           COLLEGE
     WIFED           < HS             5.00 ( 1.30)         3.47 (  .90)     1.5295       .8210        1.0818
     WIFED           HS OR JC        59.00 (15.36)        58.68 (15.28)     .3151        .0411         .1594
     WIFED           COLLEGE          .00 (  .00)          .00 (  .00)      .0000        .0000         .0000
     WIFED           GRAD DEG         4.00 ( 1.04)         5.84 ( 1.52)    -1.8445      -.7630        -1.2593

   HUSED           GRAD DEG
     WIFED           < HS             2.00 (  .52)         2.50 (  .65)     -.5040      -.3185        -.3863
     WIFED           HS OR JC        41.00 (10.67)        42.34 (11.02)    -1.3406      -.2060        -.7058
     WIFED           COLLEGE         29.00 ( 7.55)        27.16 ( 7.07)     1.8445       .3540        1.2593
     WIFED           GRAD DEG         .00 (  .00)          .00 (  .00)      .0000        .0000         .0000
```

```
Goodness-of-Fit test statistics

     Likelihood Ratio Chi Square =    2.99300    DF = 4   P =   .559
                 Pearson Chi Square =    2.98686    DF = 4   P =   .560
```

```
Estimates for Parameters

HUSED

Parameter        Coeff.       Std. Err.      Z-Value      Lower 95 CI    Upper 95 CI

      1       -.1633790844       .12325      -1.32561        -.40495        .07819
      2        .5976368139       .16018       3.73106         .28369        .91159
      3       -.8950079354       .12962      -6.90487       -1.14906       -.64095

WIFED

Parameter        Coeff.       Std. Err.      Z-Value      Lower 95 CI    Upper 95 CI

      4        .2489999000       .15437       1.61301        -.05366        .55156
      5       1.3946797275       .14979       9.31103        1.10110       1.68826
      6       -.7316830779       .15862      -4.61287       -1.04257       -.42079

DISTANCE

Parameter        Coeff.       Std. Err.      Z-Value      Lower 95 CI    Upper 95 CI

      7      -1.6821952195       .20332      -8.27375       -2.08070       -1.28369
```

MANOVA

MANOVA can be used to analyze many different types of designs. The following examples, although not exhaustive, demonstrate some of the more commonly used models. Most of these examples have been obtained from books and articles.

Example 1: Analysis of Covariance Designs

An analysis of covariance design is a specialized analysis of variance which allows you to parcel out the effect of a covariate. In this example, from Winer (1971), there is one factor, A, which represents three methods of training and one covariate, X, which is an aptitude test score. The dependent variable, Y, is the score on an achievement test administered after the training program. Thus, this design allows you to determine the effect of a factor (training method), on achievement, controlling for the effect of a covariate (aptitude). The SPSS commands are

```
COMMENT THE DATA COME FROM WINER'S STATISTICAL PRINCIPLES
 IN EXPERIMENTAL DESIGN, PAGE 776
     Y IS A DEPENDENT VARIABLE
     X IS A COVARIATE
     A IS A FACTOR.
DATA LIST / A 1 X Y 2-5.
BEGIN DATA
data lines
END DATA.
COMMENT I - THE FIRST MANOVA PORTION DOES A ONEWAY
  ANALYSIS OF VARIANCE.
MANOVA Y BY A(1,3)
 /DESIGN.
COMMENT II - THE SECOND MANOVA PORTION DOES A DEFAULT ANALYSIS
  OF COVARIANCE (NOTE:  THE DEFAULT ASSUMES HOMOGENEOUS SLOPES).
MANOVA Y BY A(1,3) WITH X
 /PMEANS
 /DESIGN
   /* III - THE THIRD MANOVA PORTION TESTS THE FACTOR BY COVARIATE
   /* INTERACTION TERM.  THIS TESTS WHETHER THE PARALLEL SLOPES
   /* ASSUMPTION IS WARRANTED
 /ANALYSIS=Y
 /DESIGN= X, A, A BY X
   /* IV - THE FOURTH MANOVA PORTION SHOWS HOW TO FIT SEPARATE
   /* SLOPES.  YOU WOULD DO THIS IF THE FACTOR BY COVARIATE
   /* INTERACTION TERM IS SIGNIFICANT
 /DESIGN= X WITHIN A, A.
```

- The DATA LIST command reads the three variables, A, X, and Y, from the data included in the command file.
- The first MANOVA command specifies a one-way analysis of variance using the default DESIGN subcommand.
- The second MANOVA command specifies the second through fourth models. The second model is a default analysis of covariance using the default DESIGN subcommand. The default analysis fits covariates, factors, and factor-by-factor interactions if you specify more than one factor, and assumes homogeneous slopes.
- The PMEANS subcommand displays predicted means for the second through fourth models.
- The third analysis shows how to test the assumption of homogeneous slopes. The ANALYSIS subcommand indicates the dependent variable. The DESIGN subcommand indicates effects, including the factor-by-covariate interaction.
- The fourth analysis shows how MANOVA can be used to analyze nested designs. The WITHIN keyword on the DESIGN subcommand fits separate regression models within each of the three groups of factor A.

Portions of the display output are shown in Figures 1 through 5.

- Figure 1 shows the default display for the first analysis. The display includes an analysis of variance table.
- Figure 2 shows the default display for the second analysis, which includes the covariate X. MANOVA displays the analysis of variance table and regression statistics associated with X.

- Figure 3 shows the table of actual and predicted means for the second analysis requested with the PMEANS subcommand. MANOVA displays the observed means, the adjusted means, which are adjusted for the covariate, and the estimated means, which are the cell means estimated with knowledge of A.

- Figure 4 shows the analysis of variance table for the third analysis. Since the A by X interaction is not significant (significance of F = 0.605), we do not reject the hypothesis of parallel slopes. That is, we can assume that the effect of change in the covariate X on the dependent variable Y is the same across all three levels of the factor A.

- Finally, Figure 5 shows the analysis of variance table for the fourth analysis. The X WITHIN A effect is the joint effect of the separate regressions. Since the third analysis shows the factor-by-covariate interaction to be nonsignificant, the second analysis is the preferred solution.

Figure 1 Results for first analysis

```
Tests of Significance for Y using UNIQUE sums of squares
Source of Variation            SS      DF        MS          F  Sig of F

WITHIN CELLS                26.86      18      1.49
A                           36.95       2     18.48      12.38      .000
```

Figure 2 Results for second analysis

```
Tests of Significance for Y using UNIQUE sums of squares
Source of Variation            SS      DF        MS          F  Sig of F

WITHIN CELLS                10.30      17       .61
REGRESSION                  16.56       1     16.56      27.32      .000
A                           16.93       2      8.47      13.97      .000

- - - - - - - - - - - - - - - - - - - - - - - - - - - - - - - - - - - - - - - -
Correlations between Covariates and Predicted Dependent Variable
          COVARIATE

VARIABLE        X

Y                    1.00000

- - - - - - - - - - - - - - - - - - - - - - - - - - - - - - - - - - - - - - - -
Averaged Squared Correlations between Covariates and Predicted Dependent Variable

VARIABLE        AVER. R-SQ

X                    1.00000
Regression analysis for WITHIN CELLS error term
---- Individual Univariate .9500 confidence intervals
Dependent variable .. Y

COVARIATE           B          Beta      Std. Err.      t-Value    Sig. of t    Lower -95%    CL- Upper

X           .7428571429   .7851199742      .14213      5.22671      .000         .44300      1.04272
```

Figure 3 Actual and predicted means for second analysis

```
Adjusted and Estimated Means
Variable .. Y
        Factor          Code         Obs. Mean    Adj. Mean    Est. Mean    Raw Resid.    Std. Resid.

        A                1            4.42857      4.88844      4.42857      .00000        .00000
        A                2            7.57143      7.07619      7.57143      .00000        .00000
        A                3            6.71429      6.74966      6.71429      .00000        .00000
```

Figure 4 Analysis of variance table for third analysis

```
Tests of Significance for Y using UNIQUE sums of squares
Source of Variation            SS      DF        MS          F  Sig of F

WITHIN+RESIDUAL              9.63      15       .64
X                           15.67       1     15.67      24.40      .000
A                            6.69       2      3.35       5.21      .019
A BY X                        .67       2       .33        .52      .605
```

Figure 5 Analysis of variance table for fourth analysis

```
Tests of Significance for Y using UNIQUE sums of squares
Source of Variation       SS       DF       MS          F   Sig of F

WITHIN+RESIDUAL          9.63      15      .64
X WITHIN A             17.22       3     5.74        8.94     .001
A                       6.69       2     3.35        5.21     .019
```

Example 2: Multivariate One-Way ANOVA

A multivariate one-way analysis of variance with one three-level factor and four dependent variables was performed. In addition to the standard test for the difference in means, you can obtain a canonical discriminant analysis. When analyzing data structures of this type, you can consider turning the problem around and using the DISCRIMINANT procedure.

The data are the iris data from Fisher (1936). Fisher collected four measures on each of three species of irises. The four measures are the four dependent variables and the species is the factor variable. There are 50 observations in each species group. The SPSS commands are

```
TITLE 'IRISDATA - TO DO ANYTHING WITH FISHER'S IRIS DATA'.
COMMENT FISHER'S IRIS DATA IS THE CLASSICAL DISCRIMINANT
 ANALYSIS EXAMPLE.  WE WILL USE IT TO ILLUSTRATE
 MULTIVARIATE ONEWAY ANALYSIS OF VARIANCE.
DATA LIST / SEPALLEN 1-2 SEPALWID PETALLEN PETALWID 3-11 TYPE 12-13.
VARIABLE LABELS SEPALLEN 'SEPAL LENGTH'
   SEPALWID 'SEPAL WIDTH'
   PETALLEN 'PETAL LENGTH'
   PETALWID 'PETAL WIDTH'
   TYPE 'TYPE OF IRIS'.
VALUE LABELS TYPE 1 'SETOSA' 2 'VERSICOLOR' 3 'VIRGINICA'.
BEGIN DATA
data lines
END DATA.
MANOVA SEPALLEN SEPALWID PETALLEN PETALWID BY TYPE(1,3)
 /PRINT=SIGNIF(EIGEN)
      CELLINFO(MEANS)
      HOMOGENEITY(BOXM)
      ERROR(COR)
 /DISCRIM(RAW STAN ESTIM COR)
 /DESIGN.
```

- The TITLE command prints a title on each page of the display output, and the COMMENT command inserts comments that print back with the commands on the display.

- The DATA LIST command reads five variables—SEPALLEN, SEPALWID, PETALLEN, PETALWID, and TYPE—from the data in the command file.

- The VARIABLE LABELS and VALUE LABELS commands assign labels that are printed on the display output.

- The MANOVA specification lists four dependent variables (SEPALLEN, SEPALWID, PETALLEN, PETALWID) and one factor (TYPE) with three levels.

- The PRINT subcommand requests several types of displays.

- SIGNIF(EIGEN) displays the eigenvalues and canonical correlations.

- CELLINFO(MEANS) displays the group means for each of the dependent variables (see Figure 6).

- HOMOGENEITY(BOXM) displays Box's M statistic, which is a multivariate test for homogeneity of variance (see Figure 7).

- ERROR(COR) displays the error correlation matrix, the standard deviations of the dependent variables, and Bartlett's test of sphericity (see Figure 8).

- The DISCRIM subcommand requests a canonical discriminant analysis relating the four dependent variables to the TYPE factor. RAW displays discriminant function coefficients, STAN displays standardized discriminant function coefficients, ESTIM displays effect estimates in discriminant function space, and COR displays correlations between the dependent variables and the canonical variables defined by the discriminant functions (see Figure 10).

Figures 6 through 10 show portions of the display.

- Figure 6 shows the cell means and standard deviations displayed with CELL-INFO(MEANS). There are large differences in both means and standard deviations for the four dependent variables by the type of iris.
- Figure 7 shows the tests for homogeneity-of-dispersion matrices displayed with HOMOGENEITY(BOXM). Both the F approximation and the chi-square approximation indicate rejection of the hypothesis of homogeneity.
- Figure 8 shows the results of specifying ERROR(COR). The within-cells correlations are the pooled within-groups correlations between the four dependent variables; that is, differences in TYPE are taken into account. MANOVA displays the standard deviations of the four variables on the diagonal. The Bartlett test of sphericity tests whether the within-cells correlation matrix is the identity matrix. Given the low significance level, this assumption is rejected. The F_{max} statistic tests whether the four within-cells variances are equal. A table for the F_{max} distribution is found in Winer (1971).
- Figure 9 shows the default display of multivariate significance for the hypothesis that all group means are equal. All test statistics, Pillais, Hotellings, Wilks, and Roys, indicate rejection of the hypothesis. The S, M, and N in the top righthand corner of the multivariate results are degrees of freedom measures. For more information about these measures, see *SPSS Update 7-9*. The Eigenvalues and Canonical Correlations display shows that the canonical discriminant analysis has two dimensions. This follows the standard criterion, which takes the lesser of the number of dependent variables and number of groups minus one as the maximum dimensionality of a problem. The first of the two dimensions, with an eigenvalue of 32.19, is overwhelmingly predominant. The figure also shows the univariate tests of significance.
- Figure 10 shows the results of specifying the DISCRIM subcommand. The correlations between dependent and canonical variables show that the first function is primarily the petal measures, whereas the second function is primarily the width measures.

Figure 6 Cell statistics

```
              CELL NUMBER
              1    2    3
Variable
  TYPE        1    2    3

Cell Means and Standard Deviations
Variable .. SEPALLEN     SEPAL LENGTH
    FACTOR         CODE          Mean   Std. Dev.      N    95 percent Conf. Interval

  TYPE           SETOSA          50.060    3.525        50     49.058    51.062
  TYPE           VERSICOL        59.360    5.162        50     57.893    60.827
  TYPE           VIRGINIC        65.880    6.359        50     64.073    67.687
For entire sample                58.433    8.281       150     57.097    59.769

Variable .. SEPALWID     SEPAL WIDTH
    FACTOR         CODE          Mean   Std. Dev.      N    95 percent Conf. Interval

  TYPE           SETOSA          34.280    3.791        50     33.203    35.357
  TYPE           VERSICOL        27.700    3.138        50     26.808    28.592
  TYPE           VIRGINIC        29.740    3.225        50     28.823    30.657
For entire sample                30.573    4.359       150     29.870    31.277

Variable .. PETALLEN     PETAL LENGTH
    FACTOR         CODE          Mean   Std. Dev.      N    95 percent Conf. Interval

  TYPE           SETOSA          14.620    1.737        50     14.126    15.114
  TYPE           VERSICOL        42.600    4.699        50     41.265    43.935
  TYPE           VIRGINIC        55.520    5.519        50     53.952    57.088
For entire sample                37.580   17.653       150     34.732    40.428

Variable .. PETALWID     PETAL WIDTH
    FACTOR         CODE          Mean   Std. Dev.      N    95 percent Conf. Interval

  TYPE           SETOSA           2.460    1.054        50      2.160     2.760
  TYPE           VERSICOL        13.260    1.978        50     12.698    13.822
  TYPE           VIRGINIC        20.260    2.747        50     19.479    21.041
For entire sample                11.993    7.622       150     10.764    13.223
```

Figure 7 Tests for homogeneity-of-dispersion matrices

```
-------------------------------------------------------------------------

Multivariate test for Homogeneity of Dispersion matrices


Boxs M =                        146.66325
F WITH (20,77566) DF =            7.04526, P =   .000 (Approx.)
Chi-Square with 20 DF =         140.94305, P =   .000 (Approx.)
```

Figure 8 Within-cells correlations results

```
WITHIN CELLS Correlations with Std. Devs. on Diagonal

                    SEPALLEN        SEPALWID        PETALLEN        PETALWID

SEPALLEN             5.14789
SEPALWID              .53024         3.39688
PETALLEN              .75616          .37792         4.30334
PETALWID              .36451          .47053          .48446         2.04650


Statistics for WITHIN CELLS correlations

Log(Determinant) =                      -1.61179
Bartlett test of sphericity = 233.44151 with 6 D. F.
Significance =                           .000

F(max) criterion =                      6.32755 with (4,147) D. F.
```

Figure 9 Multivariate, canonical, and univariate test results

```
EFFECT .. TYPE
  Multivariate Tests of Significance (S = 2, M = 1/2, N = 71 )

  Test Name            Value        Approx. F      Hypoth. DF       Error DF       Sig. of F

  Pillais            1.19190        53.46649           8.00          290.00          .000
  Hotellings        32.47732       580.53210           8.00          286.00          .000
  Wilks               .02344       199.14534           8.00          288.00          .000
  Roys                .96987
  Note.. F statistic for WILK'S Lambda is exact.

  --------------------------------------------------------------------------------
  Eigenvalues and Canonical Correlations

  Root No.      Eigenvalue         Pct.       Cum. Pct.      Canon Cor.

       1         32.19193       99.12126       99.12126        .98482
       2           .28539         .87874      100.00000        .47120

  --------------------------------------------------------------------------------
  EFFECT .. TYPE (CONT.)
  Univariate F-tests with (2,147) D. F.

  Variable      Hypoth. SS         Error SS      Hypoth. MS       Error MS               F       Sig. of F

  SEPALLEN     6321.21333       3895.62000     3160.60667       26.50082       119.26450          .000
  SEPALWID     1134.49333       1696.20000      567.24667       11.53878        49.16004          .000
  PETALLEN    43710.28000       2722.26000    21855.14000       18.51878      1180.16118          .000
  PETALWID     8041.33333        615.66000     4020.66667        4.18816       960.00715          .000
```

Figure 10 Canonical discriminant results

```
-------------------------------------------------------------------------
Correlations between DEPENDENT and canonical variables
          Canonical Variable

Variable             1               2

SEPALLEN         -.22260         -.31081
SEPALWID          .11901         -.86368
PETALLEN         -.70607         -.16770
PETALWID         -.63318         -.73724
```

Example 3: Multivariate Multiple Regression, Canonical Correlation

MANOVA can be used to do both multivariate multiple regression and canonical correlation analyses. Multivariate multiple regression is a procedure which allows you to predict values of one set of variables given the values of another set of variables. Canonical correlation is a similar procedure which analyzes the relationship between two sets of variables. MANOVA produces multivariate results, individual regression results, and analysis of residuals although residual analysis is not as extensive in MANOVA as in REGRESSION. Since there is no canonical correlation procedure in SPSS, use MANOVA to do canonical correlation analysis.

The data for this example come from Finn (1974). The data were obtained from tests administered to 60 eleventh-grade students in a western New York metropolitan school. There are two dependent variables—synthesis and evaluation—which measure achievement. The independent variables are of three types. First, there is *general intelligence*, as measured by a standard test. Second, there are three measures of creativity. *Consequences obvious* "involves the ability of the subject to list direct consequences of a given hypothetical event." *Consequences remote* "involves identifying more remote or original consequences of similar situations." *Possible jobs* "involves the ability to list a quantity of occupations that might be represented by a given emblem or symbol" (p. 11). Third, in his analysis, Finn uses multiplicative interactions of the three creativity measures with intelligence to assess whether creativity has a greater effect on the achievement of individuals having high intelligence than on individuals of low intelligence. Finn uses standard scores for the independent variables. The SPSS commands are

```
TITLE 'FINN'S MULTIVARIATE MULTIPLE REGRESSION'.
DATA LIST  / SYNTH 1 EVAL 3 CONOBV 5-8(1) CONRMT 9-12(1)
 JOB 14-17(1) INTEL 19-23(1).
MISSING VALUES SYNTH TO INTEL(9.9).
BEGIN DATA
data lines
END DATA.
DESCRIPTIVES INTEL CONOBV CONRMT JOB
 /MISSING=LISTWISE
 /SAVE.
COMMENT USE COMPUTE TO CREATE INTERACTION TERMS.
COMPUTE CI1=ZCONOBV*ZINTEL.
COMPUTE CI2=ZCONRMT*ZINTEL.
COMPUTE CI3=ZJOB*ZINTEL.
MANOVA  SYNTH EVAL WITH ZINTEL ZCONOBV ZCONRMT ZJOB CI1 CI2 CI3
 /PRINT=
   ERROR(SSCP COV COR)
   SIGNIF(HYPOTH STEPDOWN EIGEN)
 /DISCRIM(RAW,STAN,ESTIM,COR,ALPHA(1.0))
 /RESIDUALS=PLOT
 /DESIGN.
```

- The TITLE command prints a title at the top of each page of the display output.
- The DATA LIST command defines six variables. SYNTH and EVAL are the dependent variables, and CONOBV, CONRMT, JOB, and INTEL are the independent variables.
- The SAVE subcommand on the DESCRIPTIVES procedure computes standardized scores for the intelligence and creativity measures. The new variables—ZINTEL, ZCONOBV, ZCONRMT, and ZJOB—are automatically added to the active system file. The MISSING subcommand on DESCRIPTIVES specifies listwise deletion of missing values for the calculation.
- The COMPUTE commands compute three interaction variables—CI1, CI2, and CI3—from the standardized variables created with DESCRIPTIVES.
- The MANOVA specification names SYNTH and EVAL as joint dependent variables and specifies seven covariates—ZINTEL, ZCONOBV, ZCONRMT, ZJOB, CI1, CI2, and CI3.
- The PRINT subcommand requests several displays. The ERROR keyword prints the error sums-of-squares and cross-products matrix, the error variance-covariance matrix, and the error correlation matrix with standard deviations on the diagonal (see Figure 11).

- The SIGNIF keyword has three specifications. HYPOTH displays the hypothesis sums-of-squares and cross-products matrices (see Figure 11). STEPDOWN displays the Roy-Bargmann step-down F tests for the dependent variables (see Figure 12). EIGEN displays the eigenvalues and canonical correlations (see Figure 12).

- The DISCRIM subcommand requests a canonical analysis. The results correspond to canonical correlation analysis since a set of continuous dependent variables is related to a set of continuous independent variables. The RAW keyword displays canonical function coefficients; the STAN keyword displays standardized canonical function coefficients; the ESTIM function produces effect estimates in canonical function space; the COR keyword displays correlations between the original variables and the canonical variables defined by the canonical functions; the ALPHA keyword, which specifies 1, sets a cutoff value of the canonical functions in the analysis to 1. Thus, the discriminant analysis will be displayed regardless of the significance of each effect. The maximum possible number of canonical functions in this analysis is two (see Figures 13 and 14).

- The RESIDUALS subcommand produces plots of the observed and predicted values and case number against standardized residuals and normal and detrended normal probability plots for the standardized residuals (see Figures 16 through 18).

Portions of the output are shown in Figures 11 through 18.

- Figure 11 shows within-cells statistical results. The correlation of 0.37978 is the partial correlation of SYNTH and EVAL, taking into account the independent variable set. The two standard deviations, 1.37049 and 1.51256 are located on the diagonal and are adjusted. Figure 11 also shows the adjusted variance-covariance matrix, the error SSCP matrix, and the hypothesis SSCP matrix for the regression effect.

- Figure 12 shows the default display and the step-down display. Both the multivariate and univariate test results indicate that the predictor set has statistically significant impact on the dependent variables. While two dimensions are fit, it appears that one dimension will suffice. Of the two eigenvalues, the first eigenvalue has most of the variance associated with it, while the second eigenvalue has relatively little variability associated with it. Likewise, the first canonical correlation is moderately sized, while the second canonical correlation is negligible in magnitude. Provided that you accept the ordering of the criterion variables—SYNTH, then EVAL—the step-down F tests show that after taking SYNTH into account EVAL does not contribute to the association with the predictors.

- Figure 13 shows canonical results for the two dependent variables. Recall that only the first canonical function is statistically significant. Correlations between the dependent variables and the first canonical variable are of similar magnitude. The part of the figure labeled **VARIANCE EXPLAINED BY CANONICAL VARIABLES OF DEPENDENT VARIABLES** provides a *redundancy analysis* (Cooley & Lohnes, 1971).

- Figure 14 shows the analogous canonical results for the covariates. The correlations between covariates and the first canonical variable load most heavily on intelligence (ZINTELL).

- Figure 15 shows the default display of the regression results for the two dependent variables.

- Figure 16 shows two plots. The plot of the observed versus predicted values for SYNTH reflects the multiple R for the model. The plot of the observed values versus the residuals shows the way in which residuals vary in sign and magnitude across values of the dependent variable.

- Figure 17 shows two plots: the plot of the residuals versus the predicted values and the plot of case number versus residuals. The latter plot is useful when there is some meaning to the order of cases in your file.

- Finally, Figure 18 shows the normal plot of the residuals and the detrended normal plot of the residuals.

Figure 11 Within-cells results and hypothesis SSCP

```
Adjusted WITHIN CELLS Correlations with Std. Devs. on Diagonal

                 SYNTH            EVAL

SYNTH           1.37049
EVAL             .37978          1.51256

- - - - - - - - - - - - - - - - - - - - - - - - - - - - - - - - - - - - - - - -

Statistics for ADJUSTED WITHIN CELLS correlations

Log(Determinant) =                  -.15575
Bartlett test of sphericity =       7.86554 with 1 D. F.
Significance =                       .005

F(max) criterion =                  1.21806 with (2,52) D. F.

- - - - - - - - - - - - - - - - - - - - - - - - - - - - - - - - - - - - - - - -

Adjusted WITHIN CELLS Variances and Covariances

                 SYNTH            EVAL

SYNTH           1.87825
EVAL             .78726          2.28783

- - - - - - - - - - - - - - - - - - - - - - - - - - - - - - - - - - - - - - - -

Adjusted WITHIN CELLS Sum-of-Squares and Cross-Products

                 SYNTH            EVAL

SYNTH          97.66914
EVAL           40.93736        118.96726

- - - - - - - - - - - - - - - - - - - - - - - - - - - - - - - - - - - - - - - -

Adjusted Hypothesis Sum-of-Squares and Cross-Products

                 SYNTH            EVAL

SYNTH          81.18086
EVAL           69.41264         67.21607
```

Figure 12 Test results and dimensionality statistics

```
- - - - - - - - - - - - - - - - - - - - - - - - - - - - - - - - - - - - - - - -
Multivariate Tests of Significance (S = 2, M = 2 , N = 24 1/2)

Test Name          Value       Approx. F      Hypoth. DF      Error DF      Sig. of F

Pillais            .55946       2.88501          14.00          104.00        .001
Hotellings        1.05995       3.78553          14.00          100.00        .000
Wilks              .47077       3.33286          14.00          102.00        .000
Roys               .49886
Note.. F statistic for WILK'S Lambda is exact.

- - - - - - - - - - - - - - - - - - - - - - - - - - - - - - - - - - - - - - - -
Eigenvalues and Canonical Correlations

Root No.      Eigenvalue        Pct.        Cum. Pct.     Canon Cor.     Sq. Cor

   1            .99544        93.91374      93.91374        .70630        .49886
   2            .06451         6.08626     100.00000        .24617        .06060

- - - - - - - - - - - - - - - - - - - - - - - - - - - - - - - - - - - - - - - -
EFFECT .. WITHIN CELLS Regression (CONT.)

Univariate F-tests with (7,52) D. F.

Variable    Sq. Mul. R     Mul. R     Adj. R-sq.    Hypoth. MS     Error MS          F      Sig. of F

SYNTH         .45390       .67372       .38039       11.59727      1.87825      6.17450       .000
EVAL          .36102       .60085       .27500        9.60230      2.28783      4.19712       .001

- - - - - - - - - - - - - - - - - - - - - - - - - - - - - - - - - - - - - - - -
Roy-Bargman Stepdown F - tests

Variable    Hypoth. MS     Error MS     StepDown F     Hypoth. DF     Error DF     Sig. of F

SYNTH        11.59727      1.87825       6.17450           7            52          .000
EVAL          2.32700      1.99625       1.16569           7            51          .339
```

Figure 13 Canonical results for dependent variables

```
Raw canonical coefficients for DEPENDENT variables
        Function No.

Variable                    1                   2

SYNTH                    .40444            -.59708
EVAL                     .22637             .66958
- - - - - - - - - - - - - - - - - - - - - - - - - - - - - - - - - - - - - - - - - - - - - - - - - -
Standardized canonical coefficients for DEPENDENT variables
        Function No.

Variable                    1                   2

SYNTH                    .70415           -1.03956
EVAL                     .40212            1.18946
- - - - - - - - - - - - - - - - - - - - - - - - - - - - - - - - - - - - - - - - - - - - - - - - - -
Correlations between DEPENDENT and canonical variables
        Function No.

Variable                    1                   2

SYNTH                    .94733            -.32027
EVAL                     .82794             .56081
- - - - - - - - - - - - - - - - - - - - - - - - - - - - - - - - - - - - - - - - - - - - - - - - - -
Variance explained by canonical variables of DEPENDENT variables

CAN. VAR.     Pct Var DEP     Cum Pct DEP     Pct Var COV     Cum Pct COV

    1           79.14597        79.14597        39.48249        39.48249
    2           20.85403       100.00000         1.26379        40.74628
```

Figure 14 Canonical results for the covariates

```
Raw canonical coefficients for COVARIATES
        Function No.

COVARIATE                   1                   2

ZINTEL                   .84825            -.10334
ZCONOBV                  .26535             .22951
ZCONRMT                  .19301             .47229
ZJOB                    -.06403            -.27927
CI1                     -.01367            1.03503
CI2                     -.07571            -.32373
CI3                      .20707            -.04665
- - - - - - - - - - - - - - - - - - - - - - - - - - - - - - - - - - - - - - - - - - - - - - - - - -
Standardized canonical coefficients for COVARIATES
        CAN. VAR.

COVARIATE                   1                   2

ZINTEL                   .84825            -.10334
ZCONOBV                  .26535             .22951
ZCONRMT                  .19301             .47229
ZJOB                    -.06403            -.27927
CI1                     -.01172             .88718
CI2                     -.10086            -.43125
CI3                      .21699            -.04889
- - - - - - - - - - - - - - - - - - - - - - - - - - - - - - - - - - - - - - - - - - - - - - - - - -
Correlations between COVARIATES and canonical variables
        CAN. VAR.

Covariate                   1                   2

ZINTEL                   .94646            -.09081
ZCONOBV                  .30260            -.06104
ZCONRMT                  .56188             .41804
ZJOB                     .57787            -.12674
CI1                      .17980             .86843
CI2                      .49440            -.01020
CI3                      .44879             .06254
- - - - - - - - - - - - - - - - - - - - - - - - - - - - - - - - - - - - - - - - - - - - - - - - - -
Variance explained by canonical variables of the COVARIATES

CAN. VAR.     Pct Var DEP     Cum Pct DEP     Pct Var COV     Cum Pct COV

    1           15.07395        15.07395        30.21700        30.21700
    2            .83195         15.90590        13.72818        43.94518
```

Figure 15 Regression results

```
Regression analysis for WITHIN CELLS error term
--- Individual Univariate .9500 confidence intervals
Dependent variable .. SYNTH

COVARIATE          B            Beta        Std. Err.    t-Value    Sig. of t    Lower -95%    CL- Upper

ZINTEL      1.0023512430    .5757069427     .21712     4.61656      .000        .56667       1.43804
ZCONOBV      .2776146958    .1594498026     .23559     1.17836      .244       -.19514        .75037
ZCONRMT      .1600206225    .0919088832     .23801      .67232      .504       -.31759        .63763
ZJOB        -.0362511873   -.0208211047     .26665     -.13595      .892       -.57132        .49882
CI1         -.1579989581   -.0777852272     .23587     -.66986      .506       -.63130        .31530
CI2         -.0437613943   -.0334827218     .21472     -.20380      .839       -.47463        .38711
CI3          .2476316265    .1490442859     .25225      .98169      .331       -.25855        .75381
- - - - - - - - - - - - - - - - - - - - - - - - - - - - -,- - - - - - - - - - - - - - - - - - - - - -
Regression analysis for WITHIN CELLS error term  (CONT.)
Dependent variable .. EVAL
COVARIATE          B            Beta        Std. Err.    t-Value    Sig. of t    Lower -95%    CL- Upper

ZINTEL       .8558201889    .4817682025     .23963     3.57146      .001        .37497       1.33667
ZCONOBV      .3319337197    .1868559699     .26002     1.27659      .207       -.18982        .85369
ZCONRMT      .3163316155    .1780730529     .26269     1.20422      .234       -.21079        .84345
ZJOB        -.1350002789   -.0759959190     .29429     -.45873      .648       -.72554        .45554
CI1          .2396401468    .1156316040     .26032      .92057      .362       -.28273        .76201
CI2         -.1580420000   -.1185157835     .23698     -.66690      .508       -.63358        .31749
CI3          .2036655892    .1201436854     .27840      .73156      .468       -.35498        .76231
```

Figure 16 Observed values vs. predicted values and residuals

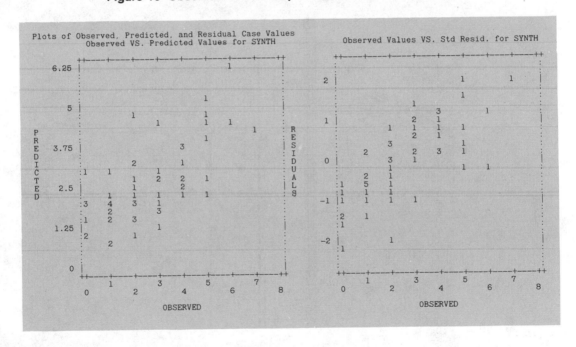

Figure 17 Residuals vs. predicted values and order

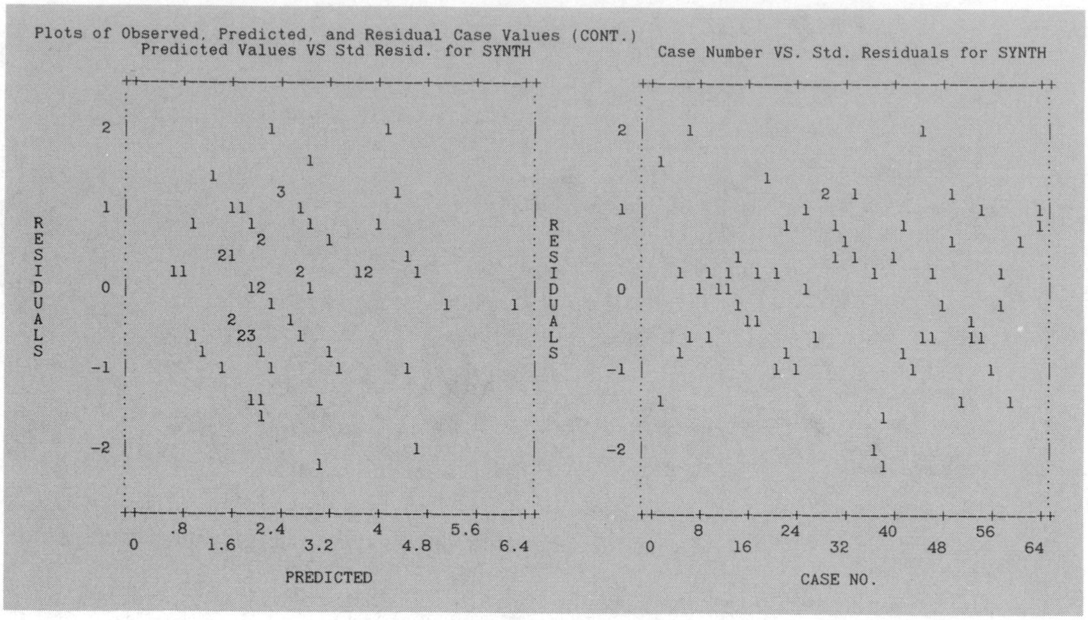

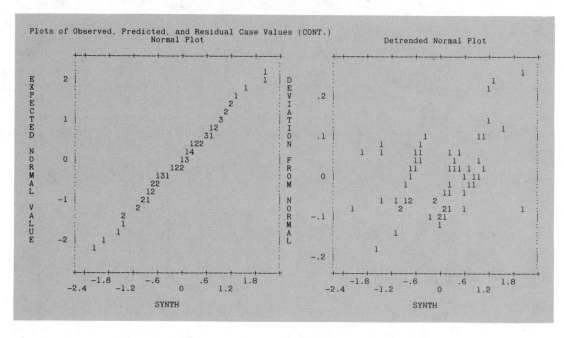

Figure 18 Normal plot and detrended normal plot

Example 4: Basic Repeated Measures

The following is a basic repeated measures example.

MANOVA provides extensive facilities for repeated measures analysis. This example is, to a great degree, a simple generalization of the paired t-test situation. Instead of measurements on two occasions, however, there are measurements on four occasions. The same subjects are measured on each occasion, so a simple one-way analysis of variance is inappropriate. This analysis takes advantage of the *multivariate setup*, in which all of a subject's scores across occasions reside in the same SPSS case. That is, the data have the following structure:

Case	Subject	Score 1	Score 2	Score 3	Score 4
1	1	30	28	16	34
2	2	14	18	10	22

This is in contrast to the *univariate setup*, in which a subject's scores across occasions spill down the cases, as in

Case	Subject	Score
1	1	30
2	1	28
3	1	16
4	1	34
5	2	14
6	2	18
7	2	10
8	2	22

On balance, we recommend the multivariate setup because the univariate setup has certain drawbacks. First, the univariate setup forces you to spread your data over many more cases, and you pay for processing time by the case. Second, analysis of the univariate setup implies that you are using a mixed-model analysis of variance approach to the data. That is, *subject* is a random effect nested under between-subjects factors, when the latter are present. In this approach, certain *symmetry conditions* must be met (Huynh & Mandevill,1979), and in practice these conditions are quite restrictive. Third, specification of the DESIGN subcommand in the univariate mixed model can be very complicated. Fourth, the univariate setup is computationally inefficient, in the sense that it can take much more memory and processing time than the equivalent multivariate setup. Fifth, in most cases, the univariate results are fully retrievable from a MANOVA command that uses the multivariate setup.

You should note that while all repeated measures examples shown in this document use the multivariate setup for the data, you will see references to statistics produced using the multivariate approach and statistics produced using the univariate approach. The latter set of statistics are produced using a multivariate setup, but they are the same statistics that MANOVA would produce if the univariate approach had been used. These univariate statistics are displayed by default and are labeled **AVERAGED TESTS OF SIGNIFICANCE**.

There are a few situations where you might turn to the univariate setup. When assumptions are met, the univariate approach has greater power. Under certain data configurations, the univariate mixed model makes fuller use of the data, such as in the following situations: too small a number of subjects in the model, too many empty cells in the repeated measures model, or the imposition of certain designs on the repeated measures, such as latin square order.

The data used for this example is an experiment which studies the effects of four drugs upon reaction time to a series of tasks (Winer, 1971). The subjects are trained in the tasks prior to the experiment, so that the learning of the tasks does not confound the analysis. There are five subjects in the analysis. The experimenter observes each subject under each drug, and the order of administration of drugs is randomized. The SPSS commands are

```
TITLE  'A BASIC REPEATED MEASURES EXAMPLE'.
COMMENT THE DATA REPRESENT 4 MEASURES ON 5 INDIVIDUALS
   THIS IS A SIMPLE REPEATED MEASURES DESIGN
   THE DATA COME FROM WINER, PAGE 268.
DATA LIST / DRUG1 DRUG2 DRUG3 DRUG4 (4F3.0).
BEGIN DATA
  30 28 16 34
  14 18 10 22
  24 20 18 30
  38 34 20 44
  26 28 14 30
END DATA.
MANOVA DRUG1 TO DRUG4
/WSFACTORS=TRIAL(4)
/CONTRAST(TRIAL)=SPECIAL(4*1, 1,-1,0,0,
                        1,1,0,-2, 1,1,-3,1)
/WSDESIGN=TRIAL
/PRINT=CELLINFO(MEANS)
  TRANSFORM
  ERROR(COR)
  SIGNIF(UNIV)
/DESIGN.
```

- The TITLE command prints a title at the top of each page of display output, and the COMMENT command inserts comments that print back with the commands on the display.

- The DATA LIST command defines four variables from the data in the command file.

- The MANOVA specification names DRUG1 to DRUG4 as four joint dependent variables. There are no between-subjects factors or covariates in the analysis.

- The WSFACTORS subcommand defines TRIAL as a within-subjects factor. A *4* is placed in parentheses after the factor name since there are four drugs. MANOVA builds the indicated orthonormal transformation matrix and uses this matrix to transform the original response variables. MANOVA then cycles through the within-subjects effects defined by the WSDESIGN subcommand and represented by sets of the transformed variables.

- The CONTRAST subcommand specifies a special set of contrasts for comparisons of the means across scores. The within-subjects factor requires *orthogonal* contrasts, so you could specify difference, helmert, or polynomial contrasts. The example uses SPECIAL, supplying contrasts among the means. If you do not specify orthogonal contrasts for the within-subjects factor, MANOVA takes your specified contrasts and orthonormalizes them. The first row of the special matrix is always the contrast for the overall mean and is typically a set of 1s. The remaining rows of the matrix contain the special contrasts signifying the desired comparisons between levels of the factor. From an inspection of the four means, we decide on the following comparisons: (1) the mean of DRUG1 versus the mean of DRUG2; (2) the means of DRUG1 and DRUG2 versus the mean of DRUG4; and (3) the means of DRUG1, DRUG2, and DRUG4 versus DRUG3.

- The WSDESIGN subcommand specifies TRIAL, the one within-subjects factor.

- The PRINT subcommand has four specifications. CELLINFO displays the means (see Figure 19). TRANSFORM displays the orthonormalized transformation matrix, which directly reflects the contrasts on the within-subjects factor (see Figure 20). ERROR(COR) displays the error correlation matrix along with some ancillary statistics. Assessment of the statistics tells whether or not it is appropriate to work with the univariate approach statistics (see Figure 24). SIGNIF(UNIV) displays the univariate statistics (i.e. single degree of freedom contrasts — see Figure 26).

- Finally, the DESIGN subcommand specifies the model for the between-subjects factor. Since there is no between-subjects factor in this model, the DESIGN subcommand simply triggers the analysis.

Portions of the display output are shown in Figures 19 through 26.

- Figure 19 shows the cell means and standard deviations. Inspection of the cell means provides a rationale for the special contrast used in the analysis. Notice that the means for DRUG1 and DRUG2 have the smallest difference. Then, the mean for DRUG4 has a smaller difference from these two than does the mean for DRUG3. Finally, the mean for DRUG3 is most different from the others.

- Figure 20 shows the orthonormalized transformation matrix with contrasts on the means. The original contrasts on the CONTRAST subcommand are orthogonal. MANOVA normalizes the contrasts so that the sum of squares of any column of the matrix is 1.

- Figure 21 shows the beginning of the default display of the multivariate repeated measures analysis. MANOVA tells you that it is using transformed variables in the analysis; this is signified in the Note.

- Figure 22 shows the test of significance for the between-subjects effect, which in this example is just the overall constant.

- Figure 23 shows the next cycle of the analysis, which is the test for the TRIAL within-subjects effect. MANOVA jointly tests the three transformed variables, making this a multivariate test.

- Figure 24 shows the results from specifying ERROR(COR). Mauchly's test of sphericity tests whether the covariance matrix of the transformed variables has a constant variance on the diagonal and zeroes off the diagonal. The observed significance level of the test, 0.470, does not reject the null hypothesis of sphericity, so, we assume that the variances of the transformed variables are equal. If the observed significance level is small, and the sphericity assumption appears to be violated, an adjustment to the numerator and denominator degrees of freedom can be made. Two estimates of this adjustment, called Huynh-Feldt and Greenhouse-Geisser epsilon, are available in MANOVA. To obtain this adjustment, specify PRINT=SIGNIF(HF) for the Huynh-Feldt epsilon, or PRINT=SIGNIF(GG) for the Greenhouse-Geisser epsilon. The Greenhouse-Geisser epsilon tends to be more conservative than the Huynh-Feldt epsilon especially for small sample sizes. The lowest value possible for epsilon is also displayed. When the Huynh-Feldt epsilon exceeds the value of one, MANOVA displays a value of one. To use either of these adjustments, multiply degrees of freedom in both the numerator and the denominator of the F-ratio by epsilon, and then evaluate *the significance of the* F-ratio with the new degrees of freedom. Given that there is no between-subjects factor, these data satisfy the *symmetry conditions* that must be met if you wish to apply the univariate-approach statistical results.

- Figure 25 shows the multivariate tests of significance of the trial within-subjects effect. The multivariate tests are significant at the 0.05 level.

- Figure 26 shows the univariate tests of significance where variable T2 represents the second contrast specified with the contrast subcommand, comparing trials one and two (1,-1,0 0). Similarly, variables T3 and T4 represent the third and fourth contrasts specified by the contrast subcommand, comparing trial 4 to trials 1 and 2 (1,1,0 2) and comparing trial 3 to trials 1, 2,and 4 respectively.

- Finally, Figure 27 shows the averaged test of significance for the drug effect; these are the *univariate approach* statistics. There are 12 error degrees of freedom for this test, while there are two error degrees of freedom for the multivariate tests. Given the error correlation results above, the averaged test is appropriate. The observed level of significance of this test is less than 0.0005, so the averaged F test corroborates the multivariate test results.

Figure 19 Cell means and standard deviations

```
Cell Means and Standard Deviations
Variable .. DRUG1
                               Mean  Std. Dev.       N   95 percent Conf. Interval

For entire sample              26.400    8.764        5     15.519     37.281

- - - - - - - - - - - - - - - - - - - - - - - - - - - - - - - - - - - - - - - - - -
Variable .. DRUG2
                               Mean  Std. Dev.       N   95 percent Conf. Interval

For entire sample              25.600    6.542        5     17.477     33.723

- - - - - - - - - - - - - - - - - - - - - - - - - - - - - - - - - - - - - - - - - -
Variable .. DRUG3
                               Mean  Std. Dev.       N   95 percent Conf. Interval

For entire sample              15.600    3.847        5     10.823     20.377

- - - - - - - - - - - - - - - - - - - - - - - - - - - - - - - - - - - - - - - - - -
Variable .. DRUG4
                               Mean  Std. Dev.       N   95 percent Conf. Interval

For entire sample              32.000    8.000        5     22.067     41.933
```

Figure 20 Orthonormalized Transformation Matrix

```
Orthonormalized Transformation Matrix (Transposed)

                    T1              T2              T3              T4

DRUG1             .50000          .70711          .40825          .28868
DRUG2             .50000         -.70711          .40825          .28868
DRUG3             .50000          .00000          .00000         -.86603
DRUG4             .50000          .00000         -.81650          .28868
```

Figure 21 Transformed Variables for Between-subject effect

```
Order of Variables for Analysis

  Variates      Covariates

   T1

   1 Dependent Variable
   0 Covariates

- - - - - - - - - - - - - - - - - - - - - - - - - - - - - - - - - - - - - - - - - -
Note..  TRANSFORMED variables are in the variates column.
        These TRANSFORMED variables correspond to the
        Between-subject effects.
```

Figure 22 Analysis of variance for CONSTANT

```
Tests of Between-Subjects Effects.

Tests of Significance for T1 using UNIQUE sums of squares
Source of Variation           SS       DF       MS         F   Sig of F

WITHIN CELLS               680.80       4     170.20
CONSTANT                 12400.20       1   12400.20     72.86     .001
```

Figure 23 Transformed Variables for the Within-subject effect

```
Order of Variables for Analysis

  Variates    Covariates

    T2
    T3
    T4

   3 Dependent Variables
   0 Covariates
- - - - - - - - - - - - - - - - - - - - - - - - - - - - - - - - - - - - - - -
Note..  TRANSFORMED variables are in the variates column.
        These TRANSFORMED variables correspond to the
        'TRIAL' WITHIN-SUBJECT effect.
```

Figure 24 Correlation and Sphericity statistics

```
WITHIN CELLS Correlations with Std. Devs. on Diagonal

               T2              T3              T4

T2          2.56905
T3          -.64875        1.73205
T4           .29109         .14199         4.31277

- - - - - - - - - - - - - - - - - - - - - - - - - - - - - - - - - - - - - - -
Tests involving 'TRIAL' Within-Subject Effect.


Mauchly sphericity test, W =      .18650
Chi-square approx. =             4.57156 with 5 D. F.
Significance =                    .470

Greenhouse-Geisser Epsilon =      .60487
Huynh-Feldt Epsilon =            1.00000
Lower-bound Epsilon =             .33333

AVERAGED Tests of Significance that follow multivariate tests are equivalent to
univariate or split-plot or mixed-model approach to repeated measures.
Epsilons may be used to adjust d.f. for the AVERAGED results.
```

Figure 25 Multivariate tests of significance

```
EFFECT .. TRIAL
Multivariate Tests of Significance (S = 1, M = 1/2, N = 0)

Test Name          Value       Exact F      Hypoth. DF      Error DF     Sig. of F

Pillais            .97707     28.41231          3.00           2.00        .034
Hotellings       42.61846     28.41231          3.00           2.00        .034
Wilks              .02293     28.41231          3.00           2.00        .034
Roys               .97707
Note.. F statistics are exact.
```

Figure 26 Univariate tests of specified contrasts

```
- - - - - - - - - - - - - - - - - - - - - - - - - - - - - - - - - - - - - - -
EFFECT .. TRIAL (CONT.)
Univariate F-tests with (1,4) D. F.

Variable   Hypoth. SS    Error SS    Hypoth. MS     Error MS           F      Sig. of F

T2            1.60000    26.40000       1.60000      6.60000      .24242        .648
T3          120.00000    12.00000     120.00000      3.00000    40.00000        .003
T4          576.60000    74.40000     576.60000     18.60000    31.00000        .005
- - - - - - - - - - - - - - - - - - - - - - - - - - - - - - - - - - - - - - -
```

Figure 27 Averaged Test of Significance   •

```
Tests involving 'TRIAL' Within-Subject Effect.

AVERAGED Tests of Significance for DRUG using UNIQUE sums of squares
Source of Variation          SS     DF      MS        F  Sig of F

WITHIN CELLS              112.80    12     9.40
TRIAL                     698.20     3   232.73    24.76      .000
```

Example 5: Basic Repeated Measures with Polynomial Contrast

The data for this example appear in Elashoff (1981). An introductory discussion is found in the annotated example for MANOVA. There is one between-subjects factor, GROUP, with two levels. There are two within-subjects factors: two types of drugs are administered at each of three doses. This study aims to estimate the relative potency of the two drugs in inhibiting a response to a stimulus. Subjects in Group 1 received the three doses of Drug 1 first and the three doses of Drug 2 second. Subjects in Group 2 received Drug 2 first and then Drug 1. Every subject has six response scores. The multivariate setup supplies all relevant statistics. This example also shows a test of the symmetry assumption.

The univariate results of the analysis of repeated measures designs are by-products of the multivariate computations. To use the univariate results, which have greater statistical power, the following two conditions must be met:

• The covariance matrices for the associated set of orthonormal variables are identical across all levels of the between-subjects factors. This is the usual homogeneity-of-variance assumption.

• The common covariance matrix has a sphericity pattern, that is, equal variances on the diagonal and zero covariances off the diagonal.

These two conditions are termed the *symmetry conditions*, and they are necessary and sufficient conditions. Note that both conditions are based on the orthonormal transformed variables and not on the original repeated measures variables. The SPSS commands are

```
TITLE 'A REPEATED MEASURES DESIGN EXAMPLE'.
COMMENT THIS EXAMPLE HAS 2 WITHIN-SUBJECTS FACTORS
 AND 1 BETWEEN SUBJECT FACTOR.
DATA LIST / Y1 Y2 Y3 Y4 Y5 Y6 1-18 GROUP 20.
BEGIN DATA
 19 22 28 16 26 22 1
 11 19 30 12 18 28 1
 20 24 24 24 22 29 1
 21 25 25 15 10 26 1
 18 24 29 19 26 28 1
 17 23 28 15 23 22 1
 20 23 23 26 21 28 1
 14 20 29 25 29 29 1
 16 20 24 30 34 36 2
 26 26 26 24 30 32 2
 22 27 23 33 36 45 2
 16 18 29 27 26 34 2
 19 21 20 22 22 21 2
 20 25 25 29 29 33 2
 21 22 23 27 26 35 2
 17 20 22 23 26 28 2
END DATA.
MANOVA Y1 TO Y6 BY GROUP(1,2)
/WSFACTOR=DRUG(2) DOSE(3)
/CONTRAST(DOSE)=POLYNOMIAL(1,2,6)
/WSDESIGN=DRUG, DOSE,DRUG BY DOSE
/PRINT=TRANSFORM
   HOMOGENEITY(BOXM)
   ERROR(COR)
   SIGNIF(AVERF)
/DESIGN.
```

- The TITLE command prints a title at the top of each page of display output, and the COMMENT command inserts comments that print back with the commands on the display.
- The DATA LIST command defines seven variables from the data in the command file.
- The MANOVA specification names six joint dependent variables—Y1 to Y6—and one between-subjects factor—GROUP.
- The WSFACTORS subcommand defines the within-subjects factors, DRUG with 2 levels and DOSE with 3 levels. The order in which you specify the factors is crucial; you *must* specify them in the order corresponding to the dependent variable list. Conversely, name your dependent variables in a known and intended order. Note that the index value of the rightmost within-subjects factor increments most rapidly.
- The CONTRAST subcommand specifies a polynomial contrast for DOSE. The spacing 1,2,6 reflects the levels of administered doses in the experiment. CONTRAST must be specified before the WSDESIGN subcommand.
- The WSDESIGN subcommand specifies the full factorial model for the within-subjects factors. This subcommand is optional because MANOVA assumes a full factorial model by default.
- The PRINT subcommand specifies several useful statistics. TRANSFORM displays the orthonormalized transformation matrix, which shows how MANOVA transforms the dependent variables to build the within-subjects effects (see Figure 29). HOMO-GENEITY(BOXM) displays a multivariate test for the homogeneity-of-dispersion matrices. Data for which the homogeneity assumption is not rejected meet the first condition for symmetry indicated above (see Figure 28). ERROR(COR) displays within-cells correlations and standard deviations when more than one transformed variable corresponds to a within-subjects effect (see Figures 32 and 36. SIGN-IF(AVERF) displays the average F, which is a univariate approach statistic (see Figure 35).
- The DESIGN subcommand specifies the between-subjects design. By default, MANOVA enters the one between-subjects factor.

Portions of the display output are shown in Figures 28 through 38.

- Figure 28 shows the multivariate test for homogeneity-of-dispersion matrices. Given the large significance levels, the test does not reject the hypothesis of homogeneity. The data do not appear to violate the first symmetry condition.
- Figure 29 shows the orthonormalized transformation matrix. Column 1 is the constant effect; column 2 is the drug effect; column 3 is the dose-linear effect; column 4 is the dose-quadratic effect; column 5 is the drug-by-dose-linear interaction; and column 6 is the drug-by-dose-quadratic interaction.
- Figure 30 shows the default display of tests of significance for T1, the transformed-Y1, which is the constant within-subjects effect. The constant within-subjects effect tests the between-subjects factor.
- Figure 31 shows the default display of tests of significance for T2, the transformed-Y2, which is the drug within-subjects effect. This effect tests drug and group by drug.
- Figure 32 shows the within-cells correlations and standard deviations for T3 and T4, the transformed-Y3 and transformed-Y4 variables respectively, which jointly correspond to the dose within-subjects effect. Mauchly's test of sphericity is nonsignificant, so the data do not appear to violate the second symmetry condition for the dose within-subjects effect. Since the first symmetry condition was also met (see Figure 28), you can use *univariate* test results in assessing the dose-related effects.
- Figures 33 and 34 show the default display of multivariate test results for dose-related effects. Figure 35 shows the univariate approach (averaged) test results for the dose-related effects.
- Figure 36 shows the within-cells correlations and related statistics for T5 and T6, the transformed-Y5 and transformed-Y6 variables respectively, which jointly correspond to the drug-by-dose interactions. This time, test statistics lead to rejection of the second symmetry condition. Therefore, you should use the *multivariate* test results in assessing effects.
- Figures 37 and 38 show the default display of multivariate test results for the drug-by-dose effects. Given the observed levels of significance, no effects are statistically significant.

Figure 28 Symmetry condition 1

```
            CELL NUMBER
              1    2
Variable
   GROUP       1    2

Cell Number .. 1

Determinant of Variance-Covariance matrix =        4138.01612
LOG(Determinant) =                                    8.32797

- - - - - - - - - -

Cell Number .. 2

Determinant of Variance-Covariance matrix =       23150.55748
LOG(Determinant) =                                   10.04977

- - - - - - - - - -


Determinant of pooled Variance-Covariance matrix   329610.63417
LOG(Determinant) =                                   12.70567


- - - - - - - - - - - - - - - - - - - - - - - - - - - - - - - - - - - - - - - -

Multivariate test for Homogeneity of Dispersion matrices


Boxs M =                          49.23512
F WITH (21,720) DF =               1.21162, P =    .233 (Approx.)
Chi-Square with 21 DF =           26.87836, P =    .175 (Approx.)
```

Figure 29 Within-subjects design

```
Orthonormalized Transformation Matrix (Transposed)

                T1            T2            T3            T4            T5            T6
Y1            .40825        .40825       -.37796        .43644       -.37796        .43644
Y2            .40825        .40825       -.18898       -.54554       -.18898       -.54554
Y3            .40825        .40825        .56695        .10911        .56695        .10911
Y4            .40825       -.40825       -.37796        .43644        .37796       -.43644
Y5            .40825       -.40825       -.18898       -.54554        .18898        .54554
Y6            .40825       -.40825        .56695        .10911       -.56695       -.10911
```

Figure 30 Constant within-subjects effect

```
Tests of Between-Subjects Effects.

Tests of Significance for T1 using UNIQUE sums of squares
Source of Variation          SS        DF        MS         F   Sig of F

WITHIN CELLS              532.98        14      38.07
CONSTANT                55632.51         1   55632.51   1461.32      .000
GROUP                     270.01         1     270.01      7.09      .019
```

Figure 31 DRUG within-subjects effect

```
Tests involving 'DRUG' Within-Subject Effect.

Tests of Significance for T2 using UNIQUE sums of squares
Source of Variation          SS        DF        MS         F   Sig of F

WITHIN CELLS              375.65        14      26.83
DRUG                      348.84         1     348.84     13.00      .003
GROUP BY DRUG             326.34         1     326.34     12.16      .004
```

Figure 32 Symmetry condition 2 for DOSE effect

```
-------------------------------------------------------------------------------
WITHIN CELLS Correlations with Std. Devs. on Diagonal

                     T3              T4

T3                3.75557
T4                -.10921          2.58427

- - - - - - - - - - - - - - - - - - - - - - - - - - - - - - - - - - - - - - - -


Tests involving 'DOSE' Within-Subject Effect.


   Mauchly sphericity test, W =        .86193
   Chi-square approx. =               1.93158 with 2 D. F.
   Significance =                      .381

   Greenhouse-Geisser Epsilon =        .87868
   Huynh-Feldt Epsilon =              1.00000
   Lower-bound Epsilon =               .50000

   AVERAGED Tests of Significance that follow multivariate tests are equivalent to
   univariate or split-plot or mixed-model approach to repeated measures.
   Epsilons may be used to adjust d.f. for the AVERAGED results.

- - - - - - - - - - - - - - - - - - - - - - - - - - - - - - - - - - - - - - - -
```

Figure 33 GROUP by DOSE multivariate tests

```
EFFECT .. GROUP BY DOSE
Multivariate Tests of Significance (S = 1, M = 0, N = 5 1/2)

Test Name           Value        Exact F      Hypoth. DF      Error DF      Sig. of F

Pillais            .18262       1.45223          2.00          13.00          .270
Hotellings         .22342       1.45223          2.00          13.00          .270
Wilks              .81738       1.45223          2.00          13.00          .270
Roys               .18262
Note.. F statistics are exact.
```

Figure 34 DOSE multivariate test results

```
EFFECT .. DOSE
Multivariate Tests of Significance (S = 1, M = 0, N = 5 1/2)

Test Name           Value        Exact F      Hypoth. DF      Error DF      Sig. of F

Pillais            .79534      25.26075          2.00          13.00          .000
Hotellings        3.88627      25.26075          2.00          13.00          .000
Wilks              .20466      25.26075          2.00          13.00          .000
Roys               .79534
Note.. F statistics are exact.
```

Figure 35 DOSE and GROUP by DOSE univariate results

```
Tests involving 'DOSE' Within-Subject Effect.

AVERAGED Tests of Significance for Y using UNIQUE sums of squares
Source of Variation         SS        DF        MS          F    Sig of F

WITHIN CELLS             290.96       28       10.39
DOSE                     758.77        2      379.39      36.51     .000
GROUP BY DOSE             42.27        2       21.14       2.03     .150
```

Figure 36 Symmetry condition 2 for DRUG by DOSE effect

```
- - - - - - - - - - - - - - - - - - - - - - - - - - - - - - - - - - - - - - - - - - - - - -
WITHIN CELLS Correlations with Std. Devs. on Diagonal

                    T5                 T6

T5                3.31754
T6                 .57501            2.58715

- - - - - - - - - - - - - - - - - - - - - - - - - - - - - - - - - - - - - - - - - - - - - -
Tests involving 'DRUG BY DOSE' Within-Subject Effect.


  Mauchly sphericity test, W =       .62962
  Chi-square approx. =               6.01422 with 2 D. F.
  Significance =                      .049

  Greenhouse-Geisser Epsilon =       .72973
  Huynh-Feldt Epsilon =              .85129
  Lower-bound Epsilon =              .50000

AVERAGED Tests of Significance that follow multivariate tests are equivalent to
univariate or split-plot or mixed-model approach to repeated measures.
Epsilons may be used to adjust d.f. for the AVERAGED results.

- - - - - - - - - - - - - - - - - - - - - - - - - - - - - - - - - - - - - - - - - - - - - -
```

Figure 37 GROUP by DRUG by DOSE results

```
EFFECT .. GROUP BY DRUG BY DOSE
Multivariate Tests of Significance (S = 1, M = 0, N = 5 1/2)

Test Name         Value        Exact F      Hypoth. DF     Error DF      Sig. of F

Pillais           .14314       1.08583        2.00          13.00          .366
Hotellings        .16705       1.08583        2.00          13.00          .366
Wilks             .85686       1.08583        2.00          13.00          .366
Roys              .14314
Note.. F statistics are exact.
```

Figure 38 DRUG by DOSE results

```
EFFECT .. DRUG BY DOSE
Multivariate Tests of Significance (S = 1, M = 0, N = 5 1/2)

Test Name         Value        Exact F      Hypoth. DF     Error DF      Sig. of F

Pillais           .12604        .93739        2.00          13.00          .417
Hotellings        .14421        .93739        2.00          13.00          .417
Wilks             .87396        .93739        2.00          13.00          .417
Roys              .12604
Note.. F statistics are exact.
```

Example 6: Repeated Measures with a Constant Covariate

This example shows repeated measures analysis with a constant covariate. You must specify as many covariates as dependent variables. If the covariate is constant across the repeated measures factor, use COMPUTE to create as many replicates of the covariate as you need.

The data are obtained from a 2×2 factorial experiment with repeated measures on factor B (Winer, 1971). Variables Y1 and Y2 are scores for the two occasions. Factor A is the between-subjects factor. There are four subjects under each level of factor A. The covariate measure X is obtained before the administration of any of the treatments, and it is therefore constant for both levels of the within-subjects factor B. The SPSS commands are

```
TITLE 'COVARIATE CONSTANT OVER TRIALS:  WINER, PAGE 803'.
DATA LIST / A, X, Y1, Y2 (4F3.0).
BEGIN DATA
data lines
END DATA.
COMPUTE X2 = X.
MANOVA Y1, Y2 BY A(1,2) WITH X, X2
 /WSFACTORS = B( 2 )
 /WSDESIGN = B
 /PRINT= TRANSFORM
 /DESIGN = A.
```

- The TITLE command prints a title at the top of each page of display output.
- The DATA LIST command defines four variables from the data in the command file.
- The COMPUTE command computes X2, which is a copy of the covariate X.
- The MANOVA specification specifies Y1 and Y2 as joint dependent variables, A as the between-subjects factor, and X and X2 as covariates. In the general case, the number of covariates *must* be an integer multiple of the number of dependent variables. In this case, the number of variables in the two sets is equal.
- The WSFACTORS subcommand specifies B as the within-subjects factor.
- The WSDESIGN subcommand specifies the within-subjects design, which here simply names B.
- The PRINT subcommand specifies display of the orthonormalized transformation matrix (see Figure 39).
- The DESIGN subcommand specifies the between-subjects design.

Portions of the display output are shown in Figures 39 through 41.

- Figure 39 shows the orthonormalized transformation matrix. Note the block diagonal structure of the transformation matrix. MANOVA uses the same transformations on dependent variable–covariate pairs. Column 1 is the transformation producing new Y1; column 2 is the transformation producing new Y2; column 3 is the transformation producing new X; and column 4 is the transformation producing new X2.
- Figure 40 shows the default display of the test for the between-subjects effect. MANOVA uses transformed-Y1 and transformed-X in the analysis. The analysis of variance table shows a test of significance for the between-subjects factor, A, adjusted for covariate X. Differences in means on the between-subjects factor are not statistically significant. The second table shows that the correlation between the covariate, X (transformed into T3) and the predicted dependent variable, Y1 (transformed into T1), is 1.00. If there is only one covariate, this correlation will always be 1. If there were multiple covariates, this display would show the relative importance of the covariates in their predicted values. The third table shows that the squared correlation between the variables in the second table, Y1(T1) and X(T3), is also 1.00. Again, this display allows you to evaluate the relative importance of multiple covariates. The fourth table shows that the regression coefficient for X(T3) is 1.022.
- Figure 41 shows the default display of the test for the B within-subjects effect. The analysis of variance table contains tests of significance for B and the A by B interaction.

Figure 39 Orthonormalized transformation matrix

```
Orthonormalized Transformation Matrix (Transposed)

                        T1              T2              T3              T4

Y1                   .70711          .70711          .00000          .00000
Y2                   .70711         -.70711          .00000          .00000
X                    .00000          .00000          .70711          .70711
X2                   .00000          .00000          .70711         -.70711
```

Figure 40 Between-subjects effects

```
Tests of Significance for T1 using UNIQUE sums of squares
Source of Variation          SS      DF      MS        F    Sig of F

WITHIN CELLS              61.30      5    12.26
REGRESSION              166.58      1   166.58    13.59     .014
CONSTANT                400.67      1   400.67    32.68     .002
A                        44.49      1    44.49     3.63     .115
 _ _ _ _ _ _ _ _ _ _ _ _ _ _ _ _ _ _ _ _ _ _ _ _ _ _ _ _ _ _ _ _ _ _ _ _ _ _ _ _
Correlations between Covariates and Predicted Dependent Variable
         COVARIATE

VARIABLE        T3

T1              1.00000
 _ _ _ _ _ _ _ _ _ _ _ _ _ _ _ _ _ _ _ _ _ _ _ _ _ _ _ _ _ _ _ _ _ _ _ _ _ _ _ _
Averaged Squared Correlations between Covariates and Predicted Dependent Variable

VARIABLE        AVER. R-SQ

T3              1.00000
Regression analysis for WITHIN CELLS error term
---- Individual Univariate .9500 confidence intervals
Dependent variable .. T1

COVARIATE          B         Beta      Std. Err.    t-Value   Sig. of t   Lower -95%   CL- Upper

T3       1.0219435737   .8549858355    .27724      3.68611      .014        .30927      1.73462
 _ _ _ _ _ _ _ _ _ _ _ _ _ _ _ _ _ _ _ _ _ _ _ _ _ _ _ _ _ _ _ _ _ _ _ _ _ _ _ _
```

Figure 41 B Within-subjects effect

```
Tests involving 'B' Within-Subject Effect.

Tests of Significance for T2 using UNIQUE sums of squares
Source of Variation          SS      DF      MS        F    Sig of F

WITHIN CELLS               6.37      6     1.06
B                         85.56      1    85.56    80.53     .000
A BY B                      .56      1      .56      .53     .494
```

Example 7: Repeated Measures with a Varying Covariate

You can use MANOVA to perform repeated measures analysis with a varying covariate. The model is a 3×2 factorial experiment with repeated measures on factor B (Winer, 1971). There are three subjects in each group. You can obtain regression coefficients for both the between-subjects effect and the within-subjects effect. See Winer for a discussion of a statistic which tests the equality of these two regression coefficients. In this analysis, since there are only two levels of the within-subjects factor, the univariate and multivariate approaches are identical. However, for a model which has more than two levels on any of the within-subjects factors with covariates varying over the repeated measures trials, interpret the multivariate results with caution. In certain models, there may be some question concerning the propriety of controlling for all covariates. The SPSS commands are

```
TITLE 'COVARIATE VARYING OVER TRIALS:  WINER, PAGE 806'.
DATA LIST / GROUP, B1X, B1Y, B2X, B2Y (5F3.0).
VALUE LABELS GROUP 1 'A1' 2 'A2' 3 'A3'.
BEGIN DATA
   1   3   8   4  14
   1   5  11   9  18
   1  11  16  14  22
   2   2   6   1   8
   2   8  12   9  14
   2  10   9   9  10
   3   7  10   4  10
   3   8  14  10  18
   3   9  15  12  22
END DATA.
MANOVA B1Y, B2Y BY GROUP(1,3) WITH B1X, B2X
  /WSFACTOR = B( 2 )
  /WSDESIGN
  /PRINT = TRANSFORM
  /DESIGN.
```

- The TITLE command prints a title at the top of each page of display output.
- The DATA LIST command defines five variables from the data in the command file, and the VALUE LABELS command assigns labels to the values for variable GROUP.
- The MANOVA command specifies B1Y and B2Y as joint dependent variables, GROUP as a three-level between-subjects factor, and B1X and B2X as covariates. The two dependent variables and two covariates contain pairs of scores obtained on two occasions.
- The WSFACTORS subcommand specifies B as the two-level within-subjects factor.
- The WSDESIGN subcommand specifies the single within-subjects factor.
- The PRINT subcommand displays the orthonormalized transformation matrix (see Figure 42).
- The DESIGN subcommand specifies the between-subjects design.

Portions of the display output are shown in Figures 42 through 45.

- Figure 42 shows the orthonormalized transformation matrix, which is block diagonal. Columns 1 and 2 correspond to transformations of the dependent variables, while columns 3 and 4 correspond to transformations of the covariates.
- Figure 43 shows the tests of significance for the between subjects effects. The REGRESSION, and CONSTANT effects are significant whereas GROUP is not significant.
- Figure 44 shows the tests of significance for the B within-subjects effect. REGRESSION and the B effects are significant, while the GROUP BY B interaction is not.

Figure 42 Orthonormalized transformation matrix

```
Orthonormalized Transformation Matrix (Transposed)

                          T1              T2              T3              T4

B1Y                   .70711          .70711          .00000          .00000
B2Y                   .70711         -.70711          .00000          .00000
B1X                   .00000          .00000          .70711          .70711
B2X                   .00000          .00000          .70711         -.70711
```

Figure 43 Constant between-subjects effect

```
Tests of Between-Subjects Effects.

Tests of Significance for T1 using UNIQUE sums of squares
Source of Variation          SS        DF        MS          F     Sig of F

WITHIN CELLS              44.37         5       8.87
REGRESSION               132.63         1     132.63      14.95      .012
CONSTANT                 128.79         1     128.79      14.51      .013
GROUP                     54.26         2      27.13       3.06      .136
```

Figure 44 Within-subjects effect

```
Tests involving 'B' Within-Subject Effect.

Tests of Significance for T2 using UNIQUE sums of squares
Source of Variation          SS        DF        MS          F     Sig of F

WITHIN CELLS               3.00         5        .60
REGRESSION                10.00         1      10.00      16.68      .010
B                         31.55         1      31.55      52.61      .001
GROUP BY B                 2.34         2       1.17       1.95      .236
```

Example 8: A Doubly Multivariate Repeated Measures Design

This example illustrates how to analyze a doubly multivariate repeated measures design using the multivariate setup. The data consist of 53 subjects with 15 response variables recorded for each subject. Each of five types of tests are administered on three occasions to the subjects. Therefore, time is a within-subjects factor. There are two between-subjects factors: a two-level sex variable and a three-level group variable.

The model is multivariate in two senses. First, when a subject is measured across occasions with respect to a given item, the multivariate setup specifies each of the scores on the same SPSS case. Second, each subject is measured with respect to more than one item at each occasion, thereby inducing multivariate considerations. This example illustrates the use of the MEASURE subcommand to label the results of the univariate approach.

Use the following rules when performing this type of analysis with MANOVA:

- Specify variables measuring a given attribute across occasions consecutively and in order.
- The number of dependent variables in the MANOVA specification must be an integer multiple of the number of within-subjects levels.

The SPSS commands are

```
TITLE  'A MULTIVARIATE REPEATED MEASURES DESIGN'.
COMMENT THIS A DOUBLY MULTIVARIATE REPEATED MEASURES DESIGN WITH
  THE DATA AS FOLLOWS:
                                        TIME

             1                 2                 3

          PREDIS            POSTDIS           FOLODIS
          PREPROB           POSTPROB          FOLOPROB
          PRESELF           POSTSELF          FOLOSELF
          PRENEG            POSTNEG           FOLONEG
          PRETHER           POSTTHER          FOLOTHER

DATA LIST / GROUP, SEX, PREDIS, PREPROB, PRESELF, PRENEG,
  PRETHER, POSTDIS, POSTPROB, POSTSELF, POSTNEG, POSTTHER,
  FOLODIS, FOLOPROB, FOLOSELF, FOLONEG, FOLOTHER
  (2F1.0,4X,2F6.3,3F3.0,2F6.3,3F3.0,2F6.3,3F3.0).
BEGIN DATA
data lines
END DATA.
MANOVA PREDIS POSTDIS FOLODIS PREPROB POSTPROB FOLOPROB
    PRESELF POSTSELF FOLOSELF PRENEG POSTNEG FOLONEG
    PRETHER POSTTHER FOLOTHER BY SEX(1,2), GROUP(1,3)
 /WSFACTOR = TIME( 3 )
 /MEASURE = DIS PROB SELF NEG THER
 /CONTRAST(TIME) = POLYNOMIAL(1 2 3)
 /WSDESIGN = TIME
 /PRINT = SIGNIF(HYPOTH)
 /DESIGN.
```

- The TITLE command prints a title at the top of each page of display output, and the COMMENT command inserts comments that print back with the commands on the display.
- The DATA LIST command defines 17 variables from the data in the command file.
- The MANOVA command specifies the 15 dependent variables and the two between-subjects factors. The prefixes PRE, POST, and FOLO indicate the three occasions. The root names DIS, PROB, SELF, NEG, and THER indicate the five types of measures. Notice the order of the variables. All DIS variables appear first, then all PROB variables, and so on. Within each group of three variables, the order of time is the same.
- The WSFACTORS subcommand specifies TIME as a within-subjects factor. The number of dependent variables in the MANOVA specification is an integer multiple of the number of levels of the within-subjects factor.
- The MEASURE subcommand lists five names, which MANOVA uses for labeling univariate results.
- The CONTRAST subcommand specifies a polynomial contrast for TIME.

- The WSDESIGN subcommand specifies the within-subjects factor, TIME. This command specification is optional because MANOVA assumes a full factorial model by default.
- The PRINT subcommand displays the hypothesis SSCP matrices (Figure 48) and the averaged statistics corresponding to the univariate approach (Figure 50). AVERF does not need to be specified as the averaged *F* statistics and will be displayed as the default for all repeated measures designs.
- The DESIGN subcommand specifies the between-subjects design.

Portions of the display output are shown in Figures 45 through 51.

- Figures 45, 46, and 47 show the multivariate tests of significance for the SEX by GROUP interaction, the GROUP effect, and the SEX effect respectively.
- Figure 48 shows the adjusted hypothesis SSCP matrix for the SEX by GROUP by TIME effect, and Figure 49 shows the default multivariate-approach test statistics for the SEX by GROUP by TIME effect.
- Figure 50 shows the "averaged" adjusted hypothesis SSCP matrix for the SEX by GROUP by TIME effect. This matrix results from the univariate approach to the data. MANOVA uses the names supplied on the MEASURES subcommand to label the pooled effects. Compare this matrix with the one in Figure 48. In the averaged hypothesis SSCP matrix, for example, the DIS sum of squares is 0.49423. This number is the trace of the submatrix in Figure 48 formed by all DIS effects, that is, POSTDIS and FOLODIS. In other words, 0.49423 is the sum of 0.16123 and 0.33300. MANOVA similarly combines submatrix trace elements of the multivariate-approach adjusted hypothesis SSCP matrix to compute the rest of the elements of the univariate-approach adjusted hypothesis SSCP matrix. Although not shown, the averaged error SSCP matrix is similarly computed.
- Finally, Figure 51 shows the univariate-approach test statistics for the SEX by GROUP by TIME effect. Compare this with Figure 49.

Figure 45 SEX by GROUP effect

```
EFFECT .. SEX BY GROUP
AVERAGED Multivariate Tests of Significance (S = 2, M = 1 , N = 20 1/2)

Test Name          Value         Approx. F       Hypoth. DF       Error DF        Sig. of F

Pillais            .14819         .70421          10.00            88.00           .718
Hotellings         .16349         .68665          10.00            84.00           .734
Wilks              .85594         .69560          10.00            86.00           .726
Roys               .11102
Note.. F statistic for WILK'S Lambda is exact.
```

Figure 46 GROUP effect

```
EFFECT .. GROUP
AVERAGED Multivariate Tests of Significance (S = 2, M = 1 , N = 20 1/2)

Test Name          Value         Approx. F       Hypoth. DF       Error DF        Sig. of F

Pillais            .21069         1.03618         10.00            88.00           .420
Hotellings         .24626         1.03428         10.00            84.00           .422
Wilks              .79657         1.03574         10.00            86.00           .421
Roys               .16727
Note.. F statistic for WILK'S Lambda is exact.
```

Figure 47 SEX effect

```
EFFECT .. SEX
AVERAGED Multivariate Tests of Significance (S = 1, M = 1 1/2, N = 20 1/2)

Test Name          Value         Exact F         Hypoth. DF       Error DF        Sig. of F

Pillais            .20556         2.22525         5.00             43.00           .069
Hotellings         .25875         2.22525         5.00             43.00           .069
Wilks              .79444         2.22525         5.00             43.00           .069
Roys               .20556
Note.. F statistics are exact.
```

**Figure 48 Hypothesis SSCP matrix
for SEX by GROUP by TIME effect**

```
EFFECT .. SEX BY GROUP BY TIME
Adjusted Hypothesis Sum-of-Squares and Cross-Products

                 T2            T3            T5            T6            T8            T9           T11

T2           .16123
T3          -.19762        .33300
T5           .14595       -.04226        .33777
T6          -.13805        .13589       -.17512        .13043
T8           .15726       -.92824       -.96459        .13527       6.11199
T9          -.28690        .89645        .56024        .04571      -4.69360       3.77997
T11         3.86160       -6.37783       1.02034       -2.70282     17.09124     -16.74162     122.28503
T12        -1.13667        1.42390       -.98278        .96199      -1.35733       2.20682     -27.78012
T14         3.35852       -7.96836      -2.75699       -1.46204     34.48205     -29.09195     150.22274
T15         1.97603        -.26219       5.03949       -2.48460    -15.57064       9.44523       8.19825

                T12           T14           T15

T12         8.02386
T14       -24.97956      233.39190
T15       -13.20086      -50.47842      75.60308
```

Figure 49 Multivariate approach for SEX by GROUP by TIME effect

```
EFFECT .. SEX BY GROUP BY TIME
Multivariate Tests of Significance (S = 2, M = 3 1/2, N = 18 )

Test Name          Value       Approx. F     Hypoth. DF      Error DF      Sig. of F

Pillais           .47001       1.19806         20.00          78.00          .279
Hotellings        .63755       1.17947         20.00          74.00          .296
Wilks             .58008       1.18930         20.00          76.00          .287
Roys              .30669
Note.. F statistic for WILK'S Lambda is exact.
```

Figure 50 Averaged hypothesis SSCP matrix

```
EFFECT .. SEX BY GROUP BY TIME
Adjusted Hypothesis Sum-of-Squares and Cross-Products

                 DIS           PROB          SELF          NEG           THER

DIS           .49423
PROB          .28184        .46820
SELF         1.05372        -.91888       9.89196
NEG          5.28550        1.98233      19.29806      130.30889
THER         3.09633       -5.24159      43.92728      137.02188     308.99498
```

Figure 51 Univariate approach for SEX by GROUP by TIME effect

```
EFFECT .. SEX BY GROUP BY TIME
AVERAGED Multivariate Tests of Significance (S = 4, M = 0, N = 44 )

Test Name          Value       Approx. F     Hypoth. DF      Error DF      Sig. of F

Pillais           .23198       1.14512         20.00         372.00          .301
Hotellings        .25801       1.14172         20.00         354.00          .305
Wilks             .78311       1.14534         20.00         299.45          .302
Roys              .12791
```

Example 9: Profile Analysis

In the previous repeated measures examples, we imposed a design on the dependent variables using an implicit orthonormal transformation of the dependent variables. The distinct dependent variables were really measures of the same items across occasions. However, not all analyses require a formal treatment structure on the dependent variables; instead, you may simply be interested in making specific kinds of comparisons among nonrepeated dependent variables. Such analyses are termed *profile analyses*.

Data in profile analysis consist of p commensurable responses that have been collected from independent sampling units grouped according to k treatments or experimental conditions. In profile analysis, there are three questions of interest:

- *Parallelism of profiles.* Are the population-mean profiles similar, in the sense that the line segments of adjacent tests are parallel?
- *Equal treatment levels.* Assuming parallelism, are the treatment levels equal?
- *Equal response means.* Assuming parallelism, are the response means equal?

The analysis proceeds very much along the same lines as that for repeated measures data. That is, you transform the data to new variables which incorporate the effects of interest. The difference from repeated measures analysis lies in the nature of the data themselves: profile analysis does not assume any correspondence between treatment interventions and dependent variables. Also, the pooled results are generally not of interest. You should *not* request orthonormalization of the new variables in profile analysis. This example appears in Morrison (1976). Three scales—A, B, and C—measuring certain maternal attitudes are administered to 21 mothers participating in a study of child development. As part of the study, each mother has been assigned to one of four socioeconomic status (SES) groups. Thus, there are three responses, four treatment levels, and 21 subjects. The three hypotheses to be tested are

- Are the scale profiles in the four SES groups parallel?
- Given 1, are class effects equal over all responses?
- Given 1, are response means equal?

To conduct the tests, first transform the observations to the differences of scales A and B and scales B and C. The SPSS commands are

```
TITLE 'PROFILE ANALYSIS'.
COMMENT THIS EXAMPLE IS FROM MORRISON, P.209.
DATA LIST / SOCLASS 1 A 3-4 B 6-7 C 9-10.
BEGIN DATA
1 19 20 18
1 20 21 19
1 19 22 22
1 18 19 21
1 16 18 20
1 17 22 19
1 20 19 20
1 15 19 19
2 12 14 12
2 15 15 17
2 15 17 15
2 13 14 14
2 14 16 13
3 15 14 17
3 13 14 15
3 12 15 15
3 12 13 13
4  8  9 10
4 10 10 12
4 11 10 10
4 11  7 12
END DATA.
REPORT VARS=A B C   /BREAK=SOCLASS   /SUM=MEAN.
MANOVA A,B,C BY SOCLASS(1,4)
  /TRANSFORM= REPEATED
  /RENAME= AVERAGE,AMINUSB,BMINUSC
  /PRINT=TRANSFORM
  /ANALYSIS =(AMINUSB, BMINUSC/AVERAGE)
  /DESIGN.
```

- The TITLE command prints a title at the top of each page of display output, and the COMMENT command inserts comments that print back with the commands on the display.
- The DATA LIST command defines four variables from the data in the command file.
- REPORT displays the means on the three response variables within each of the four SES groups (see Figure 52).

- The MANOVA command names A, B, and C as three response variables and SOCLASS as a four-level factor.
- TRANSFORM creates three transformed variables: an average effect and two adjacent differences, A-B and B-C.
- The RENAME subcommand names the transformed variables for use on the display output.
- The PRINT subcommand displays the transformation matrix (see Figure 53).
- The ANALYSIS subcommand specifies two analyses. In the first analysis, AMINUSB and BMINUSC are joint dependent variables, and in the second analysis, AVERAGE is the dependent variable. The first analysis tests Hypotheses 1 and 3 stated above; the second analysis tests Hypothesis 2.
- The DESIGN subcommand indicates the default design, which enters the SOCLASS effect.

Portions of the display output are shown in Figures 52 through 56.

- Figure 52 shows the output from REPORT. The rows of means are the four "profiles" corresponding to the four levels of SES.
- Figure 53 shows the transposed transformation matrix. Column 1 is the average effect; column 2 is the A-B difference; and column 3 is the B-C difference.
- Figure 54 shows the variables used for the first analysis. Transformed and renamed variables AMINUSB and BMINUSC are joint dependent variables in the first analysis.
- The first portion of Figure 55 shows the tests of significance of the SOCLASS effect on the joint dependent variables. This portion of the output shows a test for Hypothesis 1—the test of parallelism. The second portion shows nonsignificant test statistics which indicate that AMINUSB and BMINUSC are the same across SES levels, in which case you can assume that the profiles are parallel. In the output, the significance levels of the test statistics are indeed large enough to assume parallelism.
- Figure 56 shows the results for the second analysis specified on the ANALYSIS subcommand. The dependent variable is AVERAGE. If there are no significant differences in the means of AVERAGE across the four levels of SOCLASS, then we do not reject Hypothesis 2—the test of equal class effects. However, the highly significant F statistic for SOCLASS leads to rejection of the hypothesis of equal means. The SOCLASS parameter estimates, while not exhausting the comparisons that can be made, show that the mean of level 1 differs significantly from the means of the other levels.

Figure 52 REPORT output showing mean profiles

```
PROFILE ANALYSIS

    SOCLASS            A           B           C
        1
        Mean          18          20          20
        2
        Mean          14          15          14
        3
        Mean          13          14          15
        4
        Mean          10           9          11
```

Figure 53 Transformation matrix

```
Transformation Matrix (Transposed)
                   AVERAGE        AMINUSB        BMINUSC
A                  .33333        1.00000         .00000
B                  .33333       -1.00000        1.00000
C                  .33333         .00000       -1.00000
```

Figure 54 Model 1 variables

```
Order of Variables for Analysis

  Variates      Covariates

  AMINUSB
  BMINUSC

  2 Dependent Variables
  0 Covariates
- - - - - - - - - - - - - - - - - - - - - - - - - - - - - - - - - - - - -
Note..  TRANSFORMED variables are in the variates column.
```

Figure 55 Test of parallelism

```
EFFECT .. SOCLASS
Multivariate Tests of Significance (S = 2, M = 0, N = 7 )

Test Name         Value       Approx. F    Hypoth. DF    Error DF    Sig. of F

Pillais          .48726       1.82526        6.00         34.00        .123
Hotellings       .68534       1.71336        6.00         30.00        .152
Wilks            .56333       1.77253        6.00         32.00        .136
Roys             .33724
Note.. F statistic for WILK'S Lambda is exact.

- - - - - - - - - - - - - - - - - - - - - - - - - - - - - - - - - - - - -
EFFECT .. SOCLASS (CONT.)
Univariate F-tests with (3,17) D. F.

Variable     Hypoth. SS     Error SS     Hypoth. MS     Error MS          F     Sig. of F

AMINUSB       24.60952      51.20000       8.20317       3.01176    2.72371       .077
BMINUSC       24.30952      61.50000       8.10317       3.61765    2.23990       .121
```

Figure 56 Test of equality of class effects

```
Order of Variables for Analysis

  Variates      Covariates

  AVERAGE

  1 Dependent Variable
  0 Covariates

- - - - - - - - - - - - - - - - - - - - - - - - - - - - - - - - - - - - -
Note..  TRANSFORMED variables are in the variates column.
- - - - - - - - - - - - - - - - - - - - - - - - - - - - - - - - - - - - -
Tests of Significance for AVERAGE using UNIQUE sums of squares
Source of Variation      SS      DF      MS        F  Sig of F

WITHIN CELLS           19.81     17     1.17
SOCLASS               247.97      3    82.66     70.93     .000
```

MATRIX   The following two examples illustrate MATRIX applications.

Example 1   This example shows the calculation of least-squares regression statistics and the standard error of the regression from data in the active file. The first variable in the file is assumed to be the dependent variable.

```
MATRIX.
GET DATA.
COMPUTE N      = NROW(DATA).
COMPUTE K      = NCOL(DATA).
COMPUTE Y      = DATA(:,1).
COMPUTE X      = {MAKE(N,1,1), DATA(:,2:K)}.
COMPUTE COEF = SOLVE(T(X)*X, T(X)*Y).
COMPUTE PRED = X*COEF.
COMPUTE RESD = Y - PRED.
COMPUTE ERS    = CSSQ(RESD).
COMPUTE SERR = SQRT(ERS/(N-K)).
COMPUTE LABS = {"Const:";"    X1:";"    X2:";"    X3:";"    X4:";
               "    X5:";"    X6:";"    X7:";"    X8:";"    X9:"}.
PRINT COEF /TITLE = "Regression Coefficients" /FORMAT=F12.6
    /RNAMES=LABS /SPACE=NEWPAGE.
PRINT SERR /TITLE = 'Standard Error' /FORMAT=F12.6.
PRINT {Y, PRED, RESD}(1:10,:)
    /TITLE = "Casewise listing" /FORMAT=F15.4
    /CLABELS="Obs" "Pred" "Resid".
END MATRIX
```

• The GET statement reads the active system file into a MATRIX variable named DATA.

• The first two COMPUTE statements establish N, the number of cases, from the number of rows in the data matrix, and K, the number of variables, from the number of columns in the data matrix.

• The next COMPUTE statement extracts Y, the dependent variable, from the first column of the data matrix.

• The next COMPUTE statement forms the X matrix by creating a column of 1's (with the MAKE function) and concatenating it to the remainder of the data matrix.

• The coefficients are calculated with a single use of the SOLVE function.

• The predicted values are calculated by multiplying X by the regression coefficients, and the residuals are calculated by subtracting the predicted values from Y.

• The error sum of squares (ERS) is the sum of the squared residuals, as returned by the CSSQ (column sum-of-squares) function, and the standard error of the regression is easily calculated from this.

• The final COMPUTE statement creates a vector of string constants for use in labeling the regression coefficients. This vector will suffice for up to 9 independent variables; if the active system file had more than 10 variables in it, the LABS vector would have to be extended, or the final regression coefficients would be unlabeled.

• The first PRINT statement prints the regression coefficients, using the LABS vector as row labels. The second PRINT statement prints the standard error of the regression.

• The final PRINT statement prints casewise results for the first 10 cases. Note that the MATRIX expression consists of three concatenated column vectors inside braces, and a subscript expression that specifies the first 10 rows. The columns are labeled with literal strings supplied on the CLABELS specification.

Example 2   This example illustrates some of the programming features in the MATRIX language. A number, and then a symmetric matrix of the size indicated by the number, are read from a text file. The program then prints eigenvalues greater than or equal to 1 and their corresponding eigenvectors.

```
MATRIX.
READ SIZE /FILE=MATXFILE /SIZE=1 /FIELD=1 TO 10.
READ DATA /FILE=MATXFILE /SIZE={SIZE,SIZE} /FIELD=1 TO 80 BY 10
    /MODE=SYMMETRIC.

PRINT DATA /TITLE "Matrix read:" /SPACE=NEWPAGE /FORMAT=E10.2.

CALL EIGEN(DATA, EIGENVEC, EIGENVAL).
COMPUTE FOUND = 0.
LOOP I=1 TO SIZE.
+  DO IF (EIGENVAL(I) >= 1).
+      COMPUTE FOUND = FOUND+1.
+      PRINT EIGENVAL(I) /TITLE "Eigenvalue:" /SPACE=4.
+      PRINT T(EIGENVEC(:,I)) /TITLE "Eigenvector:".
+  END IF.
END LOOP.
DO IF (FOUND = 0).
+  PRINT /TITLE "No eigenvalues are greater than 1.".
END IF.
END MATRIX.
```

- The READ statements establish the size of the symmetric matrix, from a number on the first record in the file referenced by MATXFILE, and the contents of the matrix, from additional records in that file. MATRIX reads only the lower half of the matrix, because of the MODE=SYMMETRIC specification.

- The first PRINT statement prints back the matrix, using an exponential format to allow for very large or small values.

- The call to the EIGEN procedure passes the data matrix and two MATRIX variable names, one for the eigenvectors and one for the eigenvalues.

- A LOOP statement processes each element of the EIGENVAL vector. Within the loop, a DO IF statement checks whether the eigenvalue is greater than or equal to 1. If so, the eigenvalue and the corresponding column of the matrix of eigenvectors are printed. To avoid wasting space printing a column vector, its transpose is printed.

- At the end of the loop, a message is printed if no eigenvalues greater than or equal to 1 were found.

MEANS

The following example analyzes personnel data from Hubbard Consultants Inc., a small industrial consulting firm with headquarters in Chicago and a branch office in St. Louis. MEANS is used to examine salaries in 1981 by sex within department and job grade. The SPSS commands are

```
GET  FILE=HUB.
RECODE  GRADE81 (1 THRU 4=1) (5 THRU 7=2) (8 THRU 15=3) (ELSE=COPY)
    INTO GRADE81S.
VALUE LABELS  GRADE81S  (1) GRADES 1-4 (2) GRADES 5-7
    (3) GRADES 8-15.
MISSING VALUES  GRADE81S(0).
MEANS  SALARY81 BY DEPT81 BY GRADE81S BY SEX.
```

- The GET command defines the data to SPSS and selects the variables needed for analysis.

- The RECODE command collapses the fifteen values of GRADE81 into three values and contains them in variable GRADE81S.

- The VALUE LABELS command assigns labels to the new variable GRADE81S.

- The MISSING VALUES command defines 0 as the missing value for GRADE81S.

- The MEANS command specifies a three-way breakdown of salaries in general mode. SALARY81 is the dependent variable.

- Since no missing-value option is specified, MEANS deletes cases with missing values on a tablewide basis.

Output from MEANS

```
              - - Description of Subpopulations - -

Summaries of    SALARY81    YEARLY SALARY IN 1981
By levels of    DEPT81      DEPARTMENT CODE IN 1981
                GRADE81S
                SEX         EMPLOYEE'S SEX


Variable        Value  Label              Mean      Std Dev   Cases

For Entire Population                   15096.2125  8074.3872   160

DEPT81            1    ADMIN            15537.8421  9810.5522    38
  GRADE81S     1.00    GRADES 1-4       10076.8333  1685.2658    12
    SEX           1    MALE             10106.5455  1764.2221    11
    SEX           2    FEMALE            9750.0000     .0000      1

  GRADE81S     2.00    GRADES 5-7       11952.7333  2019.7453    15
    SEX           1    MALE             13910.0000     .0000      1
    SEX           2    FEMALE           11812.9286  2019.2662    14

  GRADE81S     3.00    GRADES 8-15      26384.0909 12759.5664    11
    SEX           1    MALE             34125.0000 15498.1047     5
    SEX           2    FEMALE           19933.3333  4858.3605     6

DEPT81            2    PROJECT DIRECTORS 15314.4286  8146.9522    28
  GRADE81S     1.00    GRADES 1-4       11340.5625  1999.6042    16
    SEX           1    MALE             10583.9000  1143.2161    10
    SEX           2    FEMALE           12601.6667  2566.9469     6

  GRADE81S     2.00    GRADES 5-7       12826.6667  2015.3494     3
    SEX           2    FEMALE           12826.6667  2015.3494     3

  GRADE81S     3.00    GRADES 8-15      23208.3333 10558.8272     9
    SEX           1    MALE             28613.0000 11587.9159     5
    SEX           2    FEMALE           16452.5000  2953.7674     4

DEPT81            3    CHICAGO OPERATIONS 14925.3016  7705.3167   63
  GRADE81S     1.00    GRADES 1-4        9922.1765  1536.2349    17
    SEX           1    MALE             10458.5000   836.5073     2
    SEX           2    FEMALE            9850.6667  1612.6409    15

  GRADE81S     2.00    GRADES 5-7       12334.7500  2190.5735    16
    SEX           1    MALE             13641.3333  3333.0827     3
    SEX           2    FEMALE           12033.2308  1903.0008    13

  GRADE81S     3.00    GRADES 8-15      19142.0333  9294.0232    30
    SEX           1    MALE             28418.0000 15680.5949     5
    SEX           2    FEMALE           17286.8400  6471.7384    25

DEPT81            4    ST LOUIS OPERATIONS 14705.0968  6624.5319   31
  GRADE81S     1.00    GRADES 1-4        9445.4286   680.5620     7
    SEX           1    MALE              9197.5000   873.2769     2
    SEX           2    FEMALE            9544.6000   679.0183     5

  GRADE81S     2.00    GRADES 5-7       12340.0000  1925.6254    13
    SEX           1    MALE             11700.0000  1357.2398     3
    SEX           2    FEMALE           12532.0000  2087.3897    10

  GRADE81S     3.00    GRADES 8-15      20847.2727  7667.4707    11
    SEX           1    MALE             21775.0000     .0000      1
    SEX           2    FEMALE           20754.5000  8075.7134    10

  Total Cases = 275
Missing Cases = 115 or  41.8 Pct
```

MULT RESPONSE

This example analyzes a 465-case sample from a survey about magazine readership and organizational memberships. The variables are

- TIME, NEWSWEEK, U.S.NEWS, STONE, REPUBLIC—dichotomous variables, coded 1=no or 2=yes, which show whether the respondent regularly read *Time*, *Newsweek*, *U.S. News and World Report*, *Rolling Stone*, or *New Republic* magazines.

- PROB1, PROB2, PROB3—multiple response variables created from a multiple response item asking the respondent to name three national problems from a list of nine problems coded 1 to 9.

- EDUC—the respondent's education, coded in three categories, 1=Grade school, 2=High school, 3=College.

- SEX—the respondent's sex, coded 1=male, 2=female.

This example examines the distribution of magazine readership and national problem concerns by education and sex. The SPSS commands are

```
GET   FILE=MRESFILE.
MULT RESPONSE   GROUPS=MAGS 'Magazines Read' (TIME TO REPUBLIC (2))
   PROBS 'National Problems Mentioned' (PROB1 TO PROB3 (1,9))
  /VARIABLES=EDUC (1,3) SEX (1,2)
  /TABLES=MAGS PROBS BY EDUC SEX
  /CELLS=COLUMN.
```

- The GET command defines the data to SPSS and selects the variables needed for analysis.
- The MULT RESPONSE command creates a multiple dichotomy group, MAGS, from the multiple dichotomy variables between and including TIME and REPUBLIC; it also creates a multiple response group, PROBS, from the multiple response variables between and including PROB1 and PROB3.
- Two other individual variables, EDUC and SEX, are named on the VARIABLES subcommand.
- The TABLES subcommand requests four crosstabulations: MAGS by EDUC, MAGS by SEX, PROBS by EDUC, and PROBS by SEX.
- The CELLS subcommand requests column percentages in the tables.

Output from MULT RESPONSE

```
     * * *  C R O S S T A B U L A T I O N  * * *              * * *  C R O S S T A B U L A T I O N  * * *

  MAGS (tabulating 2)  Magazines Read                     MAGS (tabulating 2)  Magazines Read
by EDUC  Highest Educational Attainment of Respon       by SEX  Observed Sex of Respondent


                  EDUC                                                   SEX

           Count IGrade  High    College                        Count IMale   Female
           Col pct Ischool school                 Row           Col pct I                        Row
                I                                 Total                I                         Total
                I    1 I    2 I    3 I                                I    1 I    2 I
MAGS            +------+------+------+               MAGS            +------+------+
          TIME  I   23 I   46 I  108 I    177              TIME  I   82 I   95 I    177
 Reads Time regularly I 50.0 I 31.7 I 60.0 I   47.7   Reads Time regularly I 39.4 I 53.1 I   45.7
                +------+------+------+                                +------+------+
       NEWSWEEK I   23 I   60 I  108 I    191           NEWSWEEK I  119 I   72 I    191
 Reads Newsweek Regul I 50.0 I 41.4 I 60.0 I   51.5   Reads Newsweek Regul I 57.2 I 40.2 I   49.4
                +------+------+------+                                +------+------+
       U.S.NEWS I    0 I   37 I  144 I    181           U.S.NEWS I   64 I  117 I    181
 Reads U.S. News & Wo I   .0 I 25.5 I 80.0 I   48.8   Reads U.S. News & Wo I 30.8 I 65.4 I   46.8
                +------+------+------+                                +------+------+
          STONE I    0 I  115 I    0 I    115              STONE I   92 I   39 I    131
 Reads Rolling Stone  I   .0 I 79.3 I   .0 I   31.0   Reads Rolling Stone  I 44.2 I 21.8 I   33.9
                +------+------+------+                                +------+------+
        REPUBLIC I    0 I   30 I   63 I     93           REPUBLIC I   66 I   27 I     93
 Reads New Republic R I   .0 I 20.7 I 35.0 I   25.1   Reads New Republic R I 31.7 I 15.1 I   24.0
                +------+------+------+                                +------+------+
         Column      46    145    180    371               Column     208    179    387
          Total     12.4   39.1   48.5  100.0               Total     53.7   46.3  100.0

Percents and totals based on respondents               Percents and totals based on respondents

371 valid cases;  94 missing cases                     387 valid cases;  78 missing cases
```

```
* * * C R O S S T A B U L A T I O N * * *            * * * C R O S S T A B U L A T I O N * * *

  PROBS (group)  National Problems Mentioned           PROBS (group)  National Problems Mentioned
by EDUC  Highest Educational Attainment of Respon     by SEX  Observed Sex of Respondent
```

		Grade school	High school	College	Row Total
	Count Col pct	1	2	3	
Recession	1	32 / 25.8	60 / 41.4	27 / 15.0	119 / 26.5
Inflation	2	0 / .0	108 / 74.5	36 / 20.0	144 / 32.1
Lack of religion	3	23 / 18.5	37 / 25.5	90 / 50.0	150 / 33.4
Watergate	4	0 / .0	30 / 20.7	99 / 55.0	129 / 28.7
Racial conflict	5	69 / 55.6	23 / 15.9	0 / .0	92 / 20.5
Unions too strong	6	0 / .0	0 / .0	9 / 5.0	9 / 2.0
Big business	7	32 / 25.8	55 / 37.9	54 / 30.0	141 / 31.4
Communist aggression	8	0 / .0	30 / 20.7	108 / 60.0	138 / 30.7
Weather	9	39 / 31.5	0 / .0	27 / 15.0	66 / 14.7
Column Total		124 / 27.6	145 / 32.3	180 / 40.1	449 / 100.0

```
Percents and totals based on respondents

449 valid cases;  16 missing cases
```

		Male	Female	Row Total
	Count Col pct	1	2	
Recession	1	37 / 16.0	82 / 37.6	119 / 26.5
Inflation	2	78 / 33.8	66 / 30.3	144 / 32.1
Lack of religion	3	87 / 37.7	63 / 28.9	150 / 33.4
Watergate	4	84 / 36.4	45 / 20.6	129 / 28.7
Racial conflict	5	62 / 26.8	30 / 13.8	92 / 20.5
Unions too strong	6	9 / 3.9	0 / .0	9 / 2.0
Big business	7	93 / 40.3	48 / 22.0	141 / 31.4
Communist aggression	8	66 / 28.6	72 / 33.0	138 / 30.7
Weather	9	39 / 16.9	27 / 12.4	66 / 14.7
Column Total		231 / 51.4	218 / 48.6	449 / 100.0

```
Percents and totals based on respondents

449 valid cases;  16 missing cases
```

NLR/CNLR

The following examples show how to use CNLR and NLR to do nonlinear estimation in a variety of settings. A theme running through the examples is showing how to get good initial estimates for CNLR and NLR.

Example 1: A Basic Nonlinear Model

Draper and Smith (1981) pose the following exercise. Under adiabatic conditions, the wind speed Y is given by the nonlinear model

$$Y = a^1 \ln(b^1 X + c) + e$$

where

X = the nominal height of the anemometer
a = friction velocity
b = 1 + (zero point displacement)/(roughness length)
c = 1/(roughness length)

The data are as follows:

```
   X      Y

  40   490.2
  80   585.3
 160   673.7
 320   759.2
 640   837.5
```

To arrive at good initial values, consider the model without the error term:

$$Y = a^1 \ln(b^1 X + c)$$

Simple algebraic manipulation transforms the model into linear form. First, divide both sides by *a*:

$$Y/a = \ln(b^1 X + c)$$

Then, use the EXP function, which is the inverse of the natural logarithm:

$$\exp(Y/a) = b^1 X + c$$

The model is now in linear form. The dependent variable, $\exp(Y/a)$ should be regressed on X to obtain estimates of b and c. To determine the value to use for a, you need to consider the magnitudes of the Y values. Recall that the transcendental number e is 2.7183 to four decimal places. Thus e raised to the Y power, represented as $\exp(Y)$, will be outside the bounds of machine storage if Y is at all large, as is the case here. Considering the scale of the Y variable, we decide to set a equal to 100 initially. If you choose naive initial values for a, b, and c, chances are you will get CNLR off to a bad start. Having gone through the above exercise, however, we can confidently supply initial values to CNLR.

The following SPSS commands show how to arrive at initial estimates for CNLR:

```
TITLE 'NLRDS7--EXAMPLE G'.
SET WIDTH=80.
DATA LIST / X 1-3 Y 5-9(1).
BEGIN DATA
 40 490.2
 80 585.3
160 673.7
320 759.2
640 837.5
END DATA.

PLOT PLOT=Y WITH X.
* LET A=100 SO THAT EXP DOESN'T PRODUCE TOO LARGE NUMBERS.
COMPUTE EY=EXP(Y/100).
REGRESSION VAR=EY,X/DEP=EY/ENTER.
```

Figure 1 shows the plot of the Y versus X association. The relationship is nonlinear.

Figure 1 The functional form

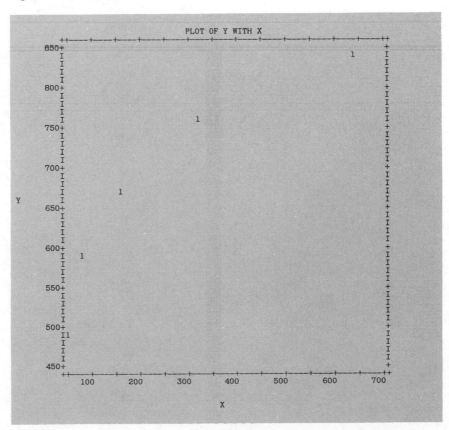

Figure 2 shows the regression used to get initial values for *b* and *c*.

Figure 2 Regression results

```
Multiple R            .99940
R Square              .99879
Adjusted R Square     .99839
Standard Error      69.22830

Analysis of Variance
                     DF      Sum of Squares        Mean Square
Regression            1      11886580.22650     11886580.22650
Residual              3         14377.67112         4792.55704

F =    2480.21675      Signif F =  .0000


------------------ Variables in the Equation ------------------

Variable              B          SE B        Beta        T   Sig T

X               7.065892      .141880     .999396   49.802   .0000
(Constant)   -223.259958    46.867778               -4.764   .0176
```

Recall that we set *a* to 100. The initial values for *b* and *c* are 7.06 and -223, respectively. The following commands show how to use CNLR to estimate the model. Because this is an unconstrained model, you can also use NLR to estimate the model parameters.

```
MODEL PROGRAM
 A=100 B=7.06 C=-223.26.
COMPUTE PRED=A*LN(B*X+C).
CNLR Y WITH X/PRED=PRED/SAVE PRED.
PLOT
  FORMAT=OVERLAY
 /PLOT=PRED WITH X;Y WITH X.
```

Figure 3 shows the iteration history from CNLR. CNLR takes some time to get to a final solution, but an inspection of values as they change across iterations reveals that nothing is awry.

Figure 3 Iteration history

```
Iteration  Residual SS            A          B           C

   0.1     6822.703884   100.000000   7.06000000  -223.26000
   1.1     6118.219759   100.003582   7.12842901  -223.25826
   2.1     5980.044858    99.3079691  7.18318715  -223.18102
   3.1     2189.215593    99.8751558  7.25081504  -203.17519
   4.1      969.0682157   99.8829723  7.03269110  -178.53483
   5.1      346.3380776   99.9820119  6.63396701  -146.30177
   6.1      241.2809321  100.221852   6.34390202  -126.98157
   7.1      233.1632074  100.394696   6.22140934  -120.56186
   8.1      228.9660802  100.567447   6.12718119  -116.91714
   9.1      210.6108403  101.510838   5.64880982  -100.76343
  10.1      191.6216324  103.042276   4.94957998   -79.980740
  11.1      153.9276211  103.806125   4.71805881   -76.312618
  12.1      112.9684153  106.405708   3.96720857   -64.516989
  13.1      101.8552912  106.152748   4.11125134   -69.138780
  14.1       85.09714967 106.154607   4.07803645   -64.325743
  15.1       70.26699518 106.994246   3.85660498   -58.647174
  16.1       54.07086976 108.832385   3.36853918   -46.433765
  17.1       39.48809011 109.300201   3.30711370   -45.456518
  18.1       27.88877849 110.894789   2.96953110   -37.284674
  19.1       17.59942496 111.803782   2.81864042   -33.199641
  20.1       13.63701498 112.864153   2.63353107   -29.260726
  21.1       10.60925934 113.656352   2.54067173   -28.092029
  22.1        8.256672638 114.694027   2.36235821   -23.152804
  23.1        8.072032652 114.278682   2.43409724   -24.442493
  24.1        7.315334149 114.556909   2.39300009   -23.887380
  25.1        7.154980179 114.885783   2.34353251   -22.746051
  26.1        7.060824167 114.965846   2.33415995   -22.554616
  27.1        7.014235706 115.119098   2.31424523   -22.106372
  28.1        7.013278395 115.143743   2.31105767   -22.038259
  29.1        7.013265870 115.146801   2.31065500   -22.028887
  30.1        7.013265849 115.146881   2.31064486   -22.028764

Run stopped after 30 major iterations.
Optimal solution found.
```

Figure 4 shows the remaining CNLR results. The ANOVA for the regression shows that the fit of the final solution is very good. Using 5 data points to estimate a 3-parameter model yields a highly parameterized situation. This is reflected in the high correlations of the estimates. The standard error of the c coefficient is relatively large. This dovetails with the iteration history shown in Figure 3, wherein CNLR began with an initial value of -223 and ended up with a final value of -22.

Figure 4 CNLR results

```
Nonlinear Regression Summary Statistics      Dependent Variable Y

  Source                    DF  Sum of Squares  Mean Square

  Regression                 3   2314527.69673  771509.23224
  Residual                   2         7.01327        3.50663
  Uncorrected Total          5   2314534.71000

  (Corrected Total)          4     75525.34800

  R squared = 1 - Residual SS / Corrected SS =      .99991

                                           Asymptotic 95 %
                              Asymptotic   Confidence Interval
  Parameter    Estimate      Std. Error   Lower        Upper

  A          115.14688147   2.040557217  106.36707239 123.92669055
  B            2.310644855   .280311478    1.104561908   3.516727803
  C          -22.02876418   6.409410588  -49.60623215   5.548703779

  Asymptotic Correlation Matrix of the Parameter Estimates

                   A         B         C

  A            1.0000    -.9963     .9666
  B            -.9963    1.0000    -.9802
  C             .9666    -.9802    1.0000
```

Figure 5 shows a plot of PRED versus X superimposed on a value of Y versus X. The fit is very good.

Figure 5 The fitted function

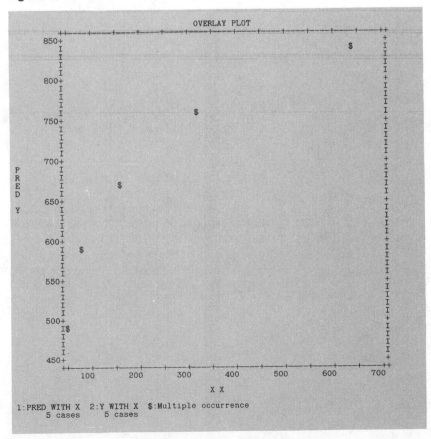

**Example 2: Grafted
Polynomials: A Segmented
Model**

In this example, we look at a time series consisting of United States wheat yields from 1908 to 1971. The example comes from Fuller's *Introduction to Statistical Time Series* (1976).

Figure 6 is a plot of the data. The plot shows that wheat yields were more or less level for the first 20 to 30 years and then increased over the rest of the span. It is not at all clear what functional form would describe the behavior of the plot in its entirety. One approach is to use SPSS Trends procedures such as CURVEFIT or EXSMOOTH to model the series. The approach used here is to model pieces or segments of the series using low-order functional forms, such as linear functions and quadratic functions.

Figure 6 Plot of wheat yields

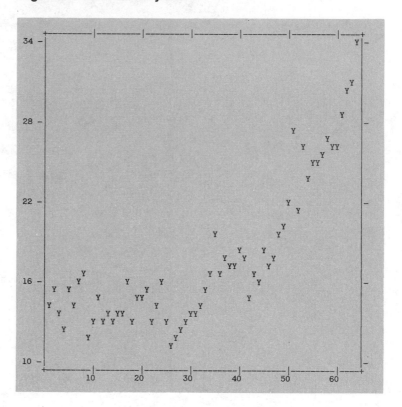

Following Fuller, the use of grafted polynomials assumes that "the time series may be divided into periods of length A such that the mean function in each period is adequately approximated by a quadratic in time. Furthermore, the mean function possesses a continuous first derivative" (p. 394). To approximate the trend line of wheat yields, we fit a function that is constant for the first 25 years, increases at a quadratic rate until 1961, and is linear for the last 10 years. In general, an examination of the plot of the series should suggest the number of pieces, the join points, and the functional forms in the pieces. In this example, we are fixing the join points. Subsequently, we will show how to estimate them.

The following SPSS commands fit grafted polynomials to the U.S. wheat yield series:

```
TITLE 'NLRFUL2A--GRAFTED POLYNOMIALS WITH FIXED JOIN POINTS'.
SET WIDTH=80.
* THIS EXAMPLE COMES FROM PAGE 396 AND FOLLOWING OF FULLER,
    "INTRODUCTION TO STATISTICAL TIME SERIES";
    DATA ARE UNITED STATES WHEAT YIELDS--1908 TO 1971.
DATA LIST FREE / Y.
COMPUTE Y=Y/10.

COMPUTE T=$CASENUM.

BEGIN DATA
                              143 155 137
124 151 144 161 167 119 132 148 129 135
127 138 133 160 128 147 147 154 130 142
163 131 112 121 122 128 136 133 141 153
168 195 164 177 170 172 182 179 145 165
160 184 173 181 198 202 218 275 216 261
239 250 252 258 265 263 259 284 306 310
339
END DATA.
TSPLOT VAR=Y.
TEMPORARY.
SELECT IF T <= 25.
DESCRIPTIVES Y.

MODEL PROGRAM
 B0=14 B1=0.01.
DO IF T <= 25.
COMPUTE PRED=B0.
ELSE IF T > 25 AND T <= 54.
COMPUTE PRED=B0+B1*(T-25)*(T-25).
ELSE IF T > 54.
COMPUTE PRED=B0+B1*((54-25)*(54-25)+54*(T-54)).
END IF.

CNLR Y WITH T/SAVE PRED.
TSPLOT VAR=PRED,Y.
```

- The variable T is simply "time" expressed by sequential integers. We need variable T in order to do trend regression.

- TSPLOT, a procedure available with SPSS Trends, produces a horizontal sequential plot of the wheat yield series.

- The block of commands TEMPORARY, SELECT IF, and DESCRIPTIVES is used to obtain an initial estimate for the level at the beginning of the series.

- The MODEL PROGRAM command specifies the initial values for the parameters to be estimated and signals the beginning of a block of commands culminating in a nonlinear regression.

- The DO IF/END IF structure specifies the segmented model. Years 25 and 54 are the join points. For T less than or equal to 25, the model is a level regression with parameter B0. For T between 25 and 54, the model is a quadratic in time with parameters B0 and B1. For T greater than 54, the model is a linear function of time with parameters B0 and B1. As you might guess, there is an art to specifying statements of this sort. Notice that at the first join point, T=25, the model statements for the level segment and the quadratic segment produce the same predicted value, and at the second join point, T=54, the model statements for the quadratic segment and the linear segment produce the same predicted value.

- The CNLR command specifies Y as the dependent variable and T as the independent variable. It also uses SAVE to save predicted values.

- The final TSPLOT command produces a plot in which the fitted trend is superimposed on the observed series.

Figure 7 shows the resulting CNLR output. CNLR converges quickly. This is because we have used CNLR to solve a problem that can be done using ordinary regression. To see this, you might build an independent variable X as follows:

$$X = \begin{cases} 0, & 1<=t<=25 \\ (t-25)**2, & 25<=t<=54 \\ 841+54*(t-54), & 54<=t<=64 \end{cases}$$

where t=1 for 1908. Then, use REGRESSION and regress Y on X including an intercept term. The equation for the estimated trend line is

predicted Y = 13.97 + .0123*X

just as we obtained here. Figure 8 shows the fitted trend line.

Figure 7 CNLR results

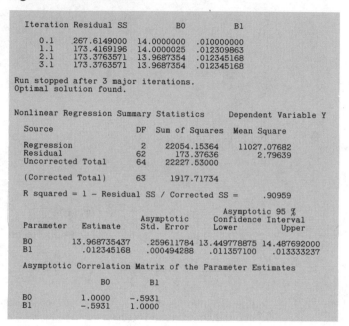

```
 Iteration Residual SS          B0            B1

    0.1    .267.6149000    14.0000000    .010000000
    1.1    173.4169196    14.0000025    .012309863
    2.1    173.3763571    13.9687354    .012345168
    3.1    173.3763571    13.9687354    .012345168

Run stopped after 3 major iterations.
Optimal solution found.


Nonlinear Regression Summary Statistics       Dependent Variable Y

  Source                 DF  Sum of Squares  Mean Square

  Regression              2     22054.15364   11027.07682
  Residual               62       173.37636       2.79639
  Uncorrected Total      64     22227.53000

  (Corrected Total)      63      1917.71734

  R squared = 1 - Residual SS / Corrected SS =      .90959

                                            Asymptotic 95 %
                             Asymptotic   Confidence Interval
  Parameter     Estimate     Std. Error   Lower        Upper

  B0        13.968735437    .259611784 13.449778875 14.487692000
  B1         .012345168    .000494288  .011357100   .013333237

Asymptotic Correlation Matrix of the Parameter Estimates

              B0         B1

  B0         1.0000    -.5931
  B1         -.5931    1.0000
```

Figure 8 Plot of fitted function

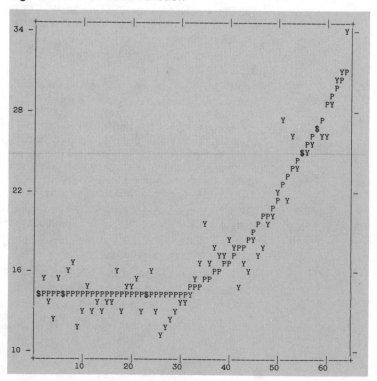

If the above example can be done in REGRESSION, why use CNLR? In this example, we assumed that we know the join points. If you want to use the data to estimate the join points, then the problem is indeed a nonlinear regression problem. It turns out that the above setup is easily modified to solve the more difficult problem of estimating the join points. The model program is:

```
MODEL PROGRAM
  B0=13.97 B1=0.0123 K1=25 K2=54.
DO IF T <= K1.
COMPUTE PRED=B0.
ELSE IF T > K1 AND T <= K2.
COMPUTE PRED=B0+B1*(T-K1)*(T-K1).
ELSE IF T > K2.
COMPUTE PRED=B0+B1*((K2-K1)*(K2-K1)+K2*(T-K2)).
END IF.

CNLR Y WITH T/PRED=PRED.
```

The rest of the example is as before. Note that there are two additional parameters—K1 and K2—representing the join points. The MODEL PROGRAM statement specifies parameter estimates from the previous run as initial values for B0 and B1, and our guesses of 25 and 54 as initial values for the join points.

Figure 9 shows the CNLR output produced by the above specification. The resulting solution has a slightly smaller residual sum of squares. The parameter estimates B0 and B1 have not changed much. The initial guesses of 25 and 54 turn out to have been good ones.

Figure 9 Iteration history

```
Iteration Residual SS        B0          B1          K1          K2

    0.1    173.4102016   13.9700000   .012300000   25.0000000  54.0000000
    1.1    173.3764235   13.9700000   .012343743   25.0000000  54.0000000
    2.1    173.2412076   13.9458767   .012547336   25.2460283  54.0288124
    3.1    173.0434791   14.0180805   .012727706   25.6113083  54.0716663
    4.1    173.0417917   14.0198918   .012733675   25.6117603  54.0849659
    5.1    173.0415989   14.0199757   .012734547   25.6130378  54.1000283
    6.1    173.0409950   14.0201634   .012730088   25.6117569  54.1732263
    7.1    173.0404710   14.0202932   .012718133   25.6048813  54.2664188
    8.1    173.0401890   14.0203104   .012704466   25.5958103  54.3374559
    9.1    173.0401448   14.0202566   .012699988   25.5923167  54.3471836
   10.1    173.0401424   14.0202330   .012699809   25.5919958  54.3430999
   11.1    173.0401424   14.0202308   .012699918   25.5920510  54.3420942

Run stopped after 11 major iterations.
Optimal solution found.


Nonlinear Regression Summary Statistics      Dependent Variable Y

   Source              DF   Sum of Squares   Mean Square

   Regression           4     22054.48986      5513.62246
   Residual            60       173.04014         2.88400
   Uncorrected Total   64     22227.53000

   (Corrected Total)   63      1917.71734

   R squared = 1 - Residual SS / Corrected SS =      .90977

                                          Asymptotic 95 %
                            Asymptotic   Confidence Interval
   Parameter    Estimate    Std. Error   Lower        Upper

   B0       14.020230799   .318564556   13.383006812  14.657454785
   B1         .012699918   .003615380    .005468081    .019931755
   K1       25.592051014  3.449934328   18.691154892  32.492947136
   K2       54.342094246 17.231712420   19.873537422  88.810651070
```

Example 3: Linearizing a Problem for Good Initial Values

You must supply CNLR (and NLR) with initial values of all parameters. Specifying bad initial values can lead to bad consequences: the procedure may not converge to a solution; or the procedure may converge to a solution that does not provide the true minimum value of the residual sum of squares; or the solution may have parameter values that are physically impossible given the phenomenon at hand.

On the other hand, good initial values will often enable the procedure to converge to a solution—hopefully the right solution—and converge much faster than otherwise.

One of the best ways to arrive at good initial values is to attempt to linearize the problem and obtain estimates via REGRESSION. This is illustrated in the following example.

Draper and Smith (1981) pose this problem as an exercise. The relationship between the yield of a crop, Y, and the amount of fertilizer, X, applied to that crop has been formulated to be

$$Y = a - bp^x + e$$

where a, b, and p are parameters to be estimated, and p is bounded by 0 and 1. The values of X and Y are as follows:

```
X       Y

0    44.4
1    54.6
2    63.8
3    65.7
4    68.9
```

The basic strategy for coming up with good initial values is to try to get the model into a form where you can usefully take logarithms, since logging "transforms" exponentiation into multiplication and multiplication into addition. Thus, a term involving multiplication and exponentiation is linearized.

Consider the model omitting the error term:

$$Y = a - bp^x$$

Subtract a from both sides:

$$Y - a = -bp^x$$

Take negatives of both sides (because you cannot take a logarithm of a negative number):

$$a - Y = bp^x$$

Take logs of both sides:

$$\ln(a - Y) = \ln(bp^x)$$
$$= \ln(b) + \ln(p^x)$$
$$= \ln(b) + X*\ln(p)$$

At this point you have the desired linear form:

$$\ln(a - Y) = \ln(b) + \ln(p)*X$$

Choose a so that $(a - Y)$ is positive, and then regress $\ln(a - Y)$ on X. Antilogs of the resulting regression coefficients will supply initial values for b and p.

The following SPSS commands show how to estimate initial values using REGRESSION for use in CNLR:

```
TITLE 'NLRDS5--EXERCISE D FROM DRAPER AND SMITH CH 10'.
* RELATIONSHIP BETWEEN CROP YIELD AND AMOUNT OF FERTILIZER.
SET WIDTH=80.
DATA LIST / X 1 Y 3-6(1).
BEGIN DATA
0 44.4
1 54.6
2 63.8
3 65.7
4 68.9
END DATA.
PLOT PLOT=Y WITH X.

* ESTIMATE A BY YMAX PLUS SOMETHING--LET A=70.
COMPUTE DEPVAR=LN(70-Y).
REGRESSION VAR=DEPVAR,X/DEP=DEPVAR/ENTER.
* REGRESSION GIVES INT=3.88 SLOPE=-.76;
   ANTILOGS ARE 29 AND .47.
```

- The PLOT command produces a plot showing the form of the Y versus X association. An examination of the plot will help you determine the functional form of the relationship, as well as plausible and implausible values of the parameters.
- DEPVAR is the transformed dependent variable needed for regression. Our guess for the value of a is 70, which is larger than any Y value, thereby ensuring that the value evaluated by the LN function is positive.
- The REGRESSION command regresses DEPVAR on X. The intercept and slope estimates from this regression are used to obtain initial values for b and p.

Figure 10 shows the plot of Y versus X. The nonlinear association of Y and X is evident.

Figure 10 The functional form

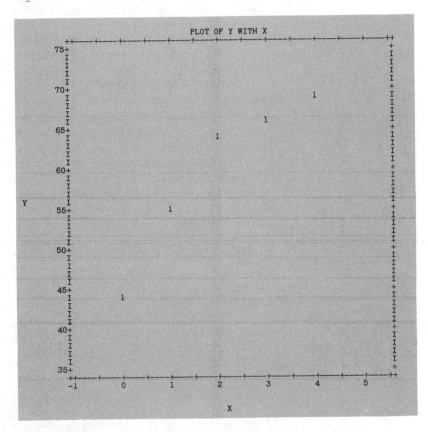

Figure 11 shows the output from REGRESSION. The antilog of 3.38 is 29.52. This becomes the initial value for b. The antilog of -0.75 is 0.469. This becomes the initial value for p.

Figure 11 Regression results

```
Multiple R              .98126
R Square                .96287
Adjusted R Square       .95049
Standard Error          .27141

Analysis of Variance
                    DF      Sum of Squares     Mean Square
Regression          1           5.73097          5.73097
Residual            3            .22099           .07366

F =      77.79854      Signif F =  .0031


--------------- Variables in the Equation ---------------

Variable              B        SE B       Beta        T    Sig T

X               -.757032    .085828    -.981260   -8.820   .0031
(Constant)      3.385150    .210234               16.102   .0005
```

The following SPSS commands run the nonlinear regression in CNLR:

```
MODEL PROGRAM
 A=70 B=29 P=.47.
COMPUTE PRED=A-B*P**X.
CNLR Y WITH X/PRED=PRED
 /BOUNDS 0 < P < 1/SAVE PRED.
PLOT
 FORMAT=OVERLAY
 /PLOT=Y WITH X;PRED WITH X.
```

- The MODEL PROGRAM command specifies initial values for the parameters and signals the beginning of a block of commands culminating in CNLR.

- The COMPUTE command specifies the model.

- CNLR specifies the regression of Y on X. The PREDICTED subcommand names variable PRED. The BOUNDS subcommand constrains the parameter estimate of *p* to lie within the interval (0,1). The SAVE subcommand saves the predicted values from the regression. Since BOUNDS is specified, you must use CNLR. If the problem were unconstrained, you could use NLR.

- The PLOT command produces an overlay plot showing Y versus X and PRED versus X. This shows how well the estimated model fits the observed values.

Figure 12 shows the output from CNLR. The iteration history shows that the initial values are good. CNLR converges quickly to a solution in the neighborhood of the initial values. CNLR prints the parameter estimates and their standard errors. Note the broad 95% confidence limits. We are estimating a model on five data points, so we should not expect much precision. With five data points and three parameters, the model is also highly parameterized, so the high correlations of the estimates are not surprising.

Figure 12 CNLR results

```
Iteration Residual SS              A            B            P

    0.2    16.49653383    70.0000000   29.0000000   .470000000
    1.1    10.74575450    70.1922983   28.4434176   .529112127
    2.2     4.480015479   70.5431977   26.5334335   .542658747
    3.1     4.172684227   71.6954703   27.3110889   .593210526
    4.1     3.720234102   71.5964337   27.4434258   .577965876
    5.1     3.616030024   71.9414089   27.8200371   .584801598
    6.1     3.570464383   72.3415954   28.1778166   .594667097
    7.1     3.568824817   72.4230603   28.2430745   .596594769
    8.1     3.568804824   72.4323386   28.2515272   .596784828
    9.1     3.568804798   72.4326326   28.2518771   .596790136

Run stopped after 9 major iterations.
Optimal solution found.


Nonlinear Regression Summary Statistics      Dependent Variable Y

  Source                   DF  Sum of Squares  Mean Square

  Regression                3     18083.09120   6027.69707
  Residual                  2         3.56880      1.78440
  Uncorrected Total         5     18086.66000

  (Corrected Total)         4       397.30800

  R squared = 1 - Residual SS / Corrected SS =     .99102

                                        Asymptotic 95 %
                            Asymptotic  Confidence Interval
  Parameter   Estimate     Std. Error   Lower        Upper

  A          72.432632595  3.186401989 58.722651381 86.142613810
  B          28.251877129  3.102811346 14.901557422 41.602196836
  P            .596790136   .080996274   .248291295   .945288977

Asymptotic Correlation Matrix of the Parameter Estimates

            A          B          P

  A       1.0000      .9131      .9434
  B        .9131     1.0000      .7901
  P        .9434      .7901     1.0000
```

Figure 13 is the plot of PRED versus X superimposed on the plot of Y versus X. The predicted points fit the observed points very well.

Figure 13 The fitted function

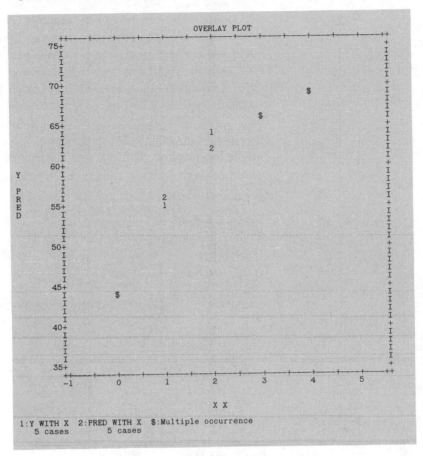

Example 4: Using CNLR to Solve Linear Programming Problems

Although CNLR is not explicitly designed to do so, you can use CNLR to solve linear programming problems. Linear programming is a special form of optimizing under constraints. If you do a lot of this sort of work, or if your problems are very large, you should acquire special-purpose software which will probably work more efficiently than CNLR. Nevertheless, we will show how to use CNLR to solve a type of problem known as a "transportation problem".

This example is found in Bruce Feiring's *Linear Programming: An Introduction* (1986) in the Sage series *Quantitative Applications in the Social Sciences.*

A plastics manufacturer has two plants, one located in Salt Lake City and one in Denver. There are three distribution warehouses, in Los Angeles, Chicago, and New York. The Salt Lake City plant can supply 120 tons per week and the Denver plant can supply 140 tons per week. The Los Angeles warehouse needs at least 100 tons each week to meet demands, Chicago needs at least 60 tons weekly, and New York needs at least 80 tons per week. Shipping costs in dollars per ton are as follows:

	To:		
	Los Angeles	Chicago	New York
From:			
Salt Lake City	5	7	9
Denver	6	7	10

The question is: How many tons of plastics should be shipped from each plant to each warehouse to minimize the total shipping cost while meeting demands and not exceeding supplies? To answer this, following Feiring, use the following variables:

- X11, the number of tons shipped from Salt Lake City to Los Angeles.
- X12, the number of tons shipped from Salt Lake City to Chicago.
- X13, the number of tons shipped from Salt Lake City to New York.
- X21, the number of tons shipped from Denver to Los Angeles.
- X22, the number of tons shipped from Denver to Chicago.
- X23, the number of tons shipped from Denver to New York.

This problem contains a set of supply-and-demand constraints that can be specified on the BOUNDS subcommand. The costs to be minimized are specified on the loss function. The following commands show how to do this:

```
TITLE 'NLRLP3--CNLR SOLVES LINEAR PROGRAMMING PROBLEM'.
SET WIDTH 80.
* EXAMPLE FROM PAGE 18 AND FF. OF FEIRING'S
   "LINEAR PROGRAMMING:  AN INTRODUCTION".
DATA LIST FREE / Y X.                    /* "DUMMY" VARIABLES
BEGIN DATA
0 0
END DATA.

MODEL PROGRAM
 X11=1 X12=1 X13=1 X21=1 X22=1 X23=1.
COMPUTE PRED=0.
COMPUTE LOSS=5*X11+7*X12+9*X13+6*X21+7*X22+10*X23.

CNLR Y WITH X
 /PRED=PRED
 /LOSS=LOSS
 /BOUNDS
  X11+X12+X13 <= 120;
  X21+X22+X23 <= 140;
  100 <= X11+X21;
   60 <= X12+X22;
   80 <= X13+X23;
    0 <= X11;
    0 <= X12;
    0 <= X13;
    0 <= X21;
    0 <= X22;
    0 <= X23; .
```

Since there are no relevant data to be read, we read in "dummy" data so that SPSS has an active system file.

- The MODEL PROGRAM command specifies initial values for the parameters and signals the beginning of a block of commands culminating in the CNLR command. You cannot use NLR to solve this problem since NLR works only for unconstrained minimization problems and does not work for loss functions other than least squares.
- The first COMPUTE command creates a variable PRED that is always 0. This is needed because CNLR expects a PRED variable. PRED is not actually used, however, since the LOSS function is only a function of X.
- The second COMPUTE creates variable LOSS, which contains the cost function to be minimized.
- The CNLR command specifies X and Y as variables, even through they aren't really used. The BOUNDS subcommand specifies the supply and demand constraints. In addition, simple non-negativity constraints are imposed.

CNLR produces the output shown in Figure 20. The display includes the iteration number, the value of the loss function, the values of the X variables, and the values of the linear constraints. Given supply-and-demand constraints and the cost function, the optimal solution is to ship 100 tons from Salt Lake City to Los

Angeles; 20 tons from Salt Lake City to New York; 60 tons from Denver to Chicago; and ship 60 tons from Denver to New York.

Figure 20 Linear programming solution

```
 Iteration  Loss funct        X11          X12           X13          X21
                              X22          X23       Lin Con  1   Lin Con  2
                          Lin Con  3   Lin Con  4   Lin Con  5

    0.1    1720.000000   99.0000000   20.0000000    1.00000000   1.00000000
                         40.0000000   79.0000000   120.000000   120.000000
                         100.000000   60.0000000    80.0000000
    1.3    1718.000004   99.9999981   18.0000038    1.99999811    .000001892
                         41.9999962   78.0000019   120.000000   120.000000
                         100.000000   60.0000000    80.0000000
    2.3    1717.000001   100.000000   17.0000006    2.99999924    .000000000
                         42.9999994   77.0000008   120.000000   120.000000
                         100.000000   60.0000000    80.0000000
    3.1    1700.000000   99.9999917    .000000000   20.0000083    .000008340
                         60.0000000   59.9999917   120.000000   120.000000
                         100.000000   60.0000000    80.0000000
    4.1    1700.000000   99.9999470    .000000000   20.0000530    .000053001
                         60.0000000   59.9999470   120.000000   120.000000
                         100.000000   60.0000000    80.0000000

Run stopped after 4 major iterations.
Optimal solution found.
```

This approach can also be used to solve nonlinear problems with general forms for the cost function and the constraints. Use the CONSTRAINED FUNCTION command and the BOUNDS subcommand to specify the nonlinear programming model in question.

NONPAR CORR

This example analyzes a 500-case sample from the 1980 General Social Survey. The variables are

- PRESTIGE—the respondent's occupational prestige scale score.
- SPPRES—the spouse's occupational prestige scale score.
- PAPRES16—the father's occupational prestige scale score when the respondent was growing up.
- DEGREE, PADEG, MADEG—the highest educational degree earned by the respondent, the father, and the mother, respectively. Each of these variables has four categories to code high school, junior college, college, and graduate degrees.

This example determines the degree to which variation in three measures of occupational prestige and three measures of educational attainment are related. NONPAR CORR computes nonparametric correlation coefficients for the ranked data. The SPSS commands are

```
GET  FILE GSS80 /KEEP PRESTIGE SPPRES PAPRES16 DEGREE PADEG MADEG.
NONPAR CORR VARIABLES=PRESTIGE TO MADEG
  /MISSING=LISTWISE
  /FORMAT=SERIAL
  /PRINT=BOTH.
```

- The GET command defines the data to SPSS and selects the variables needed for the analysis.
- The NONPAR CORR command requests correlation coefficients for one simple variable list. This form of the NONPAR CORR command produces a lower-triangular matrix.
- The MISSING subcommand excludes missing values listwise. Cases missing on any of the six variables are not used in the calculation of any coefficients.
- The FORMAT subcommand prints each lower-triangular matrix in serial format.
- The PRINT subcommand requests both Kendall and Spearman correlation matrices.

Output from the NONPAR CORR command

```
- - - - - - - - - - - - K E N D A L L   C O R R E L A T I O N   C O E F F I C I E N T S - - - - - - - - - - - -

VARIABLE        VARIABLE        VARIABLE        VARIABLE        VARIABLE        VARIABLE
PAIR            PAIR            PAIR            PAIR            PAIR            PAIR
_____        _____        _____        _____        _____        _____


PRESTIGE   .2354   PRESTIGE   .1970   PRESTIGE   .4564   PRESTIGE   .1618   PRESTIGE   .1987   SPPRES     .1386
WITH    N( 192)   WITH    N( 192)   WITH    N( 192)   WITH    N( 192)   WITH    N( 192)   WITH    N( 192)
SPPRES  SIG .000   PAPRES16 SIG .000   DEGREE  SIG .000   PADEG   SIG .003   MADEG   SIG .000   PAPRES16 SIG .003


SPPRES     .2875   SPPRES     .0975   SPPRES     .0707   PAPRES16   .2642   PAPRES16   .2875   PAPRES16   .1949
WITH    N( 192)   WITH    N( 192)   WITH    N( 192)   WITH    N( 192)   WITH    N( 192)   WITH    N( 192)
DEGREE  SIG .000   PADEG   SIG .047   MADEG   SIG .116   DEGREE  SIG .000   PADEG   SIG .000   MADEG   SIG .001


DEGREE     .3434   DEGREE     .3141   PADEG      .5545
WITH    N( 192)   WITH    N( 192)   WITH    N( 192)
PADEG   SIG .000   MADEG   SIG .000   MADEG   SIG .000

" . " IS PRINTED IF A COEFFICIENT CANNOT BE COMPUTED.

- - - - - - - - - - - - S P E A R M A N   C O R R E L A T I O N   C O E F F I C I E N T S - - - - - - - - - - - -

VARIABLE        VARIABLE        VARIABLE        VARIABLE        VARIABLE        VARIABLE
PAIR            PAIR            PAIR            PAIR            PAIR            PAIR
_____        _____        _____        _____        _____        _____


PRESTIGE   .3374   PRESTIGE   .2694   PRESTIGE   .5547   PRESTIGE   .1996   PRESTIGE   .2435   SPPRES     .1971
WITH    N( 192)   WITH    N( 192)   WITH    N( 192)   WITH    N( 192)   WITH    N( 192)   WITH    N( 192)
SPPRES  SIG .000   PAPRES16 SIG .000   DEGREE  SIG .000   PADEG   SIG .003   MADEG   SIG .000   PAPRES16 SIG .003


SPPRES     .3613   SPPRES     .1175   SPPRES     .0851   PAPRES16   .3332   PAPRES16   .3440   PAPRES16   .2368
WITH    N( 192)   WITH    N( 192)   WITH    N( 192)   WITH    N( 192)   WITH    N( 192)   WITH    N( 192)
DEGREE  SIG .000   PADEG   SIG .052   MADEG   SIG .120   DEGREE  SIG .000   PADEG   SIG .000   MADEG   SIG .000


DEGREE     .3710   DEGREE     .3387   PADEG      .5774
WITH    N( 192)   WITH    N( 192)   WITH    N( 192)
PADEG   SIG .000   MADEG   SIG .000   MADEG   SIG .000

" . " IS PRINTED IF A COEFFICIENT CANNOT BE COMPUTED.
```

NPAR TESTS

The following example requests two chi-square tests on inline data. First, the frequencies for all categories of POSTPOS are compared against equal expected frequencies. The second CHISQUARE subcommand specifies eight expected proportions. The SPSS commands are:

```
TITLE  'CHISQUARE TEST, SIEGEL, P. 45'.
DATA LIST  /POSTPOS 1-2 NWINS 4-5.
VAR LABELS  POSTPOS 'POST POSITION'.
WEIGHT  BY NWINS.
BEGIN DATA
 2 19
 7 15
 4 25
 5 17
 8 11
 3 18
 6 10
 1 29
END DATA.
NPAR TESTS  CHISQUARE = POSTPOS
   /CHISQUARE = POSTPOS /EXPECTED=22,20,4*18,16,14.
```

• The TITLE command prints a title on each page of the display output.

- The DATA LIST command defines two variables, POSTPOS and NWINS. Because the FILE subcommand is omitted, data must be inline.
- The VARIABLE LABELS command assigns a label to variable POSTPOS.
- The WEIGHT command weights cases according to the values of variable NWINS.
- NPAR TESTS requests two chi-square tests. The first test assumes equal expected frequencies because the EXPECTED subcommand is omitted. The second test uses the proportions specified on EXPECTED.

The output is shown below. For each test, the display shows the number of observed cases and expected cases in each category of variable POSTPOS; the residual (observed minus expected) for each category; and the chi-square statistic, degrees of freedom, and significance of the chi-square.

One-sample chi-square test

```
- - - - - Chi-Square Test

  POSTPOS    POST POSITION

               Cases
  Category   Observed   Expected   Residual

       1         29      18.00      11.00
       2         19      18.00       1.00
       3         18      18.00        .00
       4         25      18.00       7.00
       5         17      18.00      -1.00
       6         10      18.00      -8.00
       7         15      18.00      -3.00
       8         11      18.00      -7.00
                ----
  Total         144

       Chi-Square          D.F.          Significance
        16.333              7                 .022

- - - - - Chi-Square Test

  POSTPOS    POST POSITION

               Cases
  Category   Observed   Expected   Residual

       1         29      22.00       7.00
       2         19      20.00      -1.00
       3         18      18.00        .00
       4         25      18.00       7.00
       5         17      18.00      -1.00
       6         10      18.00      -8.00
       7         15      16.00      -1.00
       8         11      14.00      -3.00
                ----
  Total         144

       Chi-Square          D.F.          Significance
         9.316              7                 .231
```

ONEWAY   This example analyzes a 500-case sample from the 1980 General Social Survey. The variables are

- WELL—the respondent's score on a scale measuring sense of well-being. WELL is the dependent variable, computed from measures of happiness, health, life, helpfulness of others, trust of others, and satisfaction with city, hobbies, family life and friendships.
- EDUC—the respondent's education in six categories, where the original codes are years of education completed.

In this example we determine the degree to which sense of well-being differs across educational levels. The SPSS commands are

```
GET FILE GSS80/KEEP EDUC HAPPY HEALTH LIFE HELPFUL TRUST
                 SATCITY SATHOBBY SATFAM SATFRND.
COUNT  X1=HAPPY HEALTH LIFE HELPFUL TRUST SATCITY SATHOBBY
           SATFAM SATFRND(1).
COUNT  X2=HAPPY HEALTH SATCITY SATHOBBY SATFAM SATFRND(2).
COUNT  X3=HEALTH HELPFUL TRUST (3).
COUNT  X4=SATCITY SATHOBBY SATFAM SATFRND(6).
COUNT  X5=HAPPY LIFE (3).
COUNT  X6=SATCITY SATHOBBY SATFAM SATFRND(7).
COMPUTE WELL=X1 + X2*.5 - X3*.5 - X4*.5 - X5 - X6.
VAR LABELS  WELL 'SENSE OF WELL-BEING SCALE'.
RECODE  EDUC (0 THRU 8=1)(9,10,11=2)(12=3)(13,14,15=4)
             (16=5)(17,18,19,20=6) INTO EDUC6.
VAR LABELS  EDUC6 'EDUCATION IN 6 CATEGORIES'.
VALUE LABELS  EDUC6 1 'GRADE SCHOOL OR LESS'
             2 'SOME HIGH SCHOOL' 3 'HIGH SCH GRAD'
             4 'SOME COLLEGE' 5 'COLLEGE GRAD'
             6 'GRAD SCH'.
ONEWAY  WELL BY EDUC6(1,6)
   /POLYNOMIAL = 2
   /CONTRAST = 2*-1, 2*1
   /CONTRAST = 2*0, 2*-1, 2*1
   /CONTRAST = 2*-1, 2*0, 2*1
   /RANGES = SNK
   /RANGES = SCHEFFE (.01)
   /STATISTICS  ALL.
```

- The GET command defines the data to SPSS and selects the variables needed for analysis.
- The COUNT and COMPUTE commands create variable WELL by counting the number of "satisfied" responses for each variable on the scale and computing a weighted sum of these responses.
- The RECODE command creates the variable EDUC6 which contains the recoded six categories of education.
- The VAR LABELS and VALUE LABELS commands assign labels to the new variables, WELL and EDUC6.
- The ONEWAY command names WELL as the dependent variable and EDUC6 as the independent variable. The minimum and maximum values for EDUC6 are 1 and 6 (see Figure 1).
- The POLYNOMIAL subcommand specifies second-order polynomial contrasts. The sum of squares using the unweighted polynomial contrasts is calculated because the analysis design is unbalanced (see Figure 2).
- The CONTRAST subcommands request three different contrasts (see Figure 3).
- The RANGES subcommands calculate multiple comparisons between means using the Student-Newman-Keuls and Scheffe tests. (see Figures 4 and 5).
- The STATISTICS subcommand requests all the optional statistics (see Figure 6).

Figure 1 Analysis of variance table from ONEWAY

```
- - - - - - - - - - - - - - - - - - - - - - - - - - - - - - - O N E W A Y - - - - - - - - - - - - - - - - - - - - - - - - - - - - -

     Variable  WELL      SENSE OF WELL-BEING SCALE
     By Variable EDUC6   EDUCATION IN 6 CATEGORIES

                          ANALYSIS OF VARIANCE

                                   SUM OF      MEAN       F      F
             SOURCE        D.F.    SQUARES    SQUARES    RATIO   PROB.

BETWEEN GROUPS              5     361.3217    72.2643   11.5255  .0000

WITHIN GROUPS            494    3097.3463     6.2699

TOTAL                   499    3458.6680
```

Figure 2 Polynomial contrasts

```
- - - - - - - - - - - - - - - - - - - - - - - - - - - - - O N E W A Y - - - - - - - - - - - - - - - - - - - - - - - - - - - - - - - - -


      Variable  WELL        SENSE OF WELL-BEING SCALE
      By Variable  EDUC6     EDUCATION IN 6 CATEGORIES

                            ANALYSIS OF VARIANCE


                               SUM OF          MEAN          F        F
           SOURCE        D.F.  SQUARES        SQUARES      RATIO    PROB.

   BETWEEN GROUPS          5   361.3217       72.2643     11.5255   .0000

      UNWEIGHTED  LINEAR TERM   1   257.3422   257.3422   41.0439   .0000
      WEIGHTED    LINEAR TERM   1   307.2051   307.2051   48.9966   .0000
      DEVIATION FROM  LINEAR    4    54.1166    13.5291    2.1578   .0727

      UNWEIGHTED  QUAD. TERM    1     6.6073     6.6073    1.0538   .3051
      WEIGHTED    QUAD. TERM    1    16.6406    16.6406    2.6540   .1039
      DEVIATION FROM  QUAD.     3    37.4759    12.4920    1.9924   .1142

   WITHIN GROUPS         494  3097.3463        6.2699

   TOTAL                 499  3458.6680
```

Figure 3 Contrasts

```
- - - - - - - - - - - - - - - - - - - - -     - - - - - - - - - - O N E W A Y - - - - - - - - - - - - - - - - - - - - - - - - - - - - -


      Variable  WELL        SENSE OF WELL-BEING SCALE
      By Variable  EDUC6     EDUCATION IN 6 CATEGORIES

   CONTRAST COEFFICIENT MATRIX

           Grp 1      Grp 3      Grp 5
              Grp 2      Grp 4      Grp 6

   CONTRAST 1  -1.0  -1.0   1.0   1.0   0.0   0.0

   CONTRAST 2   0.0   0.0  -1.0  -1.0   1.0   1.0

   CONTRAST 3  -1.0  -1.0   0.0   0.0   1.0   1.0
```

			POOLED VARIANCE ESTIMATE				SEPARATE VARIANCE ESTIMATE			
	VALUE	S. ERROR	T VALUE	D.F.	T PROB.	S. ERROR	T VALUE	D.F.	T PROB.
CONTRAST 1	3.3207	0.5230	6.349	494.0	0.000	0.5401	6.148	252.5	0.000
CONTRAST 2	1.1517	0.6613	1.742	494.0	0.082	0.6108	1.886	123.2	0.062
CONTRAST 3	4.4724	0.6990	6.398	494.0	0.000	0.6984	6.404	172.7	0.000

Figure 4 Multiple group comparisons

```
- - - - - - - - - - - - - - - - - - - - - - - - -     - - - - - - - - - - O N E W A Y - - - - - - - - - - - - - - - - - - - - - - - - -


      Variable  WELL        SENSE OF WELL-BEING SCALE
      By Variable  EDUC6     EDUCATION IN 6 CATEGORIES

   MULTIPLE RANGE TEST


   SCHEFFE PROCEDURE
   RANGES FOR THE 0.010 LEVEL -

        5.53   5.53   5.53   5.53   5.53

   THE RANGES ABOVE ARE TABLE RANGES.
   THE VALUE ACTUALLY COMPARED WITH MEAN(J)-MEAN(I) IS..
       1.7706 * RANGE * DSQRT(1/N(I) + 1/N(J))

     (*) DENOTES PAIRS OF GROUPS SIGNIFICANTLY DIFFERENT AT THE 0.010 LEVEL


                          G G G G G G
                          r r r r r r
                          p p p p p p
         Mean    Group    1 2 3 4 5 6

        2.6462   Grp 1
        2.7737   Grp 2
        4.1796   Grp 3    * *
        4.5610   Grp 4    * *
        4.6625   Grp 5    * *
        5.2297   Grp 6    * *
```

Figure 5 Homogeneous subsets

```
- - - - - - - - - - - - - - - - - - - - - - - - - - - O N E W A Y - - - - - - - - - - - - - - - - - - - - - - - - - - - - - - - -


        Variable   WELL       SENSE OF WELL-BEING SCALE
        By Variable  EDUC6     EDUCATION IN 6 CATEGORIES


MULTIPLE RANGE TEST


STUDENT-NEWMAN-KEULS PROCEDURE
RANGES FOR THE 0.050 LEVEL -

        2.81   3.34   3.65   3.88   4.05

HARMONIC MEAN CELL SIZE =      62.7235
THE ACTUAL RANGE USED IS THE LISTED RANGE *        0.3162

   (*) DENOTES PAIRS OF GROUPS SIGNIFICANTLY DIFFERENT AT THE 0.050 LEVEL


                         G G G G G G
                         r r r r r r
                         p p p p p p

         Mean     Group   1 2 3 4 5 6

         2.6462   Grp 1
         2.7737   Grp 2
         4.1796   Grp 3    * *
         4.5610   Grp 4    * *
         4.6625   Grp 5    * *
         5.2297   Grp 6    * *


     HOMOGENEOUS SUBSETS   (SUBSETS OF GROUPS, WHOSE HIGHEST AND LOWEST MEANS
                           DO NOT DIFFER BY MORE THAN THE SHORTEST
                           SIGNIFICANT RANGE FOR A SUBSET OF THAT SIZE)


SUBSET  1

GROUP      Grp 1       Grp 2
MEAN       2.6462      2.7737
- - - - - - - - - - - - - - - - - -

SUBSET  2

GROUP      Grp 3       Grp 4       Grp 5       Grp 6
MEAN       4.1796      4.5610      4.6625      5.2297
- - - - - - - - - - - - - - - - - - - - - - - - - - - -
```

Figure 6 Statistics available with ONEWAY

GROUP	COUNT	MEAN	STANDARD DEVIATION	STANDARD ERROR	MINIMUM	MAXIMUM	95 PCT CONF INT FOR MEAN	
Grp 1	65	2.6462	2.7539	.3416	-4.0000	8.5000	1.9638 TO	3.3285
Grp 2	95	2.7737	2.8674	.2942	-5.0000	8.5000	2.1896 TO	3.3578
Grp 3	181	4.1796	2.4220	.1800	-4.0000	9.0000	3.8243 TO	4.5348
Grp 4	82	4.5610	2.1450	.2369	-.5000	9.0000	4.0897 TO	5.0323
Grp 5	40	4.6625	2.3490	.3714	-1.0000	8.0000	3.9113 TO	5.4137
Grp 6	37	5.2297	2.3291	.3829	-1.5000	9.0000	4.4532 TO	6.0063
TOTAL	500	3.8920	2.6327	.1177	-5.0000	9.0000	3.6607 TO	4.1233
FIXED EFFECTS MODEL			2.5040	.1120			3.6720 TO	4.1120
RANDOM EFFECTS MODEL				.4492			2.7374 TO	5.0466

```
RANDOM EFFECTS MODEL - ESTIMATE OF BETWEEN COMPONENT VARIANCE        0.8491

Tests for Homogeneity of Variances

       Cochrans C = Max. Variance/Sum(Variances) =  .2209, P =  .093 (Approx.)
       Bartlett-Box F =                             1.905 , P =  .090
       Maximum Variance / Minimum Variance          1.787
```

PARTIAL CORR This example analyzes 1979 prices and earnings in 45 cities around the world, compiled by the Union Bank of Switzerland. The variables are

- RENT—the average gross monthly rent in the city, expressed as a percentage above or below that of Zurich, where Zurich equals 100%.
- FOOD—the average net cost of 39 different food and beverage items in the city, expressed as a percentage above or below that of Zurich, where Zurich equals 100%.
- PUBTRANS—the average cost of a three-mile taxi ride within city limits, expressed as a percentage above or below that of Zurich, where Zurich equals 100%.
- NETPRICE—the city's net price level, based on more than 100 goods and services weighted by consumer habits. NETPRICE is expressed as a percentage above or below that of Zurich, where Zurich equals 100%.
- NETPURSE—the city's net purchasing power level, calculated as the ratio of labor expended (measured in number of working hours) to the cost of more than 100 goods and services weighted by consumer habits. NETPURSE is expressed as a percentage above or below that of Zurich, where Zurich equals 100%.
- NETSALRY—the city's net salary level, calculated from net average hourly earnings in 12 occupations. NETSALRY is expressed as a percentage above or below that of Zurich, where Zurich equals 100%.

In this example we determine the degree to which the costs of rent, food, and public transportation are related to each other, while adjusting for the effects of prices, purchasing power, and salary levels. We use PARTIAL CORR to first compute the zero-order correlations between all six variables and then compute three matrices of first-order partials that remove the effects of NETPRICE, NETPURSE, and NETSALRY, respectively. The SPSS commands are

```
GET  FILE=CITY
    /RENAME (NTCPRI NTCPUR NTCSAL = NETPRICE NETPURSE NETSALRY)
    /KEEP RENT FOOD PUBTRANS NETPRICE NETPURSE NETSALRY.
PARTIAL CORR VARIABLES=RENT TO PUBTRANS BY NETPRICE TO NETSALRY(1)
    /STATISTICS=CORR DESCRIPTIVES
    /FORMAT=CONDENSED.
```

- The GET command defines the data to SPSS, renames three variables, and selects the variables needed for analysis.
- The PARTIAL CORR command requests three sets of first-order partial correlations for all pairs of variables implied by RENT, FOOD, and PUBTRANS. The first set of partials controls for NETPRICE, the second set controls for NETPURSE, and the third set controls for NETSALRY.
- The STATISTICS subcommand on PARTIAL CORR requests the mean, standard deviation, and number of nonmissing cases for each variable and the zero-order correlation coefficients for each pair of variables implied by the correlation list and the control list.
- The FORMAT subcommand on PARTIAL CORR suppresses the printing of the degrees of freedom and significance levels in the zero-order correlation matrix and the first-order partial correlation matrices.
- Since no missing-value option is specified, listwise deletion of missing cases is in effect.

Output from PARTIAL CORR

```
VARIABLE           MEAN      STANDARD DEV     CASES

RENT            121.7500        94.6455         44
FOOD             71.0000        18.6123         44
PUBTRANS         48.8182        24.6381         44
NETPRICE         82.1591        19.7731         44
NETPURSE         58.7045        28.8062         44
NETSALRY         50.3409        24.2946         44


- - - - - - - - - - - - - - P A R T I A L   C O R R E L A T I O N   C O E F F I C I E N T S - - - - - - - - - - - - - - -
ZERO ORDER PARTIALS


                RENT       FOOD     PUBTRANS    NETPRICE    NETPURSE     NETSALRY

RENT          1.0000      .2434     -.0346      .7646**     -.1288       .1531
FOOD           .2434     1.0000      .5639**     .7224**      .2952       .5800**
PUBTRANS      -.0346      .5639**   1.0000       .3953*       .6234**     .7247**
NETPRICE       .7646**    .7224**    .3953*     1.0000        .0976       .4824**
NETPURSE      -.1288      .2952      .6234**     .0976       1.0000       .9012**
NETSALRY       .1531      .5800**    .7247**     .4824**      .9012**    1.0000


 * - SIGNIF. LE .01     ** - SIGNIF. LE .001           (" . " IS PRINTED IF A COEFFICIENT CANNOT BE COMPUTED)


- - - - - - - - - - - - - - P A R T I A L   C O R R E L A T I O N   C O E F F I C I E N T S - - - - - - - - - - - - - -

CONTROLLING FOR..   NETPRICE


                RENT       FOOD     PUBTRANS

RENT          1.0000     -.6933**   -.5690**
FOOD          -.6933**   1.0000      .4382*
PUBTRANS      -.5690**    .4382*    1.0000


 * - SIGNIF. LE .01     ** - SIGNIF. LE .001           (" . " IS PRINTED IF A COEFFICIENT CANNOT BE COMPUTED)


- - - - - - - - - - - - - - P A R T I A L   C O R R E L A T I O N   C O E F F I C I E N T S - - - - - - - - - - - - - -

CONTROLLING FOR..   NETPURSE


                RENT       FOOD     PUBTRANS

RENT          1.0000      .2970      .0590
FOOD           .2970     1.0000      .5085**
PUBTRANS       .0590      .5085**   1.0000


 * - SIGNIF. LE .01     ** - SIGNIF. LE .001           (" . " IS PRINTED IF A COEFFICIENT CANNOT BE COMPUTED)


- - - - - - - - - - - - - - P A R T I A L   C O R R E L A T I O N   C O E F F I C I E N T S - - - - - - - - - - - - - -

CONTROLLING FOR..   NETSALRY


                RENT       FOOD     PUBTRANS

RENT          1.0000      .1921     -.2136
FOOD           .1921     1.0000      .2558
PUBTRANS      -.2136      .2558     1.0000


 * - SIGNIF. LE .01     ** - SIGNIF. LE .001           (" . " IS PRINTED IF A COEFFICIENT CANNOT BE COMPUTED)
```

PLOT   This example plots the values from a derived formula for the relationship of age, weight, and, systolic blood pressure. The variables are

- AGE—age in years.
- WEIGHT—weight in pounds.
- PRESSURE—systolic blood pressure.

The SPSS commands are

```
INPUT PROGRAM.
+ LOOP #I=15 TO 85 BY 1.
+   LOOP #J=100 TO 350 BY 10.
+     COMPUTE AGE=#I.
+     COMPUTE WEIGHT=#J.
+     COMPUTE PRESSURE=59.4+0.909*AGE
        -0.0005*AGE*AGE+0.1*WEIGHT+.00085*WEIGHT*WEIGHT
        -.0004*AGE*WEIGHT.
+   END CASE.
+   END LOOP.
+ END LOOP.
+END FILE.
END INPUT PROGRAM.
VARIABLE LABELS PRESSURE 'SYSTOLIC BLOOD PRESSURE'.
PLOT HSIZE = 40
  /VSIZE = 25
  /SYMBOLS = '.-+oxOXNPX' '          0#'
  /TITLE='PRESSURE WITH WEIGHT'
  /HORIZONTAL='WEIGHT IN POUNDS'
  /PLOT = PRESSURE WITH WEIGHT
  /FORMAT = CONTOUR
  /TITLE='WEIGHT WITH AGE BY PRESSURE'
  /HORIZONTAL='YEARS OF AGE' MIN(10) MAX(90)
  /PLOT = WEIGHT WITH AGE BY PRESSURE.
```

- The commands between INPUT PROGRAM and END INPUT PROGRAM create the data to plot.
- The VARIABLE LABELS command assigns a label to PRESSURE.
- The PLOT command requests two separate 25×40 plots. Each plot uses 10 symbols, two of which are overprinted (see Figure 1).
- The first TITLE and HORIZONTAL subcommands label the plot and one axis.
- The first PLOT subcommand specifies plotting variables PRESSURE and WEIGHT. In the absence of a FORMAT specification, a bivariate scatterplot is produced (see Figure 2).
- The FORMAT subcommand specifies that the next plot is a contour plot (see Figure 3).
- The second TITLE subcommand produces a title different from that in the first.
- The second HORIZONTAL subcommand specifies a horizontal axis label and minimum and maximum values to include on the axis.

Figure 1 Data information

```
Data    Information
          1846 unweighted cases accepted.

Size of the plots

    Horizontal size is 40
       Vertical size is 25

Frequencies and symbols used (not applicable for control or overlay plots)

          1 - .
          2 - -
          3 - +
          4 - o
          5 - x
          6 - O
          7 - X
          8 - N
          9 - P
              O
         10 - X
              #
```

Figure 2   Bivariate scatterplot

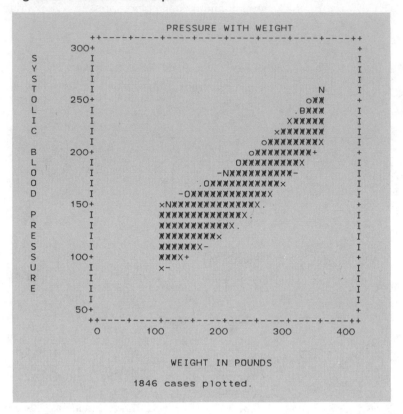

Figure 3   Contour plot

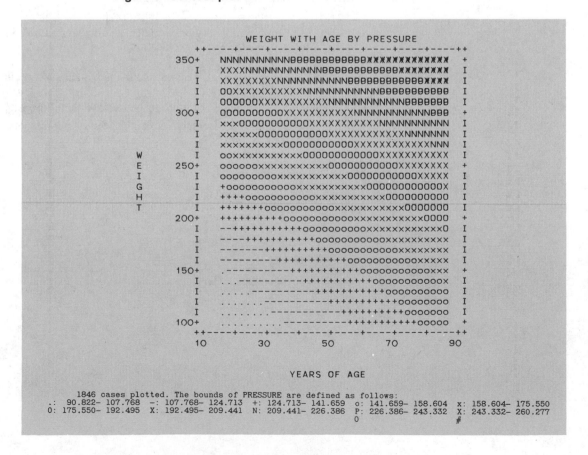

PROBIT You can use PROBIT for a variety of dichotomous response models. The examples shown here illustrate two of the most common applications: dose-response models and logistic regression models.

Example 1 The following (based on a dose-response model) shows the use of the PROBIT procedure to analyze an example from Finney (1971).

```
SET WIDTH = 80.
TITLE    "PROBIT ANALYSIS. DATA FROM 'PROBIT' BY FINNEY P.132".
DATA LIST / ROOT 1 X 3-7 N 9-11 R 13-15.
BEGIN DATA
1 148.0 142 142
1 100.0 127 126
1  48.0 128 115
1  12.0 126  58
2  62.0 125 125
2  46.0 117 115
2  31.0 127 114
2  14.8  51  40
2   3.8 132  37
2   0.0 129  21
END DATA.
PROBIT  R OF N BY ROOT(1,2) WITH X
 /MODEL = BOTH
 /NATRES
 /PRINT = ALL.
```

- The SET command restricts the output to 80 columns.
- The TITLE command sets up a title for the run.
- The DATA LIST command reads the variables ROOT, X, N, and R from the data included in the command file.
- The PROBIT command specifies that the number of responses is in variable R and the number of observations is in N. The response rate will be predicted from variable X. Two groups are defined by variable ROOT.
- The MODEL subcommand specifies both probit and logit response models.
- The NATRES subcommand requests an estimate of the natural response rate (or threshold) for each model. This specification requires that a control level be entered with the data.
- The PRINT subcommand requests all available output.
- The first data case shows 142 responses for the 142 observations with an X of 148.0 in the first group. The second-to-last case shows 37 responses for the 132 observations with an X of 3.8 in the second group. The last case has a value of 0.0 for predictor X, so the response rate used as the control level is 21 out of 129.

Figure 1 shows the case and model information displayed by PROBIT. When both models are estimated, all output for the logit model is printed before that for the probit model. Selected output from the logit model and all the output from the probit model are shown in Figures 1 through 9.

Figure 1 PROBIT case and model information

```
DATA  Information

        9 unweighted cases accepted.
        0 cases rejected because of out-of-range group values.
        0 cases rejected because of missing data.
        0 Cases rejected because of LOG-transform can't be done.


GROUP Information

     ROOT     Level  N of Cases    Label
                1         4          1
                2         5          2


MODEL Information

     BOTH Probit and Logit models are requested.


Natural Response rate to be estimated

     The number of  subjects in the CONTROL group   129.0
     The number of responses in the CONTROL group    21.0
```

Figure 2 shows the parameter estimates from the logit model. Figure 3 shows these estimates from the probit model. The number of iterations required to reach the convergence criterion and the final value for the criterion are printed first. The default cutoff values for these terms are 20 iterations and a convergence criterion of 0.001. If the convergence criterion had failed to reach the cutoff value in the allotted iterations, PROBIT would have printed an appropriate message and the estimates from the iterations that were completed.

Figure 2 Parameter estimates and covariances for logit model

```
ML converged at iteration  6.  The converge criterion =   .00095

Parameter Estimates (LOGIT model:  (LOG(p/(1-p))/2 + 5) = Intercept + BX ):
                    Note 5 added to intercept and logit divided by 2.

          Regression Coeff.  Standard Error    Coeff./S.E.

   X            2.45569          .19850         12.37135


          Intercept  Standard Error  Intercept/S.E.  ROOT

            2.02382      .30064         6.73182         1
            2.59473      .28483         9.10988         2

Estimate of Natural Response Rate = .172976  with  S.E. =   .03147

Pearson  Goodness-of-Fit  Chi Square =       8.966    DF = 6   P =  .176
         Parallelism Test Chi Square =        .048    DF = 1   P =  .826

Since Goodness-of-Fit Chi square is NOT significant, no heterogeneity
factor is used in the calculation of confidence limits.

- - - - - - - - - - - - - - - - - - - - - - - - - - - - - - - - - - - - - -


Covariance(below) and Correlation(above) Matrices of Parameter Estimates

                 X    NAT RESP

X            .03940     .42344
NAT RESP     .00264     .00099
```

Figure 3 Parameter estimates and covariances for probit model

```
ML converged at iteration  6.  The converge criterion =   .00063

Parameter Estimates (PROBIT model:  (PROBIT(p) + 5) = Intercept + BX ):
                    Note 5 added to intercept.

          Regression Coeff.  Standard Error    Coeff./S.E.

   X            2.78382          .20654         13.47809


          Intercept  Standard Error  Intercept/S.E.  ROOT

            1.59842      .33212         4.81282         1
            2.26158      .30366         7.44765         2

Estimate of Natural Response Rate = .168731  with  S.E. =   .03177

Pearson  Goodness-of-Fit  Chi Square =       5.933    DF = 6   P =  .431
         Parallelism Test Chi Square =        .050    DF = 1   P =  .823

Since Goodness-of-Fit Chi square is NOT significant, no heterogeneity
factor is used in the calculation of confidence limits.

- - - - - - - - - - - - - - - - - - - - - - - - - - - - - - - - - - - - - -


Covariance(below) and Correlation(above) Matrices of Parameter Estimates

                 X    NAT RESP

X            .04266     .46719
NAT RESP     .00307     .00101
```

Next, PROBIT prints parameter estimates with their standard errors (see Figures 2 and 3). Three kinds of parameters are estimated: a regression coefficient, group intercepts, and a natural response rate. Probit and logit models produced similar estimates. The regression coefficient for X is positive and large relative to its standard error. PROBIT produces separate intercept estimates for each group. Because no value labels are defined for ROOT, the actual values of the variable are used to label the subgroup intercepts. The second group has the greater response rate. Finally, PROBIT produces the estimate of the threshold or natural response rate.

Following the parameter estimates, PROBIT reports two chi-square statistics and their associated probabilities. The goodness-of-fit test prints by default. It tests whether residuals are distributed homogeneously about the regression line. If this test is significant, PROBIT uses a heterogeneity factor to calculate confidence limits. A large chi-square can indicate that a different response model or predictor transformation is required. In this example, the probit model has the better fit. The PRINT subcommand requests all output, which includes the parallelism chi-square. This test indicates whether regression slopes differ between subgroups. Since the test is not significant, the regression slopes are treated as equivalent.

PROBIT estimated more than one parameter (excluding intercepts), so it automatically prints their covariance/correlation matrix. The diagonal entries (variances) simply equal the squares of the standard errors. The off-diagonal correlation and covariance terms indicate how much the estimate of the natural response rate depends on the estimate of the coefficient for X, and vice versa. Here, the two estimates are moderately correlated. In multiple predictor models, this matrix is useful for examining multicollinearity.

Figures 4 and 5 show the observed and predicted frequencies from logit and probit models. PROBIT prints one row for each input case. The first column labels each case with the value of the grouping variable, ROOT. The second column shows the values for the predictor, X. PROBIT can display values for no more than six predictors when WIDTH is set to 132 columns, even though all predictors are used in the calculations. The procedure prints the number of observations and the number of responses in the next two columns. The following two columns contain the number of responses predicted by the response model ("Expected Responses") and the differences between the observed number of responses and those predicted ("Residual"). The probit response model in this example has smaller residual values than the logit, indicating a better fit to the data. The final column ("Prob") contains the predicted probability (or proportion) of responses for the predictor and group values in each row.

Figure 4 Observed and predicted frequencies for logit model

Observed and Expected Frequencies

ROOT	X	Number of Subjects	Observed Responses	Expected Responses	Residual	Prob
1	2.17	142.0	142.0	140.728	1.272	.99105
1	2.00	127.0	126.0	124.406	1.594	.97958
1	1.68	128.0	115.0	116.388	-1.388	.90928
1	1.08	126.0	58.0	43.158	14.842	.34252
2	1.79	125.0	125.0	122.735	2.265	.98188
2	1.66	117.0	115.0	113.057	1.943	.96630
2	1.49	127.0	114.0	117.491	-3.491	.92512
2	1.17	51.0	40.0	36.644	3.356	.71850
2	.58	132.0	37.0	16.255	20.745	.12314

Figure 5 Observed and predicted frequencies for probit model

```
Observed and Expected Frequencies

                   Number of    Observed    Expected
ROOT          X    Subjects     Responses   Responses    Residual    Prob
     1      2.17     142.0        142.0       141.411        .589    .99586
     1      2.00     127.0        126.0       125.075        .925    .98485
     1      1.68     128.0        115.0       115.136       -.136    .89950
     1      1.08     126.0         58.0        43.540      14.460    .34556

     2      1.79     125.0        125.0       123.477       1.523    .98782
     2      1.66     117.0        115.0       113.566       1.434    .97065
     2      1.49     127.0        114.0       116.994      -2.994    .92121
     2      1.17      51.0         40.0        35.611       4.389    .69825
     2       .58     132.0         37.0        17.215      19.785    .13042
```

Figure 6 displays the plot of probit-transformed response proportions against log-transformed values of the predictor, X. The plotting character (1 or 2) is the number of the group in which the observation appears. Because output width is restricted to 80, the plot appears in compact form. In this plot, the relation of the variables appears linear, and the response rate appears greater in the second group.

Figure 6 PROBIT plot for single-predictor probit model

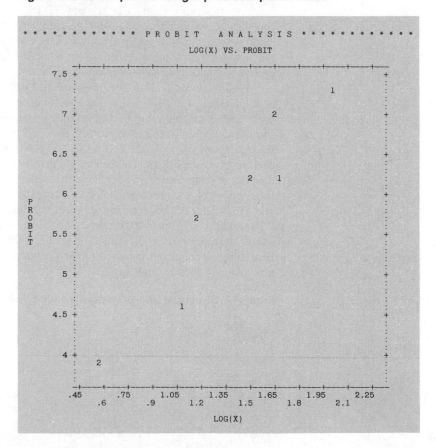

Figures 7 and 8 present the confidence intervals for estimated effects of the predictor, X. For each group, PROBIT prints a table of estimated values for X to produce selected response rates from 0.01 to 0.99. Ninety-five percent fiducial confidence intervals are provided for these estimates (Finney, 1971). If the chi-square test had been significant, PROBIT would have used a heterogeneity factor to calculate the limits. The stimulus tolerance (the predictor estimate for a response rate of 0.50) is 16.66914 in the first group and 9.63145 in the second. If an output width of 132 is in effect, PROBIT also prints effective levels and confidence limits for the log-transformed predictor.

Figure 7 Confidence intervals for effects by group in probit model

```
Confidence Limits for Effective X


ROOT        1         1

                          95% Confidence Limits
Prob        X            Lower          Upper

.01      2.43358        1.49073        3.54171
.02      3.04907        1.93470        4.32588
.03      3.51801        2.28205        4.91252
.04      3.91772        2.58346        5.40658
.05      4.27613        2.85742        5.84556
.06      4.60690        3.11310        6.24774
.07      4.91792        3.35578        6.62356
.08      5.21417        3.58886        6.97966
.09      5.49906        3.81465        7.32052
.10      5.77505        4.03482        7.64936
.15      7.07305        5.08714        9.18084
.20      8.30973        6.11123       10.62212
.25      9.54165        7.14783       12.04574
.30     10.80286        8.22256       13.49459
.35     12.11989        9.35637       15.00163
.40     13.51780       10.56970       16.59764
.45     15.02357       11.88506       18.31571
.50     16.66914       13.32937       20.19508
.55     18.49495       14.93677       22.28584
.60     20.55513       16.75274       24.65562
.65     22.92596       18.84086       27.40085
.70     25.72099       21.29482       30.66690
.75     29.12076       24.26177       34.68812
.80     33.43794       27.99319       39.87663
.85     39.28435       32.97398       47.05259
.90     48.11391       40.33717       58.20446
.91     50.52864       42.31936       61.31620
.92     53.28947       44.57021       64.90462
.93     56.49958       47.16756       69.11658
.94     60.31387       50.22763       74.17417
.95     64.97941       53.93463       80.43461
.96     70.92390       58.60507       88.52214
.97     78.98231       64.85143       99.66931
.98     91.12938       74.10608      116.83386
.99    114.17768       91.23083      150.43803
```

Figure 8 Confidence intervals for effects by group in probit model

```
Confidence Limits for Effective X


ROOT        2         2

                          95% Confidence Limits
Prob        X            Lower          Upper

.01      1.40612         .83171        2.10009
.02      1.76176        1.07972        2.56433
.03      2.03271        1.27386        2.91142
.04      2.26367        1.44239        3.20359
.05      2.47075        1.59564        3.46308
.06      2.66188        1.73871        3.70072
.07      2.84158        1.87455        3.92270
.08      3.01275        2.00506        4.13295
.09      3.17737        2.13153        4.33413
.10      3.33683        2.25489        4.52814
.15      4.08682        2.84506        5.43077
.20      4.80137        3.42031        6.27872
.25      5.51318        4.00355        7.11474
.30      6.24190        4.60933        7.96390
.35      7.00289        5.24966        8.84530
.40      7.81060        5.93636        9.77656
.45      8.68064        6.68260       10.77649
.50      9.63145        7.50419       11.86722
.55     10.68641        8.42131       13.07685
.60     11.87678        9.46096       14.44321
.65     13.24665       10.66101       16.02005
.70     14.86163       12.07738       17.88828
.75     16.82601       13.79805       20.17822
.80     19.32048       15.97345       23.11903
.85     22.69855       18.89332       27.16715
.90     27.80029       23.23349       33.43063
.91     29.19552       24.40515       35.17469
.92     30.79073       25.73677       37.18463
.93     32.64554       27.27463       39.54249
.94     34.84944       29.08777       42.37234
.95     37.54519       31.28554       45.87376
.96     40.97993       34.05583       50.39565
.97     45.63609       37.76202       56.62695
.98     52.65468       43.25367       66.22119
.99     65.97202       53.41327       85.00558
```

You can compute the relative median potency (RMP) as the ratio of the stimulus tolerances in the two groups. The tolerances (from Figures 7 and 8, for Prob = 0.50) are 16.66914 and 9.63145, which have a ratio of 1.73070. The RMP and its confidence limits appear in Figure 9. The confidence limits do not include 1, so the difference is significant.

Figure 9 Estimates of relative median potency (RMP) from probit model

```
Estimates of Relative Median Potency

                            95% Confidence Limits
    ROOT        Estimate    Lower       Upper

    1 VS.  2    1.7307      1.34843     2.30803
```

Example 2 You can use PROBIT to perform logistic regression by specifying the LOGIT response model with no log transformation of the predictors. Because the data are likely to be in uncollapsed form, you must compute an observation count variable whose value is equal to 1 for every case. You can avoid printing a case listing of observed and predicted frequencies by using the PRINT subcommand.

The General Social Survey for 1982 provides data for predicting whether a person feels safe and secure at home. The data can be analyzed by the following SPSS commands:

```
GET FILE=GSS82 / KEEP = PRESTIGE AGE EDUC SEX INCOME82 FEARHOME
                        BURGLR ROBBRY OWNGUN NEWS TVHOURS.
RECODE OWNGUN FEARHOME (0=9) (1=1) (2,3=0).
COMPUTE ONECASE = 1.
MISSING VALUES OWNGUN FEARHOME (8,9).
PROBIT FEARHOME OF ONECASE WITH AGE SEX EDUC PRESTIGE INCOME82
       OWNGUN BURGLR ROBBRY NEWS TVHOURS
 /MODEL = LOGIT
 /LOG = NONE
 /PRINT = NONE.
```

- The GET command accesses the file and keeps only those variables that will be used in this session.

- The first RECODE command changes FEARHOME so that 1 represents the response of feeling safe and secure in one's home, and 0 represents fear and insecurity. RECODE also changes OWNGUN to 1 for gun owners and 0 otherwise.

- COMPUTE produces an observation count variable, ONECASE, which indicates there is only one observation per case.

- The MISSING VALUES command specifies that 0 will be accepted as valid for FEARHOME and OWNGUN.

- The PROBIT specification identifies FEARHOME (with a value of 0 or 1) as the response count and ONECASE (always 1) as the observation count. The PROBIT command also specifies 10 predictors, including variables representing age and sex, socioeconomic status, gun ownership, recent victimization by crime, and exposure to communications media.

- The MODEL subcommand requests only the logit response model.

- The LOG subcommand indicates that predictor variables will not be transformed logarithmically.

- Because PRINT specifies NONE, no optional display output will be produced. Only the case and model information and the parameter estimates and covariances will be printed.

Figure 10 displays the case and model information that was printed. Only 184 of 1,506 input cases were omitted because of missing values for the response variable or one of the predictors. The type of model is stated.

Figure 10 Case and model information for logistic regression

```
DATA  Information

      1322 unweighted cases accepted.
       184 cases rejected because of missing data.

MODEL Information

      ONLY Logistic Model is requested.
```

Figure 11 presents the parameter estimates for the logistic regression model, their standard errors, and their covariances. The reported goodness-of-fit test is incorrect. For logistic regression, chi-square is not a meaningful measure. Three predictors—SEX, BURGLR, and ROBBRY—had large coefficients relative to their standard errors. These results indicate that persons who are male and were not crime victims in the preceding year are more likely to feel safe and secure in their homes. PROBIT prints the covariance matrix of parameter estimates whenever there is more than one predictor or when NATRES is specified. You can use this matrix to detect problems of collinearity among the predictors.

Figure 11 Parameter estimates and covariances

```
ML converged at iteration  7.  The converge criterion =   .00000

Parameter Estimates (LOGIT model:  (LOG(p/(1-p))/2 + 5) = Intercept + BX ):
               Note 5 added to intercept and logit divided by 2.

           Regression Coeff.   Standard Error    Coeff./S.E.

AGE             -.00086            .00263          -.32695
SEX             -.35930            .09224         -3.89515
EDUC             .03351            .01830          1.83053
PRESTIGE         .00172            .00391           .43997
INCOME82         .01549            .01053          1.47110
OWNGUN           .00472            .08803           .05360
BURGLR           .59751            .11864          5.03634
ROBBRY           .55632            .20559          2.70599
NEWS            -.00985            .03730          -.26414
TVHOURS         -.01676            .01932          -.86778


           Intercept  Standard Error   Intercept/S.E.

            3.78163        .53380         7.08429

Goodness-of-Fit  Chi Square =   1259.523    DF = 1311   P =   .843

Since Goodness-of-Fit Chi square is NOT significant, no heterogeneity
factor is used in the calculation of confidence limits.

- - - - - - - - - - - - - - - - - - - - - - - - - - - - - - - - - - - - - - - - - - -

Covariance(below) and Correlation(above) Matrices of Parameter Estimates

             AGE       SEX      EDUC   PRESTIGE  INCOME82   OWNGUN    BURGLR    ROBBRY     NEWS    TVHOURS

AGE         .00001   -.05523    .40984   -.19823    .10917    .03340   -.09191   -.00387    .27129   -.01735
SEX        -.00001    .00851   -.10309   -.00163    .10448    .13886   -.02411   -.05503    .01335   -.02420
EDUC        .00002   -.00017    .00034   -.46592   -.20142    .08113   -.00197    .04466    .17719    .02864
PRESTIGE    .00000   -.00000   -.00003    .00002   -.17934    .01144    .01359   -.04624    .01670    .07635
INCOME82    .00000    .00010   -.00004   -.00001    .00011   -.18728   -.01083   -.07506    .12304    .15946
OWNGUN      .00001    .00113    .00013    .00000   -.00017    .00775   -.01696    .00771   -.00129    .00628
BURGLR     -.00003   -.00026    .00000    .00001   -.00001   -.00018    .01408   -.11673    .01536    .06326
ROBBRY      .00000   -.00104    .00017   -.00004   -.00016    .00014   -.00285    .04227    .03882   -.10154
NEWS        .00003    .00005    .00012    .00000    .00005    .00000    .00007    .00030    .00139    .00160
TVHOURS     .00000   -.00004    .00001    .00001    .00003    .00001    .00014   -.00040    .00000    .00037
```

PROXIMITIES

This example shows how PROXIMITIES can produce matrix materials for input to CLUSTER.

```
SET WIDTH=80.

TITLE     'Crime Rates for Selected Cities 1979'.
SUBTITLE 'Data from  Uniform Crime Reports for the United States'.

DATA LIST / CITY 1-17(A) MURDER 18-21 RAPE 23-25 ROBBERY 27-30
            ASSAULT 32-34 BURGLARY 36-39 LARCENY 41-44
            MOTOR 46-49.

VARIABLE LABELS MURDER  'Murders per 100,000 People'
                RAPE    'Forcible Rapes per 100,000 People'
                ROBBERY 'Robberies per 100,000 People'
                ASSAULT 'Aggravated Assaults per 100,000 People'
                BURGLARY 'Burglaries, B & E per 100,000 People'
                LARCENY 'Larceny, thefts per 100,000 People'
                MOTOR   'Motor Thefts per 100,000 People'.

BEGIN DATA
San Francisco     17.0 101 1016 542 2618 5149 1290
Dallas            34.8 111  505 647 2997 5443  890
Baltimore         31.0  71 1072 788 2139 4367  856
Los Angeles       27.4  88  714 685 2596 3549 1373
Detroit           35.9 109  907 619 2598 2820 1708
Houston           40.4  91  575 171 3022 3335 1517
New York          24.4  55 1161 622 2506 3106 1262
San Diego         11.6  40  348 256 2406 4730  902
Cleveland         45.6 102  958 514 2412 2364 2251
Washington, D.C.  27.4  75 1055 452 2051 4393  550
Indianapolis      17.9  85  400 310 1664 3683  672
San Antonio       20.6  44  204 224 1990 3588  560
Chicago           28.0  54  473 354 1091 3074 1027
Milwaukee          9.8  44  247 171 1325 3498  655
Philadelphia      21.9  48  503 255 1193 1927  752
END DATA.

PROXIMITIES MURDER TO MOTOR
  /VIEW=VARIABLE
  /MATRIX=OUT(*).

CLUSTER
  /MATRIX=IN(*)
  /PRINT=DISTANCE SCHEDULE.
```

- PROXIMITIES specifies the variables MURDER through MOTOR for computing the data matrix.
- The VIEW subcommand indicates that proximities are to be computed between variables, not cases.
- The MATRIX subcommand writes the computed matrix to the active system file for CLUSTER to read. Since the MEASURE subcommand does not appear, the computed matrix will consist of Euclidean distances between variables.
- CLUSTER omits the variable list. All variables from the input matrix are therefore used in the cluster analysis. CLUSTER will find clusters of the variables, since PROXIMITIES wrote a matrix of distances between variables.
- The MATRIX subcommand indicates that matrix data are in the active system file.
- The PRINT subcommand requests the cluster agglomeration schedule as well as the computed distances between cases.

The computed dissimilarity matrix for variables

```
* * * * * * * * * * * * * P R O X I M I T I E S * * * * * * * * * * * * * *

Data Information

         15 unweighted cases accepted.
          0 cases rejected because of missing value.

Euclidean measure used.

- - - - - - - - - - - - - - - - - - - - - - - - - - - - - - - - - - - - - -

Euclidean Dissimilarity Coefficient Matrix

Variable        MURDER          RAPE         ROBBERY        ASSAULT        BURGLARY

RAPE           202.0030
ROBBERY       2788.8428     2610.9871
ASSAULT       1772.7927     1590.8474     1233.7617
BURGLARY      8627.9258     8436.2539     6185.6484     7027.9414
LARCENY      14588.4023    14400.4453    12220.1641    13007.3242     6743.8477
MOTOR         4466.1953     4283.5117     2283.2639     3020.9238     4708.1719

Variable       LARCENY

MOTOR        11043.0586

- - - - - - - - - - - - - - - - - - - - - - - - - - - - - - - - - - - - - -
```

QUICK CLUSTER

These two examples show how an analysis with QUICK CLUSTER compares with a known classification and how QUICK CLUSTER can be used with an extremely large number of cases.

Example 1

The following example uses Fisher's classic data on irises to group the irises into clusters. The clusters are then compared with the actual botanical classification.

```
TITLE   'CLUSTERING  FISHER'S IRIS DATA WITH QUICK CLUSTER'.

COMMENT      FISHER'S IRIS DATA PROVIDE THE CLASSIC EXAMPLE
             OF CLASSIFICATION. THIS PROGRAM USES THE DATA
             TO ILLUSTRATE SPSS QUICK CLUSTER.

DATA LIST / SEP.LEN 1-2 SEP.WID PET.LEN PET.WID 3-11 IRISTYPE 13.
VARIABLE LABELS  SEP.LEN  'SEPAL LENGTH'
                 SEP.WID  'SEPAL WIDTH'
                 PET.LEN  'PETAL LENGTH'
                 PET.WID  'PETAL WIDTH'
                 IRISTYPE 'TYPE OF IRIS'.
VALUE LABELS   IRISTYPE (1) SETOSA (2) VERSICOLOR (3) VIRGINICA.

SUBTITLE 'CLUSTERING IRISES BY DEFAULT METHOD'.
*  DO A DEFAULT QUICK CLUSTER ANALYSIS AND SAVE THE CLUSTER
   MEMBERSHIP AS A VARIABLE, CLUSTMEM, ON THE ACTIVE SYSTEM FILE.

BEGIN DATA
50 33 14 02 1
 . . .
53 37 15 02 1
END DATA.

QUICK CLUSTER  SEP.LEN TO PET.WID
  /CRITERIA = CLUSTER(3)
  /PRINT = INITIAL  ANOVA
  /SAVE = CLUSTER(CLUSTMEM).

VARIABLE LABELS CLUSTMEM 'CLUSTERS FROM DEFAULT METHOD'.

SUBTITLE 'VALIDITY OF CLUSTERS OBTAINED BY DEFAULT METHOD'.
COMMENT      COMPARE DERIVED CLUSTERS WITH ACTUAL IRIS TYPES.

CROSSTABS VARIABLES = IRISTYPE CLUSTMEM (1,3)
  /TABLES = IRISTYPE BY CLUSTMEM
  /STATISTICS = CHISQ LAMBDA UC.
```

- DATA LIST defines five variables, and the VARIABLE LABELS command labels them.
- VALUE LABELS assigns labels to the three values of variable IRISTYPE—three actual types of irises.
- QUICK CLUSTER specifies clustering based on the values of four variables: SEP.LEN, SEP.WID, PET.LEN, and PET.WID.
- The CRITERIA subcommand specifies three clusters.
- The PRINT subcommand specifies initial cluster centers and an analysis of variance table describing differences between clusters for each of the four clustering variables.
- SAVE saves the cluster membership of each case in a new variable, CLUSTMEM, on the SPSS active system file.
- CROSSTABS crosstabulates the cluster membership variable with variable IRIS-TYPE, which identifies the actual type of iris.
- The STATISTICS subcommand requests a chi-square test of significance plus two measures of the predictability of iris types from the cluster types.

The output from QUICK CLUSTER appears in Figure 1. The classification and final cluster centers and the number of cases in each cluster always print.

Figure 1 The QUICK CLUSTER output for the iris data

```
Initial Cluster Centers.

   Cluster      SEP.LEN      SEP.WID      PET.LEN      PET.WID

        1       58.0000      40.0000      12.0000       2.0000
        2       77.0000      38.0000      67.0000      22.0000
        3       49.0000      25.0000      45.0000      17.0000


Classification Cluster Centers.

   Cluster      SEP.LEN      SEP.WID      PET.LEN      PET.WID

        1       51.0091      35.5029      13.5981       2.3147
        2       72.7018      34.1981      63.3840      21.8201
        3       59.9192      27.5660      47.4896      16.9838


Final Cluster Centers.

   Cluster      SEP.LEN      SEP.WID      PET.LEN      PET.WID

        1       50.0600      34.2800      14.6200       2.4600
        2       70.8696      31.2609      60.1304      21.4348
        3       60.1558      27.9610      45.7532      15.3636


Analysis of Variance.

   Variable     Cluster MS   DF      Error MS      DF           F     Prob

   SEP.LEN       3645.6374    2       19.9018    147.0    183.1817   .000
   SEP.WID        611.6477    2       10.9347    147.0     55.9365   .000
   PET.LEN      21598.9198    2       22.0048    147.0    981.5565   .000
   PET.WID       3734.5515    2        8.0809    147.0    462.1462   .000


Number of Cases in each Cluster.

   Cluster    unweighted cases   weighted cases

        1            50.0             50.0
        2            23.0             23.0
        3            77.0             77.0
   Missing            0
   Total            150.0            150.0
```

Figure 2 presents output from the CROSSTABS procedure. The SAVE subcommand of QUICK CLUSTER added variable CLUSTMEM to the SPSS file. CLUSTMEM indicates the cluster membership of each case. IRISTYPE contains the actual botanical classification of each case. (Usually the actual classifications are unknown. Classifying the cases is the purpose of clustering.) The CROSSTABS output shows that the clusters are strongly associated with the actual classifications.

Figure 2 Comparing clusters to the actual botanical classifications

```
                         CLUSTMEM
                COUNT  I
                       I                                 ROW
                       I                                 TOTAL
                       I     1I      2I      3I
        IRISTYPE  -----+-------+-------+-------+
                     1 I   50  I       I       I    50
        SETOSA         I       I       I       I   33.3
                  -----+-------+-------+-------+
                     2 I       I       I   50  I    50
        VERSICOLOR     I       I       I       I   33.3
                  -----+-------+-------+-------+
                     3 I       I   27  I   23  I    50
        VIRGINICA      I       I       I       I   33.3
                  -----+-------+-------+-------+
                COLUMN     50      27      73     150
                TOTAL     33.3    18.0    48.7   100.0


   CHI-SQUARE     D.F.      SIGNIFICANCE        MIN E.F.      CELLS WITH E.F.< 5
   ----------     ----      ------------        --------      ------------------

   205.47945        4           0.0              9.000              NONE


                                                  WITH IRISTYPE    WITH CLUSTMEM
             STATISTIC              SYMMETRIC      DEPENDENT        DEPENDENT
             ---------              ---------      ---------        ---------

   LAMBDA                            0.74011        0.77000          0.70130
   UNCERTAINTY COEFFICIENT           0.74895        0.72398          0.77571

   NUMBER OF MISSING OBSERVATIONS =        0
```

Example 2 The following program produces a clustering based on a sample of cases:

```
TITLE 'CLUSTERING CASES'.

GET FILE=CLUSDATA.
COMPUTE SAMPFLAG = UNIFORM(1).

TEMPORARY.
SELECT IF  SAMPFLAG < 0.10.
QUICK CLUSTER  A B C D E F G H
 /CRITERIA = CLUSTER(5)
 /OUTFILE = CLUSCENT.

QUICK CLUSTER  A B C D E F G H
 /FILE = CLUSCENT
 /CRITERIA = CLUSTER(5) NOUPDATE
 /SAVE = CLUSTER(CLUSTMEM).

SAVE FILE = CLUSMEMS.
```

- The data are from SPSS file CLUSDATA.
- The TEMPORARY and SELECT IF commands select cases based on the value of variable SAMPFLAG, which is generated from a pseudo-uniform distribution. (This avoids the potential biases of sampling, say, a set of cases that happen to be first in the large group.) Approximately 10% of the cases are included.
- The first QUICK CLUSTER command clusters the sampled cases based on the values of eight variables, A through H.
- The CRITERIA subcommand specifies five clusters.
- The OUTFILE subcommand saves the final cluster centers on the file CLUSCENT.
- The second QUICK CLUSTER command reads inital cluster centers from the file CLUSCENT. These are the final cluster centers from the preceding analysis on a sample of the cases.

- The CRITERIA subcommand specifies five clusters and skips the cluster-center update phase of the clustering procedure.
- The program produces only default output. No PRINT subcommand is included.
- The program saves the cluster membership of each case in a new variable, CLUST-MEM, on the SPSS active system file.
- The SAVE command saves the data, including the new variable, on the SPSS system file CLUSMEMS.

REGRESSION

In this example of regression, the task is to predict the average aggregate personal savings rate of a country as a function of the age distribution of the population, the average level of real per capita disposable income, and the average percentage growth rate of real per capita disposable income. The data are 50 cases taken from an example in Belsley, Kuh, and Welsch (1980).

The variables are

- SAVINGS—the average aggregate personal savings rate in a country during the period 1960–1970.
- POP15—the average percentage of the population under 15 years of age during the period 1960–1970.
- POP75—the average percentage of the population over 75 years of age during the period 1960–1970.
- INCOME—the average level of real per capita disposable income during the period 1960–1970, measured in United States dollars.
- GROWTH—the average percentage growth rate of INCOME during the period 1960–1970.

The SPSS commands are

```
DATA LIST FILE=COUNTRY/COUNTRY 1-8(A) SAVINGS POP15 POP75
              INCOME GROWTH 11-60.
VAR LABELS    SAVINGS 'Avg Agg Personal Savings Rate'
              POP15 'Avg % Pop under 15 years old'
              POP75 'Avg % Pop over 75 years old'
              INCOME 'Avg level real per-cap disposable inc'
              GROWTH 'Avg % growth rate of dpi'.
PRINT FORMATS  SAVINGS TO GROWTH(F7.2).
REGRESSION  VARS=SAVINGS TO GROWTH/DEP=SAVINGS/ENTER
  /RESID=DEFAULT SIZE(SMALL) ID(COUNTRY)
  /CASEWISE=DEFAULT ALL MAHAL COOK SRESID SDRESID LEVER
  /SCATTERPLOT (*RES,*PRE)/PARTIALPLOT.
```

- The DATA LIST command defines the variables in file handle COUNTRY. The VAR LABELS command assigns labels to the variables. The PRINT FORMATS command assigns a print format to the variables.
- The REGRESSION command requests a direct-entry regression analysis with variable SAVINGS as the dependent variable.
- The RESIDUALS subcommand requests the default residuals results. In addition, the SIZE(SMALL) keyword overrides the default plot sizes so that small plots are displayed. The ID(COUNTRY) keyword specifies that the values for variable COUNTRY are to be used to label outlier plots. Figure 1 shows the residuals statistics and outlier plots. Figure 2 displays the histogram of the standardized residuals and the normal probability plot.
- The CASEWISE subcommand requests a casewise plot of the standardized residuals for all cases. The dependent variable and the temporary variables PRED, RESID, MAHAL, COOK, SRESID, and SDRESID are also listed for all cases. Because of the page width limitation, the specified variable LEVER is not displayed. The output is shown in Figure 3.
- The SCATTERPLOT subcommand requests a plot of the residuals against the predicted values. Since *RES is specified first, it is plotted along the vertical axis. Figure 4 shows the plot.
- The PARTIALPLOT subcommand requests separate partial regression plots of the residuals of the dependent variable SAVINGS against the residuals of each indepen-

dent variable when both variables are regressed on the rest of the independent variables. The output is shown in Figure 5.

Figure 1 Residuals statistics and outliers

```
Residuals Statistics:

                Min         Max      Mean   Std Dev   N

*PRED          5.5874    15.8185    9.6710   2.6066   50
*ZPRED        -1.5666     2.3584     .0000   1.0000   50
*SEPRED         .7344     2.7722    1.1481    .3612   50
*ADJPRED       5.2366    14.9290    9.7052   2.6865   50
*RESID        -8.2422     9.7509     .0000   3.6441   50
*ZRESID       -2.1675     2.5642     .0000    .9583   50
*SRESID       -2.2091     2.6509    -.0031   1.0053   50
*DRESID       -8.5616    10.4213    -.0342   4.0378   50
*SDRESID      -2.3134     2.8536     .0000   1.0293   50
*MAHAL          .8476    25.0613    3.9200   3.9842   50
*COOK D         .0000      .2681     .0229    .0440   50
*LEVER          .0173      .5115     .0800    .0813   50

Total Cases =        50


Durbin-Watson Test =    1.68579


Outliers - Standardized Residual

   Case #   COUNTRY      *ZRESID

      50   Zambia        2.56423
       7   Chile        -2.16749
      36   Philippi      1.75534
      35   Peru          1.71969
      18   Iceland      -1.63321
      34   Paraguay     -1.61093
      24   Korea        -1.60598
      10   Denmark       1.42014
      23   Japan         1.38890
       9   Costa Ri      1.34776
```

Figure 2 Histogram and normal probability plot

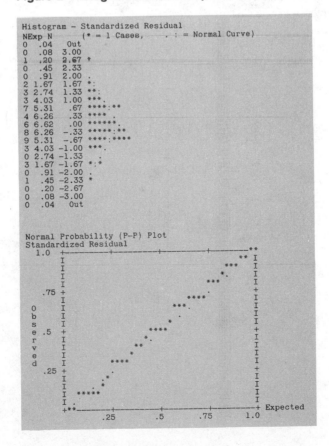

Figure 3 Casewise plot for 50 nations

```
                        * * * *   M U L T I P L E   R E G R E S S I O N   * * * *

Equation Number 1    Dependent Variable..   SAVINGS   AVG AGG PERSONAL SAVINGS R

Casewise Plot of Standardized Residual

*: Selected   M: Missing
```

		-3.0 0.0 3.0						
Case #	COUNTRY	0:......:......:0	SAVINGS	*PRED	*RESID	*SRESID	*SDRESID	*MAHAL	*COOK D
1	Australi	. * .	11.43	10.5663	.8637	.2352	.2328	2.3379	.0008
2	Austria	. * .	12.07	11.4538	.6162	.1728	.1709	4.9187	.0008
3	Belgium	. * .	13.17	10.9511	2.2189	.6108	.6065	3.3066	.0072
4	Bolivia	. *. .	5.75	6.4484	-.6984	-.1925	-.1904	3.4041	.0007
5	Brazil	. * .	12.88	9.3271	3.5529	.9686	.9679	2.4283	.0140
6	Canada	. * .	8.79	9.1066	-.3166	-.0908	-.0898	6.7815	.0003
7	Chile	. * . .	.60	8.8422	-8.2422	-2.2091	-2.3134	.8476	.0378
8	Colombia	. *. .	4.98	6.4317	-1.4517	-.3932	-.3895	1.8278	.0019
9	Costa Ri	. . * .	10.78	5.6549	5.1251	1.4017	1.4173	2.7179	.0321
10	Denmark	. . * .	16.85	11.4497	5.4003	1.4669	1.4865	2.0932	.0288
11	Ecuador	. *. .	3.59	5.9957	-2.4057	-.6538	-.6496	2.1426	.0058
12	Finland	. *. .	11.24	12.9210	-1.6810	-.4639	-.4598	3.5301	.0044
13	France	. * .	12.64	10.1646	2.4754	.7004	.6964	5.6940	.0155
14	Germany	. * .	12.55	12.7306	-.1806	-.0497	-.0492	3.3005	.0000
15	Greece	. *. .	10.67	13.7863	-3.1163	-.8622	-.8597	3.7544	.0159
16	Guatemal	. *. .	3.01	6.3653	-3.3553	-.9103	-.9086	1.9841	.0107
17	Honduras	. * .	7.70	6.9900	.7100	.1926	.1905	1.9639	.0005
18	Iceland	. *. .	1.27	7.4805	-6.2105	-1.6940	-1.7312	2.4743	.0435
19	India	. *. .	9.00	8.4914	.5086	.1388	.1373	2.5212	.0003
20	Ireland	. . * .	11.34	7.9490	3.3910	1.0047	1.0048	9.4195	.0544
21	Italy	. . * .	14.28	12.3533	1.9267	.5244	.5201	2.2790	.0039
22	Jamaica	. *. .	7.72	10.7385	-3.0185	-.8564	-.8538	5.9172	.0240
23	Japan	. . * .	21.10	15.8185	5.2815	1.5760	1.6032	9.9621	.1428
24	Korea	. *. .	3.98	10.0870	-6.1070	-1.6571	-1.6910	1.9992	.0356
25	Libya	. *. .	8.89	11.7195	-2.8295	-1.0871	-1.0893	25.0614	.2681
26	Luxembou	. *. .	10.35	12.0208	-1.6708	-.4597	-.4556	3.2511	.0040
27	Malaysia	. *. .	4.71	7.6805	-2.9705	-.8080	-.8048	2.2178	.0091
28	Malta	. . * .	15.48	12.5052	2.9748	.8153	.8123	2.9108	.0115
29	Netherla	. * .	14.65	14.2244	.4256	.1174	.1161	3.4601	.0003
30	New Zeal	. . * .	10.67	8.3845	2.2855	.6180	.6137	1.6767	.0044
31	Nicaragu	. *. .	7.30	6.6536	.6464	.1744	.1725	1.4872	.0003
32	Norway	. *. .	10.25	11.1217	-.8717	-.2349	-.2325	1.3687	.0006
33	Panama	. *. .	4.44	7.7342	-3.2942	-.8837	-.8815	.9297	.0063
34	Paraguay	. *. .	2.02	8.1458	-6.1258	-1.6699	-1.7049	2.4193	.0416
35	Peru	. . * .	12.70	6.1606	6.5394	1.7785	1.8239	2.2074	.0440
36	Philippi	. . * .	12.78	6.1050	6.6750	1.8146	1.8638	2.1685	.0452
37	Portugal	. *. .	12.49	13.2586	-.7686	-.2127	-.2104	3.7803	.0010
38	South Af	. *. .	11.14	10.6569	.4831	.1314	.1299	2.2101	.0002
39	South Rh	. .* .	13.30	12.0087	1.2913	.3707	.3671	6.8996	.0053
40	Spain	. *. .	11.77	12.4413	-.6713	-.1838	-.1818	2.8091	.0006
41	Sweden	. *. .	6.86	11.1201	-4.2601	-1.1970	-1.2029	5.0955	.0406
42	Switzerl	. . * .	14.13	11.6431	2.4869	.6795	.6754	2.6262	.0073
43	Taiwan	. . * .	11.90	9.3639	2.5361	.6945	.6905	2.8399	.0082
44	Tunisia	. *. .	2.81	5.6280	-2.8180	-.7703	-.7668	2.6738	.0096
45	Turkey	. *. .	5.13	7.7957	-2.6657	-.7153	-.7114	.9625	.0042
46	U.K.	. *. .	7.81	10.5025	-2.6925	-.7533	-.7496	4.7290	.0150
47	U.S.	. *. .	7.56	8.6712	-1.1112	-.3580	-.3545	15.3703	.0128
48	Uruguay	. *. .	9.24	11.5040	-2.2640	-.6269	-.6226	3.8193	.0085
49	Venezuel	. . * .	9.22	5.5874	3.6326	.9994	.9993	3.2478	.0189
50	Zambia	. . *.	18.56	8.8091	9.7509	2.6509	2.8536	2.1722	.0966
Case #	COUNTRY	0:......:......:0	SAVINGS	*PRED	*RESID	*SRESID	*SDRESID	*MAHAL	*COOK D

```
                        -3.0  0.0  3.0
```

Figure 4 Residuals against predicted values

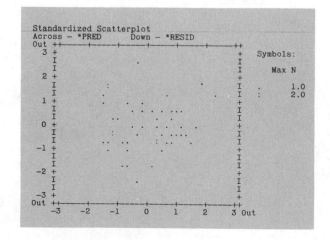

Figure 5 Partial regression plots

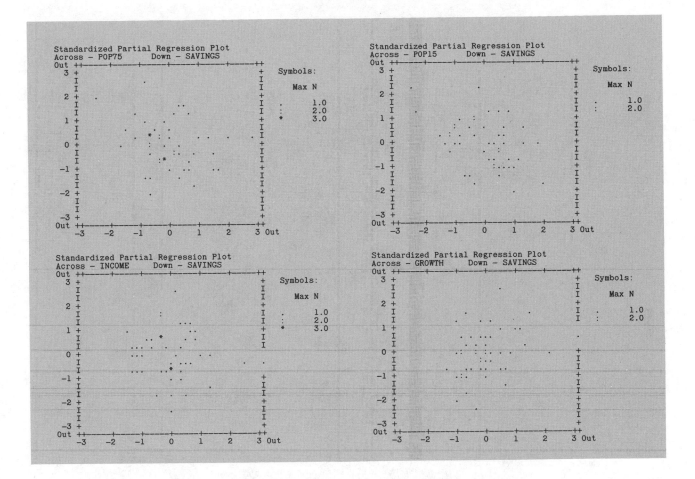

RELIABILITY   The following example demonstrates the use of RELIABILITY to analyze an attitude scale of confidence in institutions in the United States. The data come from a 500-case sample of the 1980 General Social Survey. Respondents were asked how much confidence they have in the people running the following institutions: banks and financial institutions, major companies, organized religion, education, the executive branch of the federal government, organized labor, the press, medicine, television, the United States Supreme Court, the scientific community, Congress, and the military. The SPSS commands are

```
GET  FILE=GSS80/KEEP CONFINAN TO CONARMY.
RELIABILITY  VARIABLES=ALL
  /MODEL=STRICTPARALLEL
  /SUMMARY=TOTAL
  /STATISTICS=ANOVA TUKEY HOTELLING.
```

- The GET command defines the data to SPSS and selects the variables needed for analysis.
- The RELIABILITY command analyzes the scale formed from the 13. confidence variables and uses the STRICTPARALLEL model
- The SUMMARY subcommand produces item-total statistics.
- The STATISTICS subcommand produces the analysis of variance table, the Tukey test for additivity, and Hotelling's T^2.

RELIABILITY display

```
                              R E L I A B I L I T Y   A N A L Y S I S   -   S C A L E   (C O N F I N D)

      1.    CONFINAN     BANKS & FINANCIAL INSTITUTIONS
      2.    CONBUS       MAJOR COMPANIES
      3.    CONCLERG     ORGANIZED RELIGION
      4.    CONEDUC      EDUCATION
      5.    CONFED       EXECUTIVE BRANCH OF FEDERAL  GOVERNMENT
      6.    CONLABOR     ORGANIZED LABOR
      7.    CONPRESS     PRESS
      8.    CONMEDIC     MEDICINE
      9.    CONTV        TELEVISION
     10.    CONJUDGE     U.S.   SUPREME COURT
     11.    CONSCI       SCIENTIFIC COMMUNITY
     12.    CONLEGIS     CONGRESS
     13.    CONARMY      MILITARY

      # OF CASES =     415.0
```

ITEM-TOTAL STATISTICS

	SCALE MEAN IF ITEM DELETED	SCALE VARIANCE IF ITEM DELETED	CORRECTED ITEM- TOTAL CORRELATION	SQUARED MULTIPLE CORRELATION	ALPHA IF ITEM DELETED
CONFINAN	22.8361	17.8958	.4550	.2989	.7831
CONBUS	22.8410	18.6317	.3556	.2424	.7918
CONCLERG	22.8554	18.3172	.3693	.1671	.7912
CONEDUC	22.8458	18.0679	.4652	.2321	.7823
CONFED	22.4578	18.0459	.4692	.2961	.7820
CONLABOR	22.5181	18.4242	.3763	.2102	.7902
CONPRESS	22.7108	18.8147	.3215	.2220	.7947
CONMEDIC	23.1036	18.0158	.4962	.2740	.7798
CONTV	22.5518	18.5909	.3670	.1938	.7908
CONJUDGE	22.7446	17.5771	.5061	.3125	.7783
CONSCI	23.1036	18.6632	.3910	.2185	.7887
CONLEGIS	22.4145	18.0790	.5277	.3481	.7779
CONARMY	22.7952	17.7381	.4930	.2903	.7796

ANALYSIS OF VARIANCE

SOURCE OF VARIATION	SUM OF SQ.	DF	MEAN SQUARE	F	PROB.
BETWEEN PEOPLE	669.7412	414	1.6177		
WITHIN PEOPLE	1858.9231	4980	.3733		
BETWEEN MEASURES	240.9631	12	20.0803	61.6571	.0000
RESIDUAL	1617.9600	4968	.3257		
NONADDITIVITY	.0041	1	.0041	.0125	.9109
BALANCE	1617.9559	4967	.3257		
TOTAL	2528.6643	5394	.4688		

```
GRAND MEAN =        1.8960


TUKEY ESTIMATE OF POWER TO WHICH OBSERVATIONS
MUST BE RAISED TO ACHIEVE ADDITIVITY       =      0.9778


HOTELLINGS T-SQUARED =    694.5944      F =    56.3449     PROB. =    .0000
   DEGREES OF FREEDOM:              NUMERATOR =    12    DENOMINATOR =     403


    TEST FOR GOODNESS OF FIT OF MODEL STRICTLYPARALLEL

    CHI SQUARE =      965.6186     DEGREES OF FREEDOM =   101
    LOG OF DETERMINANT OF UNCONSTRAINED MATRIX =     -13.674300
    LOG OF DETERMINANT OF CONSTRAINED MATRIX   =     -11.318964
    PROBABILITY =   .0000


    PARAMETER ESTIMATES

    ESTIMATED COMMON MEAN      =      1.8960
    ESTIMATED COMMON VARIANCE =      0.4697
            ERROR VARIANCE =      0.3733
             TRUE VARIANCE =      0.0965
    ESTIMATED COMMON INTERITEM CORRELATION =   0.2037

    ESTIMATED RELIABILITY OF SCALE  =   .7688
    UNBIASED ESTIMATE OF RELIABILITY =   .7704
```

REPORT   The following two examples illustrate the use of procedure REPORT to produce summary and listing reports.

Example 1   This example produces a report that summarizes information from a retail company's personnel file. It reports summary statistics for employees in each division of the company within each store. The SPSS commands are

```
GET FILE=CHIGDATA.
SET CASE=UPLOW.

PRINT FORMATS SALARY(DOLLAR7.0).

SORT CASES  BY STORE DIVISION.
REPORT FORMAT=AUTOMATIC MARGINS(1,72) LENGTH(1,24) BRKSPACE(-1)
 /VARIABLES=AGE TENURE JTENURE SPACE(DUMMY)' '(4) SALARY
 /TITLE='Chicago Home Furnishing'
 /FOOTNOTE=LEFT 'Tenure measured in months'
 /BREAK=STORE
   /SUMMARY=MEAN 'Average:'
   /SUMMARY=VALIDN '  Count:'(AGE)
 /BREAK=DIVISION 'Product' 'Division' (SKIP(0))
   /SUMMARY=MEAN.
```

- The GET command retrieves the system file containing information on the employees in the company.
- The SET command ensures that any variable or value labels that were defined in upper and lower case are printed in upper and lower case in the display file.
- The PRINT FORMATS command ensures that summaries on variable SALARY are printed with the dollar format.
- The SORT CASES command sorts the file into the order required for REPORT.
- The FORMAT subcommand specifies a summary report. The AUTOMATIC keyword implements REPORT's automatic format settings. The MARGINS keyword sets the left margin at column 1 and right margin at column 72. The LENGTH keyword sets the top of the report on the first line and the last line of the page on line 24. The BRKSPACE keyword places the summary for each break of DIVISION on the same line as each label of DIVISION.
- The VARIABLES subcommand defines four columns in the body of the report. AGE, TENURE, and JTENURE and SALARY are SPSS variables. SPACE defines a dummy column for spacing purposes.
- The TITLE subcommand defines a one-line centered title.
- The FOOTNOTE subcommand defines a one-line left-justified footnote.
- The first BREAK subcommand defines the major break in this two-break report. Variable STORE breaks the file into two categories: the downtown store and the suburban store. Value labels for STORE are printed in the break column.
- The first two SUMMARY subcommands print two lines of summary statistics for each store. The first SUMMARY subcommand computes means for AGE, TENURE, JTENURE and SALARY. The second SUMMARY subcommand computes the number of employees in each store. Summary titles are assigned to each summary function.
- The second BREAK subcommand breaks the file into divisions within each store. The SKIP specification suppresses blank lines between the summary for each division. A column heading is defined for DIVISION.
- The last SUMMARY subcommand computes means for AGE, TENURE, JTENURE, and SALARY for each division.

Summary report

```
                        Chicago Home Furnishing

                                   Tenure    Tenure
        Branch    Product            in        in
        Store     Division    Age   Company   Grade      Salary--Annual


        Suburban  Carpeting   26.75   4.37     3.42          $12,625
                  Appliances  30.20   4.05     3.77          $14,395
                  Furniture   35.29   4.71     4.32          $12,975
                  Hardware    32.00   4.33     4.33          $22,500

        Average:              31.59   4.42     3.95          $13,871
          Count:                17

        Downtown  Carpeting   32.75   3.87     3.25          $11,318
                  Appliances  32.25   3.52     3.25          $10,150
                  Furniture   38.25   4.86     3.86          $13,500
                  Hardware    37.25   4.67     4.62          $16,350

        Average:              35.25   4.28     3.68          $12,689
          Count:                24

        Tenure measured in months
```

Example 2   This example produces a report using data from the October 1980 issue of *Runner's World* magazine. It lists the top-rated shoes in the survey organized by manufacturer. Measures used by the raters to determine an overall evaluation for each shoe are reported. The SPSS commands used to produce this report are

```
TITLE            'RUNNER''S WORLD 1980 SHOE SURVEY'.
DATA LIST        FIXED /1 TYPE 1 MAKER 2-3 QUALITY 5-9
                 REARIMP FOREIMP FLEX SOLEWEAR 10-29
                 REARCONT SOLETRAC 31-40 WEIGHT 42-46 LASTYEAR 48
                 PREFER 50-53 STARS 55 NAME 57-72 (A).
VARIABLE LABELS  TYPE 'Type' MAKER 'Manufacturer' QUALITY 'Quality'
                 REARIMP 'Rearfoot Impact' FOREIMP 'Forefoot Impact'
                 FLEX 'Flexibility' SOLEWEAR 'Sole Wear'
                 REARCONT 'Rearfoot Control' SOLETRAC 'Sole Traction'
                 WEIGHT 'Weight' LASTYEAR '1979 Stars'
                 PREFER 'Reader Preference' STARS 'Rating' NAME
'Shoe'.
VALUE LABLES     MAKER (1)Adidas (2)Autry (3)Brookfield (4)Brooks
                 (5)Converse (6)Reebok (7)New Balance (8)Puma (9)Osaga
                 (10)Pony (11)Etonic (12)Nike (13)Saucony
                 (14)Wilson-Bata (15)Vol Shoe Corp
                 (16)Specs International (17)Power Sport
                 (18)Thom McAn Jox (19)Regal Shoes (20)Shoe Corp
                 (21)Asics (22)Intl Footwear (23)Eb Sport Intl
                 (24)Van Doren/
                 TYPE(1)Male (2)Female/
                 STARS(6)****** (5)*****.
PRINT FORMATS    QUALITY (F5.3)/REARIMP FOREIMP SOLEWEAR (F4.1)/
                 FLEX SOLETRAC (F4.2)/REARCONT WEIGHT (F5.1)/
                 PREFER (F4.3).
SELECT IF        STARS GE 5.
BEGIN DATA
1 4 3.965  8.3 11.0 1.33 10.0 -13.6   .55 232.4 5 .531 6 Vantage
1 4 3.965  8.5 10.9 1.31 10.0 -16.5   .58 239.1 5      6 Vantage
Supreme
  . . .
217 3.692 12.9 18.6 2.90  3.5   0.9   .68 280.6 0         LDT 138
221 4.920 13.2 17.6 2.34  2.1   8.6   .63 244.0 0 .026 Tigress 80
END DATA.

SORT CASES BY MAKER STARS(D).
REPORT FORMAT=AUTOMATIC MISSING ' ' LIST(4) TSPACE(3)
      /VARS =TYPE(LABEL) NAME STARS(LABEL) REARIMP
              FOREIMP FLEX 'Flexi-' 'bility'
              SOLEWEAR REARCONT SOLETRAC
              WEIGHT LASTYEAR(LABEL) PREFER(LABEL)
       /TITLE='Ratings of Training Shoes'
              'Runner''s World Magazine - October, 1980'
    /FOOTNOTE=LEFT '****** Highly recommended'
             '*****   Recommended'
           RIGHT ' ' 'Page )PAGE'
       /BREAK=MAKER.
```

- The TITLE command supplies a title for the session.
- The DATA LIST command defines the variables to be used in the report. The data are inline.
- The VARIABLE LABELS command supplies variable labels for all the variables. These labels are used as default column headings in the report.
- The VALUE LABELS command supplies value labels for the manufacturer, type of shoe, and rating. These labels are used in the report columns.
- The PRINT FORMATS command overrides the default print formats.
- The SELECT IF command selects shoes with the top two ratings.
- The BEGIN DATA command signals the beginning of the inline data and the END DATA command signals the end of the data.
- The SORT CASES command sorts cases in descending order of ranking for each manufacturer. They are sorted by manufacturer since the report groups them by manufacturer. They are sorted by descending order of ranking so that the top-rated shoes for the manufacturer are listed first.
- The FORMAT subcommand specifies a case listing that displays cases in groups of four. The AUTOMATIC keyword implements REPORT's automatic format settings. The MISSING keyword prints a blank in place of the period for variables with missing values. The TSPACE keyword inserts three blank lines between the report title and the column headings.
- The VARIABLES subcommand names all the SPSS variables being listed. Value labels are printed in place of values for variables TYPE and STARS.
- The TITLE subcommand prints a two-line centered title.
- The FOOTNOTE subcommand prints a two-line left-justified footnote and a two-line right-justified footnote. The first line of the right-justified footnote is blank; the second line uses the special keyword)PAGE to print page numbers.
- The BREAK subcommand groups the shoes by manufacturer and prints the manufacturers' names (which were supplied on the VALUE LABELS command).

Listing report

Ratings of Training Shoes
Runner's World Magazine — October, 1980

Manufacturer	Type	Shoe	Rating	Rearfoot Impact	Forefoot Impact	Flexi- bility	Sole Wear	Rearfoot Control	Sole Traction	Weight	1979 Stars	Reader Preference
Saucony	Male	TC84	******	9.3	15.1	1.56	6.5	5.2	.85	278.0	0	.028
	Male	Hornet 84	******	9.9	13.1	2.65	7.6	3.0	.68	265.0	4	.097
	Female	MS Trainer	******	10.2	13.3	1.58	6.4	22.4	.86	237.7	5	.053
	Male	Jazz	*****	8.9	12.7	2.04	7.6	−7.0	.64	270.8	0	
	Male	Trainer 80	*****	10.5	14.5	2.18	4.1	11.5	.82	307.6	5	.232
	Female	Jazz	*****	9.0	12.2	1.86	6.1	−7.5	.63	223.0	0	.013
	Female	TC 84	*****	9.3	14.6	1.46	7.5	1.3	.77	231.1	0	
	Female	MS Hornet	*****	9.8	13.2	2.59	6.4	6.5	.67	224.0	4	.046
Nike	Male	Daygreak	******	10.8	15.4	2.17	3.7	7.8	.54	304.2	5	.602
	Male	Yankee	*****	10.9	13.7	1.93	2.0	9.8	.66	276.6	0	
	Female	Liberator	*****	10.6	14.7	2.20	5.8	6.5	.52	254.2	5	.503
Etonic	Male	Eclipse Trainer	******	10.0	12.9	1.65	10.0	−2.6	.51	237.4	0	
	Female	Eclipse Trainer	******	9.6	12.8	1.78	10.0	1.4	.57	204.1	0	
	Male	Stabilizer	*****	10.3	15.5	2.25	1.2	−.6	.53	283.1	4	.232
	Male	Streetfighter	*****	10.8	15.5	2.28	1.4	−.4	.61	266.1	4	.222
	Female	Streetfighter	*****	10.7	15.5	1.66	.7	−7.7	.70	214.1	4	.344
	Female	Stabilizer	*****	10.8	14.4	2.09	2.6	−6.9	.67	235.3	4	.298
Pony	Male	Targa Flex	******	9.6	14.3	1.32	2.5	−22.7	.86	253.0	3	
	Male	Shadow	*****	9.9	13.8	1.53	2.5	−17.9	.77	270.2	0	
	Female	Lady Shadow	*****	10.6	17.4	.91	3.0	−7.1	.90	211.8	0	
Osaga	Male	Fast Rider	*****	10.5	14.0	2.48	4.9	1.9	.66	296.7	5	.025
	Female	KT-26	*****	10.7	17.3	1.66	5.5	8.1	.60	223.1	2	
New Balance	Male	420	*****	9.8	14.8	2.09	1.8	−17.7	.46	267.9	0	.516
	Male	620	*****	12.0	14.6	2.73	1.1	−3.5	.41	242.0	5	.475
	Female	420	*****	9.9	13.9	1.94	1.6	−.7	.46	219.3	0	.411
Reebok	Male	Aztec	******	10.9	12.6	2.07	2.5	3.7	.65	260.8	5	.065
	Male	Shadow I	*****	10.7	13.1	1.79	1.9	−8.7	.63	253.0	0	
	Female	Shadow III	*****	10.2	12.9	1.63	2.4	−24.6	.66	212.8	0	
	Female	Aztec Princess	*****	10.2	12.8	2.18	5.9	−20.3	.70	221.3	5	.033
Converse	Male	Arizona 84	*****	10.1	13.6	1.90	6.6	−5.1	.55	302.9	4	.006
	Female	World Class 84	*****	9.4	14.0	2.19	4.3	−.3	.65	234.7	3	.020
Brooks	Male	Vantage	******	8.3	11.0	1.33	10.0	−13.6	.55	232.4	5	.531
	Male	Vantage Supreme	******	8.5	10.9	1.31	10.0	−16.5	.58	239.1	5	
	Male	Hugger GT	******	8.5	11.2	1.32	9.4	−11.7	.60	234.5	5	.488
	Male	Nighthawk	******	8.7	13.5	1.57	3.1	−8.6	.45	216.7	0	
	Male	Super Villanova	******	10.0	14.1	1.07	10.0	14.4	.61	238.7	5	.155
	Female	Vantage	******	8.1	11.0	1.27	10.0	−13.1	.58	199.9	5	.563

****** Highly recommended
***** Recommended

Ratings of Training Shoes
Runner's World Magazine — October, 1980

Manufacturer	Type	Shoe	Rating	Rearfoot Impact	Forefoot Impact	Flexi- bility	Sole Wear	Rearfoot Control	Sole Traction	Weight	1979 Stars	Reader Preference
Brooks	Female	Hugger GT	******	8.2	11.1	1.28	10.0	−12.7	.60	203.8	0	.126
	Female	Vantage Supreme	******	8.2	11.1	1.34	10.0	.6	.62	201.4	3	.205
	Female	Super Villanova	******	9.0	13.4	1.01	10.0	11.9	.62	195.1	5	.298
	Female	Nighthawk	*****	8.6	13.1	1.54	2.4	−9.3	.45	189.0	0	
Brookfield	Male	Colt	*****	12.4	17.4	2.31	3.5	21.5	1.13	289.3	4	
Autry	Male	Mach III	*****	8.7	13.0	2.13	3.0	−37.6	.66	250.2	4	
	Male	New Jet	*****	9.1	14.5	1.88	4.0	−37.9	.69	242.4	4	
	Male	Concorde	*****	9.2	13.2	2.41	2.0	−33.9	.61	261.7	5	.023
	Female	Cloud 9	*****	9.4	17.6	1.79	2.3	−27.3	.63	198.6	3	
Adidas	Male	TRX Trainer	*****	10.5	16.8	2.07	2.1	−.6	.72	309.0	5	.143
	Male	Marathon Trainer	*****	13.0	17.2	2.75	10.0	14.5	.63	302.3	5	.315
	Female	Marathon Trainer	*****	11.7	16.5	2.14	10.0	17.5	.58	243.6	5	.298

****** Highly recommended
***** Recommended

SURVIVAL   The data in this example are from a study of 647 cancer patients. The variables are

- TREATMNT—the type of treatment received.
- ONSETMO, ONSETYR—month and year cancer was discovered.
- RECURSIT—indicates whether a recurrence took place.
- RECURMO, RECURYR—month and year of recurrence.
- OUTCOME—status of patient at end of study, alive or dead.
- DEATHMO, DEATHYR—month and year of death, or, for those who survived, the date the study ended.

Using these date variables and the YRMODA function, the number of months from onset to recurrence and from onset to death or survival are calculated. These new variables become the survival variables with TREATMNT as the single control variable. The SPSS commands are

```
SET WIDTH=132.
DATA LIST  FILE = SURVDATA/ 1 TREATMNT 15 ONSETMO 19-20
              ONSETYR 21-22 RECURSIT 48 RECURMO 49-50 RECURYR 51-52
              OUTCOME 56 DEATHMO 57-58 DEATHYR 59-60.
COMMENT   TRANSFORM ALL DATES TO RUNNING CALENDAR DAYS.
COMPUTE   ONSDATE=YRMODA(ONSETYR,ONSETMO,15).
COMPUTE   RECDATE=YRMODA(RECURYR,RECURMO,15).
COMPUTE   DEATHDT=YRMODA(DEATHYR,DEATHMO,15).

COMMENT   NOW COMPUTE SURVIVAL VARIABLES.
COMPUTE   ONSSURV = (DEATHDT-ONSDATE)/30.
IF   RECURSIT EQ 0 RECSURV = ONSSURV.
IF   RECURSIT NE 0 RECSURV = (RECDATE-ONSDATE)/30.

VARIABLE LABELS   TREATMNT 'PATIENT TREATMENT'
                  ONSSURV 'MONTHS FROM ONSET TO DEATH'
                  RECSURV 'MONTHS FROM ONSET TO RECURRENCE'.
VALUE LABELS   TREATMNT 1 'TREATMENT A' 2 'TREATMENT B'
              3 'TREATMENT C'.
SURVIVAL   TABLES = ONSSURV,RECSURV BY TREATMNT(1,3)
  /STATUS = RECURSIT(1,9) FOR RECSURV
  /STATUS = OUTCOME(3,4) FOR ONSSURV
  /INTERVALS = THRU 50 BY 5 THRU 100 BY 10
  /PLOTS /COMPARE /CALCULATE=CONDITIONAL PAIRWISE.
```

- The SET command sets the page width to 132.
- The onset, recurrence, and death dates are transformed to running days, using the YRMODA function in the COMPUTE command. The constant 15 is used as the day argument for YRMODA since only month and year were recorded, not the actual day.
- ONSSURV, the first survival variable, is calculated by taking the difference between the date of death (or survival) and the date the cancer was discovered (ONSDATE). The difference is divided by 30 to convert it from days to months.
- RECSURV, the second survival variable, is calculated conditionally using the IF command. For cases with RECURSIT values of 0, indicating no recurrence took place, RECSURV is set equal to ONSSURV.
- The TABLES subcommand in SURVIVAL specifies two survival variables, ONSSURV and RECSURV, and one control variable, TREATMNT. The life table for ONSSURV is shown in Figure 1.
- The status variable for RECSURV is RECURSIT with codes 1–9, indicating that the termination event, recurrence, took place. OUTCOME is the status variable for ONSSURV with codes 3 and 4 signaling the terminal event, death.
- The INTERVALS subcommand groups the first 50 months into 5-month intervals and the remaining 50 months into 10-month intervals.
- The default plots are requested using PLOTS. Figure 2 contains the plot of the survival function for ONSSURV.
- COMPARE with no specifications requests all comparisons. The subgroup comparisons for ONSSURV are shown in Figure 3.
- Keyword CONDITIONAL on the CALCULATE subcommand requests approximate comparisons if memory is insufficient for exact comparisons. Keyword PAIRWISE requests the pairwise output.

Figure 1 Life table

```
LIFE TABLE
   SURVIVAL VARIABLE   ONSSURV   MONTHS FROM ONSET TO DEATH
                   FOR    TREATMNT   PATIENT TREATMENT                            =     1  TREATMENT A

          NUMBER  NUMBER   NUMBER   NUMBER                    CUMUL                       SE OF   SE OF
          ENTRNG  WDRAWN   EXPOSD    OF     PROPN   PROPN    PROPN    PROBA-            CUMUL   PROB-
   INTVL  THIS    DURING   TO       TERMNL  TERMI-  SURVI-   SURV     BILITY   HAZARD   SURV-   ABILTY  SE OF
   START  INTVL   INTVL    RISK     EVENTS  NATING  VING     AT END   DENSTY   RATE     IVING   DENS    HAZRD
   TIME                                                                                                 RATE

     0.0  501.0     0.0    501.0     3.0   0.0060  0.9940   0.9940   0.0012   0.0012   0.003   0.001   0.001
     5.0  498.0     1.0    497.5    16.0   0.0322  0.9678   0.9620   0.0064   0.0065   0.009   0.002   0.002
    10.0  481.0     1.0    480.5    26.0   0.0541  0.9459   0.9100   0.0104   0.0111   0.013   0.002   0.002
    15.0  454.0     0.0    454.0    17.0   0.0374  0.9626   0.8759   0.0068   0.0076   0.015   0.002   0.002
    20.0  437.0     0.0    437.0    23.0   0.0526  0.9474   0.8298   0.0092   0.0108   0.017   0.002   0.002
    25.0  414.0     1.0    413.5    25.0   0.0605  0.9395   0.7796   0.0100   0.0125   0.019   0.002   0.002
    30.0  388.0     1.0    387.5    22.0   0.0568  0.9432   0.7354   0.0089   0.0117   0.020   0.002   0.002
    35.0  365.0     1.0    364.5    24.0   0.0658  0.9342   0.6870   0.0097   0.0136   0.021   0.002   0.003
    40.0  340.0     0.0    340.0    24.0   0.0706  0.9294   0.6385   0.0097   0.0146   0.022   0.002   0.003
    45.0  316.0     1.0    315.5    14.0   0.0444  0.9556   0.6101   0.0057   0.0091   0.022   0.001   0.002
    50.0  301.0     1.0    300.5    34.0   0.1131  0.8869   0.5411   0.0069   0.0120   0.022   0.001   0.002
    60.0  266.0     0.0    266.0    22.0   0.0827  0.9173   0.4963   0.0045   0.0086   0.022   0.001   0.002
    70.0  244.0     2.0    243.0    15.0   0.0617  0.9383   0.4657   0.0031   0.0064   0.022   0.001   0.002
    80.0  227.0     3.0    225.5    24.0   0.1064  0.8936   0.4161   0.0050   0.0112   0.022   0.001   0.002
    90.0  200.0     2.0    199.0    18.0   0.0905  0.9095   0.3785   0.0038   0.0095   0.022   0.001   0.002
   100.0+ 180.0   104.0    128.0    76.0   0.5938  0.4063   0.1538     **       **     0.019     **      **

**      THESE CALCULATIONS FOR THE LAST INTERVAL ARE MEANINGLESS.

THE MEDIAN SURVIVAL TIME FOR THESE DATA IS  69.18
```

Figure 2 Plot output for survival function

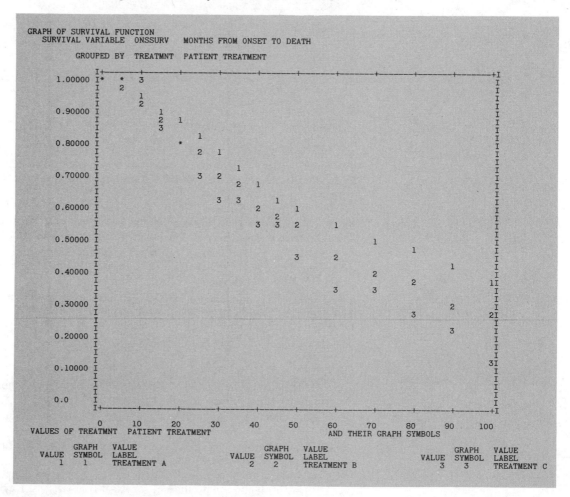

Figure 3 Subgroup comparisons

```
COMPARISON OF SURVIVAL EXPERIENCE USING THE LEE-DESU STATISTIC
   SURVIVAL VARIABLE  ONSSURV   MONTHS FROM ONSET TO DEATH
        GROUPED BY  TREATMNT  PATIENT TREATMENT

OVERALL COMPARISON    STATISTIC      9.001  D.F.    2    PROB.  0.0111

GROUP  LABEL              TOTAL N    UNCEN    CEN   PCT CEN   MEAN SCORE

    1  TREATMENT A            501      383    118     23.55       20.042
    2  TREATMENT B             97       82     15     15.46      -67.412
    3  TREATMENT C             26       24      2      7.69      -134.69
```

Figure 4 Pairwise comparisons

```
COMPARISON OF SURVIVAL EXPERIENCE USING THE LEE-DESU STATISTIC
   SURVIVAL VARIABLE  ONSSURV   MONTHS FROM ONSET TO DEATH
        GROUPED BY  TREATMNT  PATIENT TREATMENT

OVERALL COMPARISON    STATISTIC      9.001  D.F.    2    PROB.  0.0111

GROUP  LABEL              TOTAL N    UNCEN    CEN   PCT CEN   MEAN SCORE

    1  TREATMENT A            501      383    118     23.55       20.042
    2  TREATMENT B             97       82     15     15.46      -67.412
    3  TREATMENT C             26       24      2      7.69      -134.69

PAIRWISE COMPARISON   STATISTIC      5.042  D.F.    1    PROB.  0.0247

GROUP  LABEL              TOTAL N    UNCEN    CEN   PCT CEN   MEAN SCORE

    1  TREATMENT A            501      383    118     23.55       13.603
    2  TREATMENT B             97       82     15     15.46      -70.258

PAIRWISE COMPARISON   STATISTIC      4.768  D.F.    1    PROB.  0.0290

GROUP  LABEL              TOTAL N    UNCEN    CEN   PCT CEN   MEAN SCORE

    1  TREATMENT A            501      383    118     23.55        6.4391
    3  TREATMENT C             26       24      2      7.69      -124.08

PAIRWISE COMPARISON   STATISTIC      0.766  D.F.    1    PROB.  0.3814

GROUP  LABEL              TOTAL N    UNCEN    CEN   PCT CEN   MEAN SCORE

    2  TREATMENT B             97       82     15     15.46        2.8454
    3  TREATMENT C             26       24      2      7.69      -10.615
```

T-TEST

The example illustrating T-TEST analyzes 1979 prices and earnings in 45 cities around the world, compiled by the Union Bank of Switzerland. The variables are

- WORLD—the economic class of the country in which the city is located. The 45 cities are divided into three groups: cities in economically developed nations such as the United States and most European nations, cities in nations that are members of the Organization for Petroleum Exporting Countries (OPEC), and cities in underdeveloped countries. These groups are coded from 1 to 3 and are labeled 1ST WORLD, PETRO WORLD, and 3RD WORLD, respectively.

- NTCPRI—the city's net price level, based on more than 100 goods and services weighted by consumer habits. NTCPRI is expressed as the percentage above or below that of Zurich, where Zurich equals 100%.

- NTCSAL—the city's net salary level, calculated from average net hourly earnings in 12 occupations. NTCSAL is expressed as a percentage above or below that of Zurich, where Zurich equals 100%.

- NTCPUR—the city's net purchasing power level, calculated as the ratio of labor expended (measured in number of working hours) to the cost of more than 100 goods and services, weighted by consumer habits. NTCPUR is expressed as a percentage above or below that of Zurich, where Zurich equals 100%.

- WCLOTHES—the cost of medium-priced women's clothes, expressed as the percentage above or below that of Zurich, where Zurich equals 100%.

- MCLOTHES—the cost of medium-priced men's clothes, expressed as the percentage above or below that of Zurich, where Zurich equals 100%.

In this example we compare mean price, salary and purchasing power for cities grouped by economic class. We also compare the mean costs of women's and men's clothes. The SPSS commands are:

```
GET  FILE=CITY/KEEP=NTCPRI, NTCSAL, NTCPUR, WCLOTHES, MCLOTHES,
WORLD.
VAR LABELS  WCLOTHES, MEDIUM—PRICED WOMEN'S CLOTHES
            /MCLOTHES, MEDIUM—PRICED MEN'S CLOTHES.
T—TEST  GROUPS=WORLD (1,3)/VARIABLES=NTCPRI NTCSAL NTCPUR
    /PAIRS=WCLOTHES MCLOTHES/NTCPRI WITH NTCPUR NTCSAL.
```

- The GET command defines the data to SPSS and selects the variables needed for analysis.
- The VAR LABELS commands assign new labels to the variables WCLOTHES and MCLOTHES.
- The T-TEST command requests an independent-samples test and a paired-samples test. For the independent-samples test, the variable WORLD specifies a grouping criterion that compares cities in first-world countries to cities in third-world countries. Cities in petro-world countries are not included.

Output from T-TEST command

```
t-tests for independent samples of  WORLD   ECON CLASS FOR COUNTRY

GROUP 1 - WORLD  EQ        1: 1ST WORLD
GROUP 2 - WORLD  EQ        3: 3RD WORLD
```

Variable	Number of Cases	Mean	Standard Deviation	Standard Error	F Value	2-tail Prob.	Pooled Variance estimate t Value	Degrees of Freedom	2-tail Prob.	Separate Variance Estimate t Value	Degrees of Freedom	2-tail Prob.
NTCPRI NET PRICE LEVEL												
GROUP 1	25	83.8400	13.309	2.662								
					1.23	.637	3.50	36	.001	3.38	22.28	.003
GROUP 2	13	67.3077	14.773	4.097								
NTCSAL NET SALARY LEVEL												
GROUP 1	25	64.4000	19.026	3.805								
					2.06	.210	6.33	35	.000	7.18	30.07	.000
GROUP 2	12	25.6667	13.241	3.822								
NTCPUR NET PURCHASING LEVEL												
GROUP 1	25	76.7600	21.491	4.298								
					1.50	.493	6.28	35	.000	6.74	26.26	.000
GROUP 2	12	31.9167	17.573	5.073								

```
Multiple skips deleted
```

```
                - - - t-tests for paired samples - - -
```

Variable	Number of Cases	Mean	Standard Deviation	Standard Error	(Difference) Mean	Standard Deviation	Standard Error	Corr.	2-tail Prob.	t Value	Degrees of Freedom	2-tail Prob.
WCLOTHES MEDIUM—PRICED WOMEN'S CLOTHES												
		80.7111	30.195	4.501								
	45				-6.3333	17.916	2.671	.807	.000	-2.37	44	.022
		87.0444	26.192	3.905								
MCLOTHES MEDIUM—PRICED MEN'S CLOTHES												
NTCPRI NET PRICE LEVEL												
		82.1591	19.773	2.981								
	44				23.4545	33.310	5.022	.098	.528	4.67	43	.000
		58.7045	28.806	4.343								
NTCPUR NET PURCHASING LEVEL												
NTCPRI NET PRICE LEVEL												
		82.1591	19.773	2.981								
	44				31.8182	22.753	3.430	.482	.001	9.28	43	.000
		50.3409	24.295	3.663								
NTCSAL NET SALARY LEVEL												

References

Aldrich, J. H., and F. D. Nelson. 1984. *Linear probability, logit, and probit models.* In series Quantitative applications in the social sciences. Beverly Hills, California: Sage Publishing.

Belsley, D. A., E. Kuh, and R. E. Welsch. 1980. *Regression diagnostics: Identifying influential data and sources of collinearity.* New York: John Wiley & Sons.

Bishop, Y., S. Feinberg, and P. Holland. 1975. *Discrete multivariate analysis: Theory and practice.* Cambridge: MIT Press.

Cooley, W. W., and P. R. Lohnes. 1971. *Multivariate data analysis.* New York: John Wiley & Sons.

Draper, N., and H. Smith. 1981. *Applied regression analysis.* 2d ed. New York: John Wiley & Sons.

Elashoff, J. D. 1981. Data for the panel session in software repeated measures analysis of variance. *Proceedings of the Statistical Computing Section.* American Statistical Association.

Feiring, B. 1986. *Linear programming: An introduction.* In series Quantitative applications in the social sciences. Beverly Hills, California: Sage Publishing.

Finn, J. D. 1974. *A general model for multivariate analysis.* New York: Holt, Rinehart & Winston.

Finney, D. J. 1971. *Probit analysis.* Cambridge: Cambridge University Press.

Fisher, R. A. 1936. The use of multiple measurements in taxonomic problems. *Annals of Eugenics* 7:179-88.

Fuller, W. A. 1976. *Introduction to statistical time series.* New York: John Wiley & Sons.

Goodman, L. A. 1971. The analysis of multidimensional contingency tables: Stepwise procedures and direct estimation methods for building models for multiple classifications. *Technometrics* 13:33-61.

——. 1975. The relationship between modified and usual multiple-regression approaches to the analysis of dichotomous variables. *Sociological Methodology.* San Francisco: Jossey-Bass.

Haberman, S. J. 1978. *Introductory topics.* Vol. 1 of *Analysis of qualitative data.* New York: Academic Press.

——. 1979. *New developments.* Vol. 2 of *Analysis of qualitative data.* New York: Academic Press.

Hoaglin, D. C., F. Mosteller, J. W. Tukey. 1983. *Understanding robust and exploratory data analysis.* New York: John Wiley & Sons.

——. 1985. *Exploring data tables, trends, and shapes.* New York: John Wiley & Sons.

Huynh, H., and G. K. Mandevill. 1979. Validity conditions in repeated measures designs. *Psychological Bulletin* 86:964-73.

Montgomery, D. C., and E. A. Peck. 1982. *Introduction to linear regression analysis.* New York: John Wiley & Sons.

Morrison, D. F. 1976. *Multivariate statistical methods.* 2d ed. New York: McGraw-Hill.

Stouffer, S. A., E. A. Suchman, L. C. Devinney, S. A. Star, and R. M. Williams, Jr. 1949. *The American soldier: Adjustments during army life.* Vol. 1 of *Studies in social psychology in World War II.* Princeton: Princeton University Press.

Weisberg, H. F., and J. G. Rusk. 1970. Dimensions of candidate evaluation. *The American Political Science Review* 64:1167-85.

Winer, B. J. 1971. *Statistical principles in experimental design.* 2d ed. New York: McGraw-Hill.

Appendixes

- Command Order
- IMPORT/EXPORT Character Sets
- Obsolete Specifications

- Computer Cards
- Variable Format Types

Appendix A

Command Order

Command order in SPSS is determined only by the system's need to know and do certain things in logical sequence. One overriding rule that occurs throughout the system is that a variable must exist before it can be mentioned for labeling, transformation, analysis, and so forth. Otherwise, command order is a matter of your own style and of your understanding of how SPSS works. This appendix describes the program states SPSS goes through as it reads your command groups and executes them.

You can use this appendix to construct your SPSS command file if you wish, but you will find that putting your commands together in an order that seems logical to you is probably the best method. However, this appendix will help you considerably if you encounter a problem and are trying to determine why SPSS doesn't seem to want to accept your command order or seems to be carrying out your instructions incorrectly.

A.1
PROGRAM STATES

You should assemble your commands in groups that define your active system file, transform the data, and analyze it. This order conforms very closely to the order of tasks SPSS must go through as it processes your commands. Specifically, SPSS checks command order according to the *program state* through which it passes. The program state is a characteristic of the program before and after a command is encountered. There are four program states. Each SPSS session starts in the *initial state*. The *input program state* enables SPSS to read data. The *transformation state* allows data modifications. The *procedure state* enables the program to begin executing a procedure. Figure A.1a shows how SPSS moves through these states. SPSS determines the current state from the commands that it already has encountered and then identifies which commands are allowed in that state.

Figure A.1a   Program states

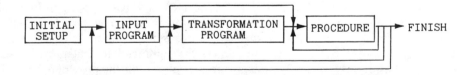

An SPSS session must go through initial, input program, and procedure steps to be a complete session. Since all sessions start in the initial state, you need to be concerned primarily with what commands you need to define your active system file and to analyze the data. The following commands define a very minimal session:

```
GET FILE=DATAIN.
FREQUENCIES VARIABLES=ALL.
```

The GET command defines the active system file and the FREQUENCIES command reads the data file and analyzes it. Thus, SPSS goes through the required three states: initial, input, and procedure.

Typically, an SPSS session also goes through the transformation state, but it can be skipped as shown in the example above and in the diagram in Figure A.1a. Consider the example in Figure A.1b. SPSS starts in the initial state, where it processes the TITLE command. It then moves into the input state upon encountering the DATA LIST command. SPSS can then move into either the transformation or procedure state once the DATA LIST command has been processed.

Figure A.1b   An SPSS session

```
TITLE  'PILOT FOR COLLEGE SURVEY'.

DATA LIST  FILE=TESTDATA
  /AGE 1-3 ITEM1 TO ITEM3 5-7.

VARIABLE LABELS  ITEM1 'OPINION ON LEVEL OF DEFENSE SPENDING'
   ITEM2 'OPINION ON LEVEL OF WELFARE SPENDING'
   ITEM3 'OPINION ON LEVEL OF HEALTH SPENDING'.
VALUE LABELS  ITEM1 TO ITEM3 -1 'DISAGREE' 0 'NO OPINION' 1 'AGREE'.
MISSING VALUES  AGE(-99,-98) ITEM1 TO ITEM3 (9).
RECODE  ITEM1 TO ITEM3 (0=1) (1=0) (2=-1) (9=9) (ELSE=SYSMIS).
RECODE  AGE (MISSING=9) (18 THRU HI=1) (LO THRU 18=0) INTO VOTER.
PRINT /$CASENUM 1-2 AGE 4-6 VOTER 8-10.
VARIABLE LABELS  VOTER 'ELIGIBLE TO VOTE'.
VALUE LABELS  VOTER 0 'UNDER 18' 1 '18 OR OVER'.
MISSING VALUES  VOTER (9).
PRINT FORMATS  VOTER(F1.0).

FREQUENCIES VARIABLES=VOTER,ITEM1 TO ITEM3.
```

In this example, SPSS remains in the transformation state after processing each of the commands from VARIABLE LABELS through PRINT FORMATS. SPSS then moves into the procedure state to process the FREQUENCIES command. As shown in Figure A.1a, SPSS can repeat the procedure state if it encounters a second procedure. SPSS can return to the transformation state if it encounters additional transformation commands following the first procedure. Finally, in some sessions SPSS can return to the input program state upon encountering commands such as FILE TYPE or MATCH FILES.

A.2
DETERMINING
COMMAND ORDER

Table A.2 shows where specific commands can go in the command file in terms of program states and what happens when SPSS encounters a command in each of the four program states. If a column contains a dash, the command is accepted in that program state and it leaves the program in that state. If one of the words INPUT, TRANS, or PROC appears in the column, the command is accepted in the program state indicated by the column heading but it moves the program into the state shown in the column. Asterisks in a column indicate errors when SPSS encounters the command in that program state. Commands marked with the dagger in the column for the procedure state clear the active system file.

The table shows six groups of commands: utility commands (which can go anywhere), file definition commands, input program commands, data transformation commands, restricted transformations, and procedure commands. These groups are discussed in Sections A.3 through A.9.

Table A.2 Commands and program states

	INIT	INPUT	TRANS	PROC
UTILITY COMMANDS				
CLEAR TRANSFORMATIONS	**	PROC	PROC	—
COMMENT	—	—	—	—
DISPLAY	**	—	—	—
DOCUMENT	**	—	—	—
DROP DOCUMENTS	**	—	—	—
EDIT	—	—	—	—
END DATA	—	—	—	—
FILE HANDLE	—	—	—	—
FILE LABEL	—	—	—	—
FINISH	—	—	—	—
HELP	—	—	—	—
INCLUDE	—	—	—	—
INFO	—	—	—	—
MACRO	—	—	—	—
N OF CASES	—	—	—	TRANS
NEW FILE	—	INIT	INIT	INIT†
NUMBERED, UNNUMBERED	—	—	—	—
PROCEDURE OUTPUT	—	—	—	—
SET, SHOW	—	—	—	—
TITLE, SUBTITLE	—	—	—	—
FILE DEFINITION COMMANDS				
ADD FILES	TRANS	**	—	TRANS
DATA LIST	TRANS	—	—	TRANS†
FILE TYPE	INPUT	**	INPUT	INPUT†
GET	TRANS	**	—	TRANS†
GET BMDP	TRANS	**	—	TRANS†
GET OSIRIS	TRANS	**	—	TRANS†
GET SAS	TRANS	**	—	TRANS†
GET SCSS	TRANS	**	—	TRANS†
GET TRANSLATE	TRANS	**	—	TRANS†
HOST	—	—	—	—
IMPORT	TRANS	**	—	TRANS†
INPUT PROGRAM	INPUT	**	INPUT	INPUT†
KEYED DATA LIST	TRANS	—	—	TRANS
MATCH FILES	TRANS	**	—	TRANS
MATRIX DATA	TRANS	**	—	TRANS†
RENAME VARIABLES	**	—	—	TRANS
UPDATE	TRANS	**	—	TRANS
INPUT PROGRAM COMMANDS				
END CASE	**	—	**	**
END FILE	**	—	**	**
END FILE TYPE	**	TRANS	**	**
END INPUT PROGRAM	**	TRANS	**	**
POINT	**	—	**	**
RECORD TYPE	**	—	**	**
REPEATING DATA	**	—	**	**
REREAD	**	—	**	**
TRANSFORMATION COMMANDS				
ADD VALUE LABELS	**	—	—	TRANS
COMPUTE	**	—	—	TRANS
CONSTRAINED FUNCTIONS	**	**	—	TRANS
COUNT	**	—	—	TRANS
DERIVATIVES PROGRAM	**	**	—	TRANS
DO IF—END IF	**	—	—	TRANS
DO REPEAT—END REPEAT	**	—	—	TRANS
ELSE	**	—	—	TRANS
ELSE IF	**	—	—	TRANS
FORMATS	**	—	—	TRANS
IF	**	—	—	TRANS
LEAVE	**	—	—	TRANS
LOOP—END LOOP, BREAK	**	—	—	TRANS
MISSING VALUES	**	—	—	TRANS
MODEL PROGRAM	**	**	—	TRANS
NUMERIC	**	—	—	TRANS
PRINT	**	—	—	TRANS

TRANSFORMATION COMMANDS	INIT	INPUT	TRANS	PROC
PRINT EJECT	**	—	—	TRANS
PRINT FORMATS	**	—	—	TRANS
PRINT SPACE	**	—	—	TRANS
RECODE	**	—	—	TRANS
SPLIT FILE	**	—	—	TRANS
STRING	**	—	—	TRANS
VALUE LABELS	**	—	—	TRANS
VARIABLE LABELS	**	—	—	TRANS
VECTOR	**	—	—	TRANS
WEIGHT	**	—	—	TRANS
WRITE	**	—	—	TRANS
WRITE FORMATS	**	—	—	TRANS
XSAVE	**	—	—	TRANS
RESTRICTED TRANSFORMATIONS				
REFORMAT	**	**	—	TRANS
SAMPLE	**	**	—	TRANS
SELECT IF	**	**	—	TRANS
TEMPORARY	**	**	—	TRANS
PROCEDURES				
BEGIN DATA	**	**	PROC	—
EXECUTE	**	**	PROC	—
EXPORT	**	**	PROC	—
LIST	**	**	PROC	—
SAVE	**	**	PROC	—
SAVE SCSS	**	**	PROC	—
SAVE TRANSLATE	**	**	PROC	—
SORT CASES	**	**	PROC	—
procedures	**	**	PROC	—

To read the table, first locate the command that concerns you. If you simply want to know where in the SPSS command stream it can go, look for columns without asterisks. For example, the COMPUTE command can be used when the program is in the input program state, the transformation state, or the procedure state, but it will cause an error if you try to use it in the initial state. If you want to know what can follow a command, look at each of the four columns next to the command. If the column is dashed, any commands not showing asterisks in the column for that program state can follow the command. If the column contains one of the words INPUT, TRANS, or PROC, any command not showing asterisks in the column for the program state indicated by that word can follow the command. For example, if you are concerned with what commands can follow the INPUT PROGRAM command, note first that it is allowed only in the initial or procedure states. Then note that INPUT PROGRAM puts SPSS into the input program state wherever it occurs legally. This means that commands with dashes or words in the INPUT column can follow the INPUT PROGRAM command. This includes all the utility commands, the DATA LIST command, input program commands, and transformation commands like COMPUTE. Commands that are not allowed after the INPUT PROGRAM command are most of the file definition commands that are their own input program (such as GET), restricted transformations (such as SELECT IF), and procedures.

A.3
Unrestricted Utility Commands

The utility commands can appear in any state. Table A.2 shows this by the absence of asterisks in the columns next to the EDIT through TITLE commands. For example, the EDIT command can appear at any point in the command file.

The dashed lines indicate that after a utility command is processed, the program remains in the same state it was in before the command. The only exception is the N OF CASES command. If SPSS is in the procedure state, N OF CASES moves the program to the transformation state. The FINISH command terminates SPSS command processing wherever it appears. Any commands appearing after FINISH will not be read and therefore will not cause an error.

A.4
File Definition Commands

You can use all the file definition commands in the initial state, the transformation state, and in the procedure state. Most of these commands cause errors if you try to use them in the input program state. You can, however, use DATA LIST, and KEYED DATA LIST in the input program state since there can be and often are multiple DATA LIST or KEYED DATA LIST commands in input programs.

After they are read, the system file commands (ADD FILES, GET, GET SCSS, IMPORT, MATCH FILES, GET BMDP, GET OSIRIS, GET SAS, GET TRANSLATE and UPDATE) move SPSS directly to the transformation state since these commands are the entire input program. FILE TYPE and INPUT PRO-GRAM both move SPSS into the input program state and require input program commands to complete the input program. Commands in Table A.2 marked with a dagger clear the active system file.

A.5
Input Program Commands

The commands associated with the complex file facility (FILE TYPE, RECORD TYPE, and REPEATING DATA) and commands associated with the INPUT PROGRAM command are allowed only in the input program state.

The RECORD TYPE command for the complex file facility, the POINT command for reading key sequenced data sets, and END CASE, END FILE, REPEATING DATA, and REREAD for specially written input programs leave SPSS in the input program state. The two that move SPSS on to the transformation state are END FILE TYPE for input programs initiated with FILE TYPE and END INPUT PROGRAM for those initiated with INPUT PROGRAM.

A.6
Transformation Commands

The entire set of transformation commands from ADD VALUE LABELS to XSAVE can appear in the input program state as part of an input program, in the transformation state, or in the procedure state.

When you use transformation commands in the input program state or the transformation state, SPSS remains in the same state it was in before the command. When the program is in the procedure state, these commands move SPSS back to the transformation state.

A.7
Taxonomy of Transformation Commands

SPSS transformation commands can be categorized according to whether they are *declarative, status-switching,* or *executable.* Declarative commands alter the active system file dictionary but do not affect the data. Status-switching commands change the SPSS program state but do not affect the data. Executable commands alter the data.

Table A.7 shows an alphabetic list of the SPSS transformation commands and indicates which of the three categories applies to each command.

Table A.7 Taxonomy of transformation commands

Command	Type	Command	Type
ADD FILES	Exec*	LOOP	Exec
ADD VALUE LABELS	Decl	MATCH FILES	Exec*
BREAK	Exec	MISSING VALUES	Decl
COMPUTE	Exec	MODEL PROGRAM	Stat*
CONSTRAINED FUNCTIONS	Stat	N OF CASES	Decl
COUNT	Exec	NUMERIC	Decl
DATA LIST	Exec*	POINT	Exec
DERIVATIVES PROGRAM	Stat	PRINT	Exec
DO IF	Exec	PRINT EJECT	Exec
DO REPEAT	Decl†	PRINT FORMATS	Decl
ELSE	Exec	PRINT SPACE	Exec
ELSE IF	Exec	RECODE	Exec
END CASE	Exec	RECORD TYPE	Exec
END FILE	Exec	REFORMAT	Exec
END FILE TYPE	Stat	REPEATING DATA	Exec*
END IF	Exec	REREAD	Exec
END INPUT PROGRAM	Stat	SAMPLE	Exec
END LOOP	Exec	SELECT IF	Exec
END REPEAT	Decl†	SPLIT FILE	Decl
FILE TYPE	Stat**	STRING	Decl
FORMATS	Decl	TEMPORARY	Stat
GET	Exec*	VALUE LABELS	Decl
GET OSIRIS	Exec*	VARIABLE LABELS	Decl
IF	Exec	VECTOR	Decl
INPUT PROGRAM	Stat	WEIGHT	Decl
KEYED DATA LIST	Exec*	WRITE	Exec
LEAVE	Decl	WRITE FORMATS	Decl
		XSAVE	Exec

*This command is also declarative.
**This command is also executable and declarative.
† This command does not fit into these categories; however, it is neither executable nor status-switching, so it is classified as declarative.

A.8
Restricted Transformations

Commands REFORMAT, SAMPLE, SELECT IF, and TEMPORARY are restricted transformation commands because they are allowed in either the transformation state or the procedure state but cannot be used in the input program state.

If you use restricted transformation commands in the transformation state, the program remains in the transformation state. If you use them in the procedure state, they move SPSS back to the transformation state.

A.9
Procedures

The procedures and the procedure-like commands (BEGIN DATA, EXECUTE, EXPORT, LIST, SAVE, SAVE SCSS, SAVE TRANSLATE and SORT CASES) cause the data to be read. These commands, including all procedures, are allowed in either the transformation state or the procedure state.

When the program is in the transformation state, these commands move SPSS to the procedure state. When you use these commands in the procedure state, the program remains in that state.

Appendix B

IMPORT/EXPORT Character Sets

Communication-formatted portable files do not use positions 1–63 in the following table. Tape-formatted portable files use the complete table. (See the EXPORT command for an explanation of the two types of files.)

POSITION	GRAPHIC	IBM EBCDIC	BURROUGHS EBCDIC	ASCII 7-BIT	ISO 8-BIT	CDC DISPLAY CODE	HIS 6-BIT	ASCII 6-BIT
0	NUL	0	0	0	0			
1	SOH	1	1	1	1			
2	STX	2	2	2	2			
3	ETX	3	3	3	3			
4	SEL	4			156			
5	HT	5	5	9	9			
6	RNL	6			134			
7	DEL	7	7	127	127			
8	GE	8			151			
9	SPS	9			141			
10	RPT	10			142			
11	VT	11	11	11	11			
12	FF	12	12	12	12			
13	CR	13	13	13	13			
14	SO	14	14	14	14			
15	SI	15	15	15	15			
16	DLE	16	16	16	16			
17	DC1	17	17	17	17			
18	DC2	18	18	18	18			
19	DC3	19	19	19	19			
20	DC4	60	60	20	20			
21	NL	21	21		133			
22	BS	22	22	8	8			
23	DOC	23			135			
24	CAN	24	24	24	24			
25	EM	25	25	25	25			
26	UBS	26			146			
27	CU1	27			143			
28	(I)FS[1]	28	28	28	28			
29	(I)GS	29	29	29	29			
30	(I)RS	30	30	30	30			
31	SM,SW	42			138			
32	DS	32			128			
33	SOS	33			129			
34	FS[2]	34			130			
35	WUS	35			131			
36	CSP	43			139			
37	LF	37	37	10	10			
38	ETB	38	38	23	23			
39	ESC	39	39	27	27			
40	(I)US	31	31	31	31			
41	BYP	36			132			
42	RES	20			157			
43	ENQ	45	45	5	5			
44	ACK	46	46	6	6			
45	BEL	47	47	7	7			
46	SYN	50	50	22	22			
47	IR	51			147			
48	PP	52			148			

POSITION	GRAPHIC	IBM EBCDIC	BURROUGHS EBCDIC	ASCII 7-BIT	ISO 8-BIT	CDC DISPLAY CODE	HIS 6-BIT	ASCII 6-BIT
49	TRN	53			149			
50	NBS	54			150			
51	EOT	55		55	4	4		
52	SBS	56			152			
53	IT	57			153			
54	RFF	58			154			
55	CU3	59			155			
56	NAK	61		61	21	21		
57	SUB	63		63	26	26		
58	SA	40			136			
59	SFE	41			137			
60	MFA	44			140			
61	reserved							
62	reserved							
63	reserved							
64	0	240	240	48	48	27	0	16
65	1	241	241	49	49	28	1	17
66	2	242	242	50	50	29	2	18
67	3	243	243	51	51	30	3	19
68	4	244	244	52	52	31	4	20
69	5	245	245	53	53	32	5	21
70	6	246	246	54	54	33	6	22
71	7	247	247	55	55	34	7	23
72	8	248	248	56	56	35	8	24
73	9	249	249	57	57	36	9	25
74	A	193	193	65	65	1	17	33
75	B	194	194	66	66	2	18	34
76	C	195	195	67	67	3	19	35
77	D	196	196	68	68	4	20	36
78	E	197	197	69	69	5	21	37
79	F	198	198	70	70	6	22	38
80	G	199	199	71	71	7	23	39
81	H	200	200	72	72	8	24	40
82	I	201	201	73	73	9	25	41
83	J	209	209	74	74	10	33	42
84	K	210	210	75	75	11	34	43
85	L	211	211	76	76	12	35	44
86	M	212	212	77	77	13	36	45
87	N	213	213	78	78	14	37	46
88	O	214	214	79	79	15	38	47
89	P	215	215	80	80	16	39	48
90	Q	216	216	81	81	17	40	49
91	R	217	217	82	82	18	41	50
92	S	226	226	83	83	19	50	51
93	T	227	227	84	84	20	51	52
94	U	228	228	85	85	21	52	53
95	V	229	229	86	86	22	53	54
96	W	230	230	87	87	23	54	55
97	X	231	231	88	88	24	55	56
98	Y	232	232	89	89	25	56	57
99	Z	233	233	90	90	26	57	58
100	a	129	129	97	97			
101	b	130	130	98	98			
102	c	131	131	99	99			
103	d	132	132	100	100			
104	e	133	133	101	101			
105	f	134	134	102	102			
106	g	135	135	103	103			
107	h	136	136	104	104			
108	i	137	137	105	105			
109	j	145	145	106	106			
110	k	146	146	107	107			
111	l	147	147	108	108			
112	m	148	148	109	109			
113	n	149	149	110	110			

POSITION	GRAPHIC	IBM EBCDIC	BURROUGHS EBCDIC	ASCII 7-BIT	ISO 8-BIT	CDC DISPLAY CODE	HIS 6-BIT	ASCII 6-BIT
114	o	150	150	111	111			
115	p	151	151	112	112			
116	q	152	152	113	113			
117	r	153	153	114	114			
118	s	162	162	115	115			
119	t	163	163	116	116			
120	u	164	164	117	117			
121	v	165	165	118	118			
122	w	166	166	119	119			
123	x	167	167	120	120			
124	y	168	168	121	121			
125	z	169	169	122	122			
126	space	64	64	32	32	45	16	0
127	.	75	75	46	46	47	27	14
128	<	76	76	60	60	58	30	28
129	(	77	77	40	40	41	29	8
130	+	78	78	43	43	37	48	11
131	|	79	79					
132	&	80	80	38	38	55	26	6
133	[	173	74	91	91	49	10	59
134	]	189	90	93	93	50	28	61
135	!	208	33	33	54	63	61	
136	$	91	91	36	36	43	43	4
137	*	92	92	42	42	39	44	10
138	)	93	93	41	41	42	45	9
139	;	94	94	59	59	63	46	27
140	¬ or ∧ or ↑	95	95	94	94	62	32	62
141	−	96	96	45	45	38	42	13
142	/	97	97	47	47	40	49	15
143	=	106		124	124			
144	,	107	107	44	44	46	59	12
145	%	108	108	37	37	51*	60	5
146	_	109	109	95	95	53	58	63
147	>	110	110	62	62	59	14	30
148	?	111	111	63	63	57	15	31
149	`	121		96	96			
150	:	122	122	58	58	0|51	13	26
151	ʅ	123	123	35	35	48	11	3
152	@	124	124	64	64	60	12	32
153	'	125	125	39	39	56	47	7
154	=	126	126	61	61	44	61	29
155	"	127	127	34	34	49	62	2
156	≤	140	140					
157	□	156	156					
158	±	158	158					
159	■	159	159					
160	°		161					
161	†	143						
162	~	161		126	126			
163	⌐	160	160					
164	⌊	171	171					
165	⌈	172	172					
166	≥	174	174					
167	0	176	176					
168	1	177	177					
169	2	178	178					
170	3	179	179					
171	4	180	180					
172	5	181	181					
173	6	182	182					
174	7	183	183					
175	8	184	184					
176	9	185	185					
177	⌟	187	187					
178	⌉	188	188					
179	≠	190	190					

POSITION	GRAPHIC	IBM EBCDIC	BURROUGHS EBCDIC	ASCII 7-BIT	ISO 8-BIT	CDC DISPLAY CODE	HIS 6-BIT	ASCII 6-BIT
180	—	191	191					
181	(	141	141					
182	)	157	157					
183	+³	142	192					
184	{	192	139	123	123			
185	}	208	155	125	125			
186	\	224		92	92	61	31	
187	¢	74	224					
188	•	175	175					
189-255 reserved								

¹file separator
²field separator
³not the plus sign

Appendix C

Obsolete Specifications

Procedures in SPSS that prior to Release 3.0 used OPTIONS and STATISTICS commands to make specifications now use subcommand and keyword alternatives for the same specifications. In addition, those procedures that handle matrix materials use a MATRIX subcommand to read and write matrix materials. Old syntax for handling matrix materials has not been recognized since Release 3.0.

The following is a list of the procedures affected by these changes.

ANOVA	NONPAR CORR
CORRELATIONS	NPAR TESTS
CROSSTABS	ONEWAY
DESCRIPTIVES	PARTIAL CORR
DISCRIMINANT	RELIABILITY
MEANS	SURVIVAL
MULT RESPONSE	T-TESTS

OPTIONS that are obsolete on the procedures are:

Command	Obsolete Specification
CORRELATIONS	OPTIONS 4 and 7
DISCRIMINANT	OPTIONS 2 and 3
NONPAR CORR	OPTION 4
ONEWAY	OPTIONS 4, 7, and 8
PARTIAL CORR	OPTIONS 4, 5, and 6
RELIABILITY	OPTIONS 4 through 13, 17

The following sections discuss the changes specific to each procedure. A cross-reference is presented (when applicable) to show the former OPTION or STATISTIC number and the new subcommand or keyword that replaces it. The term *obsolete* in the cross-references means the OPTION is no longer recognized by SPSS. The term *none* means the OPTION has not been replaced by an alternative subcommand or keyword but is still recognized by SPSS. OPTIONS replaced by the MATRIX subcommand are no longer recognized.

Except as otherwise noted; the old OPTIONS or STATISTICS commands will run if they are in a command file that you process through your operating system; they will not run if you run commands through the SPSS Manager or if you run SPSS in a prompted session. (See your SPSS *Operations Guide* for information on running SPSS on your system.)

Note to SPSS/PC+ Users. To run an SPSS/PC+ command file in SPSS systems such as SPSS for OS/2 you must change your OPTIONS and STATISTICS subcommands to the subcommands and keywords shown in this appendix. For the relevant SPSS/PC+ commands, the cross-references use an asterisk (*) if the specification is *not* available for SPSS/PC+ options.

C.1
ALSCAL

Generally, "data" read by ALSCAL are already in matrix form. This matrix can be created in either PROXIMITIES or CLUSTER. You do not need to use the MATRIX subcommand to read this file, simply use the VARIABLES subcommand to indicate the variables (or columns) to be used. However, for consistency with other procedures that read matrices, ALSCAL recognized the MATRIX subcommand with one keyword, IN, which you can use for reading matrix materials.

C.2
ANOVA

Subcommands and keywords used as alternatives to OPTIONS and STATISTICS numbers.

Subcommands and keywords and their equivalent OPTIONS and STATISTICS numbers:

OPTION*	subcommand:	keyword:
1	MISSING	INCLUDE
2	FORMAT	NOLABELS
3	MAXORDERS	NONE
4,5,6	MAXORDERS	n
7	COVARIATES	WITH
8	COVARIATES	AFTER
9	METHOD	UNIQUE
10	METHOD	HIERARCHICAL

* OPTION 11 from SPSS/PC+ is not in SPSS.

STATISTIC	subcommand:	keyword:
1	STATISTICS	MCA
2	STATISTICS	REG
3	STATISTICS	MEAN

C.3
CLUSTER

CLUSTER now uses the MATRIX subcommand with keywords IN and OUT to read and write matrix materials. The READ and WRITE subcommands, along with their keyword specifications, are no longer recognized.

C.4
CORRELATIONS (alias PEARSON CORR)

Subcommands and keywords used as alternatives to OPTIONS and STATISTICS numbers. The old OPTIONS and STATISTICS numbers dealing with matrix material are no longer recognized.

Subcommands and keywords and their equivalent OPTIONS and STATISTICS numbers:

OPTION	subcommand:	keyword:
1	MISSING	INCLUDE
2**	MISSING	LISTWISE
3	PRINT	TWOTAIL
4	MATRIX	OUT
5	PRINT	NOSIG
6*	FORMAT	SERIAL
7*	obsolete	

* Not available for SPSS/PC+ options

** OPTION 2 in SPSS/PC+ is replaced with MISSING=PAIRWISE

STATISTIC	subcommand:	keyword:
1	STATISTICS	DESCRIPTIVES
2	STATISTICS	XPROD

- N of cases is printed with keyword SIG and is not printed with NOSIG.
- FORMAT=SERIAL overrides PRINT=NOSIG.

C.5
CROSSTABS

Subcommands and keywords used as alternatives to OPTIONS and STATISTICS numbers.

Subcommands and keywords and their equivalent OPTIONS and STATISTICS numbers:

OPTION	subcommand:	keyword:
1	MISSING	INCLUDE
2	FORMAT	NOLABELS
3	CELLS	ROW
4	CELLS	COLUMN
5	CELLS	TOTAL
6	FORMAT	NOVALLABS
7*	MISSING	REPORT
8	FORMAT	DVALUE
9*	FORMAT	INDEX
10*	WRITE	CELLS
11*	WRITE	ALL
12	FORMAT	NOTABLES
13	CELLS	COUNT
14	CELLS	EXPECTED
15	CELLS	RESIDUALS
16	CELLS	SRESID
17	CELLS	ASRESID
18	CELLS	ALL

* Not available for SPSS/PC+ options

STATISTIC	subcommand:	keyword:
1	STATISTICS	CHISQ
2	STATISTICS	PHI
3	STATISTICS	CC
4	STATISTICS	LAMBDA
5	STATISTICS	UC
6	STATISTICS	BTAU
7	STATISTICS	CTAU
8	STATISTICS	GAMMA
9	STATISTICS	D
10	STATISTICS	ETA
11	STATISTICS	CORR

- The COUNT keyword on the CELLS subcommand now adds the count rather than removing it (as it did in the old syntax).

C.6
DESCRIPTIVES (alias CONDESCRIPTIVES)

Subcommands and keywords used as alternatives to OPTIONS and STATISTICS numbers.

Subcommands and keywords and their equivalent OPTIONS and STATISTICS numbers:

- The old syntax for specifying znames on the initial varlist is still accepted. Any varname mentioned on the SAVE subcommand without a zname is assigned a Z-score name. No variable can be mentioned on the SAVE subcommand that is not declared on the initial varlist.
- SKEWNESS and KURTOSIS include the standard errors.
- If you specify /STATISTICS with no keywords, you get the DEFAULT statistics.

OPTION	subcommand:	keyword:
1	MISSING	INCLUDE
2	FORMAT	NOLABELS
3	SAVE	
4*	FORMAT	INDEX
5	MISSING	LISTWISE
6	FORMAT	SERIAL
7	none	

* Not available for SPSS/PC+ options

STATISTIC	subcommand:	keyword:
1	STATISTICS	MEAN
2	STATISTICS	SEMEAN
5	STATISTICS	STDDEV
6	STATISTICS	VARIANCE
7	STATISTICS	KURTOSIS
8	STATISTICS	SKEWNESS
9	STATISTICS	RANGE
10	STATISTICS	MINIMUM
11	STATISTICS	MAXIMUM
12	STATISTICS	SUM
13	STATISTICS	DEFAULT

C.7
DISCRIMINANT

Subcommands and keywords used as alternatives to OPTIONS and STATISTICS numbers. The old OPTIONS and STATISTICS numbers dealing with matrix materials are no longer recognized.

The subcommand PRINT has been changed to HISTORY and keywords TABLE and NOTABLE of this subcommand have been changed to END and NOEND.

Subcommands and keywords and their equivalent OPTIONS and STATISTICS numbers:

OPTION	subcommand:	keyword:
1	MISSING	INCLUDE
2*	MATRIX	OUT
3*	MATRIX	IN
4	HISTORY	NOSTEP
5	HISTORY	NOEND
6	ROTATE	COEFF
7	ROTATE	STRUCTURE
8	CLASSIFY	MEANSUB
9	CLASSIFY	UNSELECTED
10	CLASSIFY	UNCLASSIFIED
11	CLASSIFY	SEPARATE

* Not available for SPSS/PC+ options

STATISTICS	subcommand:	keyword:
1	STATISTICS	MEAN
2	STATISTICS	STDDEV
3	STATISTICS	COV
4	STATISTICS	CORR
5	STATISTICS	FPAIR
6	STATISTICS	UNIVF
7	STATISTICS	BOXM
8	STATISTICS	GCOV
9	STATISTICS	TCOV
10	PLOT	MAP
11	STATISTICS	RAW
12	STATISTICS	COEFF
13	STATISTICS	TABLE
14	PLOT	CASES
15	PLOT	COMBINED
16	PLOT	SEPARATE

- On the MATRIX subcommand, at least one keyword (OUT or IN) must be specified. Both keywords can be used on the same MATRIX subcommand if you are reading and writing matrices.

C.8
FACTOR

The new MATRIX subcommand has been added to handle matrices. The old READ and WRITE subcommands are no longer recognized. Syntax for the new MATRIX subcommand is:

```
FACTOR VARIABLES=varlist

    [/MATRIX=[IN({COR=*   })]]  [OUT({COR=*   })]]
                 {COR=file}          {COR=file}
                 {FAC=*   }          {FAC=*   }
                 {FAC=file}          {FAC=file}
```

C.9
INPUT MATRIX

The INPUT MATRIX command is obsolete and no longer recognized as of Release 3.0. It was formerly used to specify an input matrix file for procedures that read matrix materials. For more information on the new format for matrix system files, see Universals.

C.10
MANOVA

As of Release 3.0, the MATRIX subcommand has been added to handle matrices. The old READ and WRITE subcommands are no longer recognized.

C.11
MEANS (alias BREAKDOWN)

Subcommands and keywords used as alternatives to OPTIONS and STATISTICS numbers.

Subcommands and keywords and their equivalent OPTIONS and STATISTICS numbers:

OPTION	subcommand:	keyword:
1	MISSING	INCLUDE
2	MISSING	DEPENDENT
3	FORMAT	NOLABELS
4*	FORMAT	TREE
5	CELLS	COUNT
6	CELLS	SUM
7	CELLS	STDDEV
8	FORMAT	NOCATLABS
9	FORMAT	NONAMES
10	FORMAT	NOVALUES
11	CELLS	MEAN
12	CELLS	VARIANCE

* Not available for SPSS/PC+ options

STATISTIC	subcommand:	keyword:
1	STATISTICS	ANOVA
2	STATISTICS	LINEARITY

- Keyword NOCATLABS for the FORMAT subcommand means no category (value) labels.
- CELLS keywords COUNT, STDDEV, and MEAN reverse the logic of present options. The old OPTIONS 5, 7, and 11 suppressed the information, but with the new format, specifying the equivalent keywords causes the information to be reported.

C.12
MULT RESPONSE

Subcommands and keywords used as alternatives to OPTIONS and STATISTICS numbers.

Subcommands and keywords and their equivalent OPTIONS and STATISTICS numbers:

OPTION	subcommand:	keyword:
1	MISSING	INCLUDE
2	MISSING	MDGROUP
3	MISSING	MRGROUP
4	FORMAT	NOLABELS
5	BASE	RESPONSES
6	none	
7	FORMAT	CONDENSE
8	FORMAT	ONEPAGE

STATISTIC	subcommand:	keyword:
1	CELLS	ROW
2	CELLS	COLUMN
3	CELLS	TOTAL

- Keyword TABLE of the MISSING subcommand excludes user missing values.
- Keyword TABLE of the FORMAT subcommand uses more than one page to print frequencies with more than 20 categories.
- The CASES keyword of the BASE subcommand bases percentages on respondents.

C.13
NONPAR CORR

Subcommands and keywords used as alternatives to OPTIONS and STATISTICS numbers. The old OPTIONS and STATISTICS numbers dealing with matrix materials are no longer recognized.

Subcommands and keywords and their equivalent OPTIONS and STATISTICS numbers:

OPTION	subcommand:	keyword:
1	MISSING	INCLUDE
2	MISSING	LISTWISE
3	PRINT	TWOTAIL
4	MATRIX	OUT
5	PRINT	KENDALL
6	PRINT	SPEARMAN
7	SAMPLE	
8	PRINT	NOSIG
9	FORMAT	SERIAL

- N of cases is printed with SIG and not printed with NOSIG.
- /PRINT keyword BOTH does not cause /MATRIX to write both.
- FORMAT=SERIAL overrides PRINT=NOSIG.

C.14
NPAR TESTS

Subcommands and keywords used as alternatives to OPTIONS and STATISTICS numbers.

Subcommands and keywords and their equivalent OPTIONS and STATISTICS numbers:

OPTION	subcommand:	keyword:
1	MISSING	INCLUDE
2	MISSING	LISTWISE
3	varlist	(PAIR)
4	SAMPLE	

STATISTIC	subcommand:	keyword:
1	STATISTICS	DESCRIPTIVES
2	STATISTICS	QUARTILES

- The (PAIR) keyword is relevant only on a variable list that allows keyword WITH.
- MISSING = ANALYSIS excludes missing cases on an analysis-by-analysis basis.

C.15
ONEWAY

Subcommands and keywords used as alternatives to OPTIONS and STATISTICS numbers. The old STATISTICS and OPTIONS numbers dealing with matrix materials are no longer recognized.

Subcommands and keywords and their equivalent OPTIONS and STATISTICS numbers:

OPTION	subcommand:	keyword:
1	MISSING	INCLUDE
2	MISSING	LISTWISE
3	none	
4*	MATRIX	OUT
6	FORMAT	LABELS
7*	MATRIX	IN
8	none	
10	HARMONIC	ALL

* Not available for SPSS/PC+ options

STATISTIC	subcommand:	keyword:
1	STATISTICS	DESCRIPTIVES
2	STATISTICS	EFFECTS
3	STATISTICS	HOMOGENEITY

- Keywords IN and OUT can both be used on the same MATRIX subcommand.
- Keyword ANALYSIS on subcommand MISSING omits cases with missing values on an analysis-by-analysis (pairwise) basis.

C.16
PARTIAL CORR

Subcommands and keywords used as alternatives to OPTIONS and STATISTICS numbers. The old STATISTICS and OPTIONS numbers dealing with matrix materials are no longer recognized.

Subcommands and keywords and their equivalent OPTIONS and STATISTICS numbers:

OPTION	subcommand:	keyword:
1	MISSING	INCLUDE
2	MISSING	ANALYSIS
3	SIGNIFICANCE	TWOTAIL
4	MATRIX	IN
5	MATRIX	OUT
6	obsolete	
7	FORMAT	CONDENSED
8	FORMAT	SERIAL

STATISTIC	subcommand:	keyword:
1	STATISTICS	CORR
2	STATISTICS	DESCRIPTIVES
3	STATISTICS	BADCORR

- The VARIABLES subcommand can be repeated; the VARIABLES keyword is optional.
- OPTION 6 is obsolete and no longer recognized as of Release 3.0.

C.17
PROCEDURE OUTPUT

The PROCEDURE OUTPUT command was formerly used by many procedures (for example CLUSTER and DISCRIMINANT) to specify an output file for matrix materials. Because of the changes in the way SPSS handles matrix materials, it is no longer used in that context. Beginning with Release 3.0, PROCEDURE OUTPUT can only be used to specify output files for cell totals from CROSSTABS, display files from FREQUENCIES, and life table records from SURVIVAL.

C.18
PROXIMITIES

The new MATRIX subcommand has been added to handle matrices. The old READ and WRITE subcommands are no longer recognized.

C.19
QUICK CLUSTER

QUICK CLUSTER now writes final cluster centers to a system file rather than a procedure output file. You use the OUTFILE subcommand to specify the system file; the former WRITE subcommand is no longer recognized. In addition, you no longer need the PROCEDURE OUTPUT command to specify the output file.

To use those final cluster centers as the initial cluster centers in a subsequent QUICK CLUSTER command, use the FILE subcommand. The former READ subcommand is no longer recognized. In addition, you no longer need the INPUT MATRIX command to specify the input file.

C.20
REFORMAT

```
REFORMAT   {ALPHA  } = varlist [/...]
           {NUMERIC}
```

REFORMAT became available in SPSS Release 1.0 to convert SPSS files to files with SPSS format. In Release 3.0, it can also be used to convert BMDP files. Instructions from the *SPSS-X User's Guide,* 2nd ed., for using REFORMAT with SPSS files are repeated here for your convenience.

In SPSS, all variables were printed as integers unless you used a PRINT FORMATS command to specify that the variable was alphanumeric or to specify the number of decimal places. If you did not use a PRINT FORMATS command when you saved a system file with SPSS, the print formats for alphanumeric and decimal variables are indicated incorrectly on the SPSS system file as integer. When you read an SPSS system file using SPSS, these variables have dictionary print and write formats of F8.0. The missing-value specifications are also expressed as integers.

To change the print formats, write formats, and missing-value specifications for variables from alphanumeric to numeric, or from numeric to alphanumeric, use ALPHA and NUMERIC subcommands of the REFORMAT command, as in:

```
REFORMAT ALPHA=NAME1 TO NAME6/ NUMERIC=HOURLY79 TO HOURLY82.
```

This command declares NAME1 to NAME6 as alphanumeric variables with dictionary print and write formats of A4. HOURLY79 TO HOURLY82 are declared to be numeric variables with dictionary print and write formats of F8.2 (or the format you specify using the SET command). Missing-value specifications for variables named with both the ALPHA and NUMERIC keywords are also changed to conform to the new formats.

After you have reformatted variables from your SPSS system file, you should create an SPSS system file by using a SAVE command (or XSAVE). This will save you the time and trouble of having to reformat these variables each time you wish to use them.

REFORMAT always assigns the print and write format F8.2 (or the format specified using the SET command) to variables specified after the NUMERIC keyword, and A4 to variables specified after the ALPHA keyword. However, you might want to declare a different total length for the variable or a different number of decimal places. For numeric variables, use the PRINT FORMATS, WRITE FORMATS, or FORMATS commands to change the format specifications.

You cannot use the PRINT FORMATS, WRITE FORMATS, or FORMATS commands to change the length of string variables in SPSS. To change the length of string variables, you must declare new string variables and use the COMPUTE command to assign the values of the original variable to the new variable. The following commands declare formats of A2 for the variable MMN and A3 for VISDAY:

```
GET FILE R9FILE.
STRING XMMN (A2)/XVISDAY (A3).
COMPUTE XMMN=MMN.
COMPUTE XVISDAY=VISDAY.
SAVE OUTFILE=NEWXFILE/DROP=MMN VISDAY
  /RENAME=(XVISDAY=VISDAY) (XMMN=MMN).
```

The above commands do the following:

- GET accesses the SPSS system file.
- STRING declares XMMN as a string variable with two positions and XVISDAY as a string variable with three positions.
- COMPUTE commands are used to transfer the information from the old system-file variables MMN and VISDAY to the SPSS string variables XMMN and XVISDAY.
- The SAVE command saves a new SPSS system file. The DROP subcommand drops the SPSS system-file variables with the inappropriate formats. RENAME renames the new SPSS string variables to the original names, MMN and VISDAY.

C.21
REGRESSION

The new MATRIX subcommand has been added to handle matrices. The old READ and WRITE subcommands are no longer recognized. If the MATRIX subcommand is used, it must precede all other subcommands.

C.22
RELIABILITY

Subcommands and keywords used as alternatives to OPTIONS and STATISTICS numbers. The old STATISTICS and OPTIONS numbers dealing with matrix materials are no longer recognized.

The FORMAT subcommand has a new meaning and syntax. It no longer has anything to do with matrix material; instead, it controls the printing of labels in your output. Use the MATRIX subcommand to handle matrix material.

Subcommands and keywords and their equivalent OPTIONS and STATISTICS numbers:

OPTION	subcommand:	keyword:
1	MISSING	INCLUDE
3	FORMAT	NOLABELS
4	obsolete	
5*	MATRIX	IN
6*	MATRIX	IN
7*	MATRIX	IN
8	obsolete	
9	obsolete	
10*	MATRIX	OUT NOPRINT
11	obsolete	
12	obsolete	
13	obsolete	
14	METHOD	COV
15	STATISTICS	FRIEDMAN
16	STATISTICS	COCHRAN
17	obsolete	

* Not available for SPSS/PC+ options

STATISTIC	subcommand:	keyword:
1	STATISTICS	DESCRIPTIVES
2	STATISTICS	COV
3	STATISTICS	CORR
4	STATISTICS	SCALE
5	SUMMARY	MEAN
6	SUMMARY	VARIANCE
7	SUMMARY	COV
8	SUMMARY	CORR
9	SUMMARY	TOTAL
10	STATISTICS	ANOVA
11	STATISTICS	TUKEY
12	STATISTICS	HOTELLING

• If there is no SCALE subcommand for a variable list, the default is: SCALE(all) = ALL. (Previously the SCALE subcommand was required.)

C.23
SURVIVAL

Subcommands and keywords used as alternatives to OPTIONS and STATISTICS numbers.

Subcommands and keywords and their equivalent OPTIONS and STATISTICS numbers:

OPTION	subcommand:	keyword:
1	MISSING	INCLUDE
2	MISSING	LISTWISE
3	CALCULATE	COMPARE
4	PRINT	NOTABLE
5	CALCULATE	CONDITIONAL
6	CALCULATE	APPROXIMATE
7	CALCULATE	PAIRWISE
8	WRITE	TABLES
9	WRITE	BOTH

C.24
T-TEST

Subcommands and keywords used as alternatives to OPTIONS and STATISTICS numbers.

Subcommands and keywords and their equivalent OPTIONS and STATISTICS numbers:

OPTION	subcommand:	keyword:
1	MISSING	INCLUDE
2	MISSING	LISTWISE
3	FORMAT	NOLABELS
4	none	
5	varlist	(PAIRED)

- Keyword (PAIRED) can be used on the PAIRS subcommand to indicate that the lists before and after WITH are to be paired with each other.

Appendix D

Computer Cards

This appendix is for sites that still use computer cards to collect data.

D.1
COLUMN BINARY FORMAT

The amount of information a computer card or input record can hold varies considerably according to how the information is stored. When stored in the usual manner, with one character per column, the maximum number of data items that can occupy a single card is 80. An alternate way to store data is to allow punches in each of the 12 rows, thereby increasing the maximum number of items by as much as a factor of 12. Data stored in this manner are called *column binary,* or *multipunch,* data.

Column binary format makes it possible to store more than one variable in the same column rather than spanning several columns. This format was especially popular when information was stored almost exclusively on computer cards, making it desirable to compress the data into as small a space as possible. For example, a variable with three possible values could be stored in just two rows of a single column (one punch for each of two values and a zero value if neither row is punched), leaving nine rows for other variables.

SPSS only processes multipunch data that have been read by IBM card readers attached to IBM 360-compatible computers. These readers produce a particular representation of the punches. Consult your operations guide to determine how multipunch data are handled by SPSS for your computer.

D.2
Column Binary Data and the FILE HANDLE Command

Although the advantages of the column binary format are obvious, it is often difficult to get at data stored in this manner. To read column binary data, use the keywords MODE=MULTIPUNCH on the FILE HANDLE command, as in:

```
FILE HANDLE ELE48 MODE=MULTIPUNCH   file specifications
```

This tells SPSS that the file ELE48 contains multiple punches. The FILE HANDLE command is required for reading column binary data.

D.3
Variable Definition on DATA LIST

Once a file has been specified as column binary, variables must then be defined in a DATA LIST command, giving starting and ending rows as well as columns. The general format for each variable is

```
varname   starting column:starting row - ending column:ending row
```

The starting column and row are required and must be separated by a colon. The ending row and column are optional if they are the same as the starting row and column. For example, the commands

```
FILE HANDLE  ELE48  MODE=MULTIPUNCH   file specifications
DATA LIST FILE=ELE48
       /1 PARTY      18
          SEX        19:1
          EMPSTAT    20(A)
          SES        48:4-6
          RELIGION   48:7-10
          OCCUPAT    50:11-51:2.
```

tell SPSS to read SEX in row 1 of column 19; SES in rows 4 through 6 of column

903

48; RELIGION in rows 7 through 10 of column 48; and OCCUPAT in column 50, row 11 through column 51, row 2. Since columns 18 and 20 were not multipunched, the column numbers alone are sufficient to define the location of PARTY and EMPSTAT.

Each computer card contains 12 rows that are numbered from top to bottom as 1 through 12. This row numbering differs from the way that punch numbers are assigned: a 12 punch goes in the top row; an 11 punch, in the second row; and the third through twelfth rows are reserved for 0 through 9 punches (see Figure D.3). Thus, row 1 is reserved for a 12 punch; row 2, for an 11 punch; and rows 3 through 12 are used for 0 through 9 punches.

Figure D.3   Row numbering versus assignment of punches

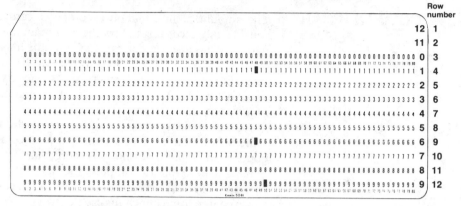

Variables that occupy a single row of one column, such as SEX in the above example, result in a value of 1 if a punch is present, and 0 if a punch is absent. A 12 punch in that instance could indicate a male, and a blank, a female. The variables that take up a series of adjacent rows (SES, RELIGION, and OCCUPAT) are assigned values as follows:

For SES:
1 if row 4 of column 48 is punched
2 if row 5 of column 48 is punched
3 if row 6 of column 48 is punched
0 if there is no punch in rows 4–6 of column 48

For RELIGION:
1 if row 7 of column 48 is punched
2 if row 8 of column 48 is punched
3 if row 9 of column 48 is punched
4 if row 10 of column 48 is punched
0 if there is no punch in rows 7–9 of column 48

For OCCUPAT:
1 if row 11 of column 50 is punched
2 if row 12 of column 50 is punched
3 if row 1 of column 51 is punched
4 if row 2 of column 51 is punched
0 if there is no punch in rows 11–12 of column 50 or in rows 1–2 of column 51

The punches in Figure D.3 indicate a value of 1 for SES, 3 for RELIGION, and a value of 2 for OCCUPAT.

No more than one punch is allowed in any given field. Any attempt to read fields that contain more than one punch will produce an error, resulting in the system-missing value for the variable. In situations where more than one response is permitted to a question, each response must be coded as a separate variable.

D.4
Column Binary Data on Tape or Disk

Column binary data may have originated on computer cards, but you normally find such data on magnetic tape or disk. On these media, column binary data occur in fixed-length records containing an even number of bytes, normally 160. Each column of the original input card is recorded in two adjacent bytes of a record. Thus, the second column of the original input card is recorded in the third and fourth bytes of the record. The top six rows of the first column of the original card are represented by the rightmost six bits of the first byte, and the bottom six rows of the first column are represented by the rightmost six bits of the second byte. The first two bits (leftmost) of each byte are always set to zero (see Table D.4). For example, a 2 punch (bit 7 of the first byte) is represented as B'00000010', and a 5 punch (bit 4 of the second byte) is represented as B'00010000'.

Table D.4   Bit, row, and punch correspondences

	First byte						Second byte					
Bit	3	4	5	6	7	8	3	4	5	6	7	8
Row	1	2	3	4	5	6	7	8	9	10	11	12
Punch	12	11	0	1	2	3	4	5	6	7	8	9

D.5
Limitations

Multipunched files can only be referenced on three commands: DATA LIST, REPEATING DATA, and REREAD. Cases may not be defined via FILE TYPE. For example, you may not specify FILE TYPE MIXED.

Appendix E

Variable Format Types

This appendix defines the variable format types available on most implementations of SPSS. For some formats (particularly Z, PIBHEX, RBHEX, and RB formats), the description of the format is system-dependent and the standard definitions below refer you to your operations guide for a machine-specific description. VAX/VMS users in particular should consult their operations guide for a VMS-specific description of each of the formats listed below.

E.1
INPUT AND OUTPUT FORMATS

Table E.1a shows the *input* data formats available in SPSS. Input formats are the formats SPSS uses when it reads data. Table E.1b shows the *output* data formats available in SPSS. Output formats are the formats SPSS uses to display output or to write data to other software programs. In both tables, *w* represents the variable width and *d* represents the number of decimal places.

When format types are specified with column-style specifications on DATA LIST, the column locations determine the variable width, so you do not specify a width. To include decimal positions in column-style specification, use a comma to separate the format type from the number of decimal positions, as in DOLLAR,2.

- Based on the input formats, SPSS automatically generates output formats. For some formats (for example, A format or F format with freefield data), SPSS generates output formats that are identical to the input formats. For others (for example, DOLLAR or PCT format, or F format with fixed data), SPSS automatically increases the width of the output format to accommodate punctuation. For example, an input format of PCT4.1 specifies a variable with a maximum width of 4. SPSS generates an output format of PCT6.1 to allow for a four-digit number plus one decimal point and one percent sign.

- To change the output formats for a variable, use the FORMATS, PRINT FORMATS, or WRITE FORMATS commands. Formats can also be specified for printed and written output on the PRINT and WRITE commands.

- Decimal positions in the format specification affect the way SPSS displays values in output; they do not affect calculations. For example, assume format F5.0 is specified for both variables V1 and V2, and that both V1 and V2 have the value 100.5. In a case listing, the displayed value for both V1 and V2 is 101, since F5.0 format specifies zero decimal places and, for display purposes, SPSS rounds off each value to the nearest whole number. If V3 is computed as the sum of V1 and V2, however, V3 nevertheless equals 201 because the display format does not affect calculations.

Implied Decimal Positions. Decimal positions can be *implied* when they are not coded in the data. This can be done only for fixed-format data. Decimal places cannot be implied for freefield data.

- By default, SPSS assumes the data are whole numbers or that decimal points have been recorded on the data file.

- *For fixed data:* If a value has no coded decimal point but the input format specifies decimal positions, the rightmost positions are interpreted as *implied* decimal digits. For example, if the input format specifies two decimal digits, the value 1234 is interpreted as 12.34. However, the value 123.4 is interpreted as 123.40.

- *For freefield data:* If a value has no coded decimal point but the input format specifies decimal positions, SPSS reads numbers as whole numbers. Decimal points must be coded in the value if decimal positions are to be read. For example, if the input format specifies two decimal digits, the value 1234 is interpreted as 1234.00, the value 123.4 is interpreted as 123.40.

Table E.1a Input data formats

Input format	Min w	Max w	Implied d (max)	Input blank	Default output type	Notes
Printable numerics						
Fw.d	1	40	16	SET	same	
Nw	1	40		SET	F	
Nw.d	1	40	16	SET	F	
Ew.d	1	40	15	SET	same	w is the greater of w, d+7, or 10
Ew	1	40		SET	same	w is the greater of w or 10
COMMAw.d	1	40	16	SET	same	
COMMAw	1	40		SET	same	
DOTw.d	1	40	16	SET	same	
DOLLARw.d	1	40	16	SET	same	
DOLLARw	1	40		SET	same	
PCTw.d	1	40	16	SET	same	
PIBHEXw	2	8		SET	F	w must be an even number
PIBHEXw	2	16		SET	F	w must be an even number
RBHEXw	4	16		SET	F	w must be an even number
PIBOCTw†	1	11		SET	F	
Zw.d	1	40	16	SET	F	
Zw	1	40		SET	F	
Nonprintable numerics						
IBw.d	1	8	16	value	F	w is in bytes, d is decimal digits
IBw	1	8		value	F	w is in bytes
PIBw.d	1	8	16	value	F	w is in bytes, d is decimal digits
PIBw	1	8		value	F	w is in bytes
Pw.d	1	16	16	SET	F	
Pw	1	16		SET	F	
PKw.d	1	16	16	value	F	
PKw	1	16		value	F	
RBw	2	8		value	F	width must be an even number
LEFTSEPw.d, LEFTSEPw†	1	31	w	SET	F	
LEFTOVRw.d, LEFTOVRw†	1	31	w	SET	F	
RIGHTSEPw.d, RIGHTSEPw†	1	31	w	SET	F	
RIGHTOVRw.d, RIGHTOVRw†	1	31	w	SET	F	
UNSIGNEDw.d, UNSIGNEDw†	1	31	w	SET	F	
BYTE, BYTE.d, BYTEw.d†	1	16	3	SET	F	
WORD, WORD.d, WORDw.d†	2	2	5	SET	F	
LONG, LONG.d, LONGw.d†	4	4	9	SET	F	
QUAD, QUAD.d, QUADw.d†	8	8	20	SET	F	
OCTA, OCTA.d, OCTAw.d†	16	16	31	SET	E	
UBYTE, UBYTE.d UBYTEw.d†	1	1	3	SET	F	
UWORD, UWORD.d UWORDw.d†	2	2	5	SET	F	
ULONG, ULONG.d ULONGw.d†	4	4	9	SET	F	
UQUAD, UQUAD.d, UQUADw.d†	8	8	20	SET	F	
UOCTA, UOCTA.d, UOCTAw.d†	16	16	38	SET	E	
FLOAT†	4	4		SET	F	
DFLOAT†	8	8		SET	F	

Input format	Min w	Max w	Implied d (max)	Input blank	Default output type	Notes
GFLOAT†	8	8		SET	F	
HFLOAT†	16	16		SET	F	
CIT†	12	12		SET	F	
Strings						
Aw	1	255		blank	same	
AHEXw	2	254		blank	A	w must be an even number
EBCDICw†	1	255		blank	A	
VARYING†	1	253		blank	A	
Bit						
column:row				SET	F	column binary format
byte:bit				SET	F	UPIB format
Spacing						
Tn	1	n/a*				tabs to column n
nX	1	n/a*				skips n columns
Date and time						**Input form**
DATEw	9	40		SET	same	dd/mmm/yy
ADATEw	8	40		SET	same	mm/dd/yy
JDATEw	5	40		SET	same	yyddd
QYRw	4	40		SET	same	qQyy
MOYRw	6	40		SET	same	mm/yyyy
WKYRw	6	40		SET	same	wkWKyy
TIMEw	5	40		SET	same	hh:mm:ss.ss
DTIMEw	11	40		SET	same	d hh:mm:ss.ss
DATETIMEw	17	40		SET	same	dd/mmm/yy hh:mm:ss.ss
WKDAYw	2	40		SET	same	dd
MONTHw	3	40		SET	same	mmm
ASCTIME†	1	255		SET	same	dd/mmm/yy hh:mm:ss.ss
ASCDELTA†	1	255		SET	same	dd/mmm/yy hh:mm:ss.ss
BINTIME†				SET	ASCTIME	
BINDELTA†				SET	ASCDELTA	
UIC formats						
UICw†	1	255		SET	same	
RIGHTSIDw†	1	255		SET	same	

* Not applicable

† Available only on VAX/VMS operating systems

Table E.1b Output data formats

Format type	PRINT	Min w	Max w	Max d
Numeric				
Fw, Fw.d	yes	1*	40	16
COMMAw, COMMAw.d	yes	1*	40	16
DOTw, DOTw.d	yes	1*	40	16
DOLLARw, DOLLARw.d	yes	2*	40	16
CCw, CCw.d	yes	2*	40	16
PCTw, PCTw.d	yes	1*	40	16
PIBHEXw	yes	2**	16**	
RBHEXw	yes	4**	16**	
PIBOCTw†	yes	1	11	
Zw, Zw.d	yes	1	40	16
IBw, IBw.d	no	1	8	16
PIBw, PIBw.d	no	1	8	16
Nw	yes	1	40	
Pw, Pw.d	no	1	16	16
Ew, Ew.d	yes	6	40	
PKw, PKw.d	no	1	16	16
RBw	no	2	8	
LEFTSEPw.d, LEFTSEPw†	no	1	31	w
LEFTOVRw.d, LEFTOVRw†	no	1	31	w
RIGHTSEPw.d, RIGHTSEPw†	no	1	31	w
RIGHTOVRw.d, RIGHTOVRw†	no	1	31	w
UNSIGNEDw.d, UNSIGNEDw†	no	1	31	w
BYTE, BYTE.d, BYTEw.d†	no	1	16	3
WORD, WORD.d, WORDw.d†	no	2	2	5
LONG, LONG.d, LONGw.d†	no	4	4	9
QUAD, QUAD.d, QUADw.d†	no	8	8	20
OCTA, OCTA.d, OCTAw.d†	no	16	16	31
UBYTE, UBYTE.d UBYTEw.d†	no	1	1	3
UWORD, UWORD.d UWORDw.d†	no	2	2	5
ULONG, ULONG.d ULONGw.d†	no	4	4	9
UQUAD, UQUAD.d, UQUADw.d†	no	8	8	20
UOCTA, UOCTA.d, UOCTAw.d†	no	16	16	38
FLOAT†	no	4	4	
DFLOAT†	no	8	8	
GFLOAT†	no	8	8	
HFLOAT†	no	16	16	
CIT†	no	12	12	
String				
Aw	yes	1	254	
AHEXw	yes	2**	510	
EBCDICw†	yes	1	255	
VARYING†	yes	1	253	

Format type	PRINT	Min w	Max w	Max d	Result form
Date and time					
DATEw	yes	9	40		dd-mmm-yy
		11			dd-mmm-yyyy
ADATEw	yes	8	40		mm/dd/yy
		10			mm/dd/yyyy
JDATEw	yes	5	40		yyddd
		7			yyyyddd
QYRw	yes	6	40		q Q yy
		8			q Q yyyy
MOYRw	yes	6	40		mmm yy
		8			mmm yyyy
WKYRw	yes	8	40		ww WK yy
		10			ww WK yyyy
WKDAYw	yes	2+	40		
MONTHw	yes	3+	40		
TIMEw	yes	5++	40		hh:mm
TIMEw.d	yes	10	40	16	hh:mm:ss.s
DTIMEw	yes	8++	40		dd hh:mm
DTIMEw.d	yes	13	40	16	dd hh:mm:ss.s
DATETIMEw	yes	17++	40		dd-mmm-yyyy hh:mm
DATETIMEw.d	yes	22	40	16	dd-mmm-yyyy hh:mm:ss.s
ASCTIME†	yes	1	255		dd-mmm-yyyy hh:mm:ss.s
ASCDELTA†	yes	1	255		dd-mmm-yyyy hh:mm:ss.s
BINTIME†	yes				
BINDELTA†	yes				
UIC formats					
UICw†	yes	1	255		
RIGHTSIDw†	yes	1	255		

† Available only on VAX/VMS operating systems

*Add number of decimals plus one if number of decimals is more than one. Total width cannot exceed 40 characters.
**Must be a multiple of two.
+As the field width is expanded, the output string is expanded until the entire name of the day or month is produced.
++Add three to display seconds.

E.2
Printable Numeric Formats

Generally, each of the printable numeric formats adheres to the conventions discussed below:

The following conventions apply to input formats:

- *For fixed data:* Blank fields read with any of the printable numeric formats are set to system- missing by default or to the value specified on the BLANK subcommand on the SET command.
- *For freefield data:* A blank in the data is interpreted as the end of the value.
- *For fixed data:* Decimal positions can be implied in the format.
- *For freefield data:* Decimal positions cannot be implied.

The following conventions apply to output formats:

- The default PRINT and WRITE FORMATS include enough space for printing and writing punctuation characters (decimal points, commas, dollar signs, etc.).
- Formats specified on PRINT FORMATS, WRITE FORMATS, FORMATS, or in PRINT and WRITE commands must allow enough positions to include any punctuation characters such as decimal points, commas, dollar signs, or date and time delimiters. SPSS *does not* automatically expand the output formats you assign. The column labeled **Max d** in Table E.1b indicates the maximum number of decimal places allowed for each format type.

- Even if a data value exceeds its width specification, SPSS makes an attempt to produce some value. It takes out punctuation characters, then it tries scientific notation, and then, if there is still not enough space, it produces asterisks indicating that a value is present which cannot be printed in the assigned width.
- By default, SPSS translates restricted numeric, hexadecimal numeric, and zoned input formats to output formats of standard numeric (F). All other printable input formats retain the same output format type (see Table E.1a).

E.3
Fw.d (Standard Numeric)

The F format reads standard numeric values. Each input value can include a maximum of one decimal point. Dollar signs, commas, and percent signs cannot be coded in the data.

For fixed data, if a value has no coded decimal point but the input format specifies decimal positions, the rightmost positions are interpreted as *implied* decimal digits. For example, if the input format specifies two decimal digits, the value 1234 is interpreted as 12.34. However, the value 123.4 is still interpreted as 123.4. For freefield data, decimal digits cannot be implied.

The F format accepts numbers in scientific notation, provided the data values include E or D, the sign, and the power of 10. For example, the data value 543E+3 can be read under an F6 format. If a value is coded in scientific notation, an implied decimal specification is ignored.

The default output formats are type F. Thus, assuming there are no implied decimal positions in the input format, the value 1234 is displayed in output as 1234.

E.4
Nw.d (Restricted Numeric)

The format is used to specify fields containing unsigned integers. Leading, trailing, and imbedded blanks are not allowed. You can specify the number of digits that follow an implied decimal point. Coded decimal values are not allowed. This format is useful for reading and checking values that you know should be only integers with leading zeros.

For example, N2 defines a two-column variable. The value 2 must be input as 02. Leading blanks are not allowed. A completely blank field is assigned the system-missing value.

The default output formats are type F.

E.5
Ew.d (Scientific Notation)

The E format reads all forms of scientific notation numbers. As an input format, E format can read an imbedded E or D symbol and an imbedded + or − sign. If the sign is omitted, + is assumed. If the sign is coded in the data, the E or D can be omitted. In addition, E format can read any value that is acceptable to F format. Thus, assuming the input format E9, the input values 1.234E+03, 1.234E3, 1.234+3, and 1234 are equivalent.

The input value can be up to 40 columns wide and can include up to 15 decimal positions. For fixed field data, the decimal positions can be implied. For example, assuming an E4.3 input format and keyword FIXED on DATA LIST, the value 1234 is interpreted as 1.234E+00. For freefield data, decimal positions cannot be implied. For example, assuming an E4.3 input format and keyword FREE on DATA LIST, the value 1234 is interpreted as 1.234E+03. Decimal points cannot be coded in the exponent portion of the value.

The default output formats are type E with a minimum width of ten columns, three of which are decimal positions (E10.3). For the output width, SPSS uses either the specified input width, the number of specified decimal positions plus seven $(d+7)$, or ten, whichever is greater. Thus, the input format E12.4 is unchanged as an output format. The input format E7.4 generates the output format E11.4. The input format E4.3 generates the output format E10.3. Whether zero, one, or two decimal positions are specified in the input format, SPSS uses three decimal positions in the output format. Thus, the input format E11.2 generates the output format E11.3.

Output formats assigned on FORMATS, PRINT FORMATS, and WRITE FORMATS are not altered. The assigned output width for E format must be at least six columns, and the assigned width minus the number of assigned decimal positions must be equal to or greater than 6.

E.6
COMMAw.d (Commas in Numbers)

As an input format with fixed data, COMMA is identical to F format, except that it can read numeric values with or without imbedded commas. For example, assuming keyword FIXED on DATA LIST, the values 1,234, 12,34 and 123,4 are all interpreted as 1234. In other words, the commas in the input values are ignored.

As an input format with freefield data, COMMA is identical to F format; thus, commas *cannot* be coded in the data (a comma in freefield data is interpreted as a delimiter).

The default output formats are COMMA, whether the input values have imbedded commas, and whether data are fixed or freefield. Thus, assuming there are no implied decimal positions in the input format, the input value 1234 is displayed in output as 1,234.

E.7
DOTw.d (Dots in Numbers)

The DOT format is similar to COMMA format, except the roles of the comma and the dot (period) are reversed. This is useful for reading and displaying numbers according to European conventions.

For input, DOT should be used only with fixed format data.

The default output formats are DOT. Thus, assuming there are no implied decimal positions in the input format, the input value 1234 is displayed as 1.234.

E.8
DOLLARw.d (Dollar Sign and Commas in Numbers)

As an input format with fixed data, DOLLAR is identical to F format, except that it can read numeric values with or without dollar signs and commas. For example, assuming keyword FIXED on DATA LIST, the values $1,234, 12,34 and 123,4 are all interpreted as 1234. In other words, dollar signs and commas in the input values are ignored. Only one leading dollar sign with no imbedded blanks can be coded into each value.

As an input format with freefield data, DOLLAR is identical to F format; thus, dollar signs and commas *cannot* be coded in the data (commas in freefield data are interpreted as delimiters).

The default output formats are DOLLAR, whether the input values have imbedded dollar signs and commas, and whether data are fixed or freefield. Thus, assuming there are no implied decimal positions in the input format, the input value 1234 is displayed in output as $1,234. (See the SET command for customizing currency formats for output.)

E.9
PCTw.d (Percent Sign after Numbers)

As an input format with fixed data, PCT is identical to F format, except that it can read numeric fields with or without a trailing percent sign. For example, assuming keyword FIXED on DATA LIST, the values 12 and 12% are both interpreted as 12. In other words, percent signs in the input values are ignored.

Only one trailing percent sign with no imbedded blanks can be coded into each value.

As an input format with freefield data, PCT is identical to F format; thus, percent signs *cannot* be coded in the data.

The default output formats are PCT, whether the input values have imbedded percent signs, and whether data are fixed or freefield. Thus, assuming there are no implied decimal positions in the input format, the input value 12 is displayed in output as 12%.

The PCT format *does not* compute percentages, it just adds the percent sign to the value. The result of 1 divided by 2, for example, is displayed as 0.5% if PCT format is specified.

E.10
PIBHEXw (Hexadecimal of PIB)

The PIBHEX format interprets a series of hexadecimal characters as an unsigned integer. For example, F0 is interpreted as 250 and FFFF is interpreted as 65,535. Consult the definition of PIBHEX format in your operations guide to see how hexadecimal characters are interpreted on your operating system.

The values must be positive, and the width must be an even number. The maximum width specification is 16 columns. You cannot specify implied decimal digits.

The default output formats are an equivalent F format.

E.11
PIBOCTw (Octal of PIB)

The PIBOCT format (available only on VAX/VMS operating systems) represents any positive integer between 0 and 9E18 (approximately). It can be used to interpret an octal value on input or to list, print, or write the octal representation of a positive integer binary value on output. Since this format is based on the positive integer binary representation of a value, its format width is equal to the physical byte width of the field. The maximum PIB width that can be represented with PIBOCT is PIB4.

E.12
RBHEXw (Hexadecimal of RB)

The RBHEX format interprets a series of hexadecimal characters as a number that represents a floating-point number. This representation is highly implementation dependent. If the field width is less than twice the width of a floating-point number, padding with binary zeros occurs on the right. The values are real numbers, and the width must be an even number. Consult the definition of RBHEX format in your operations guide to see if there is additional information on how floating- point numbers are represented on your operating system.

The default output formats are an equivalent F format.

E.13
Zw.d (Zoned Decimal)

The Z format reads data values that contain zoned decimal data. Such numbers may be generated by COBOL systems using DISPLAY data items, by PL/1 systems using PICTURE data items, or by ASSEMBLER systems using zoned decimal data items.

The general format of a zoned decimal number varies by operating system. The general format is one digit per byte. Each byte other than the last contains a hexadecimal "F" in the four leftmost bits and a single digit in the rightmost four bits. The last byte contains a hexadecimal "F" (or "C") in the leftmost four bits for positive numbers or a hexadecimal "D" (or "E") for negative numbers. Leading blanks and coded decimal points are allowed. Zoned decimal is simply a formatted field in which the sign is an overpunch in the rightmost position.

The default output format is an equivalent F format.

Z format is not available on all operating systems. Consult your operations guide to see if it is available on your system, and whether there is any additional information on zoned decimal format.

E.14
Nonprintable Numeric Input Formats

Nonprintable numeric input formats apply to data that is readable only by machines. Generally, these formats adhere to the following conventions:

- Input blanks are treated as values and are not assigned the system-missing value.
- Each input format is converted to an equivalent F format for output.

E.15
LEFTSEPw.d (Numeric Left Separate) and RIGHTSEPw.d (Numeric Right Separate)

For both of these data types (available only on VAX/VMS operating systems) one byte is always reserved for the sign (positive or negative); thus, the variable width (the number of digits) will always be one less than the actual physical field width. This difference is important when considering the use of column-style format specifications on the DATA LIST, WRITE, or PRINT commands. For example, a variable with the format LEFTSEP7 will require an eight-byte physical field when specifying its column location on input or output. Thus, the following two DATA LIST statements are equivalent:

```
DATA LIST  /VARA VARB (LEFTSEP11,RIGHTSEP2).
DATA LIST  /VARA 1-12 (LEFTSEP) VARB 1-3 (RIGHTSEP).
```

E.16
LEFTOVRw.d (Numeric Left Overpunch) and RIGHTORw.d (Numeric Right Overpunch)

These decimal data types (available only on VAX/VMS operating systems) overpunch the sign in the leftmost and rightmost bytes, respectively. All values representable with the standard numeric format can be represented with the LEFTOVR and RIGHTOVR formats.

E.17
UNSIGNEDw.d (Numeric Unsigned)

This decimal data type (available only on VAX/VMS operating systems) only accepts positive values between 0 and 1E38. Negative values will be converted to SYSMIS.

E.18
IBw.d (Integer Binary)

The IB format reads fields which contain fixed point binary (integer) data. The data might be generated by COBOL using COMPUTATIONAL data items, by FORTRAN using INTEGER*2 or INTEGER*4, or by ASSEMBLER systems using fullword and halfword items. The general format of binary items is a binary number of 16 or 32 bits in length using twos-complement notation for negative quantities.

For the IB format, w is the field width in bytes (omitted for column-style specifications) and d is the number of decimal digits to the right of the decimal point. Widths of 2 and 4 represent standard halfword and fullword integers, respectively. Single byte fields are treated as signed. For example, hexadecimal FF is read as -1.

E.19
BYTE.d, WORD.d, LONG.d, QUAD.d, and OCTA.d (Signed Integers)

These integer binary data types (available only on VAX/VMS operating systems) have a format width equal to the physical byte width of the field. The integer values representable by each data type are the following:

BYTE (IB1)	-128 thru $+127$
WORD (IB2)	-32768 thru $+32767$
LONG (IB4)	-2147483648 thru $+2147483648$
QUAD (IB8)	$-3.69E19$ thru $+3.69E19$
OCTA (IB16)	$-1.06E37$ thru $+1.06E37$

E.20
PIBw.d (Positive Integer Binary)

The PIB format is essentially the same as IB, except that negative numbers are not allowed. This restriction allows one additional bit of magnitude.

E.21
UBYTE.d, UWORD.d, ULONG.d, UQUAD.d, and UOCTA.d (Unsigned Integers)

These positive integer binary data types (available only on VAX/VMS operating systems) have a format width equal to the physical byte width of the field. Only positive integers can be represented with these formats. The values representable by each type are the following:

UBYTE (PIB1)	0 thru $+255$
UWORD (PIB2)	0 thru $+65535$
ULONG (PIB4)	0 thru $+4294967296$
UQUAD (PIB8)	0 thru $+7.38E19$
UOCTA (PIB16)	0 thru $+1.40E38$

E.22
Pw.d (Packed Decimal)

The P format is used to read fields with packed decimal numbers. Such numbers are generated by COBOL systems using COMPUTATIONAL–3 data items, and by ASSEMBLER systems using packed decimal data items. The general format of a packed decimal field is two four-bit digits in each byte of the field except the last. The last byte contains a single digit in its four leftmost bits and a four- bit sign in its rightmost bits. The number of digits in a field is $(2*w-1)$ where w is the field width in bytes. The sign is X'F' for positive values and X'D' for negative values (C zone equals F and E zone equals D). Remember, when defining a variable under P format, w is the number of bytes (not digits) and d is the number of digits to the right of the implied decimal point.

E.23
PKw.d (Unsigned Packed Decimal)

The PK format is essentially the same as P, except that there is no sign. That is, even the rightmost byte contains two digits, and negative data cannot be represented. One byte under PK format can represent numbers from 0 to 99, while under PIB one byte can represent numbers from 0 through 255.

E.24
RBw (Real Binary)

The RB format is used to read data values which contain internal format floating-point numbers. Such numbers are generated by COBOL systems using COMPUTATIONAL–1 or COMPUTATIONAL–2 data items, by PL/1 systems using FLOATING DECIMAL data items, by FORTRAN systems using REAL or REAL*8 data items, or by ASSEMBLER systems using floating-point data items.

The general format of a floating number varies by operating system. Consult the definition of RB format in your operations guide to see if there is any information about the general format of a floating number on your operating system.

Normally, a width specification of 8 is used to read double precision values, and a width of 4 is used to read single precision values. The width specification must be an even number between 2 and 8.

E.25
FLOAT, DFLOAT, GFLOAT, HFLOAT (Floating Point)

These floating point data types (available only on VAX/VMS operating systems) have format widths equal to their physical byte width. Each data type can represent any floating point value between $-1.7E38$ and $-.29E-38$, the value 0, and any value between $.29E-38$ and $1.7E38$. Each type, however, represents a different degree of precision. The precision of each format type is listed below:

FLOAT (RB4)   7 digits
DFLOAT (RB8)   16.5 digits
GFLOAT (8 bytes)   15 digits
HFLOAT (16 bytes)   16.5 digits

E.26
CIT (Cobol Intermediate Type)

The CIT format is a special data type (available only on VAX/VMS operating systems) produced and used by COBOL. The format width for this type is always 12, the same as its physical byte width. Values that this type can represent are $-10E99$ to $-10E-99$, 0, and $10E-99$ to $10E99$. This format has 16.5 digits of precision (17 digits outside of SPSS) and has its own missing value, known as the COBOL indeterminate value. When missing values are output from SPSS using this data type, they are converted to this COBOL indeterminate value.

E.27
String Formats

The string input formats are used to read character data. The values are either alphanumeric characters or the hexadecimal representation of alphanumeric characters. String formats conform to the following rules:

- Blank fields are interpreted as valid, not assigned the system-missing value.
- The default print and write formats are type A.

E.28
Aw (Standard Characters)

The A format is used to read standard characters. Characters can include letters, numbers, punctuation marks, blanks, and most other characters on your keyboard. This format defines a variable as a *string* variable; numbers entered as values for string variables cannot be used in calculations.

E.29
AHEXw (Hexadecimal Characters)

The AHEX format is used to read the hexadecimal representation of standard characters. On input, each set of two characters represents one standard character. The *w* specification must be an even number. By default, the output formats are of type A.

E.30
EBCDICw (EBCDIC Characters) and VARYING (Varying Length Character String)

The EBCDIC and VARYING string formats are available only on VAX/VMS operating systems. EBCDIC format has a one-to-one correspondence between the variable width and physical byte width. Since varying length strings store the length of the string in the first two bytes, the variable width is also expressed in terms of characters represented with an actual physical byte width equal to the number of characters plus two.

E.31
Date and Time Input Formats

Date and time formats are used to read values representing dates and times or date-time combinations. These formats translate values to "special" internal representations. The internal representation is up to 20 characters indicating the number of seconds from a fixed date (October 14, 1582), the number of seconds in a time interval, or an ordinal number.

- Date and time formats cannot be used with freefield input.
- There are eleven defined format codes. Each produces either a date, a time interval, or an ordinal number.

E.32
DATE

This format reads international dates in the form dd/mmm/yyyy. The following conventions apply:

- Two-digit years are assumed to be prefixed by 19.
- Months may be represented in digits, Roman numerals, three-character abbreviations, or fully spelled out: 10, X, OCT, OCTOBER, or October.
- Dashes, periods, commas, slashes, or blanks can be used as delimiters. For example, the date "December 2, 1984" can be expressed as 02-December-1984; 02.December.84; 02,December,1984; 02/December/1984; or 02 December 1984.
- The width defined on the DATA LIST command must be at least nine characters; however, data values of fewer characters are correctly evaluated.

E.33
ADATEw (American Date)

The ADATE format reads American format dates of the general form mm/dd/yyyy. As with DATE format, years may be represented as either two or four digits. Acceptable delimiters are blanks, dashes, periods, commas, or slashes. Months may be fully spelled out or represented as digits, Roman numerals, or three-character abbreviations. The width defined on the DATA LIST command must be at least eight characters. However, data values that have fewer characters are correctly evaluated.

E.34
JDATEw (Julian Date)

The JDATE format reads Julian-formatted dates in the form yyddd. If the number of digits read is five, a two-digit year is assumed, and 1900 will be added. A four-digit year is assumed if the number of digits is seven. The days field can be any number between 001 and 366. Leading zeros are required in the day field. No delimiters are allowed between the year and day fields. For example, the Julian equivalent of September 6, 1954, can be expressed as 1954249 but not as 1954/249.

E.35
QYRw (Quarter and Year)

The QYR format reads fields containing the quarter and the year in the form qQyyyy. The quarter is expressed as 1, 2, 3, or 4, and the year is represented by two or four digits. If two digits are used, 1900 is added. The quarter and year are separated by the letter Q. Blanks may be used as additional delimiters. The month is 3*(quarter−1)+1, and the day is 1. For example, April 1, 1958 is in the second quarter of 1958 and can be represented either as 2 Q 1958 or as 2Q1958.

E.36
MOYRw (Month and Year)

The MOYR format reads values in the form mm/yyyy. Months can be expressed as digits, Roman numerals, three-character abbreviations (as in JAN, FEB, and so on), or they may be spelled out. The year is expressed as either two or four digits. If it is two digits, 1900 is added. Blanks, dashes, periods, commas, or slashes can be used as delimiters. The "days" portion of the date is assumed to be 1. The width defined on the DATA LIST command must be at least six characters; however, data values of fewer characters are correctly evaluated.

E.37
WKYRw (Week and Year)

The WKYR format reads dates in the form wkWKyyyy. A week is expressed as a number from 1 to 53. The year is a two- or four-digit number. Week 1 is assumed to begin on 1 JAN, week 2, on 8 JAN, and so forth. The week and year are separated by the string WK. Blanks can be used as additional delimiters. For example, you can express the 14th week of 1984 as either 14 WK 1984 or as 14WK1984. The width defined on the DATA LIST command must be at least six characters; however, data values of five characters are correctly evaluated.

E.38
TIMEw (Time)

The TIME format is used to read a time of day or a time interval into a datum of type time interval. The input field is of the form hh:mm:ss.ss. The following conventions apply:

- Colons, blanks, or periods may be used as delimiters between hours, minutes, and seconds. A period is required to separate seconds from fractional seconds.

- Input fields must contain hours and minutes. Seconds and fractional seconds may be omitted and will default to zeros. Thus, the field 23:59 when read under TIME format will result in 23:59:00.

- Data values can contain a sign.

- Fractional seconds must have the decimal point coded in the data value.

- Hours may be of unlimited magnitude. The maximum for minutes is 59; for seconds, 59.99....

E.39
DTIMEw (Days and Time)

The DTIME format is used to read a time interval which includes days in the form ddd hh:mm:ss.ss, such as 12 23:44:01.58 or 144 18:40. The number of days is separated from the hours by an acceptable TIME delimiter: a blank, a period, or a colon. A preceding sign ($+/-$) may be used. The remainder of the field must conform to required specifications for the TIME format. Fractional seconds must have the decimal point coded in the data value.

E.40
DATETIMEw (Date and Time)

The DATETIME format is used to read values containing a date and a time. The date must be written as an international date (dd-mmm-yyyy) followed by a blank and then a time in the form hh:mm:ss.ss, such as 14-OCT-1977 14:12:51.10. The time conforms to a twenty-four hour clock. Thus the maximum subfields for time are 23 for hours, 59 for minutes, and 59.999... for seconds.

Fractional seconds must have the decimal point coded in the data value. The width defined on the DATA LIST command must be at least 17 characters; however, data values of fewer characters are correctly evaluated.

E.41
WKDAYw (Day of the Week)

The WKDAY format is used to read the day of the week expressed as a character string. Only the first two characters are significant, and the minimum field width is two. Remaining characters are optional: Sunday could be expressed as SUNDAY or as SU. Though the input values must be entered as strings, SPSS translates them to integers between 1 and 7, where Sunday equals 1 and Saturday equals 7. Thus, the values are numeric and cannot be treated as strings. For example, you cannot use the string function CONCAT to concatenate WKDAY with MONTH. The output values are displayed as strings. To display the values as integers, use FORMATS to define F formats for the output.

E.42
MONTHw (Month)

The MONTH format is used to read the month of the year expressed as a character string. Names may be fully spelled out, for example OCTOBER, or abbreviated to three characters. For example, OCTOBER could be written as OCT. In addition, input values can be entered as integers between 1 and 12, where January equals 1 and December equals 12. Whether the values are entered as strings or integers, SPSS translates them to integers between 1 and 12. Thus, the values are numeric and cannot be treated as strings. For example, you cannot use the string function CONCAT to concatenate WKDAY with MONTH. The output values are displayed as strings. To display the values as integers, use FORMATS to define F formats for the output.

E.43
ACSTIME (ASCII time), ASCDELTA (ASCII delta time), BINTIME, and BINDELTA

The VAX/VMS version of SPSS includes four data types specifically for the VAX/VMS binary and ASCII absolute and delta times. The format widths for the binary formats are fixed and cannot be changed. The format widths for ASCII absolute and delta times can range between 1 and 255. The date and time delimiters (− and :) are included when calculating the correct format widths.

E.44
UIC Formats

Two additional data types (formats) are available on VAX/VMS operating systems: UIC and RIGHTSID. These formats turn an unsigned integer value into an alpha string.

E.45
UICw (VMS User Identification Code)

On output, UIC format (available only on VAX/VMS operating systems) will turn a numeric value (such as those obtained for variable UIC in GET VMS ACCOUNTING) into a string of the form [group,member]. If no equivalent alpha string is found, the numeric form [m,n] will be output. SYSMIS is output as all blanks. On input, UIC will turn an alpha string of one of the forms [group,member], [member], or [m,n] into a numeric value. Strings of the form [member] or [group,member] for which no numeric equivalent is found will be set to SYSMIS.

Field widths can be specified on UIC and format. The default field width is 16.

E.46
RIGHTSIDw (VMS Rights Identifier)

The RIGHTSID format (available only on VAX/VMS operating systems) behaves in a similar manner to the UIC format, except that numeric values are turned into rights identifiers (alpha strings such as DAVIS or SPSSXNET) on output. If no identifier is found, the hexadecimal numeric value is output, and SYSMIS is output as all blanks. Rights identifiers are turned into numeric values on input (if the identifier is not found, the value is set to SYSMIS).

Field widths can be specified on RIGHTSID format. The default field width is 16.

E.47
T AND X FORMAT ELEMENTS

The T and X format elements skip columns you do not want to define. The T and X elements are available only as input formats for fixed data. If T and X elements are specified with freefield data, the element specifications are ignored.

- The element *Tn* tabs to the column number specified by *n*. The next format element defines the variable to be read beginning in that column.
- The T format element can be used to move backward and forward within the same record.
- The element *nX* skips *n* columns. The next format element defines the variable to be read beginning with the column *following* the skip.
- If two or more variables are recorded in adjacent columns of the same record and have the same format type, width, and number of implied decimal places, they can be defined by specifying the number of adjacent variables before the format element.
- Several format elements can be combined into a *format list* within the same set of parentheses to define a list of variables. The variable list can include individual variable names and variable names defined using keyword TO. The format element or format list enclosed in parentheses follows the variable name or variable list to which it applies.

Example.

```
DATA LIST  FILE=HUBDATA RECORDS=3
  / MOHIRED (T12,F2.0).
```

- Variable MOHIRED is located in columns 12 and 13.

Example.

```
DATA LIST  FILE=HUBDATA RECORDS=3
  /MOHIRED (11X,F2.0).
```

- The X element is used to make the same specification made by the T element in the previous example.

Example.

```
DATA LIST  FILE=HUBDATA RECORDS=3
  /1 ID (T19,F3.0) LNAME (T12,A20)
  /2 MOHIRED, YRHIRED, DEPT1 TO DEPT4 (T12,2F2.0,4F1.0).
```

- The first defined variable on record 1 is ID, located in column 19. Variable ID is a numeric variable with a width of three characters. The second variable on record 1 is LNAME, located in columns 12 through 31. Variable LNAME is a string variable with a width of 20 characters.
- The next set of the defined variables are located on record 2. The T12 format element in the format list positions the next data format element in column 12.
- The first variable, MOHIRED, is a two-column integer variable located in columns 12 and 13. The second variable, YRHIRED, also a two-column integer variable, is located in columns 14 and 15. The next four variables, DEPT1 through DEPT4, are single-column variables located in columns 16 through 19.

E.48
COLUMN BINARY FORMAT

Column binary formats are used to define data stored on computer cards, tapes, or disks that use the *column binary* (also called *multipunch*) method of storing data. The general format for each variable with a column binary format is

```
varname  starting column:starting row - ending column:ending row
```

SPSS only processes multipunch data that have been read by IBM card readers attached to IBM 360-compatible computers. These readers produce a particular representation of the punches.

- The FILE HANDLE command is required for reading column binary data. The file handle must match the handle named on the FILE subcommand on DATA LIST. In addition, MODE=MULTIPUNCH must be specified on FILE HANDLE to specify the file as column binary. Variables can then be defined on DATA LIST.

- Once a file has been specified as column binary, variables must then be defined on the DATA LIST command (or a REPEATING DATA, or REREAD command). Starting and ending rows as well as columns must be specified for each variable. The starting column and row are required and must be separated by a colon. The ending row and column are optional if they are the same as the starting row and column.

- No more than one punch is allowed in any given field. Any attempt to read fields that contain more than one punch will produce an error, resulting in the system-missing value for the variable. In situations where more than one response is permitted to a question, each response must be coded as a separate variable.

- Although multipunch columns can be read only by using column binary format, all other formats can be used to read single-punched columns in the same data file.

- Frequently, data stored in column binary format use the 11 punch and the 12 punch (in EBCDIC these are minus signs and ampersands) to represent responses like "don't know," "no answer," or "non- applicable." When using a non-column binary format, variables containing these values must be read in as string variables. Use the keyword CONVERT on the RECODE command to transform the alphanumeric values '&' and '−' to the numeric values 11 and 12, as in

```
RECODE V1 ('-'=11) ('&'=12) (CONVERT) INTO V2.
```

E.49
Limitations

- Multipunched files can only be referenced on three commands: DATA LIST, REPEATING DATA, and REREAD. Cases cannot be defined with FILE TYPE. For example, you cannot specify FILE TYPE MIXED.

Example.

```
FILE HANDLE  ELE48  MODE=MULTIPUNCH
   /NAME='E:\DATA\ELECTION.RES'.
DATA LIST FILE=ELE48
     /1 PARTY     18
        SEX       19:1
        EMPSTAT   20(A)
        SES       48:4-6
        RELIGION  48:7-10
        OCCUPAT   50:11-51:2.
RECODE EMPSTAT (CONVERT) ('-'=11)('&'=12) INTO EMPSTAT2.
```

- The FILE HANDLE command defines handle ELE48 for the data. MODE = MULTIPUNCH identifies data as column binary data. The NAME subcommand locates the data on device E: in the directory E:\DATA. The file is identified as ELECTION.RES.

- The DATA LIST command defines variables for the file referenced by the handle ELE48. Variable SEX is located in row 1 of column 19, SES in rows 4 through 6 of column 48, RELIGION in rows 7 through 10 of column 48, and OCCUPAT in column 50:row 11 through column 51:row 2. Since columns 18 and 20 were not multipunched, the column numbers alone are sufficient to define the location of PARTY and EMPSTAT.

- A standard numeric format is used to read the variable PARTY.

- All numbers in string variable EMPSTAT are recoded to numbers for target variable EMPSTAT2. In addition, the minus sign is changed to 11 and the ampersand to 12.

E.50
Column Binary Data on Disk

Column binary data occur in fixed-length records containing an even number of bytes, normally 160. Each column of the original input card is recorded in two adjacent bytes of a record. Thus, the second column of the original input card is recorded in the third and fourth bytes of the record. The top six rows of the first column of the original card are represented by the rightmost six bits of the first byte, and the bottom six rows of the first column are represented by the rightmost six bits of the second byte. The first two bits (leftmost) of each byte are always set to zero (see Table E.50). For example, a 2 punch (bit 7 of the first byte) is represented as B'00000010', and a 5 punch (bit 4 of the second byte) is represented as B'00010000'.

Table E.50 Bit, row, and punch correspondences

	First byte						Second byte					
Bit	3	4	5	6	7	8	3	4	5	6	7	8
Row	1	2	3	4	5	6	7	8	9	10	11	12
Punch	12	11	0	1	2	3	4	5	6	7	8	9

E.51
UNALIGNED POSITIVE INTEGER BINARY FORMAT

Unaligned positive integer binary format (known as UPIB format) permits you to read positive integer binary (PIB) fields that do not begin and end on byte boundaries. This feature allows you to read individual bits within fields or to read fields that contain a combination of punches as one variable.

- Fields are defined according to starting and ending byte and bit locations.
- If multiple adjacent fields containing equal numbers of bits are to be read, the location information follows the list of variable names.

Note: UPIB formats that span byte boundaries should not be used.

E.52
UPIB versus Column Binary Format

The UPIB format also reads multipunched data. Fields to be read under UPIB format are specified with a syntax identical to that used for column binary. In fact, when used to read single-bit dichotomies, the two formats produce results that are identical. The determination of which type of field the user specified is made by examining the declared data mode of the input field. If the data mode was declared to be MULTIPUNCHED on the FILE HANDLE command, the field is assumed to be column binary. If the data mode was not specifically declared to be multipunched, the field is assumed to be unaligned binary. There are three additional differences between column binary and unaligned positive integer binary:

- The column binary format specifies which rows are to be read from virtual card columns. The UPIB format specifies which bits are to be read from actual bytes.
- The column binary format is restricted to records containing a maximum of 80 virtual card columns. The UPIB format can be used when reading a record of any length supported by SPSS.
- For each field, the column binary format expects at most a single punch on a given case and returns the ordinal position of the punch that occurs. The UPIB format accepts any combination of bits and returns the binary integer represented by the bits that are on.

E.53
Limitations

- Unaligned binary input field specifications are valid only on DATA LIST, KEYED DATA LIST, and REPEATING DATA.
- The maximum number of bits that can be specified for any single variable is 64. On machines that support OS, DOS, and CMS operating systems, a maximum of 56 significant bits will be retained when reading fields over 56 bits in width.
- Fields to be read as unaligned binary integers are always treated as positive. No parenthesized format type is permitted following the location information. The variables defined are assigned print and write formats of F.

Example.

```
DATA LIST FILE=FILEIN
   / USERTYPE 1:1-2
     CPUTIME  1:3-4:7
     V1 TO V5 10:3-7.
```

- Variable USERTYPE is in bits 1 and 2 of byte 1; CPUTIME is defined as a series of bits that begins in bit 3 of byte 1 and ends in bit 7 of byte 4.
- For variables V1 to V5, five single-bit variables will be read from bits 3 through 7 of column 10 of the input record. The contents of each field are read as the positive integer represented in binary by the combination of bits within the field.

Example.

```
DATA LIST   FILE=PSWS
    /PERMASK 1:2          /*Program Event Recording Mask
     TRANSMODE            /*Translation Mode
     IOMASK               /*Input/Output Mask
     EXTMASK 1:6-8        /*External Mask
     PROTKEY 2:1-4        /*Protection Key
     ECMODE               /*EC Mode=1
     MCMASK               /*Machine Check Mask
     WAIT                 /*Wait State
     PROB    2:5-8        /*Problem State
     CC      3:3-4        /*Condition Code
     FXOVMASK             /*Fixed Point Overflow Mask
     DCOVMASK             /*Decimal Overflow Mask
     EXUFMASK             /*Exponent Underflow Mask
     SIGMASK 3:5-8
     ADDRESS 5-8 (PIB).   /*Instruction Address
```

- This example illustrates interpreting the IBM machine Program Status Word (EC mode). The protection key is four bits long, the condition code is two bits, and the instruction address is three bytes long. All the other fields are single bits.

Index

Index

A (format)
fixed-format data, 120
A (keyword)
  DESCRIPTIVES command, 126
  SORT CASES command, 680
ABS (function), 18
  MATRIX command, 415
ABSOLUTE (keyword)
  PROXIMITIES command, 552
active system file
  defined, 6-7
  in ADD FILES command, 35
  in MATCH FILES command, 402
  in UPDATE command, 706-707
ADD (function)
  REPORT command, 640
ADD FILES (command), 33-38
  active system file, 35
  BY subcommand, 36
  DROP subcommand, 37
  FILE subcommand, 35
  FIRST subcommand, 37-38
  IN subcommand, 37
  KEEP subcommand, 37
  LAST subcommand, 37-38
  MAP subcommand, 38
  RENAME subcommand, 35-36
  with DATA LIST command, 35
  with DROP DOCUMENTS
    command, 34
  with SORT CASES command, 35, 681
ADD VALUE LABELS (command),
  39-40
  limitations, 40
  string variable, 40
additive scales, see RELIABILITY
  (command)
ADEVICE (subcommand)
  SET command, 674
  SHOW command, 679
ADJPRED (keyword)
  REGRESSION command, 599
AFREQ (keyword)
  FREQUENCIES command, 221
AFTER (keyword)
  ANOVA command, 64
AGGREGATE (command), 41-47
  BREAK subcommand, 43
  DOCUMENT subcommand, 44
  function arguments, 45-46
  functions, 44-46
  MISSING subcommand, 46-47
  OUTFILE subcommand, 43
  PRESORTED subcommand, 44
  variable definitions, 44-46
  with MATCH FILES command,
    42-43
  with MISSING VALUES command,
    46-47
  with SORT CASES command, 681
  with SPLIT FILE command, 42, 682

aggregate functions, 44-46
  arguments, 45-46
  REPORT command, 637-640
aggregated data
  in SURVIVAL command, 694-695
aggregation functions
  GRAPH command, 251-253
aggregation of groups of cases, 41-47
AIC (keyword)
  FACTOR command, 188
AINDS (keyword)
  ALSCAL command, 54
ALIGN (keyword)
  REPORT command, 630
ALL (function)
  MATRIX command, 415
ALL (keyword)
  ALSCAL command, 56
  ANOVA command, 64, 67
  CORRELATIONS command, 94
  CROSSTABS command, 103-107
  DESCRIPTIVES command, 125
  DISCRIMINANT command, 133-135
  LOGISTIC REGRESSION
    command, 319
  MEANS command, 461-462
  MULT RESPONSE command, 470
  NPAR TESTS command, 504
  ONEWAY command, 512-513
  PARTIAL CORR command, 520
  RELIABILITY command, 607-608
ALPHA (keyword)
  FACTOR command, 191
  MANOVA command, 390
  RELIABILITY command, 607
ALPHA (subcommand)
  REFORMAT (command), 584, 900
alpha device
  SPSS Graphics, 273
alphanumeric variable, 120
ALSCAL (command), 48-60
  annotated examples, 735-743
  CONDITION subcommand, 51-52
  CRITERIA subcommand, 54-55
  FILE subcommand, 52-54
  INPUT subcommand, 50
  LEVEL subcommand, 51
  limitations, 50
  matrix input, 50
  matrix output, 56-57
  MATRIX subcommand, 58-59
  METHOD subcommand, 54
  missing values, 50
  MODEL subcommand, 54
  model types, 54
  OUTFILE subcommand, 56-57
  PLOT subcommand, 56
  PRINT subcommand, 55-56
  SHAPE subcommand, 51
  VARIABLES subcommand, 50
  with obsolete commands, 892

ANALYSIS (keyword)
  NPAR TESTS command, 505
  ONEWAY command, 513
  PARTIAL CORR command, 520
  T-TEST command, 703
ANALYSIS (subcommand)
  DISCRIMINANT command, 130
  FACTOR command, 187
  MANOVA command, 371-372,
    384-385
analysis of covariance, 796-798
analysis of variance, 62-68, 509-516
  in MEANS command, 461
AND (keyword)
  logical operator, 31-32
ANOVA, see also MANOVA (command)
ANOVA (command), 62-68
  annotated example, 743-744
  cell means, 67
  covariates, 67
  COVARIATES subcommand, 64
  FORMAT subcommand, 68
  interaction effects, 64
  limitations, 63
  MAXORDERS subcommand, 64
  METHOD subcommand, 64-66
  MISSING subcommand, 68
  multiple classification analysis, 67-68
  references, 68
  sums of squares, 64-66
  VARIABLES subcommand, 63-64
  with AUTORECODE command, 70
  with obsolete commands, 892
ANOVA (keyword)
  MEANS command, 461
  QUICK CLUSTER command, 566
  REGRESSION command, 590
  RELIABILITY command, 607
ANY (function), 19, 28
  MATRIX command, 415
APPEND (subcommand)
  MCONVERT command, 456
APPROXIMATE (keyword)
  MANOVA command, 379, 391
  SURVIVAL command, 693-694
AR (keyword)
  FACTOR command, 192
arcsine, 18
arctangent, 18
AREA (keyword)
  GRAPH command, 263-264
area line chart, 263-264
arguments
  complex, 17, 88-89
  defined, 17-18
  in macros, 347-349
  missing values, 26-27
arithmetic operators, 17
ARSIN (function), 18
  MATRIX command, 415

ARTAN (function), 18
  MATRIX command, 415
ASCAL (keyword)
  ALSCAL command, 54
ASRESID (keyword)
  CROSSTABS command, 103
assignment expression
  in COMPUTE command, 86-89
  in IF command, 285-286
ASSOCIATION (keyword)
  HILOGLINEAR command, 282
asterisk (file name)
  in ADD FILES command, 35
  in MATCH FILES command, 402
  in UPDATE command, 707
ASYMMETRIC (keyword)
  ALSCAL command, 51
AUTOMATIC (keyword)
  REPORT command, 629
automatic fit
  in REPORT command, 625-626
AUTORECODE (command), 69-71
  compared to RECODE, 69
  DESCENDING subcommand, 71
  examples, 744-747
  INTO subcommand, 71
  missing values, 69
  PRINT subcommand, 71
  VARIABLES subcommand, 71
  with ANOVA command, 70
  with MANOVA command, 70-71
  with TABLES command, 70
AVALUE (keyword)
  CROSSTABS command, 105
AVERAGE (function)
  REPORT command, 640
AVERF (keyword)
  MANOVA command, 396
AVONLY (keyword)
  MANOVA command, 396

BACKWARD (keyword)
  HILOGLINEAR command, 279
  REGRESSION command, 589
BADCORR (keyword)
  PARTIAL CORR command, 520
  REGRESSION command, 594
balanced design
  in MANOVA, 365
BAR (subcommand)
  GRAPH command, 253-259
bar chart
  change character displayed in output,
    669
  GRAPH command, 253-259
BARCHART (subcommand)
  FREQUENCIES command, 222
BART (keyword)
  FACTOR command, 192
Bartlett-Box F
  in ONEWAY command, 513
Bartlett's test of sphericity, 189, 389
BASE (subcommand)
  MULT RESPONSE command, 470
BASIS (keyword)
  MANOVA command, 386
BAVERAGE (keyword)
  CLUSTER command, 78
BCON (keyword)
  LOGISTIC REGRESSION
    command, 319

BCOV (keyword)
  REGRESSION command, 590
BEGIN DATA (command), 72-73
  in a prompted session, 72
  with INCLUDE command, 72
BEUCLID (keyword)
  PROXIMITIES command, 558
binary data
  in PROXIMITIES, 554-559
BINOMIAL (subcommand)
  NPAR TESTS command, 496-497
blank
  delimiter, 5
  reading, 111, 666, 676
BLANK (keyword)
  FACTOR command, 188
  REPORT command, 634
BLANKS (subcommand)
  SET command, 666
  SHOW command, 676
!BLANKS (function)
  macro facility, 354
BLKSIZE (subcommand)
  SHOW command, 676
BLOCK (function)
  MATRIX command, 416
BLOCK (keyword)
  CLUSTER command, 78
  PROXIMITIES command, 554
BLOCK (subcommand)
  GRAPH command, 267-268
  SET command, 669
  SHOW command, 676
block diagram, 267-268
BLWMN (keyword)
  PROXIMITIES command, 559
BMPD to SPSS data conversion
  in GET BMDP (command), 229
BOOTSTRAP (subcommand)
  CNLR command, 487-488
BOTH (keyword)
  NONPAR CORR command, 491
  SET command, 668
  SURVIVAL command, 695
BOUNDARY (subcommand)
  GRAPH command, 271
BOUNDS (subcommand)
  CNLR command, 486-487
BOX (keyword)
  CROSSTABS command, 105
BOX (subcommand)
  SET command, 669-670
  SHOW command, 676
Box's M test
  in DISCRIMINANT command, 133
  in MANOVA command, 389
BOXM (keyword)
  DISCRIMINANT command, 133
  MANOVA command, 389
BREAK (command), 74
  with DO IF command, 74
  with LOOP command, 74
BREAK (statement)
  MATRIX command, 425
BREAK (subcommand)
  AGGREGATE command, 43
  REPORT command, 634-637
!BREAK (command)
  macro facility, 355-356
BREAKDOWN (command), see
  MEANS

BRIEF (keyword)
  MANOVA command, 389
BRKSPACE (keyword)
  REPORT command, 630
BSEUCLID (keyword)
  PROXIMITIES command, 558
BSHAPE (keyword)
  PROXIMITIES command, 558
BSTEP (keyword)
  LOGISTIC REGRESSION
    command, 317
BTAU (keyword)
  CROSSTABS command, 104
BTUKEY (keyword)
  ONEWAY command, 512
BUFFNO (subcommand)
  SHOW command, 677
BY (keyword)
  ANOVA command, 63-64
  CROSSTABS command, 100-102
  LOGISTIC REGRESSION
    command, 314
  LOGLINEAR command, 325-326
  LOOP command, 339
  MEANS command, 459
  MULT RESPONSE command,
    468-470
  NPAR TESTS command, 496
  PARTIAL CORR command, 517-518
  PROBIT command, 545
  SORT CASES command, 680
  SPLIT FILE command, 682
  SURVIVAL command, 690
  WEIGHT command, 720
BY (subcommand)
  ADD FILES command, 36
  MATCH FILES command, 403-404
  UPDATE command, 707
!BY (keyword)
  macro facility, 355-356

CALCULATE (subcommand)
  SURVIVAL command, 693-695
CALL (statement)
  MATRIX command, 421-422
canonical correlation analysis, 801-806
CASE (keyword)
  FILE TYPE command, 207-209
  PROXIMITIES command, 551-552
CASE (subcommand)
  FILE TYPE command, 205-207
  RECORD TYPE command, 581
  SET command, 669
  SHOW command, 677
$CASENUM (system variable)
  defined, 12
  in PRINT EJECT command, 538
  in PRINT SPACE command, 541
  with SELECT IF command, 662
CASES (keyword)
  DISCRIMINANT command, 135
  MULT RESPONSE command, 470
CASEWISE (subcommand)
  LOGISTIC REGRESSION
    command, 320-321
  REGRESSION command, 601-602
CATEGORICAL (subcommand)
  LOGISTIC REGRESSION
    command, 314-315
CC (keyword)
  CROSSTABS command, 104

CC (subcommand)
  SET command, 670-671
  SHOW command, 670-671, 677
CDFNORM (function), 20
  MATRIX command, 416
CELLINFO (keyword)
  MANOVA command, 372-373
CELLS (keyword)
  CROSSTABS command, 107
CELLS (subcommand)
  CROSSTABS command, 103
  MATRIX DATA command, 449
  MEANS command, 461
  MULT RESPONSE command, 470
CENTER (keyword)
  REPORT command, 643-644
CENTROID (keyword)
  CLUSTER command, 78
CFVAR (function), 18
CHA (keyword)
  REGRESSION command, 590
CHALIGN (keyword)
  REPORT command, 630
!CHAREND (keyword)
  macro facility, 349
CHDSPACE (keyword)
  REPORT command, 630
CHEBYCHEV (keyword)
  CLUSTER command, 78
  PROXIMITIES command, 553
chi-square test, 104
CHICDF (function)
  MATRIX command, 416
CHISQ (keyword)
  CROSSTABS command, 104
  PROXIMITIES command, 554
CHISQUARE (subcommand)
  NPAR TESTS command, 497
CHOL (function)
  MATRIX command, 416
choosing a sort program
  with SET command, 671
CHOROPLETH (keyword)
  GRAPH command, 271
CI (keyword)
  PROBIT command, 547
  REGRESSION command, 590
CINTERVAL (subcommand)
  MANOVA command, 379-380, 391
CKDER (keyword)
  CNLR command, 483-484
  NLR command, 485-486
CLABELS (keyword)
  MATRIX command, 423
classification options
  in DISCRIMINANT command,
    134-135
classification plots, 135
CLASSIFY (subcommand)
  DISCRIMINANT command, 134-135
CLASSPLOT (subcommand)
  LOGISTIC REGRESSION
    command, 320
CLEAR TRANSFORMATIONS
  (command), 75
CLUSTER (command), 76-83
  annotated example, 747-751
  ID subcommand, 79
  limitations, 77
  matrix input, 81
  matrix output, 81

MATRIX subcommand, 81-83
MEASURE subcommand, 77-78
METHOD subcommand, 78
MISSING subcommand, 80
PLOT subcommand, 80
PRINT subcommand, 79-80
references, 83
SAVE subcommand, 78-79
variable list, 77
with obsolete commands, 892
with PROXIMITIES command,
  860-861
CLUSTER (keyword)
  CLUSTER command, 79
  QUICK CLUSTER command,
    565-566
CMAX (function)
  MATRIX command, 416
!CMDEND (keyword)
  macro facility, 349-351
CMIN (function)
  MATRIX command, 416
CNAMES (keyword)
  MATRIX command, 423
CNLR (command), 475-488
  annotated examples, 830-843
  BOOTSTRAP subcommand, 487-488
  BOUNDS subcommand, 486-487
  CONSTRAINED FUNCTIONS
    command, 477, 480
  CRITERIA subcommand, 483-484
  DERIVATIVES command, 477,
    479-480
  FILE subcommand, 481
  iteration criteria, 483-484
  linear constraint, 486
  LOSS subcommand, 487
  MODEL PROGRAM command, 477,
    478-479
  nonlinear constraint, 486-487
  OUTFILE subcommand, 480-481
  PRED subcommand, 481-482
  SAVE subcommand, 482-483
  simple bounds, 486
  weighting cases, 477
  with CROSSTABS command, 841
  with PLOT command, 837-840
  with PROBIT command, 841
  with REGRESSION command, 833,
    841
COCHRAN (keyword)
  RELIABILITY command, 607
COCHRAN (subcommand)
  NPAR TESTS command, 498
Cochran's C
  in ONEWAY command, 513
CODE (subcommand)
  GET BMDP command, 230
COEFF (keyword)
  DISCRIMINANT command, 133
  REGRESSION command, 590
coefficient of variation, 18
COLCONF (keyword)
  ALSCAL command, 53
COLLECT (keyword)
  REGRESSION command, 588
COLLIN (keyword)
  REGRESSION command, 590
COLLINEARITY (keyword)
  MANOVA command, 374
COLSPACE (keyword)
  REPORT command, 630

COLUMN (keyword)
  CROSSTABS command, 103
  MULT RESPONSE command, 470
COLUMN (subcommand)
  REREAD command, 646-648
column binary format
  on DATA LIST command, 903-905
column heading alignment
  REPORT command, 633, 635
column style formats
  in DATA LIST command, 110-111
column titles
  REPORT command, 632-633, 635
column widths
  REPORT command, 625, 633,
    635-636
COLUMNWISE (keyword)
  AGGREGATE command, 46-47
COMBINED (keyword)
  DISCRIMINANT command, 135
combining system files, 33-38, 399-405
COMM (keyword)
  EXPORT command, 180
  IMPORT command, 290
comma
  delimiter, 5
COMMA (keyword)
  REPORT command, 641-642
command
  order, 1-3
  syntax, 3-4
command file
  defined, 6
commands
  processed through your operating
    system, 4
  run within SPSS, 4
  that read data, 1-3
  that take effect immediately, 1-3
COMMENT (command), 84
COMPARE (keyword)
  SURVIVAL command, 694
COMPARE (subcommand)
  EXAMINE command, 172
  SURVIVAL command, 693
COMPLETE (keyword)
  CLUSTER command, 78
complex files
  with FILE TYPE command, 199-204
  with INPUT PROGRAM command,
    151-152
composite functions
  REPORT command, 639-640
COMPOSITIONAL (keyword)
  GRAPH command, 255
COMPRESSED (subcommand)
  SAVE command, 655
  XSAVE command, 731
compression
  of scratch file, 672
COMPRESSION (subcommand)
  SET command, 672
  SHOW command, 677
COMPUTE (command), 85-91
  arithmetic functions, 85-91
  arithmetic operators, 85-91
  functions, 85-91
  missing values, 85-91
  with DO IF command, 88, 146
  with FREQUENCIES command,
    89-90
  with STRING command, 91

COMPUTE (statement)
  MATRIX command, 414-421
CONCAT (function), 29
!CONCAT (function)
  macro facility, 353
concentration statistic, 325
CONDENSE (keyword)
  FREQUENCIES command, 221
  MULT RESPONSE command, 471
CONDENSED (keyword)
  PARTIAL CORR command, 520
CONDITION (subcommand)
  ALSCAL command, 51-52
CONDITIONAL (keyword)
  MANOVA command, 384-385
  SURVIVAL command, 694
conditional probabilities
  in PROXIMITIES, 556-557
conditional processing
  macro facility, 355
CONFIG (keyword)
  ALSCAL command, 52
conformable matrices
  MATRIX command, 410
CONSTANT (keyword)
  MANOVA command, 368
constants, 17
CONSTRAIN (keyword)
  ALSCAL command, 55
CONSTRAINED FUNCTIONS
    (command)
  CNLR command, 477, 480
CONTENT (subcommand)
  GET BMDP command, 230
CONTENTS (subcommand)
  MATRIX DATA command, 450-452
contingency coefficient, 104
CONTINUED (subcommand)
  REPEATING DATA command,
    620-623
continuous variables on DESIGN
    subcommand
  MANOVA command, 367
CONTOUR (keyword)
  PLOT command, 525
CONTRAST (keyword)
  MANOVA command, 386
CONTRAST (subcommand)
  LOGISTIC REGRESSION
    command, 315-316
  LOGLINEAR command, 329-331
  MANOVA command, 369-370,
    397-398
  ONEWAY command, 511
control scatterplot
  PLOT command, 524-525
CONVERGE (keyword)
  ALSCAL command, 54
  HILOGLINEAR command, 280
  PROBIT command, 546
CONVERT (keyword)
  RECODE command, 575-576
converting database files, 243
converting spreadsheet files, 242-243
COOK (keyword)
  LOGISTIC REGRESSION
    command, 320
  REGRESSION command, 599
COR (keyword)
  MANOVA command, 389-390

CORR (keyword)
  CROSSTABS command, 104
  DISCRIMINANT command, 133
  LOGISTIC REGRESSION
    command, 319
  MATRIX DATA command, 450
  PARTIAL CORR command, 519
CORRELATION (keyword)
  FACTOR command, 188
  PROXIMITIES command, 553
  REGRESSION command, 594
  RELIABILITY command, 607-608
CORRELATIONS (command), 92-96
  annotated example, 751-752
  FORMAT subcommand, 94-95
  limitations, 93
  matrix output, 95-96
  MATRIX subcommand, 95-96
  MISSING subcommand, 94
  PRINT subcommand, 93-94
  significance tests, 93-94
  STATISTICS subcommand, 94
  with obsolete commands, 892-893
COS (function), 18
  MATRIX command, 416
COSINE (keyword)
  CLUSTER command, 78
  PROXIMITIES command, 553
COUNT (command), 97-98
  missing values, 97
  range, 97
  string variable, 97
  with DO IF command, 146
COUNT (function)
  GRAPH command, 252
COUNT (keyword)
  CROSSTABS command, 103
  MATRIX DATA command, 450
  MEANS command, 461
  MULT RESPONSE command, 470
COV (keyword)
  DISCRIMINANT command, 133
  MANOVA command, 388-390
  MATRIX DATA command, 450
  REGRESSION command, 594
COVARIANCES (keyword)
  RELIABILITY command, 607-608
COVARIATES (subcommand)
  ANOVA command, 64
CPI (subcommand)
  SET command, 674
  SHOW command, 679
Cramer's V, 104
CRITERIA (subcommand)
  ALSCAL command, 54-55
  CNLR command, 483-484
  FACTOR command, 190-191
  HILOGLINEAR command, 279-280
  LOGISTIC REGRESSION
    command, 319-320
  LOGLINEAR command, 331
  NLR command, 483, 485-486
  PROBIT command, 546-547
  QUICK CLUSTER command, 565
  REGRESSION command, 591-592
CROSSBREAK (subcommand)
  MEANS command, 461
CROSSTABS (command), 99-108
  annotated example, 753-754
  cell contents, 103
  cell percentages, 103

CELLS subcommand, 103
  expected values, 103
  FORMAT subcommand, 105
  indexing tables, 105
  integer mode, 102-103
  limitations, 101
  MISSING subcommand, 104-105
  reproducing tables, 107-108
  residuals, 103
  STATISTICS subcommand, 104
  TABLES subcommand, 101-102
  VARIABLES subcommand, 103
  with CNLR command, 841
  with obsolete commands, 893
  with PROCEDURE OUTPUT
    command, 105-107
  with WEIGHT command, 107-108
  WRITE subcommand, 105-108
  writing tables, 105-107
crosstabulation
  in MEANS command, 461
CRSHTOL (keyword)
  CNLR command, 484
CSSQ (function)
  MATRIX command, 417
CSUM (function)
  MATRIX command, 417
CTAU (keyword)
  CROSSTABS command, 104
CTIME.DAYS (function), 23
CTIME.HOURS (function), 23
CTIME.MINUTES (function), 23
CUFREQ (function)
  GRAPH command, 252
cumulative distribution function, 20
CUPCT (function)
  GRAPH command, 252
custom currency formats
  in FORMATS command, 216
  in PRINT FORMATS command, 539
  in WRITE FORMATS command, 726
  SET command, 670-671
CUSUM (function)
  GRAPH command, 252
CUTOFF (keyword)
  ALSCAL command, 55
CUTPOINTS (subcommand)
  PLOT command, 525-527
CWEIGHT (subcommand)
  HILOGLINEAR command, 280-281
  LOGLINEAR command, 327

D (keyword)
  CROSSTABS command, 104
  DESCRIPTIVES command, 126
  PROXIMITIES command, 557
  SORT CASES command, 680
d, Somers', 104
data
  inline, 72-73
DATA (keyword)
  ALSCAL command, 55
DATA (subcommand)
  GET OSIRIS command, 234
  GET SAS command, 238
  REPEATING DATA command, 619
data formats
  column binary data, 903-905
  column style, 110-111
  FORTRAN-like, 111-112
  in DATA LIST command, 110-111,
    119-121

in FORMATS command, 216-218
in PRINT FORMATS command,
    539-540
in WRITE FORMATS command,
    726-727
multipunch data, 903
DATA LIST (command), 109-121
column binary data, 903-905
column style formats, 110-111
END subcommand, 115-117
FILE subcommand, 112
FIXED keyword, 113-114
fixed-format data, 111
FORTRAN-like formats, 111-112
FREE keyword, 113-114
freefield data, 111
inline data, 112
LIST keyword, 113-114
multipunch data, 903
NOTABLE subcommand, 114
RECORDS subcommand, 114-115
TABLE subcommand, 114
variable definition, 117-121
variable formats, 119-121
variable locations, 117-118
variable names, 117
with ADD FILES command, 35
with INPUT PROGRAM command,
    151-152, 343
with MATCH FILES command, 402
with UPDATE command, 706-707
data types, 906-923
GET TRANSLATE command, 243
date and time output formats, 216-218
date functions, 20-21
DATE.DMY (function), 21
DATE.MDY (function), 21
DATE.MOYR (function), 22
DATE.QYR (function), 21-22
DATE.WKYR (function), 22
DATE.YRDAY (function), 21
$DATE (system variable)
    defined, 13
)DATE (argument)
    REPORT command, 643
dates, 20-21
DEFAULT (keyword)
    DESCRIPTIVES command, 125
    FACTOR command, 192
    LOGISTIC REGRESSION
        command, 318
    MEANS command, 461
!DEFAULT (keyword)
    macro facility, 352
DEFINE (command)
    macro facility, 345-357
delimiter, 5
    blank, 5
    comma, 5
    special, 5
DELTA (keyword)
    FACTOR command, 190
    HILOGLINEAR command, 280
DENDROGRAM (keyword)
    CLUSTER command, 80
DENSITY (keyword)
    SURVIVAL command, 692
DEPENDENT (keyword)
    MEANS command, 462
DEPENDENT (subcommand)
    REGRESSION command, 587-588

DERIVATIVES (command)
    CNLR/NLR command, 477, 479-480
DESC (keyword)
    RELIABILITY command, 607
DESCENDING (subcommand)
    AUTORECODE command, 71
DESCRIPTIVES (command), 122-126
    annotated example, 754-755
    compared to FREQUENCIES, 125
    FORMAT subcommand, 124-125
    limitations, 123
    MISSING subcommand, 126
    SAVE subcommand, 123-124
    STATISTICS subcommand, 122-125
    with obsolete commands, 894
    with SET WIDTH command,
        124-125
    Z scores, 123-124
DESCRIPTIVES (keyword)
    CORRELATIONS command, 94
    NPAR TESTS command, 504
    ONEWAY command, 513
    PARTIAL CORR command, 519
DESCRIPTIVES (subcommand)
    REGRESSION command, 594
design
    balanced, in MANOVA, 365
DESIGN (function)
    MATRIX command, 417
DESIGN (keyword)
    MANOVA command, 374
DESIGN (subcommand)
    HILOGLINEAR command, 282-283
    LOGLINEAR command, 326-327
    MANOVA command, 365-368
DET (function)
    MATRIX command, 417
DET (keyword)
    FACTOR command, 188
DEV (keyword)
    LOGISTIC REGRESSION
        command, 320
DEVIATION (keyword)
    LOGISTIC REGRESSION
        command, 315
    MANOVA command, 386
DEVIATION contrasts
    MANOVA command, 370
DFBETA (keyword)
    LOGISTIC REGRESSION
        command, 320
DFE (keyword)
    MATRIX DATA command, 450
DFREQ (keyword)
    FREQUENCIES command, 221
DIAG (function)
    MATRIX command, 417
DIAGONAL (keyword)
    MATRIX DATA command, 446
DIAGONAL (subcommand)
    FACTOR command, 189-190
DICE (keyword)
    PROXIMITIES command, 556
dictionary
    formats, 111
    system file, 652, 728
DICTIONARY (keyword)
    DISPLAY command, 141
DICTIONARY (subcommand)
    GET OSIRIS command, 234
dictionary formats
    defined, 216-218

in GET SCSS command, 240
in PRINT command, 534-535
in WRITE command, 723-724
DIFFERENCE (keyword)
    GRAPH command, 264-265
    LOGISTIC REGRESSION
        command, 315
    MANOVA command, 386-387
DIFFERENCE contrasts
    MANOVA command, 370
difference line chart, 264-265
difference scores
    in MANOVA command, 387
DIGITS (subcommand)
    EXPORT command, 181
DIMENR (keyword)
    MANOVA command, 389
DIMENS (keyword)
    ALSCAL command, 55
direct access files, 301-305
DIRECTIONS (keyword)
    ALSCAL command, 55
DISCRIM (subcommand)
    MANOVA command, 390-391
DISCRIMINANT (command), 127-140
    analysis phase, 129-133
    ANALYSIS subcommand, 130
    annotated example, 756-757
    classification phase, 133-135
    classification plots, 135
    CLASSIFY subcommand, 134-135
    classifying cases, 133-135
    display options, 133
    FIN subcommand, 131
    FOUT subcommand, 131
    FUNCTIONS subcommand, 132
    GROUPS subcommand, 129
    HISTORY subcommand, 133
    inclusion levels, 139-140
    limitations, 128
    matrix input, 136-137
    matrix output, 136-137
    MATRIX subcommand, 136-139
    MAXSTEPS subcommand, 132
    METHOD subcommand, 130
    MISSING subcommand, 135
    PIN subcommand, 131
    PLOT subcommand, 135
    POUT subcommand, 131
    PRIORS subcommand, 134
    ROTATION subcommand, 133
    SAVE subcommand, 135-136
    SELECT subcommand, 129-130
    STATISTICS subcommand, 132-133
    TOLERANCE subcommand, 131
    VARIABLES subcommand, 129
    VIN subcommand, 131
    with MATRIX DATA command, 442
    with obsolete commands, 894-895
DISPER (keyword)
    PROXIMITIES command, 558
DISPLAY (command), 141-142
    VARIABLES subcommand, 142
DISPLAY (statement)
    MATRIX command, 437-438
display file
    box characters, 668-670
    defined, 6
    length, 668
    setting case, 668-669
    width, 668

DISTANCE (keyword)
  CLUSTER command, 79
  QUICK CLUSTER command, 566
distance model, 794-795
DIVIDE (function)
  REPORT command, 640
DO IF (command), 145-152
  concatenating raw data files, 150-151
  missing values, 147-148
  nested, 151
  string variables, 146-147
  with INPUT PROGRAM command,
    151-152
  with PRINT command, 535
  with PRINT EJECT command,
    537-538
  with PRINT SPACE command,
    541-542
  with SAMPLE command, 651
  with SELECT IF command, 663
DO IF (statement)
  MATRIX command, 424
DO REPEAT (command), 153-156
  with INPUT PROGRAM command,
    154-155
  with LOOP command, 154-155
!DO (command)
  macro facility, 355-356
DOCUMENT (command), 143-144
DOCUMENT (subcommand)
  AGGREGATE command, 44
documentation, 293-295
DOCUMENTS (keyword)
  DISPLAY command, 141
!DOEND (command)
  macro facility, 355-356
DOLLAR (keyword)
  REPORT command, 641-642
domain errors
  defined, 26
  numeric expressions, 26
DOUBLE (keyword)
  FREQUENCIES command, 221
  MULT RESPONSE command, 471
doubly multivariate repeated measures,
  820-822
DOWN (keyword)
  SORT CASES command, 680
DRAW (subcommand)
  SET command, 674
  SHOW command, 679
DRESID (keyword)
  REGRESSION command, 599
DROP (subcommand)
  ADD FILES command, 37
  EXPORT command, 180
  GET BMDP command, 230
  GET command, 226
  GET OSIRIS command, 234
  GET SAS command, 238-239
  GET TRANSLATE command, 245
  IMPORT command, 290
  MATCH FILES command, 404
  SAVE command, 654
  SAVE SCSS command, 657
  SAVE TRANSLATE command, 660
  UPDATE command, 708-709
  XSAVE command, 729-730
DROP DOCUMENTS (command), 157
  with ADD FILES command, 34
  with MATCH FILES command, 400
  with UPDATE command, 705

DUMMY (keyword)
  REPORT command, 632
DUNCAN (keyword)
  ONEWAY command, 512
DUPLICATE (subcommand)
  FILE TYPE command, 207-209
  RECORD TYPE command, 582
DURBIN (keyword)
  REGRESSION command, 601
DVALUE (keyword)
  CROSSTABS command, 105
  FREQUENCIES command, 221

ECONVERGE (keyword)
  FACTOR command, 190
EDIT (command), 158-159
EFFECTS (keyword)
  ONEWAY command, 513
EFSIZE (keyword)
  MANOVA command, 373, 396
EIGEN (keyword)
  FACTOR command, 189
  MANOVA command, 389
  MATRIX command, 421-422
element
  VECTOR command, 713-719
ELSE (command), see DO IF command
ELSE (keyword)
  RECODE command, 574
ELSE (statement)
  MATRIX command, 424
ELSE IF (command), see DO IF
  command
ELSE IF (statement)
  MATRIX command, 424
!ELSE (keyword)
  macro facility, 355
!ENCLOSE (keyword)
  macro facility, 349
END (keyword)
  DISCRIMINANT command, 133
  REGRESSION command, 591
END (subcommand)
  DATA LIST command, 115-117
END CASE (command), 160-166
  complex files, 164-165
  with DO REPEAT command, 163
  with END FILE command, 342
  with LOOP command, 342
  with VECTOR command, 161-163,
    340
END DATA (command), 72-73
END FILE (command), 167-169
  concatenating raw data files, 169
  with DO REPEAT command, 168
  with END CASE command, 168-169,
    342
  with LOOP command, 342
END FILE TYPE (command), see FILE
  TYPE command
END IF (command), see DO IF
  command
END IF (statement)
  MATRIX command, 424
END INPUT PROGRAM (command),
  see INPUT PROGRAM
  command
END LOOP (command), 333-343
  IF keyword, 334
  logical expressions, 334
  missing values, 341-342

END LOOP (statement)
  MATRIX command, 424-425
END MATRIX (command), see
  MATRIX command
end of file processing
  END subcommand, 115-117
END REPEAT (command), 153-156
  PRINT subcommand, 155-156
ENDCMD (subcommand)
  SET command, 672-673
  SHOW command, 677
!ENDDEFINE (command)
  macro facility, 345-357
ENTER (keyword)
  LOGISTIC REGRESSION
    command, 317
  REGRESSION command, 589
entropy statistic, 325
EOF (function)
  MATRIX command, 417
EPS (keyword)
  LOGISTIC REGRESSION
    command, 319
EQ (keyword)
  relational operator, 31
EQUAMAX (keyword)
  FACTOR command, 192
  MANOVA command, 390
equiprobability model, 326-327, 782-784
ERROR (keyword)
  MANOVA command, 374, 388-389
ERROR (subcommand)
  MANOVA command, 368-369
error terms for specific effects
  MANOVA command, 368
errors
  setting maximum, 666-667
ERRORS (subcommand)
  SET command, 668
  SHOW command, 677
ESTIM (keyword)
  HILOGLINEAR command, 282
  MANOVA command, 390
ESTIMATION (keyword)
  MANOVA command, 378
ETA (keyword)
  CROSSTABS command, 104
eta coefficient, 104, 461
EUCLID (keyword)
  ALSCAL command, 54
  CLUSTER command, 78
  PROXIMITIES command, 553
EVAL (function)
  MATRIX command, 417
!EVAL (function)
  macro facility, 354
EVERY (keyword)
  PLOT command, 526
EXACT (keyword)
  MANOVA command, 379, 391
  SURVIVAL command, 693
EXAMINE (command), 170-176
  annotated example, 757-761
  COMPARE subcommand, 172
  FREQUENCIES subcommand, 173
  ID subcommand, 173
  MESTIMATORS subcommand,
    175-176
  MISSING subcommand, 176
  PERCENTILES subcommand,
    173-174
  PLOT subcommand, 174-175

SCALE subcommand, 172
STATISTICS subcommand, 175
VARIABLES subcommand, 171-172
EXCLUDE (keyword)
ANOVA command, 68
DISCRIMINANT command, 135
MANOVA command, 380
PARTIAL CORR command, 520
RELIABILITY command, 608
EXECUTE (command), 177
EXP (function), 18
MATRIX command, 417
EXPECTED (keyword)
CROSSTABS command, 103
EXPERIMENTAL (keyword)
ANOVA command, 64-65
EXPORT (command), 178-181
DIGITS subcommand, 181
DROP subcommand, 180
KEEP subcommand, 180
MAP subcommand, 181
OUTFILE subcommand, 180
RENAME subcommand, 180-181
TYPE subcommand, 180
EXTERNAL (subcommand)
LOGISTIC REGRESSION
command, 321
EXTRACTION (keyword)
FACTOR command, 189
EXTRACTION (subcommand)
FACTOR command, 191

F (keyword)
MANOVA command, 379
REGRESSION command, 591
FACILITIES (keyword)
INFO command, 294
FACTOR (command), 182-196
ANALYSIS subcommand, 187
annotated example, 761-764
CRITERIA subcommand, 190-191
DIAGONAL subcommand, 189-190
EXTRACTION subcommand, 191
FORMAT subcommand, 188
limitations, 186
matrix input, 193-194
matrix output, 193-194
MATRIX subcommand, 193-195
MISSING subcommand, 186-187
PLOT subcommand, 189
PRINT subcommand, 188-189
ROTATION subcommand, 191-192
SAVE subcommand, 192-193
syntax, 185
VARIABLES subcommand, 186
WIDTH subcommand, 187
with obsolete commands, 895
with PROXIMITIES command, 562
FACTORS (keyword)
FACTOR command, 190
MATRIX command, 436-437
FACTORS (subcommand)
MATRIX DATA command, 448-449
FCDF (function)
MATRIX command, 418
FGT (function)
AGGREGATE command, 45
FIELD (keyword)
MATRIX command, 426-429
FIELDNAMES (subcommand)
GET TRANSLATE command, 244-245

SAVE TRANSLATE command, 660
file, 6
FILE (keyword)
MATRIX command, 426, 430,
433-434
FILE (subcommand)
ADD FILES command, 35
ALSCAL command, 52-54
CNLR/NLR command, 481
DATA LIST command, 112
FILE TYPE command, 205
GET BMDP command, 229
GET command, 226
GET TRANSLATE command, 244
IMPORT command, 289
INCLUDE command, 292
KEYED DATA LIST command, 304
MATCH FILES command, 401-402
MATRIX DATA command, 445
POINT command, 531
QUICK CLUSTER command, 565
REPEATING DATA command, 620
UPDATE command, 706-707
file definition, 6
FILE HANDLE (command), 197
MODE subcommand, 197
FILE LABEL (command), 198
file specifications, 197
FILE TYPE (command), 199-211
CASE subcommand, 205-207
DUPLICATE subcommand, 207-209
FILE subcommand, 205
GROUPED keyword, 203-204
MISSING subcommand, 209-210
MIXED keyword, 203-204
NESTED keyword, 203-204
ORDERED subcommand, 210-211
RECORD subcommand, 205
summary table, 204
WILD subcommand, 207
with REPEATING DATA command,
613
file types
GET TRANSLATE command, 244
SAVE TRANSLATE command,
659-660
FIN (function)
AGGREGATE command, 45
FIN (keyword)
REGRESSION command, 592
FIN (subcommand)
DISCRIMINANT command, 131
FINISH (command), 212
FIRST (function)
AGGREGATE command, 45
FIRST (keyword)
ANOVA command, 64
FIRST (subcommand)
ADD FILES command, 37-38
MATCH FILES command, 405
Fisher's exact test, 104
FIXED (keyword)
DATA LIST command, 113-114
FLIP (command), 213-215
NEWNAMES subcommand, 214-215
VARIABLES subcommand, 214
flow of control
DO IF command, 146
LOOP command, 333-343
FLT (function)
AGGREGATE command, 45

FNAMES (keyword)
MATRIX command, 436
FOOTNOTE (subcommand)
GRAPH command, 250-251
REPORT command, 643-644
FOR (keyword)
SURVIVAL command, 691
foreign files, 6
FORMAT (keyword)
MATRIX command, 422-423,
428-430
FORMAT (subcommand)
ANOVA command, 68
CORRELATIONS command, 94-95
CROSSTABS command, 105
DESCRIPTIVES command, 124-125
FACTOR command, 188
FREQUENCIES command, 221
MATRIX DATA command, 445-447
MEANS command, 462
MULT RESPONSE command,
471-472
NONPAR CORR command, 492
ONEWAY command, 513
PARTIAL CORR command, 520
PLOT command, 525
RELIABILITY command, 608
REPORT command, 629-630
SET command, 668-669
SHOW command, 677
T-TEST command, 703
formats, 13-16, 906-923
in DATA LIST command, 110-111,
119-121
in FORMATS command, 216-218
in PRINT FORMATS command,
539-540
in WRITE FORMATS command,
726-727
input, 109-121
output, 216-218
FORMATS (command), 216-218
FORTRAN-like formats
in DATA LIST command, 111-112
in PRINT command, 534
in WRITE command, 723
FORWARD (keyword)
REGRESSION command, 589
FOUT (function)
AGGREGATE command, 45
FOUT (keyword)
REGRESSION command, 592
FOUT (subcommand)
DISCRIMINANT command, 131
FPAIR (keyword)
DISCRIMINANT command, 133
FPRECISION (keyword)
CNLR command, 484
FRACTION (subcommand)
RANK command, 571
FREE (keyword)
DATA LIST command, 113-114
MATRIX DATA command, 446
FREQ (function)
GRAPH command, 252
FREQ (keyword)
FREQUENCIES command, 222
HILOGLINEAR command, 282
PROBIT command, 547
frequencies
in MULT RESPONSE command, 465

FREQUENCIES (command), 219-224
  annotated example, 765-766
  BARCHART subcommand, 222
  compared to DESCRIPTIVES, 125
  FORMAT subcommand, 221
  general mode, 220
  HBAR subcommand, 223
  HISTOGRAM subcommand, 222-223
  indexing tables, 221
  integer mode, 220
  limitations, 220
  MISSING subcommand, 224
  NTILES subcommand, 223
  PERCENTILES subcommand, 223
  STATISTICS subcommand, 223-224
  VARIABLES subcommand, 219-221
  with COMPUTE command, 89-90
  with LOOP command, 336-337
  with NLR command, 843
  with PROCEDURE OUTPUT
    command, 221
  with VECTOR command, 714
  writing tables, 221
FREQUENCIES (subcommand)
  EXAMINE command, 173
  MULT RESPONSE command, 468
FREQUENCY (function)
  REPORT command, 639
FRIEDMAN (keyword)
  RELIABILITY command, 607
FRIEDMAN (subcommand)
  NPAR TESTS command, 498
FROM (keyword)
  SAMPLE command, 650
FSCORE (keyword)
  FACTOR command, 189
FSTEP (keyword)
  LOGISTIC REGRESSION
    command, 317
FTOLERANCE (keyword)
  CNLR command, 484
FTSPACE (keyword)
  REPORT command, 630
FULL (keyword)
  MATRIX DATA command, 446
functions, 85-91
  MATRIX command, 415-421
  numeric variables, 17-26
  REPORT command, 637-640
  string variables, 28-30
FUNCTIONS (subcommand)
  DISCRIMINANT command, 132

gamma, 104
GAMMA (keyword)
  CROSSTABS command, 104
GCMDFILE (subcommand)
  SET command, 675
  SHOW command, 679
GCOV (keyword)
  DISCRIMINANT command, 133
GDATA (subcommand)
  SET command, 675
  SHOW command, 679
GDEVICE (subcommand)
  SET command, 675
  SHOW command, 679
GE (keyword)
  relational operator, 31
GEMSCAL (keyword)
  ALSCAL command, 54
general linear models, 359-398

general log-linear model, 778-780
GET (command), 225-227
  DROP subcommand, 226
  FILE subcommand, 226
  KEEP subcommand, 226
  limitations, 226
  MAP subcommand, 227
  RENAME subcommand, 226-227
  SPSS system files, 900
GET (statement)
  MATRIX command, 430-432
GET BMDP (command), 228-231
  case selection, 228-229
  CODE subcommand, 230
  CONTENT subcommand, 230
  DROP subcommand, 230
  FILE subcommand, 229
  formats, 229
  KEEP subcommand, 230
  LABEL subcommand, 230
  limitations, 229
  MAP subcommand, 231
  missing values, 229
  RENAME subcommand, 230-231
  SCAN subcommand, 229
  subcommand order, 228
  variable names, 229
GET OSIRIS (command), 232-235
  DATA subcommand, 234
  DICTIONARY subcommand, 234
  DROP subcommand, 234
  KEEP subcommand, 234
  limitations, 233
  MAP subcommand, 235
  RENAME subcommand, 234-235
GET SAS (command), 236-239
  DATA subcommand, 238
  DROP subcommand, 238-239
  KEEP subcommand, 238-239
  MAP subcommand, 239
  RENAME subcommand, 239
  SASLIB subcommand, 238
GET SCSS (command), 240-241
  $ convention, 241
  MASTERFILE subcommand, 240
  missing values, 240
  renaming variables, 241
  reserved keywords, 241
  VARIABLES subcommand, 241
  WORKFILE subcommand, 241
GET TRANSLATE (command),
  242-245
  database files, 243
  DROP subcommand, 245
  FIELDNAMES subcommand,
    244-245
  FILE subcommand, 244
  KEEP subcommand, 245
  limitations, 244
  RANGE subcommand, 245
  spreadsheet files, 242-243
  TYPE subcommand, 244
GG (keyword)
  MANOVA command, 396
GINV (function)
  MATRIX command, 418
GLS (keyword)
  FACTOR command, 191
GMEMORY (subcommand)
  SET command, 675
  SHOW command, 679
Goodman and Kruskal's tau, 104

GRAPH (command), 246-274
  aggregation functions, 251-253
  BAR subcommand, 253-259
  basic specifications, 251
  BLOCK subcommand, 267-268
  BOUNDARY subcommand, 271
  CASEFILE subcommand, 272
  count functions, 252
  FOOTNOTE subcommand, 250-251
  HISTOGRAM subcommand, 268
  limitations, 250
  LINE subcommand, 261-265
  MAP subcommand, 271-272
  NAME keyword, 270-271
  PIE subcommand, 259-261
  PYRAMID subcommand, 265-267
  REGION subcommand, 271-272
  SCATTERPLOT subcommand,
    269-271
  SET command, 674-675
  SHOW command, 679
  SUBTITLE subcommand, 250-251
  summary functions, 251-252
  TABLE subcommand, 272
  TITLE subcommand, 250-251
  VALUE function, 253
graphics command file, 273
graphics device
  SPSS Graphics, 274
GREAT (function)
  REPORT command, 640
GRESID (subcommand)
  LOGLINEAR command, 328
group variables
  in MULT RESPONSE command, 465
GROUPED (keyword)
  FILE TYPE command, 203-204
  GRAPH command, 256
grouped files
  defined, 204
GROUPS (subcommand)
  DISCRIMINANT command, 129
  MULT RESPONSE command, 467
  T-TEST command, 702
GROUPWISE (keyword)
  SURVIVAL command, 695
GSCH (function)
  MATRIX command, 418
GT (keyword)
  relational operator, 31
GUTTMAN (keyword)
  RELIABILITY command, 607

HAMANN (keyword)
  PROXIMITIES command, 557
HARMONIC (subcommand)
  ONEWAY command, 512
Hartley's F, 513
HAZARD (keyword)
  SURVIVAL command, 692
HBAR (subcommand)
  FREQUENCIES command, 223
!HEAD (function)
  macro facility, 353
HEADER (keyword)
  ALSCAL command, 56
HEADER (subcommand)
  SET command, 669
  SHOW command, 677
HELMERT (keyword)
  LOGISTIC REGRESSION
    command, 315
  MANOVA command, 387

HELMERT contrasts
  MANOVA command, 370
HELP (command), 275-276
HF (keyword)
  MANOVA command, 396
HICICLE (keyword)
  CLUSTER command, 80
HIERARCHICAL (keyword)
  ANOVA command, 64, 65
HIGHEST (keyword)
  COUNT command, 97
  MISSING VALUES command, 464
  RECODE command, 574
HILOGLINEAR (command), 277-283
  annotated examples, 767-770
  CRITERIA subcommand, 279-280
  CWEIGHT subcommand, 280-281
  DESIGN subcommand, 282-283
  limitations, 278
  MAXORDER subcommand, 279
  METHOD subcommand, 279
  MISSING subcommand, 283
  PLOT subcommand, 282
  PRINT subcommand, 281-282
  references, 283
  variable list, 279
histogram, 268
HISTOGRAM (keyword)
  REGRESSION command, 601
HISTOGRAM (subcommand)
  FREQUENCIES command, 222-223
  GRAPH command, 268
  SET command, 669
  SHOW command, 676
histograms
  change character displayed in output,
    669
HISTORY (keyword)
  REGRESSION command, 591
HISTORY (subcommand)
  DISCRIMINANT command, 133
HOLD (keyword)
  MATRIX command, 429
HOMOGENEITY (keyword)
  MANOVA command, 374, 389
  ONEWAY command, 513
homogeneity-of-variance tests
  in ONEWAY command, 513
HORIZONTAL (subcommand)
  PLOT command, 527-528
HOST (command), 284
HOTELLING (keyword)
  RELIABILITY command, 607
HSIZE (subcommand)
  PLOT command, 527
HYPOTH (keyword)
  MANOVA command, 389

ID (keyword)
  QUICK CLUSTER command, 566
  REGRESSION command, 601
ID (subcommand)
  CLUSTER command, 79
  EXAMINE command, 173
  LOGISTIC REGRESSION
    command, 318
  PROXIMITIES command, 559
  REPEATING DATA command, 623
IDENT (function)
  MATRIX command, 418
IF (command), 285-288
  missing values, 286

string variables, 285-286
  with ELSE command, 149
  with LOOP command, 287
!IF (command)
  macro facility, 355
!IFEND (command)
  macro facility, 355
IMAGE (keyword)
  FACTOR command, 191
implied decimal place, 119-120
IMPORT (command), 289-291
  DROP subcommand, 290
  FILE subcommand, 289
  KEEP subcommand, 290
  MAP subcommand, 291
  RENAME subcommand, 290
  TYPE subcommand, 290
IN (keyword)
  ALSCAL command, 58
  CLUSTER command, 81
  DISCRIMINANT command, 136-137
  FACTOR command, 193-194
  MANOVA command, 380-381
  ONEWAY command, 513-514
  PARTIAL CORR command, 520-521
  PROXIMITIES command, 559-560
  RELIABILITY command, 609
IN (subcommand)
  ADD FILES command, 37
  KEYED DATA LIST command, 305
  MATCH FILES command, 404
  UPDATE command, 709
!IN (keyword)
  macro facility, 356
INCLUDE (command), 292
  FILE subcommand, 292
INCLUDE (keyword)
  ANOVA command, 68
  CLUSTER command, 80
  CORRELATIONS command, 94
  CROSSTABS command, 105
  DESCRIPTIVES command, 126
  DISCRIMINANT command, 135
  FACTOR command, 187
  FREQUENCIES command, 224
  HILOGLINEAR command, 283
  MEANS command, 462
  MULT RESPONSE command, 471
  NONPAR CORR command, 492
  NPAR TESTS command, 505
  ONEWAY command, 513
  PARTIAL CORR command, 520
  PROBIT command, 548
  PROXIMITIES command, 559
  REGRESSION command, 596
  RELIABILITY command, 608
  SURVIVAL command, 695
  T-TEST command, 703
INCREMENT (keyword)
  FREQUENCIES command, 222
increment value
  in LOOP command, 339
  in LOOP statement (MATRIX),
    424-425
independent-samples test
  NPAR TESTS command, 495
INDEX (function), 28-29
INDEX (keyword)
  CROSSTABS command, 105
  DESCRIPTIVES command, 124-125
  DISPLAY command, 141
  FREQUENCIES command, 221

!INDEX (function)
  macro facility, 353
indexing clause
  in LOOP command, 335-339
  in LOOP statement (MATRIX),
    424-425
indexing strings, 28
indexing variable
  in LOOP command, 335
  in LOOP statement (MATRIX),
    424-425
INDICATOR (keyword)
  LOGISTIC REGRESSION
    command, 316
INDIVIDUAL (keyword)
  MANOVA command, 380
INDSCAL (keyword)
  ALSCAL command, 54
INFO (command), 293-295
  limitations, 294
  local documentation, 293
  new facilities, 294
  new procedures, 294
  new releases, 294-295
  OUTFILE (subcommand), 295
  update documentation, 293
INITIAL (keyword)
  FACTOR command, 188
  QUICK CLUSTER command, 566
INITIAL (subcommand)
  QUICK CLUSTER command, 565
initial state
  defined, 881-882
initial value
  in LOOP command, 335
  in LOOP statement (MATRIX),
    424-425
initialization
  in COMPUTE command, 87-88
  in DO IF command, 147
  in DO REPEAT command, 154
  in IF command, 286
  LEAVE command, 306
  numeric variables, 507
  scratch variables, 13
  string variables, 684
INLINE (keyword)
  MATRIX DATA command, 445
inline data, 72-73
INPUT (subcommand)
  ALSCAL command, 50
input data
  file, 6
  freefield format, 113
input formats
  in DATA LIST command, 110-111,
    119-121
INPUT MATRIX (command)
  obsolete, 896
INPUT PROGRAM (command),
  296-300
  concatenating raw data files, 299
  with DATA LIST command, 151-152,
    343
  with LOOP command, 342-343
  with REPEATING DATA command,
    613-617
input programs, 199-200, 296
input state, 200, 296-297
  defined, 881-882
integer mode
  in MEANS command, 460-461

INTERMED (keyword)
ALSCAL command, 55
intermediate file
GRAPH command, 249
INTERVAL (keyword)
ALSCAL command, 51
INTERVALS (subcommand)
SURVIVAL command, 690-691
INTO (keyword)
RECODE command, 575
INTO (subcommand)
AUTORECODE command, 71
INV (function)
MATRIX command, 418
INV (keyword)
FACTOR command, 188
ISTEP (keyword)
CNLR command, 484
item analysis, see RELIABILITY
(command)
ITER (keyword)
ALSCAL command, 54
CNLR command, 483
LOGISTIC REGRESSION
command, 319
NLR command, 485
ITERATE (keyword)
FACTOR command, 190
HILOGLINEAR command, 280
LOGISTIC REGRESSION
command, 319
PROBIT command, 546

JACCARD (keyword)
PROXIMITIES command, 556
$JDATE (system variable)
defined, 13
JOINT (keyword)
MANOVA command, 380
JOURNAL (subcommand)
SET command, 672-673
SHOW command, 677
journal file
defined, 6

K-S (subcommand)
NPAR TESTS command, 498-499
K-W (subcommand)
NPAR TESTS command, 499-500
KAISER (keyword)
FACTOR command, 190
Kaiser-Meyer-Olkin test, 189
KAPPA (keyword)
CROSSTABS command, 104
KEEP (subcommand)
ADD FILES command, 37
EXPORT command, 180
GET BMDP command, 230
GET command, 226
GET OSIRIS command, 234
GET SAS command, 238-239
GET TRANSLATE command, 245
IMPORT command, 290
MATCH FILES command, 404
SAVE command, 654
SAVE SCSS command, 657
SAVE TRANSLATE command, 660
UPDATE command, 708-709
XSAVE command, 729-730
KENDALL (keyword)
NONPAR CORR command, 491

KENDALL (subcommand)
NPAR TESTS command, 500
Kendall's tau-b, 104, 491
Kendall's tau-c, 104
KEY (subcommand)
KEYED DATA LIST command,
304-305
POINT command, 531
key variables
in ADD FILES command, 36, 36
in MATCH FILES command,
403-404
in UPDATE command, 707-708
KEYED DATA LIST (command),
301-305
direct access files, 301
FILE subcommand, 304
IN subcommand, 305
KEY subcommand, 304-305
keyed files, 301-302
NOTABLE subcommand, 305
TABLE subcommand, 305
keyed files
KEYED DATA LIST command,
301-305
POINT command, 529-531
keyword arguments
macro facility, 348
keywords
reserved, 12
syntax, 4
KMO (keyword)
FACTOR command, 189
Kolmogorov-Smirnov test
one sample, 498-499
two sample, 499
KRONEKER (function)
MATRIX command, 418
Kruskal-Wallis test
NPAR TESTS command, 499-500
KURTOSIS (function)
REPORT command, 638
KURTOSIS (keyword)
DESCRIPTIVES command, 125-126
FREQUENCIES command, 224
K1 (keyword)
PROXIMITIES command, 556
K2 (keyword)
PROXIMITIES command, 556-557

LABEL (keyword)
REPORT command, 632, 635
LABEL (subcommand)
GET BMDP command, 230
LABELS (keyword)
ANOVA command, 68
CROSSTABS command, 105
DESCRIPTIVES command, 124
DISPLAY command, 141
MEANS command, 462
MULT RESPONSE command, 471
RELIABILITY command, 608
T-TEST command, 703
LAG (function), 19, 28-29
lambda, 104
LAMBDA (keyword)
CROSSTABS command, 104
PROXIMITIES command, 557
LAST (function)
AGGREGATE command, 45
LAST (subcommand)

ADD FILES command, 37-38
MATCH FILES command, 405
LCON (keyword)
LOGISTIC REGRESSION
command, 319
LE (keyword)
relational operator, 31
LEAST (function)
REPORT command, 640
LEAVE (command), 306-308
with END CASE command, 307-308
LEFT (keyword)
REPORT command, 643-644
LENGTH (function), 29
LENGTH (keyword)
REPORT command, 629
LENGTH (subcommand)
REPEATING DATA command, 620
SET command, 668
SHOW command, 677
$LENGTH (system variable)
defined, 13
!LENGTH (function)
macro facility, 353
!LET (command)
macro facility, 357
LEVEL (subcommand)
ALSCAL command, 51
LEVER (keyword)
LOGISTIC REGRESSION
command, 320
REGRESSION command, 599-600
LFTOLERANCE (keyword)
CNLR command, 484
LG10 (function), 18
MATRIX command, 418
life tables
in SURVIVAL command, 688
LIMIT (keyword)
FREQUENCIES command, 221
limitations, see entries under individual
procedures
LINE (keyword)
DESCRIPTIVES command, 125
REGRESSION command, 591
LINE (subcommand)
GRAPH command, 261-265
line chart, 261-265
linear logit model, 330-331, 784-786
LINEARITY (keyword)
MEANS command, 462
LIST (keyword)
DATA LIST command, 113-114
MATRIX DATA command, 446
REPORT command, 629, 644
LISTING (keyword)
SET command, 668
LISTWISE (keyword)
CLUSTER command, 80
CORRELATIONS command, 94
DESCRIPTIVES command, 126
FACTOR command, 187
HILOGLINEAR command, 283
NONPAR CORR command, 491-492
NPAR TESTS command, 505
ONEWAY command, 513
PARTIAL CORR command, 520
PROBIT command, 548
PROXIMITIES command, 559
REGRESSION command, 596
SURVIVAL command, 695
T-TEST command, 703

LN (function), 18
  MATRIX command, 418
local documentation
  INFO command, 293
LOG (subcommand)
  PROBIT command, 546
logical expressions, 27, 30-32
  defined, 30-31
  in DO IF, 145-147
  in ELSE IF, 149-150
  in END LOOP, 31, 334
  in IF, 285-286
  in LOOP, 31, 334
  in SELECT IF, 31, 661-663
  missing values, 32, 662
  order of evaluation, 32
  string variables, 27-28, 87
logical functions, 19
logical operators, 31-32
  defined, 31-32
  missing values, 32, 147-148, 286
logical variables
  defined, 31
logistic regression, see LOGISTIC
    REGRESSION (command)
  PROBIT (command), 858-859
LOGISTIC REGRESSION (command),
    312-322
  CASEWISE subcommand, 320-321
  CATEGORICAL subcommand,
    314-315
  CLASSPLOT subcommand, 320
  CONTRAST subcommand, 315-316
  CRITERIA subcommand, 319-320
  EXTERNAL subcommand, 321
  ID subcommand, 318
  METHOD subcommand, 316-317
  MISSING subcommand, 321
  NOORIGIN subcommand, 318
  ORIGIN subcommand, 318
  PRINT subcommand, 318-319
  SAVE subcommand, 321
  SELECT subcommand, 318
  VARIABLES subcommand, 314
LOGIT (keyword)
  PROBIT command, 546
logit model, 325, 775-778
  multinomial, 780-781
  simultaneous linear, 326
LOGLINEAR (command), 323-332,
    774-795
  annotated examples, 774-795
  cell covariates, 325
  cell weights, 327
  CONTRAST subcommand, 329-331
  covariates, 326-327
  CRITERIA subcommand, 331
  CWEIGHT subcommand, 327
  DESIGN subcommand, 326-327
  dispersion, analysis of, 325
  distance model, 794-795
  equiprobability model, 326-327,
    782-784
  factor, defined, 329
  frequency table models, 782-784
  general log-linear model, 325, 778-780
  GRESID subcommand, 328
  interactions, 326
  log-linear time-trend model, 782-784
  logistic regression on category
    variables, 331, 786-789
  logit model, 325, 775-778

logit model, linear, 330-331, 784-786
logit model, multinomial, 330,
    780-781
main effects model, 326
measures of association, 325
MISSING subcommand, 332
multinomial response models,
    789-793
NOPRINT subcommand, 328-329
PLOT subcommand, 329
PRINT subcommand, 328-329
simultaneous linear logit model, 326
single-degree-of-freedom partitions,
    326
statistics, 328-329
structural zeros, 327
variable list, 325-326
WIDTH subcommand, 331
LOGSURV (keyword)
  SURVIVAL command, 692
long string variable, 5
LOOP (command), 333-343
  IF keyword, 334
  indexing clause, 335-339
  logical expressions, 334
  missing values, 341-342
  nested, 334, 337
  with FREQUENCIES command,
    336-337
  with INPUT PROGRAM command,
    342-343
  with SET MXLOOPS command,
    333-335, 666-667
  with VECTOR command, 71?
LOOP (statement)
  MATRIX command, 424-425
looping constructs
  macro facility, 355-356
LOSS (keyword)
  CNLR command, 482
LOSS (subcommand)
  CNLR command, 487
LOWER (function), 28-29
LOWER (keyword)
  MATRIX DATA command, 446
LOWEST (keyword)
  COUNT command, 97
  MISSING VALUES command, 464
  RECODE command, 574
LPAD (function), 28, 29
LPI (subcommand)
  SET command, 674
  SHOW command, 679
LRESID (keyword)
  LOGISTIC REGRESSION
    command, 320
LSD (keyword)
  ONEWAY command, 512
LSTOLERANCE (keyword)
  CNLR command, 484
LTRIM (function), 29

M-W (subcommand)
  NPAR TESTS command, 500-501
macro argument terminators, 349-352
macro definition, 345
macro facility, 344-357
  !BLANKS function, 354
  !BREAK command, 355-356
  !BY keyword, 355-356
  !CHAREND keyword, 349
  !CMDEND keyword, 349-351

!CONCAT function, 353
conditional processing, 355
!DEFAULT keyword, 352
DEFINE command, 345-357
!DO command, 355-356
!DOEND command, 355-356
!ELSE keyword, 355
!ENCLOSE keyword, 349
!ENDDEFINE command, 345-357
!EVAL function, 354
!HEAD function, 353
!IF command, 355
!IFEND command, 355
!IN keyword, 356
!INDEX function, 353
keyword arguments, 348
!LENGTH function, 353
!LET command, 357
looping constructs, 355-356
macro argument terminators, 349-352
macro definition, 345
macro invocation, 345
!NOEXPAND keyword, 352
!NULL function, 354
!OFFEXPAND keyword, 352
!ONEXPAND keyword, 352
positional arguments, 348-349
!POSITIONAL keyword, 347-349
!QUOTE function, 354
SET command, 354-355, 673
string manipulation functions,
    353-354
!SUBSTRING function, 353
!TAIL function, 353
!THEN keyword, 355
!TO keyword, 355-356
!TOKENS keyword, 349
!UNQUOTE function, 354
!UPCASE function, 354
with MATRIX command, 438
macro invocation, 345
MACROS (keyword)
  DISPLAY command, 141
MAGIC (function)
  MATRIX command, 419
MAHAL (keyword)
  REGRESSION command, 599
main effects model
  in LOGLINEAR, 326
MAKE (function)
  MATRIX command, 419
Mann-Whitney test
  NPAR TESTS command, 500-501
MANOVA (command), 358-398
  analysis of covariance, 796-798
  ANALYSIS subcommand, 371-372,
    384-385
  annotated examples, 796-825
  canonical correlation analysis,
    801-806
  CELLINFO keyword, 372-373
  CINTERVAL subcommand, 379-380,
    391
  CONSTANT keyword, 368
  continuous variables on DESIGN
    subcommand, 367
  CONTRAST subcommand, 369-370
  DESIGN keyword, 374
  DESIGN subcommand, 365-368
  DEVIATION contrasts, 370
  DIFFERENCE contrasts, 370
  difference scores, 387

DISCRIM subcommand, 390-391
doubly multivariate repeated
    measures, 392, 396, 820-822
ERROR keyword, 374
ERROR subcommand, 368-369
error terms for specific effects, 368
ESTIMATION keyword, 378
HELMERT contrasts, 370
HOMOGENEITY keyword, 374
matrix input, 380-381
matrix output, 380-381
MATRIX subcommand, 380-382
MEASURE subcommand, 396
METHOD subcommand, 377-379
MISSING subcommand, 380
MODELTYPE keyword, 377-378
multivariate applications, 383-391
multivariate multiple regression,
    801-806
multivariate one-way ANOVA,
    798-800
multivariate syntax, 384
MUPLUS keyword, 366
MWITHIN keyword, 366
nested effects, 365-366
NOPRINT subcommand, 372,
    388-389
OMEANS subcommand, 374-375,
    385-388
orthogonal contrasts, 370
PARAMETERS keyword, 373
PARTITION subcommand, 371
partitioning method for sums of
    squares, 377
partitions on DESIGN subcommand,
    366-367
PCOMPS subcommand, 390
PLOT subcommand, 376-377, 389
PMEANS subcommand, 375-376
POLYNOMIAL contrasts, 370
POOL keyword, 367
pooled effects, 366
POWER subcommand, 379, 391
PRINT subcommand, 372-374,
    388-389, 395-396
profile analysis, 822-825
RENAME subcommand, 385, 388,
    398
REPEATED contrasts, 370
repeated measures analysis, 392-398,
    806-819
repeated measures, doubly
    multivariate, 820-822
RESIDUAL keyword, 368-369
RESIDUALS subcommand, 377
reverse Helmert contrasts, 370
SIGNIF keyword, 373-374
SIMPLE contrasts, 370
SPECIAL (user-defined) contrasts, 370
specification of between-subject
    factors, 364
specification of covariates, 364-365
specification of dependent variable,
    364
SSTYPE keyword, 365, 377
TRANSFORM subcommand,
    385-387
transformations, 385-387
variables specification, 364-365, 384
VS keyword, 368
with AUTORECODE command,
    70-71

with obsolete commands, 896
WITHIN keyword, 365-366, 368-369
within-subjects factors, 392
WSDESIGN subcommand, 395
WSFACTORS subcommand, 394-395
MANUAL (keyword)
    REPORT command, 629
map
    choropleth, 271
    prism, 271
MAP (keyword)
    DISCRIMINANT command, 135
MAP (subcommand)
    ADD FILES command, 38
    EXPORT command, 181
    GET BMDP command, 231
    GET command, 227
    GET OSIRIS command, 235
    GET SAS command, 239
    GRAPH command, 271-272
    IMPORT command, 291
    MATCH FILES command, 405
    SAVE command, 655
    UPDATE command, 709
    XSAVE command, 730-731
MARGINS (keyword)
    REPORT command, 629
MASTERFILE (subcommand)
    GET SCSS command, 240
MAT (keyword)
    MATRIX DATA command, 450
MATCH FILES (command), 399-405
    active system file, 402
    BY subcommand, 403-404
    common variables, 404
    dictionary information, 404
    DROP subcommand, 404
    duplicate cases, 403-404
    FILE subcommand, 401-402
    FIRST subcommand, 405
    IN subcommand, 404
    KEEP subcommand, 404
    LAST subcommand, 405
    MAP subcommand, 405
    RENAME subcommand, 402-403
    TABLE subcommand, 402
    table-lookup files, 402
    with AGGREGATE command, 401
    with DATA LIST command, 402
    with DROP DOCUMENTS
        command, 400
    with SORT CASES command, 401,
        681
matching coefficients
    in PROXIMITIES, 555-556
matrices, see also MATRIX (command)
    correlation, 92-96, 136-139, 193-195,
        380-382, 489-493, 519-522
    covariance, 94
    factor loading, 193-195
MATRIX (command), 406-438
    BREAK statement, 425
    CALL statement, 421-422
    COMPUTE statement, 414-421
    DISPLAY statement, 437-438
    DO IF statement, 424
    ELSE IF statement, 424
    ELSE statement, 424
    END IF statement, 424
    END LOOP statement, 424-425
    GET statement, 430-432
    LOOP statement, 424-425

MGET statement, 433-434
MSAVE statement, 434-437
PRINT statement, 422-424
READ statement, 426-428
RELEASE statement, 438
SAVE statement, 432-433
with macro facility, 438
WRITE statement, 428-430
MATRIX (keyword)
    ALSCAL command, 52
    CORRELATIONS command, 94
    NONPAR CORR command, 492
    PARTIAL CORR command, 520
MATRIX (subcommand)
    ALSCAL command, 58-59
    CLUSTER command, 81-83
    CORRELATIONS command, 95-96
    DISCRIMINANT command, 136-139
    FACTOR command, 193-195
    MANOVA command, 380-382
    MCONVERT command, 455
    NONPAR CORR command, 492-493
    obsolete commands, 891-902
    ONEWAY command, 513-515
    PARTIAL CORR command, 520-522
    PROXIMITIES command, 559-562
    REGRESSION command, 595-596
    RELIABILITY command, 608-611
MATRIX DATA (command), 439-453
    active system file, 439
    CELLS subcommand, 449
    CONTENTS subcommand, 450-452
    data-entry format, 446
    entering data, 440, 444-450
    FACTORS subcommand, 448-449
    FILE subcommand, 445
    FORMAT subcommand, 445-447
    formats, print and write, 440-441
    matrix shape, 446-447
    N subcommand, 453
    record order, 450
    ROWTYPE_and subcommand
        settings, 440
    ROWTYPE_variable, 440, 444-445,
        448-452
    scientific notation, 440
    SPLIT subcommand, 447-448
    subcommands in relation to
        ROWTYPE_, 440
    VARIABLES subcommand, 443-445
    VARNAME_variable, 444
    with DISCRIMINANT command,
        442
    with ONEWAY command, 443, 515
    with REGRESSION command,
        442-443
MATRIX functions, 415-421
MATRIX language, 406-438
    operators, 411-412
    statements, 413
    syntax, 408-409
    terminology, 407-408
    variables, 408
matrix output
    with SPLIT FILE command, 682
matrix system files, 7-11
    defined, 7-8
    format, 8-11
    matrix input, 8
    MATRIX subcommand, 8
Mauchly's test of sphericity, 392

MAX (function), 18, 28-29
  AGGREGATE command, 45
  REPORT command, 638
MAX (keyword)
  DESCRIPTIVES command, 125-126
  PROXIMITIES command, 552
MAXIMUM (function)
  GRAPH command, 252
MAXIMUM (keyword)
  FREQUENCIES command, 222-224
MAXORDER (subcommand)
  HILOGLINEAR command, 279
MAXORDERS (subcommand)
  ANOVA command, 64
MAXSTEPS (keyword)
  HILOGLINEAR command, 280
  REGRESSION command, 592
MAXSTEPS (subcommand)
  DISCRIMINANT command, 132
MCA (keyword)
  ANOVA command, 67
MCNEMAR (subcommand)
  NPAR TESTS command, 501
MCONVERT (command), 454-456
  APPEND subcommand, 456
  MATRIX subcommand, 455
  REPLACE subcommand, 455
MDGROUP (keyword)
  MULT RESPONSE command, 471
MDIAG (function)
  MATRIX command, 419
MEAN (function), 18
  AGGREGATE command, 44
  GRAPH command, 252
  REPORT command, 638
MEAN (keyword)
  ANOVA command, 67
  DESCRIPTIVES command, 125-126
  DISCRIMINANT command, 133
  FREQUENCIES command, 223
  MATRIX DATA command, 450
  MEANS command, 461
  PROXIMITIES command, 552
  REGRESSION command, 594
MEANS (command), 457-462
  annotated example, 827-828
  CELLS subcommand, 461
  CROSSBREAK subcommand, 461
  crosstabulation, 461
  FORMAT subcommand, 462
  integer mode, 460-461
  limitations, 459
  MISSING subcommand, 462
  narrow output, 458
  STATISTICS subcommand, 461-462
  TABLES subcommand, 459-460
  VARIABLES subcommand, 460-461
  with obsolete commands, 896
MEANS (keyword)
  RELIABILITY command, 608
MEANSUBSTITUTION (keyword)
  DISCRIMINANT command, 135
  FACTOR command, 187
  REGRESSION command, 596
MEASURE (subcommand)
  CLUSTER command, 77-78
  MANOVA command, 396
  PROXIMITIES command, 552-559
MEDIAN (function)
  GRAPH command, 252
  REPORT command, 638-639

MEDIAN (keyword)
  CLUSTER command, 78
  FREQUENCIES command, 223
MEDIAN (subcommand)
  NPAR TESTS command, 501-502
memory
  SPSS Graphics, 274
MESSAGES (subcommand)
  SET command, 668
  SHOW command, 677
MESTIMATORS (subcommand)
  EXAMINE command, 175-176
METHOD (subcommand)
  ALSCAL command, 54
  ANOVA command, 64-66
  CLUSTER command, 78
  DISCRIMINANT command, 130
  HILOGLINEAR command, 279
  LOGISTIC REGRESSION
    command, 316-317
  MANOVA command, 377-379
  REGRESSION command, 588-590
  RELIABILITY command, 608
MEXPAND (subcommand)
  SET command, 354, 673
  SHOW command, 677
MGET (statement)
  MATRIX command, 433-434
MIN (function), 18, 28-29
  AGGREGATE command, 45
  REPORT command, 638
MIN (keyword)
  DESCRIPTIVES command, 125-126
MINEIGEN (keyword)
  FACTOR command, 190
  MANOVA command, 390
MINIMUM (function)
  GRAPH command, 252
MINIMUM (keyword)
  FREQUENCIES command, 222-224
MINKOWSKI (keyword)
  PROXIMITIES command, 554
MINORITERATION (keyword)
  CNLR command, 483
MISSING (function), 19
  SELECT IF command, 662
MISSING (keyword)
  COUNT command, 97
  MATRIX command, 431
  RECODE command, 574
  REPORT command, 630
MISSING (subcommand)
  AGGREGATE command, 46-47
  ANOVA command, 68
  CLUSTER command, 80
  CORRELATIONS command, 94
  CROSSTABS command, 104-105
  DESCRIPTIVES command, 126
  DISCRIMINANT command, 135
  EXAMINE command, 176
  FACTOR command, 186-187
  FILE TYPE command, 209-210
  FREQUENCIES command, 224
  HILOGLINEAR command, 283
  LOGISTIC REGRESSION
    command, 321
  LOGLINEAR command, 332
  MANOVA command, 380
  MEANS command, 462
  MULT RESPONSE command,
    470-471
  NONPAR CORR command, 491-492

NPAR TESTS command, 505
ONEWAY command, 513
PARTIAL CORR command, 520
PLOT command, 528
PROBIT command, 548
PROXIMITIES command, 559
QUICK CLUSTER command, 567
RANK command, 571
RECORD TYPE command, 581-582
REGRESSION command, 596-597
RELIABILITY command, 608
REPORT command, 644
SURVIVAL command, 695
T-TEST command, 703
missing values, see entries under
    individual procedures
  functions, 19
  in arguments, 26-27
  in END LOOP command, 341-342
  in logical expressions, 32, 662
  in LOOP command, 341-342
  in numeric expressions, 26
  in SELECT IF command, 662
  MISSING function, 19
  NMISS function, 19
  suffix, 18
  SYSMIS function, 19
  VALUE function, 19
  with logical operators, 32, 147-148,
    286
MISSING VALUES (command),
    463-464
  string variable, 463
  value range, 464
  with AGGREGATE command, 46-47
MITERATE (subcommand)
  SET command, 354, 673
  SHOW command, 677
MIXED (keyword)
  FILE TYPE command, 203-204
mixed files
  defined, 203
ML (keyword)
  FACTOR command, 191
MMAX (function)
  MATRIX command, 419
MMIN (function)
  MATRIX command, 419
MNEST (subcommand)
  SET command, 354, 673
  SHOW command, 677
MOD (function), 18
  MATRIX command, 419
MODE (function)
  GRAPH command, 252
  REPORT command, 639
MODE (keyword)
  FREQUENCIES command, 223
  MATRIX command, 427-429
MODE (subcommand)
  FILE HANDLE command, 197
MODEL (subcommand)
  ALSCAL command, 54
  PROBIT command, 545-546
  RELIABILITY command, 607
MODEL PROGRAM (command)
  CNLR/NLR command, 477, 478-479
MODELTYPE (keyword)
  MANOVA command, 377-378
MODLSD (keyword)
  ONEWAY command, 512

MOSES (subcommand)
NPAR TESTS command, 502
MPRINT (subcommand)
SET command, 354, 673
SHOW command, 677
MRGROUP (keyword)
MULT RESPONSE command, 471
MSAVE (statement)
MATRIX command, 434-437
MSE (keyword)
MATRIX DATA command, 450
MSSQ (function)
MATRIX command, 419
MSUM (function)
MATRIX command, 419
MULT RESPONSE (command),
465-472
annotated example, 828-830
BASE subcommand, 470
cell percentages, 470
CELLS subcommand, 470
FORMAT subcommand, 471-472
FREQUENCIES subcommand, 468
group variables, 465
GROUPS subcommand, 467
limitations, 466-467
MISSING subcommand, 470-471
multiple-response items, 465
PAIRED keyword, 470
statistics, 470
TABLES subcommand, 468-470
VARIABLES subcommand, 468
with obsolete commands, 897
multidimensional scaling, 48-60
multinomial logit model, 330, 780-781
multinomial response models, 789-793
MULTIPLE (keyword)
GRAPH command, 262-263
multiple classification analysis
in ANOVA command, 67-68
multiple comparisons, see ONEWAY
(command)
multiple-response items
defined, 465
in MULT RESPONSE command, 465
MULTIPLY (function)
REPORT command, 640
MULTIPUNCH (keyword)
FILE HANDLE command, 197
multipunch data, 197
multipunch format
on DATA LIST command, 903
MULTIV (keyword)
MANOVA command, 389
MULTIVARIATE (keyword)
MANOVA command, 391
multivariate analysis of variance,
359-398
multivariate F tests, 389
multivariate multiple regression,
801-806
multivariate one-way ANOVA, 798-800
MUPLUS (keyword)
MANOVA command, 366
MWITHIN (keyword)
MANOVA command, 366
MXERRS (subcommand)
SET command, 666-667
SHOW command, 677
MXLOOPS (subcommand)
SET command, 666-667
SHOW command, 677
with LOOP command, 333-335

MXWARNS (subcommand)
SET command, 666-667
SHOW command, 677

N (function)
AGGREGATE command, 45
GRAPH command, 252
n (keyword)
ANOVA command, 64
MATRIX DATA command, 450
REGRESSION command, 594
N (subcommand)
MATRIX DATA command, 453
RANK command, 569
SHOW command, 677
N OF CASES (command), 473-474
with SAMPLE command, 473
with SELECT IF command, 473
N_MATRIX (keyword)
MATRIX DATA command, 450
N_SCALAR (keyword)
MATRIX DATA command, 450
N_VECTOR (keyword)
MATRIX DATA command, 450
NAME (keyword)
DESCRIPTIVES command, 126
GRAPH command, 270-271
REPORT command, 636
NAMES (keyword)
DISPLAY command, 141
MATRIX command, 431
MEANS command, 462
NATRES (subcommand)
PROBIT command, 547
NCOL (function)
MATRIX command, 419
NCOMP (keyword)
MANOVA command, 390
NE (keyword)
relational operator, 31
NEGATIVE (keyword)
ALSCAL command, 55
NESTED (keyword)
FILE TYPE command, 203-204
nested effects
MANOVA command, 365-366
nested files
defined, 204
NEWNAMES (subcommand)
FLIP command, 214-215
NEWPAGE (keyword)
FREQUENCIES command, 221
Newton-Raphson algorithm, 331
NFTOLERANCE (keyword)
CNLR command, 484
NGT (function)
GRAPH command, 252
NIN (function)
GRAPH command, 252
NLR (command), 475-486
annotated examples, 830-843
CRITERIA subcommand, 483,
485-486
DERIVATIVES command, 477,
479-480
FILE subcommand, 481
iteration criteria, 485-486
missing values, 477-478
MODEL PROGRAM command, 477,
478-479
OUTFILE subcommand, 480-481
PRED subcommand, 481-482
SAVE subcommand, 482-483

weighting cases, 477
with FREQUENCIES command, 843
NLT (function)
GRAPH command, 252
NMISS (function), 19
AGGREGATE command, 45
NO (keyword)
SET command, 666
NOBOX (keyword)
CROSSTABS command, 105
NOCATLABS (keyword)
MEANS command, 462
NODIAGONAL (keyword)
MATRIX DATA command, 446
NOEND (keyword)
DISCRIMINANT command, 133
!NOEXPAND (keyword)
macro facility, 352
NOINDEX (keyword)
CROSSTABS command, 105
DESCRIPTIVES command, 124-125
NOINITIAL (keyword)
QUICK CLUSTER command, 565
NOKAISER (keyword)
FACTOR command, 190
NOLABELS (keyword)
ANOVA command, 68
CROSSTABS command, 105
DESCRIPTIVES command, 124
FREQUENCIES command, 221
MEANS command, 462
MULT RESPONSE command, 471
RELIABILITY command, 608
T-TEST command, 703
NOLIST (keyword)
REPORT command, 629
NOMINAL (keyword)
ALSCAL command, 51
NONAME (keyword)
REPORT command, 636
NONAMES (keyword)
MEANS command, 462
NONE (keyword)
ANOVA command, 64, 67
CLUSTER command, 79-80
CROSSTABS command, 103-104, 107
HILOGLINEAR command, 282
MEANS command, 462
ONEWAY command, 512-513
PARTIAL CORR command, 519
REPORT command, 644
SET command, 668
SURVIVAL command, 695
NONMISSING (keyword)
DISCRIMINANT command, 134
NONPAR CORR (command), 489-493
annotated example, 843-844
FORMAT subcommand, 492
limitations, 490
MATRIX subcommand, 492-493
MISSING subcommand, 491-492
PRINT subcommand, 491
random sampling, 491
SAMPLE subcommand, 491
significance tests, 491
VARIABLES subcommand, 490
with obsolete commands, 897
with WEIGHT command, 720
NOORIGIN (subcommand)
LOGISTIC REGRESSION
command, 318

NOPRINT (subcommand)
LOGLINEAR command, 328-329
MANOVA command, 372, 388-389
NORMAL (function), 19
NORMAL (keyword)
FREQUENCIES command, 222
NORMAL (subcommand)
RANK command, 569
NORMPLOT (keyword)
HILOGLINEAR command, 282
NORMPROB (keyword)
REGRESSION command, 601
NOROTATE (keyword)
FACTOR command, 192
MANOVA command, 390
NOSIG (keyword)
CORRELATIONS command, 94
NONPAR CORR command, 491
NOSTEP (keyword)
DISCRIMINANT command, 133
NOT (keyword)
logical operator, 32
NOTABLE (keyword)
CROSSTABS command, 105
FREQUENCIES command, 221
SURVIVAL command, 692
NOTABLE (subcommand)
DATA LIST command, 114
KEYED DATA LIST command, 305
PRINT command, 536
REPEATING DATA command, 623
WRITE command, 725
NOULB (keyword)
ALSCAL command, 55
NOUPDATE (keyword)
QUICK CLUSTER command, 565
NOVALLABS (keyword)
CROSSTABS command, 105
NOVALUES (keyword)
MEANS command, 462
NOWARN (keyword)
FILE TYPE command, 207-209
RECORD TYPE command, 582
NPAR TESTS (command), 494-505
annotated example, 844-845
limitations, 496
MISSING subcommand, 505
pairing variables, 501
random sampling, 505
references, 505
SAMPLE subcommand, 505
STATISTICS subcommand, 504
with obsolete commands, 898
with WEIGHT command, 720
NROW (function)
MATRIX command, 419
NTILES (subcommand)
FREQUENCIES command, 223
NTILES(k) (subcommand)
RANK command, 570
NU (function)
AGGREGATE command, 45
!NULL (function)
macro facility, 354
NULLINE (subcommand)
SET command, 672-673
SHOW command, 677
NUMBER (function), 29
NUMBERED (command), 506
NUMBERED (subcommand)
SHOW command, 677

NUMERIC (command), 507-508
with INPUT PROGRAM command, 508
NUMERIC (subcommand)
REFORMAT (command), 584, 900
numeric expressions, 17-26
missing values, 26
numeric variable
in DATA LIST command, 119-120
RECODE command, 574-575
NUMISS (function)
AGGREGATE command, 45
NVALID (function), 19

OBLIMIN (keyword)
FACTOR command, 192
OCCURS (subcommand)
REPEATING DATA command, 618-619
OCHIAI (keyword)
PROXIMITIES command, 558
OF (keyword)
PROBIT command, 545
OFF (keyword)
SPLIT FILE command, 682
WEIGHT command, 720
!OFFEXPAND (keyword)
macro facility, 352
OFFSET (keyword)
REPORT command, 633, 636
OMEANS (subcommand)
MANOVA command, 374-375, 385-388
one-sample test
NPAR TESTS command, 495
one-way analysis of variance, 509-516
ONEPAGE (keyword)
FREQUENCIES command, 221
MULT RESPONSE command, 472
ONETAIL (keyword)
CORRELATIONS command, 94
NONPAR CORR command, 491
PARTIAL CORR command, 519
ONEWAY (command), 509-516
analysis design, 510
annotated example, 845-846
CONTRAST subcommand, 511
FORMAT subcommand, 513
HARMONIC subcommand, 512
limitations, 510
matrix input, 513-514
matrix output, 513-514
MATRIX subcommand, 513-515
MISSING subcommand, 513
POLYNOMIAL subcommand, 510-511
RANGES subcommand, 511-512
references, 516
STATISTICS subcommand, 513
with MATRIX DATA command, 443, 515
with obsolete commands, 898
!ONEXPAND (keyword)
macro facility, 352
OPTIMAL (keyword)
MANOVA command, 373
OPTIONS (command)
obsolete commands, 891-902
OPTOLERANCE (keyword)
CNLR command, 484
OR (keyword)
logical operator, 31-32

order of commands, 1-3
defined, 882-884
file definition commands, 885
input programs, 885
procedure commands, 886
program states, 882-884
restricted transformation commands, 886
transformation commands, 885
unrestricted utility commands, 884-885
order of operations
numeric expressions, 17
ORDERED (subcommand)
FILE TYPE command, 210-211
ORDINAL (keyword)
ALSCAL command, 51
ORIGIN (subcommand)
LOGISTIC REGRESSION command, 318
REGRESSION command, 592-593
orthogonal contrasts
MANOVA command, 370
ORTHONORM (keyword)
MANOVA command, 386
OSIRIS to SPSS data conversion
in GET OSIRIS (command), 233
OTHER (keyword)
RECORD TYPE command, 579-580
OUT (keyword)
CLUSTER command, 81
CORRELATIONS command, 95
DISCRIMINANT command, 136-137
FACTOR command, 193-194
MANOVA command, 380-381
NONPAR CORR command, 492-493
ONEWAY command, 513-514
PARTIAL CORR command, 520-521
PROXIMITIES command, 559-560
RELIABILITY command, 609
OUTFILE (keyword)
MATRIX command, 428, 432, 436
OUTFILE (subcommand)
AGGREGATE command, 43
ALSCAL command, 56-57
CNLR/NLR command, 480-481
EXPORT command, 180
INFO command, 295
PRINT command, 536
PRINT SPACE command, 541
QUICK CLUSTER command, 566
REPORT command, 631-632
SAVE command, 654
SAVE SCSS command, 657
SAVE TRANSLATE command, 659
WRITE command, 725
XSAVE command, 729
OUTLIERS (keyword)
LOGISTIC REGRESSION command, 321
REGRESSION command, 601-602
output
routing, 667-668
output file
defined, 6
output formats
in FORMATS command, 216-218
in PRINT FORMATS command, 539-540
in WRITE FORMATS command, 726-727
OUTS (keyword)
REGRESSION command, 590

OVERLAY (keyword)
  PLOT command, 525
OVERVIEW (keyword)
  INFO command, 294

P (keyword)
  HILOGLINEAR command, 280
  PROBIT command, 546-547
padding strings, 28
PAF (keyword)
  FACTOR command, 191
PAGE (keyword)
  REPORT command, 636
page layout
  REPORT command, 631
page size, see SET command
)PAGE (argument)
  REPORT command, 643
PAGE1 (keyword)
  REPORT command, 629
PAIRED (keyword)
  MULT RESPONSE command, 470
  NPAR TESTS command, 496
  T-TEST command, 703
PAIRED (subcommand)
  NPAR TESTS command, 501
paired crosstabulations
  in MULT RESPONSE command, 470
PAIRS (subcommand)
  T-TEST command, 702-703
PAIRWISE (keyword)
  CORRELATIONS command, 94
  FACTOR command, 187
  NONPAR CORR command, 491
  REGRESSION command, 596
  SURVIVAL command, 694
PARALL (keyword)
  PROBIT command, 548
PARALLEL (keyword)
  RELIABILITY command, 607
PARAMETERS (keyword)
  MANOVA command, 373
PARTIAL CORR (command), 517-522
  annotated example, 849-850
  control variables, 518
  correlation list, 518
  FORMAT subcommand, 520
  limitations, 518
  matrix input, 520-521
  matrix output, 520-521
  MATRIX subcommand, 520-522
  MISSING subcommand, 520
  order values, 518
  SIGNIFICANCE subcommand, 519
  STATISTICS subcommand, 519-520
  VARIABLES subcommand, 518-519
  with obsolete commands, 899
partial correlation coefficient, see
  PARTIAL CORR
PARTIALPLOT (subcommand)
  REGRESSION command, 602-603
PARTITION (subcommand)
  MANOVA command, 371
partitions on DESIGN subcommand
  MANOVA command, 366-367
PATTERN (keyword)
  PROXIMITIES command, 558
PA1 (keyword)
  FACTOR command, 191
PA2 (keyword)
  FACTOR command, 191

PC (keyword)
  FACTOR command, 191
PCOMPS (subcommand)
  MANOVA command, 390
PCON (keyword)
  NLR command, 485
PCT (function)
  GRAPH command, 252
  REPORT command, 640
PEARSON CORR, see
  CORRELATIONS
Pearson correlation coefficient, 104, 462
PERCENT (function)
  REPORT command, 639
PERCENT (keyword)
  FREQUENCIES command, 222
PERCENT (subcommand)
  RANK command, 569
PERCENTILES (subcommand)
  EXAMINE command, 173-174
  FREQUENCIES command, 223
period missing value specification
  suffix, 18
PGROUP (keyword)
  LOGISTIC REGRESSION
    command, 320
PGT (function)
  AGGREGATE command, 45
  GRAPH command, 252
  REPORT command, 639
PHI (keyword)
  CROSSTABS command, 104
  PROXIMITIES command, 558
phi coefficient, 104
PH2 (keyword)
  PROXIMITIES command, 554
PIE (subcommand)
  GRAPH command, 259-261
pie chart, 259-261
PIN (function)
  AGGREGATE command, 45
  GRAPH command, 252
  REPORT command, 639
PIN (keyword)
  LOGISTIC REGRESSION
    command, 319
  REGRESSION command, 592
PIN (subcommand)
  DISCRIMINANT command, 131
PLAIN (keyword)
  REPORT command, 641-642
PLOT (command), 523-528
  annotated example, 851-852
  CUTPOINTS subcommand, 525-527
  FORMAT subcommand, 525
  HORIZONTAL subcommand,
    527-528
  HSIZE subcommand, 527
  limitations, 524
  MISSING subcommand, 528
  missing values, 528
  PLOT subcommand, 524-525
  SYMBOLS subcommand, 525-527
  TITLE subcommand, 528
  VERTICAL subcommand, 527-528
  VSIZE subcommand, 527
  with CNLR command, 837-840
PLOT (keyword)
  REGRESSION command, 602
PLOT (subcommand)
  ALSCAL command, 56
  CLUSTER command, 80

DISCRIMINANT command, 135
EXAMINE command, 174-175
FACTOR command, 189
HILOGLINEAR command, 282
LOGLINEAR command, 329
MANOVA command, 376-377, 389
PLOT command, 524-525
SURVIVAL command, 691-692
PLT (function)
  AGGREGATE command, 45
  GRAPH command, 252
  REPORT command, 639
PMEANS (subcommand)
  MANOVA command, 375-376
POINT (command), 529-531
  FILE subcommand, 531
  KEY subcommand, 531
  keyed files, 529
POLYNOMIAL (keyword)
  LOGISTIC REGRESSION
    command, 315-316
  MANOVA command, 387
POLYNOMIAL (subcommand)
  ONEWAY command, 510-511
POLYNOMIAL contrasts
  MANOVA command, 370
POOL (keyword)
  MANOVA command, 367
POCLED (keyword)
  DISCRIMINANT command, 135
  REGRESSION command, 601
pooled effects
  MANOVA command, 366
population pyramid, 265-267
portable file, 178-181, 289-291
  defined, 178-179
  Kermit, 179
  with WEIGHT command, 178, 289,
    720
portable files
  defined, 6
positional arguments
  macro facility, 348-349
!POSITIONAL (keyword)
  macro facility, 347-349
POUT (function)
  AGGREGATE command, 45
POUT (keyword)
  LOGISTIC REGRESSION
    command, 319
  REGRESSION command, 592
POUT (subcommand)
  DISCRIMINANT command, 131
POWER (keyword)
  CLUSTER command, 78
  PROXIMITIES command, 554
POWER (subcommand)
  MANOVA command, 379, 391
precedence of commands, see order of
  commands
PRED (keyword)
  LOGISTIC REGRESSION
    command, 320
  REGRESSION command, 599
PRED (subcommand)
  CNLR/NLR command, 481-482
predictability measures
  in PROXIMITIES, 557
PRESERVE (command), 532
  macro facility, 354-355
PRESORTED (subcommand)
  AGGREGATE command, 44

PREVIOUS (keyword)
  REPORT command, 642
PRINT (command), 533-536
  formats, 534-535
  line specifications, 536
  missing values, 534
  NOTABLE subcommand, 536
  OUTFILE subcommand, 536
  RECORDS subcommand, 536
  string variables, 535
  TABLE subcommand, 536
  variable list, 533-535
  with DO IF command, 535
  with SORT CASES command, 681
PRINT (statement)
  MATRIX command, 422-424
PRINT (subcommand)
  ALSCAL command, 55-56
  AUTORECODE command, 71
  CLUSTER command, 79-80
  CORRELATIONS command, 93-94
  END REPEAT command, 155-156
  FACTOR command, 188-189
  HILOGLINEAR command, 281-282
  LOGISTIC REGRESSION
    command, 318-319
  LOGLINEAR command, 328-329
  MANOVA command, 372-374,
    388-389, 395-396
  NONPAR CORR command, 491
  PROBIT command, 547-548
  PROXIMITIES command, 559
  QUICK CLUSTER command,
    565-566
  RANK command, 571
  SURVIVAL command, 692
PRINT EJECT (command), 537-538
  $CASENUM system variable, 538
  missing values, 538
print formats
  in PRINT command, 534
  in PRINT EJECT command, 538
  REPORT command, 641-642
  setting default, 668-669
PRINT FORMATS (command),
    539-540
  with PRINT command, 534
  with PRINT EJECT command, 538
PRINT SPACE (command), 541-542
  $CASENUM system variable, 541
  number of lines, 541-542
  OUTFILE subcommand, 541
  with DO IF command, 541-542
PRINTBACK (subcommand)
  SET command, 668
  SHOW command, 678
PRIORS (subcommand)
  DISCRIMINANT command, 134
PRISM (keyword)
  GRAPH command, 271
PROBIT (command), 543-548
  annotated examples, 853-859
  case-by-case form, 545
  CRITERIA subcommand, 546-547
  limitations, 544
  LOG subcommand, 546
  logistic regression, 858-859
  MISSING subcommand, 548
  MODEL subcommand, 545-546
  NATRES subcommand, 547
  PRINT subcommand, 547-548
  response rate, 547

variable specification, 545
  with CNLR command, 841
PROBIT (function), 20
PROBIT (keyword)
  PROBIT command, 546
PROCEDURE OUTPUT (command),
    549
  with CROSSTABS command, 105-107
  with FREQUENCIES command, 221
  with obsolete commands, 899
  with SURVIVAL command, 695
procedure state
  defined, 881-882
procedures
  update documentation, 294
PROCEDURES (keyword)
  INFO command, 294
profile analysis, 822-825
program states
  defined, 881-882
  order of commands, 882-884
PROPORTION (subcommand)
  RANK command, 569
PROX (keyword)
  MATRIX DATA command, 450
PROXIMITIES (command), 550-562
  annotated example, 860-861
  binary data, 554-559
  continuous data, 553-554
  frequency count data, 554
  ID subcommand, 559
  limitations, 551
  matrix input, 560
  matrix output, 560
  MATRIX subcommand, 559-562
  MEASURE subcommand, 552-559
  MISSING subcommand, 559
  PRINT subcommand, 559
  STANDARDIZE subcommand,
    551-552
  variable specification, 551
  VIEW subcommand, 552
  with CLUSTER command, 860-861
  with FACTOR command, 562
  with obsolete commands, 899
PROXIMITIES (keyword)
  PROXIMITIES command, 559
PTILE (function)
  GRAPH command, 252
PYRAMID (subcommand)
  GRAPH command, 265-267

Q (keyword)
  PROXIMITIES command, 557
quartiles, 504
QUARTILES (keyword)
  NPAR TESTS command, 504
QUARTIMAX (keyword)
  FACTOR command, 192
  MANOVA command, 390
QUICK CLUSTER (command),
    563-567
  annotated examples, 861-864
  CRITERIA subcommand, 565
  FILE subcommand, 565
  INITIAL subcommand, 565
  MISSING subcommand, 567
  OUTFILE subcommand, 566
  PRINT subcommand, 565-566
  SAVE subcommand, 566-567
  standardization, 565
  variable list, 565

with large number of cases, 564
  with obsolete commands, 899
!QUOTE (function)
  macro facility, 354

r, see CORRELATIONS
R (keyword)
  REGRESSION command, 590
RADIAL (keyword)
  GRAPH command, 260-261
radial pie chart, 260-261
random numbers
  setting seed, 671
RANGE (function), 19, 28-29
RANGE (keyword)
  DESCRIPTIVES command, 125-126
  FREQUENCIES command, 224
  GRAPH command, 258-259
  PROXIMITIES command, 552
RANGE (subcommand)
  GET TRANSLATE command, 245
range bar chart, 258-259
RANGES (subcommand)
  ONEWAY command, 511-512
RANK (command), 568-572
  FRACTION subcommand, 571
  MISSING subcommand, 571
  N subcommand, 569
  NORMAL subcommand, 569
  NTILES(k) subcommand, 570
  PERCENT subcommand, 569
  PRINT subcommand, 571
  PROPORTION subcommand, 569
  RANK Function subcommands,
    569-570
  RANK subcommand, 569
  RFRACTION subcommand, 569
  SAVAGE subcommand, 570
  TIES subcommand, 570-571
RANK (function)
  MATRIX command, 419
RANK (subcommand)
  RANK command, 569
rank-order correlation coefficients, see
    NONPAR CORR
RATIO (keyword)
  ALSCAL command, 51
RAW (keyword)
  DISCRIMINANT command, 133
  MANOVA command, 390
RCON (keyword)
  NLR command, 485
RCONVERGE (keyword)
  FACTOR command, 190
READ (statement)
  MATRIX command, 426-428
reading ASCII/EBCDIC matrix
    materials, 439-453
RECODE (command), 573-576
  compared to AUTORECODE, 69
  CONVERT keyword, 575-576
  INTO keyword, 575
  limitations, 574
  missing values, 574
  numeric variables, 574-575
  string variables, 574-576
  target variable, 575
  with DO IF command, 146
RECORD (subcommand)
  FILE TYPE command, 205

RECORD TYPE (command), 577-583
  CASE subcommand, 581
  DUPLICATE subcommand, 582
  MISSING subcommand, 581-582
  OTHER keyword, 579-580
  SKIP subcommand, 580
  SPREAD subcommand, 582-583
RECORDS (subcommand)
  DATA LIST command, 114-115
  PRINT command, 536
  WRITE command, 724
RECTANGULAR (keyword)
  ALSCAL command, 51
REDUNDANCY (keyword)
  MANOVA command, 374
REFORMAT (command), 584, 900
REG (keyword)
  ANOVA command, 67
  FACTOR command, 192
REGRESSION (command), 585-603
  annotated example, 864-867
  CASEWISE subcommand, 601-602
  CRITERIA subcommand, 591-592
  DEPENDENT subcommand, 587-588
  DESCRIPTIVES subcommand, 594
  limitations, 587, 600
  MATRIX subcommand, 595-596
  METHOD subcommand, 588-590
  MISSING subcommand, 596-597
  ORIGIN subcommand, 592-593
  PARTIALPLOT subcommand,
      602-603
  REGWGT subcommand, 593-594
  RESIDUALS subcommand, 600-601
  SAVE subcommand, 603
  SCATTERPLOT subcommand, 602
  SELECT subcommand, 594-595
  STATISTICS subcommand, 590-591
  VARIABLES subcommand, 587-588
  WIDTH subcommand, 587, 597
  with CNLR command, 833, 841
  with MATRIX DATA command,
      442-443
  with obsolete commands, 901
REGRESSION (keyword)
  PLOT command, 525
REGWGT (subcommand)
  REGRESSION command, 593-594
related-samples test
  NPAR TESTS command, 495
relational operators, 31
  defined, 31
RELEASE (statement)
  MATRIX command, 438
RELIABILITY (command), 605-611
  ALL keyword, 607-608
  ALPHA keyword, 607
  annotated example, 867-868
  ANOVA keyword, 607
  COCHRAN keyword, 607
  CORRELATIONS keyword, 607-608
  COVARIANCES keyword, 607-608
  DESC keyword, 607
  EXCLUDE keyword, 608
  FORMAT subcommand, 608
  FRIEDMAN keyword, 607
  GUTTMAN keyword, 607
  HOTEL keyword, 607
  INCLUDE keyword, 608
  LABELS keyword, 608
  limitations, 606
  MATRIX subcommand, 608-611

  MEANS keyword, 608
  METHOD subcommand, 608
  MISSING subcommand, 608
  MODEL subcommand, 607
  NOLABELS keyword, 608
  PARALLEL keyword, 607
  SCALE keyword, 607
  SCALE subcommand, 606-607
  SPLIT keyword, 607
  STATISTICS subcommand, 607-608
  STRICTPARALLEL keyword, 607
  SUMMARY subcommand, 608
  TOTAL keyword, 608
  TUKEY keyword, 607
  VARIABLES subcommand, 606
  VARIANCE keyword, 608
  with obsolete commands, 901
remainder function, 18
REMOVE (keyword)
  REGRESSION command, 589
RENAME (subcommand)
  ADD FILES command, 35-36
  EXPORT command, 180-181
  GET BMDP command, 230-231
  GET command, 226-227
  GET OSIRIS command, 234-235
  GET SAS command, 239
  IMPORT command, 290
  MANOVA command, 385-388, 398
  MATCH FILES command, 402-403
  SAVE command, 654-655
  SAVE SCSS command, 657
  UPDATE command, 707-708
  XSAVE command, 730
RENAME VARIABLES (command),
      612
REPEATED (keyword)
  LOGISTIC REGRESSION
      command, 316
  MANOVA command, 387
REPEATED contrasts
  MANOVA command, 370
repeated measures analysis, 392-398,
      806-819
repeated measures, doubly multivariate,
      392, 396
REPEATING DATA (command),
      613-623
  CONTINUED subcommand, 620-623
  DATA subcommand, 619
  FILE subcommand, 620
  ID subcommand, 623
  LENGTH subcommand, 620
  NOTABLE subcommand, 623
  OCCURS subcommand, 618-619
  STARTS subcommand, 617-618
  with DATA LIST command, 613
  with FILE TYPE command, 613
  with INPUT PROGRAM command,
      613-617
REPLACE (subcommand)
  MCONVERT command, 455
REPORT (command), 624-644
  aggregate functions, 637-640
  annotated examples, 869-872
  automatic fit, 625-626
  AUTOMATIC vs. MANUAL, 626
  BREAK subcommand, 634-637
  column titles, 632-633, 635
  column widths, 625, 633, 635-636
  composite functions, 639-640
  FORMAT subcommand, 629-630

  intercolumn spacing, 625
  MISSING subcommand, 644
  OUTFILE subcommand, 631-632
  page layout, 631
  print formats, 641-642
  STRING subcommand, 633-634
  SUMMARY subcommand, 637-642
  summary titles, 640-641
  titles and footnotes, 643-644
  VARIABLES subcommand, 632-633
  with SORT CASES command, 680
REPORT (keyword)
  CROSSTABS command, 105
REPR (keyword)
  FACTOR command, 189
REREAD (command), 645-648
  COLUMN subcommand, 646-648
REREAD (keyword)
  MATRIX command, 427-428
RESCALE (keyword)
  PROXIMITIES command, 552-553
reserved keywords, 12
  in SAVE SCSS command, 656
RESHAPE (function)
  MATRIX command, 419
RESID (keyword)
  CROSSTABS command, 103
  HILOGLINEAR command, 282
  LOGISTIC REGRESSION
      command, 320
  REGRESSION command, 599
RESIDUAL (keyword)
  MANOVA command, 368-369
RESIDUALS (subcommand)
  MANOVA command, 377
  REGRESSION command, 600-601
RESPONSES (keyword)
  MULT RESPONSE command, 470
RESTORE (command), 649
  macro facility, 354-355
result files
  in UPDATE command, 705
resulting files
  in ADD FILES command, 34
RESULTS (subcommand)
  SET command, 668
  SHOW command, 678
REVERSE (keyword)
  PROXIMITIES command, 552
reverse Helmert contrasts
  MANOVA command, 370
RFRACTION (subcommand)
  RANK command, 569
RIGHT (keyword)
  REPORT command, 643-644
RINDEX (function), 28-30
RISK (keyword)
  CROSSTABS command, 104
RLABELS (keyword)
  MATRIX command, 423
RMAX (function)
  MATRIX command, 419
RMIN (function)
  MATRIX command, 419
RMP (keyword)
  PROBIT command, 547-548
RNAMES (keyword)
  MATRIX command, 423
RND (function), 18
  MATRIX command, 420
RNKORDER (function)
  MATRIX command, 420

ROTATE (keyword)
  MANOVA command, 390
ROTATION (keyword)
  FACTOR command, 189
ROTATION (subcommand)
  DISCRIMINANT command, 133
  FACTOR command, 191-192
routing SPSS output, 667-668
ROW (keyword)
  ALSCAL command, 52
  CROSSTABS command, 103
  MULT RESPONSE command, 470
ROWCONF (keyword)
  ALSCAL command, 53
ROWS (keyword)
  ALSCAL command, 50
Roy-Bargmann stepdown F test, 389
RPAD (function), 30
RR (keyword)
  PROXIMITIES command, 556
RSSQ (function)
  MATRIX command, 420
RSUM (function)
  MATRIX command, 420
RT (keyword)
  PROXIMITIES command, 556
RTRIM (function), 28, 30
run commands
  through your operating system, 4
  within SPSS, 4
RUNS (subcommand)
  NPAR TESTS command, 502-503

SAMPLE (command), 650-651
  placement, 651
  with DO IF command, 651
SAMPLE (subcommand)
  NONPAR CORR command, 491
  NPAR TESTS command, 505
SAS to SPSS data conversion
  in GET SAS command, 236-237
SASLIB (subcommand)
  GET SAS command, 238
SAVAGE (subcommand)
  RANK command, 570
SAVE (command), 652-655
  COMPRESSED subcommand, 655
  DROP subcommand, 654
  KEEP subcommand, 654
  MAP subcommand, 655
  OUTFILE subcommand, 654
  RENAME subcommand, 654-655
  UNCOMPRESSED subcommand,
    655
  with TEMPORARY command, 699
SAVE (statement)
  MATRIX command, 432-433
SAVE (subcommand)
  CLUSTER command, 78-79
  CNLR/NLR command, 482-483
  DESCRIPTIVES command, 123-124
  DISCRIMINANT command, 135-136
  FACTOR command, 192-193
  LOGISTIC REGRESSION
    command, 321
  QUICK CLUSTER command,
    566-567
  REGRESSION command, 603
SAVE SCSS (command), 656-657
  DROP subcommand, 657
  KEEP subcommand, 657
  missing values, 656

OUTFILE subcommand, 657
  RENAME subcommand, 657
  reserved keywords, 656
SAVE TRANSLATE (command),
  658-660
  DROP subcommand, 660
  FIELDNAMES subcommand, 660
  KEEP subcommand, 660
  limitations, 659
  OUTFILE subcommand, 659
  TYPE subcommand, 659-660
SCALE (keyword)
  RELIABILITY command, 607
SCALE (subcommand)
  EXAMINE command, 172
  RELIABILITY command, 606-607
scale analysis, see RELIABILITY
  (command)
SCAN (subcommand)
  GET BMDP command, 229
scatterplot, 269-271
  PLOT command, 525
SCATTERPLOT (subcommand)
  GRAPH command, 269-271
  REGRESSION command, 602
SCHEDULE (keyword)
  CLUSTER command, 79
SCHEFFE (keyword)
  ONEWAY command, 512
SCOMPRESSION (subcommand)
  SHOW command, 678
SCRATCH (keyword)
  DISPLAY command, 141
scratch file
  compression, 672
scratch variables
  defined, 13
scree plot
  in FACTOR command, 189
SD (function), 18
  AGGREGATE command, 44
SD (keyword)
  MATRIX DATA command, 450
  PROXIMITIES command, 552
SDRESID (keyword)
  REGRESSION command, 599
SEED (subcommand)
  SET command, 671
  SHOW command, 678
SEKURT (keyword)
  FREQUENCIES command, 224
SELECT (subcommand)
  DISCRIMINANT command, 129-130
  LOGISTIC REGRESSION
    command, 318
  REGRESSION command, 594-595
SELECT IF (command), 661-663
  limitations, 662
  MISSING function, 662
  missing values, 661-663
  VALUE function, 662
  with $CASENUM, 662
  with DO IF command, 663
SEMEAN (keyword)
  DESCRIPTIVES command, 125-126
  FREQUENCIES command, 223
SEPARATE (keyword)
  DISCRIMINANT command, 135
SEPRED (keyword)
  REGRESSION command, 599
SERIAL (keyword)
  CORRELATIONS command, 94-95
  DESCRIPTIVES command, 125

NONPAR CORR command, 492
  PARTIAL CORR command, 520
SES (keyword)
  REGRESSION command, 590
SESKEW (keyword)
  FREQUENCIES command, 224
SET (command), 664-675
  ERRORS subcommand, 668
  MESSAGES subcommand, 668
  PRINTBACK subcommand, 668
  RESULTS subcommand, 668
  square plots, 674
  with DESCRIPTIVES command,
    124-125
  with T-TEST command, 703
SETDIAG (keyword)
  MATRIX command, 422
SEUCLID (keyword)
  CLUSTER command, 78
  PROXIMITIES command, 553
SHAPE (subcommand)
  ALSCAL command, 51
short string variable, 5
SHOW (command), 676-679
SIG (keyword)
  CORRELATIONS command, 94
  FACTOR command, 188
  NONPAR CORR command, 491
  REGRESSION command, 594
SIGN (subcommand)
  NPAR TESTS command, 503
SIGNIF (keyword)
  MANOVA command, 373-374, 389,
    396
SIGNIFICANCE (subcommand)
  PARTIAL CORR command, 519
SIMPLE (keyword)
  GRAPH command, 253-262
  LOGISTIC REGRESSION
    command, 315
  MANOVA command, 387
SIMPLE contrasts
  MANOVA command, 370
SIN (function), 18
  MATRIX command, 420
SINCE (keyword)
  INFO command, 294-295
SINGLE (keyword)
  CLUSTER command, 78
SINGLEDF (keyword)
  MANOVA command, 373, 389
SIZE (keyword)
  MATRIX command, 427
  PROXIMITIES command, 558
  REGRESSION command, 600-603
SKEWNESS (function)
  REPORT command, 638
SKEWNESS (keyword)
  DESCRIPTIVES command, 125-126
  FREQUENCIES command, 224
SKIP (keyword)
  REPORT command, 636, 642
SKIP (subcommand)
  RECORD TYPE command, 580
SM (keyword)
  PROXIMITIES command, 556
SNAMES (keyword)
  MATRIX command, 437
SNK (keyword)
  ONEWAY command, 512
SOLVE (function)
  MATRIX command, 420
Somers' d, 104

SORT (keyword)
   FACTOR command, 188
SORT CASES (command), 680-681
   with ADD FILES command, 35, 681
   with AGGREGATE command, 681
   with MATCH FILES command, 401,
     681
   with PRINT command, 681
   with REPORT command, 680
   with SPLIT FILE command, 682
   with UPDATE command, 681, 706
SORTED (keyword)
   DISPLAY command, 142
sorting data
   choosing a sort program, 671
SPACE (keyword)
   MATRIX command, 423
SPEARMAN (keyword)
   NONPAR CORR command, 491
Spearman correlation coefficient, 104
Spearman's rho, 491
SPECIAL (keyword)
   LOGISTIC REGRESSION
     command, 316
   MANOVA command, 387
SPECIAL (user-defined) contrasts
   MANOVA command, 370
SPLIT (keyword)
   MATRIX command, 437
   RELIABILITY command, 607
SPLIT (subcommand)
   MATRIX DATA command, 447-448
SPLIT FILE (command), 682-683
   with AGGREGATE command, 42,
     682
   with ALSCAL command, 50
   with SORT CASES command, 682
   with TEMPORARY command, 682
split-file processing
   with matrix system files, 10
SPREAD (subcommand)
   RECORD TYPE command, 582-583
spreadsheet files
   GET TRANSLATE command,
     242-243
SPSS Graphics, interface to, 246-274
SQRT (function), 18
   MATRIX command, 420
square root, 18
SRESID (keyword)
   CROSSTABS command, 103
   LOGISTIC REGRESSION
     command, 320
   REGRESSION command, 599
SSCON (keyword)
   NLR command, 485
SSCP (function)
   MATRIX command, 420
SSCP (keyword)
   MANOVA command, 388
SSTYPE (keyword)
   MANOVA command, 365, 377
SS1 through SS5 (keywords)
   PROXIMITIES command, 556-558
STACKED (keyword)
   GRAPH command, 257
STAN (keyword)
   MANOVA command, 390
stand-in variable
   DO REPEAT command, 153
standard deviation function, see also
     SD, STDDEV, 18

STANDARDIZE (subcommand)
   PROXIMITIES command, 551-552
STARTS (subcommand)
   REPEATING DATA command,
     617-618
states, see program states
STATISTICS (command)
   obsolete commands, 891-902
STATISTICS (subcommand)
   CORRELATIONS command, 94
   CROSSTABS command, 104
   DESCRIPTIVES command, 122-123
   DISCRIMINANT command, 132-133
   EXAMINE command, 175
   FREQUENCIES command, 223-224
   MEANS command, 461-462
   NPAR TESTS command, 504
   ONEWAY command, 513
   PARTIAL CORR command, 519-520
   REGRESSION command, 590-591
   RELIABILITY command, 607-608
STATUS (subcommand)
   SURVIVAL command, 691
STDDEV (function)
   GRAPH command, 252
   REPORT command, 638
STDDEV (keyword)
   DESCRIPTIVES command, 125-126
   DISCRIMINANT command, 133
   FREQUENCIES command, 223
   MATRIX DATA command, 450
   MEANS command, 461
   REGRESSION command, 594
STEP (keyword)
   DISCRIMINANT command, 133
STEPDOWN (keyword)
   MANOVA command, 389
STEPLIMIT (keyword)
   CNLR command, 484
STEPWISE (keyword)
   REGRESSION command, 589
STIMWGHT (keyword)
   ALSCAL command, 53
STRESSMIN (keyword)
   ALSCAL command, 54
STRICTPARALLEL (keyword)
   RELIABILITY command, 607
string
   syntax, 5
STRING (command), 684-685
   with INPUT PROGRAM command,
     685
STRING (function), 30
STRING (subcommand)
   REPORT command, 633-634
string expressions
   defined, 27
string functions, 28-30
string manipulation functions
   macro facility, 353-354
string variable, 120
   in ADD VALUE LABELS command,
     40
   in COMPUTE command, 87
   in COUNT command, 97
   in DATA LIST command, 119-121
   in DO IF command, 146-147
   in IF command, 285
   in MISSING VALUES command, 463
   in PRINT command, 535
   in RECODE command, 574-576
   in SAVE SCSS command, 656

   in VALUE LABELS command, 711
   in WRITE command, 724
   syntax, 5
string variables
   in logical expressions, 27-28, 87
STRINGS (keyword)
   MATRIX command, 433
Student-Newman-Keuls test, 512
Student's t, see T-TEST
subcommand
   syntax, 4
SUBJWGHT (keyword)
   ALSCAL command, 53
SUBSTR (function), 28, 30
!SUBSTRING (function)
   macro facility, 353
substrings, 28
SUBTITLE (command), 686
SUBTITLE (subcommand)
   GRAPH command, 250-251
SUBTRACT (function)
   REPORT command, 640
suffix
   missing values, 18, 26
SUM (function), 18
   AGGREGATE command, 44
   GRAPH command, 252
   REPORT command, 638
SUM (keyword)
   DESCRIPTIVES command, 125-126
   FREQUENCIES command, 224
   MEANS command, 461
SUMMARY (keyword)
   LOGISTIC REGRESSION
     command, 318
SUMMARY (subcommand)
   RELIABILITY command, 608
   REPORT command, 637-642
summary function
   GRAPH command, 251-252
summary functions, multiple
   GRAPH command, 252
summary titles
   REPORT command, 640-641
sums of squares, method of partitioning
   MANOVA command, 377
SUMSPACE (keyword)
   REPORT command, 630
SURVIVAL (command), 687-697
   aggregated data, 694-695
   annotated example, 873-875
   CALCULATE subcommand, 693-695
   COMPARE subcommand, 693
   comparisons, 693-695
   INTERVALS subcommand, 690-691
   life tables, 688
   limitations, 688
   MISSING subcommand, 695
   output file, 695-697
   PLOTS subcommand, 691-692
   PRINT subcommand, 692
   STATUS subcommand, 691
   TABLES subcommand, 690
   value range, 691
   with obsolete commands, 902
   with PROCEDURE OUTPUT
     command, 695
   WRITE subcommand, 695-697
SURVIVAL (keyword)
   SURVIVAL command, 692
SVAL (function)
   MATRIX command, 420

SVD (keyword)
  MATRIX command, 422
SWEEP (function)
  MATRIX command, 421
SYMBOLS (subcommand)
  PLOT command, 525-527
SYMMETRIC (keyword)
  ALSCAL command, 51
syntax, 1-5
  diagrams, 1
SYSMIS (function), 19
  in SELECT IF command, 662
SYSMIS (keyword)
  COUNT command, 97
  MATRIX command, 431-432
  RECODE command, 574
SYSMIS (subcommand)
  SHOW command, 678
$SYSMIS (system variable)
  defined, 12
system file
  GET command, 225
  SAVE command, 652
  updating, 704-709
  WEIGHT command, 225-226, 720
  XSAVE command, 728
system files
  combining, 33-38, 399-405
  defined, 6
system variables, 12-13
system-missing value, 111, 119

T (function)
  MATRIX command, 421
T (keyword)
  MANOVA command, 379
t test, see T-TEST
T-TEST (command), 701-703
  annotated example, 875-876
  FORMAT subcommand, 703
  GROUPS subcommand, 702
  independent samples, 702
  limitations, 702
  MISSING subcommand, 703
  paired samples, 702
  PAIRS subcommand, 702-703
  VARIABLES subcommand, 702
  with obsolete commands, 902
  with SET command, 703
TABLE (keyword)
  CROSSTABS command, 105
  DISCRIMINANT command, 133
  MEANS command, 462
  MULT RESPONSE command, 471
  SURVIVAL command, 692
TABLE (subcommand)
  DATA LIST command, 114
  GRAPH command, 272
  KEYED DATA LIST command, 305
  MATCH FILES command, 402
  PRINT command, 536
  WRITE command, 725
table-lookup files
  MATCH FILES (command), 402
TABLES (command)
  SET command, 673-674
TABLES (keyword)
  CROSSTABS command, 105
  SURVIVAL command, 695
TABLES (subcommand)
  CROSSTABS command, 101-102
  MEANS command, 459-460

MULT RESPONSE command,
  468-470
  SURVIVAL command, 690
!TAIL (function)
  macro facility, 353
TAPE (keyword)
  EXPORT command, 180
  IMPORT command, 290
target variable
  in COMPUTE command, 86
  in COUNT command, 97
  in IF command, 285-286
  in RECODE command, 575
target variables
  in COMPUTE command, 27
tau statistics, 104, 491
taxonomy of transformation commands,
  885-886
TBFONTS (subcommand)
  SET command, 673-674
  SHOW command, 678
TB1 and TB2 (subcommands)
  SET command, 673-674
  SHOW command, 678
TCDF (function)
  MATRIX command, 421
TCOV (keyword)
  DISCRIMINANT command, 133
TEMPORARY (command), 698-699
  limitations, 698
  with SAVE command, 699
  with SPLIT FILE command, 682
  with XSAVE command, 699
TERMINAL (keyword)
  SET command, 668
terminal value
  in LOOP command, 335
TEST (keyword)
  REGRESSION command, 589-590
test of linearity, 462
!THEN (keyword)
  macro facility, 355
THRU (keyword)
  COUNT command, 97
  MISSING VALUES command, 464
  RECODE command, 574
  SURVIVAL command, 690
TIES (subcommand)
  RANK command, 570-571
TIESTORE (keyword)
  ALSCAL command, 55
time and date output formats, 216-218
time functions, 20-21
time intervals, 20-21
TIME.DAYS (function), 22
TIME.HMS (function), 22
$TIME (system variable)
  defined, 13
TITLE (command), 700
TITLE (keyword)
  MATRIX command, 423
TITLE (subcommand)
  GRAPH command, 250-251
  PLOT command, 528
  REPORT command, 643-644
TO (keyword)
  LOOP command, 335
  variable list, 12
!TO (keyword)
  macro facility, 355-356
tokens
  macro facility, 349

!TOKENS (keyword)
  macro facility, 349
TOLERANCE (keyword)
  REGRESSION command, 591-592
TOLERANCE (subcommand)
  DISCRIMINANT command, 131
TOTAL (keyword)
  CROSSTABS command, 103
  MULT RESPONSE command, 470
  RELIABILITY command, 608
  REPORT command, 636
TRACE (function)
  MATRIX command, 421
TRANSFORM (keyword)
  MANOVA command, 389
TRANSFORM (subcommand)
  MANOVA command, 385-387
transformation commands
  taxonomy, 885-886
transformation state
  defined, 881-882
transformations
  in MANOVA command, 385-387
  in PROXIMITIES, 552-553
TRANSPOS (function)
  MATRIX command, 421
transposing files
  FLIP command, 213-215
treatment effects, defined, 67
TREE (keyword)
  MEANS command, 462
trimming strings, 28
TRUNC (function), 18
  MATRIX command, 421
TSPACE (keyword)
  REPORT command, 630
TUKEY (keyword)
  ONEWAY command, 512
  RELIABILITY command, 607
TWOTAIL (keyword)
  CORRELATIONS command, 93
  NONPAR CORR command, 491
  PARTIAL CORR command, 519
TYPE (keyword)
  MATRIX command, 434-436
TYPE (subcommand)
  EXPORT command, 180
  GET TRANSLATE command, 244
  IMPORT command, 290
  SAVE TRANSLATE command,
    659-660

UC (keyword)
  CROSSTABS command, 104
ULS (keyword)
  FACTOR command, 191
uncertainty coefficient, 104
UNCLASSIFIED (keyword)
  DISCRIMINANT command, 134
UNCOMPRESSED (subcommand)
  SAVE command, 655
  XSAVE command, 731
UNCONDITIONAL (keyword)
  ALSCAL command, 52
  MANOVA command, 384-385
UNDEFINED (subcommand)
  SET command, 666
  SHOW command, 678
undefined data, 119
UNDERSCORE (keyword)
  REPORT command, 630, 636

UNIFORM (function), 19
  MATRIX command, 421
UNIQUE (keyword)
  ANOVA command, 64-65
UNIV (keyword)
  MANOVA command, 389
UNIVARIATE (keyword)
  FACTOR command, 188
  MANOVA command, 380
UNIVF (keyword)
  DISCRIMINANT command, 133
UNNUMBERED (command), 506
!UNQUOTE (function)
  macro facility, 354
UNSELECTED (keyword)
  DISCRIMINANT command, 134
UP (keyword)
  SORT CASES command, 680
UPCASE (function), 28, 30
!UPCASE (function)
  macro facility, 354
UPDATE (command), 704-709
  active system file, 706-707
  BY subcommand, 707
  DROP subcommand, 708-709
  FILE subcommand, 706-707
  IN subcommand, 709
  KEEP subcommand, 708-709
  MAP subcommand, 709
  RENAME subcommand, 707-708
  with DATA LIST command, 706-707
  with DROP DOCUMENTS
      command, 705
  with SORT CASES command, 681,
      706
update documentation
  INFO command, 293
updating system files, 704-709
UPPER (keyword)
  MATRIX DATA command, 446

V, Cramer's, 104
VALIDN (function)
  REPORT command, 638
value
  syntax, 4-5
VALUE (function), 19
  GRAPH command, 253
  SELECT IF command, 662-663
VALUE (keyword)
  REPORT command, 632, 635
value labels
  case, 669
VALUE LABELS (command), 710-711
  limitations, 710-711
  string variable, 711
VALUES (keyword)
  MEANS command, 462
VAR (keyword)
  REPORT command, 644
)var (argument)
  REPORT command, 643
variable
  in MATRIX language, 408
  syntax, 12-16
VARIABLE (keyword)
  DESCRIPTIVES command, 126
  PROXIMITIES command, 551-552
variable labels
  case, 669
VARIABLE LABELS (command), 712
  limitations, 712

variable names
  rules for assigning, 12
VARIABLES (keyword)
  DISPLAY command, 141
  MATRIX command, 430-436
VARIABLES (subcommand)
  ALSCAL command, 50
  ANOVA command, 63-64
  AUTORECODE command, 71
  CROSSTABS command, 103
  DISCRIMINANT command, 129·
  DISPLAY command, 142
  EXAMINE command, 171-172
  FACTOR command, 186
  FLIP command, 214
  FREQUENCIES command, 219-221
  GET SCSS command, 241
  LOGISTIC REGRESSION
      command, 314
  MATRIX DATA command, 443-445
  MEANS command, 460-461
  MULT RESPONSE command, 468
  NONPAR CORR command, 490
  PARTIAL CORR command, 518-519
  REGRESSION command, 587-588
  RELIABILITY command, 606
  REPORT command, 632-633
  T-TEST command, 702
VARIANCE (function), 18
  GRAPH command, 252
  REPORT command, 638
VARIANCE (keyword)
  DESCRIPTIVES command, 125-126
  FREQUENCIES command, 224
  MEANS command, 461
  PROXIMITIES command, 558
  REGRESSION command, 594
  RELIABILITY command, 608
VARIMAX (keyword)
  FACTOR command, 192
  MANOVA command, 390
$VARS (subcommand)
  SHOW command, 678
VECTOR (command), 713-719
  short form, 717-718
  with AGGREGATE command, 719
  with END CASE command, 716-717
  with FREQUENCIES command, 714
VECTOR (keyword)
  DISPLAY command, 141
VERTICAL (subcommand)
  PLOT command, 527-528
VICICLE (keyword)
  CLUSTER command, 80
VIEW (subcommand)
  PROXIMITIES command, 552
VIN (subcommand)
  DISCRIMINANT command, 131
VS (keyword)
  MANOVA command, 368
VSIZE (subcommand)
  PLOT command, 527

W-W (subcommand)
  NPAR TESTS command, 503-504
Wald-Wolfowitz test
  NPAR TESTS command, 503-504
WARD (keyword)
  CLUSTER command, 78
WARN (keyword)
  FILE TYPE command, 207-209
  RECORD TYPE command, 582

warnings
  setting maximum, 666-667
  suppressing messages, 666
WAVERAGE (keyword)
  CLUSTER command, 78
WEIGHT (command), 720-721
  limitations, 721
  missing values, 720
  with CROSSTABS, 107-108
  with NONPAR CORR, 720
  with NPAR TESTS, 720
WEIGHT (subcommand)
  SHOW command, 678
weighting data
  noninteger weights, 720
WIDTH (subcommand)
  FACTOR command, 187
  LOGLINEAR command, 331
  REGRESSION command, 587, 597
  SET command, 668
  SHOW command, 678
$WIDTH (system variable)
  defined, 13
WILCOXON (subcommand)
  NPAR TESTS command, 504
WILD (subcommand)
  FILE TYPE command, 207
WITH (keyword)
  ANOVA command, 64
  CORRELATIONS command, 95
  LOGISTIC REGRESSION
      command, 314
  LOGLINEAR command, 326-327
  NONPAR CORR command, 490-492
  NPAR TESTS command, 496, 501
  PARTIAL CORR command, 518
  PROBIT command, 545
  T-TEST command, 702
WITHIN (keyword)
  MANOVA command, 365-366,
      368-369
within-subjects factors
  in MANOVA command, 392
WORKFILE (subcommand)
  GET SCSS command, 241
WRITE (command), 722-725
  formats, 723-724
  line specifications, 724
  missing values, 723
  NOTABLE subcommand, 725
  OUTFILE subcommand, 725
  RECORDS subcommand, 724
  strings, 724
  TABLE subcommand, 725
  variable list, 722-724
WRITE (keyword)
  FREQUENCIES command, 221
WRITE (statement)
  MATRIX command, 428-430
WRITE (subcommand)
  CROSSTABS command, 105-108
  SURVIVAL command, 695-697
write formats
  in WRITE command, 722
  setting default, 668-669
WRITE FORMATS (command),
      726-727
  with WRITE command, 722
WSDESIGN (subcommand)
  MANOVA command, 395
WSFACTORS (subcommand)
  MANOVA command, 394-395

XDATE.DATE (function), 25
XDATE.HOUR (function), 24
XDATE.JDAY (function), 25
XDATE.MDAY (function), 24
XDATE.MINUTE (function), 24
XDATE.MONTH (function), 24
XDATE.QUARTER (function), 25
XDATE.SECOND (function), 24
XDATE.TDAY (function), 25
XDATE.TIME (function), 25
XDATE.WEEK (function), 25
XDATE.WKDAY (function), 24-25
XDATE.YEAR (function), 24
XPROD (keyword)
  CORRELATIONS command, 94
  REGRESSION command, 594
XSAVE (command), 728-731
  COMPRESSED subcommand, 731
  DROP subcommand, 729-730

KEEP subcommand, 729-730
MAP subcommand, 730-731
OUTFILE subcommand, 729
RENAME subcommand, 730
UNCOMPRESSED subcommand,
  731
with TEMPORARY command, 699
XSORT (subcommand)
  SET command, 671
  SHOW command, 678
XTX (keyword)
  REGRESSION command, 590

Y (keyword)
  PROXIMITIES command, 557
Yates' corrected chi-square test, 104
YES (keyword)
  SET command, 666
YRMODA (function), 23

Z (keyword)
  PROXIMITIES command, 552
Z scores
  in DESCRIPTIVES command,
    123-124
ZCORR (keyword)
  MANOVA command, 389
ZPP (keyword)
  REGRESSION command, 590
ZPRED (keyword)
  REGRESSION command, 599
ZRESID (keyword)
  LOGISTIC REGRESSION
    command, 320
  REGRESSION command, 599